Behavioral Economics

Over the last few decades behavioral economics has revolutionized the discipline. It has done so by putting the human back into economics, by recognizing that people sometimes make mistakes, care about others, and are generally not as cold and calculating as economists have traditionally assumed. The results have been exciting and fascinating, and have fundamentally changed the way we look at economic behavior.

This textbook introduces all the key results and insights of behavioral economics to a student audience. Ideas such as mental accounting, prospect theory, present bias, inequality aversion, and learning are explained in detail. These ideas are also applied in diverse settings such as auctions, stock market crashes, charitable donations, and health care, to show why behavioral economics is crucial to understanding the world around us. Consideration is also given to what makes people happy, and how we can potentially nudge people to be happier.

This new edition contains expanded and updated coverage of neuroeconomics, emotions, deception, and the contrast between group and individual behavior, among other topics, to ensure that readers are kept up to speed with this fast-paced field. A companion website is also now available containing a test bank of questions and worked examples allowing users to see for themselves how changing the parameters can change the outcomes. This book remains the ideal introduction to behavioral economics for advanced undergraduate and graduate students.

Edward Cartwright is a Senior Lecturer in Economics at the University of Kent, Canterbury, United Kingdom.

A range of further resources for this book are available on the companion website: www.routledge.com/cw/cartwright.

Routledge advanced texts in economics and finance

1. **Financial Econometrics**
   Peijie Wang

2. **Macroeconomics for Developing Countries (2nd edition)**
   Raghbendra Jha

3. **Advanced Mathematical Economics**
   Rakesh Vohra

4. **Advanced Econometric Theory**
   John S. Chipman

5. **Understanding Macroeconomic Theory**
   John M. Barron, Bradley T. Ewing and Gerald J. Lynch

6. **Regional Economics**
   Roberta Capello

7. **Mathematical Finance**
   Core theory, problems and statistical algorithms
   Nikolai Dokuchaev

8. **Applied Health Economics**
   Andrew M. Jones, Nigel Rice, Teresa Bago d'Uva and Silvia Balia

9. **Information Economics**
   Urs Birchler and Monika Bütler

10. **Financial Econometrics (2nd edition)**
    Peijie Wang

11. **Development Finance**
    Debates, dogmas and new directions
    Stephen Spratt

12. **Culture and Economics**
    On values, economics and international business
    Eelke de Jong

13. **Modern Public Economics (2nd edition)**
    Raghbendra Jha

14. **Introduction to Estimating Economic Models**
    Atsushi Maki

15. **Advanced Econometric Theory**
    John Chipman

16. **Behavioral Economics**
    Edward Cartwright

17. **Essentials of Advanced Macroeconomic Theory**
Ola Olsson

18. **Behavioral Economics and Finance**
Michelle Baddeley

19. **Applied Health Economics (2nd edition)**
Andrew M. Jones, Nigel Rice, Teresa Bago d'Uva and Silvia Balia

20. **Real Estate Economics**
A point to point handbook
Nicholas G. Pirounakis

21. **Finance in Asia**
Institutions, regulation and policy
Qiao Liu, Paul Lejot and Douglas Arner

22. **Behavioral Economics (2nd edition)**
Edward Cartwright

Behavioral Economics

Second edition

Edward Cartwright

LONDON AND NEW YORK

First published 2011
by Routledge
This edition published 2014 by Routledge
2 Park Square, Milton Park, Abingdon, Oxon OX14 4RN

and by Routledge
711 Third Avenue, New York, NY 10017

Routledge is an imprint of the Taylor & Francis Group, an informa business

British Library Cataloguing in Publication Data
A catalogue record for this book is available from the British Library

Library of Congress Cataloging in Publication Data
Cartwright, Edward.
Behavioral economics/Edward Cartwright.
pages cm
Revised edition of the author's Behavioral economics published in 2011.
Includes bibliographical references and index.
1.Economics—Psychological aspects. I. Title.
HB74.P8C37 2014
330.01'9—dc23

2013038838

ISBN: 978–0–415–73761–6 (hbk)
ISBN: 978–0–415–73764–7 (pbk)
ISBN: 978–1–315–81789–7 (ebk)

Typeset in Times New Roman
by RefineCatch Limited, Bungay, Suffolk

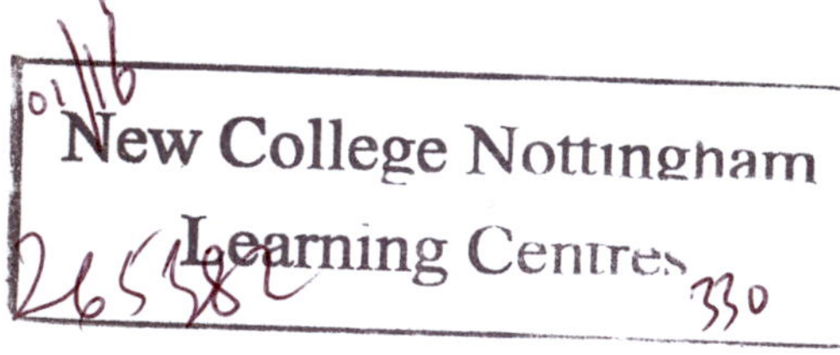

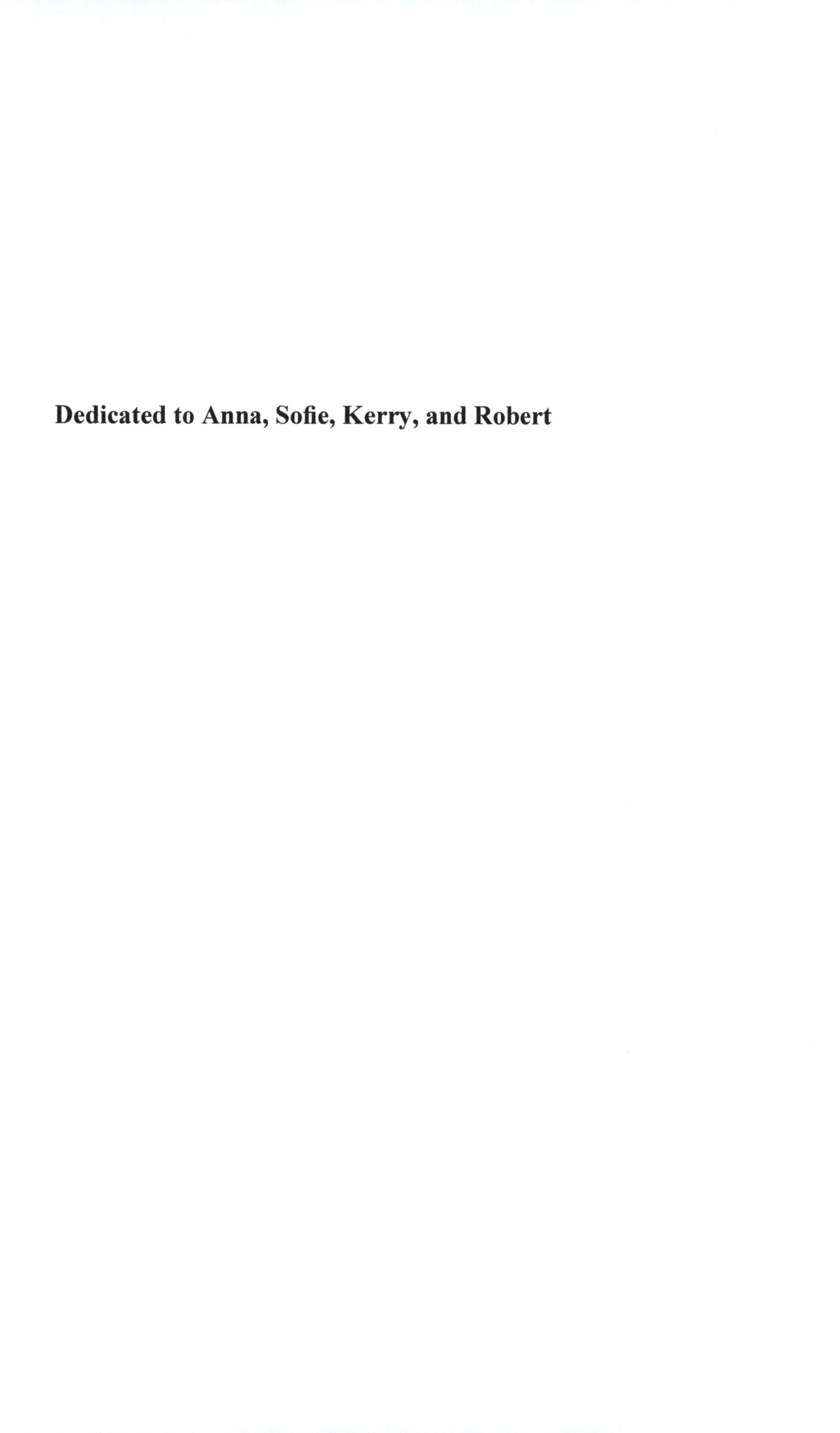

Dedicated to Anna, Sofie, Kerry, and Robert

Contents

Figures

Tables

Preface

The first edition of this book came about from teaching a course called Strategy and Games to first-year undergraduates. The idea of the course was to illustrate through classroom experiments some of the basic ideas of economics and game theory. In teaching that course my interest and knowledge of behavioral economics grew a lot; as did my frustration at the limited resources available to students wanting to learn more about this fascinating area of economics. Eventually, I decided it was time to write a book.

My basic objective when writing the book was to convey both the excitement and the importance of behavioral economics. I wanted to explain the basic principles, ideas, and results of behavioral economics and show how fascinating they are. I also wanted to illustrate through applications why behavioral economics is fundamentally important in understanding the world around us. I wanted a book that was accessible to a general reader, not just those trained in economics and comfortable with algebra.

This second edition builds on the first edition. Behavioral economics is an evolving subject and so there is always new material to add, and updates to take note of. There are, for example, new sections on deception and on team decision making. A host of new applications are also considered, including tax evasion, development economics, environmental economics, and industrial organization.

I could not have written this book without those who have contributed to the literature on behavioral economics and given me such great material to work with. Particular thanks are due to those who made my job so easy by writing papers over many years that, when put together, gave very clear insights into economic behavior. I would also like to thank the many people who have given me useful feedback on the first edition of the book. I should, though, make clear that the opinions expressed in this book are mine, and not necessarily those of the researchers whose work I refer to.

A lot of thanks is due to my wife Anna, who has helped so much in writing this and the earlier edition of the book. On a personal level, she has been patient and supportive while I wrote them. On a practical level, she is my greatest critic, never happy until everything is explained as fully and clearly as possible; she is also a great source of new ideas and new ways of thinking about old ideas. I should also thank all the students and colleagues connected with the Strategy and Games course, for teaching me so much. Finally, I want to give a big thanks to Myrna Wooders who, as well as being a fantastic person to know, has long been, and continues to be, a great inspiration and mentor.

Part I

Introduction

1 An introduction to behavioral economics

> However beautiful the strategy, you should occasionally look at the results.
>
> Sir Winston Churchill

It seems natural to start the book by asking, what is behavioral economics? That's a tough question, but I will give you three answers. You might think that this is two too many, but, if we put all three together, we get a definition of behavioral economics that I am happy with. So, here's the first answer:

> Behavioral economics is about understanding economic behavior and its consequences. It's about understanding why someone buys a hotdog, goes to work, saves for retirement, gives to charity, gets a qualification, sells an old car, gambles on a horse race, cannot quit smoking, etc. It's also about understanding whether people make good or bad choices, and could be helped to make better choices.

I like this definition, because I want to know the answer to all those questions. The problem is that we end up with far too broad a definition to be very useful. So, we need something a bit different.

For that something different, we can use the fact that economists already have a fantastic model with which to try and understand economic behavior and its consequences. You can find this **standard economic model** in any economics textbook, and it gives us a beautiful story of how things *might* work. We can, for example, derive demand and supply curves, solve for equilibrium prices and quantities, and design mechanisms or policy to increase efficiency and social welfare.

The potential problem with this standard economic model is that it is based on some strong assumptions. For example, it assumes people can be approximated by a **homo economicus** who is rational, calculating and selfish, has unlimited computational capacity, and never makes systematic mistakes. It also assumes **market institutions** work and so, for instance, prices should converge, as if by magic, to equilibrium. There is no obvious reason why humans can be well approximated by homo economicus, or why market institutions should work. This leads to my second definition:

> Behavioral economics is about testing the standard economic model on humans, seeing when it works and when it does not, and asking whether it can be tweaked, or given an overhaul, to better fit what we observe.

This is a more practical and specific definition, but it does leave open the question of how we are going to test and tweak the model. After all, surely economists have been testing the model all along? Well, unfortunately, we now know the standard economic model is flexible enough that it can be manipulated to explain just about any anomaly we ever observe. We somehow need to step out of this trap. That leads to my third and final definition:

> Behavioral economics is about applying insights from laboratory experiments, psychology, and other social sciences in economics.

We will, therefore, be guided by the evidence on human behavior and psychology, both in testing and in tweaking or overhauling the standard economic model. In short, we will replace homo economicus with homo sapiens.

If you combine all three definitions, I think we can strike a nice balance. Behavioral economics is about working constructively with the standard economic model to get a better understanding of economic behavior. The objective is definitely not to criticize the standard economic model, or accentuate the negatives. Testing the standard model is a means to an end, and that end is to understand economic behavior as best we can.

Behavioral economics has really come of age in the last 40 years or so, and so a lot of progress has been made. Various things could have happened as we started to put the standard economic model to the test. The model could have worked perfectly; that would have been fantastic news for economics, but not so exciting for the future of behavioral economics. At the other extreme, the model could have proved useless; that would be bad news all round (except for those who like to poke fun at economics). What has actually happened is an exciting mix in which the model sometimes seems to work very well, sometimes to work very badly, but most of the time is not far off, and with a bit of tweaking gets a lot better.

This is exciting because it means that behavioral economics can teach us a lot. It can tell us when the standard economic model does a good job and when not, and it can tell us how to change the model to get a better fit with reality. That is progress, and that is why behavioral economics is revolutionizing economics and our ability to understand economic behavior. In this book I hope to talk you through some of the main results and insights of behavioral economics in order that you can see for yourself how exciting and informative it is.

This chapter will set the scene a little by introducing some basic ideas and concepts, before previewing the rest of the book.

1.1 The history and controversies of behavioral economics

Behavioral economics has an interesting and checkered history. I will not delve too deeply into that history here, but an overview is useful because it will allow me to expand on the motivations behind behavioral economics. I will also explain some of the controversies and debates that surround it.

These controversies and debates still rumble on, and so it is helpful to have some understanding of them before you see what behavioral economics has to offer.

It is difficult to say when behavioral economics began, but I am going to credit Adam Smith with being its founder. Any student of economics should be familiar with Adam Smith's book *An Inquiry into the Causes of the Wealth of Nations*, first published in 1776. In that book Smith famously explained the invisible hand of the market. Less well known to most economists is a book that Smith first published in 1759, called *The Theory of Moral Sentiments*. It was actually in this book that the invisible hand first made an appearance. More interesting, for our purpose, is how Smith explains that people are not motivated solely by self-interest, but also feel a natural sympathy with others, and have a natural sense of virtue.

In short, in *The Theory of Moral Sentiments*, Smith talks about many things that in the last 30 years or so have become major issues in behavioral economics. For example, a theme through many parts of his book is the importance of reward and punishment (something we will pick up on in Chapter seven). Another theme is the influence of custom and fashion (which we will pick up on in Chapter five). In my mind Adam Smith comfortably does enough to be the father of behavioral economics. The intriguing question is why we had to wait over 200 years for the ideas that he talked about to be taken seriously by economists.

That turns out to be slightly the wrong question, because psychology did go hand in hand with economics for a long time after Adam Smith. Early economists gave much weight to emotions, impulses, stimulus, morals, and the like. For example, the law of diminishing marginal utility, one of the most fundamental principles of the standard economic model, was based on psychological ideas; economists would often appeal to the work of psychologists in supporting and developing their work. At the beginning of the twentieth century, however, economics turned away from psychology, and behavioral economics, if we can call it that, disappeared for over half a century.

This shift was initiated by Vilfredo Pareto. In a letter dated 1897 Pareto writes: 'Pure political economy has therefore a great interest in relying as little as possible on the domain of psychology.' This is presumably why, when he published a paper in 1900 outlining a new approach to the theory of choice, he claims as one of its main achievements that 'every psychological analysis is eliminated' (these quotes taken from Bruni and Sugden 2007). Why would we want to rid economics of psychology, and how is it possible to do so?

It is easier to start with the latter question. Psychology can be taken out of economics by focusing on choice rather than desire. Instead of trying to work out why people do things, we can make inferences based solely on what they do. To quote again from Pareto: 'I am not interested in the reason why man is indifferent between [one thing and another]: I notice the pure and naked fact.' This approach makes a lot of sense, because it allowed Pareto, and subsequent economists, to abstract away from difficult psychological questions and develop a mathematical theory of rational choice. If people are rational then they will reveal their desires through their choices and so we only need focus on choice.

Asking, as Pareto did, what happens if people are rational is a good, logical thing to do because it provides a natural benchmark to work with. The same could be said of asking, as Adam Smith did in discussing the invisible hand, what happens if people are selfish. Assuming for mathematical convenience that people are rational and selfish clearly does not, however, mean that people actually are rational or selfish. Adam Smith clearly recognized this, and Pareto did so too by distinguishing when rational choice should or should not be expected to approximate what people do.

The problem is that these caveats can easily be forgotten in the beauty or simplicity of the argument. Adam Smith's conjecture that someone, 'by pursuing his own interest, frequently promotes that of the society more effectually than when he intends to promote it', is truly intriguing. Similarly, Pareto's new theory of choice seemed widely applicable. In the face of such appeal and convenience it became easy to overlook the fact that people are neither rational nor selfish; homo economicus became king, and economics became very distant from psychology.

Interestingly, homo economicus became ever cleverer as the twentieth century progressed, Pareto's caveats long since forgotten. The assumption of rational expectations, for instance, meant that homo economicus knew far more about the workings of the economy than any economist. As behavioral economist Richard Thaler wrote, while behavioral economics was still in its relative infancy (1990: 203):

> The problem seems to be that while economists have gotten increasingly sophisticated and clever, consumers have remained decidedly human. This leaves open the question of whose behavior we are trying to model. Along these lines, at an NBER conference a couple of years ago I explained the difference between my models and Robert Barro's by saying that he assumes the agents in his model are as smart as he is, while I portray people as being as dumb as I am.

In my mind, to assume people are like rational and selfish homo economicus is the most natural, objective place to begin thinking about modeling economic behavior. Indeed, in many of the chapters that follow I will start by asking what a selfish, rational person would do; so you will hopefully see why it's a good place to start. The crucial point, though, is that it is the start point and not the end point. It is the best way to start thinking about modeling economic behavior but not necessarily the best way to model economic behavior. A crucial distinction!

The standard economic model does, though, march ever onwards, and behavioral economics has so far done relatively little to quell the tide. Many economists continue to derive ever more complicated and elaborate results based on the standard economic model. Whether these results are any use in understanding what happens on planet Earth, I am not so sure. That's why we need behavioral economics, and that's why the time would inevitably come for behavioral economics to be reborn.

1.1.1 Behavioral economics is reborn

From the 1960s onwards, psychology gradually made a return to economics. I would suggest four distinct elements to its comeback. Let's look at each in turn.

The first element I would call the 'you cannot be serious attack', and give the main credit to Herbert Simon. Simon seriously questioned the sense of approximating people by homo economicus. For example, in a paper published in 1955, he solves for how a rational person should behave before stating: 'My first empirical proposition is that there is a complete lack of evidence that, in actual human choice situations of any complexity, these computations can be, or are in fact, performed.' Instead, Simon suggested looking at the information and computational capacities that humans possess, and using this as the starting point for economic models. Recognizing the limitations faced by humans led to the term, 'bounded rationality'.

Simon won the Nobel Prize in Economics in 1978 for his 'pioneering research into the decision-making process within economic organizations'. His calls, however, to replace homo economicus with something more human-like fell largely on deaf ears. Symptomatic of this was Herbert Simon leaving the Graduate School of Industrial Administration at Carnegie Mellon University for the psychology department. In his autobiography (Simon 1991) he writes: 'My economist friends have long since given up on me, consigning me to psychology or some other distant wasteland.'

One thing notably lacking in much of what Simon wrote was proof that homo economicus is not a good approximation of how people behave. He may have thought this was obvious (many do), but the lack of any formal proof made it easy for economists to ignore his work. The same could not be said of the second element I want to talk about. I will call this the 'your assumptions are wrong attack', and give the main credit to Daniel Kahneman and Amos Tversky. The approach here is one of demonstrating that people really are very different to homo economicus. One way to make the point is to get people, including economists, to answer simple questions such as this (which I took from Thaler and Sunstein 2008):

> A bat and ball cost $1.10 in total. The bat costs $1.00 more than the ball. How much does the ball cost?

If you said ten cents, then you are like most people, but you need to think again, because the answer is five. Here's another famous example from Tversky and Kahneman (1983):

> Bill is 34 years old. He is intelligent, but unimaginative, compulsive, and generally lifeless. In school, he was strong in mathematics but weak in social studies and humanities.
>
> Rank the following eight statements from most probable to least probable:
>
> Bill is a physician who plays poker for a hobby.
> Bill is an architect.
> Bill is an accountant.
> Bill plays jazz for a hobby.
> Bill surfs for a hobby.
> Bill is a reporter.
> Bill is an accountant who plays jazz for a hobby.
> Bill climbs mountains for a hobby.

If you are like most then you said it is more likely Bill is an accountant, than Bill is an accountant who plays jazz for a hobby, than Bill plays jazz for a hobby. Now, how can it be more likely that Bill is an accountant who plays jazz, than Bill plays jazz? It cannot.

If most people make mistakes like this, how can we possibly expect them to do the complex calculations that homo economicus routinely does? With this, and many other examples, very clear evidence was provided that people are not like homo economicus, or at least not like the version assumed in the standard economic model. Different assumptions, therefore, seemed sensible. To quote from a paper that Tversky *et al.* published in 1981 (p. 453):

> The definition of rationality has been much debated, but there is general agreement that rational choices should satisfy some elementary requirements of consistency and coherence. In this article we describe decision problems in which people systematically violate the requirements of consistency and coherence, and we trace these violations to the psychological principles that govern the perception of decision problems and the evaluation of options.

Daniel Kahneman won the Nobel Prize in Economics in 2002 for 'having integrated insights from psychological research into economic science, especially concerning human judgment and decision-making under uncertainty' (Amos Tversky was, unfortunately, no longer alive). Even so, I am not so sure their work, and that of others in a similar vein, was ultimately that crucial in the comeback of psychology in economics. That's because the attack was still too easy to dodge for economists confident in the standard economic model. After all, was it not obvious that people are not like homo economicus? The real issue is whether models in which people are approximated by homo economicus made good predictions. The early work of Kahneman, Tversky, and others had less to say on this issue.

To illustrate the point we can get to the third element, which I will call the 'markets work revelation', and give the main credit to Vernon Smith. Starting in 1955 Smith performed a series of experiments to see whether basic predictions of the standard economic model about markets would prove correct. We will look at these experiments in more detail in the next chapter, but basically the predictions proved good. A stunning result! Maybe, therefore, it does not matter if people are not like homo economicus; the standard economic model can still work.

These initial experiments led to a continuing line of research on market institutions that to my mind provide the most important results to have come out of behavioral economics. In 2002 Vernon Smith won the Nobel Prize in Economics 'for having established laboratory experiments as a tool in empirical economic analysis, especially in the study of alternative market mechanisms'. I am still though reluctant to think that this work had too much of a hand in the comeback of psychology in economics. That's because, while moving beyond the standard economic model, it largely confirmed that the standard economic model was getting something right. Why, therefore, would we need behavioral economics?

While all three of the elements I have discussed so far were instrumental in the comeback of behavioral economics, you have probably guessed by now that it is to the last element that I would give most importance. This final element I will call the 'what equilibrium to choose problem', and give the main credit to Reinhard Selten. The problem became apparent with the rapid progress of game theory in the 1950s and 1960s. Game theory looks to capture behavior in strategic situations, and meant the demands on homo economicus became ever more stringent. Not only should he or she be selfish, rational, and more clever than any economist, homo economicus also needs to be telepathic in order to predict what others will do (and even that is not enough). Basically, in strategic situations, it usually becomes ambiguous what homo economicus should do; it is ambiguous what is the rational thing to do.

The technical way to express this problem is to say that there are multiple equilibria. Somehow we need to try and say which of the equilibria 'makes more sense' or 'seems more likely to occur'. That's a bit like throwing darts at a dartboard while blindfold. To have any chance of success it makes sense to question how people might think or reason in such strategic situations and observe what people do when they play games. In other words, it made sense to draw a little on psychology and to run controlled experiments.

In the late 1950s Selten began running experiments. These first experiments were primarily concerned with industrial economics and ultimately led to important theoretical ideas like subgame perfection, something we will look at in Chapter six. The main thing, though, was that experiments increasingly became seen as a useful way to learn more about economic behavior. To quote from an autobiographical sketch by Selten (1994),

> More and more I came to the conclusion that purely speculative approaches like that of our paper of 1962 are of limited value. The structure of boundedly rational economic behavior cannot be invented in the armchair, it must be explored experimentally.

Selten won the Nobel Prize in Economics in 1994 together with John Nash and John Harsanyi 'for their pioneering analysis of equilibria in the theory of non-cooperative games'. More than anything else I think that game theory was instrumental in the rebirth of behavioral economics. That's because it meant that the next logical step in developing the standard economic model was to draw from psychology and use experiments. The standard economic model had hit a dead end and behavioral economics was needed to move it forward.

If we put together these four different elements in the rebirth of behavioral economics, it is no surprise that it has made a strong comeback. Behavioral economics has the potential to improve our understanding of economic behavior from so many different angles, and this eventually shone through. (Before moving on, it would be remiss of me not to mention that it did so through the work of many more than just the five people to whom I gave credit above.)

1.1.2 Behavioral economics and policy

If behavioral economics can improve our understanding of the economy, then we would be able to put it to good use. Consequently, I will add a fifth element into the mix. This fifth element has little to do with the rebirth of behavioral economics but is proving instrumental in its rapid growth. I will call it the 'policies that work problem'. By its nature economics is an applied subject; it should inform on how to alleviate poverty, avoid unemployment, regulate industry, and so on. Many, however, have become frustrated by the inability of economists to provide good answers to the important policy questions!

Increasingly, this problem is being traced back to an over-reliance on the standard economic model. The standard economic model suggests that intervention is only needed where markets fail because of things like externalities, imperfect information, or imperfect competition; if markets work, then people make the rational decision. So, if people do not save for retirement, then they clearly want to end their life in poverty. If someone buys a mortgage they cannot afford, then they knowingly gambled everything on house prices rising. Similarly, if someone becomes addicted to heroin, then they chose to do so taking into account their financial constraints. To anyone other than economists these kinds of statements sound weird. They also sound weird to a behavioral economist.

Once we take into account the mistakes people make and the difficulties of coordinating on an equilibrium, then the rationale for intervention becomes stronger. But, it is important to realize that behavioral economics does not prescribe big government, rather it prescribes clever government! I would distinguish two distinct elements to this.

One thing behavioral economics does is give fresh insight on what policies will work and what will not. For instance, the traditional approach to increase saving for retirement has been complex tax breaks; these are the kinds of things that appeal to homo economicus but are ignored by homo sapiens. A behavioral economics approach suggests things like the save more tomorrow plan that I will look at in Chapter eleven; these are the kinds of things that appeal to homo sapiens but are ignored by not homo economicus.

Another thing that behavioral economics does is make us question the purpose of policy. This is because the emphasis turns more towards measuring happiness, than measuring rational choice. In fact, we shall see that choice can be influenced by all kinds of context effects like a 50-percent-off sticker or TV advert on the consequences of evading tax; this makes the very notion of rational choice become somewhat meaningless. Suppose, for instance, Anna 'loves a bargain' and cannot resist buying a handbag that she has absolutely no need for, because the price is reduced 50 percent. We might call this a 'mistake' because Anna was only won over by the 50-percent-off sticker. But, if buying the handbag makes her happy then was it a mistake? Is Anna going to be any happier if we point out to her that she has just been duped into buying a handbag she does not need? Will she be any happier if the government bans misleading price offers? Similarly, suppose Anna always pays her taxes because she overestimates the probability of being caught evading tax. Will she be any happier if we point out to her that she has been duped by the advertising of the tax authorities? Clever policy should make people happier, and behavioral economics gives us a better picture of what makes people happier.

Behavioral economics, therefore, offers a fresh approach to economic policy. Indeed, it is arguably in terms of policy prescription that behavioral economics differs most from the standard economic model. Behavioral economics has started to deliver on its promise and make a real difference, not only in economics, but to people's lives.

This seems as good a point as any to also highlight that behavioral economics is not just about microeconomics and finance. It can easily seem that way given that the focus is on individual decision making. Behavioral economics, however, has a lot to offer across the spectrum of economics, including macroeconomics. This is forcefully argued by George Akerlof and Robert Shiller in their book *Animal Spirits: How human psychology drives the economy, and why it matters for global capitalism*. Concepts such as wage and price stickiness, money illusion, fairness, and social norms are fundamental to understanding how the aggregate economy works. Behavioral economics can have a big role, therefore, in informing macroeconomic policy. For instance, one thing we have learnt is that being unemployed makes people particularly unhappy. This suggests that reducing unemployment should take center stage in designing policy.

1.1.3 The different faces of behavioral economics

In suggesting, as I have, that there were four distinct elements in the rebirth of behavioral economics, it is not too surprising that behavioral economics is somewhat splintered into subtly different sub-fields. In this book I am going to use a very broad and encompassing notion of behavioral economics that tries to cut across any arbitrary divisions. Divisions do exist, however, and it is worth knowing something about these, and some terms used to describe them that you may come across.

I will start with the notion of **bounded rationality** that we already came across in talking about Herbert Simon. The idea here is to recognize the constraints that people face, in terms of computational capacity, memory, information, time, and the like. We should not, for instance, assume that homo economicus can do mathematical calculations that a human cannot do, or can remember more things than a human can. This sounds clear enough, but there are two quite different ways in which the idea has been put into practice.

Today, the term bounded rationality is commonly reserved for work in which the constraints people face are explicitly modeled. The approach is thus one of solving for what a rational person will do if she has, say, limited memory. For instance, what password should Anna use on her computer if she knows she might forget it? With this approach it is still assumed that people can be approximated by a selfish and rational homo economicus: just one with a bit less memory and mathematical ability. Such an approach is prone to something called the infinite regress problem, that I will talk about in the next chapter, but does give us an idea of how a person can optimally cope with their limitations, or bounded rationality.

This common usage of the term is somewhat removed from what Herbert Simon originally envisaged. More in keeping with his work is the idea of **simple heuristics that make us smart**. This approach starts with the idea that people use heuristics, or 'rules of thumb', to make decisions. For example, Anna might use the same password whenever she is asked to give a password; this way she is less likely to forget the password for her computer. Whether or not heuristics like this are optimal is not really considered important. More important is to find what heuristics people do use, and to think about the consequences.

This approach most naturally fits with the work of psychologists, like Daniel Kahneman and Amos Tversky. Heuristics, however, tend to come with biases, and sometimes it's the bias that gets more of the headlines. For example, a reasonable heuristic in repetitive situations is: 'do what I did last time'. Anna, for instance, might always go grocery shopping in the same store. Sensible though this may be, it can lead to a **status quo bias** in which she fails to change her behavior 'often enough'. Maybe she keeps going to the same store even though a cheaper and better store opened nearer to her house. Such biases usually go by the name **cognitive biases**.

In exploring the connection between simple heuristics and cognitive bias it is useful to introduce the notion of **ecological rationality**. This recognizes that a heuristic can be smart or dumb depending on the environment in which it is used. For example, Anna may use one heuristic when shopping in her local superstore and a completely different one when shopping at a bazaar in the Middle East. Each heuristic is matched to the context. Cognitive bias is most likely to result when a heuristic is used out of context or in an environment for which it was not designed. Haggling, for example, is unlikely to get you a great deal at the local supermarket.

Cognitive biases are simplest to see in well-designed experiments, and experiments have long been the most common form of research method in psychology. In economics the story is a bit different, with experiments basically unheard of until the early ones involving Vernon Smith and Reinhard Selten. Since then they have become progressively more common, but the proportion of academic economists who have run an experiment is still way below the corresponding proportion of psychologists. Where I work at the University of Kent, for example,

I estimate the respective proportions at 15 percent and 100 percent; this is typical. Consequently, one still often sees the term **experimental economics** as referring to any economic research based on experiments.

As more and more economists use experimental methods, however, the term experimental economics becomes ever more non-descriptive. Experiments are now being used in very different ways and in very different subject areas. Sometimes, for instance, as with the market experiments of Vernon Smith, the focus is on institutions or aggregate behavior, and there may be relatively little interest in individual behavior. Other times, as with the experiments of Reinhard Selten, there is a greater focus on individual behavior and testing theories of individual behavior. Experiments have also been run across the subject boundaries of economics from game theory to macroeconomics.

The contrasts between game theory and bounded rationality on the one side and experimental economics and research on cognitive biases on the other can be quite stark. As far as I am concerned, however, it is all behavioral economics. Good behavioral economics can involve theoretical research with no experiments. It can also involve experimental research with little or no theory. It seems natural, therefore, to split things according to subject of investigation and not method of investigation. That's how I will do things in this book, trying to mix theory and experiment. It's notable, however, that some big gaps in our knowledge still exist between theory and experiment; these are the kinds of gaps that will hopefully be filled by the next generation of behavioral economists.

Before I finish, a few more terms you may come across seem worth mentioning. I will start with economic psychology. In principle, **economic psychology** is a subdiscipline of psychology that deals with the psychology of economic decision making. For example, it might ask what cognitive processes were used in deciding to buy this book. The difference between behavioral economics and economic psychology is sometimes a little subtle, and I will come back to the difference shortly. But it seems fair to say that a lot of what has historically been called behavioral economics would probably be more appropriately called economic psychology. The trouble is that behavioral economics needs to draw heavily on economic psychology, and that's why the dividing line becomes a bit blurred. It's also why a lot of what I am going to talk about would probably be more appropriately called economic psychology!

The next term I want to mention is behavioral finance. As the name suggests, **behavioral finance** is, in principle, a subset of behavioral economics that deals with financial decision making and financial behavior. I say 'in principle' because in reality behavioral finance has taken on something of a life of its own. As detailed more in Section 1.3.2, I will cover key issues and results of behavioral finance. Indeed, many of the applications I will look at will be from behavioral finance.

Finally, I want to introduce neuroeconomics. **Neuroeconomics** gets its own chapter in the book, and so probably needs little mention here. But I will mention that it is the latest development in behavioral economics, and brings neuroscience to bear on economics. It seems safe to say that neuroeconomics has contributed more to neuroscience than it has to economics, so far. For that reason it remains somewhat controversial, but only time will tell whether it can significantly advance economics. And behavioral economics is not short of controversy, as I now want to explain.

1.1.4 Debate and controversy

Yes, behavioral economics does have its controversy and disputes. Economists question whether we need behavioral economics, and whether we need economic experiments. Behavioral economists question the methods and techniques of others, such as the need for neuroeconomics. There is nothing unusual in academics disagreeing, but it can be useful to know something about the disagreements. Here are four interesting debates for you to think about, both now and while you read through the remainder of the book.

Let's start with the big question, one that I talked about a little in tracing the decline and rebirth of behavioral economics:

> Is it enough to assume people can be approximated by homo economicus, or do we need psychologically grounded assumptions?

Common sense might suggest that we do need psychologically grounded assumptions. The **methodology of positive economics**, advocated by Milton Friedman, suggests things are not so obvious. The basis of this methodology is that a model and theory should be judged on its predictions and not its assumptions. Friedman (1953: 40–41) writes:

> One confusion that has been particularly rife and has done much damage is confusion about the role of 'assumptions' in economic analysis. A meaningful scientific hypothesis or theory typically asserts that certain forces are, and other forces are not, important in understanding a particular class of phenomena. . . .
>
> Such a theory cannot be tested by comparing its 'assumptions' directly with 'reality.' Indeed, there is no meaningful way in which this can be done.
>
> Complete 'realism' is clearly unattainable, and the question whether a theory is realistic 'enough' can be settled only by seeing whether it yields predictions that are good enough for the purpose in hand or that are better than predictions from alternative theories.

That people are not like homo economicus is not, therefore, reason to *assume* they are not like homo economicus. We need to look at the predictions. To illustrate this distinction, suppose we see Anna go into the bookstore and are interested in whether she will buy this book. We come up with two models of what she does; call them the 'cognitive model' and the 'choice model'. Suppose that the cognitive model better describes the thought processes that Anna will go through when deciding to buy the book. Suppose that the choice model better predicts whether or not Anna will buy the book. Which model is better?

You might say that this is a trick question, because something that better describes her thought processes should better predict what she does. Unfortunately, however, the need to use models that are tractable abstractions from a complex reality makes it common to face such a dilemma. So, you do need to make your choice!

To a psychologist, the cognitive model is surely best, because it gives a better description of what Anna was thinking; this is good economic psychology. To an economist, the choice model is surely best because we get a more accurate economic prediction; this is good behavioral economics. It is not so obvious, therefore, that psychologically grounded assumptions are better for economics, and we will see examples in this book where models with psychological grounded assumptions do a lot worse than the standard economic model.

Search though we might, therefore, for the 'perfect model' that combines the best elements of both the cognitive and choice model, we may not find it. Behavioral economics needs to prove itself by coming up with good economic predictions, and better predictions than that of the standard economic model.

This leads on to the second debate that I want to talk about:

> Should more emphasis be put on things that the standard economic model does well or badly?

An interesting example of this debate playing itself out came after the Behavioral Foundations of Economic Theory conference held in 1985. The conference organizers stressed 'a growing body of evidence – mainly of an experimental nature – that has documented systematic departures from the dictates of rational economic behavior' (Hogarth and Reder 1987). Vernon Smith (1991), who was present at the conference, preferred to stress 'a growing body of evidence that is consistent with the implications of rational models'! Elsewhere, Smith (1998: 105) wrote that 'Our scientific advance is handicapped by our failure to pursue the exciting implications of the fact that things sometimes work better than we had a right to expect from our abstract interpretations of theory'.

It is clear that the argument carries on to this day. Some behavioral economists prefer to emphasize the good, and some the bad. Why no agreement? One reason is probably the distinction between assumptions and predictions. Behavioral economists from an economics background, like Vernon Smith, have usually been the ones emphasizing what the standard economic model does well, and that's probably because they more naturally focus on the predictions, not the assumptions. Those coming from a psychology background seem more prone to emphasize what the standard economic does badly, probably because they more naturally focus on the limitations of the assumptions. If the assumptions of the standard economic model are pretty bad but the predictions are often pretty good, then we can see why there may be grounds for disagreement.

This is far from the end of the story, however, because people can also disagree on how to evaluate predictions. This partly stems from how far people are prepared to push the standard model. As game theorist and experimental economist Ken Binmore (2008: F249) explains:

> At one end of the spectrum, there are conservative experimenters who defend traditional economic theory by looking at situations in which it predicts fairly well. At the other end of the spectrum, there are radical experimenters who seek to show that traditional economic theory does not work at all by looking at situations in which its predictions fail.

Even on relatively safe ground, however, there can be disagreement. To see why, consider this question:

> What should we conclude if the standard economic model only predicts well what experienced people do, i.e. people familiar with a task or decision?

This turns out to be a tough question to answer. The problem is that in many instances we find that the standard economic model gives a poor prediction of what happens the first time someone faces a particular situation, but a much better prediction the fourth, fifth, sixth time they face the same situation. This is the **discovered preference hypothesis**, that the standard economic model is a good predictor if people have had ample opportunity to learn from experience.

There is debate over the validity of the discovered preference hypothesis, and we shall see situations where no amount of experience helps the standard economic model predict well. This, however, gets us back to a half-full or half-empty debate. More interesting is to ask what we should conclude if the discovered preference hypothesis is correct. This will depend on whether people have ample opportunity to learn from experience in most of the things we are interested in. Arguably they do not because there are many important things that a person only does once or a few times in their life, like retiring, choosing a career, buying a house, and so on. We want to be able to predict what will happen in these situations too, so maybe the standard economic model is not so great after all? I shall conveniently avoid that question and finish with a much easier one:

> Should behavioral economics look to rewrite economics from a psychological perspective, or adapt the standard economic model to take account of psychological insight?

Some would probably like to start from scratch, and scrap the standard economic model. Maybe that is what you expected of behavioral economics. This is not, however, what behavioral economics is about. Behavioral economics is very much about working with the standard economic model, whether it is a good predictor or not. That's because, as mentioned earlier, it is the natural starting point. Daniel Kahneman writes (2003: 1449), for example, about his work with Amos Tversky that: 'The rational-agent model was our starting point and the main source of our null hypotheses.' To quote from two other leading behavioral economists, Colin Camerer and George Loewenstein (2004: 3): 'At the core of behavioral economics is the conviction that increasing the realism of the psychological underpinnings of economic analysis will improve economics on its own terms.'

1.1.5 Too far or not far enough

Disagreement on the kinds of questions we have just discussed means that behavioral economics has no shortage of critics. Some criticize it for not being radical enough. Others criticize it for going too far! As you learn more about behavioral economics it is useful to be aware of this criticism and see how it relates back to the questions above.

Pretty much all criticism stems from the same basic concern, namely that behavioral economics is too much like the standard economic model. As we have seen, behavioral economics takes the standard economic model as its starting point. In practice, this means that behavioral models are almost always the standard economic model plus something new. That something new might be a reference point, loss aversion, greater weight on the present than the future, a desire to earn no less than others, and so on. The basic assumptions of the standard economic model are still, however, retained.

This means that behavioral models retain many non-psychologically grounded assumptions. Put another way, behavioral economics is firmly based on the methodology of positive economics. Some suggest that a more radical approach is needed. For example, in a recent critique of behavioral economics Berg and Gigerenzer (2010) write:

> The unrealistic models now being defended [in behavioral economics] are endowed with additional parameters given psychological labels, resting on the claim that people behave as if they are solving a complicated constrained optimization problem with bounds on self-interest, willpower, or computational capacity explicitly modeled in the objective function or constraint set. . . . To become more genuinely helpful in improving the predictive accuracy and descriptive realism of economic models, more attention to decision process will be required.

This brings us back to the debate on the methodology of positive economics: Will more attention to the decision process result in improved predictive accuracy? I cannot answer that question. I will, however, use this as an opportunity to warn against some of the hyperbole that surrounds behavioral economics, and a lot of hyperbole does surround behavioral economics! While behavioral economics is revolutionizing economics, it is not as radical a departure from the standard economic model as some would have you believe.

Let us turn now to those who criticize behavioral economics for going too far. If behavioral economics is the standard economic model plus something else, then it is no surprise that we can get a better fit. The danger is one of **over-fitting**. The basic critique goes something like this: The behavioral economist observes behavior that 'should not happen', according to the standard economic model, like

Anna borrowing at a high interest rate on a credit card while simultaneously saving for retirement at a low interest rate. We then come up with something that can 'explain' this anomaly, like an impulsive desire to buy expensive handbags while out shopping. We then congratulate ourselves on a better fit.

There are three related problems here. (i) Can we really be sure there is an anomaly? Maybe Anna will learn over time to not borrow so much on her credit card. (ii) If there is an anomaly, then maybe other things could explain it. How can we be sure an impulsive desire to buy handbags is the real cause? (iii) It is easy to come up with ad hoc explanations for observed anomalies. More difficult is to come up with **novel testable predictions** that are subsequently proved correct. Those who criticize behavioral economics for going too far would say that the extent of anomalies is overblown, the derived models are too ad hoc, and there is not enough focus on novel testable predictions. For instance, in an article critical of the methods being used in behavioral economics, Ken Binmore and Avner Shaked (2010) write:

> [T]he scientific gold standard is prediction. It is perfectly acceptable to propose a theory that fits existing experimental data and then use the data to calibrate the parameters of the model. But, before using the theory in applied work, the vital next step is to state the proposed domain of application of the theory and to make specific predictions that can be tested with data that was used neither in formulating the theory nor in calibrating its parameters. . . . [S]ome events are easier to predict than others. A good theory will successfully predict events that are difficult to predict. Choosing events that a theory is to predict in a manner that favors the theory – especially if done after the test experiment has been run – is unacceptable.

A further, related concern is the **external validity** of laboratory experiments. Behavioral economics draws heavily on lab experiments when looking for the existence of anomalies, comparing models, and testing predictions. Given, however, that lab experiments are typically very context specific, the concern is that we cannot infer much from them about real behavior. In a recent review of lab experiments Levitt and List (2007) write:

> Perhaps the most fundamental question in experimental economics is whether the findings from the lab are likely to provide reliable inferences outside of the laboratory. – [W]e argue that lab experiments generally exhibit a special type of scrutiny, a context that places extreme emphasis on the process by which decisions and allocations are reached, and a particular selection mechanism for participants. In contrast, many real-world markets are typified by a different type of scrutiny, little focus on process, and very different forms of self-selection of participants.

The issue here is not whether we should do experiments; the broad consensus is that experiments are an important tool of economic analysis. The issue is the balance between experiment and theory. Experiments are inevitably going to be somewhat artificial. For instance, experiments done in the field, rather than in the lab, are arguably even more context specific (a point I will return to in Chapter eight when looking at development economics). The key thing to guard against, therefore, is becoming over-reliant on experiments. Some would argue that behavioral economics is too quick to draw conclusions from lab experiments. This can easily lead to ad hoc models and overblown claims of anomalies.

What to make of all this criticism? It should definitely be taken seriously. There is a danger that behavioral economics is not focused enough on decision processes, that it is too ad hoc, and that it is over-reliant on experiments. Some 'findings' of behavioral economics will inevitably not stand the test of time. Taken as a whole, however, I think it is clear that behavioral economics has delivered. In particular, it has come up with many novel testable predictions that have proved correct, not only in the lab but also in real application. Indeed, over the last few decades behavioral economics has come under closer scrutiny than any other area of economics, and it has survived the test well. So, take note of the criticism but also be reassured that you can learn a lot from behavioral economics!

1.2 Some background on behavioral economics methods

We have already seen that behavioral economics involves both theory and experiment. In this section I want to briefly sketch a little more about the methods of behavioral economics and in particular give some background on economic experiments. Before doing so, I want to make clear that my objective is not to explain how to run experiments, or to perform statistical tests on the experimental data. These warrant books on their own and there are lots of good books out there (see the further reading at the end of the chapter). All I want to do is explain enough that you will be able to follow the rest of this book. That means, in particular, getting straight some terminology that I am going to use.

Rather than talk abstractly about experiments and theory I thought it would be more interesting to talk through some research that I did (with Federica Alberti and Anna Stepanova) while writing this book. This will give me a chance to introduce all the concepts you need at this stage. Other concepts will be introduced as and when needed or relevant in 'research methods boxes' that you will find throughout the book.

I will use the term **study** for a particular piece of research. The objective of our study was to see whether the amount of money people are endowed with in a threshold public good game has any affect on their ability to coordinate. That might not make much sense at this point, but do not worry because it should make more sense shortly. A study may be part of a more general **project**. Our ongoing project is to see how people can better coordinate in threshold public good games. The main part of this study involved running experiments, and so I will talk about that first.

1.2.1 Some background on experiments

To run an experiment we need people who are willing to take part. Those that do are given the title **subject** or participant. In order to recruit subjects we sent e-mails and placed adverts and eventually got the 120 volunteers we needed. Most of these were students at the University of Kent. Each subject was asked to come to a particular **experimental session** and we ran six sessions in all, with 20 people invited to come to each session. (We actually invited a few more, because the chance that 20 students will turn up on time in the right place is clearly quite small!) All the sessions took place in a computer lab at the University.

When the subjects arrived, after a brief introduction, they were each allocated to a computer. After this there was no talking until the experiment ended, and a subject could only see their own computer screen. Things were, therefore, completely anonymous, and subjects were reassured this would be the case. Beside their computer each subject would find an instruction sheet, which read something like this:

> In this experiment you will make decisions, and earn an amount of money that depends on what you and others choose. The money will be given to you at the end of the experiment in an envelope. Only you will know how much money you earned.
>
> You have been organised into groups of five. Each group will consist of the same five people for the duration of the experiment. The experiment will last for 25 rounds. In each period you will be required to make a decision, and your total earnings will depend on your decisions in all rounds.
>
> At the beginning of every round you, and all other members of your group, will receive 55 tokens. Each of you must decide, on your own, how many of the 55 tokens to allocate to a group account.
>
> If the total number of tokens allocated to the group account is 125 or more then you will each receive an additional 50 tokens.
>
> If the total number of tokens allocated to the group account is less than 125 then you will receive no additional tokens but will get back any tokens you allocated to the group account.
>
> So, at the end of the round:
>
> If the total number of tokens allocated to the group account ≥ 125, your earnings = initial 55 tokens − tokens allocated to group account + additional 50 tokens.
>
> If the total number of tokens allocated to the group account < 125, your earnings = initial 55 tokens.
>
> At the end of the session, you will be asked to fill in a short questionnaire. You will be paid in cash the total amount that you earned for all rounds in the session plus £2. Each token will be worth 0.5 pence.

Once all subjects had read the instructions the experiment would commence with everything taking place on computer (using an experimental economics program called z-tree). So, the first thing that would happen is each subject was asked to input how many tokens they wanted to allocate to the group account. To illustrate, in group one, subject one input 25, subject two input zero, and subjects three to five input 50, 25 and 10. The total number allocated was, therefore, 110 which was short of the 125 target. The subjects were told this and told their earnings were 55. That was the end of round one.

Similar happened in rounds two to 25. This did not take long and so the experiment was over after around 30 to 45 minutes. Once the last round had finished we worked out how much money each subject had earned and paid them in cash. The average subject earned around £10, which is not bad for 30 minutes.

One thing I want to highlight is that, in an experiment, subjects are typically asked to do the same thing several times. In this case they were asked to play the same threshold public good game 25 times. There are various reasons for doing this, of which the main one is to see how people learn with experience. For instance, the group I have just talked about were short of the target in round one and we might wonder how they will respond. In fact the total number of tokens allocated in round two went up to 161, well above the target. As you may have seen by now the term **round** keeps track of how far subjects have progressed through the experiment. (The word period is also used, but I will try and avoid this because we will use period for something slightly different.)

Hopefully, this gives you some idea of what a threshold public good game is (we are going to talk about them in more detail in Chapter six). Hopefully, it also gives you some idea of what an experiment is, and what it's like to take part in one. But what were we hoping to get out of this experiment?

The primary thing of interest in a threshold public good game is whether group members give enough to the group account to reach the threshold of 125. If this all seems a little abstract, then imagine five housemates who want to buy a new TV that costs $125. Between them they need to find enough to buy the TV or they go without. Broadly speaking, it is in their interests to reach the threshold, but there are good reasons why they may fall short. From prior research we know groups can be quite unsuccessful at reaching the threshold.

The specific question that motivated our study was whether groups will be more successful at achieving the threshold if they have more tokens to start with. The instructions above correspond to the case where subjects got 55 tokens, which you can think of as each housemate having $55 of spending money. What if they have $30 or $70; will they be any more or less successful at reaching the threshold?

This is relatively easy to test with experiments, because we can just give some groups 55 tokens to start with, some 30, some 70, and record how often groups reach the threshold. That's basically what we did. The term **experimental treatment** is used to distinguish these different versions of the experiment. We had five treatments, but I will just focus on the three of them that I have already mentioned. These are summarized in Figure 1.1, and correspond to subjects having 55, 30 or 70 tokens.

It is common to have one treatment called the **baseline treatment**, which serves as a reference point for comparison. In our study the treatment where subjects got 55 tokens was the baseline. We chose this as the baseline because it had already been used many times by other researchers. We thus have an expectation of what

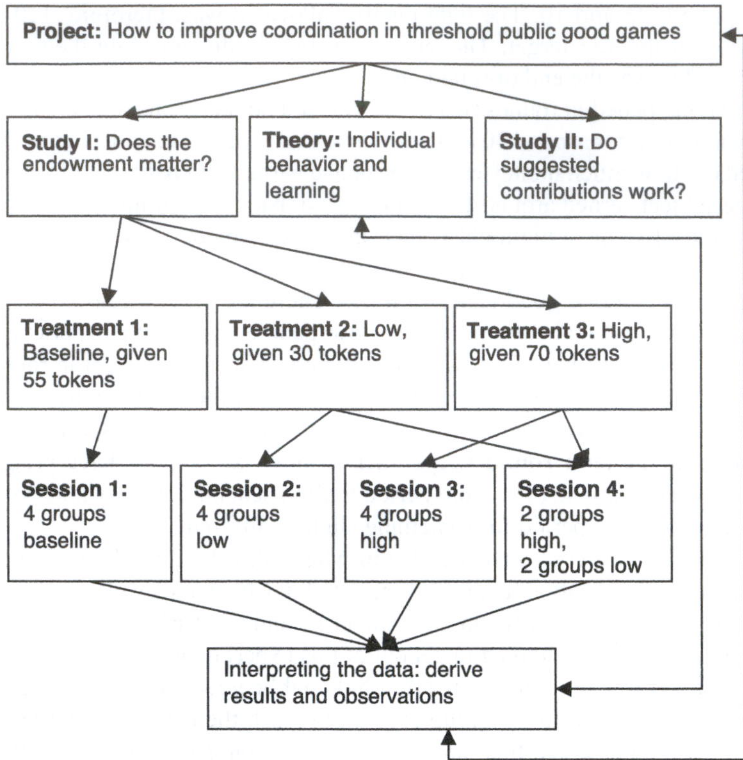

Figure 1.1 An overview of the project.

should happen in this treatment, and can more easily relate our results to the results of other researchers. This is invaluable in making good scientific progress, and so the baseline typically corresponds to a treatment that has already been done in previous studies.

One thing I want to make clear is the distinction between experimental session and experimental treatment. **Experimental session** refers to a particular instance in time and space when an experiment was run; for instance, we had a 2.00 p.m. session on Friday, 29 January. Experimental treatment refers to a specific version of the experiment used; for instance, we had the baseline treatment where subjects got 55 tokens. Session and treatment are quite different. You might have, as we did, one session with multiple treatments, or multiple sessions with the same treatment. In session four, for example, we had four groups, two of which were in the high treatment so subjects in these groups got 70 tokens, and two were in the low treatment so subjects got 30 tokens.

Another thing I want to mention is deception. In psychology it is not unknown to see **deception** in experiments, meaning the experimenter basically lies to subjects about what they are doing. (Afterwards they are told that they were lied to.)

This is a definite no-no in economics, where we are not allowed to deceive subjects in any way. So, if the instructions say there will be 25 rounds, or say one token is worth 0.5p, then it really is so. That subjects cannot be deceived does not, however, mean that they have to be told everything. Indeed, a basic requirement of most experiments is that they be **single blind**, meaning subjects are not biased by knowing too much. For instance, we did not want the subjects in our experiment to know that the objective of our study was to vary the number of tokens given. If they knew this, it might have biased how they behaved. So, while subjects cannot be deceived, they can be given a minimum amount of information.

Before moving on to look at theory I should point out that the experiment I have described above is not untypical, but experiments do vary considerably. For example, some experiments are done with pen and paper rather than via computer. Some do not involve interaction between subjects in any way. Others allow subjects to communicate with each other, possibly via computer chat. Some use schoolchildren as subjects, or experienced financial traders. Some are done outside the lab in a supermarket, or at a sports show. There are many other possibilities, and I will talk about some of these as and when we get to them.

1.2.2 Some background on theory

As we have already noted, experiments are not much use without some theory behind them. So, I also want to give a little background information about basic theoretical concepts that we are going to need. Let's start by thinking what someone called Edward does when he is in the experiment described above. To keep things simple, imagine for now that there is only one round.

All Edward has to do is to decide how many tokens to allocate to the group account. He can choose any integer between 0 and 55. We call this the **set of actions** or **set of possible options**, and he needs to pick one action or choose one option from this set. An **action** thus describes what he does, for instance, 'allocate 20 tokens to the group account'.

I now want to contrast action with strategy. You can think of a **strategy** as a description of how Edward decides what action to choose. To explain what this means it's useful to talk briefly about a second study we did. In this study, one person in the group could suggest how much others should allocate to the group account, before others choose how much they will allocate to the group. If Edward is not the one giving the suggestion, then his set of actions is the same as before; he needs to choose an integer between 0 and 55. His strategy can, however, be conditional on what was suggested. For instance, his strategy might be 'allocate as many tokens as was suggested'. With this strategy his action will be 'allocate 20 tokens' if the suggestion is to allocate 20 tokens, but 'allocate 25 tokens' if the suggestion was to allocate 25, and so on.

Actions and strategies are, therefore, different, and you might have noticed that actions are observable but strategies need not be. For instance, we observe how many tokens Edward gave but generally speaking will not know how many tokens he would have given if, say, the suggestion had been different.

The next thing to introduce is the payoff function. Edward's **payoff function** says what payoff he will get for any possible combination of strategies he and everyone else uses. For instance, if everyone allocates 20 to the group account, his payoff is 55. There are various different notations for the payoff function. One is to write $u_E(s_1, s_2, s_3, s_4, s_5)$ for Edward's payoff as a function of the strategies of the five group members, including him. Another is to write $u_E(s_E, s_{-E})$ for his payoff as a function of his strategy and the strategy of others. The payoff function in the experiment we are looking at is:

$$u_E(s_E, s_{-E}) = \begin{cases} 55 - s_E + 50 & \text{if } s_1 + s_2 + s_3 + s_4 + s_5 \geq 125 \\ 55 & \text{if } s_1 + s_2 + s_3 + s_4 + s_5 < 125 \end{cases}$$

For simplicity, it's not uncommon, as I have just done, to substitute action for strategy when working out the payoff function.

It is useful to be aware of a slightly troublesome thing about the interpretation of payoff. Easiest is to think of payoff as the amount of money earned. Given that subjects were paid money for every token they earned during the experiment, this is the approach I have taken above when writing down the payoff function; payoff equals money. The problem with this approach is that we typically want to equate payoff with utility, a subjective measure of happiness. In Chapter ten we'll see that money and happiness are quite different things. Doubling the amount of money earned need not lead to a doubling in the amount of increased happiness. So, why not just write down a payoff function that reflects utility? Measuring utility is difficult, while measuring money is simple. The norm, therefore, is to wish the problem away and equate utility with money. I shall do the same here. I will, at least, point out that this is done mainly for convenience rather than any good economic reason! But, be reassured that I shall return to this issue at various points during the book.

If we have a group of people and know the set of actions and strategies and payoff function of each person, then we have a **game**. Recall that subjects in an experiment typically play a game several times. What happens in any one round is called the **stage game** or **base game** or **constituent game**. So, the stage game in our experiment was the threshold public good game. The whole experiment, i.e. the 25 rounds, constitutes the **game**. The reason to make this distinction is that someone may want to make their action in round two conditional on what happened in round one, and so on. For instance, a strategy might be, 'if we reached the threshold in round one, I will allocate the same number of tokens to the group account in round two'.

Normally, the distinction between stage game and game is not so important, but it can be useful if the stage game changes at some point during the experiment. For example, we shall see experiments where subjects play one stage game for ten rounds and then a different stage game for a subsequent ten rounds.

I should also briefly mention that a game can be between **teams** of people as well as between individuals. In this case each team chooses an action and strategy with the members of a team collectively deciding what they should do. We'll return to this distinction in Chapter six.

The final concepts I want to talk about are possible outcomes of a game. Two particularly important concepts are Pareto efficiency and Nash equilibrium. Let's do Pareto efficiency first. We say that an outcome is **Pareto efficient** if no one could be made better off without making someone worse off. To see why this is interesting, imagine an outcome that was not Pareto efficient. Then we would be able to do something that made at least one person better off and no one worse off. This looks like a good thing to do. In the threshold public good game, if everyone were to allocate 25 tokens to the group account, everyone would get a payoff of 80 tokens. This is Pareto efficient. If everyone were to allocate zero tokens to the group account, they would get a payoff of 55. This is not Pareto efficient. Pareto efficiency is thus one way to formalize the idea of something that is desirable versus something that is not.

Contrast this with Nash equilibrium. A **Nash equilibrium** is a strategy for each person such that no one could change their strategy and increase their own payoff. Again, imagine this were not the case. Then someone can change their strategy and increase their payoff. We might expect them to do so. A formulation you might come across is that Nash equilibrium requires:

$$u_i\,(s_i, s_{-i}) \geq u_i\,(s, s_{-i})$$

for any person i where s_i is the strategy they do choose, and s is any other strategy they might have chosen. In the threshold public good game, everyone allocating 25 tokens to the group account is a Nash equilibrium. Everyone allocating 24 tokens to the group account is not a Nash equilibrium because the total will fall short of the threshold by five, and if one person were to give 29 rather than 25, their payoff would increase.

Interestingly, everyone allocating zero tokens to the group account is also a Nash equilibrium, because no one person on their own can do anything to reach the threshold. This illustrates that a Nash equilibrium need not be Pareto efficient. It's also true that a Pareto-efficient outcome need not be a Nash equilibrium (see if you can find an example in the threshold public good game). Nash equilibrium and Pareto efficient are, thus, two very different things.

I will finish this section by making a connection with some of the ideas I talked about in the last section. In many ways Nash equilibrium is the epitome of the standard economic model. It is pretty much always assumed in standard economic analysis that behavior can be captured by Nash equilibrium. But there can be many Nash equilibria. I have already shown you that there are at least two in the threshold public good game, and there are actually many more. The standard economic model has nothing to say about which of these is supposed to happen. That renders it pretty useless (for me at least). We need to know which equilibrium, if any, is most likely to happen and that, as I have discussed above, inevitably leads us into behavioral economics. Experiments can help us to understand what happens when people play such a game. This can give us the clues to improve our theoretical ability to model economic behavior, and better understand how people reason and learn.

1.3 How to use this book

To put things in some context I should give a brief preview of the rest of the book. Before I do that, I want to talk a little about my approach in writing this book.

As I said in the preface, my objective in writing the book was to explain the basic principles, ideas, and results of behavioral economics and also illustrate through applications how these can help us understand the world around us. This will be reflected in the make-up of each chapter. The first half of each chapter will be dedicated to explaining the basic principles, ideas, and results, while the second half will give various applications. Hopefully, this will give a nice mix of theory and practice.

The approach I have taken throughout is to pick a few experiments and theoretical papers that I think best illustrate the more general lessons that have been learnt. I like this approach because it gives me a chance to look in a bit more detail at some studies and give a better flavor of what behavioral economics is all about. One downside is that it can give the impression that our knowledge hangs on the results of one or two experiments or theoretical examples (that you might spot a potential flaw in). Sometimes this impression would not be far wrong, but for the most part it is a long way off. Most of the ideas I will talk about in this book are robust. In terms of experiments, that primarily means the results have been replicated in many other similar studies. In terms of theoretical examples this means the examples can be generalized to give the same conclusions. The further reading, at the end of each chapter, as well as the online resources, gives you the chance to check this and explore things in a bit more depth.

To make the book as accessible as possible, I have tried to keep algebra and notation to the minimum. Algebra, though, is part and parcel of behavioral economics, so a few equations are unavoidable to get a full grasp of the main issues. I also do not like discriminating against those who do like a bit of algebra. So, sometimes you will see [Extra] written, which is a cue that the rest of the paragraph will contain some algebra but can be skipped without missing anything.

Also, each chapter contains theoretical examples. Essentially this is about illustrating a model by giving a specific example that you can work through. We shall look at Anna shopping for breakfast cereal, Alan buying car insurance, Maria deciding when to go to the movies, and so on. In order to focus on behavioral economics, rather than algebra, I will not give a blow-by-blow account of where the numbers in these examples come from. The more advanced and confident you are, the more I would encourage you to try working through the examples yourself. In case you get stuck the companion website contains a lot more detail on all the examples.

Finally, I have little time for the politically correct issue of whether to use he or she, or she or he. So, each chapter will be based on one or two characters and the language will reflect the sex of those characters. The fact that the characters share the same names as my wife and colleagues is pure coincidence.

1.3.1 Chapter previews

The book will be split into three further parts, of which the next part will be by far the biggest, looking at what behavior we observe and how we can model it. It begins, in Chapter two, with an introduction to heuristics and context effects. The main message I want you to get from this chapter is that people can be influenced in a systematic way by the context or setting in which choices are made. This might seem obvious enough, but it is quite a big step away from the standard economic model.

In Chapter three I will look at choice with risk, and in Chapter four at choice over time. The basic approach in both chapters will be the same: to start with a simple and standard way to model behavior, namely expected utility and exponential discounting, and then to propose various modifications to the model so that we can better fit the behavior we observe. This will bring us to some of the more important concepts in behavioral economics like prospect theory and time inconsistency.

A theme throughout chapters two to four will be the importance of reference dependence and context. In particular, we shall see that behavior often depends on whether outcomes are perceived as a loss or gain relative to some reference point. We shall also see that the reference point a person has in mind can change a lot depending on the context.

In chapters five and six the focus switches to how people use information. In Chapter five the focus will be on how people can learn from the information around them, including what they get from other people. In Chapter six the focus will be on learning and behavior in interactive situations, where it's necessary to predict the behavior of others. I think the basic message that comes out of these two chapters is that people are clever and do learn, but also struggle to cope with more complex situations. We are going to see, for example, some worrying biases in how people learn from new information.

Chapter seven continues the theme of Chapter six in looking at interactive situations, but has a very different focus. The focus here will be on looking at whether people are selfish and, if not, how we can model this. We shall see that it is necessary to take account of people's preferences for fair and just outcomes, and there are various ways we can do this. One of the more important lessons from this chapter will be the heterogeneity of behavior. We'll see that some people give, some not, and what is considered fair or just can vary from one person to the next and one context to the next.

The next part of the book will consist of two chapters that look at the origins of behavior. That is, we shall try to answer questions like why people are risk averse, are loss averse, value fairness, and so on. Chapter eight will focus on the role of evolution and culture in shaping economic behavior. Chapter nine will look at neuroeconomics and recent attempts to see what is going on in the brain as people make economic decisions. We'll see that an evolutionary and neuroscience perspective provides some fascinating insights into economic behavior, and really does tell us something about why people are risk averse and the like.

In the final part of the book my focus will primarily be on whether behavioral economics can help us do something useful in improving the happiness of people. In Chapter ten I will look at what makes people happy and whether they know what makes them happy. We are going to see that people do not always do the thing that would make them happiest, and may be willing to pre-commit or delegate choice to others. It's clear, however, that people still desire some choice or self-determination.

Chapter eleven follows this up by looking at how behavioral economics can help inform policy. I will look at both the design of institutions and policies aimed more at individual incentives. Making the world a better place is always easy on paper, but I am going to argue that behavioral economics does give us some nice tools to improve policy for the better.

1.3.2 Behavioral finance

As I have already mentioned, behavioral finance has taken on something of a life of its own alongside behavioral economics. Given that this is a textbook on behavioral economics, rather than behavioral finance, there will naturally not be a comprehensive treatment of behavioral finance. The key ideas of behavioral finance are, however, covered. For those interested in behavioral finance I shall briefly point out three key things to watch out for.

Of primary importance is the efficiency of markets. This will be a theme in Chapter two (see sections 2.5 and 2.7). Particularly relevant for finance is the efficiency of markets in the presence of uncertainty. This is covered in Chapter five (see section 5.6), including a discussion of bubbles and busts. Chapter three (see section 3.6) focuses on some specific finance 'puzzles' such as the equity premium puzzle.

An often neglected area of finance is the interaction between traders. Two important concepts for behavioral finance are information cascades and beauty contests. Information cascades help us study how one trader may learn from another (see section 5.3). The beauty contest helps us study the incentives of traders (see section 6.1 to 6.4).

The saving and investment decisions of individuals will be a recurring theme throughout the book. See in particular section 2.8 on the life cycle hypothesis, sections 2.9 and 10.6 on retirement saving, and section 4.5 on borrowing.

1.4 Further reading

Many have given good introductions to what behavioral economics is all about: Mullainathan and Thaler (2000), Camerer (2003), and Camerer and Loewenstein (2004) is a small selection. The excellent review articles by Conlisk (1996), Rabin (1998), and DellaVigna (2009) are also worth a mention at this point. For more on the methodology of experiments, the books by Cassar and Friedman (2004) and Bardsley and co-authors (2010) are recommended. For more on the history of behavioral and experimental economics, see Roth (1995), Sent (2004), and Bruni and Sugden (2007).

1.5 Review questions

1.1 Why is the standard economic model a good thing, and why is it a bad thing, in trying to understand economic behavior?

1.2 Why do we need to run economic experiments?

1.3 Why does a heuristic usually come hand in hand with a cognitive bias? Should we emphasize how clever people are for having good heuristics, or how dumb they are for being biased?

1.4 Why does it make sense to mix up experimental treatments and sessions, i.e. to have multiple treatments in each session and multiple sessions for each treatment?

1.5 Is it good that experiments usually involve students as subjects?

1.6 What are the objectives of behavioral economics?

1.7 What are the objectives of studying the standard economic model?

Part II

Economic behavior

2 Simple heuristics for complex choices

> Rule No. 1 is never lose money. Rule No. 2 is never forget rule number one.
>
> Warren Buffet

Even the most innocuous of economic choices are in principle very complicated. For example consider a shopper in a grocery store looking at rows of breakfast cereal and deciding which one to buy. Should she buy the cereal she usually buys? Should she try a new cereal the store has just introduced? Should she buy the cereal on special offer? Will the cereal she usually buys be on special offer next week? Will it be cheaper in another store? Should she be tempted by the cereal with the chance to win a holiday in the Caribbean?

Clearly, most of us do not spend much time considering all these issues. Indeed, most of us simply buy the cereal that we usually buy. That way we can make a quick decision that will probably keep us happy. This is an example of a heuristic. A **heuristic** is any 'rule of thumb' or simple rule of behavior by which a person solves a problem. The shopper can solve their problem of what cereal to buy with the heuristic, 'buy what I usually do'. Almost all the economic decisions we make are based on such heuristics, otherwise life would get far too complicated. This means we need to know how heuristics work and what their consequences can be.

Heuristics, and the biases they give rise to, are going to be a recurring theme throughout the book, and are the primary focus of this chapter. I will start by giving some examples, but the main thing I want to do is provide some structure for how to think about the consequences of heuristics. In doing this we shall come across some of the key concepts and ideas in behavioral economics.

2.1 Utility and search

I will start by taking up the story of a shopper called Anna in a grocery store deciding what breakfast cereal to buy. There is a large selection of potential choices, all with different characteristics, but we will narrow things down to the four listed in Table 2.1. How can she decide what to buy?

The standard way of thinking about this in economics is to assume that Anna has a **utility function** that says how much utility she gets from particular

Table 2.1 Cereals for sale, and their characteristics, where 1 = low, 2 = medium and 3 = high

Product	*Price*	*Taste quality*	*Health quality*
Budget	\$1	1	1
Nutty	\$3	2	2
Honey	\$4	3	2
Superior	\$6	3	3

combinations of money, and goods. In this context we would write $u(x, TQ, HQ)$ as the utility she gets from having money x and a cereal with taste quality TQ and health quality HQ. One important point to note is that, in the standard description, utility should be a function of money wealth, and so when evaluating each choice we need to focus on how much money Anna will have after buying the cereal. To illustrate, Table 2.2 works through an example where she initially has \$100 and her utility function is:

$$u(x, TQ, HQ) = 20\sqrt{x} + 2TQ + HQ.$$

She can buy no cereal, keep wealth \$100 and have utility 200, or pay \$1 for Budget, have wealth \$99 and utility 202, and so on.

You might be wondering what it means to say that Anna's utility is 200, or 204. The interpretation we should give to utility is crucial but ultimately very tricky and so, on the basis that we have plenty of other things to worry about at this stage, I am going to dodge that question for now. In Chapter ten we will look at it in some detail. In the meantime you can think of utility as a general measure of happiness or satisfaction. So, more utility is better, and Anna wants to choose the cereal with highest utility. We are also not going to get far unless we think in terms of **cardinal utility**. What this means is that the differences in utility should mean something. So, we can say things like: 'Honey is better than Budget by the same amount as Budget is better than no cereal.'

In the example we can see that Honey offers the highest utility and so looks like the best choice. It does so because it offers the best trade-off of quality for price. Anna is willing to pay the extra \$1 to \$4 that Honey costs over other choices in

Table 2.2 The utility of each cereal if initial wealth is \$100

Choice	*Wealth*	*TQ*	*HQ*	*Utility*
No cereal	\$100	0	0	200
Budget	\$99	1	1	202
Nutty	\$97	2	2	203
Honey	\$96	3	2	204
Superior	\$94	3	3	203

order to improve the taste and health quality, but is not willing to pay a further $2 to get the highest quality. We have, therefore, a prediction of what Anna should buy: she should buy Honey.

This is fine, if Anna knows what maximizes her utility. Realistically, however, she probably will not know. Maybe she has never tried Budget or Superior, or maybe she did try them once but has forgotten what they tasted like, her preferences have changed, or the manufacturers have subsequently improved the quality.

This lack of knowledge is crucial, and means that it is not enough for us to say that Anna should do the thing that maximizes her utility. She does not know what that is, and so we need to delve a little deeper. Two things that become relevant when we do so are search and choice arbitrariness. I will look at each in turn.

2.1.1 How to search

If Anna does not know the quality of goods, or her utility function, then she can gather more information in order to become better informed; we call this search. A **search heuristic** specifies what Anna should do in order to become better informed. There are lots of possible search heuristics, and I shall look at five to give you some idea of what they, and heuristics in general, look like.

The most obvious search heuristic is to 'try everything'. For example, Anna could try a different cereal every week until she has tried them all, and then subsequently buy the one she liked the most. This means she will end up knowing a lot about cereals. The process will, however, be potentially costly. To see why, suppose that in the first week she tries Honey and can tell that she likes it a lot. If she sticks to her heuristic then in subsequent weeks she will have to buy and try cereals that are not going to give her as much utility. She would have been better off just sticking with Honey (if you will excuse the pun).

In this case search proves costly in terms of **forgone utility**. Search can also be costly in terms of time and money. A good search heuristic needs to trade off the benefits of acquiring more information with these costs. Characterizing optimal, or good, search algorithms has a long history in mathematics, computer science, and economics. Optimal search algorithms are, however, typically very complicated, so we need to think what search heuristics people could realistically use that come close to the optimum. Three such heuristics are satisficing, elimination by aspects, and directed cognition.

The basic idea behind **satisficing** is that a person sets some **aspiration level** for what they are looking for, and continues to search until they find something above the aspiration level. For example, Anna may decide she wants something that tastes good and is reasonably healthy. This determines her aspiration level, and she will keep on trying cereals until she tries Honey or Superior. Satisficing relaxes the objective from finding the optimal choice, to merely finding a choice that is good enough. This means a person may not end up with the best, but they will end up with something relatively good, while avoiding the costs of excessive search. If Anna, for instance, tries Superior before Honey, then she will never get to know how good Honey is, but she might also avoid knowing how bad Budget is.

How close satisficing comes to the optimum will depend on the aspiration level. This is where satisficing become slightly more tricky, because it is not trivial what the aspiration level should be, or how it should change. If, for example, Anna's aspiration is to find a cereal costing less than $7, then she may end up with Budget; the aspiration level looks too low. If her aspiration is to find a very tasty and healthy cereal for less than $5, then she will be disappointed because no such cereal exists; the aspiration level looks too high. Anna will need, therefore, to set the aspiration level appropriately and revise it as she goes along; it's just not clear how exactly she will do so.

A heuristic that partly addresses this problem is that of directed cognition. The idea behind **directed cognition** is that a person treats each chance to gather information as if it is the last such chance before they have to make a choice. Typically, it will not actually be their last chance. Directed cognition simplifies Anna's task, because she does not need to forward plan. To illustrate, suppose she knows only the characteristics of Nutty. Using directed cognition she should ask herself, Shall I try one alternative cereal and, if so, which one? This is a much simpler question than would be needed with forward planning. With forward planning there are many more permutations that need to be considered, such as, Shall I try Budget and, if that tastes nice, try Honey and, if not, try Superior, and then Honey?

The final search heuristic I want to look at, for now, is that of elimination by aspects. The basic idea of **elimination by aspects** is to consider the aspects of possible choices one by one and sequentially eliminate choices that fall below some aspiration level. For example, if Anna's aspirations are to buy a medium taste and health quality cereal for under $5, then on the price aspect she would eliminate Superior, and on the quality aspects eliminate Budget. This would leave a choice between Honey and Nutty.

Elimination by aspects is different from the previous two heuristics in that it compares across aspects, such as price, rather than across choices, such as Honey or Nutty. Conceptually it is simpler to compare across aspects because there is likely to be a simple ordering from best (e.g. least expensive) to worst (most expensive). The problem is that comparing across aspects presupposes that the person has information about all the possible choices. With aspects like price and health quality this is plausible because the prices and ingredients will be displayed on the box. With an aspect like taste quality it is difficult to know the differences without trying them all. Elimination by aspects can, therefore, only take us so far in explaining search, but it does offer vital clues on how a person can choose what to try next and what to not try at all.

The three heuristics that we have discussed should be seen as complementary rather than alternatives, as summarized in Table 2.3. Satisficing, for instance, suggests how long Anna should search, but offers no clues as to what she should try. Directed cognition has less to say about how long to search, but can offer clues as what to try next. Together, therefore, they give us a picture of how people might search. In general, no one heuristic is ever going to be perfect, and so we can expect people to use different combinations of heuristics for different tasks. Indeed, Anna may have a heuristic to say what heuristic to use (see Research Methods 2.1).

Table 2.3 Five search heuristics with a very brief statement of how they can help with search

Heuristic	*What it does well*	*What it does not do so well*
Try them all	Make the person well informed	Minimize the cost of search
Satisficing	Say when to stop search	Say what choice to try next
Directed cognition	Suggest what choice to try next	Give a forward-looking plan of search
Elimination by aspects	Say what choices not to try	Say when to stop searching
Search for x minutes	Give certainty how long search will last	React to success or failure in search

Research Methods 2.1

The infinite regress problem

We began by talking about Anna's problem of 'what cereal to choose' and suggested she should choose the cereal that maximized her utility. Having noted that she will probably not know what cereal maximizes her utility, we got the additional problem, 'how to find out what cereal maximizes utility'. This has to be a harder problem to solve than the original one, but we have not finished yet. That is because there are lots of ways to search for information about preferences, so we get a further additional problem, 'how to find out, how to find out what cereal maximizes utility'. I could go on: 'how to find out, how to find out, how to find out . . .', and so on.

More generally, finding the optimal answer to a problem involves finding the optimal way to find the optimal answer, and the optimal way to find the optimal way, and so on. This is known as the **infinite regress problem**. Clearly, if Anna, or anyone else, is going to make a decision, they need some way to break the loop. Heuristics, emotions, and intuition (which we shall get to shortly) are one way to do this because they provide simple rules to make decisions. That answer is not, however, entirely satisfactory, because Anna will need heuristics to choose what heuristic to use, and then we are back in the cycle again!

In short, the problem is not going to go away, and so we need to be aware of it when we try to model behavior. Behavioral economists have primarily focused on basic heuristics, i.e. heuristics designed to solve a specific problem. Some attention, but much less, has been given to heuristics for choosing heuristics, and we will get to them in later chapters. The problem of how people choose heuristics for choosing heuristics is ignored, but in Chapter eight I will suggest that evolution might do that job.

To get a feel for how people search we can look at the results of a study by Gabaix and co-authors (2006). In the study, subjects were asked to choose between eight options where the payoff of each option was the sum of ten numbers. One of the numbers was visible, but to find the value of each of the other nine numbers the subjects had to click on the screen. To relate this back to our earlier example, imagine that the price is visible, but to find the health quality Anna has to pick up the box and look up the ingredients. Software called mouselab can track what information subjects choose to look up and gives us some idea how subjects searched (see Research Methods 6.1).

There are lots of things we can look at in the data in terms of how much information subjects choose to look up, what sequence they choose to look it up, and so on. One way to see if subjects were using a particular heuristic is to compare how much information subjects should have looked up about each choice, if they were using, say, directed cognition, and how much information they did look up. This measures how well the search heuristic fits observed search behavior. A second thing we can do is to see how well the search heuristic fits the final choice made. This measures how well the search heuristic fits observed choice behavior.

Figure 2.1 summarizes the results of the study. We see that directed cognition does a good job of fitting how subjects search, while elimination by aspects does less well. In terms of fitting choice, all algorithms do roughly as well as each other, and the choice is what we would have expected around 50 percent of the time. A 50 percent success rate at predicting what subjects will choose is much better than we could have done by guessing (remember there were eight possible choices), but still not as high as we might like. It looks like we are missing something.

One thing that becomes apparent is that subjects were not as selective in what information they looked for as the three heuristics suggested they should have been. In different ways they looked up both too much and too little. First, the too much: if one choice ranks poorly on the visible aspect, then it pays to not search

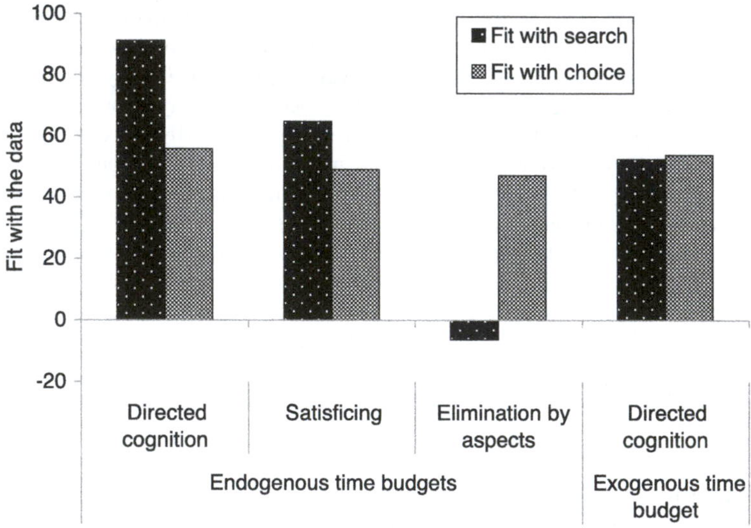

Figure 2.1 How well search heuristics fit the observed search and choices in a search experiment. The fit is measured relative to what could have been expected by chance. Directed cognition and satisficing give the best fit.

Source: Gabaix *et al.* (2006).

for other information about that choice. For example, if Superior is too expensive, then there is little point in looking at the health quality. Subjects tended to look up more information than we might expect in such instances (see Research Methods 2.2). Next, the too little: it does not matter how long the search has gone on; if the search has not yet uncovered something useful, it pays to carry on searching. Subjects, however, seemed to stop searching if they had looked up a lot of information, even if that information had not been very informative.

Research Methods 2.2

How long should an experiment take?

One slightly troublesome issue in running experiments is how much time to give subjects to make decisions.

On a practical level this issue is important if we do not want some subjects to be delayed by others. In particular, it immediately becomes apparent when running an experiment that some people take a lot longer to make decisions than others! If the experiment can only proceed when each subject has made a decision, this can leave some subjects twiddling their thumbs for a long while. On the one hand this may be good if it means some subjects spend a bit more time thinking about the experiment. On the other hand it can lead to boredom and less thinking about the experiment.

On a theoretical level it may be important how much time subjects have, if we are interested in the consequences of time pressure. Time is very relevant in search and so important to take into account. Gabaix and co-authors did this by comparing an exogenous and endogenous time budget. In an exogenous time budget treatment, subjects are given a fixed amount of time during which they can look at a particular set of eight choices. In an endogenous time budget treatment, subjects are given 25 minutes to look at as many sets of eight choices as they wish.

This distinction turns out to be potentially informative. In particular, subjects were more selective about what information they looked up with an endogenous than exogenous budget. So, the low success at predicting search with an exogenous time budget (see Figure 2.1) may reflect subjects having too much time. Optimally, they should have found out more information about the current best-looking choices, but maybe they had already made up their mind and so were filling in time.

Putting these observations together suggests a fifth search heuristic: a person decides how much time to spend on search and then searches for that long. This may mean that Anna would search too long, if she initially tried something she liked, or search too little, if she has yet to try anything she really likes. But it does mean search will last a definite length of time, and this may be a useful thing.

There are many more possible search heuristics and many more studies (see the suggested reading) that look at how people search. We will, however, come back to search elsewhere in the book, notably Chapter five, and so I will leave the issue for now. The main thing I wanted you to see at this stage is how people can use simple (or not so simple) heuristics to solve complex search problems. Hopefully, this gives you some idea of how people can search effectively, and gives some feel for what heuristics in general look like. Now I want to look at choice arbitrariness, which raises some quite different issues.

2.1.2 Choice arbitrariness

In the process of search, Anna is going to face some fairly arbitrary choices. That's because she does not yet know what maximizes her utility but still has to choose something. For example, she may have narrowed her choice to Nutty or Honey, and there is no real reason to try one ahead of the other. Which one to try first? Her choice will be arbitrary, and she might as well toss a coin to decide. Arbitrary does not, however, have to mean random. For instance, Anna might be attracted by the bright red packaging of Honey, the '50 percent off' sticker on Nutty, or choose Budget because she just saw it advertised on TV. In each of these cases choice is systematic. The crucial thing is that choice is influenced by factors that just happened to be like that and could have been different: this is **choice arbitrariness**. Let's look at some examples.

I will start by looking at the difference between conflicting and non-conflicting choices. We say a set of choices are **conflicting** if one choice is better on one aspect and a different choice better on some other aspect. For example, Budget is better on the price aspect but Superior is better on the health quality aspect, and so these are conflicting choices. A set of choices are **non-conflicting** if one choice is better on all aspects. For example, if Superior were on sale for $0.50 then there would be a non-conflicting choice.

To illustrate the potential consequences of conflicting versus non-conflicting choice, consider this example from a study by Tversky and Shafir (1992). Subjects were asked to imagine that they want to buy a CD player, and walk past a shop with a one-day clearance sale. Some subjects were given the conflicting choices of a Sony player for $99 and a top-of-the-range Aiwa player for $169. Some were given the non-conflicting choice of the Sony player for $99 or an inferior Aiwa player for $105. Others were just given the option of the Sony player for $99. All subjects were asked whether they would buy one of the players or wait and learn more about the models. Figure 2.2 summarizes the choices made.

We see that more people buy the Sony when the choice is non-conflicting than when it is conflicting. Also, more choose the Sony when the choice is non-conflicting than when there is no choice at all. This latter observation violates the **regularity condition** of choice that an increase in the number of available options should not increase the share buying a particular option. It seems that the presence of an inferior option increased the likelihood of buying the Sony.

What we have just seen suggests that one alterative can look more or less desirable depending on what it is compared to. A slightly different possibility is that particular aspects of an alternative can look more or less desirable depending on what they are compared to. To illustrate, let's suppose Anna has narrowed her choice to either Nutty or Honey and there are only three cereals on display: Nutty, Honey, and one of Budget or Superior. Honey looks relatively cheap when contrasted with Superior but relatively expensive when contrasted with Budget.

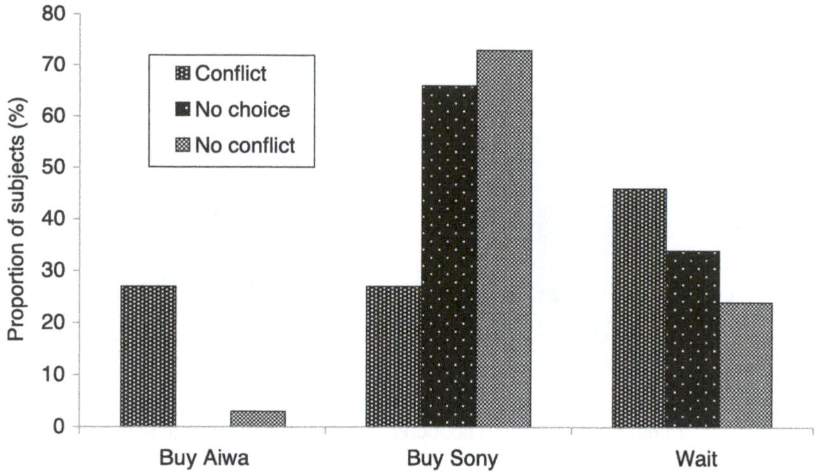

Figure 2.2 The decision that subjects made when the choice is conflicting or non-conflicting, compared to when there is no choice. Subjects were more likely to wait, the more conflicting the choice.

Source: Shafir *et al.* (1993).

She might, therefore, be more likely to buy Honey when it is contrasted with Superior. This would be an example of trade-off contrast. The **trade-off contrast hypothesis** is that a product with a desirable quality will appear cheaper if contrasted with a product where that desirable quality is more expensive.

A study by Simonson and Tversky (1992) shows the relevance of trade-off contrast. In one part of the study, subjects were asked to choose between coupons and cash, where each coupon could be redeemed for books or CDs at local stores. In a background stage subjects were exposed to choices where a coupon cost either $15 or $5. After this they were all exposed to the same choices where a coupon cost $10. Figure 2.3 summarizes the results. The first choice offered to subjects was $47 and five coupons, or $37 and six coupons (the extra coupon costing $10). We see that those exposed to a background stage where coupons cost $15 were more likely to choose the extra coupon, while those exposed to a background stage where coupons cost $5 were not. This is consistent with the trade-off contrast hypothesis; the $10 coupon looks cheap, or expensive, depending on whether coupons previously cost $15 or $5.

Let us now go back to the scenario where there are two or three cereals on display out of Budget, Nutty, and Honey. Budget has the advantage of being cheap, Honey has the advantage of being tasty, but Nutty strikes a good compromise. Maybe, therefore, Anna will buy Nutty because it's 'in the middle'. If true, this means she should be more likely to buy Nutty when all three cereals are on display than just two. This would be an example of **extremeness aversion with comprise**. There is another possibility. It may be that the presence of Honey or Budget on

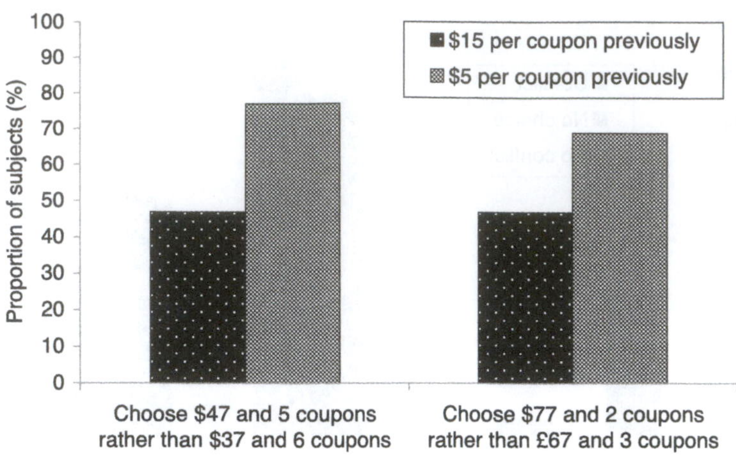

Figure 2.3 Whether subjects prefer an extra coupon to $10 depends on whether they were exposed to a background stage where coupons cost $15 or $5.

Source: Simonson and Tversky (1992).

display emphasizes the importance of quality. So, the presence of Honey on display increases the likelihood that Anna will buy Nutty, but the presence of Budget on display decreases the likelihood that Anna will buy Nutty, because she switches to Honey. This would be an example of **extremeness aversion with polarization**. Table 2.4 distinguishes these possible effects with examples.

To give an example of extremeness aversion we can return to the study of Simonson and Tversky, and a different scenario. Subjects were given information about three radio-cassette players, a mid-quality Emerson, mid-quality Sony and top-quality Sony. In Figure 2.4 we see the proportion that chose the mid-quality Sony. Adding the top-quality Sony decreases the proportion choosing the mid-quality Sony compared to the Emerson. Also, adding the Emerson increases the proportion choosing the mid-quality Sony compared to the top-quality Sony. This

Table 2.4 Examples of how Anna's choice may be influenced by the three psychological effects

Psychological effect	*Example of what Anna may choose*
Trade-off contrast	If choices are Budget, Nutty, and Honey, buys Nutty. If choices are Nutty, Honey, and Superior, buys Honey.
Extremeness aversion with compromise	If choices are Nutty and Honey, buys Honey. If choices are Budget and Nutty, buys Budget. If choices are Budget, Nutty, and Honey, buys Nutty.
Extremeness aversion with polarization	If choices are Nutty and Honey, buys Nutty. If choices are Budget and Nutty, buys Budget. If choices are Budget, Nutty, and Honey, buys Honey.

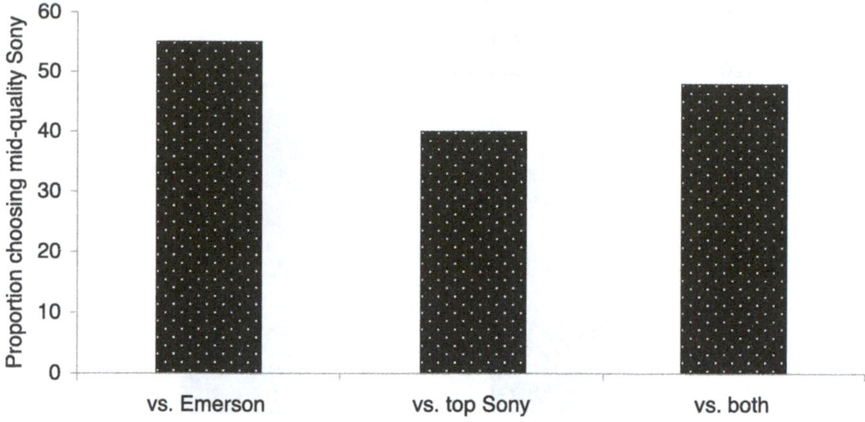

Figure 2.4 The proportion choosing a mid-level Sony radio-cassette player when the alternative was an Emerson player, a top-quality Sony player, or both the Emerson and Sony. We observe extremeness aversion with polarization.

Source: Simonson and Tversky (1992).

is an example of extremeness aversion with polarization. It is also a second example violating the regularity condition.

In the next example we push extremeness aversion a bit further. First, imagine that Anna asks herself, 'What cereal shall I buy?'. She might say Superior because it is more extreme, higher quality. Now imagine she asks herself, 'What cereal shall I not buy?' She might say Superior because it is more extreme, more expensive. In both cases the fact that Superior is more extreme makes it more salient. That means it is the first thing she considers, and so might be the first thing she accepts and/or rejects. This can lead to a **choose-reject discrepancy** where a person chooses the same thing whether asked what she wants or what she does not want.

Here is an example from a study by Shafir *et al.* (1993). Subjects were given two choices for a vacation. Spot A was relatively neutral: average weather, average beaches, average nightlife, etc. Spot B was more extreme: lots of sunshine, gorgeous beaches, very strong winds, no nightlife. Some subjects were asked which they would prefer to book. Other subjects were told they have a provisional booking at each location and now have to decide which to cancel. In Figure 2.5 we see that most subjects preferred spot B over A but were equally split on whether to cancel A or B. Overall the proportion of choices for spot B exceeded 100 percent. This basically means that some people would both prefer spot B and want to cancel spot B!

To give a final example, suppose that on going into the grocery store Anna is stopped and asked to do a survey. One question they ask is whether she would be willing to pay $8 for a new cereal they are trialing. After that, Superior may look relatively cheap at $6. If the question had said $4, then maybe Superior would look expensive. This is an example of an **anchoring effect**, where a person's choice is influenced by some prior cue or anchor. This might look like a trade-off

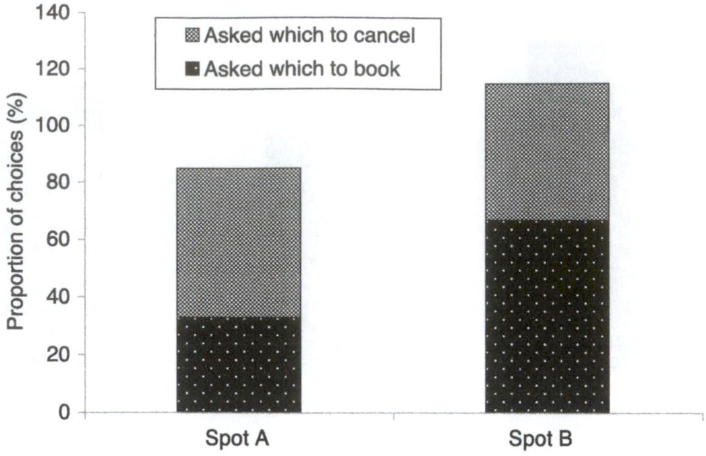

Figure 2.5 The proportion who chose spot A and B to book and to cancel. Both columns should add up to 100 percent, because if, say, 30 percent prefer spot A, 70 percent should reject spot A.

Source: Shafir *et al.* (1993).

contrast. In trade-off contrast, however, two or more different products are compared, while, with the anchoring effect, a person's thoughts on a particular product are influenced by some prior event.

To illustrate how the anchoring effect can happen, we shall look at part of a study by Ariely, Loewenstein, and Prelec (2003). Subjects were first asked whether they would buy a box of Belgian chocolates, and some other items, for more than the last two digits of their social security number. For example, if the last two digits are 25 they are asked whether they would pay more than $25. They were then asked how much they would be willing to pay. The last two digits of a social security number are random, but did matter, as we see in Figure 2.6. On average those asked whether they were willing to pay, say, $55 subsequently said they were willing to pay a higher price than those who were asked to pay, say, $15 (but see Research Methods 2.3).

Research Methods 2.3

Can you replicate it?

The study by Ariely, Loewenstein, and Prelec, of which the box of chocolates experiment is just one small part, is one of the best known and most widely cited in behavioral economics. Why? In large part it is because an anchoring effect should not exist according to the standard economic model, and so the study raises new questions. The popularity of the study is also, inevitably, helped by there being some 'fun' and 'quirky' results. Who would have thought the last two digits of someone's social security number influences how much they are willing to pay for a box of chocolates?

Herein, however, we potentially have a problem. The profession and society like revolutionary, quirky results! To see why this is a problem, suppose that 100 research teams did the exact same box of chocolates experiment and only one team found any effect. The team that found an effect can publish their results in a top academic journal and get the publicity. The 99 that found no effect will throw their results away because the 'social security number does not influence willingness to pay for chocolates' result is hardly exciting.

Interestingly, the anchoring effect results are now so widely accepted that showing 'social security number does not influence willingness to pay for chocolates' has become revolutionary and quirky! A recent study by Fudenberg, Levine, and Maniadis (2012) reports a series of experiments showing no evidence of any anchoring effect. In this case, though, we do not know if there were 99 research teams that did the same experiment and found evidence of an anchoring effect.

To be really confident of experimental results we need independent **replication** of findings and the publication of those findings. There are no incentives, however, within the profession for this to happen. Running replication studies is a dead-end career path, and top journals will not publish them. The simple truth, therefore, is that some of the experimental results I will discuss in this book are likely to be flukes rather than representative of the truth! Do not, however, be too disheartened because knowledge generally goes on an upward path (see e.g. Research Methods 2.4 and 3.4). There are enough studies, for instance, for us to be confident that anchoring effects are a reality. What is less clear is how big the effects are.

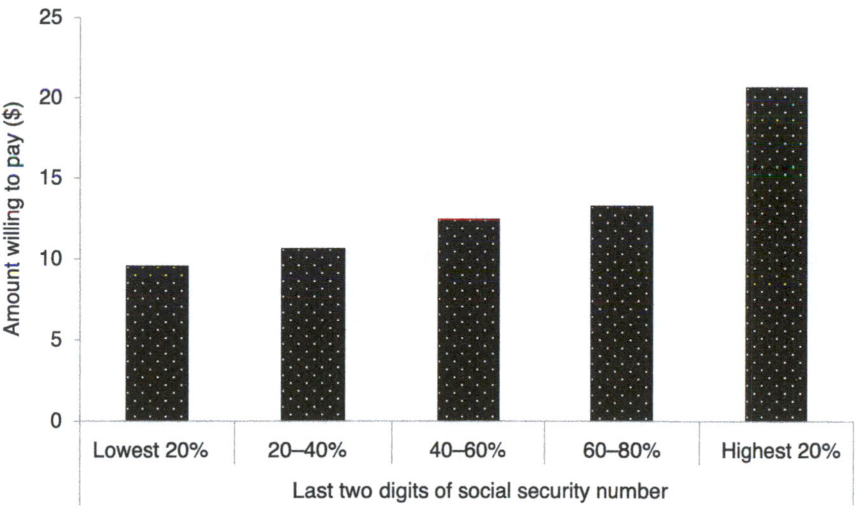

Figure 2.6 The amount that subjects were willing to pay for a box of chocolates was higher for those with a higher social security number.

Source: Ariely *et al.* (2003).

The five psychological effects we have looked at are the consequences of choice heuristics, like 'pick the one in the middle' or 'pick the most extreme'. They result in choice arbitrariness. Put another way, they cause **context effects**, a general name I shall give to any external factors, like the other choices on offer that influence choice. Recall that this all comes about because people are unlikely to know what maximizes their utility. We should expect, therefore, context effects in just about any economic choice a person ever makes. This means choice arbitrariness and context effects are important. Important enough, that I shall devote the next section to trying to understand them in more detail.

Before doing that I want to make one point clear. Some would have you believe that things like trade-off contrast and extremeness aversion are evidence of people not being rational and not being like homo economicus. This is not true. In a complicated world where there are lots of decisions to make it may be optimal to 'pick the one in the middle' or 'pick the most salient' or 'be influenced by the other choices on offer'. We are not, therefore, going to spend time wondering whether such things are evidence for or against the standard economic model. Indeed, even the more bizarre effects, like choice being influenced by the last two digits of a social security number, can be consistent with rational behavior. Such effects just mean that the heuristics that people use are not always well adapted to some of the things experimenters have us do in the lab!

2.2 Mental accounting and framing

What I want to do now is question why context effects exist: Why is it that external factors can influence the choice someone makes? A good starting point is to focus on a subset of context effects called framing effects.

Framing effects are where essentially equivalent descriptions of the same thing lead to different choices. That some people would choose to go to spot B for their vacation but also choose to not go to spot B for their vacation is an example of a framing effect: what people choose is dependent on the way the question is asked, or framed. If we can explain why people choose different things when offered the same set of choices, it should be simple to see why they may choose different things when offered a slightly different set of choices.

To understand why we observe framing (and context) effects I want you to look at the simple classification of cognitive processes summarized in Figure 2.7. (In Chapter nine we will revisit this classification to see how accurate it is and see that, while not perfect, it is more than good enough for our purposes.) The classification suggests that, when we initially see something, perception and intuition kick in automatically to give us impressions of what we are looking at. This process happens spontaneously and the person has no or very little control over it. Anna, for example, may make a choice purely based on intuition. More generally, however, particularly for the kinds of choices of interest in economics, she might use reasoning to think through options and make a more deliberate, informed judgment. In this case she will use reasoning processes.

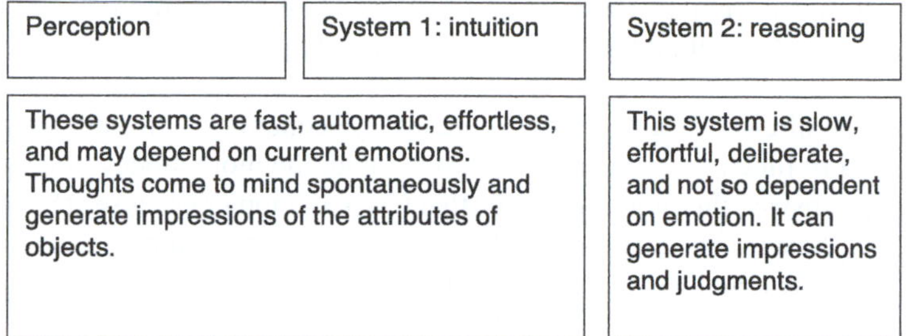

Figure 2.7 A representation of different brain processes.

Now, here's the key thing we learn from this classification: even if Anna does use reasoning, her initial perception and intuition will inevitably influence the starting point for her subsequent reasoning. Initial perceptions and intuition will, therefore, matter. How a choice is framed will likely affect perception and intuition, which will in turn affect reasoning. To see this in action recall the example of trade-off contrast. If someone was led to think a coupon costs $15, then being asked to pay $10 will be perceived as a good deal and maybe one worth taking. If they were led to think it costs $5, then it looks like a bad deal.

That context and framing influence perception and intuition, which influences reasoning, is one of the most important ideas in behavioral economics. Homo economicus only ever uses reasoning. So recognizing the role played by perception and intuition gives us a completely different perspective on why people behave the way they do compared with the standard economic model. Furthermore, this explanation of context and framing effects means that they are inevitable, and not just a quirk of some experiment. Every time a person makes a choice, that choice has to be framed in a particular way, and how it is framed will likely affect perception, intuition, reasoning, and the choice made. If we want to understand economic behavior, we therefore need to understand framing effects. This, as I shall now explain, means we need to understand reference points.

2.2.1 Reference-dependent utility

Some attributes of an object are more **accessible** than others when we first perceive it. Such **natural assessments** of an object include size, distance, loudness, temperature, similarity, and whether it is good or bad. Importantly, a natural assessment will usually be a relative rather than absolute one. It is far more natural for us to say what is bigger, longer, louder, hotter, and better, without knowing the exact volume, length, temperature, etc. To be able to judge relative magnitude we need some standard of comparison, and this is called the **reference point** or **reference level**.

To illustrate why the distinction between absolute and relative can be important for economic behavior consider this question, taken from Kahneman (2003):

> Two persons get their monthly report from a broker. Carol is told that her wealth went from \$4 million to \$3 million. Amanda is told that her wealth went from \$1 million to \$1.1 million. Who is happier?

As we have already discussed, the standard in economics is to measure utility using a utility function $u(x)$ where x is money and, the more money, the higher is utility. The answer, therefore, should be that Carol is happier because $u(\$3\ million) > u(\$1.1\ million)$. Things, however, do not seem quite this simple, because many of us may be tempted to think that Amanda would be the happier. She might be the happier because her wealth is bigger than before, while Carol's is smaller than before.

This example suggests that we need to take seriously the distinction between relative and absolute measures. The simplest way to do this is to suppose some reference point about which outcomes are measured. So, we can use a utility function or **value function** $v(x - r)$ that measures the utility of outcome x relative to some reference point r. If the reference point is $r = 0$, then the value function will coincide with the original formulation, but if r is different, say, wealth last year, then we get something different. Setting r as wealth last year we see that Carol would get $v(-\$1\ million)$ and Amanda would get $v(\$0.1\ million)$. With this formulation it seems that Amanda should be happier because $v(\$0.1\ million) > v(-\$1\ million)$.

Now Amanda is happier. Things still seem, however, a little incomplete because Carol does have more money than Amanda. A more general formulation is the **reference dependent utility function:**

$$u^r(x) = \eta u(x) + v(x - r)$$

where η is some parameter and r is the reference point. Total utility is now a weighted sum of utility from total wealth and the utility from a relative gain or loss. With this we can capture Carol being potentially happier because she has more wealth and potentially less happy because her wealth has decreased.

Judging things relative to a reference point raises the important distinction between gains and losses. Intuitively there is something distinctly different about being above the reference point, a gain, or being below the reference point, a loss. A large amount of evidence, which we shall get to shortly, backs this up and points towards something called loss aversion. Someone is **loss averse** if a loss causes a bigger fall in utility than a similar sized gain causes an increase in utility. In terms of the value function loss aversion implies that $v(-g) < -v(g)$ for any $g > 0$. Basically, losses are worse than gains are good.

We are going to see that reference dependence and loss aversion have big implications for economic behavior. Before we look at this in more detail I want to briefly preview why reference dependence is so important.

At first glance it might look as though we have just rewritten the utility function to include an extra parameter r called the reference point. If this were the case, then economists could carry on modeling utility and utility maximization the way they traditionally have done and not a great deal would need to change. This is not how it is! That's because the reference point a person uses when making a particular decision can be relatively arbitrary and will likely be determined by perception and intuition. In other words the reference point can depend on the context, causing important framing and context effects. This is why reference dependence is more than just adding a parameter to the utility function. The ways in which the reference point can depend on context will be a recurring theme in the rest of this chapter and those to follow.

2.2.2 The endowment effect

One important consequence of reference dependence and loss aversion is the endowment effect. To explain what this is, we shall look at a study by List (2004). The study was conducted on the floor of a sports card show in the US. Subjects were recruited throughout the day and completed a short survey before being asked to choose whether they would like to take a coffee mug or chocolate bar as reward for doing the survey. Both the mug and chocolate bar retailed at around $6. The key thing about the experiment was to vary the perception of ownership. Some people were physically given a mug and told they could swap for a chocolate bar, some were given the chocolate bar and told they could swap for a mug, others were either given both or neither and asked to choose.

Figure 2.8 details the proportion of subjects who chose the mug. Look first at the non-dealers, who were people attending the show. Here we see the same has been observed in many other experiments: those given the chocolate bar do not want to

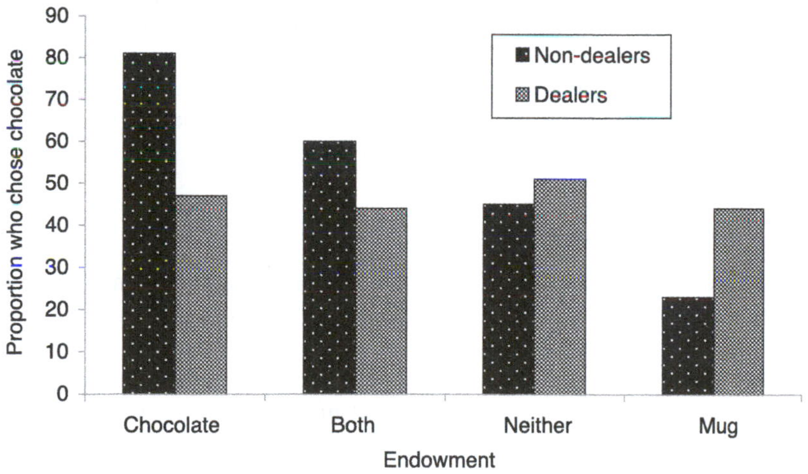

Figure 2.8 Whether subjects chose chocolate depended on the endowment. Those given chocolate were more likely to choose chocolate and those given a mug to choose the mug.

Source: List (2004).

swap for a mug, and those given a mug do not want to swap for a chocolate bar! It is highly unlikely that this is just an accident of giving chocolate to those who like chocolate and mugs to those who like coffee. Instead it seems that people are biased by physically having the good in their hand, a framing effect. This is clear from the 'both' and 'neither' cases, where approximately 50 percent swap.

That people value more highly goods that they have some ownership over is called the **endowment effect**. If the endowment effect shows up in people who randomly possess for a few seconds a mug they probably do not want, then economists need to take it seriously, because ownership and trading of goods is at the heart of economics.

One way to explain the endowment effect is through reference dependence and loss aversion. If Anna has the coffee mug in her hand, then she may feel that she already owns that coffee mug. To give it away would be a loss. By contrast, if she does not have the chocolate bar in her hand then she feels no sense of ownership over it. To get the chocolate would be a gain. We have suggested that losses are weighted more heavily than gains. If so, Anna would be reluctant to swap the mug in her hand for a chocolate bar, even if she would have marginally preferred a chocolate bar.

Being overly possessive of a mug does not seem particularly useful. In some situations, however, the endowment effect may be beneficial, as we shall see when we talk about housing and saving. In situations where it is not beneficial, we should expect more experienced people to have learned to avoid the effect. This is what we generally do observe. To illustrate, look at what dealers, people with booths at the show, did when offered a mug. Dealers had more market experience in trading (sports cards) than non-dealers, and showed no signs of being biased.

Interestingly, however, people may learn to redirect the endowment effect, rather than suppress it. This follows from an appreciation of opportunity cost. To someone familiar with the concept of opportunity cost, to keep the coffee mug in your hand is a loss, because of the value that can be got from swapping the mug. The distinction between what is a loss and what is a gain can thus be blurred. In this way the endowment effect is lessened and we get our first suggestion that the reference point depends on the person and context.

2.2.3 Willingness to pay or accept

One place the endowment effect shows up is contingent valuation. **Contingent valuation** is an often used technique to get people to reveal how much they value things like health, safety, or the environment. Two basic methods of contingent valuation are willingness to pay (WTP) and willingness to accept (WTA). In the first, **willingness to pay**, people are asked how much money they would be willing to pay to get an extra unit of some good; that is, they are asked how much they would pay to consume $c + 1$ rather than c units of the good. In the second, **willingness to accept**, people are asked how much money they would be willing to accept for having one unit less of the good; that is, they are asked how much they would accept to consume c rather than $c + 1$ units. In both cases we get a valuation on the $c + 1$st unit of the good.

Given what we know of loss aversion and the endowment effect, we should not be surprised that WTA and WTP can lead to different valuations. WTP makes the person think of losing money and they may not be willing to pay much, i.e. lose a lot of money, to get an extra unit of the good. WTA, by contrast, makes the person think of losing the good, and they may want a lot of money to compensate for getting less of the good. This is consistent with what we do observe. The valuation of a good based on willingness to accept typically exceeds one based on willingness to pay, and this difference can be large. This is a **violation of procedural invariance**, in that the answer we get to a question depends on the procedure we use to find the answer, a specific form of framing effect.

To illustrate, Figure 2.9 provides some data from a study by Bateman and co-authors (2005) in which subjects were asked to put a contingent valuation on ten chocolates. For now, just focus on the WTA and WTP. The WTA valuation is around 60 percent more than the WTP valuation. This difference is a problem for anyone who wants to obtain a reliable estimate of the value that people put on goods. Should they use the WTP or WTA measure?

It also raises some fundamental questions about how people value goods. That's because when talking about the endowment effect it is natural to have in mind physical ownership of a good. So, we think of the subject owning a mug or owning a box of chocolates, if only for a few seconds. The WTA and WTP measures, however, get subjects to think about potentially owning a good. This seems enough to trigger an endowment effect and shift of the reference point.

One place where this becomes relevant is in thinking through the **no loss in buying hypothesis**. The idea behind this hypothesis is that, when people are deciding whether to buy a good, they mentally deduct money from their current income and then decide whether to gain the good or (re)gain the money they

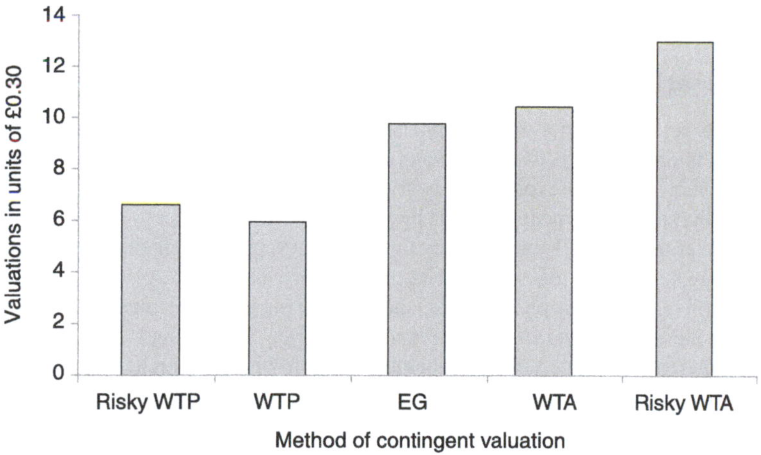

Figure 2.9 The valuation put on ten chocolates. The WTP exceeds the WTA but not the EG.

Source: Bateman *et al.* (2005).

would spend buying the good. For example, if Anna usually buys Honey cereal for $4 then she feels no loss in spending $4 buying Honey because she expected to pay $4. We can rephrase this in terms of the reference point. Is the reference point current income, and so buying Honey involves a loss of $4, or is it current income minus the amount needed to buy Honey, meaning that not buying the good involves regaining $4?

For me, it is more natural to think of the latter. For example, I might say that 'Anna's reference point for Honey is $4'. What I really mean is that Anna expects to spend $4 on Honey, and so has mentally deducted that from her wealth to give a reference point of wealth minus $4. The study by Bateman and co-authors, however (see Research Methods 2.4), put the no loss in buying hypothesis to the test and found little support for it. What to make of this result?

The no loss in buying hypothesis essentially assumes that people take account of the opportunity cost of money, as we suggested experienced traders might do to avoid the endowment effect. This suggests that experience is important. If people are inexperienced in a particular task, which is likely when finding the WTP and WTA of goods that the person rarely if ever buys, then buying may be interpreted as a loss. By contrast, if people are more experienced in a task, like Anna buying Honey every week, then buying may not be interpreted as a loss, unless the price is more than she expected.

The interesting thing this illustrates is that it can be quite ambiguous what a person thinks they own or do not own, or what is counted as a gain or a loss. For instance, when Anna walks into the grocery store, does she own $4, or the box of Honey that she expects to buy for $4? That depends on how she thinks. That means it's somewhat arbitrary and subject to perception, intuition, and framing. We will look next at why this matters.

Research Methods 2.4

Adversarial collaboration

Often, observed behavior can be explained by two or more competing theories, with no way to distinguish between the theories using existing data. That means that we need a more nuanced experiment to try and evaluate one theorem over another. Typically, such experiments are done by researchers who historically have supported one side of the debate. Typically, they find data that supports their side of the debate. This may be for pure reasons, such as confirmatory bias which we shall explain in Chapter five, or for less pure reasons, such as wanting to further their career. Either way, it does not often seem the most constructive way to do things.

An alternative is adversarial collaboration. This is where researchers on both sides of a debate get together and jointly design and evaluate an experiment to test respective theories. In the study we have been looking at, a team, loosely based at the University of East Anglia, joined with Daniel Kahneman to explore the no loss in buying hypothesis. Given that both sides are given equal chances to influence the design of the experiment and look at and evaluate the data, the conclusions should be free of systematic bias. This seems, therefore, a much more constructive way of doing things.

For completeness I should briefly explain what the researchers did. A third valuation method is **equivalent gain** (EG), in which a person is asked the smallest amount of money that would be equivalent to one more unit of the good. Like WTA, this question asks about consuming c rather than $c + 1$ units of the good. The difference is the endowment point. In WTA the person should feel as though they are endowed with $c + 1$ units and are being asked to give up a unit. With EG the person should feel as though they are endowed with c units and have a choice between more money or an extra unit of the good.

All agree that WTA will exceed EG. The more interesting question is whether EG exceeds WTP. If giving up money in exchange for a good is counted as a loss then EG should exceed WTP, if it is considered a forgone gain then EG and WTP should be equal. This seems to provide a simple test. What happens, however, if WTA is a 'lot bigger' than EG and EG only 'slightly bigger' than WTP? This is the kind of thing open to different interpretations. So, valuation methods called risky WTP and risky WTA are also used. For reasons we will skip, this gives a test of the no loss in buying hypothesis:

$$\text{if } \frac{EG}{WTP} > 1 \text{ and } \frac{WTP}{risky\ WTP} = 1 \text{ evidence that exchange is a loss of money}$$

$$\text{if } \frac{EG}{WTP} = 1 \text{ and } \frac{WTP}{risky\ WTP} > 1 \text{ evidence that exchange is a forgone gain of money}$$

Other checks that things are working well include that risky WTA equals the WTA. The data, summarized in Figure 2.9, suggests that exchange is a loss of money.

2.2.4 Transaction utility

If reference dependence fundamentally affects how much we value goods, as loss aversion and the endowment effect suggest it does, then it should influence our decisions to buy or not. To illustrate, suppose that Anna is on holiday and wants to buy Nutty, so goes into the local grocery store. How much should she be willing to pay? There are two things worth considering. First is the maximum she is willing to pay for a box, ignoring any possible psychological effects. Let's suppose that she likes Nutty a lot, so this is \$8. Next is the reference point, and given that she normally pays \$3, we can start with a reference point of r = \$3. Remember that what this actually means is, 'the reference point is wealth minus \$3'.

We can then distinguish between acquisition and transaction utility. **Acquisition utility** measures the net gain from buying something for less than it is valued, so in this case is $v(8 - p)$. **Transaction utility** measures the net gain or loss from buying something for less or more than expected, so is $v(r - p)$. The total value from buying the box of cereal is therefore $v(8 - p) + v(3 - p)$. If p = \$2, then she will feel a double gain: she buys something she likes and pays less than she expected to! If $p = \$4$, then she will probably buy but will feel a loss of paying more than she expected. If $p = \$6$, then she will probably not buy because the loss from 'paying too much' exceeds the gain from buying the cereal she likes.

Transaction utility is the key thing here in that it captures how Anna may feel good about buying a bargain, or bad about being charged too much. This can influence whether or not she buys Nutty. But this in itself is not so fundamental. What is fundamental is that the reference point she has will likely depend on perception and intuition. Whether she perceives Nutty as a bargain or a rip-off will depend on the context. An example from Thaler (2008a) illustrates:

> You are lying on the beach on a hot day. All you have to drink is water. For the last hour you have been thinking about how much you would enjoy a nice cold bottle of your favorite brand of beer. A companion gets up to go make a phone call and offers to bring back a beer from the only nearby place where beer is sold, a fancy resort hotel. He says that the beer might be expensive and so asks how much you are willing to pay for the beer. . . . What price do you tell him?
>
> Now, substitute 'a small, run-down grocery store' instead of 'a fancy resort hotel'.

People surveyed by Thaler said they would pay on average \$2.65 in the fancy hotel and \$1.50 in the store. The difference probably reflects concerns for fairness, which we shall look at in Chapter seven, but the key point is that there is a difference. The reference point, and thus the perception of what is a bargain or a rip-off, depended on the context. Indeed the reference point by which transaction utility is judged can seemingly change quite easily. We are back to framing effects and choice arbitrariness. Someone might buy a beer from a fancy resort hotel but not from a small, run-down grocery store, even if it's the same beer at the same price.

The notion of transaction utility may seem intuitive, but we do hit a snag. Anna might have a reference price for Nutty, or beer, but it is unlikely she has a reference price for everything she might buy. It is also unlikely she knows for sure what things she is going to buy. It is even more unlikely she keeps track of each gain or loss of transaction utility when buying 100 or more different products in a grocery store. We have, therefore, some work to do in order to apply the notion of transaction utility.

2.2.5 Narrow framing

It could be that Anna enters the grocery store with a reference point for various things she might buy, like 'I will probably spend \$3 on Nutty'. More likely, however, is that Anna has an expectation of how much she should spend in the grocery store, or how much she should spend a week on food. The important reference point will thus be something like '\$200 a week on food'. If Nutty is cheaper than \$3, then great, but that will soon be counteracted if apples are more expensive than usual. It is the final total at the checkout that matters most.

What's happening here is that things are being grouped together, or not, so that Anna can keep track of what is going on. This way she knows whether she is spending more or less than she wanted. She can keep track of spending on individual items, like a box of Honey, and keep track of the total amount spent in the store.

The process of grouping things together not only brings some things together but also separates those that end up in different groups. This can cause **narrow framing**, wherein a choice or outcome is seen in isolation rather than being integrated with other things. For instance, spending on food items might be seen as separate from spending on leisure. Here's another example:

> Question one. Imagine that you have decided to see a play where admission costs $10 per ticket. As you enter the theater you discover that you have lost a $10 bill. Would you pay $10 to watch the play?
>
> Question two. Imagine that you have bought the ticket to see a play where admission costs $10. As you enter the theater, you discover you have lost the ticket and there is no way to recover it. Would you pay $10 for another ticket?

Tversky and Kahneman (1981) report that 88 percent of subjects asked question one said they would pay, but only 46 percent asked question two said they would pay. In both cases the loss is $10, so where the loss comes from clearly matters.

To capture such things we can introduce mental accounting. **Mental accounting** is the process of coding, categorizing, and evaluating choices and outcomes. The primary component of mental accounting is to put any spending or income into separate accounts for specific purposes. For example, Anna might have a 'go to the theater account', a 'loose change account', and a 'food account'. Outcomes will be perceived and experienced relative to the particular account that is brought to mind. Losing a $10 bill brings to mind the loose change account, whereas losing the theater ticket brings to mind the theater account. Losing the $10 bill has, therefore, no implications for the theater account, and so should not influence Anna's choice to go to the theater; she expected to pay $10 and so should still pay $10 to watch, and she just might look to save $10 somewhere else to bring the loose change account back below the reference point. By contrast, losing the ticket does matter for the theater account; she expected to watch for no extra cost but now has to pay an additional $10. This makes the cost to go to the theater feel like $20 and that may put her off going.

A pertinent question is how narrowly defined accounts are. For example, is there a 'theater account', an 'entertainment account', or just a general 'current spending account'? To get some idea, we can look at a study by Heath and Soll (1996). In the study, subjects were asked how their spending would likely be affected by a related purchase, a gift, or an unrelated purchase. For instance, subjects were asked whether they would purchase a $25 theater ticket if they had ((a), related purchase) already bought a $50 sports ticket, or ((b), gift) been given for free a sports ticket worth $50, or ((c), unrelated purchase) heard of a flu epidemic and had to spend $50 on a flu inoculation. Of particular interest are people who answer no, yes, and yes. That they answer yes to (b) and (c) means they would be willing to go to both the theater and sports event and can afford to do so even if they have already spent $50. That they answer no to (a) is evidence of narrow framing.

Table 2.5 summarizes what proportion of subjects answered no, yes, yes for various combinations of the good being purchased and the related purchase. For instance, 38 percent did so for our example question of buying a theater ticket after having purchased a sports ticket. We see that a high proportion of subjects said no, yes, yes and so there is evidence of narrow framing. By comparing goods we can also see how narrowly defined mental budgets appeared to be. The combinations in bold were considered by subjects to not be related purchases. For example, buying a sweatshirt was not considered related to buying a sports ticket. In these cases the proportion of no, yes, yes answers goes down. This suggests that mental accounts can be quite narrowly defined. Spending on a sweatshirt does not come out of the same account as spending on a sports ticket, boat tour, party snacks, etc.

More generally, the evidence suggests that people use mental accounts to keep track of income and spending, and that gains or losses are coded relative to an account reference point. One interesting thing about this is that we now have two dimensions to the arbitrariness of the reference point. There is the question of what reference point will be brought to mind; will Anna think of the 'Nutty is usually $3' reference point or the 'I should spend $200 on food' reference point?; will the person on the beach think of the '$2 for beer is expensive' reference point or the 'I have $8 loose change' reference point? There is then the question of what level the reference point should be: a person might pay $2.50 from a fancy resort hotel but only $1.50 from a small, run-down grocery store. This gives lots of room

Table 2.5 The proportion of subjects (%) who answered no, yes, yes to purchasing a good when the alternative was a related purchase, gift, or unrelated purchase. The numbers in bold indicate that the related purchase was not considered in the same mental account as the good being purchased

The 'related' purchase	*The good being purchased*		
	Theater ticket (entertainment)	*Chinese takeaway (food)*	*Sweatshirt (clothes)*
Sports ticket	38	**12**	**12**
Boat tour	41	**16**	**6**
Party snacks	21	12	**6**
Salmon	21	24	**0**
Dinner out	32	32	**6**
Wine	15	18	**3**
Jeans	**0**	**0**	12
Watch	15	**3**	9
Costume	38	**9**	9

Source: Heath and Soll (1996).

for perception and intuition to matter. No wonder we get framing effects and choice arbitrariness. But can we go even further?

2.2.6 Hedonic editing

So far we have primarily been thinking of a person responding to external factors beyond their control that influence perceptions, intuition, the reference point, and possibly behavior. Mental accounting, however, suggests that people may have some control of such factors. Anna can potentially choose what mental accounts she has, the reference point for each account, and how she codes gains and losses.

To illustrate, suppose that Anna buys one box of Nutty for herself and a box of Superior for her son. She goes to the shop and fortunately finds that both are in a half-price sale. This means she gains \$1.50 on the box of Nutty and \$3 on the box of Superior. This could be coded as two separate gains or as one big gain. If the outcomes are **segregated**, they are valued separately to give v (\$1.50) + v (\$3). If they are **integrated** they are combined together to give v (\$4.50). We are going to show in the next chapter that the value function is probably concave, which means that v(\$1.50) + v(\$3) > v (\$4.50). Thus, it would be better for Anna to segregate the gains in her mind.

Suppose that a month later, the sale long over, Anna goes to the store and finds that the prices of the Nutty and Superior have increased by 50 percent. This means she needs to spend an extra \$1.50 on Nutty and \$3.00 on Superior. Segregating these losses gives v(−\$1.50) + v (−\$3), while integrating the losses gives v(−\$4.50). We shall show that the value function is probably convex in losses, which means that v(−\$1.50) + v (−\$3) < v(−\$4.50). This means that Anna would do best to integrate losses.

So, if Anna has a choice how to code gains and losses, then: multiple gains should be segregated, multiple losses should be combined, and gains should be used to cancel small losses. Does such integration and segregation make sense? Intuitively it does seem to, as an example by Thaler (2008a) illustrates:

> Mr A was given tickets to some lotteries. He won \$50 in one lottery and \$25 in the other. Mr B was given a ticket for another lottery and won \$75. Who was happier?

Most people say that A will be happier. As Thaler suggests, 'Moral: don't wrap all the Christmas presents in one box'! We call this process of categorizing gains or losses as **hedonic editing**. It suggests that people can partly manipulate how they perceive or interpret things in order to make themselves feel better. Another way to do this is choice bracketing.

2.2.7 Choice bracketing

The focus in this final section is on the coding of losses and gains over time. Often there is a delay between paying for a good and consuming it, or consuming it and paying. For example, Anna might buy some frozen food she does not expect to eat for a month or two, but also might put everything on credit, meaning that she does not need to pay for a month or two. Such things mean that losses and gains will appear in accounts at different points in time. People can choose how narrowly or broadly they want to group together events spread over time, an example of **choice bracketing**.

I will look first at the implications of a delay between paying and consumption, using a study by Shafir and Thaler (2006) to illustrate. They first asked subscribers to a wine newsletter how they would think about giving away as a gift, drinking, or dropping and breaking, a bottle of wine that cost \$20 and now sells for \$75. Figure 2.10 summarizes the results. Overall we see a fairly mixed response. Many, however, thought that giving away or drinking the bottle of wine costs them nothing, or even saves them money. This suggests the cost must be accounted for when the bottle is bought. Further questioning, however, suggested that, when buying the wine, most framed the purchase as an investment rather than a cost. This motivates the title of Shafir and Thaler's paper, 'Invest now, drink later, spend never'. It is as if delayed consumption allows people to frame the initial purchase as an investment which has depreciated by the time the consumption takes place. This is a convenient way to never feel any loss! Only if the bottle is broken does the loss become apparent.

We can next look at what happens when there is a delay between consumption and paying, with a study by Siemens (2007). In the study, subjects were paid \$5

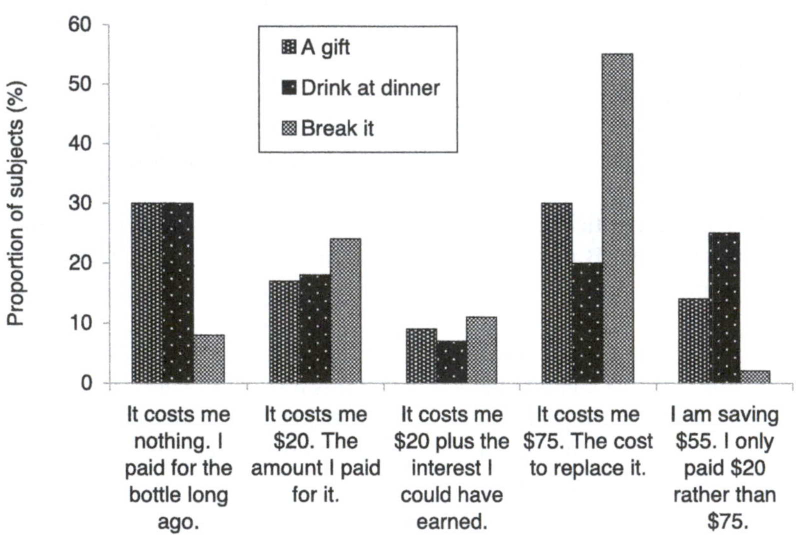

Figure 2.10 How subjects valued a bottle of wine that cost \$20 and is now worth \$75 depending on whether they drank it, gave it as a gift, or broke it.

Source: Shafir and Thaler (2006).

for doing a 30-minute survey. All subjects were given the $5 immediately. What differed was when they did the study. Some did it immediately, some three days later, some a week later and some two weeks later. Having finished the survey, subjects were asked what they thought about the task. Figure 2.11 summarizes the results. We see a fairly clear and consistent drop-off in perceived satisfaction, fairness, and willingness to do the task again, the more the delay between getting the $5 and doing the survey.

Both of these studies give a consistent picture in which the costs and benefits, or losses and gains, diminish over time. So, the cost of buying the wine is forgotten by the time it is drunk, and the gain of $5 is forgotten by the time the task has to be done.

One interesting thing to take from this is that we now have a third dimension to the arbitrariness of the reference point, namely how far forward or back a person looks. For instance, Anna's entertainment account could be '$50 a week', or '$200 a month'. The former option means she will probably only go to one event a week. The latter option allows her to attend a few events one week if she makes up for that with subsequent weeks of abstinence. What time frame comes to mind at any one time will likely depend on her perception and intuition of the situation.

Hopefully, by now you have got the idea that reference points matter and are somewhat arbitrary. They are likely to depend on the context and the way that someone perceives a particular situation. This is a very important idea to keep in mind as you read through the rest of the book.

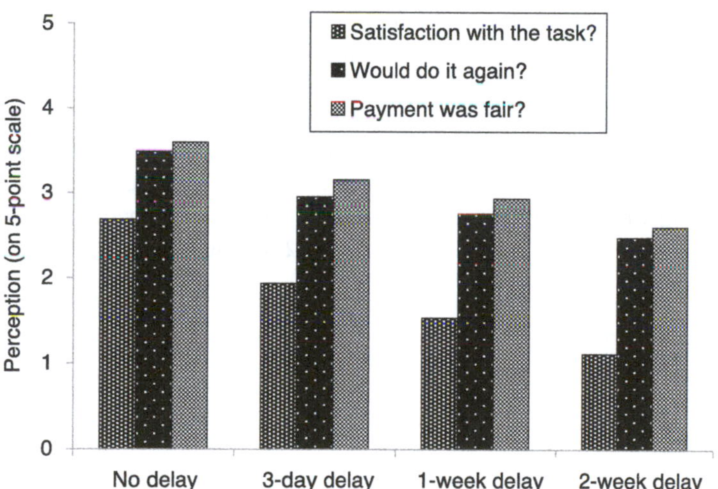

Figure 2.11 How subjects felt about a task depending on how long they did it after getting paid. Answers measured on a five-point scale from unpleasant, definitely would not, extremely unfair (1) to pleasant, definitely would, extremely fair payment (5).

Source: Siemens (2007).

2.3 The role of emotions

All the heuristics mentioned so far have been relatively practical ones, like 'do the same as last time', 'spend no more than $200 a week on food', and 'pick the one in the middle'. It is important to recognize that heuristics can also have a much more emotive and moral character. One particularly interesting example is the heuristic 'do not lie'.

Clearly, the decision whether or not to lie has various moral, religious, and philosophical undertones. That, though, does not stop it being a crucial component in many economic interactions. The saleswoman can lie about the quality of her product, the job candidate can lie about her qualifications, the buyer can lie about her ability to pay, and so on. Whether or not the person lies, and whether or not others trust her to not lie, are fundamental to how such interactions will play out. Heuristics like 'do not lie' and 'trust others to not lie' are, therefore, easily as relevant to economics as heuristics like 'do the same as last time'.

Indeed, emotions are a vital part of what makes us different to homo economicus. We get excited, angry, sad, upset, and happy, while homo economicus just keeps on maximizing objective functions. Emotions inevitably influence choice and so behavioral economics needs a way to take account of that. What I want to do here is illustrate how emotions naturally fit within the system of mental accounting and framing developed in the previous section. In order to do that, I shall focus on the 'do not lie' heuristic.

2.3.1 Aversion to lying

Homo economicus would lie whenever she can benefit from doing so. Homo sapiens, however, do not like lying. To illustrate the point I'll look at an experimental study by Mazar and co-authors (2008). Subjects were given a test sheet containing 20 matrices, like the one in Figure 2.12, and asked to find, for each matrix, the two numbers that add to ten. In the matrix shown, for instance, the answer is 4.81 and 5.19. Subjects had four minutes to solve as many matrices as possible and were asked to record the number solved on a separate answer sheet. They were subsequently paid either $0.50 or $2 for each matrix solved.

1.69	1.82	2.91
4.67	4.81	3.05
5.82	5.06	4.28
6.36	5.19	4.57

Figure 2.12 A matrix for the adding to 10 task. Subjects had to find the two numbers that add up to 10.

Source: Mazar *et al.* (2008).

Three treatments were compared. In the 'answers will be checked' treatment subjects had to hand in both the test sheet and answer sheet. The experimenter would then verify how many matrices the subject solved. In the 'chance to lie' treatment subjects had to hand in only the answer sheet. The experimenter, therefore, had no opportunity to check how many matrices the subject really had solved. Finally, in the 'honor code' treatment subjects had the chance to lie but were asked to sign below a statement that read 'I understand that this short survey falls under MIT's honor system'. This set-up captures three basic ways in which employers can monitor workers. They can closely monitor worker output, let the worker self-report, or let the worker self-report with reminders of moral obligations.

Letting a worker self-report may seem bizarre. What is to stop, for instance, someone in the chance to lie treatment saying they solved all 20 matrices? They walk away with the maximum payout and the employer (or experimenter in this case) is short-changed. Self-reporting is, however, very common in the workplace, particularly in skilled professions. A professor, for example, does most of her work behind the closed, or half-closed, door of her office. She might be carefully marking students' work, or she might be rushing through the marking with one eye on the football that is streaming live on the internet. Monitoring performance is very difficult, and that means we rely on the honesty of the professor. Figure 2.13 shows why that may not be such a bizarre thing to do.

Figure 2.13 summarizes the number of matrices that subjects reported to have solved. Subjects in the chance to lie treatment did on average 'solve' more than

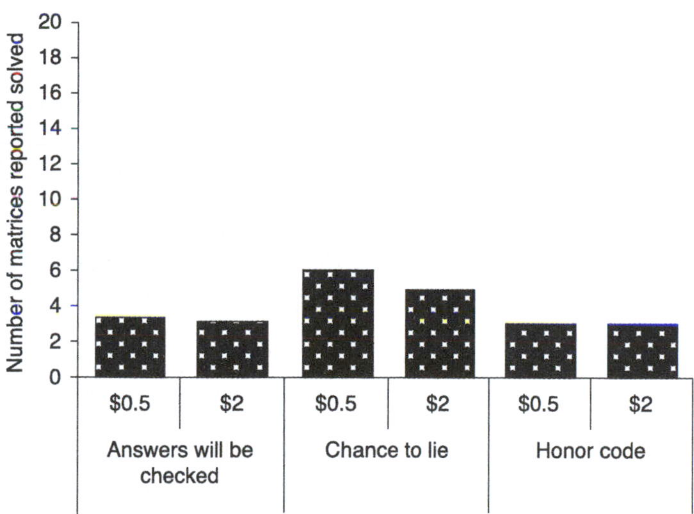

Figure 2.13 Number of matrices that subjects reported to have solved. In the chance to lie treatment, subjects 'solved' more correctly. But, cheating was well below that possible. Subjects could have reported 20 solved matrices.

Source: Mazar *et al.* (2008).

those in the answers will be checked treatment. This suggests that some cheating went on. The numbers are, however, way below the maximum of 20. So, subjects did not cheat anywhere near as much as they could have done. Also, getting subjects to sign up to the honor code was enough to eliminate any cheating. And increasing the rewards to cheating from $0.5 to $2 decreased the amount of cheating. It seems as though subjects did use a 'do not lie' heuristic.

2.3.2 Deception

In the discussion so far we have focused on a person who could lie for financial gain and has to choose whether or not to do so. For example, the worker can misreport output and, for sure, earn a higher payout. In reality things are rarely so simple. A more realistic exchange would be one where the worker reports output and the employer decides whether or not to believe that report. Or, where the saleswoman reports on the quality of her product and the buyer decides whether or not to trust her. Such interrelationships bring us to the issue of **deception**. To illustrate the ideas we can look at a so-called **cheap-talk sender-receiver game**.

The game involves two options, called A and B, and two people, called the sender and receiver. The sender gets to see the payoffs from each option. She learns that option A would give her $5 and the receiver $15, and that option B would give her $15 and the receiver $5. Clearly, option A looks better for the receiver and option B looks better for her. Having seen these payoffs she then has to send a message to the receiver. She can either send the message 'Option A will earn you more money than option B', or 'Option B will earn you more money than option A'. The first message is honest and the second is dishonest. The receiver, without knowing anything about payoffs, must choose option A or B.

To put the game in context you can think of a saleswoman trying to sell a student a calculator. Model A is the better model but not very profitable for the seller. Model B is not so good, but a lot more profitable for the seller. The saleswoman must choose whether to be honest and say model A is best. The student must decide whether to believe the saleswoman's claims. The saleswoman has no material incentive to be honest. So, why should the student believe anything she says? Well, if people have an aversion to lying then it may make sense to trust her word.

A study by Gneezy (2005) had subjects play this cheap-talk game and others in which the payoffs from options A and B differed. Subjects also played a dictator version of the game in which the sender chose between options A and B. The dictator game is important for comparison purposes because people, as we'll see in Chapter seven, often voluntarily give money to others. Figure 2.14 illustrates the main results of the study.

To make sense of the results let us start by looking at the games where option A yields $5 and $15 and option B yields $15 and $5. In the dictator version of the game around 90 percent of senders chose option B. This is not surprising given that the sender chooses to have $15 rather than $5. In the cheap-talk version of the

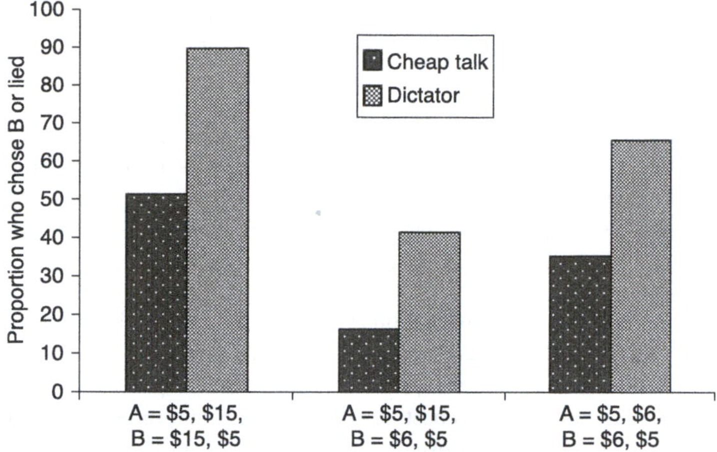

Figure 2.14 The proportion of subjects who chose option B or lied that option B will earn more money. Subjects showed an aversion to lying as shown by a lower proportion in the cheap-talk game than the dictator game.

Source: Gneezy (2005).

game only around 50 percent of senders sent the 'B will earn you more money' message. The drop from 90 percent to 50 percent could be an aversion to lying. Senders did not want to lie to receivers about which option was best (see Research Methods 2.5).

Research Methods 2.5

Eye tracking and lie detection

In a study by Wang and co-authors (2010) subjects played a sender–receiver game not too unlike the one already described. The main differences were that there were five options instead of two and the receiver had some information about payoffs. These differences mean that strategy is more of an issue. I don't, however, want to focus on this. Instead I want to focus on the fact that the eye movements of senders were monitored as they made their decision.

This was possible with an eye-tracking device that can tell where subjects are looking (or on what their eyes are fixated). For example, we know that senders spent an average 3.99 seconds looking at what their own payoff would be for each option, and only 2.72 seconds looking at what the payoff of the receiver would be. The device can also tell how dilated the pupil is. This is fascinating, because pupils are known to dilate during stress or while doing cognitively difficult tasks. As expected, the pupils of senders become more dilated the more they attempt to deceive the receiver.

So, what do we gain from eye tracking? Without eye tracking we only observe the choice of the sender. We then have to try and infer why the sender made the choice they did and how they felt about it. That can be a difficult, if not impossible, task. Eye tracking gives us a lot more information to go on. By analyzing the things they chose to look at we can potentially piece together the strategy they were using (see also Research Methods 6.1). By measuring pupil dilation we get some limited insight on how they felt about the decision (see also Chapter nine). To prove the point, the authors of the study showed that information on eye movements and dilation was enough to relatively accurately predict the truth. A lie detector test!

For the two other payoff combinations senders were less likely to choose option B. This is understandable given the change in payoffs and a willingness to give money to others. We still, though, see a clear drop in the proportion of senders who lied by saying that option B was best. Again, this suggests some aversion to lying.

Interpreting behavior is, however, a little bit tricky in sender-receiver games given their strategic element. For instance, suppose the saleswoman expects the student will use the heuristic 'never trust a saleswoman'. Then the saleswoman may recommend the best model A in the hope that the student's mistrust will cause her to buy model B. In this case, the saleswoman attempts to deceive the student by telling the truth! Such strategic concerns are more the topic of later chapters (see, in particular, Research Methods 7.4), but I want to give you some idea of how prevalent such 'false truth telling' can be. To do that, I turn to a study by Sutter (2009).

The key thing about this study was that senders were asked which option they expected receivers to choose. This allows us to pick out the four types of behavior summarized in Table 2.6. We are particularly interested in the sophisticated truth teller. This is someone who 'tells the truth' expecting the receiver to not trust her. Figure 2.15 details the proportion of senders that could be classified as liars and sophisticated truth tellers (hardly anyone was a benevolent liar). The study contrasted the situation where the sender was an individual with the situation where the sender was a team of two or three that made a joint decision.

Focus first on individuals. Previously, in Figure 2.14 in particular, we only picked out the liars. You can see that the proportion of liars is similar in this study by Sutter to that of Gneezy. We can now also see, however, that around 20 to 30 percent of subjects were sophisticated truth tellers. In teams, the proportion is much higher (see Research Methods 2.6). Such evidence shows that we need to take seri-

Table 2.6 Four different types of behavior possible in cheap talk sender-receiver game

Behavior of sender	*Recommends to receiver*	*Expects receiver to choose*
Benevolent truth teller	A	A
Sophisticated truth teller	A	B
Liar	B	B
Benevolent liar	B	A

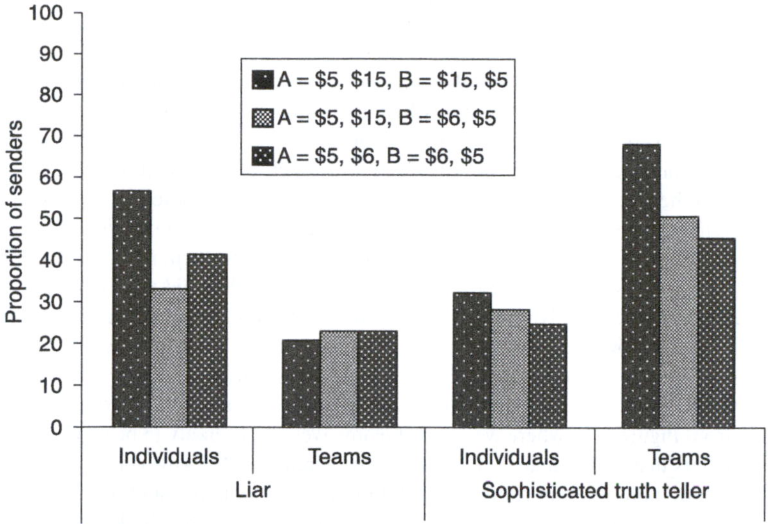

Figure 2.15 Proportion of senders who were liars and sophisticated truth tellers distinguished into individuals and groups. A large proportion of individuals were sophisticated truth tellers. An even larger proportion of groups were sophisticated truth tellers.

Source: Sutter (2009).

ously the idea that people can deceive by telling the truth. Once we take account of sophisticated truth tellers the proportion of senders who do not attempt to deceive (benevolent truth tellers) falls to around 30 percent. This is still a large proportion, but it is clear that people feel less aversion to deceiving than to lying. An aversion to lying does not necessarily, therefore, translate into always telling the truth.

This qualification should not, though, detract from the basic message that senders reveal much more information than homo economicus would. It is also clear that receivers are a lot more trusting of the information sent than homo economicus would be. For example, in both the studies by Gneezy and Sutter, over 70 percent of receivers followed the advice of the sender. So, the heuristic 'trust others to not lie' seems to fit much better than 'never trust a saleswoman'.

Research Methods 2.6

Videoing team decision making

There are various reasons why a sender might look like a sophisticated truth teller but not want to deceive. For example, she might think that the receiver is going to choose B no matter what she says. Or, she might be averse enough to lying that she says A is best but doesn't want the receiver to choose B. In neither case is her objective in choosing A the deliberate deception of the receiver. It would be nice, therefore, to know what is going through the mind of sophisticated truth tellers when they send message A. Are they really trying to deceive the receiver?

This is impossible to tell from the choices that senders make. So, in order to gain some insight on this question the study by Sutter looked at decision making in teams. The teams were videoed reaching their decision. By analyzing the discussion between team members it is possible to get a much clearer picture of how they arrived at their decision. Of the 37 sender teams that were classified as sophisticated truth tellers, 34 explicitly discussed the argument that sending option A would increase their payoff because the receiver would not believe them and choose option B. This strongly suggests that most sophisticated truth tellers did want to deceive.

Here we see a clear advantage of using teams in the laboratory. By eavesdropping on the conversation between team members we can get a clearer picture of each subject's thought processes. This can help us understand why a particular decision was made. The drawback is that teams may behave differently to individuals. This is clear from Figure 2.15 where we see that teams were more likely to be sophisticated truth tellers than individuals. It does not seem unreasonable, however, to argue that the deception observed in teams is a good indication that many sophisticated truth-telling individuals also set out to deceive. In Chapter six we shall look at team decision making in more detail.

2.3.3 Honesty and framing

The general picture we get, from many different studies, is that the 'do not lie', 'do not deceive', and 'trust others to not lie' are important heuristics in economic decision making. This is not to say that people do not lie and deceive. They clearly do. The collapse of Enron and doping in professional sport are two powerful examples of people's willingness to lie for financial gain. The point is: people lie and deceive a lot less than they could do.

So, why are people so honesty? A leading explanation is that honesty helps a person maintain a **positive self-concept**. The person wants to feel that she is a good person and by not lying she can help maintain a positive opinion of herself. If this is true, then we should be able to observe some interesting framing effects. We have already seen one example: the honor code reminds a person of the importance of honesty and so brings the 'do not lie' heuristic to mind. On the flip side may be possibilities to lie without harming self-concept. For example, if a person perceives that 'everyone is lying', then it may excuse her lying. People may also be more willing to lie in order to avoid a loss than to achieve a gain. And they may be even more willing to lie in order to avoid a loss of something they feel they have earned. We'll come back to some of these issues when we look at tax avoidance in Chapter three.

The differences we observed between deception and lying can also arise from a framing effect. In a sender-receiver game strategic interaction is foremost. This more easily allows a person to maintain positive self-concept by passing on the blame to others. Should, for instance, a sophisticated truth teller feel any guilt from recommending A? After all, she told the truth. The receiver can only lose out if she mistrusts what she is told. Similarly, should a liar feel any guilt from recommending B? In this case the receiver loses out because of naively trusting what she is told.

Such reasoning can explain why people appear more willing to deceive than lie. Given, however, that lying is inherently an interpersonal process, passing the blame is always possible. For example, the professor who self-reports output can say that the university is naive to believe she will report honestly! The difference is that some contexts, and frames, make it easier for a person to lie and maintain self-concept by passing the blame than others.

In bringing this section to a close I want to highlight the key thing you should take away: heuristics, perception, and intuition can have a moral and emotional dimension to them. A person feels guilt from lying. She feels pride from being honest. She feels pleasure when someone tells the truth. She feels angry when she is deceived. Not all heuristics, therefore, are about simple, hard-headed, cost-benefit calculation. Instead, emotions often drive perception and intuition, meaning that context effects can be caused by the mood that the context generates.

We can already see the consequences of emotions in things like loss aversion, the endowment effect, and transaction utility. Paying $2.50 for a beer from a fancy resort hotel is fine, but being asked to pay $2.50 in a run-down grocery store makes a person angry. That anger means she would rather stay thirsty than buy the beer.

In the remainder of the book we shall see more and more examples of the role that emotions play in choice. For instance, emotions are particularly important when analyzing interpersonal choice. A person can only lie if they have someone to lie to; they feel guilty for having deceived the other person. In later chapters we shall see heuristics like 'punish those that harm me' and 'reward those that help me'. Such heuristics can only be understood if we take account of the emotions that harm and help arouse in the person.

2.4 Summary

We have already covered a lot of important ideas, so it's high time that I put things into context with a short summary.

I started with the observation that saying someone should maximize her utility does not get us far if, as seems reasonable, she does not know what maximizes her utility. This lack of knowledge means she needs to search for more information about what she likes and dislikes. It also means that her choices will be somewhat arbitrary until she becomes better informed. Indeed, her choice can be influenced by all sorts of external factors, including the way things are framed. We called these context effects.

I then argued that people focus more on relative rather than absolute judgments. In terms of economic behavior this means there will be a focus on gains or losses relative to some reference point. People seem particularly averse to losses, resulting in things like the endowment effect.

We then saw that the reference point can be a very subjective thing. It is essentially what someone expected or thought would or should happen and the person is free to think different things. She is also free to change the viewpoint from, say, what will happen this week to what will happen this month.

One step up from this is a person using 'creative accounting' to manipulate the reference point or viewpoint to increase their utility. This we called hedonic editing. Most of the time, however, the reference point will probably be influenced by subconscious processes like intuition and perception. So, context influences perception and intuition, which influences the reference point, which influences choice. Framing matters and the reference point matters!

The final thing we looked at is the importance of emotions. Heuristics can have a moral and emotive character to them, such as the heuristic, 'do not lie'. Also, perception and intuition will often be influenced by the emotions that a context generates.

That there are context effects, and that emotions and framing matter, might seem obvious, particularly if you have studied some psychology, but it does mean a fairly fundamental departure from the standard economic model. Specifically, there are two new and crucial things we need to add to the model: (i) that utility depends on outcomes relative to some reference point, and (ii) that the reference point and choice will depend on the context in which the decision is made in somewhat arbitrary ways. The first thing is relatively easy to add to the standard economic model, the second less so, but we will see more on that in the next chapter. What I want to do now is look through some applications where heuristics, search, and reference dependence have a role to play.

2.5 Demand, supply, and markets

Through much of this chapter I have used the example of Anna in the grocery store choosing a breakfast cereal. This is illustrative of a **market** where potential buyers of a good, such as Anna, interact with people who are collectively willing to provide that good (the owners and workers of the store, farm that supplies the wheat for the cereal, etc.). Markets are at the heart of economics, so they seem an apt place to begin looking at applications of what we have learned.

It's easiest to start with a laboratory market. The standard way to create a market in the experimental lab begins by randomly allocating subjects to the role of buyer or seller. Each buyer is given a card that has written on it the value to him or her of buying one unit of a fictitious good that will be traded in the experiment. Each seller is given a card that has written on it the value to him or her of selling one unit of the good. Different subjects are given different values and only they know their value. Buyers and sellers are then able to interact and do a deal. The profit of a buyer is her value minus the price she bought for. The profit of a seller is the price she sold for minus her value. So, in principle, buyers want to buy as cheap as possible and sellers to sell as dear as possible.

If we know the values of all sellers and buyers we can derive a demand and supply curve. To illustrate, suppose that the values given to buyers and sellers are as in Table 2.7. For example, one buyer is given a value of $2.30, meaning that, if she bought for $2, she would make a profit of $0.30. To derive the **supply curve** we have to look at all possible prices and ask how many sellers would sell at each price. If the price is less than $1.50 then no one should sell. If the price is between $1.50 and $2 then there is one person who should sell, namely the seller with value $1.50. If the price is between $2 and $2.50 then there are two people who should sell, namely the sellers with value $1.50 and $2. Carrying this on, we obtain the supply curve in Figure 2.16. To derive the **demand curve** we have to look at all possible prices and ask how many buyers would buy at each price. If the price is more than $3.10 then no one should buy. If the price is between $2.80 and $3.10 then there is one person who should buy, namely the buyer with value $3.10. Carrying this on, we obtain the demand curve.

Demand and supply curves are one of the most basic ideas in economics, and these curves are no different to those you may be familiar with. For instance, the demand curve must slope down and the supply curve slope up. (You might be used to smooth curves rather than the stepped ones drawn here, but this is just because it is usually more convenient to think of a smooth curve.) The **market equilibrium**

Table 2.7 The number of sellers and buyers before and after a shift in demand

Type	*Distribution of values*
Sellers	There are five sellers with values $1.50, $2, $2.50, $2.50, and $3.
Buyers	There are five buyers with values $1.80, $2.30, $2.60, $2.80, and $3.10.
Buyers after change	There are five buyers with values $1.50, $1.70, $2.20, $2.20, and $3.

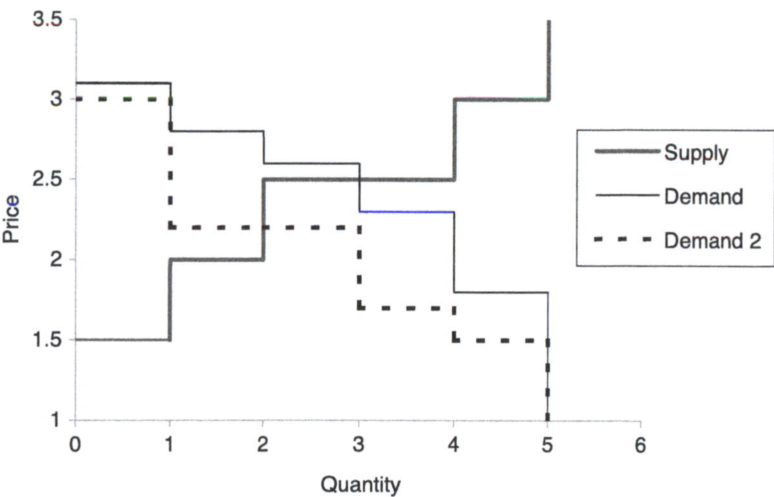

Figure 2.16 The demand and supply curves before and after a shift in demand.

Table 2.8 The market is most efficient in equilibrium as evidenced by the high total profit

	Trades			*Profit*		
	Buyer value	*Seller value*	*Price*	*Buyer*	*Seller*	*Total*
Equilibrium	$3.10	$1.50	$2.50	$0.60	$1.00	$1.60
	$2.80	$2.00	$2.50	$0.30	$0.50	$0.80
	$2.60	$2.50	$2.50	$0.10	$0.00	$0.10
						$2.50
Maximum trades	$1.80	$1.50	$1.65	$0.15	$0.15	$0.30
	$2.30	$2.00	$2.15	$0.15	$0.15	$0.30
	$2.60	$2.50	$2.55	$0.05	$0.05	$0.10
	$2.80	$2.50	$2.65	$0.15	$0.15	$0.30
	$3.10	$3.00	$3.05	$0.05	$0.05	$0.10
						$1.10
Maximum seller	$3.10	$1.50	$2.79	$0.31	$1.29	$1.60
Profit	$2.80	$2.00	$2.79	$0.01	$0.79	$0.80
						$2.40

price and **quantity** are where demand equals supply. In the example, that is where price is $2.50 and quantity is three. In practice this means we should expect there to be three trades, each at a price of $2.50. If we change the demand curve, we see that the equilibrium price drops to $2.20 and the equilibrium quantity to two. Thus, a shift in demand and supply should change the market price in a predictable way.

One remarkable thing about market equilibrium is that total profit is maximized at the equilibrium. Table 2.8 illustrates how this works by contrasting the equilibrium with two other possible sets of trades. In equilibrium there are three trades at $2.50 and total profit is $2.50. In the second scenario all ten people trade and make a profit, but total profit is only $1.10. There are lots of other possible combinations of trades we should check, but none will give as high a profit as the equilibrium. This is an illustration of the celebrated **First Fundamental Theorem of Welfare Economics**, that any market equilibrium is Pareto efficient. Notice, however, that the equilibrium need not be 'fair'. For instance, one seller makes $1 while several sellers would make $0.

This stylized example illustrates why demand and supply analysis is so fundamentally important in economics: it is a tool to predict what may happen in markets, and should tell us what the most efficient outcome is.

One thing we have not done is specify how people interact in order to make trades. Three of the more common ways we observe are:

1 A **negotiated price institution** where buyers and sellers are free to talk to each other and try to do a deal. This is similar to bartering in a local market.
2 A **double auction institution** where buyers submit bids of what they are willing to pay and sellers submit asks of what they are willing to sell for. All bids and asks are displayed on a screen for all to see. A buyer can buy by

accepting the lowest ask price. A seller can sell by accepting the highest bid price. This institution is used in most financial, commodity, and currency markets.

3 A **posted offer institution** where each seller displays a take it or leave it price. Buyers can go to any seller and agree to trade at the displayed price. This institution is what we are familiar with when we go to the grocery store or most shops.

That is enough background information. I now want to get on and look at some data on how markets work. I will start with markets in the experimental lab and work progressively towards real markets.

2.5.1 Double auction markets in the lab

All three of the institutions above have been used in the laboratory, but the double auction is most common, so I will start by looking at that.

In one of the earliest economic experimental studies, Vernon Smith (1962) ran ten experimental double auction markets. Each market was repeated up to six periods and had different demand and supply curves. Figure 2.17 summarizes the data from four of the sessions. For each market the equilibrium price is represented by a circle. We can then see the observed quantity and average price over the periods.

Market 6 is the easiest to explain, because there we see the average price increase over the periods from 5.29 in period 1 to 7.17, 9.06, and finally 10.9 in

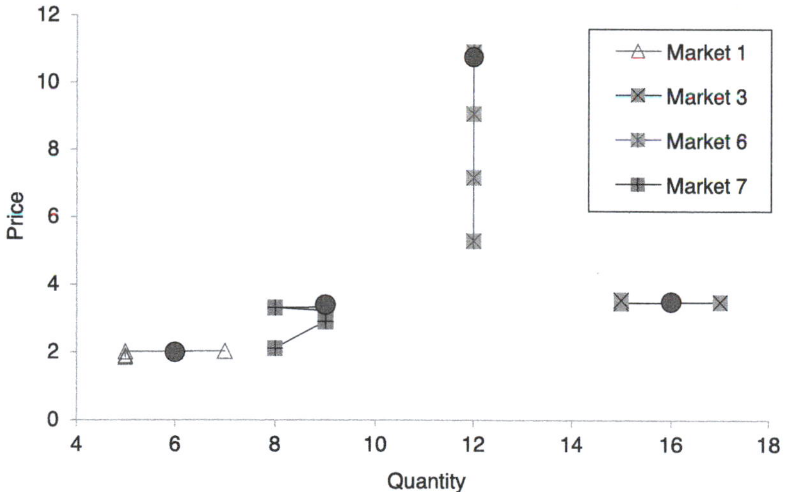

Figure 2.17 Convergence of market price and quantity to equilibrium in four double auction markets. The circles show the equilibrium.

Source: Smith (1962).

period 4. The quantity traded is 12 in every period. The equilibrium price was 10.75 and quantity was 12, and so by period 4 the market was trading at equilibrium. In the other three sessions I have plotted there is not much to see, and the same could be said of all of the sessions run in the study, but that's the beautiful thing! The average price and average quantity traded were remarkably close to the market equilibrium in all periods.

The closeness between market and observed prices also holds when demand and supply are changed from period to period. This is illustrated in Figure 2.18, where the equilibrium and average price are plotted for a market that lasted 15 periods, with the equilibrium price changing each period. The match between equilibrium and observed average prices is nearly perfect!

Basically, the average price and quantity observed in experimental double auction markets almost always get close to the market equilibrium with repeated trading, and typically start close. The price and quantity also change as predicted by changes in demand and supply.

This is a fantastic result. It suggests that demand and supply are reliable predictors of what will happen in a market, which is good news for economists. It also suggests that markets are a great way to allocate resources, which is good news for everyone. Indeed, this result goes further than the First Fundamental Theorem of Welfare Economics, because the Theorem is agnostic about how prices will be determined, but the double auction gives us an institution to determine prices and achieve efficiency.

The efficiency of double auction markets is arguably the most important lesson so far from behavioral economics. The reason that double auction markets work so well is that subjects only need use simple heuristics. Recall that the only thing

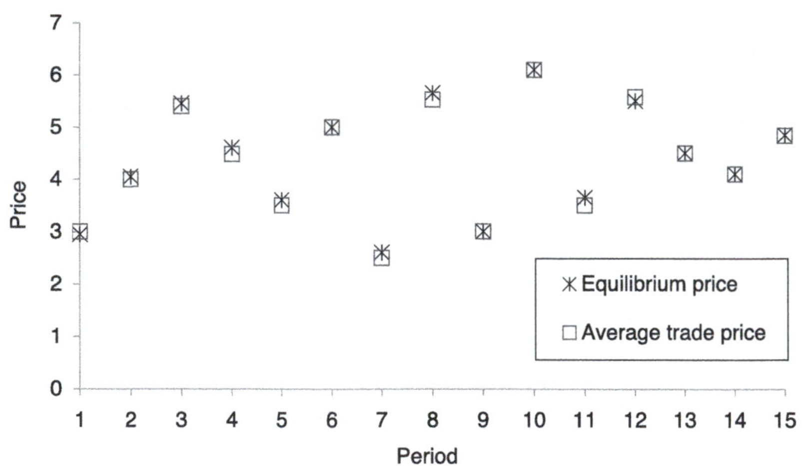

Figure 2.18 The equilibrium price and average price traded in a market that lasted 15 periods.

Source: Smith (2002).

a subject knows at the start is her own value to buy or sell. So she simply needs to buy for less or sell for more than her value to make a profit, and this is something very familiar to most of us (see Research Methods 2.7).

Research Methods 2.7

Intelligent institutions or people?

There are broadly two reasons why double auction markets work: subjects are very clever, or double auction markets are very clever. It is probably a bit of both. To illustrate why, we can look at a study by Gode and Sunder (1993). They compared what happens in double auction markets if choices are made by 'zero-intelligence' computer programs rather than human subjects.

They use two versions of zero intelligence. In the first, each trader randomly generated bids or offers, and so there was no sense to behavior at all. This really does look like a zero-intelligence trader. In the second, each trader randomly generated bids or offers, but would never do a deal that would lose them money. So a seller never sold for less than value, and a buyer never sold for more than value. I will call this a 'don't sell at a loss' trader. Table 2.9 gives a snapshot of the results by comparing the efficiency of markets with humans to those with zero-intelligence traders. The main result is that 'don't sell at a loss' seems enough to get high efficiency.

Table 2.9 The market efficiency of five experimental markets, comparing human participants to zero-intelligent traders

Participants	*Market efficiency (%) in market*				
	1	*2*	*3*	*4*	*5*
Zero intelligence	90.0	90.0	76.7	48.8	86.0
Don't sell at a loss	99.9	99.2	99.0	98.2	97.1
Human	99.7	99.1	100.0	99.1	90.2

Source: Gode and Sunder (1993)

How should we interpret this result? It would appear to demonstrate the relevance of heuristics because the simple, 'don't sell at a loss' heuristic is enough to achieve market efficiency. We need to be a little careful, however, to distinguish institutions from individuals. This is because an individual trader may want to use something more subtle than this heuristic, and there was good evidence that human subjects did do that. The main lesson, therefore, is that some institutions can work well even if people use only the most basic of heuristics. This does not imply that people do use only the most basic of heuristics, but it does mean that institutions can be clever, and potentially make up for a lack of subtlety in people's strategy or behavior.

Having given the good news, it is time for some of the bad. Markets are not always so efficient, for a variety of reasons. In Chapter five we shall see how efficiency can decrease if buyers and sellers have some uncertainty about the value of the good. Here I shall look at a host of other reasons why efficiency may be less, starting with a brief look at posted offer markets.

2.5.2 Posted offer markets and market power

To give an illustration of what happens in posted offer markets I will look at a study by Ketcham, Smith, and Williams (1984). Figure 2.19 summarizes the differences between prices and quantities observed in double auction and posted offer markets averaged over the 12 experimental markets of the study. As expected, in the double auction, price and quantity converged over the periods towards the equilibrium. The same cannot be said in the posted offer market. In this case prices stayed consistently above the equilibrium and quantity below the equilibrium, and there is no evidence that this would change if the market were to be repeated more times.

It is not too much of a surprise that we do not always see convergence to the market equilibrium in posted offer markets. This is because suppliers have an incentive to try and keep the price high. To illustrate, we can look back at the third set of possible trades in Table 2.8. In this case the price is pushed above the equilibrium and, while total profit is less than at equilibrium, the profit of sellers is higher than at equilibrium, at $2.08 compared to $1.50. Things are not that simple, because sellers do not share the profit and so have an incentive to compete amongst each other for their share of the profit. The basic incentive to push prices higher exists, however, and a posted offer market gives sellers more possibility to do so.

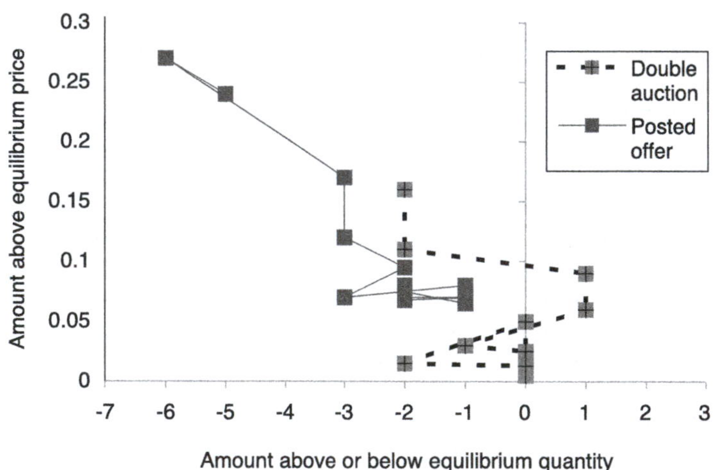

Figure 2.19 The deviation from equilibrium price and quantity in experimental double auction and posted offer markets.

Source: Smith (2002).

Sellers can keep prices high because they have the power to set prices. They can signal to each other from one period to the next through the prices they offer and potentially collude on higher prices. Prices are, therefore, higher because sellers have market power. More generally, market power can move the price away from the market equilibrium. This is a point I'll return to in Chapter six, when we look at industrial organization.

2.5.3 The law of one price

The final institution to look at is negotiated price. In looking at this type of market it is pertinent to mention the law of one price. The **law of one price** is that all items should be sold at the same price in market equilibrium. For instance, in Figure 2.16 we predict that all items are sold at $2.50. In a double auction this is what we typically do see, and this is not surprising, given that all buyers and sellers automatically have access to the same information. If we consider institutions where buyers and/or sellers have to search for information, then things change.

We can illustrate by looking at a negotiated price market from one of the first ever recorded economic experiments by Chamberlin (1948). Recall that, in this institution, buyers and sellers move around the room, interact personally, and try to do a deal on a one-to-one basis. This makes it possible that people on one side of the room could be agreeing a different price to people on the other side of the room. Figure 2.20 summarizes what happened in the market. The equilibrium

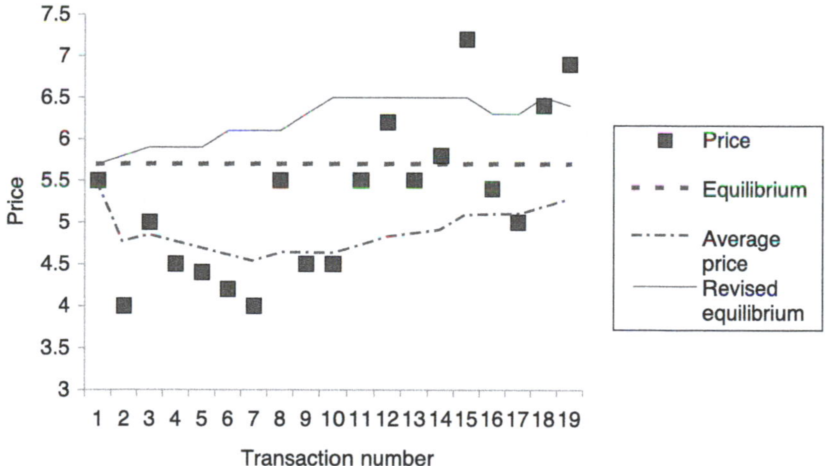

Figure 2.20 The prices traded in a negotiated price market. The prices vary a lot but the average ends up close to equilibrium. As trades are being done and buyers and sellers leave the market, the demand and supply curve changes, so we should concentrate more on the revised equilibrium price than equilibrium price.

Source: Chamberlin (1948).

price was 5.7, but we can see that actually the prices traded vary considerably from as low as 4 to as high as 7.2. The law of one price does not hold in this market. Interestingly, however, the average price comes out at 5.3, which is not that far from the equilibrium.

This large variation of individual prices but an average price close to the equilibrium is what we typically observe in this type of market. So, demand and supply are still reliable predictors of what will happen in the market but are not so reliable a predictor of what will happen in a specific transaction. Why?

The person who sold at $4 and the person who bought at $7.20 could have come together and agreed a price of $5.60. This would mean both make an extra profit of $1.60 and would mean the traded price would have been a lot closer to the equilibrium. Why did they not do that? Presumably they never met to talk about this possibility. Both could have searched a bit longer, or harder, for a better deal. The problem is that such search is costly, not only in time and effort, but also in potentially missing out on a good deal. For example, selling at $4 might look like a good deal to the seller; remember he or she has no idea what the market demand is, so should they risk losing that deal to search for a better one? Potentially not, and so search costs and reference points are a good reason why we should not expect to see the law of one price.

Search costs are clearly relevant in many markets. You might have an idea what the price of a textbook is, but you cannot know for sure the price of different sellers without a little bit of effort. We should not be surprised, therefore, to see variation in prices for an identical good that is sold at more than one location. This is the case irrespective of the institution used to sell the good. To illustrate the point, Pratt, Wise, and Zeckhauser (1979) randomly opened the Yellow Pages of the Boston telephone directory to select 39 products, and then rang all the advertised sellers for each product to see how much they charged. Figure 2.21 illustrates the large variability in prices across sellers. The maximum price was often twice that of the minimum.

The data in Figure 2.21 is arranged in order of increasing price. Carnations are cheapest, with a price of $0.33, and a boat the most expensive, with a price of $602.87. One slightly curious thing is that the relative variability in price does not decline for more expensive items. To better understand why this is curious, consider this question:

> You are about to purchase a jacket for $125 and a calculator for $15. The salesman tells you that the calculator is $5 cheaper at another branch of the store 20 minutes' drive away. Would you make the trip to the other store?
>
> Now imagine the jacket costs $15 and the calculator $125.

Tversky and Kahneman (1981) report how 68 percent of those they surveyed would make the trip to save $5 on an item costing $15, but only 29 percent would make the trip to save $5 on something costing $125. Either way, the person will save $5 and so it is slightly strange that it matters whether the saving is on a cheap or expensive item. Put another way, however, the person will save 33 percent in

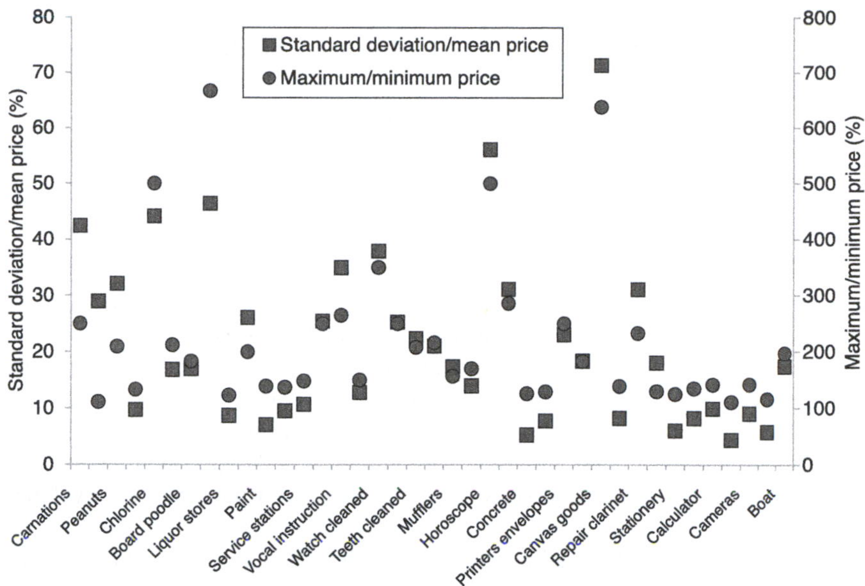

Figure 2.21 The law of one price does not hold in many markets. The standard deviation in price is typically more than 10 to 20 percent of the mean price. The maximum price is typically twice or more the minimum price available.

Source: Pratt *et al.* (1979).

the one case and 4 percent in the other, so if we have a heuristic that says 4 percent is not a good saving but 33 percent is, then things become easier to explain.

Now let's return to search costs. There is no reason to suppose the cost of search depends on the price of the item being sold. So, if someone puts the same effort into searching for a $1 saving on all goods, we should see less variability in the relative price of expensive items. We do not see this. If someone puts the same effort into searching for a 1 percent saving on all goods, then the variability in relative prices should not depend on the price of the good. That is what we do seem to observe.

This focus on relative rather than absolute savings is the first indication we have seen in this section that framing and perceptions can influence a person's willingness to trade. What I want to do now is look at two specific markets where we might expect a bit more evidence that framing and perceptions matter.

2.6 Labor supply and reference dependence

The story told in the previous section is largely one where it is obvious if someone has made a profit, and so gains and losses are easy to calculate. The buyer wants to sell for less than she values the good, and the seller wants to sell for more than the cost of the good. In some markets that story is all we need, but in others it misses something, because it may not be obvious what counts as a gain or a loss, or selling at a profit. In other words, it may not be clear what the relevant reference point is. This can have implications for how the market works. I shall illustrate by looking at labor supply in this section and the housing market in the next section.

2.6.1 A target income and target wage

In the labor market it is natural to think of people deciding how many hours they want to work at the going wage. For example, if Anna is an accountant, then she needs to decide how many clients to take on, whether to work full time or part time, and so on. Anna may have a reference level of hours that she wants to work, or a reference level of income that she wants to earn. This reference level could be determined by a variety of things, but what has previously happened, or what friends and peers are doing, are two likely candidates. Before we look at some data it is useful to have a model of labor supply to see how the reference level may matter.

The standard way of modeling labor supply is to think of the utility function $u(x, H)$ which depends on wealth x and the number of hours spent working H. To measure the benefit of working, we need the hourly wage rate w. Anna trades wealth for leisure time and if we solve for the optimal amount of hours she should work we get a condition like:

$$-\frac{du}{dH} = w\frac{du}{dx}. \tag{2.1}$$

This means that the disutility from an extra hour of work should be offset by the utility she gets from the money earned by working an extra hour.

Figure 2.22 gives two examples of how Anna's utility may change as she works more or less. The marginal disutility of working is assumed to increase the more she works in both examples. What differs is that in one she has a reference level for working eight hours a day. This causes a big change in the disutility of working at eight hours. Anna is relatively happy to continue work if she has worked less than eight hours, but is relatively unhappy to continue work if she has already worked more than eight hours. Consequently, equation (2.1) is likely to be satisfied when she works eight hours and labor supply is likely to be insensitive to changes in the wage.

The story when there is a target level of income is relatively similar. Figure 2.23 illustrates what may happen if Anna has \$10,000 in wealth and wants to increase her income by \$160. Extra income is worth relatively more when she has earned less that the target than when she is above the target. Consequently, amount earned will be relatively insensitive to changes in the disutility of working. The number of hours worked would, however, change if the wage rate changes. A higher wage would mean Anna can work fewer hours and still reach her target, while a lower wage would mean Anna needs to work more hours to reach the target.

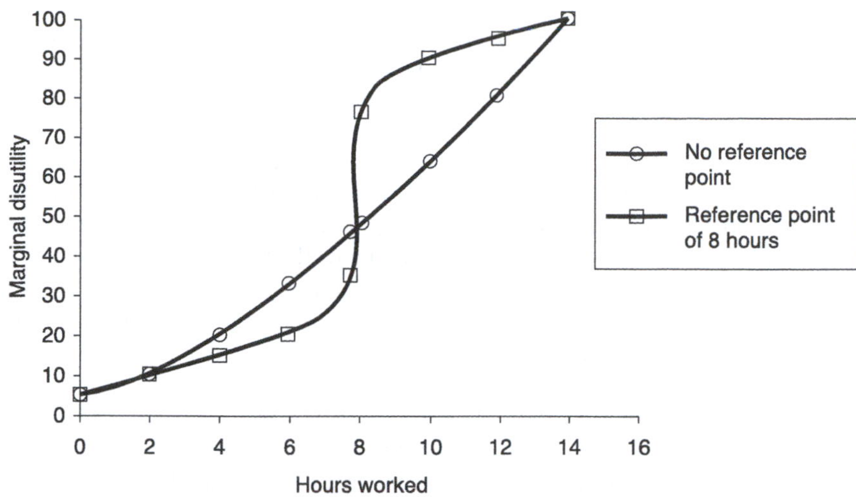

Figure 2.22 Two possible utility functions. If there is a reference level of eight hours' work, the utility function becomes S-shaped and the number of hours worked will not change much as the wage changes.

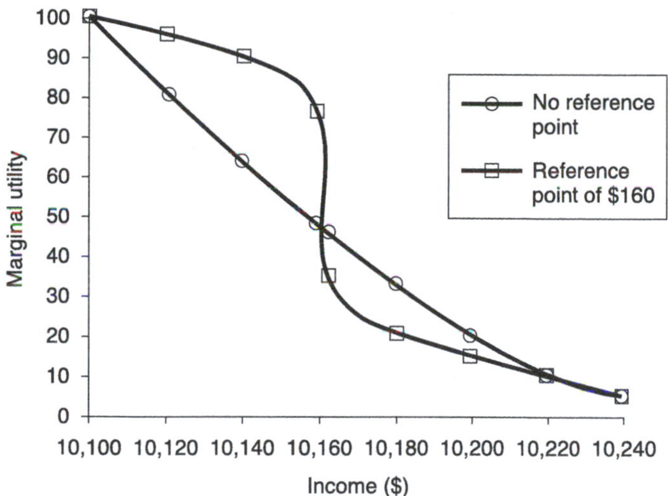

Figure 2.23 If there is a reference level of earning $160, the utility function becomes S-shaped. An increase in wages will cause a decrease in hours worked because the target of $160 can be achieved more easily.

2.6.2 Taxicab drivers

In practice we might expect that Anna has both a target income and target number of hours she wants to work. This comes out in the first set of data I want to look at. The people who arguably have most control over how many hours they work are self-employed workers. An example that has attracted some interest amongst economists is that of taxicab drivers. Many taxicab drivers lease a cab from a taxi-leasing company and keep any money they make from fares or tips, net of fuel costs. By choosing when to start and end the shift, and how many breaks to have, the driver has complete control over how long he works and some control over his income. In New York City, taxicab drivers are required to fill out trip sheets which record details on all the trips done during a shift, including times, locations, and fares. The trip sheets are a great source of data to look at labor supply. To illustrate, I will look at a study by Farber (2005, 2008) of 21 New York City taxicab drivers working in 1999 and 2000.

What we can focus on is the probability that a driver ends his shift at a particular point in time. Factors that might influence that decision are the hours already worked, income already earned, and things like the weather and time of day. Demand for taxicabs varies a lot across days and within the course of a day, meaning that the wage rate w will fluctuate a lot day to day and during the day. We saw that, if drivers focus on a reference level of hours that they want to work, fluctuations in the wage should make little difference to the number of hours they work. By contrast, if drivers focus on a target level of income, changes in the wage should affect hours worked.

To see what does happen, we can estimate the probability that a driver will stop after each trip. Figure 2.24 summarizes what we get from estimating this probability. It shows the change in the probability that a driver ends his shift, compared to if he has worked nine hours and earned \$150–\$175. We see that drivers are far more likely to stop after having worked ten or more hours. By contrast, income earned has very little effect. [Extra] These probabilities were estimated by writing the probability that driver i on day j will stop after trip t by:

$$P_{ijt} = \Phi(X_{ijt}\,\beta)$$

where Φ is the cumulative normal distribution and $X_{ijt}\,\beta$ is a term that includes things like the number of hours worked and the time of day.

Figure 2.24 suggests that drivers primarily stop after having worked a certain number of hours, and not after reaching a target level of income. Clearly, this is consistent with a reference level of hours worked (but see Review question 2.10). It does not, however, completely rule out there being a subsidiary target level of income. To check this, we can plug a target income into the equation that we estimate and see whether we get a better fit with the data. Doing this suggests that drivers do indeed have a target level of income. Somewhat strangely, however, we also find that the target fluctuates a lot from day to day. In particular, the mean target was \$196 but the standard error \$91. So, a driver might have a target income

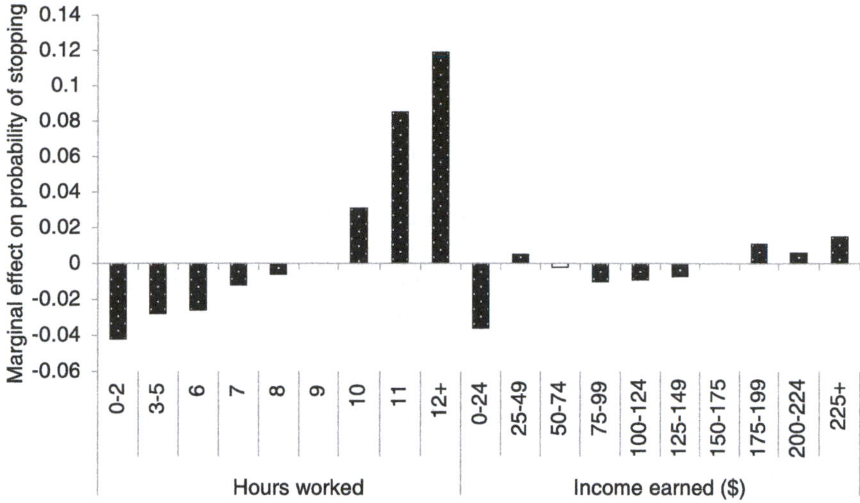

Figure 2.24 The probability that a driver stops his shift compared to when he has worked nine hours and earned \$150–\$175. Drivers were significantly more likely to stop if they had worked ten or more hours. The decision to stop was not influenced much by income already earned.

Source: Farber (2005).

of \$120 one day, \$250 the next, and so on. It is not so easy to interpret what this means.

[Extra] To check whether drivers have a target income, we can slightly change the equation estimated to:

$$P_{ijt} = \begin{cases} \Phi(X_{ijt}\beta + \delta) & \text{if } y_{ijt} \geq r_{ij} \\ \Phi(X_{ijt}\beta) & \text{if } y_{ijt} < r_{ij} \end{cases}$$

where r_{ij} is a reference level of income for driver i on day j and y_{ijt} is current income. If current income is above the reference point, $y_{ijt} \geq r_{ij}$, then, the larger is δ, the higher the probability the driver will stop. Term δ therefore measures the potential importance of a target level of income. We can assume that the reference point is determined by:

$$r_{ij} = R_i + \varepsilon_{ij}$$

where R_i is the average reference level of driver i, which may fluctuate day to day. On estimating δ, R_i, and β it turns out that δ is significantly greater than zero and so there does appear to be a target level of income.

2.6.3 Female labor supply

The overall picture we get from the taxicab data is that drivers might have a target level of income, but the number of hours they have worked seems a more dominant factor. I now want to look at some data that gives a slightly different perspective. Most workers do not have as much flexibility as taxi drivers in how many hours a day they work. Often choices are restricted to a more discrete choice of whether to work full time or part time, or to work at all. But this still raises some interesting issues. For instance, Figure 2.25 plots the growth in labor force participation of women in the US and UK since the Second World War. Clearly there is a significant rise in the number of women choosing to work. Why?

If we look at equation (2.1), then either the wage increased, the utility of money increased, or the disutility of working decreased. Changes in wages and the disutility of work can account for a lot of the increase in participation. For example, lower fertility and the growth of the service sector are two reasons why the disutility of work could have decreased for women. I want to focus more, however, on the possibility that the utility of money has changed. Why would it have? If people want to earn a similar amount to friends and family, then the fact that some women enter employment (because of the higher wages and decreased disutility of work) could spur other women to enter employment so as to not fall behind.

Neumark and Postlewaite (1998) explore this possibility with data on a sample of US women who become of employable age in the 1980s. They question whether a woman is more likely to work if her sister-in-law works, or if her sister's husband earns more than her husband.

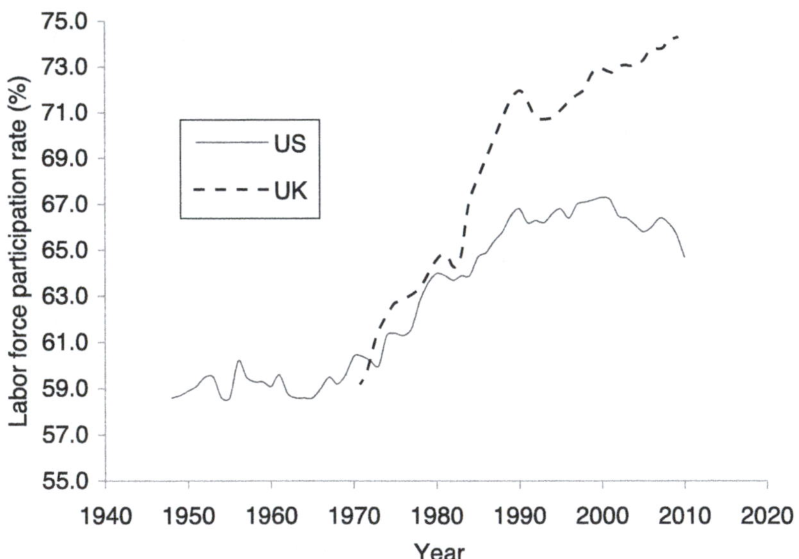

Figure 2.25 The participation rate of women aged 16 and above in the US and UK.

Sources: Bureau of Labor Statistics and Office for National Statistics.

[Extra] To see how this is done, let P_{it} denote the probability that woman i is employed at time t. To see whether a woman is more likely to work if her sister-in-law also works we can fit equation

$$P_{it} = \Lambda(X_{it}\,\beta + \gamma SL)$$

where $X_{it}\,\beta$ captures things like education, Λ is the logistic cumulative probability distribution and SL is one or zero depending on whether the sister-in-law works. The bigger is γ, the more likely a woman will work if her sister-in-law works. To see whether a woman is more likely to work if her sister's husband earns more than her husband, we can fit

$$P_{it} = \Lambda(X_{it}\,\beta + \gamma HM)$$

where HM is one or zero depending on whether the sister's husband earns more.

Figure 2.26 summarizes the main results. We see that a woman's choice to work was significantly affected by what her sister or sister-in-law was doing. She was more likely to work if her sister-in-law worked, and a lot more likely to work if her sister worked and her sister's husband earned more than her husband! This is consistent with a person, or family, being influenced by a reference level of income that depends on what others are earning.

We have now seen evidence that workers can have a reference level of hours they want to work and a reference or target level of income they want to earn. This is important in understanding individual labor supply but also important in

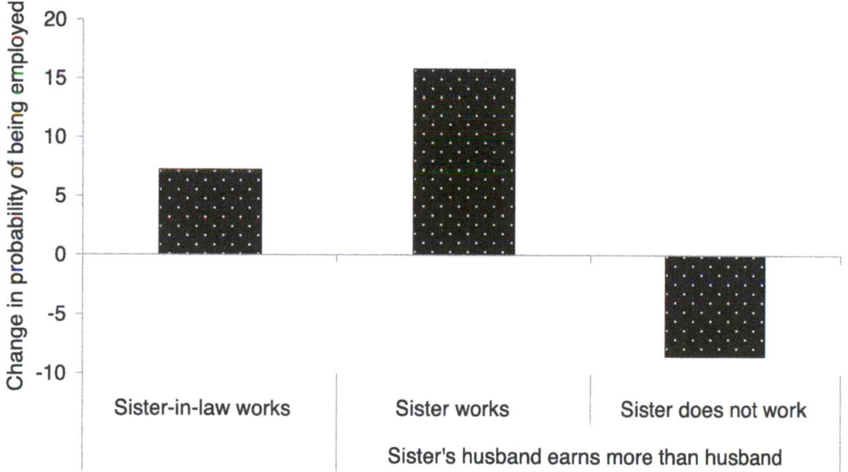

Figure 2.26 The change in probability of a woman being in employment depends on whether her sister-in-law works and her sister's husband earns more than her husband.

Source: Neumark and Postlewaite (1998).

understanding how the labor market works. That's because the reference point will partly determine what is counted as a gain or loss and so also partly determine the equilibrium price and quantity. We see this in the large increase in the number of women working, and in the price of a taxicab in the middle of the night.

2.7 The housing market

The second market I want to look at is the housing market. Buying property is one of the bigger decisions most people will make in their life and can be thought of as both a consumption and investment decision. People want somewhere nice to live, but are also aware that the value of a house can increase or decrease, and the more it increases the better. Figure 2.27 plots the average property price and number of sales by month in England and Wales between January 1995 and December 2010. The price clearly increases over this time, but not without periods of decline. Knowing when to sell or buy, and what price to ask or bid, are financially important and complicated decisions. But what is an appropriate reference point to say what is a gain or loss?

2.7.1 Reluctance to sell

Let's look first at what price Anna might want to sell her apartment. She could use two natural reference prices: the price that other similar properties are selling for, or the price she originally paid for her apartment. For instance, selling for less than she originally paid might be interpreted as a loss, while selling for more is inter-

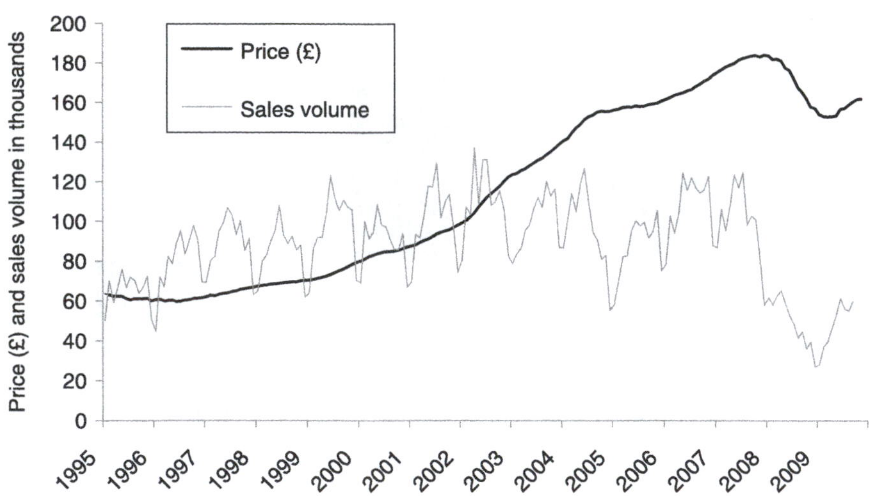

Figure 2.27 The average selling price of residential property and sales volume in England and Wales.

Source: Land Registry.

preted as a gain. To see the implications of this, suppose that Anna bought her apartment for $80,000 while John bought an almost identical apartment for $100,000. Both are looking to sell, and the price of other similar apartments is $90,000. For Anna, selling at $90,000 feels like a gain, so she might be happy to sell at this price, or maybe even slightly less. For John, selling at $90,000 feels like a loss. Loss aversion might mean he tries selling his apartment at something like $95,000, or even decides to not sell his apartment at all.

A study by Genesove and Mayer (2001) puts this prediction to the test with data from downtown Boston in the 1990s. They use data from over 5,000 apartments put up for sale between 1990 and 1997. Most importantly, they have data on the price someone bought an apartment for and the price they first listed it when trying to sell. They also have estimates of market value and any outstanding loan at sale. This latter number is important in order to rule out people being reluctant to sell below the price they paid because they have to repay the loan used for purchase.

What Genesove and Mayer find is that someone, like John, who is expected to make a loss, asks for a higher price and has to wait longer to sell, but does sell at a higher price. It seems, therefore, that sellers may be averse to selling a house for less than they paid for it. This helps us better understand the housing market. In particular, one puzzling thing we observe in housing data, and that can be seen in Figure 2.27, is that sales volume falls during a slump in prices. If prices fall, we might expect demand to pick up, not fall. This becomes easier to explain once we account for loss aversion. If prices fall, and people are unwilling to sell at a loss, then we can predict less property being put up for sale and prices being above what they should be. This clearly suggests lower sales.

What is less clear is whether loss aversion benefits a potential seller. To put the magnitude of loss aversion into context, we can plug the numbers estimated by Genesove and Mayer into the Anna and John example. Anna would have asked for $90,000 and sold for this after around 60 days. John would have tried to recoup 25–35 percent of his 'loss' and so would have asked for around $93,000 and actually recouped 3–18 percent of the loss by selling for, say, $91,000. He would have had to wait around 6 percent longer, but this only equates to an extra four days. It seems as though John does not do so badly!

It is not as simple as that, however, because people who sell also, typically, buy. A slump in the market may be a good opportunity to sell, even if at a loss, and upsize to a more expensive property. Someone who does not want to sell at a loss could miss this opportunity. Or perhaps they need to do a bit of hedonic editing and alter their reference point to focus on the gain they can make on the property they will buy, rather than the loss on the property they will sell.

2.7.2 What are buyers willing to pay?

This brings us on to the buyers. What price should someone be willing to pay for property? The price of similar property may be the most natural reference point in this case. A nice way to see whether it is, is to follow people who relocate from one area of the country to another. To illustrate, suppose Anna currently lives in an area where a good apartment costs $90,000 and she is going to relocate due to work. If, where she is moving to, apartments cost around $70,000, they will look cheap, but if they average $120,000 they will look expensive. Reference dependence suggests that she might be happy to buy something for less than $90,000 but be averse to spending anything more than $90,000.

A study by Simonsohn and Loewenstein (2006) puts this prediction to the test by looking at data on people in the US relocating between 1983 and 1993. They question whether the average rent or house price in the location a person moved from significantly affects the price they pay where they move to. They find that it does matter. A 10 percent difference in the median rent or property price at the location moved from causes an increase of around 2 percent in the rent paid or purchase price at destination. You might say that this could be because of preferences or something else. They also find, however, that, when people move for a second time, this time in the same area, any differences disappear. It seems, therefore, as if the reference point readjusts as people live in the area for some time. Reference dependence can, therefore, really matter.

To finish this section I want to show that anchoring can matter as well. The point was nicely illustrated in a study by Northcraft and Neale (1987). They had subjects view two different properties for sale in Tucson, Arizona. All subjects were given a detailed ten-page brochure full of facts about the property. The only thing that differed between subjects was the reported list price. The properties were actually listed for $74,900 and $134,900, but subjects were given prices around 5 and 12 percent either side of this. For example, some subjects were told the $74,900 property was listed for $65,900 and some that it was listed at $83,900. After viewing the property subjects were asked what value they would put on the property.

Figure 2.28 summarizes the results. An increase in the list price led to a significant increase in the value subjects put on the property. Keep in mind that subjects could view the property and had a host of information at their fingertips. The list price still affected judgment. This is a great example of anchoring and of a framing effect. The study also allows comparison of amateurs at real estate (i.e. students) with professional real estate agents. The amateur subjects were more biased than the experts, but not by much. A more interesting difference showed up when subjects were asked to describe how they came to an estimated value. The experts were less likely to admit that the list price affected judgment than the amateur subjects. This illustrates how blissfully ignorant we often are of framing effects!

2.8 The behavioral life cycle hypothesis

Having spent some time looking at markets I now want to move on to another of the more important and controversial ideas in economics, the life cycle hypothesis. The **life cycle hypothesis** comes in various different guises but the basic idea is relatively simple: a person should take a long-term view about their future income and smooth consumption over their lifetime to maximize expected utility. Figure 2.29 gives a stylized illustration of the model. We see that income goes through large variation over the life cycle, as Anna earns little when a student, has increased income as she

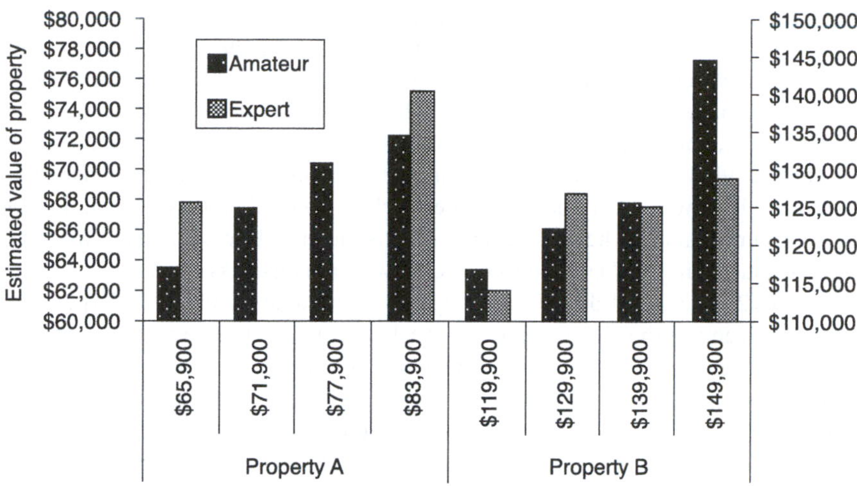

Figure 2.28 The estimated value of two properties depending on the reported list price. If the list price was higher, subjects estimated the value as higher.

Source: Northcraft and Neale (1987).

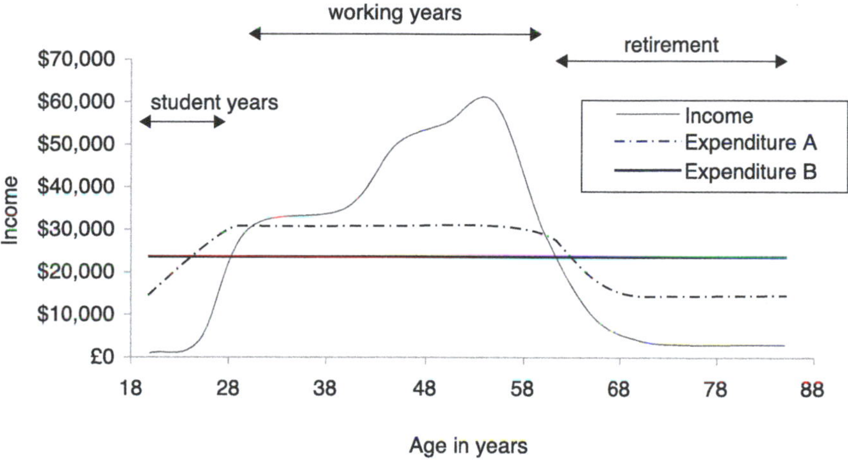

Figure 2.29 An illustration of consumption smoothing. Income varies a lot with age, but consumption can be completely smoothed, as in schedule A, or partly smoothed, as in schedule B.

works and gets promoted, and then little income again when she retires. Presumably she will want her standard of living and consumption to be more stable than this (something we shall discuss in Chapter four). Consequently she may smooth consumption by borrowing in her student years, saving during her working years, and using her savings during retirement. Smoothing consumption completely would give schedule A. More realistic is something like schedule A, where consumption does change with age because, for example, of having children.

Rather than rely on the stylized illustration in Figure 2.29 we can look at some actual data. When we look at consumption over the lifetime we typically find an inverted U shape like that in Figure 2.30. This inverted U shape has been observed in different countries, and for all types of workers, education background, etc. An alternative view is obtained by looking at consumption over calendar time. Figure 2.31 shows what typically happens when we do this. It is very noticeable that consumption is cyclical and changes by as much as 11 percent from trough to peak. Unsurprisingly, these cycles coincide with the business cycle.

Figures 2.30 and 2.31 do not look very consistent with the life cycle hypothesis. Instead it seems as though consumption tracks income with little sign of consumption smoothing. If we factor in the effects of children and a desire to be prudent, or to not want to spend uncertain and unearned future income, then we could argue that the data in Figures 2.30 and 2.31 is consistent with the life cycle hypothesis. But, that essentially amounts to arguing that the optimal thing is to not smooth consumption! This seems an unsatisfactory conclusion.

A more realistic perspective is to acknowledge that people undeniably do smooth consumption over their lifetime by saving for retirement, borrowing when a student, or borrowing to buy a first home. But they do not smooth consumption as much as we might expect. Instead, consumption seems to track current income more closely and be more sensitive to macroeconomic cycles than would seem optimal. We need to try and understand why this is the case. One potential contributory factor is mental accounting.

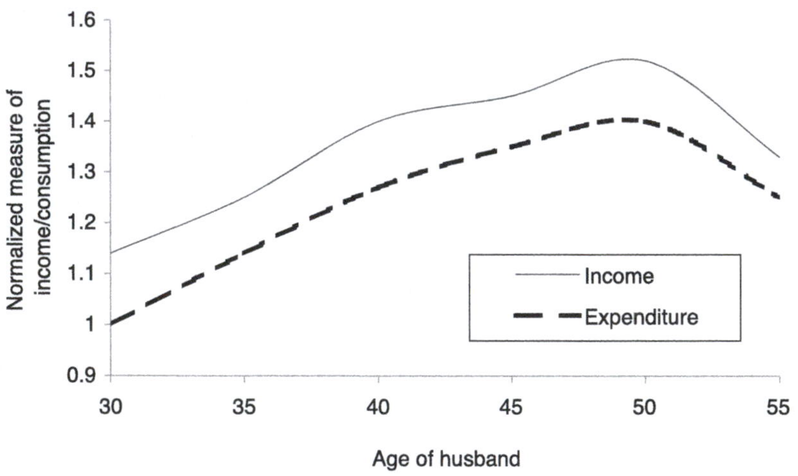

Figure 2.30 An inverse U-shaped consumption and income pattern derived from UK couples with a husband born between 1936 and 1943. Cyclical and growth effects are removed from the data.

Source: Browning and Crossley (2001).

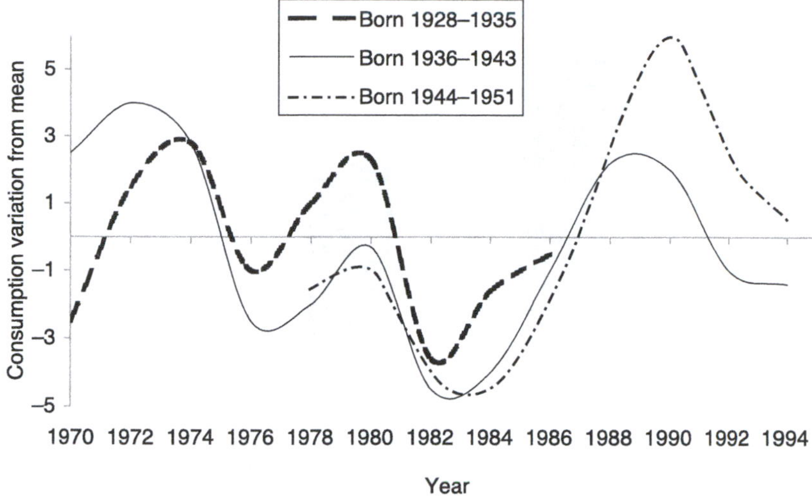

Figure 2.31 Consumption patterns over time derived from UK data.

Source: Browning and Crossley (2001).

2.8.1 Fungibility and mental accounting

Mental accounting and narrow framing are very important in thinking about the life cycle hypothesis. That's because the life cycle hypothesis assumes **fungibility**, meaning that all money is treated the same, no matter where it came from. If people keep mental accounts, then money is likely to be segregated according to how it was obtained and so is not fungible.

To illustrate, consider these three scenarios:

> You have been given a special bonus at work, meaning you will receive $200 a month over the next year.
>
> You have been given a special bonus at work, meaning you will receive a lump sum payment of $2,400.
>
> You have been told of a distant relative who has left you an after-tax inheritance of $2,400, but you will not receive the money for five years.

In all three scenarios your wealth will increase by $2,400. Fungibility requires that the use to which you put this extra money should not depend on where it came from. You should just think how you will spend the $2,400 over the rest of your lifetime. In reality things seem different, as the results of a study by Shefrin and Thaler (1988) illustrate. Figure 2.32 shows a stark difference in how much of the extra $2,400 people said they would consume over the following year. If the money came from the regular payment, people planned to consume half of it in one year, but, if it came from a future inheritance, would spend none of it.

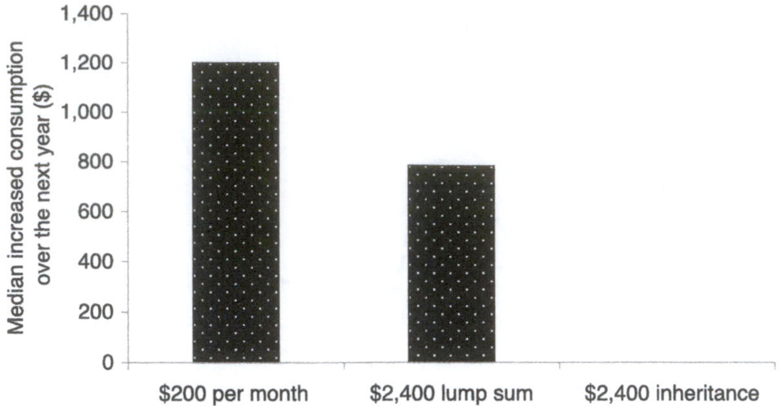

Figure 2.32 The amount of the $2,400 that subjects thought they would spend in the next year. The origin of the money significantly affects the amount that subjects expected to spend.

Source: Shefrin and Thaler (1998).

Broadly speaking we can think that households keep in mind three basic mental accounts: a current income account, an asset account, and a future income account. The **current income account** is for day-to-day spending. We would expect that the **marginal propensity to consume** from this account, or the proportion of the money spent, is relatively high, because the money is there to be spent. The **asset account** is for saving and investing for things like retirement or a new house. We would expect a much lower marginal propensity to consume from this account. Indeed, its purpose may be to commit the household to save adequately. Finally, the **future income account** includes predictable future income such as from a pension, inheritance, or expected salary increases. The marginal propensity to consume from this account is likely to be very low if people are reluctant to spend income they do not have.

These predicted differences in the marginal propensity to consume are not consistent with fungibility. They are, however, consistent with the data in Figure 2.32. A regular payment of $200 a month is more likely to be added to the current income account. A lump sum payment may be saved in the asset account. The inheritance is clearly put in the future income account. This can help explain the decreasing marginal propensity to consume.

Fortunately we have a wealth of expenditure data with which to move beyond hypothetical surveys to real choices. I will look at three examples.

The first example concerns a tax rebate in the US in 2001. Most US households over a ten-week period received a rebate of either $300 or $600. The rebate could have been predicted because the policy was widely publicized and was part of a long-term change in tax policy. There was, therefore, a gap between a person knowing they would get $300 or $600 and actually getting the money. Fungibility requires that people should start spending the money as soon as they know they will get it, and not when they actually get it (unless they have insufficient money). Mental accounting would suggest that receipt of the money moves it from the future income account to either the current income or asset account, and so the money is treated differently once it is received.

Johnson and co-authors (2006) looked at expenditure data on what households did with the money, and paid particular attention to whether receiving the rebate made any difference to spending. Figure 2.33 shows the change in spending in the three months after the rebate arrived compared to the three months before the rebate. Different households received the money at different times, so there is no possibility that this difference is due to some seasonal effect. It looks like receipt of the money did make a difference to spending. This is consistent with mental accounting, not fungibility.

Another interesting thing about this rebate is that what households did with it seemed slightly at odds with what they planned to do with it. For example, Shapiro and Slemrod (2003) surveyed households about what they planned to do with the rebate. Only 22 percent of those surveyed expected to spend the rebate. Most expected to pay back debt. This suggests that households planned to put the money in the asset account. And it seemingly confirmed by Agarwal and co-authors (2007), who showed that households did initially 'save' the money by paying off debt, such as credit card debt. Soon after, however, their spending rose.

We can pick up on this distinction between the current and asset account in the second example I will look at. In this example the focus is on Israeli recipients of German restitution payments in the late 1950s. Families received a lump sum 'wind-

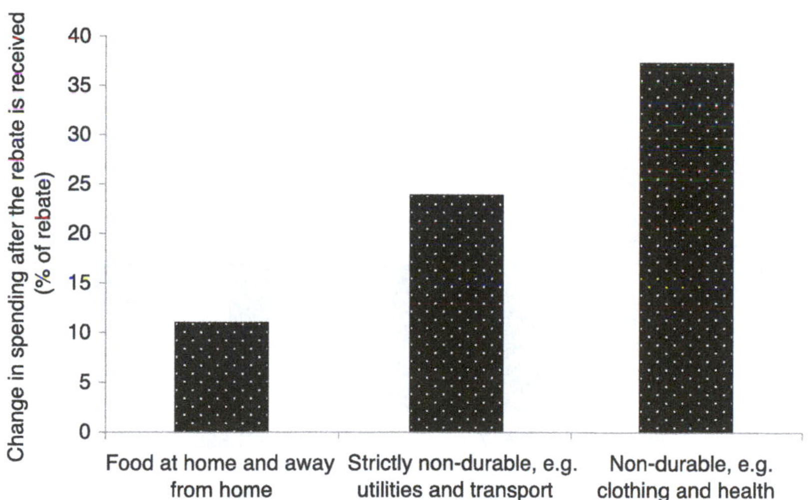

Figure 2.33 The change in spending in the three months after receiving the rebate compared to the three months before receiving the rebate.

Source: Johnson *et al.* (2006).

fall payment' of varying amounts. Landsberger (1966) looked at what people did with the money and compared it to normal spending. The results are summarized in Figure 2.34. The difference between the marginal propensity to consume from normal income and the windfall is large. As with the tax rebate this suggests a lack of fungibility. More interesting is how the size of the windfall seemed to matter in terms of how much a family spent of the money. A small payment was spent twice over! A large payment was primarily saved. This illustrates how the amount of money can matter in terms of what mental account it is put into. A small windfall is added to the current account and a big windfall added to the savings account.

The final example I want to look at is very different to the previous two. It demonstrates how accounts can be more narrowly defined than the three accounts I have mentioned so far. Often, government benefits are given for a specific reason. For example, child benefit is given to families with children. Fungibility would suggest that households should ignore the reason they got the money. Mental accounting suggests they may not. Kooreman (2000) looks at data from the Dutch child benefit system from 1978 to 1994.

Over these years various changes to the benefit system allow us to try and estimate whether child benefit is used to buy things for children. In the study, the focus was put on the amount spent on clothing in families with one child. Figure 2.35 summarizes the main finding. The marginal propensity to consume child clothing out of child benefit was much larger than that from other income. By contrast, the marginal propensity to consume adult clothing out of child benefit is much less than that from other income. It seems that child benefit was spent on the child.

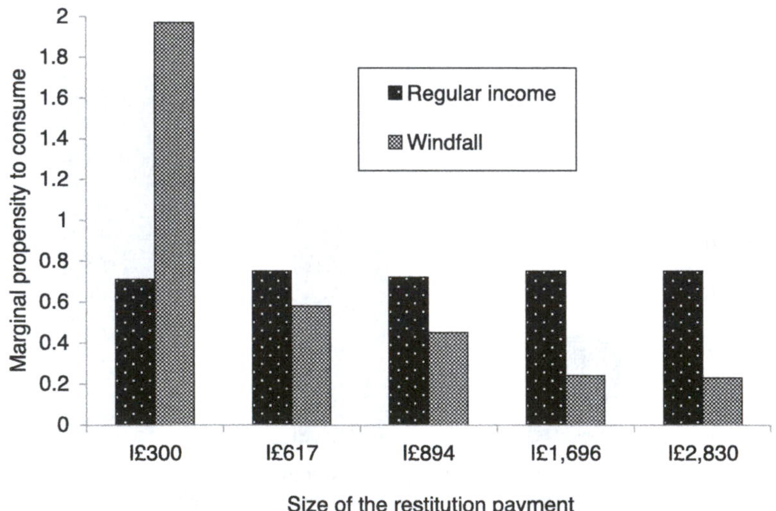

Figure 2.34 The marginal propensity to consume the windfall gain compared to normal income of Israeli recipients of German restitution payments.

Source: Landsberger (1966).

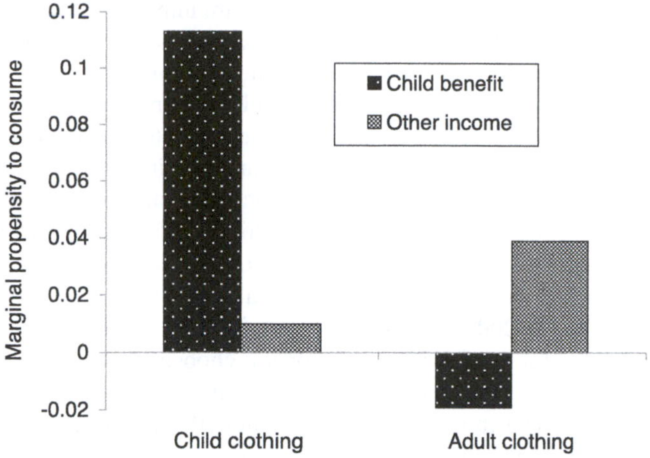

Figure 2.35 The marginal propensity to consume clothing our of normal income and child benefit.

Source: Kooreman (2000).

All three of these examples show a lack of fungibility. Households treat money differently depending on where it comes from, how much it was, and for what purpose it was given. There are lots of other examples I could give to demonstrate the same basic conclusion (see Review question 2.12). But, given what we saw in section 2.2 it should come as no surprise that money is not fungible. If people keep mental accounts then it is natural that money should not easily flow from one account to the next. The question we need to get back to is what implications this has for the life cycle hypothesis.

One thing we have seen is that people seem reluctant to spend future unearned income. Only when they got the money did households spend the tax rebate and restitution payment. We know, more generally, that people do spend unearned income. Student debt and families taking out a mortgage to buy a house are ample evidence of this. The point is, however, that people may spend less of their unearned income than the life cycle hypothesis might suggest they should. Given that most people get increasing amounts of money through their lifetime this would mean spending tracks income more than would be predicted by the life cycle hypothesis. This is what we observe.

2.9 Saving for the future

One particularly important aspect of the life cycle hypothesis is saving. People need to save enough for retirement, to buy a house, or new car, and so on. A survey of faculty and staff at the University of Southern California by Benartzi and Thaler (1999) found that 58 percent of those surveyed spent less than one hour determining their contribution rate and investment decisions to a savings plan. This is presumably quite typical, but these are important, complicated decisions, and so it is slightly worrying that so little time is spent making them! Put another way, however, people must be using simple heuristics to help them make decisions so quickly. Maybe these heuristics help them make the right decisions.

To illustrate the heuristics we do observe, Figure 2.36 plots the distribution of contribution rates of those joining a large retirement savings plan in 2001 or 2002. The contribution rate is the proportion of income that people allocate to the savings plan. Three heuristics are apparent in this data. First is to **pick a multiple of five** as seen in the notable spikes at 5, 10, and 15 percent. Second is to **pick the maximum allowed**. In 2001 the maximum allowed in this contribution plan was16 percent, but in 2002 the maximum was increased to 100 percent. We can see that this caused a big fall in the proportion choosing 16 percent. Finally, in most contribution plans, the employer will match the contribution of an employer up to some limit. The third heuristic is to **pick the maximum to get a full employer match**. In this plan that maximum was 6 percent, explaining why so many chose this contribution rate.

With these three heuristics we can get a good feel for why the contribution rate is distributed as in Figure 2.36. Next I want to look in a bit more detail at one important kind of heuristic we have not yet seen.

2.9.1 Let's diversify

As well as deciding how much to save, an investor also needs to decide where to save, or invest. The typical contribution retirement savings plan will give the

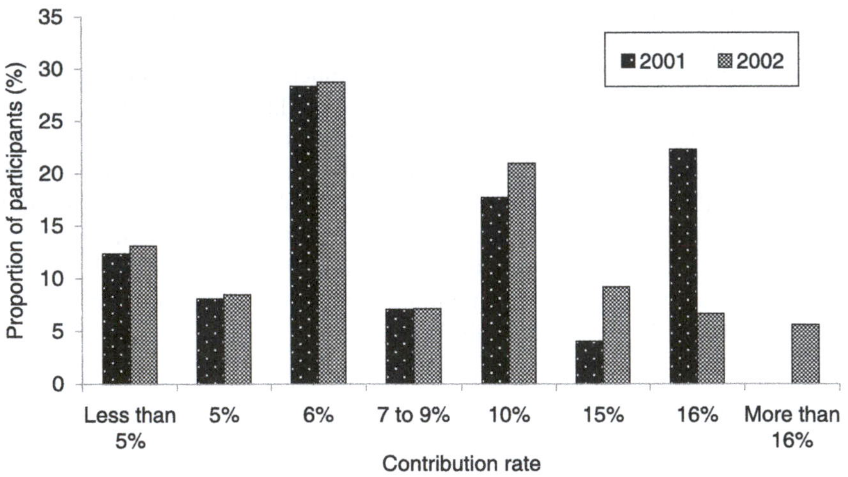

Figure 2.36 The contribution rate of people enrolled in a large defined contribution plan.
Source: Benartzi and Thaler (2007).

saver a set of funds or investment opportunities that they can invest the money into. For example, Benartzi and Thaler (2001) look at a database from the Money Market Directories that covers 170 retirement savings plans with 1.56 million participants. The average number of investment options available in a plan was around six to seven. For example, a plan might allow participants to split investments between an equity, international equity, corporate bonds, balanced growth, government bonds, and money market funds.

Deciding where to invest is a complex choice. One option is to use a simple **diversification strategy**, called the 1/n heuristic. The **1/n heuristic** is to split the amount to be saved or invested equally among the available funds. A simple heuristic, but one that leaves the saver exposed to any bias in the options on offer. For example, compare a plan that has three equity options and one money option to one with two equity options and two money options. In the first, someone using the 1/n heuristic would invest 75 percent in equity, and in the second, they would invest 50 percent. That's a big difference.

Do we observe people using the 1/n heuristic? Benartzi and Thaler categorized the investment plans in their data as having a low, medium, or high proportion of equity fund options. Figure 2.37 compares the proportion of equity fund options with the proportion invested in equities. We can immediately see that things are not as simple as the 1/n heuristic would suggest because the proportion invested is more consistent across plans than the proportion of equity fund options offered. Even so, those in a plan with a larger number of equity fund options do invest significantly more in equities.

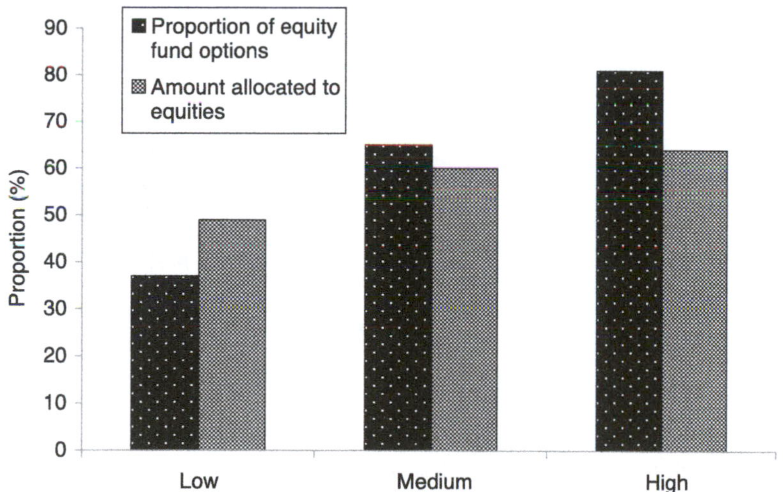

Figure 2.37 The proportion of funds that were based on equities and the proportion of savings that savers invested in equity. Those in plans with more equity funds invested more in equity.

Source: Benartzi and Thaler (2001).

It is hard to justify such a systematic difference in investments without people being biased by the options they have to choose from. To illustrate this further Benartzi and Thaler analyze data from a specific company. The company is interesting because at the end of 1994 and 1996 the fund options available to investors were changed. Figure 2.38 charts the change in investment patterns over time. In 1994 four new fund options were made available. In 1996 the bond fund was withdrawn. You can see that by the end of 1997 investments are quite evenly split amongst the remaining possible funds. The remarkable thing about this is that it means there was a huge shift in exposure to equity funds. In 1993 only 18 percent of investments were in equity but by 1997 that had risen to 76 percent. It is highly unlikely that this shift is because of a change in preferences or the optimal portfolio!

2.9.2 Let's not diversify

The 1/n heuristic makes most sense if n is not very large, i.e. the number of options is small. What if the number of options is large? Then we might get a **conditional 1/n heuristic** of picking a small number of funds and dividing investments equally amongst these. Huberman and Jiang (2006) looked at the investment decisions of over half a million participants of defined contribution plans in 2001. Figure 2.39 compares the number of funds participants chose to invest in versus the number of funds offered. The majority of participants were in plans with over ten funds to choose from. Despite this, the majority of participants chose to invest in only one to five of the possible funds. Investors were clearly, therefore, selective in where they invested, consistent with the first part of the conditional 1/n heuristic.

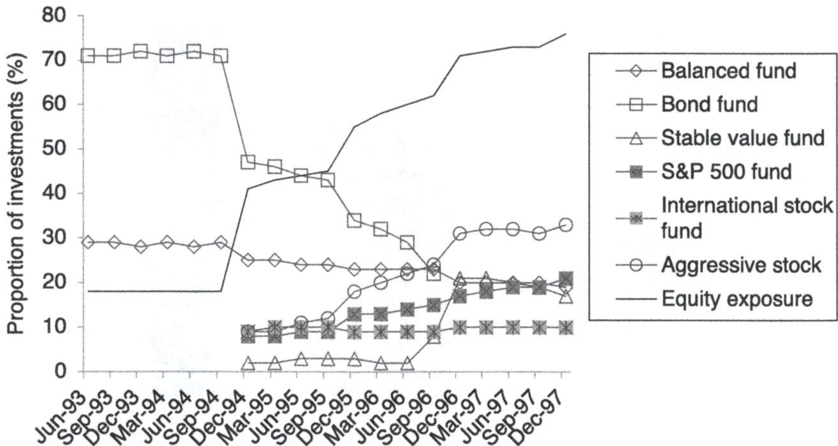

Figure 2.38 The proportion of investments in each fund of a company's contribution savings plan. In 1994 new funds are added and in 1996 the bond fund withdrawn. The amount invested in equities increases a lot as a consequence.

Source: Benartzi and Thaler (2001).

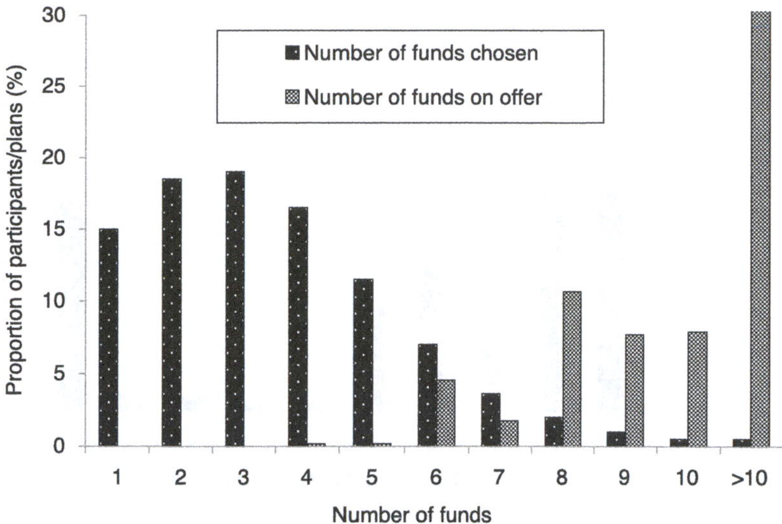

Figure 2.39 The number of funds that savers invest in and are on offer in a large sample of defined contribution plans. A typical plan offers ten or more funds. Most savers invest in one to five funds.

Source: Huberman and Jiang (2006).

To check the second part of the conditional 1/n heuristic we need to see how participants allocated their investments between the funds they did invest in. This is not simple to do, because the value of funds goes up or down over time, and so even if an investor did split her investments equally across funds initially, it may not look this way a few years later. To compensate for this, Huberman and Jian look at new participants. Figure 2.40 summarizes for each choice of number of funds the proportion of new participants that invest consistent with the 1/n heuristic. We see that a high proportion of those investing in two, four, five, and ten funds do seem to use the 1/n heuristic. Intuitively this makes sense because then 1/n is a round number. Figure 2.40 is misleading as to the total proportion who use the 1/n heuristic because we need to factor in the proportion of participants who chose one, two, and three funds, etc. Doing this we find that over 70 percent of participants behaved consistent with a conditional 1/n heuristic.

Figure 2.37 suggested investors may be biased towards investing in equity if the proportion of equity funds offered is high. It was clear, however, that the differences in investments chosen were smaller than those of investments offered. Huberman and Jiang draw a similar conclusion, finding only a small positive correlation between the number of equity funds offered and the number chosen. One possibility is that when the number of offered funds is small, as in Figure 2.38, investors are biased by the number of equity funds on offer, but if the number of funds is large, investors are not so biased by the proportion of equity funds.

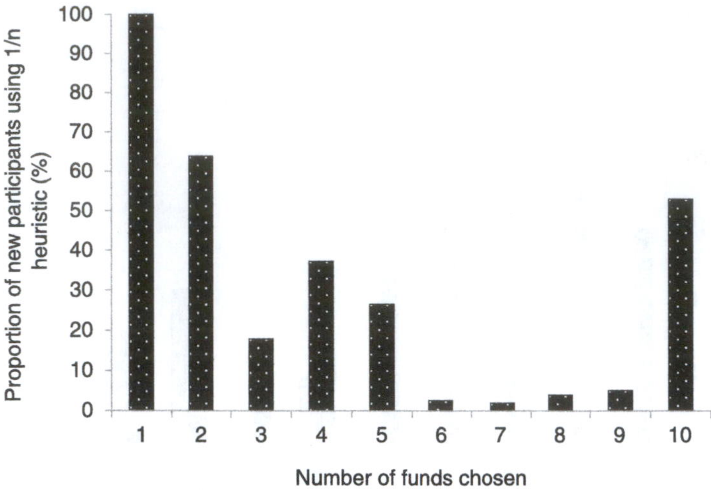

Figure 2.40 The proportion of new participants who behave consistent with the conditional 1/n heuristic, i.e. split their investments equally between the funds they invest in.

Source: Huberman and Jiang (2006).

Whether this is true or not, the picture we get is one of investors using simple heuristics to make complex choices. What's not so clear is whether these heuristics are optimal for the investor. It's hard to believe that, by some happy coincidence, a contribution rate of 10 percent, or a split of 75 to 25 percent between equities and money, is optimal. Maybe, however, a contribution rate of 10 percent is nearly as good as the true optimum of, say, 9.34 or 11.28 percent. Maybe it is not so bad that investors increase their exposure to equity because of a change in the funds on offer. These are important questions, and so we will come back to them in subsequent chapters.

2.10 Further reading

There is an overlap between this chapter and the next in terms of further reading for sections 2.1 and 2.2. That said, the articles by Tversky and Kahneman (1981, 1986), Kahneman and Tversky (1983), Rabin (1998), Kahneman (2003) and Thaler (2008) are particularly worth a look. The book by Kahneman (2011) is a must read! One issue I covered relatively briefly is search; the paper by Schunk (2009) provides an interesting recent addition to the literature connecting search with loss aversion. For more on markets the papers by Vernon Smith (2002, 2003) are a good starting point. For more on the life cycle hypothesis and savings you could start with Shefrin and Thaler (1998), Thaler (1990), Browning and Crossley (2001), and Benartzi and Thaler (2007).

2.11 Review questions

2.1 If you wanted to find a new mobile phone, outfit, car, house, job, how would you search for one?

2.2 Why might a company wanting to advertise a product be interested in the trade-off contrast hypothesis and extremeness aversion?

2.3 Is it possible that Anna could be influenced by both trade-off contrast and extremeness aversion simultaneously?

2.4 Why is time important in reference-dependent utility? Compare how happy Carol and Amanda will feel the day they get the report from their broker, the next day, after a month, etc.

2.5 List all the heuristics that have appeared in the chapter.

2.6 Argue that, if true, the 'no loss in buying' hypothesis means the WTP valuation is more reliable than the WTA valuation.

2.7 Why would we expect EG to be greater than WTA?

2.8 Suppose someone's willingness to pay for a good is $10 and their reference point is $20. If the good is $13 will they buy it? What does this tell us about sales and 'bargain buys'?

2.9 Write down a list of occasions where you could have gained from lying or deception. Why can context influence whether or not you lie?

2.10 Does the fact that a taxi driver works nine hours a day mean he has a reference level of hours he wants to work? [Hint: it could be that his utility function just becomes steep at nine hours. A reference level of hours worked should be determined by some exogenous factor such as how many hours his friends work. But, is it always possible to distinguish exogenous factors from his preferences?]

2.11 Using search, contrast effects, and reference dependence suggest why a person who lives in an area where apartments cost around $200,000 may be reluctant to buy when she moves to an area where apartments cost around $300,000.

2.12 Suppose that Anna owns her own house and house prices go up. Should she spend more? Now, suppose she has money invested in the stock market and share prices go down. Should she spend less?

3 Choice with risk

> The safest way to double your money is to fold it over once and put it in your pocket.
>
> Kin Hubbard

Economic choices are almost always made with some uncertainty as to what the outcome will be. A person buys groceries without knowing for sure how tasty they will be. He buys a new car without knowing how it will perform or how long it will last, a plane ticket without knowing whether the plane will be delayed, house insurance because he does not know whether his house will be burgled, and invests in shares without knowing whether they will increase or decrease in value. In the last chapter we saw that uncertainty can lead to choice arbitrariness and all the consequences that entails. What I want to do in this chapter is look in more detail at some other important consequences of risk.

Before we get started there is one distinction I need to explain. We say that someone faces a **situation of risk** if they know what could happen and how likely it is. An example would be someone who bets $10 on the toss of a coin; they know that there is a 50:50 chance it could be heads or tails, and, if it's heads, they win $10 and, if it's tails, they lose $10. We say that someone faces a **situation of uncertainty** if they do not know some of the possible outcomes or how likely they are. An example would be someone booking a plane ticket, who is unlikely to know all the possible delays or problems that could happen to change his experience of the flight.

Most of the situations we face are ones of uncertainty. Even the toss of a coin could be biased in many different ways. It is, however, more difficult to model situations of uncertainty than ones of risk, and without knowing the consequences of risk we cannot get very far thinking about uncertainty. It is traditional, therefore, to focus on situations of risk, and that is what I shall do in this chapter. That makes our task manageable and, as we shall see, still gives us a lot to think about. But do not be too disappointed, because in Chapters five and nine we will come back to look at choice with uncertainty.

3.1 Expected utility

To illustrate some of the issues, imagine someone called Alan deciding whether or not to insure his car. Table 3.1 summarizes the choice he has to make. This is a choice with risk, because he cannot know for sure whether the car will be stolen, or will be in an accident, or whether he will be asked to prove he has insurance. He begins with \$20 in money and his car is worth an additional \$50 (you can multiply these numbers by \$1,000 if you wish). Full insurance costs \$9 and guarantees his final wealth will be \$61 = 20 + 50 − 9. Insurance against theft costs only \$6 but does not insure against an accident. No insurance costs nothing but leaves him vulnerable to theft, an accident, or being fined \$40 by the police for having no insurance. Should he insure his car?

More generally we shall be interested in things called prospects. A **prospect** is a list of probabilities that things will happen, together with the monetary payoff if they do happen. In the insurance example there are three prospects. The 'full insurance prospect' gives probability one of having \$61. We can write this as (1, \$61). The 'insurance against theft prospect' gives probability 0.95 of \$64 and 0.05 of \$14. We can write this as (0.95, \$64; 0.05, \$14). Finally, the 'no insurance prospect' gives probability 0.1 of \$20, 0.1 of \$30 and 0.8 of \$70, which we write as (0.1, \$20; 0.1, \$30; 0.8, \$70). In general we would summarize a **prospect** with the list $(p_1, x_1; p_2, x_2; \ldots; p_n, x_n)$ where p_i is the probability of getting monetary payoff x_i.

The reason we are interested in prospects is that this is what a person must choose. In the insurance example Alan must decide whether to choose the 'full insurance', 'insurance against theft', or 'no insurance prospect'. We need, therefore, a model of how people choose prospects. The standard way to do this is to use expected utility.

To calculate expected utility we make use of a utility function u that translates money into utility. This is the same utility function as we saw in the last chapter; it is just that, to make life easier for ourselves, we ignore things other than money. So, if Alan has x in money, his utility is $u(x)$. The **expected utility of a prospect** $A = (p_1, x_1; p_2, x_2; \ldots; p_n, x_n)$ is then found using the formula:

$$U(A) = \sum_{i=1}^{n} p_i u(x_i). \tag{3.1}$$

We can then predict that people will choose the prospect with the highest expected utility. This gives us a simple way to predict choice with risk.

Table 3.1 The possible consequences of Alan buying insurance

	Car is stolen	*Car is in an accident*	*Stopped by police*	*No theft, accident, or police*
Probability	0.05	0.05	0.10	0.80
Final wealth if buys full insurance	\$61	\$61	\$61	\$61
Insurance against theft	\$64	\$14	\$64	\$64
No insurance	\$20	\$20	\$30	\$70

To see how this works in the insurance example I shall contrast the choices Alan would make for three different possible utility functions. Table 3.2 provides the numbers and Figure 3.1 plots them. With a linear function we see that insurance against theft gives the highest expected utility. If the utility function is sufficiently concave, then full insurance gives the highest expected utility, and if it is sufficiently convex, no insurance gives the highest expected utility.

The example illustrates how the prospect that gives the highest expected utility will depend on the shape of the utility function. To explain why, I should first define the **expected value of a prospect A** as:

$$V(A) = \sum_{i=1}^{n} p_i x_i. \tag{3.2}$$

Table 3.2 Alan's expected utility depends on his utility function

Utility function	*Expected utility if chose:*			*Predicted choice*
	Full insurance	*Insurance for theft*	*No insurance*	
Linear: $u(x) = x$	61.0	61.5	61.0	Insurance for theft
Concave: $u(x) = 10\sqrt{x}$	78.1	77.9	76.9	Full insurance
Convex: $u(x) = x^2/50$	74.4	78.0	81.0	No insurance

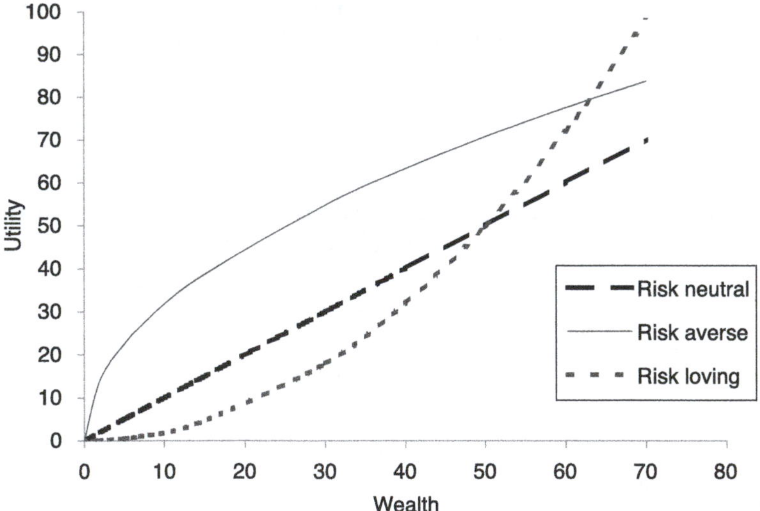

Figure 3.1 Three possible utility functions: one is concave, which would imply Alan is risk averse, and one convex, which would imply Alan is risk loving.

The only difference between equations (3.1) and (3.2) is that we do not transform monetary payoffs into utility payoffs. This means that we obtain expected monetary payoff rather than expected utility payoff. In the example, insurance for theft has the highest expected value. It is not clear, however, that choosing the prospect with the highest expected value is best. This is because Alan will want to also take into account the riskiness of the prospect.

The relevant trade-offs are illustrated in Table 3.3. With full insurance, Alan knows his payoff will be $61. There is no risk, and Alan might like this. Indeed he might like it so much that he is willing to sacrifice $0.50 of expected value to get it. In this case we would say that he is risk averse. Someone is **risk averse** if they prefer a certain amount of money to a prospect with the same expected value; they would rather avoid risk. Going to the other extreme, it may be that Alan likes to gamble and prefers to choose no insurance because that is where the risk is highest. In this case we would say that he is risk loving. Someone is **risk loving** if they prefer a risky prospect to the expected value of the prospect for sure; they would prefer risk.

Whether or not Alan is risk averse or risk loving will depend in a simple way on the curvature of his utility function. If his utility function is concave, Alan loses relatively more if his wealth goes down than he gains if his wealth goes up, so he would rather not risk a loss for a gain, and he is risk averse. If his utility function is convex, then he loses relatively less if his wealth goes down than he gains if his wealth goes up, so he would risk a loss for a gain and he is risk loving. The curvature of the utility function tells us, therefore, a lot.

There are two commonly used ways to measure this: one measures **absolute risk aversion** and the other **relative risk aversion**. It's not so important that you know exactly what these are, but for completeness the formulas are:

$$\text{absolute risk aversion: } r_u^a = -\frac{u''(x)}{u'(x)}; \text{ relative risk aversion: } r_u^r = -x\frac{u''(x)}{u'(x)}$$

where $u'(x)$ denotes the derivate and $u''(x)$ the second derivate of $u(x)$. If Alan is risk neutral, then $u(x) = x$ and so $r_u^a, r_u^r = 0$. But if he is risk averse, $r_u^a, r_u^r > 0$, and the more risk averse he is, the larger is r_u^a and r_u^r. Various methods can be used to measure risk aversion (see Research Methods 3.1).

Table 3.3 The expected value and risk of different choices

	Expected value	*Minimum possible*	*Maximum possible*	*Probability wealth below expected value*
Full insurance	$61	$61	$61	0.00
Insurance against theft	$61.5	$14	$64	0.05
No insurance	$61	$20	$70	0.20

Economists like things simple, and so two utility functions are of particular note because they imply respectively **constant absolute risk aversion** (CARA) or **constant relative risk aversion** (CRRA). It's even less important that you know what these are, but here they are:

$$\text{CARA: } u(x) = -e^{-r_u^a x}; \quad \text{CRRA: } u(x) = \frac{x^{1-r_u^r}}{1-r_u^r}$$

The beauty of the CARA or CRRA functions is that we only need to know one number, the level of risk aversion, and then we can model choice with risk, because we know what the utility function is and can use expected utility to find what maximizes utility. No wonder that expected utility has become the standard way of modeling choice with risk: If we know Alan's level of risk aversion then we can predict his choice over any set of risky prospects!

Research Methods 3.1

Measuring risk aversion

Given the risk inherent in many economic choices, it is important to know the level of risk aversion, even if our primary interest is not how a person reacts to risk. There are lots of methods that have been used to measure risk aversion and we will see many of them as we go through the rest of the chapter. The basic idea behind most methods is the same: choices are observed and fed into either the CARA or CRRA utility function to estimate the parameter r_u^a or r_u^r. The differences between methods are the choices observed. Needless to say the experimental laboratory is one setting that has been used. In this case we look at prospects with relatively small amounts of money. Empirical settings where we can measure risk aversion include asset and insurance markets. In this case we can observe choices over prospects with both relatively small and large amounts of money (see section 3.7).

An intriguing and slightly different way to measure risk aversion was suggested by Chetty (2006). This method does not use choices over prospects but instead looks to directly estimate the curvature of the $u(x)$ function. This is, after all, what we need to calculate r_u^a or r_u^r because the more curved is $u(x)$ the more risk averse a person is. The curvature of $u(x)$ is estimated by looking at labor supply. To explain how this works: the more curved is $u(x)$ the quicker a person becomes relatively satiated with money, that is, has enough money to not want more; if someone is satiated with money then they will not want to risk losing money to gain more, they are risk averse, and they have no desire to increase their income, so can work less if the wage rate increases. By looking at how people react to changes in wages we can therefore estimate risk aversion.

The problem that economists face is that different studies have given very different estimates for the level of risk aversion, and we are not talking small differences. For example, Chetty estimates that r_u^r must be less than two, but we shall see estimates later in this chapter as high as 1,000. This suggests that there is no real measure of risk aversion, just measures that are appropriate for particular situations.

Expected utility does give us, therefore, a very simple and transparent way to model and understand how people make choices when there is risk. Maybe, however, it is a bit too simple. Is it possible to capture all the things that can influence choice, and that we are interested in predicting and modeling, in just one number? The only way to find out is to look at some data and see. To get us started on this I am going to give a series of examples that suggest that expected utility cannot explain everything we typically observe. These examples will serve as a precursor to us thinking more generally about how to move beyond expected utility. As we go through the examples, I would strongly encourage you to 'play along' and think what you would choose and why.

3.1.1 The Allais Paradox

Consider the prospects in Table 3.4. When asked to choose between prospects A and B, most people choose prospect B. When asked to choose between prospects C and D, most people choose prospect C. This seems entirely sensible but is not consistent with expected utility theory: the **Allais Paradox**.

To see why this is a paradox, first observe that prospect C is obtained from prospect A, and prospect D is obtained from prospect B, by removing a 0.66 chance of winning $2,400. Now, if Alan chooses B over A (and put $u(0) = 0$),

$$u(2{,}400) > 0.33u(2{,}500) + 0.66u(2{,}400),$$

which (removing the 0.66 chance of winning $2,400) means that

$$0.34u(2{,}400) > 0.33u(2{,}500). \tag{3.3}$$

If, however, he chooses prospect C over D:

$$0.33u(2{,}500) > 0.34u(2{,}400). \tag{3.4}$$

Equations (3.3) and (3.4) cannot both be true.

So, what causes the Allais Paradox? There is a sense in which removing the 0.66 chance of winning $2,400 matters more for prospect B than A because changing a sure thing to a risk matters more than changing a risk to a risk. Generalizing from this, the evidence suggests that people favor outcomes that are perceived certain rather than probable or possible. This is called the **certainty effect**.

Interestingly, the certainty effect can be relevant even if outcomes are not theoretically certain. To illustrate, consider Table 3.5, with four more prospects. Most people choose prospect F over E and prospect G over H. This is again inconsistent with expected utility theory. It does seem consistent with a certainty effect because a 0.9 chance might look relatively certain compared to a 0.45 chance. What is perceived as certain can thus depend on the context.

Table 3.4 The Allais Paradox. Many people prefer B to A and C to D

Prospect	*Amount with probability of outcome*		
A	$2,500 with probability 0.33	$2,400 prob. 0.66	$0 prob. 0.01
B	$2,400 for sure.		
C	$2,500 with probability 0.33		$0 with probability 0.67
D	$2,400 with probability 0.34		$0 with probability 0.66

Table 3.5 The near-certainty effect. Many people choose F over E and G over H

Prospect	*Amount with probability of outcome*	
E	$6,000 with probability 0.45	$0 otherwise
F	$3,000 with probability 0.9	$0 otherwise
G	$6,000 with probability 0.001	$0 otherwise
H	$3,000 with probability 0.002	$0 otherwise

3.1.2 Risk aversion

Next consider the prospects in Table 3.6. Anyone who prefers prospect I to prospects J to N is risk averse. They prefer $0 for sure to a prospect with expected value greater than $0. The further we go down the list of prospects, the more risk averse someone would have to be to prefer prospect I. Many people choose prospect I over prospect J (see Research Methods 3.2). More generally, many people display risk aversion for relatively small gambles.

This, in itself, is consistent with expected utility. The problem comes when we try to infer what such a choice implies a person would do when choosing amongst prospects with bigger stakes.

Research Methods 3.2

Money or something else

Experimental subjects are almost always given financial incentives. This means that at the end of the experiment they are given cash, and the knowledge that they will be given cash is supposed to be incentive enough to think about their choices. For economists this is easy to justify, because money is a unit of exchange and easily substituted for other goods. Maybe, however, subjects would behave differently if the incentive were something other than money? We have already encountered an experiment that gave chocolates as well as money, but this does not really answer the question of interest here. What we need is an experiment where subjects are provided with a monetary incentive in one treatment and a different incentive in another treatment.

Harrison and co-authors (2007) did such a study on risk aversion. The study was done at the Central Florida Coin Show and involved subjects choosing amongst prospects that had either monetary or coin outcomes. In a monetary treatment the possible prize was money and in a coin treatment it was a collectable coin. The coins that could be won had a retail value of \$40, \$125, \$200, and \$350. The money prizes were set to match these amounts.

The study showed very similar estimates of risk aversion whether subjects chose amongst prospects with a monetary or coin prize. The answer to our question, at least on the basis of this study, would, therefore, be that subjects did not behave differently when the incentive was something other than money. There is, however, one important caveat to this conclusion.

Two versions of the coin treatment were considered in the study. In one, the grade of the coins that could be won was clear to subjects, and in the other it was not. The grading is important in determining the value of the coin. When the grade of coin is clear, someone who knows about coins would be able to give a relatively accurate value of the coin. When the grade is not clear, the valuation would be more uncertain. Risk attitudes were the same whether the prize is money or a coin of known grade. But, when the grade was not clear, subjects were more risk averse. This suggests that people may be more risk averse if there is background uncertainty about the value of possible outcomes. This also suggests that estimates of risk aversion based on monetary incentives may understate risk aversion for the many contexts where people do face background uncertainty. Note that we could only know this by using non-monetary prizes. That is because there cannot be background uncertainty in a monetary prize: for instance, a subject in the US has a pretty good idea what a \$10 note is worth.

To explain, suppose that Alan has a wealth of \$100 and prefers prospect I to prospect K. This means that:

$$u(100) > 0.5u(0) + 0.5u(225).$$

If $u(0) = 0$ and $u(100) = 100$, it must be that $u(225) < 200$. Knowing that Alan prefers prospect I to prospect K thus tells us something about the utility he gets from having wealth of \$225. Now, suppose that Alan has wealth of \$225 and still prefers prospect I to prospect K. We can then infer something about the utility he gets from having wealth of \$350; see below. Continuing in this way, we get a picture of what the utility function must be like if Alan continues to prefer prospect I to K for higher and higher levels of wealth. Figure 3.2 gives such a picture.

Table 3.6 Prospects that can lead to extreme risk aversion

Prospect	*Amount with probability of outcome*	
I	\$0 for sure	
J	\$100 loss with probability 0.5	\$105 gain otherwise
K	\$100 loss with probability 0.5	\$125 gain otherwise
L	\$100 loss with probability 0.5	\$200 gain otherwise
M	\$225 loss with probability 0.5	\$375 gain otherwise
N	\$600 loss with probability 0.5	\$36 million gain otherwise

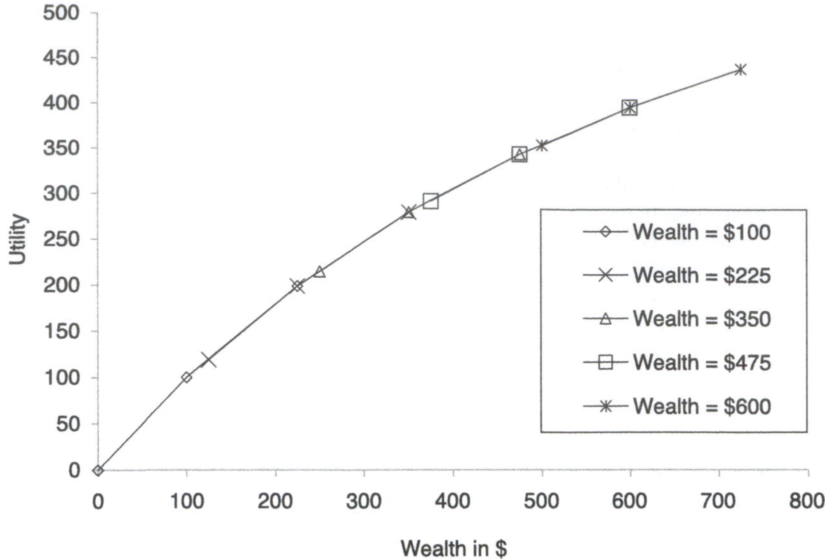

Figure 3.2 What can we infer about the utility function of someone who prefers prospect I to prospect K for increasing levels of wealth?

[Extra] I should explain how to get this picture. Let us say that u (225) = 199, and so Alan just prefers prospect I to K when his wealth is $100. If Alan has wealth of $225 and would still prefer prospect I to prospect K:

$$u\ (225) > 0.5u\ (125) + 0.5u\ (350).$$

We do not know $u(125)$, but we do know that $u(100) = 100$ and $u(225) = 199$, so can infer that $u(125) > 119$. This means $u(350) \leq 279$. Suppose that $u(350) = 279$. Now imagine that Alan has wealth of $350 and would still prefer prospect I to prospect K. This means that:

$$u\ (350) > 0.5u\ (250) + 0.5u\ (475).$$

Again, we do not know $u(250)$, but we can infer that $u(250) > 215$, so $u(475) \leq 343$. We can go on and on doing this.

The key point to notice in Figure 3.2 is how the utility function has already curved a lot. Going from $0 to $100 is worth 100 utility, but going from $600 to $700 is worth only 40 utility. We need the utility function to bend like this for low levels of wealth in order to understand why Alan would prefer prospect I. The problem is that, once we have started bending it, we have to carry on bending it. This relative bending of the utility function has implications for bigger gambles.

Table 3.7 The amount a person would need to gain on a 50:50 bet to take the bet, if risk averse for small gambles

Potential loss	*Potential gain needed to take the bet if:*	
	Prefers prospect I to J	*Prefers prospect I to K*
$400	$420	$1,250
$600	$730	$36,000,000,000
$800	$1,050	$90,000,000,000
$1,000	$1,570	$160,000,000,000
$20,000	$71,799,110	$540,000,000,000,000,000,000

Source: Rabin (2000).

To illustrate, if $u(225) = 199$, and if you carry on the reasoning above, you should find that $u(600) < 400$. Consequently, if Alan had a wealth level of $225, he would prefer prospect I to prospect M. This may well be the case, but we see that the difference between the relative gain and loss has increased quite a lot. If we were to look at realistic wealth levels of $50,000 to $300,000, then this effect would become very pronounced.

To demonstrate, Table 3.7 details the amount of money: Alan would need as potential gain in order to take on a 50:50 gamble, if he had a wealth level of $290,000 and would prefer prospect I to J or K, for any level of wealth below $300,000. By this stage we see that the differences between relative gain and loss have become huge, implausibly huge. For example, it must be that anyone who would prefer prospect I to prospect K must prefer prospect I to prospect N. This is possible, but seems highly unlikely, suggesting that expected utility cannot explain risk aversion for small gambles (see Research Methods 3.3).

Research Methods 3.3

Risk aversion and incentives in the lab

In many economic experiments we are interested in something other than attitudes to risk. The outcome may, however, be inherently risky. For example, in Chapters six and seven we shall look at behavior in strategic contexts where one person's payoff will depend on what others do. Our focus will be on things like a person's ability to predict what another will do, or his desire to be fair. His payoff will, however, depend on what another subject does, and so there is an element of risk. This complicates things. For example, we shall have to try and determine whether he gave something to another to be fair or because he is risk averse. What we would like is that the subject's choice does not depend on his attitude to risk.

If subjects are risk neutral then the problem goes away. If, however, subjects are risk averse (or risk loving) then things are not so simple. One potential solution is to frame choices in a slightly different way. Instead of asking subjects to make choices that might increase their payoff from, say, $5 to $10 we can offer them choices that increase the probability of winning, say, $100 from 0.05 to 0.10. If a subject maximizes expected utility then this approach should make attitudes to risk irrelevant. If, however, the subject maximizes expected utility, then risk aversion should not matter anyway for the small sums of money in a typical experiment! It is not clear, therefore, how much such alternative framings really help.

Indeed, there seems to be no simple way to disentangle the consequences of risk and uncertainty from other things we might be interested in. This means that we need to be mindful of attitudes to risk in interpreting any experimental results.

3.1.3 Risk loving for losses

The next set of prospects are in Table 3.8. Most people choose prospect P rather than O, and prospect Q rather than R. This suggests that people are risk averse for gains, preferring the $3,000 for sure, but risk loving for gambles, preferring to gamble on losing $0.

Such choices are theoretically possible while maximizing expected utility, but only by pushing things to the limit. Recall that utility should be measured according to the absolute level of wealth. So, we would need that, when asked to choose amongst these options, a person's current wealth just happened to be at a point where the utility function is concave for higher levels of wealth, and convex for lower levels of wealth. This is possible, but seems a bit too much of a coincidence. More plausible, particularly given what we saw in the last chapter, is that choices are made, in part, by measuring relative deviations from current wealth. This is called the **reflection effect**.

To illustrate the possible consequences of the reflection effect, consider the next set of prospects given in Table 3.9. In principle, prospect S is equivalent to U and prospect T equivalent to V. Despite this, most people choose prospect T rather than prospect S and prospect U rather than prospect V. This can be explained by the reflection effect. In prospect T the $500 is perceived as a gain, while in prospect V the $500 is perceived as a loss.

Table 3.8 Prospects with gains and losses. Many prefer P to O and Q to R

Prospect	*Amount with probability of outcome*	
O	$4,000 with probability 0.8	$0 otherwise
P	$3,000 for sure	
Q	$4,000 loss with probability 0.8	$0 otherwise
R	$3,000 loss for sure	

Table 3.9 Framing of losses versus gains. Many prefer T over S and U over V

Prospect	*In a preliminary stage given*	*Subsequently get amount with probability of outcome*	
S	\$1,000	\$1,000 gain with probability 0.5	\$0 otherwise
T	\$1,000	\$500 for sure	
U	\$2,000	\$1,000 loss with probability 0.5	\$0 otherwise
V	\$2,000	\$500 loss for sure	

3.1.4 When expected utility will work

Expected utility provides a brilliantly simple way to model choice with risk. We have already seen, however, that it can be a bit too simple to capture all that we observe. No model will work all the time and so this is no great surprise, and it does not mean that we should ditch expected utility. If you want a model that can reliably capture how a person behaves for particular types of gamble, then expected utility may be good enough. If, though, you want a single model that can capture all the risky choices a person may make, whether it be big or small gambles, gambles with losses or with gains, then expected utility is probably not good enough. It is natural, therefore, to look for a model that can do a better job. A useful first step in doing this is to question when expected utility does provide a good model of choice. This can hopefully help pinpoint what expected utility misses.

The first thing we need for expected utility to work well is transitivity. A person's **preferences are transitive** if, for any three prospects X, Y, and Z,

$$\text{if } X \geq Y \text{ and } Y \geq Z \text{ then } X \geq Z$$

where the notation $X \geq Y$ means that the person prefers prospect X to prospect Y or is indifferent between prospects X and Y. In other words, there should be a natural ordering to preferences, with a best, X in this case, and worst, Z.

The second thing we need is independence. A person's **preferences satisfy independence** if, for any three prospects X, Y, and Z,

$$\text{if } X \geq Y \text{ then } (p, X; 1-p, Z) \geq (p, Y; 1-p, Z)$$

for any number p between zero and one. In other words, if Alan prefers prospect X to Y, then he must also prefer a prospect that mixes X with some other prospect Z to one that mixes Y with the same prospect Z.

If preferences satisfy independence and transitivity (as well as two other properties of completeness and continuity), then preferences and choice can be modeled using expected utility. Expected utility would then be the best way to model choice. This is useful to know in trying to work out why expected utility may not work so well. In the following sections I shall take up in turn the possibility that preferences do not satisfy independence and that they do not satisfy transitivity. With this we shall see how to adapt expected utility to better account for choice with risk.

3.2 Independence and fanning out

I want to start this section by revisiting the Allais Paradox. To help us understand the paradox we can use a probability triangle diagram like that in Figure 3.3. On the horizontal axis we measure the probability of having \$0, and on the vertical axis we measure the probability of having \$2,500. Any point in the triangle is a prospect. This becomes clear by plotting on the four prospects in the Allais Paradox. Prospect B guarantees \$2,400 for sure so goes at the bottom left corner where $p_1 = p_3 = 0$. Prospect A gives \$0 with probability 0.01 and \$2,500 with probability 0.33, so goes where $p_1 = 0.01$ and $p_3 = 0.33$. We can also plot on prospects C and D. Drawing this diagram makes clear that prospects C and D are similar to A and B but 'moved across' by adding a 0.66 chance of getting \$0.

What we now want to start to do is represent preferences on the probability triangle diagram. While we are doing this I want to clarify two different notions of utility. First, there is **outcome utility**. This is the utility we talked about in the previous chapter and can capture with the function *u*. It tells us the utility that Alan will get from a particular outcome such as winning \$0, \$2,400, and \$2,500. Next is the **utility of a prospect**. You can think of this as the utility that Alan gets

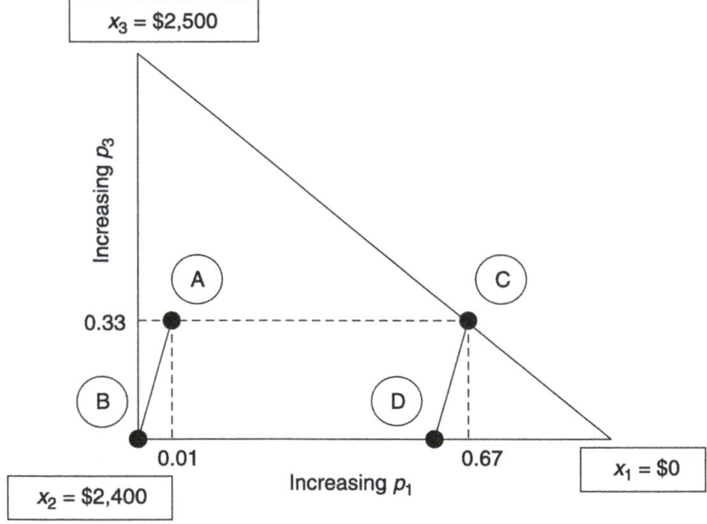

Figure 3.3 A probability triangle diagram of the Allais Paradox. The horizontal axis is the probability of winning \$0 and the vertical axis the probability of winning \$2,500. The other possibility is to win \$2,400.

from a prospect before he knows the outcome of that prospect. We capture this with the function *U*, and to understand the Allais Paradox we need to know the utility of prospects A to D. Expected utility is one way of getting at this (see equation (3.1)), but we now want to consider alternatives.

If we know the utility that Alan would get from any possible prospect, then we can start to draw indifference curves in the probability triangle diagram. An **indifference curve** should show prospects that give the same utility. So, all we need to do is fix a level of utility, and find the prospects, that is, points in the probability triangle diagram, that give this utility. Figure 3.4 illustrates what indifference curves may look like. Indifference curves will likely slope up because a higher probability of the worst outcome $0 needs to be offset by a higher probability of the best outcome $2,500. This also means that the steepness of the indifference curves measures attitude to risk. The more risk averse someone is, the more the probability of getting $2,500 has to increase to compensate for any increase in the probability of getting $0. Thus, the steeper the indifference curve, the greater the risk aversion.

It turns out that, if preferences satisfy independence, the indifference curves must be straight parallel lines like those in Figure 3.4. Figure 3.5 illustrates the implications of this by combining parallel indifference curves with the four prospects. If the lines between prospects A and B, and C and D are parallel, and the indifference curves are also parallel, then Alan should choose either A and C or B and D. As I have drawn it he would choose A and C. Recall, however, that most people chose B and C. This is the paradox.

From this we learn two things. First, the Allais Paradox is probably caused by preferences not satisfying independence. Second, to explain the Allais Paradox

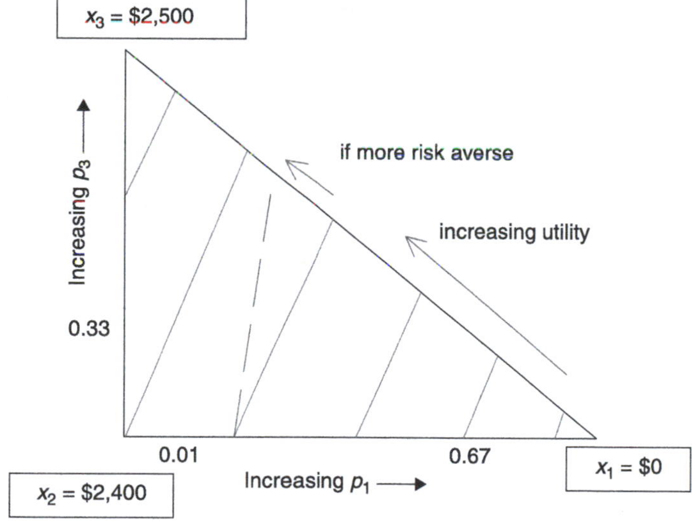

Figure 3.4 Indifference curves in a probability triangle diagram. The steeper the indifference curve the more risk averse.

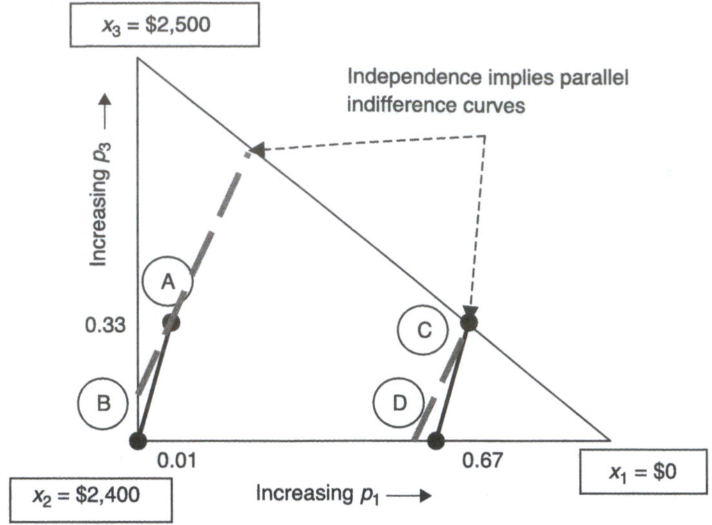

Figure 3.5 The Allais Paradox. If preferences satisfy independence, the person should prefer either A and C, or B and D.

we will need indifference curves that are not parallel but instead **fan out** like those in Figure 3.6. The key thing about fanning out is that indifference curves get steeper the closer to the vertical axis, meaning that people are more risk averse the closer they get to being guaranteed $2,400 or more. This is consistent with the certainty effect and can explain why someone prefers B over A, and C over D.

There are lots of ways that have been suggested for how to model the fanning out of indifference curves. Basically, if we want indifference curves to fan out, then we can write down an equation for the utility of prospects that will give us what we want. More constructive is to develop models based on some intuition for why indifference curves might fan out. I shall look at two such models, one with disappointment and one with rank-dependent expected utility. In section 3.3 we shall look at other, more radical models that also cause fanning out.

3.2.1 Disappointment

One explanation for why Alan might dislike prospect A in the Allais Paradox is that, if he chooses A and gets a payoff of zero, he will likely be very disappointed (you might want to substitute some stronger word here). Such disappointment can be avoided by choosing prospect B and getting a guaranteed high payoff. A way to capture such disappointment and its consequences was proposed by Loomes and Sugden (1986).

The basic idea is to measure outcome utility relative to some prior expectation of what utility will be. If outcome utility is below the expected level, then Alan experi-

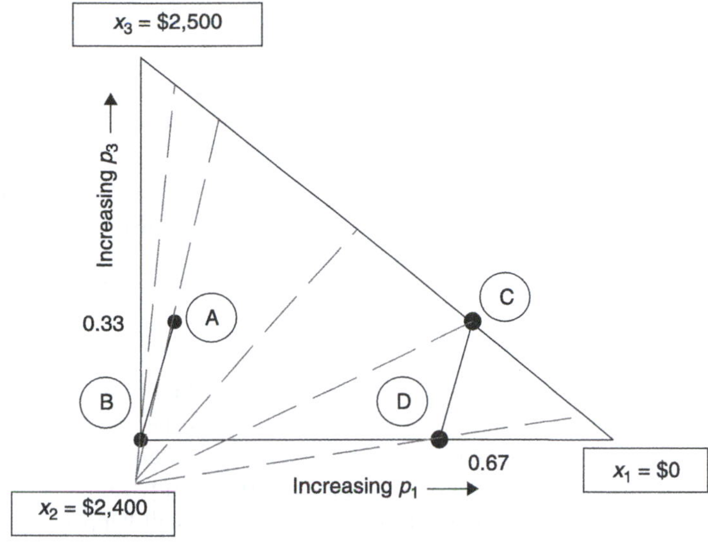

Figure 3.6 The Allais Paradox can be explained by the fanning out of indifference curves. Where indifference curves get steeper, the closer the person is to being guaranteed $2,400 or more.

ences **disappointment**. If the outcome utility is above the expected level, then he experiences **elation**. Elation and disappointment are captured by some function, D. So, if the outcome is x his utility will be $u(x) + D(u(x) - \text{prior})$, the outcome utility plus or minus elation or disappointment. The utility of a prospect X is then written:

$$U(X) = \sum_{i=1}^{n} p_i[u(x_i) + D(u(x_i) - prior)].$$

This is the same as expected utility, but taking into account disappointment and elation of being below or above the prior expectation. The prior expectation can be context specific but a natural candidate is the expected utility of a prospect, calculated using equation (3.1). It is also natural to impose assumptions on D including that $D(g) \geq 0$ if $g > 0$ and $D(l) \leq 0$ if $l < 0$, so elation is good and disappointment bad.

To demonstrate the implications of disappointment, we can work through the Allais Paradox. Suppose that $u(x) = x$ and

$$D(g) = \begin{cases} \theta g^2 \text{ for any } g > 0 \\ -\theta l^2 \text{ for any } l < 0 \end{cases} \tag{3.5}$$

where $\theta \geq 0$ measures the importance of disappointment. Table 3.10 details the utility of each prospect for different values of θ. When $\theta = 0$ we have a standard

Table 3.10 The Allais Paradox can be explained by disappointment. If $\theta = 0$, prospect A is preferred to B, and C to D. If $\theta = 0.0002$, prospect B is preferred to A, and C to D

Prospect	*Utility of the prospect*		*Value of D(.)*			*Net D(.)*
	$\theta = 0$	$\theta = 0.0002$	*IF \$0*	*IF\$2,400*	*IF \$2,500*	
A	2,409	2,398	−1,161	0	+2	−11
B	2,400	2,400	—	0	—	0
C	825	919	−136	—	+561	+94
D	816	899	−133	+502	—	+83

expected utility model and Alan would choose prospect A over B, and C over D. If disappointment is given weight $\theta = 0.0002$, we see that prospect B becomes preferred to prospect A. Why? The expected utility of prospect A is \$2,409 and so if he gets \$0 his disappointment is 1,161 = $2409^2\theta$, which is relatively large. For example, the elation he feels if he gets \$2,500 is only 1.66 = $91^2\theta$. These numbers must be weighted by the probability that they will happen, because he will only be disappointed with probability 0.01. Even so, we get a net effect of $-0.01 \times 2409^2\theta - 0.66 \times 9^2\,\theta + 0.33 \times 91^2\,\theta = -11$. This is enough to just swing things in favor of prospect B.

The small probability of being very disappointed if he chooses prospect A can be enough for Alan to prefer prospect B. The Allais Paradox can thus be caused by people avoiding potential disappointment. If we plot the indifference curves when $\theta = 0.0002$, we find that they do indeed fan out similarly to in Figure 3.6.

Disappointment provides, therefore, a plausible explanation of the Allais Paradox and fanning out. It can also point to other things that we might want to be aware of. For example, if we increase the weight given to disappointment, we can get indifference curves with weirder shapes. Figure 3.7 illustrates what happens when $\theta = 0.002$. There is still a preference for prospects B and C, but the indifference curves are no longer fanning out. In fact we obtain, counter-intuitively, that an increase in p_1, the probability of getting \$0, can increase the utility of a prospect! The explanation is that, when p_1 is relatively large, Alan is not so disappointed if he gets \$0, because he expected it. He might, therefore, prefer less chance of winning because this means less disappointment if he does not win. Maybe not so counter-intuitive after all?

3.2.2 Rank-dependent expected utility

A model of disappointment deviates from expected utility by changing how utility is perceived. An alternative possibility is to change how probabilities are perceived. This is the approach taken by rank-dependent expected utility. I should probably warn you, before launching into the explanation, that the primary virtue of rank-dependent expected utility is that it works. It's not so intuitive why it works, so a little bit of faith is needed.

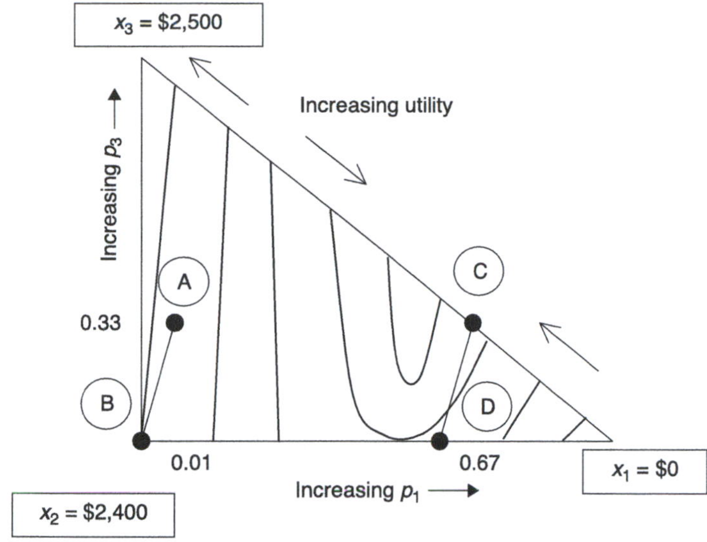

Figure 3.7 Indifference curves no longer fan out if disappointment is very strong.

One crucial component we need is a function π that **weights probabilities**. A commonly used function is:

$$\pi(p) = \frac{p^{\gamma}}{(p^{\gamma} + (1-p)^{\gamma})^{\frac{1}{\gamma}}} \tag{3.6}$$

where γ is some number between zero and one. The main reason for using this function is that it gives the nice S-shaped probability weights illustrated in Figure 3.8. You can see that if $\gamma = 1$ then $\pi(p) = p$, and so there is essentially no weighting of probabilities. When γ is less than one, there are two things that happen. First, there is an **overweighting of small probabilities,** in the sense that a small probability is given a relatively bigger weight. Second, there is an underweighting of large probabilities. We will come back later to why we would want these two things.

Now that we know how to weight probabilities, we can find the utility of a prospect. The first thing we need to do is rank the outcomes so that x_1 is the worst outcome and x_n is the best. For now we shall assume that $x_1 \geq 0$, and so the worst outcome is not a loss. The **rank-dependent expected utility** of a prospect X is then given by:

$$U(\mathrm{X}) = \sum_{\mathrm{i=1}}^{\mathrm{n}} \mathrm{w_i u(x_i)}.$$

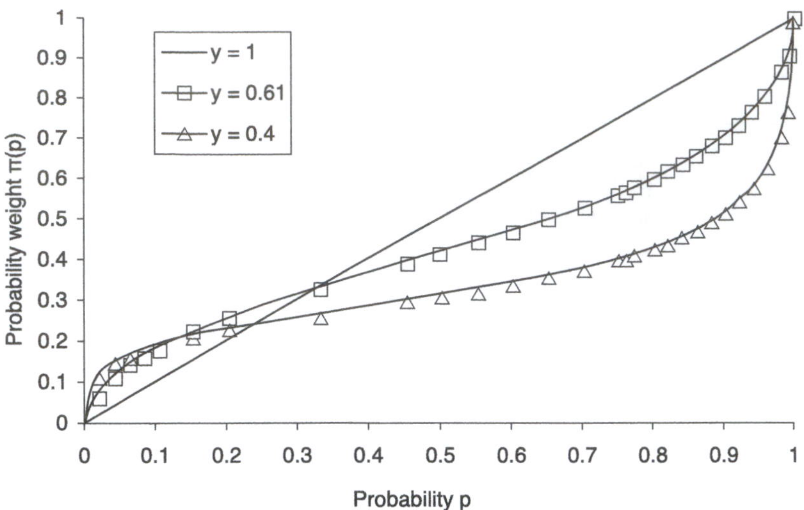

Figure 3.8 An illustration of probability weighting.

where the **decision weights** are:

$$w_i = \pi(p_i + \ldots + p_n) - \pi(p_{i+1} + \ldots + p_n)$$

for all i. In interpretation, $\pi(p_i + \ldots + p_n)$ is the weighted probability of getting an outcome equal to or better than i, and $\pi(p_{i+1} + \ldots + p_n)$ is the weighted probability of an outcome better than i.

Rank-dependent expected utility is easy enough to work out if we know u and π. It's slightly harder to know why it works or why we would want to do it. I can, though, try to provide some intuition. If $\pi(p) = p$, then $w_i = p_i$ and we have standard expected utility. More generally, decision weights allow us to capture pessimism and optimism. To illustrate, consider prospect $X = (0.5, \$0; 0.5, \$100)$ where Alan has a 50:50 chance of winning $100. The decision weights will be $w_1 = 1 - \pi(0.5)$ and $w_2 = \pi(0.5)$. If $\pi(0.5) < 0.5$, then $w_1 > w_2$. This suggests that Alan is **pessimistic** because he puts a higher decision weight on the worst outcome. If $\pi(0.5) > 0.5$ then $w_1 < w_2$. This suggests Alan is **optimistic** because he puts a higher decision weight on the best outcome. Figure 3.8 illustrates that, with the weighting given by equation (3.6), we primarily observe pessimism with a little bit of optimism over small probabilities.

To illustrate rank-dependent expected utility, Table 3.11 works through the Allais Paradox when $u(x) = x$. We can see that for the most part the weighting of probabilities has little effect. The important exception is prospect A, where the 0.01 probability of the worst outcome is increased in decision weight to 0.088. This is pessimism and is enough to make prospect B be preferred to prospect A. The Allais Paradox could thus be explained by pessimism and the overweighting of a small probability of getting $0.

Table 3.11 Rank-dependent utility and the Allais Paradox, when $u(x)=x$. If $\gamma=1$, prospect A is preferred to B, and C to D. If $\gamma=0.61$, prospect B is preferred to A, and C to D

Prospect	*If γ = 1*				*If γ = 0.61*			
	w1	*w2*	*w3*	*Utility*	*w1*	*w2*	*w3*	*Utility*
A	0.01	0.66	0.33	2,409	0.088	0.577	0.334	2,221
B	0	1	0	2,400	0	1	0	2,400
C	0.67	0	0.33	825	0.666	0	0.334	836
D	0.66	0.34	0	816	0.661	0.339	0	815

For completeness we should have a look at the indifference curves we get in the probability triangle diagram. Figure 3.9 illustrates what they look like. They are not as exciting as with disappointment, but even here we see that the story is not as simple as fanning out. The indifference curves have an S shape.

My focus throughout this section has been on the Allais Paradox, but hopefully you can see that there is enough intuition behind the models of disappointment and rank-dependent utility that we should be able to meaningfully apply them more generally. Indeed, given that both models capture something intuitively appealing, a next step is to combine them together and try to account for things other than the Allais Paradox. This is the direction we shall take in the next section.

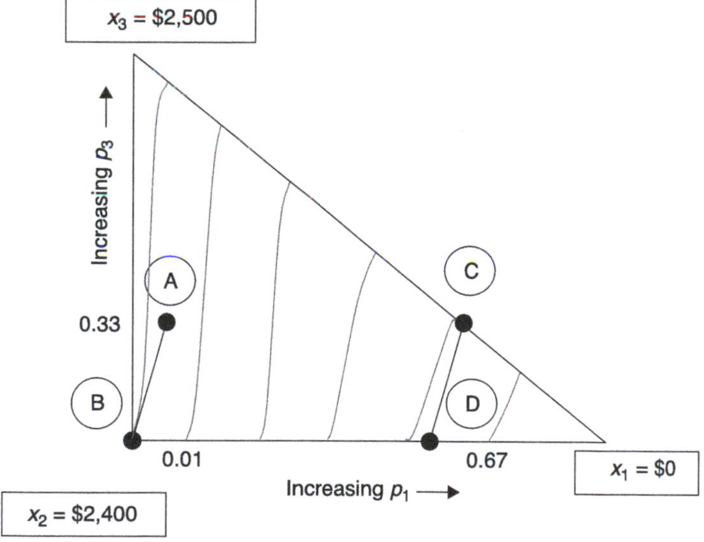

Figure 3.9 Indifference curves in the Allais Paradox with rank-dependent utility.

3.3 Reference dependence and prospect theory

A theme through much of the previous chapter was the relevance of reference points and a potential asymmetry between losses and gains. I now want to show how we can extend that to choice with risk. Doing so brings us to **prospect theory** (see Research Methods 3.4). Prospect theory can be as general or as specific as one wants it to be. Given that I have already talked about reference dependence a fair bit in the previous chapter, I am going to focus on a specific formulation of the theory here.

Research Methods 3.4

The development of an idea

In 1979 Kahneman and Tversky published a paper on 'Prospect theory: An analysis of decision under risk'. This paper went on to become one of the most cited papers in economics, and prospect theory became arguably behavioral economics' most well-known idea.

The first half of the 1979 paper was a critique of expected utility. Kahneman and Tversky used hypothetical choice problems to demonstrate phenomena (like the Allais Paradox) that violated expected utility theory. The second part proposed a theory that could explain these phenomena and, therefore, provide a better account of decision making with risk. The theory consisted of two parts, an editing phase in which prospects would be organized and reformulated, and then an evaluation phase where probabilities are weighted and the value of a prospect evaluated. The editing phase could account for things like framing effects and the evaluation phase for things like loss aversion.

The theory originally proposed by Kahneman and Tversky in 1979 was hard to apply. It was formulated only for prospects with two outcomes, and essentially set out what properties a model of decision making with risk should have, rather than proposing a specific model. In 1992 a second paper was published that proposed a parameterized model of prospect theory that could more easily be applied. This is commonly referred to as second-generation prospect theory. The key step was to make use of rank-dependent weighting of probabilities.

The second-generation model was simpler and focused on the evaluation phase, with the editing phase almost completely forgotten. This lack of an editing phase left it unclear what the reference point should be. Recent models address this by allowing for a changing and probabilistic reference point. This is commonly referred to as third-generation prospect theory, and brings the attention back a little on the editing phase. Combined together, this work pointed out the shortcomings of standard economics while also, crucially, proposing something else that might work instead. That is progress, and prospect theory has rightly become a celebrated idea.

Unsurprisingly, one key ingredient of prospect theory is a reference point about which outcomes are judged. We then talk of gains or losses relative to the reference point. If x is final wealth and r is the reference level of wealth, then $x \geq r$ is a gain and $x < r$ is a loss. Outcomes are judged relative to the reference point using utility function or value function:

$$v(x) = \begin{cases} (x-r)^{\alpha} & \textit{if } x \geq r \\ -\lambda(r-x)^{\beta} & \textit{if } x < r \end{cases} \tag{3.7}$$

where α, β, and γ are parameters. In interpretation this value function is exactly the same as that which I talked about in the previous chapter. The only difference is that I have now given a specific functional form for what it might look like.

The thing we do need to do, that we did not do in the last chapter, is think about risk. To do this we shall use rank-dependent expected utility. One slight twist is that, when weighting probabilities, we should distinguish gains from losses. So, when we rank outcomes from worst x_1 to best x_n, we also need to distinguish outcomes that are losses, say x_1 to x_L, and gains x_{L+1} to x_n. Gains are then given decision weight:

$$w_i = \pi_g(p_i + \ldots + p_n) - \pi_g(p_{i+1} + \ldots + p_n)$$

as before, and losses are given decision weight:

$$w_i = \pi_l(p_1 + \ldots + p_i) - \pi_l(p_1 + \ldots + p_{i-1})$$

where

$$\pi^g(p) = \frac{p^{\gamma}}{(p^{\gamma} + (1-p)^{\gamma})^{\frac{1}{\gamma}}}, \quad \pi^l(p) = \frac{p^{\delta}}{(p^{\delta} + (1-p)^{\delta})^{\frac{1}{\delta}}}$$

are the probability weights for gains and losses. This formulation might look a little messy, but it is just a natural extension of what we did before to capture the asymmetry whereby gains are good and losses are bad.

With equations (3.6), (3.7), and this weighting of probabilities, we can work out easily enough the utility of any prospect, if we know r, α, β, λ, γ, and δ. The overriding motivation for this formulation is that it is relatively simple but has the potential to explain what we observe. For instance, if $\lambda > 1$, then we capture loss aversion because losses are given more weight than gains. If $1 > \alpha, \beta > 0$, then we capture risk aversion over gains and risk loving over losses. Finally, if $\gamma, \delta < 1$, then we can capture the certainty effect.

But, to see whether this formulation really does work, we need to go and estimate the parameters λ, α, β, γ, and δ. Tversky and Kahneman (1992) did this by recruiting 25 graduate students from Berkeley and Stanford and having them choose amongst a series of prospects. Before giving the headline numbers I want to point out that these estimates are based on the median responses and we should not ignore the possibility that different subjects behave very differently. Now for the headline numbers: they were $\lambda = 2.25$, $\alpha, \beta = 0.88$, $\gamma = 0.61$, and $\delta = 0.69$. Thankfully, these numbers are consistent with what is needed to capture loss aversion and the like.

Figure 3.10 plots the utility function for parameters $\lambda = 2.25$ and $\alpha, \beta = 0.88$. The asymmetry between losses and gains is apparent, and comes from losses being given over twice the weight of gains. You might also notice, however, that there is not much curvature to the utility function. It is marginally concave for gains and convex for losses, but this is quite hard to see. This is because the estimates of $\alpha, \beta = 0.88$ are close enough to one for the utility function to be nearly linear above and below the x axis. Indeed, to simplify things, it is not uncommon to use $\alpha, \beta = 1$.

This lack of curvature might suggest that we are going to struggle to explain risk aversion over small gambles. The utility function in Figure 3.10, for example, is a lot flatter than that in Figure 3.2. Loss aversion, however, can help us out. That's because the kink in the utility function at zero means that the utility function curves a lot when we compare negative and positive amounts. Loss aversion can, for example, explain why Alan would prefer prospect I in Table 3.6 to prospect J. This line of thinking does raise some questions, which I will come back to, about what the reference point should be and what should be coded as a gain and a loss. For now though let's focus on the good news: prospect theory has allowed us to capture everything we came across in sections 3.1.1 to 3.1.3.

3.3.1 Reference-dependent utility

To put prospect theory in context, we can write down a more general model that includes as special cases all the models we have seen so far. This extends the reference-dependent utility function that I introduced in the previous chapter. The **rank-dependent, reference-dependent expected utility** of a prospect X is:

$$U(X) = \sum_{i=1}^{n} w_i[\eta u(x_i) + h(x_i, r)] \tag{3.8}$$

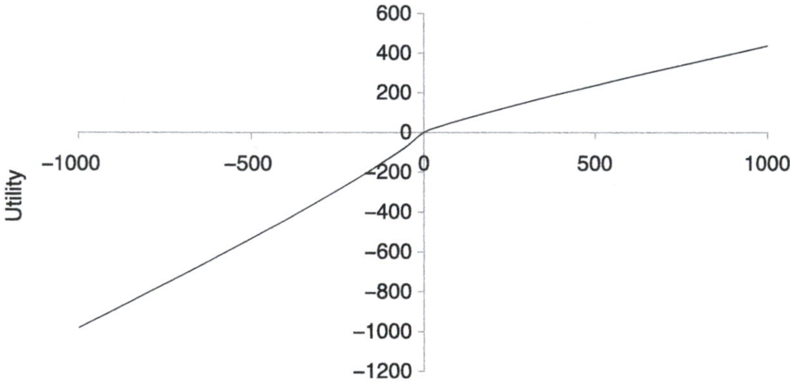

Figure 3.10 A prospect theory utility function for money with parameters $\lambda = 2.25$, $\alpha, \beta = 0.88$, $\gamma = 0.61$ and $\delta = 0.69$.

where h is some function that depends on a reference point r and η is some parameter. The three special cases we have looked at can be explained as follows.

If $\eta = 1$, $w_i = p_i$, and h is the same as the disappointment function D in equation (3.5), then we have a model of disappointment. In this case there is no weighting of probabilities, but there is disappointment or elation if the utility of the outcome is above or below the prior expected level of utility.

If $\eta = 1$ and $h(x, r) = 0$ for all x, then we have rank-dependent expected utility. If $w_i = p_i$, then this reduces to expected utility. Another way to get at the same thing is have $\eta = 0$, $u(r) = 0$, and h the same as the utility function u. In this case outcomes are not judged relative to a reference level, but there is weighting of probabilities.

Finally, if $\eta = 0$ and h is the same as the value function v in equation (3.7), then we have prospect theory. In this case utility is determined by the loss or gain relative to the reference point, and there is weighting of probabilities.

The reference-dependent utility function (3.8) gives us, therefore, a framework to compare models. We see that they are all different, and all point to different ways that we might want to move beyond expected utility. This is summarized in Table 3.12. Clearly, when we combine the three models we also obtain a very general model to think about choice with risk. The model, however, is probably a bit too general to be very practical. So, in practice it is necessary to start thinking about narrowing things down a little by asking what features are most important or most important in particular contexts.

That is an exercise I leave for you to think about because what I want to do now is focus on two things that we looked at in some detail in the last chapter but are worth briefly revisiting here. First, equation (3.8) is going to depend crucially on reference point r, and so we need to think about that. Second, attitudes to risk will depend on how potential risks are bracketed or perceived relative to existing risk.

3.3.2 *The reference point and expectations*

We have seen so far, in this chapter, three candidates for the reference point: they are the current level of wealth (prospect theory), zero wealth (expected and

Table 3.12 How disappointment theory, rank-dependent expected utility, and prospect theory differ from expected utility

Model	*Differences to expected utility*
Disappointment	There is disappointment or elation if the utility of the outcome is below or above the prior expectation.
Rank-dependent utility	There is weighting of probabilities to take account of pessimism or optimism.
Prospect theory	There is weighting of probabilities, and the utility of the outcome is determined solely by the gain or loss relative to the reference point.

rank-dependent expected utility), and the expected utility of the prospect (disappointment theory). In the last chapter we looked at other things that might influence the reference point, such as the no loss in buying hypothesis, and said that these things primarily reflected expectations. For instance, if Anna expected to pay \$3 for a box of Nutty cereal, then paying \$3 for a box was not counted as a loss. In choice with risk, expectations of what may happen can become even more important.

To illustrate the implications of expectations let's return to the insurance example and consider the choice between full insurance and insurance against theft. Recall that the insurance against theft prospect is AT = (0.05, \$14; 0.95, \$64), full insurance is prospect FI = (1, \$61), and Alan's wealth is \$70. Suppose that Alan has the reference-dependent utility function:

$$u^r(x) = \begin{cases} 10\sqrt{x} + (x - r) & \text{if } x \geq r \\ 10\sqrt{x} - 2.25(r - x) & \text{if } x < r \end{cases}$$

where r is the reference point. I shall now contrast three scenarios worked through in Table 3.13.

First, suppose that it was a complete surprise to Alan that he was asked to make this choice, and once he has made the choice he will immediately find out the outcome. For example, the renewal letter arrives in the post when he is not expecting it, he needs to reply that day, and the next day he will find out whether his son is going to use the car. This sounds a bit contrived but is the scenario that most closely fits what we have been analyzing so far, and happens in a typical experiment. In this case the current level of wealth seems the most relevant reference point. Paying for insurance is thus seen as a loss, and Alan would prefer insurance against theft.

Next, suppose, more realistically, that Alan was still surprised to get the renewal letter but will only have to pay for the insurance after some delay and will not find out the outcome, i.e. whether the car is in an accident, for some time. In this case it makes sense for the reference level to be the expected outcome of the prospect that Alan chooses, because he will have time to change his expectations of wealth before anything happens. His reference point will thus depend on what he chooses. In this case Alan will prefer full insurance because by the time he pays for it he will not think of it as a loss. With insurance against theft, by contrast, he could still lose if the car is in an accident.

Finally, suppose that Alan was expecting the renewal letter. He presumably had some expectation of what he would choose and has already factored this into his reference point. The reference point will, therefore, depend on whether he expected to choose insurance against theft or full insurance. In both cases he prefers full insurance. We see, however, that full insurance looks relatively better if he expected to buy full insurance and insurance against theft looks relatively better if he expected to buy insurance against theft. This can lead to self-fulfilling expectations where the thing that Alan expected to choose looks better because he expected to choose it.

Table 3.13 How the utility of Alan will depend on his expectations. The expected utility from gains and losses measures the expected utility from gains and losses relative to the reference point

Framing	*Reference point*	*Expected utility from gains and losses*		*Reference-dependent utility*	
		AT	*FI*	*AT*	*FI*
Unexpected choice, immediate outcome	$70	−19.1	−20.3	58.8	57.9
Unexpected choice, delayed outcome, chooses AT	$61.5	−3.0	—	74.9	—
Unexpected choice, delayed outcome, chooses FI	$61	—	0.0	—	77.9
Expected choice of AT	$61.5	−3.0	−1.1	74.9	77.0
Expected choice of FI	$61	−2.4	0.0	75.4	77.9

Two general points are apparent in this example. First, whether or not Alan expected to face risk will influence how he deals with that risk. For instance, he is not willing to pay for full insurance when the renewal letter was a surprise, but is when the renewal letter was expected. Second, if risk was expected, the optimal choice can depend on what Alan expected to choose. Kőszegi and Rabin (2007) capture this with the idea of a **personal equilibrium**. The expected choice of full insurance is a personal equilibrium because it makes sense for Alan to choose full insurance if he expected to choose it. The expected choice of insurance against theft is not a personal equilibrium because Alan would want to choose full insurance even if he expected to choose insurance against theft.

The picture we get is one where expectations and context can matter a lot in determining the reference point and hence the perception of gains and losses. This naturally builds on the things we talked about in the previous chapter, but the presence of risk adds even more things to the mix. There is even more ambiguity about how things will be perceived and what the reference point may be. This clearly raises some challenges in trying to model choice with risk. One small part of meeting this challenge requires asking how people might perceive interrelated gambles.

Research Methods 3.5

TV game shows

The objective in most economic experiments is complete anonymity. The exact opposite is surely a TV game show where contestants make choices in front of millions of viewers. Game shows provide, therefore, an interesting alternative to an economic experiment, particularly as the stakes are typically a lot higher.

Post and co-authors (2008) are one group of several researchers to study the show 'Deal or no deal?'. In the game, a contestant has to choose one of 26 briefcases. Each briefcase contains an amount of money from €0.01 to €5,000,000 (in the Dutch edition). Having chosen a briefcase, the contestant is sequentially told what is in the other briefcases, and given a walk-away offer. If he or she continues to turn down the offers they eventually get to see how much money is in the briefcase they first chose, and they can keep it! The walk-away offer depends on the expected value of the remaining suitcases.

The issue that Post and co-authors focus on is whether choice is path dependent. Specifically, did the contestants' risk attitudes change as they began to see what was in the briefcases? They find that they did. Contestants became less risk averse when either high amounts (which is unlucky) or low amounts (which is lucky) were in the briefcases they did not choose. For example, one contestant called Frank was unlucky but carried on gambling, eventually rejecting a sure €6,000 in favor of a 50:50 gamble of €10 or €10,000. He won €10. A second contestant, Susanne, was lucky and rejected a sure €125,000 to eventually win €150,000. It is doubtful we would see such risk taking without the prior process of sequentially seeing what was in the other briefcases.

Post and his co-authors show that such behavior can be explained by prospect theory with a reference point based largely on prior expectations of the likely prize.

3.3.3 Combined gambles

Most people are constantly exposed to existing risks because they have money invested in the stock market, might lose their job, have already bought a lottery ticket, etc. This raises interesting issues about how a person should evaluate a new risk.

To get us started I will demonstrate that it may be in Alan's interest to take on a small gamble, as a form of diversification, if he is exposed to existing risk. Consider the prospects in Table 3.14. Suppose that Alan is already committed to prospect X, because, say, he has money invested in the stock market. He now needs to decide whether to take on prospect Y or Z. As you can see, the outcome of prospects may be revealed now or in one week's time. Suppose that his current wealth is \$20,000 and his utility function is:

$$u^r(x) = \begin{cases} x - 20{,}000 & \text{if } x \geq 20{,}000 \\ -2(20{,}000 - x) & \text{if } x < 20{,}000. \end{cases}$$

With these preferences Alan would not prefer prospect Y or Z to prospect W. More relevant, however, is to compare prospect Z with prospect X, because both will be resolved in a week's time. If he chooses prospect Z, then this should be combined with the existing prospect X to give a combined prospect X + Z. It turns out that prospect X + Z is preferred to prospect X.

The key point of the example is that Alan should choose prospect Z if he is already exposed to prospect X. That's because any new risk should be considered in the light of existing risk. This holds more generally than this simple example.

People should be less risk averse over prospects for small amounts of money if they are already exposed to risk.

Another thing the example illustrates is how the delay before knowing the outcome of a prospect should influence choice, if there are existing risks. Alan would do well to choose prospect W rather than Y, but also choose prospect Z. Or should he? If there is no escape from being told the outcome of prospect Y immediately then, yes, he should choose prospect W rather than Y. Suppose, however, he could somehow arrange that he will not be told the outcome of prospect Y until one week's time. Then he should do this. This brings to the fore the question of how often a person should choose to observe the outcome of prospects. If Alan is loss averse it may be beneficial for him to delay or combine finding the outcomes of existing prospects so as to avoid too much 'bad news'.

These issues of how to combine prospects are the same as those we looked at in Chapter two in terms of mental accounting, hedonic editing, narrow framing, and the like.

A pertinent question is whether people do take existing risks, and delay, into account. Narrow framing would suggest they do not, but we also know there is a question of how narrowly people like to bracket things together. I will come back to some evidence on this later when looking at investing in the stock market. In the meantime, here are two things for you to think about. Let's start with the puzzle of low stock market participation. Historically, though things have changed now, relatively few people invested in the stock market. If people are risk averse this may seem reasonable. If, however, we take into account all the other risks that people were exposed to, such as becoming unemployed, being in an accident, etc., then it becomes much harder to explain such low participation. This suggests narrow framing. On the other hand, it is not unknown for people to delay opening a letter that may bring bad news until they can also open a letter that will, it is hoped, have good news!

3.4 Preference reversals

Recall that in section 3.1.4 I said that expected utility should be appropriate if preferences satisfy independence and transitivity. Up until now our focus has primarily

Table 3.14 Risk aversion for small gambles is less if there is existing risk. Alan is already exposed to prospect X and so by choosing prospect Z would obtain prospect X + Z, which is preferred to prospect X

Prospect	*Probability and value*	*Timing*	*Expected utility*
W	(1, $0)	Now	0
X	(0.5, –$10,000; 0.5, $30,000)	One week	5,000
Y	(0.5, –$500; 0.5, $550)	Now	–225
Z	(0.5, –$500; 0.5, $550)	One week	–225
X + Z	(0.25, –$10,500; 0.25, –$9,450; 0.25, $29,500; 0.25, $30,550)	One week	5,037.5

been on independence. For instance, preferences consistent with reference-dependent expected utility need not satisfy independence but must satisfy transitivity. What I want to do now is change focus a little by questioning whether preferences satisfy transitivity. In order to do this I shall revisit the disparity between willingness to accept and willingness to pay, that we looked at in the previous chapter.

Research Methods 3.6

Behavioral economics' longest saga

Preference reversals have created a lot of debate over the years. Things got started with work by Lichtenstein and Slovic published in the late 1960s and early 1970s. Most widely cited is a paper they published in 1971, entitled 'Reversals of preferences between bids and choices in gambling decisions'. Since then debate has continued unabated about whether preference reversals are real, what causes them, whether they disappear with experience, and so forth.

One interesting aspect of the debate has been the different methods used to think about the issue. Psychologists have largely focused on the issue of procedural invariance. Lots of different ways to model and explain procedural invariance have been suggested. Some economists have focused on whether preference reversals are real, questioning whether the experimental methods used are reliable enough. Others have pointed out that preference reversals could be obtained by a violation of the independence axiom, while others, as we shall see, that they can be obtained by a violation of the transitivity axiom. A more recent literature has looked at what happens if the willingness to accept is elicited from markets, and subjects have chance to learn over time.

This mix of approaches looks fantastic, but can end up seeming a little antagonistic. At times it seems as though the debate is one in which some argue that preference reversals are not real and others respond by showing they are. On the plus side this has given us a lot of evidence to suggest that preference reversals really exist. It can, however, detract slightly from some of the more subtle underlying issues that tend to get muddled together. For example, we need to ask if the willingness to accept a sure thing is different to the willingness to pay, and if so why? How does willingness to accept or pay change for risky prospects? How does willingness to accept or pay change when we use different methods (e.g. markets to elicit choices)? Why can we observe cyclical choices in experiments when the willingness to accept or pay is not considered at all?

Look at the prospects in Table 3.15. Prospects AA and AB have the same expected value but get there in different ways: the **P bet** offers a high probability of winning a low payoff and the **$ bet** a low probability of winning a high payoff. Suppose that we elicit the willingness to accept for each of the prospects. You can refer back to the last chapter for a definition of willingness to accept, but basically we shall ask Alan the minimum amount of money he would accept rather than have prospect AA, or prospect AB, and shall interpret this as the price Alan puts on the prospect. Subsequently we can ask Alan what he would rather choose, prospect AA or prospect AB.

Figure 3.11 summarizes the results of a study by Tversky, Slovic, and Kahneman (1990) where subjects were asked to do this. Many put a higher price on the $ bet than the P bet, but then choose the P bet over the $ bet. This is an example of a **preference reversal**. Another example is to value the P bet more than the $ bet yet choose the $ bet over the P bet. This is rarer.

Preference reversals are puzzling. To see why, suppose that Alan prices the $ bet at $9 and the P bet at $7 and also says he would choose the P bet over the $ bet. You could sell him the $ bet for $9, then offer to swap that for the P bet, and then buy the P bet off him for $7. We are back where we started, except you are $2 richer and he is $2 poorer. It looks like a good deal for you!

Because they are so puzzling, many have questioned whether preference reversals really exist. The evidence, however, suggests that they definitely do exist (see Research Methods 3.6 and 3.7). The more important question, therefore, is why they exist. It might be because preferences are non-transitive. After all, it looks like Alan has preferences $AA \geq AC$ and $AC \geq AB$ yet $AB \geq AA$. These preferences would be non-transitive. We saw enough in the last chapter, however, about

Table 3.15 Prospects that can lead to a preference reversal. Many value the $ bet higher than the P bet but choose the P bet over the $ bet

Prospect	*Amount with probability of outcome*	
AA, the '$ bet'	$100 gain with probability 0.08	$0 otherwise
AB, the 'P bet'	$10 with probability 0.8	$0 otherwise
AC, sure thing	$8 with probability one	

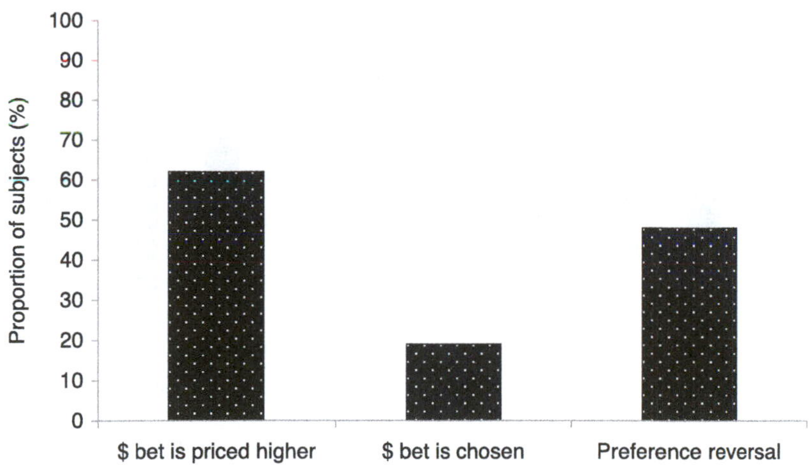

Figure 3.11 The proportion of subjects who price the $ bet higher, choose the $ bet, and exhibit a preference reversal.

Source: Tversky *et al.* (1990).

framing effects and procedural invariance to suggest that this might also be the cause. Maybe Alan perceives prospects differently depending on how they are presented to him. We need to think about both of these possibilities.

Research Methods 3.7

Do incentives matter?

A perennial issue in experimental economics is how to incentivize subjects to make the choices that really capture their preferences. For example, when asking a subject to state a willingness to accept a $ bet, how can we be sure he tells us what he would really want?

In psychology it is common to ask subjects hypothetical questions, and so a subject is asked about his willingness to accept, knowing that his answer is ultimately not going to matter. Economists are generally skeptical about such an approach and prefer monetary incentives. So, having asked the subject his willingness to accept, a real game is played. For example, we could generate a random number between 0 and 10. If the random number is above his willingness to accept he gets to keep that amount of money (e.g. if his minimum willingness to accept is $8 and the number comes up 9, he gets $9). If the random number is below his willingness to accept, the $ bet is played out and he either wins $100 or gets $0. Knowing that this game will happen should get a subject to reveal his true willingness to accept.

A study by Berg and co-authors (2010) looks back over the many studies on preference reversals and tries to pick out whether it matters what the incentives are for subjects. In some studies choices are hypothetical and in others monetary incentives are provided that should get subjects to reveal their true preferences. In an intermediate category subjects are given monetary incentives but the procedure used may not get subjects to reveal their true preferences. Figure 3.12 summarizes some of their data. It

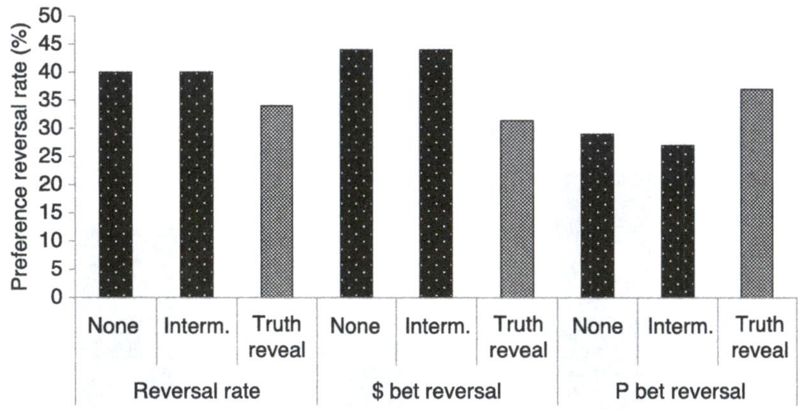

Figure 3.12 Whether the rate of preference reversal differs if there are no, truth revealing, or intermediate incentives. The overall reversal rate does not significantly change, but the rate of $ and P reversals becomes more similar.

Source: Berg *et al.* (2010).

turns out that the overall preference reversal rate does not change much if there are truth-revealing incentives: it does go down, but not by a significant amount. This might suggest that incentives do not matter much.

If we look a little deeper, however, we do see that incentives start to matter. This is most apparent when comparing the $ bet reversal rate (the percentage of those subjects who priced the $ bet higher and subsequently chose the P bet) and the P bet reversal rate (the percentage of those subjects who priced the P bet higher and subsequently chose the $ bet). With non-truth-revealing preferences there is a systematic tendency for more $ bet reversals than P bet reversals. With truth-revealing preferences this disappears. This is important, because a systematic tendency for reversals of one kind and not another suggests something we can model and explain. If reversals are non-systematic they could be just due to mistakes or errors.

This study is not going to close the debate on preference reversals. We now have lots of evidence that there are systematic tendencies in preference reversals even with truth-revealing preferences. The study is also not going to close the debate on whether incentives matter (and we shall return to this issue a few times in the rest of the book). The study does, however, illustrate the care needed in running and interpreting experimental results. The incentives that subjects are given do matter, but possibly in quite subtle ways that are not immediately apparent.

3.4.1 Procedural invariance

When describing prospect theory we focused on something Kahneman and Tversky called the **evaluation phase** and ignored the editing phase (see Research Methods 3.4). The editing phase is, though, important. In the **editing phase** Alan will organize and reformulate prospects to make them simpler to understand. This can consist of various operations. For example, in a coding phase he classifies outcomes as gains or losses. In a simplification phase he may round probabilities and outcomes up or down. It is basically a combination of mental accounting and the use of simplifying heuristics.

This editing and reformulating of prospects means that the way in which prospects are presented to Alan can affect his interpretation of them. We already saw this in Table 3.9, where a different framing of the same prospect meant that outcomes were coded differently as gains or losses. A similar type of thing could explain preference reversals, because there is a big difference between asking Alan to price a prospect and asking him to choose between the prospect and another.

To pursue this possibility further, Tversky, Slovic, and Kahneman also included the sure-thing prospect AC (see Table 3.15) and asked subjects whether they would prefer prospect AA or AC, and prospect AB or AC. To see why this is useful, suppose that Alan chose prospect AB over AA while pricing prospect AA more than $8 and prospect AB less than $8. This is a preference reversal. Table 3.16 summarizes four different ways to get such a reversal. For instance, if Alan chooses prospect AA over AC and AC over AB, then it looks as though his preferences are intransitive. If, by contrast, he chooses prospect AC over both AB and AA, then it looks as though his preferences are transitive but he just put too high a price on $ bet, prospect AA.

Table 3.16 Four possible explanations for a preference reversal and the number of choices by subjects fitting each explanation. The sample is restricted to those who chose AB > AA, and price AA > $8 > price AB

Explanation	*Choices*	*Times observed (%)*
Intransitivity	*AA* > *AC* and *AC* > *AB*	10.0
Overpricing of $ bet, AA	*AC* > *AA* and *AC* > *AB*	65.5
Underpricing of P bet, AB	*AC* > *AA* and *AB* > *AC*	6.1
Both overpricing of $ bet and underpricing of P bet	*AC* > *AA* and *AB* > *AC*	18.4

Source: Tversky *et al.* (2000).

I have also put in Table 3.16 the percentage of choices by subjects in each category. We see that most preference reversals in this study could be explained by an overpricing of the $ bet. Only 10 percent of preference reversals suggested intransitive preferences. It is plausible, therefore, that preference reversals are caused, in large part, by procedural invariance. To back this up it would be nice to have a good explanation for why there is procedural invariance. Two context effects that seem relevant are scale compatibility and the prominence effect.

Scale compatibility is where the importance of one aspect of an option (e.g. the probability or money that can be earned on a prospect), is enhanced by compatibility with the decision a person is asked to make. So, when Alan is asked to put a price on the $, bet his attention is drawn to the relatively large payoff, causing him to overprice it. The **prominence effect** is where one aspect of an option becomes more prominent depending on the task. For example, the probabilities in a prospect may become more prominent when Alan is comparing prospects. So, when asked to choose between the P bet and the $ bet he may focus on the higher probability winning with the P bet.

Procedural invariance clearly seems relevant in explaining why we observe preference reversals. But, have we done enough yet to completely rule out intransitive preferences?

3.4.2 Regret theory

In the study by Tversky, Slovic, and Kahneman, around 10 percent of choices were suggestive of intransitive preferences. This might seem a relatively small percentage. If we think in a different way, however, we can get a much bigger percentage. For example, Loomes, Starmer, and Sugden (1991) asked subjects to choose amongst several prospects like those in Table 3.15 and found that only 36 percent of subjects always made choices consistent with transitive preferences. Most subjects, therefore, made choices suggestive of intransitive preferences, some of the time.

You may be skeptical of this approach. Is it not a case of asking subjects to choose amongst so many prospects that they eventually make a mistake that we then interpret as intransitive preferences? It is probably not. The main evidence that it is not is the fact that subjects were far more likely to choose *AA* > *AC, AC*

> *AB*, and *AB* > *AA*. It was more rare to observe *AA* > *AB, AB* > *AC*, and *AC* > *AA* or any other form of intransitivity. If subjects were making random mistakes we should not see such a systematic tendency for one set of choices. It seems, therefore, that preferences can be intransitive.

None of the models of choice that we have considered so far in this chapter can lead to intransitive preferences (although I will come back to prospect theory later), so we need something new. One possibility is **regret theory**. Regret theory is most easy to apply when comparing two prospects, so, let's compare prospects AA and AB from Table 3.15.

The key to regret theory is a function $R(x, y)$ that assigns a number to any pair of payoffs x and y. In interpretation $R(x, y)$ is the **regret** or **rejoice** that Alan experiences from getting payoff x if he would have got payoff y by choosing the other prospect. One slight complication is that by choosing, say, prospect AA, Alan will, generally speaking, not know what his payoff would have been if he had chosen AB. We can get around this by thinking of distinct states of the world and saying what the outcome would be in each state of the world, ordering outcomes according to payoffs, as in Figure 3.13. So, for example, there is 0.08 chance he will rejoice $R(100,10)$, a 0.72 chance he will regret $R(0,10)$, and a 0.2 chance he will have no regret $R(0,0)$. We then say that prospect AA is preferred to AB if $0.08R(100,10) + 0.72R(0,10) + 0.2R(0,0) > 0$. That is, prospect AA is preferred if the expected rejoice exceeds the expected regret.

Generalizing from this example, given any two prospects X and Y, we can distinguish possible states of the world (in the example there were three). We then say that:

$$X > Y \text{ if and only if} \sum_i p_i R(x_i, y_i) > 0$$

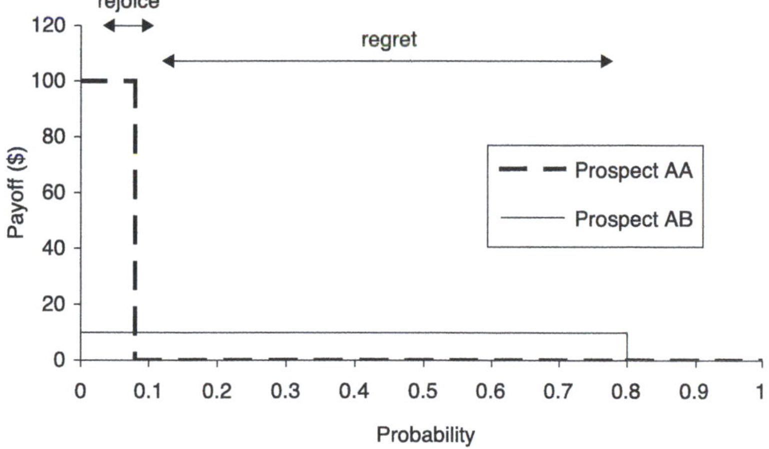

Figure 3.13 The expected regret and rejoice from choosing prospect AA rather than AB.

where i are possible states of the world and x_i and y_i are the outcomes of the respective prospects. Three assumptions are natural for the function R: (i) $R(x, y) = -R(y, x)$ that implying, regret is the opposite of rejoice. This also implies $R(0,0) = 0$; (ii) $R(x, z) > R(y, z)$ if $x > y > z > 0$, implying that regret and rejoice are increasing in the difference in outcomes; (iii) $R(x, z) > R(x, y) + R(y, z)$ if $x > y > z > 0$, implying that a large difference in outcomes is regretted or causes rejoice more than two smaller differences combined.

Of primary interest for us is to see whether and why regret can lead to non-transitive preferences. The short story is that it can, and in particular preferences $AA > AC$, $AC > AB$, and $AB > AA$ are consistent with regret theory, while choices $AA > AB$, $AB > AC$, and $AC > AA$ are not. Remember, it was the first type, of choices that are most often observed, so this is a really nice result.

[Extra] If you want the slightly longer story, then here it is. Applying regret theory, we get:

$AA > AB$ if and only if $0.08R(100,10) + 0.72R(0,10) > 0$.
$AC > AA$ if and only if $0.08R(8,100) + 0.92R(8,0) > 0$.
$AB > AC$ if and only if $0.8R(10,8) + 0.2R(0,8) > 0$.

Now, let's consider whether it is possible that $AA > AB$, $AB > AC$, and $AC > AA$. Using symmetry we know that $0.92R(8,0) + 0.2R(0,8) = 0.72R(8,0)$. It will also be convenient to write $0.8R(10,8) = 0.08R(10,8) + 0.72R(10,8)$. Doing this, we require the following to hold:

$$0.08[R(100,10) + R(8,100) + R(10,8)] + 0.72[R(0,10) + R(8,0) + R(10,8)] > 0.$$

We can rewrite this as:

$$0.08[R(100,10) + R(10,8) - R(100,8)] + 0.72[R(8,0) + R(10,8) - R(10,0)] > 0.$$

If we now apply condition (iii), we see that this is not possible (use $x = 100$, $y = 10$, $z = 8$, and $x = 10$, $y = 8$, $z = 0$). So, we cannot get preferences $AA > AB$, $AB > AC$, and $AC > AA$. In showing this, however, we have shown that we can get preferences $AB > AA$, $AA > AC$, and $AC > AB$!

Regret theory can explain why we observe non-transitive choices and can explain why we observe some choice cycles and not others. But, what's the intuition behind this? Risk aversion could easily explain why prospect AB is preferred to AA and prospect AC is preferred to AB. What we need to do is explain why prospect AA is preferred to AC. That Alan would regret not having a gamble on prospect AA is one possible explanation. Essentially, he would regret missing out on \$92. So, prospect AA is preferred to AC because of **regret aversion**. Regret theory does, therefore, give a plausible explanation for why preferences may be non-transitive.

3.4.3 Prospect theory and preference reversals

For another plausible explanation of preference reversals I am going to revisit prospect theory. To make this work we are going to rethink what the reference point might be if someone is endowed with a risky prospect.

Suppose that Alan is asked the minimum price for which he will give up the $ bet, prospect AA. Given that he is being asked to sell prospect AA, it makes sense, recalling the endowment effect, to think of that as his reference point. The problem is how to interpret a risky prospect as a reference point. What does it mean to say the reference point is $100 with probability 0.08 and $0 with probability 0.92? The simplest way to deal with this is to say that, if he accepts some amount of money, say, $9, then with probability 0.08 he will be down $91 on his reference point and with probability 0.92 he will be up $9. This is quite similar to regret and rejoice.

The minimum price he is willing to sell the $ bet, prospect AA, will then be where the expected gain equals the expected loss. Putting this into the standard prospect theory model with parameters $\lambda = 2.25$, $\alpha = 0.5$, $\gamma = 0.61$, and $\delta = 0.69$ gives a selling price of $16.7. If we do the same for the P bet, prospect AB, we get a selling price of $9.7. So, the $ bet is priced above the P bet.

[Extra] To see how we can get these numbers let p_{AA} denote the price Alan puts on the $ bet. Setting the gains equal to the losses gives:

$$\pi^g(0.92) \times p_{AA}^{\alpha} = \lambda\pi^l(0.08) \times (100 - p_{AA})^{\alpha}.$$

Using parameters $\lambda = 2.25$, $\alpha = 0.5$, $\gamma = 0.61$, and $\delta = 0.69$ implies that

$$0.74 \times p_{AA}^{0.5} = 2.25 \times 0.15 \times (100 - p_{AA})^{0.5}.$$

Squaring both sides gives:

$$0.55p_{AA} = 0.11(100 - p_{AA})$$

and $p_{AA} = \$16.7$ works. So, he would be willing to sell the $ bet for $16.7. Using the same logic for the P bet, prospect AB, we get that he would sell for p_{AB} where:

$$\pi^g(0.2) \times p_{AB}^{\alpha} = \lambda\pi^l(0.8) \times (10 - p_{AB})^{\alpha}.$$

Working through the algebra gives $p_{AB} = \$9.7$.

Finally, we can ask whether he should choose prospect AA or prospect AB. In this case the relevant reference point would appear to be his current wealth. So, he chooses the P bet if:

$$\pi^g(0.08) \times 100^{0.5} < \pi^g(0.8) \times 10^{0.5}.$$

If you work this out, it comes to 1.5 < 2.1, which it clearly is. So he would choose the P bet.

To recap, Alan priced the $ bet above the P bet and yet would choose the P bet over the $ bet. We have a preference reversal! Furthermore, we have done so because of an overpricing of the $ bet, consistent with the data in Table 3.16 (although $p_{AB} > \$8$). Basically, Alan would be reluctant to sell the $ bet both because of the overweighting of the small probability of winning, and the large potential loss from selling a prospect that could have yielded him a high payoff.

Thus, prospect theory provides another plausible explanation for preference reversals. Is this explanation procedural invariance or intransitive preferences? I would say it is a bit of both. Framing is clearly relevant here because the explanation relies on Alan perceiving that he does or does not have ownership of a prospect. The explanation also, however, captures something of preferences; Alan puts a higher price on the $ bet because he does not want to regret missing out on a potentially big win.

3.4.4 Why preference reversals matter

We have seen that a combination of things seem to come together to make preference reversals a reality. But, why is it important that we observe preference reversals? We saw in the last chapter that choice can depend on context effects for a host of different reasons; have we not just seen a further example of this? I want to finish this section by arguing that preference reversals go beyond being just another context effect.

To motivate the point, let's think back to the last chapter and Anna deciding what cereal to buy. According to Table 2.2 she would maximize her utility by choosing the Honey cereal. Maybe her preferences will change, but at that point in time the best thing she could do would be to buy Honey. The problem is, she may not know that this is the best thing to do, and because of context effects choose something different. For instance, if she is attracted to the bright-red packaging of Superior she might choose that. This does not change the fact that Honey was what she should have chosen.

Now, let's think about Alan deciding what insurance to buy. Maybe we can say that full insurance is definitely the best thing for him to choose but because of context effects he might choose something else. This would be analogous to the story with Anna. If, however, his preferences are intransitive, we get a quite different picture. Suppose, for example, that Alan prefers full insurance to no insurance, $FI \geq NI$, prefers no insurance to insurance against theft, $NI \geq AT$, and insurance against theft to full insurance, $AT \geq FI$. This does not seem so crazy.

With such preference it should come as no surprise that Alan's choice would depend on context effects. There is, however, a deeper issue here of what is best for Alan. Whatever choice he makes we can find a choice that he seemingly prefers! There is no best thing he can do. This kind of thing plays havoc with the standard economic model. It also raises some interesting policy questions concerning what is in Alan's best interest. Intransitive preferences and preference reversals, therefore, matter and raise some fundamental questions. In choice with risk they might also be not so uncommon.

3.5 Summary

We started with the idea that the utility of a prospect is equal to the expected utility of the prospect. This is the standard way of modeling choice with risk in economics and is a simple, transparent way of doing so. It must be a good way to do so if preferences are transitive and satisfy independence.

We subsequently saw evidence that expected utility is a bit too simple to capture all that we observe. The Allais Paradox, risk aversion for small gambles, risk-loving behavior over losses, and preference reversals are all hard to reconcile with expected utility. This motivated adapting how we model choice with risk.

One thing we considered was to take account of disappointment and elation when measuring the utility of a prospect. A second possibility was to weight probabilities to take account of pessimism and optimism. This is enough to explain the Allais Paradox.

We subsequently looked at prospect theory and reference-dependent utility and showed that this can explain all the other deviations from expected utility that we looked at. We also saw how the presence of risk suggests additional reasons, to those we looked at in the previous chapter, why the reference point can depend on context effects. Expectations of what might happen are particularly important.

Finally we looked at preference reversals and the possibility that preferences are intransitive. Regret theory is one way to explain this.

There can be no denying that the things we have looked at in this chapter give us a much better understanding of choice with risk. The one minor problem is that we have lots of different ways of thinking that individually make sense and can explain a lot, but not everything. For example, rank-dependent expected utility can explain the Allais Paradox but not preference reversals. Regret theory can explain preference reversals but not why someone would be risk loving over losses. On this score, prospect theory looks like a clear winner because it can explain all that we have seen. Arguably, however, this is only because we have the flexibility to change the reference point to something that works. The search still goes on, therefore, for a unified theory of choice with risk. Until we have such a theory it's important to think carefully which model or way of thinking is the one best adapted to the question you are interested in.

3.6 Financial trading

The first application I want to look at in this chapter is financial trading. Investing in stocks and shares is clearly an inherently risky business, and so the models and ideas that we have developed in this chapter should be able to tell us something useful about it. To illustrate that they can, I have picked out three interrelated things to talk about: the equity premium puzzle, disposition effect, and ostrich effect. A particular reason for choosing these three things is that in looking at them we not only learn something useful about investor behavior, but also need to think more about the importance of time and risk, an issue we only briefly looked at in section 3.3.3.

3.6.1 The equity premium puzzle

The **equity premium puzzle** is that the real rate of return on stocks is much higher than the return on 'safer assets' like treasury bills. Figure 3.14 gives some data to illustrate the size of these differences. Such differences in annual return can multiply to huge differences over a few years. For example, $1 invested in stocks in the US in 1926 would have been worth over $2,500 by the year 2000, while the same amount invested in treasury bills would have been worth less than $20. Given such numbers, why would anyone invest in treasury bills?

The obvious answer would be that investors are risk averse and so only invest in stocks, the riskier of the two, if the average return is higher. The equity premium that we observe could not, however, be explained solely by risk aversion, because to do so would require a coefficient of relative risk aversion of around 30, which is implausibly high. We need a different explanation. One explanation that does work is loss aversion and prospect theory. To make it work, however, we are going to have to think about a complicating factor: time.

The prices of stocks are changing minute by minute during a working day, and in principle an investor could change his investments at any time. There is, therefore, no definite moment in time where the outcome of investing in the stock market is known. Instead, an investor must choose how long to leave his investments before he evaluates how they are doing. We call this length of time the

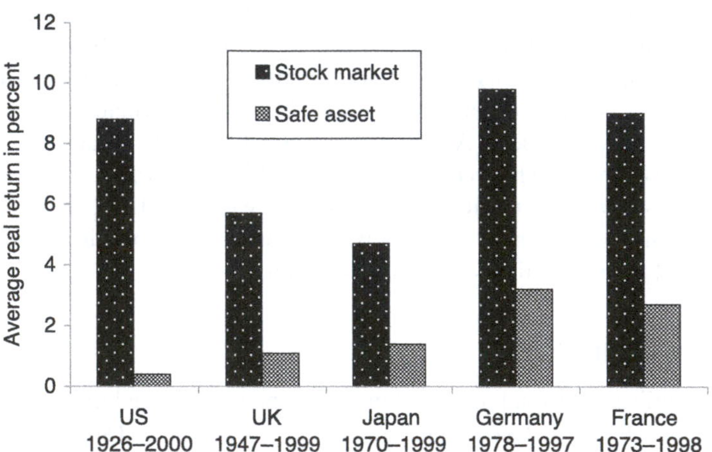

Figure 3.14 The equity premium puzzle. The average annual return on money invested stock exceeds that invested in a safe asset like treasury bills.

Source: Mehra and Prescott (2003).

evaluation period. It seems sensible to assume that the investor gets utility when he evaluates his investments at the end of each evaluation period. For example, Alan might check how his investments are doing every Friday morning and it's then that he perceives any loss or gain.

The evaluation period is going to be crucial. To explain why, it is easiest to work through an example. In Figure 3.15 I have plotted the value over time of $100 invested in two hypothetical assets. In any month the risky asset could fall or rise by $10 while the safe asset grows by a steady $1. If we just look at the value of the investment, in the top half of the figure, then the risky asset looks a clear winner. Things, however, are not so simple when we look at the investor's utility.

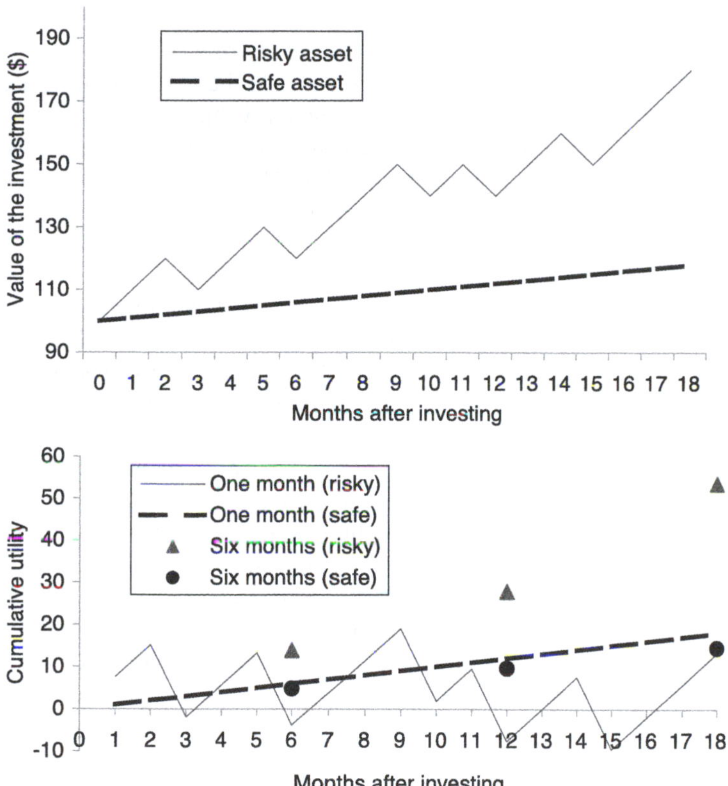

Figure 3.15 The returns in money and utility from investing in two hypothetical assets. If the evaluation period is one month, the investor gets more cumulative utility from the safe asset because he avoids the frequent falls in the risky asset. If the evaluation period is six months, the investor gets more cumulative utility from the risky asset.

Let's look first at the case where the evaluation period is one month and Alan invested in the risky asset. In the first month the value of the asset went up \$10. If we plug a gain of \$10 into the prospect theory equation (3.7) with values $\alpha = 0.88$, then we get a utility of $10^{0.88} = 7.6$. The same thing happened at the end of month two. What about at the end of month three? In the third month the asset fell in value by \$10. If we plug a loss of \$10 into equation (3.7) with values $\lambda = 2.25$ and $\beta = 0.88$, then we get a utility of $-2.25 \times 10^{0.88} = -17.1$. This is bad, and bad enough to wipe out the positive utility of the previous two months. Given Alan's loss aversion, his cumulative utility after three months would have been higher if he had invested in the safe asset and avoided this loss. The same can be said after 18 months.

Now suppose the evaluation period is six months. At the end of every six months the value of the risky asset has gone up. Consequently, the cumulative utility from the risky asset works out to be a lot higher than that from the safe asset.

What we see in this example is how the volatility of a risky asset can make it undesirable for someone who is loss averse, even if the overall returns are high. For every month that the investment goes down in value there needs to be three months of gain to compensate Alan for the disutility of the bad month. This effect is lessened by lengthening the evaluation period. The longer the evaluation period the less chance the investment will have decreased in value, and so the less chance that Alan feels a loss. This means there should be an evaluation period where he is relatively indifferent between the risky and safe asset.

Benartzi and Thaler (1995) asked how long the evaluation period would have to be to explain the equity premium that we do observe. That is, how long the evaluation period would have to be to make the expected utility on safe assets the same as on stocks. They evaluate this by simulating the utility an investor would have got from investing in US stocks, bonds, or treasury bills for various time intervals between 1926 and 1990. As in our stylized example they find that, with an evaluation period of one month, estimated utility would be higher from investing in safe assets. With an evaluation period of 18 months, it would be higher from stocks. The point where the estimated utility from safe assets and stocks are equal is an evaluation period of 12 months.

The estimate of 12 months is remarkably plausible! It does seem intuitive that ordinary investors might use a one-year period to evaluate returns on investments. Managers of pension and investment funds might also be evaluated on their year-by-year performance. We have, therefore, an explanation for an equity premium. This explanation is based on people being both loss averse and **myopic** in the sense that the evaluation period is shorter than it could be.

3.6.2 The disposition effect

Our next puzzle is why investors prefer to sell stocks that are trading at a gain and hold on to stocks trading at a loss. To explain, suppose that Alan sells a stock on a particular day. We can ask whether there was a **realized gain** – the stocks were sold for more than was paid for them – or a **realized loss** – the stocks were sold for less than was paid for them. We can also look at all the other stocks in his portfolio that are not sold and ask whether there was a **paper gain** – the stocks could have been sold for more than was paid for them – or a **paper loss** – the stocks could only have been sold for less than was paid for them. Next we calculate two ratios:

$$\text{proportion of gains realized} = \frac{\text{number of realized gains}}{\text{number of realized gains} + \text{number of paper gains}}$$

$$\text{proportion of losses realized} = \frac{\text{number of realized losses}}{\text{number of realized losses} + \text{number of paper losses}}$$

The **disposition effect** is that the proportion of gains realized is significantly greater than the proportion of losses realized. In other words, investors prefer to sell stocks that will give them a realized gain than to sell stocks that will give them a realized loss. To give some numbers, we can look at a study by Odean (1998), who analyzed the trading activity from 1987 to 1993 of 10,000 households who held accounts at a large brokerage firm. He found that the proportion of gains realized was 0.148 and the proportion of losses realized only 0.098.

You might be thinking that the disposition effect is just good investing. For example, if a stock has gone up in price, meaning realized gains, maybe it will subsequently fall in price and so it is better to sell while the going is good. Unfortunately the evidence suggests otherwise. Odean found, for instance, that stocks that were sold for a realized gain earned on average 3.4 percent more over the subsequent year than stocks that were not sold for a realized loss. Again, we need a different explanation. Given that prospect theory did so well at explaining the equity premium puzzle maybe it can work again?

I shall stick with a very similar story to that that we used to think about the equity premium puzzle. So, imagine assets that every month either go up or down in value. At the end of the year Alan will evaluate his portfolio. The utility he feels at that point depends on the gain or loss on his portfolio and is consistent with the prospect theory equation (3.7) with $\lambda = 2.25$ and $\alpha, \beta = 0.88$. Up until now, everything is the same as when we looked at the equity premium puzzle. Here is the new thing: during the year Alan can check how his portfolio is doing and buy or sell assets if he wishes to. When he checks on his investments he does not feel any loss or gain; that only comes at the end of the evaluation period.

Now, suppose that Alan checks how his investments are doing six months into the year. If his investments have gone down during the first six months then, because of loss aversion, he will be very eager to regain those losses before the evaluation period ends. By contrast, if his investments have gone up during the first six months, then he may be keen to guarantee those gains to avoid any loss. This looks like a possible explanation for the disposition effect, but we need to check that (see Research Methods 3.8). Barberis and Xiong (2009) do that by working out the optimal strategy of an investor in such a situation, and then simulating asset prices to calculate the proportion of gains realized and losses realized that we would expect to see.

Figure 3.16 plots some of the data from the study. Recall that we are trying to explain why the proportion of gains realized is larger than the proportion of losses realized. Figure 3.16 suggests that prospect theory will actually give us the opposite! For the most part we predict that the proportion of losses realized should exceed the proportion of gains realized.

To try and understand why we obtain this result we can work through an example illustrated in Figure 3.17. Suppose that Alan will evaluate his portfolio after 12 months and check it once after six months (the $T = 2$ case in Figure 3.16). He is only interested in one asset, which starts the year at price $25 and every six months either goes up in value by $5 or down by $2.50. Alan buys two shares at the start of the year, investing $50. We need to ask what he will do after six months if the price has gone up or down.

First, suppose that it has gone up. This means he is at point G in Figure 3.17. He could sell at this point and be guaranteed a gain by the end of the year, but why stop there? He could buy two more shares, still be guaranteed to not make a loss, and have the chance to be at point 2G if the price goes up again. It turns out that, if he was willing to invest at the start of the year (when there was the chance of

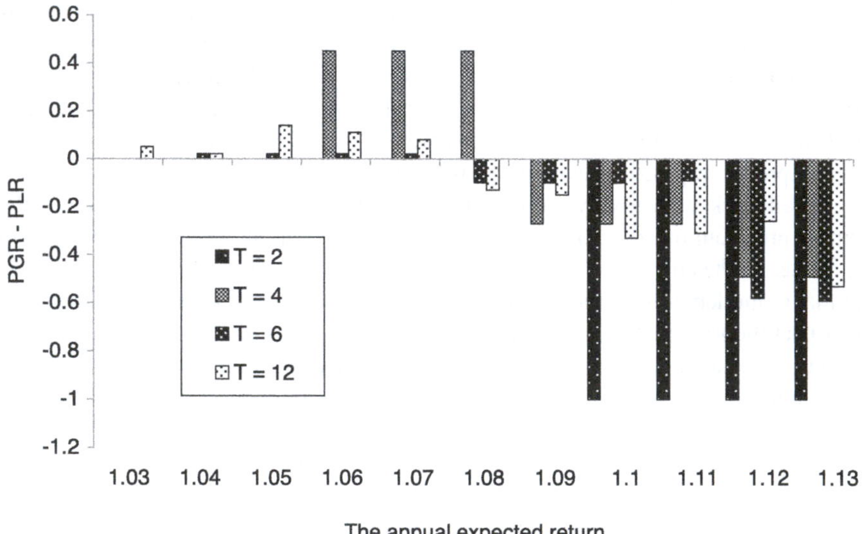

Figure 3.16 The proportion of gains realized (PGR) minus the proportion of losses realized (PLR) in simulated investments. T is the number of times that the investor looks up his portfolio during the evaluation period. The disposition effect is that the proportion of gains realized exceeds the proportion of losses realized. Prospect theory appears to give the opposite.

Source: Barberis and Xiong (2009).

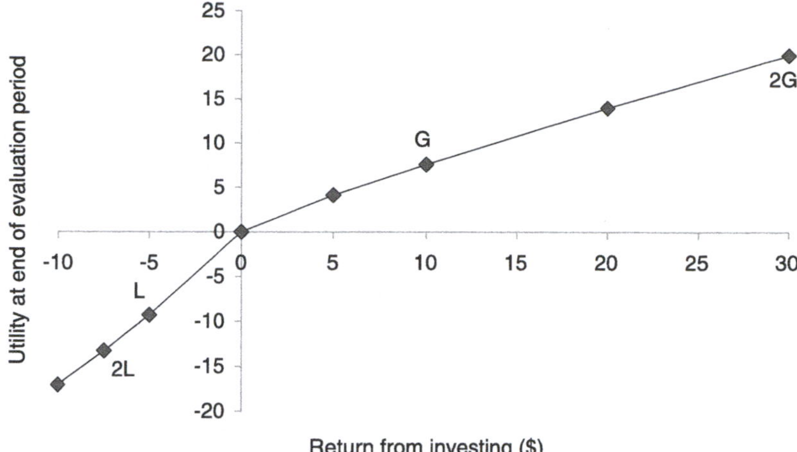

Figure 3.17 Why prospect theory does not cause the disposition effect. If the investor is at point G after six months, he should increase his investment and aim for 2G. If the investor is at point L after six months, he should decrease his investment to make sure he does no worse than 2L.

making a loss), then he must want to increase his investment at this stage (now that he is guaranteed not to make a loss).

Now, suppose the price has gone down after six months. This means he is at point L. He would like to regain his losses, but also wants to avoid further losses. This is possible by selling one share and keeping the other. If the price goes up then he will be back to zero by the end of the year and if the price goes down a second time he will at least only be at point 2L with losses of $7.50. Again, this will be the optimal thing to do.

We see through this example that prospect theory fails to explain the disposition effect on both counts. If Alan had realized gains then he should increase his investment, and if he had realized losses he should decrease his investment. You might say this result is dependent on the asymmetry whereby the price of the asset increases by more than it decreases. This, however, is what we do tend to observe about asset prices. Furthermore, if Alan was willing to invest at all, despite his loss and risk aversion, then there must have been this asymmetry, because he will only invest in stocks that are more likely to go up than down.

Prospect theory does not, therefore, seem a convincing explanation for the disposition effect. Indeed, it suggests we have even more of a puzzle to solve than we might have first imagined. Not all hope is lost, because we might argue that the investor will feel a loss or gain in utility every time he looks at the value of his portfolio and not just at the end of the evaluation period. Perhaps, however, it is better to accept reality. Prospect theory was able to explain the equity premium puzzle without any trouble, but raises more questions about the disposition effect than it solves. In Chapter five we shall come back and try to answer these questions.

3.6.3 The ostrich effect

In both the previous puzzles, time has played a pivotal role. First, we looked at the evaluation period over which gains and losses are judged. Then, we looked at how often an investor may check up on and trade within the evaluation period. The point I shall pick up on now is that the evaluation period and frequency of trade are not only pivotal but also typically chosen by the investor. This raises the issue of how often Alan should pay attention to his investments.

To get some insight on this issue, imagine that Alan periodically hears news about the performance of the stock market. This news gives him some idea what may be happening to his investments. It is only by looking up his investments, however, that he can definitively find out what has happened to them. What should he do after he has watched the news?

Research Methods 3.8

Don't always trust intuition

Ronald Reagan once said: 'One definition of an economist is somebody who sees something happen in practice and wonders if it will work in theory.' A nice quote which sums up a lot of what economics is about. Many question whether this formalism is of any use, as is clear in a second quote from Alfred Knopf: 'An economist is a man who states the obvious in terms of the incomprehensible.' This study by Barberis and Xiong is one illustration of why economists believe it is good to check that things work in theory.

Prospect theory was an intuitive solution to the disposition effect. If a stock has risen in value it takes an investor to the concave risk-averse area of her utility function and if it falls in value it takes her to the convex risk-loving area of her utility function. Consequently, she should take more risks on stocks that have fallen in value than gained in value. It was so intuitive an explanation that it became the most commonly mentioned explanation for the disposition effect. Barberis and Xiong took on the task of checking that the explanation does work in theory (to make the obvious incomprehensible). Their conclusion was that prospect theory is not so great an explanation for the disposition effect. Sometimes, therefore, intuition and common sense can lead us astray. That's why it's important to write down models and check that things really do work like they seem to.

If he only feels the loss or gain of investing when he evaluates his investments at the end of the year, then he should look up his investments, because he has got nothing to lose. Realistically, however, he is going to feel something when he checks on his investments, even if the biggest effect is at the end of the evaluation period. We can distinguish, therefore, two effects. First, there is an **impact effect**, whereby looking up his investments makes it more likely he will feel the gain or loss on his investments. Second, there is a **reference point updating effect**, whereby he is more likely to change the reference point by which he will evaluate his investments at the end of the evaluation period.

These two effects work in opposite directions. If the news is good, then the investor would be tempted to look up his investments and feel happy about the gain that he is likely to observe. But, he would also be reluctant to see the gain, increase his reference point, and subsequently be more likely to experience a loss relative to this higher reference point. There are similar trade-offs if the news is bad. Intuitively, however, the reasons to look up the investments after good news seem a bit stronger than those to look up after bad news. This suggests the **ostrich effect**, whereby the investor is more likely to look up his investments following good news rather than bad.

A study by Karlsson and co-authors (2009) looked at data from Norway and Sweden on how often investors do look up their investments. They compare the daily number of investors who look up their portfolio to the performance of the relevant stock market index in the previous week. Figure 3.18 summarizes the data and shows that there did indeed appear to be an ostrich effect. When the stock market index was going up (good news), investors were more likely to look up their investments than when it was flat or going down (neutral or bad news).

The consequences of an ostrich effect are interesting to hypothesize about. In discussing the equity premium puzzle, we suggested that investors may have too short an evaluation period. The ostrich effect partly alleviates this. In discussing the disposition effect we suggested that investors may not do the best thing when they look up a portfolio with gains and losses. The ostrich effect may be a way to

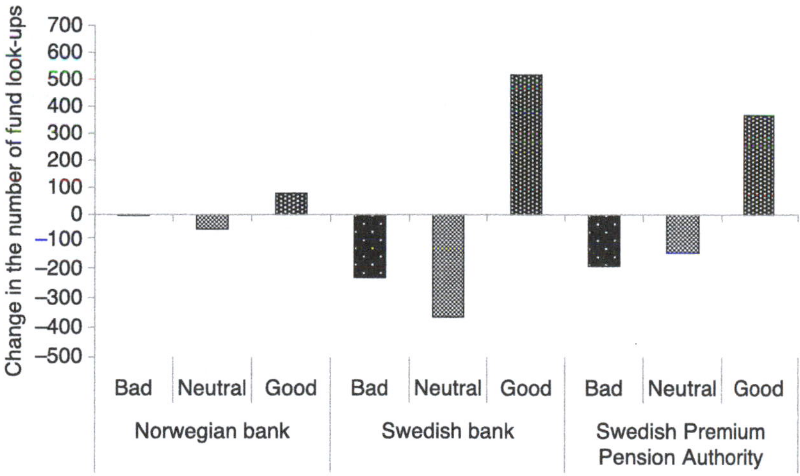

Figure 3.18 The change in the number of investors looking up their investments depending on whether the stock market was up, down, or neutral over the previous week.

Source: Karlsson *et al.* (2009).

avoid this. Might selective attention, therefore, be a good way of managing loss aversion and the like?

3.7 Insurance

I started this chapter with the example of Alan buying insurance, so it seems apt to look at some real data on insurance. One basic observation is that people seem to want insurance. Most people buy at least one of the following: house insurance, life insurance, car insurance, health insurance, travel insurance. In some instances this is because insurance is compulsory, but that can only explain so much. It seems, therefore, that people like insurance, and this clearly suggests that people are risk averse for big gambles. That should be no surprise, given that we observe risk aversion for small gambles, and so it is not too hard to explain why people might want insurance.

What I will focus on, therefore, is a more subtle question of how much insurance people choose to have. One particularly interesting issue is that of the deductible. The **deductible** is the amount of any insurance claim that a person would have to pay themselves. So, for example, if Alan's car is involved in an accident with total damage of $2,000 and his deductible is $500, then Alan pays the first $500 and the insurance company the remaining $1,500.

Insurance companies typically give some choice of deductible, and a policy with a lower deductible will have a higher premium. In choosing the level of deductible, Alan faces a clear trade-off: by spending, say, $10 more in premium he will have to pay, say, $100 less if he makes a claim. The choice of deductible is, therefore, a nice thing to look at. It can give us a picture of how people choose insurance and also give us some general insights on choice with risk.

Sydnor (2010) looked at a sample of 50,000 standard policies from a large home insurance provider in the US. Customers could choose a deductible of $1,000, $500, $250, or $100. Table 3.17 summarizes some of the data and shows that the majority chose the $500 or $250 deductible. The exact amount of premium

Table 3.17 Choice of deductible on home insurance. Few households chose the $1,000 deductible, but this is hard to explain using expected utility because it requires extreme levels of risk aversion

Deductible	*Proportion who chose it (%)*	*Average extra premium*	*Claim rate (%)*	*Expected saving with $1,000 Deductible*	*Lower bound on risk aversion using CRRA*
$1,000	17.0	$0	2.5	—	—
$500	47.6	$100	4.3	$80	1,719
$250	35.0	$159	4.9	$127	4,000
$100	0.3	$243	4.7	—	—

Source: Sydnor (2010).

would depend on the house value, location, etc., but on average people paid around \$100 or \$150 extra to lower the deductible.

There was evidence, which we cannot see in Table 3.17, that households were price sensitive, in the sense that those buying the \$250 deductible paid on average less extra premium than those who chose the \$500 deductible would have had to do. Even so, the amount that households spent to lower the deductible looks high. We can say this with some confidence because we know the actual claim rate of the customers and so know how much they would have benefited from the lower deductible. The costs of the deductible do not seem to justify the benefits, and the estimated level of risk aversion to justify such choices is way above what is plausible.

How can we explain the preference for a lower deductible? One likely factor is an overestimation of the likelihood of making a claim. If the claim rate is 20 percent, then the estimates of risk aversion come down to around ten. This, in itself, is still not enough, however, because an expected claim rate of 20 percent would be too pessimistic, and a coefficient of risk aversion of ten is still too high. A second likely factor is loss aversion.

Care is needed, however, in applying loss aversion to insurance because paying the premium might be interpreted as a loss. It can, therefore, become even harder to explain why someone would incur for sure the loss of, say \$100, to lower the probability that they will subsequently lose \$500. Indeed, this would directly contradict the evidence that people are risk loving over losses. One way out of this puzzle is to apply the 'no loss in buying' hypothesis that we looked at in the last chapter. Recall that this hypothesis says giving up money to buy something is perceived as a forgone gain rather than loss. So, spending an extra \$100 on insurance is not perceived as a loss. Recall also the example in section 3.3.2.

If we accept the 'no loss in buying' hypothesis and apply the standard formulation of prospect theory with $\lambda = 2.25$, $\alpha, \beta = 0.88$, and $\delta = 0.69$, we find that a 4 percent claim rate would be weighted as 12 percent and a person would pay \$100 for a \$500 deductible. A combination of loss aversion and overestimating the probability of making a claim can easily, therefore, explain the choice of deductible that people made. Prospect theory again comes up trumps.

Things may not be quite so simple, however. To give a first hint why, we can look at a study by Cohen and Einav (2007). They looked at the deductible choices of over 100,000 individuals buying car insurance in Israel between 1994 and 1999. Again people could choose from four deductible levels, called regular, low, high, or very high. This time the premium and deductible were percentages of the regular premium and deductible. For example, someone opting for a low deductible paid 6 percent more than the regular premium and got 60 percent of the regular deductible. Table 3.18 gives some numbers to compare with those of Table 3.17.

The financial trade-offs that people faced were roughly similar to those of the previous study, with one notable exception: namely the claim rate is much higher. Unfortunately, it is difficult to calculate a precise estimate of risk aversion from the data. If we focus on the fact that the vast majority of people chose the regular deductible, and not the high or very high deductible, then we would obtain high

Table 3.18 Deductible choice in Israeli car insurance (monetary amounts were converted from the actual New Israel Shekels by dividing by 3.5, the average exchange rate over the period)

Deductible chosen	*Average deductible*	*Proportion who chose it (%)*	*Extra premium*	*Claim rate (%)*
Very high	$1,075	0.5	0	13.3
High	$745	0.6	$69	12.8
Regular	$415	81.1	$182	23.2
Low	$250	17.8	$237	30.1

Source: Cohen and Einav (2007).

estimates of risk aversion, similar to those in the study by Syndor, and too high to be plausible. Cohen and Einav noted, however, that customers may not have been informed about the high and very high deductible options when deciding what to do. In this case we should focus on the fact that people chose the regular and not the low deductible. Doing this, we find low and plausible estimates of risk aversion of less than four.

We are simply unable to tell from this data what the attitudes to risk were. That, in itself, though, is informative because it emphasizes that many things other than attitudes to risk will likely influence an insurance decision. It is surely not a coincidence that so many chose the regular option. Indeed, Syndor also found considerable inertia in his study, with many choosing the same deductible as they had in the past. To carry on this story we need to look at choice over time, which is the focus of the next chapter.

3.8 Tax evasion

Benjamin Franklin famously said that 'In this world nothing can be said to be certain, except death and taxes.' It might have been more accurate to say that nothing can be certain except death, taxes, and people not paying their taxes. You typically don't have to wait long before the latest story of tax evasion hits the headlines. Usually, it is a politician, movie star, sports star, or rich businessman caught underdeclaring income or moving money offshore. Tax evasion is not, however, solely the domain of the rich. It goes a lot deeper than that. And that's why it is a big concern in many countries.

Tax evasion has two bad consequences. First, it is unfair that one person honestly pays their taxes while another illegally avoids doing so. Second, it creates uncertainty at the macroeconomic level because a government has less security of income. This latter problem became all too clear in the Euro crisis where large-scale tax evasion in some countries made it very difficult to know how a change in policy (e.g. an increase in tax rates) would feed through into government revenue. Eliminating tax evasion is, therefore, an important goal. In this section we shall look at how behavioral economics can inform on the reasons why people evade taxes, and the things that might stop them doing so.

Before getting into the theory it is interesting to get a feel for how big a problem tax evasion is. Measuring tax evasion is inevitably difficult, given that evaders have a strong incentive to cover their tracks. Various indirect ways to measure tax evasion have, however, been developed. Most reliable are measures that take account of a combination of different indicators of unreported activity. The kinds of indicators to look for are aggregate spending above reported income, debt out of line with reported income, a discrepancy between official employment statistics and the number of people seemingly in work, and the use of cash rather than cheques or bank cards.

Figure 3.19 provides estimates on the size of the shadow economy between 1999 and 2007 in a wide selection of countries. The shadow economy measures that part of the economy that goes unreported, and so is a good proxy for tax evasion. In Brazil, Mexico, Nigeria, and Russia the shadow economy is estimated at a whopping 40 percent of the economy. Even at the other end of the scale, in countries like the US and Japan, the shadow economy is still estimated at around one-tenth of the economy. Table 3.19 focuses on Greece and looks at the estimated tax evasion of self-employed workers by profession. Here we can more clearly see the potential unfairness that results from tax evasion. Some professions are seemingly able to 'get away' with more than others.

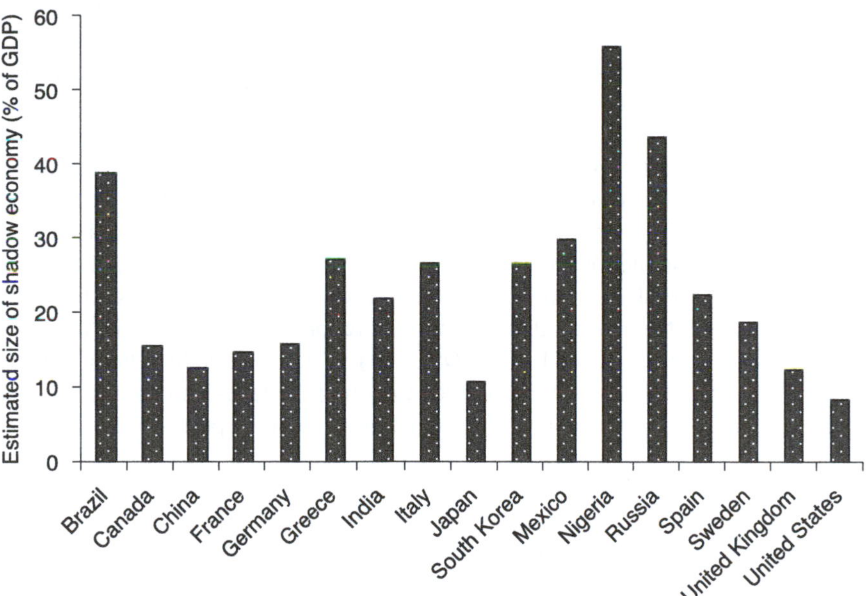

Figure 3.19 The estimated size of the shadow economy between 1999 and 2007 as a percentage of GDP.

Source: Buehn and Schneider (2012).

Table 3.19 Estimated tax evasion by profession. The income multiplier measures how much lenders are estimated to multiply reported income in order to obtain a more realistic estimate of true income.

Profession	*Average tax evasion (€)*	*Income multiplier*
Doctors and medicine	29,343	2.45
Engineering and science	28,625	2.40
Education	24,742	2.55
Accounting and financial services	24,572	2.22
Law	24,032	2.24
Lodging and restaurants	15,884	1.99
Construction	13,919	1.85
Agriculture	9,288	1.75
Retail	5,215	1.27

Source: Artavanis *et al.* (2012).

3.8.1 Standard model of tax evasion

We begin our efforts to model tax evasion with the standard model, based around expected utility maximization. To explain the model let us look at Alan's choices. Suppose that Alan earns an income of $\$M$. He must decide how much of that income to report to the tax authorities. For every dollar he reports he is taxed at rate t. Every dollar he doesn't report is his to keep, provided he is not caught evading taxes. With probability p, the tax authorities will audit Alan and discover all his unreported income. For every dollar he did not report he is fined $f > t$.

Alan must decide how much income to report. Equivalently he must decide amongst an array of prospects. He could choose to be fully compliant with the tax authorities, meaning he chooses prospect (1, $\$M(1 - t)$). In this case, it doesn't matter whether he is audited or not because he did not break the rules. At the other extreme he could try to evade all taxes, meaning he chooses prospect ($1 - p$, \$M; p, $\$M(1 - f)$). In this case, if he is not audited then he avoids paying tax, but if he is audited he has to pay a fine that is more than his taxes would have been. In general, let $\$R$ denote the amount of income Alan chooses to report and $\$D = M - R$ the amount that he does not report. Then, he chooses prospect ($1 - p$, $\$R(1 - t) + D$; p, $\$R(1 - t) + D(1 - f)$). If he is not audited he only pays taxes on reported income. If he is audited then he pays taxes on reported income and a fine on unreported income. The expected value of the prospect is:

$$V(R, D) = R(1 - t) + D(1 - pf).$$

To see more clearly how things work let's put in some realistic numbers. Suppose that Alan has a wealth of \$1 million and has an income, on top of that, of \$100,000. The tax rate is 40 percent, $t = 0.4$, the probability of an audit is 2 percent, $p = 0.02$, and the fine is 300 percent of unreported income, $f = 3$. Table 3.20 looks through three levels of reported income that Alan could choose. He is supposed to pay \$40,000 in tax. By trying to avoid this tax he increases expected value. This is primarily because it is unlikely he will be audited. Avoiding tax does, however, carry the risk of a big fine in the case that he is audited.

To see what Alan will choose we could calculate expected utility. I will assume that Alan has a constant relative risk aversion utility function (CRRA) with risk aversion parameter r_u^r. This means that the expected utility of the prospect where \$*R* is reported is:

$$U(R,D) = (1-p)\frac{(R(1-t)+D)^{1-r_u^r}}{1-r_u^r} + p\frac{\left(R(1-t)+D(1-f)\right)^{1-r_u^r}}{1-r_u^r}.$$

This is easy enough to work out given specific values. Figure 3.20 plots expected utility as a function of reported income for different values of the risk aversion

Table 3.20 A summary of the outcome if Alan reports all, half, or none of his income when $t = 0.4$, $p = 0.02$ and $f = 3$. Expected value is increasing in the amount not reported, but not reporting increases the risk of a big fine

				Total wealth	
Income reported	*Taxes paid*	*Fine if audited*	*Expected value*	*Not audited*	*Audited*
100,000	40,000	0	60,000	1,060,000	1,060,000
50,000	20,000	150,000	77,000	1,080,000	930,000
0	0	300,000	94,000	1,100,000	800,000

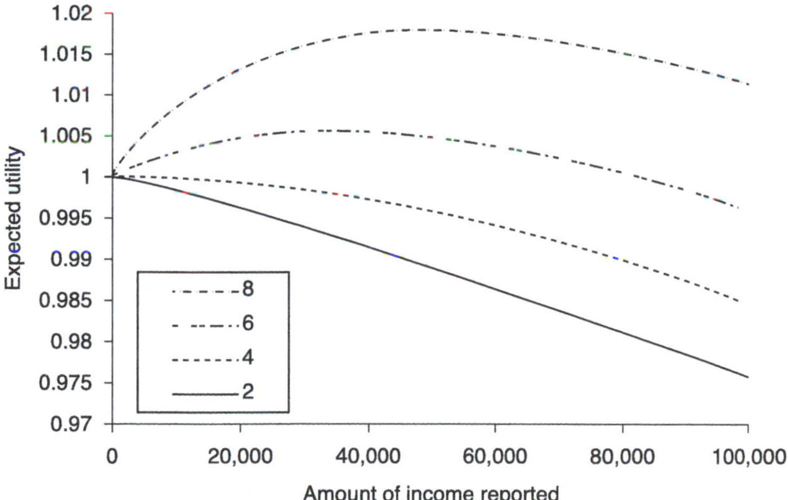

Figure 3.20 Expected utility (rescaled) for different amounts of income reported and for different values of the risk aversion parameter r_u^r.

parameter. Most realistic is a risk aversion parameter of two. We can see in this case that Alan will not report any income because his expected utility is decreasing in the amount of income that he reports. If Alan is more risk averse, then his expected utility is maximized by reporting some of this income. Even, however, for the implausibly large risk aversion parameter of eight he would only report half of his income.

This specific example illustrates a general problem with the standard model of tax evasion. For plausible parameter values it predicts that everybody should be doing a lot of tax evasion. It is difficult to reconcile this prediction with the largely honest reporting that we observe in many countries; many evade taxes but many do not. Put another way, the standard model says that the tax authorities are not tough enough. The probability of audit and the size of fine are predicted to be an insufficient deterrent against tax evasion. Again, this prediction doesn't seem to fit the facts. So, what are we missing?

3.8.2 Behavioral theories of tax evasion

In Chapter two we looked at evidence that people do not like to lie or deceive. Maybe this can explain why people honestly report income. It may be part of the story, but it is unlikely to be the whole story. That is because a person must have a pretty big aversion to lying in order to file an honest tax return. If Alan, for example, does not report any income he gains an expected $34,000. A lot of people would be willing to tell a lie for $34,000!

For a more likely explanation of honest reporting we can look at things like disappointment, reference dependence, and the overweighting of small probabilities. To illustrate, let's see what happens if we apply the reference-dependent utility approach. To do that, we need to think about expectations and the reference point. I will compare three different scenarios.

First, suppose that Alan never pays his taxes and resents having to give money to the government. In this case his reference point is a final wealth of $1,100,000. Paying any amount of tax is interpreted as a loss. Following the approach of section 3.3, we shall first rank outcomes. The worst outcome is clearly that he gets audited, and the best outcome is that he does not get audited. So, the decision weight on being audited will be:

$$w_1 = \frac{p^\delta}{(p^\delta + (1-p)^\delta)^{\frac{1}{\delta}}}$$

and the decision weight on not being audited will be $w_2 = 1 - w_1$. If we put in values of $p = 0.02$ and $\delta = 0.69$, then we get $w_1 = 0.06$ and $w_2 = 0.94$. So, a 2 percent probability of being audited gets converted into a 6 percent decision weight, because of the overweighting of small probabilities.

This overweighting of the probability of being audited should push Alan more towards reporting his income, but is it enough? The next thing to do is to look at his utility function. I'll assume the utility function is given by:

$$u(x) = \begin{cases} \sqrt{x} + (x-r)^{0.88} & \text{if } x \geq r \\ \sqrt{x} - 2.25(r-x)^{0.88} & \text{if } x < r \end{cases}$$

where x is final wealth and r is the reference point. Putting in $r = 1{,}100{,}000$ we can work out expected utility for any prospect. Figure 3.21 shows what we get. And you can see that Alan still maximizes his utility by not reporting any income. So, the overweighting of probabilities is not enough in itself.

Now let us suppose that Alan always pays his taxes and believes in big government. In this case it is natural to think of his reference point as a final wealth of $1,060,000. Alan could potentially gain by evading tax. But, the only way he can lose is to evade tax and be caught. Given Alan's desire to avoid losses this change in reference point makes a huge difference to his incentive to report taxes. The decision weights also change. The decision weight on being audited remains the same as before at 0.06. Given, however, that being not audited now counts as a gain, the decision weight will be:

$$w_2 = \frac{(1-p)^\gamma}{(p^\gamma + (1-p)^\gamma)^{\frac{1}{\gamma}}}.$$

Setting $p = 0.02$ and $\gamma = 0.01$ gives $w_2 = 0.87$. This effectively means that the decision weight on being audited becomes even higher. We can see in Figure 3.21 that these effects combined mean that Alan maximizes his utility by reporting all his income. We have a viable story of why Alan may honestly pay his taxes.

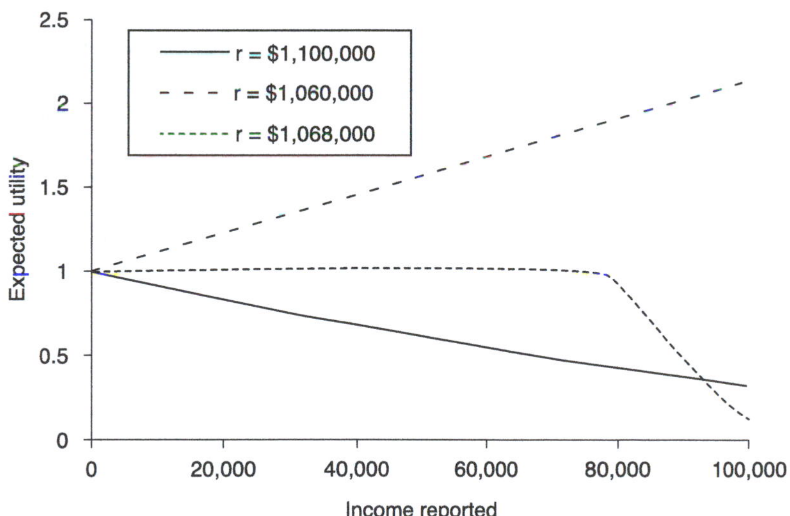

Figure 3.21 Expected utility (rescaled) for different amounts of income reported depending on the reference level.

I want to consider a final possibility. This is arguably the most realistic in looking at tax evasion. Suppose that Alan has a salary of $80,000 and is used to paying tax on that. In addition, he earns $20,000 'on the side'. For example, he does a bit of consultancy, gets royalties from books he wrote, or does odd jobs for friends and neighbors. Paying tax on this additional $20,000 seems to Alan like a loss. In this case the natural reference point is the $1,068,000 that results from paying a $32,000 tax on his salary. The only way Alan can avoid a loss is to not report the $20,000 he earns on the side. In this case, we can see in Figure 3.21 that we get a kink in the expected utility at $80,000. For the numbers I have chosen Alan's utility is maximized when he reports around $50,000 of income. The more general point, however, is that he will not report more than the $80,000 that he is 'willing' to pay tax on.

3.8.3 Taxes and reference points

We have seen that reference-dependent expected utility can explain why Alan, or anyone else, would honestly report their income. But we have also seen that the reference point is crucial. If Alan is used to paying all his taxes, then he maximizes his utility by paying taxes. If he is used to not paying taxes then he maximizes his utility by not paying taxes. To meaningfully apply the theory we, therefore, need to think carefully about what the reference point will be in particular contexts.

As we have already seen several times in the book so far, the reference point is likely to depend on framing. Suppose, for instance, that Alan works for a big employer who automatically takes tax out of his income. In this case the reference point is surely one of paying taxes. Alan essentially doesn't notice that the money going on taxes disappears from his pay. Or, relating back to the endowment effect, he never owns the money to lose it. Contrast this with the situation where Alan is self-employed. Now all the money he earns passes through his hands and it is up to him to pay his taxes. The framing is very different and this may be reflected in a reference point of tax evasion.

Another side to the story is desire to pay taxes. If Alan thinks his tax money will be used wisely, then that may increase the reference amount of income that he reports. Similarly, if Alan dislikes being threatened and harassed about taxes, then, the more pressure the authorities put on him, the lower may be the reference amount of income that he reports. Alan may be more likely to honestly report his income if the government positively promotes the societal benefits of paying taxes, than if they threaten him for not paying. Changing the frame can potentially do a lot more than changing the probability of audit.

A final framing effect I want to discuss is that of social influence. We shall look at social influence a lot more in Chapter five, but it is worth briefly touching on the issue here. The basic idea is that a person's reference point may be influenced by what others are doing. So, if all Alan's friends and colleagues are evading taxes, this may lower the reference amount of tax that Alan reports. Similarly, if all his friends honestly report, then it may increase the reference amount of tax he reports.

There are different reasons why we may observe such influence. One possibility is that Alan simply likes doing the same as others. Another possibility is that he learns from others the trade-offs of evading taxes. The outcome, however, is likely to be the same whatever the cause, in that we shall observe social reference points.

3.8.4 Tax evasion in the laboratory

As I have already said, it is not easy to measure tax evasion. It is not the kind of thing that people openly admit to doing! This makes it very difficult to know how a change in, say, the probability of audit affects the level of tax evasion. The experimental laboratory is, therefore, an invaluable place to learn more about tax evasion. In the laboratory we can directly measure evasion and much more easily see what effect things like the probability of audit have on reported income (see Research Methods 3.9).

To illustrate what we can learn from tax evasion experiments I will talk about a study by Alm and co-authors (2010). This is an interesting study for us to look at because it highlights another crucial aspect of tax evasion. We have taken it as given, so far, that Alan knows how much tax he is supposed to pay. The reality is almost always that a person does not know how much tax they are supposed to pay! For just about any country you choose to look at, the tax code will be impenetrable. Different income is taxed at different rates, there are deductibles, entitlements to benefits, tax credits, etc. This complexity can make filing a tax return into a nightmare.

In the study by Alm and co-authors, subjects had to pay tax on income earned during a simple task. To capture some of the complexity of tax reporting a subject could claim a tax deduction (a reduction in taxable income) and a tax credit (extra money that declined with the level of income). If someone did not file a tax return then they paid no tax, but also missed out on claiming any tax credit. In a baseline treatment, subjects were made fully aware of the rules for deduction and tax credit. In an uncertainty treatment, subjects were left guessing how much tax deduction and tax credit they could claim. Only if they were audited would they find out exactly how much tax they needed to pay. In an information treatment, subjects were left guessing how much income they should report but could press a button to find out exactly how much they should report.

One could argue that the uncertainty treatment most closely reflects the reality for many individuals filing their tax return. There is almost inevitably a little bit of guesswork in knowing how much tax should be paid. This could result in a person paying more tax than they are supposed to, in order to avoid any chance of a fine, or paying less, because of annoyance with the tax system. The latter possibility seems more likely, and so there is an increasing recognition that tax authorities need to provide services to taxpayers. Their job is not only to audit and catch tax evaders, but also to help compliant individuals more easily declare their income. This translates into good, user-friendly online systems, helpdesks that work, and so on.

Figure 3.22 summarizes the main results of the study. It allows us to compare across treatments the proportion of subjects who filed a tax return and the proportion of income that was declared. We can see that the filing rate and compliance rate was higher in the information treatment. It is not dramatically higher, but a small increase in reported income can add up to a large change in tax revenue when aggregated over millions of taxpayers.

This result may seem bizarre. The benchmark and information treatments are basically identical. All that differs is the frame. So, making the tax code more complex and then offering a solution to the problem increases compliance! The lesson to take away from this study is not, however, that we should be increasing the complexity of the tax code; tax codes are complex enough as it is. Instead, we learn that tax compliance can increase if the tax authorities provide a service to taxpayers. Moreover, this effect may be largely due to framing. Alan, for instance, is more likely to declare his income if he feels he gets something for his money. A nice, online interface that makes it effortless to file a tax return may convince Alan that he does get something for his money. A clunky system that doesn't work might leave Alan infuriated and unconvinced his taxes are worth paying.

This study on tax services is only one of many. Other studies have looked at how tax compliance varies with the probability of audit, size of fine, etc. The study nicely illustrates, however, the role that experiments can play in studying tax evasion. Improving tax authority services is not simple or cheap. Experiments like this can inform on whether it is worth doing, and how best to do it. More generally, we have seen in this section that understanding tax compliance requires

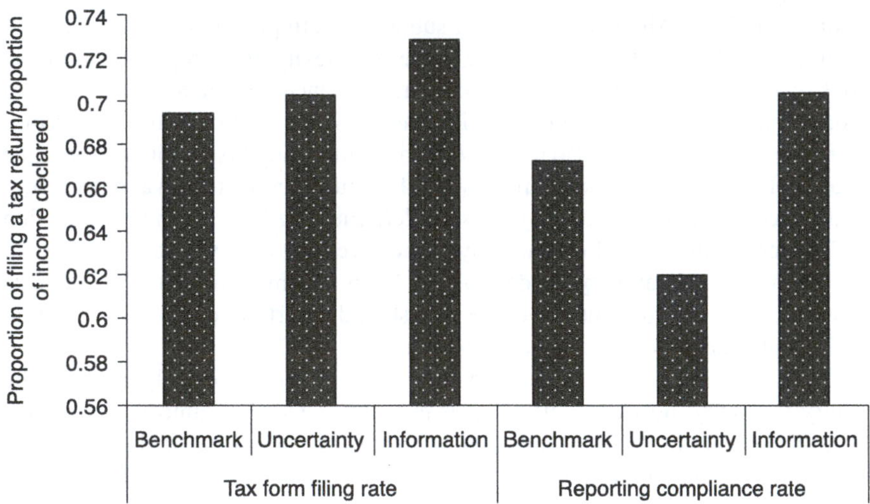

Figure 3.22 The proportion of subjects who filed a tax return (tax form filing rate) and the proportion of income that is declared (reporting compliance rate), by treatment. The filing rate and compliance rate is highest in the information treatment.

Source: Alm *et al.* (2010).

taking on board many of the things we have looked at in the last two chapters. Framing effects, endowment effects, reference points, weighting of probabilities are all key in the decision to evade taxes or not.

Research Methods 3.9

External validity, something is better than nothing

Tax evasion experiments clearly raise issues of external validity. In a laboratory experiment we can have a student who has never filed a tax return in his life making decisions about $10 he earned in five minutes on a simple game. In the real world we can have a seasoned adult making decisions about $100,000 earned through a year of hard work, facing jail if he misreports. How can the one possibly tell us anything about the other?

A first response to this concern is to say that something is better than nothing. In order to inform policymakers it is really important that we have some clear evidence to back up the theory. Improving tax authority services, for instance, costs millions of dollars and so should not be done on a whim. If it is difficult, or impossible, to get evidence from the real world, then we have to rely on laboratory studies. This is a strong argument. And it not only applies to tax evasion, but to many areas of policy.

Difficulty in obtaining field data is not in itself, however, enough to justify laboratory experiments. We also need to have some confidence that behavior in the laboratory is something like behavior in the real world. Otherwise we are wasting our time, or worse, misinforming policymakers. This is why tax evasion experiments are one of the few occasions in experimental economics where an explicit frame is used. In the study by Alm and co-authors, subjects earned money, were asked to file a tax return, and were given an interface that is not unlike filing a tax return.

That, however, may not be enough, and checking external validity is impossible if we cannot accurately measure real tax evasion. There are no easy answers to such problems. This does not mean experiments are not useful, but it does mean we should not become overly reliant on them. We need good theory to complement experimental studies.

3.9 Legal settlements

Economics and law may seem like two very different subjects. There is, however, a considerable amount of overlap between the two. Tax evasion illustrates one reason for this: many crimes, like tax evasion, theft, smuggling, corruption, and fraud, are motivated by financial gain. So, committing the crime is an economic gamble and, as we have seen in the previous section, can be modeled as such. Other crimes, like vandalism, minor assault, negligence, workplace discrimination, careless driving, and drink driving are not motivated by financial gain. The likely punishment, however, is a financial one in the form of a fine or of compensation to the victim. In this section we shall look at how behavioral economics can inform on the 'bargaining' process between the prosecution and defense.

To guide us through the issues I will consider the following example. Alan has been accused by one of his employees, Anna, of sex-discrimination in the workplace. With probability p Alan will be found guilty, in which case he will have to pay compensation of \$5,000 to Anna. With probability $1 - p$, Alan will be found not guilty and have to pay no compensation. Suppose that both Alan and Anna start with wealth of \$100,000. They would like to reach an out-of-court settlement, and thereby avoid legal costs and emotional strain. But will they be able to agree?

Looked at from an individual point of view, Alan faces prospect (p,\$95,000; $1 - p$,\$100,000) and Anna faces prospect (p,\$105,000;$1 - p$,\$100,000). The fascinating thing, however, is the connection between the two prospects. Alan's loss is Anna's gain. In order to reach agreement they will, therefore, need to find a settlement that *both* prefer compared to their existing prospect. This provides an ideal opportunity to introduce a key feature of prospect theory that I have so far neglected – the fourfold pattern of risk attitudes.

3.9.1 Fourfold pattern of risk attitudes

Before we delve into some equations let me ask you what you would do. Here are some scenarios.

> Scenario A: Imagine you are in the place of Alan. There is a 5 percent chance you will be found guilty and have to pay \$5,000. Anna offers to settle out of court for a payment of \$250. Would you agree to settle?
>
> Scenario B: Now, imagine you are in the place of Anna. There is a 50 percent chance you will win the case and get \$5,000. Alan offers you \$2,500 to settle out of court?
>
> Scenario C: Still in the place of Anna. There is a 5 percent chance you will win the case and get \$5,000. Alan offers you \$250 to settle out of court?
>
> Scenario D. You are back in the place of Alan. There is a 50 percent chance you will lose the case and have to pay \$5,000. Anna offers to settle out of court for a payment of \$2,500?

Any set of answers is possible. But, if you are like most people, your answers will have fitted the fourfold pattern of risk attitudes summarized in Table 3.21. You will have settled in scenarios A and B and not settled in scenarios C and D. The predictions in the case of B and D should need little explanation; in section 3.1.3 we already discussed that people are typically risk averse over gains and risk loving over losses. The more interesting cases are A and C. These cases are characterized by the probability of a guilty verdict being relatively small. Why would this matter?

We have seen that people overweight small probabilities. So, when the probability of a guilty verdict is only 5 percent, Alan and Anna will likely overweight its probability. This overweighting of probability acts as a counterweight to the natural tendency to be risk averse over gains and risk loving over losses. Anna, for instance, will overweight the probability of winning the \$5,000 and so be reluctant

Table 3.21 The fourfold pattern of risk attitudes in litigation

	Low probability	*Medium to high probability*
Gains	**Risk loving** (scenario C). Will go to court unless offered a generous settlement.	**Risk averse** (scenario B). Happy to settle out of court.
Losses	**Risk averse** (scenario A). Happy to settle out of court.	**Risk loving** (scenario D). Will go to court unless offered a generous settlement.

to settle out of court. Alan, by contrast, will overweight the probability of losing the $5,000 and be happy to settle out of court. Low probability events can, thus, cause a switching of risk attitudes.

To formalize the idea let us work through a model of reference-dependent utility. The overweighting of probabilities is crucial, and so I will start with this. Following the logic of section 3.3 we can work out the decision weight Anna and Alan put on a guilty verdict. Anna stands to gain from going to court, and the best outcome is that she wins the case. So, the decision weight on winning the case will be:

$$w_2 = \frac{p^\gamma}{(p^\gamma + (1-p)^\gamma)^{\frac{1}{\gamma}}}.$$

The decision weight on not winning is $w_1 = 1 - w_2$. Table 3.22 illustrates how the decision weight varies with p when $\gamma = 0.61$. We see that a 5 percent chance of winning the case is converted into a 13 percent decision weight. Alan stands to lose from going to court, and the worst outcome is that he is found guilty. So, the decision weight on losing the case will be:

$$w_1 = \frac{p^\delta}{(p^\delta + (1-p)^\delta)^{\frac{1}{\delta}}}.$$

Table 3.22 Outcomes of going to court or settling out of court

	Probability of Anna winning the case			
	0.05	*0.10*	*0.25*	*0.50*
Expected value	$250	$500	$1,250	$2,500
Anna's decision weight on guilty verdict	0.13	0.19	0.29	0.42
Alan's decision weight on guilty verdict	0.11	0.17	0.29	0.45
Anna's expected utility if go to court	3410	3512	3708	3951
Anna's expected utility if fair settlement	3295	3407	3717	4179
Alan's expected utility if go to court	2702	2460	1950	1288
Alan's expected utility if fair settlement	2868	2620	1947	922

The decision weight on winning the case is $w_2 = 1 - w_1$. Setting $\delta = 0.69$, we get the decision weights given in Table 3.22. Notice how Alan's decision weights differ from those of Anna.

We can look next at expected utility. I'll assume that Alan and Anna have the utility function:

$$u(x) = \begin{cases} 10\sqrt{x} + (x-r)^{0.88} & \text{if } x \geq r \\ 10\sqrt{x} - 2.25(r-x)^{0.88} & \text{if } x < r \end{cases}$$

where x is final wealth and r is the reference point. The natural reference point here is a not-guilty verdict, meaning r = \$100,000. Observe that there is nothing dodgy about the utility function. Alan and Anna have diminishing marginal utility of wealth, are risk averse for gains and are risk loving for losses. So, any switching of risk attitudes cannot be caused by the payoff function.

Table 3.22 details the expected utility of Anna and Alan if they go to court. It also details their utility from settling out of court with a payment equivalent to expected value. We can see that Anna's utility is higher from going to court if the probability of a guilty verdict is low. Alan's utility is higher from going to court if the probability of a guilty verdict is high. We get the predicted fourfold pattern of risk attitudes.

3.9.2 Frivolous litigation

The switching of risk attitudes due to an overweighting of small probabilities means that we can expect very different outcomes in a case depending on the probability of a guilty verdict. If the probability of a guilty verdict is moderate to high, then Anna is more willing to settle out of court than Alan. So, the defense has more bargaining power. Any settlement is likely to be for less than expected value. For example, if $p = 0.5$, the expected value of going to court is \$2,500, but Anna may be willing to settle out of court for, say, \$2,000. Of course, the amount for which Anna is willing to settle may be too much for Alan and so they take their chances in court. The point, though, is that, if they reach a settlement, it will be favorable to Alan.

If the probability of a guilty verdict is low, then Alan is more willing to settle out of court. The prosecution has more bargaining power. Any settlement is likely to be for more than expected value. For example, if $p = 0.05$, the expected value of going to court is \$250, but Alan may be willing to settle out of court for, say, \$400. Again, Anna and Alan may still take their chances in court. But this time, if they reach a settlement, it will be favorable to Anna.

A study by Fobian and Christensen-Szalanski (1993) illustrates this fourfold pattern of risk attitudes in action. They asked subjects to consider genuine medical liability cases. Subjects were also given advice 'from their lawyer' on the probability of winning the case and the amount of money they would win. The probability was either 0.1 or 0.9 and the amount was either \$100,000 or \$1 million. Figure 3.23 details the average amount of money that the prosecution and defense were willing to accept and pay to settle out of court. Focus first on the case where

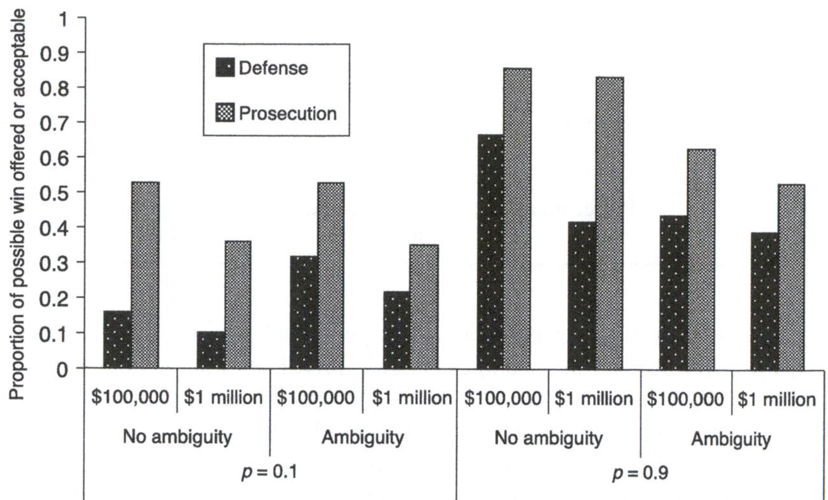

Figure 3.23 The amount of money the defense was willing to offer and the prosecution was willing to accept for settling out of court (as a proportion of the claim amount).

Source: Fobian and Christensen-Szalanski (1993).

$p = 0.1$ and there is no ambiguity. We see that the defense was willing to pay just over expected value; they were risk averse. The prosecution, by contrast, demanded way over expected value; they were risk loving. Consider now the case where $p = 0.9$. This time the defense was willing to pay a lot less than expected value; they were risk loving. The prosecution was willing to settle for slightly less than expected value; they were risk averse.

These results perfectly illustrate the fourfold pattern of risk attitudes. They also illustrate the difficulty for parties to reach agreement. An out-of-court settlement is only possible if the defense offers more than the prosecution will accept. We can see in Figure 3.23 that the two parties are often a long way from agreement! Ambiguity meant the lawyer (while still predicting $p = 0.1$ or 0.9) expressed a lack of confidence in his belief about the probability of winning because of uncertainties with the case. This brought the claims a bit closer together, which is important, because ambiguity is almost inevitable in legal cases. Is it, however, good news that agreement is more likely?

Table 3.23 summarizes what we have seen so far. The fourfold pattern of risk attitudes lets us make sense of out-of-court settlements. A more normative question is whether we should use this knowledge to advocate reform of the legal system. You might argue that if Anna and Alan reach an out-of-court settlement then they do so voluntarily and so we should not intervene. Things, however, are not necessarily so simple. A genuine case is likely to fit the category of moderate to high probability of a guilty verdict and we see that the prosecution

Table 3.23 A summary of outcomes of litigation

Probability of a guilty verdict	*Best bargaining position*	*If settle out of court*	*Implication*
Moderate to high	Defense	Less than expected value	In genuine cases the victim gets less than a fair amount.
Low	Prosecution	More than expected value	Frivolous litigation is encouraged.

will settle for less than expected value. So, people who genuinely are discriminated against will walk away short-changed. Frivolous, non-genuine cases are likely to fit the category of low probability and we see that the prosecution gets more than expected value. So, people who make up claims walk away with money! In both cases one can motivate intervention, and it is clear from Figure 3.23 that ambiguity may make matters worse.

The fourfold pattern of risk attitudes not only, therefore, gives us a means to understand out-of-court settlements, it also gives us a mandate for policy change. Frivolous litigation, for instance, is particularly costly for the court system. If we know why it happens, then we are in a better position to do something about it. In Chapter eleven we shall look in detail at how framing can be used as a policy tool to change behavior. In this instance a different frame may avoid the overweighting of small probabilities, or turn perceived losses into gains. This almost certainly means fighting against a 'compensation culture' that encourages a perception of easy money to be made from frivolous claims. In Chapter five we shall see the difficulties of overcoming such biased beliefs.

3.10 Further reading

The survey paper by Starmer (2000) is a great place to start. Much of the material in this chapter owes its origins to the work of Robert Sugden and co-authors. Some of the relevant papers are Loomes and Sugden (1982, 1983, 1986), Loomes *et al.* (1991) and Schmidt *et al.* (2008). Most of the rest of the material owes its origins to Kahneman and Tversky, including their 1979 and 1992 papers I mentioned earlier (much of the suggested reading for Chapter two is relevant here as well). I also want to mention Rabin (2000), who first appreciated the issues in section 3.1.2, and on the issue of measuring risk aversion the paper by Holt and Laury (2002) is a useful reference. For more on tax evasion see the review articles by Alm (2012) and Hashimzade *et al.* (2013)

3.11 Review questions

3.1 Explain why the indifference curves in a probability triangle diagram are straight lines if preferences satisfy expected utility theory. [Hint: we can write the expected utility of a prospect as $U(x) = p^1u(x^1) + (1 - p^2 - p^3)u(x^2) + p^3u(x^3)$.]

3.2 Show why it is inconsistent with expected utility that most people choose prospect F over E, and prospect G over H, when the prospects are as in Table 3.5.

3.3 Using the model of disappointment with $\theta = 0.002$, consider the following three prospects: A = (0.5, \$2,400; 0.5, \$0), B = (0.7, \$2,400; 0.3; \$0), and C = (0.3, \$2,400; 0.7; \$0). Work out the utility of each prospect and comment on the result.

3.4 Using prospect theory, say whether a person would prefer prospect I or prospects J to N from Table 3.6.

3.5 In 1963 Paul Samuelson wrote about a colleague who said that he would turn down the prospect (0.5, −\$100; 0.5, \$200) but would accept 100 such prospects. Suppose that his utility function is $u(x) = x - w$ if $x \geq w$ and $u(x) = -2.5(w - x)$ if $w > x$ where w is his wealth. Show why he turned down the prospect. Now, imagine two prospects will be done in turn and he will adjust his wealth level after each prospect. Show that he should turn down the two prospects. Finally, imagine that he only adjusts his wealth level after seeing the outcome of both prospects. Should he take on the two prospects? Should he take on 100 prospects?

3.6 What do you think is the relevant reference point of a prospect? How might the certainty effect be related to reference dependence?

3.7 One set of prospects considered by Loomes *et al.* (1991) was the following: A = (0, \$10; 0.6, \$3), B = (0.7, \$7.50; 0.3, \$1), and C = (1, \$5). What would you choose between A and B, B and C, and A and C? How can regret theory help us explain choices in this case?

3.8 What would happen to the equity premium if investors were less loss averse or the evaluation period was longer? How often should you evaluate your investments?

3.9 I argued in section 3.7 that, applying the standard formulation of prospect theory, with $\lambda = 2.25$, $\beta = 0.88$, and $\gamma = 0.61$, a person would pay \$110 for an extra deductible of \$500 if the claim rate was 4 percent. How much would a person be willing to pay to reduce the deductible by \$165 if the claim rate is 25 percent? Comment on the numbers in Table 3.18.

3.10 Is expected utility theory of any practical revelance?

3.11 Why may a person's decision to evade taxes be influenced by what his friends and colleagues are doing?

3.12 Carefully explain why the overweighting of low probabilities can lead to tax evasion and frivolous litigation.

3.13 In many court cases there is no clear-cut defense and prosecution (e.g. divorce disputes). What does the fourfold pattern of risk attitudes predict in such cases?

4 Choosing when to act

The only way to get rid of a temptation is to yield to it.
I can resist everything except temptation.

Oscar Wilde

Time is important in most economic decisions because the choices we make will have future consequences. Should a person do the shopping today, or tomorrow? Should she buy a new TV, or save for retirement? Should she look for a new job? Should she go to university and get a qualification? Should she eat healthily and join a gym? The answer to all these questions involves weighing future benefits and costs with present benefits and costs. We need to think about how people do that, and that's the focus of this chapter.

4.1 Exponential discounting

To illustrate some of the issues, consider Maria planning when to do her homework. The homework was set on Friday and must be handed in on Monday morning. She can do it on Friday, Saturday, Sunday, or Monday. Table 4.1 gives her day-by-day utility, depending on when she does the homework. For example, if she does it on Friday she pays a cost on Friday, gets to enjoy Saturday and Sunday, and on Monday gets to know how well she did. Doing the homework on a weekend is more costly but also means she does it better. When should Maria do the homework?

Clearly she has to weigh up the benefits and costs of doing the homework on each possible day. Before we see how she might do this, it is worth introducing some general notation for thinking about choice over time. We can think of time as running from period one to period T. In the example, period one is Friday and period $T = 4$ is Monday. Maria needs to plan what she will do in each period between now and T, and, given a plan, she can work out what her utility will be in each period. We can think of the utility in a period as determined by the same utility function that we came across in Chapters two and three, and I will use u_t to denote the utility in period t. (Just to clarify, in some parts of the book I have used u_i to denote the utility of person i, but not in this chapter.) In the example, a plan

Table 4.1 The day-by-day utility for Maria of doing her homework on different days

Plan	*Utility on*			
	Friday	*Saturday*	*Sunday*	*Monday*
Do it Friday	−5	5	10	4
Do it Saturday	0	−5	10	10
Do it Sunday	0	5	−5	10
Do it Monday	0	5	10	−5

is when to do the homework, and we see, for example, that the utility in period three is $u_3 = 10$ if Maria plans to do the homework on Friday.

To try and model Maria's choice we can use an **inter-temporal utility function** that combines utility from each period to one measure of overall utility. The simplest way to do this would be to just add together the utility from each time period. Generally, however, she might want to **discount**, that is, give less weight to future utility. This suggests a **utility function with exponential discounting**. The inter-temporal utility of getting u_1 in period 1, u_2 in period 2, and so on is then:

$$u^T(u_1, u_2, \ldots, u_T) = u_1 + \delta u_2 + \delta^2 u_3 + \ldots, +\delta^{T-1} u_T = \sum_{t=1}^{T} \delta^{t-1} u_t \qquad (4.1)$$

where δ is a number called the **discount factor**. Inter-temporal utility is, therefore, a simple weighted sum of the utility in each period. If $\delta < 1$ then less weight is given to the utility in a period the further away that period is. So, the smaller is δ, the more future utility is discounted.

If we know the utility in each period of each plan then we can work out the inter-temporal utility of each plan. A prediction would be that Maria should choose the plan with highest inter-temporal utility. Table 4.2 illustrates what happens when we do this for three different discount factors. We can see that, the higher is δ, the more impatient Maria becomes. If $\delta = 1$, she is willing to sacrifice an enjoyable Saturday in order to get a higher mark on Monday. If $\delta = 0.7$, she is more impatient to enjoy herself and does not do the homework until Monday.

Table 4.2 The inter-temporal utility of each plan for three different discount factors

Plan	*Inter-temporal utility*		
	$\delta = 1$	$\delta = 0.9$	$\delta = 0.7$
Do it Friday	14	10.5	4.7
Do it Saturday	15	10.9	4.8
Do it Sunday	10	7.7	4.5
Do it Monday	10	9.0	6.7

Exponential discounting is a very simple way to model choice over time. All we need to know is the discount factor, and then we can easily predict choice. For that reason exponential discounting is by far the most common way used in economics to model choice over time. What we need to do is ask whether it is sophisticated enough to capture all the things we observe. Before we do that, it is important that we fully understand what the model and, in particular, the discount factor, implies, and so there are a couple of things I want to mention.

The first thing I want you to think about is the units of measurement: a period and utility. Maria's choice is going to have a stream of future consequences, and we somehow need to measure those consequences. What I have done is split the future into days and say what her utility will be on each day, but there is inevitably something arbitrary about how we split things up. For instance, I could have split into hours and said what her utility will be in each hour, or seconds, etc. One sensible approach is to split things up as Maria perceives them, and so, if she thinks in terms of what will happen each day, then that is how we should split things. How Maria perceives things will, however, likely depend on the context. This is already enough to suggest important context effects.

The second thing I want to clarify is the distinction between discount factor and discount rate. If the **discount factor** is 0.8, then '\$10 worth of utility' next period is equivalent to \$8 today. More generally, \$10 next period is equivalent to δ\$10 today. The smaller the discount factor, the more impatient Maria is. Given a discount factor δ, we can work out a **discount rate** ρ using the relation:

$$\delta = \frac{1}{1+\rho} \quad or \quad \rho = \frac{1-\delta}{\delta}.$$

For example, if the discount factor is 0.8, then the discount rate is 0.25. In interpretation a discount rate of 0.25 means Maria would require an interest rate of 25 percent to delay until next period. So, instead of \$8 today she would want 1.25 × \$8 = \$10 next period. The higher the discount rate, the more impatient she is. It does not matter whether we use discount rate or discount factor, and so to be consistent I will use discount factor throughout this book. If you follow up the further reading, however, expect many to use the term discount rate. [Extra] If you are wondering why the name 'exponential discounting': in continuous time, equation (4.1) becomes:

$$u^T = \int_O^T e^{-\rho t} u_t$$

where ρ is the discount rate.

4.1.1 The discount factor

To better understand exponential discounting we need to see what values for the discount factor seem most appropriate. In the experimental lab the discount factor can be estimated by giving subjects questions of the form: 'Would you prefer $100 today or $150 in a year's time?' If they answer $100 today then the discount factor is smaller than 0.66 (but see Review question 4.1!). I will look next at a study by Benzion and co-authors (1989), where subjects were asked questions a bit like this. More precisely, subjects were asked questions of the four basic types given below. As you look through these questions, please think about what your answer would be.

- **Postpone receipt**: You have just earned $200 but have the possibility to delay receiving it by one year. How much money would you need to get after a year in order to want to delay payment?
- **Postpone payment**: You need to pay back a debt of $200 but have the possibility to delay payment by one year. How much money would you be willing to pay back after a year if payment is delayed?
- **Expedite receipt**: You will get $200 in one year but have the chance to receive the money immediately. How much money would you accept now rather than have to wait a year?
- **Expedite payment**: You need to pay back a debt of $200 in one year but can pay it now. How much would you be willing to pay now rather than pay off the debt after one year?

In specific questions the time period was changed from six months to four years and the amount of money from $40 to $5,000. Figure 4.1 summarizes the implied annual discount factor that we get from subjects' responses to each question. There is a lot to look at in Figure 4.1. One thing, however, stands out immediately and that's that the discount factor appears to depend a lot on context. We can see this in how the discount factor varies a lot depending on the length of time, amount of money, payment versus receipt, and expedite versus postpone.

In looking in a little more detail at Figure 4.1 I want to point out five things. First, notice that the discount factor is relatively low, around 0.8–0.9, suggesting that the subjects were relatively impatient. Next, notice that the discount factor is higher, the longer it is necessary to wait, suggesting **short-term impatience**. For example, subjects wanted on average almost as much compensation to postpone receipt by six months as to postpone by four years. A third thing to note is that the larger the sum of money, the larger the estimated discount factor, suggesting people are more patient for larger amounts. This is called the **absolute magnitude effect**.

Next I want to compare payment versus receipt and loss versus gain. If you look from top to bottom in Figure 4.1, then you can see a **gain-loss asymmetry** where the estimated discount factor is smaller for gains than for losses. For example, the discount factor is higher in the case of postponing payment (which would require a loss of money) than for postponing receipt (which would involve a gain of money). Similarly, the discount factor is higher in the case of expediting receipt (which would require a loss of money) than for expediting payment (which would involve a gain of money). This is consistent with loss aversion because it suggests that subjects were reluctant to lose money in order to postpone or expedite.

The final thing I want you to do is compare postponing versus expediting. If you look from left to right in Figure 4.1 then you can see a **delay-speed-up asymmetry** where the estimated discount factor is higher to postpone than to expedite payment, and higher to expedite than postpone receipt. This is because subjects were willing to pay relatively less money to postpone a payment than they demanded to expedite payment. Similarly, they demanded relatively more to postpone receipt than they were willing to pay to expedite receipt.

To really work well, exponential discounting requires that the discount factor should not change depending on context. In other words, in Figure 4.1 we should see overlaying horizontal lines all at the same discount factor. We clearly do not, and this is not good news for anyone wanting to use exponential discounting. By now, however, you should be getting used to the idea that context matters. Indeed, the gain-loss asymmetry is consistent with loss aversion, and the delay-speed-up asymmetry is suggestive of mental accounting.

The existence of such large context effects does not mean that exponential discounting is necessarily a bad way to model choice. What it does mean is that we have to be very careful in thinking about what the appropriate discount factor should be for a particular situation. There is no such thing as 'Maria's discount

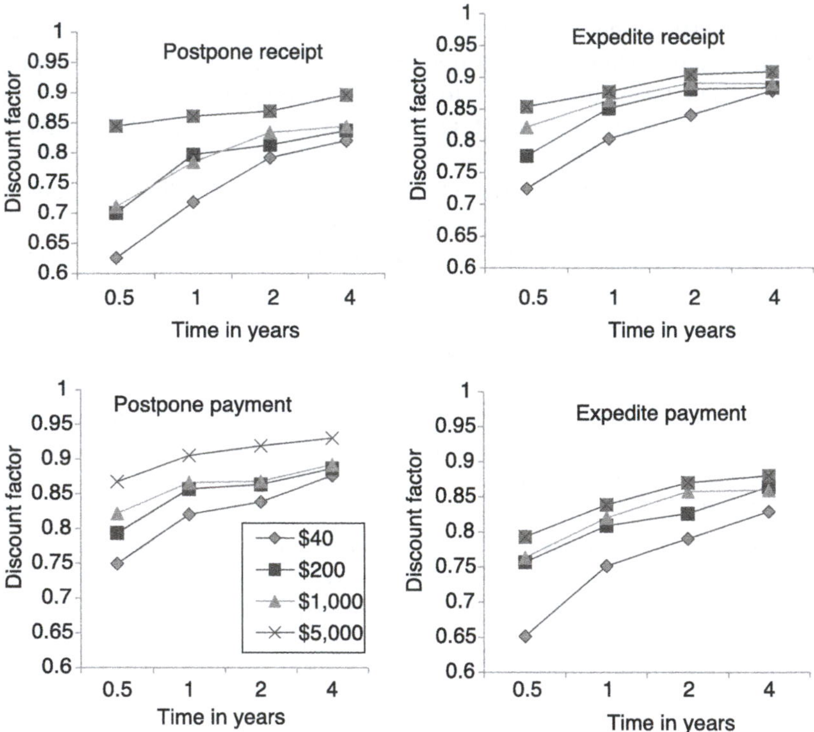

Figure 4.1 Estimated discount factors for four types of choices.

Source: Benzion *et al.* (1989).

factor'. Instead, Maria will likely have different discount factors for different things. For example, she might be impatient to repay \$10 she borrowed from one friend, but more patient to get back a CD she lent to another friend. Before we explore the implications of this there is one more important context effect that we have yet to consider.

Research Methods 4.1

Empirical versus lab evidence

Inter-temporal choice is one area where the experimental lab does seem inadequate to answer many of the questions we are interested in, because we want to know how people trade off money over relatively large time periods. How can we create delay over relatively large time periods in the experimental lab? One option is to use hypothetical scenarios, as in the study by Benzion and co-authors. This, however, leads to the objection that subjects are not making real choices. If we do use real choices, then we cannot realistically delay payment beyond a few months, and certainly not years. It is also questionable whether subjects would find delayed payment credible.

This means that empirical studies in which we observe people making choices with long-term trade-offs are very useful. We can illustrate with a study by Warner and Pleeter (2001). In 1992 the US Department of Defense needed to reduce the size of the US military. They offered selected servicemen two possible packages for leaving the military: (i) a lump sum payment of around \$25,000 for privates and NCOs, and \$50,000 for officers; (ii) an annuity that would pay some fraction of current basic pay for twice the length the person had worked for the military.

Serviceman had, therefore, the choice between a one-off payment and deferred payments. For a particular serviceman it is possible to work out the discount factor such that the serviceman should be indifferent between the two options. Formally, we find the δ^* such that:

$$LS(1-T_{LS}) = \sum_{t=1}^{2YOS} \delta^{*t-1} A(1-T_A)$$

where LS is the lump sum payment, A the annuity payment, YOS the years of service, and T the respective tax rates. A serviceman should choose the lump sum payment if and only if they are more impatient than is implied by δ^*, i.e. only if their discount factor is $\delta < \delta^*$. With data on what a person chose and by calculating δ^*, we can therefore estimate a person's discount factor. This is what Warner and Pleeter do. Estimates of the mean discount factor were around 0.85.

The estimate of 0.85 is consistent with what we see in Figure 4.1, which provides reassurance that the numbers obtained from the study by Benzion and co-authors are not unrealistic. I think this nicely illustrates how empirical studies can complement experimental studies. Experimental studies allow us to investigate relatively easily the comparative statics of changing things like the amount of money and time frame. This is simply not possible with empirical studies because events such as the US military downsizing are rare and only give a point estimate of the discount factor. Empirical studies do, though, serve as a useful check that results obtained in the lab are meaningful.

4.1.2 The utility of sequences

Imagine now that instead of asking someone whether they would prefer $100 today or $150 in a year's time, we ask them whether they would prefer $100 today and $150 in a year's time, or $150 today and $100 in a year's time. This gets us thinking how people interpret **sequences** of events. To illustrate how people tend to respond to such questions, I will look at how subjects answered two questions asked in a study by Loewenstein and Prelec (1993).

In the first question people were asked to imagine two planned trips to a city they once lived in but do not plan to visit again after these two trips. During one trip they need to visit an aunt they do not like, and in the other visit friends they do like. Those asked were given three scenarios for when the trips might be (e.g. one this weekend and the other in 26 weeks) and asked to say who they would rather visit first. The results are in Figure 4.2.

One thing to pick out from Figure 4.2 is a **preference for an improving sequence** in which subjects visit the aunt first and then friends later. This might seem natural, but is the opposite of what exponential discounting would predict. If someone uses exponential discounting, with a discount factor less than one, then they would maximize their inter-temporal utility by visiting the friends first because they are impatient for higher utility. This impatience does become apparent when the gap between the trips is made bigger because then more subjects wanted to visit friends first.

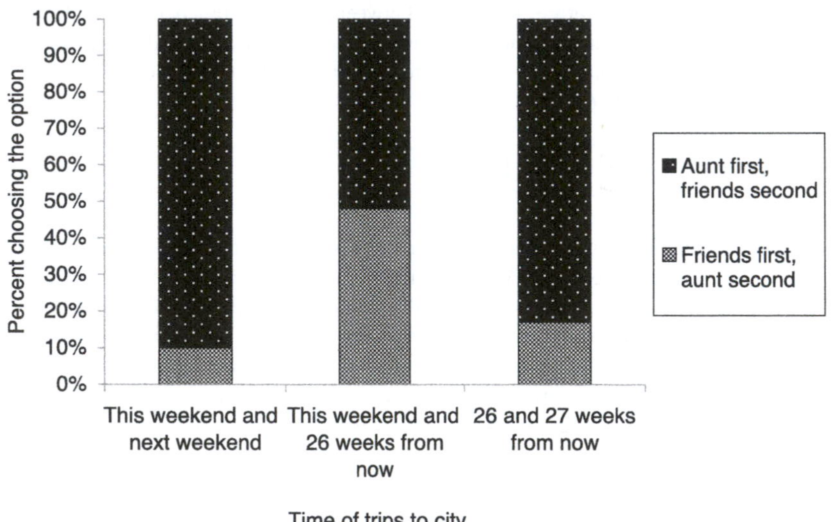

Figure 4.2 Choice of when to visit an aunt and friends. If the two trips were close together, most subjects chose to visit the aunt first. If the two trips were far apart, more subjects chose to visit friends first.

Source: Loewenstein and Prelec (1993).

In the second question I want to look at people who were asked to choose when over the next three weeks they would like to eat out at restaurants called Fancy French and Fancy Lobster. The results are in Table 4.3. When asked to choose between options A and B, we see the same preference for an improving sequence that we saw for the previous question. When asked to choose between options C and D, however, many subjects preferred to spread the good events over the sequence. Again, this might seem natural, but is not consistent with exponential discounting. This switch in choices should not happen because the utility in period three should not affect the optimal choice in periods one and two. It clearly may do.

Overall, therefore, we see a preference for improving sequences coupled with a preference for spreading events evenly throughout the sequence. None of this seems consistent with exponential discounting. The only way to make it consistent is to distinguish sequences from disjoint events. This can work. For instance, we could say that the relevant time period for deciding when to visit the aunt and friends is one month. If, therefore, the two trips are consecutive weekends they should be bundled together and seen as a sequence, while if they are 26 weeks away they should be seen as disjoint events and discounted. Table 4.4 illustrates how this might work to explain what we see in Figure 4.2.

Table 4.3 Choice of when to eat at a restaurant. When asked to choose between options A and B, most subjects prefer to delay eating at Fancy French restaurant. When asked to choose between options C and D, most subjects prefer not to delay eating at Fancy French restaurant

Option	*This weekend*	*Next weekend*	*Two weekends away*	*Choices (%)*
A	Fancy French	Eat at home	Eat at home	16
B	Eat at home	Fancy French	Eat at home	84
C	Fancy French	Eat at home	Fancy Lobster	54
D	Eat at home	Fancy French	Fancy Lobster	46

Source: Loewenstein and Prelec (1993).

Table 4.4 Maria deciding when to visit an aunt and friends. Events in weeks one to four and weeks 24 to 28 are bundled together as a sequence. Events in weeks 24 to 28 are seen as disjoint from those in weeks one to four and discounted with a factor of 0.8

Events		*Inter-temporal utility*
Weeks 1–4	*Weeks 24–28*	
Visit aunt then friends		10
Visit friends then aunt		5
Visit aunt		0
Visit friends		15
Visit aunt	Visit friends	12
Visit friends	Visit aunt	15
	Visit aunt then friends	8
	Visit friends then aunt	4

This approach works perfectly if we can distinguish a length of time and say that events happening over a shorter period of time are a sequence and everything happening over a larger period of time are separate events. In general, however, this is not going to be easy, because we need to know how the person perceives things. Does Maria perceive the events before she hands in her homework as separate, or a sequence? Will she be thinking, 'Today I want to play sport so other things can wait till tomorrow', or 'If I do my homework today, then tomorrow I can go out and play sport'? It will likely affect her choice, but it is not obvious how she might think. There is certainly no simple rule to say when something is a sequence or not. It is more likely to depend on the context.

Clearly, context will matter in thinking about and modeling inter-temporal choice. What I want to do now is question what the implications of this may be, and whether we need a different model to that of exponential discounting in order to capture it.

4.2 Hyperbolic discounting

We clearly see in Figure 4.1 that the discount factor is larger for longer time intervals. This means that people are impatient over the short term but more patient over the long term. To give another example, in a study by Thaler (1981), subjects were asked the amount of money they would require in one month, one year or ten years to make them indifferent to receiving $15 now. The average responses of $20, $50, and $100 seem entirely sensible, but imply an annual discount factor of 0.22, 0.45, and 0.84 respectively. Relatively speaking, therefore, subjects were asking a lot to wait one month but not very much to wait ten years. Such decreasing impatience is called **hyperbolic discounting**.

One way to capture hyperbolic discounting is to modify the model of exponential discounting and allow for different discount factors in different periods. In equation (4.1) we assume exponential discounting where payment in t time periods from now is discounted by an amount:

$$D(t) = \delta^{t-1}.$$

One of many possible alternatives is to assume:

$$D(t) = \frac{1}{1-\alpha(t-1)} \tag{4.2}$$

where α is a parameter that can capture changes in the discount factor over time. I will call this a **model of hyperbolic discounting**. In either case equation (4.1) is generalized to:

$$U^T(x_1, x_2, \ldots, x_T) = \sum_{t=1}^{T} D(t)\, x_t. \tag{4.3}$$

To illustrate, Figure 4.3 plots $D(t)$ and the annualized discount factor assuming exponential discounting with factor $\delta = 0.85$ and hyperbolic discounting with $\alpha = 0.25$. We see that hyperbolic discounting does give a higher discount factor for longer periods and looks a bit more like what we saw in Figure 4.1.

We are, therefore, able to accommodate a changing discount factor without too much change to a standard exponential discounting model. But are we really capturing decreasing impatience? To explain why we might not be, consider the following set of choices:

> Do you want \$100 today or \$110 tomorrow?
>
> Do you want \$100 in 30 days or \$110 in 31 days?

When asked such questions, many people choose the \$100 today and \$110 in 31 days. This can be consistent with a model of hyperbolic discounting. The

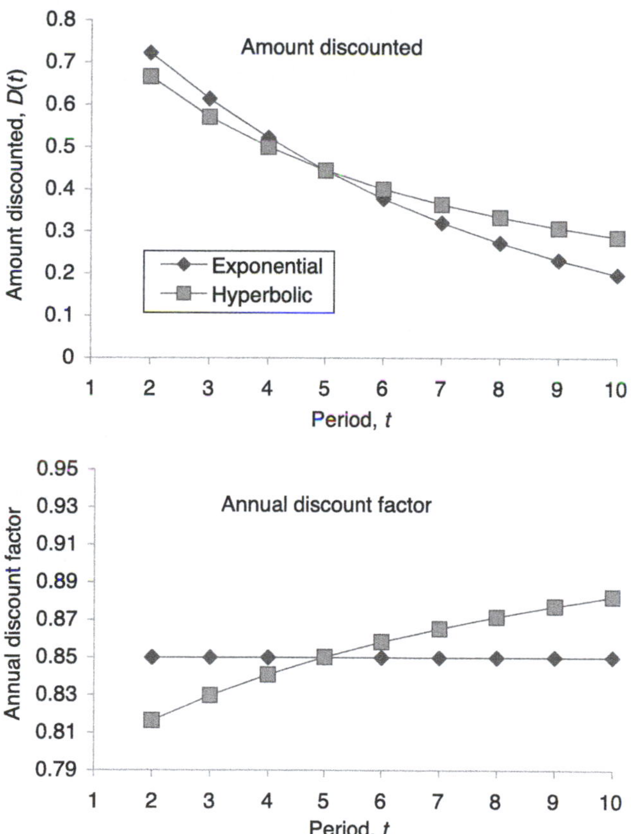

Figure 4.3 Hyperbolic discounting compared to exponential discounting. With hyperbolic discounting, the discount factor is lower for shorter time periods.

potential problem comes if we ask the same question after 30 days and get the same answer. That is, suppose Maria says she would prefer \$110 in 31 days to \$100 in 30 days, but then after 30 days says that she prefers \$100 today to \$110 tomorrow. This is not consistent with a model of hyperbolic discounting, because the model requires choices to be consistent over time. Maria should not change her mind. If she says that she prefers \$110 in 31 days' time to \$100 today, then after 30 days she should still prefer \$110 tomorrow to \$100 today.

[Extra] To illustrate this with some numbers, let me first explain why it can be consistent with a model of hyperbolic discounting to choose the \$100 today and \$110 in 31 days' time. Suppose the time period is a day and $D(2) = 0.9$, $D(30) = 0.85$, and $D(31) = 0.84$. Then \$110 tomorrow is worth \$99 today, \$100 in 30 days is worth \$85 today, and \$110 in 31 days is worth \$92.4 today, so it makes sense to choose \$100 today and \$110 in 31 days' time. What happens after 30 days? Given that $D(30) = 0.85$ and $D(31) = 0.84$ we should, after 30 days, calculate a revised discount factor of $D(2) = 0.99$. With this value of $D(2)$ it is optimal to choose the \$110 tomorrow rather than \$100 today.

It seems plausible that someone who chooses the \$100 today and \$110 in 31 days might also choose the \$100 today and \$110 in 31 days when asked 30 days later. We need, therefore, a different model to that of hyperbolic discounting.

4.2.1 Quasi-hyperbolic discounting

With exponential and hyperbolic discounting, a time period should be interpreted as a specific date. For instance, in the homework example we thought of period one as Friday and period four as Monday. If today is Friday then the discount factors $D(t)$ are specific to that day, and on Saturday we need to update them. For example, if $D(2) = 0.9$ and $D(3) = 0.9$ on Friday, then Maria does not discount between Saturday and Sunday, and on Saturday we should get $D(2) = 1$. Consequently, in a model of hyperbolic discounting, decreasing impatience means that a person gets less impatient as they get older, even if only by a few days.

An alternative interpretation of decreasing impatience is that a person is more impatient for short-term gains relative to long-term gains, and this has nothing to do with age. We can capture this by interpreting $D(2) = 0.9$ and $D(3) = 0.9$ as constant over time and showing how much future amounts are discounted relative to today. So, if today is Friday, then $D(2) = 0.9$, and if today is Saturday, then $D(2) = 0.9$. In this interpretation Maria chooses the \$100 today because she is always impatient for a possible immediate gain. The distinction is illustrated in Figure 4.4.

If it makes more sense to think of the discount factor as relative to today rather than calendar time, we say that there are **present-biased preferences**. In this case Maria does not postpone her homework today, or choose the \$100 today, because today is Friday, 1 May and on Friday, 1 May she is impatient; she is always impatient for immediate gains.

To model present biased preferences we can reuse equation (4.2) but now interpret t as how many time periods from today rather than a specific point in

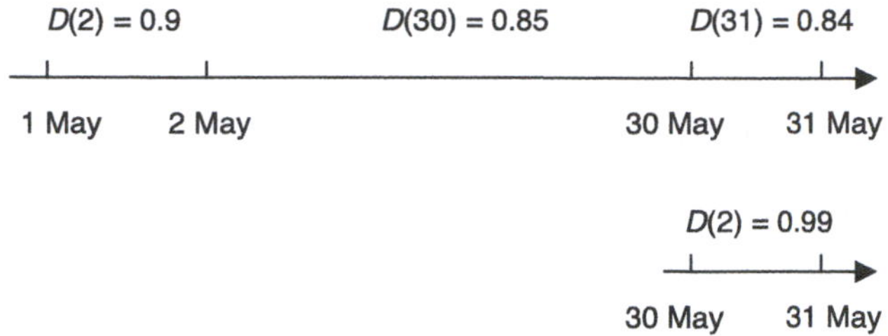

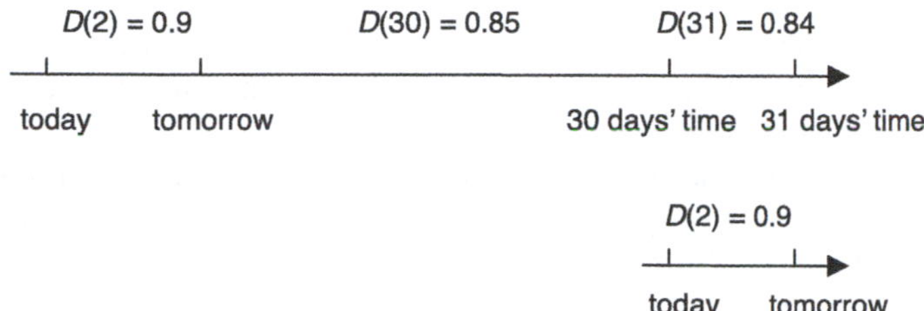

Figure 4.4 The difference between time-consistent and present-biased preferences. In the model of hyperbolic discounting, period refers to a specific moment of calendar time. In the model of quasi-hyperbolic discounting, period refers to a delay from now.

time. But, we still need to capture decreasing impatience. A simple way to do this is to use a model of **quasi-hyperbolic discounting** or **(β,δ) preferences** where:

$$U^T(x_1, x_2, \ldots, x_T) = x_1 + \beta \sum_{t=2}^{T} \delta^{t-1} x_t \quad (4.4)$$

and where β is some number between zero and one. The β is crucial here because it measures **present bias**. If $\beta = 1$, then there is no bias, and equation (4.4) is equivalent to (4.1). If $\beta < 1$, then more weight is given to today than to the future. This means that there is a present bias and decreasing impatience. For instance, if $\beta = 0.7$ and $\delta = 0.99$, then \$110 in 31 days is always preferred to \$100 in 30 days, but \$100 today is always preferred to \$110 tomorrow.

To see how (β, δ) preferences work, we can return to the example of Maria deciding when to do her homework. Table 4.5 summarizes the payoffs that she gets if she does or does not have a present bias. First, look at what happens if $\beta = 1$ and so she does not have a present bias. On Friday, she should plan to do her homework on Saturday, and on Saturday, she also thinks this way, and so would do the homework. The same is true when $\beta = 0.9$. Next, look at what happens if

Table 4.5 Quasi-hyperbolic discounting in the homework example. If the present bias is high, Maria plans to do the homework on Saturday, but on Saturday would rather do it on Monday

	$\beta = 1, \delta = 0.9$		$\beta = 0.9, \delta = 0.9$		$\beta = 0.8, \delta = 0.9$	
Plan	*On Friday*	*Saturday*	*On Friday*	*Saturday*	*On Friday*	*Saturday*
Do it Friday	10.5	—	9.0	—	7.4	—
Saturday	10.9	12.1	9.8	10.4	8.7	8.7
Do it Sunday	7.7	8.6	7.0	8.2	6.2	7.9
Monday	9.0	10.0	8.1	9.5	7.2	9.0

$\beta = 0.8$ and so the present bias is relatively large. On Friday she would plan to do the homework on Saturday. The interesting thing is that, when Saturday comes, she would rather do it on Monday.

We say that there is a **time inconsistency** if someone plans to do something in the future but subsequently changes her mind. Planning to do the homework on Saturday but then on Saturday deciding to do it on Monday, and planning to wait an extra day for $110 but when the time comes taking the $100, are examples of time inconsistency. There cannot be time inconsistency in a model of exponential or hyperbolic discounting, but there can be in a model of quasi-hyperbolic discounting. Time inconsistency is potentially very important in terms of welfare and policy because it suggests that people plan to do something but then end up doing something else. I am, therefore, going to spend some time on the issue in Chapters ten and eleven when we look at welfare and policy. At this point I want to show you how time inconsistency can have important consequences for behavior.

4.2.2 The consequences of time inconsistency

The consequences of time inconsistency will depend on whether people know they are time inconsistent or not. For example, does Maria realize on Friday that, if she plans to do the homework on Saturday, when Saturday comes she might think differently? This could clearly be important in deciding what she does do on the Friday.

We say that someone is **naïve** if they are unaware that they have present-biased preferences. In this case, Maria would plan on Friday to do the homework on Saturday and not expect to think differently on Saturday. By contrast, we say that someone is **sophisticated** if they know that they have present-biased preferences. In this case Maria will realize on Friday that if she leaves the homework until Saturday she will probably end up doing it on Monday.

I'll look first at what happens if Maria is naïve. It's easiest to start with cases where the costs of an activity precede the benefits, as in the homework example.

We saw in the example that on Friday Maria will expect to do the homework on Saturday, but on Saturday might decide to do it on Monday. This means that she can end up doing the homework later than she expected and later than she would have done without a present bias. To delay doing something in this way is called **procrastination**. Maria procrastinates because she puts off doing the costly thing. What happens if the benefits come before the costs?

To help illustrate, I will use a second example. Imagine it costs $10 to go to the movies and Maria only has $11 spending money. There are movies on Friday, Saturday, and Sunday. Table 4.6 shows that she will prefer the movie on Sunday to that on Saturday and that on Saturday to that on Friday. Table 4.7 summarizes her inter-temporal utility (these tables can be compared to 4.1 and 4.5). If Maria has time-consistent preferences then she would plan to go to the movie on Sunday. If she has present-biased preferences, then on Friday she would to plan to go on Sunday, but on Saturday would change her mind and go that day. Again we see a time inconsistency. The difference is that this time Maria does something earlier than she expected and earlier than she would have done with no present bias. To bring forward something in this way we can call to **preproperate**.

In both the homework and the movie example, Maria is impatient for benefits. In the homework example this causes her to put off something that is costly. In the movie example it causes her to do early something that is pleasurable. Will someone who is sophisticated and knows they are time inconsistent avoid such problems? The answer is a bit surprising.

The surprise is not in the homework example. If Maria knows that on Saturday she will delay until Monday, then on Friday she knows the real choice is between

Table 4.6 Payoffs from Maria going to watch a movie

	Payoff on		
Plan	*Friday*	*Saturday*	*Sunday*
Go on Friday	5	0	0
Go on Saturday	0	6	0
Go on Sunday	0	0	8

Table 4.7 Inter-temporal utility in the movie example with time-consistent and present-biased preferences

	$\beta = 1, \delta = 0.9$		$\beta = 0.8, \delta = 0.9$	
Plan	*On Friday*	*On Saturday*	*On Friday*	*On Saturday*
Go on Friday	5.0	—	5.0	—
Go on Saturday	5.4	6.0	4.3	6.0
Go on Sunday	6.5	7.2	5.2	5.8

doing her homework now, giving utility 7.4, or on Monday, giving utility 7.2. So, she will do the homework on Friday and behave as if time consistent. Being sophisticated thus allows Maria to avoid any time inconsistency. So far, so good. But what about the movie example? In this case Maria knows that if she does not go on Friday she will go on Saturday. On Friday she therefore knows that the real choice is between going today or tomorrow. She will go today. Being sophisticated, therefore, means that Maria preproperates more than if she was naïve. She knows that she will not be able to resist going to the movies and so goes even earlier!

Table 4.8 summarizes the choices made. We see that, in the case of delayed benefits, sophistication helps overcome the problems associated with present bias, but in the case of delayed costs it makes things worse. It is not obvious what is better or worse in terms of utility because it is not clear whether to take into account the present bias or not. What we do see, however, is that a present bias has important implications for choice, even if someone is sophisticated.

The movie example shows that being sophisticated can make things worse because Maria anticipates her future present bias. This, however, misses part of the story. That is because someone who is sophisticated may use **commitment** to constrain her future choice. For instance, Maria could pre-order her movie ticket on Friday for Sunday. She would be willing to pay to do such a thing because it means she is committed to making the best choice. If she was naïve, she would see no need to do so. Someone who is sophisticated will thus be looking for ways that they can commit and avoid future temptation.

4.2.3 Temptation and self-control

The model of quasi-hyperbolic discounting is a nice simple model that has allowed us to capture important aspects of inter-temporal choice. One thing that it does not capture so well is the potential benefits of commitment. An approach suggested by Gul and Pesendorfer (2001) provides us with a more elegant way to capture this. To illustrate how it works I will continue the homework example.

On Saturday Maria can either do the homework or play sport. What I want you to imagine now is the possibility that on Friday Maria can commit to what she will do on Saturday. So, she can commit to doing the homework or to playing sport by,

Table 4.8 A summary of the two examples: choice and utility (calculated as inter-temporal payoff on Friday with no present bias)

	Delayed benefits (homework)		*Delayed costs (movie)*	
	Choice	*Payoff*	*Choice*	*Payoff*
Time consistent	Saturday	10.9	Sunday	6.5
Sophisticated	Saturday	10.9	Friday	5.0
Naïve	Monday	9.0	Saturday	5.4

for example, arranging things with friends. This means that on Friday Maria has three choices: commit to doing the homework on Saturday, commit to playing sport on Saturday, or not commit and decide what to do on Saturday.

If Maria has time-consistent preferences then the possibility to commit is irrelevant. If she thinks it is best to do the homework on Saturday then she will be indifferent between committing to do the homework on Saturday and not committing, because she will do the homework on Saturday either way. If Maria has present-biased preferences then things are different.

If Maria thinks it is best that she does the homework on Saturday but knows that on Saturday she may not do it, then it may be good for her to commit on the Friday to doing the homework on Saturday. What's interesting is that we can now distinguish two distinct reasons for her to commit. Most obvious is that Maria knows on Saturday she will choose to play sport and wants to stop this happening. Looking back at Table 4.5 this makes sense if $\beta = 0.8$. The second possibility is that Maria knows she would do the homework on Saturday but only after overcoming the temptation to play sport. That is, she would do the homework but only after exercising **self-control**, which is psychologically costly. She may be able to avoid this cost by committing on Friday to do the homework on Saturday. This fits the case where $\beta = 0.9$.

We can formalize this in a simple model. We already have u_2 to measure the utility of Maria on Saturday. If she does her homework, she gets utility $u_2(H) = -5$, and if she plays sport she gets utility $u_2(S) = 5$. We are now going to add to this a cost of temptation. The cost of temptation should reflect Maria's psychological cost of not doing something she might have wanted to do. So, let $m(H)$ denote the **temptation** to do homework and $m(S)$ the temptation to do sport. The **cost of temptation** from doing action a is then calculated as follows:

$$C(a) = m(a) - max_{b=H,S}m(b).$$

For instance, if the temptation to do sport is greater than that of doing homework, then $m(S) \geq m(H)$ and so the cost of temptation from doing the homework is $C(H) = m(H) - m(S)$. This is the psychological cost of doing the homework when Maria would rather be playing sport.

What if we add together Maria's basic utility plus the cost of temptation? Then we get that if she has not committed on Friday to do something on Saturday, her overall utility on Saturday can be of two forms. First, Maria could exercise self-control, and so the payoff from not committing includes the cost of overcoming temptation. We can write this:

$$u_2^m(H,S) = max_{a=H,S}\{u(a) + m(a)\} - max_{b=H,S}\, m(b). \tag{4.5}$$

Or, it could be that Maria has not exercised self-control and so chooses the action that gives highest utility. We can write this:

$$u_2^m(H,S) = max_{a=H,S}u(a) \text{ subject to } m(a) \geq max_{b=H,S}\, m(b). \tag{4.6}$$

We can, therefore, distinguish the two reasons that Maria may want to commit.

Equations (4.5) and (4.6) might look a little over the top for what we need. The neat thing, though, is that, if Maria would want to pre-commit, we can say for certain that her overall utility must be like that in (4.5) or (4.6). More generally, if someone wants to be able to pre-commit then we must be able to represent their preferences with a utility function u and temptation function m like this (see Research Methods 4.2). This means that a desire to pre-commit must come hand in hand with temptation.

Research Methods 4.2

Axioms and behavior

Gul and Pesendorfer analyzed a much more general setting than that which we have discussed here and obtained a stronger result than I have suggested so far. They showed that preferences satisfy four 'intuitive' axioms if and only if preferences can be represented by functions like u, m and u^m. As well as being a beautiful mathematical result, this is also an interesting illustration of the axiomatic approach to modeling choice.

In an axiomatic approach a researcher basically questions what properties of preferences are consistent with a particular way of modeling choice. Gul and Pesendorfer look at four axioms. Informally these are that preferences (i) be complete and transitive, (ii) be continuous, (iii) satisfy independence, in the sense that a third option would not change the choice between two others, and (iv) satisfy a preference for commitment, meaning that if someone would rather they did one action than another, then they prefer to commit to doing that action. Their results show that, if you think a person's preferences satisfy these axioms, then you have to think functions u, m and u^m are a good way to model choice. Similarly, if you think u, m and u^m are a good way to model choice, then you have to think these axioms are reasonable.

The axiomatic approach has a very long history in economics. In principle, it seems entirely consistent with behavioral economics in trying to match plausible assumptions on preferences with observed choices. In reality, something of a divide has emerged between behavioral economics and the axiomatic approach. This is probably because axioms that seemed sensible have not held up to scrutiny in the experimental laboratory, transitivity being one example. The axiomatic approach does, however, give definitive answers about when ways of modeling choice are appropriate and so clearly does have its place, as Gul and Pesendorfer show.

To illustrate, Table 4.9 follows through what Maria's preferences may look like. If there is no present bias, then there is no temptation, and so it is natural to think that $m(S) = m(H) = 0$. It does not matter whether she commits or not. If there is a relatively small present bias, $\beta = 0.9$, then Maria will do the homework on Saturday. If she does not pre-commit, however, she will have a cost of temptation. If $m(S) = 0.5$ and $m(H) = 0$ then by pre-committing to do her homework she can avoid the cost of this temptation and increase the utility she gets on Saturday.

Table 4.9 The utility of Maria on Saturday. The basic utility u^T is the same as in Table 4.5, the temptation is given by m, and the overall utility, taking into account the cost of temptation, is given by u^{T^m}. By committing to the homework, she avoids the cost of temptation when $\beta = 0.9$ and avoids procrastinating when $\beta = 0.8$

	$\beta = 1, \delta = 0.9$			$\beta = 0.9, \delta = 0.9$			$\beta = 0.8, \delta = 0.9$		
	u^T	m	u^{T^m}	u^T	m	u^{T^m}	u^T	m	u^{T^m}
Committed to homework	12.1	0	12.1	10.4	0	10.4	8.7	0	8.7
Committed to sport	10.0	0	10.0	9.5	0.5	9.5	9.0	0.5	9.0
Decide on Saturday	12.1	—	12.1	10.4	—	9.9	9.0	—	9.0

If there is a larger present bias, $\beta = 0.8$, then Maria will delay doing the homework unless she commits to doing it on Saturday. This is motive enough to commit.

This model allows us to nicely capture the benefits of commitment. In particular, it illustrates how someone may make consistent choices yet still desire commitment, in order to avoid the psychological costs of temptation. Altogether,therefore, we now have some useful ways to model decreasing impatience and present bias. We have, however, only addressed one of the issues raised in section 4.1. Now, it is time to consider some of the others.

4.3 Loss aversion and sequences

What I want to do now is look back on things like the delay-speed-up asymmetry and see if we can better understand them. In doing so, I will draw heavily on work by Loewenstein and Prelec (1992, 1993).

4.3.1 Reference dependence

We can begin by applying the idea of reference dependence to inter-temporal choice. This means writing the inter-temporal utility function as:

$$u^T(x_1, x_2, \ldots, x_T) = \sum_{t=1}^{T} D(t)v(x_t - r_t)$$

where $D(t)$ is the discount factor, $v(x)$ is some value function, and r_t is the reference point in period t. We shall not say much about the discount factor because everything we did in section 4.2 is relevant here. Our focus, therefore, will be on the value function.

As we saw in Chapters two and three, the most important thing about the value function is that it measures consumption relative to some reference point. So, instead of thinking of x_t as the payoff in period t we need to think of $x_t - r_t$ as the loss or gain relative to the reference point. This raises familiar questions about what the reference point should be, but we can assume for now that the reference point is current income. What does the value function need to look like for us to capture the behavior I talked about in section 4.1.1?

To answer that question, suppose that Maria is indifferent between getting \$$q$ now rather than \$$y > q$ in some future period t. This means $v(q) = D(t)v(y)$. Recall that the **gain-loss asymmetry** implies that she should be relatively reluctant to postpone payment compared to postponing receipt. So, she should prefer to pay \$$q$ now instead of having to pay \$$y$ in period t. For instance, if she is indifferent between getting \$10 today or \$11 tomorrow, she would prefer to pay \$10 today than \$11 tomorrow. This means $v(-q) > D(t)v(-y)$. The gain-loss asymmetry requires, therefore, that:

$$\frac{v(q)}{v(y)} < \frac{v(-q)}{v(-y)}. \tag{4.7}$$

Recall that the **absolute magnitude effect** means that the larger the amount, the more patient she is. So, Maria should prefer getting \$$\alpha y$ in period t rather than \$$\alpha q$ now, if $\alpha > 1$ captures some proportional increase in the amounts to be paid. This means that $v(\alpha q) < D(t)v(\alpha y)$. The absolute magnitude effect requires, therefore, that:

$$\frac{v(q)}{v(y)} > \frac{v(\alpha q)}{v(\alpha y)}. \tag{4.8}$$

Finally, we come to the **delay-speed-up asymmetry**. Speed-up is naturally thought of as expediting a receipt, in order to get \$$q > 0$ now rather than \$$y > 0$ in some future period t. One can think of the reference level as zero now and \$$y$ in the future. By expediting the receipt Maria loses, therefore, \$$y$ in the future but gains \$$q$ now. If she is indifferent between doing this, then $-D(t)v(-y) = v(q)$. We can estimate a discount factor for speeding up t periods using $q = \delta^{speed\ up}\, y$ to give:

$$\delta^{speed\ up} = \frac{q}{y} = \frac{v^{-1}(-D(t)v(-y))}{y}.$$

Delay is naturally thought of as delaying a receipt so as to get \$$y > 0$ at some future period t rather than \$$q > 0$ now. This time we can think of the reference level as \$$q$ now and zero in the future. By delaying receipt Maria loses \$$q$ now but gains \$$y$ in the future. If she is indifferent to do this, then $-D(t)v(y) = v(-q)$. We can estimate a discount factor for delaying t periods using $q = \delta^{delay}\, y$ to give:

$$\delta^{delay} = \frac{q}{y} - \frac{v^{-1}(-D(t)v(y))}{y}.$$

Suppose we compare these two discount factors and, for simplicity, assume that $D(t) = 1$. Then, $\delta^{speed\ up} > \delta^{delay}$ if:

$$v^{-1}(-v(-y)) > -v^{-1}(-v(y)).$$

If you stare at this long enough you might see that we require $-v(-y) > v(y)$, but this is what we get with loss aversion. So, all we need to explain the delay-speed-up asymmetry is loss aversion.

A model with reference-dependent preferences can, therefore, capture a lot of the things we observe in inter-temporal choice. Unfortunately, things do not work out as perfectly as we might hope, because the formula for the value function we looked at in Chapter three (see equation (3.7)) does not satisfy either relations (4.7) or (4.8)! But we could easily tweak it and sort that out. As in Chapters two and three, therefore, reference dependence helps a lot in understanding behavior.

As you might expect, however, by now we do need to think a bit more about the reference point. To illustrate why, let's return to the homework example and suppose Maria must do the homework on Saturday or Monday. Furthermore, suppose that it is rare for homework to be set over the weekend, and so this is not her reference point. Instead, her reference point is to doing something on Saturday. One possibility is that on a Saturday she usually plays sport. Another is that she usually has to visit an aunt she does not like. This gives the reference-dependent utility in Table 4.10.

Irrespective of the reference point, Maria faces the same trade-off between a relatively large drop in utility on Saturday, a difference of 10, for a gain on Monday, a difference of 15. The reference point will matter in how she perceives this trade-off. Let's go through each reference point in turn. If she normally plays sport on Saturday, then doing the homework on Saturday will feel like a loss. This might make her reluctant to do the homework. If:

$$D(2)v(-10) + D(4)v(10) < D(4)v(-5)$$

Table 4.10 The homework example with reference-dependent preferences. If the reference point is to play sport, doing the homework on Saturday feels like a loss, but if the reference point is to visit an aunt, doing the homework on Saturday feels like a gain

	Utility on		
	Saturday	*Sunday*	*Monday*
Payoff x_t if do homework Saturday	−5	10	10
Payoff x_t if do homework Monday	5	10	−5
Reference point is to play sport			
Reference payoff r_t	5	10	0
Reference-dependent utility if do homework Saturday	−10	0	10
If do homework Monday	0	0	−5
Reference point is to visit aunt			
Reference payoff r_t	−10	10	0
Reference-dependent utility if do homework Saturday	5	0	10
If do homework Monday	15	0	−5

then she will leave the homework until Monday. If she normally visits her aunt on Saturday, then doing the homework on Saturday will feel like a gain. This might make her more likely to the homework. If:

$$D(2)v(5) + D(4)v(10) > D(2)v(15) + D(4)v(-5)$$

then she would want to do the homework on Saturday.

To focus on the issue at hand, suppose that $D(2) = D(4) = 1$. Then we need to know whether $v(-10) + v(10) < v(-5)$ and whether $v(5) + v(10) > v(15) + v(-5)$. These equations may or may not be satisfied but suppose, by way of illustration, that $v(5) = 3, v(10) = 5, v(15) = 6, v(-5) = -7$, and $v(-10) = -13$. Then she would not do her homework on Saturday if the reference point is playing sport, but she would do her homework on Saturday if the reference point is to visit her aunt. The reference point and context can, therefore, influence behavior.

4.3.2 Preferences for sequences

What I want to look at next is how to model preferences over sequences. For now we shall ignore the question of when a set of events is viewed as a sequence rather than separate. So, what we need to do is measure the overall utility of a sequence of payoffs such as $\{x_1, x_2, \ldots, x_T\}$.

One way we do so is to compare this sequence with one that gives the same payoff in each period. That is, we compare the actual sequence to the smoothed sequence $\{\bar{x}, \bar{x} \ldots, \bar{x}\}$ where:

$$\bar{x} = \frac{1}{T}\sum_{t=1}^{T} x_t.$$

For every period t let:

$$d_t = t\bar{x} - \sum_{t=1}^{t} x_i$$

be the difference in utility, up to and including period t, between the smoothed sequence and actual sequence. We then get a nice way to think about the utility of a sequence by saying that utility is given by:

$$u^q(\{x_1, x_2, \ldots, x_T\}) = \sum_{t=1}^{T} x_t + \beta \sum_{t=1}^{T} d_t + \sigma \sum_{t=1}^{T} | d_t |. \quad (4.9)$$

To see why this is a nice way to think about things I need to introduce two further concepts.

We say that the **anticipated utility** of receiving sequence $\{x_1, x_2, \ldots, x_T\}$ is given by:

$$AU = \sum_{t=1}^{T} (t-1)x_t.$$

The story is that if Maria is going to receive payoff x_t in period t then she spends $t-1$ periods anticipating this. So, she gets $(t-1)x_t$ anticipated utility. Summing this over all periods gives total anticipated utility.

Following a similar logic we say that the **recollected utility** of the sequence is:

$$RU = \sum_{t=1}^{T} (T-t)x_t.$$

If Maria received payoff x_t in period t then she has $T-t$ periods to recollect it, and so gets $(T-t)x_t$ recollected utility.

A bit of rearranging shows that:

$$\sum_{t=1}^{T} d_t = 0.5(AU - RU).$$

So, positive values of Σd_t are associated with more anticipated than recollected utility. This means that a high Σd_t goes hand in hand with an improving sequence in which the x_ts increase with t.

Now we can go back to equation (4.9) and make some sense of it. We can see that a $\beta > 0$ means a preference for an improving sequence and a $\beta < 0$ a preference for a worsening sequence. We also see that $\sigma < 0$ indicates a preference for a smoothed sequence while $\sigma > 0$ indicates a preference for a one-sided sequence. To illustrate what this means, Table 4.11 has some example sequences. If σ is small and β positive, then Maria would prefer sequence C with lots of anticipation utility. If σ is negative and β positive, then she may prefer sequence E which still has anticipation utility but is more smoothed over time.

Table 4.11 Preference over sequences of outcomes with the anticipated and recollected utility

	Period					*AU*	*RU*	Σd_t
	1	*2*	*3*	*4*	*5*			
Sequence A	1	1	1	1	1	10	10	0
Sequence B	5	0	0	0	0	0	20	−10
Sequence C	0	0	0	0	5	20	0	10
Sequence D	2	1	1	1	0	6	14	−4
Sequence E	0	1	1	1	2	14	6	4
Sequence F	2	0	1	0	2	10	10	0

The evidence we looked at in section 4.1.2 would suggest that $\beta > 0$ and $\sigma < 0$. With the help of Table 4.12 we can see what this means in the homework example. Doing the homework on Saturday gives the most improving sequence, but not a very smooth one. To do the homework on Friday or Sunday may, therefore, be optimal. Indeed, if σ is very negative, Monday may be optimal as it gives the most smooth sequence.

The homework example brings us back to the troubling question of when period payoffs are seen as part of a sequence and when they are not. Will Maria think of the weekend as one sequence of events, or think of each day as separate from another? We see now that this might affect her choice. Unfortunately, there is no simple rule as to when a person will think of periods as separate or part of a sequence. The further apart are two events, then the more likely it intuitively seems that they will be seen as two separate events rather than as a sequence of events. This logic can only take us so far, however, as we shall see shortly in looking at habit formation.

4.4 Summary

I began by looking at a utility function with exponential discounting. The basic idea here is that inter-temporal utility, and choice, can by captured by assuming people discount the future at a constant rate. If true, this would make our life easier. Unfortunately, we saw that preferences seem to depend a lot on context, and exponential discounting is not well placed to pick this up. For example, we observe things like a gain-loss asymmetry, delay-speed-up asymmetry, absolute magnitude effect, and preference for improving sequences.

In looking at alternatives to exponential discounting we focused first on the fact that people seem impatient for short-term gain. We saw that there are two distinct ways to think about this. We can think in terms of a model of hyperbolic discounting with time-consistent preferences, or we can think in terms of quasi-hyperbolic discounting with time-inconsistent or present-biased preferences. The latter looked the better way to go.

Present bias, and time inconsistency, raises some interesting possibilities. A person may procrastinate by putting off doing something costly, preproperate by doing early something pleasant, or fight to overcome temptation. What happens

Table 4.12 Preferences over sequences in the homework example

	Payoff on:				*AU*	*RU*	Σd_t
Plan	*Friday*	*Saturday*	*Sunday*	*Monday*			
Do it Friday	−5	5	10	4	37	5	16
Do it Saturday	0	−5	10	10	45	0	22.5
Do it Sunday	0	5	−5	10	25	5	10
Do it Monday	0	5	10	−5	10	20	−5

can depend on whether the person is naïve or sophisticated in knowing about their present bias.

We next added reference dependence and loss aversion to the mix and showed this can explain things like the delay-speed-up asymmetry and gain-loss asymmetry. We also saw that perceptions of the reference point can influence choice.

Finally, we looked at how we can capture the utility from a sequence of events using anticipated and recollected utility.

A recurring theme in Chapters two and three was that context mattered. It would influence perceptions which would then influence choice because of things like the reference point. In thinking about inter-temporal choice we can come up with many other good reasons why context will matter. For instance, whether someone perceives a series of events as a sequence or separated can have a huge impact on behavior; in the one they are impatient for gain and in the other they want to delay for the future. Context effects will be less of a theme in the rest of the book (although they will crop up again in Chapter seven). So, before we move on I do want to emphasize their importance.

Most economic choices involve choice arbitrariness, risk, and time, all mixed up together. The potential context effects are, therefore, huge, and behavior will depend a lot on the context, and perceptions of the context. It's vital to be aware of and try to account for this. It's a key part of being a behavioral economist. What this means in practice is questioning things like what is the reference point, and what is a loss or a gain, in the different contexts that you are interested in understanding. This is a matter of judgment.

4.5 Borrowing and saving

In Chapter two we spent some time looking at the life cycle hypothesis and saving. Clearly these are inter-temporal issues, and so it is natural to think back to them now that we have a means to model inter-temporal choice. In doing so there are two new issues I want to pick out: habit formation and consumer debt.

4.5.1 Saving equals growth or growth equals saving?

A high savings rate usually goes together with a high growth rate. What is not so clear is why. A standard life cycle model of consumption predicts that higher expected income should lead to less saving, because the higher expected income means less income needs to be saved now in order to smooth future consumption. The prediction, therefore, would be that high saving causes high growth, and not the other way around. A lot of evidence, however, tends to suggest that things do go the other way around. It seems that high growth tends to proceed and cause high saving.

Habit formation is one possible way to account for this, as shown by Carroll and co-authors (2000). I am going to look at habit in more detail in Chapter ten, but the basics are all we need here. In a **model of habit formation** the utility of today's consumption depends on past consumption. One possible reason for this is that a person wants to maintain consumption at past levels. They have got used to a certain standard of living and would rather keep to, or improve upon, that standard. This fits with the idea that people want an improving sequence. People want to see their income and standard of living improving and not getting worse.

To capture this, assume that Maria has a habit level of consumption h. The habit evolves over time according to:

$$\frac{dh}{dt} = \rho(c - h)$$

where c is consumption and ρ determines to what extent habit depends on the recent past. The larger ρ is, the more quickly Maria's habits adapt to recent consumption.

A simple utility function we could use would be:

$$u(c, h) = \frac{c}{h^{\gamma}}$$

where γ measures the importance of habit. If $\gamma = 0$, then habits are irrelevant and we have a standard model where utility depends on consumption. If $\gamma = 1$, then utility depends only on whether consumption is more or less than the habit level. For intermediate γ, utility depends on both the absolute level of consumption and whether it is more or less than the habit level. For example, if $\gamma = 0.5$, then consumption of two with a habit level of one gives the same utility as if both consumption and the habit level are four.

It is possible to show, with some reasonable assumptions, that savings will increase with income if and only if the importance of habit γ is sufficiently large. Thus, habit can cause high savings if there is a high growth rate of income. The intuition for this is that a habit level of consumption means less reason to devote any increase in income to consumption. As long as consumption is above the habit level and the standard of living is rising, Maria will get relatively high utility. So, she does best to increase her consumption slowly over time and always have a rising standard of living. What she would not want to do is devote all the increased income to consumption. This would risk a subsequent fall in consumption below her new habit level with a consequent fall in living standards and utility.

Table 4.13 illustrates how this may work. We can see that income is going to increase over the four periods and can compare a smoothed consumption schedule A to an increasing schedule B. The increasing schedule gives higher utility because Maria does relatively well compared to what she has become used to. It also guards against any potential fall in the income she might get in period four.

We see, therefore, that habit and a preference for an improving sequence can explain why people save rather than spend, even if they expect future income growth. That people may think about their lifetime earnings as a sequence also highlights the problems of trying to distinguish when events are seen as separated rather than as a sequence. Here we are thinking of someone potentially seeing year-to-year earnings as a sequence!

Table 4.13 Two sequences of consumption compared in a model of habit formation. Consumption schedule B gives the highest utility

	Period				*Total utility*
	1	*2*	*3*	*4*	
Income	15	15	30	100	
Consumption A	40	40	40	40	
Habit A	15.0	27.5	33.75	36.9	
Utility A	10.3	7.6	6.9	6.6	31.4
Consumption B	25	35	45	55	
Habit B	15.0	20.0	27.5	36.0	
Utility B	6.5	7.8	8.6	9.1	32.0

4.5.2 Why save when you have debts?

One of the more puzzling aspects of saving behavior is that many people borrow on credit cards at a high interest rate to buy consumer goods, while simultaneously saving for the future at lower interest rates. To give some figures, in March 2009, US consumer debt, made up primarily of credit card debt, was about $950 billion, and around 14 percent of disposable income went to paying off this debt. At the same time the savings rate was around 4 percent of disposable income. One might argue that some people are saving while others are borrowing, but this does not seem to be the case; many people are both saving and borrowing. Why?

In trying to explain this puzzle the key thing to recognize is that people typically borrow for the short term (i.e. to buy a new dress) while saving for the long term (i.e. to buy a new house or retire). This distinction between short term and long term leads naturally to thoughts of quasi-hyperbolic discounting and time inconsistency. Several studies have indeed shown that this can help explain what is going on. For example, Laibson and co-authors (2007) try fitting the (β, δ) preferences model to data from US households. Having taken account of risk attitudes, they find that the model with parameters $\beta = 0.90$ and $\delta = 0.96$ fits the data well. This equates to a long-run discount rate of 4.1 percent and a short-term rate of 14.6 percent.

Why does a model with (β, δ) preferences work? First, a consumer with a long-run discount rate of 4.1 percent would be happy to save over the long term at a savings rate of, say, 5 percent per year. Second, a consumer with a short-term discount rate of 14.6 percent would be happy to borrow money to buy something now if she can pay that back at a rate of, say, 14 percent per year. Basically, the consumer wants to save but because of time inconsistency may also be unwilling to wait to buy that new dress.

Clearly banks and credit card companies can profit from this, which brings us nicely on to the next topic.

4.6 Exploiting time inconsistency

We have seen that present-biased preferences and time inconsistency can result in someone procrastinating. They keep on delaying something they need to do. Could a company exploit this? To see why this question is pertinent I am going to look at a study by Della Vigna and Malmendier (2006). The study was published with the title 'Paying not to go to the gym', which somewhat gives away the punch line.

4.6.1 Time inconsistency and consumer behavior

DellaVigna and Malmendier look at attendance data for over 7,000 health club members at three health clubs in New England between April 1997 and July 2000. People going to the gym had four basic options: (i) pay $12 per visit, (ii) pay $100 every 10 visits, (iii) sign a monthly contract with a fee of around $85 per month, and (iv) sign an annual contract with a fee of around $850. One difference between the monthly and annual contract is that the monthly contract was automatically renewed, while the annual contract was not. Those on a monthly contract could cancel at any time, but needed to do so in person or in writing. Those on an annual contract needed to sign up again at the end of the term, or their membership would stop.

This difference between the monthly and annual contract is a difference of what happens if the member does nothing, or is in the **default position**. The default position with a monthly contract is that a member needs to **opt out** of being a member. With the annual contract a member needs to **opt in** to being a member. Why should we worry about this distinction? Possibly we should not, because it costs very little to make a phone call, or write a letter, to opt in or opt out. There is, however, potential for time inconsistency. A person may want to cancel, or rejoin, but put it off until tomorrow, and then put it off until the next day, and so on. Similarly, a person may think they will go to the gym often, but typically find some excuse to go tomorrow rather than today. Let's look at the data.

Any of the four payment options could make sense to a particular consumer. They may go rarely, so the pay per visit makes sense; they may know they will go often, so the annual contract makes sense; or they may be unsure how often they will go, so prefer the flexibility of the monthly option. The interesting question is whether consumers do choose the option that is best for them. The study finds that basically they do not. To give a first illustration of this, Figure 4.5 plots the average price per attendance of new members. We see that in the first six months of membership the average cost per visit was relatively high. Indeed, 80 percent of monthly members would have been better off paying for every ten visits.

Figure 4.5 is suggestive of customers not choosing the best option, but does not capture the whole picture. That is because we need to see whether people learn and readjust. It may have been optimal for someone to sign a monthly contract but then switch to paying per visit once they realized how much (or how little) they used the gym. There is little evidence, however, of readjustment. This

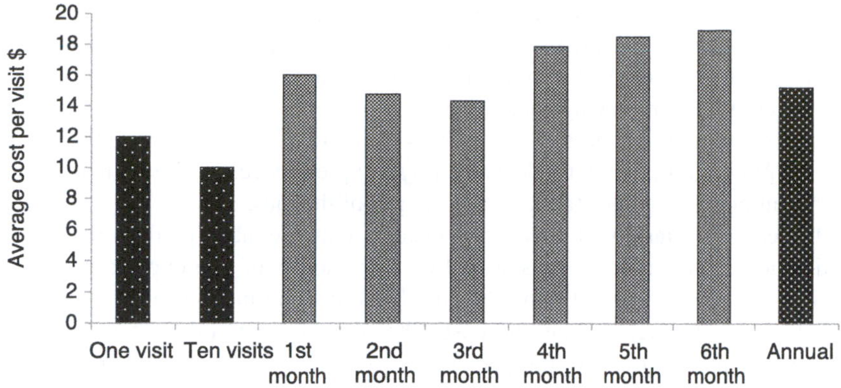

Figure 4.5 Average cost per visit to the gym for the first six months of monthly membership or year of annual membership. Monthly members pay on average more per visit than if they had paid per visit.

Source: DellaVigna and Malmendier (2006).

is particularly the case for those on the monthly contract. Many monthly members appeared to consistently overestimate their future usage and put off canceling their membership. Particularly telling is the average lag of over two months between the last time a person attends the gym and the moment they cancel membership! Such a delay is costly. Looking over the whole period of membership, the average loss for someone on the monthly contract was $614. For those on the annual contract it was just $1.

In trying to make sense of these results, DellaVigna and Malmendier suggest the most likely explanations are overestimation of future usage, time inconsistency, and naïvety. A model of naïve consumers with (β, δ) preferences where $\beta = 0.7$ and $\delta = 0.9995$ can explain the data, including the average delay of over two months in cancelation.

4.6.2 Firm pricing

In the gym example the loss made by a consumer on the monthly contract was the firm's gain. This raises the question of whether firms use a pricing strategy that maximizes the profit they can make from consumers. To answer this question we first need to know how firms should price if consumers have a present bias. To do so I will work through a model of gym membership based on that by DellaVigna and Malmendier (2004).

There are three periods. In period one the gym proposes a **two-part tariff** (L, p) that consists of a **lump sum membership fee** L and a **user fee** p that is paid every visit. If Maria joins the gym, then in period two she pays the membership fee and decides whether or not to use the gym. If she uses the gym then she pays the user fee, p plus some personal cost to attend, c. Maria does not know the personal cost until after joining. If she does go to the gym, then in period three she receives some benefit, B. Figure 4.6 summarizes what happens. The key to the model are the delays. There is a delay between joining and using the gym, so Maria needs to predict future usage when joining. There is also a delay between using the gym and benefitting from having used the gym.

This delay gives scope for present bias to matter. So, let's assume that Maria has (β, δ) preferences, but thinks she has ($\hat{\beta}$, δ) preferences. If $\hat{\beta} > \beta$, then she has a present bias but underestimates the strength of the bias.

To see what Maria will do we first need to imagine that we are in period one and Maria is predicting what she will do in period two. She expects that when period two comes she will think the payoff from using the gym is $\delta\hat{\beta} B - p - c$, the discounted benefit minus the cost. She, thus, expects that she will use the gym if $c < \delta\hat{\beta} B - p$. From the perspective of period one the benefit from using the gym is $\delta\hat{\beta}(\delta B - p - c)$. So, if Maria signs the contract, she should expect net benefit:

$$NB = \delta\hat{\beta}\left(-L + \int_0^{\delta\hat{\beta}B-p} (\delta B - p - c)dc\right). \tag{4.10}$$

The integral term captures her uncertainty about what the personal cost of using the gym could be.

The next thing we need to do is question what Maria will actually do in period two. She will only use the gym if $c < \delta\beta B - p$. If, therefore, $\hat{\beta} > \beta$ she is biased in overestimating her likelihood of going to the gym, and because of this overestimates the benefits of joining the gym. This is consistent with what we saw in Figure 4.5.

Now we can consider the firm. Suppose the firm pays production cost K whenever anyone joins and per-unit cost a if anyone uses the gym. They know that a consumer will use the gym in period two if $c < \delta\beta B - p$. The objective of the firm is to choose L and p to maximize profits,

$$max_{L,p}\left(L - K + \int_0^{\delta\beta B-p} (p-a)\,dc\right).$$

The one caveat is that the net benefit NB must be greater than zero, or no one would join. If you solve this maximization problem (see below) then the optimal price is:

$$p = a - \delta B(1 - \hat{\beta}) - \delta B(\hat{\beta} - \beta). \tag{4.11}$$

I'll look at this in three stages, summarized in Table 4.14.

If customers have no present bias, $\beta = 1$, the firm should set the per-usage fee equal to the cost, $p = a$. This result should be familiar to those who have studied price discrimination in a microeconomics course. The optimal thing for the gym to do is charge as high a membership fee as customers will pay and then make zero profit from customer use.

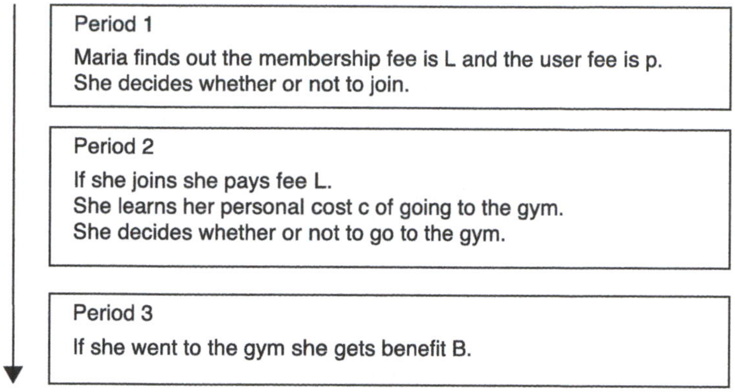

Period 1

Maria finds out the membership fee is L and the user fee is p.
She decides whether or not to join.

Period 2

If she joins she pays fee L.
She learns her personal cost c of going to the gym.
She decides whether or not to go to the gym.

Period 3

If she went to the gym she gets benefit B.

Figure 4.6 The timeline of the model of gym pricing.

If customers do have a present bias, $\beta < 1$, then the firm should set the per-usage fee below the cost, $p < a$. That means the gym makes a loss every time a customer uses the gym! Why would that make sense? It depends on whether the customer is sophisticated or naïve. If Maria is sophisticated, she knows that, because of her present bias, she may put off going to the gym. Thus, she wants something that makes it more likely she will go. A lower user fee serves that purpose. Maria would, therefore, be willing to pay a higher membership fee in order to have a lower usage fee. The gym does not profit from Maria having a present bias, but it does need to charge different prices.

If Maria is naïve, then she may overestimate how much she will use the gym. The lower the usage fee, the more she thinks she will use the gym, and consequently the higher the membership fee she is willing to pay. In this case the gym

Table 4.14 The consequences of optimal pricing in the gym example with present-biased preferences

Preferences	*Consumer*	*Firm*
No present bias, $\beta = 1$	Correctly predicts when will use the gym.	Makes a profit on membership fees. Makes no profit when members use the gym.
Present bias and sophisticated, $\beta = \hat{\beta}$	Knows will possibly not use the gym because of present bias.	Needs to charge a lower user fee to attract customers. Makes a loss when people use the gym but this is compensated for by a higher lump sum fee. Does not profit from consumers' present bias.
Present bias and naïve, $\beta < 1$ and $\hat{\beta} = 1$	Does not realize will possibly not go to the gym because of a present bias.	Charges a lower user fee to exploit customers. Makes a loss when people use the gym but this is compensated for by a higher lump sum fee and some customers not using the gym. Profits from consumers' naivety.

can profit from Maria's present bias. By offering a low usage fee it can charge a high membership fee and gain on people who join but subsequently do not use the gym. The larger the naïvety of consumers, the more profit the gym can make.

[Extra] To see how to get equation (4.11): If we set $NB = 0$, we can substitute in for L from equation (4.10) to rewrite the firm's problem as:

$$max_p\left(\int_0^{\delta\hat{\beta}B-p}(\delta B-p-c)dc-K+\int_0^{\delta\beta B-p}(p-a)dc\right).$$

This can be rewritten:

$$max_p\left(\int_0^{\delta\beta B-p}(\delta B-a-c)dc-K+\int_{\delta\beta B-p}^{\delta\hat{\beta}B-p}(\delta B-p-c)dc\right)$$

and:

$$max_p\left((\delta\beta B-p)(\delta B-a)+\delta B(\hat{\beta}-\beta)(\delta B-p)-K-\int_0^{\delta\hat{\beta}B-p}cdc\right).$$

Evaluating the last integral and differentiating with respect to p gives the result!

There are two important lessons from this simple model. First, firms should take account of present bias when setting an optimal price. This is particularly pertinent if consumers are sophisticated. In this case, the firm cannot profit from the present bias but does need to price differently to make the same profits as without a present bias. Second, firms can profit by exploiting naïve consumers. They can charge a high membership fee and offer a low usage fee, knowing that some customers will not take advantage of the lower usage fee.

The data we have for gym membership would suggest that firms are aware of this. The user fee for members was zero, which must be below the gym's per-unit cost. We also did see underuse of the gym. Let's look at another example.

4.6.3 Choosing the correct calling plan

If the title of DellaVigna and Malmendier's paper, 'Paying not to go to the gym', gave away the punch line, the title of a paper by Miravete (2003), 'Choosing the wrong calling plan?,' leaves things more open.

Miravete looks at consumers' choice of telephone calling plans following a tariff change by company South Central Bell in 1986. Customers had the choice between a flat-rate tariff of \$18.70 per month, or a measured tariff of \$14.02 per month plus call charges. Such choices (and utility payments in general) are often suggested as fertile ground for present bias. That's because it may be best for a customer to switch tariff, and she may know that, but delays doing so because of present bias. This study aimed to put that anecdotal hunch to the test.

Key to the study was a survey of 5,000 customers that included questions on expected telephone usage. If we know how much customers expected to use the telephone then we can hope to identify customers who should have expected the other tariff to be less costly, but did not switch.

Around 30 percent of the consumers surveyed chose the measured option and 70 percent stayed with the flat rate. So, did consumers make the correct choice and, more importantly, did they switch if it looked like they had initially made a wrong choice? Table 4.15 provides some relevant data to see what happened. There was a high proportion of people over/underestimating the number of calls they would make. This should feed through to some making the wrong choice of calling plan. Of interest to us is how many of those who were in the wrong plan in October switched by December to the better plan. Overall, around 40 percent of customers were in the wrong plan in October, falling to 33 percent in December. There is also evidence that those with the most to gain from switching were the ones to switch.

This study gives an interesting contrast to the one on gym membership. Recall that, with gym membership, it was those opting for the 'flat' monthly tariff that were most often making the wrong choice. In this telephone example those choosing the flat rate are on average making the right choice. It is those choosing the 'variable' per-use tariff that are most often making the wrong choice. It would be hard, therefore, to argue that people are on average biased towards a flat versus variable tariff or vice versa. It just seems that people are bad at predicting future usage and therefore end up making the wrong choice.

Present bias can give a plausible explanation for all of this. People might overestimate how much they will use the gym and underestimate how much they will use the telephone because of time inconsistency. Furthermore, they may put off changing plan once they have realized it's wrong because of procrastination. Present bias gives us a good story, but is it the whole story?

Probably not. In the gym case, those who are paying too much do eventually change their membership. Similarly, in the telephone case the number of customers choosing the wrong tariff does fall over time. What appears to be time inconsistency and procrastination may, therefore, just be people taking time to learn their

Table 4.15 Choices of calling plan, estimates of usage, and the proportion of customers making the wrong choice

Choice in October	*Flat*	*Flat*	*Measured*	*Measured*
Choice in December	*Flat*	*Measured*	*Flat*	*Measured*
Number of customers	953	43	41	375
Underestimated calls by 20% or more	26%	28%	32%	33%
Overestimated calls by 20% or more	59%	49%	61%	49%
Made wrong choice in October	11%	44%	100%	57%
Made wrong choice in December	6%	7%	0%	67%

Source: Miravete (2003).

preferences and make the best choice. This is not to say that present bias is not important, it is just to highlight that other things are clearly going on as well. These other things will be a theme of the next two chapters as we look at how people interpret new information and how they learn over time.

4.7 Environmental economics

Up until now we have focused on an individual making choices about her future. For example, when should Maria do the homework, or go to the cinema, or visit the aunt she does not like? Many important economic decisions, however, involve decisions that will affect future generations. For example, if Maria builds up too much debt, then her children, and grandchildren, may be expected to pay that off. In this section I want to briefly look at how we can understand such long-term trade-offs.

In doing so I shall focus on environmental protection. This is natural given that the most pressing examples of long-term trade-offs concern the environment. Many scientists paint a depressing picture of the future unless we reduce or control carbon emissions. Similar fears surround many related issues such as deforestation, overfishing, radioactive waste, pollution of rivers, etc. I will use, therefore, the example of protecting the environment to illustrate the more general ways that behavioral economics can inform debate on long-term trade-offs.

4.7.1 Inter-generational discount factor

Debate on climate change was blown open in 2006 by the Stern *Review on the Economics of Climate Change*. The *Review*, commissioned by the UK government, advocated immediate action to reduce CO_2 and other greenhouse emissions. It warned of dire long-run consequences unless we acted *now*. This advice was in stark contrast to conventional economic thinking. Most economists advocated a **climate-policy ramp** in which policies to slow global warming would increasingly ramp up over time. So, why did the *Review* reach such a radical conclusion?

To help explain the issues, consider the entirely made-up numbers in Table 4.16. These show the utility of an average person now and after 50 to 200 years, depending on the climate change policy enacted. If we do nothing we risk catastrophe. The climate-policy ramp advocates gradual action in the future. If we

Table 4.16 The long-run consequences of four climate change policies

	Utility				
Policy	*Now*	*50 years*	*100 years*	*150 years*	*200 years*
Do nothing	100	100	0	0	0
Climate-policy ramp	100	95	80	90	100
Immediate action	90	90	100	100	100

act immediately then we lower current utility for the sake of the future. Which policy should we choose?

Table 4.16 is similar to Tables 4.1 and 4.6, which detailed Maria's utility from doing her homework or going to the movies. The same techniques we used to analyze those choices can be used to decide on a climate change policy. But there is one fundamental difference. As Maria decides when to do her homework she is trading off her utility now for her utility in the future. We need to know her personal discount factor, present-day bias, preference for an increasing sequence, and so on. When society decides on a climate change policy we are trading off the utility of the current generation for the utility of future generations. This means we need some way of making inter-generational choices. We need a discount factor and preference over sequences that measure society's long-term desires (see Research Methods 4.3).

Research Methods 4.3

Inter-generational lab experiments

I have already remarked that long-run trade-offs are hard to measure in a laboratory experiment (see Research Methods 4.1). Looking at inter-generational trade-offs would seem even more impossible. Economists, however, are an ingenious bunch and inter-generational experiments have been run. Given that such experiments involve games that we are not going to look at until later in the book, I will not go through them in detail here, but the basic design can be illustrated with a study by Chaudhuri and co-authors (2009).

Groups of eight subjects were brought into the lab and played the weakest link game for ten rounds (see Chapter six for more on this game). Once the ten rounds were up, each subject was replaced by a new subject, her laboratory descendant. The new group of eight subjects played the weakest link game for a further ten rounds. This continued for up to nine generations. When a subject handed over to her descendant she was allowed to leave a message. Depending on the treatment, the descendant was allowed to see this message and the recent history of her parent. The final thing to point out is that a subject was paid based on her own performance and the performance of her descendant. A subject, thus, had an incentive to send a good message.

Experiments like this cannot tell us much about inter-generational discount factors. They can, however, tell us some interesting things about how advice is passed down and acted on from generation to generation. For example, subjects in the study tended to send pessimistic advice, which the next generation initially ignored but soon followed. The outcome was inefficiency. In terms of protecting the environment, this suggests that we need to be wary of a 'don't bother, it's hopeless' message being passed down the generations.

There are three basic approaches to tackling this problem. The approach taken by the Stern *Review* sees deciding on an appropriate discount factor and preference over sequences as a philosophical and ethical issue. What we know about personal discount factors is deemed irrelevant, because they are person specific. We need to think of future generations, and the *Review* argued that one generation should not unduly advantage itself at the cost of future generations. It, thus, advocated a discount factor near one and a smoothing of utility over time. Indeed, they argued that the only reason why the discount factor should differ from one is because of the threat of extinction; we need to take account of the fact that a meteor might wipe out humanity before 200 years are up.

Table 4.17 shows that, when we put in a discount factor of 0.999, immediate action is the optimal policy. The high discount factor means we should make immediate sacrifice for future generations. It did not take long, however, for economists to criticize such a high discount factor.

An alternative approach is based on revealed preference. This approach basically says that we should look to personal discount factors when deciding policy because these reveal how much we actually care about future generations. If Maria does not save for the future, then she reveals that she does not care too much about her children and grandchildren! Moreover, this approach argues that decisions to invest in climate change abatement technology should be based on current rates of return.

Table 4.17 shows that, if we put in a discount factor of 0.95, then the climate-policy ramp is optimal. If the discount factor is any lower, then doing nothing is optimal. The radical conclusions of the Stern *Review* follow, therefore, from the relatively high weight put on the future. Crisis over!

Well, the material in this chapter should leave you somewhat skeptical of the revealed preference approach. We have seen that personal discount factors are highly context dependent. We have also seen that people are time inconsistent and happy to pre-commit. They borrow at high interest rates while saving at low interest rates and buy gym memberships they do not need. Against this backdrop it seems hard to argue that current rates of return can be taken all that seriously when deciding on the optimal inter-generational discount factor. Indeed, the climate-policy ramp looks remarkably like present bias.

Fortunately, there is a third approach that can help reconcile views. This approach takes as its starting point the huge uncertainty about climate change. If we do not know what discount factor to choose, then let us build that into our thinking. This might sound like fudging the issue, but it turns out not to. To see

Table 4.17 The discount factor for which each policy is optimal, and the inter-temporal utility of each policy for different discount factors

Policy	*δ when optimal*	*Inter-temporal utility*			
		$\delta = 0.999$	*0.95*	*0.9745*	*uncertain*
Do nothing	0.945 or less	195.1	107.7	127.5	151.4
Climate-policy ramp	0.945 to 0.996	422.1	107.8	134.6	264.9
Immediate action	0.996 to 1	434.0	97.6	124.9	265.8

why, let us say the appropriate discount factor is either 0.999 or 0.95. We put 50 percent probability on each possibility. At first glance this may seem equivalent to a discount factor half-way between 0.999 and 0.95, but Table 4.17 makes clear that it is not. If we are uncertain about the discount factor, then immediate action is the optimal policy. Basically, some probability that we should use a high discount factor is enough to advocate immediate action.

All three approaches summarized above have their critics, and it is up to you to decide which approach makes most sense to you. The point I would emphasize is that behavioral economics can inform your opinion, particularly about the reliability of using revealed preference. I want to show next that behavioral economics can also help us tackle climate change and reduce CO_2 emissions.

4.7.2 Reducing CO_2 emissions

Just about all economists agree that climate change requires action at some point in the future. That will require people to change their behavior. We need to pollute less, consume less, and so on. The standard economic model suggests that a change in behavior will only come about when there are changes in prices. Attention has, thus, focused on things like a carbon tax or subsidies for renewable energy. Behavioral economics, however, points to many ways in which behavior can be changed without disturbing economic fundamentals. I will look at two examples to illustrate the point. In Chapter eleven I shall look at the general approach to behavior change in more detail.

Suppose that Maria is persuaded by the need to protect the environment and is committed to reducing her CO_2 emissions. She needs a new car and decides to buy an environmentally friendly one. Suppose that she drives 10,000 miles per year for work, and this cannot be changed. The standard model of car she would like to buy does 15 miles per gallon and costs $20,000. It is possible to buy alternative models that differ only in fuel efficiency, ranging from 20 miles per gallon up to 60 miles per gallon. How much should Maria pay for greater fuel efficiency?

Note that this question is partly about saving money. By buying a more fuel-efficient car Maria not only helps the environment but also can save money on fuel. It is potentially a win-win situation where no sacrifice is needed in order to reduce CO_2 emissions. But this is only going to happen if Maria makes the right choice. A study by Larrick and Soll (2008) put subjects in the position of Maria and asked them how much they would pay for the fuel savings. Figure 4.7 summarizes the results. We can see that the subjects' willingness to pay followed a linear pattern. They were willing to pay as much to reduce fuel consumption from 45 to 55 miles per gallon as they were to reduce consumption from 25 to 35 miles per gallon. This, however, is a basic misunderstanding of how the miles per gallon ratio works.

To see things more clearly it is convenient to convert miles per gallon into gallons per 100 miles. A change from 25 to 35 miles per gallon means a reduction from 4 to 2.86 gallons per 100 miles. A change from 45 to 55 miles per gallon means a reduction from only 2.22 to 1.81 gallons per 100 miles. Remember that Maria was going to do 10,000 miles per year. So, buying the model that does

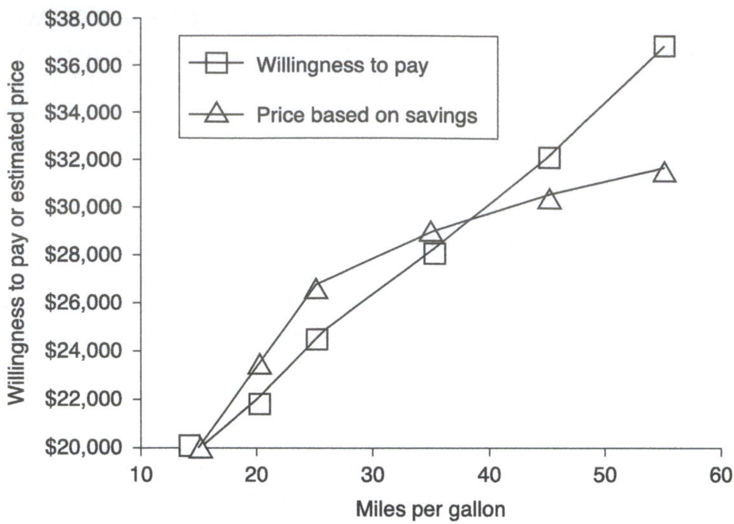

Figure 4.7 Willingness to pay for a more fuel-efficient car and the estimated price taking into account predicted fuel savings.

Source: Larrick and Soll (2008).

35 rather than 25 miles per gallon saves her 114 gallons of fuel. Buying the model that does 55 instead of 45 miles per gallon only saves 40 gallons of fuel. The linear willingness to pay schedule that we see in Figure 4.7 overestimates the benefit of going from 45 to 55 miles per gallon, while it underestimates the benefit of going from 25 to 35.

The bias we see here results from the use of simple heuristics. The framing in terms of miles per gallon makes most people think that any saving in ten miles per gallon is equivalent. If things are reframed in terms of gallons per 100 miles then people will be far less biased. The message, therefore, is simple. If we want people to make informed decisions we should use the amount of fuel per unit of output (as Europe typically does), rather than the amount of output per unit of fuel (as the US and UK typically do).

Having bought a fuel-efficient car, Maria now looks to cut down on her domestic energy usage. Her local utility company starts sending her Home Energy Report letters from a company called OPOWER. The report compares her energy use to that of 100 similar neighbors. She is rated as great, good, or below average and offered tips on energy reduction. Will this motivate, or inform her, to reduce energy consumption?

Allcott (2011) evaluated the consequences of sending such letters to over half a million energy customers across the US. In households that received the letters energy consumption was reduced by around 2 percent. That may not sound much, but it is a large reduction. For example, we can estimate that a price rise of around 11 to 20 percent would be needed to bring about such a fall in usage. Most of the reduction was caused by day-to-day changes such as turning off lights and adjusting thermostats. Again, we see that Maria can help the environment and save money at the same time.

These two examples illustrate once more the importance of framing and context effects. The new thing I want to emphasize is how such effects are amplified by procrastination. When it comes to reducing gas emissions, procrastination is potentially a very dangerous thing. If Maria, and everyone else, continually puts off protecting the environment until tomorrow, then it may not be long before there is no environment left to protect. This point makes clear that, for all the talk of the Stern *Review*, climate-policy ramps, and inter-generational discount factors, gas emissions will only be reduced if individuals change behavior. Procrastination is a major reason that people will not change behavior, even if they 'want' to.

Climate change policy, therefore, needs to look for ways of overcoming procrastination. A change in the way decisions are framed may help do that. For example, Maria may partly put off getting a fuel-efficient car because she underestimates the gains she would make from doing so. Similarly, receiving a letter with tips on energy reduction may help overcome her procrastination on reducing home energy usage. Small changes in framing can have big, long-run consequences!

4.8 Further reading

The survey article by Frederick *et al.* (2002) is a good place to start. The papers by O'Donoghue and Matthew Rabin (1999, 2000, 2006) are recommended reading on time inconsistency. As is the pioneering article by Strotz (1956). Note that we will return to time inconsistency in Chapter eleven, and so much of the further reading there is also relevant here. For an interesting look at the desire for wages to increase over time see Frank and Hutchens (1993). For more on applying behavioral economics in industrial organization see Ellison (2006). For more on behavioral environmental economics see Shogren and Taylor (2008) and Allcott and Mullainathan (2010).

4.9 Review questions

4.1 Inter-temporal utility (as defined in equation 4.1) is about measuring streams of utility over time. To make life easier for themselves, however, economists normally think about streams of money over time. This should be OK if we think in terms of, say, '\$10's worth of utility', but could be problematic if we really mean 'a \$10 note'. To illustrate, if someone says they are indifferent between \$150 in one year's time to \$100 today, what is the discount factor, when the utility function is $u(x) = x$ and $u(x) = \sqrt{x}$ and x is money? Think about the implications of this.

4.2 Explain the difference between time-consistent and present-biased preferences. Why is this distinction not important in a model of exponential discounting?

4.3 In section 4.3, I showed that $\delta^{speed\text{-}up} > \delta^{delay}$ in the case of a receipt. Show that $\delta^{speed\text{-}up} < \delta^{delay}$ in the case of a payment.

4.4 Looking back at Table 4.10, what would happen if Maria's reference point was to do her homework on Saturday, and what if it was to do it on Monday? How is this related to the concept of personal equilibrium that we looked at in the last chapter?

4.5 Looking back over this chapter and the previous two, come up with examples of context effects.

4.6 What is the expression for $D(t)$ with quasi-hyperbolic discounting?

4.7 What context effects do you think make it more likely that someone will think of a series of events as a sequence rather than separated?

4.8 What are the implications of habit formation for the life cycle hypothesis?

4.9 What is the relationship between a model of habit formation and reference-dependent utility?

4.10 Why do many firms, like gyms, charge a two-part tariff with a zero user fee?

4.11 Is there a difference between firms exploiting a customer's bias and changing their strategy to take account of a customer's bias?

4.12 What strategy can firms use to take account of other cognitive biases and heuristics that we have looked at, like loss aversion and risk aversion?

4.13 How can people overestimating how much they will use the gym and underestimating how much they will use the telephone both be caused by time inconsistency?

4.14 Compare the three approaches, looked at above, for deriving an intergenerational discount factor. Why is it so difficult to agree on the best approach?

5 Learning from new information

> He is accelerating all the time. That last lap was run in 64 seconds compared to the one before in 62 seconds.
>
> David Coleman, sports commentator

A theme in Chapters two and three was uncertainty and risk. For instance, in Chapter two I talked about Anna not knowing whether she would prefer the Nutty breakfast cereal or the Honey cereal. In Chapter three I talked about Alan deciding whether or not to fully insure his car without knowing whether his car would be stolen. New information should remove some of this uncertainty. For example, if Anna tastes the breakfast cereals, or Alan finds out the number of cars stolen in his area in recent years, then they should be able to make more informed decisions. This looks like a good thing.

It should, therefore, be a good thing that we are continually bombarded with new information from the TV, radio, internet, newspapers, friends, family, colleagues, and our own experiences. New information is only useful, however, if it is used wisely. There can be no doubt that new information influences behavior in significant ways. Why else would firms spend so much money on advertisements? Why else would someone ask friends, or look on the internet, for advice before making a decision? What we need to think about is how wisely people use new information, and the consequences this has for how they behave. That will be the focus of this chapter.

5.1 Bayesian updating and choice with uncertainty

Imagine someone called John, who is thinking of buying a new car and has narrowed it down to two choices, a 'Sporty' car or a 'Comfort' car. Either car is approximately the same price, but John does not know which will give him higher utility. In the process of deciding, he tries to become better informed by asking his friends, doing a test drive, searching for advice on the internet, and so on. What should he do with this new information?

The benchmark for what he should be doing is **Bayesian updating**. Let p denote the **prior probability** that John puts on the Sporty giving the higher utility.

Any new information he gets we call a **signal**. For example, a signal might be his friend saying, 'buy the Comfort' or him doing a test drive and 'liking the Sporty'. Let θ denote the **signal precision** or probability that he would have got the signal if Sporty does give the higher utility. The value ofθ should capture things like the trust that John puts in his friend's opinion or expertise, or how relevant he thinks a test drive is. If John uses **Bayes' rule**, then the **posterior probability** that he should put on the Sporty giving the higher utility is:

$$\Pr(\text{Sporty is best} \mid \text{signal}) = \frac{\theta p}{\theta p + (1-\theta)(1-p)}. \tag{5.1}$$

For example, if John started relatively indifferent between the two, say, $p = 0.4$, but his friend said that Sporty is better and he trusts his friend's opinion, say, $\theta = 0.9$, then he should put posterior probability 0.86 on the Sporty being better for him. This new information changes his beliefs and in doing so may change his behavior from buying the Comfort to buying the Sporty.

Bayesian updating is what John should do if he wants to make the most informed decision. For every new piece of information he gets, it makes sense to use Bayes' rule. We have, therefore, a prediction for how John should use any new information. Bayes updating can, however, be a bit more complicated than equation (5.1) might suggest. To explain why, it is useful to relate John's choice to what we did in Chapters two and three.

We can think of John as not knowing what car will give him highest utility and so he searches for more information to become better informed. He is never going to be completely sure what is best, but new information allows him to update his beliefs and eventually make a more informed decision. Throughout this process John is making risky choices, particularly when he finally buys a car. For example, we can think of there being a 'Sporty prospect' and a 'Comfort prospect', where each prospect details the possible outcomes from buying that car. New information allows John to change the numbers in one or more of the prospects. For example, if he test drives the Comfort he can update the Comfort prospect. Once he has updated the Comfort prospect he can then update his beliefs that Comfort is best. Table 5.1 illustrates how this might work in practice if John test drives the Comfort.

Framing things in this way, we can see two potential issues. First, it becomes complicated to update beliefs. When I introduced Bayes updating, the focus was on the probability that the Sporty is best for John. Now, we are starting to get down to finer details about each car. This seems natural but means that John has some work to do in order to turn new information into updated beliefs. He has to update his beliefs about the merits of each car, and then update his belief about which car is best. This can easily get quite complicated. Can John realistically be expected to do it? We will get back to that question in section 5.2.

A second issue is that of ambiguity and uncertainty. At the start of Chapter three I mentioned the distinction between risk and uncertainty, and you might recall that if a person has a choice with uncertainty then they may not know the probability of possible outcomes. John can presumably predict that he could like the Comfort, not like the Comfort, and so on. What would be much harder for him to do is to put

Table 5.1 John updates his beliefs after a test drive. The Comfort is best if it is worth $12,000. Initially he puts probability 0.7 on this being the case, so Sporty is best with probability 0.3. He test drives the Comfort and does not like it. This lowers the probability that he puts on the Comfort being worth $12,000 down to 0.6

Event	*John's opinion*	*Summary*
Initial prior	The Sporty is worth $10,000 with probability 0.9 and $9,000 with probability 0.1. The Comfort is worth $12,000 with probability 0.7 and $4,000 with probability 0.3.	Sporty is best with probability 0.3.
Test drives the Comfort and gets signal 'did not like the Comfort'	The signal precision (i.e. probability that this would happen if the Comfort is worth $12,000) is 0.39. He updates his beliefs about the Comfort to being worth $12,000 with probability 0.6 and $4,000 with probability 0.4.	Sporty is best with probability 0.4.

specific numbers on, say, the probability that he will like the Comfort, and the value he would put on it if he did like it. This means that John's choice of car is a choice with uncertainty. It also means we need to think about where the numbers in Table 5.1 could come from because without them we cannot possibly expect John to use Bayesian updating. We need, therefore, to think about choice with uncertainty.

5.1.1 Models of choice with uncertainty

I shall start by talking about a relatively simple example to illustrate the most important issues, and then relate things back to John buying a car. Imagine a box containing ten balls. One of the balls is going to be drawn randomly from the box, and you have to bet on what color the ball will be. If you get it correct, you win $2. Now contrast these two different possibilities:

> Box 1: Contains five red balls and five black balls.
> Box 2: Contains an unknown number of red balls and black balls. It could be zero red and ten black, ten red and zero black, or anything in between. What box would you rather bet on?

Box 1 provides a simple choice with risk like that we looked at in Chapter three. If John bets on black, he faces the prospect (0.5, $2; 0.5, $0), so with a 50 percent chance he will be correct and win the $2. His expected utility is then:

$$U\text{(black)} = 0.5\text{u (w + 2)} + 0.5\text{u (w)}$$

where w is his wealth. What about box 2? This time I cannot write down the prospect, because I cannot say what probability John has of winning if he bets on black. The probabilities are **ambiguous**. If the probabilities are ambiguous, then we cannot work out John's expected utility, use prospect theory, or do anything else we did in Chapter three. We need something new.

The simplest thing we can do is use **subjective expected utility** in which we go with what John thinks will happen. If John thinks that box 2 will contain four red balls and six black balls, then his subjective probability of drawing a black ball is 0.6 and his subjective expected utility is:

$$U\text{(black)} = 0.6\text{u}(\text{w} + 2) + 0.4\text{u}(\text{w}).$$

That looks like a simple solution! The problem is that John could have any beliefs he wanted and not be wrong. He could believe that none of the balls are black, all of them are black, and we have no way to tie down what his beliefs should be, or are likely to be.

Consider now another possible box:

> Box 3: A number between zero and ten will be randomly drawn and determine the number of red balls in the box. The rest of the ten balls will be black.

Does this box provide a choice with risk or with uncertainty? The correct answer is that it provides a choice with risk. It does, however, look different to box 1. That's because it involves a compound lottery. A **compound lottery** is when there are two or more consecutive lotteries to determine the outcome. Box 3 is a compound lottery because there is a lottery to determine how many balls are in the box, and then a lottery when John comes to pick a ball. Just to confuse, the final stage, where John picks a ball, is typically called the **first order lottery** or **second stage lottery**. The preliminary stage, where the number of balls in the box is determined, is called the **second order lottery** or **first stage lottery**. Two stages are enough in this case, but there can be three or more stages in a compound lottery.

To try and capture the lottery of box 3 we could write down one long prospect. For instance, if he chooses black, he faces prospect (0.09, \$2; 0.09, (0.9, \$2; 0.1; \$0); 0.09, (0.8, \$2; 0.2, \$2); . . .) where we recognize that there is a one in 11 chance that all the balls are black and John wins \$2, a one in 11 chance that nine of the balls are black and John wins \$2 with probability 0.9, and so on. This looks a bit messy. We could, therefore, try **reducing the compound lottery** to a simple lottery. To do this we work out the overall probability that a ball will be black or red. If you do this you should find that there is a 50 percent chance a ball will be black and a 50 percent chance it will be red. This suggests betting on black with box 3 gives the same prospect (0.5, \$2; 0.5, \$0) as it did with box 1!

It is not clear, however, that we should be reducing compound lotteries to a simple lottery. For instance, we could do something called **recursive expected utility** and work out the expected utility of each lottery and compound them together. To do this, we start with the first order lottery where John picks a color.

If there is one black ball and nine red balls, his expected utility of betting on black is:

$$U\,(\text{black} \mid \text{one black}) = 0.1\text{u}(\text{w} + 2) + 0.9\text{u}(\text{w}).$$

We need to do this for all possible combinations of black and red balls. We then go to the second order lottery where the number of balls is determined. For reasons we do not need to worry about, Kilbanoff and co-authors (2005) show that his expected utility can be written:

$$U\,(\text{black}) = 0.09\phi\,(U\,(\text{black} \mid \text{no black})) + 0.09\phi\,(U\,(\text{black} \mid \text{one black})) + \ldots$$

where ϕ is some function that captures preferences over second order lotteries.

The key to this way of doing things is that we may want to distinguish risk attitudes towards first and second order lotteries. In particular, we shall see that there are good arguments for why John may be more risk averse in a second order lottery than a first order lottery. If so, we should not be reducing compound lotteries but instead using recursive expected utility. It also means that John will be more reluctant to bet on box 3 than box 1 because he essentially does not like compound lotteries.

It is now interesting to go back and look again at box 2. When the probabilities are ambiguous, as they are in box 2, it seems more natural to think in terms of a compound lottery. That is, it seems natural to think of John having subjective beliefs about an additional stage in which balls are added to the box. For example, he might put subjective probability 0.5 on there being five red and five black balls, and probability 0.25 that all the balls are black, and so on. It may, therefore, be most apt to use **recursive subjective expected utility** to think about choice with uncertainty. To see whether that is the case we need to look at some data.

5.1.2 The Ellsberg Paradox

I am going to look at the results of a study by Halevy (2007). In the study, subjects were asked to bet on boxes 1 to 3, and a fourth box:

> Box 4: A fair coin will be tossed to determine whether all the balls in the box are black, or all of them are red.

The interesting thing about box 4 is that all risk is resolved in the first stage. So, we have box 1 where risk is resolved in the second stage, box 4 where it is resolved in the first stage, and box 3 which is a true compound lottery. If people are more risk averse about second order risk, we should be able to pick this up.

In the study, rather than just have subjects bet on a color, subjects were given the chance to sell bets by saying the amount they were willing to accept to forgo

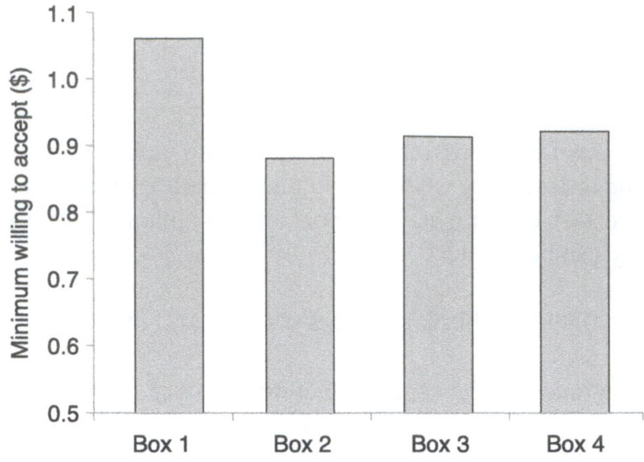

Figure 5.1 The willingness to sell a bet on each of the boxes. The Ellsberg Paradox is why subjects want less to sell a bet on box 2 than on box 1.

Source: Halevy (2007).

the bet. Figure 5.1 plots the average, minimum amount subjects were willing to accept. Remember they would win $2 if they won the bet, so a risk-neutral person would want $1. The most important thing to pick out is the greater willingness to sell a bet on box 2 than a bet on box 1. This difference was first pointed out by Ellsberg (1961), and so goes by the name of the **Ellsberg Paradox**. (For another Ellsberg Paradox, see Review question 5.2.) The Paradox is why people do not like betting on box 2. It seems that people are **ambiguity averse** in preferring a choice with risk to one with uncertainty. The results for boxes 3 and 4 suggest, however, that we need to qualify this somewhat because subjects also seem averse to a second order lottery.

To delve a little deeper, Halevy looks at the choices of individual subjects and tries to classify those choices. Table 5.2 summarizes his findings. Let's go through the table row by row.

First, there were subjects willing to sell a bet on any box at the same price. They did not seem to be bothered by ambiguity or a second order lottery and so their choices seem consistent with subjective expected utility maximization.

Second are those who were more willing to sell a bet on box 4 than on box 3 than on box 1. These subjects seemed to be risk averse about a second order lottery and so their choices are most consistent with recursive expected utility.

Third are those who are willing to sell a bet on boxes 1 and 4 at the same price but more willing to sell a bet on box 3. It does not look as though these subjects are risk averse about a second order lottery, otherwise they would be more willing to sell a bet on box 4. Instead, it seems they disliked the

Table 5.2 The proportion of subjects fitting each model of preferences and the average willingness to sell

Model of preferences	*Proportion of subjects (%)*	*Willingness to accept to forgo bet*			
		box 1	*box 2*	*box 3*	*box 4*
Subjective expected utility	19.2	1.03	1.03	1.03	1.03
Recursive expected utility	40.3	1.04	0.78	0.96	0.79
Recursive non-expected utility	39.4	1.11	0.91	0.85	1.07
Maxmin expected utility	0.1	0.90	0.80	0.90	0.90

Source: Halevy (2007).

compounding of lotteries with box 3. I will not go into the details, but this is consistent with recursive non-expected utility in which a person uses rank-dependent utility (as introduced in Chapter three).

Finally, we come to those who simply do not like ambiguity. In his original paper Ellsberg suggested that, when there is ambiguity, people are pessimistic and go with the worst thing that can happen. Hence we get a story of maximizing the minimum. Only one subject in this study behaved like that in being more willing to sell box 2, but not boxes 3 or 4.

Let's go back now and think about John deciding what car to buy. First of all, we now know that we should view the numbers in Table 5.1 as John's subjective beliefs about what he thinks might happen. We can also now see that it is natural to think of his choice as a compound lottery where, say, the quality of each car is determined in a second order lottery and the car he would most prefer is determined in a first order lottery.

The subjective nature of John's beliefs means it will be very hard for us to know why John would choose one car over another and whether he made the best choice. We can see, however, in Table 5.2 that the majority of people do not seem to like compound lotteries, or are ambiguity averse. This does have clear implications: John may be reluctant to gamble on which car is best, and so he may put off buying a car; he should also be eager to become better informed about each car in order to reduce the ambiguity or second order risk that he faces. It is this last possibility I want to focus on first.

5.2 Two cognitive biases

If John does not like ambiguity or second order risk, then he needs to become better informed, and so he should be on the lookout for new information. What we need to ask is whether he will use that information wisely. Will he, for example, use Bayes' rule? To do so would be quite complicated and so it would not be a huge surprise to see some mistakes and biases in how he does interpret new information. In this section I will look at two of the more common biases that we seem to observe: the confirmatory bias and law of small numbers.

5.2.1 Confirmatory bias

Suppose John asks his friend's advice and is told: 'The Comfort is a great car, but the Sporty is more eco-friendly.' This may be useful information, but it is not obvious how John should interpret it. The basic problem is that the information is ambiguous, in the sense that any interpretation of it will be subjective, and different people might interpret it in different ways. Some might focus on 'the Comfort is a great car' and others on 'the Sporty is more eco-friendly'.

This ambiguity is common in a lot of information we get and can easily lead to a biased interpretation of information. We say that there is **confirmatory bias** if a person has a tendency to interpret ambiguous, new information as consistent with his initial beliefs and opinions. Two psychology studies will help illustrate.

In a study by Lord and co-authors (1979), subjects were asked to read two reports on the deterrent effect of the death penalty and then asked to use their own 'evaluative powers' in thinking whether the reports provided support for or against the death penalty. They were initially given a brief description of the first report and asked questions about their attitudes and change in attitudes having seen the report. They were then given a more detailed description and asked questions about how well they thought the research in the report had been conducted and how convincing it was. The whole process was then repeated for the second report.

Some weeks before doing this experiment, subjects had filled in a questionnaire where half of the subjects invited to the experiment had appeared proponents of capital punishment and the other half opponents. The reports given to subjects could also be classified as having a pro- or anti-deterrence conclusion.

The main results of the experiment are summarized in Table 5.3. We see that brief descriptions of a study change attitudes in the way we would expect.

Table 5.3 Evidence of confirmatory bias in attitudes to capital punishment. Mean evaluations on a −8 to +8 scale where +8 meant agree with capital punishment or convincing and well done and −8 meant disagree with capital punishment or not convincing and not well done

Question	*Report*	*Evaluation*	
		Proponents	*Opponents*
Brief description changes my attitude to capital punishment	Pro-deterrence	1.3	0.4
	Anti-deterrence	−0.7	−0.9
How convincing the research was	Pro-deterrence	1.4	−2.1
	Anti-deterrence	−1.8	0.1
How well the research was conducted	Pro-deterrence	1.5	−2.1
	Anti-deterrence	−1.6	−0.3
Detailed description changes my attitude to capital punishment	Pro-deterrence	0.8	−0.9
	Anti-deterrence	0.7	−0.8

Source: Lord *et al.* (1979).

After a detailed description, however, attitudes diverge. Proponents of the death penalty rate pro-deterrence studies as convincing and well conducted, while anti-deterrence studies are not convincing or well conducted. Vice versa for opponents. Thus, subjects had a tendency to rate positively evidence that was consistent with their opinion, and rate negatively evidence inconsistent with their opinion! This is **confirmatory bias**. The consequence is a **polarization of attitudes**, with proponents of the death penalty becoming more in favor and opponents less in favor, despite having read the same evidence.

In the second study by Darley and Gross (1983), subjects were asked to evaluate the academic capabilities of a fourth-grade child. All subjects were given some basic information about the child. Half of the subjects were given the impression that she was from a low-income background and the other half that she was from a middle-class background. Half of the subjects then watched a video of the child answering questions. The video was designed to be relatively uninformative about the child's ability. Subjects were finally asked to evaluate the child's capabilities.

The results of the experiment are summarized in Table 5.4. We see that those who did not watch the video and believed she was from a middle-class background have a higher expectation of ability than those who believed she was from a low-income background. Whether or not this might be justifiable is not our main concern. Of interest to us is that watching the video lowered perceptions of ability if the child was believed to be from a low-income background but increased perceptions of ability if she was believed to be from a middle-class background. How subjects interpreted the same video depended, therefore, on initial information about the child. Those primed to think she might be low ability had their belief confirmed by the video, and those primed to think she might be high ability had this different belief confirmed by the same video! This is confirmatory bias.

In neither of these studies were subjects asked to make economic choices. Clearly, however, confirmatory bias can potentially influence economic behavior. If John was favoring the Comfort, then confirmatory bias suggests the main thing he will take from his friend's advice is 'the Comfort is a great car'. This could

Table 5.4 Evidence of confirmatory bias in assessing the ability of a child. Predicted grade placement goes down after watching a video if the child was perceived to be from a low-income background, and goes up if she was perceived to be from a middle-class background

Watched the video or not?	*Information provided*	*Grade level placement in:*		
		Mathematics	*Reading*	*Liberal arts*
Did not	Low income	3.98	3.90	3.85
	Middle class	4.30	4.29	4.03
Did	Low income	3.79	3.71	3.04
	Middle class	4.83	4.67	4.10

Source: Darley and Gross (1983).

mean that he is over-confident when making his choice. To explore this further it is useful to have a model, and for that I will turn to the work of Rabin and Schrag (1999).

5.2.2 A model of confirmatory bias

Imagine that every week John reads a magazine or looks up some review on the internet and gets a signal of which car is better. The signals are correct with probability $\theta \in (0.5,1)$. So, if the Comfort is best for John, then with probability θ a review will suggest the Comfort is best, and with probability $1 - \theta$ it will suggest the Sporty is best.

To capture confirmatory bias we assume that John does not always correctly interpret signals. To see how this works, suppose that he currently believes the Comfort is best. If he reads a review that suggests the Comfort is best, he always correctly interprets the review as supportive of the Comfort. But if he reads a review that suggests the Sporty is best, he incorrectly interprets the review as supportive of the Comfort with probability q. This captures confirmatory bias because John has a bias to interpret information as consistent with his prior belief. If he thinks that the Comfort is best, he is likely to think a review is supportive of the Comfort even though it is not. Similarly, if his prior belief is that the Sporty is best, he is likely to think a review is supportive of the Sporty even though it is not. The larger is q, then the larger the bias. If $q = 0$ there is no bias because all signals are correctly interpreted. If $q = 1$ then there is complete bias because whatever John reads he will think is supportive of what he believes.

Suppose John uses Bayes' rule based on the signals he thinks he has received. If he started indifferent between the two cars, and after t weeks thinks he has read S_t reviews supportive of Sporty and C_t reviews supportive of Comfort, then his posterior belief should be:

$$prob(\text{Sporty is best} \mid S_t, C_t) = \frac{\theta^{S_t}(1-\theta)^{C_t}}{\theta^{S_t}(1-\theta)^{C_t} + (1-\theta)^{S_t}\theta^{C_t}}.$$

What are the consequences of confirmatory bias?

We can first look at whether it leads to John having wrong beliefs more often. By wrong beliefs I mean he thinks one car is better when actually the other car is better. Table 5.5 details the proportion of times he has the wrong belief after reading 10 or 100 reviews. Remember that if $q = 0$ there is no confirmatory bias and so we see the unbiased probability of John being wrong. Confirmatory bias has two consequences: (i) John has wrong beliefs more often, as seen by the larger proportion of errors as q increases; (ii) He does not correct these beliefs over time, as seen by the error rates being similar after reading 100 reviews and 10 reviews, the higher is q.

We can see that these two effects combine to make wrong beliefs much more likely. To get some intuition for why this is the case, suppose that the Sporty is the

Table 5.5 The probability of an incorrect belief (%) after reading 10 or 100 reviews. The higher the confirmatory bias q, the higher the probability that John has wrong beliefs and the less difference it makes if he reads more reviews

q	θ			
	0.6	*0.7*	*0.8*	*0.9*
0	25, 2	7, 0	2, 0	0, 0
0.1	25, 5	10, 0	2, 0	1, 0
0.3	32, 27	13, 5	6, 0	2, 0
0.5	35, 34	20, 18	9, 7	5, 3
0.7	36, 36	24, 24	15, 15	7, 7
0.9	40, 40	27, 27	19, 19	10, 10

best car for John and he receives signals *C,C,S,C,S,S,S* so the first two reviews are supportive of the Comfort, the next of the Sporty, and so on. If John has no confirmatory bias he will correctly think that three reports are supportive of the Comfort and four of the Sporty, and four beats three, so overall the Sporty looks best. If he has confirmatory bias, however, he may become biased by the first few reports that are supportive of the Comfort. Specifically, he will correctly think the first, second, and fourth reviews were supportive of the Comfort. So, he only needs to wrongly think one of the third, fifth, sixth, or seventh reviews were supportive of the Comfort and he will have wrong beliefs. The higher is q, the more this becomes likely.

Confirmatory bias can, therefore, lead John astray. This means we might want to be careful of anything he tells us. Suppose, for instance, John tells you that 'I think the Comfort is best because 11 of the 15 reviews I have read are supportive of the Comfort.' What should you believe if you suspect confirmatory bias? It is possible to show that you should believe that John is correct but be less confident than he is. For instance, if he says that 11 of the 15 reviews he has read are supportive of the Comfort, then it would be sensible for you to think that around nine or ten were actually supportive. This is because the confirmatory bias will, on average, make him overestimate the number of times he read a supportive review.

Next, suppose John tells you: 'The Comfort is best, but I have recently read some reviews supportive of the Sporty', or he says: 'The Comfort is best, but I used to think the Sporty was.' In the first case you should probably put less faith in his belief, because there are signs that confirmatory bias is causing him to overestimate Comfort. Indeed, if there is a strong confirmatory bias, the fact that he has recently read some reviews supportive of the Sporty might imply you should think the Sporty is best. In the second case, we have cause to be confident in John's belief. That he recently changed his mind, despite confirmatory bias, suggests you should be more confident than John that the Sporty is best.

Things are now starting to get a bit messy and complicated. Indeed we now see that John should be thinking about the confirmatory bias of the people writing the reviews that he is reading! The main point, however, is simple: confirmatory bias means people may not correctly interpret new information, and so we may want to be skeptical of what they say they have learnt.

5.2.3 Law of small numbers

Suppose, continuing the previous thread, John tells you that 75 percent of the reviews he has read are supportive of the Comfort. If you do not suspect confirmatory bias, how should you interpret this information?

A Bayesian updater wouldn't do anything without asking first: how big was the sample size? That three out of four reviews are supportive of the Comfort should be much less persuasive than hearing that 15 out of 20 reviews were supportive. For instance, if $\theta = 0.6$, a Bayesian updater would put probability 0.69 on the Comfort being best for John in the first case, and 0.98 in the latter.

There is evidence, however, that many people fail to recognize the importance of sample size. They expect small samples to be more representative of the population than they likely are. This is the **law of small numbers**. There are two sides to the law of small numbers that we need to look at. I'll start with something called the gambler's fallacy.

If John expects a small sample to be representative of the population, then he may expect random events to be self-correcting. For example, if ten tosses of a coin have been heads, there may be a tendency to think the next one 'must be tails'. This is known as the **gambler's fallacy**. We see interesting evidence for the gambler's fallacy in betting on lottery numbers. To illustrate, I will look at studies by Clotfelter and Cook (1991) and Terrell (1994) which analyzed data from the state lotteries of Maryland and New Jersey. In both lotteries a better must correctly guess a three-digit winning number. In Maryland any winner gets $500. In New Jersey a prize fund is split between all those who guess the right number, meaning that a person wins more the fewer guess the winning number.

In both Maryland and New Jersey there was clear evidence of people betting less on a number that had recently won. This is consistent with the gambler's fallacy, 'if number 525 has just won it cannot win again'. In Maryland the gambler's fallacy does not affect expected winnings because all numbers are equally likely and every winner gets $500. In New Jersey, however, the gambler's fallacy does matter because winnings are higher the fewer pick the number. If others are unlikely to pick a number that has just won, then that is actually a good number to pick.

Table 5.6 demonstrates that winners in New Jersey did indeed get more when betting on numbers that had recently won. The difference is large, with a person choosing a number that won in the previous week winning on average $89, or 34 percent more than the average winner! The gambler's fallacy thus lowered a person's expected winnings. This suggests that we should see less evidence of the gambler's fallacy in New Jersey, where it did reduce earnings, than in Maryland, where it could not. Table 5.6 partly supports this by estimating the payout that there would have been in Maryland if winners were paid as in New Jersey. There we see slightly larger differences in potential winnings, but only slightly larger.

Table 5.6 Payouts to winners in state lotteries. Fewer people bet on numbers that have just won, so the payout is higher in New Jersey, where the winnings are shared, and would be higher in Maryland, if the winnings were shared

Winning number repeating	*Average payout in New Jersey*	*Estimated average payout in Maryland*
Within 1 week	$349	$396
Between 1 and 2 weeks	$349	–
Between 2 and 3 weeks	$308	–
Between 3 and 8 weeks	$301	$382
Not within 8 weeks	$260	$289

Source: Terrell (1994).

That the gambler's fallacy would reduce winnings did not, therefore, seem to make much difference to the strength of the bias.

The flip side to the gambler's fallacy is the **hot hand fallacy**. Here there is an expectation that streaks will continue, and it has particularly come to be associated with professional sport. For instance, a basketball player who is 'on form' or 'on a roll' is expected to keep on shooting well.

In a famous study, Gilovich and co-authors (1985) put the hot hand fallacy to the test by looking at the performance of professional and college basketball players. This included following the fortunes of the Philadelphia 76ers during the 1980 to 1981 season. As Table 5.7 shows, supporters and players expressed a belief in a hot hand. They thought that a player would be more likely to make a shot if he had just made one. The data on actual performance painted a different picture. There was no evidence for a hot hand. This study has now been replicated in other sports, with similar results. Sports fans, it seems, are not good at judging whether a sequence is random or not!

At first sight, the gambler's fallacy seems very different to the hot hand fallacy. In the one, 'five heads means the next must be tails', while, in the other, 'five successes must mean he will be successful again'. It is important, therefore, to understand why the gambler's fallacy and hot hand fallacy can both result from

Table 5.7 Evidence (or lack of it) for the hot hand fallacy. Supporters and players expected performance in the recent past to be a predictor of future performance – but it was not

	Probability of making a field goal shot	
	If just missed one (%)	*If just made one (%)*
What supporters expected	42	61
What players expected	50	63
What the data says	54	51

Source: Gilovich *et al.* (1985).

the same law of small numbers. The key difference is whether the probability of each outcome is known.

The gambler's fallacy can occur when the probability of the outcome is known. It occurs if someone trying to predict the next draw from a sequence expects a small sequence to match the known probability. For example, we know that a fair coin has a 50 percent chance of landing heads, and so John might expect 50 percent of coin tosses to be heads. This means he would think five heads in a row is unlikely, and likely to be balanced out by a subsequent tail. Similarly, a lottery number should not occur two weeks in a row.

The hot hand fallacy can occur when there is uncertainty over the probability of the outcomes. Someone trying to predict the probability of the next draw expects a small sequence to be a good predictor of what will happen next. So, a basketball shooter who has got five in a row must be on form and likely to get the next. Similarly, if John has read four reviews in a row supportive of Comfort, he might expect the next one will also be supportive of Comfort.

One interesting way to illustrate how these two fallacies can fit together is to look at sequences of random events, such as coin flips. Here are three possible sequences of coin flips. Which do you think are really generated by a coin?

hhTThTThhhTTThhTTThTThTTTThhhhThTThThTTThThhTTTh
hTThhhTThTThThhThTTThhThhhThTThhThTTThhThhTTThThhT
hhhhhTThThhTThhhhhhhThTTThTThhTThThhTTThThhhhhhTT

The top and bottom really were random and the middle one a figment of my imagination. To try to understand why you might think the middle one is random it is useful to use the **proportion of alternations**. For a sequence of n signals you need to count the number of **streaks**, or unbroken sub-sequences, r and then calculate:

$$\text{proportion of alternations} = \frac{r-1}{n-1}.$$

If the sequence is random, the proportion should be 0.5, and in the top and bottom sequences it is 0.49 and 0.43. The evidence, however, is that many people think sequences with a proportion of around 0.6 are actually random, and in the middle sequence the proportion is 0.59.

That we expect the proportion of alternations to be high is consistent with the gambler's fallacy; we do not expect five heads in a row. That we think sequences with a low proportion of alternations cannot be random is consistent with the hot hand fallacy; if we do see five heads in a row then the coin cannot be fair. (Basketball fans may be interested to know that Gilovich and co-authors (1985) found the proportion of alternations of professional basketball players was very close to that expected if the sequence of hits and misses was random.)

In looking at the consequences of the law of small numbers it is useful to have a model. This time we turn to Rabin (2002).

5.2.4 A model of the law of small numbers

Imagine again John reading car reviews. As before, let θ be the probability that a review is supportive of the Comfort and $1 - \theta$ the probability that a review is supportive of the Sporty. John wants to know θ because then he can better know what car is best.

First, let's think about the gambler's fallacy. In this case it is most apt to think that John is confident that he knows θ. The bias comes when he tries to predict what a review will say. We can capture this by assuming that John thinks signals are randomly drawn **without replacement** from a box containing N balls. On θN of the balls are written 'Comfort is best' and on $(1 - \theta)N$ are written 'Sporty is best'. I have emphasized the 'without replacement' because that is what causes the bias. If you substitute 'with replacement', then there would be no bias. To see why, suppose that $N = 2$ and John thinks $\theta = 0.5$. Then John thinks the box contains one review supportive of Sporty and one supportive of Comfort. So, if he reads a review supportive of Sporty he would think the next report must be supportive of Comfort. If $N = 4$ then there are two reviews supportive of Sporty and two supportive of Comfort. If he reads a review supportive of Sporty he would think there is a two-in-three chance that the next report will be supportive of the Comfort.

This nicely captures the gambler's fallacy because John expects that a sample of size N will be representative. The smaller is N, then the more biased he is. There is, however, a problem with the model: what happens when he has read more reviews than there are balls in the box? To overcome this, we assume that the box is replaced after he reads every other review. This makes the model work in a way that we can still capture the gambler's fallacy. Can it also capture the hot hand fallacy?

To capture the hot hand fallacy we need to add some uncertainty about θ. Suppose John thinks that $\theta = 0.25$, 0.5, or 0.75 are equally likely. He then reads two reviews in a row that are supportive of the Comfort. How will he update his beliefs about θ? Table 5.8 compares what he will think if he is unbiased and biased. We see that when he is biased he ends up overestimating the probability that reviews are supportive of Comfort. Indeed, he infers that it is impossible that reviews are more likely supportive of Sporty. This example is representative of

Table 5.8 Beliefs when there is the law of small numbers. If John is biased, he overestimates the significance of two C signals

		θ		
		0.25	*0.5*	*0.75*
The likelihood of two C signals	Unbiased, N large	0.0625	0.25	0.5625
	Biased, N = 4	0	0.166	0.495
Updated beliefs after two C signals	Unbiased, N large	0.071	0.286	0.643
	Biased, N = 4	0	0.251	0.749

what will happen more generally. John will overestimate how much he can learn from reading a small number of reviews. This is the hot hand fallacy.

One implication of the law of small numbers is that John's beliefs are too sensitive to the signals he gets. Whether he reads good reviews about the Comfort or the Sporty will lead to a bigger swing in his beliefs than is justified. This can have a knock-on effect in how much variation he perceives in the quality of cars. For example, suppose he compares other pairs of cars besides Sporty and Comfort. If $\theta = 0.5$ for all the pairs, then in around half of the pairs he is likely to read two reviews supportive of one of the cars. The hot hand fallacy means that John will read too much into this and come away believing there is more variation in cars than there actually is. In other words, some cars are naturally going to have a run of bad or good reviews, but John will overinterpret this as due to differences in quality rather than chance.

5.2.5 Generating random sequences

One interesting implication of the law of small numbers is that people may be bad at generating random sequences. For example, Rapoport and Budescu (1997) asked subjects to imagine a sequence of 150 draws with replacement from a deck of cards with five black and five red cards. They were asked to call aloud the sequence. Table 5.9 summarizes how subjects were biased towards switching too often and balancing out the sequence. If the sequence really is random, the probability of calling out black should always be 50 percent. We see, however, that subjects called out black more often if they had just called out red, and called out black less often if they had recently called out black more often.

It might seem a bit artificial to ask a person to generate a random sequence, but there are strategic situations where this is a useful skill. One such setting is competitive sports, where a player wants to keep an opponent guessing. For example, in tennis a server does not want his opponent to be able to predict where in the court he will serve. Similarly, in soccer or hockey a penalty-taker does not want the goalkeeper to know which side he will shoot. We might think that professional sportsman would learn to generate random sequences when competing. Do they?

One study, by Walker and Wooders (2001), looked at serving in ten important tennis matches and analyzed how often players served left versus right. There are

Table 5.9 Probability of calling out a sequence of blacks and reds in a deck of cards with five black and five red cards

Last few calls	*Probability of calling out black (%)*
Red	58.5
Black, red	46.0
Black, black, red	38.0
Black, black, black	29.8

Source: Rabin (2002).

two things that it is interesting to check with the data: whether a player was serving left and right with a probability that maximized his chance of winning, and whether sequences of serves were random. They found that players did serve left and right with appropriate probabilities but, on average, there was too much switching for the sequences to be random. To illustrate, Table 5.10 summarizes the famous 1982 Wimbledon final between Jimmy Connors and John McEnroe. Connors won the match, but that would be hard to guess from the data! McEnroe wins roughly as many points to the left and right, showing that he was serving left and right with the correct probability. He also had an appropriate number of streaks (or proportion of alternations), indicating that the sequence of serves looked random. Connors, by contrast, should have served more to the right from the ad court and more to the left from the deuce court than he did. He also had too many streaks for the sequence to look random, suggesting he was switching from left to right too often.

We see, therefore, that learning and experience does not necessarily mean that people can generate random sequences. It does seem clear, however, that people become better at generating random sequences with experience. For example, Walker and Wooders compared the performance of the tennis players with subjects in a previous lab experiment, and the data from the tennis players was starkly different from that of the lab subjects. Less clear is whether people experienced at generating random sequences in one setting, such as a tennis game, are able to carry that skill over to a different setting, such as a game of poker.

5.2.6 Do biases matter?

To briefly summarize what we have seen in this section, it is helpful to first recall how Bayesian updating requires both correctly interpreting signals and updating probabilities according to Bayes' rule. Confirmatory bias means that people are biased in interpreting signals. The law of small numbers means that people do not update probabilities according to Bayes' rule. Overall, therefore, we get a somewhat pessimistic picture of people's ability to use new information appropriately.

Table 5.10 Data from the 1982 Wimbledon final. If maximizing their payoff, players should win approximately as many points to the left and right. A high number of streaks tells us if players were switching from left to right more often than a random sequence

		Serves			*Points won*		*Streaks*	
Player	*Court*	*Total*	*Left (%)*	*Right (%)*	*Left (%)*	*Right (%)*	*Number*	*Prob. if random*
Connors	Ad	78	41	59	50	70	49	0.001
	Deuce	91	84	16	67	53	31	0.042
McEnroe	Ad	71	45	55	72	62	36	0.563
	Deuce	79	44	56	69	68	36	0.848

Source: Walker and Wooders (2001).

And the bad news does not stop there, because there are many other biases that I have not mentioned here (some of which we shall see later).

Do such biases matter? Some important consequences of the biases we have seen include: (i) over-confidence and wrong beliefs; (ii) a belief that there is more variation in a population than there actually is; (iii) a polarization of views, despite people seeing similar information. These look like pretty important things. For example, over-confidence can cause John to make a relatively uninformed choice of car and not choose the car that is best for him. Polarization can lead to prejudice and discrimination. It is clear, therefore, that we do need to take seriously possible biases in interpreting new information. This will be further illustrated when we look at health care and the stock market later in this chapter.

5.3 Learning from others

One issue that we need to consider in a bit more detail is how to interpret information that comes from other people. Often this is how we get new information, for example, John asking his friend or reading a magazine review. The complication I want us to think about is that John only sees the choice or decision of the other person and not the reason for that choice. For example, if John sees a friend driving the Sporty car, then he can never really know why his friend chose it. Instead he has to try and infer his friend's motives and then question whether this tells him anything useful.

When trying to infer motives many complicating questions arise, such as: (i) how biased is my friend?; (ii) does he have similar preferences or tastes to me?; and (iii) is he deliberately trying to manipulate me? We need to have some answers to all these questions.

5.3.1 To conform or not

To get us started, imagine that John test drives both the Sporty and Comfort and decides he prefers the Sporty. Before he makes a final decision, however, he goes out and looks at what others are driving. If he sees lots of others driving Comfort should he change his mind?

To answer that question it is useful to work through a simple model. Suppose that everyone has the same preferences. So, either the Comfort is the best car for everyone or the Sporty is the best car for everyone. Let β be the probability that Comfort is the best. Before anyone buys a car they test drive both cars and form an independent opinion of which car is best. If Comfort really is the best car, there is a θ_C chance a person will prefer Comfort on the test drive, and if Sporty is the best car, there is a θ_S chance they will prefer Sporty on the test drive. To see what happens I will set $\beta = 0.5$ and $\theta_C = \theta_S = 0.67$ and work through the possible choices. Table 5.11 summarizes what is going on.

Anna is first to buy a car. She has no choice but to buy the car she preferred on the test drive. Imagine she preferred the Comfort and bought it.

Alan is the next to buy a car. He does the test drive and sees that Anna has bought the Comfort. If he preferred the Comfort on the test drive, then he has an

Table 5.11 An information cascade. Anna and Alan both prefer Comfort when they test drive it, so buy it. Emma preferred Sporty but can see that the other two have bought Comfort, so also buys Comfort. Same for John. If three friends each prefer the Sporty, their three signals outweigh the two choices of Anna and Alan

	Order to buy a car					
	1st	*2nd*	*3rd*	*4th*	*5th to 9th*	*10th*
Person	Anna	Alan	Emma	John	–	3 friends
Signal	Comfort	Comfort	Sporty	Sporty	–	3 Sporty
Choice	Comfort	Comfort	Comfort	Comfort	Comfort	Sporty

easy choice. If he preferred the Sporty, he has a more difficult choice; it makes sense, however, to choose the Sporty. Imagine that Alan actually preferred the Comfort on the test drive and bought it.

The choice of both Anna and Alan tells a lot about what car they preferred on the test drive. In particular, it should be possible to infer their signal from their choice. If Anna buys the Comfort she must have preferred the Comfort on the test drive. If Alan buys the Sporty he must have preferred the Sporty on the test drive. This means that observing what they bought is useful information.

Emma is the third person to buy a car. She can see that two people have bought the Comfort and from this infers that two people must have preferred the Comfort on the test drive. What does that mean? Even if Emma does a test drive and prefers the Sporty, it is still two against one in favor of the Comfort. Using Bayes' rule, these two observations should outweigh her one signal. She should choose Comfort.

Irrespective of what she thinks on the test drive, Emma should choose Comfort. This means that she should ignore her own signal. Equivalently, her choice tells us nothing about her signal. We call this an **information cascade**. The same is true of John and all those after him. They should buy Comfort.

Finally, suppose that three friends decide to all buy a car simultaneously. They each test drive the cars and say what they prefer. Imagine that all three preferred the Sporty. Do these three signals that Sporty is best outweigh seeing nine people driving Comfort? Yes, they do, because the friends should know that they cannot infer anything from Emma, John, and those that follow buying Comfort. They only bought Comfort because Anna and Alan did. So, it is three signals versus two observations and they should buy the Sporty.

What we see here is that an information cascade can be **fragile**. That three, four, five, or more bought Comfort conveys no new information. Thus, someone with a more precise signal may want to go with their signal rather than what others have been observed doing.

What can we learn from this model? First of all we see that a person's choice may convey a lot of information about what they know. This is the case for Anna, Alan, and the three friends. We also see, however, that a person's choice may convey very little information about what they know, because they are conforming to others. This is the case for Emma and John. It is very important, therefore, to try and work out how much information someone's choice conveys before drawing too many inferences from it. In practice this can be complicated to do, particularly if $\theta_C \neq \theta_S$ or different people have different θ_S. But it is more important for us to start questioning how people behave when faced with such situations.

5.3.2 Cascade experiments

There have now been a variety of experimental studies to see whether information cascades happen as predicted. Anderson and Holt (1997) were one of the first to do so and Figure 5.2 summarizes some of their results. There are two things that these results try to pick up. The first is how close subjects got to the payoff they would have achieved using Bayes' rule. This is measured by actual efficiency. When $\theta_S = \theta_C = 0.67$ we see that subjects were pretty close to using Bayes' rule, but in the more complicated game where $\theta_S = 0.86$, $\theta_C = 0.71$ there is a bigger gap. The next question is how well subjects would have done by just following their own signal. This is measured by private efficiency. We see that in both cases subjects did a lot better than they would have done from following their own signal. It is clear from this, and other studies, that people learn from observing others – actual efficiency is above private efficiency – but not everyone uses Bayes' rule – actual efficiency is less than 100 percent.

If John knows that others are likely to be biased in some way, then he should

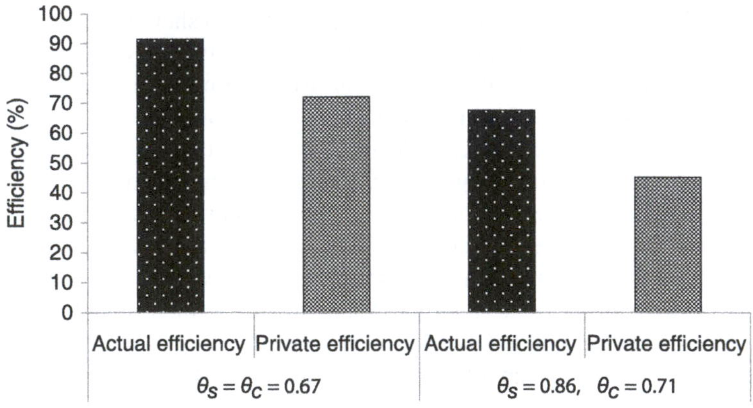

Figure 5.2 A cascade experiment. The payoff that subjects got relative to what they would have got if they had followed Bayes' rule, actual efficiency. The payoff they would have got if they had followed their own signal relative to that they would have got with Bayes' rule, private efficiency.

Source: Anderson and Holt (1997).

rethink what choices say about signals. For example, if he suspects that Emma will follow her own signal and ignore that Anna and Alan chose Comfort, then her choice is more informative than it would be if she was following Bayes' rule. We can test whether subjects do take this into account by looking at choices relative to the **empirical optimum** (see Research Methods 5.1). For example, we can look at all situations where a subject has observed three others choosing C. On average, does a subject in this situation get a higher payoff choosing S or C? We call the answer the empirical optimum and then ask how many subjects follow the optimum.

Research Methods 5.1

Empirical optima versus Nash equilibrium

A Nash equilibrium details a strategy for each person such that it is optimal for a person to follow his strategy if all other people follow theirs. That is, it consists of a strategy s_i for each person such that she can do no better,

$$u_i(s_i, s_{-i}) \geq u_i(x, s_{-i})$$

by playing another strategy x if others play strategies s_{-i}. In a cascade experiment there is one Nash equilibrium and so it is simple to say whether a subject behaved consistently with the Nash equilibrium.

The problem is that, if one person does not behave consistently with Nash equilibrium, because of some bias, then it may no longer be optimal for others to follow their Nash equilibrium strategy. For example, Anna is supposed to buy the car she preferred on the test drive. If she randomly decides what to buy, then it is optimal for others to ignore what she does. So, if Anna does not follow her Nash equilibrium strategy, neither should anyone else!

This makes it difficult to judge whether people are behaving optimally. Does a person deviate from his Nash equilibrium strategy because he is biased or because he expects others to be biased?

This will be a recurring question over the next few chapters, and calculating the **empirical optimum strategy** is one way to address it. First we calculate the strategies that others typically follow. Denote by e_i the strategy the person usually plays. We then ask whether person i is maximizing his payoff,

$$u_i(e_i, e_{-i}) \geq u_i(x, e_{-i})$$

given that others are playing e_{-i}. If yes, then we say that i is playing the empirical optimum strategy. If all people play the empirical optimum strategy, we get back to a Nash equilibrium.

Weizsäcker (2010) did this for a collection of previous experimental studies (see Research Methods 5.2) and the results are summarized in Table 5.12. Let's focus first on the choice rate. This tells us that on those occasions where subjects would

Table 5.12 Did subjects play the empirical optimal strategy in cascade experiments? The choice rate tells us the percentage of times subjects played the optimal strategy. The success rate tells us the percentage of times they chose the best option

Some possible scenarios	*Choice rate*	*Success rate*	
		Actual	*Empirical optima*
Should not follow own signal	44	53	64
Should follow own signal	91	73	75
Signal different to majority choice	–	54	–
Signal same as majority	–	89	–
Signal different to what many and all have previously chosen	–	73	

Source: Weizsäcker (2010).

have maximized their expected payoff by not following their own signal they did so only 44 percent of the time. The conclusion is, therefore, clear: subjects followed their own signal more often than they should have done. By looking at the success rate we can see how much this lowers their payoff. When it is optimal for them to not follow their own signal, they choose the best option 53 percent of the time, but if they were to follow the empirical optimal strategy, they would choose the best option 64 percent of the time.

This drop in success rate shows that subjects did not learn enough from what others were doing. The second part of Table 5.12 shows us that subjects were only successful in learning from others if a lot had all chosen the same thing. Put another way, for the average subject to not follow his signal there needed to be a more than 67 percent chance that not following his signal was optimal. This ratio should have been 50 percent. We need to ask why subjects were reluctant to learn more from the choices of others.

Research Methods 5.2

Meta-data analysis

A typical experimental study will involve around 50 to 150 participants. If each participant makes between 10 and 20 decisions, this gives 500 to 3,000 data points. This should give enough statistical power to test some important hypotheses, but not all. Ideally we would want more data points and more variety of locations and subjects. One way around this is to be a bit more inventive in recruiting subjects, for example, using the internet or newspapers. Another way is to compile meta-data sets in which results from similar studies are combined together. This is what Weizsäcker (2010) did for his study. The results from 13 cascade experiments, including those by Anderson and Holt, were combined to give almost 30,000 data points. With such a large data set it is possible to ask questions that cannot be asked with a single study.

5.3.3 What happened to conformity?

The basic conclusion from the cascade experiments is that subjects follow their own signal more often than they should. This is interesting because it seemingly goes against psychological evidence that people tend to conform to the choices of others more than they should. In famous experiments by Soloman Asch, for instance, subjects given a very simple visual task seemingly conformed to the choices of others (see Research Methods 5.3). So, what role does conformity play?

Research Methods 5.3

Deception in experiments

In Chapter one I briefly talked about the issue of deception. In economic experiments, everything that subjects are told should be true (but there might be things they are not told). In a psychology experiment it is not considered so bad to mislead or deceive subjects about the true experiment. This is apparent in the studies by Asch.

In these experiments, subjects were asked to say which of three lines was the same length as a fourth. In a control experiment only one subject ever gave a wrong answer, so this was a very simple task. In the real experiment there was one subject and a number of **confederates**, people told what to do by the experimenter. In turn, the confederates would say which line they thought was the same length, and then the subject would say. Note that the subject did not know that the others were confederates, hence the deception. On some occasions the confederates were told to give the wrong answer, with the objective of seeing whether the subject would conform to the obviously wrong choice of others. Three-quarters of subjects did conform at least once during the experiment.

As I have already said, the deception in this experiment was to give the impression that confederates were genuine subjects. Economists do not like deception for a number of reasons. A most basic concern is whether choices will be reliable if the subject fears deception, or the situation appears implausible. In the Asch experiments it is simply not possible that a string of people would have given the wrong answer. The subject is, thus, faced with a non-credible situation that can create a sense of discomfort and unease because 'something is not right'. How reliable are choices made in such a context? The study by Goeree and Yariv does not raise such a concern because all choices are made by genuine subjects.

A study by Goeree and Yariv (2007) shows that conformity can matter. In their study, subjects had to choose between S and C, as in a cascade experiment, but without seeing an informative signal. Specifically, the first three subjects make their choice seeing only the choices of those before them. This would equate to Anna, Alan, and Emma choosing without the benefit of a test drive. They seemingly have no option but to randomly choose a car. Subsequent subjects were then given the choice to see a private informative signal or to see the choices made by those who had not received a signal. So, John could either do a test drive or find out what Anna, Alan, and Emma had chosen.

If a subject's objective is to choose the best option, then this is a simple choice: they should get the informative signal. As Figure 5.3 shows, however, this is not what a significant proportion of subjects did. Two treatments were considered. In the first, a subject is paid solely for choosing the best option. In this case 34 or 50 percent of subjects, depending on the stakes, chose to see what others did and 84 or 88 percent of those copied the majority choice. In the second treatment, subjects were paid if the majority of subjects chose the best option. Here there is at least some rationale for looking at others' choices in order to go against the majority and balance out the uninformed choices of others. We see, however, that most subjects still conformed to the majority choice. The end result of this was lower success rates. In the high stakes treatment, subjects missed out on an average of $16.80 each, compared to the optimal strategy!

Overall, therefore, we get a mixed picture: the cascade experiments suggest people often overweight private information, while this study and others suggest people conform too much to the choices of others. These two things need not be incompatible, but just how much choices are determined by own information, or those of others, remains an open question.

5.3.4 Signaling games

Before we finish this section there is one important complication I want to mention. In the cascade experiments Anna, Alan, and everyone else has no incentive other than to try and buy what they think is the best car. Sometimes, however, a person may have an incentive to try and influence others through her actions. For instance,

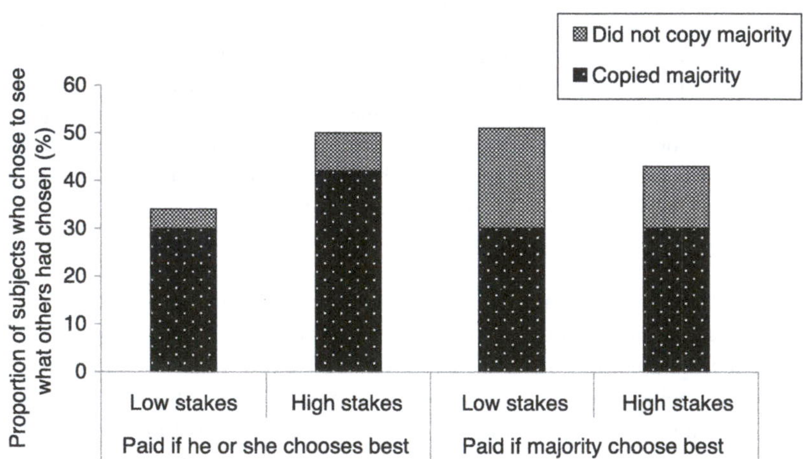

Figure 5.3 The proportion of subjects who chose to see what others had done and then copied or not the majority.

Source: Goeree and Yariv (2007).

if Maria's job is to sell Comfort cars, then it is not a surprise that she drives one. It would also not be a surprise if she says to John that 'it is a fantastic car, far better than Sporty'. She might be telling the truth, but she clearly has an incentive to say such a thing, even if it is not the truth.

To model such situations we can use a signaling game. The basic idea of a **signaling game** is that one person, called a **sender**, does some action, like, say, how wonderful the Comfort car is, and another person, called the **receiver**, tries to infer information from that, like how good Comfort really is. Signaling games are very useful for modeling strategic interaction, and so we shall come across them a few times in the next couple of chapters. Here I shall look at a study by Brandts and Holt (1992) to illustrate the issues that arise.

Rather than talk of car saleswomen, I want you to imagine signaling in the labor market. Figure 5.4 schematically depicts the game in a game tree. It looks a bit messy but is not that bad if we think one stage at a time. Start at the middle. Chance decides whether the worker, John, is low ability or high ability. John then chooses how hard to work in his education. He can work hard and get A grades, taking him to the left of Figure 5.4, or work less hard and get B grades, taking him to the right of Figure 5.4. Knowing the grades of John, but not knowing his innate ability, the employer, Anna, must decide whether to give John an executive job or a manual job. The numbers give the payoffs to John and Anna for any combination of decisions.

The payoffs mean that, *ceteris paribus*, John prefers the executive job to the manual job, but prefers to get A grades when high ability and B grades when low ability. Anna would like to put a low-ability worker in a manual job and a high-ability worker in an executive job.

What makes the game interesting is that John knows whether he is high or low ability but Anna does not. She would like to know and so has to try to infer

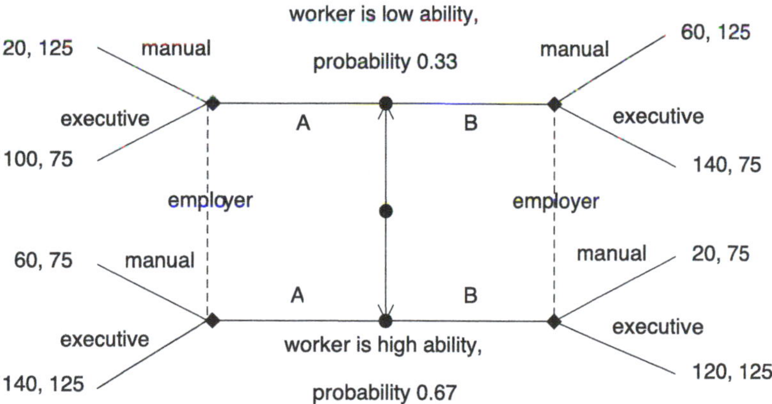

Figure 5.4 The game tree of a signaling game. Chance decides the type of the worker. The worker then chooses A or B and the employer manual or executive. The worker knows his type but the employer does not.

something from John's actions. John, however, has an incentive to appear as though he is high skilled. He potentially, therefore, has an incentive to mislead. It is this incentive to mislead that has been absent from everything we have done so far in this chapter.

There are two Nash equilibria in this game, one given the technical name of intuitive and the other unintuitive. The **intuitive equilibrium** is that John works hard and gets an A grade whether he is high or low ability and is then given an executive job; if John did get a B grade, he would be given a manual job. The **unintuitive equilibrium** is that John works less hard and gets a B grade whether he is high or low ability and is given an executive job; if John did get an A grade, he would be given a manual job.

In both cases there is **pooling**, in the sense that John will do the same irrespective of his type. This means that the employer will not be able to distinguish whether John is high or low ability. The reason that one of the equilibria is called intuitive and the other unintuitive should, hopefully, need little explanation. It seems far more natural that John should have to sacrifice a little when he is of the low-ability, undesirable type, than when he is of the high-ability, desirable type. A priori, however, we cannot rule out the unintuitive equilibrium.

Table 5.13 summarizes results from the study by Brandts and Holt in which subjects played this and similar games. In the top row we see that subjects did not initially play either the intuitive or unintuitive equilibrium. Instead, high-ability workers chose A and low-ability workers chose B. Employers, however, did behave consistently with the intuitive equilibrium by assigning workers with an A grade to executive jobs and those with a B grade to manual jobs. Workers learnt from this, and by rounds 9–12 both types of worker were choosing A.

In some subsequent experiments the payoffs of the game were revised to make workers more indifferent whether they chose A or B but to give employers more incentive to predict worker type. One objective was to see whether the unintuitive equilibrium would ever emerge. To see whether it did, we look to the bottom two rows of Table 5.13. Intriguingly we do see that most workers choose B and

Table 5.13 Play in a signaling game (%). In the standard game, behavior converges towards an intuitive equilibrium. In the revised game, behavior is closer to that of the unintuitive equilibrium

Game	*Round*	*Worker choice given type*		*Employer choice given worker choice*	
		A if high	*A if low*	*Exec. if A*	*Manual if B*
Standard game	1–4	100	21	98	74
Standard game	9–12	100	75	98	60
Revised game	1–6	39	52	45	15
Revised game	7–12	15	38	56	13

Source: Brandts and Holt (1992).

high-ability workers are less likely to choose A than low-ability workers. This is consistent with the unintuitive equilibrium. Employer behavior is not, however, consistent, because those getting an A grade are still more likely to be allocated an executive job. We do not, therefore, see the unintuitive equilibrium, but are far from seeing the intuitive equilibrium either.

This study by Brandts and Holt illustrates some of the more general lessons that have emerged from looking at signaling games. The most important lesson is that people do seem to behave strategically and expect others to behave strategically. For instance, the low-ability worker may work hard to get A grades in order to appear high ability, but the employer will probably realize this and be skeptical whether those with A grades are high ability. Similarly, the car salesman may say 'Comfort is best', even if she knows it is not, but the buyer is likely to be skeptical of such claims.

It seems, however, that people do need a bit of experience before they start behaving strategically. At first, the employer may think that all those with A grades must be hard-working, and John may believe the car salesman's claims. With experience they learn to be more skeptical. One consequence of such learning is that it becomes hard to predict what will happen. We can predict that people will learn, but we cannot predict quite what they will learn; it could depend on all sorts of random things. This makes it hard to know for sure whether the intuitive or unintuitive equilibrium will be the one to emerge in a particular situation.

In the next chapter we shall explore these issues of strategy and learning in a lot more detail. The key thing I want you to see at this point is how complicated it can be to try to infer information from someone's actions, particularly if there is an incentive for them to mislead. Things get even more complicated when we realize that confirmatory bias, the law of small numbers, and conformity are clearly relevant in signaling games. For example, an employer who has some workers who got A grades and some B grades might suffer from confirmatory bias, and think that those with A grades are more productive than they really are. Also, because of the law of small numbers, and a few bad experiences with workers who got B grades, he may only hire those with A grades. Learning from new information is complicated, and learning from what others do is even more complicated!

5.4 Summary

We started by looking at Bayesian updating as the most appropriate way to learn from new information.

I next suggested that choices often involve compound lotteries or ambiguity. This led us to look at recursive expected utility and ambiguity aversion. We saw that most people seem to be averse to ambiguity and/or second order risk. This means that people should be eager to get new information.

We saw, however, that people can be biased in how they interpret new information. Confirmatory bias means someone can misinterpret new information and the law of small numbers means they can infer too much from new information.

Next, we saw that people can also be biased when learning from what others do. In some situations people seem to learn less from others than they could have done, and in other situations they conform more to others than seems sensible.

Finally, we saw that if one person has the incentive to mislead another, then we can use a signaling game to capture this, but things can quickly become quite complex. So, it becomes hard to know how a person should interpret new information.

Overall, this presents a somewhat depressing picture of how wisely people use new information. Are things that bad? On the one hand, I think they are; the assumption that people use Bayes' rule I would comfortably put as the dodgiest assumption in the standard economic model. On the other hand, things are probably not so bad; in particular, people can still make good choices even if they do not use information wisely. One reason for this is the aversion to ambiguity and second order risk. Such an aversion may mean that people simply avoid making choices when they are poorly informed and we saw some evidence for this in Chapters two and four.

5.5 Health care

Health care is one area of life where information is fundamentally important. To see why, let's think about the decisions that are made. A patient will decide things like: whether to take out private medical insurance, whether to seek treatment if ill, where to go for treatment, what to tell the doctor or nurse, whether to follow their recommendations, and whether to seek a second opinion. Doctors and other medical practitioners decide things like: which patients to prioritize, what tests to perform, what treatments to recommend, and what to tell a patient. Each of these decisions requires good use of available information, and the stakes could not be higher because lives are involved. What evidence do we have that patients and practitioners make these decisions wisely? I will look at patients first and practitioners second.

5.5.1 Patients

Recent years have seen dramatic increases in the amount of information available to patients in many Western countries, the internet being one reason for this. For example, patients in the UK can go to a website (www.nhs.uk), put in their address, and instantly find a wealth of information about doctors and hospitals in their area. Everything is rated, from the quality of hospital food to mortality rates. Similar information is available in the US (www.HospitalCompare.hhs.gov). Do people use such information?

The evidence suggests not. The Kaiser Family Foundation routinely surveys people in the US about attitudes to health care. In the 2008 survey only 30 percent of people had seen information comparing health care providers in the last year and only 14 percent used this information. Instead people were more likely to rely on family and friends; an earlier survey found that 59 percent think that the opinions of family and friends are a good source of information compared to just 36 percent who thought that family and friends do not have enough knowledge and experience to advise. Figure 5.5 gives some more evidence to think about. Here we see a strong, but declining, desire for familiarity rather than higher expert ratings.

One might argue that family and friends are a potentially good source of information. The evidence, however, suggests otherwise. For instance, patients are good at judging aspects of quality such as whether the doctor was respectful, attentive, clear in explaining issues, and had a clean and efficient office. Unfortunately, they are not so good at judging aspects such as whether the doctor supplied appropriate, evidence-based treatment! It also seems that patients have high levels of trust in practitioners and are willing to put errors down to things beyond the practitioner's control, even if it be that the practitioner is stressed and overworked.

The evidence does, therefore, point towards the biases we looked at in section 5.2. For instance, we see evidence for the law of small numbers given that patients are content to rely on past experience and the experience of friends; such experience is likely to be a fairly small sample on which to draw inferences. We see evidence for confirmatory bias in the trust that patients put in practitioners and treatments; if they think their doctor is good or medication is working, then ambiguous information may be interpreted in a way to support this belief. The considerable ambiguity of information about health care exasperates these two biases. For instance, if a patient gets better, was that because of the medication or nature taking its course? The answer is ambiguous enough that a patient could believe whatever they want.

That we observe the law of small numbers and confirmatory bias is not so surprising. What is more surprising is that patients have alternative sources of

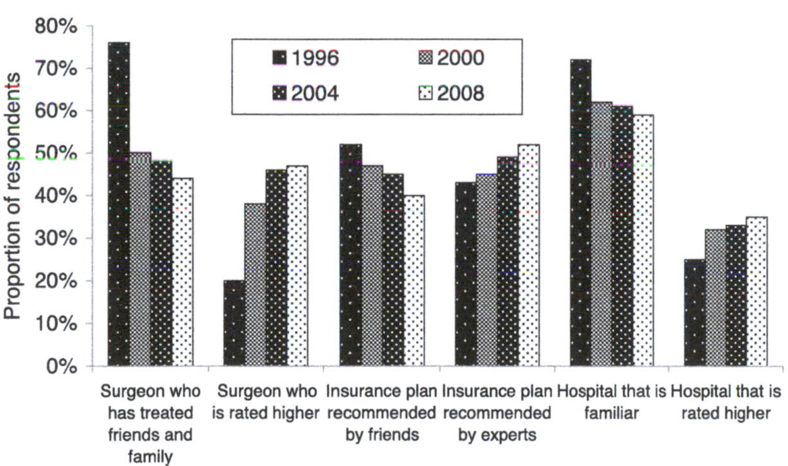

Figure 5.5 Preferences of respondents in surveys of patients in 1996, 2000, 2004, and 2008. Most people prefer things that are familiar or recommended by friends and family, rather than things recommended by experts.

Source: Kaiser Family Foundation (2008).

information that they seem to ignore. Why would patients choose not to use the wealth of information that is available about health care based on large samples and scientifically based experiments?

One possibility is the availability heuristic. The **availability heuristic** could be summarized: if you remember something, it must be important. One consequence of this heuristic is that more vivid and memorable experiences can seem more important. For instance, John is more likely to remember his grandfather living to 100 despite smoking all his life, than he is to remember the statistics on lung cancer. Similarly, he is more likely to remember the great treatment he got at a hospital, rather than a report showing that the average performance of the hospital was poor.

A nice illustration of the availability heuristic is provided by Lichtenstein and co-authors (1978). In the study they look at whether subjects knew the likely causes of death in the US. In one part of the study subjects were told that on average 50,000 people per year die in the US because of motor vehicle accidents and were then asked to say how many they thought died from 40 other possible causes. Table 5.14 gives some of the results. There is a primary bias to

Table 5.14 Approximate number of deaths in the US and estimated number of deaths from different causes

	Actual number	*Estimated number*	*Newspaper inches*
Fireworks	6	331	0
Whooping cough	15	171	0
Venomous bite or sting	48	535	0
Tornado	90	688	153.5
Lightning	107	128	0.8
Non-venomous animal	129	298	33.8
Flood	205	863	41.8
Pregnancy, childbirth and abortion	451	1,932	0
Appendicitis	902	880	0
Electrocution	1,025	586	42.2
Train collision	1,517	793	0
Asthma	1,886	769	1.9
Firearm accident	2,255	1,623	28.2
TB	3,690	966	0
Fire and flames	7,380	3,814	320.7
Drowning	7,380	1,989	247
Leukemia	14,555	2,807	14.8
Homicide	18,860	8,441	5,042.9
Accident falls	17,425	2,585	124.8
Breast cancer	31,160	3,607	0
Diabetes	38,950	2,138	0
Motor vehicle accidents	55,350	50,000	1,440.5
Lung cancer	75,580	9,723	35.9
Heart disease	738,000	25,900	303.4

Source: Lichtenstein *et al.* (1978).

overestimate the number dying from less likely causes. More interesting is a secondary bias in which two things that actually cause a similar number of deaths are thought to cause very different numbers of deaths. They find that this bias correlates with things that might influence availability, including newspaper coverage and whether the subject had direct experience of someone dying from the cause.

When put together, the law of small numbers, confirmatory bias, and availability heuristic present a depressing picture of how wisely patients may use information and make choices. One particular situation where the negative consequences of such biases are abundantly clear is health scares. For example, a study published in 1998 in the UK suggested that a vaccine against measles, mumps, and rubella (the MMR vaccine) caused autism in children. For one reason or another, this story hit the headlines, and despite all the experts saying that the MMR vaccine was safe, the number of parents who gave their children the vaccine fell dramatically. By 2009 the UK had one of the highest rates of measles in Europe. Given that one in 15 children suffer complications from having measles, this is a serious problem that could have been avoided. An inability to correctly interpret new information caused this health scare.

5.5.2 Practitioners

That patients may be biased is not great, but surely we can expect better of medical practitioners? Unfortunately, the evidence here is not good either.

The possibilities for bias are not hard to imagine. For instance, we might imagine a doctor is reluctant to use a treatment that did not save one of his previous patients. More generally, we might imagine a doctor relies more on his own experience with treatments than the results of scientific tests. The law of small numbers, confirmatory bias, and the availability heuristic all come into play again. And now we have a new factor to add into the mix: conformity. If a doctor is in a hospital where other doctors use a particular treatment, will he be the one to do something different? But, this is just conjecture. What does the data say?

One thing that it is very easy to find data on is whether patients receive the same treatment for the same illness in different parts of the country. To a rough approximation, they should. Often they do not. Table 5.15 gives some examples of the differences in the number of people treated in different areas. Such variation is known as **small area variation**. To give a more specific example, Figure 5.6 summarizes some data from a study by Baicker and co-authors (2006) into the prevalence of Cesarean sections in different US cities. The variation may not look that big, but, given the number of births in these cities, there is no way that this could be random variation.

If it is not random variation, then what is it? One suggestion is that practitioners in certain areas conform to the norms of their peers or learn from their peers. This can be exaggerated by the education of new doctors if different teaching hospitals emphasize different methods. For instance, Phelps and Mooney (1993) quote a physician from New Haven: ‘The academic flavor in Boston, the teaching

Table 5.15 The highest and lowest rates of performing a treatment (per 10,000 people) in different areas of the US

Procedure	*Highest rate*	*Lowest rate*
Injection of hemorrhoids	17	0.7
Knee replacement	20	3
Cartoid endarterectomy	23	6
Bypass surgery	23	7
Heart catheterization	51	22
Hip replacement	24	8
Appendix removal	5	2
Hernia repair	53	38

Source: McCall (1996).

atmosphere, has a much stronger tradition of bringing people into the hospital. . . . [When Boston-trained physicians relocate in New Haven] they bring their bad habits with them, but peer pressure changes that.'

Such variation cannot be efficient, because treatment is expensive. So, either patients are getting undertreated in some regions or overtreated in others. In a thorough review published in 2001, the Institute of Medicine gave a fairly damning verdict: 'Americans should be able to count on receiving care that meets their needs and is based on the best scientific knowledge. Yet there is strong evidence that this frequently is not the case.' They do indeed find evidence of under- and overtreatment. They also find that physicians regularly departed from

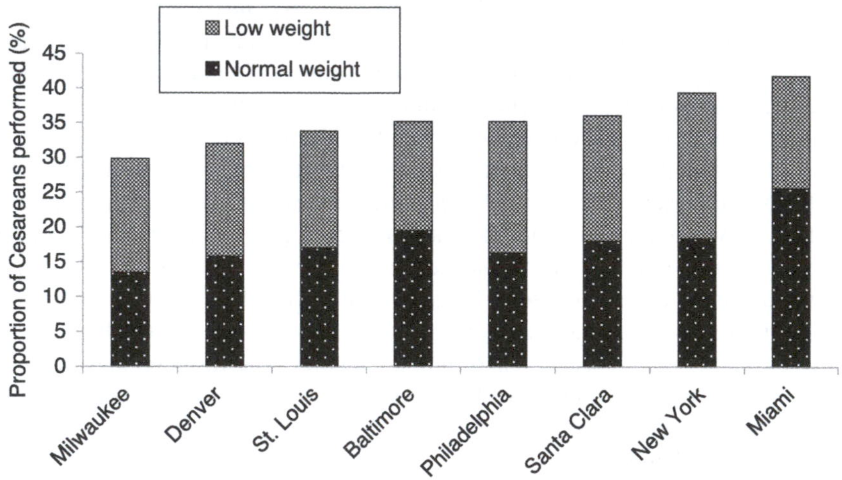

Figure 5.6 Cesarean rates in different counties of the US for normal-weight and low-weight babies.

Source: Baicker *et al.* (2006).

best practice in treating conditions like diabetes, depression, and asthma, and were reluctant to use drugs widely shown to have improved health outcomes.

My objective is not to scare you about the state of the US health system, or any other health system. But we do need to be realistic. Health care practitioners are no better or worse than anyone else, and so they are likely to be biased in interpreting information. Recognizing this provides a means to progress. If we have the tools to understand biases, and we have seen some in this chapter, then we can potentially mitigate the problems they cause.

5.6 Bubble and bust

Bubbles and crashes are familiar in many markets, like the housing and financial markets. It is headline news when markets crash, and bad news for many. This is why crashes are often etched into the history books as a black day: 'black Friday' on September 24, 1869, 'black Thursday' and 'black Tuesday' on October 24 and 29, 1929, 'black Monday' on October 19, 1987, 'black Wednesday' on September 16, 1992, and 'black week' beginning October 6, 2008! What I want to look at in this section is why we get such extreme swings in the prices of goods.

I will primarily focus on stock markets. The **efficient markets hypothesis** says that the price of stock should be equal to its fundamental value. The **fundamental value** is basically the expected future returns from the stock, in the form of dividends. We cannot predict for certain what these future returns will be, and so the fundamental value is uncertain. The share price should, however, take into account all the information available at the time. It follows that the share price should only change if there is some new information about fundamental value.

So, information is key. Given, therefore, that new information is likely arriving all the time, is it any surprise that prices fluctuate? That turns out to be a tricky question. The consensus, however, is that the fluctuations we observe in share prices seem too large to be caused solely by new information.

To explain: mathematical logic says that the fluctuations in the fundamental value must exceed fluctuations in the expectation of the fundamental value. This means that share prices should be less volatile than fundamental value. The intuition for this is that, if people do not know all the relevant information, the share price should vary less, on average, than it would have done if they had known everything. What we observe is the opposite. To illustrate, Figure 5.7 plots the price of the S&P 500 index, compared to the estimated fundamental value. Prices clearly fluctuate more than the fundamental value.

There are lots of reasons to question the data in Figure 5.7. For instance, the fundamental value at a particular time is found by looking at the discounted value of dividends that accrues after that time, and we could argue what discount rate should be used. The data also looks at a composite index, rather than individual assets. Even if we take this into account, however, the evidence points to more volatility in share prices than we might expect. We observe **bubbles**, where price exceeds fundamental value, **busts**, where price is below fundamental value, as well as sudden rises and falls in prices.

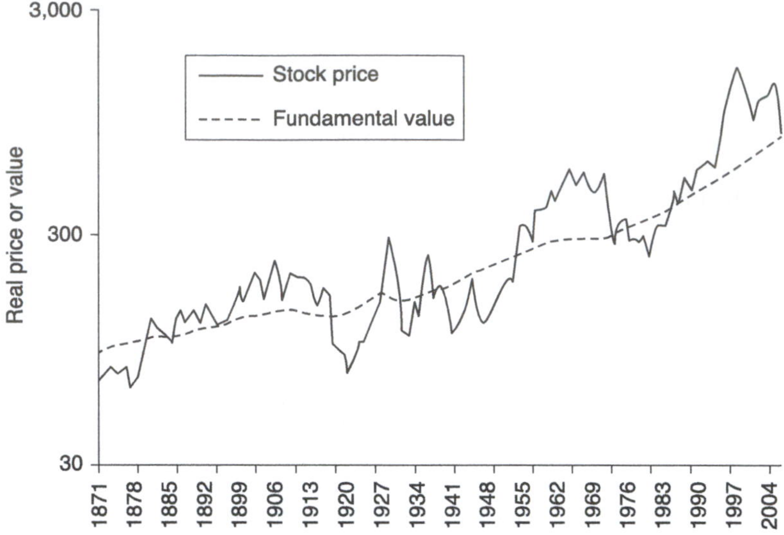

Figure 5.7 Price of the S&P 500 index compared to the estimated fundamental value. The fundamental value at a particular time is calculated by looking at what the dividends were in the following years.

Source: Shiller (2003).

Before we get on to why this happens, it's useful to step into the experimental lab to see whether we observe bubbles and busts there.

5.6.1 Bubbles in the lab

In Chapter two we saw that double auction markets appeared to work well in that the price and quantity traded was close to the efficient amount where supply equals demand. In those experiments, subjects were either a buyer or a seller, knew their value for the good, and traded once at a time. This is a good representation of many markets, such as the labor market or new car market, but is not so good a representation of many other markets, such as the stock market. In a stock market we observe traders who sometimes buy and sometimes sell, do not know the value of the good they are trading, and trade over consecutive periods. What happens when we add such things to experimental markets?

To illustrate, I shall look at some results of a study by Smith and co-authors (1988) in which subjects took part in an experimental asset market. To explain how these experiments worked I will talk though an example, with Figure 5.8 to help. There are three subjects or traders. At the start of the experiment each trader is given an initial amount of money and some units of the asset. There are then 15 market periods, lasting at most 240 seconds each. In each period traders can sell any units of the asset they hold, or buy units if they have sufficient money. This

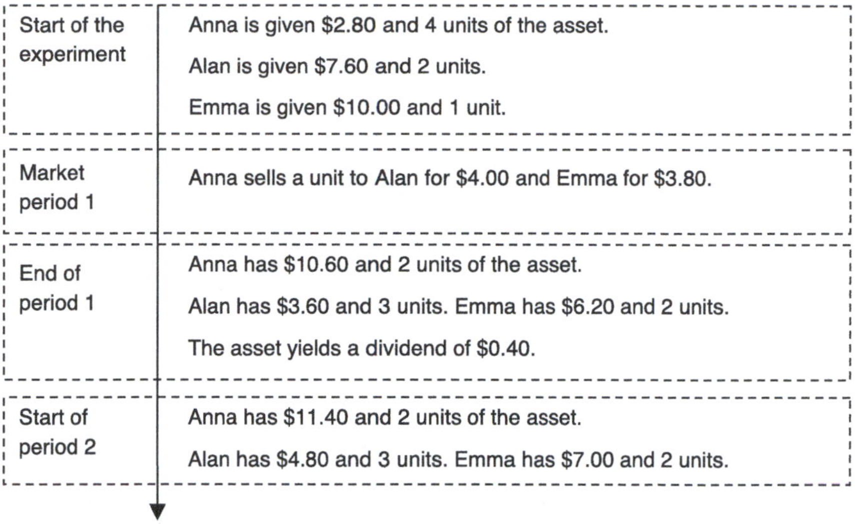

Start of the experiment	Anna is given \$2.80 and 4 units of the asset. Alan is given \$7.60 and 2 units. Emma is given \$10.00 and 1 unit.
Market period 1	Anna sells a unit to Alan for \$4.00 and Emma for \$3.80.
End of period 1	Anna has \$10.60 and 2 units of the asset. Alan has \$3.60 and 3 units. Emma has \$6.20 and 2 units. The asset yields a dividend of \$0.40.
Start of period 2	Anna has \$11.40 and 2 units of the asset. Alan has \$4.80 and 3 units. Emma has \$7.00 and 2 units.

Figure 5.8 A description of an experimental asset market that can give rise to bubbles.

buying and selling takes place via a double auction. At the end of each period the asset yields a randomly determined amount of money called a dividend. Traders receive this dividend and the next period begins. Thus, traders can accumulate money and assets over the 15 periods. At the end of the fifteenth period, traders take home any money they have accumulated, and the assets become worthless.

Given that assets will be worthless by the end of the experiment, the primary reason to hold an asset is the dividend it may yield. Suppose that the dividend could be \$0.00, \$0.08, \$0.16, or \$0.40 with equal probability. The expected dividend is \$0.16 per period and so the expected value of holding the asset in period one is 15 × \$0.16 = \$2.40, the expected value in period two is 14 × \$0.16 = \$2.24, and so on. By the final period the expected value is just \$0.16. The maximum dividend is \$0.40 per period and so the maximum value of holding the asset in period one is 15 × \$0.40 = \$6.00, the maximum value in period two is 14 × \$0.40 = \$5.60, and so on.

Figure 5.9 illustrates what happened in an experimental market the same as we have described but with 12 rather than three subjects. What we see is a spectacular bubble and crash! The price rises in the first eight periods with relatively large amounts of trading. It reaches a price far higher than can be justified by the value of the asset, even on the most optimistic hopes of future dividends. Then, after period ten, the volume of trade slows down and the price crashes towards zero.

What we observe in Figure 5.9 is startling, and to my mind one of the most fascinating insights of behavioral economics to date. This was a very simple market to understand, with a minimal amount of uncertainty. Yet, we observe

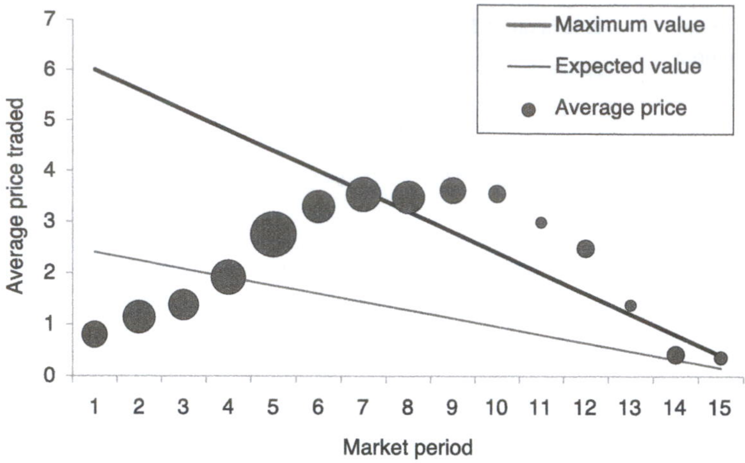

Figure 5.9 A bubble in an experimental asset market. The size of the average price circle indicates the number of trades done. The efficient markets hypothesis would suggest average price should track expected value or, at least, not go above maximum value.

Source: Smith *et al.* (1988).

trading at prices well below and well above the fundamental value of the asset. If we get such bubble and bust in so simple an environment, then no wonder we see bubble and bust in more complicated financial and goods markets.

You might think that bubbles would stop happening if we change the market institution. For example, what if we allow **short selling**, where a trader can sell assets they do not own? Or, what about **futures trading**, where traders can trade, say, period eight assets ahead of schedule? The basic conclusion seems to be that institutions sometimes dampen bubbles, but they do not stop them happening. Bubbles, it seems, are hard to stop, even in these simple experimental markets.

5.6.2 Experience and bubbles

One thing that might stop bubbles happening is experience. When the price crashed, in Figure 5.9, some of the subjects lost money. Will they be reluctant to fall for the same trap a second time? Figure 5.10 plots what happened when nine subjects from the session that generated the data in Figure 5.9 came back to take part in a second asset market (see Research Methods 5.4). As we can see, the bubble and bust is much reduced. In general, it seems that experience is enough to stop bubbles in some situations. For instance, bubbles are rare if subjects have taken part in two previous asset markets in the same group. It is

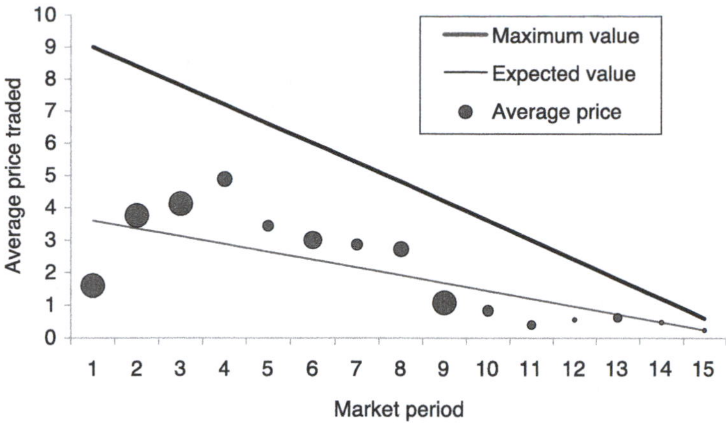

Figure 5.10 The second time that the group takes part in an experimental asset market the bubble is much reduced.

Source: Smith *et al.* (1988).

clear, however, that experience in itself is not enough to always stop bubbles happening.

Research Methods 5.4

Experienced trader versus experienced group

In most experiments we want subjects who have no prior experience. They have not taken part in the experiment before, they do not know the other subjects, they have not studied the experiment in an economics class, and so on. Sometimes, though, it is useful to have something different. For instance, there may be practical reasons for inviting experienced subjects who have, say, some experience of double auctions. That way, it is not necessary to spend so long on the instructions, and still be unsure how much subjects really understood. In the study by Smith and co-authors all subjects had taken part in a double auction before taking part in this study. More importantly, though, it may be interesting to see how more experienced subjects play the game. There are various ways that this can be done, as the study by Smith and co-authors demonstrates.

In one experimental session, business people from the Tucson community were subjects. In this case subjects were experienced in 'real world' trading.

In some sessions, nine of the 12 who took part in an earlier session took part again. In this case the subjects had experience of trading, and of trading with other people in that group.

In two further sessions, subjects were given experience in an environment where bubbles could not happen before being put in an environment where bubbles could happen. In this case there is experience of the mechanisms of the market but not of the possibility of bubble and bust.

Finally, other sessions involved a combination of inexperienced subjects and subjects who had taken part in at least two previous asset markets and performed well. Here it is possible to combine subjects who had previous experience of bubbles, or no previous experience of bubbles.

There are lots of possible combinations and permutations. All of them are interesting.

To illustrate, I will look at a study by Hussam and co-authors (2008). Subjects were invited to take part in three experimental sessions. In the first session they were all inexperienced. In the second session everything was kept the same as the first session, both the market and the other subjects. In the third session the market was changed (e.g. the expected dividend was changed), and subjects were put into a new group. So, subjects were given time to learn and then put in a very different environment. Would bubbles reappear in the new environment? As a control it is necessary to have some subjects who interacted together in all three sessions. This gives three treatments as shown in Table 5.16.

A snapshot of the results is provided in Figure 5.11. The figure shows what happened in three sessions, one from each treatment, after subjects had become experienced. In the baseline treatment we see no bubble, and so it looks like experience does matter. In the rekindle treatment, however, we see a bubble, and so it seems that bubbles can reappear if the environment changes. This could be due to a change in the market or change in group, and the extreme treatment suggests it is a bit of both. Here we also see a bubble that is as big but lasts less time.

It is a little bit cheeky to give the data from just three sessions, but I chose these sessions, trust me, because they illustrated the more general pattern we observe. Experience in the same environment reduces the duration of bubbles but not their amplitude. Sometimes this is enough to stop bubbles happening, but not always. Experience, therefore, does not stop bubbles happening. Indeed, nothing seems guaranteed to stop bubbles happening (see Research Methods 5.5).

Table 5.16 The three different treatments in an experiment with experienced subjects

Treatment	*1st session*	*2nd session*	*3rd session*
Baseline	Basic market	Basic market	Basic market, same group
Extreme	Extreme market	Extreme market	Extreme market, same group
Rekindle	Basic market	Basic market	Extreme market, different group

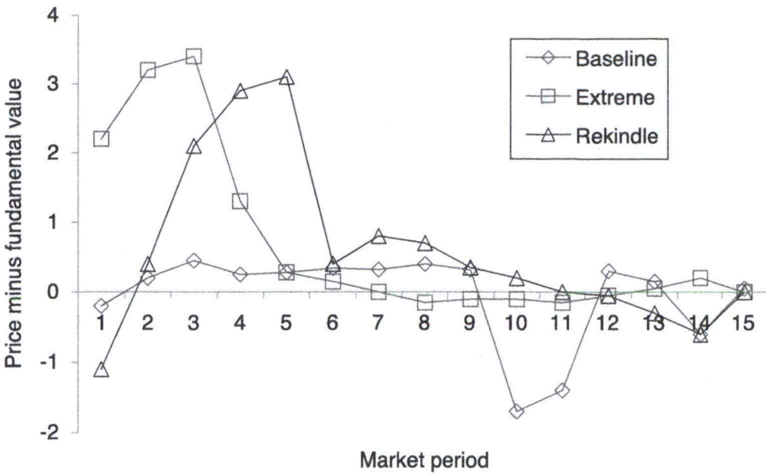

Figure 5.11 The deviation of price from fundamental value when subjects have already experienced two markets. In the baseline market there is no bubble. In the extreme market there is a bubble. In the rekindle market there is a bubble of longer duration.

Source: Hussam *et al.* (2008).

Research Methods 5.5

Why do experiments?

The experimental work on asset market bubbles provides a good example of why experiments are worth doing. Bubbles and crashes are ubiquitous and matter, so we need to know why they happen. But trying to discern this from real markets seems like a hopeless task, because they are so complicated. In the experimental laboratory we can simplify down to something that is manageable.

I think that to most people it is surprising how easily bubbles can be created in very simple markets, even with experienced traders. It is this surprise that shows why experiments are worth doing. Economics is full of very complicated theories for why we might get bubbles. These might be correct, but we observe bubbles in experiments with markets far too simple for these theories to make sense. So, something more basic is going on. Realizing that seems fundamental to making any progress in truly understanding why bubbles happen.

This logic does, however, only work if the bubbles we get in the laboratory resemble those in real markets. Fortunately, they appear to. For instance, Henker and Owen (2008) look at data from the Australian stock exchange and find similarities with the laboratory data.

5.6.3 Explaining bubbles

Having seen bubbles, we now need to try and work out why they happen. Let's start by saying that the bubbles we have seen are not necessarily damning evidence against the efficient market hypothesis. That is because the trading price does eventually equal the fundamental value. For instance, it gets there by period 14 in Figure 5.9, period 13 in Figure 5.10, and period 12 in Figure 5.11. So, we could argue that subjects just take time to learn. This is particularly plausible if subjects start with different initial beliefs and it takes time for these beliefs to converge.

There are, however, good reasons to think that bubbles are caused in part by biases in interpreting new information. The law of small numbers would suggest that, if the price has gone up three or four periods in a row, it should keep on rising. Confirmatory bias would suggest that, if people expect prices to rise, they will interpret a slight fluctuation in price as a signal that this is going to happen. Putting these and other biases together gives something called feedback theory. The basic idea of **feedback theory** is that prices rise because people expect them to rise, and they expect them to rise because they have been rising! A rising price translates, therefore, to a rising price.

Feedback theory can explain bubbles, and comes about because people are biased by what they see happening to the price. What it cannot do is explain the crash. Why do prices not keeping on rising? Well, there are only so many investors, and so prices cannot keep on going higher and higher, because eventually no one is left to buy. In the laboratory, a crash is usually preceded by a period with fewer trades (see Figures 5.9 and 5.10). Bubbles, therefore, basically run out of steam. In real markets there is a less pronounced drop-off in volume than in the laboratory, presumably because real markets are not going to end after a known 15 periods, but the logic still holds.

To give a bit more substance to the feedback theory, I want to finish with an interesting study by Barber and Odean (2008). They looked at data from individual and institutional investors to see whether the news matters. The news might matter because of various reasons, but one is the availability heuristic. When choosing where to invest, people might remember seeing a stock in the news and choose that one. If stocks get into the news because their price has increased this can cause a feedback of prices rising because prices are rising.

One key to Barber and Odean's empirical strategy is the difference between buying and selling. When investing, the investor has thousands of stocks to choose from, but when he comes to sell, he only has to look at those stocks he has invested in, and these probably number at most 100. So, we should expect investors to be more influenced by the news when they buy than when they sell. For institutional investors this is less likely to matter because they can short sell stocks they do not own. More generally, we might expect professional, institutional investors to be less influenced by the news.

If we expect buying to be influenced by the news and selling to not be, then the buy–sell imbalance is a useful measure. For a particular stock on a particular day this is calculated as follows:

$$\text{buy–sell imbalance} = \frac{\text{number of buys} - \text{number of sells}}{\text{number of buys and sells}}.$$

Barber and Odean consider various measures of a stock being in the news, but we will just consider one: whether the stock appeared on the daily news feed from the Dow Jones News Service on a particular day. Figure 5.12 summarizes the result. We see that for private investors there is a large difference in the buy–sell imbalance depending on whether the stock was in the news or not that day. For institutional investors there is no such difference. It would appear, therefore, that people are influenced by what stocks have appeared on the news when deciding where to invest. Interestingly this effect becomes even more pronounced if the stock went down in value that day (i.e. the news was likely to be bad) than if it went up!

That people are more likely to buy stocks that have appeared on the news brings us nicely on to something called the beauty contest, which we shall look at in detail in the next chapter. A slightly different form of beauty contest is voting in elections.

5.7 Voting in elections

Over $2 billion was spent on campaigning for the 2012 US Presidential Election. This is a staggering amount of money. Was it worth it? An argument to defend such spending might go something like this. It is crucial we elect the

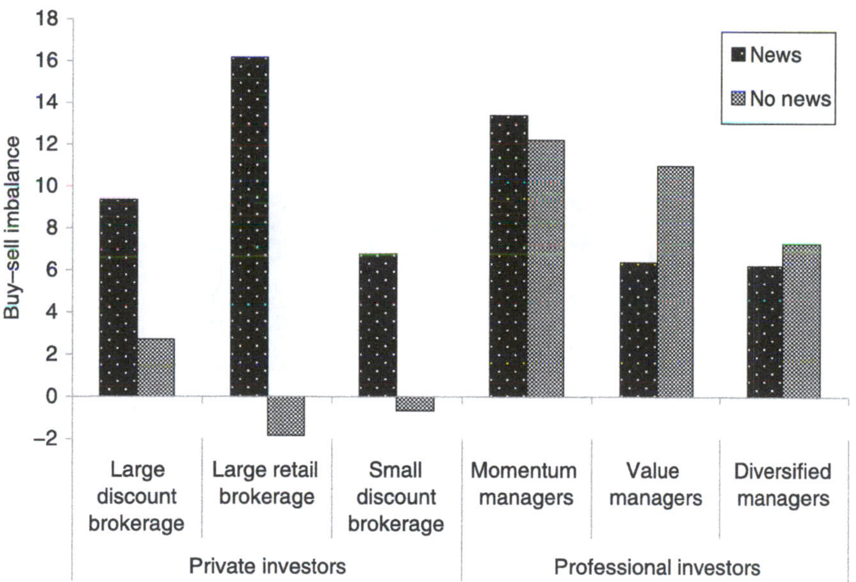

Figure 5.12 The buy–sell imbalance for different types of investors depending on whether the stock appeared in the news or not.

Source: Barber and Odean (2008).

best candidate for office and so all of the money spent on political rallies, TV adverts, campaign leaflets, and the like is essential to inform the electorate. This argument might have some merit if the electorate are ready to be informed, but we have seen plenty of examples in this chapter that people have problems coping with new information. So, do people form an informed opinion before going out to vote?

There are now a collection of studies that provide a reliable way of predicting election outcomes. The method is to show people photos of the two candidates for a second or less and ask them who they think will win. You do not need to give any information about political persuasion, or political views, experience, etc. One glance is all it takes!

To illustrate how this works, consider first a study by Todorov and co-authors (2005). They showed subjects the faces of rival candidates for one second and asked them to say who was more competent. Inferences of competence were far better than chance at predicting the election outcomes for both the US Senate and House of Representatives; the results are given on the left-hand side of Figure 5.13. They also found that the inferred difference in competence was able to predict the margin of election victory. Clearly, such findings are controversial, but they seem robust. For instance, judgments on other traits, such as intelligence, leadership, honesty, trustworthiness, charisma, and likability, do not predict the election outcome. Only competence seems to matter.

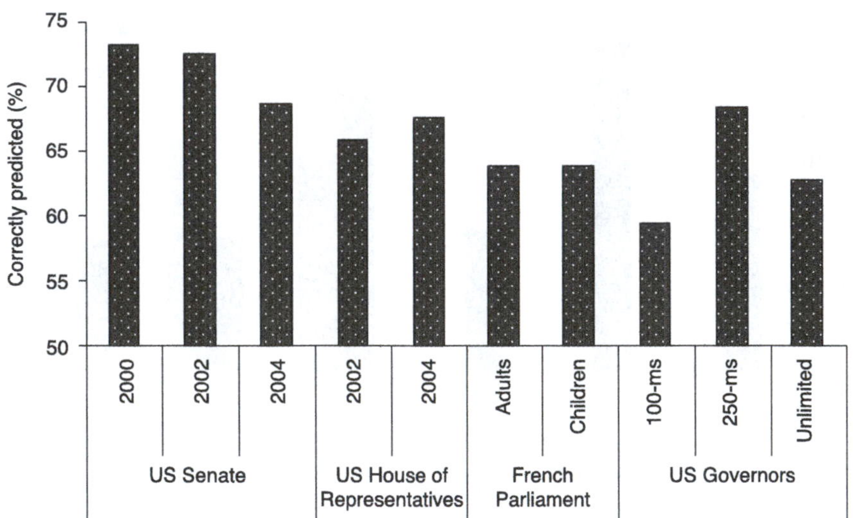

Figure 5.13 The proportion of outcomes that were correctly predicted by looking at photos of the two candidates. In the US Governors elections, subjects were given either 100ms (a tenth of a second), 250ms, or unlimited time.

Sources: Todorov *et al.* (2005), Ballew and Todorov (2007), Anotonakis and Dalgas (2009).

In order to demonstrate the robustness of these findings, a study by Antonakis and Dalgas (2009) is particularly worth a mention. They showed that children aged 13 or below were able to predict the outcomes of French Parliamentary elections (see Figure 5.13 for the results). This shows that the ability to predict elections is innate and not a quirk of the US electoral system (the children in the study were from Switzerland). Also, it is gut instinct that seems to matter, as shown in a study by Ballew and Todorov (2007). They gave some subjects 100ms, or one-tenth of a second, to look at the photos. Others got 250ms, or a quarter of a second, and yet others got as long as they wanted. As shown on the right-hand side of Figure 5.13, a quarter of a second was enough. Having time to think decreased predictive power!

What to make of such findings? They do not imply that people go to vote without taking account of what the candidates say and stand for. Many people take voting as a serious responsibility. Recall, though, the distinction between system one and system two brain processes introduced in Chapter two. Making a judgment on the basis of appearance is clearly a system one process: it is automatic and based on spontaneous judgment. When we go out to vote, or listen to a candidate speak, system two processes begin to work as we reason through the pros and cons of each candidate. Crucially, however, this reasoning is inevitably influenced by the perceptions and intuition gained from first impressions. System two starts from where system one leaves it. So, a candidate who does not look competent has some catching up to do.

Will he be able to catch up? We have primarily focused on system two reasoning processes throughout this chapter. What we have seen suggests that it may be very difficult for a candidate to play catch-up. Take confirmatory bias, for instance: if a candidate is inferred as less competent, then any new information can easily be interpreted as confirming initial impressions. Those inferred as competent will appear more competent than they really are and those inferred as not competent will appear less competent than they really are. Or, consider conformity: if a voter talks to friends about the election, he may be swayed by their views, even though those views are based on first impressions. Do not expect, therefore, thoughtful reasoning to overcome spontaneous inference. Also, do not expect the best candidate to win the election, and do not expect campaign spending to make much of a difference to the outcome.

The more general point to take away from this discussion is that bias can happen in both system one and system two brain processes. This is an important point to keep in mind because it is common to think that system one processes are the cause of all bias. To illustrate the distinction let us look at two examples. In Chapter two I discussed the endowment effect whereby physically handling a mug made people value it more. This bias can be put down to system one processes; the more a person reasons things through, the smaller the bias is likely to become. The picture is, thus, one of intuition creating a bias that reasoning corrects. Compare this to confirmatory bias in judging electoral candidates. Intuition might suggest the candidate looks good, and confirmatory bias makes him look even better. In this case, intuition creates a bias that reasoning amplifies. Reasoning can, therefore make matters worse!

5.8 Further reading

Tversky and Kahneman (1974) provide an interesting introduction to the psychology of choice under uncertainty. Camerer and Weber (1992) provide a comprehensive survey of economic research on uncertainty and ambiguity. Rabin (1998) gives a good overview of many of the biases we have looked at. Oskarsson *et al.* (2009) provide a comprehensive survey of the literature on the gambler's fallacy and hot hand beliefs. Also worth a read is Kahneman and Tversky (1973). One consequence of the law of small numbers and confirmatory bias can be prejudice and stereotyping. The book by Brown (1995) provides a fascinating and thought-provoking introduction to these issues. Bikhchandani *et al.* (1998) provide an introduction to information cascades. Chapter six by Richard Frank in Diamond and Vartiainen (2007) is a great starting point for more on health care. The book by McCall (1996) is also worth a read. For more on bubbles and stock market movements I would recommend the excellent surveys by Caginalp *et al.* (2000), Porter and Smith (2003), and Shiller (2003). See also Dufwenberg *et al.* (2005) for the first study to look at experience and bubbles.

5.9 Review questions

5.1 Why might people dislike compound lotteries or uncertainty?

5.2 Ellsberg (1961) suggested another box in which there are 90 balls. You know that 30 of the balls are red and the other 60 are some mix of black and yellow. One ball will be randomly drawn from the box. Would you prefer to 'bet the ball is red' or 'bet the ball is black'? Would you prefer to 'bet the ball is red or yellow' or 'bet the ball is black or yellow'? Were your choices consistent with subjective expected utility maximization?

5.3 Why might someone who is ambiguity averse delay making a decision? How does this relate to procrastination because of a present bias?

5.4 There are no experiments to test for confirmatory bias in economic behavior. Design one. And then do one to test for the law of small numbers.

5.5 Why might people be overinfluenced by what others do in some situations, and underinfluenced in others?

5.6 Can we trust people's opinions? Why might people trust friends over expert advice?

5.7 Consider reasons why confirmatory bias and the law of small numbers may matter in health care.

5.8 How can we address the problems caused by biases in the interpretation of new information in health care, and more generally?

5.9 When should someone buy an asset that is rising in price? When should they sell it?

5.10 Why do we see bubbles and crashes in the housing market?

5.11 What do you think happens if some traders have experience of bubble and crash but some do not?
5.12 How does the buy–sell imbalance relate to the ostrich effect?
5.13 Come up with a list of reasons why a person's opinion of electoral candidates may be biased. On what basis should the person decide whom to vote for?

6 Interacting with others

> For it is, so to speak, a game of Snap, of Old Maid, – a pastime in which he is victor who says *Snap* neither too soon nor too late, who passes the Old Maid to his neighbour before the game is over, who secures a chair for himself when the music stops.
>
> John Maynard Keynes, *General theory of employment, interest and money*

Economics is fundamentally about exchange and interaction between people. We can capture some of that by saying that people interact through markets, but a lot of the time that is not enough. We need to think how people interact with each other more directly, and that will be the theme of the next two chapters. In this chapter I want to focus on strategic behavior, which primarily means focusing on how people try to predict what others might do. For example, when should a trader sell her investments to ride the bubble but avoid the crash? What route should she take to work to avoid traffic jams? How much effort should she put into keeping her office tidy? And what should she choose for lunch at the canteen? In all these examples, the trader would do best to predict what others will do, whether they are fellow traders or the canteen chef, before making her choice. In this chapter I want to look at how she can do this.

6.1 The beauty contest

In this first section I want to set the scene a little for the rest of the chapter by looking at a game called the beauty contest. In the **simple beauty contest** people are independently asked to say which out of a set of faces is the most beautiful. The face with the most votes is declared the most beautiful, and anyone who voted for the most beautiful face is eligible for a prize. John Maynard Keynes said that this contest was a useful way to think about how stock markets behave. His basic argument was that to pick the most beautiful face is a relatively naïve strategy. More sophisticated is to pick the face you believe most others will pick. This maximizes your chances of winning the prize. The stock market is similar, except we substitute beautiful companies for beautiful faces. The fundamental value of a company may, therefore, be less relevant in determining the movement in share price than popularity.

We are going to look in more detail at a slightly different version of the beauty contest. To motivate this version, imagine that someone called Emma holds shares in a company called FlyMe. At the moment the share price is increasing, which is great, but it is also well above fundamental value. Emma knows the price is probably going to crash, but she wants to hold on to the shares while the price is still rising. The decision she has to make is how long she is going to hold on to the shares before she sells them.

What she will probably do is track the share price and see what happens. That, however, does not make for a very simple story. So, we are going to assume instead that she has to decide today when she will sell the shares, and after that she cannot change her mind. She could decide to sell them anytime between today, zero days, and 100 days from now. Suppose that everyone else who holds shares in FlyMe also has to make the same decision. When is the optimal time to sell?

The 'it' in the quote with which I started this chapter is 'investing in the stock market'. Keynes explains that a trader needs to be 'neither too soon nor too late', and we saw this when looking at bubbles and crashes in the last chapter. The crucial thing is that what is too soon or too late will depend on others, because the optimal time to sell will depend on how long others delay. A simple way to capture this is to assume that the optimal time to sell depends on the average number of days D that other investors choose to delay.

This is what happens in a **p-Beauty Contest**, where the objective is to be as close as possible to p times the average chosen by others. A p less than one makes most sense, because then Emma does best to wait less than the average, and so is selling before most others. For example, if the average trader delays 30 days and $p = 0.67$, then the optimal delay is 20 days. This way Emma does not sell too early, to avoid the entire rise in price, but sells early enough to avoid the crash. To understand what Emma should do in this game (given that she does not know what others are doing), we need to introduce some basic concepts from game theory.

6.1.1 Strategy and Nash equilibrium

One thing we shall talk a lot about in this chapter is strategy. Recall (see Chapter one) that a **strategy** is best thought of as a person's plan of what they will do. In the simple beauty contest, Emma's strategy is which face to choose. In a p-beauty contest Emma's strategy is how long to delay. Emma's payoff will depend on her strategy, and the strategy of others.

When it comes to determining payoff in the p-beauty contest there are different possibilities. In the most commonly used version the investor closest to the optimal delay earns a positive payoff and everyone else gets nothing. An alternative version will be more useful for our purposes, in order to illustrate the concepts that follow. In this version the investor gets a higher payoff the closer she is to the optimal delay. For example, in a 0.5-beauty contest with n investors, we could write the payoff of Emma as:

$$u_E(s_E, s_{-E}) = 100 - \left| s_E - 0.5 \times \left(\frac{s_1 + s_2 + \ldots + s_n}{n} \right) \right|$$

where s_E is her strategy and s_{-E} is a shorthand way of writing down the strategies of everyone but her. She wants, therefore, to be as close as possible to 0.5 times the average, and if she gets it spot on, her payoff is 100.

One of the most basic concepts in game theory is that of a dominated strategy. To illustrate the idea, let's think about the 0.5-beauty contest. Given that investors can delay at most 100 days, the highest the average delay can possibly be is 100 days. This means that the highest the optimal delay can possibly be is $0.5 \times 100 = 50$ days. Does it, therefore, make sense for Emma to delay more than 50 days? No; by delaying 50 days she is guaranteed doing at least as well as if she delays 51, 52, or more days. This does not mean she should necessarily want to delay 50 days, but it does mean she would be unwise to delay more than 50 days; the strategy of waiting 50 days dominates any strategy of waiting more than 50 days.

More generally, we say that a strategy *l* **dominates** a strategy *j* for Emma if she always gets a higher payoff from *l* than from *j*, that is:

$$u_E(l, s_{-E}) > u_E(j, s_{-E})$$

for any s_{-E}. The prediction is that people should not play a dominated strategy. Intuitively, this makes sense because strategy *l* is guaranteed to give a higher payoff than *j*, so why play *j*?

Now, suppose that Emma believes no one would ever play a dominated strategy. For instance, she does not expect anyone to delay more than 50 days in a 0.5-beauty contest. If no one is going to delay more than 50 days, then the optimal delay cannot be more than $0.5 \times 50 = 25$ days. This means that delaying 25 days seems better than delaying more than 25 days. We say that the strategy to delay more than 25 days is **one-step dominated** by a strategy to wait 25 days. The one step is there to acknowledge that Emma needed to go through one step of reasoning to get to this; first she eliminates anyone waiting more than 50 days, and then she eliminates waiting more than 25 days. But why stop there? If Emma believes that no one would ever play a one-step dominated strategy and delay more than 25 days, then there is no sense in delaying more than 12.5 days. The strategy to delay more than 12.5 days is **two-step dominated** by a strategy to wait 12.5 days.

More generally, we say that strategy *j* is **one-step dominated** by strategy *l* for Emma if she always gets a higher payoff from *l* than from *j* if no one plays a dominated strategy, that is:

$$u_E(l, s_{-E}) > u_E(j, s_{-E})$$

for all s_{-E} where no one plays a dominated strategy. Two-step dominates and three-step dominates are defined in an analogous way.

To continue in this way is called **iterated deletion of dominated strategies**. There is a logic that says people should only play strategies that **survive** iterated deletion of dominated strategies. What strategies survive iterated deletion of dominated strategies in the 0.5-beauty contest? There is only one, and that is to delay zero days. We get, therefore, a very specific prediction of what should happen in this game.

This prediction is an example of a Nash equilibrium. Recall that a **Nash equilibrium** is a list of strategies s_1 to s_n for each person such that no one could change their strategy and do better. That is,

$$u_i(s_i, s_{-i}) \geq u_i(j, s_{-i})$$

for all people i and any strategy j. A dominated strategy cannot be part of a Nash equilibrium and so, if there is only one strategy that survives iterated deletion of dominated strategies, then that strategy must be a Nash equilibrium strategy. In the 0.5-beauty contest, for example, the unique Nash equilibrium is that everyone chooses zero.

If, as in the 0.5-beauty contest, there is only one strategy that survives iterated deletion of dominated strategies, then we get a nice and simple prediction. Unfortunately, things do not always work out so nicely. Sometimes, eliminating dominated strategies does not get us very far, and we end up with multiple Nash equilibrium. We already came across this in the previous chapter where there was an intuitive and unintuitive equilibrium in a signaling game.

To give another example, think about a 1.5-beauty contest, where it is optimal to choose 1.5 times the average. What should Emma do if everyone else chooses zero? The best she can do is to also choose zero, because $0 = 1.5 \times 0$ and she will be spot on the optimal delay. What should Emma do if everyone else chooses 100 days? The best she can do is to also choose 100 because that is as close as she can get to the optimal delay of 150 days. 'Everyone delays zero days' and 'everyone delays 100 days' are both Nash equilibria, and we can tell from this that there is no dominated strategy in this game.

If there are multiple Nash equilibria, we get a less precise prediction of what will happen. But, we still get a prediction. The natural question is whether dominance and Nash equilibrium give us good predictions.

6.1.2 Choice in a beauty contest

To recap: in a p-beauty contest, the Nash equilibrium is for everyone to choose zero if $p < 1$, and either for everyone to choose zero or everyone to choose 100 if $p > 1$. Is this what people actually do? Figure 6.1 gives some data from a study by Nagel (1995). It shows what numbers subjects chose the first time they played a p-beauty contest. A couple of things stand out from this data. On the one hand it looks a mess, because there is a lot of heterogeneity in what subjects did and very few chose the Nash equilibrium strategy. On the other hand, there are clear peaks in the data that change as p varies. So, people are not playing the Nash

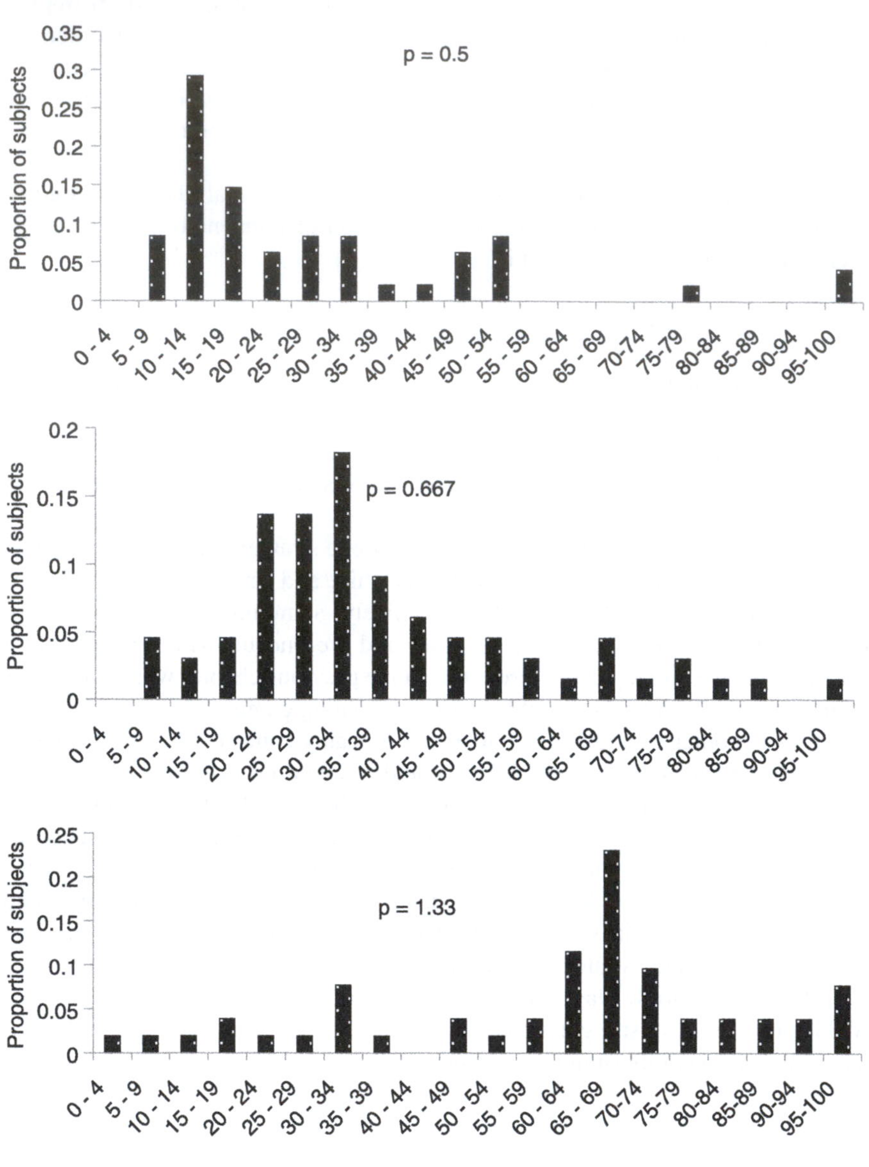

Figure 6.1 Choices the first time that subjects play a p-beauty contest.

Source: Nagel (1995).

equilibrium, but they are seemingly responding in a systematic way to the incentives of the game.

Why does the Nash equilibrium turn out to be such a bad predictor in this game? One thing we can do is to see whether people play dominated strategies or not. Let's say that a person is **type D-0** if they never play a dominated strategy, but may play a one-step dominated strategy. Similarly, someone is a **type D-k** if they never play a k-step dominated strategy, but may play a $k + 1$-step dominated strategy. By looking at Figure 6.1 we can start to work out how many subjects seemed to be of each type. A study by Ho, Camerer and Weigelt (1998) does this in a more structured way by looking at four different beauty contests. Their results are summarized in Table 6.1, where lower bounds are put on the proportion of subjects of each type. They are lower bounds because someone who does not realize that a strategy is dominated may still not play it, by accident.

The results in Table 6.1 are broadly consistent with what we see in many other games. Relatively few people play dominated strategies, but most people only go through one, two, or three steps of iterated deletion of dominated strategies. To say that people do not play dominated or iterated dominant strategies does, therefore, give us some power to predict what people will do, but we are going to need more than this to fully understand what is going on (see also Research Methods 6.1). For example, looking at Figure 6.1, we have an explanation for why so few people choose more than 50 when $p = 0.5$ or 0.667, or less than 50 when $p = 1.33$. We are still lacking an explanation for the choices people did make. This, though, is arguably natural enough, because the focus in looking at dominated strategies is on what strategies people will not use, and not on what they will.

6.1.3 Learning in a beauty contest

The next issue I want to look at is what happens when the same game is played a second, third, and fourth time. Figure 6.2 illustrates what happened in the study by Nagel. There is a clear downward trend in the average number chosen. This suggests that subjects learnt from experience, and behavior is converging towards

Table 6.1 Proportion of subjects of each type in four p-beauty contests

Game	*Type (%)*					
	Played dominated	*D-0*	*D-1*	*D-2*	*D-3*	*D-4 +*
$p = 1.3$	15.7	36.4	36.1	11.8		
$p = 1.1$	4.3	3.2	5.1	9.8	35.0	42.6
$p = 0.9$	4.4	2.6	8.4	6.2	12.0	63.4
$p = 0.7$	15.0	23.2	18.9	12.5	13.9	16.5

Source: Ho *et al.* (1998).

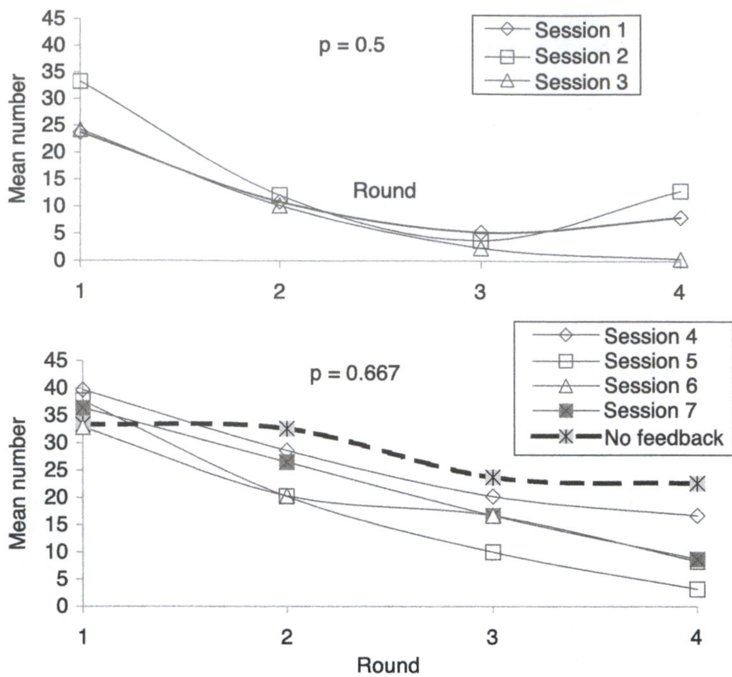

Figure 6.2 The mean number chosen when playing a p-beauty contest four consecutive times, for each of the experimental sessions.

Sources: Nagel (1995), Weber (2003).

the Nash equilibrium. The Nash equilibrium becomes, therefore, a better predictor if people have some experience with the game. Just to illustrate how intriguing this issue can be, in Figure 6.2 I also included data from a no-feedback treatment from a study by Weber (2003). In the experiments by Nagel, subjects were told after each round what the winning number was before they played again. Most subjects guessed too high and so lowered their choice next round, making things converge towards the Nash equilibrium. In the no-feedback treatment, subjects were not told the winning number before playing again. Subjects could not, therefore, have known that they guessed too high. Still, however, the choice decreases over the rounds!

This discussion of the beauty contest helps motivate the three key themes I want to focus on in the rest of the chapter. First, I want us to think more about what people do the first time they play a game, like the beauty contest. How can we explain the data in Figure 6.1? Second, I want us to think more about how people learn when playing a game several times. How can we explain the data in Figure 6.2? Third, I want us to think more about the relevance of the Nash equilibrium, particularly in situations when there are multiple Nash equilibria. Once we have done all that we should have a good picture of how people behave in strategic situations.

6.2 Playing for the first time

I will begin by looking at how we can model what people do when they play a game for the first time. A useful starting point for doing that is something called level-k thinking.

6.2.1 Level-k thinking

The basic idea behind level-k thinking is that someone, like Emma, forms an expectation of what others will do and tries to be 'one step ahead of them'. In a p-beauty contest this is nice and easy to apply: Emma is assumed to form an expectation of the average delay of others and then guesses p times that average. For example, if she thinks the average will be 50, she will guess $50p$, and if she thinks the average will be $50p$ she will guess $50p^2$.

In a general model of **level-k thinking** we start with people of **type L-0** who are assumed to choose without thinking too much about what others will do (more on this below). We then say that someone like Emma is of **type L-1** if she thinks that all others will be of type L-0, and maximizes her payoff given this belief. We say that she is of **type L-k** if she thinks that all others will be of type L-*k*-1, and maximizes her payoff given this belief.

The type L-0s are crucial here because they determine what the L-1 types will do, which determines what the L-2 types will do, and so on. Unfortunately there is no simple rule for saying what the L-0 types will do. Two possibilities are: (i) A **type L-0 randomly chooses** a strategy because they are maybe confused, misunderstood the game, or are simply uninterested; (ii) A **type L-0 chooses some salient or focal strategy** such as the Nash equilibrium. In neither case does a type L-0 take account of what others will do. We shall see, however, that a different assumption about type L-0s can lead to very different conclusions about what everyone else will do.

To illustrate, we can work through the p-beauty contest with the help of Table 6.2. If type L-0s choose randomly, then on average they will choose 50. This means that Emma will choose $50p$ if of type L-1 and $50p^2$ if of type L-2, which equals 25 and 12.5 in a 0.5-beauty contest. Now, suppose, by contrast, the

Table 6.2 Level-k thinking in the p-beauty contest if type L-0s choose randomly, compared to choosing the Nash equilibrium

Type	*Type L-0s choose randomly*			*Type L-0s choose Nash equilibrium*		
	p = 0.5	*p = 0.67*	*p = 1.33*	*p = 0.5*	*p = 0.67*	*p = 1.33*
L-0	50	50	50	0	0	100
L-1	25	33.5	66.5	0	0	100
L-2	12.5	22.45	88.44	0	0	100
L-3	6.25	15.03	100	0	0	100

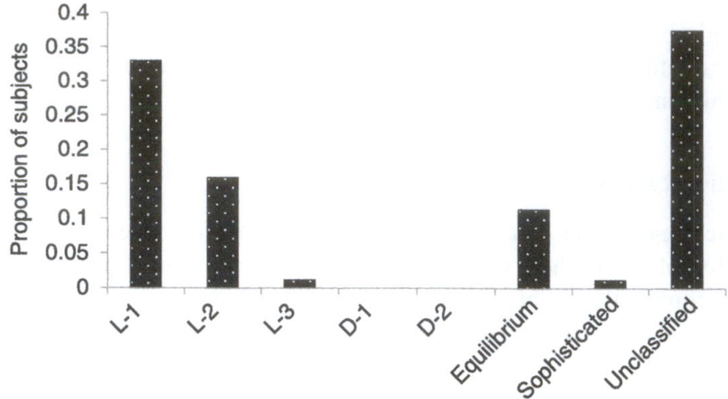

Figure 6.3 Classifying subjects by type after they had played 16 different games. Many subjects were best classified as of type L-1 or L-2.

Source: Costa-Gomes and Crawford (2006).

L-0 types choose the Nash equilibrium of 0 or 100. Maybe, for instance, they have just gone to a game theory class and been told this is the equilibrium. Then Emma should also choose the Nash equilibrium, and we get a very different prediction. Clearly some thought needs to go into what the type L-0s will do, and different situations will suggest different ways they might behave. Having done this, however, we have a simple way to make predictions of what people will do. Are these predictions any good?

You may already have noted that the spikes in Figure 6.1 at 12.5, 33.33, and 66.67 suggest that we are on the right track. A study by Costa-Gomes and Crawford (2006) provides a more detailed test. In the study, 88 subjects played 16 two-player guessing games similar to a beauty contest. The 16 games were chosen to try and distinguish how subjects were reasoning and classify them as of type L-k, D-k, someone who plays the Nash equilibrium, or someone who is sophisticated (which I shall explain below). Figure 6.3 summarizes the main results.

We see that many subjects were best classified as of type L-1 or L-2. It seems, therefore, that level k-thinking does a relatively good job of capturing what people do. By contrast, no one was best classified as of type D-1 or D-2. This is not inconsistent with what I said in section 6.1.2 about dominated strategies, because a level-k thinker will never play a dominated strategy. So, we are still correct in saying that most people do not play a dominated strategy; we just now have a sharper prediction of what they will play. Before we question more how good a prediction that is, I should explain what is meant by someone being sophisticated.

Research Methods 6.1

Seeing how subjects choose

In behavioral economics we are often interested in how people decide what to do. Experiments, however, typically only show us what people do, and not why they did it. It is routine to add questionnaires to the end of an experiment asking subjects why they chose as they did. But it is also routine to ignore such questionnaires as unreliable because subjects may not know why they did what they did. Technology is starting to offer more possibilities.

The study by Costa-Gomes and Crawford used a program called MouseLab that can track where subjects click or put the cursor on the computer screen. This makes it possible to know what subjects would have known when making their choice and what they wanted to know before making their choice. This is useful in trying to understand how people decide, and in Figure 6.3 we report results that make use of this data. More technologically demanding ways of recording what subjects do include eye tracking (see Research Methods 2.5) and brain imaging (see Chapter nine).

6.2.2 Sophisticated beliefs

One slightly concerning aspect of k-step elimination of dominated strategies and level-k thinking is that the higher *k* is, the worse a person will typically be at predicting what others will do. This is because a type D-k believes that all others will be of type D-k-1and a type L-k believes that all others are of type L-k-1. The higher k is, the less sensible this might be. For example, in a 0.5-beauty contest, if Emma is of type D-3, she would think that no one will choose more than 12.5 and, if of type L-3, would expect the average choice to be 12.5. These are relatively low numbers. Is it reasonable that Emma expects everyone else to be one level lower than her?

It might be, but equally it might not. Indeed, it seems more intuitive for me that she would expect some to be, say, level-0 thinkers, some to be level-1 thinkers, some to play the Nash equilibrium, and so on. This leads us to the idea of sophisticated and semi-sophisticated types.

To illustrate, we can look at the **cognitive hierarchy model** of Camerer and co-authors (2004a). The model starts with type L-0s and L-1s exactly as I defined them above. But, now we need to keep track of how many people are of each type, so let $f(0)$ be the proportion of type L-0s in the population, $f(1)$ be the proportion of type L-1s, and $F(1) = f(1) + f(0)$ be the proportion of type L-0s and L-1s.

We then say that someone is of **type C-2** if she expects that proportion $f(0)/F(1)$ of others will be of type L-0 and proportion $f(1)/F(1)$ will be of type L-1, and maximizes her payoff given this belief. Thus, if Emma is of type C-2, she expects that some will be of type L-0 and some will be of type L-1. This is different to a type L-2 who expects all others to be of type L-1. Furthermore, if she is of type C-2, she correctly predicts the proportion of type L-0s relative to type L-1s. What she does not do is account for the possible existence of type L-2s, C-2s, or beyond.

But there is no need to stop with a type C-2. Let $f(2)$ be the proportion of type C-2s and $F(2) = f(1) + f(2) + f(3)$ be the proportion of types L-0, L-1, and C-2 in the population. Emma is of **type C-3** if she expects proportion $f(0)/F(2)$ to be type L-0, $f(1)/F(2)$ to be type L-1, and proportion $f(2)/F(2)$ to be type C-2, and chooses the optimal strategy given this belief. Continuing in this way, we can define type C-4, and so on. Table 6.3 illustrates how this works in the 0.5-beauty contest.

We can say for sure that, if Emma is of type C-3, she will be better at predicting what others will do than someone of type C-2. Similarly, if she is of type C-4 she will be better than someone of type C-3. The higher, therefore, k is, the better Emma is at predicting what others will do, creating a natural cognitive hierarchy.

Someone of type C-k is, however, still only **semi-sophisticated**, because they fail to predict people at the same (or higher) cognitive level than themselves. The final step is to consider someone who is **sophisticated** and correctly predicts what all others, including other sophisticated people, will do. That is, if Emma is sophisticated, she will correctly predict the proportion of people of type D-k, L-k, and C-k, the proportion of people who play the equilibrium, are sophisticated, and so on. This means that she will play the empirical Nash equilibrium and best respond to what others are doing (see Research Methods 5.1).

The issue of sophisticated and semi-sophisticated people brings into sharp focus the relative proportions of each type in the population. That's because we need to clarify what it means to correctly predict the proportions of people at lower, or the same, cognitive levels. For Emma to correctly predict the actual proportions would be asking too much, unless she is telepathic! More sensible is that she predicts the average proportions that one might expect to see. We need, therefore, to think what these proportions might be.

Camerer and co-authors suggested that the higher k is, the less likely there are to be people of type C-k. One way to capture this is to assume that:

$$\frac{f(k)}{f(k-1)} \propto \frac{1}{k}.$$

Table 6.3 Level-k thinking in the 0.5-beauty contest compared to a model of cognitive hierarchy. For example, a type C-2 believes 37.5% of others are type L-0 and 62.5% are type L-1, so chooses 17.19

Level-k thinking		*Cognitive hierarchy*				
Type	*Choice*	*Type*	*Proportion (%)*	*Type C-2 beliefs (%)*	*Type C-3 beliefs (%)*	*Choice*
L-0	50	L-0	30	37.5	33.3	50
L-1	25	L-1	50	62.5	55.6	25
L-2	12.5	C-2	10	0	11.1	17.19
L-3	6.25	C-3	10	0	0	16.23

This implies that $f(k)$ is characterized by a Poisson distribution with parameter τ, and we can write:

$$f(k) = \frac{e^{-\tau}\tau^k}{k!}.$$

Figure 6.4 illustrates what proportion of people will be of each type for three different values of τ. We see that the higher it is, the more levels of reasoning the average person is expected to do. To put this in some perspective, if $\tau = 1.5$, then someone of type C-2 would expect 40 percent of others to be type L-0 and 60 percent to be type L-1.

The neat thing about this model is that everything now depends on just one parameter. If we know τ, then we know how many people to expect of each type, and if we know how many people to expect of each type, we can predict what everyone will do. With just one parameter we can estimate the full distribution of choices. Fantastic, if it works!

Camerer and co-authors estimated τ for a variety of games, including the p-beauty contest, and suggested $\tau = 1.5$ as a reasonable value to assume. Without going into the details, the cognitive hierarchy model with $\tau = 1.5$ seems to work quite well for some games, and so can give us a very simple and parsimonious way to model choices. For other games the model seems a bit too restrictive and we need to better capture the mix of L-k, D-k, C-k, and sophisticated types. This, though, can easily be done by changing assumptions about the distribution of types. We can, therefore, create models that are as simple or complicated as needs dictate.

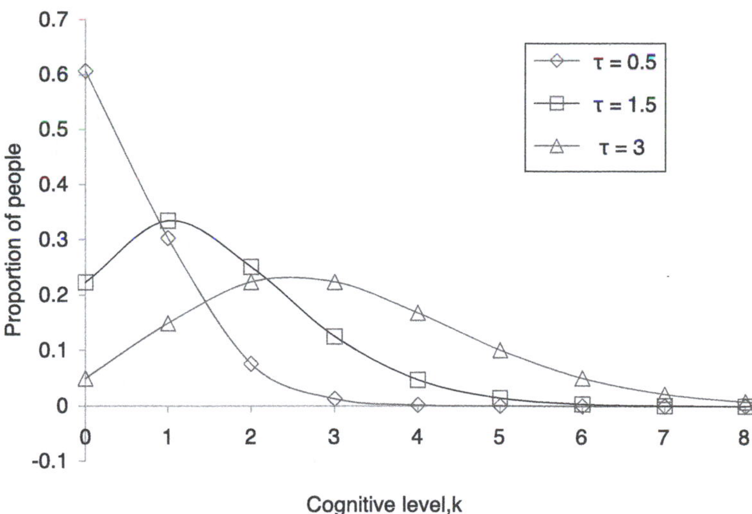

Figure 6.4 The proportion of people at each cognitive level in a cognitive hierarchy.

Let's not, however, get too carried away just yet. If you look back at Figure 6.3 you will see that the biggest spike is over 'unclassified'. With the notions of type D-k, L-k, and C-k we are able to better understand and model what a lot of people seem to be doing, but we are still some way from a complete picture. We have also yet to tackle the problem of multiple equilibria. It is to this problem that I now turn.

6.2.3 Focal points

Consider the simple beauty contest that I introduced towards the start of the chapter. Recall that people were asked to pick which of a set of faces they thought most beautiful, and anyone who voted for the most popular face was eligible for a prize. If we know that Emma is of type L-k, or D-k, or sophisticated, can we predict what she will do? Not really; at least, not without doing a bit of work first. That's primarily because there are multiple Nash equilibria.

To explain: in the simple beauty contest, if everyone chooses, say, face two, then the optimal thing that Emma can do is to also choose face two. The same if everyone chooses face one, three, etc. There are, therefore, as many Nash equilibria as faces (plus some ones we don't need to worry about). Basically, it does not matter to anyone what they choose, they just want to choose the same as everyone else. This is called a **pure coordination game**. If people are not allowed to communicate with each other, then it can seem a pretty hopeless task to coordinate in a pure coordination game. Is Emma supposed to just choose one of the faces at random and hope for the best?

Maybe not, if there exists a focal point. Thomas Schelling highlighted the remarkable power of focal points in his book *The Strategy of Conflict*. For example, Schelling asked people to imagine that they had to meet someone in New York, but are unable to communicate with that person. Where should they go in the hope of meeting? New York is a big city, so this seems like a difficult problem, but most people named the same place, Grand Central Station. As a further example, Schelling asked people to independently choose between the words 'Heads' or 'Tails' trying to match someone else's choice. Most people (36 out of 42) said 'Heads'.

The point Schelling was trying to make is that people are able to coordinate much better than can be due to pure chance. So, Emma does not need to pick a face randomly. But, she does need to know the secret of how to coordinate. There are, at least, three plausible explanations for what this secret is.

The **primary salience hypothesis** is that people choose the option that is most salient to them, and because the same option is salient to many people, people coordinate by accident. For example, people might have said Grand Central Station simply because it is their favorite place in New York. Similarly, Emma could just say which face she thinks is most beautiful and expect to coordinate with others.

The **secondary salience hypothesis** is that people expect others to use primary salience and so choose the option they think will have primary salience for others.

For example, if Emma's favorite place in New York is the Yankee Stadium, but she expects the favorite place of most others to be Grand Central Station, then using secondary salience she will choose Grand Central Station. Similarly, if she really likes face three but thinks that others will like face two, she should choose face two.

Secondary salience may sound like level-k thinking. That's no accident, given that it basically assumes everyone will be of type L-1. It does, however, a little bit more than this because it ties down what someone of type L-0 will do. Someone of type L-0 is assumed to (iii) choose their favorite option, or the option that is primary salient. Recall that when discussing the p-beauty contest we assumed that type L-0s would choose randomly or choose the equilibrium. We now have, therefore, a third possible assumption for what type L-0s might do. The assumption that it seems most apt to use will likely depend on the context. For instance, it is hard to think of a 'favorite option' in the p-beauty contest.

The third possible secret to coordination is the Schelling salience hypothesis. The **Schelling salience hypothesis** is that people ignore what is primary or secondary salient and look for some key or clue to how to coordinate. For example, Grand Central Station may not be the favorite place of anyone, but somehow stands out as the best choice. Similarly, no one may like face four but it stands out, because, say, it is the only male face. Schelling salience may not look much like level-k thinking, but it is not really that different. That's because we can again think of it as assuming that people will be of type L-1. The difference now is that someone of type L-0 is assumed to (iv) choose the **focal point** or the option that stands out the most. We do, of course, need to think what the focal point might be, but let us look at some examples first.

In a study by Mehta and co-authors (1994) subjects were asked questions like 'Write down any year, past, present, or future', and 'Write down any positive number'. Some subjects were given no incentive to match the choices of others, while others were given the objective of trying to match the choices of others. Table 6.4 summarizes the results for two of the questions. The answers of those with no incentive to match should tell us what was primary salient. For example, when asked to 'Write down a year', many chose their year of birth. There is a lot of variety in the answers, and we can infer that coordination due to primary salience would be low. There is much more consistency in the responses of subjects who were given an incentive to match.

These examples illustrate the ability of people to coordinate when needed. That the incentive to coordinate changed responses so much also means that we can rule out primary salience as an explanation for coordination. The data points more towards Schelling salience or secondary salience. Distinguishing between these two is, however, much harder. In the 'write down any number' example it looks like Schelling salience is at work, because many chose number one when they had an incentive to coordinate and very few without this incentive. In the pick-a-year example, it is harder to tell. The majority of students chose the then current year 1990 when they had an incentive to coordinate, and so we might think of this is a focal point. But 1990 was also a relatively popular

Table 6.4 The answers subjects gave, and the proportion giving each answer, to two questions. The answers depend on whether the subjects did or did not have an incentive to match with others

Question	*No incentive to match*		*Incentive to match*	
	Response	*Proportion*	*Response*	*Proportion*
'Write down any year'	1971	8.0	1990	61.1
	1990	6.8	2000	11.1
	2000	6.8	1969	5.6
	1968	5.7		
'Write down any positive number'	7	11.4	1	40.0
	2	10.2	7	14.4
	10	5.7	10	13.3
	1	4.5	2	11.1

Source: Mehta *et al.* (1994).

response for those with no incentive to coordinate, so secondary salience also looks plausible.

More generally, it seems that an ability to coordinate can come from either secondary salience or Schelling salience. Which fits better seems to change, depending on the context. One thing, however, is clear, which is that the notion of focal point and Schelling salience is compelling. In some situations we are able to coordinate with others because there exists some focal option. If we are going to predict what people do in such situations, then we need to be able to predict the focal point. This, though, is no easy task (see Research Methods 6.2).

Research Methods 6.2

Algebra has limits?

In particular situations it can be 'obvious' to most people what the focal point is. The problem is that, to make good economic predictions, we need to abstract away from particular situations to get a more general model. This is hard to do. It is hard to say in general why, and when, 'things stand out' or 'seem obvious'. This presents a particular problem for economists, who have an insatiable desire to capture things in models with equations. The idea of a focal point may be something that equations simply cannot capture. Framing effects may be another. Does this matter?

It should not. Just because we cannot write down a nice equation does not mean we should not take focal points or framing seriously or be able to model them. We just need to be content with a more descriptive theory. Daniel Kahneman commented:

> psychological theories of intuitive thinking cannot match the elegance and precision of formal normative models of belief and choice, but this is just another way of saying the rational models are psychologically unrealistic.
>
> (Kahneman 2003: 1449)

Sugden (1995) proposed one means to try to capture focal points by introducing the idea of a **collectively rational recommendation** (CRR). The basic idea behind a CRR is to imagine two people being recommended rules by which to make a choice; if one or more of them do not use a recommended rule, then they all get strictly less than if they used the rules. To illustrate the concept, consider these three different scenarios:

> Scenario A: Emma and Alan are independently handed five discs that are identical except for the numbers one to five written on the underside of the discs. Both are asked to choose one of the discs with the objective of matching the choice of the other. They cannot see the numbers but an independent witness can, and can therefore verify whether they choose the same disc. The discs are presented to each of them in a random order.

In this scenario there is simply no way that Emma and Alan can improve their chances of coordinating. For example, if both use the recommendation 'pick the one furthest to the left' the random way that they are presented means the chances of matching are still only 20 percent. In this game any recommendation is a CRR.

> Scenario B: Now suppose that the discs have the numbers written visibly on the topside.

In this scenario it is much easier for them to coordinate. For instance, if they both use the recommendation 'choose disc one', then they coordinate for sure. The problem is that they need to coordinate on a recommendation. This means that there is no CRR. For example, recommending that they 'choose disc one' cannot be a CRR because they could both ignore the recommendation, use their own rule, 'choose disc two', and do just as well.

> Scenario C: Finally, suppose that the numbers are written on the non-visible underside but two disks are blue and three are red.

This scenario combines elements of both scenarios A and B. Specifically there is the chance to coordinate (as in scenario B) using color, but this will not guarantee coordination (as in scenario A) because there is more than one disc of each color. The CRR in this scenario is for both 'to choose a blue disc'. This does not guarantee coordination but does mean a better chance of success than both choosing red. In this scenario blue is a focal choice.

Can we use the concept of a CRR to capture why so many people choose Grand Central Station and Heads? Yes. That is because in many coordination games it turns out that the only CRR is to recommend 'choose the option most frequently mentioned in everyday life'. This is basically because a lot more people are likely to agree on what is the most frequently mentioned option than to agree on what is, say, the tenth or eleventh or 235th most frequently mentioned option. The chances of coordination are thus maximized if everyone chooses the most frequently mentioned option. Closely related is the **recognition heuristic** of 'if in doubt, choose the one you recognize, or are most familiar with'. For example, subjects in the study by Mehta and co-authors were also asked to name a mountain, and 89 percent of subjects named Everest.

The notion of a focal point is a hard one to tie down and the concept of a CRR is only going to make sense in some situations. It does, though, give us some insight. And predicting what people will do in pure coordination games is inevitably going to be very tough, given that people are completely indifferent to what they do as long as they coordinate. In games with a bit more structure, where people are not so indifferent to what they do, our task may be a little easier.

6.2.4 Equilibrium refinement

So far we have looked in some detail at the p-beauty contest where there is a unique Nash equilibrium and the simple beauty contest where there are many Nash equilibria and little to choose among them. Between these two extremes there is a limitless supply of different games that are interesting for us to look at. What I want to do here is select three of those games to illustrate some concepts that are useful in thinking about how people might behave and reason when playing games.

Let's start by looking at the game depicted in Table 6.5. If you have never seen a matrix game before the idea is very simple. Alan and Emma both need to decide at the same time whether to choose high or low effort. The numbers indicate the possible payoffs. So, if they both choose high effort they get $13 each. In section 6.6 I am going to look in more detail at why these payoffs fit a story of high or low effort. For now, I want you to think what Alan should do.

There are two Nash equilibria in this game (plus another one I will ignore). There is one where they both choose low effort and another where they both choose high effort. You could argue that the equilibrium where they put in high effort stands out as more salient because it gives a higher payoff. To capture this we say that a **Nash equilibrium is Pareto dominant** if it gives a higher payoff to everyone than any other Nash equilibrium. The high-effort Nash equilibrium is Pareto dominant in this game. Will Emma and Alan coordinate on the Pareto-dominant Nash equilibrium?

Table 6.5 A matrix game. For example, if Alan chooses low effort and Emma chooses high effort, Alan gets $7 and Emma gets $0. The Nash equilibrium of low effort is risk dominant and high effort is Pareto dominant

		Emma	
		Low effort	*High effort*
Alan	Low effort	$7, $7	$7, $0
	High effort	$0, $7	$13, $13

If Alan chooses low effort he is guaranteed \$7, while if he chooses high effort he could get \$13, but might also get \$0. If he is worried about getting \$0, then he may prefer to play it safe and guarantee himself \$7. To capture this we say that a **Nash equilibrium is risk dominant** if each person is choosing the strategy that would maximize their payoff if they cannot predict what others will do. To see how this works, suppose that Alan cannot predict what Emma will do and so says there is a 50 percent chance she will choose high effort and a 50 percent chance she will choose low effort. Given this, his payoff from choosing low effort is \$7 and that from high effort is $0.5 \times \$0 + 0.5 \times \$13 = \$6.5$; \$7 beats \$6.5 and so Alan should choose low effort. The low effort Nash equilibrium is risk dominant.

We see that there are good arguments why Alan should choose high effort, and good arguments why he should choose low effort. That's the problem of multiple equilibria! In this case there is a tension between the Pareto-dominant equilibrium, that gives a high payoff, and the risk-dominant equilibrium, that is less risky. It is only by observing what people do that we can hope to pull apart when people favor one or the other. We will come back to that in section 6.7 and look at some data.

I next want us to look at sequential games. In a **sequential game** one person chooses before another. To illustrate, we can look at versions of the battle of the sexes game. Figure 6.5 summarizes a standard version. In this case Alan decides whether to buy tickets for the football or ballet. His friend, Emma, sees what tickets he bought and then decides whether to go to the football or ballet. The numbers indicate the respective payoffs, with Alan first. You can see that they both want to go together but Alan prefers football and Emma prefers ballet. What should Alan choose?

In this game there are three Nash equilibria. In describing the Nash equilibria we need to be a little careful because, recall, a strategy should be a complete plan of what to do. So, Emma needs to say what she will do if Alan buys football tickets and what she will do if he buys ballet tickets. The simplest strategy is where Emma says: 'If he buys football tickets I go to the football and if he buys

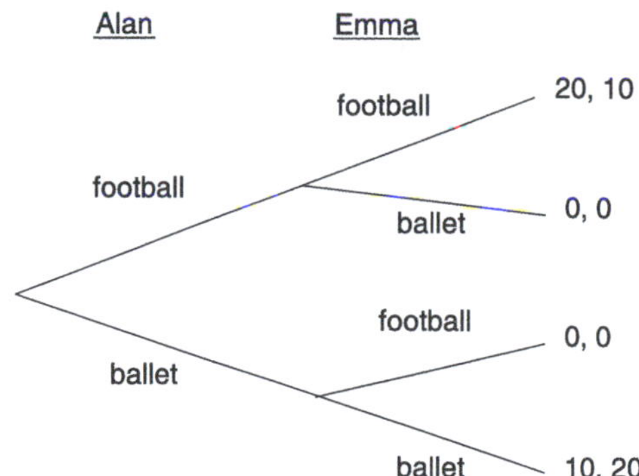

Figure 6.5 A sequential battle of the sexes game. Alan chooses to buy football or ballet tickets and then Emma decides whether to go to the football or ballet. For instance, if they both choose football, Alan gets payoff 20 and Emma payoff 10.

ballet tickets I go to the ballet.' If she does this and Alan chooses football, then we have our first Nash equilibrium.

In this case it does not really matter what Emma would have done if Alan had bought a ballet ticket. There is, therefore, a second Nash equilibrium where Alan buys a football ticket and Emma says:, 'I will go to the football if he buys football or ballet tickets.' The final equilibrium is similar. This time Emma says: 'I am going to the ballet whether he buys football or ballet tickets.' You could think of this as a threat that she will go to the ballet. In this case the best thing Alan can do is buy a ballet ticket, and this gives us our third Nash equilibrium. The three equilibria are summarized in Table 6.6.

How can we choose amongst these three equilibria? One of them probably stands out as more sensible. That's the first one, where Emma does what Alan does. The second equilibrium seems strange given that Emma would go to the football if Alan buys ballet tickets! The third equilibrium is more intuitive but there is a problem. The threat of Emma to go to the ballet if Alan buys football tickets is not a **credible threat** because she would get a higher payoff going to the football.

One technique we can use to justify the first equilibrium as more sensible is **backward induction**. We start with Emma's choice and ask what it is optimal for her to do. If Alan buys football tickets, it is optimal she chooses football, and if he buys ballet tickets, it is optimal she chooses ballet. We then assume that Alan knows this. If he knows that Emma will choose football if he buys football tickets then it is optimal for him to buy football tickets. Another way to describe this is to say that the first equilibrium is **sub-game perfect** because if we look at any part of the game, people are behaving optimally. The first equilibrium is the unique sub-game perfect equilibrium of this game. If we look at the third equilibrium, for instance, Emma is not behaving optimally in the part of the game where we imagine Alan has chosen football.

A complement to backward induction is forward induction. To motivate this, consider a modified battle of the sexes game, like that in Figure 6.6. What I have done is give Emma the option of choosing whether or not to go out with friends before she contacts Alan and asks him if they should go somewhere together. How does this change things? If you use backward induction you will find that there is a unique sub-game perfect Nash equilibrium and that involves Emma going with friends. If she goes with Alan they will end up going to the football and she gets a payoff of 10, which is less than if she goes with friends. This looks like a bad outcome.

Table 6.6 The Nash equilibria in the sequential battle of the sexes

Equilibrium	*Alan's strategy*	*Emma's strategy*
1	Football	Football if Alan chooses football and ballet if he chooses ballet.
2	Football	Football no matter what Alan chooses.
3	Ballet	Ballet no matter what Alan chooses.

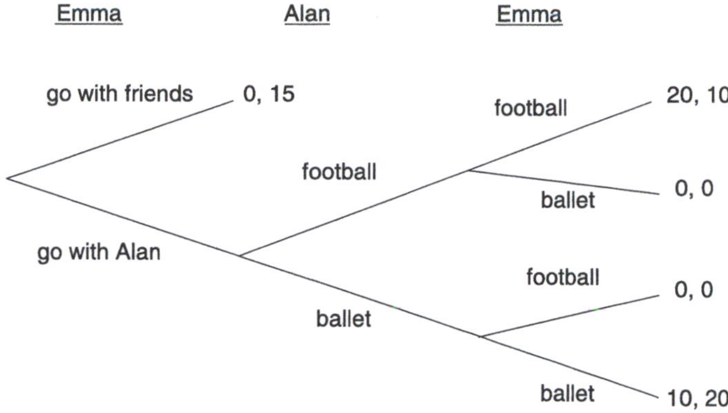

Figure 6.6 A sequential battle of the sexes game with an outside option. Emma decides first whether or not to go with friends or with Alan.

What would happen if Emma were to choose to go with Alan? Alan might reason that she could only possibly have chosen to go with him if she expects they will go to the ballet. That is the only thing that could justify her choice. If they go to the ballet he gets payoff 10, which is better than he would have got if Emma went with friends. This might, therefore, look like a good deal. This is an example of **forward induction**, where we start with the first choice and ask what will happen if a certain choice is made. Forward induction gives a Nash equilibrium where Emma chooses to go with Alan and threatens to choose ballet whether Alan buys football or ballet tickets. The fact that she chose to go with Alan arguably makes the threat more credible.

Hopefully, you are getting the idea that there are lots of ways we can model how people might reason when playing games. Risk dominance, Pareto dominance, backward induction, sub-game perfection, and forward induction are just some of the concepts that game theorists have dreamt up to deal with the complication of multiple equilibria. In the latter half of this chapter and the next we will look at lots of examples to see whether these concepts are any good at predicting what people actually do. All the concepts we have looked at so far, though, are called equilibrium refinements (see Research Methods 6.3); to finish I want to give one example of equilibrium selection.

Research Methods 6.3

Equilibrium refinements and selection

If there are multiple Nash equilibria it seems natural to ask if one equilibrium seems more likely to be observed than others. This has led to various suggestions of how to refine and select equilibria.

A Nash equilibrium is **refined** by adding an extra condition that must be satisfied. For example, a sub-game perfect Nash equilibrium is required to be a Nash equilibrium of every possible sub-game of the original game. A Pareto-dominant Nash equilibrium is required to give higher payoffs to everyone than any other Nash equilibrium. Refining the set of Nash equilibria can be done using ideas from behavioral economics. The problem is that there may be multiple or no equilibria that satisfy the refinement. So, the original problem of saying which equilibrium will be observed need not be resolved.

Equilibrium **selection** tackles the problem of multiple equilibria head-on by providing an algorithm to select a unique equilibrium for a general class of games. We shall see that quantal response equilibrium can be applied to do this. Clearly this approach provides a specific prediction of what people will do. The problem is that the behavioral justification for the algorithm may have to give way to the analytical need to pick one equilibrium. Put another way, it may be natural to think of multiple or no equilibria as possible outcomes of the game, and equilibrium selection does not allow that.

6.2.5 Nash equilibrium with mistakes

In section 6.1 we saw that Nash equilibrium was a poor predictor of what people would do when they play the p-beauty contest for the first time. In section 6.2.3 we saw that the Nash equilibrium was a slightly better predictor in pure coordination games, but still far from perfect. Trust me, we are going to see before too long that the Nash equilibrium is not always as bad. Even so, it seems as though we should be looking at deviations from the Nash equilibrium. One way to do this is to assume that people sometimes make mistakes. There are different ways this can be done, but I will focus on one possibility called quantal response equilibrium, for which we need to thank McKelvey and Palfrey (1995).

The basic idea behind **quantal response equilibrium** (QRE) is that people choose their optimal strategy with some error. The main thing we need to know is that at a QRE the probability person i will choose strategy l is given by:

$$\sigma_i^*(l) = \frac{e^{\lambda u_i(l,\sigma_{-i}^*)}}{\sum_j e^{\lambda u_i(j,\sigma_{-i}^*)}} \tag{6.1}$$

for all i and l where λ is a precision parameter that measures the size of errors. This equation looks a bit messy but it does turn out to be a nice way to capture mistakes. That's because: if $\lambda = 0$ then everyone chooses at random, and the larger is λ the fewer errors people make. As λ tends to infinity, QRE converges to a Nash equilibrium.

To illustrate how to find a QRE, consider the matrix game in Table 6.7. The only Nash equilibrium here is what's called a Nash equilibrium in mixed strategies, where Alan and Emma are supposed to randomize what they do. To find the QRE, let p_L denote the probability that Emma chooses left and q_U denote the probability that Alan chooses up. Plugging this into equation (6.1) we get:

$$q_U = \frac{e^{9\lambda p_L}}{e^{9\lambda p_L} + e^{\lambda(1-p_L)}} \text{ and } p_L = \frac{e^{\lambda(1-q_U)}}{e^{\lambda q_U} + e^{\lambda(1-q_U)}}.$$

We now need to find the values of q_U and p_L such that both equations hold. This will depend on λ. For example, if $\lambda = 1$, then we get $q_U = 0.89$ and $p_L = 0.31$ (check it and see). Figure 6.7 plots the values of q_U and p_L for different values of λ.

One way to interpret the QRE here is that, because of mistakes, Emma is likely to choose left more often that she would do with the Nash equilibrium. Consequently Alan should play up more often than with the Nash equilibrium. QRE thus gives us a prediction of where the Nash equilibrium might go wrong. The really clever thing, however, is that it also gives us a means to select equilibria. This is how it works: if $\lambda = 0$, there is a unique QRE. The trick is then to increase λ and keep track of how this QRE changes. Doing this gives a unique QRE for each λ and ultimately (when $\lambda = \infty$) selects a unique Nash equilibrium. Analytically this is very neat. Does it work?

Table 6.7 A matrix game

		Emma	
		Left	*Right*
Alan	Up	\$9, \$0	\$0, \$1
	Down	\$0, \$1	\$1, \$0

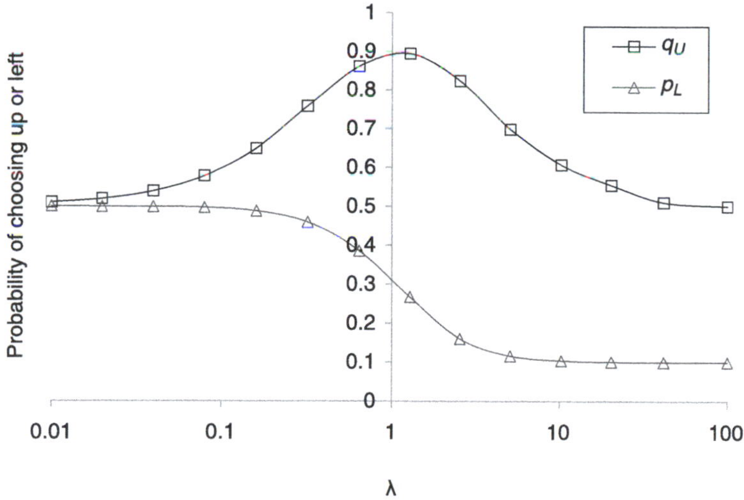

Figure 6.7 The QRE for the game in Table 6.7. The equilibrium depends on λ, where a high λ means fewer mistakes are made.

McKelvey, Palfrey, and Weber (2000) had subjects play the game in Table 6.7 and two others. In these other games the payoffs of Alan and Emma were four times as big. This increase in payoffs does not change the Nash equilibrium but it does change the QRE. Indeed one of the main predictions of QRE is that people should make smaller errors, and be expected to make smaller errors, when payoffs are bigger.

McKelvey and co-authors found that QRE did a lot better at predicting what subjects do than Nash equilibrium or an alternative of Nash equilibrium with mistakes. The news was not all good, however. To see why, Figure 6.8 plots the estimated distribution of λ for each of the games. The way to interpret this distribution is that some people make more mistakes than others, and the distribution shows the probability that a random person is best characterized by the different values of λ. The main concern is that the distribution of λ is different for each game. This makes it hard to apply QRE because we cannot know what the distribution of λ will be for the particular game we are interested in.

Let's finish this section by focusing on the good news. We have now looked at lots of different ways to think about how people might play games. Most of them are complementary. For example, level-k thinking requires us to think what the type L-0s will do, and the equilibrium refinements and selections we have looked at give us some clue as to what they might do. What we need to do now is get a feel for which way of thinking is best for particular games. Before getting started on that, however, I want to look at how people can learn from experience.

[Extra] If you are desperate to know where equation (6.1) comes from, then here is one motivation. Suppose Emma's perception of the payoff she will get is

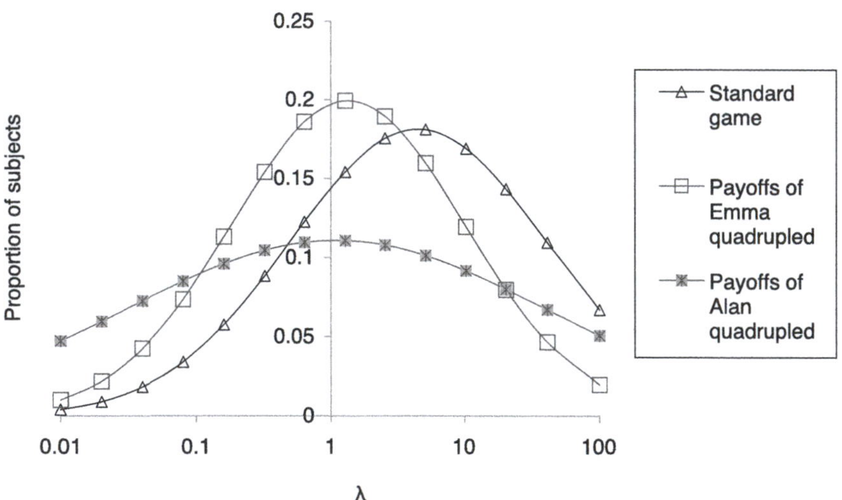

Figure 6.8 The estimated distribution or λ across subjects for each of the three games.
Source: McKelvey *et al.* (2000).

slightly wrong. We denote by $u_E^P(l, s_{-E})$ the payoff she thinks she will get from choosing l if others choose s_{-E}. This will be her actual payoff plus an error, i.e.:

$$u_E^P(l, s_{-E}) = u_E(l, s_{-E}) + \varepsilon_l$$

where ε_l is the size of the error. Suppose that size of the error ε_l is determined randomly according to probability distribution f. If Emma believes others will use strategy σ_{-E}, then she will maximize her expected payoff by choosing l if $u_E^P(l, \sigma_{-i}) \geq u_E^P(j, \sigma_{-i})$ or $u_E(l, \sigma_{-E}) + \varepsilon_l \geq u_E(j, \sigma_{-E}) + \varepsilon_j$ for all j. The probability that she will choose l is, therefore:

$$\sigma_E^*(l) = \int_{R_l(\sigma_{-E})} f(\varepsilon)\, d\varepsilon \qquad (6.2)$$

where $R_l(\sigma_{-E})$ is the set of errors ε_l for which she would choose strategy l. A QRE is obtained when everyone has correct beliefs of what others will do. That is, strategy vector $\sigma^* = (\sigma_1^*, \ldots, \sigma_N^*)$ is a QRE if each σ_i^* satisfies (6.2) with $\sigma_{-i} = \sigma_{-i}^*$. If f is something called the extreme value distribution, then it is possible to derive equation (6.1). The main thing to take from this exercise is that we can justify QRE as a likely outcome if people are uncertain of their payoff function. In Chapter two I suggested people may be uncertain of their payoff function, so QRE has an intuitive appeal.

6.3 Learning from experience

I now want to look at what happens if Emma has the chance to play a game a few times and so learn from experience. In this context it is natural to think of the *probability* that she will play a strategy; she may, for instance, want to try a new strategy to see what happens, or stick with a strategy that has done well in the past. What we need to determine, therefore, is the probability $P^l(t)$ that Emma will play strategy l the t'th time she plays a game. There are two key elements to doing this.

First are initial beliefs. In the previous section we were effectively questioning what $P^l(1)$ is, that is, the probability Emma will play each strategy the first time she plays the game. What she plays will depend on her **initial beliefs**. For example, Emma may have no idea what her payoff function is, or what others will do, and so chooses a strategy randomly. In other situations, she may know her payoff function and, having read section 6.2, be sure what strategy she wants to choose. Initial beliefs are important, but primarily the subject of the last section, and so I will mention them only briefly. Instead I want to focus on the second element of learning.

Once she has played the game Emma will almost certainly want to **update her beliefs** and change the probability that she chooses each strategy. In modeling how this works it is useful to measure the attractiveness of a strategy. I shall denote by $Q^l(t)$ the **attractiveness of strategy** l for Emma the t'th time she plays the game. What a learning model needs to do is specify the **learning rule** or **updating rule** whereby we can determine $Q^l(t)$ from $Q^l(t-1)$. That is, we need to know the rule determining how attractive each strategy will look for Emma.

Once we know the learning rule and the attractiveness of each strategy we can then work out the probability that Emma will choose each strategy. As you might expect, we will assume that more attractive strategies will be more likely to be chosen. The simplest way to do this is to set:

$$p^l(t) = \frac{Q^l(t)}{\sum_j Q^j(t)}.$$

In other words, we assume that Emma chooses a strategy with a probability **proportional to its attractiveness**. This way is simplest but not necessarily best. Other ways include use of an exponential, power, or probit formula. For example, using an **exponential** formula we get:

$$p^l(t) = \frac{e^{\omega Q^l(t)}}{\sum_j e^{\omega Q^j(t)}}. \tag{6.3}$$

The parameter ω allows us to vary how sensitive Emma's choice is to the attractiveness of a strategy. The higher is ω, the more likely is Emma to choose the strategy with the highest attractiveness.

The focus of this section will mainly be on the learning rule, and there are three main models of learning that we need to look at.

6.3.1 Reinforcement learning

Abundant psychological evidence has shown that choices that led to good outcomes in the past are likely to be repeated. This is called the **law of actual effect**. For example, if Emma is playing the 0.5-beauty contest, delays 20 days, and does well, then she is likely to delay around 20 days the next time. Models of **reinforcement learning** or **adaptive learning** are designed to capture this. To illustrate how such models work, I shall work through a model based on that of Roth and Erev (1995).

Imagine that the t'th time Emma played a game she chose strategy l and got payoff $u_E(l, s_{-E}(t))$. Also imagine that she has an **aspiration level** of a (which you can think of in the same way as the aspiration level I introduced in Chapter two). We then assume that she updates the attractiveness of each strategy using learning rule:

$$Q^j(t+1) \propto \begin{cases} Q^l(t) + [u_E(l, s_{-E}(t)) - a] & \text{if } j = l \\ Q^j(t) & \text{if } j \neq l \end{cases}. \tag{6.4}$$

There are two key things about this rule. First, a strategy can only become more attractive if Emma plays it and it gives a higher payoff than her aspiration level. Second, the higher the payoff above the aspiration level, the more attractive it becomes next time.

This means that Emma will tend over time to choose those strategies that she has played in the past and gave her a relatively high payoff. She is less likely to choose those strategies that gave her a relatively low payoff. That looks like a reasonable plan. To see how it works, Table 6.8 illustrates what might happen as Emma plays the 0.5-beauty contest with an aspiration level of 90. Recall that her payoff could be between zero and 100, and an aspiration of 90 means she wants to be within 10 of the optimum. To keep things simple I assume that Emma only considers waiting 20 days or 30 days and the probability of choosing either is proportional to the attractiveness. After playing the game four times she has become more likely to wait 30 days (see also Review question 6.5).

This basic model can be adapted in various ways. One interesting extension is **local experimentation**. In this case, for every strategy l we associate a set of strategies $L(l)$ that we consider near to or similar to l. Assuming an aspiration level of zero, the updating rule is then modified to:

$$Q^j(t+1) \propto \begin{cases} Q^l(t) + u_E(l, s_{-E}(t)) & \text{if } j = l \\ Q^j(t) + \varepsilon u_E(l, s_{-E}(t)) & \text{if } j \in L(l) \\ Q^j(t) & \text{otherwise} \end{cases}$$

where ε measures the extent of local experimentation. The additional feature that this adds is that a strategy becomes more attractive if a nearby strategy earned a high payoff. Thus, Emma would be willing to, say, experiment with a delay of 29 days if 30 days has worked in the past.

The main advantage of reinforcement learning is that Emma need only know her own payoff. She just tries things and sees what happens. She does not need to know what others did, what their payoffs were, what payoffs she would have got for doing something else, etc. Reinforcement learning can, therefore, be very

Table 6.8 Emma using reinforcement learning in the 0.5-beauty contest. Her choice and the optimum are hypothetical, but, given this hypothetical experience, we can see what happens to the attractiveness and probability of her choosing each strategy

Round	*Attractiveness Q^l*		*Probability of choosing P^l*		*Outcomes*	
	20 days	*30 days*	*20 days*	*30 days*	*Chooses*	*Optimum*
1	30	30	0.5	0.5	20	40
2	20	30	0.4	0.6	20	25
3	25	30	0.45	0.55	30	30
4	25	40	0.38	0.62	30	35

generally applied and has a good chance to capture learning when someone is relatively uninformed about a game. If, however, Emma does know something about the game, reinforcement learning gives no scope for her to exploit what she knows. Belief-based learning, which I shall look at next, does.

6.3.2 Belief-based learning

As well as reflecting on past payoffs it may be appropriate to reflect on the past behavior of others and try to predict what they will do in the future. For example, if it would have been optimal for Emma to delay 25 days last time, then maybe she should delay 25 days next time. Models of **belief-based learning** capture this. To illustrate, I will work through a model based on that of Cheung and Friedman (1997).

The main thing we need to do is determine Emma's beliefs about what others will do. For example, how long she thinks others will delay. Let $B^c(t)$ denote the probability with which she thinks others will play strategy combination s^c_{-E} the t'th time the game is played. Beliefs will likely depend on what happened in the past, and so we assume that Emma keeps track of what others have done. Let $\#^c(t)$ denote the number of times that strategy combination s^c_{-E} has been chosen by others in the first t plays of the game. In a p-beauty contest this would require Emma to keep count of the number of times that the optimal delay was one day, two days, etc.

If $s_{-E}(t)$ denotes what others did in the t'th game, we assume that beliefs are updated using rule:

$$B^c(t+1) \propto \begin{cases} \rho\#^c(t)+1 & \text{if } s_{-E}(t)=s^c_{-E} \\ \rho\#^c(t) & \text{if } s_{-E}(t)\neq s^c_{-E} \end{cases}$$

where ρ is a parameter. To understand this rule it is useful to think about two special cases. If $\rho = 0$, Emma would expect others to do in the future what they did last time. This is called **best reply** or **Cournot**, and means beliefs are based solely on the last time the game was played. If $\rho = 1$, Emma believes the probability that a strategy combination will be chosen by others in the future is equal to the relative frequency with which it has been chosen in the past. This is called **fictitious play** and means beliefs are based on the average of what has happened in all plays of the game. The parameter ρ measures, therefore, how far into the past Emma wants to look. The lower ρ is, the quicker the past is ignored, or the quicker she forgets. Table 6.9 illustrates what Emma may do in the 0.5-beauty contest when $\rho = 0.5$.

From the beliefs $B^c(t)$ we need to get to attractiveness. We can do this by equating attractiveness with expected payoff. Given beliefs $B^c(t)$, Emma's expected payoff from choosing strategy l is proportional to:

$$Q^l(t)=\sum_c u_E(l,s^c_{-E})B^c(t). \qquad (6.5)$$

Table 6.9 Emma using belief-based learning in the 0.5-beauty contest with $\rho = 0.5$. Her beliefs keep track of what has happened in the past. The attractiveness is worked out using equation 6.5. For simplicity I only give the attractiveness of three possible strategies

Round	*Beliefs* B^c			*Attractiveness* Q^l			*Others' choice*
	10	*20*	*30*	*5*	*10*	*15*	
1	0	0	0	–	–	–	30
2	0	0	1	90	95	100	20
3	0	1	0.5	140	147.5	145	10
4	1	0.5	0.25	170	168.75	162.5	20

In this case Emma is more likely to choose a strategy that would have been a relatively good strategy to have chosen in the past. If $\rho = 1$, she will choose the strategy that would have been best the last time the game was played. If $\rho = 0$, she will choose the strategy that would have been best averaging over all the times she has played the game. Again, these seem like sensible things to do. [Extra] Equation (6.5) is good enough for our purposes but if we substitute in for $B^c_i(t)$ we can get the updating rule:

$$Q^l(t+1) \propto \rho Q^l(t) \sum_c \#^c(t) + u_E(l, s^c_{-E}(t)). \tag{6.6}$$

Crucial in the model is the value of ρ. In the study by Cheung and Friedman they report experiments that allow us to estimate ρ for different subjects and different games (see Research Methods 6.4 for more on this). The estimates are given in Figure 6.9 (and for completeness I also give estimates from Camerer and Ho

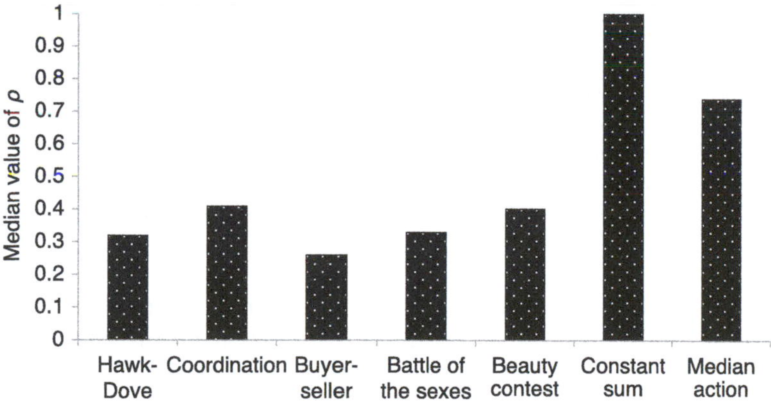

Figure 6.9 A model of belief-based learning. Estimates of the median ρ for different matrix games.

Sources: Cheung and Friedman (1997), Camerer and Ho (1999).

(1999) that we shall discuss below). Overall, we see relatively low values of ρ suggesting that the average player looks mainly to the recent past. There was, however, a lot of heterogeneity. Of those subjects they could classify, Cheung and Friedman estimated 56 percent used Cournot (with $\rho = 0$), 33 percent used fictitious play (with $\rho = 1$), and 11 percent were adaptive (with $\rho \in (0,1)$). Most subjects, therefore, took a short-term view, but many took a long-term view. Crucially, though, the distribution of ρs was similar across the games considered, which is useful for applying the model to predict what will happen in other games.

Research Methods 6.4

Estimating learning models

A learning model is typically fitted to experimental data using **maximum likelihood estimation**. Basically, for any given set of parameters it is possible to calculate the likelihood of the experimental data given the particular set of parameters and model. For example, in the EWA model, we can fix values for δ, β, φ, $P^1(0), \ldots, P^K(0)$ and #(0) and then say how likely a particular set of experimental data was, given the EWA model. We then search for the parameters that maximize the (log) likelihood to see how well a model can fit the data.

A real concern when doing this is that some models have more parameters than others and so a priori are likely to have a better chance of fitting the data. Put another way, a model with too many parameters may over-fit the data. There are various sophisticated ways to check for such things, but a more basic solution is to do an **out of sample forecast**. To do this, maximum likelihood estimates are derived using, say, 70 percent of the data and then the estimated model is used to predict what should happen in the other 30 percent of the data. If the model does a great job of fitting the original 70 percent but a poor job of predicting the other 30 percent, then there is evidence of over-fitting.

A related issue is how to capture heterogeneity. To assume that all subjects will have the same parameters seems a little extreme because we might imagine that some people learn more by reinforcement learning and others by belief-based learning, etc. If, however, we allow different subjects to have different parameter values we are likely to over-fit the data. A **latent class approach** allows there to be one, two, or more types of people, where each person of a particular type is assumed to have the same parameter values. The amount of data should be used to determine how many types seem reasonable. Camerer and Ho consider two latent types; Friedman and Cheung let each individual have different parameters.

Friedman and Cheung also provided interesting insight on the choices of subjects and whether subjects choose the strategies with highest attractiveness. They use equation (6.3) to estimate choices from attractiveness. Recall that a high ω means that someone is more likely to choose attractive strategies. Figure 6.10 gives estimates of ω for two of the games but four different treatments. In a **mean matching experiment** each subject is matched to play every other subject in each round, while in a **random experiment** each subject plays one randomly selected subject

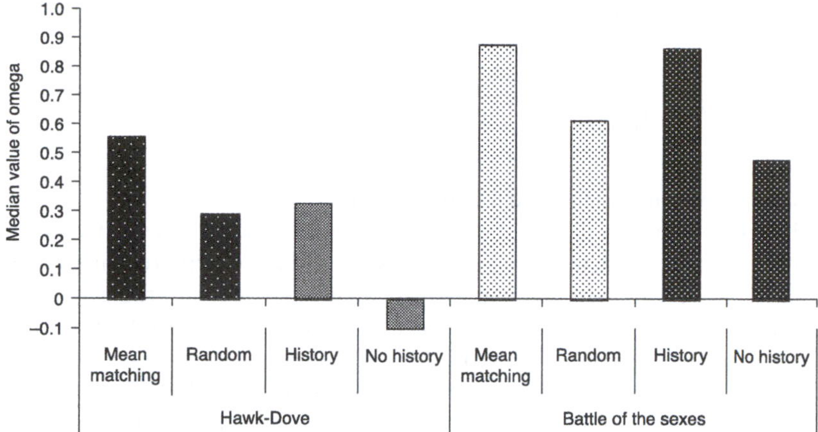

Figure 6.10 Median estimates of ω in a belief-based model of learning. The higher ω in situations with mean matching and history suggests subjects were more influenced by what others have done in the past in these situations.

Source: Cheung and Friedman (1997).

per round. In a **history experiment** the distribution of past choices in previous rounds is displayed and in a **no-history experiment** it is not. In a mean matching and history experiment a subject has relatively more information on what others have done in the past. This should help form beliefs. Consistent with this we see, from the higher ω, that choice was more likely to be informed by beliefs in the mean matching and history experiments.

6.3.3 Experience-weighted learning

Reinforcement and belief-based learning nicely complement each other. Reinforcement learning means Emma looks at whether a strategy did give a high payoff; with belief-based learning she looks at whether it would have given a high payoff. Reinforcement learning means Emma updates beliefs about the payoff of each strategy; with belief-based learning she updates beliefs about what others will do. Is there any way to combine the two and get the best of both worlds?

Camerer and Ho (1999) showed that this is possible with **experience-weighted attraction learning** or EWA. Similar to a belief-based model, we need a variable $\#(t)$ that keeps count of past experience and is updated using rule

$$\#(t) = \beta\#(t-1) + 1$$

where β is some number called the **depreciation rate**. To see how $Q^j(t)$ is updated, suppose that in period t Emma chooses strategy l and others choose $s_{-E}(t)$. She gets payoff $u_E(l, s_{-E}(t))$, but for every other strategy j misses out on the payoff

$u_E(j, s_{-E}(t))$ she could have got. Emma is assumed to weight received payoffs by $1 - \delta$ and missed payoffs by δ. The updating rule is then:

$$Q^j(t+1) \propto \begin{cases} \varphi\#(t)Q^l(t) + u_E(l, s_{-E}(t)) & \text{if } j = l \\ \varphi\#(t)Q^j(t) + \delta u_E(j, s_{-E}(t)) & \text{if } j \neq l \end{cases}$$

where ω is some number called the **decay rate**.

This looks a bit complicated, but you do not need to worry too much about that because the beauty of the EWA model is its ability to capture reinforcement learning and belief-based learning as special cases. It does so primarily through the parameter δ which measures the relative weight given to missed payoffs rather than received payoffs. If $\delta = 0$, $\#(0) = 1$, $\varphi = 1$ and $\beta = 0$, then we obtain a model of reinforcement learning like that in equation (6.4). That's because when $\delta = 0$ Emma focuses exclusively on the payoff she did receive and ignores the payoffs she missed out on. If $\delta = 1$ and $\beta = \varphi = \rho$, then we obtain a model of belief-based learning similar to that of equation (6.6). That's because when $\delta = 1$ Emma focuses equally on the payoff she missed out on compared to the payoff she did receive. If δ is between 0 and 1, we get a mix of reinforcement learning and belief-based learning.

Camerer and Ho fitted the EWA model to a variety of data and compared fit to that with reinforcement and belief-based learning. Table 6.10 summarizes the estimates they find for the various parameters and Figure 6.11 plots an estimate of goodness of fit. As we would expect, EWA does relatively well. More interesting is how reinforcement learning does relatively well in the beauty contest and median action game, while belief-based learning does better in constant sum games. We can give an ex-post rationalization for this but the main point is that people might learn in different ways in different games, and EWA is well placed to pick this up. Indeed, with the three models of learning we now have, we are well placed to better understand how people learn from experience. But is this enough?

Table 6.10 EWA parameter estimates

Game	*Learning*	δ	β	φ	ω
Beauty contest	Reinforcement	0	0	1.38	0.22
	Belief based	1	0.40	0.40	0.94
	EWA	0.23	0.94	1.33	2.58
Constant sum	Reinforcement	0	0	0.96–1.01	0.03–0.10
(4 different games)	Belief based	1	0.99–1.00	0.99–1.00	0.46–1.81
	EWA	0.00–0.73	0.93–0.96	0.99–1.04	0.18–0.65
Median action	Reinforcement	0	0	0.930	1.19
	Belief based	1	0.74	0.738	16.73
	EWA	0.85	0.00	0.800	6.82

Source: Camerer and Ho (1999).

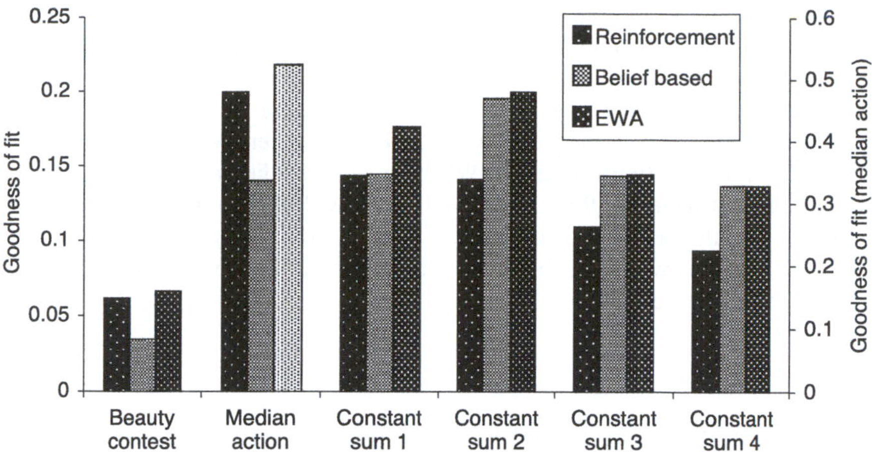

Figure 6.11 The adjusted R^2 for the three different learning models in six games.

Source: Camerer and Ho (1999).

6.3.4 Learning and prediction

A model of learning says what Emma will do, conditional on what has happened previously. This is great for looking back and trying to make sense of what she did. But is it so useful in trying to look forward and predict what she will do? One thing we could do is combine the ideas of sections 6.2 and 6.3, get a prediction of what will happen the first time a game is played, and then use a learning model to see what will happen after, say, ten plays of the game. But how confident can we be in the answer? Looking back at Tables 6.8 and 6.9, which trace through what happens as Emma learns in the 0.5-beauty contest, we can see that the prediction we will get depends a lot on chance events like what Emma randomly chooses to do.

Another approach is to ask whether play will **converge**, and if so to what. To do this, we ask what happens after people have played the game, say, 1,000 times. If we always get the same answer, then we say that play converges and then use this as a prediction of what will happen. This puts the focus firmly on what will happen in the long run. But maybe it also gives a good prediction of what will happen in the short run after, say, ten plays of the game. Unfortunately, this approach does not work so well for the three learning models we have seen so far. That's because play need not converge, and if it does converge, it converges to a Nash equilibrium. So we are basically just using a kind of equilibrium refinement. There are, though, alternatives, and in this section I will consider three.

I will start with something called **payoff sampling**. Suppose that for each possible strategy, Emma samples the payoff she got from choosing that strategy on, say, six previous occasions. Remember, we are assuming Emma has played the game lots of times and so she can do this. She then chooses the strategy that gave her the highest payoff. This is a type of reinforcement learning and lets us predict what Emma will do. Indeed, we can find a **payoff sampling equilibrium** that tells us the probability that she will choose each strategy in the long run if everyone uses payoff sampling.

To illustrate how it works, consider the matrix game in Table 6.11. Suppose that when Alan samples the payoff from choosing up there were U_L times that he got 10 and $6 - U_L$ times he got 0. When he samples the payoff from choosing down he must have got 9 all six times. So, he will choose up if $10U_L > 9 \times 6 = 54$. This could only happen if $U_L = 6$. If p_L is the probability that Emma chooses left, this happens with probability $p_L{}^6$. So, letting q_U denote the probability that Alan chooses up we get:

$$q_U = prob(U_L = 6) = p_L{}^6.$$

We can now do the same to derive p_L as a function of q_U. When Emma samples her payoff from choosing left, she gets 9. Suppose that when she samples her payoff from choosing right there were R_U times that she got 18 and $6 - R_U$ times she got 8. She will choose left if $9 \times 6 > 18R_U + 8(6 - R_U)$ or $6 > 10R_U$. This can only be satisfied if $R_U = 0$. Thus:

$$p_L = prob(R_U = 0) = (1 - q_U)^6.$$

We now know the probability that Alan chooses up as a function of the probability that Emma chooses left, and vice versa. To obtain a payoff sampling equilibrium we look for the point where these two probabilities are consistent. That is, where $q_U = ((1 - q_U)^6)^6$ and $p_L = (1 - p_L{}^6)^6$. Values $q_U = 0.071$ and $p_L = 0.643$ work. This is a prediction of what Alan and Emma might do.

Before we see how good this prediction is, I want to go through the other two possibilities. Next up is **action sampling**. Imagine now that Emma samples what Alan chose on, say, seven previous occasions. She then chooses the strategy that would have maximized her payoff given what Alan did. This gives a form of belief-based learning. By finding an **action sampling equilibrium**, using similar techniques to that which we used to find a payoff sampling equilibrium, we get a prediction of what Emma will do. If we work through the game in Table 6.11 then we get the values $q_U = 0.057$ and $p_L = 0.664$.

Table 6.11 A matrix game to illustrate payoff sampling

		Emma	
		Left	*Right*
Alan	Up	\$10, \$9	\$0, \$18
	Down	\$9, \$9	\$9, \$8

[Extra] To see where these numbers come from. Alan should choose up if $10p_L > 9$ or $p_L > 0.9$. So, he should choose up if and only if he observed Emma choosing left all seven times he samples. So:

$$q_U = prob(\text{observes left seven times}) = p_L{}^7.$$

Emma should choose left if $9 > 18q_U + 8(1 - q_U)$ or $q_U < 0.1$. So she should choose left if Alan never chose up on the seven times she samples. Thus:

$$p_L = prob(\text{does not observe up}) = (1 - q_U)^7.$$

To obtain an action sampling equilibrium we look for the point where these two probabilities are consistent. That is, $q_U = ((1 - q_U)^7)^7$ and $p_L = (1 - p_L{}^7)^7$. The values $q_U = 0.057$ and $p_L = 0.664$ work this time.

The final possibility I want to look at is called **impulse balance**. What we do here is calculate a **security level** of payoff that Emma can guarantee herself. For instance, in the game in Table 6.11, Emma can guarantee a payoff of $9 by choosing left. Taking into account loss aversion we then say that gains above the security level are treated as less than losses below the security level. For example, we might say that a loss counts twice as much as a gain. Table 6.12 shows what happens when we do this. For instance, if Alan chooses up and Emma chooses right, the payoff of $0 is $9 short of the security level and so would feel to Alan like $9 - 2 \times 9 = -9$.

The final thing we do is to say that Emma would have an **impulse** in the direction of a particular strategy if choosing that strategy would have earned a higher payoff. The size of the impulse is given by the payoff difference. Table 6.13 shows the impulses in the example. An impulse of 0 means she has no incentive to change strategy, and the higher the number, the stronger the impulse to change. There is an **impulse balance equilibrium** if these impulses to change strategy cancel out.

To see how this works we can work through the example. Given that Emma chooses left with probability p_L and he chooses up with probability q_U, Alan's expected impulse from up to down is $18q_U(1 - p_L)$ and his expected impulse from

Table 6.12 Transforming the payoffs to take into account loss aversion. Losses relative to the security payoff of $9 count twice as much

		Emma	
		Left	*Right*
Alan	Uup	10, 9	−9, 18
	Down	9, 9	9, 7

Table 6.13 Impulses after taking into account loss aversion. For instance, if Alan chose up and Emma chooses left, he has no impulse to change strategy, but if he had chosen down he would have had an impulse of 1 to change strategy

		Emma	
		Left	*Right*
Alan	Up	0, 9	18, 0
	Down	1, 0	0, 2

down to up is $(1 - q_U)p_L$. At an impulse balance equilibrium we want these to be the same, so $18q_U(1 - p_L) = (1 - q_U)p_L$, or

$$q_U = \frac{p_L}{18 - 17p_L}.$$

Similarly, Emma's expected impulse from left to right is $9q_U p_L$ and from right to left is $2(1 - q_U)(1 - p_L)$. Setting these equal gives:

$$p_L = \frac{1 - q_U}{3.5q_U + 1}.$$

Solving these two equations gives the equilibrium. In this case $q_U = 0.1$ and $p_L = 0.67$. Impulse balance combines elements of both reinforcement learning and belief-based learning because it favors strategies that give a relatively high payoff. The most appealing thing about it, however, is that it can capture the loss aversion we saw in Chapters two and three. It says that people will be drawn away from strategies that are likely to cause a loss. Given the evidence we saw for loss aversion this looks like a great thing to be trying to model.

The nice thing about payoff sampling equilibrium, action sampling equilibrium, and impulse balance equilibrium is that there is only one of them. They give us, therefore, a nice prediction of what should happen in the long run as people learn. Furthermore, they are relatively easy to calculate because we do not need to model the learning process itself. But are the predictions any use?

In a study by Selten and Chmura (2008) subjects played 12 different games similar to that in Table 6.11. Figure 6.12 gives a measure of how good different equilibria were at fitting the data. We see that QRE, action sampling, payoff sampling, and impulse balance did a much better job than the Nash equilibrium. This is a clear signal that we need to take seriously deviations from the Nash equilibrium. Whether the three equilibria we have looked at in this section are an improvement over QRE is a more subtle and controversial point. But it is safe to say that they do no worse.

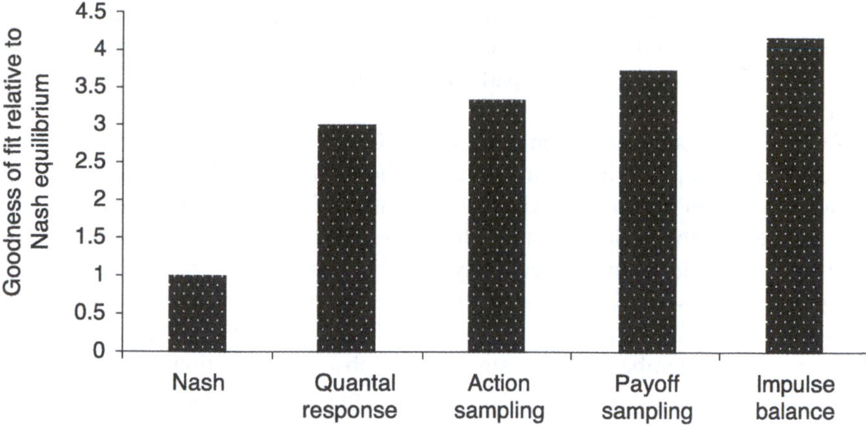

Figure 6.12 Assessing the goodness of fit of various equilibria relative to the Nash equilibrium.

Source: Brunner *et al.* (2011).

An important question to ask in interpreting these results is how many times subjects played the games. There were 12 games and a subject played for 200 rounds, so they played each game around 16 or 17 times. The results, though, are the same if we focus on just the first 100 rounds. This is good news because it means these equilibrium predictions look as though they work even if people have had little or no chance to learn from experience. That does present something of a conundrum as to why they work so well, but maybe they just capture nicely how people reason when playing games. That seems a positive note upon which to finish the section.

6.4 Teams make decisions

The focus throughout the chapter so far has been on how individuals choose a strategy, or learn from experience. This reflects the norm in economics of focusing on individuals. The reality, however, is that many economic decisions are made by teams. A board of directors decides on the strategy of the firm. A committee of politicians and experts designs policy. A husband and wife decide whether to sell their house and move on. In all of these examples the collective decision is made after team members have discussed things through with each other and reached a joint decision. The decisions that teams make could differ substantially from the decisions that individuals make. If so, an almost exclusive focus on individual behavior is misplaced!

In this section I want to begin to look in more detail at whether the decisions made by teams differ from those of individuals. I also want to illustrate how the theory we have learnt so far in the chapter can be applied to team decision making. More examples will then follow over the next few chapters. Before we get started let me clarify definitions, and in particular, clarify the distinction between a team and group.

When I introduced the notion of a game in Chapter one I used the example of a group of five people trying to finance a threshold public good. Why is this not an example of team decision making? Particularly, if group members can discuss amongst each other, bargain, etc.? The answer is that each group member ultimately makes a decision independently of the others. If there are five members of the group, we observe five actions in the game, or five contributions to the public good. This is different to saying that a team of people reach a collective decision. If there are five members of the team, we only observe one action. For example, a household of husband, wife, and three children may make one contribution to the public good.

To avoid confusion I shall talk of decision makers. For each **decision maker** we will see an action. A decision maker may be an **individual** or a **team** of people. Decision makers may belong to a **group**. For example, we might have five decision makers in a group trying to finance a public good where each decision maker is a household of two or more people. To give another example, we may have five decision makers in an industrial group trying to make profit, where each decision maker is a company board of directors.

This distinction between groups and teams is convenient. But is it convincing? The reason I ask this question is that, when a team of people try to make a collective decision, they are playing a game. The husband and wife arguing over how much to contribute to the public good are playing a game. Similarly, company directors trying to pull the company one way or another are playing a game. The outcome of this game determines the action of the team. The picture is, therefore, somewhat like that in Figure 6.13. The figure shows a schematic of competition between two airlines, FlyMe and YouFly. Within FlyMe there is a game between directors over the direction the firm should take. Something similar is happening within YouFly. The outcomes of these two games determine pricing decisions that feed into the airline pricing game.

The key point to take from this is that team decision making is a game in itself with all the strategic interaction that this entails. It may be the whole game, such as a household deciding where to go on holiday. Or, it may be a small part of a bigger game, such as the directors of YouFly deciding on pricing strategy. Recognizing the strategic interaction between team members does not, however, mean the distinction between teams and groups is not important. It is often very useful to treat the strategic interaction between team members as a black box that we do not need to worry ourselves about. For example, when analyzing the competition between FlyMe and YouFly we do not want to get bogged down looking at the dynamics within the boardroom. But for this to work we need general insight on how a team, black box, works and how we can appropriately model it.

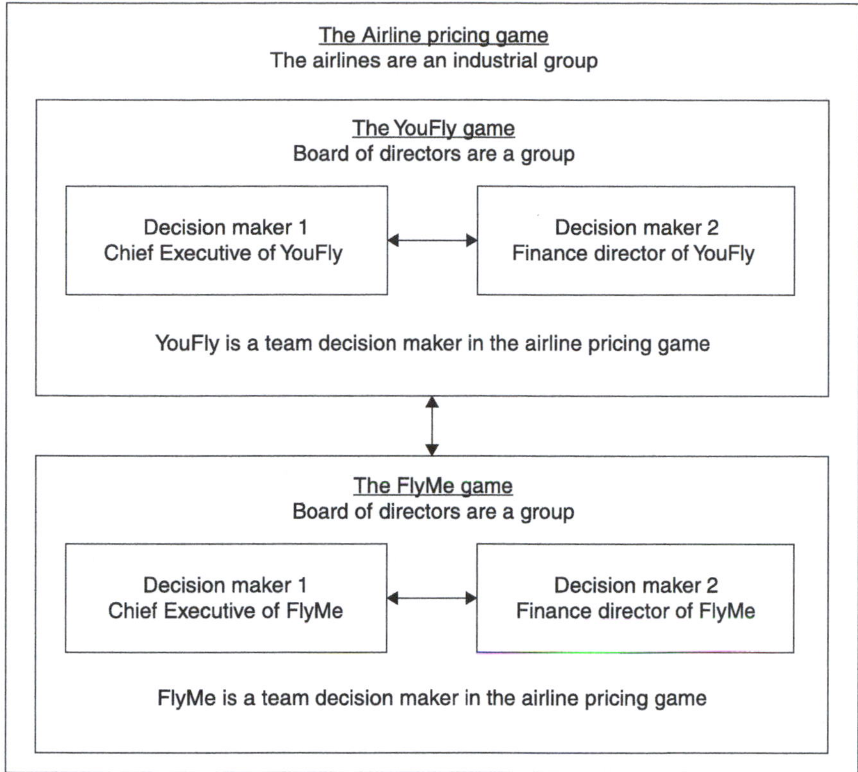

Figure 6.13 Within FlyMe and YouFly the board of directors play a game. The outcome of each game determines the strategy of each firm, or team, in the airline pricing game.

6.4.1 Teams and the beauty contest

The p-beauty contest is an ideal place to begin comparing teams against individuals in a simple strategic environment. It also provides an interesting window onto financial markets where individual investors are routinely pitted against teams of investors. At the same time, for instance, as Emma is deciding when to sell her shares in FlyMe, you can be sure a fund managed by a team of investors is also deciding when to sell their shares. Does a team of investors outperform an individual?

To give some insight on how teams perform in the 0.67-beauty contest I will look at studies by Kocher and Sutter (2005) and Sutter (2005). In these studies a team consisted of two to four individuals who have five minutes to discuss with each other face to face before making a joint decision of what to do.

The first thing we can look at is how teams versus teams compare to individuals versus individuals. Figure 6.14 summarizes the outcomes from four sessions. The

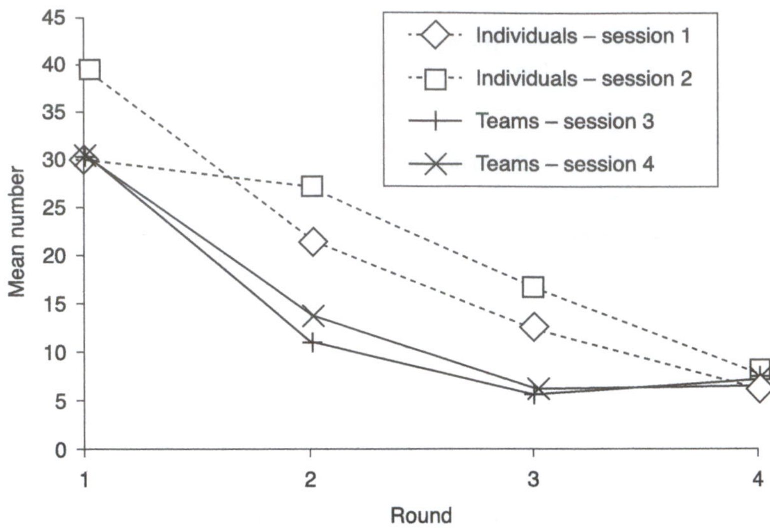

Figure 6.14 The mean number chosen when playing a 0.67-beauty contest four consecutive times, comparing individuals versus individuals and teams versus teams.

Source: Kocher and Sutter (2005).

outcomes when individuals played with individuals (sessions one and two) are as we would expect (see Figure 6.2). Compare this with how teams played with teams (sessions three and four). There is no difference between individuals and teams in round one or round four. There is, however, a difference between teams and individuals in rounds two and three. This suggests that teams learnt quicker than individuals.

To explore things in a little more detail we can apply some of the models introduced earlier in the chapter. Let us start by looking at choices in round one. Figure 6.15 details the proportion of decision makers, individuals or teams, that could be classified as level-k thinkers. The proportion of individuals that were type L-1 is similar to the proportion of teams that were type L-1. This can help explain why individuals and teams made similar choices in round one. It is noticeable, however, that there was a lower proportion of L-0 types and a higher proportion of L-2 types in teams.

In this setting, a type L-0 is someone who randomly chooses what to do. This presumably means they did not understand the game to some extent. A team is much less likely to fit this description because one member of the team can explain the game to others. To be type L-0 we, therefore, need all three members of the team to misunderstand the game! Three heads are better than one. And speaking much more generally, we typically find that teams perform better than individuals on **intellective tasks** where there is a clear problem to solve. This makes intuitive sense because team members can feed off each other and collectively work

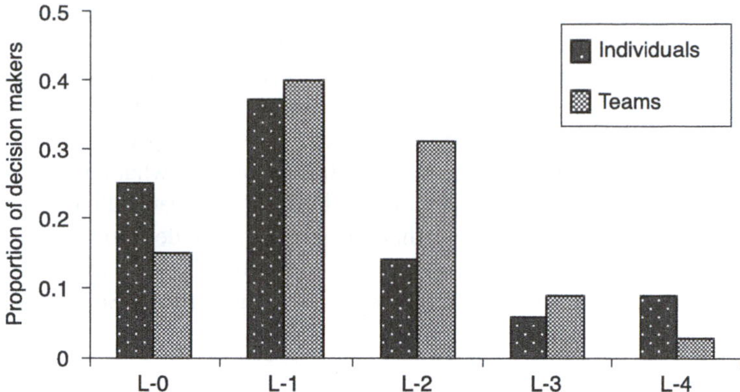

Figure 6.15 The proportion of individuals and teams of each type of level-k thinking.

Source: Kocher and Sutter (2005).

towards a solution. It only needs one member to solve the problem for the team to have solved the problem.

The p-beauty contest, however, is more than an intellective task. It is also a **judgmental task** because there is a need to predict what others will do. The general evidence is that teams are no better than individuals at solving such tasks. To give some intuition for why this makes sense, you need to recall issues covered in the previous chapter like information cascades and conformity. One member of the team can easily drag others off in a strange direction. And, because there is no right or wrong answer, the team cannot tell it is going wrong. This can help explain why teams did not think too much ahead of individuals in the first round of the beauty contest.

In the second round of the contest it is clear that teams reacted more to experience than individuals. To capture this Kocher and Sutter fitted the EWA model to the data. The results are given in Table 6.14 (and can be compared with Table 6.10). Teams had a noticeably lower decay rate φ than individuals, meaning teams adapted faster. Teams also had a higher δ, meaning missed payoffs were weighted the same as received payoffs, as is the case in belief-based learning. This would

Table 6.14 EWA parameter estimates comparing individuals and teams

Decision makers	*Learning*	δ	β	φ	ω
Individuals	Belief based	1	0	0.70	1.06
	EWA	0.88	0	0.71	0.59
Teams	Belief based	1	0	0.64	0.52
	EWA	1	0.09	0.64	0.53

Source: Kocher and Sutter (2005).

suggest that teams more quickly learnt to think one step ahead. It takes individuals time to catch up.

If teams are one step ahead of individuals, then they should earn a higher payoff. This makes it particularly interesting to see how teams perform against individuals. Recall that, until now, teams were pitted against other teams. The study by Kocher and Sutter (2005) also looked at what happens when a team of three play against two individuals. Sutter (2005) looked at what happens when a team of four, a team of two, and an individual play against each other. Figure 6.16 details the average number of times that different types of decision makers 'won' by being closest to the optimal number. The conclusion is clear: teams did better than individuals, and teams of four did better than teams of two. So, you would be better to trust your investment decisions to a team!

6.4.2 The sophistication of teams

The clear lesson from the p-beauty contest seems to be that teams outperform individuals. The victory, however, is far from overwhelming. In particular, it rests on teams learning faster than individuals. In round one there is no big difference between individuals and teams. To broaden the picture, it is interesting to look at a study by Sutter and co-authors. (2013). In the study subjects played 18 different games, with some subjects playing as an individual and some in a team of three. Each game was only played once and so the focus is very much on initial play rather than learning.

In all of the 18 games played there was a unique Nash equilibrium, but the games differed in complexity. In some games there was a dominant strategy, in

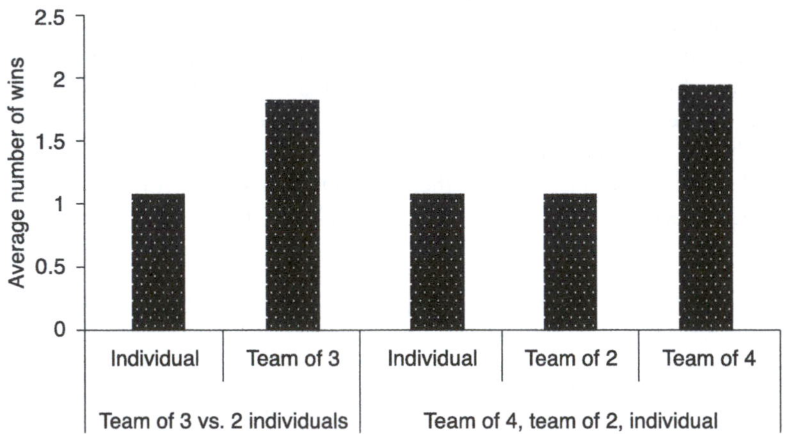

Figure 6.16 The average number of times (out of four rounds) that different types of decision maker were closest to the optimal number.

Sources: Kocher and Sutter (2005) and Sutter (2005).

others not. In some games the Nash equilibrium could be found by iterated deletion of dominated strategies, in others it could not. In some games it took three steps of elimination of dominated strategies, in others one or two. Figure 6.17 shows the proportion of decision makers that chose consistent with the Nash equilibrium for progressively more complex games.

The simplest situation is where a decision maker has a dominant strategy and so one step of elimination of dominated strategies reveals the Nash equilibrium strategy. This situation is simple enough that most decision makers, individuals or teams, played the Nash equilibrium strategy. At the other extreme are games that are not solvable by elimination of dominated strategies, or where three steps of elimination are required to reveal the Nash equilibrium. This situation appeared complex enough that few decision makers, individuals or teams, played the Nash equilibrium.

The difference between teams and individuals comes when two steps of elimination of dominated strategies are required to reveal the Nash equilibrium. In these situations of intermediate complexity, teams are significantly more likely to choose the Nash equilibrium strategy. This is a fascinating result that allows us to pinpoint when teams can outperform individuals the first time they play a game. Teams are better than individuals provided the game is not too simple or too complex. Note that the p-beauty context would be counted as complex because more than three steps of elimination are needed to reveal the Nash equilibrium. So, it makes sense that we found no big difference between teams and individuals in the first round.

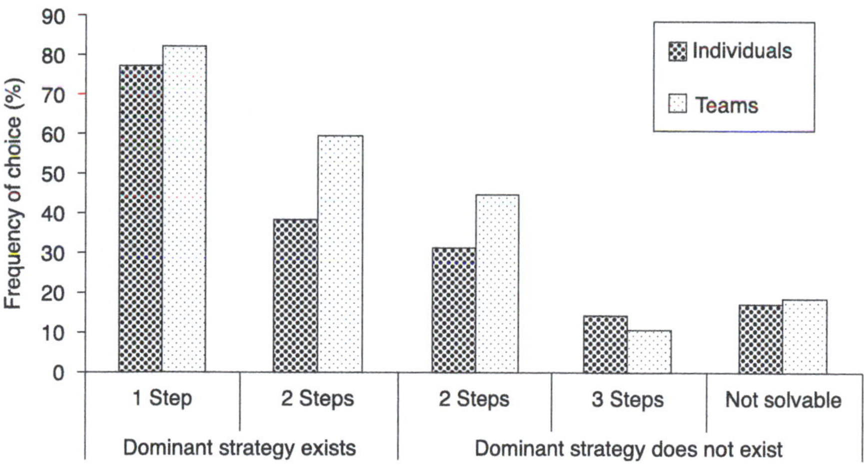

Figure 6.17 The proportion choosing the Nash equilibrium strategy depending on whether a dominant strategy existed or not and whether the game was solvable in one, two, three, or no steps of iterated deletion of dominated strategies.

Source: Sutter *et al.* (2013).

The study by Sutter and co-authors also asked subjects what they thought the opponent would do. Specifically, the individual or team were asked what action they expected their opponent to choose – **first order belief** – and what action they expected their opponent would expect them to choose – **second order belief**. Eliciting such beliefs can tell us something about the sophistication of the decision maker. For example, we can see if the action chosen is a best reply to the first order belief. Consistent with what we see in Figure 6.17, teams appeared more sophisticated. Teams were more likely to best reply to their first order belief and more likely to expect the Nash equilibrium outcome. It is not by accident, therefore, that teams chose the Nash equilibrium strategy. Teams seemed to reason through the game more than individuals.

6.4.3 Are teams smarter?

As already mentioned, I shall periodically come back to the distinction between teams and individuals through the remainder of the book. We have already seen enough, however, to know that the behavior of teams can be different to that of individuals. Clearly, therefore, it is important to take seriously the fact that many economic decisions are taken by teams. To put things in context two observations seem pertinent.

The first thing to observe is that teams appear to behave more like homo economicus than do individuals. So, teams better fit the standard economic model. In the p-beauty contest, for instance, teams converged quicker towards the Nash equilibrium. In the games we have just been looking at teams were initially more likely to play the Nash equilibrium. Teams, therefore, fit somewhere between the 'rationality' of homo economicus and the heuristically driven homo sapiens.

But let us not get carried away. The second thing to observe is that teams are not much different to individuals. In the first and fourth round of the p-beauty contest, for instance, teams and individuals are indistinguishable. We have just seen that teams and individuals are also indistinguishable in relatively simple or complex games. On the scale of rationality between homo economicus and homo sapiens, teams, therefore, are sitting somewhere next to homo sapiens. This should not be a surprise given that teams are, of course, composed of individuals!

To draw this section to a close I remind that it is often very useful to treat the strategic interaction between team members as a black box that we do not need to worry ourselves about. The fact that teams appear to behave similarly to individuals a lot of the time should reassure that we can get away with this. We, hopefully, do not miss much by approximating a team with an individual. We have also seen, however, that in some contexts teams can differ from individuals. It is important to keep this in mind, particularly in applications. See, for example, section 6.8 on monetary policy by committee.

6.5 Summary

In trying to understand strategic behavior we started with the notion of the Nash equilibrium and elimination of dominated strategies. A basic premise is that people should not play dominated strategies. A slightly more involved premise is that they should play a Nash equilibrium strategy. In some games this gives us a very nice prediction, in principle, of what people should do because there is a unique Nash equilibrium or a unique strategy that survives iterated elimination of dominated strategies.

Evidence on how people behaved in the p-beauty contest was enough to suggest, however, that the Nash equilibrium and elimination of dominated strategies is not enough to explain behavior. This led us to the ideas of level-k thinking as well as semi-sophisticated and sophisticated behavior. The focus here is to model the various ways that people might reason in strategic situations and not 'get as far as' the Nash equilibrium. On a related note we looked at quantal response equilibrium, which tries to model what happens if people make mistakes.

In many contexts the notion of the Nash equilibrium and elimination of dominated strategies does not get us very far, because there are several Nash equilibria. That means that we need to think how people might reason which equilibrium 'makes more sense'. By looking at focal points, risk and Pareto dominance, and backward and forward induction, we have seen that there are various ways to do this.

We then looked at how people might learn with experience, contrasting reinforcement learning and belief-based learning. We also looked at how learning models can be used to predict what will happen after people have learnt.

Finally we contrasted behavior in teams with that of individuals. When looking at teams we have two levels of strategic interaction, that within the team and that between teams. The ways we have seen to model individual behavior can be applied to model behavior within the team and between teams.

One thing you may have noticed by now is that modeling behavior in strategic contexts is not easy. There is a lot going on, because we have all the choice arbitrariness, risk, and uncertainty that we had in Chapters two to five compounded by the interdependence between people. Also, different games raise very different issues. For this reason anyone expecting a unified theory of behavior in strategic contexts is probably going to be disappointed. Sometimes level-k thinking will work well, sometimes not; sometimes backward induction will work well and sometimes not. This though, is not bad news. We now have lots of different ways to help us think about strategic behavior.

6.6 Auctions

A nice example of where strategy matters is bidding at an auction. We have already encountered auctions a few times, in Chapters two and four, but now I want to look at them in a bit more detail. It seems apt to start by saying that auctions are one of the most important ways that goods are sold. Examples are as diverse as the selling of antique furniture or paintings at Sotheby's, livestock at a cattle market, cars, houses, goods on eBay, and governments selling tracts of land for oil drilling. Here I want to focus on two particularly interesting aspects of auctions: revenue equivalence and the winner's curse. In Chapter eleven we will look at some other aspects.

6.6.1 Revenue equivalence

There are various different types of **auction format**. I will look at four of the more common formats here (and a few more in Chapter eleven).

In an **English auction** the auctioneer starts the bidding at a low price and incrementally increases the price until only one bidder is willing to pay that price. This is the most common auction format and is what you would see, for instance, at Sotheby's. In a **Dutch auction** the auctioneer starts the bidding at a high price and incrementally lowers the price until someone is willing to buy at that price. This auction gets its name from the way tulips and other flowers are sold in Holland.

In a **first price sealed bid auction** potential bidders are asked to submit simultaneously and independently the amount they are willing to pay for the item. The highest bidder wins and pays the price he bid. This is a standard format for government tendering.

Finally, in a **second price sealed bid auction** everything is the same as the first price sealed bid auction, except that the highest bidder only has to pay the amount bid by the second highest bidder. Ebay is a combination of this and an English auction.

A natural question for anyone looking to sell using an auction is which type of auction will maximize the revenue from the sale. Auction theory offers a specific and intriguing answer to this question: the **Revenue Equivalence Theorem** says that in many cases all four auction formats result in the same revenue if bidders behave optimally.

One case where this theorem applies is an **independent, privately known value auction**. In such an auction different bidders may value the item differently, but each bidder knows her own value, and knows that her own value does not tell her anything about the likely values of others. This is the situation found in many common auctions such as the auctioning of an antique, car, house, or consumer item on eBay. For example, consider a painting up for auction that Emma is thinking of bidding for. She knows that different people will likely value the painting differently, some liking it and some not, but she only knows her own preferences, and not those of others.

If Emma decides she wants the painting, and values it at \$1,000, how much should she bid? The optimal way to bid in this type of auction depends on the auction format.

In an English or second price sealed bid auction, she should bid up to the amount she values the item, i.e. \$1,000. There is no point bidding more because she might end up paying more than she thinks it's worth. There is no point bidding less because she will only have to pay the amount the second highest bidder is willing to pay. For example, if Alan is the second highest bidder at \$950, she only has to pay $950 (even if she bid $1,000) and so there would have been no gain in bidding, say, $980 rather than $1,000.

Things are different in the Dutch and first price sealed bid auctions. Now Emma needs to bid below the amount she values the item, say, $980. This is called **shading the bid**. If she does not shade her bid, then she can never make any profit, because she will have to pay what she bids. But, she does need to bid high enough to have a good chance of winning. It is quite complicated knowing exactly how much to bid given these competing incentives, but we do not need to worry too much about that.

Let's now go back to the Revenue Equivalence Theorem. We can see now why the English and second price auction should give the same revenue, and the Dutch and first price should give the same revenue. What remains to be shown is that a first price or Dutch auction gives the same revenue as a second price or English auction. In a first price auction Emma needs to shade her bid, and so bids less than she would in a second price auction. If she wins a second price auction, however, she only has to pay the amount bid by the second highest bidder. The neat thing is that these two effects cancel each other out: the highest bid in a first price auction will, on average, equal the second highest bid in a second price auction! Thus, all four auctions give the same expected revenue. Well, that's the theory.

Lucking-Reiley (1999) put the theory to the test in a field experiment that involved selling 'Magic cards' to online devotees of a game called 'Magic: The Gathering'. Four different collections of cards were independently auctioned using two of the four different auction formats. The results are summarized in Table 6.15. Collections one and two allow us to compare first price and Dutch auctions. We see that the Dutch auctions raised more revenue than the first price

Table 6.15 Bidding in the Magic game. The Dutch auction appears to raise more revenue than the first price auction. There is no difference between the English and second price auctions

	First price		*Dutch*		*No. of cards sold at higher price*		
	Revenue	*Bidders*	*Revenue*	*Bidders*	*1st price*	*Neither*	*Dutch*
Collection 1	$431.25	32	$446.35	56	12	12	63
Collection 2	$327.05	42	$348.45	88	22	5	59
	Second price		*English*		*No. of cards sold at higher price*		
	Revenue	*Bidders*	*Revenue*	*Bidders*	*2nd price*	*Neither*	*English*
Collection 3	$85.50	27	$79.50	40	38	8	20
Collection 4	$517.05	43	$600.40	38	24	9	65

Source: Lucking-Reiley (1999).

auctions, with more cards selling for a high price. Collections three and four allow us to compare second price and English auctions. Here we see no significant differences in revenue. Overall, therefore, we see somewhat mixed support for the Revenue Equivalence Theorem. A similar conclusion has been found in laboratory studies, but with different results. Indeed, in the laboratory, first price auctions have been seen to raise more revenue than Dutch auctions, and second price auctions more than English auctions (see Research Methods 6.5).

Anyone selling an item might, therefore, want to think more closely about which auction format to use than the Revenue Equivalence Theorem might suggest. The popularity of the English auction is possibly a signal as to what many sellers think is best. To progress beyond such conjectures we need to know more about how people typically bid in auctions. We will get some insight into this as we look at the winner's curse.

Research Methods 6.5

Field experiments

Given that auctions are so common and easy to take part in, they seem one natural setting for field experiments or source of field data. In this study, Lucking-Reiley needed to find a setting flexible enough that he could auction the same things using four different auction formats. The online community of 'Magic: The Gathering' offered such an opportunity because there was already use of the English, first price and Dutch auctions, so only the second price auction would be new to bidders.

The usual potential advantages of field experiments over laboratory experiments are seemingly present in this study, namely, the subjects should be experienced in valuing the items and bidding for them. The results illustrate why this can prove important. That the Dutch auction raised more revenue than a first price auction goes against what has been observed in laboratory experiments. The probable explanation is that more people wanted to take part in the Dutch auction. This, unpredictable, increase in the number of bidders could not have happened in a lab experiment where the number of bidders is fixed by how many subjects the experimenter invites to the lab.

6.6.2 Winner's curse

Recall that in a privately known value action, Emma knew how much the item was worth to her but not to others. The opposite extreme is a **common value auction.** In this type of auction a bidder will not know how much the item is worth until she has got it, but does know that others will value it as much as her. An example of this would be drilling rights to a tract of land that may or may not have oil. Only having purchased the land and drilled for oil can it be known for sure whether there is oil, but, if there is, then any oil company would have wanted to buy the land. A slightly more mundane example would be people entering a charity auction at the local fete not knowing what the mystery winning prize is.

In a privately known value auction the bidder who wins is likely to be the one who most valued the item. For example, the one who most liked the painting. In a common value auction the bidder who wins is likely to be the one who was most optimistic about the value of the item. Optimism is sometimes a dangerous thing. If the bidder is more optimistic than others, then she may be too optimistic and may pay more for the item than it is actually worth. This is called the **winner's curse**. Examples of the winner's curse abound. Oil companies have overpaid for land, telephone companies have overpaid for the rights to transmit signals, TV channels have overpaid for the rights to televise sporting events, and many have been disappointed by the prize they won at the local fete.

To look in more detail at why the winner's curse can happen, it is useful to first look at how a person should bid in a common value auction. So, imagine Emma is entering a charity English auction for a prize of unknown value. She likely gets some signal of how much the prize might be worth. From this she gets an initial expectation of the value of the item. For example, she might have an initial expectation that the prize is worth $20. Surely she should bid up to $20? No. She should reason that if she wins she must have had the most optimistic initial expectation. For example, if she wins bidding $20, then everyone else must have thought the prize was worth less than $20. If everyone else thinks the prize is worth less than $20, maybe she was overoptimistic? She should lower her expectations, and so bid up to something less than her initial expected value.

With this we can now list some distinct reasons why Emma might suffer the winner's curse: (i) She could be a risk-loving person who bids high knowing that the probability that the prize is worth so much is small, but she is happy to take the risk. Ultimately the gamble does not pay off; ii) She bids optimally, and so lowers her bid below her initial expectation, but still proves unlucky because the prize turns out to have a lower value than most expected; (iii) She naïvely bids up to her initial expectation and is unlucky; (iv) She bids an irrationally high amount. This is most likely in a second price auction if she expects the second highest bid will be relatively low.

I now want to look at two studies. The first, by Crawford and Iriberri (2007), looks to explain the winner's curse using level-k thinking. The focus, therefore, is on the behavior of inexperienced bidders. The second, by Selten and co-authors (2005), uses impulse balance and so puts the focus more on learning from experience.

We know that in level-k thinking it is crucial what we assume about type L-0s. Crawford and Iriberri consider two alternatives. First, that type L-0s bid randomly; or second, they bid naïvely their initial expectation. In different auction formats bidding behavior will differ, but Table 6.16 summarizes the main predictions of level-k thinking by comparing level-k bidding with the equilibrium bidding that would happen if everyone used the optimal strategy.

We see that if people of type L-0 bid randomly, then people of type L-0 and L-1 are particularly vulnerable to the winner's curse. If people of type L-0 bid initial expectations, then people of type L-0 and L-2 are vulnerable. Figure 6.18 details the percentage of subjects that Crawford and Iriberri estimated were of each type

Table 6.16 Bidding strategies of a type L-k comparing what happens with two different assumptions about type L-0s

Type	*Random*	*Initial expectation*
L-0	Bids randomly.	Bids up to her initial expectation.
L-1	Bids up to her value, and more than the equilibrium amount. Because type L-0s are bidding randomly, that she wins tells her nothing about the expected values of others. So, she sees no reason to lower her bid.	Bids less than her value, and less than the equilibrium amount. Because type L-0s are bidding more than in equilibrium, she thinks that if she wins she must have been very optimistic about the expected value. So, she lowers her bid to compensate.
L-2	Bids less than her value, and less than the equilibrium amount. Because type L-1s are bidding more than in equilibrium, she thinks that if she wins she must have been very optimistic about the expected value. So, she lowers her bid to compensate.	Bids more than an L-1 type and possibly more than the equilibrium amount. Because type L-1s are bidding less than in equilibrium, she thinks that if she did win she was not necessarily optimistic. So, there is less need to lower her bid.

in four different auctions. It's fairly clear that most subjects were classified as being type L-1 with an expectation that type L-0s bid randomly. These types are vulnerable to the winner's curse because they naïvely ignore the information that the bids of others convey. They fail to take into account that, if they win, they must have been relatively optimistic about the expected value.

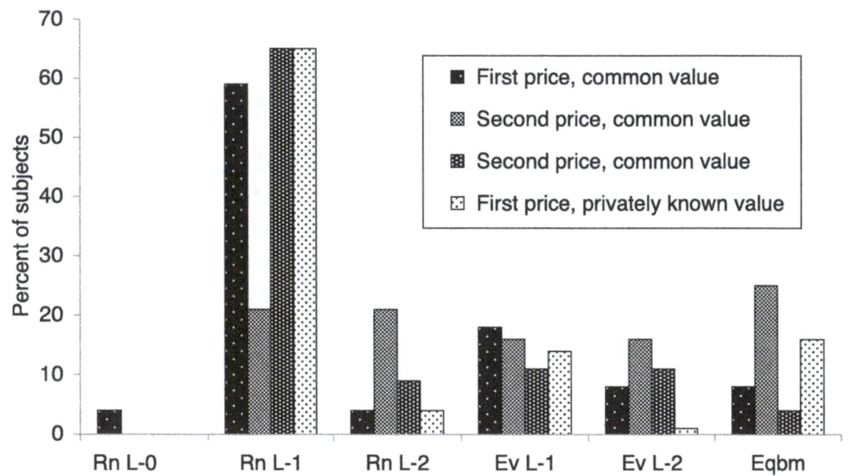

Figure 6.18 Percentage of subjects of each type in four auction experiments. Rn assumes type L-0s choose randomly and Ev means they choose initial expectation.

Source: Crawford and Iriberri (2007).

If people are vulnerable to the winner's curse because of naïve bidding, then we might expect that they should learn with experience. Things are not so simple, however, because Emma, say, could bid 'too much' but be lucky and win a great prize, or bid 'the optimal amount' and be unlucky because the prize is less than everyone expected. This makes it potentially difficult to learn from experience.

The study of Selten and co-authors uses impulse balance equilibrium and a closely related idea of learning direction theory to try and understand how people learn when playing auctions several times. The basic idea of **learning direction theory** is that someone goes with their impulse and moves in the direction of improved payoffs. In the context of an auction the person who wins almost certainly bids more than they needed to and so will lower their bid subsequently. The person who does not win might regret not bidding more and so increase their bid subsequently. This gives an interesting contrast between overpaying and a missed opportunity.

They find that learning direction theory and impulse balance equilibrium fits well how subjects behaved in the experiments. This means that bids did not converge over time to that predicted by equilibrium, but instead tended to fluctuate as subjects overpaid some periods but then regretted not bidding more in other periods. This is despite playing 100 successive auctions. To see this a bit more clearly, Figure 6.19 shows what happens if we try to put subjects into categories depending on how they bid. Clearly, a lot of subjects were adapters, and this is the category that most closely fits learning direction theory. Of the other categories, gamblers are worth a mention. Gamblers were seemingly interested in high gains and seemed to fall for the gambler's fallacy. If they overpaid one auction they tended to bid more next time, possibly thinking their luck must change.

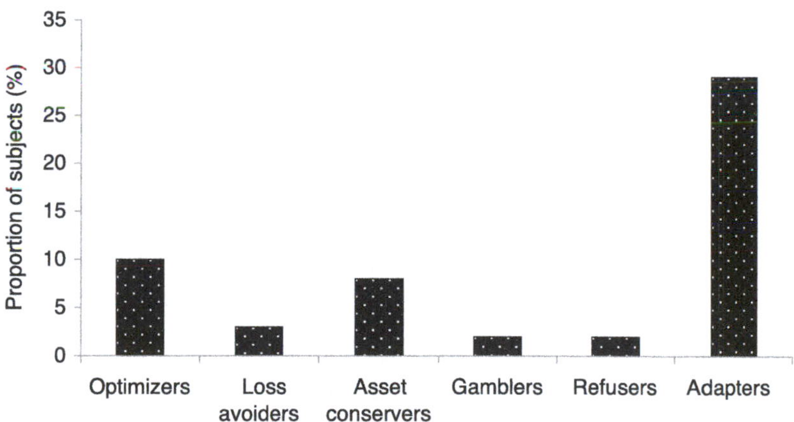

Figure 6.19 Categories of bidder. Adapters behaved consistently with learning direction theory, increasing their bid if they previously missed out and lowering their bid if they previously paid too much.

Source: Selten *et al.* (2005).

Such gambling is the opposite of what is predicted by learning direction theory. So, learning direction theory cannot capture what everyone does, but it does do a good job of capturing what many do. It also gives us an explanation of why the winner's curse does not disappear with experience. Namely, naïve bidding sometimes pays off, and so people need not realize that it is not the best thing to do.

This is an important point, not only in looking at auctions, because it demonstrates that learning need not converge to Nash equilibrium. The reason it did not do so here is because payoffs were random. If payoffs are going up and down, through good luck and bad luck, quicker than Emma learns the optimal way to bid, she might never learn the optimal way to bid. Auctions, therefore, are one area of life where it pays to read the economic textbook and not rely on trial and error!

6.7 Learning to coordinate

The next thing I want to do is go back and look in a bit more detail at **coordination games** – games where people want to coordinate their strategies to mutual benefit. Coordination is vital in many areas of life, whether it be the world deciding how to tackle climate change or two friends trying to meet in a crowded cafeteria. So, it is very interesting to look at coordination games and see what we can learn. In section 6.2.3 we saw some evidence that people can coordinate using focal points, and in section 6.2.4 we saw how people might use forward or backward induction to coordinate. In this section I want to ask more generally how well people can coordinate. In doing so we shall look at two very different types of coordination problem (see also section 6.9.2).

6.7.1 Weakest link games

In a **weakest link game** or **minimum effort game** a group of people independently must decide how much effort to put into a group task. Higher effort is costly, but the output of the group is determined by the smallest effort that someone puts in. A nice example to illustrate is going somewhere by plane. To get to her destination on time Emma would probably need lots of people to put in effort: the taxi driver to get her to the airport, the pilot to be there, the cleaner to clean the plane, the serviceman to put in the fuel, etc. If anyone puts in low effort, Emma may not leave on time. The plane is going nowhere, for instance, if the pilot turns up late.

Table 6.17 gives the payoffs that are usually used in weakest link game experiments. In this case people need to choose effort between one and seven. The best thing for the group and the individual, the Pareto-dominant Nash equilibrium, is for all members of the group to put in high effort. This gives the highest payoff of 13. The safest thing for the individual, however, the risk-dominant Nash equilibrium, is to put in low effort. This guarantees a payoff of 7. Choosing higher effort is risky, because it only takes one member of the group to choose low effort for the high effort to be wasted and costly.

The weakest link game has the tension between the Pareto-dominant and risk-dominant Nash equilibrium that we looked at in section 6.2.4. Indeed, the payoffs

Table 6.17 Payoffs in a weakest link game

Your choice of effort	*Smallest choice of effort in the group*						
	7	*6*	*5*	*4*	*3*	*2*	*1*
7 (high)	13	11	9	7	5	3	1
6		12	10	8	6	4	2
5			11	9	7	5	3
4				10	8	6	4
3					9	7	5
2						8	6
1 (low)							7

in Table 6.5 are a condensed version of Table 6.17. Ideally we want people to coordinate on the Pareto-dominant Nash equilibrium.

Figure 6.20 gives a fairly typical picture of what happens in a weakest link game experiment. In this case there were four players who played together for ten rounds. We see that there was coordination failure. That subject 2 chose low effort in every round meant that the high effort of subjects 1, 3, and 4 was wasted. Over the rounds the effort of these three subjects falls as they learn effort is not going to pay. Figure 6.21 summarizes some aggregate results from a series of experiments by van Huyck and co-authors (1990). The dramatic rise in the proportion of subjects choosing low effort clearly demonstrates coordination failure. Nearly 80 percent of subjects are choosing low effort by round ten!

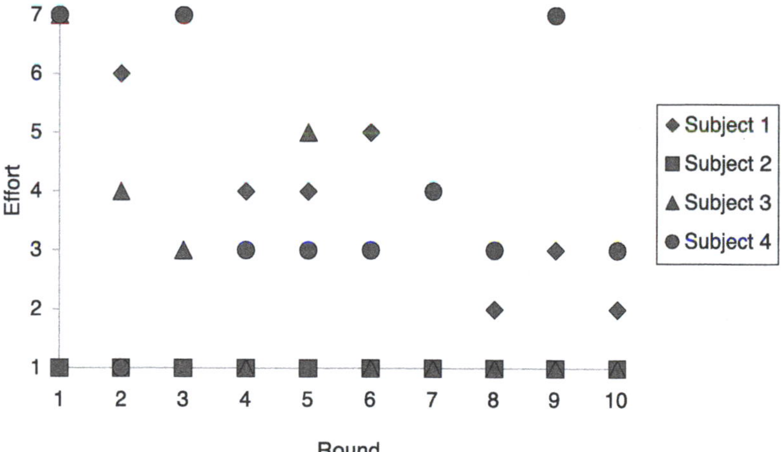

Figure 6.20 An example of coordination failure in a weakest link game. That subject 2 chose an effort level of 1 meant the high effort of the other three was wasted.

Source: Cartwright *et al.* (2013).

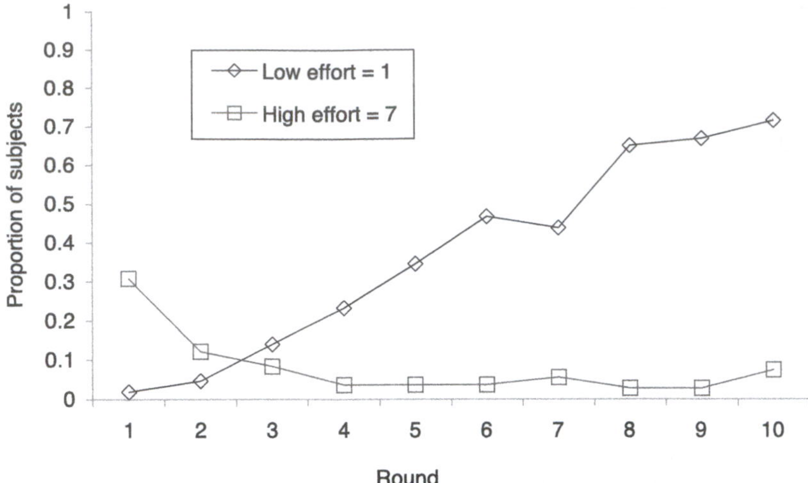

Figure 6.21 The proportion of players choosing 1 and 7 in weakest link games. There is a large rise in the proportion choosing low effort.

Source: van Huyck *et al.* (1990).

Such coordination failure is not good. With results like this I would not be betting on Emma's plane leaving on time. So, how can we make things better? Many suggestions have been tried out in the laboratory, with varying degrees of success. I shall look at some shortly (see also Research Methods 6.6). First, however, it is useful to get a better idea of why there is coordination failure.

Research Methods 6.6

Money versus real effort

A common interpretation of choice in the weakest link game is a choice of effort. Experimental subjects, however, are usually asked how much money to give. Do we get different results if subjects are asked to put in effort rather than give money? This is a question about the external validity of weak link game experiments. Bortolotti and co-authors (2009) go some way to answering this question by getting subjects to do a real effort task. Subjects were asked to sort and count, within a given time interval, a bag of one, two, five, and ten cent euro coins. Group payment was based on the worst performance in the group. They found that there was significant coordination failure in the first few rounds, but increasing coordination over time. This suggests that real effort might be different to money, because of, say, social norms around working versus shirking. The effort task used was, however, still very particular and so concerns about external validity can never be completely removed. Also, significant coordination failure was still observed, just less than in standard experiments.

To do this we can use the models we looked at in sections 6.2 and 6.3. I will start by looking at initial choices. Costa-Gomes and co-authors (2009) looked at how well things like level-k reasoning did at matching first round choices in the weakest link game. Figure 6.22 gives the log likelihood of each model which is an estimate of goodness of fit. To give some interpretation to the numbers, the first two bars show what numbers we would get with a perfect fit and assuming subjects choose randomly. The clear winner is that subjects played the Pareto-dominant equilibrium of high effort. How can that be? How can people be choosing the Pareto optimum of high effort, yet we get coordination failure? The answer is that we need just one person to choose low effort to get coordination failure. Most subjects do choose high effort but there is typically at least one subject who chooses low effort, as in Figure 6.20. This causes coordination failure.

Next we can look at how subjects learn with experience. Crawford (1995) showed that a model of belief learning, similar to that discussed in section 6.3.2, can do a good job of explaining the change in behavior over time. In the model people update their beliefs about what the minimum effort will be over time. A person who expected others to choose high effort but observes low effort will lower her future estimate of expected effort. If less effort is expected from others, then she puts in less effort herself. This means that the low effort of one person can drag down the effort of everyone in the group. That's also what we see in Figure 6.20.

The picture we get is one of coordination failure being caused by a small minority of people who choose low effort. Most do try high effort but the one or

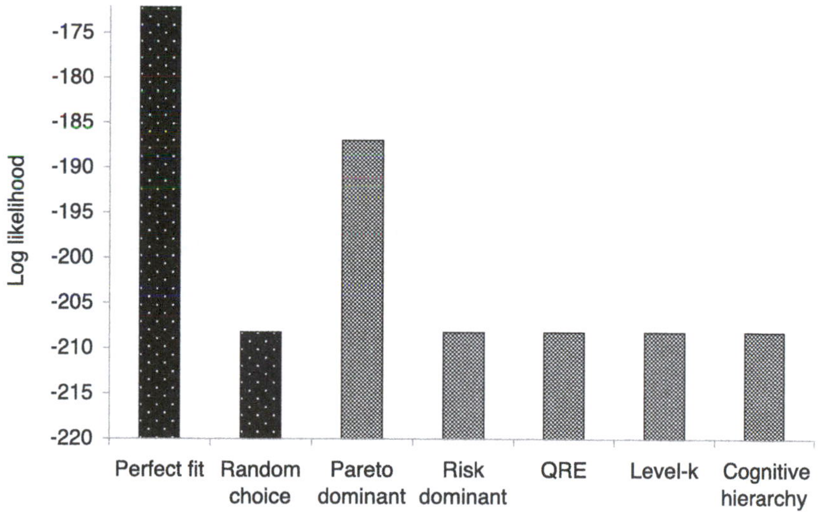

Figure 6.22 How well various models fit data from the weakest link game. Perfect fit and random choice given us an upper and lower bound on how good fit could be.

Source: Costa-Gomes *et al.* (2009).

two people choosing low effort means that this is wasted. That suggests that we might be able to overcome coordination failure if we can stop this minority of people choosing low effort.

One way that seems to work quite well is to have people work in teams. Specifically, a study by Feri and co-authors (2010) looked at what happens when decisions are made by teams of three. Figure 6.23 shows that average effort was a lot higher when decisions were made by teams than if they were made by individuals. More importantly, there is also no sign that average effort is declining over time. Teams, therefore, seem better able to coordinate on high effort. This is further evidence that teams can behave differently to individuals.

The design of the study allows us to explore why this was. Before first interacting with fellow team members, each subject was asked what effort they intended to choose. These intentions did not differ from the choices made by individual decision makers. So, being part of a team, in itself, made no difference. The difference comes from the interaction between team members. After this interaction many team members chose a higher effort than they had intended. So, team interaction does something to eliminate the minority of people choosing low effort. The way that the team reached a decision, whether by voting, leadership, or consensus, seemed to make little difference (see section 6.8 for a similar result).

So, team decision making seems to work. Is there any other way to keep effort high? I will look next at a series of studies by Brandts and Cooper. Not content with the challenge of maintaining high effort, they asked if coordination failure can be overcome. They did so by looking at a **turnaround game** in which we can think of a manager trying to get a group of workers to increase effort. In the first

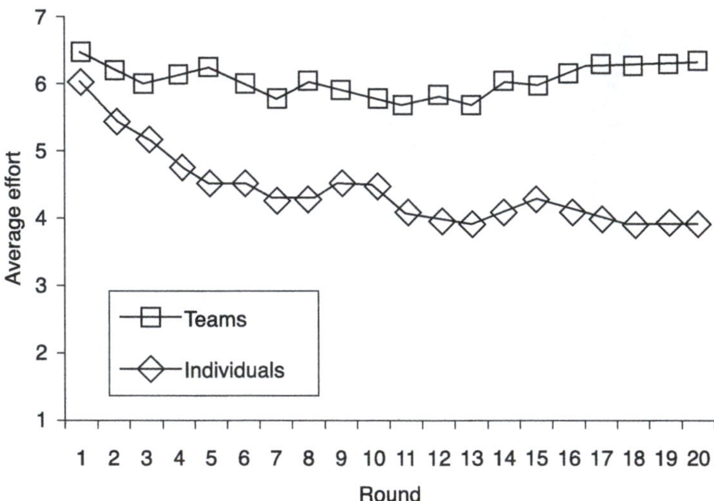

Figure 6.23 Average effort in a weakest link game comparing teams and individuals.
Source: Feri *et al.* (2010).

ten periods the group plays the weakest link game and effort typically falls to a low level. In period 11 the manager steps in and tries things to increase effort. For example, the manager can talk to the group or increase the payoff incentives for high effort.

Let's look first look at what happens if the payoff incentives to high effort are changed. Figure 6.24 plots minimum effort from round ten onwards as the bonus from coordinating is increased from 6 to more than 6. The first thing to observe is that effort is low in period ten and does not improve if the bonus remains at 6. By contrast, if the bonus is increased, we observe a rise in effort. Interestingly the change in the bonus to 8 increases effort more than a change to 10 or *14*. So, it is not the size of the incentive that seems to matter, but that incentives were changed.

The most plausible explanation for the increased effort is that the change in incentives provides a focal event around which members of the group can escape from low effort. One critical part of this story is that subjects observe the effort of all members of the group, called **full feedback**. If they only observe the minimum effort in the group, called **limited feedback**, then things do not work so well. This is apparent in Figure 6.25, where we can compare full feedback and limited feedback. With limited feedback the increase in effort is much less. The story we get, therefore, is one where the change in bonus is a focal event around which enough people increase effort to persuade others to increase effort. This time it is the subjects putting in high effort that drags up the effort of others.

Another possibility the manager could use is communication. With one-way communication the manager can talk to the group and try to encourage high effort. With two-way communication, members of the group can talk to the manager, and perhaps suggest what might work well, and then the manager talks to the group.

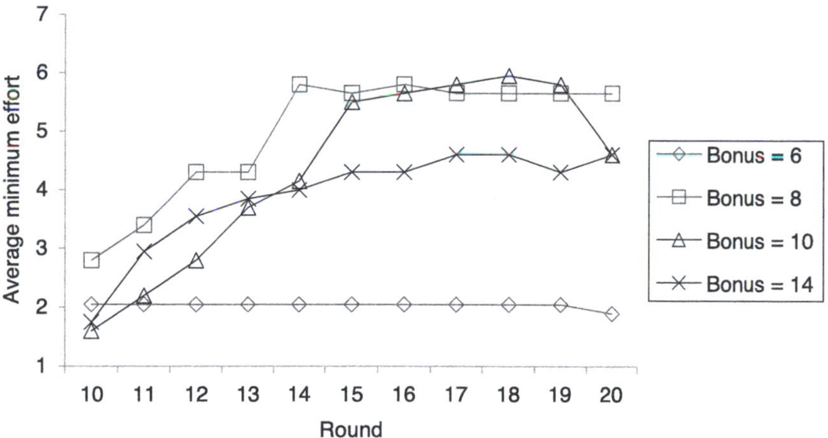

Figure 6.24 The minimum effort in the turnaround game. A change in the bonus to coordination allows groups to escape from low effort.

Source: Brandts and Cooper (2006).

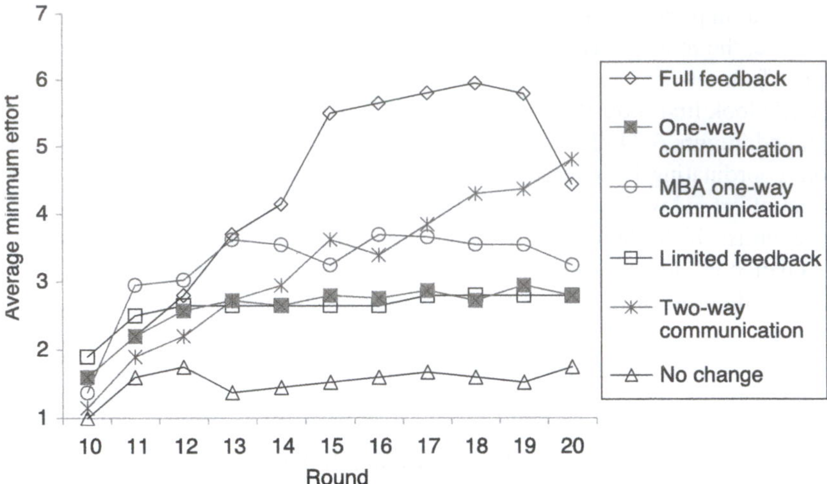

Figure 6.25 Average effort in the turnaround game. It is easier to overcome coordination failure with full feedback than with limited feedback, and with two-way communication than with one-way communication.

Sources: Brandts and Cooper (2007), Cooper (2006).

Figure 6.25 plots some results that allow us to see how well communication performs (see also Research Methods 6.7). Overall we see that one-way communication was not very successful, but two-way communication was. This, however, masked the fact that saying the right thing did usually work. Saying the right thing meant asking for a specific effort level and stressing the benefits of coordination. This usually led to an increase in average effort, when coupled with an increase in the bonus.

Research Methods 6.7

Artefactual field experiments

An **artefactual field experiment** is performed in the lab but with subjects likely to have **task-specific experience**. A study by Cooper (2006) provides an interesting example by comparing the performance in the turnaround game of undergraduate students to that of managers on an executive MBA program. People on the program had at least ten years' work experience, including five years as managers, and had average annual earnings over $120,000. The main findings of the study were that those on the MBA were very successful at turning things around and did so faster than students. They did so because they knew how to effectively communicate to people in the group better than students. These results offer reassurance that the turnaround game does capture things going on in the workplace.

It is possible, therefore, to get people to coordinate in a weakest link game, but it is not easy. It will be a similar story for the next type of game that I want to look at.

6.7.2 Threshold public good games

The basic idea of a **threshold public good game** is that a good will be provided for the benefit of everyone if and only if people contribute enough to exceed some **threshold**. For example, if a church roof needs replacing and doing so costs $100,000, then members of the church somehow need to raise the $100,000 threshold. Or if flatmates have to clean a flat to the standard their landlord requires, between them they need to put in time cleaning the flat to the threshold standard. In this game there is no trade-off between risk dominance and Pareto dominance. The best outcome is that they contribute enough to exceed the threshold. The problem now is a **conflict of interest** over how much each should contribute. For instance, one flatmate may do little to clean the flat, in the hope that another flatmate will do lots.

The main question is whether people can coordinate by contributing enough, despite the conflict of interest. Figure 6.26 gives the results of a typical experiment. In this experiment subjects were put in groups of five, and were given 55 tokens. To produce the public good they needed to contribute between them 125 tokens (see Chapter one for more on this). We see that the group was not as good at coordinating as we might have hoped. In nine of the 25 rounds the total contribution was less than the threshold and things get worse as time goes on. This

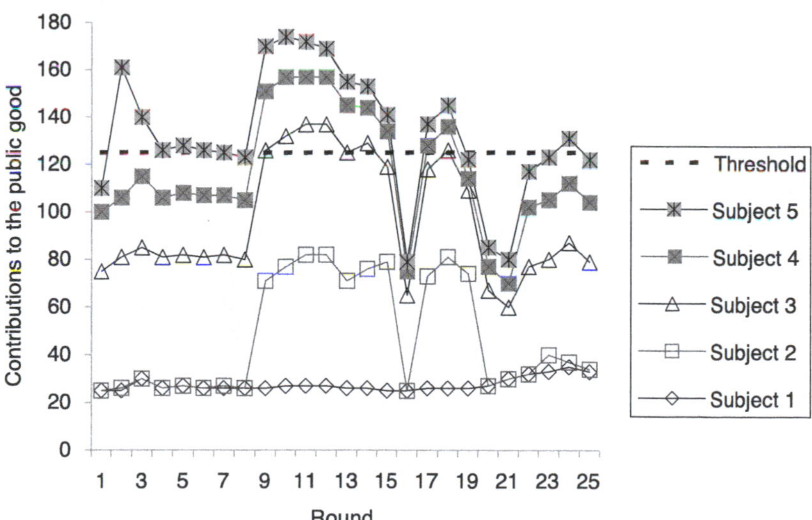

Figure 6.26 A typical threshold public good experiment.

Source: Alberti and Cartwright (2010).

is primarily because subjects 2, 4, and 5 give less and try to free ride on the contributions of the others.

Yet again we see that people are not great at coordinating. Yet again, we need to ask what might help people coordinate better. One thing that might matter is the institution in place to collect contributions. For example, if contributions fall short of the threshold, then we might be able to give people a **refund** on their contribution. Sometimes this is not possible; for instance, flatmates cannot get back the time they have spent cleaning. But sometimes it is possible; for instance, the church could give back donations if insufficient funds are raised. Another possibility is to give a **rebate** if contributions exceed the threshold.

Figure 6.27 gives for comparison the success rates of providing the public good observed in various experiments with various institutions. We want the success rate to be 100 percent, meaning that the public good is always provided. In the base case, where there is a refund, no rebate, and contributions are made simultaneously, the success rate is a disappointing 40 to 60 percent. Can we do any better?

The most dramatic drop in the success rate comes from removing the possibility of a refund. In this case the success rate drops to around 20 percent! So, refunds work. The consequences of a rebate seem to depend on the type of rebate. I have given data for two types of rebate in Figure 6.27. With a proportional rebate, contributions above the threshold are given back in proportion to how much a person contributed. This does not seem to increase the success rate. What works better is a utilization rebate whereby excess contributions are used in some way to increase the value of the public good. An example of this type of rebate would be the church using any money it raises above the $100,000 to, say, paint the walls. Another thing that seems to work well is sequential choice. In this case people can

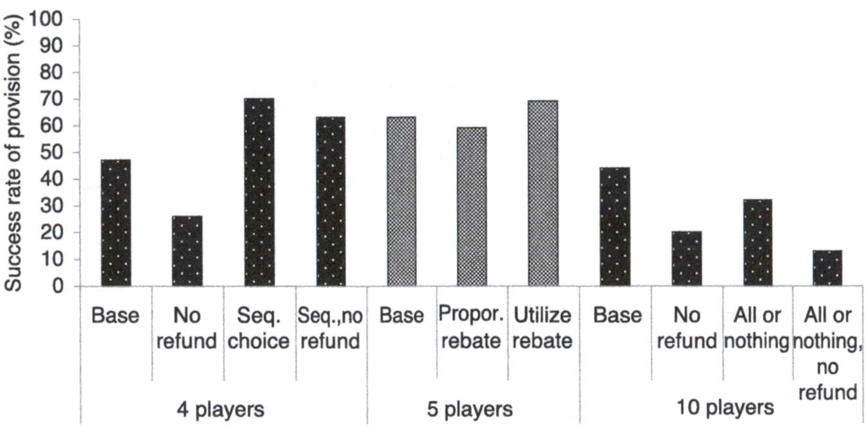

Figure 6.27 Success at providing a threshold public good depends on the institution.

Sources: Croson and Marks (2001), Marks and Croson (1998), Coats *et al.* (2009), Cadsby and Maynes (1999).

see contributions as they happen. For example, the church might put a chart on the wall to see how close they are to the target.

I could go on talking about various other institutions that have been looked at, but I think that we have done enough to illustrate the main points. In both the weakest link game and the threshold public good game we have seen that it can be a problem to coordinate. We need to understand why, and ask how to make things better. The benefits of doing so could be huge: Emma gets her plane on time, the church gets its new roof, the flat gets cleaned, and much more besides. When looking at the weakest link game I focused on how people within or connected to the group could possibly make things better. When looking at the threshold public good game I have focused on how the broader institution can possibly make things better. Together, therefore, we have a variety of ways that might help people coordinate.

The main lesson, however, seems to be that coordinating is not easy: the best we have seen are success rates of around 70 percent. This is a depressing way to finish a section! Fortunately, the next chapter is a bit more optimistic in showing that people can cooperate better than we might have expected.

6.8 Monetary policy by committee

The most important component of monetary policy is undoubtedly the interest rate. A change in the interest rate affects everyone, from savers, borrowers, and investors, to traders; it has long-term consequences for inflation, wages, jobs, and growth. Indeed, it is hard to think of another routinely made policy decision that has such wide-ranging implications. So who would you choose to make the crucial decisions? I'll simplify your task by giving you some possibilities.

Traditionally, interest rates in the UK were decided by one individual, the Chancellor of the Exchequer (i.e. finance minister). In 1997 that all changed when responsibility for setting interest rates was devolved to the Bank of England's Monetary Policy Committee (MPC). The Committee is composed of eight members, four from the Bank and four independent members, and meets once a month. Decisions are made by majority vote, with the Governor's vote counting double. In the US, interest rates have long been set by the Federal Open Market Committee (FOMC). The FOMC is similar to the MPC but there are some notable differences. It has a few more members, meets a bit less often, and requires a consensus or unanimous verdict.

So, the three basic possibilities are: (i) an individual, (ii) a team that must reach a majority decision, (iii) a team that must reach a unanimous decision. You could also mess around with the number of team members and frequency of decision. What is best? The fact that the UK and many other countries have changed to a committee system might lead you to believe that teams must be best. The change towards committee was not, however, motivated by evidence that teams are best! Fortunately, a study by Blinder and Morgan (2005) gives us more evidence to go on. In so doing, it also provides a nice illustration of why the distinction between individuals and teams is important to take seriously.

The study compared individuals and teams in an explicit context of monetary policy. The economy was simulated using the standard model you can find in any macroeconomic textbook. Subjects were put in the role of a monetary policymaker trying to keep unemployment at 5 percent and inflation at 2 percent. Each round of the experiment consisted of ten periods, which you can think of as ten months of policymaking. Every month the economy was subject to minor shocks. But, in one randomly selected month there was a major shock. Roughly speaking, it was best to keep interest rates unchanged in the face of minor shocks and adjust in the case of a major shock. The skill is distinguishing a major shock from a minor shock (or an accumulation of minor shocks) and to move interest rates in the right direction by the right amount.

In each round the monetary policy was scored on how close unemployment and inflation were kept to target. Figure 6.28 shows how average score varied during the 40 rounds of the experiment. In the first ten rounds subjects acted as individuals. In the second set of ten rounds, subjects were put into teams of five. Some teams were told to decide by majority vote and others by consensus. We can see that the introduction of teams in round 11 led to an immediate jump in score. It is clear that this was not due to any learning effect, given the abruptness of the jump; teams simply performed better than individuals. In the third set of ten rounds, subjects go back to making decisions as individuals. The experience of being in a team seemed to make subjects better monetary policymakers! In the final set of ten rounds, subjects were again put back into teams of five. We see a further jump in performance.

We have already seen evidence in this chapter that teams are better than individuals. Each context, however, is different, and so it is reassuring to see specific

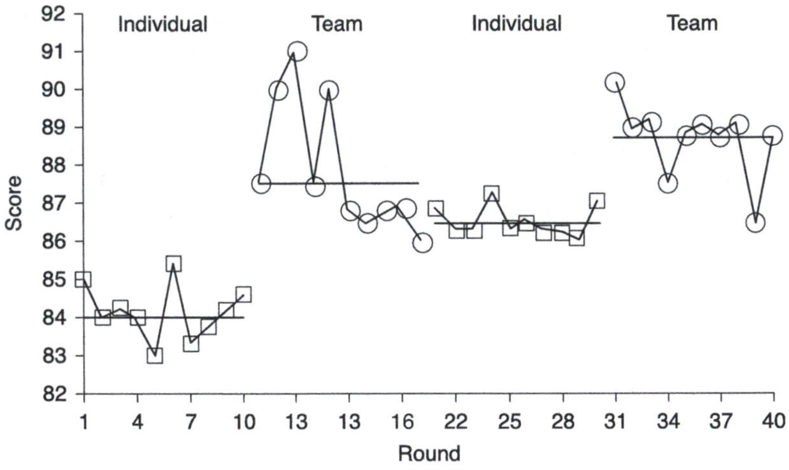

Figure 6.28 The score of monetary policymakers trying to keep unemployment and inflation on target. Teams perform better than individuals.

Source: Blinder and Morgan (2005).

evidence that monetary policy by committee makes sense. Indeed, one interesting factor present in this context, that has been absent from everything we have looked at so far, is time. A particular concern of many macroeconomists was that decision making by committee would lead to inertia, or a hesitation to act until sufficient evidence was accumulated. Such inertia could be costly and seems especially likely if consensus is required. The study by Blinder and Morgan, however, found that teams changed the interest rate *quicker* than individuals following the shock. Teams waited an average of 2.3 periods, or months, versus 2.45 periods for individuals. There was also no evidence that requiring consensus was any different to having a majority vote.

6.9 Industrial organization

It is natural in a chapter on strategic interaction to look at industrial organization, a field of economics that analyzes the firm and market structure. Just about any decision a firm makes should involve thinking through the reaction of others. For instance, when deciding on what price to charge, whether to build a new factory, how much to advertise, and whether to invest in research and development the firm needs to anticipate how rivals and customers will react. There are plenty of examples in this book of how behavioral economics can help us understand better the relationship between a firm and its customers (see, in particular, sections 4.6.2 and 7.6.4).

What I want to do in this section is focus on the relationship between a firm and its rival. Given that industrial organization is a huge field, I need to be somewhat selective in what I cover. The issues of limit pricing, market entry, and quantity leadership are the topics I have chosen to briefly look at.

Before we get started I want to make one point of clarification. To date, behavioral economics has probably learnt a lot more from industrial organization than industrial organization has learnt from behavioral economics. When studying the relationship between a firm and its rival we come up with novel games, and it is interesting to see how people play those games. So, behavioral economics has learnt from industrial organization. With time, the relationship will, hopefully, become more reciprocal. Certainly, an understanding of how people reason through strategic interaction can potentially inform on how a firm may interact with its rival. That will, hopefully, become clear as we proceed.

6.9.1 Limit pricing

To begin, let us imagine we have a market with a monopoly supplier. For example, suppose your local town has only one superstore. It is called BuyFood. Monopoly power gives BuyFood the chance to make maximum profit; but such profits may look attractive to rival firms. One such rival, called CheapFood, is deciding whether to enter the market by building its own superstore in the town.

The **incumbent monopolist**, BuyFood, would rather the **potential entrant**, CheapFood, did not enter the market. But is there anything BuyFood can do to deter entry? One possibility is called limit pricing. Essentially, it means that BuyFood pre-commits to low prices and thereby makes the market look unattractive to CheapFood. Low prices result in BuyFood making less profit, but it may still make more profit than it would have done if CheapFood had entered the market. Whether or not limiting pricing can work will depend on how easily BuyFood can make the market look unattractive to CheapFood.

The timeline of a simple limit pricing game is depicted in Figure 6.29. The extra thing added into the mix is some uncertainty. BuyFood may be a low-cost seller, in which case it can easily lower prices without sacrificing profit. Or, it may be a high-cost seller, in which case lower prices would require a big drop in profit. If CheapFood knew the costs of BuyFood, then things would be simple: it would enter the market if BuyFood is high cost, and stay out of the market if BuyFood is low cost. But it is more realistic to assume that CheapFood does not know the cost of BuyFood.

The lack of information on cost turns the limit pricing game into a signaling game. The size of extension that BuyFood builds sends a signal to CheapFood about its likely costs. As we have already seen in Section 5.3.4, things can get complicated pretty quickly when looking at signaling games. Plus, there are many different permutations of possible costs for BuyFood and ease with which CheapFood can enter. So, I will keep things simple by looking at the two possible equilibrium outcomes summarized in Table 6.18 based on two different scenarios.

In the first scenario it is hard for CheapFood to enter the market. Hard enough that the firm should only enter if it can be confident that BuyFood has high costs. What if BuyFood chooses the same size of extension irrespective of its costs? That way CheapFood cannot infer anything about the costs of BuyFood and stays

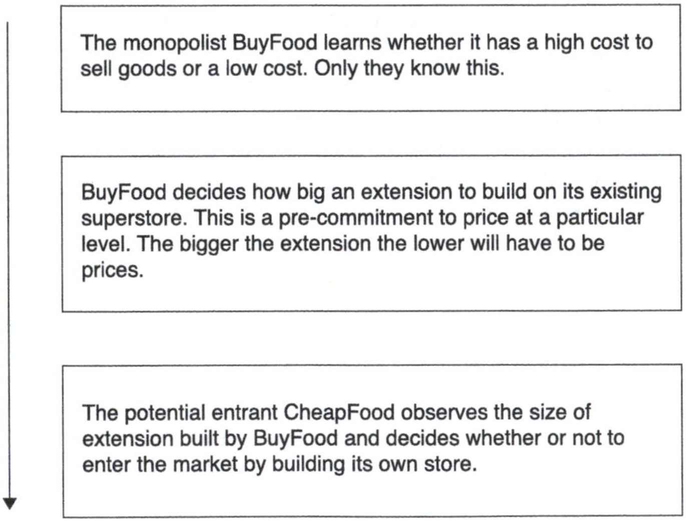

Figure 6.29 Timeline in a limit price entry game.

Table 6.18 Possible equilibria in the limit price entry game

Scenario	*Equilibrium*	*Monopolist*	*Entrant*
Hard to enter	Pooling	Chooses a medium-sized extension irrespective of cost	Stays out
Easy to enter	Separating	Chooses a large extension if low cost and small extension if high cost	Stays out if a large extension and enters if a small extension

out of the market. We get a pooling equilibrium. The key thing here is that BuyFood builds a bigger extension than it would ideally like when it is high cost. It does so to deter entry.

In the second scenario it is easy for CheapFood to enter the market. Easy enough that the firm will enter unless it knows for sure that BuyFood has low costs. In this scenario, pooling no longer makes sense because BuyFood will need to signal that it has low costs. So, it will build a large extension if it is low cost and a small extension if high cost. CheapFood can, thus, infer the cost of BuyFood and we get a separating equilibrium. This time BuyFood builds a bigger extension than it would ideally like when it is low cost.

The equilibria in Table 6.18 are a hint of how complex and subtle a limit pricing game can be. Industrial organization textbooks churn out the equations that help find the optimal strategy. But how realistic is it to expect managers to follow the strategy? We saw in the previous chapter how easily people can be biased when interpreting information. What kinds of biases can we expect when managers interpret the behavior of rival firms? It is questions like these that illustrate the important role that behavioral economics can play in industrial organization.

Two reasons to put some faith in managers are that they have the chance to learn from experience, and typically work in teams. With that in mind let us look at a study by Cooper and Kagel (2005) in which subjects played a limit price entry game. Some subjects played as individuals and some in teams of two. The main results are summarized in Figure 6.30. Focus first on the dashed lines. These tell us what happened when subjects repeatedly played a version of the game where entering the market was easy. In this case strategic play required the monopolist to build a large extension to signal low cost. In the first 12 rounds we see that few behaved strategically. With experience, the proportion of strategic play rises. Teams were also a lot more strategic than individuals. Experience and teamwork seem to do the trick!

Focus now on the solid lines. In the first 32 rounds, subjects played a version of the game where entering the market was hard. In this case strategic behavior equated to a pooling equilibrium. We can see that there was a larger proportion of strategic play than when entering was easy. The really interesting thing, however, is what happens from round 33 onwards. At this point the game changed to one where entering was easy. Strategic behavior, thus, equated to a separating equilibrium. The remarkable thing to note is that subjects adapted quickly to the new

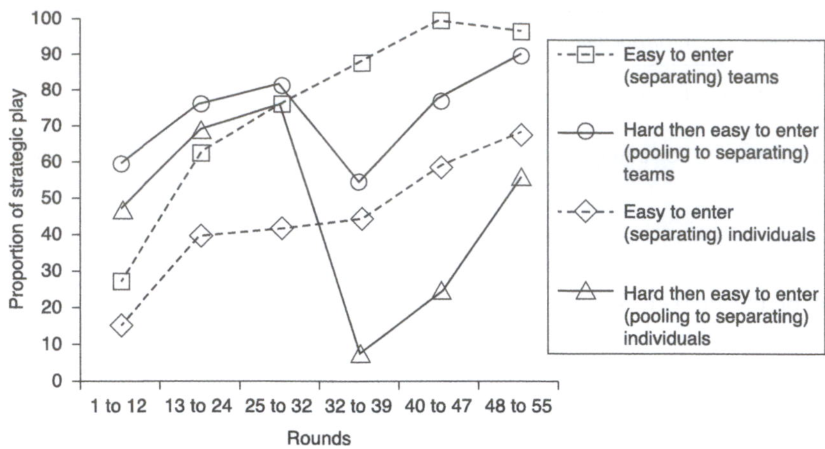

Figure 6.30 The proportion of strategic play in a limit pricing game. Each cycle lasted 12 or eight rounds.

Source: Cooper and Kagel (2005).

setting and teams adapted particularly quickly. Indeed, teams in this 'crossover' treatment were much more strategic than teams in the comparator treatment were for similar levels of experience.

We have another example of how teams can outperform individuals. The interesting thing in this case is how experience in one setting translated into an improved performance in a different setting. Teams adapted to a change in the game more quickly than individuals did. Again, however, we should be careful to not get too carried away. It took a lot of experience before subjects were consistently behaving strategically. Moreover, there are other variants of the limit pricing game where teams do not come close to strategic behavior even with experience.

The general lesson, therefore, is that firms will sometimes deviate from the optimal strategy. In this context that means firms may not do all they could to deter potential entrants.

6.9.2 Market entry

In the limit pricing game an incumbent monopolist is pitted against a potential rival. Consider now a new market with no existing firms. To stick with the superstore example, you might think of a new town, or town that is rapidly expanding, and is not currently served by any store. I am going to use the slightly different example of a new technology. Something called a Widget is invented that will revolutionize home entertainment. Imagine that you own a firm in the home entertainment business. Should you enter the Widget market?

Your first reaction might be to say: of course I should enter, it is an exciting new opportunity and I should not miss out. The problem with this line of reasoning is that other firms in the home entertainment business are probably thinking the same thing. And, if all firms enter the market, there will be oversupply and someone is going to lose out. That someone might be you. Somehow, therefore, the 'right' number of firms need to enter the market. If too few enter, those in the market make bumper profits. If too many enter, some are going to make losses. We have a **market entry coordination game**. Firms need to coordinate on who enters and who stays out of the Widget market.

A market entry game is relatively complex and it seems difficult to know how firms could coordinate on who enters the market. Subjects in the laboratory, however, seem good at solving this problem. To illustrate I am going to look at a study by Rapoport and co-authors (2002). This study is particularly interesting because it considers firm asymmetry. For some firms it is less costly to start producing Widgets than for others. This asymmetry seemingly offers a simple solution to the coordination problem, namely those with the lowest cost to produce Widgets should be the ones to enter the market. This is not how things turned out!

First let us look at Figure 6.31, which illustrates how good subjects are at coordinating. In the games considered there were 20 firms in a group and the capacity of the market could be anything between one and 19. Over 100 rounds, subjects were exposed to all the possible capacities ten times. In Figure 6.31 we see that the average number of firms entering the market compared to the equilibrium prediction. Every group is basically spot on the prediction! So, subjects learned to coordinate very well.

When we analyze how subjects learnt to coordinate, things get somewhat intriguing. Figure 6.32 shows what happened in one of the groups in the final rounds of the experiment. Subjects 1 to 4 had the lowest cost to enter and subjects

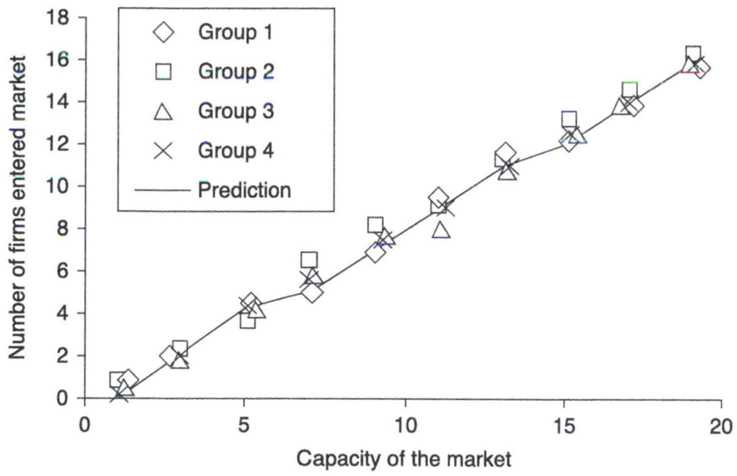

Figure 6.31 The predicted number of entrants in a market entry game compared to the average number of entrants in four groups.

Source: Rapoport *et al.* (2002).

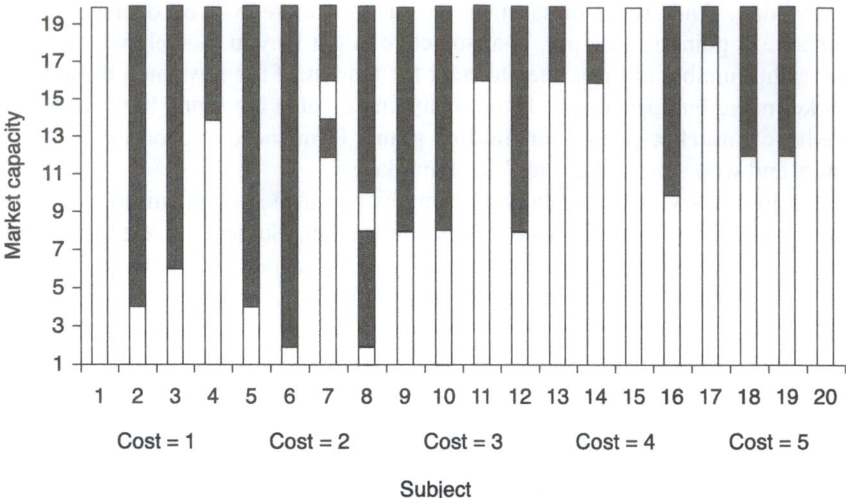

Figure 6.32 The behavior of subjects in a market entry game. The filled-in blocks show the subject entered, and the empty blocks that they stayed out.

Source: Rapoport *et al.* (2002).

17 to 20 the highest cost. The filled-in blocks show for which market capacity a subject entered. Subject 2, for instance, stayed out of the market if capacity was one or three, but entered if capacity was five or more. Recall, we would predict that those with the lowest cost should be the ones to enter. That did not happen! Subject 1, for instance, always stayed out, while subject 18 entered if capacity was 13 or above.

Clearly subjects found a way to coordinate other than through cost. The authors of the study show that a model of reinforcement learning can explain how they do so. The key to the model is to equate strategy with a rule, 'enter the market if capacity is x or above'. With experience, a subject revises the value of x, meaning that over time subjects come to coordinate. This result reiterates the point that people can be good at coordinating, but not necessarily on the most efficient outcome. It also suggests that market entry may be based more on history and precedent than on costs. Firms with a history of entering new markets in the past may be the most likely to enter the market for Widgets, even if they are no good at producing Widgets.

On the topic of market entry I will briefly mention a fascinating study by Goldfarb and Xiao (2011). They looked at entry in local US telephone markets after the 1996 Telecommunications Act. This Act opened up local telecommunications to competition and so created a swathe of market entry games. Goldfarb and Xiao looked at how the strategic decision of firms related to the characteristics of the firm's manager. They found that experienced and 'better educated' CEOs made better decisions. In particular, they entered markets with fewer competitors.

Reassuringly, having an economics or business degree was a big component of being 'better educated'! Indeed, an economics or business degree was a substitute for experience.

Results like these reiterate the basic point. Firms are run by managers and managers are inevitably going to be subject to all the cognitive biases and limited strategic reasoning that we have seen so far in this book. As mentioned in the previous section, the fact that decisions are made by teams of experienced managers is only going to go a little way to eliminating such bias and improving strategic reasoning. So, do not expect firms to be as strategic as they could be when entering the Widget or telecommunications market. But do expect behavioral economics to have an increasing impact in the field of industrial organization.

6.9.3 Quantity leadership

It would be rude to discuss industrial organization and not mention Cournot, Stackelberg, and Bertrand. These three names are etched in history for having given us the three classic models of firm competition. Conveniently ignoring the Bertrand model, I shall look at the Cournot and Stackelberg models. In both models, firms independently choose a level of output. To fix ideas we can think of BuyFood and CheapFood deciding how big a superstore to have, or how many tins of tuna to order for resale. In the Cournot model, BuyFood and CheapFood choose their own quantity without knowing the quantity of the rival. In the Stackelberg model, a leader firm chooses its quantity and, having observed this, the follower firm chooses its quantity.

Figure 6.33 illustrates how the models work. The two superstores choose to produce either a low, medium, or high amount of output. The best for them, not for customers, is that they produce a low output and each get profit 72. This collusive outcome is, however, unlikely because each firm would have an incentive to increase output. The **Cournot equilibrium** is to produce medium output and each get profit 64. This is an equilibrium because neither store can gain by producing more or less, given the output of its rival. Finally, we come to the two **Stackelberg equilibria**. If BuyFood produces a high output, then CheapFood's optimal

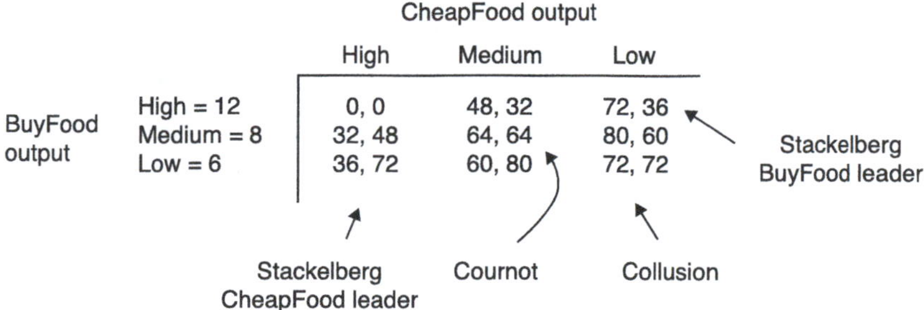

Figure 6.33 Profits in a quantity-setting game and classification of outcomes.

response is to produce low output. This is the best that BuyFood can do and so is the Stackelberg equilibrium outcome. If CheapFood is the leader, then we get the analogous equilibrium.

A study by Huck and co-authors (2001) looked at whether the predictions of the Cournot and Stackelberg model are borne out in the laboratory. It also looked at the potential for collusion by comparing a setting where subjects interacted with a random opponent each round with a setting where subjects repeatedly interacted with the same opponent each round. Repeated interaction is much more conducive to collusion. In order to connect the results of the study with the numbers in Figure 6.33 we need to equate high output with a choice of 12, medium with 8 and low with 6. Subjects could choose any output between 3 and 15, but the equilibria were still as given in Figure 6.33.

The results of the study are summarized in Figure 6.34. Consider first the outcome when firms choose simultaneously, as in the Cournot model. The equilibrium prediction is that each firm produces output eight. This prediction is spot on. Output is slightly lower with repeated interaction, but not by much. This suggests little collusion. Look next at the outcome where firm 1 chooses before firm 2, as in the Stackelberg model. The equilibrium prediction is for firm 1 to produce 12 and firm 2 to produce 6. This prediction is off the mark. Total output is near to that predicted, but firm 1 produces significantly less than predicted. I will come back to an explanation for this shortly. Again, output is slightly lower with repeated interaction, but not by much.

In the Cournot and Stackelberg models 'fate' decides whether a firm chooses output with or without knowing the output of the other. In reality, firms have considerable control over when they decide on output. BuyFood, for example, may decide to delay extending its superstore until it sees what CheapFood does.

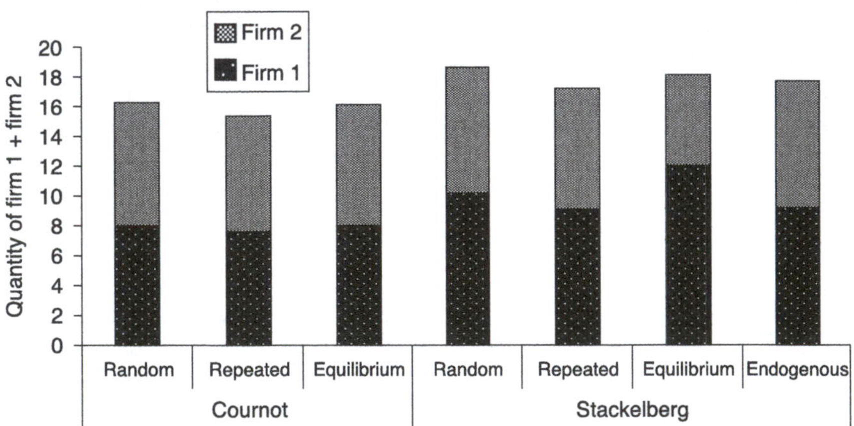

Figure 6.34 The output of firm 1 and firm 2 combined in Cournot and Stackelberg markets compared to the equilibrium.

Source: Huck *et al.* (2001, 2002).

This brings us on to models of **endogenous timing**. One of the many possible models of endogenous timing goes something like this. There are two periods, today and tomorrow. Today, each firm can choose what output to produce or they can decide to wait and decide tomorrow. Tomorrow, any firm that waited must choose output.

If both firms decide to wait until tomorrow then we should get the Cournot equilibrium outcome, because both firms are choosing simultaneously. But this means that both firms will not wait until tomorrow. If, for instance, BuyFood expects CheapFood to wait, then it would do better to choose high output today and 'force' the Stackelberg equilibrium outcome. We can also rule out both firms choosing output today. If, for instance, BuyFood expects CheapFood to choose output today, then it cannot possibly lose anything by waiting to see what output CheapFood will choose. The prediction, therefore, is that we should get the Stackelberg equilibrium outcome. One firm should lead and the other should follow.

A study by Huck and co-authors (2002) tests this prediction. And they do not find good support for it. One reason was that too few subjects waited. The prediction would be that 50 percent will wait, but only 39 percent did so. Another issue was that those choosing output today chose significantly less than the Stackelberg outcome. This finding fits the results of the earlier study. Indeed, the final bar of Figure 6.34 shows the average output of subjects that chose today (firm 1) and those that decided to wait (firm 2); endogenous timing seems to make little difference.

Both of the studies we have looked at seem to suggest that the Stackelberg model is missing something. With both exogenous and endogenous timing we see systematic deviations from the predicted output. This is mainly because leaders choose less than they should. Why did they do that? Figure 6.35 shows the

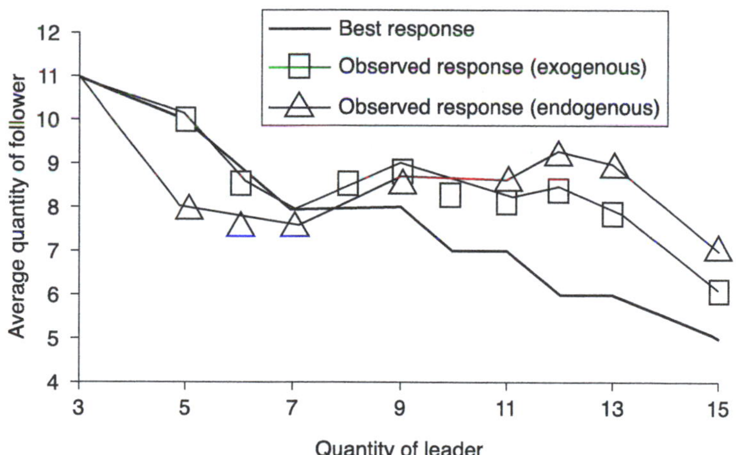

Figure 6.35 The best response and observed response of followers to the output of a Stackelberg leader.

Source: Huck *et al.* (2002).

response of followers to the output of the leader. We can see that, if leaders chose a high output, then followers responded by choosing medium to high output. They were supposed to choose low output. Leaders, therefore, were wise to not choose a large output! The question becomes why followers chose a larger output than predicted.

Look back to the numbers in Figure 6.33. If BuyFood is leader, then the Stackelberg outcome gives CheapFood a lot less profit than BuyFood. By choosing medium instead of high output, CheapFood loses a little, but dramatically closes the gap with BuyFood. If, therefore, CheapFood is willing to sacrifice some profit to make things more equal with BuyFood, it is no surprise that we see a systematic deviation from the Stackelberg equilibrium.

This brings us neatly onto the next chapter on social preferences. In the chapter we shall discuss the overwhelming evidence that people do not like inequality. If this distaste for inequality extends to firm managers, and there is no reason why it should not, then we have good reason to question the predictions of the Stackelberg model. Firms that lead in the market may not be able to exploit their position quite as much as the model predicts.

6.10 Further reading

We have covered a lot of ground in this chapter, so there are plenty of sources for further reading. The book by Colin Camerer (2003) is the most natural place to start. For a recent reinterpretation of behavior in the p-beauty contest, see Breitmoser (2012). Additional material on equilibrium selection and equilibrium refinements can be found in any good game theory textbook, of which there are many. For more on focal points, coordination games, and strategic interaction more generally, the book by Schelling (1990) is definitely recommended. The further reading for Chapter eleven contains references to more on auctions. One issue I have ignored is that people rarely play the same game multiple times, and so more realistically have to learn from their own or others' experiences of playing 'similar' games. This raises questions about what is similar, and so on. Case-based decision theory (see Gilboa and Schmeidler, 1995) and analogy-based expectation equilibrium (see Jehiel, 2005), are two potential ways to deal with this. For more on team decision making see Charness and Sutter (2012).

6.11 Review questions

6.1 When is the best time to sell an asset as a function of what other investors will do?

6.2 Suppose you are playing the p-beauty contest with a group of people who have only just been told about the game. Is what you have learnt in this chapter any help to you? What about in the simple beauty contest?

6.3 Does it make any difference if people can communicate with each other before playing a game?

6.4 Does risk dominance or Pareto dominance seem more relevant to you in predicting what people will do? What about forward or backward induction?
6.5 Look back at Table 6.8. I assumed an initial attractiveness of 30 for both strategies. What happens if the initial attractiveness of both is 10 or is 100? What has this got to do with initial beliefs?
6.6 Look back at Table 6.9. What would happen if $\rho = 0$ or $\rho = 1$?
6.7 I said that it does not always make sense to set the probability of choosing a strategy proportional to its attractiveness. Can you explain why?
6.8 How can we change the models of reinforcement learning and belief-based learning to take account of loss aversion?
6.9 What do you think are the consequences of the law of small numbers and confirmatory bias for learning in games?
6.10 Given what we see in Figures 6.13 and 6.14, which auction format do you think will raise the most revenue?
6.11 Why do you think it matters if there is the possibility of a refund or rebate when contributing to a threshold public good?
6.12 How can leadership help people coordinate in the weakest link game and threshold public good game? You might want to think about forward induction.

7 Social preferences

> Charity collector: I want you to give me a pound and then I go away and give it to the orphans.
> Merchant banker: Yes.
> Charity collector: Well that's it.
> Merchant banker: No, no, no. I don't follow this at all. I mean, I don't want to seem stupid but it looks to me as though I'm a pound down on the whole deal.
>
> Monty Python's merchant banker sketch

You may recall from Chapter one my saying that homo economicus is both rational and selfish. Up until now we have primarily been questioning whether it makes sense to assume that people are as rational as homo economicus. Now it's time to look at whether it makes sense to assume they are as selfish. That people behave as if selfish is one of the most basic assumptions in the standard economic model. The evidence suggests, however, that most people do care about others. Why else would millions of dollars be given to charity every year? Why else would someone feel envious of a work colleague earning a higher salary than them? If the utility of one person depends on the utility of another, then we say that there are **social** or **interdependent preferences**. In this chapter our task is to review the evidence for social preferences, look at how we can model them, and look at what consequences they can have.

7.1 The experimental evidence for social preferences

There have been literally thousands of experiments suggesting that people have social preferences in one shape or another. In this section I am going to look at a selection of these experiments in order to illustrate the main things that we observe. At this point, I shall not try to explain why people behave as they do (that comes in sections 7.2 to 7.4), but you might want to be asking yourself this question when you look at the evidence. To try to help you through the maze of different games that I will look at, Table 7.1 gives a basic description of each game.

Table 7.1 A brief overview of the games I will look at

Game	*Stage 1*	*Stage 2*
Dictator game	Proposer splits $10	—
Trust game	Investor can invest up to $10	Invested money is tripled and proposer can give back to the investor
Gift exchange game	Employer pays the worker a wage	Worker chooses how hard to work
Ultimatum game	Proposer splits $10	Receiver accepts or rejects
Dictator game with third-party punishment	Proposer splits $10	Third party can punish proposer
Linear public good game	Contribute to a public project	—
Linear public good game with punishment	Contribute to a public project	Can punish others after seeing contributions
Moonlighting game	Proposer invests or takes from responder	Responder gives or takes from proposer
Ultimatum game with responder competition	Proposer splits $10	Many receivers can try to accept
Ultimatum game with proposer competition	Many proposers say how they would split $10	Receiver can accept best offer

7.1.1 The nice side of social preferences

I shall begin with three games that show the nice side of social preferences. That is, they show people voluntarily giving money to others.

The dictator game is an obvious place to start. A **dictator game** involves two people: a proposer and receiver. The **proposer** is given a sum of money, say, $10, and asked how much of that $10 he would like to give to the **receiver**. There the game ends! The receiver gets what she is given and the proposer keeps the rest. You may well have played this game yourself in a restaurant you will never visit again. In that case you play the role of proposer, deciding what tip to leave the waiter before you leave the restaurant. If the proposer only cares about his own payoff, then he should simply walk off with the $10 and give nothing to the receiver. What proposers actually do is quite different.

Figure 7.1 summarizes what happened in a series of comparable experiments by Forsythe and co-authors (1994), Hoffman and co-authors (1994) and Hoffman and co-authors (1996). Each treatment varied the way that the game was run (see Research Methods 7.1 for more information), but we can ignore that here. The size of the bubble in the figure indicates what proportion of proposers offered a particular share to the responder, so the larger the bubble, the more offered that amount.

By looking up from zero we can see that lots of proposers gave zero to the receiver; the proportion of subjects varies from around 20 percent in the standard experiments to 60 percent in the double blind experiments. Clearly, however, not everyone gives

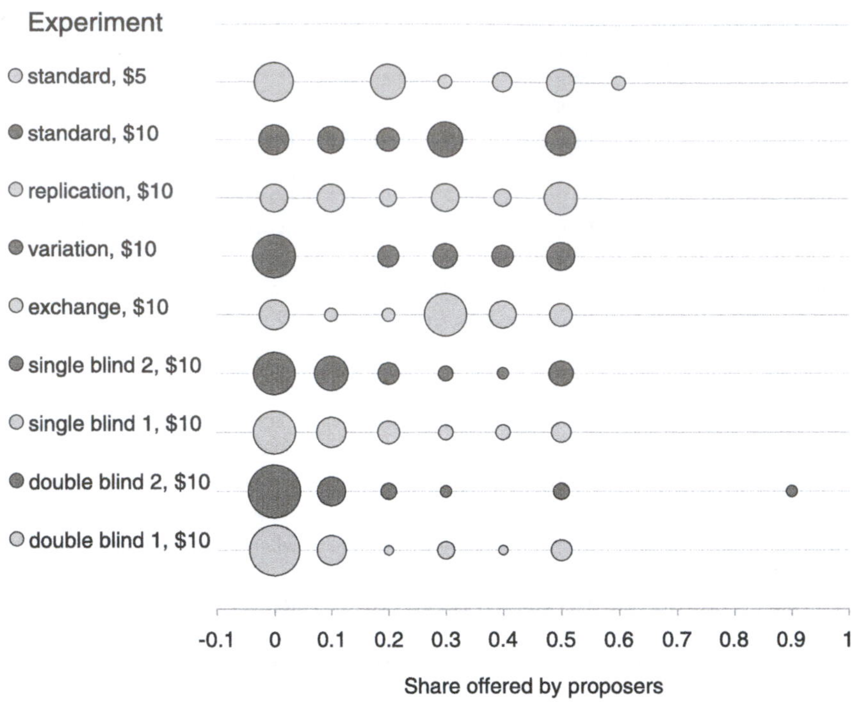

Figure 7.1 The amount that proposers gave in dictator experiments. The size of the bubble indicates the proportion of subjects offering each share. Many do give zero, but the majority give more than zero.

Sources: Forsythe *et al.* (1994), Hoffman *et al.* (1994), Hoffman *et al.* (1996), Camerer (2003).

zero, and lots of proposers give money to the receiver. The amount they give varies, but there is always at least some willing to give away half of the money.

Research Methods 7.1

Single and double blind, anonymity versus reality?

The dictator game is a **one-shot** game, in that it is played just once and anonymously. So, in principle there is no point in a subject thinking about reputation or what others, including the researcher, might think about them. In reality, particularly when experiments are done on university campuses with students and faculty, can we expect subjects to behave as if the game is one shot and anonymous? Or does it cross their mind that, 'if I take all the money the researcher will think that I am mean, and he will probably be marking my exam soon'?

In a series of experiments, Hoffman, McCabe, Schachat, and Smith varied the **social distance** between subjects and researcher to try to answer such questions.

The results are summarised in Figure 7.1. I shall not explain all the nuances of the different treatments, but here are the basic differences.

In the standard and replication treatments, the instructions contain **sharing language** such as 'has been provisionally allocated' $10 and 'the amount to be divided'. In the variation treatment, the sharing language is dropped. In the exchange treatment, the game is framed as a seller (the proposer) setting a price which the buyer (receiver) must pay.

In the single blind 2 treatment, once they have written down their choice, the proposers put any money they will give to the receiver into a sealed envelope along with some blank pieces of paper (so that all envelopes have the same weight/size) and drop this envelope into a box. All proposers put their envelopes into the same box. Receivers randomly pick an envelope from the box. This guarantees anonymity between proposer and receiver and so is called **single blind**. In the single blind 1 treatment, a proposer no longer has to write down their choice but does let the researcher look inside the envelope before it is sealed.

In the double blind 2 treatment, proposers put envelopes into the box and leave. Only then does the researcher look inside the envelopes and record how much was left. This guarantees anonymity between proposer and researcher and so is called **double blind**. In the double blind 1 treatment the recording of offers is made by a randomly assigned student monitor (not the researcher) and two dummy envelopes containing no money are also put in the box. This means that a receiver who gets $0 cannot know whether there was a proposer who left $0 or they were just unlucky and got a dummy envelope. Anonymity between proposer and receiver and proposer and researcher is maximized.

The further we go down the line, the greater the social distance between the proposer and receiver, and the proposer and researcher. This should make the proposers more readily believe that the game is one shot and anonymous. Figure 7.1 suggests that this is the case, given that we see less giving with more social distance. Note, however, that a significant proportion of proposers still give money, even in the double blind 1 treatment. Care is also needed in creating too much social distance because it could leave subjects doubting the experiment is real. For example, proposers might start doubting whether there really is a receiver waiting in another room to pick up the envelope!

The next game I want to look at is called the trust game. A **trust game** involves an investor and a proposer. Both investor and proposer are given $10. The **investor** is told that he can give as much of his $10 as he likes to the proposer. Any amount that he gives will be tripled in value before being given to the proposer. The proposer can then give as much money as she likes back to the investor.

As in the dictator game, a proposer who cares only about her own payoff should not give any money back to the investor. Investors, therefore, should not give money to proposers. This, however, results in inefficiency because it misses out on the tripling of money that is possible with investment. To illustrate, if the investor invests $0 then both investor and proposer get $10. If the investor invests all his $10 then the proposer would have $40 (the initial $10 plus the invested $30) and so could easily pay back the investor on his investment.

Figure 7.2 shows what subjects did in a study by Berg and co-authors (1994). For now, let's ignore the distinction between 'no history' and 'with history'. The squares show the amount that different proposers returned to investors. As in the dictator game, we see that some proposers keep all the money for themselves but many, the majority, give at least some money back. The circles tell us how much investors gave to proposers. The majority of investors were willing to invest at least half their $10 with the proposer. This could be because the investors were happy to give money away to proposers. More realistically, however, it suggests that most investors were willing to trust that proposers would return the investment. An investor who gives to a proposer expects the proposer will give something back.

This brings into focus what is expected of others and whether others fulfill expectations. The distinction between 'no history' and 'with history' takes this further. In a 'no history' experiment, subjects simply got the instructions and played the game. In the 'with history' experiment, investors and proposers were told what happened in the earlier experiment (i.e. the 'no history' side). Things could have gone potentially two ways: investors could have been put off investing by seeing that some proposers kept all the money, or investors and proposers could have been influenced by the positive investing and returning. The later effect seemed to come through in the experiment with more money being returned. Proposers perhaps

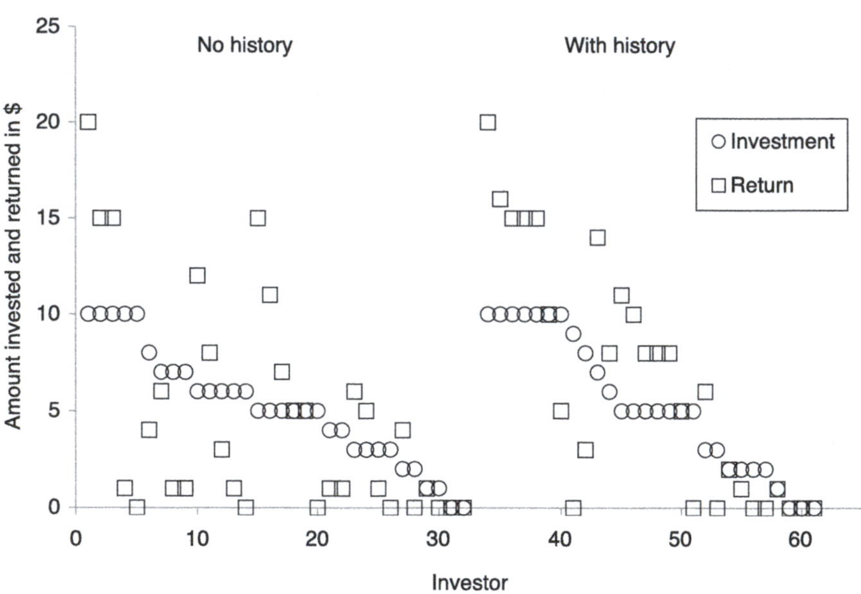

Figure 7.2 Investments and returns in a trust game with and without social history. Most investors invest something. Many proposers do not give anything back, but the majority do give something back.

Source: Berg *et al.* (1994).

better understood that they were given money on the expectation that they would give a 'fair' share back.

The third game I want to look at is a gift exchange game. A **gift exchange game** is a slight variant on a trust game. There are two people, often thought of as worker and employer. The employer is given an amount of money, say, $10, and chooses how much of this to give to the worker, as a wage. Having observed her wage, the worker chooses how much effort to put into working. Higher effort costs the worker, but also means the employer receives higher revenues.

Cost and revenue are usually designed in such a way that higher worker effort is mutually beneficial, i.e. the extra effort would earn enough extra revenue that the employer could pay a high enough wage to offset the worker's effort cost. A worker motivated solely by her own monetary payoff would not, however, put in effort, because it is too late to do anything about her wage and so all it would do is lower her payoff. Given this, why should an employer pay a high wage? He should not.

To see what happens in a typical experiment I will look at the results of a study by Gächter and Falk (2002). In this case employers could choose a wage between 20 and 120 and workers choose effort between 0.1 and 1. Figure 7.3 plots wages and effort over ten rounds of play. In a one-shot experiment, workers and

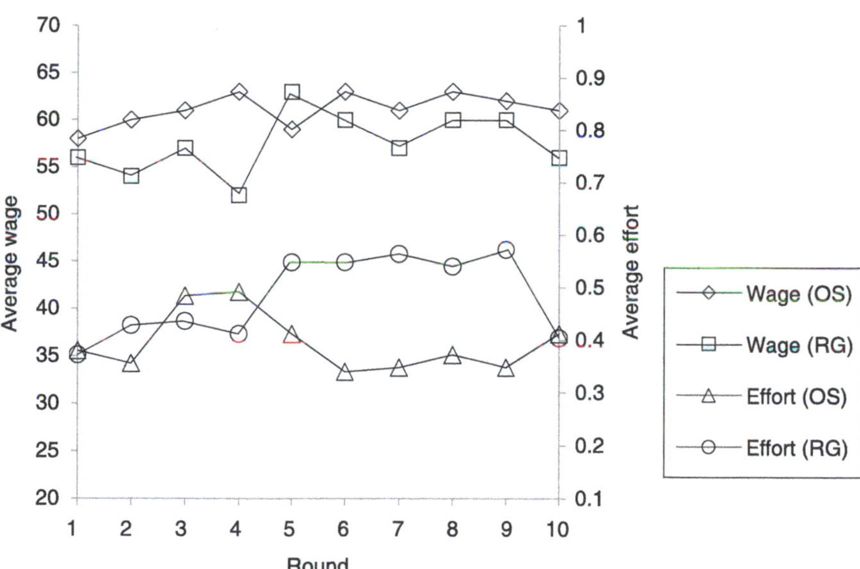

Figure 7.3 Wage and effort levels in a gift exchange experiment comparing one shot (OS) and repeated game (RG). The average wage and average effort are well above the minimum. Effort is higher in the repeated game, but falls in the last round consistent with imitation.

Source: Gächter and Falk (2002).

employers were randomly rematched each round, and so interaction was one shot. In a repeated game experiment, the same workers and employers were matched in each round. As in the trust game we see that on average employers were willing to give workers wages above the minimum, and workers reciprocated by choosing effort above the minimum.

To delve a little deeper, in the one-shot game, Gächter and Falk classified a worker as a **reciprocator** if there was a positive correlation between the wage they were offered and the effort they chose to make, and an **egoist** if they chose the minimum effort most of the time. They found that 20 percent of workers were egoists and 53 percent were reciprocators. The majority of workers, therefore, reciprocated a high wage by higher effort.

In the repeated game it becomes slightly harder to judge reciprocation, because a worker may want to build a reputation as someone who reciprocates a high wage. This way she can secure a high wage in the future. We could call such a worker an **imitator** because they imitate a reciprocator. How can we tell a reciprocator from an imitator? We look at the last round. In this round an imitator no longer has any need to reciprocate a high wage, so she should choose minimum effort. A genuine reciprocator would still reciprocate a high wage by high effort. Gächter and Falk found that 20 percent of workers were imitators, 21 percent were egoists and 48 percent were reciprocators. What we learn new, therefore, is that some people realize that it may be in their interests to look like someone who gives or reciprocates.

To summarize what we have seen so far: many people are willing to give to others at a cost to themselves, expect others will reciprocate giving, and realize it may be in their interests to look like someone who gives. But don't overlook the fact that many do not give at all.

7.1.2 The nasty side of social preferences

Now it is time to look at a more nasty side of social preferences: people taking money from others.

I will start by looking at the ultimatum game. The **ultimatum game** is a twist on the dictator game. As in the dictator game, a proposer is given a sum of money, say, $10, and asked how much of that $10 he would like to give to the receiver. The twist is that the receiver must decide to either accept the offer, in which case the receiver gets what she is given and the proposer keeps the rest, or reject the offer, in which case both get zero.

If a receiver only cares about her own payoff, she should accept any positive offer, because if she rejects the offer she gets zero. To illustrate what typically does happen, Figure 7.4 gives the proportion of subjects who would have rejected offers in experiments by Larrick and Blount (1997). (See Research Methods 7.2 for more on why I chose this study.) Clearly, a large proportion of people were willing to reject offers less than a 50:50 split. The evidence, therefore, is that some people are willing to sacrifice their own monetary payoff to decrease that of others.

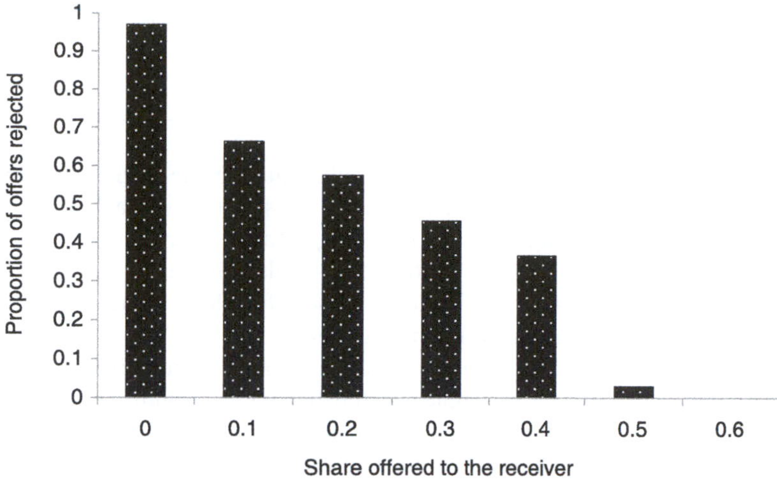

Figure 7.4 The proportion of offers rejected in an ultimatum game. Offers of a 0.5 share or better are rarely rejected, but offers of a less than 0.5 share are often rejected.

Source: Larrick and Blount (1997).

Research Methods 7.2

Finding out what you actually want to know, the strategy method

In the ultimatum game what we are particularly interested in is whether receivers reject offers. This, however, presents a problem: if all of the proposers propose a 50:50 split, then we can never know whether or not the receivers would have rejected a low offer. One way around this is the **strategy method**, where responders are asked what they would do in any possible contingency. So, receivers have to say what they would do if they were offered $0, $1, $2, and so on. Only after this do they learn how much they have actually been offered. This way we can learn if a low offer would be rejected by the receiver.

Despite this big advantage, the strategy method is rarely used. I took the results for Figure 7.3 from one study that did use this method. More typical is the **game method**, in which receivers get to see the actual offer made by proposers before deciding what to do.

In principle, the strategy method and game method frame the problem in two different ways, so we might expect different behavior. It could also be argued that the more typical framing in real life is the game method. We get to see, for example, the waiter's service before we decide the tip. The evidence, however, suggests that there is relatively little difference in conclusion depending on what method is used.

It is also not uncommon to see framing in real life similar to the strategy method. For example, a wage contract might specify what will happen for a variety of different possible effort levels. I am, therefore, at a loss to explain why the strategy method is so rarely used!

The main lesson to be learnt from the ultimatum game is the rejection of positive offers. For completeness, however, we should have a look at what proposers offer. This, though, will not take long because the evidence is relatively easy to summarize: most proposers offer a 50:50 split. Figure 7.5 illustrates some representative experiments. In Chapter nine we shall have more to say about ultimatum game giving across different cultures.

Another variant on the dictator game is the **dictator game with third-party punishment**. In this game, two people play the dictator game while being observed by a third person. This third person has no monetary interest in the game, but having observed the game has the option to reduce the payoff of the proposer. Specifically, for every $1 the third person gives up, she can lower the payoff of the proposer by $3. If she only cares about her own payoff there is no reason for the third person to punish. But many do.

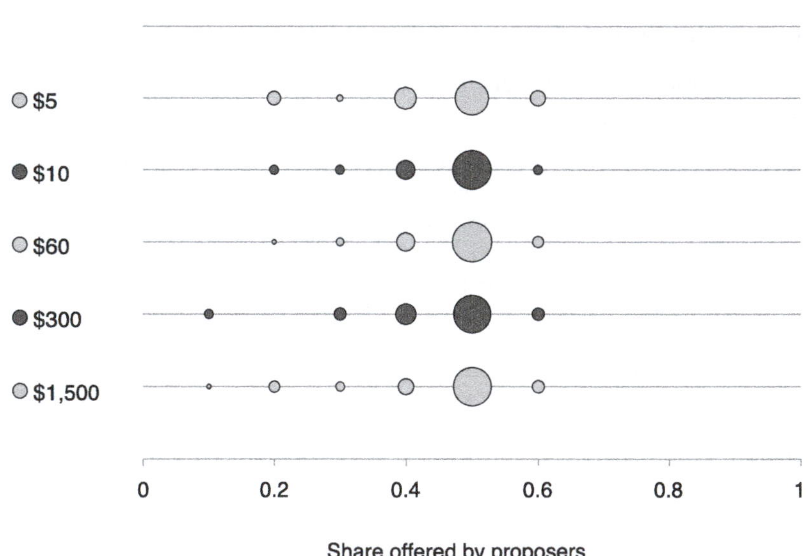

Figure 7.5 The share that proposers gave in ultimatum experiments where the amount of money given to the proposer ranged from $5 to the equivalent of $1,500.

Sources: Forsythe *et al.* (1994), Slonim and Roth (1998).

Research Methods 7.3

Does stake size matter?

A guiding rule of economic experiments is that subjects should be paid according to their decisions. Otherwise we cannot be sure that subjects take decisions seriously. But, how much do subjects need to be paid to take things seriously? The evidence seems to be that subjects do need to be paid something, but paying them more does not necessarily make much difference.

To illustrate, Figure 7.5 shows the results from experiments by Slonim and Roth (1998) in Slovakia, in which the money at stake was varied between $60 and $1,500. These can be compared with standard experiments by Forsythe and co-authors (1994) using a stake of $5 and $10. It is clear that stake size had no effect in these experiments for the amount that proposers gave. There was evidence that it had an effect on receivers, with them being less likely to reject, the higher the stake. The effect, however, was arguably still not large, with the rejection rate falling from 17.1 percent, to 12.1 percent, to 8.8 percent as the stake size went from $60, to $300, to $1,500.

Figure 7.6 illustrates what happened in a study by Fehr and Fischbacher (2004). Focus first on the dark shaded columns. These show the amount that proposers were punished as a function of the share offered. We see that low offers are punished by the third-party observer. In fact, roughly 60 percent of observers were willing to punish low offers and, the lower the offer, the more they punished. Many people, therefore, were willing to sacrifice their own payoff to lower that of someone they observe giving too little to someone else. This is a step up from the ultimatum game where people punished people giving little to them. For comparison, the lighter shaded columns in Figure 7.6 show the effective punishment in the ultimatum game as seen in Figure 7.4. Third-party observers punish less than responders, but still a relatively large amount.

7.1.3 Reciprocity

Having seen something of the nice and nasty sides of social preferences, I am now going to consider two games in which both sides seem to combine: people voluntarily giving money to some and taking from others.

In a **linear public good game** there is a group of n people, typically four in experiments, who are each given some money, say, $20, and asked how much of this $20 they wish to contribute to a group project. Any money contributed to the group project is multiplied by some multiplier M and shared equally amongst the people in the group. The key to the game is that $1 < M < n$ and so it is good for the group that a person contributes, but not in the material interests of the person to contribute.

For example, if $M = 1.6$ and someone like Anna contributes $1, then each person in the group gets $1.6/4 = $0.4 and the overall return is $1.6. This is clearly

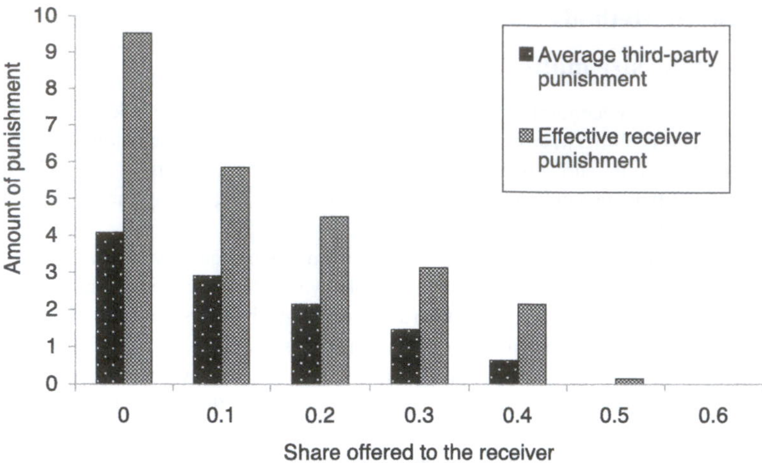

Figure 7.6 Punishment in a dictator game with third-party punishment compared to in the ultimatum game. Third-party observers punish low giving, but not as much as responders do.

Source: Fehr and Fischbacher (2004), Larrick and Blount (1997).

better than the $1 contributed. So, the best for the group, or **Pareto-efficient** outcome, is that every person contributes everything they have. For each $1 that Anna contributes, however, she only gets back $0.4 and so it is not in her material interests to contribute. A person only interested in her own material payoff would, therefore, not contribute to the public project, and the **Nash equilibrium** is for no one to contribute anything. Table 7.2 illustrates this trade-off.

As a slight aside: in general, we say that there is a **social dilemma** whenever there is a difference between the Pareto-efficient outcome, which captures what is best for the group, and the Nash equilibrium, which captures individual incentives. A linear public good game, trust game, and gift exchange game are social dilemmas.

Figure 7.7 shows what happened in a study by Fehr and Gächter (2000a). For now, focus on the left-hand side of the figure, i.e. the first ten rounds. In a partner treatment, the same four people played the game ten times. In a stranger treatment, each person is matched with three randomly chosen people each round. In both experiments we see that subjects contribute in the first round but contributions fall over time. Given what we saw in the dictator game it comes as no surprise that in the first period some subjects contribute zero and some contribute a positive amount. What is new here is the dynamic effect of falling contributions over time. This suggests that giving to others is not done unconditionally. In particular, a subject who contributes, but sees that others did not, has a tendency to lower his

Table 7.2 Some possible payoffs in a four-person linear public good game with endowment \$20 and multiplier $M = 1.6$. The group payoff is maximized if all people contribute \$20. Person 1's payoff is highest if she free-rides by contributing \$0 while all others contribute \$20

Scenario	*Contributions*	*Payoff of person*				*Total payoffs*
		1	*2*	*3*	*4*	
A	\$20, \$20, \$20, \$20	\$32	\$32	\$32	\$32	\$128
B	\$0, \$0, \$0, \$0	\$10	\$10	\$10	\$10	\$40
C	\$0, \$20, \$20, \$20	\$44	\$24	\$24	\$24	\$116
D	\$10, \$10, \$10, \$10	\$26	\$26	\$26	\$26	\$104
E	\$0, \$10, \$10, \$20	\$36	\$26	\$26	\$16	\$104

or her subsequent contributions. Maybe they do not want to give to the **free-riders** who contribute zero.

Next consider a variant of the game called the **linear public good game with punishment**. The linear public good game is played, as explained above, but then a second stage occurs. In this second stage each person can pay an amount t to punish another person by lowering that person's monetary payoff by \$1. For

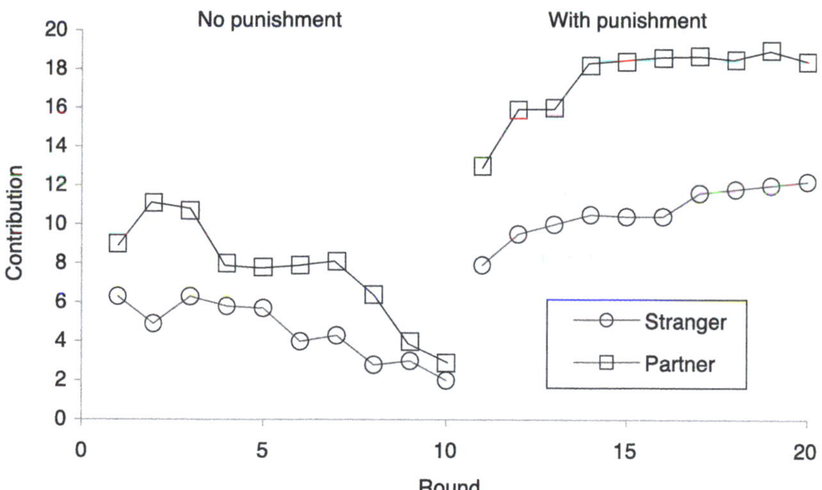

Figure 7.7 Contributions in linear public good games with and without punishment and with stranger and partner matching. Contributions fall over time without punishment and rise with punishment.

Source: Fehr and Gächter (2000a).

example, if t = \$0.33, then by paying \$1 Anna could lower the payoff of three other people by \$1 each or lower the payoff of one person by \$3. Given that punishment is costly and cannot possibly change the contributions that have already been made, no person, who maximizes their own material payoff, should ever punish. Punishment does not, therefore, change the Nash equilibrium or the fact that there is a social dilemma.

Punishment does, however, change what people typically do, as we can see on the right-hand side of Figure 7.7. With punishment, there are high and increasing investments over time. Punishment makes a difference because subjects punish those who do not contribute. Figure 7.8 illustrates by plotting the amount of punishment received by a subject depending on how much less or more they contributed relative to the average contribution of others in the group. We clearly see that those who contribute less are punished more. This is incentive enough for those who might want to free-ride to contribute.

In the linear public good game with punishment we see people willing to give money to others by contributing, but also taking money from some by punishing. Giving and taking is thus conditional on others' behavior. A game that makes this more explicit is the moonlighting game.

The **moonlighting game** combines various elements of the games considered so far. There are two people: a proposer and responder. Both are given, say, \$12. As in a trust game, the proposer can give up to \$6 to the responder and any money given will be tripled in value. The proposer can, however, also take up to \$6 from

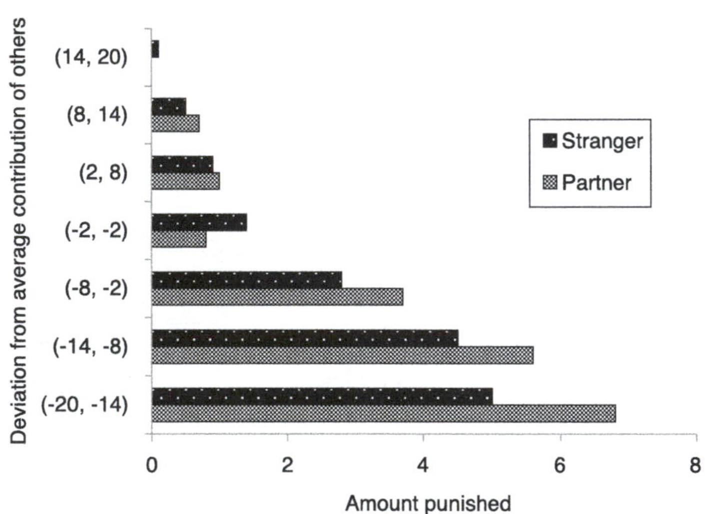

Figure 7.8 The amount of punishment depends on how much the subject contributed relative to the average contribution in the group. Those contributing less than the average are punished more.

Source: Fehr and Gächter (2000a).

the responder. Having seen what the proposer has done, the responder can reward the proposer by giving her some of her money. Or, she can punish the proposer by paying to reduce the money of the proposer. This game is the most flexible that we have considered so far in that it allows giving, taking, punishing, and rewarding.

The main lesson that we can learn from this experiment is summarized in Figure 7.9 with results from a study by Falk and co-authors (2008). Of most interest to us, at this stage, is the intention treatment. Here, as in the trust game, we see that, if a proposer gives money, then the responder reciprocates by also giving. As in the ultimatum and public good games, we see that, if a proposer offers a low share (takes money), then the responder reciprocates by punishment. In a no-intentions experiment the choice of the proposer is made randomly by a computer, and we see much less evidence of reciprocation. We will come back to this in section 7.3.

7.1.4 Fairness and competition

I want to finish with some experiments showing that, in the face of competition, giving can change. To do so, I will revisit the ultimatum game. In an **ultimatum**

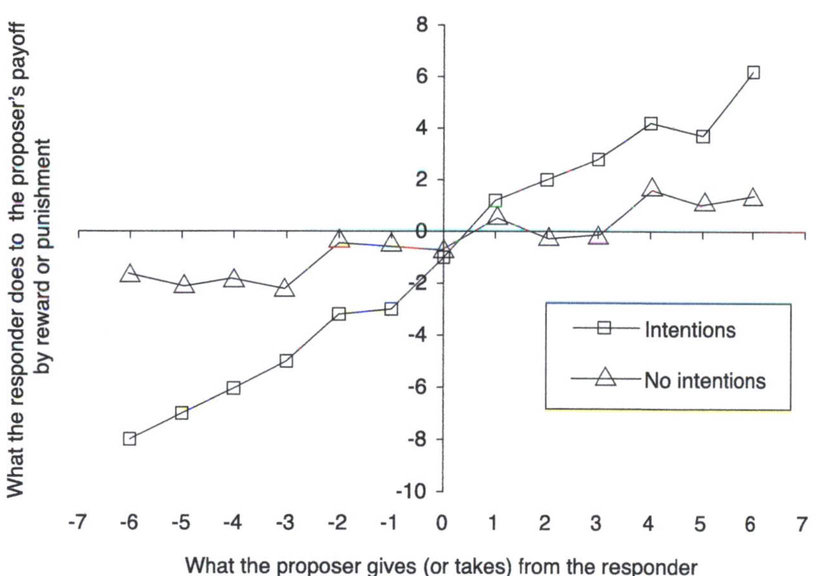

Figure 7.9 Responders' impact on proposers in the moonlighting game. If the proposer gives to the responder, the responder rewards the proposer. If the proposer takes from the responder, the responder punishes the proposer. If the computer randomly decides, the responder neither rewards nor punishes the proposer.

Source: Falk *et al.* (2008).

game with responder competition there is one proposer and many receivers. Once a proposer has made an offer, each receiver says whether she would accept the offer. One of those who said she would accept the offer is randomly chosen to actually get the offer. In an **ultimatum game with proposer competition** there are many proposers and one receiver. All proposers make an offer and the receiver can accept or reject the best offer made.

Competition would suggest that offers should be higher with proposer competition and lower with responder competition. Figure 7.10 shows that this was the case in experiments run by Roth and co-authors (1991) and Grosskopf (2003). This figure can be compared with Figure 7.5 to see that competition makes a real difference. Interestingly, however, competition does not eradicate giving. For example, with responder competition, offers are less than in the ultimatum game but still well above zero. It would seem, therefore, that proposers still wanted to give something, but gave less than in the ultimatum game.

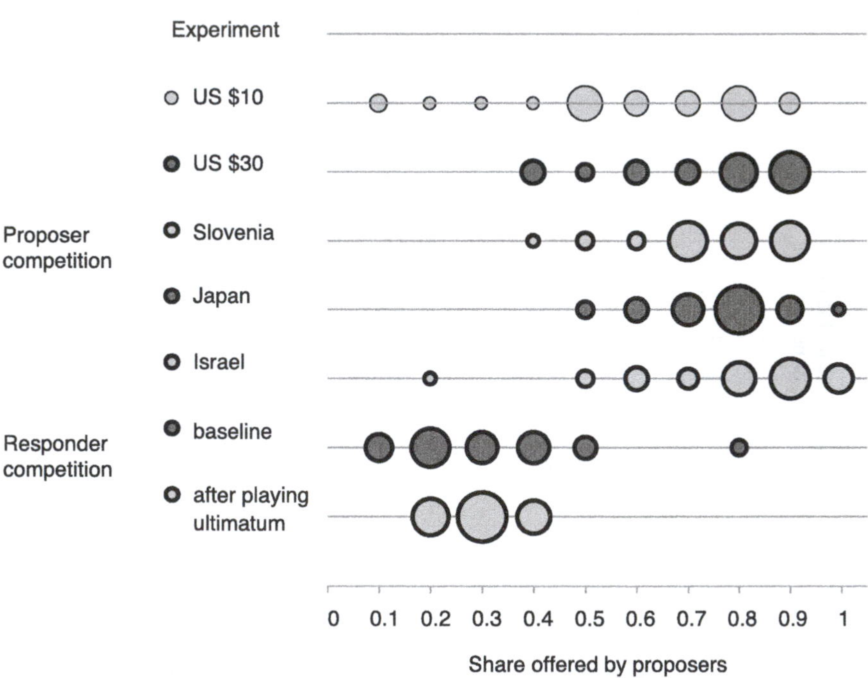

Figure 7.10 The share that proposers offer in ultimatum games with competition. Roth and co-authors find that the effect of proposer competition is the same across four countries, and Grosskopf finds that responder competition lowers offers even if subjects had played the standard ultimatum game beforehand.

Sources: Roth *et al.* (1991), Grosskopf (2003).

7.1.5 The terminology of reciprocity

I have talked through a lot of different games and results, so it seems apt to summarize what we have seen. In doing so, I will introduce some useful terminology. We saw that:

- Many people are willing to sacrifice their own monetary payoff to increase that of others (dictator game, trust game, public good game).
- Many people reciprocate the kind action of another to them by kindness of their own (trust game, gift exchange game, moonlighting game). This is **positive reciprocity**.
- Many people reciprocate the unkind action of another to them with punishment (linear public good game, moonlighting game). This is **negative reciprocity**.
- Many people show both positive and negative reciprocity (moonlighting game, linear public good game). This is **strong reciprocity**.
- Many people reciprocate the kind or unkind action of another to someone other than them (dictator game with third-party punishment). This is **indirect reciprocity**.
- There is considerable **heterogeneity** in desires for giving and reciprocity (all experiments), with many giving zero if they have the chance.

The clear picture we get is one of reciprocity, not of altruism or unconditional giving. An important question is whether such behavior is consistent with utility maximization. We know that it is inconsistent with utility maximization if a person cares only about her own payoff. But this does not mean it is inconsistent with utility maximization. Andreoni and Miller (2002) had subjects play a series of modified dictator games and asked whether choices were consistent with utility maximization (see Review question 7.3 for more details). They were, for all bar three of the 176 subjects.

This is important because it shows that interdependent preferences, reciprocity, and the like need not be inconsistent with the standard economic story of utility maximization. Our task now, therefore, is to find a utility function that can capture the type of behavior described above. In doing this, it is useful to distinguish material payoff from utility. You should think of **material payoff** as the utility from money or goods that go directly to the person; so far in the book that is what we have focused on. What we want to allow now is that utility depends on some social component as well as material payoff, giving us social preferences.

7.1.6 Social preferences and teams

Before we look at modeling social preferences it is interesting to make a brief diversion to look at giving by teams. Recall (see section 6.4) that teams are typically more like homo economicus than individuals. Our focus, however, in Chapter six was on strategic interaction. What I want to look at now is whether teams are less likely to give, punish, trust, or reciprocate than individuals.

Consider first a study by Luhan and co-authors (2009) on the dictator game. Subjects played the game as individuals, then in teams of three, and again as individuals (see Research Methods 7.4). This can be compared to a control treatment where subjects played as individuals three times. Figure 7.11 summarizes the results. We see that the share offered by teams was less than that offered by individuals. Moreover, the experience of being in a team lowered the offer that many subjects made when they subsequently played as an individual. Even so, the differences are not huge.

Research Methods 7.4

Letting subjects chat

One possibility is to let team members interact face to face when reaching a decision (see Research Methods 2.6). This, however, slightly diminishes anonymity, and when it comes to measuring social preferences this may not be a good thing. Another possibility is to let team members chat via computers. This retains anonymity and was the method used by Luhan and co-authors The chat can subsequently be analyzed to give some insight on how teams reached a decision. For example, fairness was mentioned by 17 of the 30 teams. Perhaps surprisingly, 11 teams used fairness to justify a less generous transfer! Here is an excerpt from one piece of chat:

Team member 1: Obvious decision, don't you think?
Team member 3: Sure, all for ourselves.
Team member 1: I am no good Samaritan.
Team member 3: Transfer 0.
Team member 3: Right, neither am I.
Team member 1: We are not responsible for [the receiver] are we?
Team member 1: Therefore 0.
Team member 1: OK. I'll enter it.
Team member 3: No. 2, do you share our opinion?
Team member 2: I think we should be fair.
Team member 3: I don't. Nobody has ever been fair to me.
Team member 1: 0 is fair.
Team member 2: Wait a second and don't enter anything.

After a long chat they shared 20 percent with the receiver.

Consider next studies by Bornstein and Yaniv (1998) on the ultimatum game and Kugler and co-authors (2007) on the trust game. In both studies direct comparison was made between individuals and teams of three. Figure 7.12 summarizes the results. We see that teams offered less in the ultimatum game, and invested and returned less in the trust game than individuals. Again, however, the differences are not huge.

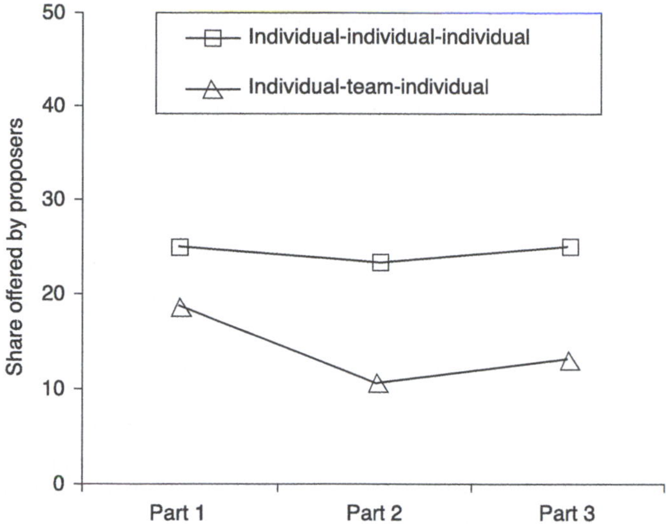

Figure 7.11 The share offered by proposers in the dictator game. In parts 1 and 3, all subjects acted as individuals. In part 2, some subjects acted as individuals and some as a team of three.

Source: Luhan *et al.* (2009).

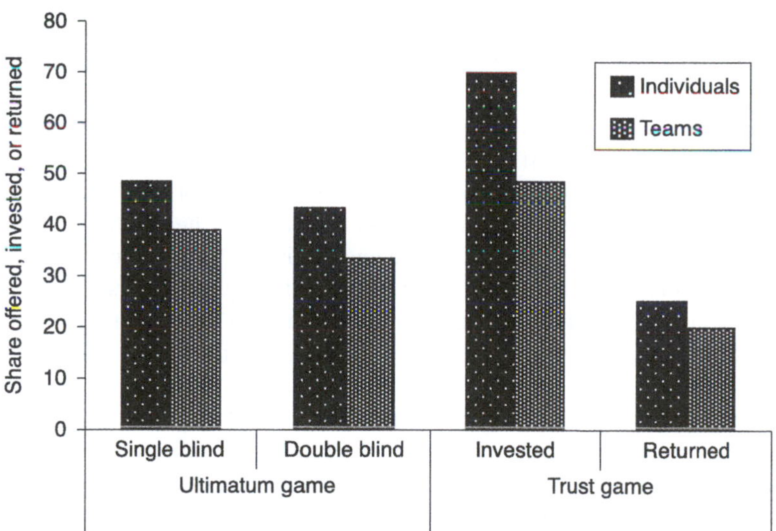

Figure 7.12 The share proposed in the ultimatum game, invested in the trust game, and returned in the trust game comparing individuals and teams of three.

Sources: Bornstein and Yaniv (1998) and Kugler *et al.* (2007).

These findings confirm and extend to social preferences the general picture that I painted in Chapter six. Teams are more consistent with the standard economic model than are individuals. The behavior of teams is also, however, a lot closer to that of individuals than it is to that of homo economicus. Teams still give, take, and reciprocate. This reiterates the need for an appropriate way to capture social preferences.

7.2 Inequality aversion

Reference dependence was a recurring theme in Chapters two, three, and four. We saw that the perceptions of an outcome are often determined by whether it was above or below some reference level. We also saw that the reference level can be determined by a multitude of factors such as past experience, an expectation of what would happen, and so on. A very natural reference point, which we only briefly touched upon in section 2.6, is what others are getting. For instance, if Alan observes his co-workers getting paid $30 an hour, then he might expect to get paid $30 an hour. Similarly, if Anna knows her friend bought a box of Nutty cereal for $4, then she might also expect to pay $4.

If the reference point is what we observe happening to others, then doing better than others is a gain while doing worse than others is a loss. Making the argument that people are averse to getting less than others seems easy enough. Making the argument that people positively gain from getting more than others, particularly given the evidence we have seen in section 7.1, is slightly harder to make. We are going to look, therefore, at something called inequality aversion. If a person is **inequality averse**, then she gets disutility from earning less than others and, possibly, gets disutility from earning more than others. This means she may be willing to sacrifice some of her material payoff to obtain a more equitable outcome with others.

What are the consequences of inequality aversion? We shall see that inequality aversion can do a good job of explaining the experimental data summarized in section 7.1. For example, if Alan is averse to earning more than others, then he would be willing to propose a positive amount in a dictator or ultimatum game. Similarly, if Anna is averse to earning less than others, she would be willing to reject a low offer in the ultimatum game and punish a free-rider in a public good game. To formalize this, we need a good model of inequality aversion.

I am going to look at two models. The principal way in which they differ is in what information they assume a person has. The first model I will look at is applicable to situations with **incomplete information**, where a person does not know the actions of others. The second model can only be applied in situations with **complete information**, where a person knows the actions of all others. To explain this distinction we can look back at Table 7.2 and contrast scenarios D and E. In a game of incomplete information, person 2 only gets to know that her payoff is $26. She can infer that total contributions to the public good must have been 40 and so the average payoff is $26, but she cannot know whether person 1 was a free-rider or not. In a game of complete information she gets to know individual contributions and so can tell whether person 1 contributed $10 or $0.

Some settings may naturally be ones of incomplete information and some of complete information. Intuitively this is going to make a difference because person 2 might think differently about scenarios D and E. That means we need a model for both possibilities. It is worth pointing out, however, that a model applicable to situations of incomplete information can also be applied to situations of complete information. The converse need not be true.

7.2.1 Inequality aversion with incomplete information

The **Equity, Reciprocity, and Competition** (ERC) model was proposed by Bolton and Ockenfels (2000) and can capture inequality aversion in settings with incomplete (or complete) information. I shall explain here a simple, special case of the more general model that they propose.

Imagine a group of n people who have played a game and earned material payoffs of $u_1, u_2, \ldots, u_n$. I will focus on one of the people, called Miguel. In calculating the utility of Miguel, the first thing we do is work out his **relative share** of the total payoff using equation:

$$s_M = \frac{u_M}{\Sigma_j u_j}.$$

The utility of Miguel is then assumed to be:

$$U_M(u_1, \ldots, u_n) = u_M - \theta_M \left(s_M - \frac{1}{n} \right)^2,$$

where θ_M measures the strength of his inequality aversion.

If Miguel does not care about inequality aversion, then $\theta_M = 0$ and his utility is simply his material payoff u_M. If he does care about inequality aversion, then he cares about how close his payoff is to the **social reference point** of an equal share.

He dislikes earning more or less than the average material payoff of others. The squared term means that the further he is away from the social reference point, the more he dislikes earning more or less than the average. So, he does not mind being a little away from the average but dislikes a lot being a long way from the average.

To better illustrate the model, we can work through the experimental games of section 7.1 and show that the model does a good job of fitting what we observe. To simplify matters a little I will equate material payoff with money received, but you need to think about whether this is a reasonable thing to do or not.

We can start with the **dictator game**. If the proposer, Miguel, splits the \$10 so that he keeps \$$p$, then his material payoff is p and his utility is:

$$U_M = p - \theta_M \left(\frac{p}{10} - \frac{1}{2} \right)^2.$$

The social reference point in this case is \$5 and inequality aversion means he gets disutility from keeping more or less than \$5. To be a bit more specific, we can maximize utility with respect to p and get equation:

$$1 = \frac{2\theta_M}{10}\left(\frac{p}{10} - \frac{1}{2}\right)$$

which can be rearranged to:

$$p = min\left\{5 + \frac{50}{\theta_M},\ 10\right\}.$$

He will, therefore, keep at least \$5 and, if $\theta_M \leq 10$, will keep \$10. If $\theta_M > 10$, then he will give some money to the receiver so as to not be earning relatively too much. For example, if $\theta_M = 25$, then he will keep \$7 and give \$3 to the receiver, consistent with what we see in Figure 7.1.

Extending this to the **ultimatum game** is relatively simple because the proposers have the same utility function as in the dictator game. We only, therefore, need to think about what responders will do and all they can do is accept or reject. Suppose that Anna is the responder. If she accepts, her utility will be:

$$U_A = 10 - p - \theta_A\left(\frac{10-p}{10} - \frac{1}{2}\right)^2$$

and if she rejects, it will be $U_A = 0$. So, she will accept if:

$$10 - p \geq \theta_A\left(\frac{10-p}{10} - \frac{1}{2}\right)^2$$

which we can rearrange to:

$$\frac{100(10-p)}{(5-p)^2} \geq \theta_A.$$

If $\theta_A = 0$, she will accept any positive offer, but the higher is θ_A, the higher needs to be the offer before she will accept. For example, if p = \$9.50 and so she is offered \$0.50, then she will reject if $\theta_A > 2.5$. This is because the material gain of \$0.50 is not enough to compensate for the disutility of earning less than Miguel. If she is offered the social reference point of \$5, then she will accept for sure.

I will finish looking at the ERC model with the **linear public good game**. Consider first the case without punishment. Going through the equations is a bit tedious. We can, however, argue quite easily that the unique equilibrium will be one where no person contributes. To see why, suppose that all people are contributing the same amount, say, c^*. What would happen if someone like Miguel contributes a tiny amount less than c^*? He gains in monetary payoff, because he has lowered his contribution, but he is now earning more than the average payoff, because he is contributing less than others. Recall, however, that there is hardly any utility loss from earning a little bit more than the average. So, provided he only contributes a little bit less than others his utility will increase by contributing less.

You can see this in Table 7.3 by comparing scenarios A and F. If Miguel lowers his contribution to \$19, he gains \$0.60 in material payoff and loses $0.75^2\theta_M = 0.56\theta_M$ because of inequality aversion. This is a good deal if $\theta_M \leq 1$. I will leave it to you to work out how high θ_M can be for him to gain from lowering his contribution by \$0.50 or \$0.01. You should find that he will gain from lowering his contribution a bit. If everyone thinks like this, then contributions will drift downwards, either for real or in the minds of people, until no one is contributing.

What if we add punishment? Punishment requires complete information about the distribution of payoffs, and so we can no longer assume incomplete information. But the model can still clearly be applied. Doing so, we find that it can be in everyone's interests to contribute \$20 provided two (or more) people are willing to punish. In explaining why, I will keep things simple by assuming it costs $t = 0.1$ to punish, and we only want to deter people from contributing \$19 rather than \$20. Suppose that Anna threatens to lower the payoff of anyone who contributes \$19 by an amount of \$2. This would cost her \$0.20. Also, suppose that Alan threatens to lower the payoff of Anna by \$2 if she contributes \$19. Will this work?

It will, as illustrated in Table 7.3. We first need to check that the threat of punishment would deter Miguel from lowering his contribution to \$19. Comparing scenarios A and G we see that, if Miguel contributes \$19 and is punished, then he

Table 7.3 The ERC model and linear public good game. If he will not be punished, Miguel gains by contributing \$19 (scenario F) rather than \$20 (scenario A). If he will be punished (scenario G), he does best to contribute \$20. Anna does better to punish Miguel for contributing \$19 (scenario G) if she sufficiently dislikes earning less than the social reference point

Scenario		*Person*				*Reference point*
		Anna	*Alan*	*3*	*Miguel*	
A	Contributions	20	20	20	20	
	Material payoff	32	32	32	32	
	Relative to reference point	0	0	0	0	32.00
F	Contributions	20	20	20	19	
	Material payoff	31.6	31.6	31.6	32.6	
	Relative to reference point	−0.25	−0.25	−0.25	+0.75	31.85
G	Contributions	20	20	20	19	
	Material payoff	31.4	31.6	31.6	30.6	
	Relative to reference point	+0.1	+0.3	+0.3	−0.9	31.3

loses both in material payoff and relative terms. This is enough to deter him from contributing \$19. We next need to check that Anna would be willing to punish. This is slightly trickier, but comparing scenarios F and G we see that, by punishing, she loses in material terms and gains in relative terms. Provided the utility gain from being closer to the social reference point exceeds the \$0.20 cost of punishing, then she will want to punish.

If, therefore, there are some people like Anna and Alan who are relatively inequality averse, high contributions can be sustained by the threat of punishment. More generally, we have seen that the ERC model can do a good job of explaining a lot of the evidence we saw in section 7.1, even in situations of complete information. Before long, however, we shall see that, when people do have complete information, their utility will likely depend on individual actions in a way that the ERC model cannot capture so well. What I want to do now, therefore, is introduce a model better suited to situations of complete information.

7.2.2 Inequality aversion with complete information

Fehr and Schmidt (1999) developed a model of inequality aversion that works when there is complete information. For want of a better name it is usually called the **Fehr-Schmidt model**. As before, imagine a group of n people who have played a game and earned material payoffs of $u_1, u_2, \ldots u_n$. To work out the utility of Miguel we first distinguish between people who earned a higher and lower material payoff than him. So, let $H_M = \{j: u_j > u_M\}$ be the set of people who earned more than him and $L_M = \{j: u_j < u_M\}$ be the set of people who earned less. The utility of Miguel is then calculated using:

$$U_M(u_1, \ldots, u_n) = u_M - \alpha_M \frac{1}{n-1} \sum_{j \in H_M} (u_j - u_M) - \beta_M \frac{1}{n-1} \sum_{j \in L_M} (u_M - u_j),$$

where $\beta_M \leq \alpha_M$ are measures of Miguel's inequality aversion.

To explain how this works, let's concentrate first on the α_M bit. This captures Miguel's disutility from earning less than others. For every person who has a higher material payoff than he, he suffers a utility loss proportional to the difference in payoff. The higher is α_M, the more he dislikes earning less than others. The β_M bit captures his disutility from earning more than others. Again, for every person who has a lower material payoff than he, he suffers a utility loss proportional to the difference in payoff. The assumption that $\beta_M \leq \alpha_M$ means that he gets more disutility from earning less than others than he does from earning more than others, which, hopefully, seems intuitive.

To better illustrate the model we can work through the same examples as for the ERC model, starting with the **dictator game**. If Miguel splits the \$10 so that he keeps \$$p$ and the receiver gets \$10 − p then his utility will be $p - \alpha_M(10 - 2p)$ if $p <$ \$5, and $p - \beta_M(2p - 10)$ if $p \geq$ \$5. Given that $\beta_M \leq \alpha_M$, there is never any incentive for him to give more than \$5, so he should maximize $p - \beta_M(2p - 10)$ with respect to p. Consequently, he should give \$0 if $\beta_M < 0.5$ and give \$5 if $\beta_M \geq 0.5$.

This is not exactly what we observe in Figure 7.1, but we do at least see a possible incentive for the proposer to share something.

In the **ultimatum game**, proposers again have the same utility function as in the dictator game, so we just need to think about what receivers will do. Assuming that proposers will at best offer an equal share (i.e. $p \geq \$5$), the utility function of the receiver, Anna, will depend on whether she accepts or rejects. If she accepts, she gets $10 - p - \alpha_A(2p - 10)$ and if she rejects, she gets zero. Thus, Anna will accept if:

$$p < 10\left(\frac{1+\alpha_A}{1+2\alpha_A}\right).$$

This means that, if Anna does not mind earning less than Miguel, $\alpha_A = 0$, she will accept any offer, but if she is more inequality averse, α_A increases, she will only accept offers closer to an equal share. For example, if $\alpha_A = 1$, she will reject anything less than a one-third share.

This possibility of rejection may make the proposer think a little. We know from looking at the dictator game that, if $\beta_M \geq 0.5$, Miguel will offer an equal share and this will be accepted. It is slightly trickier to say what he should do if $\beta_M < 0.5$. He would want to offer the minimum amount that will be accepted. The problem is, he is unlikely to know the inequality aversion of Anna and so will not know what this minimum is. Instead, he will have to form some expectation about what the responder will do and offer an appropriate share. He, therefore, faces a risky choice. In the next section we shall look in more detail at how expectations and beliefs can be captured in a model of social preferences.

To further illustrate the Fehr-Schmidt model, suppose we now add competition into the mix. In the **ultimatum game with proposer competition** it is natural to assume that the receiver will accept the best proposal. This means that there will be inequality for sure, because the receiver and one proposer will get a positive material payoff while all other proposers get zero. Given this, the objective of a proposer should be to offer an amount that will be accepted. This way he will at least be earning more than others, which is better than earning less than others. If all proposers are aiming to get their offer accepted, then they should offer almost all of the money. This is consistent with what we saw in Figure 7.10. I leave you to think about what happens with responder competition.

Finally, we can look at the **linear public good game**. Depending on how inequality averse people are, it may or may not be an equilibrium to contribute to the public good. Table 7.4 will help illustrate why. Suppose that everyone is contributing \$20. Would Anna want to contribute less? Comparing scenarios A and H, we see that, for every \$1 she decreases her contribution, she gains \$0.60 in material payoff, but increases the gap between her payoff and others by \$1. If she dislikes earning more than others, or more specifically $\beta_A > 0.6$, then she does best to contribute \$20. If she does not mind earning more than others, $\beta_A < 0.6$, then she would contribute \$0. We could, therefore, see high or low contributions depending on preferences.

Table 7.4 The linear public good game and Fehr-Schmidt model from the perspective of Anna. Anna may not want to contribute less than others (scenarios A and H) but may want to lower her contribution if someone else contributes zero (scenarios I and J). She may also be willing to punish anyone who contributes zero (scenarios I and K)

Scenario		*Person*			
		Anna	*2*	*3*	*Miguel*
A	Contributions	20	20	20	20
	Material payoff	32	32	32	32
	Relative to others	—	0	0	0
H	Contributions	19	20	20	20
	Material payoff	32.6	31.6	31.6	31.6
	Relative to others	—	+1	+1	+1
I	Contributions	20	20	20	0
	Material payoff	24	24	24	44
	Relative to others	—	0	0	−20
J	Contributions	19	20	20	0
	Material payoff	24.6	23.6	23.6	43.6
	Relative to others	—	+1	+1	−19
K	Contributions	20	20	20	0
	Material payoff	21.5	24	24	19
	Relative to others	—	−2.5	−2.5	+2.5

Most realistic, given the heterogeneity that we observed in section 7.1, is that some people have a high β and some a low β. This raises the interesting question of how many people it needs to contribute \$0 for all those with a high β to also contribute \$0. In Table 7.4 we can compare scenarios I and J to see what happens if Anna contributes \$20 or \$19 and Miguel contributes \$0. In this case, when Anna lowers her contribution to \$1, she gains \$0.60 in material payoff, gains by lowering the gap between her and Miguel, but loses by increasing the gap with the other two. Overall she gains if $\$0.60 + 0.33\alpha_A > 0.67\beta_A$. This means that β_A needs to be at least 1.8 to stop Anna also contributing \$0. It only takes, therefore, one person to contribute \$0 for it to be likely the other three will too. This is consistent with the falling contributions we observe in Figure 7.7.

[Extra] For those who like a bit of algebra, models of social preferences are fun to play around with. In a linear public good game the task is made a bit easier by the fact that, if Anna contributes c_A and Miguel contributes c_M, then, irrespective of what else happens, the difference in their material payoffs is $u_A - u_M = c_M - c_A$, the difference in contributions. So, if there are n people each endowed with \$20 and contributions are $c_1, c_2, \ldots, c_n$ the utility of Anna will be:

$$U_A = 20 - c_A + m\sum_j c_j - \alpha_A \frac{1}{n-1}\sum_{j\in H_A}(c_A - c_j) - \beta_A \frac{1}{n-1}\sum_{j\in L_A}(c_j - c_A).$$

Now suppose that K people are contributing \$0, and the rest are contributing \$20, what will Anna want to contribute? If she contributes \$20, her utility is:

$$U_A = 20m(n-K) - \alpha_A \frac{20K}{n-1}.$$

If she contributes \$0, her utility is:

$$U_A = 20 + 20m(n-1-K) - \beta_A \frac{20(n-1-k)}{n-1}.$$

So, she does better to contribute \$0 if:

$$(1-m)(n-1) > \beta_A(n-1-K) - \alpha_A K$$

or the proportion of those contributing \$0 is:

$$\frac{K}{n-1} > \frac{\beta_A + m - 1}{\alpha_A + \beta_A}.$$

This gives us a measure of how many people will need to not contribute for others to also not contribute.

As you might imagine, adding punishment only complicates the analysis. We shall, therefore, restrict ourselves to showing that it can be an equilibrium for all people to contribute when punishment is allowed. In fact, we shall show that it is enough to have just one person willing to punish. Suppose that $\beta_A > 0.6$ and so we know Anna would contribute \$20 if everyone else does. Suppose also that Anna threatens to lower the payoff of anyone who contributes \$0 by \$25 and that this will cost her \$2.50, because $t = 0.1$. Will this work? This size of punishment will clearly deter any person from contributing \$0, but will Anna be willing to pay to punish this much? In Table 7.4, by comparing scenarios I and K, we see what happens if she punishes Miguel for contributing \$0. She loses the \$2.50 in material payoff but is now only \$2.50 behind or ahead of the others rather than \$20 behind Miguel. She must be better off if $5\alpha_A - 5/6\beta_A >$ \$2.50 and, because $\alpha_A \geq \beta_A > 0.6$, we know that this must be the case. She is, therefore, willing to punish Miguel so as to narrow the gap in their material payoffs.

7.2.3 An evaluation of inequality aversion models

Both the ERC and Fehr-Schmidt model do a good job of fitting the experimental data summarized in section 7.1. In particular, they are able to account for cooperation in some contexts, such as a public good game with punishment, and a lack of cooperation in other contexts, such as a public good game without punishment. The models also have the virtue of being relatively simple and easy to apply. The news is not all good, however, because we shall see that, when pushed a bit further, both the ERC and Fehr-Schmidt models start to struggle. The models do, therefore, have their limitations and so we shall need to think of alternatives to inequality aversion. Before we do that I want to briefly show that in some situations there are different models of inequality aversion that can outperform the ERC and Fehr-Schmidt models.

Engelmann and Strobel (2004) asked subjects to play a variety of **distribution games**. In the different games, three of which are given in Table 7.5, person 2 was able to decide which of the distribution of payoffs A, B, or C should be used. Different models of inequality aversion give different predictions. In the taxation game, for example, the Fehr-Schmidt model predicts option A, while the ERC model predicts option C (but I will leave you to check this).

In the final row of Table 7.5 we have the choices actually made to compare with the predictions. It is clear that the ERC model does a relatively poor job at predicting the data. This would suggest that subjects did take account of the full distribution of payoffs. What seemed to matter most to subjects was maximizing the minimum payoff that any person would receive, which we can think of as a **maximin** notion of fairness. The Fehr-Schmidt model can pick up this effect to some extent, because it predicts that a person will get disutility from earning more than others. The model also predicts, however, that a person would be more willing to lower the payoff of those earning more, than increase the payoff of those earning less; this was not observed in these experiments, particularly the envy game.

In these distribution games, an inequality aversion model based on maximin would do a good job of fitting the data. Maximin would, however, do a lousy job of fitting the data for an ultimatum game or public good game, with or without punishment. This illustrates how different strategic settings likely call for different models. We shall now look at some models that are not based on inequality aversion.

Table 7.5 Payoffs, predictions, and choices in distribution games. Person 2 gets to choose which distribution of payoffs there should be: A, B, or C

	Taxation game			*Envy game*			*Rich game*		
Payoffs	*A*	*B*	*C*	*A*	*B*	*C*	*A*	*B*	*C*
Person 1	8.2	8.8	9.4	16	13	10	11	8	5
Person 2	5.6	5.6	5.6	7	8	9	12	12	12
Person 3	4.6	3.6	2.6	5	3	1	2	3	4
Predictions									
Efficiency	A			A			A		
ERC			C		B	C	A		
Fehr-Schmidt	A					C	A		
Maximin	A			A					C
Choices									
Percentage	84	10	6	77	13	10	27	20	53

Source: Engelmann and Strobel (2004).

7.3 Intentions and social norms

In models of inequality aversion, people are motivated solely to earn no more and no less than others. To illustrate why this sometimes appears to miss something, I will return to the ultimatum game and look at an **ultimatum game with restricted choice**. When I first explained the ultimatum game I said the proposer could propose to split the $10 in any way that he chose. Offers of an $8, $2 split were often rejected, seemingly because of the unequal payoffs. Suppose now that we constrain the proposer to offer either an $8, $2 split or a $10, $0 split. The offer of an $8, $2 split does not look quite so unfair now. But will it still be rejected?

A study by Falk and co-authors (2003) allows us to answer this. They considered four different games. In each game the proposer must choose between just two possible offers. As Table 7.6 summarizes, one of the offers is always an $8, $2 split. What we want to know is how the perception of an $8, $2 offer changes relative to the other offer a proposer could have made. If a responder cares only about inequality aversion, then the other offer should make no difference because she still gets $2 and the proposer $8. We clearly see, however, that it does make a difference. Responders are more likely to reject an $8, $2 split if the proposer could have proposed a $5, $5 split compared to if he could have proposed a $10, $0 split.

These results are not consistent with inequality aversion. Arguably, what is missing is that inequality aversion does not take into account the intentions of proposers. If Miguel offers $8, $2 when he could have offered $10, $0, then he is intending to be fair. If he offers $8, $2 when he could have offered $5, $5, he is intending to be unfair.

We have already seen something similar if you look back to Figure 7.9 and the moonlighting game. You may recall that in the no intentions experiment a computer randomly chose the proposer's offer and in this case responders did little to reward or punish proposers. Again, if a computer generates the offer, then there is no intention on the part of proposers, and this seems to matter. We need, therefore, some way to build intentions into a model of fairness.

Table 7.6 The proportion who offered and the proportion who would reject an $8, $2 split in ultimatum games with restricted choice

Game	*Proposer's choices*		*Interpretation of an $8, $2 offer*	*Proportion of $8, $2 offers (%)*	*Proportion who would reject an $8, $2 offer (%)*
	A	*B*			
(5/5)	$8, $2	$5, $5	unfair	31	44
(2/8)	$8, $2	$2, $8	relatively fair	73	27
(8/2)	$8, $2	$8, $2	no choice	100	18
(10/0)	$8, $2	$10, $0	fair	100	9

Source: Falk *et al.* (2003).

7.3.1 A model of fairness based on intentions

I shall now work through a model of fairness that takes account of intentions. The model is based on the work of Rabin (1993) and Dufwenberg and Kirchsteiger (2004). Unfortunately, the model is not as easy as the inequality aversion models, but if you stick with it, all will hopefully become clear.

Consider Miguel and someone called Federica playing a game. The key thing we want to do is think about what Miguel believes Federica will do, and what Federica believes Miguel will do. **Beliefs** are going to give us a means to think about intentions. Here is why.

Suppose that, if Miguel chooses action a_M and Federica chooses action a_F, they get material payoffs $u_M(a_M, a_F)$ and $u_F(a_M, a_F)$, respectively. Now, if Miguel believes that Federica will choose action b_F, then he should also believe that if he chooses action a_M they will get payoffs $u_M(a_M, b_F)$ and payoff $u_F(a_M, b_F)$. This suggests that we can think of Miguel as choosing payoffs for both of them from the set:

$$U(b_F) = \{u_M(a_M, b_F), u_F(a_M, b_F)|a_M \in S_M\}$$

where S_M is the set of actions that he could choose.

Ignore from set $U(b_F)$ any payoff pairs that are not Pareto efficient and let $U_F^h(b_F)$ and $U_F^l(b_F)$ be the highest and lowest payoffs that Federica could get from set $U(b_F)$. We then call:

$$U_F^e(b_F) = \frac{U_F^h(b_F) + U_F^l(b_F)}{2},$$

which is the payoff halfway between the highest and lowest, the **equitable payoff**. We now come to the crux of the model; we say that Miguel's **kindness** to Federica if he chooses action a_M and believes that Federica will choose action b_F is:

$$k_{MF}(a_M, b_F) = u_F(a_M, b_F) - U_F^e(b_F).$$

So, Miguel is **kind** if he chooses an action that he believes will give Federica more than the equitable payoff. He is **unkind** if he chooses an action that he believes will give Federica less than the equitable payoff.

We next assume that Miguel wants to be kind to Federica if Federica is kind to him. The slight problem is that Miguel cannot know whether Federica is being kind to him, because he does not know Federica's beliefs. So, Miguel will need to form a belief about whether Federica is being kind. To do this, let c_M denote Miguel's belief about b_M. That is, Miguel believes that Federica believes that he will choose action c_M. Miguel's beliefs about how kind Federica is being to him are now:

$$\lambda_{MF}(c_M, b_F) = u_M(c_M, b_F) - U_M^e(c_M).$$

This expression naturally extends kindness to beliefs about kindness.

The utility function of Miguel can finally be written as:

$$U_M(a_M, b_F, c_M) = u_M(a_M, a_F) + \mu_M k_{MF}(a_M, b_F) \cdot \lambda_{MF}(c_M, b_F)$$

where μ_M is Miguel's desire to reciprocate. If Miguel does not care about fairness, then $\mu_M = 0$ and his utility is his material payoff u_M. If he does care about fairness and believes that Federica is being kind, so, $\lambda_{MF}(c_M, b_F) > 0$, then he can increase his utility by also being kind, $k_{MF}(a_M, b_F) > 0$. If he believes that Federica is being unkind, then he would also want to be unkind. A desire for reciprocity is, therefore, built into the utility function.

It is important that beliefs correspond to reality and so we say that there is a **fairness equilibrium** if $a_M = b_M = c_M$ and $a_F = b_F = c_F$.

This model may be a bit tricky to get one's head around, but the basic idea is relatively simple. Miguel wants to be kind to Federica if Federica is kind to him, and vice versa. Where things get complicated is determining what is kind or not. This is why we needed to think about beliefs, and beliefs about beliefs. To better understand what is going on I will work through the **ultimatum game**.

We can think of the proposer, Miguel, as proposing an amount $\$a_M$ to give, while the receiver, Federica, simultaneously sets a minimum amount $\$a_F$ that she will accept. If $a_M \geq a_F$, then Federica accepts the offer. If Miguel believes that Federica will accept offers of b_F or more, then he can offer $\$10 = U_F^h(b_F)$ or $\$b_F = U_F^l(b_F)$ or anything in between and the outcome will be Pareto efficient. The equitable payoff is, therefore:

$$U_F^e(b_F) = \frac{10 + b_F}{2}.$$

Miguel's kindness is:

$$k_{MF}(a_M, b_F) = a_M - \frac{10 + b_F}{2}.$$

This means that Miguel has to give quite a lot to be considered kind. For example, if $b_F = \$2$, then an offer of \$6 or less is not kind!

If Federica believes Miguel will offer b_M, she can either reject by setting $a_F > b_M$ or accept with $a_F \leq b_M$. Rejection can never, however, be Pareto efficient. This means that $\$10 - b_M = U_M^l(b_M) = U_M^h(b_M)$. If Federica accepts, her kindness is zero, and if she rejects, her kindness is $k_{FM} = -(10 - b_M)$. Federica can never be kind in this game!

Given that Federica cannot be kind, Miguel can never gain by being kind to Federica. Miguel does, however, still have to offer enough that Federica will not reject. If Federica accepts an offer of a_M, her utility is a_M and if she rejects, it is:

$$\mu_F k_{FM}(b_M, a_F) \bullet \lambda_{FM}(b_M, c_F) = -\mu_F(10 - b_M)\left(b_M - \frac{10 + c_F}{2}\right).$$

In equilibrium, therefore, where $b_M = c_F = a_M$, Federica will accept if $2a_M \geq \mu_F (10 - a_M)^2$. An offer of zero will, therefore, be rejected if $\mu_F > 0$, but a high enough offer will be accepted.

These results are similar to those obtained in the inequality aversion models. Can this model also capture the importance of intentions? In the ultimatum game with qualified choice the model predicts that a responder may reject an \$8, \$2 split in the (5/5) and (2/8) game, but should never reject an \$8, \$2 split in the (8/2) or (10/0) game. This is because the offered split is unkind in the first two games and kind or neutral in the last two games. The model does, therefore, take account of intentions. It fails, however, to completely fit the data, because offers of an \$8, \$2 split were rejected some of the time in all the games.

7.3.2 What is fair?

The crux of the intentions-based model of fairness that we have just been looking at is the equitable payoff, because kindness is judged by whether or not utility is above or below this equitable payoff. The equitable payoff can be thought of as an example of a **fair reference point** about which losses or gains are measured. A theme in Chapters two, three, and four was the potential arbitrariness of reference points; things are no different here. The equitable payoff is that payoff halfway between the highest and lowest possible (Pareto-efficient) payoff, but why should the fair reference point be this and not something else?

The model is flexible to using any fair reference point, so we do not need to stick with the equitable payoff. But what reference point should we be using? We have looked at two candidates so far. In inequality aversion models, the fairness of a person's material payoff is judged relative to the payoff of others. So, the fair reference point is what others are earning, and the fairest outcome is one where everyone earns the same material payoff. In the intentions-based model we have just looked at, the fairness of a person's payoff is judged relative to the worst and best material payoff that she could have got. The fairest outcome is one where she gets at least halfway between this worst and best.

In a symmetric game, like the ultimatum game with unconstrained choice, these two notions of a fair reference point will turn out the same. But in general they are not the same. For example, in the ultimatum game with constrained choice (10/0), a split of \$8, \$2 is unfair by the standards of inequality aversion because the proposer gets more than the receiver, but is fair by the standards of the intentions-based model because the receiver could have got less than she did.

The results that we have for the ultimatum game with constrained choice suggest that both notions of fair reference point are important. Is it possible to combine both elements in the same model? Falk and Fischbacher (2006) showed that it is if we use an intentions-based model of fairness with a different definition of kindness.

In this revised model, the kindness of Miguel consists of two parts:

$$k_{MF}(a_M, b_F) = \delta_{MF}(a_M, b_F) \bullet \vartheta_{MF}(a_M, b_F).$$

The first part, $\delta_{MF}(a_M, b_F)$, captures inequality aversion and is calculated as follows:

$$\delta_{MF}(a_M, b_F) = u_F(a_M, b_F) - u_M(a_M, b_F).$$

This means that Miguel is **kind** if he chooses an action that he expects to give Federica a higher material payoff than him. He is **unkind** if he chooses an action that he expects to give Federica a lower material payoff than him. The second part, $\vartheta_{MF}(a_M, b_F)$, of the kindness expression captures intentions and is called the **intention factor**. Letting $u_M = u_M(a_M, b_F)$ and $u_F = u_F(a_M, b_F)$, it is calculated using:

$$\vartheta_{MF}(a_M, b_F) = \begin{cases} 1 \text{ if } u_F > u_M \text{ and there exists } a \text{ such that } u_F(a, b_F) < u_M \\ \varepsilon \text{ if } u_F > u_M \text{ and there is no } a \text{ such that } u_F(a, b_F) < u_M \\ 1 \text{ if } u_F < u_M \text{ and there exists } a \text{ such that } u_F(a, b_F) > u_M \\ \varepsilon \text{ if } u_F < u_M \text{ and there is no } a \text{ such that } u_F(a, b_F) > u_M \end{cases}.$$

This might look complicated, but it is not. The first two terms consider the case where Federica is earning a higher material payoff than Miguel. This appears kind, but we ask: did Miguel have any alternative but to be kind? If he did, then the intention factor is 1 and Miguel is considered **intentionally kind**. If he did not, then the intention factor is $\varepsilon < 1$ and so we consider Miguel **unintentionally kind**.

Similarly, the bottom two terms consider the case where Federica is earning less than Miguel. This looks unkind, but maybe Miguel had no choice? If he did, the intention factor is 1 and if he did not, the intention factor is $\varepsilon < 1$. For example, offering an \$8, \$2 split in the (10/0) game is considered **unintentional unkindness**, so is not as bad as offering an \$8, \$2 split in the (5/5) game, which is **intentional unkindness**.

This model has both inequality aversion and intentions and can do a great job of fitting the data for the ultimatum game with and without restricted choice. It demonstrates, therefore, that intentions-based models are flexible enough to consider any notion of what is fair or kind (see also Research Methods 7.5). That still leaves us asking, however, what we should consider is kind. As with models of inequality aversion, the Falk and Fischbacher model proposes that fairness is primarily judged by comparing the relative material payoffs of people. Is there any situation where fairness should be judged relative to the best and worst payoff that a person could have got?

Research Methods 7.5

Psychological game theory

A focus on beliefs and intentions is at the heart of something called psychological game theory first introduced by Geanakoplos, Pearce, and Stacchetti (1989). In 'traditional' game theory, as discussed in Chapter one, the payoffs in the game should capture the emotional as well as material payoff. The problem with this approach is that a person's emotional payoff may depend not only on what happens, but also on what the person believed would happen. For instance, emotions like envy, surprise, and disappointment happen relative to some expectation. A psychological game theory approach allows us to explicitly model this and so keep some separation between emotional and material payoffs.

To illustrate how psychological game theory can be applied in settings other than reciprocity, I'll return to the issue of honesty and deception that we first looked at in Chapter two. It was suggested in Chapter two that someone who lied would feel guilty about that. Following an approach due to Charness and Dufwenberg (2006) we can add a somewhat subtle twist to the story. We are now going to say that a person only feels guilty about lying if they were expected to tell the truth.

To fix ideas, consider the following scenario. Federica is deciding whether or not to employ Miguel to clean her windows. Miguel charges $10 to clean the windows, Federica values clean windows at $15, and the cost to Miguel of cleaning the windows is $5. If Federica decides not to employ Miguel, they both have payoff zero. If she employs him and he works hard, then both have material payoff $5. If she employs him and he slacks on the job, then Federica has lost $10 and Miguel has gained $10. Miguel clearly has an incentive to slack on the job because $10 beats $5. Suppose, however, that he promises Federica that he will do a good job, and he feels guilty if he breaks his promise?

In this case Federica must decide whether or not to employ Miguel, a_F, and Miguel must decide whether or not to work hard, a_M. When Federica makes her decision she forms some belief about what Miguel will do. Suppose that she believes he will choose b_M. When Miguel makes his decision he forms some belief about what Federica believes he will do. Suppose that he believes Federica believes he will choose c_M. Miguel will feel guilty if he believes that Federica believes he will work hard (c_M is 'work hard') and yet he slacks on the job (a_M is 'slack'). If this guilt is enough to offset the $5 gain from slacking, then Miguel will work hard, and Federica should employ him. If, however, Miguel believes that Federica believes he will slack (c_M is 'slack') then he feels no guilt from breaking his promise to work hard.

The interesting thing about this story is that Miguel is not really seen as deceiving Federica or lying to her if no one believes his promise. This generates multiple equilibria. There is an equilibrium where Miguel keeps his promises because he is expected to keep his promises, and an equilibrium where Miguel does not keep his promises because no one expects him to keep them. Psychological game theory is a really nice tool for highlighting such possibilities and allowing us to analyze them.

One issue we have not touched on yet is that of property rights. In all of the experiments we have discussed so far, subjects were randomly assigned roles in the game. In this case it seems natural that fairness should be judged by whether people earn the same material payoff. Now, suppose that people earn their material payoffs in some way and so have a stronger sense of ownership or **property rights** over their material payoff. Is it fair that a person who has earned more than another should give this away?

To start to answer that question we can look at a **dictator game with take and earnings**. Figure 7.13 provides some results from a study by List (2007). In the baseline treatment, both proposer and receiver were given $5 (a show-up fee) and the proposer was given an additional $5 that he could split with the receiver. This corresponds to the standard ($5) game of Figure 7.1 (and the results are similar). In the 'take $1' and 'take $5' treatments, the proposer could not only offer some of his or her $5 to the receiver but also take up to $1 or $5 from the receiver. In the earned $5 treatment, the proposer and receiver 'earned' their money by completing a task, including sorting and handling mailings for a charitable fundraiser.

In the baseline treatment, most proposers offer money, resulting in more equality between the proposer's and receiver's payoff. In the take $1 and take $5 experiments, many fewer proposers give money. The fact that they can take money appears to excuse not giving money. This is consistent with an

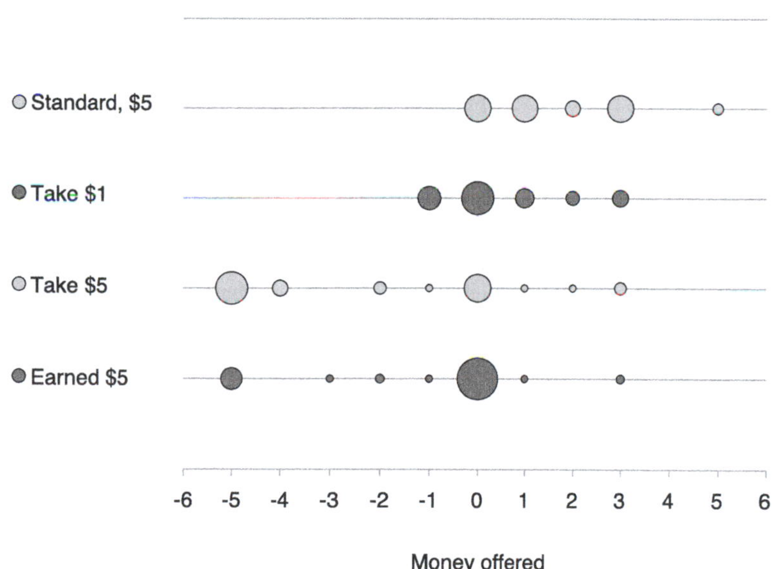

Figure 7.13 The amount shared by dictators in dictator games with take and earnings. Less is shared when there is the chance to take money, or money is earned.

Source: List (2007).

intentions-based model of fairness (like that in section 7.3.1), where the kindness of a proposer is judged by the worst that he could have done to the receiver, and not one judged by how equal proposer and receiver payoffs are. In the earned $5 experiment, we see that very few proposers take or offer money. Seemingly, money earned is money deserved.

What we learn from this study is that property rights and norms, or institutions, influence what people give and therefore presumably what is considered fair or kind. To take money is different to giving money. To have earned money is different to having been randomly given money. Other studies have similarly shown that perceptions of what is fair or kind will depend on how the problem is framed and the social norms that this brings to mind. Sometimes it is natural to judge kindness by equality of monetary payoffs. In others it is natural to judge kindness by whether a person could have done worse or better for another. There is, therefore, no set prescription for what the reference point should be. This, though, should come as no surprise given what we have seen in previous chapters.

7.4 Summary

We started by looking at a series of games and experimental studies which suggest that people have social or interdependent preferences. The evidence suggested that many people are reciprocators in that they want to be kind to those who are kind and unkind to those who are unkind.

In our first attempt to formally model such reciprocation, we looked at two models of inequality aversion. The basic idea behind both models is that a person dislikes earning less than others, and possibly dislikes earning more than others. The difference between the models that we looked at is the information a person is assumed to have. In the ERC model a person compares her payoff to the average payoff of others. In the Fehr-Schmidt model a person compares her payoff to the individual payoffs of others.

A great advantage of the ERC and Fehr-Schmidt models is that they are simple and easy to apply. We saw, however, that they only capture part of the story of social preferences. To try to fill the gap we considered models that take account of intentions. This meant that we needed to think about what is a fair reference point, what is kind or unkind, and how we can model beliefs about kindness. We saw that the answers would depend on context and framing effects.

With intentions-based models we can account for much more of the behavior that we observe, but that is primarily because the models are far more flexible. One symptom of this, which I only mentioned in Research Methods 7.5, is that we can very easily end up with ambiguous outcomes: an equilibrium where everyone is unkind because everyone is being unkind, and an equilibrium where everyone is kind because everyone is being kind. Which of these is more plausible? Again, the answer is likely to depend on context and framing effects.

In short, there is no 'perfect' model of social preferences that we can apply without much thought. What we do have, however, is a range of models and ways of thinking about social preferences that allow us to capture behavior on a case-by-case basis. In some applications the simplicity of an inequality aversion model will be appealing. In other applications it will be more important to take careful account of intentions.

Before we get on to the applications, there is one last thing I want to mention. While we have seen clear evidence that many people voluntarily give to others, we should not overplay the hand. In all of the games we have looked at there are always some who behave 'as if selfish', and even those who give only appear to give 'with strings attached'. Furthermore, in Figure 7.13, and a study I will look at in the next section, we see that many appear less likely to give if they have some excuse or wiggle room for not giving. The world is not full of altruists. But it is full of people with very diverse social preferences.

7.5 Giving to charity

A lot of people give time and money to charitable causes. For example, the World Giving Index 2012 (which collected data from 146 countries) reports that around 28 percent of people donated money to charity in 2011 and around 18 percent volunteered time. A survey by the Charities Aid Foundation in 2012 found that over 55 percent of UK adults gave to charity regularly, with donations averaging £27 per month; an estimated five million people (around one in 20) raised money by competing in a running event! The Giving USA Foundation estimated charitable contributions in the USA in 2012 to be $312 billion. These are big numbers.

To understand why so many people give so much to charity, we surely need to think about social preferences. The story that I have told so far seems, however, incomplete in understanding charitable giving. That's because the picture I have drawn is one of people helping and giving to others with strings attached. People help those who they see being kind or are earning less than them. Is there any role for pure altruism, people just helping others unconditionally? This seems plausible because many people give money and time to charity without knowing whether this will help people who are kind or not, or have more money than them.

So, why might a person give money or time to charity? There are three broad explanations: they might just want to help people; this would be **pure altruism**. They might feel good about themselves after giving, because of, say, prestige, respect, or social approval. Call this a **warm glow** or **joy of giving**. Finally, they might feel bad about themselves if they do not give, because of, say, the social disapproval of others, or guilt. These last two reasons give rise to **impure altruism** in that the person directly benefits herself from giving, and so her motives for giving are not purely altruistic. But does it matter whether a person gives for pure or impure reasons? Yes, for at least two reasons, which I shall look at in turn.

7.5.1 Crowding out

Suppose that Federica was planning to contribute to a charity but then finds out that someone else has already done so. If Federica is motivated by pure altruism she would no longer want to give, because somebody else has done the good work for her. This is **crowding out**. If Federica is motivated by impure altruism she might still want to give, indeed she may feel more incentive to give in order to compete with the other giver. There will be less crowding out.

To illustrate the issues, I will consider a special case of a **model of warm glow** developed by Andreoni (1990). Consider a group of individuals contributing to a charity or public good. The utility function of Federica is given by:

$$U_f(w_f - c_f, C, c_f) = w_f - c_f + \eta_f\sqrt{C} + \rho_f\sqrt{c_f}$$

where w_F is Federica's wealth, c_F is how much she contributes to the public good, C are the total contributions (including hers), and η_F and ρ_F are parameters. If $\rho_F = 0$, then we can say that Federica is a pure altruist because all she cares about are her wealth after contributing and total contributions to the charity. If $\rho_F > 0$, then we can say that Federica is an impure altruist because she gets utility from having contributed. If $\eta_F = 0$, then Federica contributes only to get a warm glow.

If we solve for the optimal contribution we get relation:

$$1 = \frac{\eta_F}{2\sqrt{C}} + \frac{\rho_F}{2\sqrt{c_F}}.$$

If $\rho_F = 0$ then:

$$c_F = \frac{\eta_F^2}{4} - C_{-F}$$

where C_{-F} is total contributions of those other than Federica. The pure altruist, therefore, wants $\eta_F^2/4$ to be contributed and does not care who contributes. If C_{-F} increases, then she will decrease c_F and there will be complete crowding out. If $\eta_F = 0$, then:

$$c_F = \frac{\rho_F^2}{4}$$

and so the amount given is independent of the amount given by others. There will be zero crowding out. Whether or not giving is because of altruistic or impure altruistic reasons does, therefore, matter.

Testing whether or not there is crowding out can be done in the lab or with real data on charitable giving. In the lab the results suggest that there is sizeable but not complete crowding out. For example, Andreoni (1993) and Bolton and Katok (1998) ran two very different experiments to test the extent of crowding out and found the remarkably similar results of 71.5 percent and 73.7 percent crowding out. That means that a person reduces her giving by \$0.715 or \$0.737 for every \$1 someone else gives. Real data on charitable giving shows far less crowding out.

For example, Ribar and Wilhelm (2002) looked at private donations from the US to 125 international relief and development organizations between 1986 and 1992, and found that giving by the government and other organizations crowded out private donations by only 18 percent. The evidence consistently shows, therefore, that there is crowding out, but not complete crowding out. What it is hard to agree on is just how much crowding out there is.

Can we reconcile the differences between the experimental and empirical results? Ribar and Wilhelm suggest that we can by taking into account the number of other potential givers. To explain, suppose that Federica is an impure altruist who gets utility from both pure altruism and a warm glow. Because of pure altruism she wants total donations to be sufficiently high, $\eta_F^2/4$ in the example. Because of the joy of giving she wants to give at least a certain amount herself, $\rho^2_F/4$ in the example. If there are few other potential givers, as in the experimental lab, total donations are likely to be lower, so pure altruism will most influence her decision. If there are many other potential givers, as in real life, total donations will likely be high, so the joy of giving will most influence her decision. To see this in the model, suppose that all contributors will contribute identical amounts. Then we can substitute in $C = nc$ and get:

$$c = \frac{1}{4}\left(\frac{\eta_F}{\sqrt{n}} + \rho_F\right)^2.$$

If n is large, then η_F becomes irrelevant and only a warm glow matters. If n is small, then η_F is relevant and altruism will matter.

It seems, therefore, that we observe a mixture of both a warm glow and altruistic reasons for giving; the extent of crowding out that we observe depends on the number of other potential givers.

7.5.2 Who is watching?

A pure altruist will give irrespective of whether or not someone will know she has given. Someone motivated by impure altruism may give more if their giving will be observed. This is because giving can serve as a way for someone to signal something good about themselves. For example, giving may signal generosity or wealth. That people may want to give more if being observed offers a potentially important means to increase donations, and the evidence is that some people do indeed give in order to signal. But before looking at that evidence, I think it is useful to briefly look at a simple model to see how signaling interacts with altruism and a warm glow.

Suppose that giving is seen as a signal of someone's generosity. For this to make sense we need there to actually be some variation in how generous people are. In the model of a warm glow this would mean individuals vary in their values of η and ρ, with a high η and ρ being seen as generous. For simplicity, suppose that there are only two types of individuals: the generous who have $\eta = 0$ and

$\rho = 2$, and the not generous who have $\eta = \rho = 0$. If giving is not observed, then the generous will give one and receive a warm glow, while the not generous will give zero. What happens if giving is observed?

A second ingredient of any model of signaling is that some individuals must want to appear like a different type of agent. In this case a not generous individual, say, Federica, will try to look like she is generous. She can do this by giving $c_F = 1$. Suppose that she receives a prestige bonus of P if she is perceived by others as generous, zero if she is perceived as not generous, and $0.5P$ if it is unclear whether she is generous or not. Contributing costs 1, but will gain a bonus of at least $0.5P$, so, if $0.5P > 1$, she will contribute. But what if a generous individual, called Miguel, also gets the prestige bonus? Miguel will want to contribute more in order to distinguish himself from Federica. By contributing a little bit more than $0.5P$ he does just enough to make sure Federica would not try to copy him and he can get the full bonus of P.

To summarize, if only the not generous get a bonus for being perceived as generous, then both Federica and Miguel will give one, $c_M = c_F = 1$. If generous individuals also get the bonus, then the Federica will give zero, $c_F = 0$, and Miguel will give more, $c_M = 0.5P$. Desires for appearing generous can thus increase the giving of either the not generous or the generous. In more general models the implications of signaling become more complicated, but giving is always likely to increase. So, what of the evidence that people do give, at least partially, for signaling reasons?

In short, there is a lot of evidence that signaling is important for some. The most compelling evidence is that very few donors to charity choose to remain anonymous. In public good experiments we also see that giving is less, the more anonymity there is. To illustrate this, and also to make a slightly different point, I want to look at a study by Dana and co-authors (2007).

In the study, subjects play variations of the dictator game in which proposers have reason or not to excuse not giving. The results are summarized in Table 7.7.

In all the experiments proposers could, with some variations, offer a fair \$5, \$5 split, or an unfair \$6, \$1 split. In the baseline treatment, we see what we would expect, given the evidence in section 7.1, in that most proposers chose the fair

Table 7.7 Offers in a dictator game with varying amounts of moral anonymity

Treatment	*Proportion choosing fair option (%)*	*Other details*
Baseline	74	
Hidden	38	56% of subjects chose to reveal the receiver's payoff.
Two dictators	35	
Possibly random	34	76% of participants chose before the cut-off time.

Source: Dana *et al.* (2007).

option. In all of the other treatments, proposers had some plausible reason for not choosing the fair option. We see that the proportion choosing the fair option falls dramatically.

In the hidden information treatment, a proposer knew their own payoff but had to choose to find out the payoff of the receiver. Even though this could be done without cost, nearly half of proposers chose not to find out the payoff of the receiver. A majority of those then chose the unfair option. In the two dictator treatments, the offer sent was determined by two dictators simultaneously, either of which could enforce the sending of a fair offer. In the possibly random treatment, the proposer's choice would be made randomly if he or she did not make their choice before some undisclosed cut-off time. Most did choose before the cut-off, but still chose the unfair option!

What this study nicely shows is how signaling is interrelated with intentions. In the baseline treatment, a proposer's choice made his or her intentions very clear and so they could not hide, either from the receiver or from themselves. This means that the proposer's actions would send a clear signal, so they had the incentive to send a good signal and receive a warm glow, avoid guilt, etc. In the other three treatments, a proposer's choice is much less revealing about their intentions. This lessens the incentive to send a good signal, and is enough for the majority of subjects to not choose the fair offer. We see, therefore, that a little bit of wiggle room to not give can be enough to significantly reduce the amount that is given. Signaling is the most plausible explanation for this.

7.5.3 Why do people give?

The picture we get is one of people giving for a variety of reasons. Giving does not appear to be solely due to pure altruism, but is likely a mixture of a warm glow, guilt at not giving, signaling, and pure altruism. Understanding this can be useful in getting people to give more. To illustrate these points, I shall wrap up this section by looking at a study by Alpizar and co-authors (2008).

They looked at giving by international visitors to Poas National Park in Costa Rica in 2006. A random sample of visitors was interviewed privately about their visit to the National Park, at the end of which they were asked to make a donation. Three things were varied: some were given a small gift of value \$3, some were told that 'most common donations have been' \$2, \$5, or \$10, and some made their donations without the interviewer knowing how much they gave.

The results are summarized in Table 7.8. A relatively high proportion did give, but it is noticeable that the proportion who gave is increasing in the lowness of the reference point. The contribution, conditional on giving something, is 25 percent higher in the non-anonymous compared to anonymous treatments. We also see higher contributions, the higher is the reference amount. Indeed, many givers matched the reference amount. All of these findings are impossible to reconcile with a giver motivated solely by pure altruism or one who cares only about their own payoff. Instead they suggest the mix of motives for giving that we have looked at.

Table 7.8 The proportion who contribute, the average contribution conditional on giving something, and the average contribution to Poas National Park

Treatment	*Proportion contribute (%)*	*Conditional contribution ($)*	*Average contribution ($)*
No gift	48	5.09	2.43
Gift	56	4.56	2.56
Anonymous	51	4.36	2.21
Non-anonymous	53	5.21	2.77
No reference	47	6.00	2.84
$2 reference	61	3.61	2.20
$5 reference	50	3.95	1.98
$10 reference	49	5.97	2.95

Source: Alpizar *et al.* (2008).

7.6 Price and wage rigidity

Take a look at the number of unemployed in just about any country and you will see some big numbers. The unemployment rate in the UK and US is typically above 5 percent of the workforce and in a few European countries the number can be as high as 20 percent. Some of this could be voluntary unemployment, but clearly not all of it. That means that labor markets are not clearing, at least in the short run. If there is an excess supply of labor, then the standard story would say that the price of labor, or the wage rate, should fall until the market clears, or supply equals demand. If wages do not fall for some reason, then we say there is **wage stickiness**. There are lots of reasons why we might observe wage stickiness, such as regulation and unions, but the reason I want to focus on here is that of reciprocity and fairness.

Why should reciprocity matter? The relationship between that of an employer and a worker is a **principal–agent relationship**. The employer, or principal, hires a worker, or agent, to do a job for her. Given that the employer's profit will depend on how much effort and initiative the worker puts into her job, the employer needs to find a way to motivate the worker to work hard. Crucially, however, in most jobs the employer will not be able to tell for sure how hard the worker is working. At least, the worker may have ways to make it look as though she is working harder than she is (see section 2.3). The employer, therefore, needs to think carefully about how to motivate the worker.

Now let's think about reciprocity. Positive reciprocity would imply that, if the employer is kind to the worker, the worker will be kind to the employer. Negative reciprocity would imply that, if the employer is unkind to the worker, the worker will be unkind to the employer. What is kind and unkind in this context? That will depend on the reference point. Given, however, what we have seen in Chapters two and four and this chapter, the most obvious reference points would seem to be: the wage paid previously or the wage being paid to others. To cut wages or pay a lower wage than to others would then be seen as unkind, while to increase wages or pay a higher wage than others would be seen as kind.

We might predict, therefore, that employers would pay high wages to motivate workers and appeal to positive reciprocity. They might be reluctant to cut wages and demotivate workers because of negative reciprocity. Numerous surveys of employers have found evidence for both of these effects, and particularly the latter. For example, Campbell III and Kamlani (1997) asked 184 firms why they do not cut wages as low as they could in a recession. The main concern of employers was that the most productive workers would leave (an adverse selection argument) but a close second was that worker effort would decrease (a reciprocity argument). Table 7.9, for instance, shows the percentage of employers who thought a 10 percent pay cut or increase would have an effect, and a serious effect, on worker effort. A pay rise is predicted to have some benefit, but it is clear that a wage cut is expected to have a significant negative effect.

If employers are reluctant to cut wages because it will cause negative reciprocity, then we have a plausible reason for wage stickiness. But we should test this explanation out a bit more thoroughly. I will do so by formalizing the argument a bit more, using a model of fairness, and then looking at some experimental results.

7.6.1 A model of worker reciprocity

To formalize how reciprocity can result in sticky wages I shall work through the intentions-based model of fairness that we looked at in section 7.3.1. Figure 7.14 illustrates. To keep things simple, imagine that a worker, Miguel, can put in either high or low effort $e \in \{H, L\}$, and high effort costs him some amount C. Suppose that, if effort is high, $e = H$, the employer, Federica, gets revenue R and, if effort is

Table 7.9 The percentage of employers who thought that a 10 percent wage cut or increase would change worker effort, and change it by more than 10 percent. For example, after a 10 percent wage cut it is expected that 74.7 percent of blue collar workers will decrease effort by 10 percent or more

Change in wages	*Expected change in effort*	*Proportion of workers who will change effort (%)*		
		White collar workers	*Blue collar workers*	*Less skilled workers*
10% cut	Decrease	85.8	92.0	91.3
	Decrease by 10% or more	61.7	74.7	78.8
10% increase	Increase	55.8	52.1	53.2
	Increase by 10% or more	19.4	18.7	22.5

Source: Campbell III and Kamlani (1997).

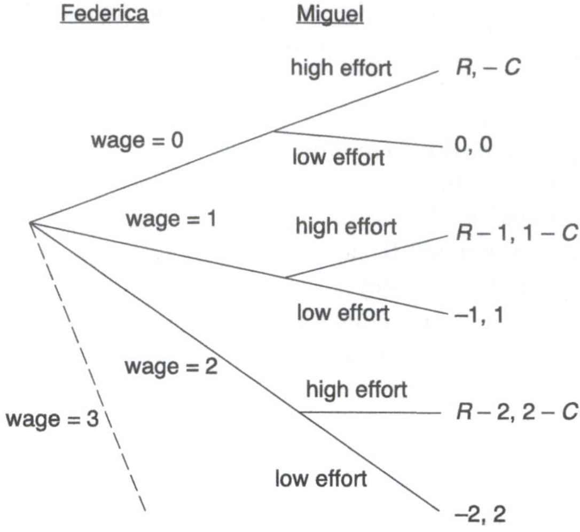

Figure 7.14 A simple model of worker reciprocity. Federica chooses a wage w and Miguel chooses effort. Federica's material payoff is revenue − w and Miguel's is w − effort cost.

low, $e = L$, she gets zero revenue. Federica chooses a wage w and makes a profit, or material payoff, of revenue minus w. Miguel gets a material payoff of w minus effort cost.

Federica does not care about fairness and so simply wants to maximize her profit. Should she pay a high wage?

Miguel can be kind by putting in high effort and unkind by putting in low effort. The revenue of Federica is R in the first case and zero in the latter, so an equitable payoff is $0.5R - w$. The kindness of Miguel is thus $0.5R$ or $-0.5R$ depending on whether he puts in high or low effort. Federica can realistically offer any wage between zero and R, so the equitable payoff is also $0.5R$ and the kindness of Federica is $w - 0.5R$.

This means that, if Miguel puts in high effort, his utility is:

$$w - C + \mu_M \left(w - \frac{R}{2} \right) \frac{R}{2}$$

and if he puts in low effort, his utility is:

$$w - \mu_M \left(w - \frac{R}{2} \right) \frac{R}{2}$$

where recall that μ_M is his desire to reciprocate. Miguel will, therefore, put in high effort if:

$$w > \frac{R}{2} + \frac{C}{\mu_M R}.$$

We can see that he may be willing to put in high effort if Federica is kind and offers a wage above the equitable payoff of $0.5R$.

Is Federica willing to pay this wage? If Miguel puts in high effort, she gains R in revenue and so she will be willing to pay any wage less than R. Setting $w < R$ gives the condition $2C < \mu_M R^2$. Thus, provided the cost of effort is sufficiently small and/or Miguel has sufficient desire to reciprocate, Federica will be willing to pay a high enough wage that Miguel will be willing to put in high effort.

In this example we see that a worker may be willing to work hard if he believes the employer is being kind and offering a higher than equitable wage. We can also see how reciprocity can cause unemployment and wage stickiness. For instance, suppose that R were to subsequently fall, but Miguel still equated kindness with his old wage, or the old value of w. We could get wage stickiness because Miguel will think a wage cut is unkind. This can lead to unemployment if Federica can no longer afford to pay the wage Miguel wants.

Do not, however, think of reciprocity as a bad thing that we could do without. Yes, it is the reason why we might get wage stickiness and unemployment, but without it Miguel would never be willing to put in high effort, and Federica would never make any profit! So, reciprocity is beneficial, but could have negative side effects.

7.6.2 Wage stickiness in the lab

The lab provides a controlled environment to try to better understand wage stickiness and has shown the importance of reciprocity. To illustrate, I will look at the study by Fehr and Falk (1999). The basic design of the experiments was similar to that of the gift exchange game that we already looked at in section 7.1. The main difference was a preliminary stage in which workers and employers were matched through a double auction. In this auction workers could say what wage they would accept, employers could say what wage they would pay, and, if a worker and employer agreed on a wage, they then played the gift exchange game. This procedure was repeated ten times, but an employer could never know who the worker was, and so there was no opportunity for reputation building. The key to the experiment was that there was an excess supply of workers, 11 workers to seven employers, so unemployment was inevitable.

Figure 7.15 summarizes the main results. The reservation wage shows what wages the seven workers posting the lowest wages were willing to accept. This is, therefore, the wage that employers could have offered and got workers. We can compare this with the wage they did pay. First, look at the treatment where effort does not count, meaning that the employer's payoff did not depend on worker effort. In this treatment there was no incentive to pay a high wage and we consequently observe that the average wage was low and similar to the reservation wage.

Now look at the treatment we are most interested in, where effort did count. We see that wages are relatively high and, most importantly, above the reservation

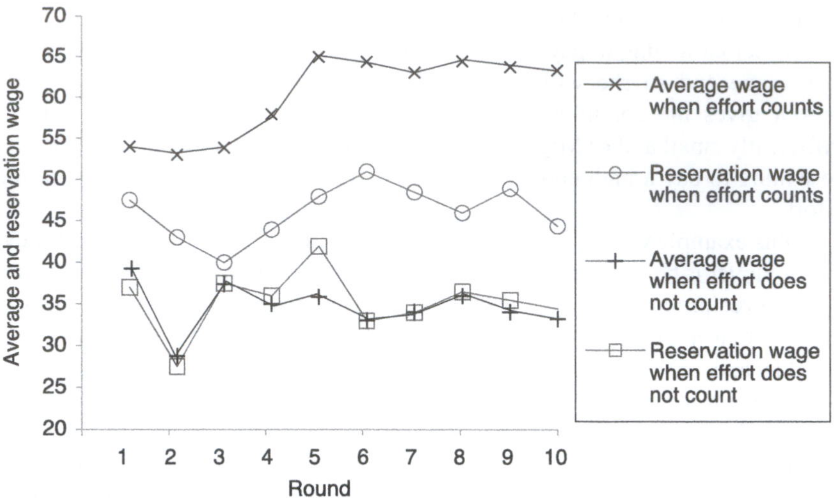

Figure 7.15 The average wage and reservation wage in experimental labor markets. In the treatment without effort the average wage is relatively low. When effort matters, we see that employers pay relatively high wages, well above the minimum that some workers were willing to accept.

Source: Fehr and Falk (1999).

wage. So, employers could have hired cheaper workers but chose not to. They chose to hire workers who wanted a high wage! Was this a good decision? Around 34 percent of workers did not make effort conditional on wage, but 66 percent did reciprocate a high wage with high effort. This was enough to mean that paying a high wage did pay back in higher profits.

This experiment demonstrates nicely how positive reciprocity from workers can make it worthwhile to pay high wages. In a second part of their study Fehr and Falk (1999) show that negative reciprocity can also make it worthwhile to pay high wages. They do this by changing the workers' effort costs, so that it is least costly for a worker to put in maximum effort. Workers paid a low wage still on average lower their effort, but now at a cost to themselves. Workers are therefore willing to sacrifice their own monetary payoff to punish a low-paying employer.

7.6.3 How long to forget a wage change?

It seems clear that reciprocity is important in the labor market and is a causal factor in wage stickiness. But, before we move on, there is one final issue that I want to touch on, that of time. We have already talked in Chapters two and four about how reference points can change over time. If an employer's wage changes, then their reference point should also eventually change. That would suggest that employers need to constantly increase the wage in order to motivate workers through positive reciprocity. This is consistent with the desire for an increasing wage profile that we talked about in Chapter four. Do we have any idea how long it takes people to adjust to new wages?

A study by Gneezy and List (2006) suggested that it does not take long to forget a wage increase. They recruited people to do routine tasks, like data entry in the university library, and door-to-door fundraising, and some were given an unexpected wage increase. Those given the increase worked harder for the first 90 minutes but after that their effort dropped to the level of those who did not receive an increase. Ultimately, the wage increase did not pay for itself.

In a similar experiment, Kube and co-authors (2006) got a similar result to that of Gneezy and List when looking at a wage increase. They also, however, consider an unexpected cut in the wage and find that this has longer lasting consequences. Maybe people soon forget a wage increase but never forget a wage cut? This emphasizes the asymmetry that we had already seen in Table 7.9, where a decrease in wages was predicted to have stronger effects on worker effort than an increase in wages. This asymmetry is consistent with loss aversion and is key to explaining why reciprocity can lead to wage rigidity. Cutting wages is worse for worker effort than increasing wages is good for effort, so firms should avoid cutting wages.

7.6.4 Firm pricing

It is not only wages that can be sticky. If there is excess demand for a good, then firms, according to a standard story, should push up prices until supply equals demand. Often, however, we observe large excess demand for goods. For example, tickets for major sporting events like the Superbowl or World Cup Final could be sold many times over. Similarly, ski resorts are bursting to capacity at Christmas and New Year. Why do prices not rise more?

There are good arguments to say that it is because of desires for fairness and reciprocity. The explanation is very similar to that for wage stickiness, so I will not spend much time on this issue. But I will talk through some of the results from a study by Kahneman and co-authors (1986) that help illustrate the key points. They conducted a household survey with questions like:

> A hardware store has been selling snow shovels for $15. The morning after a large snowstorm, they raise the price to $20. Please rate this action as: Completely fair, Acceptable, Unfair, Very unfair.

In times of excess demand, firms have a rationale to increase prices, but 82 percent of respondents in the survey considered this price increase unfair. Reciprocity would suggest that this unfairness might be enough to stop people buying a snow shovel.

As with wages, the most obvious reference price is probably the previous price or the price charged by others. This means that a price increase or relatively high price is unkind while a price decrease or relatively low price is kind. To get price stickiness, we need the asymmetry whereby raising prices is considered worse than lowering prices is considered good. This is what we seem to observe. For example, another survey question was:

> A shortage has developed for a popular model of automobile, and customers must now wait two months for delivery. A dealer has been selling these cars at list price. Now the dealer prices the model at $200 above list price.

Seventy-one percent considered this unfair. Other respondents were told:

> A dealer has been selling these cars at a discount of $200 below list price. Now the dealer sells this model only at list price.

Fifty-eight percent found this acceptable.

So, is it ever acceptable to raise prices? Most people surveyed considered it fair for a firm to pass on increases in wholesale costs to consumers. They seemed to accept that firms need to make an acceptable level of profit, and so are willing to accommodate this. What was considered unfair is for a firm to raise prices because of increased market power. This is clear in the snow shovel question. As we might expect, therefore, the reference point is a little bit more subtle than the previous price.

You may disagree on what is fair or not. The main thing is that firms must take account of customers' likely perceptions of a price rise. This is because we know that people reject in ultimatum games and so presumably are willing to not buy a product they consider overpriced. Firms may, therefore be reluctant to increase prices, with the consequence that many markets may have excess demand.

Indeed, we can be more specific about which markets will have excess demand. Primarily it will be markets where there are large fluctuations in demand, but little change in costs, and where customer loyalty is important. This is because the large fluctuations in demand will cause there to be excess demand but the importance of customer loyalty will make firms reluctant to increase prices. This is often the case in sport and entertainment events. Prices do in fact vary for sporting events and in hotels according to demand, but the evidence would suggest that they do not vary enough to stop excess demand at peak times. Kahneman and co-authors quote a skiing industry explanation: 'If you gouge them at Christmas, they won't be back in March.'

7.7 Further reading

The review articles by Thaler (1988), Camerer and Thaler (1995), and Fehr and Gächter (2000b) provide a gentle introduction to the economics of social preferences, and the article by Sobel (2005) a more in-depth survey. Much of the book by Camerer (2003) is also relevant. Interest in social preferences was sparked in large part by the ultimatum game experiments reported by Güth *et al.* (1982). See also the articles by Charness and Rabin (2002) and Binmore and Shaked (2010). For a recent advance in psychological game theory, see Battigalli and Dufwenberg (2009). For interesting insights on public goods, a classic book by Olson (1971) is recommended and I'll also recommend at this point a great book by Frank (1991). The papers by Frank, Gilovich, and Regan (1993) and Levitt and List (2007) raise some interesting issues. See Andreoni (2006) for more on the economics of charitable giving, and Shang and Croson (2009) for a recent, interesting paper that overviews relevant literature. Bewley (2007) provides a survey on fairness in wage setting.

7.8 Review questions

7.1 What is the Nash equilibrium in a dictator game? What about the trust game and ultimatum game? Be careful to distinguish sub-game perfect Nash equilibria from other Nash equilibria.

7.2 Why might payoffs be lower in a public good game with punishment even if punishment increases contributions? Is it good to have the threat of punishment or not?

7.3 In section 7.1.5 I mentioned a study by Andreoni and Miller (2002). They asked subjects to play 11 different dictator games. In each game the proposer was given a number of tokens, from 40 to 100, and asked to divide the tokens between them and a receiver. Each token was worth $0.10 to $0.40 to the proposer and $0.10 to $0.40 to the receiver. For example, a token might be worth $0.40 to the proposer and $0.10 to the receiver, or $0.20 to the proposer and $0.30 to the receiver. How do you think the share given to receivers depended on the worth of tokens? How should it depend, to be consistent with utility maximization?

7.4 Should we equate material payoff with money?

7.5 Find the general conditions such that punishment can work in a linear public good game in the ERC model and the Fehr-Schmidt model. Hint: For the ERC model find the level of punishment such that, after she has paid for punishing, Anna will have exactly the social reference point. For the Fehr-Schmidt model find the level of punishment such that the free-rider, Miguel, and punisher, Anna, will end up with the same material payoff.

7.6 Why can punishment work in a linear public good game according to the Fehr-Schmidt model if only one person is willing to punish, but in the ERC model only if two people are willing to punish?

7.7 How can an intentions-based model of fairness be adapted to take account of earned versus unearned payoff, and social norms?

7.8 In the intentions-based model of section 7.3.1, the equitable payoff was derived looking only at Pareto-efficient outcomes. Why is this sensible?

7.9 Is it better to be in a firm where you earn $50,000 and the average salary is $80,000 or in a firm where you earn $45,000 and the average salary is $30,000?

7.10 Why can loss aversion help explain why a cut in wages is worse than a rise in wages is good? How is this related to wage stickiness and habit formation?

7.11 Should employers fine poorly performing workers, or give bonuses to well-performing workers in order to provide the most effective incentives?

7.12 What can we learn from the ultimatum game about the interaction between a buyer and seller of a good?

Part III

Origins of behavior

8 Evolution and culture

> It is not the strongest of the species that survives, nor the most intelligent, but rather the one most adaptable to change.
>
> Clarence Darrow

In this, and the next, chapter our objective will shift away from trying to describe behavior to that of trying to understand the reasons for behavior. For example, we want to ask: Why are people risk averse? Why do people value fairness? Why is there reference dependence? Hopefully, you agree that these are fascinating questions. In answering them we can learn not only why people behave the way they do but can also get additional insight on how they behave. Potentially, therefore, we can learn a lot.

In this chapter I am going to take seriously the fact that anyone's behavior is shaped by our evolutionary history and the culture that we grow up and live in. I will begin by looking at the consequences of evolution and then turn to the role of culture. Note that the section on culture will make a lot more sense if you are familiar with the material in Chapter seven.

8.1 Evolution and economic behavior

I shall not go deeply into the science of evolution, but it will be useful to know the basic idea. Evolution by natural selection relies on three things: **variation**, meaning that different individuals are different in their traits, abilities, characteristics, preferences, and so on; **inheritance**, meaning that offspring inherit similar traits to their parents; and **mutation**, meaning that with random chance the traits of the individual are altered during reproduction and are slightly different to the traits of their parents. Over generations, the consequences of **natural selection** are twofold: (i) traits that result in an individual having relatively more offspring than others will become more common in the population, because of variation and inheritance; (ii) traits that increase the relative number of offspring of an individual can emerge in the population, because of mutation and inheritance.

To illustrate, consider a very stylized example in which there are two types of people, some having green hair and some blue. Those with green hair find it easier to attack prey and catch food, so survive longer and have more children. On average greens have four offspring each and blues have two. Suppose that there are ten greens and ten blues to start with. After one generation there are 40 greens and 20 blues; after two generations there are 160 greens and 40 blues; after three generations there are 640 greens and 80 blues. Clearly, the greens are becoming a larger proportion of the population, from 50 percent to 88 percent in three generations.

Now, suppose that because of some random mutation one person is born with yellow hair and another with red. A person with yellow hair finds it even easier to attack prey and so has on average six offspring, while someone with red hair is very poor at attacking prey and so has only one offspring. If you do the math you will find that it is not many generations before those with yellow hair dominate the population.

This simple example avoids many complexities that we need to think about, but it will do for the moment, and I shall provide a more nuanced picture as we proceed. The important thing at this stage is to start explaining what evolution has got to do with modern economic behavior.

8.1.1 Looking for food and finding a utility function

Food and water are essential to survival, and much time would have been spent in our evolutionary history trying to find enough of it. Indeed, finding food is still the main preoccupation of many in the developing world today. Evolution should, therefore, favor those with good strategies for finding food and water. Can this shed light on how humans behave today?

Consider a person called Edward, looking for food. Every day he leaves his cave and can go either east or west in search of food. Suppose that on day t, if he were to go west, he would find f_t^W calories of food and if he were to go east, he would find f_t^E. The more calories he finds the better. The problem is, Edward does not know f_t^W or f_t^E without going and looking, and he can only go one way per day. Which way should he go?

Let's suppose that the amount of food in either direction on any one day is random. The probability of finding f calories by going east is p_f^E and by going west is p_f^W. If:

$$\sum_{f=0}^{\infty} p_f^E f > \sum_{f=0}^{\infty} p_f^W f \tag{8.1}$$

then Edward will maximize his calorie intake by going east. Remember, however, that having children is the objective favored by natural selection, not eating a lot. Let $u(f)$ denote the expected number of extra children Edward (and his wife Anna) will have if Edward gets f calories of food on any one day. We do not need $u(f)$ to be an integer and, given that Edward will likely have far fewer children than meals, $u(f)$ will likely be a small fraction. If:

$$\sum_{f=0}^{\infty} p_f^E u(f) > \sum_{f=0}^{\infty} p_f^W u(f) \tag{8.2}$$

then Edward will maximize the expected number of children by going east.

Look at the difference between equations (8.1) and (8.2). In the first we calculate the expected number of calories, in the second the expected number of children. It may well be that going west gives the highest expected calories, but going east the highest expected number of children. For instance, the amount of food to the east may always be a nice consistent amount, while that to the west is either very high or very low. Evolution will favor those who maximize the expected number of children, and so obey equation (8.2) rather than (8.1).

This means that Edward not only needs to work out how much food there is likely to be in each direction, he also needs to work out the relationship between the amount of food he eats and the number of children he will likely have! Given that Edward will have relatively few children, this looks like a hopeless task. Suppose, however, that Edward is born with the function u already hard-wired into his brain. What I mean is that, when he sees and eats foods with a calorie content of f, he gets an enjoyment, satisfaction, or utility of $u(f)$. Does Edward's problem become simpler?

Robson (2001b) showed that it does. Edward can now maximize his expected number of children with the following heuristic: today I go east, tomorrow I go west, the next day I go east, and so on; each day I keep a cumulative count of the difference in utility between going east versus west; if this difference reaches some critical threshold, then from that moment on I always go east or west depending on which gave the highest utility. This is a simple solution to a complex problem and works because Edward is born with the utility function $u(f)$ and the heuristic of how to use it.

The utility function has two key benefits here. The first is that Edward only has to think about food. If he finds enough food to maximize his utility, then, without knowing it, he will maximize his expected number of children. This is because evolution will favor those who have the correct utility function, i.e. get satisfaction from eating food proportional to the expected number of children that eating food provides. The utility function $u(f)$ thus encapsulates the **accumulated experience of past generations**.

The second benefit of the utility function is that Edward can adapt to novelty. Over generations it will likely change whether going east or west is best. It would, therefore, not be a good evolutionary strategy to follow the actions of one's ancestors, and say go west because a parent did. The utility function allows Edward to follow the strategies of his ancestors, as given by heuristics. Again, evolution will favor those with the best heuristic, meaning that Edward, and his children, will be very **adaptable to a changing environment**.

We have already seen in Chapter three the distinction between expected utility, equations (8.2) and (3.1), and expected value, equations (8.1) and (3.2). Now we have an explanation for it, and a justification to assume that people behave as if maximizing an expected utility function. Indeed, we see that evolution may have favored people with a cardinal utility function where satisfaction from goods comes in proportion to the expected number of children such goods give. We call such goods **intermediate goods** because they are anything that increases, or decreases, the expected number of children. Food and shelter are obvious examples of intermediate goods, but status, generosity, esteem, and a host of other things may be equally relevant, as we shall see.

Is this useful in understanding modern economic behavior? Yes. It gives us important clues as to what should give us utility and what probably will not. It also gives us clues as to what we should have good heuristics for, search being one of them. What I want to do now is add time and risk to the mix to see what else we can learn.

8.1.2 Choosing when to have children

I will start by adding time to the story, by questioning when Edward (and Anna) should choose to have children. Let's suppose that Edward can have children up to T years of age. What he needs to do is to decide when to have children during those T years. In our story this choice is primarily determined by when he chooses to consume the intermediate goods such as food and shelter and not necessarily when he gets together with Anna. We represent his choice by a **reproductive profile** $x = \{x_1, \ldots, x_T\}$ that says how many children, x_t, he expects to have when age t. If all people, including Edward and his children, survive from one year to the next with probability s, what reproductive profile should Edward choose?

Again, this does not look a simple problem. It turns out, however, that, if Edward has an inter-temporal utility function hard-wired into his brain, then he can solve this problem relatively easily. Similar to before, he will not need to choose when to have children, but instead just consume intermediate goods in a way that maximizes his utility (and get together with Anna every so often). But what will the inter-temporal utility function look like? Robson and Samuelson (2009) show that evolution will favor people with the inter-temporal utility function:

$$u^T(x_1, \ldots, x_T) = \sum_{t=1}^{T} \delta^{t-1} x_t \tag{8.3}$$

where:

$$\delta = e^{-(\ln \varphi - \ln s)}$$

and $\ln \varphi$ is the population growth rate. The term $\ln \varphi - \ln s$ is equal to the population growth rate plus the population death rate. You might want to refer back to Chapter four to see in more detail what this means. But, basically it means that evolution will favor people who use exponential discounting and have consistent, non-time-varying preferences with a discount factor that depends on the population growth rate and death rate.

This gives us an explanation for exponential discounting and a prediction of what the discount factor should be. But why this specific discount factor? If Edward delays having children one year then he can expect to fall behind others because of population growth and the possibility that he does not survive the year. So, a child next year needs to be discounted by the rate of population growth and death. The higher is population growth and the lower the chance of survival, the more impatient Edward should be to consume intermediate goods and have children.

[Extra] For those curious how to derive equation (8.3), here are some of the details. Starting when Edward is zero years old, we can roll forward time and keep track of how many descendants he has of each age. Let $N_a(t)$ denote the number of descendants of age a after t years. Things will evolve according to the equation:

$$[N_1(t+1), \ldots, N_T(t+1)] = [N_1(t), \ldots, N_T(t)] \begin{bmatrix} sx_1 & s & 0 & \ldots & 0 \\ sx_2 & 0 & s & \ldots & 0 \\ \vdots & \vdots & \vdots & & \vdots \\ sx_{T-1} & 0 & 0 & \ldots & s \\ sx_T & 0 & 0 & \ldots & 0 \end{bmatrix} \quad (8.4)$$

To explain, the number of one-year-olds after $t + 1$ years is equal to the number of surviving offspring born to those who were one in year t, i.e. $N_1(t)\ sx_1$, plus the number born to those who were two in year t, i.e. $N_2\ (t)\ sx_2$, etc. The number of two-year-olds in year $t + 1$ is equal to the number of one-year-olds who survive from year t to $t + 1$, i.e. $N_1(t)\ s$, etc. The matrix in equation (8.4) is called the Leslie matrix and is crucial to finding what reproductive profile evolution will favor. Technically, evolution will favor the profile that maximizes the dominant eigenvalue of the Leslie matrix. What this means in practice is that evolution will favor the utility function in equation (8.3).

8.1.3 Aggregate risk

So far we have described Edward as maximizing expected utility using exponential discounting. In Chapters three and four we saw that people may not maximize expected utility or use exponential discounting, so how can we reconcile things a little? One way is to add aggregate risk to the story. To explain: an **idiosyncratic risk** is one that affects only one individual in the population, while an **aggregate risk** is one that will likely affect all the population. For example, a cold winter or flood is an aggregate risk, while getting attacked by a predator is more likely to be idiosyncratic. I have focused on idiosyncratic risk so far, but in our evolutionary past aggregate risk was undoubtedly relevant. With the help of four examples, I shall illustrate that it likely had important consequences.

To guide us through the examples I shall immediately preview the main insights, and also point towards Table 8.1. In the presence of aggregate risk we find that evolution may favor people who: (i) diversify, (ii) avoid aggregate risk, (iii) have a relative high discount rate and so are impatient, and (iv) have a discount rate that decreases with age consistent with decreasing impatience. Clearly, aggregate risk makes a difference. Most interestingly, it offers an explanation for both risk aversion and hyperbolic discounting. So, let's work through the four examples.

Table 8.1 The four examples involving aggregate risk

Example	*Brief description*	*Implication*
Collecting food for winter	The extended family of types who randomly determine how much food to collect will be most able to prosper in good years and survive bad years.	Risk aversion and desire to diversify.
Living together or separately	It's better they live separately. If they live together there is a small probability of the population growing very large but a large probability that the population will end up small.	Should avoid aggregate risk.
Surviving the winter	Aggregate risk should not affect how much people discount the future, because it is relative individual differences that matter, and aggregate risk affects everyone equally.	The discount rate will be relatively high, suggesting impatience.
Something happens to 24-year-olds	Before they are 24 people should be relatively impatient because the aggregate shock at 24 lowers the expected growth rate of the population.	Hyperbolic discounting, and increasing patience with age.

In the first example, think about people collecting enough food to survive winter. Winters are either long or short and people are of two types, Long types who store enough food to survive any winter, and Short types who store enough to survive a short winter but not enough to survive a long winter. Because of the extra time spent collecting food, Long types have a 0.5 chance of surviving the summer while Short types have a 0.75 chance. What will happen? Despite being better at surviving summers, the Short types are doomed to extinction because they will all die in the first long winter! Evolution, thus, favors Long types.

Consider, now, a new type of person who at the start of each summer randomly decides whether to store enough food for a long winter or short winter. The extended family of such Mixed types stand to do well because in any year some of them will collect enough for a long winter and some will not. That some of them do not collect enough for a long winter means the family can grow at a relatively quick rate. That some of them do collect enough for a long winter means the family will never be wiped out by one long winter. It turns out that evolution will favor people who store enough for a long winter with probability $3p$, where p is the probability of a long winter (see Review question 8.2).

This example shows that in the presence of aggregate risk the optimal strategy may involve randomizing. This might look like an argument for risk-loving behavior, but actually it is more of an argument for risk aversion and diversification, because it shows that risks, like a long winter, should be guarded against.

Another way to interpret this first example is that in the presence of aggregate risk it may make sense to have idiosyncratic gambling. The next example takes this point one stage further by showing that idiosyncratic risk is preferred to aggregate risk.

A group of people are now deciding where to live and have two options. They could all live together in one big village or live separately. Every year each person has two children and, no matter where they live, there is a 0.5 chance that one child will not survive the winter because, say, there is an attack by a rival tribe. The difference is that, if everyone lives together, this risk is aggregate, so there is a 0.5 chance that everyone in the group will have only one surviving child. If they all live separately, the risk is idiosyncratic, so each person independently has a 0.5 chance of having only one surviving child. Should they live together or separately?

It turns out that they should live separately (see below). The general lesson to take from this is that evolution will favor people who avoid aggregate risk. To give some intuition for why this is the case: after a few years, aggregate risk leads to a small probability of there being a very large population but a large probability of there being a very small population. It is best to avoid such a gamble, and people do that by avoiding aggregate risk. Interestingly, however, a person by himself may not be able to avoid aggregate risk because it depends on what others do. For example, Edward and Anna cannot live alone if others follow them. This creates interdependence between individuals that we shall explore a bit more later on.

[Extra] Why should they live separately? For simplicity, suppose that no adult ever survives the winter. In both cases the expected population size by year t is $N(t) = 1.5^t N(0)$, where $N(0)$ is the original population size. In terms of expected utility, therefore, both options are equivalent. In an evolutionary sense, however, they are different. If they live separately, the number of people will be very close to $N(t) = 1.5^t N(0)$ because the risk is idiosyncratic. The growth rate of the population will, therefore, be:

$$\frac{\ln N(t) - \ln N(0)}{t} = \ln 1.5.$$

If everyone lives together, the population size will be $N(t) = 2^{b(t)} N(0)$, where $b(t)$ is the number of years in which all children survived. The growth rate now is:

$$\frac{\ln N(t) - \ln N(0)}{t} = \frac{b(t)}{t} \ln 2 \rightarrow \frac{1}{2} \ln 2 = \ln \sqrt{2}.$$

The growth rate if they live separately exceeds that if they live together.

In the final two examples I want to return to the issue of when Edward should have children. First, imagine that the length of winter can be anything from $l = 100$ to 50 days long. The longer it is, the less chance that a person survives the winter where the probability of survival is $s(l) \in (0,1)$. That the probability of survival $s(l)$ depends on the random length of the winter implies that there is aggregate risk. That each person survives independently with probability $s(l)$ means that there is also idiosyncratic risk. Does the aggregate risk make any difference to how Edward should discount the future?

Robson and Samuelson (2009) showed that Edward should maximize expected utility, discounting exponentially, with a discount rate equal to $\ln \varphi - \ln s$ where $\ln \varphi$ and $- \ln s$ are the rate of population growth and death rate that there would be without aggregate risk. This sounds like equation (8.3), but there is a difference. Aggregate risk, for the same reasons as in the previous example, will lower the actual population growth rate below what it would be without aggregate risk. Some numbers will help illustrate.

Suppose that in 'normal' conditions a population grows at 2 percent a year with a death rate of 4 percent a year, numbers plausible in human evolution. Also suppose that every so often a catastrophe occurs that decimates the population and means that, in the long run, population growth is around zero a year, which is also plausible in human evolution. Evolution will favor individuals who ignore the aggregate risk of the catastrophe and have a discount rate of $2 + 4 = 6$ percent. If we had gone off equation (8.3), we would have expected a discount rate of $2 + 0 = 2$ percent.

The catastrophe proves irrelevant, in an evolutionary sense, because it is an aggregate shock that affects all in the same way. This means that it will not alter the number of children that Edward has relative to another and so he can ignore it. This makes people relatively impatient, because they should discount at, say, 6 percent rather than 2 percent a year. It also means that we should not be surprised to see higher discount rates than might seem sensible, given observed population growth and death rates.

In the final example, suppose that, for some reason, the average temperature has an effect on the survival rate of people who are 24 years old. To model this, we say that the probability of survival is $s(l) + d(\text{temp.})$ for anyone aged 24, for some function $d(\text{temp.})$, while the probability of survival for anyone not aged 24 remains $s(l)$. For instance, if $d(5) > 0$ and $d(-5) < 0$, then someone aged 24 has a higher probability of survival than others if the temperature is five, and a lower probability if it is minus five. This creates an aggregate shock that affects all 24-year-olds.

If Edward is not yet 24, the possibility of an aggregate shock when he is 24 should reduce the value he puts on children that he might have after he is 24. This is because aggregate risk, as we have seen, lowers the expected growth rate of the population. Edward should, therefore, be relatively impatient to consume intermediate goods and have children just before he is 24. Intriguingly, this is the case even if the aggregate shock at age 24 makes it is more likely that he will survive when he is 24 than at any other age!

This shows that, with age-specific aggregate risk, the discount rate will change with age. So, evolution need not necessarily favor individuals who use exponential discounting. In fact, provided the age-specific effects are relatively small, the best thing is hyperbolic discounting where the discount rate decreases with age. Thus, evolution can help explain why we see the types of time preferences discussed in Chapter four, although we have yet to see any explanation for time inconsistency.

8.1.4 Competing with others

The picture I have given so far is one of evolution as a struggle between Edward and the environment. This, however, is only half of the story because evolution is also a struggle between different people. A further two examples will help illustrate why this matters. Table 8.2 summarizes.

Suppose that some people are cooperative and some are non-cooperative. People randomly meet each other in pairs and collect food. Two cooperative people go together and share any food they collect. A non-cooperative person collects food with a cooperative person but then takes all the food. Finally, two non-cooperative people go off and steal the food from cooperative people! Payoffs are summarized in Table 8.3 (and see Research Methods 8.1 for how to interpret these payoffs).

Table 8.2 The two examples with interdependence

Example	*Brief description*	*Implication*
Cooperators and non-cooperators	If cooperators can find some way to interact more with each other than non-cooperators, then they can prosper. The result is a signaling game of hide-and-seek, where cooperators try to distinguish themselves and non-cooperators try to copy them.	Seemingly irrelevant things can become important evolutionary signals.
Different ability at finding food	Women should prefer to mate with men who are better at finding food, which means that men need to appear good at finding food.	People should be good at signaling their desirable attributes.

Table 8.3 The payoffs if people are cooperative or non-cooperative

		Person 2	
		Cooperative	Non-cooperative
Person 1	Cooperative	1, 1	0, 2
	Non-cooperative	2, 0	0.5, 0.5

Research Methods 8.1

Evolutionary game theory

Once we recognize the importance of interactions between individuals it is natural to turn to game theory. Game theory has developed tools specific for modeling evolution which we can illustrate with a hawk-dove game introduced to model animal conflict.

Consider two animals competing for food with a value of V. Each animal can either attack or share. If they share, each gets $V/2$. If one attacks and the other shares, the attacker takes all the food. If both attack, there is a conflict that costs 0.5C, and each has an equal chance of winning the food. The payoff matrix is given in Table 8.4. To put this in an evolutionary context we think of the strategy, attack or share, as a genetic trait or **phenotype** that is constant through the animal's lifetime and inherited by offspring. We also think of the payoffs as representing the net additional offspring that the animal will get from consuming the food (in a similar way to section 8.1.1).

Table 8.4 Payoffs in the hawk-dove game

		Animal 2	
		Attack	Share
Animal 1	Attack	$(V-C)/2$, $(V-C)/2$	V, 0
	Share	0, V	$V/2$, $V/2$

Imagine that the population was full of animals who share. If a mutation produces an animal with the attack strategy, this animal would have relatively many offspring. The strategy attack would, therefore, spread. Now imagine that the population was full of animals that attack. If $V < C$, an animal who shares would have relatively many offspring and the strategy share would spread. The population will be stable if the payoff from attacking is the same as sharing. If proportion p^* of animals attack, this requires:

$$\left(\frac{V-C}{2}\right)p^* + (1-p^*)V = (1-p^*)\frac{V}{2}.$$

This simplifies to $p^* = V/C$. This is known as the evolutionary stable strategy and means that we should expect to see a mix of animals that attack and share.

More generally, an **evolutionary stable strategy** details the proportion of the population that should be of each type if the population is to remain stable over time. Typically we would expect the population to converge to an evolutionary stable strategy and so these strategies tell us a lot about the likely consequences of evolution.

I will briefly note that there is an important, and intriguing, connection between an evolutionary stable strategy and symmetric Nash equilibrium. The connection is as follows: if p^* is an evolutionary stable strategy, then 'both animals choose p^*' is a Nash equilibrium; the converse need not hold. The notion of evolutionary stable strategy offers, therefore, a form of equilibrium refinement (see Research Methods 6.3). This is intriguing because the two concepts are subtly different, and have different historical routes. Recall, a Nash equilibrium is such that anyone who deviates gets a lower payoff than if he did not deviate. An evolutionary stable strategy, by contrast, is such that anyone who deviates gets a lower payoff than those who do not deviate.

Unfortunately, evolution will favor non-cooperative people because they always have a higher payoff than cooperative people. Suppose, however, that cooperative people start to grow longer noses than non-cooperative people, meaning that people can tell who is cooperative and who is not. Now the odds swing back in favor of the people who are cooperative because they can make sure they only interact with each other. This means that they can get a payoff of one, while non-cooperative people only get a payoff of 0.5. Evolution will now favor cooperative people. Unfortunately, though, the non-cooperative people might fight back by growing noses as long as the cooperative people.

This example illustrates how evolution can result in signaling games of hide-and-seek (not unlike that which we looked at in the last three chapters). Evolution will favor cooperators who can signal that they are cooperators. But it will also favor non-cooperators who can look like cooperators. This game of hide-and-seek can mean that seemingly irrelevant traits, like the length of nose, can become an important battleground of evolution.

What's going on here is something called assortative matching. We say that there is **assortative matching** if it is more likely that certain types will meet than others. If a cooperator is more likely to interact with a cooperator, then a non-cooperator is likely to interact with a cooperator, and then there is assortative matching. This is crucial if cooperators are not to be exploited by non-cooperators, and so assortative matching is crucial if evolution is to favor cooperative people.

We see interesting evidence of assortative matching in human interaction, the 'lie detector' being one example. Experimental economists and psychologists have also shown that individuals have varying abilities to predict what an opponent will do in a game even if they only meet or see that person for a few seconds. For example, Pradel and co-authors (2009) did a study in which schoolchildren, aged ten to 19, were asked to predict what their classmates would do in a dictator game (see Chapter seven for more on this game). As we would expect, there was a split of children offering nothing (8 percent of children), half the amount (49 percent of children), or something in between.

Research Methods 8.2

Experimenting with children

The study by Pradel and co-authors involved children aged ten to 19 as subjects, and I am going to talk later about two more studies that involved children. So, psychologists and behavioral economists do sometimes use children as subjects. This can be for convenience, because a school might provide a large group of willing volunteers. For the most part, though, it's because looking at how children behave can provide insight into the causes of behavior.

For instance, if we get children to play the ultimatum game and find they very rarely reject offers, then we can say that the desire to reject seems to develop later in life. Indeed, this might suggest that it is a cultural thing (although care is needed because things can develop later in life for genetic reasons, breasts being a fairly obvious example). We shall come back to such issues in section 8.2.4. Ideally we would like to experiment with very young children to see how economic behavior develops with age. That, though, poses some challenges. For example, young children need an incentive other than money and can more easily lose attention.

The most important thing for us is that the children were good, better than chance, at predicting what others would do, and were particularly good at knowing who would give nothing. This is illustrated in Figure 8.1, where we see that children were much better than chance at predicting the giving of friends and those they dislike. Furthermore, this was not just due to friends being like them, but a genuine ability to predict giving.

If we are able to predict what others will do, then assortative matching becomes very relevant in understanding human cooperation. On a related note, the next thing I want to show is that evolution can lead to a desire for Edward to signal his good attributes.

Suppose that males differ in their skill at finding food and let $y \in (0,1)$ be an unobservable measure of a man's skill. The cost to a man of type y to find f calories of food is $c(f) = (y + 1 - f)^2$. More food improves the probability of children surviving, so let the benefit of finding f calories be $b(f) = 2f$. If mating is random, a type y male will collect food until the marginal benefit of two equals the marginal cost of $2(y + 1 - f)$, so he collects $f = y$ calories. As we might expect, a male collects more food if he has more skill.

This means, however, that we should not expect to see random mating. Instead evolution will favor females who are fussy who they mate with and search out those more skilled at finding food. But then males have an incentive to signal that they are skilled at finding food, and they can do this by collecting lots of food. To illustrate, consider the most extreme case, where females will only mate with the

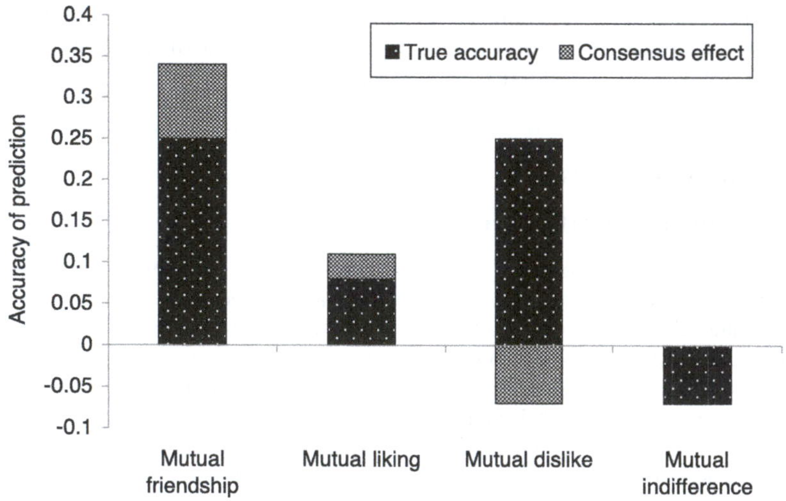

Figure 8.1 Accuracy of children's ability to predict the giving of fellow students in a dictator game, above that of guessing randomly. High accuracy could be because children expected those they like more to behave more like them, a consensus effect. Even taking this into account, however, children were good at predicting the giving of those they knew.

Source: Pradel *et al.* (2009).

male who collects the most food. This turns things into an auction which completely changes the benefit of finding f calories. Collecting $f = y$ calories no longer makes any sense because each male needs to collect more food than the others. There will be a race to the top, and a lot more food.

In this case evolution will favor those who are good at signaling their ability to find food. More generally, we see another important evolutionary struggle, sometimes called **sexual selection**, between men and women. Evolution will favor people who are fussy who they mate with and look for the partner most likely to have healthy, well-looked-after children. This means that relative traits like strength, health, and faithfulness become important. It also means that a person's ability to signal their desirable attributes becomes important. This provides an explanation why status and conspicuous consumption may be valid intermediate goods because those with higher status, who use conspicuous consumption to signal their status, may look more attractive to the opposite sex.

We have now started to touch on situations where culture will matter. This is because we have moved away from talking about intermediate goods, like food, that objectively increase the probability of having children, to goods, like stylish hair, or a new sports car, that increase the probability of having children if and only if they impress others. In different cultures different things might impress: in one place stylish hair and in another stylish clothes. So, now seems a good point to start adding culture to the mix.

8.2 Culture and multi-level selection

For the most part humans are very similar the world over. We all smile, laugh, cry, and get angry in similar ways over similar things. This is a consequence of evolution. Behavior is not, however, solely determined by our genes. It is also shaped by the culture that we live in. Elsewhere in the book I have looked in some detail at how people can be influenced by what they see others doing and saying, and so I will not spend too much time here showing why culture matters. Instead, I want to focus on how culture can interact in interesting ways with evolution. To put this into some context it is useful to start by seeing if there are cross-cultural differences.

8.2.1 Cross-culture comparisons

I am going to look at three cross-culture comparisons. In each we compare how people behave in different cultures to see if there are systematic differences. You may want to look back at the previous chapter for an explanation of the games we shall look at.

I'll start with a fascinating study by a group of economists and anthropologists, where the **ultimatum game** was played with members of 15 small-scale societies (Henrich and co-authors 2004). This can be coupled with a study by Roth and co-authors (1991), and the hundreds of other ultimatum game experiments performed around the world with university students, to give a picture of how behavior varies across cultures. Figure 8.2 shows proposer offers in a variety of different places.

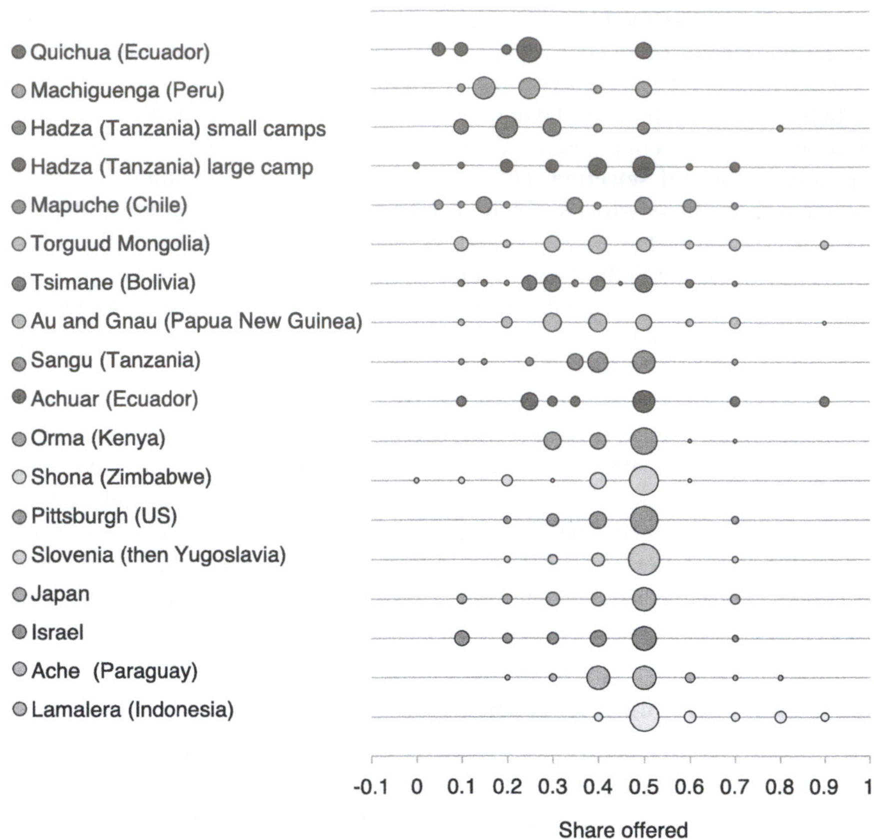

Figure 8.2 Ultimatum game offers across different cultures.

Source: Henrich *et al.* (2004), Roth *et al.* (1991).

In all cases we see that proposers give something, and so the picture we gave in Chapter seven still holds true. There is, however, clearly a large variation in how much people give. To see why, it's useful to look in a bit more detail at some of the societies.

The most giving was observed in Lamalera. This is a village located on an island in Indonesia where whale hunting is integral to village life. Whale hunting can only be done in groups and so cooperation and sharing is a big part of village life.

At the other extreme is the Machiguenga of the Peruvian Amazon. Here we observe the least giving. The Machiguenga have traditionally lived in single family units and so sharing or cooperation outside of the family is rare.

The Achuar and Quichua are two ethnic/political groups in Conambo in the Ecuadorian Amazon. To look at the data it would seem that the Quichua give less than the Achuar. It turns out, however, that the differences can largely be put down to politics. High-status males in Conambo give meat in order to maintain strong alliances, and a strong correlation was observed between meat-giving and offers in the ultimatum game. The relatively low status of the Quichua men can, therefore, explain the relatively low offers.

Finally, Au and Gnau are the languages spoken in two villages located near to each other in Papua New Guinea. The results in these villages were noticeable for the large rejection rates. The overall rejection rate was 32.8 percent, and three offers of a 0.7 share were rejected! When gifts are given by the Au and Gnau, it is understood by both the giver and receiver that the acceptor has incurred a debt that must be repaid at some future point. It can, therefore, be wise to not always accept a gift.

This gives only a snapshot of the differences across the different societies but does illustrate how behavior was influenced by everyday experience. People more used to sharing shared more, and people not used to sharing shared less, and so on. Henrich and co-authors take this one stage further by constructing two indices for each of the 15 societies they considered: payoffs to cooperation, which depends on local ecology, and aggregate market integration, which depends on things such as social complexity and settlement size. There was a strong correlation between payoffs to cooperation, aggregate market integration, and offers in the ultimatum game. Those more used to cooperating, sharing, and interacting with others offered more.

Research Methods 8.3

Statistics and lies: more, less, or just different?

Comparing behavior in the ultimatum game across countries provides a good opportunity to illustrate what data and statistical tests tell us and what they do not. Figure 8.2 plots the distribution of offers. Why not just plot the mean, mode, or median offers instead? This does not give such a complete picture of the data and can mislead. For example in the Ache, the modal offer was 0.4, which is less than the 0.5 in most other societies, including the Mapuche, but the mean offer was higher than in many other societies, including the Mapuche.

While it is tempting to want to say that giving is higher in one society than in another, in many cases this is simply impossible to do. For example, were offers higher in the Achuar, or Ache, or Sangu? There is no way to answer that question. This also means that care is needed in interpreting statistical tests. Many tests, such as the Mann-Whitney, have a null hypothesis that two samples are drawn from the same distribution and an alternative, in this instance, that one sample stochastically dominates another. The primary thing learnt from a rejected test is that the samples are drawn from different distributions. A little care is needed in interpreting the results of such tests.

A more recent study by Gächter and co-authors (2010) provides a cross-cultural comparison of behavior in a **public good game with punishment**.

The most interesting thing to come out of this was differences in the use of punishment. Figure 8.3 plots the frequency of punishment relative to whether the subject contributed more than the average, the same as the average, or less than the average by varying amounts.

As we might expect, those who contributed less were punished, and the frequency of punishment did not vary too much across the locations. More surprising was the frequency of punishment for those who contributed above average. In places such as Boston, Melbourne, and Nottingham, there was little punishment of those contributing above average. In Muscat, Athens, and Riyadh, by contrast, those giving above average were punished as much as those giving below average. The best explanation for this is **anti-social punishment**, as a form of revenge. In particular, there was a strong correlation between punishment received in one period and that given out in the next. So, those punished for giving less seemingly tried to punish those who had punished them!

The consequence of anti-social punishment was less cooperation. For example, mean contributions were 18 out of 20 in Boston and 17.7 in Copenhagen, but only 5.7 in Athens and 6.9 in Riyadh. The good news of the previous chapter, therefore, namely that a threat of punishment can increase cooperation, needs to be toned down a little. The threat of punishment does not seem to work everywhere. So, why were there such differences in punishment?

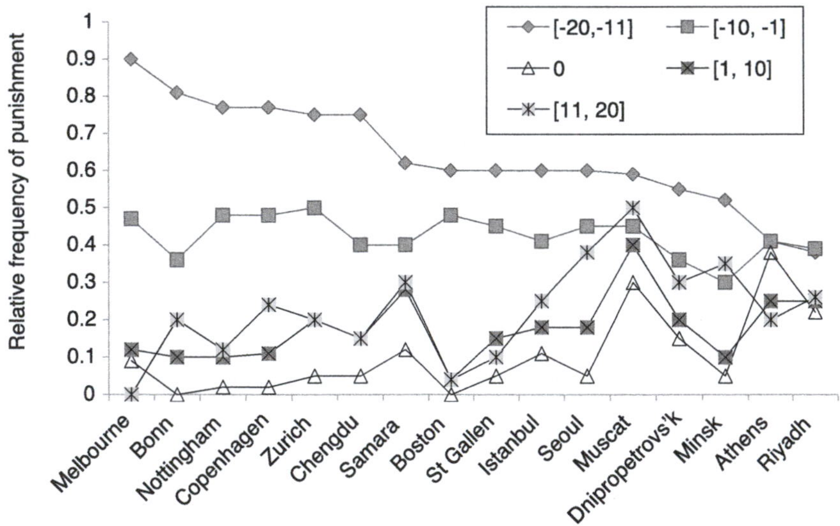

Figure 8.3 Punishment in a public good game in different locations. The proportion of times people were punished depended on whether they contributed a lot less [−20,−11], less [−10,−1], the same [0], more [1,10], or a lot more [11,20] than the person punishing.

Source: Herrmann *et al.* (2008).

One explanation is the strength of law and norms of civic cooperation in society. The stronger the rule of law, the less people might think that they need to rely on revenge, and the stronger the norms of cooperation, the less people will want to punish those behaving in a socially desirable way. Consistent with this, Gächter and co-authors show that punishment of those who contributed less is positively correlated with stronger norms of civic cooperation, while punishment of those who contributed more is negatively correlated with the strength of both law and norms of civic cooperation. Again, we see local institutions and norms making a difference.

The final cross-cultural comparison I want to look at is that of **trust**. The World Values Survey is a large-scale survey of attitudes across a very broad selection of countries. The survey was first conducted in 1981 and has been done several times since. The survey is a fantastic source of information on how values and attitudes change across time and location. One question asked is: 'Generally speaking, would you say that most people can be trusted or that you need to be very careful in dealing with people?' The possible answers are 'Most people can be trusted' or 'Can't be too careful'. Figure 8.4 details by country what proportion thought most people can be trusted in the 1981 to 2000 data.

There is clearly large variation in what proportion say they can trust. Trust is relatively low in Eastern Europe, South America and Africa, and relatively high in Scandinavia. But does this matter? In the previous chapter we saw that trust can be beneficial in simple experimental games and it appears that this does transfer over to the real economy. Knack and Keefer (1997), for example, using data up to 1991, find that a 10 percent rise in the proportion who say they can trust

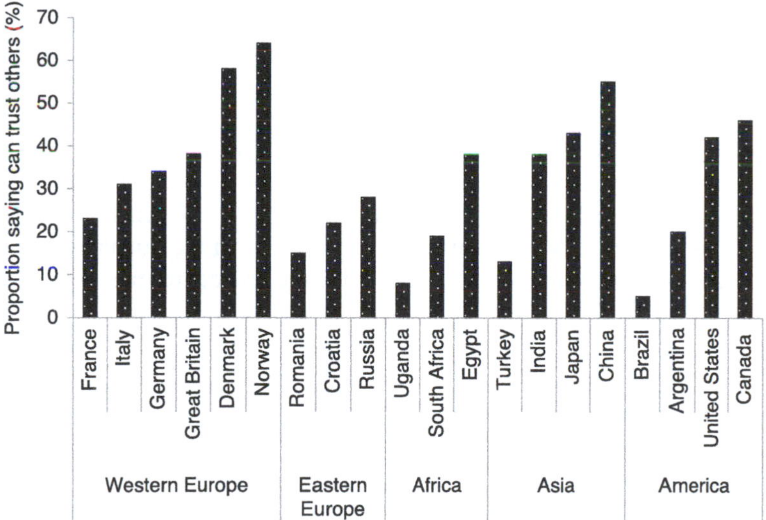

Figure 8.4 The proportion of respondents who said 'most people can be trusted'.

Source: World Values Survey (2009).

is associated with a 0.8 percent increase in economic growth. This would suggest that the level of trust is potentially very important for the economy.

So what lessons can we take from these three cross-cultural comparisons? There seem to be two main ones. First, there is significant variation in how people behave across societies and cultures. In some places we see on average more giving, more cooperation, and more trust than others. Second, this variation appears to come in large part from variation in institutions and norms. This does create a kind of chicken and egg problem of what comes first. Does behavior influence the norms and institutions that emerge, or do the institutions and norms that emerge influence behavior?

There are good reasons to think that it is at least partly the latter. The catalyst can be the environment that people live in. Some environments require cooperation for people to survive, like that of the Lamalera, while some environments allow people to be largely self-sufficient. The environment could, therefore, influence the norms and institutions that emerge which then influence behavior. The main thing, though, is that we observe cultural variation. What I want to do now is see what implications this variation might have for evolution.

8.2.2 Group selection

That there are cultural differences implies that there must be distinct groups of people for different cultures to emerge. In our evolutionary past people will clearly have been separated into groups based on kinship and geography. This can give rise to something called **group selection** in which evolution acts on the level of the group rather than on the level of the individual. We have already come across this in section 8.1, where we saw that evolution might favor groups who avoid aggregate risk. I now want to take things one stage further.

To do so I will look at a stylized model of group selection called the **haystack model**. It gets its name from thinking of mice living in haystacks, but I will frame things in terms of people living in fields. So, imagine that nature provides fields with enough food that people can survive happily. The model then consists of three recurring stages, summarized in Table 8.5. In the first stage people randomly decide what field to live in. They then live together for T generations. After T generations all the fields are destroyed and everyone in the population is mixed together, before nature provides new fields and the process repeats itself. The key

Table 8.5 The three recurring stages of the haystack model. Natural selection takes place in stage 2, but group selection takes place overall

Stage	*Description*
1	People in the population randomly decide what field to live in.
2	People who chose the same field live together as a distinct colony for T generations.
3	The fields are destroyed and everyone in the population is mixed together.

is the periodic separation of people into distinct colonies and then mixing together when the fields are destroyed. This can lead to group selection.

To see why, suppose that there are cooperative people and free-riders. Cooperative people go out and collect food which is then shared amongst others. This costs c but benefits everyone in the colony by amount b/N where N is the number of people in the colony. Free-riders do not collect any food for others. So, if $q(t)$ is the proportion of cooperators in a colony at time t, we can assume that cooperators have $a + bq(t) - c$ children and free-riders have $a + bq(t)$ children, where a is some positive number.

Suppose that $b/N < c$ but $b > c$. Then we have a linear public good game where collecting food is the public good. Because $b > c$, the more cooperators a colony has, the more children will be produced in that colony. But, because $b/N < c$, a free-rider will always have more children than a cooperator. This latter effect means that, if T is small, free-riders will have more children, and free-riders will eventually dominate the population. Fortunately, if T is large, then colonies with more cooperators will have time to grow relatively large. This means that cooperators could be dominant in the population.

To illustrate, suppose that there are two fields. Field 1 starts with ten cooperators, and field 2 with nine cooperators and one defector. Figure 8.5 plots the proportion of each type over time. In the second field the number of free-riders exceeds the number of cooperators after 18 generations. Eventually, free-riders will dominate this colony. The colony in field 1, however, grows at a higher

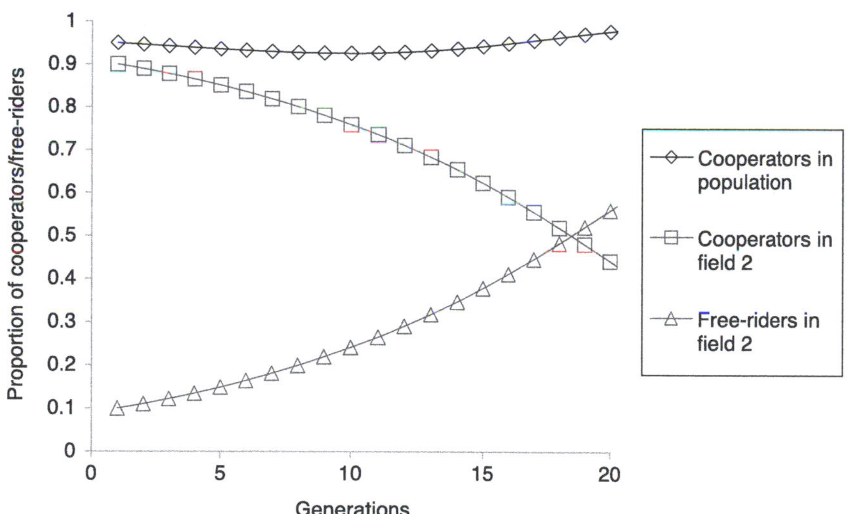

Figure 8.5 An example of the haystack model, where $a = 1$, $b = 3$, $c = 0.5$; field 1 starts with ten cooperators, and field 2 with nine cooperators and one defector. Field 2 becomes full of free-riders, but the overall population is still full of cooperators.

rate because it is full of cooperators. This means that after ten generations the proportion of cooperators in the total population is increasing. Thus, cooperation can be sustained in the population if colonies with cooperators have long enough to benefit from being cooperative.

The haystack model shows that cooperative behavior *can* be sustained through group selection. As in section 8.1.3 this is possible because of **assortative matching**. A cooperator in a colony full of cooperators is more likely to meet a cooperator than is a free-rider in a colony full of free-riders. Thus, cooperators can do relatively well despite their apparent disadvantage relative to free-riders. For this to work we need the repeating process of reproduction in distinct colonies which then disperse and intermingle.

Some care, however, is needed not to read too much into group selection. Group selection does not mean that evolution will always favor what is good for the group and in reality it is typically a relatively weak force compared to individual selection. This is apparent in the haystack model where it is very unlikely that cooperation would emerge or spread. The best to hope for is that cooperation is not overtaken by free-riding. Even this only happens in ideal conditions!

The weakness of group selection should not, though, come as much surprise given what we saw in the previous chapter. There we saw that in social dilemmas most people behave either selfishly or reciprocate. We simply do not observe the cooperative, altruistic self-sacrifice that would be best for the group. That does not mean that group selection is not important. It just means that we need to be realistic in what it can achieve. What it might be able to do is help explain reciprocal altruism, as I shall now show.

When we looked at the haystack model we assumed a linear public good game without punishment. In this case, irrespective of $q(t)$, a cooperator always has c less offspring than a free-rider. Now suppose a third type emerges, willing to punish. A punisher will collect food and also at cost k lower the payoff of any free-rider by p. Now, if there are $q(t)$ cooperators, $l(t)$ punishers, and $f(t)$ free-riders, cooperators will have $a + b(q(t) + l(t)) - c$ children, free-riders $a + b(q(t) + l(t)) - pl(t)$, and punishers $a + b(q(t) + l(t)) - c - kf(t)$. What difference does punishment make?

We can see that cooperators will have more children than free-riders if $c < pl(t)$. Thus, cooperators will have more children than free-riders if the punishment given to free-riders is sufficiently high. Evolution could favor cooperation. There is, however, a second order free-rider problem that we need to worry about. A punisher pays both the cost of collecting food and of punishing, so likely has the fewest offspring. Will, therefore, there be enough punishers to sustain cooperation, or will people free-ride on punishing?

To illustrate, suppose that women punish men who free-ride by not having children with them. In an evolutionary sense this is an extreme form of punishment that favors cooperation. But a woman who does not punish has a greater choice of men to mate with than one who does not, so will likely have more children. This means that evolution will favor women who do not punish. One partial solution is to punish women who have children with a free-rider. That is, to punish people who do not punish. But then it would be necessary to have someone to punish those who do not punish those who do not punish, and so on! This is the **second order free-rider problem**.

The second order free-rider problem means that punishing behavior could not have arisen by individual selection. Crucially, however, the numbers have now changed in a way that cooperation and punishment is easier to sustain by group selection. To explain: without punishment a cooperator always has c less offspring than a free-rider, and so a cooperator is always at a large disadvantage relative to a free-rider; group selection has a lot to do to overcome this disadvantage. With punishment, a cooperator has more offspring than a free-rider and a punisher has $kf(t)$ less offspring than a cooperator. The crucial thing this means is that a punisher is only at a disadvantage if there are free-riders. Group selection has relatively less to do to help punishers overcome any disadvantage. This can tip the balance in a way that group selection can have a realistic role to play.

So, group selection is a plausible explanation for why we observe reciprocity. The story, however, is still a little incomplete. That's because while we now have a good story for why cooperation could be sustained through punishment, we still do not have much of a story for why cooperation and punishment would emerge in the first place. For that we need to add culture.

8.2.3 Gene-cultural co-evolution

Group selection relies on people being separated into distinct groups or cultures. Behavior is still, however, determined by genetic evolution. So, Edward is, say, cooperative because he has a cooperative gene that he inherited from his parents. His payoff is influenced by those in his culture, but his behavior is not. This is consistent with cross-cultural variation but gives only a very minor role to culture itself. What happens if we start to add a bit more cultural influence?

Observing and learning from others can lead to cultural transmission, in which ideas are passed from one person to another. Ideas might be passed from parent to child, **vertical cultural transmission**, or between people of the same generation, **horizontal cultural transmission**. In the same way that good strategies or behaviors might be favored by genetic evolution, good ideas might be favored by **cultural evolution**. For example, Edward might copy or inherit the cooperative, trusting behavior he sees in a friend. Or, he might copy the latest fashion of the day.

The interaction between cultural and genetic evolution raises some fascinating questions. These are encapsulated in the **nature versus nurture debate** about whether a person's behavior is more shaped by their genes or the environment they grow up in. Is Edward more likely to be cooperative because he has a cooperative gene or grew up with cooperative people? I am not going to explore such questions here. But I think it is worth briefly thinking about how cultural evolution interacts with genetic evolution. Does cultural evolution, for example, overwhelm genetic evolution?

To me that seems unlikely. After all, genetic evolution gave us and shapes our ability to learn from others. Genetic evolution would also put a stop to certain types of cultural evolution, particularly by vertical cultural transmission. For example, a family passing from generation to generation the idea: 'use contraceptives and only have one child' is probably not destined to last very long. Neither is a family with a norm to 'smoke, drink, and exercise rarely'. Things, though, can work the other way, and cultural evolution influences genetic evolution. For example, if there is a cultural norm to mate with tall people, then the average height of the population will likely rise over generations.

It seem most apt, therefore, to think of genetic and cultural evolution as part of one big process in which they complement each other rather than dominate each other. This interaction is termed **gene-culture co-evolution**. One interesting aspect of gene-culture co-evolution that I want pick up on here is how it can increase the possible strength of group selection. Let's see why.

Suppose that there is a **conformist bias**, whereby individuals copy the most prevalent behavior in the group or culture. We saw some evidence in Chapter five that this is plausible. I now want to think through what consequence this has in the haystack model. A conformist bias means that colonies will become relatively homogenous or, at least, more homogenous than they would be without a conformist bias. For example, if most people in a colony are cooperative, then others will conform to that and so the colony as a whole becomes more cooperative.

This has two consequences. First, it means that the differences between colonies become more stark. We tend to get fewer colonies with a mixture of types, and more colonies dominated by one type, either cooperators or free-riders. The second thing it does is make colonies resistant to change. For example, a free-rider who joins a colony full of cooperators may conform and change his behavior, rather than having lots of children who subsequently turn the colony into one of free-riding.

Both of these things make the group selection explanation for reciprocation more plausible. Indeed, it may be enough for punishment and cooperation to emerge rather than just survive, because cooperation, once established in one colony, can easily spread from colony to colony through cultural transmission. Also, in a group that has a cultural norm of cooperation, genetic evolution may favor individuals who do not free-ride. Cooperation in one colony may be enough, therefore, for cooperation to spread through the population.

The exact details of how reciprocation emerged are still hotly debated, and there are certainly a lot of ifs and buts in the story that I have just told. We saw in the last chapter, however, that reciprocation is common in human behavior and so this must have an evolutionary explanation. Gene-culture co-evolution seems to offer the most promising explanation we have.

8.2.4 Reciprocity in children and chimpanzees

In Section 8.1 I focused mainly on how evolution can shape individual decision making. In looking to explain social preferences, such as reciprocation, I have drawn increasingly on the role played by culture. It is natural to take account of culture when looking at social preferences because the focus is on interpersonal decision making. There is a sense, however, in which gene-culture co-evolution can seem like a bit of a fudge. The accusation would be that we are explaining behavior like reciprocity by adding more and more things to a complex model. Can we not find a cleaner distinction between the role played by evolution and culture?

The answer is almost certainly no. Neither evolution nor culture, on their own, seem enough to explain reciprocity. What we end up with, therefore, is an inevitable interplay between the two. One interesting way to illustrate this is to look at the social preferences of children and chimpanzees. By studying children and chimpanzees we get as close as we possibly can to stripping culture out of the equation (see Research Methods 8.2). We shall see, though, that culture still plays its role.

Let me start with a study by Proctor and co-authors (2013). They looked at chimpanzees playing a restricted choice version of the dictator and ultimatum game. The basic setup of an ultimatum game experiment is depicted in Figure 8.6. Two chimpanzees are next to each other. The proposer is offered two tokens and must choose one. One of the tokens equates to an offer of three banana rewards each, and the other token equates to five banana rewards for the proposer and one for the receiver. Having chosen a token the proposer must hand it to the receiver. The receiver then decides whether to hand it back to the experimenter. If it is handed back, the receiver and proposer get some banana. In the dictator game experiment, the proposer simply chooses a token and returns it straight to the experimenter.

In the dictator game experiment, chimpanzees chose the token giving an equal payoff 11 percent of the time. In the ultimatum game experiment the proportion rose to 72 percent. In other words, the chimpanzees were far more likely to offer a fair split than to give a fair split. This is similar to what we see in human subjects. Slightly puzzling, however, was that no chimpanzee ever rejected an unfair offer.

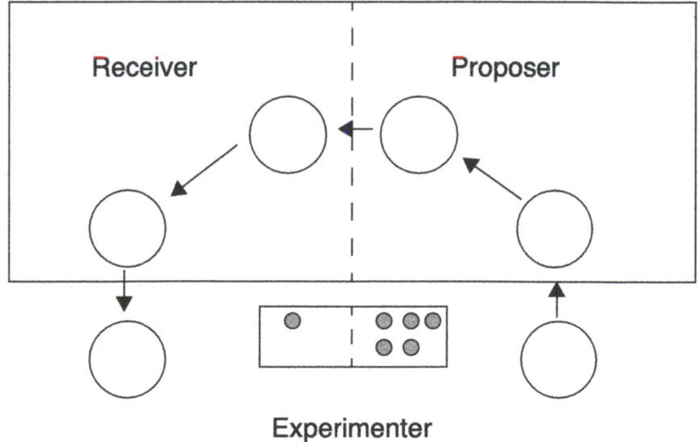

Figure 8.6 Experimental setup for an ultimatum game with chimpanzees.
Source: Proctor *et al.* (2013).

To delve a little deeper we can look at a study by Jensen, Call, and Tomasello (2007). They also had chimpanzees play a restricted choice ultimatum game. The slight twist is that they considered more games (and used raisins rather than bananas). Specifically, they looked at all of the four games in Table 7.6. Recall that in these games the responder could offer an 8 and 2 split or something else. The something else ranged from an equally unfair 2 and 8 split to an even more unfair 0 and 10 split. (We can think of the study by Proctor and co-authors as focusing on the 5/5 game.)

The left-hand side of Figure 8.7 looks at the proportion of times that chimpanzees offered the 8 and 2 split. This can be compared with human subjects. If you think carefully about the trade-offs in each game you should come to the conclusion that chimpanzees were less generous than humans. They were, however, willing to share a lot of the time. More interesting is the proportion of offers rejected. The right-hand side of Figure 8.7 shows that chimpanzees hardly ever rejected an 8 and 2 offer. This is in stark contrast to human subjects.

Both studies we have looked at show a similar pattern. Proposer chimpanzees were willing to share, but receiver chimpanzees hardly ever rejected. If, however, offers are never rejected, why were the chimpanzees willing to share in the first place? Inequality aversion may be part of the story, but comparison of the dictator and ultimatum game experiments tells us that it is only part of the story. Something else, therefore, is at work. That something else may be social norms. Chimpanzees who do not share food in the wild are more likely to be threatened or subject to a temper tantrum. Also, the ultimatum game requires both chimpanzees

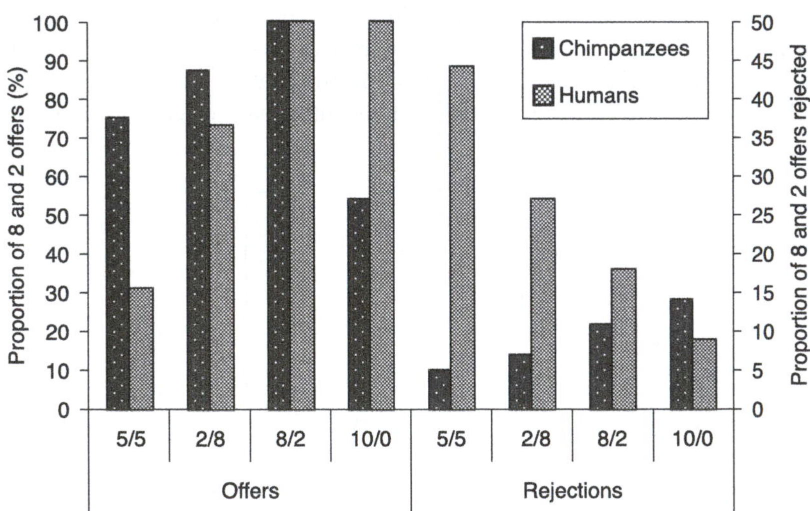

Figure 8.7 The proportion of eight and two offers by game and the proportion of 8 and 2 offers rejected.

Source: Jensen *et al.* (2007), Falk *et al.* (2003).

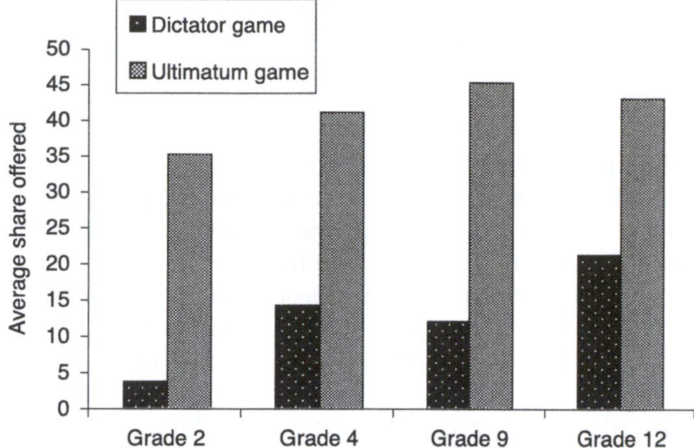

Figure 8.8 The share given in the dictator game and offered in the ultimatum game by school-aged children.

Source: Harbaugh *et al.* (2003).

to work on the task and so it may have seemed more normal to share the reward in this case than in the dictator game.

Consider next a study by Harbaugh *et al.* (2003) on giving in children. Figure 8.8 details the amount offered by children, aged between seven and 18, in a dictator and ultimatum game. We see that young children gave very little in the dictator game. Most children, however, offered a near 50:50 split in the ultimatum game. The behavior of young children looks similar to that of chimpanzees and things remain similar, although a bit more nuanced, when we look at rejection rates. Young children were willing to reject low offers, but they were less willing to reject than older children or adults.

Both chimpanzees and children used a 50:50 sharing rule. Is this due to culture or evolution? Recall from section 8.2.1 that not all cultures use a 50:50 sharing rule. We might, therefore, conclude that 50:50 sharing is a learnt social norm. This would explain why different cultures end up at different norms. It would also explain why the chimpanzees and children offered to share even though low offers were unlikely to be rejected. This story, however, has to be incomplete. Without an evolutionary advantage to sharing there is no way we would see such a universal willingness to share something (even if not always 50:50). Evolution, therefore, must play its role. Indeed, in the next chapter we shall see that giving and punishment are associated with 'older' or more 'primitive' areas of the brain.

The basic thing I am trying to illustrate here is the complex interplay between evolution and culture. Even in the seemingly simplest case of chimpanzees and children we see that there is no simple way to pull apart the influence that evolution and culture have. Over time we may find answers to some of the questions raised in this section, and this may give a somewhat clearer distinction between their respective influences. It seems clear, however, that a simple, clean distinction between the two is never going to emerge. Behavior, such as reciprocity, is shaped by a complex mix of both evolution and culture.

8.3 Summary

For most of us, finding food is now a simple task of going to the nearest supermarket, and we live well away from the savannahs of Africa. Hopefully, however, I have shown you that an evolutionary perspective is still useful in understanding modern economic behavior. Here's what we have seen.

We first saw that evolution will favor people who have good heuristics for maximizing expected utility. Intermediate goods that most increase the likelihood of having children will give most utility. We also saw that, when risks are idiosyncratic, evolution will favor people who use exponential discounting.

We also saw that the presence of aggregate risk and interdependence between people can have important implications. Aggregate risk can help explain risk aversion, impatience, and decreasing impatience with age. Interdependence between people can help explain why signaling and seemingly irrelevant traits become important; this, in turn, can help explain desires for things like status and esteem, and a keen ability to distinguish the motives or traits of others.

We next looked at the consequences of culture. Cross-cultural comparisons of behavior in the ultimatum game and public good game, and of trust, provided evidence that important cultural differences do exist. These differences seem to depend a lot on local institutions and norms. We then questioned whether group selection can help explain reciprocation, and argued that it probably can if we take account of cultural transmission. This suggests that social preferences are shaped by a mix of evolution and culture.

In sum, we have seen an evolutionary explanation for a cardinal utility function over intermediate goods, risk aversion, exponential and hyperbolic discounting, signaling and a desire for status and esteem, and reciprocity. That is by no means all the behaviors we have looked at in this book, but it is a pretty impressive list. For me, though, the most exciting thing about an evolutionary perspective is that it can suggest questions that we may have ignored without it. For example, we have seen that an evolutionary perspective predicts a big difference between aggregate risk and idiosyncratic risk. We now need to go away and ask whether we do observe this, and whether it matters. An evolutionary perspective also gives different insight on what is likely to give people high utility and what not. This will prove useful when we look at happiness in Chapter ten.

8.4 The gender gap

An issue that has always attracted much interest is the differences in opportunities and outcomes between men and women. I will not delve too deeply into how large and important these differences are, but Table 8.6 gives some figures from the World Economic Forum's Gender Gap Report 2012. Even in the highest-ranked

Table 8.6 Gender equality data

Country	*Ranking*	*Labor force participation (%)*		*Wage for similar work*	*Estimated earned income (PPP $)*		*Members of Parliament (%)*	
		Men	*Women*	*Men/Women*	*Men*	*Women*	*Men*	*Women*
Iceland	1	90	81	0.70	40,000	29,280	60	40
UK	18	82	69	0.68	40,000	29,752	78	22
US	22	80	68	0.67	40,000	37,376	83	17
Russia	59	76	69	0.62	26,877	16,609	86	14
China	69	85	74	0.66	10,156	6,592	79	21
Italy	80	74	52	0.49	40,000	21,465	78	22
Japan	101	84	62	0.60	40,000	22,096	89	11
India	105	85	35	0.62	5,635	1,530	89	11

Source: World Economic Forum, Global Gender Gap Report (2012).

country, Iceland, we see that men participate more in the labor market, earn higher wages, and are more represented in Parliament. An important question is whether such differences are due to discrimination against women or due to different preferences and choices of women. In the former case the gender gap is a problem we need to solve, but in the latter case it is not.

Maybe we can learn something about the gender gap by looking at whether men and women behave differently when making economic decisions. Let's see. Before I do that, one point is worth making. Men and women generally behave in very similar ways. There is certainly far more heterogeneity in behavior within gender than there is variation in behavior between genders. That said, there are some notable differences that we do observe between the behavior of the average woman and the average man. It is these differences in the averages that I want to look at.

8.4.1 Attitudes to risk

One difference we observe is in attitudes to risk. Women it seems are more risk averse than men. For example, several studies have shown that women are less likely than men to take risks in the economics laboratory. Other studies have shown that women are less willing to speed, more likely to wear a seat belt, brush their teeth, and have regular blood pressure checks than men. To illustrate, I shall look at one study by Jianakoplos and Bernasek (1998).

They looked at a sample of over 3,000 US households in 1989 to see whether women were less likely to invest in risky financial assets than men. The main findings are summarized in Table 8.7, which contains estimates of the share of risky assets that a household held. Across the board, single females invest less in risky assets than single men or couples. Also noteworthy is the effect of a change in wealth from $20,000 to $100,000. Both men and women are predicted to increase

Table 8.7 Predicted proportion of portfolio invested in risky assets. The baseline case is a 41- to 45-year-old white homeowner, employed, high school degree, $20,000 investment wealth, and two children

	Single females (%)	*Single males (%)*	*Married couples (%)*
Base case	43	51	48
Wealth = $10,000	35	39	39
= $20,000	43	51	48
= $100,000	62	79	69
= $500,000	81	100	89
Age = 26–30	23	63	47
= 31–35	32	42	37
Education = 6 years or less	77	79	50
Race = white	43	51	48
= black	58	49	42

Source: Jianakoplos and Bernasek (1998).

their share of risky assets, but men increase the share more than women. This is a sign of greater risk aversion in women.

In the long term risky assets give a higher rate of return and so differences in risk attitude can have large implications for investment return. For example, a return of 5 percent rather than 4.5 percent per year on a $1,000 investment will result in a $241 difference after 20 years. This can build up to a huge difference in wealth over a lifetime, suggesting that women will on average end up with less wealth than men.

Before moving on, I want to pick out three other notable things in Table 8.7. We see that young women are predicted to invest much less in risky assets than young men, while less educated, and black, women are predicted to invest more in risky assets. This is interesting, because it would suggest that differences in risk attitudes are due to culture as well as evolution. There is, for instance, no genetic reason why black women would invest so much more in risky assets.

8.4.2 Attitudes to competition

A second difference that we observe between men and women is how they respond to competition. Some studies have shown that men improve their performance when faced with competition, while women do not. Other studies have shown that, given the choice, men choose competitive environments while women do not. To illustrate, I shall look at two studies, the first by Gneezy and Rustichini (2004), the second by Niederle and Vesterlund (2007).

The Gneezy and Rustichini study was performed in a school in Israel and involved nine-to-ten-year-old children running a 40m track. First, each child ran by themselves and times were recorded. Next, pairs of children who recorded similar times were matched together and raced against each other. Finally, some children were just asked to run a second time by themselves. The results are summarized in

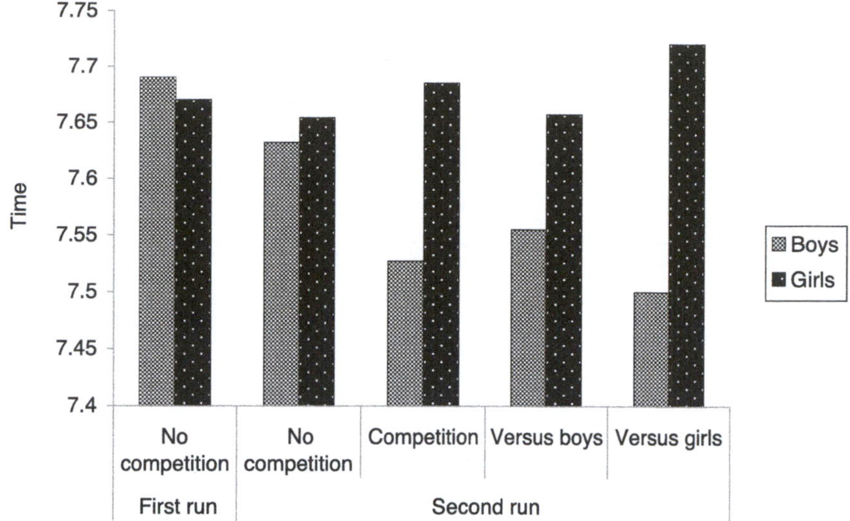

Figure 8.9 Running times of boys and girls. With no competition, there is not much difference in times. With competition, the boys get faster and the girls slower.

Source: Gneezy and Rustichini (2004).

Figure 8.9. In the first run, and when there was no competition, there are no differences between boys and girls. In a competitive environment, however, boys ran significantly faster and girls ran slower. Boys thus responded more to competition than girls. That this was observed in children maybe points more towards genes than culture?

The Niederle and Vesterlund study consisted of four parts. In the first three parts, subjects had five minutes to answer as many simple arithmetic problems as they could. In part 1 they were paid by a piece rate of $0.50 for each correct answer. In part 2 subjects were put in groups of four and payment was by tournament, the subject with the most correct answers getting $2 per correct answer. In part 3 participants could choose whether to be paid by piece rate or tournament. In part 4 subjects were asked to choose whether they wanted their part 1 performance paid by piece rate or tournament.

This sounds a bit complicated so I will go through it step by step. In the first two parts gender had no effect. Men and women were as good as each other with both the piece rate, where there was no competition, and the tournament, where there was competition. Interesting things start to happen in part 3 of the experiment, where subjects had to decide whether to be paid by piece rate or tournament. Figure 8.10 illustrates what happened by plotting the proportion of subjects who chose the tournament relative to how well they had performed. We see that men were more likely to choose the tournament than women.

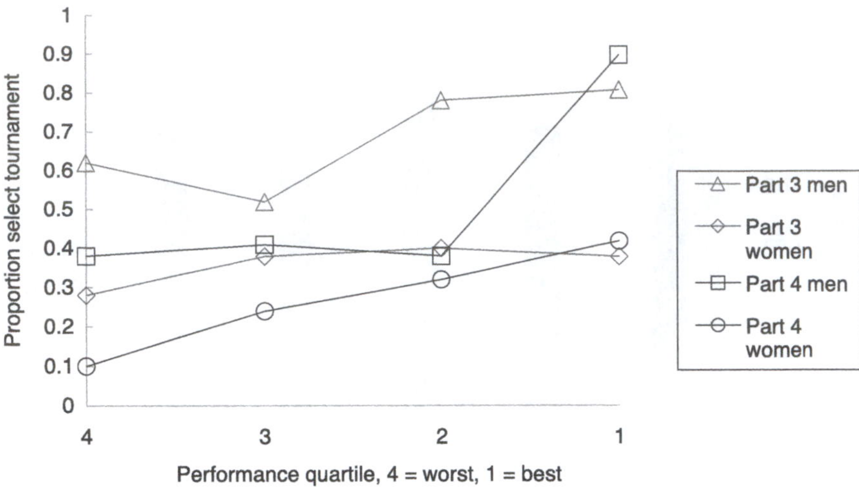

Figure 8.10 The proportion who chose competition conditional on how well they had performed.

Source: Niederle and Vesterlund (2007).

Indeed, the best-performing women, on average, chose the tournament less often than the worst-performing men! The story is similar, if slightly less dramatic, in part 4, where subjects were asked how they wanted to be paid for the first part of the experiment. Again, men were more likely to choose the tournament payment.

Research Methods 8.4

Incentives over time

If participants play the same game a number of times, issues arise about how to pay them and maintain good incentives. An obvious solution is to pay participants for every decision they make. If, however, a participant is going to make 25 decisions and be paid around $10 in total, then there is never going to be much incentive to make good choices. Also, if participants have in mind some reservation amount that they want from participating in the experiment, then choices may change if they achieve that amount. This is a real concern in the Niederle and Vesterlund (2007) study, where someone who does well in parts 1 and 2 may be more willing to take a risk in parts 3 and 4. To avoid this it is typical to pay participants for one randomly selected round or part of an experiment. This should maintain good incentives but can lead to somewhat lucky and unlucky participants!

We see, therefore, that men appear to react differently to competition than do women. I shall shortly try to explain why this might be the case. For now, however, I want to point out that much is still unknown about how competition effects interact with gender. For example, the Gneezy and Rustichini study suggests that women are less competitive with other women (see Figure 8.6). A complementary study by the same authors showed an opposite effect. We see similar complications when looking at social preferences.

8.4.3 Social preferences

In terms of social preferences there appears to be no simple relationship between gender and behavior. For example, in one set of experiments women might seem more altruistic, but then, in another, men might seem more altruistic. In specific contexts, however, gender has been shown to matter. To illustrate these points I shall compare studies by Eckel and Grossman (2001) and Solnick (2001). In both studies the ultimatum game was played between a receiver and proposer of known gender. In both cases we see that gender has an effect on receiver behavior.

In the study by Eckel and Grossman (2001), subjects had to divide \$5 and interacted in groups of four proposers and four receivers sitting opposite each other. A proposer could not know which of the four people sitting opposite would be the receiver to his or her offer, but one of them would be. Table 8.8 provides a snapshot of the results by looking at whether an offer of \$1 is accepted or rejected (according to a model that fits the data). We see that a \$1 offer from a female is more likely to be accepted than a similar offer from a male. We also see that females are more likely to accept than men. Eckel and Grossman call this chivalry and solidarity.

In the study by Solnick, subjects had to split \$10 and were not sitting opposite each other. A further difference is that receivers wrote down minimal acceptable offers before seeing the actual offer they had received (see Research Methods 7.2). Table 8.9 details the minimal acceptable offers of receivers. This time things look very different. We see that both male and female receivers set a higher minimal acceptable offer when the proposer is a female rather than a male. We also see females setting

Table 8.8 The percentage of \$1 offers accepted from a model fitted to the experimental data. For example, if the proposer was female, 36 per cent of males would accept the offer

		Responder (%)	
		Male	*Female*
Proposer	Male	20	39
	Female	36	78
	Unknown	17	42

Source: Eckel and Grossman (2001).

Table 8.9 Minimal acceptable offers. For example, if the proposer was female, the average amount that a male would accept was $3.39

		Responder	
		Male	*Female*
Proposer	Male	$2.45	$2.82
	Female	$3.39	$4.15
	Unknown	$2.71	$3.30

Source: Solnick (2001).

higher minimal acceptable offers than men. This means that, if a male offers a $7, $3 split to another male, it is likely to be accepted, while between two females it is likely to be rejected. There are no signs of chivalry or solidarity here.

The results of these two studies come to very different conclusions about receiver behavior. These differences could arise from the strategic environment. Female offers were more likely to be accepted when subjects could see each other and when they were responding to an actual offer. Female offers were less likely to be accepted when subjects could not see each other and were deciding before an offer had actually been made. Gender does, therefore, matter, but seemingly in ways that are conditional on the strategic environment.

8.4.4 Why are men and women different?

We have seen that gender seems to matter for behavior. Why? There are personality differences between men and women that could help explain the differences in economic behavior. Here are three of them.

First, women appear to experience stronger emotions than men. This could influence their behavior. For example, we saw in Chapters two and three the importance of loss aversion and risk aversion. Both of these are partly emotional responses connected to the fear of losing money or something else. Stronger emotions may also explain why women were less likely to reject when face to face with an ultimatum game opponent.

Second, men appear to be more overconfident than women, at least in some situations. This could make men more willing to gamble and to prefer competition. For example, Niederle and Vesterlund found that 75 percent of men thought that they would be the best in their group, compared to just 43 percent for women. Remember there were four in the group, so the number should have been 25 percent. Both men and women were overconfident, but men were far more overconfident!

Finally, men appear more stimulated by challenge than do women. Again, this could account for less risk aversion and a preference for competition. In the Niederle and Vesterlund study, for instance, there was less difference between men and women in part 4, which was about past behavior, than part 3, which was about a task yet to be done.

But why do we see these personality differences? Is it genetic or cultural? The answer is probably a mix of both. There are good evolutionary reasons why we could see such differences. For example, there is far more possible variation in the number of offspring that a man can have relative to a woman, so evolution could favor risk-taking, competitive men. Also, women differ from men in levels of testosterone and other hormones that are known to be correlated with things like aggression. Culture, however, can still play its part if boys and girls are raised and educated relative to stereotype. For instance, if women are expected to be less assertive, then we should not be surprised that on average women might become less assertive.

So, what about the gender gap? If men are less risk averse and more competitive than women, it is not hard to understand why a gender gap could arise. Whether the gender gap is a problem is a much more difficult question to answer. If genetic differences mean men and women want different things then maybe the gender gap is not such a problem. If the differences are cultural, then arguably there is more to be worried about. These are not questions I can answer, so I leave them for you to reflect on.

8.5 The economics of family

As I have already pointed out when looking at team decision making, it is typical in economics to focus on individuals. Occasionally we might talk about households, but it is only occasionally. Many economic decisions, however, are made as a family, or at least with the family in mind. For example, Edward and Anna might want to save money for their children's education, or save in order to bequeath something when they die. An evolutionary perspective is crucial to understanding such decisions.

One good reason to take account of evolution is kin selection. As a rough rule of thumb, half of a child's genes are inherited from the father and half from the mother. This means that evolution should favor mothers and fathers who look after their children and make sure that 'their genes' are passed on. More precisely, there is a **coefficient of relatedness** between a parent and child of 0.5, between a grandparent and child of 0.25, between brother and sister of 0.5, and so on. **Hamilton's rule** states that an individual who can, at cost C, benefit a relative by B should do so if $Br > C$ where r is the coefficient of relatedness between them. Put in its most extreme form, Anna or Edward may be willing to sacrifice their own life to save two or more of their children.

Kin selection brings the unit of selection down to the level of the gene (compared to the individual and group selection we have seen so far) and is a form of assortative matching because it means an individual tries to interact with and help family rather than unrelated individuals. This makes it much easier to understand transfers between family members. For instance, it is not really altruistic for Edward and Anna to pay for their children's education, it is just good evolutionary sense.

Kin selection matters in all species, but humans have taken it to a relatively extreme level. To see why, it's interesting to compare humans with primates, our closest relatives. Humans are distinctive in at least five ways: we (i) have bigger brains, (ii) live longer, (iii) spend longer as infants being dependent on parents, (iv) spend time in a post-reproductive age looking after grandchildren, and (v) find men supporting women and their offspring.

To illustrate, Figure 8.11 compares human consumption and production of food in three hunter-gatherer societies (Ache, Hadza, and Hiwi) and chimpanzees. In humans we see huge differences over a lifetime between production and consumption, and between men and women. In chimpanzees we see hardly any difference between consumption and production. What this means is that chimpanzees are largely self-sufficient. Humans are far from self-sufficient. Indeed, the basic story with humans is that men aged 20 to 60 acquire enough food to support those under 20 and women aged 20 to 45 who are looking after children. This involves big transfers within the family.

The leading explanation for why we see such transfers is humans' bigger brains. Bigger brains mean we need longer to develop, and that means we need the support of family when we are young. It also means that we need to live longer in

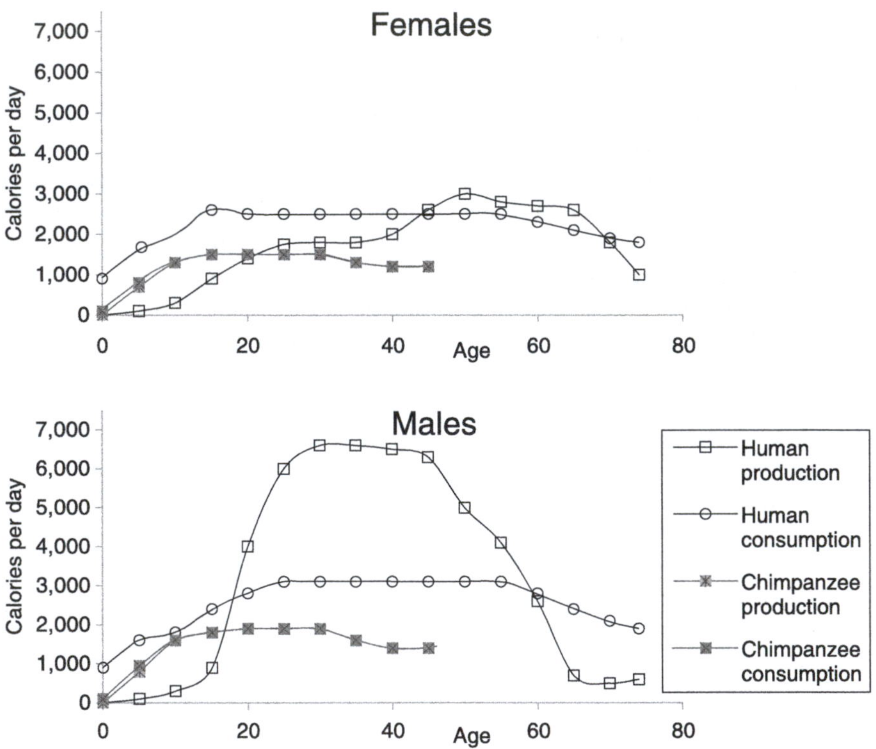

Figure 8.11 Food production and consumption by age in males and females, and in chimpanzees.

Source: Kaplan *et al.* (2000).

order to repay the debt that is accumulated in the early years of life. Luckily, a bigger brain also means that we have learnt more complicated ways to acquire food, and hence produce large amounts of food. It is a complicated mix, but everything holds together. What is not so clear is the catalyst that started the process. Did evolution favor big brains and we acquired ways to produce them? Or did evolution favor males who produced large amounts of food (see section 8.1.4) and big brains were a consequence?

What we can say for sure is that transfers within the family are an integral part of life. That is not going to stop just because food is more plentiful, for most of us, than in our evolutionary past. We should expect to see transfers between family members. This suggests we should more readily think of the household as most relevant in many economic decisions. It can also help us understand a bit better the transfers we do see, whether that be bequests, paying for education, or supporting a poor relative.

To illustrate, one recent trend of family life is the growing importance of **remittances** from migrant workers to their families back in the native country. For example, in 2007, remittances to Honduras were equivalent to 21.5 percent of that country's GDP, 13.9 percent in Serbia, 6.6 percent in Kenya, 3.3 percent in India, and 1 percent in China (figures from the World Bank). Put another way, over $45 billion was sent from the USA in 2007 in remittances. These are big numbers. Moreover, this possibility of sending back remittances has been a major motivation for individuals to seek work abroad, with the consequent increase in immigrant labor.

From an evolutionary point of view we should expect transfers to flow downwards from older to younger generations. This would suggest that remittances serve a 'helpers-at-the-nest' purpose, whereby a worker abroad, say, sends money back to his parents so that they can support younger offspring. An alternative possibility is that children are supporting relatively poorer parents and so there is a transfer from younger to older generations. This is hard to justify with an evolutionary explanation but easier to support with cultural transmission if it becomes an accepted norm for children to go abroad and support poorer parents. It is not clear yet which way the flows typically go, but a better understanding of the evolutionary and cultural forces at work may help provide the answers.

8.6 Development economics

One of the most basic goals of economics is to help alleviate poverty. The ideal would be that sound economic theory can create a world where resources are exploited efficiently and everyone has a comfortable standard of living. Unfortunately, economics does not have a great track record. While people in developed countries can have pretty much whatever they want, many in the rest of the world have to survive on next to nothing. Clearly, economics is not entirely to blame for this! There is, however, a litany of failed economic policies in developing countries. In this section I want to briefly look at how behavioral economics can explain such failure and offer alternatives.

Explaining why many economic policies have failed in developing countries is the easy bit. Development economics and economic policy has almost always been based on the standard economic model. This has led to policies that would work fine for homo economicus, but do not always work so well in reality. For instance, according to the standard economic model, people should be the same the world over, and so whatever works well in North American or Western Europe should work well anywhere. This mindset has driven policy. We have already seen, however, that this mindset is flawed because it ignores important, and systematic, cultural differences. Recall, for example, how the possibility of punishment works well to sustain cooperation in North American and Western Europe but makes things worse in the Middle East and Eastern Europe.

There is now an increasing recognition that development economics needs to take account of behavior, bias, cultural differences, and the like. Consequently, development economics is fertile ground for applying behavioral economics. It is worth highlighting that this is a two-way process, given that behavioral economics can also learn a lot from trying to tackle the problems relevant to developing countries. To illustrate the interplay between the two, I shall look at two of the more active areas of study – the education production function and microfinance.

8.6.1 The education production function

The Millenium Summit of the United Nations set eight millennium development goals to be reached by 2015. Number two on the list was to ensure that 'children everywhere, boys and girls alike, will be able to complete a full course of primary schooling'. This goal clearly recognizes the role that education can play in reducing poverty, and narrowing the gender gap. Steady progress is being made in achieving the goal, with enrolment in 2010 estimated at 90 percent, compared to 82 percent in 1999. Universal education is not, however, enough in itself. We also need the education to be of the highest possible standards. A lot of the early experimental work in development economics focused on this issue.

I shall start with a study by Glewwe and co-authors (2009). They questioned whether providing textbooks to rural Kenyan schools led to an increase in test scores. This is a particularly pertinent question given that policymakers seem to think it should. Indeed, the objective of the World Bank Free Primary Education Support Project in Kenya, that ran from 2003 to 2007 and cost $55 million, was to ensure 'an adequate supply and better use of instructional materials'. So do textbooks work? The simple answer seemed to be no. The study looked at an earlier project that began in 1995 and progressively increased the number of textbooks in 100 schools. The textbooks made no apparent difference to test scores, except for the most able students. That the textbooks are in English, the third language of most of the students, presumably did not help.

Spending money on textbooks may not, therefore, be a good idea. This is a surprising negative result. We can look next at a surprising positive result. The Primary School Deworming Project, beginning in 1998, progressively made free deworming treatment available to 75 Kenyan schools. Miguel and Kremer (2004) demonstrate that the project reduced school absenteeism by around a quarter. This was partly due to an externality effect, whereby untreated students benefited from the treatment of others because it slowed the transmission of worms. The success of the program is very good news in terms of improving child health and amount of schooling. It did not, however, translate into an improvement in test scores.

Can anything improve test scores? Let me finish this section with a study by Banerjee and co-authors (2007). They looked at two interventions in India. In one intervention the weaker students were taken out of the classroom to work with a young woman from the community for two hours per day; the teaching of this balashki (or child's friend) focused on core skills. In the other intervention all students were given access to a computer-assisted learning program adapted to their ability. Figure 8.12 provides data on the short-term effect of the program by comparing performance on a test at the start of the school year with one at the end of the year. Almost across the board, test scores were higher with the balashki and computer-assisted learning.

The improvement in test scores did drop off somewhat after a student left the project. The overall picture, however, is still a very positive one. In many ways this is a surprising finding. In particular, the balashkis are given only minimal training before entering the classroom, and many have expressed doubts about the merit of computer-assisted learning. Even so, both interventions seemed to improve upon standard teaching methods. This offers real hope for increasing the quality of education. For instance, the minimal training means that the balashki project is cheap and easy to scale up.

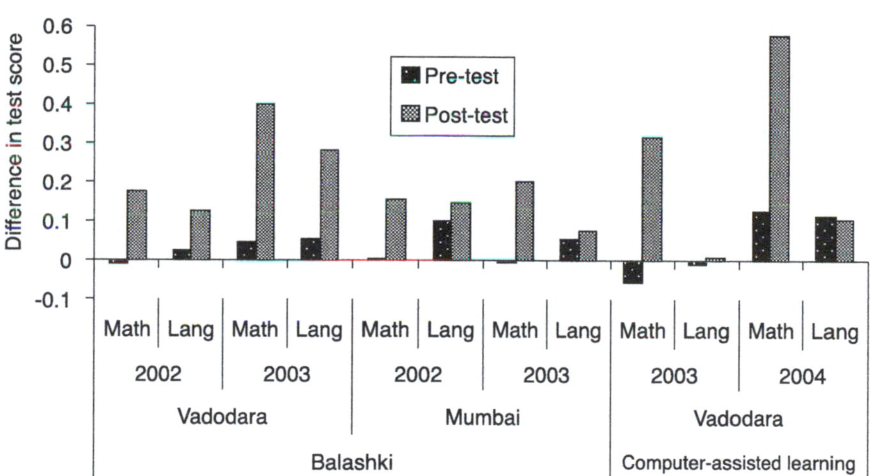

Figure 8.12 The difference in average test score comparing schools involved in the project and those not, in a particular year. Post-test scores are higher in schools involved in the project. Vadodara and Mumbai are the cities where the project took place.

Source: Banerjee *et al.* (2007).

The three studies we have looked at in this section are by no means all that have been done on the education production function. They do, however, nicely illustrate the kind of things we can learn. The main lesson seems to be that one cannot trust intuition (or the standard economic model). Some things do not work when we might have expected them to, and some things work when we might not have expected them to. This emphasizes the need for a lot more investigation of potential policy interventions (see Research Methods 8.5) if we are to alleviate poverty and not waste money.

Research Methods 8.5

Experimenting with policy

In order to properly evaluate the merits of different policy interventions we need well-designed randomized trials. The minimum this requires is an intervention and control treatment. For example, we need some randomly selected schools to implement a policy of deworming or balashki while others do not. Comparison of the schools in the intervention treatment with the control treatment allows us to draw robust conclusions about the consequences of the intervention. Randomized trials of this nature do, however, raise some difficult ethical, methodological, and practical problems.

Let us think about the ethical problems first. A basic principle in economic experiments is that of **informed consent**, which means that the subject knowingly signs up to take part. The problem we have here is that children are not in a position to make informed consent. In general, this need not be a barrier to running experiments with children. Earlier in the chapter, for instance, we looked at three experiments with children that clearly raised no real ethical issues. When it comes to an experiment with, say, deworming treatment, the ethics become a bit less clear cut. In this instance a child assigned to the control treatment would have more ill health and less education than a child in the intervention treatment. Is that ethical? The difficulty in answering this question makes it hard to do randomized trials with children, whether in development economics or medicine.

Next we can look at the methodological problems. The general rule with experiments is to add one thing at a time in order to not overly complicate matters. This approach is not well suited to a development context where money is tight, time is short, and people want to see immediate results. Multiple interventions, therefore, can be bundled together with the same population. The difficulty that this creates is in disentangling the various effects. More generally, a policy intervention in a developing country is also almost inevitably going to be quite context specific. This makes it difficult to draw general conclusions, or at least we need care in doing so. For example, if greater access to textbooks failed to improve performance in Kenya because of the specific textbooks being used, then what do we learn? The main lesson we learn is the importance of quality textbooks, not that textbooks do not matter.

Finally, we come to the practical problems. Many practical problems arise from the ethical and methodological problems already discussed. For example, the ethical issues may mean reluctance from government and aid agencies to take part in studies. There are, however, additional practical problems from working in developing countries. Most notably, the experimental environment is likely to be much less stable than in a standard experiment. Attrition rates at school, for instance, could be high. Implementation of the project may also be patchy. For example, in Mumbai, only two-thirds of the schools assigned balashkis actually received any, because of administrative difficulties. Such effects need to be carefully monitored and taken control of.

8.6.2 Microfinance

One of the most exciting things to happen in developing countries over the last decade or so has been the growth of microfinance. The basic idea is simple enough. Conventional lending does not work well for relatively poor people because the chance of default is large and there is no collateral. A microfinance scheme 'solves' these problems by lending to a group of people who collectively take responsibility for the loan. The pooling of risk within the group lowers the chance of default. This looks like a win-win solution: lenders can make a profit and poor people can borrow money to buy land, equipment, secure a job, or deal with a family emergency.

Most credit for the emergence of microfinance goes to Mohammad Yunus. In 1976 he began a project in Bangladesh lending to the poor. That project resulted in the establishment of Grameen Bank in 1983. The guiding principle was that loans are better than charity at alleviating poverty. In 2006 Yunus and Grameen Bank won the Nobel Peace Prize for 'their efforts to create economic and social development from below'. Microfinance has now spread to over 50 countries. In 2010 an estimated 137.5 million poor families had a microloan, typically of around $100. In short, microfinance looks like a resounding success story. Appearances, however, can be deceptive.

One thing we can say with some certainty is that microfinance is a profitable business. This means that group lending must work in the sense that repayment rates are high enough. To see why this is an interesting finding I will look at a study by Abbink and co-authors (2006), who ran a laboratory experiment with a microfinance game.

To explain how the game works, consider a group of four people. Each person is lent $175 for a total of $700. After one year the bank wants a repayment of $840 from the group, equating to an interest rate of 25 percent. Group members independently invest the $175 in their 'business'. With probability 0.83 that the investment is successful, the person ends up with $420. With probability 0.17, the investment is not successful and the person ends up with $0. At the end of the year each group member reports whether his investment was successful, and those with successful investments split the cost of repaying the loan. For example, if three are successful they each pay $280 each.

In order to repay the loan at least two group members must report a successful investment. The interesting word here is 'report'. It is assumed that only the person himself knows whether or not his investment was successful. In order to repay the loan, therefore, it is not enough that two or more investments are successful. We also need group members to honestly report their success. If the loan is repaid, then the bank will extend a loan in the subsequent year and the whole process is repeated. This setup captures two key elements of microfinance schemes. First, it is difficult to monitor borrowers and so there is a big reliance on self-reporting. Second, the main benefit from repaying the loan is the chance to borrow again.

The game is such that no group member has a material incentive to report a successful investment. I will not go through the full explanation, but to give the basic idea, suppose Rob's investment was successful and he is deciding what to report. If two or three of the other group members report a successful investment, then the loan will be repaid; by saying that his investment was not successful, Rob avoids repaying his share of the loan. If no other group members report a successful investment, the loan will not be repaid whatever Rob does; by reporting a successful investment Rob would have to pay his $420 but not be able to get a loan in the future. It is only if exactly one other group member reports a successful investment that Rob can possibly gain from reporting his successful investment; that is not incentive enough.

If group lending is going to work, therefore, we need group members to report successful investments. We need guilt aversion, social preferences, social norms, or something similar. Let us turn to some experimental data. Figure 8.13 shows the repayment rates that would occur given the amount of honest reporting observed in the study. Treatments were run with groups of size two, four, and eight. To explore the group element in more detail, a treatment was also run with groups composed of four friends.

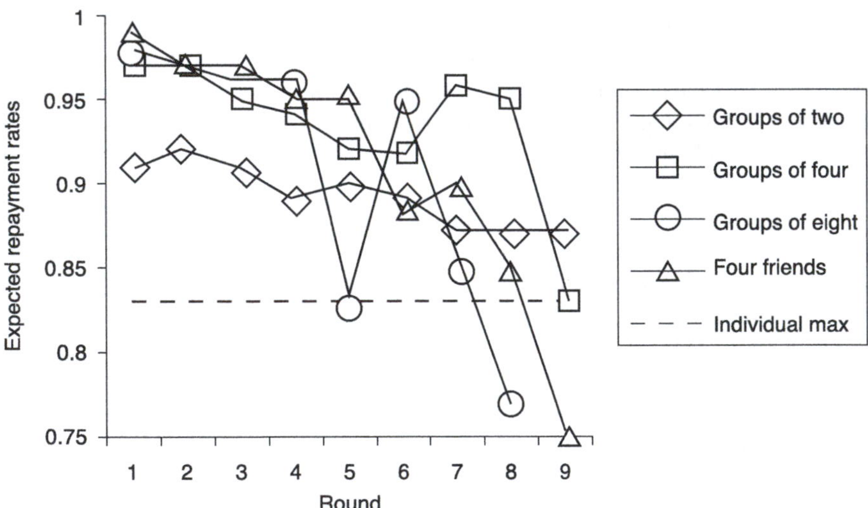

Figure 8.13 The probability of the loan being repaid given the observed levels of honest reporting.

Source: Abbink *et al.* (2006).

The main thing to note from Figure 8.13 is that enough subjects honestly reported successful investments to generate a high repayment rate. To put things in context the 'individual max' line plots the repayment rate that the bank would have expected if it loaned on an individual basis and closely monitored every loan. Lending to groups is a significant improvement over this hypothetical ideal. So, lending to groups works, and it seems that the size or composition of the group does not make much difference.

The high repayment rates we see in Figure 8.13 are an indication of why microfinance has been successful for the banks. We need to question next whether microfinance has been beneficial for borrowers. The evidence, so far, is not positive. In particular, a spate of recent studies has found little evidence of the purported benefits of microfinance. To illustrate, I will look at a study by Banerjee and co-authors (2013).

In Hyderabad, India, 52 of 104 poor neighborhoods were randomly selected for the opening of a branch by the microfinance institution Spandana. Operations were progressively rolled out between 2006 and 2007. The study surveyed a large sample of local people three times, in 2005, 2007, and 2009. Comparison of the neighborhoods with and without access to microfinance allows a relatively clean test of its consequences.

There was evidence that people used microfinance to make inter-temporal choices. Specifically, those who borrowed money appeared to spend the money on a durable good. The cost of the loan was offset by reduced consumption on 'temptation goods' and an increase in hours worked. There was no evidence, however, of microfinance lifting people out of poverty. Indeed, if it helped any, it tended to help larger businesses; the average business remained small and not very profitable. Moreover, the take-up of microfinance was not high; less than 40 percent of eligible households took out a microfinance loan, even though most borrowed from some other source.

The results from this study in India are consistent with other studies in Morocco, Mexico, Mongolia, and Bosnia. Microfinance may not, therefore, be the miracle cure for poverty. This is probably due in large part to the lack of good investment opportunities for the poorest in society. Few businesses are able to turn around a 25 percent return in one year! This is not to say that microfinance is a bad thing. If it helps people smooth consumption and pre-commit to not spending money on temptation goods, then it can have some benefits. It is not clear, however, that even these benefits are worth much. Would it not be better to find some cheaper way for people to smooth consumption, such as through saving rather than borrowing? In Chapter eleven (see in particular section 11.2.1) we shall look at an alternative to microfinance.

8.7 Further reading

For those eager to learn more: much of the material in section 8.1 was based on the work of Arthur Robson. Robson (2001a, 2001b, 2002) and Robson and Samuelson (2009) are useful references. For more on cultural differences I would suggest following up the references in the text, particularly the book by Henrich and co-authors (2004). See also Cardenas and Carpenter (2008). Sobel (2002) provides an interesting review of the literature on trust and social capital. For more on group selection, and the evolution of cooperation, Bergstrom (2002) and the book by Gintis and co-authors (2005) are worth reading, while the 8 December 2006 issue of *Science*, with articles by Boyd, Bowles, and Nowak, provides an interesting snapshot of research in this area. For an interesting earlier contribution to the debate see Güth and Yaari (1992). For more on the effects of gender see the excellent review article by Croson and Gneezy (2009) and for the economics of the family, Bergstrom (1996) is a good starting point. The fascinating article by Kaplan *et al.* (2000) explains the data on food production and consumption, while Robson and Kaplan (2003) offer an economic perspective. Webley (2004) provides interesting insights on children's understanding of economics. On a more general level the books by Frank (1991), Ridley (1997), and Laland and Brown (2005) are three that I would pick out from the host of excellent, general readership books taking an evolutionary perspective. For more on development behavioral economics and microfinance see Bertrand, Mullainathan, and Shafir (2004), Rodrik (2008), Banerjee and Duflo (2008), and Banerjee (2013).

8.8 Review questions

8.1 Give some examples of intermediate goods that may enter the utility function. Is money an intermediate good?

8.2 Let's go back to the first example of long and short winters. Suppose there are 1,600 adults of type L, 1,600 of type S, and 1,600 randomizer types. The randomizer types decide at the start of each summer whether to gather enough food for a long winter, and do gather enough with probability 0.4. Suppose we have the sequence, summer, short winter, summer, short winter, summer short winter, summer, long winter, how many of each type will likely survive?

8.3 How can evolution explain reference dependence? How about loss aversion?

8.4 Is present bias and time inconsistency a good evolutionary strategy?

8.5 Design an experiment to find out whether people dislike aggregate risk compared to idiosyncratic risk.

8.6 Is natural selection relevant in understanding modern economic behavior or is it only culture that matters?

8.7 Why is it so hard to get cooperation to emerge in the haystack model?

8.8 Does maximizing utility mean maximizing happiness?

8.9 What do you think is the main cause of the gender gap?

8.10 How can confirmatory bias help explain the gender gap?

8.11 Why do many people save money all their life in order to bequeath to their children?

8.12 Why does it not make evolutionary sense for a young person to support an older parent? Why could it happen because of cultural influence?

8.13 Why should development economics take account of cultural differences?

9 Neuroeconomics

> Giving up smoking is the easiest thing in the world. I know because I've done it thousands of times.
>
> Mark Twain

We use our brains to think and make decisions, whether consciously or unconsciously, and so, if we understand how the brain works, we should be able to better understand economic behavior. Clearly, things are not quite as simple as this, because the brain is a very complicated thing. Over the last 20 years or so our understanding of the brain, and our ability to measure brain activity, has, however, improved a lot. It has improved so much that neuroscience is now a viable tool for economists to use in interpreting economic behavior. The goal of this chapter is to see what we have learnt so far.

9.1 An introduction to the brain

We will not get very far unless we know some basics of how the brain works. I am not, though, going to go into very much depth on this subject; all we need is a simple model of the brain that is not too far from reality. The model that economists typically work with assumes modularity. The idea behind **modularity** is that the brain can be split into a number of distinct components or **brain modules** that are each responsible for specific functions like breathing, seeing, language, being altruistic, or getting angry. We can think of these brain modules as distinct areas of the brain, and so we can split the brain into areas that are responsible for different things. This is schematically shown in Figure 9.1. Controlling all of this is the **interpreter**, which monitors the output of the modules, interprets them, and reacts.

Modularity is a very crude model of how the brain works. For instance, we know that modules can work in parallel with other modules, and communicate with each other while doing so. We also know that there is nothing anywhere near as simple as an 'altruism module' or an 'anger module', and any classification is inevitably one of judgment. To a rough approximation, however, modularity does not seem too bad, and it is a very useful model for economists to work with.

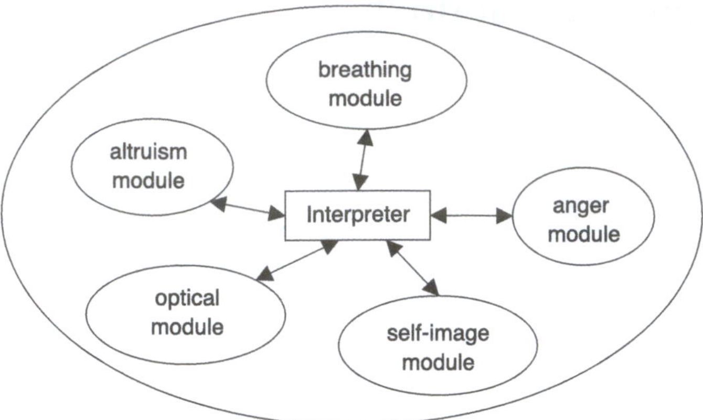

Figure 9.1 A schematic representation of modularity. The brain consists of modules that perform specific functions. An interpreter monitors and interacts with these modules.

It is useful because it potentially allows us to infer what causes a particular behavior. For example, suppose that someone called Rob has the chance to give Federica money, and does so. Furthermore, suppose that we know a brain module associated with altruism and another associated with self-image. If we monitor the brain and find that the altruism module is activated, but not the self-image module, when Rob gives money, then we could infer that he gave to be kind to others and not to promote self-image.

For this to be useful we need to measure brain activity. Historically neuroscience has learnt a lot from people who, for one reason or another, usually an accident, have brain damage in an area of the brain. If the person loses the ability to perform a function, such as get angry, then we can infer that the anger module is where the brain damage is. More recent techniques such as EEG, PET, and fMRI allow us to measure brain activity directly (see Research Methods 9.1). In principle these techniques allow us to see what parts of the brain are activated when Rob is, say, angry, and also measure the intensity of the brain activity, so we can say how angry he is.

Research Methods 9.1

Monitoring brain activity

There are three basic brain-imaging methods: electro-encephalogram (EEG), positron emission topography (PET), and functional magnetic resonance imaging (fMRI). Each of these methods uses a different technique to measure brain activity in different parts of the brain. In an experiment, brain activity is measured during some baseline task and during some experimental events, such as the person being told they have some money. It is the difference in brain activity between the baseline and experimental event that is important, because it gives us a clue as to what parts of the brain are activated, and how much they are activated, by the experimental event.

EEG is the only one of the three methods that directly measures brain activity. It does so via electrodes attached to the scalp, which pick up the electrical current that results when neurons fire.

PET and fMRI make use of the fact that active neurons need energy and they get this energy from glucose in blood. Neural activity, therefore, increases blood flow. It also, because the active neurons take glucose from the blood and not oxygen, relatively increases the oxygen content of the blood.

A **PET** scanner measures the blood flow in the brain. To do this, a radioactive tracer isotope is injected into the person's blood circulation. As this isotope decays it emits positrons which, on meeting nearby electrons, produce photons which can be detected. By counting the number of photons emitted it is possible to get an idea of how much blood and blood flow there is in different areas of the brain.

An **fMRI** scanner measures the oxygen content of blood. To do this, the head is put in a magnetic field. It so happens that the way blood interacts with this magnetic field depends on the oxygen content of the blood. This can be detected to show where in the brain the blood contains more or less oxygen and thus where there is more or less neural activity. This is the most widely used method in neuroeconomics today.

The technicalities of EEG, Pet, and fMRI are interesting, but not ultimately our main concern. One thing, however, is worth mentioning: there is no perfect way, yet, of measuring brain activity. EEGs can record very accurately the time of brain activity (down to milliseconds), but are relatively inaccurate in saying where the activity was, or at picking up activity in some parts of the brain. PET and fMRI scanners can record much more accurately where the brain activity takes place (typically to within two to three millimeters) but are much less accurate on the time of activity (seconds rather than milliseconds). Also, none of the methods is very user friendly. EEG is relatively unobtrusive and portable compared to PET and fMRI but still a lot more involved than participating in a normal economic experiment.

The idea that we can measure the intensity of brain activity is exciting, because it suggests that we can measure pleasure, pain, and utility. Care is needed in pushing this idea too far, not least because of the crudeness of the modularity model of the brain. Even so, in principle, as Rob thinks about giving away money, we could measure activity in the altruism, self-image, and selfish modules, and see whether we can predict what he will choose from the intensity of activity. For instance, if the selfish module is activated a lot, we might be able to predict him keeping the money.

This already gives us two things to look at while we watch the brain: what areas of the brain are activated, and how much they are activated. Potentially, this can help us understand a bit better the behavior we observe, and we'll see how this works in practice soon enough. Before that, there are a couple of important things that I would like to do: introduce some areas of the brain of most relevance to economists, and talk a bit about different brain processes.

9.1.1 An economist's map of the brain

Neuroscience brings with it a load of terminology that is probably alien to many; at least it is to me. An understanding of this terminology is, however, useful, and so I will try to explain the main terms you are likely to come across. On the basis that this is an economics textbook and not a medical textbook, I shall only give the most basic introduction.

It is traditional to start with the big picture and progressively narrow things down. So, I should start with the nervous system. The **nervous system** transmits signals from one part of the body to another. In doing so it allows an individual to detect changes within themselves and their environment, analyze them, and respond to them. The latter two of these are of primary importance for us, meaning that we can focus on the central nervous system. The **central nervous system** consists of seven basic parts: the spinal cord, the cerebellum, the medulla, pons and midbrain, which are collectively called the **brainstem**, plus the **diencephalon** and the **cerebrum**. These are illustrated in Figure 9.2.

While the cerebellum, midbrain, and diencephalon are of interest to economists (Table 9.1 outlines their main functions), most attention is usually given to the cerebrum. This is the big part of the brain responsible for higher-level information processing and decision making. The cerebrum is more than big enough that we need to distinguish different parts of it, and there are various ways of doing this.

The one you are probably familiar with is the distinction between **left** and **right cerebal hemispheres**, corresponding to the left and right sides of the brain.

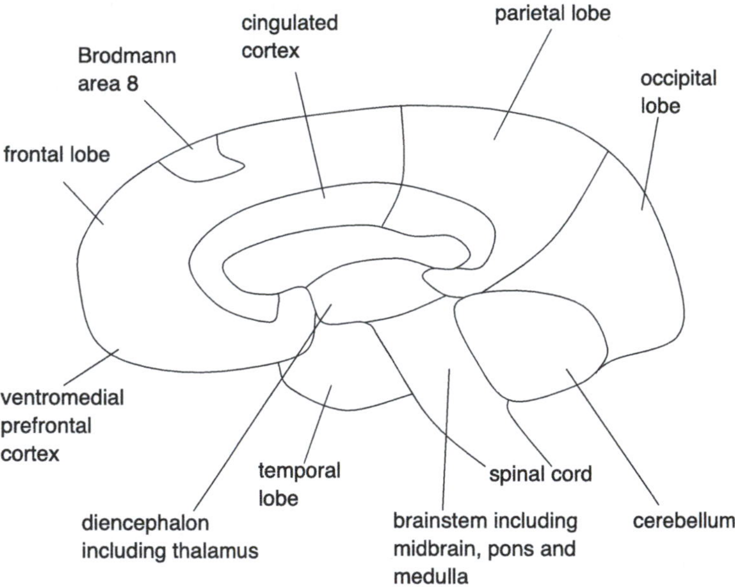

Figure 9.2 Some areas of the brain seen from the medial surface of the brain (i.e. by slicing the brain down the middle).

Table 9.1 Parts of the central nervous system and some of the main functions that go on in that part

Parts of the central nervous system	*Functions include:*
Brainstem (including pons, medulla, and midbrain)	Control of reflexes such as heart rate, breathing, and coughing. Basic aspects of reward and pleasure. Conduit of information in the system.
Cerebellum (little brain)	Sensory-motor skills necessary for smoothly coordinated movements.
Diencephalon (including thalamus)	Control of homeostatic and reproductive functions, such as body temperature, hunger, and thirst.

Equally intuitive, but probably less familiar, is a distinction between the outside and inside of the cerebrum. The **cerebral cortex** is the distinctive outside layer of the cerebrum and is essentially a crumpled sheet of neurons around two to four millimeters thick. Within that we find something called the **basal ganglia**.

As well as distinguishing left and right, and inside and outside, we need ways to pinpoint different areas of the cerebral cortex and basal ganglia. To get some intuition for how this is done, imagine a map of a country. There are natural features like mountains and rivers that we might use to pinpoint a specific location. There are also artificial features like county or city boundaries that we might want to use. Sometimes the natural and artificial features will coincide, but sometimes not. Something similar happens with mapping the cerebrum.

Let's start with the cerebral cortex and the artificial features. One classification splits it into four basic parts: the **frontal**, **parietal**, **temporal**, and **occipital lobe**. These can be further distinguished into things like the **dorsolateral prefrontal cortex** and **ventromedial prefrontal cortex** (see Research Methods 9.2). If these names seem a bit unwieldy, then you may prefer a classification originally conceived by Brodmann. In this case the cerebral cortex is split into 52 areas known as **Brodmann areas**. Each Brodmann area corresponds to a particular area of the cerebral cortex; area eight, for instance, is illustrated in Figure 9.2. These areas do not necessarily correspond to natural features of the brain, but they do allow us to pinpoint specific locations of the cerebral cortex.

Research Methods 9.2

The terminology of neuroanatomy

Various terms are used to specify locations of the brain, some of which are illustrated in Figure 9.3.

Simplest are: **anterior** and **posterior**, which indicate front and back of the head; **inferior** and **superior**, which indicate above and below; **medial** and **lateral**, which indicate toward the centre or to the side.

Other terms come from drawing the axis of the body and brain. **Dorsal** refers to the back or upper half depending on whether the focus is the body or brain. **Ventral** refers to the front or lower half. **Rostral** indicates the direction towards the nose and **caudal** towards the back.

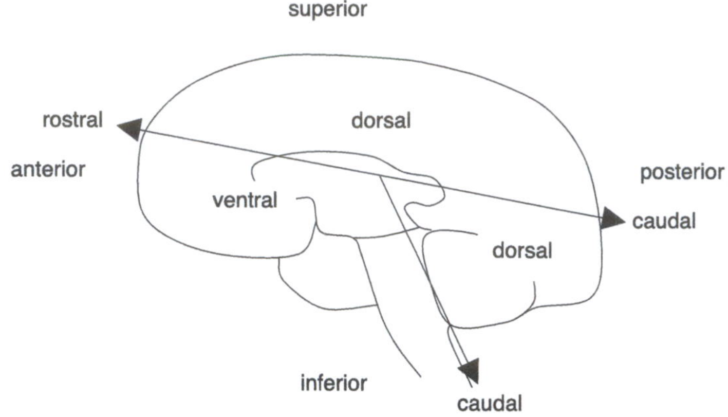

Figure 9.3 Terminology to describe location in the brain.
Source: Purves *et al.* (2008).

This is enough to understand terms like the posterior parietal cortex and anterior cingulated cortex. The only other thing you should need to know is that the frontal lobe is commonly subdivided into the prefrontal cortex (corresponding to the frontal gyri at the front of the frontal lobe) and the precentral cortex (corresponding to the precentral gyrus at the back of the frontal lobe). Now you can understand terms like dorsolateral prefrontal cortex and ventromedial prefrontal cortex.

Now for the natural features. Recall that the cerebral cortex is like a crumpled sheet. The bits of the sheet that stick out are called **gyri** (singular, **gyrus**), while the concavities between are called **sulci** (singular, **sulcus**) or **fissures**. These are the mountains and rivers of the brain and provide a natural way to pinpoint specific locations of the cererbral cortex. For example, the cingulated cortex including the cingulate gyrus and cingulate sulcus runs along the bottom of the frontal and parietal lobes, taking in Brodmann areas 23, 24, 26, 29, 30, 31, and 32.

Mixing both artificial and natural features gives us a further collection of names, some of which you may be familiar with, including the amygdala, hippocampus, and insular. These tend to be towards the middle of the brain and not necessarily in the cerebral cortex. The **amygdala**, for instance, consists of a group of **nuclei** (where a nuclei is a compact collection of neurons) at the anterior pole of the temporal lobe. The **hippocampus** is a cortical structure lying inside the temporal lobe. The **insula** is a portion of the cerebral cortex folded deep between the frontal and temporal lobes.

The final thing we need to do is distinguish parts of the basal ganglia, the area inside the cerebral cortex. Most important are two nuclei called the **caudate** and **putamen**, which are collectively referred to as the **striatum**.

Being able to pinpoint specific locations of the brain is critical in neuroscience, and so understanding the above terminology is useful in following the literature of neuroeconomics. It is not really necessary, however, for us to know exactly where, say, Brodmann area 41 is; we can leave that to the neuroscientists. More important for us is to know what different areas of the brain do. Tables 9.1 and 9.2 give you some idea as to basic functions. What I want to do now is introduce some functions of more specific interest to economists. In order to do that it's necessary to talk a bit more about brain processes.

9.1.2 Brain processes

Neuroscience is not just about filling in a map of the brain. It also helps us understand the processes by which decisions are made. To see why, it is useful to think of brain activities as fitting within a two-dimensional framework where we distinguish between controlled and automatic, and between cognitive and affective processes. This is summarized in Table 9.3.

Table 9.2 Parts of the cerebrum and some of the main functions that go on in that part

Parts of the cerebrum	*Functions include*
Frontal lobe	Controlling movement. Organizing, planning, and decision making.
Parietal lobe	Bodily sensation including aspects of vision. Aspects of language. Attending to stimuli.
Temporal lobe	Hearing. Higher order visual tasks. Recognizing stimuli.
Occipital lobe	Initial processing of visual information.
Amygdala	Aspects of emotional processing.
Insula	Visceral and autonomic functions including taste.
Hippocampus	Certain kinds of memory.

Table 9.3 Four different brain processes with an example

	Cognitive processes	*Affective processes*
	Free of emotion	*Involve emotion*
Controlled processes		
Step-by-step conscious	Thinking through a math problem.	An actor recalling being angry to better play his role in a play.
Automatic processes		
Parallel sub-conscious	Playing a golf shot.	Jumping when hearing a loud noise.

We have already briefly come across the distinction between controlled and automatic processes in Chapter two when comparing perception, intuition, and reasoning. **Controlled processes** involve step-by-step logic in which someone consciously thinks through some problem or about some event. **Automatic processes** are not accessible to consciousness and go on in parallel, allowing many tasks to be performed simultaneously. A person will typically have little conscious idea, during or after, how automatic processes work.

Affective processes involve emotions that typically result in a desire or drive to do something. For example, Rob feels fear and so runs away, or feels hungry, so eats. We can simply think of **cognitive processes** as everything else, so that thought processes are free, or almost free, of emotion, for example, Rob driving his car or preparing his dinner.

Common sense tells us that most of what we do must involve automatic processes. As I write this, I am breathing, my heart is pumping, my fingers are pressing the keyboard, my eyes are watching the screen and the fields outside, I'm listening to the cars and birds, and thinking what to write, plus a lot of other things. There is clearly no way that this could all be done consciously, and so most of it goes on at a subconscious level.

For this to work, we need to learn how to do things automatically, because the more we can do automatically, the more we can do. It is possible to do quite complicated things automatically, like hit a golf ball, or play a piano concerto. More interesting for our purpose is the reverse logic. We cannot possibly consciously decide what to do using controlled processes and so we must subconsciously decide what is 'important enough' to warrant conscious control. This leads to the idea of executive control.

In the absence of executive control we could imagine that behavior would be determined by a **default mode**. This is basically what would happen if we stopped to think consciously; life would go on with everything happening according to automatic processes. Young children and some adults with brain damage are thought to essentially be like this. Most of us, though, are not like that. Instead, we have **executive control systems** that sometimes cut in and give us control to move away from default mode.

It's natural, therefore, to think of automatic processes as inevitable and the norm, while control processes are rarer and only happen when automatic processes let them happen. This is important because it goes a long way to justifying the important chain of reasoning that I highlighted in Chapter two: framing and context influence intuition and perceptions, which influence reasoning. On first encountering an event, automatic processes, both cognitive and affective, get to work, and it's only subsequently that controlled processes are given a role.

So, whether Rob feels a loss or a gain, feels happy or angry, or perceives something as kind or unkind, will happen automatically and subconsciously. This must then influence the starting point for any subsequent reasoning that he does about how to behave. Hence, we observe context and framing effects. Stylized though it is, this is a nice way to think about economic behavior, and one good thing about neuroscience is that it allows us to put some details to the idea. In particular, we can hope to understand a bit more about how automatic and controlled processes work and interact. For that we need to know more about executive control.

9.1.3 Executive control systems

To work well, executive control systems need to perform a few intermediate processes. Most important is when to switch from automatic to control. Following that there is the need for inhibition and task switching. **Inhibition** is the suppression of automatic behavior no longer deemed appropriate while **task switching** involves starting any new behavior. An important part of this is likely to be **simulation**, in which the possible consequences of different actions are worked through.

To illustrate, one test or means to measure executive control is the **Wisconsin card sorting task**. (You can find free versions of this test on the web, and it only takes around 20 minutes, so maybe you might want to have a go before reading on.) The task requires participants to sort a deck of cards according to some rule. The color, shape, and number of symbols on the cards are different and determine the rule. For instance, the rule might be to sort cards according to color, or to sort according to number of symbols. Subjects are not told the rule, but are told whether they are sorting the cards correctly so they can learn by trial and error what the rule is. The key to the test is that, without the subject being told, the rule periodically changes. For instance, it might go from sorting by color to sorting by shape. Of interest is whether, and how quickly, subjects adapt to the new rule.

This task means that subjects learn something well enough for it to become automatic, and then at some point have to realize that the default mode is no longer working, inhibit the old rule, and switch to a new one! Some of this might happen at a conscious level, but executive control need not be conscious. For instance, while driving along the highway, Rob might swerve to avoid something before he knows he's done it.

There are a few areas of the brain thought to be involved in executive control processes including the dorsolateral prefrontal cortex and ventromedial prefrontal cortex. These areas stand out as prime candidates because they are linked to many other areas of the brain and so have the ability to control. Brain imaging allows us to confirm their role, as summarized in Table 9.4.

That these areas are important in executive control means that they are going to be important areas of interest to economists and, while the functions might look a bit abstract at first sight, underlying them are things we need to think about. For example, simulating behavioral consequences and learning the connection between stimuli and reward are fundamental parts of making economic decisions.

In following this up there are three things that I now want to look at in turn, as we start to focus more on economic behavior: how outcomes are evaluated, how people learn about the value of outcomes, and, finally, how people make decisions.

Table 9.4 Main components of executive control systems

Parts of the brain	*Functions include*
Dorsolateral prefrontal cortex (DLPFC)	Initiating and shifting behavior, e.g. to switch task or change action. Inhibition, in the sense of getting rid of irrelevant information, e.g. forgetting the old rule in Wisconsin card sorting task. Simulating behavioral consequences and abstracting from reality.
Ventromedial prefrontal cortex (VMPFC)	Inhibition, in the sense of adhering to rules of behavior, e.g. behaving appropriately in social situations. Learning when things change by following the link between stimuli and reward.
Anterior cingulated cortex	Notices conflict and decides whether to run default mode or not.
Basal ganglia	Learning the connection between stimuli and reward.

9.2 Valuing rewards and learning

In this section we are going to start looking directly at economic behavior but with a focus on automatic processes, primarily the valuation of rewards and learning. This will be a precursor to looking at the more involved controlled processes that are essential in economic decisions. The natural place to start is with the evaluation of rewards.

9.2.1 Reward evaluation

The basic question I want to start with is how people process rewards. For example, if Rob wins \$10, or loses \$10, what goes on in his brain? The action appears to start in the midbrain. The neurotransmitter **dopamine** is heavily involved in the evaluation of rewards, and there are two important structures in the midbrain that are associated with dopamine. These are called the **substantia nigra** and **ventral tegmental area (VTA)**. Most important for decision making is probably the VTA, because this has pathways projecting into other important areas of the brain. In particular it has pathways to the frontal lobe, and pathways projecting to areas important for emotional and affective processing, such as the amygdala, hippocampus, and other areas of basal ganglia. So, you might want to think of the VTA as the hub sending out messages to other areas of the brain about what has happened.

In principle, this means we should keep track of what happens in the VTA and all the areas that connect to the VTA. But you may well have had enough of terminology by now and so I am going to make life a bit easier for us. In order that we can focus unencumbered on the economics, I will primarily refer from here onwards to just two areas of the brain, summarized in Table 9.5. First is something

Table 9.5 Two areas of the brain that connect with the VTA and are important in economic valuation and decision making

Area	*Description*
Nucleus accumbens (NAcc)	In the caudate nucleus, in the basal ganglia, that is on the inside of the cerebrum.
Ventromedial prefrontal cortex (VMPFC)	Part of the frontal lobe and part of the cortex, that is on the outside of the cerebrum.

called the nucleus accumbens, which I shall call the **NAcc**, and second is the ventromedial prefrontal cortex which I shall call the **VMPFC**. Why these two areas? Both connect to the VTA; the nucleus accumbens is part of the basal ganglia, i.e. is inside the cerebrum, and is involved with reward evaluation, while the VMPFC is part of the cortex, i.e. on the outside of the cerebrum, and is important in executive control. Keeping watch on these two areas will, therefore, give us a good idea of what is going on more generally.

(Just for the record, I am going to think of the nucleus accumbens and something called the ventral striatum as the same thing, and the VMPFC and something called the orbitofrontal cortex as the same thing. They are not quite the same things, but I don't think that matters much to us.)

Let's start looking at some data. I will begin with a study by Breiter and co-authors (2001). In each round of the study a subject was shown a circle split into three equally sized sectors labeled with an amount of money. For example, the circle might have one sector labeled \$10, one labeled \$2.50, and one labeled \$0. An arrow would then spin and finally land on one of the sectors, with the subject winning the corresponding amount of money. So, if the arrow landed on the \$10 sector, the subject won \$10. There were different circles used: a good one (with labels \$10, \$2.50, and \$0), an intermediate one (\$2.50, \$0, and −\$1.50), and a bad one (\$0, −\$1.50, and −\$6). Of interest is to see how subjects reacted to seeing which circle would be used and how they reacted to knowing how much they had won.

Figure 9.4 gives us some idea of what happened in the NAcc, and Figure 9.5 in the VMPFC. We are going to see a few of these types of figures so let me explain what they show. The vertical axis shows the change in signal from the relevant area of the brain relative to some baseline level. So, a positive suggests that the area is more activated than normal, and a negative that it is less active than normal. The horizontal axis plots time relative to some start point. In this case the subject saw the circle being used after around two seconds and saw what they had won after eight seconds. We can, therefore, track changes in activation as things happen.

To keep the figures manageable, I have only plotted outcomes for the good wheel, but in both the NAcc and VMPFC we see activation on seeing the circle and then also activation when the outcome is known. Further, the activation appears related to the desirability of the circle used and amount won. The better the circle, the more activation observed, and the better the outcome, the more

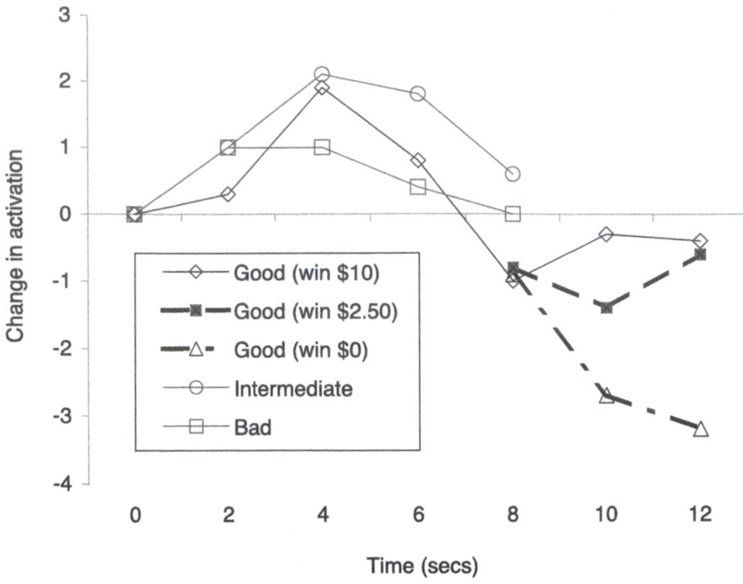

Figure 9.4 Activity in the nucleus accumbens on seeing the circle, around two seconds, and knowing how much is won, around eight seconds.

Source: Breiter *et al.* (2001).

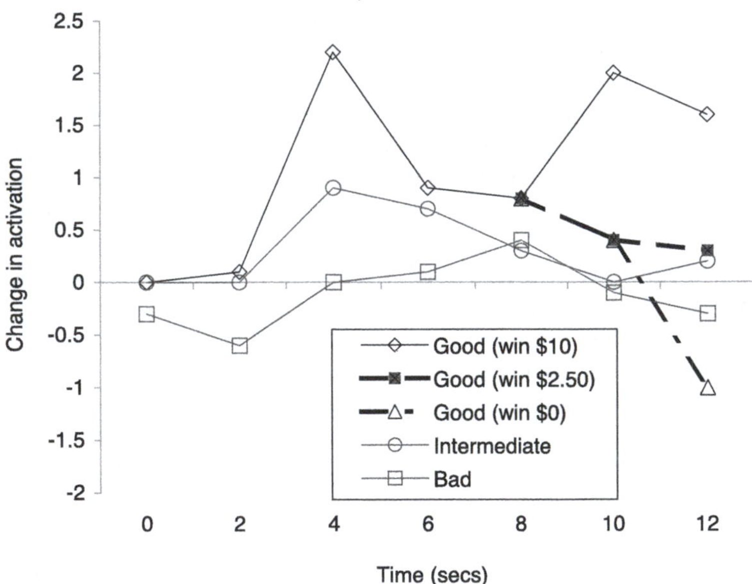

Figure 9.5 Activity in the ventromedial prefrontal cortex on seeing the circle, around two seconds, and knowing how much is won, around eight seconds.

Source: Breiter *et al.* (2001).

activation observed. One thing to note for future reference is how the activation in the VMPFC on seeing the outcome is positive, while that in the NAcc is negative.

We need to be careful of reading too much into one study (see Research Methods 9.3), but the results I have given above are representative of what is observed in other studies, namely that the NAcc and VMPFC respond to rewards and might respond by an amount related to the size of the reward. (We shall see some more examples of this as we go on.) Maybe, therefore, we have found the utility function! That would be very premature to say, but it is an exciting possibility. For it to make sense, the brain would need to learn about rewards, so that's what I want to look at next.

Research Methods 9.3

Sample sizes and confidence intervals

One criticism of neuroeconomics is the smallness of the sample sizes sometimes used. For example, the study by Breiter and co-authors (2001) used 12 subjects. This is fairly typical in neuroscience. Is 12 enough? To answer that, we need to enter the murky world of statistical tests and confidence intervals.

To get us started, think about an experiment, neuro or not, with the objective of finding what proportion of people use one heuristic or another. For example, we might be interested in what proportion of people use level one or level two reasoning (see Chapter six). We invite subjects to the lab and get them to play games over a number of rounds. From this we need to: (i) estimate the heuristic used by individual subjects, and (ii) estimate what this tells us about the general population. Then we find out what we want to know.

The word 'estimate' here is important because we cannot know for sure the answer to either of these two questions, and that's why sample size matters. I am not going to go into the technicalities of confidence intervals, but basically: (i) the more rounds a subject plays, the more confident we can be in our estimate of what heuristic he is using, and (ii) the more subjects we ask to the experiment, the more confident we can be in our estimate of what happens in the general population. So, we need lots of rounds and lots of subjects. Fortunately, the law of large numbers is on our side and so lots need not mean ridiculously many, but the more, the better, and something like 100 is great, 50 not bad, but 10 too few.

In a normal experiment we can easily invite 100 subjects and have them play as much as we want. The cost involved in brain imaging makes that impractical in neuroscience. So, while we can confidently estimate what an individual subject is doing, it is harder to confidently generalize any results to the wider population. It's not really clear at the moment whether this is a problem or not. Going on statistical logic it is a problem, but if we think that brains are fairly homogeneous across the wider population it need not be.

You might be wondering how this relates to the more standard economic experiment involving treatments. For instance, we might have one treatment where subjects play an ultimatum game to split $10, and another where they play an ultimatum game to split $100, and we are interested if behavior is different in the two treatments. Some might say that we just need to have enough subjects to spot a difference, because if we observe a difference in, say, the 100 subjects we invite to the lab, there must be a difference in the general population. Economists are prone to become fixated with such statistically significant differences, but of more interest is usually the magnitude of any difference. To estimate this with confidence, the more subjects, the better.

9.2.2 Learning about rewards

To get us started, imagine a sequence of events, like Rob putting a bet on a roulette wheel, seeing the roulette wheel stop on his number, getting the cash he won, buying a packet of chips with his winnings, and then eating the chips. Ultimately Rob should be happy. What I want us to think about now is when he feels happy. Is it when he bets, wins, or eats the chips?

This brings us to the distinction between primary and secondary reinforcers. You can think of a **primary** or **unconditioned reinforcer** as something that has been 'hard-wired' into Rob's brain, by evolution, to be important, like food, water, and sex. You can think of a **secondary reinforcer** as something that Rob has learnt to indirectly associate with a primary or other secondary reinforcer, like money. In the previous chapter we saw that evolution could have favored lots of possible intermediate goods, and so the distinction between a primary and secondary reinforcer is not necessarily an easy one. The basic principle, however, is simple enough; Rob does not need to learn about a primary reinforcer, but he does need to learn about a secondary reinforcer.

For Rob, food is a primary reinforcer, while money is a secondary reinforcer, and seeing the roulette wheel stop, or start, are even more removed secondary reinforcers. So, when does he start to get excited at winning?

To illustrate what might happen, I will briefly mention a study by O'Doherty and co-authors (2002). The study involved subjects seeing a visual cue before getting 0.5ml of either a pleasant taste, an unpleasant taste, or a neutral taste. Some areas of the brain, including the VTA and NAcc, were activated when the subject saw the cue, rather than felt the taste. Other areas, however, including the VMPFC, reacted more to the taste than to the cue. To take things one stage further, we can look at a similar study by Knutson and co-authors (2001). This study involved money rather than taste, but the results are similar. On seeing the cue of a future payment, areas like the VTA and NAcc were activated but areas of the VMPFC reacted more on seeing the reward rather than the cue.

To put a few more details to this, Figure 9.6 plots the timeline as subjects see the visual cue at zero and then find out whether they won money or not. Focus first on what happens if they win money. Then we see activation of the NAcc when they are anticipating winning, but not on knowing they have won. There is no such effect in the VMPFC. On finding out they have not won there is negative activity in both the NAcc and VMPFC. You might now want to check back and see what happens in Figures 9.4 and 9.5.

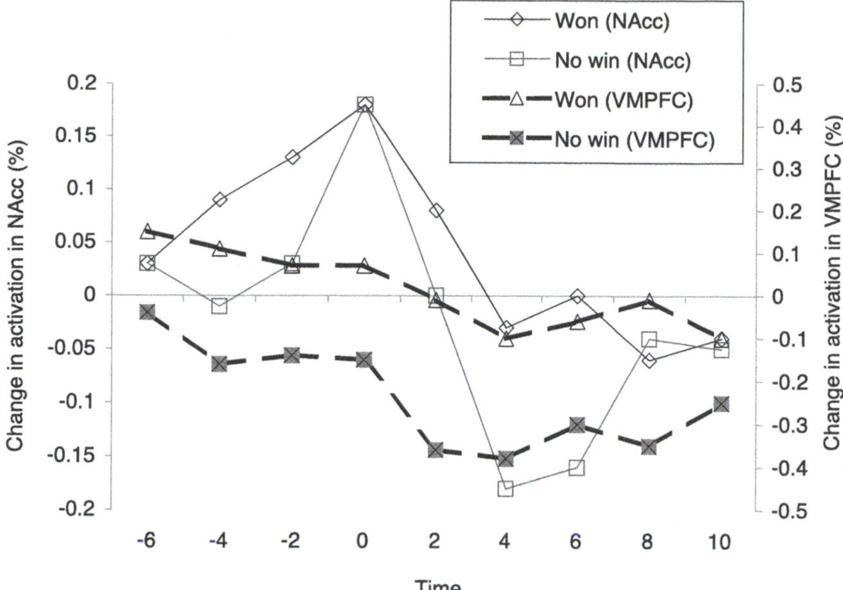

Figure 9.6 The response in the nucleus accumbens and ventromedial prefrontal cortex to anticipating, and then winning, or not winning, money.

Source: Knutson *et al.* (2001).

A stylized story of what is happening is that some areas of the brain, like the NAcc, learn to treat secondary reinforcers like primary reinforcers, while other parts, like the VMPFC, keep a check on things and so react more to receiving the reward than expecting to receive it. This fits the story of executive control that I summarized in Table 9.4 with the NAcc, in the basal ganglia, and VMPFC updating ongoing predictions about how much reward can be expected in the future from a particular secondary reinforcer.

An interesting example of this is the **Iowa gambling task** (and again, free versions are available on the web if you want to try before reading further). This task involves four decks of cards which subjects are repeatedly asked to choose from. Every card from decks A and B pays a large reward (e.g. $100) but sometimes also entails a large loss (e.g. $1,250). Every card on decks C and D pays a small reward (e.g. $50) and only sometimes entails a small loss. Overall, decks A and B have negative expected value, while decks C and D have positive expected value, and most subjects soon choose only from decks C and D. Those, however, with damage to the VMPFC continue to choose from decks A and B. It's as though the VMPFC is not doing its job of checking whether decks A and B are the good choices that the NAcc thinks they are.

On a related theme, I next want to mention a study by O'Doherty and co-authors (2001). The task that subjects did was partly like the Iowa gambling task, in that they had two choices: option A that gave large losses and small rewards, or option C that gave large rewards and small losses. Once, however, subjects had learnt that C was the best choice, the reward structure was reversed, similar to the Wisconsin card sorting task. Figure 9.7 illustrates what happened in two areas of the VMPFC while the subjects were learning that option C was best, and then after the change to option A being best.

The interesting thing here is how one area of the VMPFC (which I have labeled lateral) was activated following a loss and another (labeled medial) was activated following a reward. Figure 9.8 takes this one stage further by showing how the activation correlates with the magnitude of the reward or loss. This is not only consistent with the VMPFC being involved in learning but also suggests that different areas of the VMPFC are activated for rewards and losses. If losses and gains affect different areas of the brain, then it's no surprise that this distinction matters when modeling economic behavior.

9.2.3 Risk and uncertainty

One important issue that we need to address is that of risk. In most of the studies I have mentioned so far there has been risk. For instance, in the study by Breiter

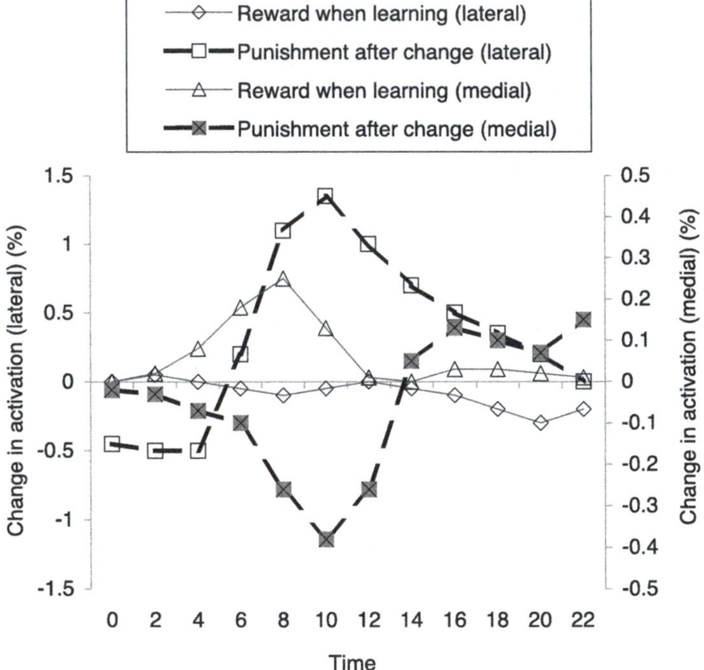

Figure 9.7 The change in activation in two areas of the VMPFC following a reward during a learning stage, or loss in a task-reversal stage.

Source: O'Doherty *et al.* (2001).

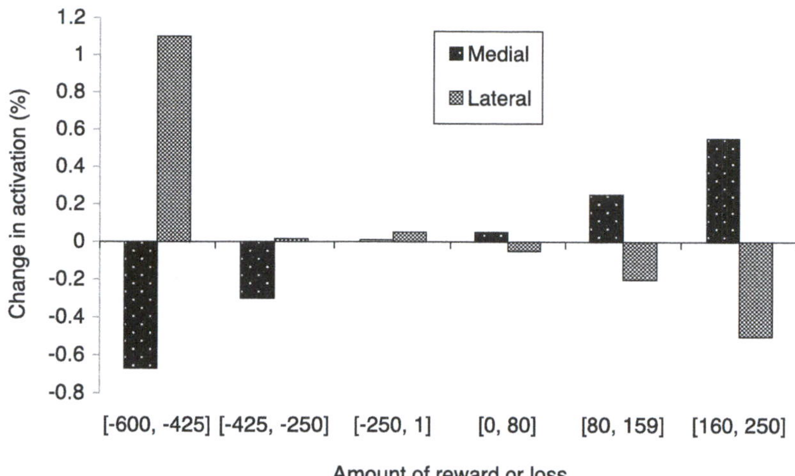

Figure 9.8 The change in activation in two areas of the VMPFC following a reward or loss of varying magnitudes.

Source: O'Doherty *et al.* (2001).

and co-authors (2001), subjects saw the arrow spin to decide what reward they would get. This raises the question of whether it's expected reward that matters, and how people learn when the outcome of an event is unknown. For example, what would be happening in Rob's brain between the roulette wheel starting to spin and stopping?

I will start by looking at a study by Preuschoff and co-authors (2006). In the study, subjects were asked to bet whether the second of two cards would have a higher or lower number than the first, the numbers ranging from one to ten. They then saw the number on the first card, followed by the number on the second card. The gap between seeing the two numbers was long enough for subjects to realize their chance of winning. For example, if the subject said the second card would be lower, and the number on the first card was nine, then he or she had a good chance of winning. If the number was five, the chance of winning was less and the risk was higher.

Figure 9.9 plots a measure of activation in the NAcc against the expected reward and the level of risk, where risk is highest if the probability of a win is 0.5. We see that activation is increasing in expected reward and is higher when there is more risk. A similar story has been told for the VMPFC. The brain, it seems, has no problem working with risk and expected values. What about uncertainty and ambiguity?

Recall that, with a risky choice, the probabilities of different outcomes are known, but with uncertainty they are not. For instance, suppose Rob is asked to bet on whether a red or blue card will be randomly drawn from a deck of 20 cards.

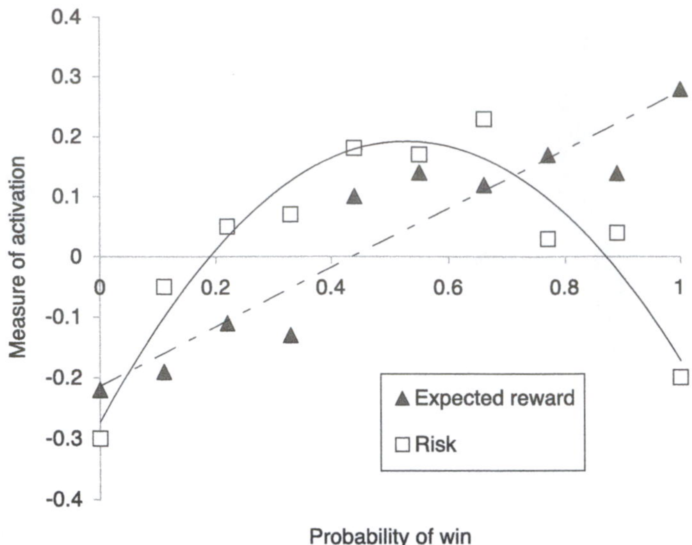

Figure 9.9 Activity in the NAcc (left ventral striatum) increases with expected value and risk.

Source: Preuschoff *et al.* (2006).

If he knows that ten of the cards are red and ten blue, then he has a choice with risk. If he does not know how many are red or blue, then he has a choice with uncertainty. In a study by Hsu and co-authors (2005), subjects were given both risky and ambiguous choices like this in order to see whether uncertainty made a difference.

Figure 9.10 plots the timeline of activation in the NAcc and an area of the VMPFC. The subject would see the choices at zero seconds, and the average decision what to choose was made at around six to seven seconds. Look first at what happens in the NAcc with a risky choice as compared to a choice with uncertainty. Clearly, once a decision has been made, the NAcc is activated much less when there is uncertainty, suggesting that the (expected or subjective) value put on an uncertain outcome is less than a risky outcome. Subjects, it appears, did not like uncertainty. Now look at what happens in the VMPFC. Here we see greater activation when there is uncertainty and when the subject is deciding what to choose. A similar pattern was observed in the amygdala, suggesting some of the areas of the brain were activated to 'try to find the missing information'.

The picture we get, therefore, is that when there is uncertainty the brain is alerted to the fact that information is missing and because of this a choice with uncertainty is not valued as much as a choice with risk. Indeed, it seemed that a choice with uncertainty was given a very low expected reward. That fits with what we looked at in Chapter five and the suggestion that people are ambiguity averse.

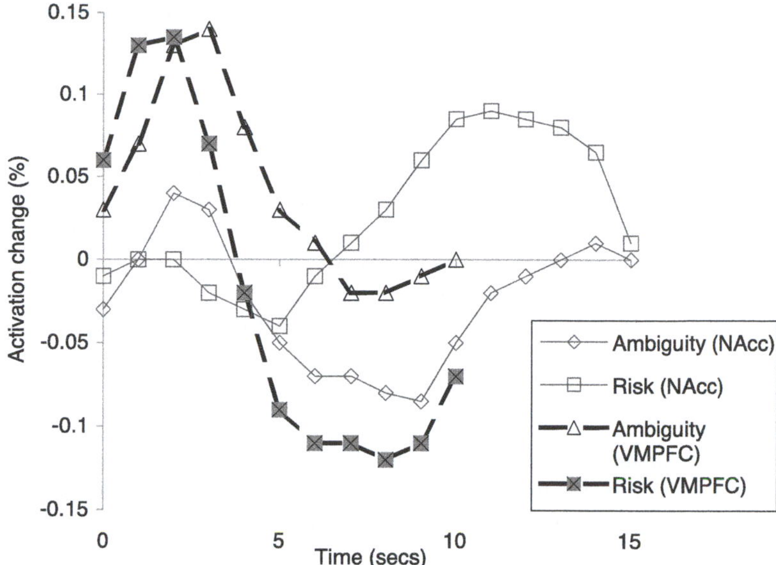

Figure 9.10 Activation in the NAcc (left striatum) and VMPFC (left orbitofrontal cortex) depended on whether the choice was with risk or uncertainty.

Source: Hsu *et al.* (2005).

(We don't know yet what happens with compound lotteries.) I will come back to the differences between risk and uncertainty shortly, but I want to finish this section by looking a bit more at different types of reward.

9.2.4 Different types of reward

We have seen that brain activation can be nicely correlated with expected reward. An important concept in taking this idea further is **reward prediction error**. Basically, this is the difference between the reward expected and what was received. So, if Rob expected to win \$5 and wins \$0 or \$10, then his prediction error is −\$5 or \$5. Reward prediction error is clearly important in determining how excited Rob should be and how he should learn for the future.

In the studies that we have looked at so far it is difficult to distinguish how the areas of the brain react to reward prediction error as opposed to expected reward. It seems, however, that NAcc is activated in proportion to the reward prediction error. To illustrate, I will look at a study by Hare and co-authors (2008).

In the study, before going into the scanner, subjects stated a willingness to pay for 50 food items and were given some 'spending money'. Once in the scanner, they were given the chance to say yes or no to purchasing food items at a randomly determined price while also learning that their spending money had randomly been increased or decreased by some amount. For example, a subject might be presented with a screen displaying a candy bar, for sale at price $2, and something to say he or she had lost $1 of spending money.

The purpose of doing this was to distinguish three things that could influence the subject's reaction and choice. First, there is the willingness to pay for the good, second, there is the difference between price and willingness to pay, and third, there is the reward prediction error. You might recall that in Chapter two I gave these first two things the names, acquisition utility and transaction utility. Figure 9.11 illustrates how much activity in three different areas of the brain correlated with the three different values. The picture we get is again consistent with different areas of the brain reacting differently to these values. The NAcc is activated by the prediction error, and areas of the VMPFC by the willingness to pay and transaction utility.

I think we have already seen some exciting results. We have seen that the distinctions made earlier in the book, between losses and gains, risk and uncertainty, and acquisition and transaction utility, really do make sense, not only in trying to model choice, but as a description of how people think. The next step is to see if this translates into choice and decision making.

9.3 Making decisions

So far the focus has been on people passively reacting to events largely out of their control. This firmly puts us in the domain of automatic processes, even if with some executive control. Now it's time to go up a gear and look at what

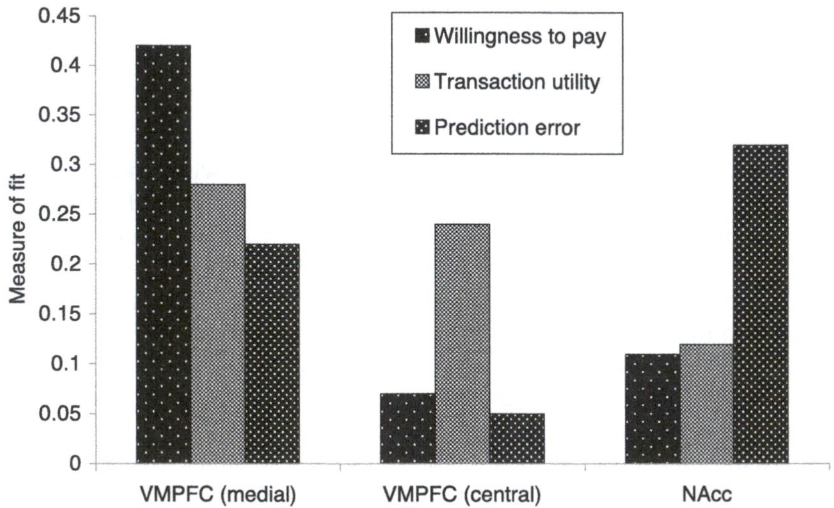

Figure 9.11 The fit between values and activity in three areas of the brain.
Source: Hare *et al.* (2008).

happens when people have some choice, and so use reasoning and control processes.

To get us started, I want to look at a study by O'Doherty and co-authors (2004) that nicely illustrates the potential differences between passive learning and choice. In the study, subjects were repeatedly exposed to two options before getting either a tasty juice or neutral reward. One of the options came with a 60 percent chance of getting the juice and the other with a 30 percent chance of getting the juice. So, subjects had to learn the correlation between option and reward. More interesting for our purpose was that sometimes subjects chose an option and sometimes the computer chose for them.

The main results of the study are summarized in Figure 9.12. Focus first on the left-hand side and the ventral striatum. For our purposes the ventral striatum and NAcc are the same and, as we have now come to expect, this area was activated in proportion to the expected reward and reward prediction error. Now look at what happens in the dorsal striatum. This time there is activation when the subject has the chance to make a choice, but not when the computer will decide. This relationship leads to **actor-critic models** in which the ventral striatum is cast in the role of critic, evaluating rewards, while the dorsal striatum is cast in the role of actor, selecting what to choose.

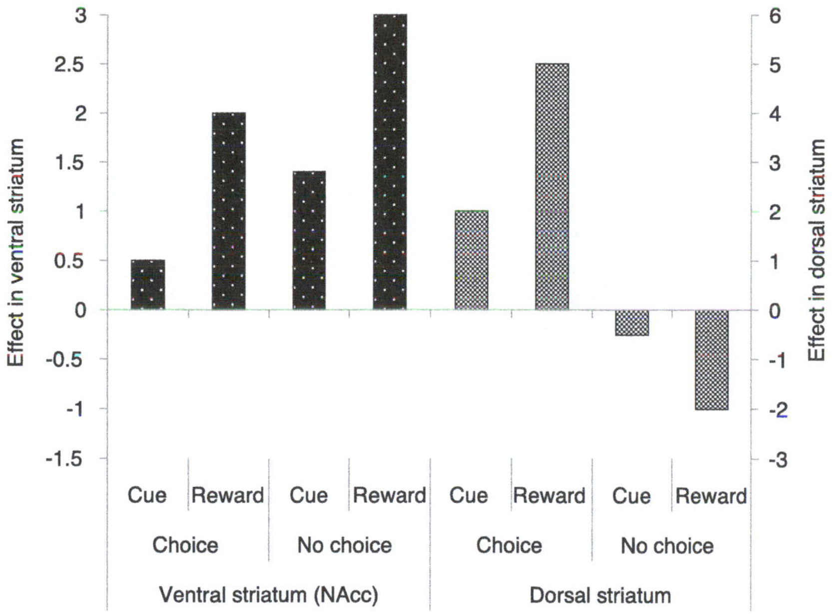

Figure 9.12 Activation in the dorsal and ventral striatum during a learning task on seeing the options or cue and getting the reward. Activation in the dorsal striatum depends on whether there is choice or not.

Source: O'Doherty *et al.* (2004).

Choice does, therefore, make a difference to what goes on in the brain as other areas are activated to seemingly help make the decision. An intriguing issue is whether we can use this to predict choice and strategy.

9.3.1 Choice and strategy

To show that the idea, we can relate choice and strategy to brain activation is not so crazy, I want to look at two studies where subjects had to choose between risky or uncertain gambles.

I'll start with a study by Huettel and co-authors (2006). In this study, subjects were presented with pairs of gambles or prospects of which some gambles involved risk and some uncertainty. For example, they might have to choose between a risky gamble that pays out $12 with probability 0.75 and $20 with probability 0.25, and an uncertain gamble that pays out $0 or $35 with unknown probability. We thus move away from asking how subjects respond to seeing risk or uncertainty to how they choose between the two.

For each subject, having seen what they chose, it is possible to construct indices of how much they seem to like (or not) ambiguity and risk. We can then see whether these preferences correlate with the brain activation observed while the subject was making choices. That is, we are trying to find a link between brain activation and choice. Figure 9.13 suggests that we can find such a link, although we are going to have to look at areas of the brain other than the NAcc and VMPFC. Figure 9.13 summarizes how ambiguity led to the greatest activation in the lateral

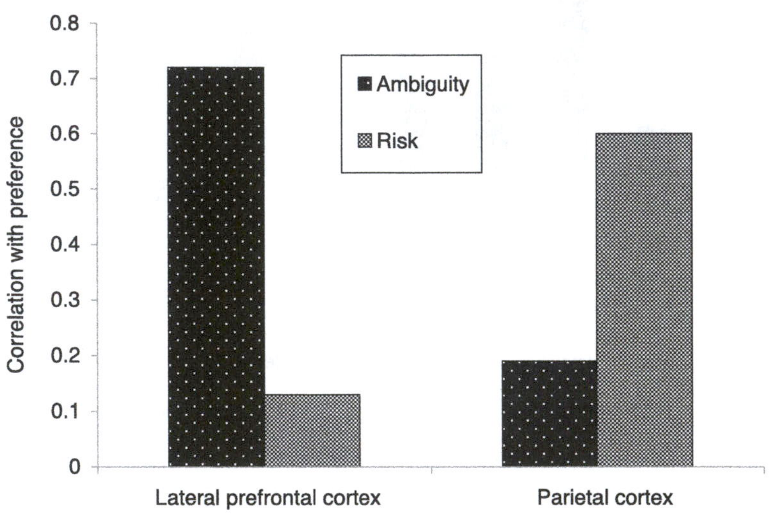

Figure 9.13 Areas of the lateral prefrontal cortex and parietal cortex are more activated in those with a preference for ambiguity and risk.

Source: Huettel *et al.* (2006).

prefrontal cortex for those whose choices suggest they like ambiguity. Similarly, risk led to the greatest activation in the parietal cortex for those whose choices suggest they are less risk averse.

We see, therefore, that not only do risk and ambiguity activate different areas of the brain, but by seeing how much the brain is activated we can potentially predict choices. Can we go one stage further and predict strategy?

To see if we can, I will look at a study by Venkatraman and co-authors (2009). In the study, subjects were first presented with a risky prospect containing five possible outcomes, for example, to win $80 with probability 0.25, lose $75 with probability 0.2, and so on. They were then given two alternatives to improve the prospect and had to choose which they wanted. For example, the alternatives might be to make it a $100 win with probability 0.25, or a $55 loss with probability 0.2.

There are two basic types of strategy that one might employ in this scenario. The 'simple strategy' is to maximize the probability of making a difference, and so, for instance, to add $20 to the $80 outcome because this is more likely to matter than adding $20 to the $75 loss. A more 'complex strategy' would be to maximize gains, by adding $20 to the $80, or minimize losses, by adding it to the $75 loss, or maximize expected utility in some other way.

In standard experiments, without brain imaging, most subjects were observed using the simple strategy but some did use a complex strategy. The main thing, though, was that subjects seemed to stick to a strategy through multiple rounds. We can, therefore, potentially disentangle choice from strategy.

Let's look first at choice. Figure 9.14 shows that choice was correlated with activation in different brain areas. For example, choosing the option that maximized the possible gain was associated with greater activity in the VMPFC,

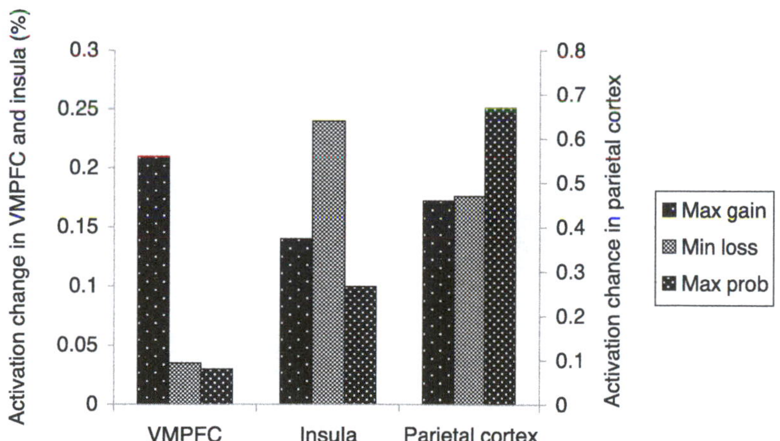

Figure 9.14 Different choices correlate with increased activation in different areas of the brain.

Source: Venkatraman *et al.* (2009).

while choosing the option that minimized the possible loss was associated with greater activity in the insula. So far, so good.

Now let's look at strategy. What we want to do here is see whether some areas of the brain are more activated when someone makes a choice not consistent with their usual strategy. That is, what happens when someone who usually uses a simple strategy decides to do something 'more complicated' like maximize the possible gain, or when someone who usually uses a complex strategy decides to do the 'simpler thing' of maximizing probability? When this happens the dorsomedial prefrontal cortex becomes more activated and, what's more, as Figure 9.15 shows, we observe greater connectivity between this and the areas associated with choice.

So, greater activation of some areas correlates with choices made, while greater activation in others correlates with strategy, or with the differences between choice and strategy. It looks, therefore, as though we can watch both choice and strategy being played out in the brain, which is fascinating stuff. Fascinating enough that I want to give you a second example.

9.3.2 Framing effects

We have already seen evidence that a gain activates a different area of the VMPFC than a loss. The question I want to look at now is whether this difference can lead to framing effects. Let us look at a study by De Martino and co-authors (2006). Subjects had to choose between a sure amount of money or a risky gamble.

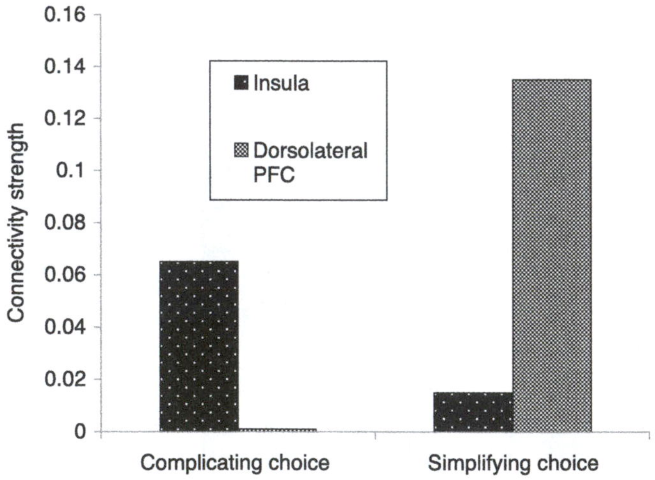

Figure 9.15 Increased connectivity is observed between the dorsomedial prefrontal cortex and the insula and parietal cortex when someone makes a choice inconsistent with their normal strategy.

Source: Venkatraman *et al.* (2009).

For example, they could take $20 or gamble with a 40 percent chance of getting $50 and 60 percent chance of getting $0. What differed is the way these options were presented. Using a gain frame, the sure thing was framed as a gain of $20. Using a loss frame, the sure thing was framed as a loss of $30.

As we would expect, subjects were more likely to choose the sure option in a gain frame than in a loss frame. Can we pick up this framing effect in the brain? Figure 9.16 shows activation in the amygdala and anterior cingulated cortex. When subjects made the 'simple' choice, the amygdala was positively activated. When subjects made the 'difficult' choice, the amygdala was negatively activated and the anterior cingulated cortex was more activated. Recall (see Table 9.2) that the amygdala is involved with emotional processing, while the anterior cingulated cortex (see Table 9.4) is involved with conflict resolution.

The picture we get, therefore, is of framing and context effects working exactly as discussed in Chapters two and three. Consistent with people being risk loving for losses (see section 3.1.3), the automatic process is to gamble on the loss frame and not to gamble on the gain frame. This automatic process, however, is potentially inhibited by the executive control system. Such inhibition activates a more reasoned choice, less subject to the framing effect. Again, we can see choice and strategy being played out in the brain.

What is new is that we can also question the sense of that strategy. Subjects varied a lot in how much they were affected by framing. Some subjects nearly always made the same choices in a gain and loss frame, while other subjects were more affected by the frame. This allowed the authors of the study to construct a

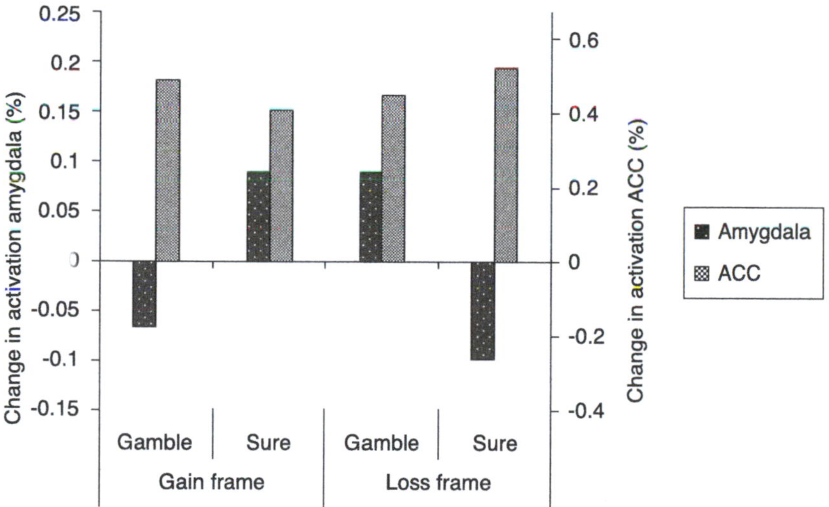

Figure 9.16 Activation in the amygdala and anterior cingulated cortex (ACC) depending on the frame and choice.

Source: De Martino *et al.* (2006).

'rationality index', where a subject less affected by framing was considered more rational. Interestingly, they found that this rationality index was highly correlated with activity in the orbital and medial prefrontal cortex (OMPFC) and VMPFC. We have not come across the OMPFC yet, but it is connected to the amygdala and known to be important in evaluating the outcomes of decisions. We also know that the VMPFC is involved in inhibition (see Table 9.4).

This suggests that some subjects were better able to recognize the potential emotional bias that the framing effect would create. In other words, the executive control system of 'rational' subjects was more aware that it needed to get involved and inhibit automatic processes. In this case a subject needed to be aware of their own bias. In strategic interaction a subject needs to think through the strategy and potential bias of others. It is to this that I now briefly turn.

9.3.3 Strategic behavior

Where better to begin looking at strategic interaction than the p-beauty contest (see Chapter six)? In a study by Coricelli and Nagel (2009), subjects played 13 different p-beauty contests where p ranged from near zero to near two. Recall (see section 6.2.1) that people playing the p-beauty context differ in their depth of reasoning. A type L-1 expects others to choose randomly, while a type L-2 expects others to be type L-1, and so on.

In order to better evaluate depth of reasoning, Coricelli and Nagel also had subjects play 13 contests with computer opponents, where the computers chose a number randomly. A type L-1 would be expected to behave the same against human opponents as computer opponents. A type L-2, however, would be expected to behave differently against humans than computers.

Figure 9.17 summarizes some of the ways in which brain activity differed between subjects classified as type L-1 and type L-2 or higher. Let us focus first on the medial prefrontal cortex (MPFC). Notice that this is strongly activated in type L-2 subjects when playing against humans. The MPFC is believed to be involved in **theory of mind** or reasoning through other people's minds. In type L-1 subjects the MPFC is not activated, but the anterior cingulated cortex is. We have focused on the anterior cingulated cortex's role in the executive control system, but it is also associated with thinking about self.

These results provide good evidence that level-k thinking is an appropriate way to model choice in the beauty contest. We see that those subjects classified as type L-2 or above thought through what others would do, while those classified as type L-1 thought more about themselves.

By comparing the distance between a subject's guesses and the guesses of others it is possible to construct an index of 'strategic rationality'. The authors found that this index correlates strongly with activity in the MPFC and VMPFC. This result is very similar to that found for the framing study, looked at in the previous section. The only change is that different areas of the brain are activated to reflect the different task involved. In the framing task, 'rational' subjects had greater activation in the OMPFC, which is associated with evaluating outcomes.

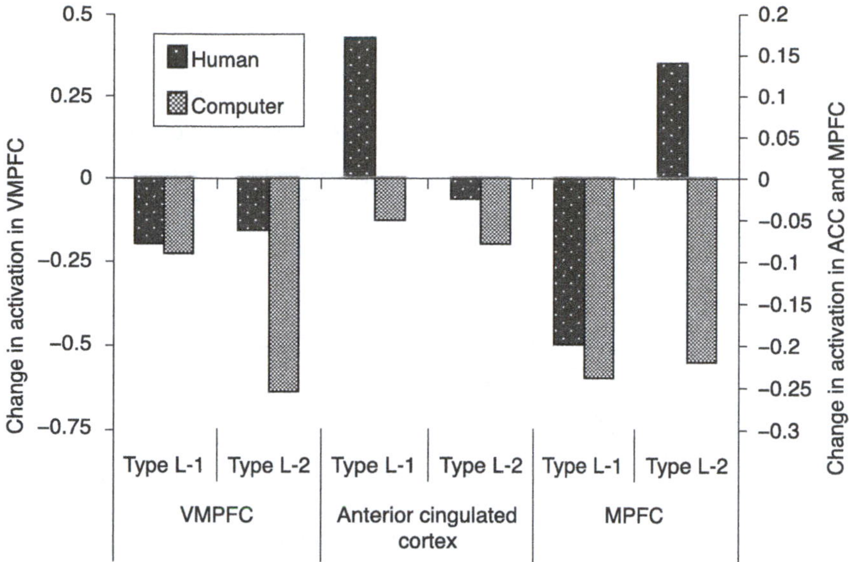

Figure 9.17 Activation in the VMPFC, anterior cingulated cortex and medial prefrontal cortex (MPFC) depending on level of reasoning and whether the opponents were humans or computers.

Source: Coricelli and Nagel (2009).

In the strategic task, 'rational' subjects had greater activation in the MPFC, which is associated with theory of mind. The VMPFC appears to play a role in both cases.

We have now seen a few examples of how choice and strategy can be picked apart and analyzed. What I want to do now is question how far this ability can take us in understanding social preferences and inter-temporal choice.

9.3.4 Fairness and norms

In getting us started with social preferences I want to talk about a study by Sanfey and co-authors (2003). The study basically involved subjects playing the ultimatum game (see Chapter seven) to see how people react to unfair and fair offers. Subjects, in the role of receiver, were offered proposed splits of \$5 and \$5, of \$9 and \$1, of \$8 and \$2, and of \$7 and \$3. The main question of interest is how subjects responded to a fair offer, \$5 and \$5, as compared to unfair offers like \$9 and \$1.

One area of the brain we have yet to talk about is the insula, but now it becomes a lot more relevant. As Figure 9.18 shows, the insula was activated more when a subject received an offer that was unfair rather than fair, and more when the proposer making the unfair offer was known to be a human rather than a computer. There was also greater activation, the more unfair the offer. Most

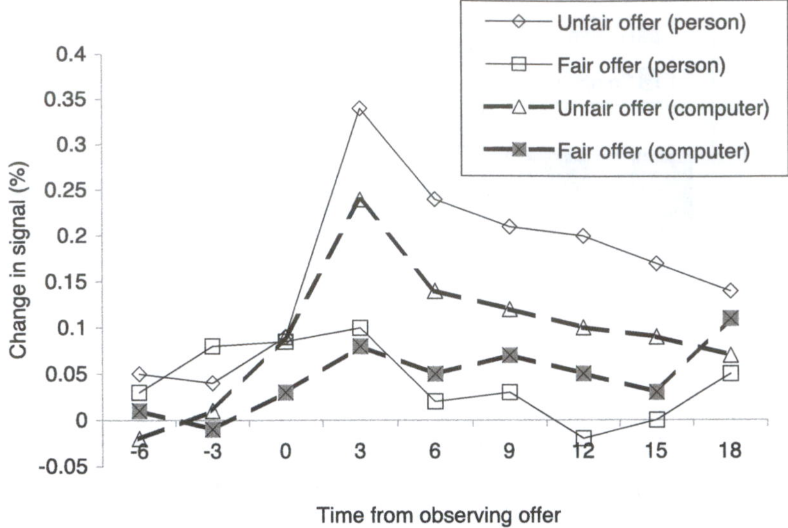

Figure 9.18 Timeline of activation in the (right anterior) insula depending on whether the offer was fair or unfair.

Source: Sanfey *et al.* (2003).

interesting is probably Figure 9.19, which compares activation in the insula and dorsolateral prefrontal cortex (DLPFC) for offers that were subsequently rejected relative to those that were accepted. We see that the rejection of an offer comes with relatively large activation of the insula. So, what is going on?

The only mention the insula has had so far is in Table 9.2, where I said that it was involved in visceral and autonomic functions like taste. In fact, things that are consistently associated with the insula include negative emotional states like pain and distress, hunger, thirst, and disgust from taste or odor. This clearly fits with a story of receivers feeling a negative emotional response on receiving an unfair offer. By contrast, we know the DLPFC is usually associated with cognitive processes and executive control and so is possibly more focused on getting as much money as possible. This suggests a potential conflict between the insula, that wants to reject, and DLPFC, that wants to accept. Figure 9.19 is certainly consistent with this. Further credence to this idea comes from increased activation of the anterior cingulated cortex for unfair offers. Remember that this is thought to be involved in conflict resolution.

So, we get a neat story. The insula is upset by an unfair offer and wants to reject, while the DLPFC wants the money, so is happy to accept. Sometimes the insula wins out and sometimes the DLPFC. Neat stories often have a catch, and this one is no exception. To see why, I want to look at a study by Knoch and co-authors (2006). In this study low-frequency repetitive transcranial magnetic

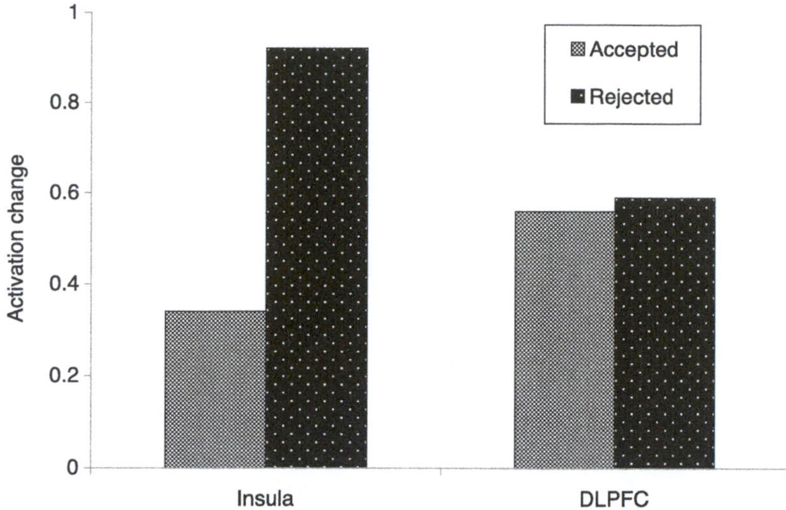

Figure 9.19 Activation in the (right) insula and (right) dorsolateral prefrontal cortex for offers that were subsequently rejected or accepted.

Source: Sanfey *et al.* (2003).

stimulation was applied to either the right or left DLPFC of subjects. This suppresses activity in that part of the brain. It basically switches off either the left or right DLPFC. So, what should happen if we switch off the DLPFC?

If the DLPFC wants to accept any offer, the insula wants to reject an unfair offer, and we switch of the DLPFC, then we should see more rejection of unfair offers. Figure 9.20 shows that we observe the complete opposite! We see far less rejection of unfair offers when the right DLPFC is switched off than when the left is switched off, or when neither is switched off. This is despite the unfair offer still being perceived as unfair.

The story we get now, therefore, is one where the DLPFC wants to reject a low offer, because of fairness norms, and other areas of the brain want to accept, and get the money. Consistent with this, stimulation of the right DLPFC had less of an effect when the low offer was received from a computer rather than human proposer. So, it's not really very clear what's going on, but either way the (right) DLPFC does seem important for reciprocity.

To explore this further, we can look at a study by Spitzer and co-authors (2007). In the study, subjects played two different games several times. One game was a variation on the dictator game, in that one subject, the proposer, was given 125 tokens and a second subject, the receiver, was given 25 tokens; the proposer could give up to 100 of his or her tokens to the receiver. The second game was a variation on the ultimatum game, in that the receiver had the chance to punish the proposer after seeing how many tokens he or she had been given; for every one

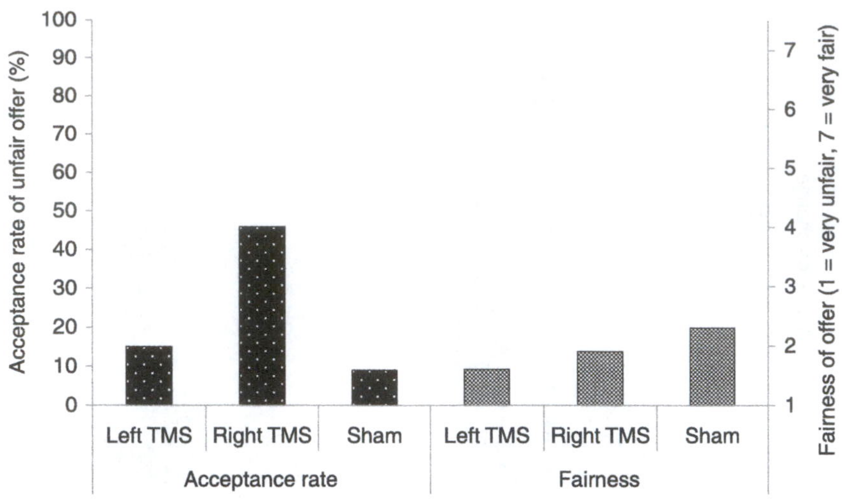

Figure 9.20 Acceptance rate and perceptions of an unfair offer in the ultimatum game. Those with stimulation (TMS) to the right DLPFC are more likely to accept, despite still thinking the offer is unfair. In the sham treatment there is no stimulation.

Source: Knoch *et al.* (2006).

token that the receiver spent punishing, five tokens would be taken from the proposer. For example, if the proposer gave no tokens to the receiver and the receiver spent 25 tokens on punishing, then both proposer and receiver would end up with zero tokens. Some subjects played the ultimatum game with another subject (and knew it), while some played against a pre-programmed computer (and knew it).

As discussed in Chapter seven, the dictator game gives us an idea of how much a subject would voluntarily give to another, while the ultimatum game gives us an idea of how much he or she would give with the threat of punishment. The focus switches, therefore, more onto the proposer than the receiver. When we compare activation during the ultimatum game to that in the dictator game we see greater activation in several areas including the DLPFC and VMPFC. Furthermore, activation was higher in these areas, and the insula, when the receiver was a person and not a computer. There was also correlation between activation and the amount offered.

The task in the ultimatum game is already getting quite complex because the proposer needs to think through both how much they want to give and how much the receiver is likely to accept. It's no surprise therefore that various areas of the brain, including the DLPFC, VMPFC, and insula, are more activated. The story we get, though, seems again to be one of the prefrontal cortex acting as a check on other areas that might want to take the money. To progress further, it's interesting to look a bit more at preferences for punishment and equality.

9.3.5 Punishment and inequality aversion

A study by De Quervain and co-authors (2004) gives us interesting insights into preferences for punishment. They looked at a trust game (see Chapter seven) in which an investor can invest zero or ten tokens with a proposer; if he or she invests, then the proposer has 50 tokens and must decide whether to return zero or 25 of those to the investor. The variation on this basic trust game is to allow the investor the option of punishing the proposer if the tokens were invested but not repaid.

Focusing solely on those cases where the investor invested but got no return, Figure 9.21 illustrates the activation in the striatum. There are four different conditions depending on whether the investor chose to punish (intentional) or the computer did, whether it was costly for the investor to punish (costly), and whether the punishment actually lowered the payoff of the proposer (costly and free, versus symbolic). Recall that the striatum is involved in reward evaluation, and so it's particularly interesting that this should be activated more in those conditions where the investor could meaningfully punish the proposer. Activation also correlated with the amount of punishment. So, do people get satisfaction from punishing?

One way to try to answer this is to compare what happens when punishment is free to when it is costly. Several subjects punished the maximum amount when punishment was free, and so we can say that any differences in activation between them were probably due to differences in a desire to punish. We then ask whether those who had higher activation when punishment was free punished more when it was costly, and they did. This suggests that people did get satisfaction from punishing! One further piece of evidence is that the VMPFC was more activated when punishment was costly, suggesting that it was trading off the desire to punish with the cost of punishing.

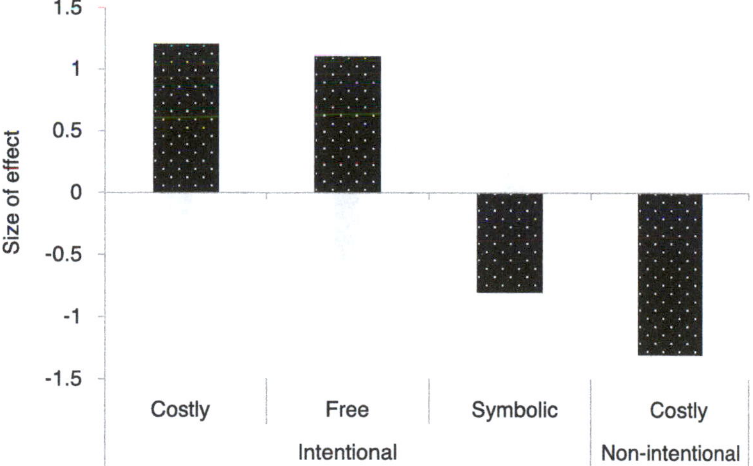

Figure 9.21 Activation in the striatum depends on the type of punishment.
Source: De Quervain *et al.* (2004).

If a preference for punishing seems a bit depressing, then a study by Tricomi and co-authors (2010) gives a slightly more upbeat conclusion. In the study, subjects participated in pairs. Having been given an initial $30 each, one subject was randomly given another $50 and the other nothing, creating a 'rich' and 'poor' subject. Subsequently, subjects were asked to evaluate future potential payments to them and the other subject. As we can see from the left-hand side of Figure 9.22, evaluations were consistent with inequality aversion: a rich subject valued a payment to them only slightly above a payment to the poor subject, while poor subjects rated relative highly payments to them and negatively payments to the rich subject. So, how did this inequality aversion translate into brain activity?

The right-hand side of Figure 9.22 shows a consistency between the valuations and activation in the NAcc and VMPFC. Most interesting is the NAcc, which we have seen is activated by expected reward. Rich subjects seemed to be more activated by transfers to the poor subject, while poor subjects seemed to be more activated by transfers to the rich subject. This suggests that inequality aversion really does exist. The role of the VMPFC is again probably to trade off the desire to equalize payoffs with the desire to get money.

It's fascinating to see that there potentially is pleasure in punishing and pleasure in redressing inequality. You might have noticed, however, that this brings us back full circle in trying to discern the competing incentives in the brain. If punishing and giving provide satisfaction, then it's not obvious whether the 'basic emotion' is to take the money or to punish. With such competing evidence we simply do not know yet what conflict the VMPFC and executive control systems

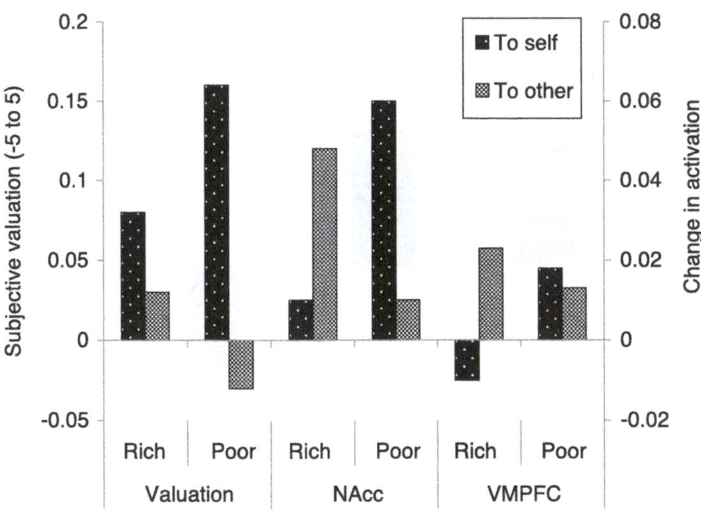

Figure 9.22 The effect of inequality on the valuation of subsequent transfers and activation in the NAcc and VMPFC.

Source: Tricomi *et al.* (2010).

have to sort out or inhibit when it comes to social preferences. But there's not much doubt that there are conflicting incentives, and it's this that I will now take up in a bit more detail.

9.3.6 Present bias and a brain in conflict

If parallel processes are going on in the brain all the while, then it is not surprising that these sometimes **conflict** in suggesting different behavior. Indeed, if the basic purpose of the executive control systems is to switch from automatic to control, and in so doing inhibit automatic processes, there is a clear potential for conflict. So, if it feels like one part of your brain is telling you one thing and another part something else, that may not be too far from reality.

We have already seen a potential tension between taking money offered or punishing in the ultimatum and trust game. It's not hard to find other examples. Someone falling asleep at the wheel despite trying to stay awake is a fairly extreme example. Another example you may be familiar with is the **Stroop task**, where a person is asked to read color words very fast and some words are in the 'wrong' color (e.g. the word blue might be colored green). People take longer to reply when the word and color are incongruent because of the conflicting signals they get, the anterior cingulated cortex sorting the conflict out.

That someone could be 'of two minds' is potentially very important, particularly in thinking about present bias and time inconsistency (see Chapter four). We could imagine, say, that Maria's automatic processes suggest she enjoys herself today, while her control processes say she should do her homework. If the automatic processes prove stronger than her control processes, then she might want to do her homework, think it was best she did her homework, but still delay it to another day. We have a plausible explanation for time inconsistency.

To see if this story fits, I will look first at a study by McClure and co-authors (2004). In the study, subjects made a series of inter-temporal choices between an early or delayed monetary reward. Sometimes the reward was available immediately, but sometimes only with some delay. This made it possible to distinguish brain areas more activated by choices involving an immediate outcome. To illustrate, Figure 9.23 compares activation in the NAcc and DLPFC. We can see that activation of the DLPFC is not influenced by the delay until getting the reward, but the NAcc is. A reward today activates this area more than a delayed reward.

In Chapter four I looked at a quasi-hyperbolic model of (β, δ) preferences where the δ captured exponential discounting and the β captured present bias. We can now see areas of the brain, like the NAcc, that possibly give us the β part, while others, like the DLPFC, give us the δ part. If so, then choice should correlate with relative activation of areas associated with each part. Figure 9.24 shows that this is exactly what was seen; when a subject chose the early option, areas of the brain that we might associate with the β part were more activated, and when they chose the delayed option, areas of the brain that we might associate with the δ part were activated.

To continue the story, I want to briefly mention a study by Diekhof and Gruber (2010). They ran experiments where, in a first stage, subjects did a task in which

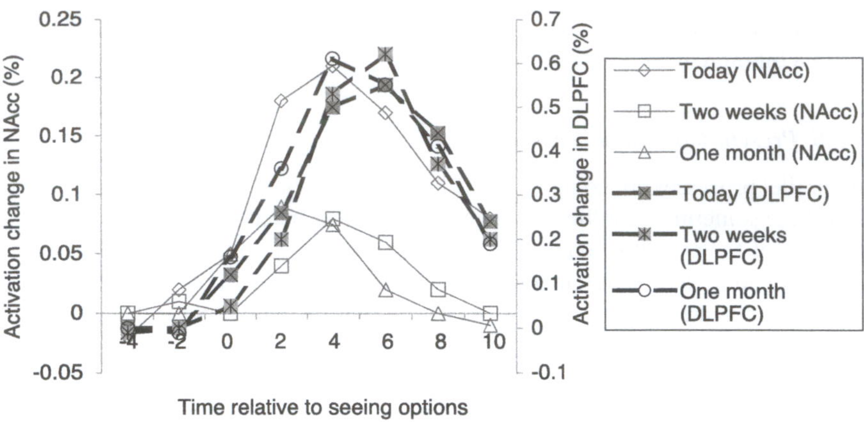

Figure 9.23 Activation in the NAcc and DLPFC depending on whether the reward was immediate or delayed.

Source: McClure *et al.* (2004).

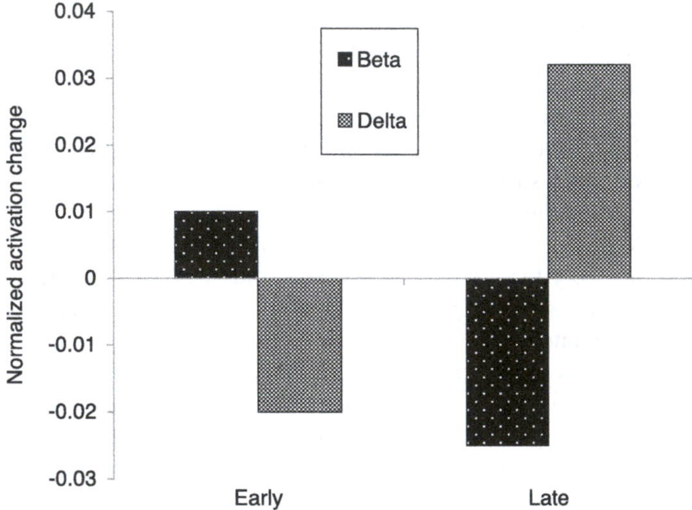

Figure 9.24 Areas associated with immediate reward (beta) are more activated when the subject chooses the early option, and areas associated with delayed reward (delta) are more activated when choosing the later option.

Source: McClure *et al.* (2004).

they learnt that choosing certain colors gave a reward. In a second stage, they were given a task that involved choosing certain colors a fixed number of times. This created a conflict between the long-term goal of collecting the right number of each color and the impulse to choose a color that gives an immediate reward. As we would expect, a color associated with a reward led to greater activation of the NAcc. The interesting thing comes during the second stage where a negative functional connectivity was observed between the NAcc and areas of the prefrontal cortex. In other words, the more the prefrontal cortex was activated, the less the NAcc. Furthermore, the stronger this negative connectivity, the more likely the subject performed the task correctly.

I think that these two studies are interesting to contrast in the way that conflict resolution appears to emerge. In the first we have the impression of two areas of the brain conflicting, with the one activated the most winning. So impulsivity might win over patience, or a desire to punish might win over a desire to take the money (as in Figures 9.19 and 9.20). The second study gives more of an impression of areas of the prefrontal cortex overseeing and directing what is going on elsewhere in the brain. So, patience subdues impulsivity or the need for money subdues the desire to punish.

Both of these ways of looking at things are really just part of the same executive control systems. On the one hand, controlled processes compete with automatic processes and, on the other hand, controlled processes direct automatic processes. One interesting implication of this, which can have important economic consequences, is that behavior can depend on the cognitive load of the executive control systems. Basically, if executive control is looking after one thing, it might let slip something else.

An interesting example of this is provided in a study by Shiv and Fedorikhin (1999). The study involved subjects having to remember either a two-digit or seven-digit number while deciding whether to choose between chocolate cake or fruit salad. Figure 9.25 shows that subjects were significantly more likely to

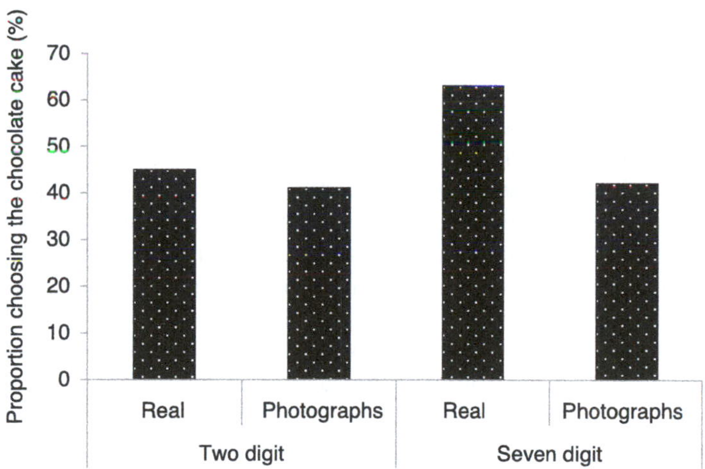

Figure 9.25 The proportion of subjects choosing chocolate cake is higher when the subject had to remember a seven-digit number and was shown the snacks for real.

Source: Shiv and Fedorikhin (1999).

choose the chocolate cake when the subject had to remember a seven-digit number and was shown the snacks for real. This is consistent with automatic processes being more likely to overpower the controlled processes if the controlled processes are busy doing something else.

9.3.7 Multiple self-models

This conflict being played out in the brain suggests why people have **self-control problems**. Recall that in Chapter four we saw that someone like Maria may want to pre-commit by, say, agreeing to meet with friends tomorrow, which means her homework has to be done today. Furthermore, she might want to pre-commit even if she does her homework today, because she still avoids the cost of overcoming temptation. This kind of thing is very hard for the standard economic model to cope with. Why would someone want to pre-commit and thereby reduce the options available to her? Now we have an explanation.

It's reassuring to have an explanation for self-control problems, but can we go further? One possibility is to explicitly model the conflict going on in the brain. This leads to the idea of **multiple-self** or **dual-self** models. I will not go into too many details here because I will work through an example of such a model when looking at addiction, but the basic idea is simple. We can think of one self, whom Thaler and Shefrin (1981) suggest calling the **planner**, who wants to maximize lifetime utility, and another self, the **doer**, who wants to maximize utility today.

The easiest way is to think of the doer as being the one who always makes the decisions what to do now. This gives a lot of the power to automatic processes and is potentially quite worrying for the individual, because the doer will always sacrifice the future for today. Fortunately, the planner is given two main ways to constrain the doer. First, it could change the preferences or incentives of the doer. For example, Maria's planner might make it that the doer likes doing homework, or bets with a friend who will get the best homework mark. Second, it could impose rules that change the constraints of the doer. For example, Maria's planner might pre-commit to playing with friends tomorrow.

This type of model is very useful in understanding and modeling precommitment and self-control. It gives a big role to automatic processes, which we shall see is apt when thinking about something like addiction. But, should we be using dual-self models a lot more? Maybe it makes sense, given the real conflict between automatic and controlled processes going on in the brain.

As ever, there can be a danger in taking an idea too far. The reason I say this is that conflict is already at the heart of the standard economic model. For example, when I wrote down Anna's utility function over breakfast cereals, $u(x, TQ, HQ)$, in Chapter two, encapsulated within that is a conflict between her wanting money and wanting the cereal of the highest quality. Anna faces a potentially tough choice in trading off money for a tasty cereal, and so she may spend some time in the grocery store being in two minds what to buy. We do not need a multiple-self model to capture that.

This is not an issue of whether there is or is not a conflict between automatic and controlled processes. Indeed, I have made a point of saying that automatic processes will influence all decisions through perception and intuition. So Anna's choice will inevitably involve both controlled and automatic processes – we just have better ways to model this. For example, Anna might get angry at a price rise, an automatic process, and then be reluctant to buy despite knowing it's still a price she is willing to pay, a controlled process. In Chapter two we saw how this can be captured by distinguishing between transaction utility and acquisition utility.

Dual-self models are probably not, therefore, so important in improving how well we can model economic behavior. We have also seen that, when it comes to things such as fairness, it is very hard to disentangle the automatic 'doer' behavior and the objectives of the controlled 'planner'. Indeed, in terms of modeling economic behavior it seems more natural to think of the dual self as a distinction between automatic processes that determine the reference point versus controlled processes that work around that reference point. That's the approach we have taken throughout most of the book.

9.4 Summary

I have only looked at a small selection of the many results from neuroscience and neuroeconomics, but I think that there is already enough here to be impressed with what we can learn.

I started by describing the idea of modularity in which we think of different brain areas as performing different tasks. We can then potentially learn something from observing what areas are activated and by how much when a person observes something or makes a particular decision.

The second idea I talked about was that of different brain processes. We contrasted automatic processes with controlled processes and gave executive control the job of knowing when to switch from automatic to control. This suggests that there can potentially be conflict in the brain as one area wants to do one thing, another area something different, and executive control has to sort this conflict out.

In looking at economic behavior, the focus to start with was on how people react to observing outcomes. We saw that some areas, like nucleus accumbens, are activated by the expectation of a reward and are potentially activated in proportion to the expected reward, or reward prediction error. We saw that other areas, like the ventromedial prefrontal cortex, are more activated on getting the reward. While it may be a step too far to say that this is like seeing the utility function in the brain, it does allow us to see what types of outcome activate different reward areas and so learn something about preferences. We saw evidence consistent with ambiguity aversion, with present bias, with the distinction between transaction and acquisition utility, and with inequality aversion.

The next step was to add an element of choice to see how the brain is activated when making decisions. We saw that additional areas were activated suggesting the actor-critic distinction between areas of the brain primarily responsible for evaluation and those responsible for action. We saw that brain activation often does correlate with the action chosen and strategy used.

In looking at social preferences we saw that people appear to react negatively to an unfair offer and get a reward from punishing. Harder is to pull apart what are the automatic and controlled processes.

As I briefly mentioned in Chapter one, neuroeconomics is a controversial topic, and so it seems natural, now that you have seen something of what it has to offer, to try to make sense of the controversy. The basic controversy is whether neuroeconomics can add anything useful to economics, and this is primarily a manifestation of the debates that we looked at in Chapter one. For instance, the main charge is that knowing how the brain works is neither necessary nor sufficient to understand, model, and predict economic behavior.

I hope to have shown you in this chapter that knowing how the brain works can definitely help us to understand economic behavior a bit better. It's fascinating to see things like inequality aversion and present bias seemingly being acted out within the brain. Seeing such things should reassure that the models I have looked at earlier in the book, taking account of things like inequality aversion and present bias, make sense.

I also believe that knowing how the brain works can potentially help us model and predict economic behavior a bit better. For example, if we can distinguish automatic from controlled processes, this could help us predict how behavior will change as the context changes: to understand better, say, when people will want to punish unfair behavior and when they will not.

It is, though, slightly worrying to have to use the phrase 'potentially help us model and predict'. While neuroeconomics is undoubtedly fascinating in understanding economic behavior, it is much harder to see how it can significantly help us to better model and predict economic behavior. It's hard to believe, for instance, that watching people's brains as they play the ultimatum game can make us any more able to predict what they will do than we have learnt from the thousands of standard experiments already run. Given that economic theories are usually judged on their ability to predict behavior, this is where neuroeconomics loses out.

So, while neuroeconomics is clearly informative and worth doing, it's unlikely to revolutionize economics. It's good – but not that good.

Where neuroeconomics can be more revolutionary is in neuroscience. While economists are unlikely to learn too much from watching people's brains as they play the ultimatum game, neuroscientists can potentially learn a lot, precisely because economists know so well how people behave when playing such games. So, while we might debate just how good neuroeconomics is for economics, it is definitely good for neuroscience.

Turning around this logic I also think economics has a lot more to learn from neuroscience. In particular, the most depressing chapter for me to write in this book was Chapter six, on interaction and learning. Our ability to predict how people learn and behave in strategic situations is still quite poor. Given that learning, memory, and social cognition are important components of neuroscience, maybe we can find some answers there.

9.5 Addiction

Addiction is a big social issue. For instance, the National Survey on Drug Use and Health suggests that, in 2008, 14.2 percent of Americans aged 12 years or older had used illicit drugs during the past year. The National Drug Intelligence Center estimated the economic cost of this at nearly $215 billion, and summarized: 'The damage caused by drug abuse and addiction is reflected in an overburdened justice system, a strained healthcare system, lost productivity, and environmental destruction' (NDIC 2010). That's before we start on cigarettes and alcohol!

You might think that addiction is not a domain for economists, but it is also a big economic issue. For instance, cigarette taxes are an important source of government revenue. The US federal government raised around $15.5 billion from cigarette taxation in 2010, while local governments raised around $17 billion. Remarkably, the UK government, despite a far smaller tax base, raised nearly as much, at $16.9 billion! A primary motivation for setting taxes high is to cut demand and lower the costs associated with addiction. The merits of such policies are, however, hotly debated. Behavioral economics is ideally placed to inform the debate.

In order to get started we need to have a definition of addiction. One definition is to say that someone like Rob is **addicted** to a good if: (i) the more he consumes the good the more he wants to consume of the good – call this **reinforcement**; (ii) the more he consumes the good, the lower his utility from consuming the good in the future – call this **tolerance**.

This is a nice definition for economists because we can easily capture reinforcement and tolerance in simple models. It is, however, probably too broad a definition for many. Indeed, according to this definition I am addicted to lots of things, including long-distance running, and watching cricket. Given, however, that I am an economist, we will go with this definition for now, possibly thinking of it more as a definition of habit than addiction. More important is to start modeling adiction.

9.5.1 A model of rational addiction

To prove that I really am an economist, I will start with a model of rational addiction (credit to Becker and Murphy 1988). It might seem strange to put rational and addiction in the same sentence, but this provides a natural starting point. Here is the model.

Rob can choose to consume an addictive good, called cigarettes, or a non-addictive good, called money. Let a_t denote the amount of cigarettes he consumes in period t and let c_t denote the amount of money he spends. We then assume that his utility from smoking will depend on his previous consumption of cigarettes. To do this we need to keep track of how much he has smoked in the past. We do that by letting:

$$S_t = d(S_{t-1} + a_{t-1})$$

denote the **stock of past consumption** where d measures the addictiveness of the good. The higher is d, the more addictive cigarettes appear to be because the more past consumption is remembered. If $d = 1$, cigarettes are very addictive because past consumption is never forgotten.

We then assume that Rob's utility in period t will depend on present consumption and the stock of past consumption:

$$u_t = \begin{cases} c_t + 10\sqrt{a_t - S_t} & \text{if } a_t \geq S_t \\ c_t - 10(S_t - a_t) & \text{if } a_t < S_t \end{cases}.$$

We also assume that he uses exponential discounting (see Chapter four) to find his inter-temporal utility:

$$u^T = u_1 + \delta u_2 + \delta^2 u_2 + \ldots + \delta^{T-1} u_T. .$$

What Rob needs to do is plan his addiction. He knows that cigarettes are addictive, but he likes them none the less, and so needs to plan how many cigarettes to consume early in his life knowing that he will subsequently become addicted. The problem Rob faces is analogous to that faced by Maria in section 4.5.1 deciding when to consume goods, knowing she will become used to that level of consumption. One slight difference is that Maria could smooth consumption freely by saving for the future. To make things more interesting we are going to assume that Rob cannot save for the future, either cigarettes or money.

Working out Rob's optimal consumption of cigarettes is a somewhat tedious exercise in math. So, I will just look at some addiction plans and see what Rob would think about them. Table 9.6 looks at three. For each one we can see what utility Rob would get depending on what happens to the price of cigarettes in period 4. If the price of cigarettes is \$1 in all four periods, then Rob does best to consume a lot of cigarettes: he prefers to consume an increasing amount and in period 4 spends all his money on cigarettes. If the price of cigarettes increases to \$2 in period 4, then Rob does best to be a little restrained: he buys fewer cigarettes in periods 1 to 3 so that he does not become too addicted before cigarettes become expensive. If the price increases to \$2.50, then he does best to abstain altogether.

All this was assuming $d = 1$, and so cigarettes are highly addictive. If $d = 0.5$, so cigarettes are less addictive, Rob still does best to consume a lot of cigarettes.

This example illustrates the main predictions that come out of a rational addiction model, namely that Rob should base his present consumption on how addictive cigarettes are, and what will likely happen to the future price of cigarettes. If cigarettes are addictive and the future price will increase, then he should not consume now so as to not become trapped wanting something he cannot afford. If cigarettes are less addictive and/or he does not expect any increase in the price, then he can consume more. We can call this **forward-looking behavior**.

Table 9.6 The utility of several different addiction plans, assuming Rob has $10 per period and a pack of cigarettes costs $1 in periods 1 to 3. In period 4 the amount of cigarettes that Rob can consume is constrained by his income. Unless stated, $d = 1$

Price in period 4	*Cigarettes in period*				*Utility*
	1	*2*	*3*	*4*	
$1	0	0	0	0	40.0
	1	2	4	10	70.3
	1	1	2	5	51.0
$2	0	0	0	0	40.0
	1	2	4	5	33.0
	1	1	2	5	46.0
$2.50	0	0	0	0	40.0
	1	2	4	4	23.0
	1	1	2	4	36
$2.50 and d = 0.5	0	0	0	0	40.0
	1	2	4	4	73.6
	1	1	2	4	70.5

Before we question the plausibility of forward-looking behavior, I want to look at some data. The data is from a study by Gruber and Köszegi (2001) that looks at whether demand for cigarettes changes when taxes are announced. Given that there is often a delay of two months or more between a government announcing that taxes will increase and taxes actually increasing, it is possible to check for forward-looking behavior. We would expect consumption of cigarettes to fall when the tax increase is announced, not when prices actually rise. We might, however, expect demand for cigarettes to increase when the tax increase is announced, because it is a chance to hoard them before prices rise.

Gruber and Köszegi look at some data on both sales and consumption of cigarettes and find the predicted effects. In the sales data there is evidence of a hoarding effect, with sales increasing after the announcement of a tax increase. For example, an increase in the tax from 10 to 35 cents in California was announced in November 1988 and become effective in January 1989. Cigarette sales jumped from an average of 6.68 packs per person in November to 8.71 packs in December, before falling back to around six packs. In the consumption data there is evidence of decreased consumption once the tax increase is announced. It seems, therefore, that consumers are using forward-looking behavior.

This suggests that Rob could be in control of his addiction, and the only rationale for policy intervention would be if Rob's smoking has a negative externality on others. Given the biases we have seen elsewhere in this book, this might seem a surprising conclusion. It is not, however, the end of the story. That's because we observe a lot of other behavior that is not so consistent with a rational model of addiction. To that I now turn.

9.5.2 Biases and addiction

The rational model of addiction suggests two important biases that we might observe. First, the rational model requires forward-looking behavior, and we have seen (in Chapter four) that people like Rob may not be able to stick with a forward-looking plan because of a present bias. He might always plan to 'quit tomorrow' but never do so. Second, the rational model says that Rob can smoke more if he thinks cigarettes are less addictive, and we have seen (in Chapter five) that he may be biased in underestimating its addictiveness. For example, because of confirmatory bias and the law of small numbers he may ignore the scientific evidence on how addictive smoking is, because his friend was able to quit smoking.

Both these biases have the same basic prediction: Rob will become more addicted and consume more cigarettes than he planned to do. Evidence of this is not too hard to find. To demonstrate, we can look at some data from a report published in the UK about smoking-related attitudes and behavior (ONS 2004). Figure 9.26 summarizes how many people surveyed wanted to quit smoking. A lot of them did. Given this, we might expect that they would try to quit. Figure 9.27 looks at how many smokers had tried to quit. Many had tried and failed. Finally, Figure 9.28 summarizes the thoughts of those who planned to quit in the next 12 months. There was some realism about the difficulties of quitting, but overall people were more optimistic than they probably should have been about their chances of quitting.

There is lots more data I could have given, and all of it is hard to reconcile with a rational model of addiction. It looks, therefore, as though people are not forward

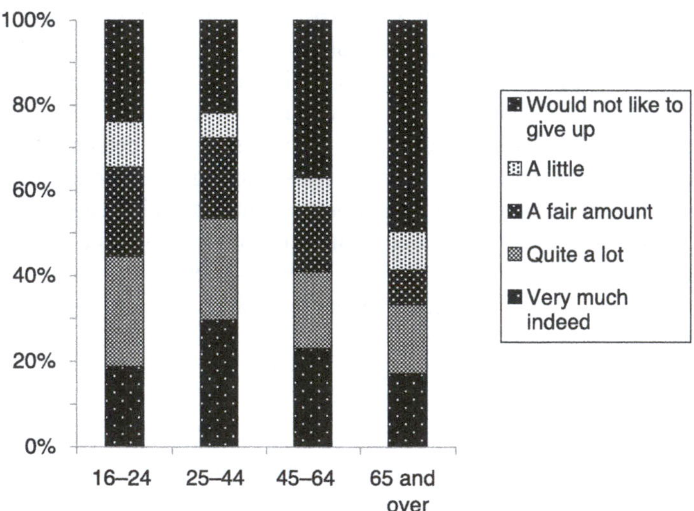

Figure 9.26 The proportion of people surveyed, by age group, who wanted to quit smoking.
Source: ONS (2004).

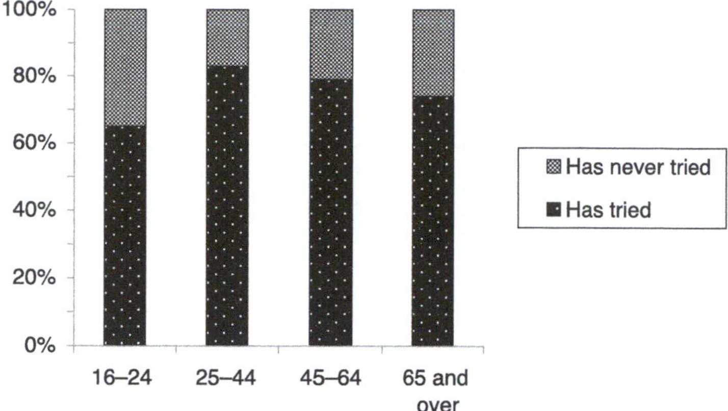

Figure 9.27 The proportion of current smokers who had tried quitting in the past.

Source: ONS (2004).

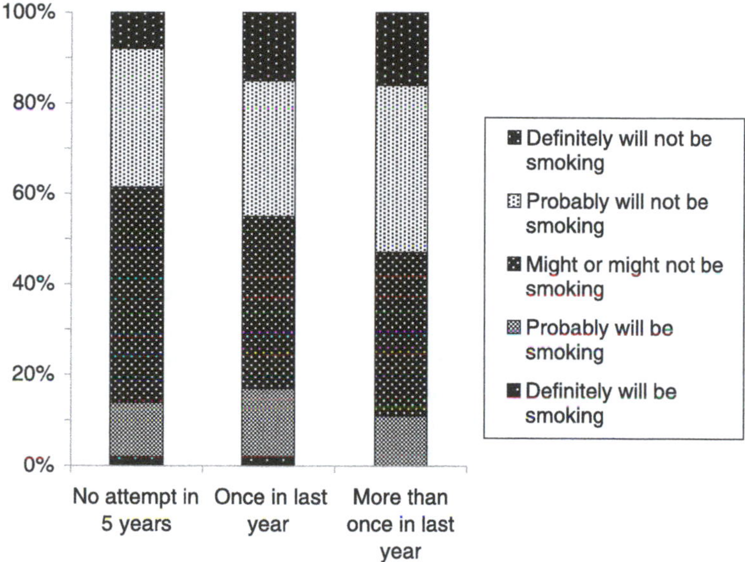

Figure 9.28 What smokers who were planning to quit in the next 12 months expected would happen after 12 months.

Source: ONS (2004).

planning very well and are underestimating difficulties of quitting smoking. More complex is to say exactly why this is. Is it because of present bias, or an underestimation of the addictiveness of cigarettes? To try to answer this question let's look in a bit more detail at how each bias would work.

Table 9.7 The consequences of underestimating the addictiveness of cigarettes, and present bias in the example

Bias	*Cigarettes in period*				*Expected utility*
	1	*2*	*3*	*4*	
None	0	0	0	0	40.0
	1	2	4	4	23.0
Thinks d = 0.5	0	0	0	0	40.0
	1	2	4	4	73.6
	1	3	4	4	73.4
	—	2	4	4	51.0
	—	3	4	4	51.2
Present bias $\beta = 0.8$	0	0	0	0	34.0
	1	2	4	4	22.2
Thinks d = 0.5 and has present bias $\beta = 0.8$	0	0	0	0	34.0
	1	2	4	4	62.6
	1	4	4	4	61.6
	—	2	4	4	44.4
	—	4	4	4	44.8

Table 9.7 illustrates the basic ideas. Imagine the price of cigarettes is expected to be $1 in periods 1 to 3 and to increase to $2.50 in period 4. Also, imagine that $d =$ 1 and so cigarettes are very addictive. Without any bias, of the profiles I am going to look at, Rob would do best to not smoke. What if he is biased?

If he thinks cigarettes are less addictive than they are, then in period 1 he would prefer a plan with only two packs of cigarettes in period 2. When he gets to period 2, however, because he is more addicted than he thought he would be, he prefers having three packs of cigarettes rather than two. He will consume more cigarettes than he planned, and more than would maximize his utility.

By contrast, if he has a present bias then not a lot happens in this example. We can see from the relative utilities that consuming cigarettes has become slightly more attractive, but still not enough to warrant smoking. You can play around with the numbers yourself, but it turns out that present bias is not going to make much difference to what Rob will do unless he has a really strong present bias. I'll come back to why this is the case later.

It looks like underestimating the addictiveness of smoking is the real problem Rob needs to be wary of. Present bias can, however, make a difference if Rob underestimates the addictiveness of smoking. We see, for instance, that if Rob underestimates the addictiveness of cigarettes and has present bias he would be happy to smoke four packs of cigarettes rather than the two he planned when he is in period 2. He will thus consume even more cigarettes than he planned and get an even lower utility. The less addictive Rob thinks smoking is, the more present bias is going to matter.

A combination of underestimating the addictiveness of smoking and present bias can, therefore, easily lead to Rob smoking more cigarettes than he planned and getting more addicted than he planned. It is no surprise, therefore, that he might end up wanting to quit but be unable to do so. The data we looked at earlier becomes a lot easier to explain. The role for government policy also changes because there becomes a clear rationale for more information on the addictiveness of smoking and it also makes sense to give people help in trying to quit. But the story we have so far is primarily one of why Rob might become addicted. What we need to do now is look more at the potential difficulties of quitting.

9.5.3 Cues and addiction

One important factor in addiction can be **cue-elicited behavior**. The idea here is that some cue, such as a particular sound, smell, or situation, makes someone crave something. For example, if Rob typically smokes a cigarette after dinner, or when he goes to the bar with friends, then his craving for a cigarette might be higher than normal at these times. We have seen how secondary reinforcers can have this effect, and such cue-elicited behavior is often cited as a reason for relapse in people trying to quit an addiction. For example, Laibson (2001) gives the story of a smoker who hadn't smoked for years, but on going to the beach one day had an intense craving to smoke. The craving was a consequence of smoking on the beach being common at one time in his life.

We can model cue-elicited behavior without too much change to the rational addiction model. All we need to add are the cues. Let's suppose that each day Rob either eats dinner at home or eats out. This will be the cue. At dinner he then decides to smoke or not. Instead of keeping stock of how many cigarettes Rob smokes, we now distinguish how many cigarettes he smokes during dinners at home and how many at dinners out.

To explain how we can do this, imagine that on day $t-1$ Rob decided to eat out. Then we let:

$$S_t^{out} = d(S_{t-1}^{out} + a_{t-1})$$

denote the stock of past consumption of cigarettes when eating out, and keep $S_t^{in} = S_{t-1}^{in}$ as the stock of past consumption of cigarettes when eating in. Similarly, if he had decided to eat in we would let:

$$S_t^{in} = d(S_{t-1}^{in} + a_{t-1})$$

denote the stock of past consumption of cigarettes when eating in, and keep $S_t^{out} = S_{t-1}^{out}$ as the stock of past consumption of cigarettes when eating out.

Rob's utility in period t then depends on where he eats and the difference between present consumption and the stock of past consumption. For instance, if he eats out his utility is:

$$u_t = \begin{cases} c_t + 10\sqrt{a_t - S_t^{out}} \text{ if } a_t \geq S_t^{out} \\ c_t - 10(S_t^{out} - a_t) \text{ if } a_t < S_t^{out} \end{cases}$$

If he eats in his utility is:

$$u_t = \begin{cases} c_t + 10\sqrt{a_t - S_t^{in}} \text{ if } a_t \geq S_t^{in} \\ c_t - 10(S_t^{in} - a_t) \text{ if } a_t < S_t^{in} \end{cases}$$

We still assume that he uses exponential discounting to find his inter-temporal utility:

$$u^T = u_1 + \delta u_2 + \delta^2 u_2 + \ldots + \delta^{T-1} u_t.$$

To better understand the model, let's start by assuming that Rob eats out every day. Then the model is exactly the same as the rational model of addiction. But, whereas I previously assumed the discount factor was $\delta = 1$, meaning there was no discounting of the future, it is now going to be important to think a bit about the discount factor. Table 9.8 looks at what happens if the discount factor is $\delta = 0.7$ rather than $\delta = 1$. We can see that the decrease in the discount factor makes smoking look relatively more attractive. The reason for this is that the costs of smoking come primarily in period 4, when Rob is very addicted. The lower the discount factor the less Rob worries about these costs.

Basically, the discount factor can matter a lot in Rob's choices. Incidentally this does not contradict me saying earlier that present bias may not have such a large effect. That's because the benefits of smoking come not just today but over the initial few periods, and so present bias discounts most of the benefits as well as the costs of smoking. The costs of smoking do, however, come after some time, and so something that discounts the future the further away it is will make a difference.

Why should we care about the discount factor? To see why the discount factor is important in understanding cues, imagine that Rob eats in six days a week and eats out on a Saturday. As Table 9.9 illustrates, when deciding whether to smoke

Table 9.8 The effect of the discount factor on Rob's desire to smoke during dinner, assuming that $d = 1$ and a pack of cigarettes costs \$2 in all periods

Cigarettes on day				*Utility*	
1	*2*	*3*	*4*	*δ = 1*	*δ = 0.7*
0	0	0	0	40.0	25.33
1	2	3	5	28	27.73

Table 9.9 The discount factor matters if there are two cues

Day of week	*Cue*	*If smoke when it will first matter*
Monday	Eat in	Tuesday
Tuesday	Eat in	Wednesday
Wednesday	Eat in	Thursday
Thursday	Eat in	Friday
Friday	Eat in	Sunday
Saturday	Eat out	Next Saturday
Sunday	Eat in	Monday

on a Monday he knows that whether or not he smokes will affect his stock of past consumption when eating in and so will affect his utility on the following day. By contrast, on a Saturday he knows that whether or not he smokes will affect his stock of past consumption when eating out and so will not affect his utility until one week. This means that the effective discount factor for eating out is a lot lower than that for eating in. For example, if the discount factor is $\delta = 0.95$, then the effective discount factor for eating in is 0.95, but for eating out it is $0.95^7 = 0.7$.

We have already seen that a low discount factor makes it optimal for Rob to smoke more cigarettes. A probable outcome, therefore, is that he would not smoke when eating in but would smoke when eating out. This is why cues matter, and why Rob may decide to smoke only when he gets certain cues. If we add present bias or an underestimation of the addictiveness of cigarettes to the story, then we can see why addictiveness can become cue dependent and why Rob may become more addicted to smoking when eating out than he wanted to.

Cue dependence is interesting in thinking about how people can quit addiction. If addiction is cue dependent, then people can avoid addiction by avoiding the cues that cause it. For example, if Rob does become too addicted to smoking when eating out, then he can simply stop eating out and solve the problem. This looks like good news for those wanting to quit because it provides a viable way to avoid addiction. It is not all good news, however, because Rob would have to sacrifice eating out, which he might like, and may remain vulnerable to reigniting his addiction if he ever does eat out. This last point may suggest why many people struggle to quit.

9.5.4 Addiction and neuroscience

Economists love simple models, and also love drawing analogies, but it's sometimes useful to check whether it all makes sense. That seems particularly pertinent in looking at addiction, where economists are a long way from familiar ground. So, are the models we have just been looking at reasonable models of addiction, and how far can we generalize them in looking at habit and more mundane consumer purchases? Neuroscience can potentially guide us to an answer.

Fortunately, we do not need to delve too deeply into the complex neuroscience of addiction in order to learn some interesting things. In terms of hard drugs we know that on initial use such drugs increase dopamine transmission, which you might recall is usually associated with a positive reward. Users are, therefore, likely to associate the drug with pleasure, and begin to associate cues that might have preceded using the drug with that pleasure. This is the same story as we looked at above in valuing rewards, and so there is little at this stage to distinguish drugs from anything else, i.e. money.

If, however, the person continues to use the drug, then they go through various stages in which the neural circuitry appears to essentially be rewired by the drug use. This leads to addiction. In the final stage of addiction, the VMPFC seems to lead the way in demanding the drug, rather than passively responding to consumption of the drug. Potentially, this can become permanent, making it very hard for an addict to ever quit. It also means that addicts will be less responsive to 'normal' rewards, and less able to make decisions.

What do we learn from this? It lends strong support to a cue-based model of addiction, because it is cues that activate the VMPFC to crave the drug. It also lends support to the potential importance of underestimating the addictiveness of drugs, because drugs really are addictive and people may underestimate their effect. Present bias, though, starts to appear less relevant, because if a person really did know the consequences of drug addiction, then any present bias would have to be very extreme for them to still use the drug. It's probably not present bias, therefore, that's at work, but a potential uncontrollable craving for the drug that is unrelated to present bias.

Knowing this gives us some idea of what a model of addiction should look like (and actually points towards a model of addiction proposed by Bernheim and Rangel (2004) that I'm not going to look at here, but I suggest you do). It also gives us a better idea how to design policy to deal with the problems of addiction. For instance, it seems clear that conventional economic incentives, like increasing the price of a drug, are liable to be relatively ineffective. Thus, taxes, while they raise a lot of government revenue, are not going to solve the problems of addiction. More apt is probably to increase awareness of the problems of addiction and to help people avoid cues that trigger their addiction.

We can also see that addiction and habit are quite different things. Thus, an analogy only gets us so far, and we probably will need different models to capture drug addiction versus a habit to watch cricket. Drawing the dividing line is not necessarily easy because drugs come in varying strengths, from heroine, to caffeine, to chocolate, but a distinction does need to be made. We thus learn better how to model addiction, and also can be reassured that things like reference dependence and present bias are probably enough to capture habit.

9.6 Further reading

Textbooks on neuroscience and cognitive neuroscience, such as Purves *et al.* (2008), are a natural place to start. The book by Glimcher (2004) gives a more general introduction to the subject. Overlapping survey articles include Camerer (2007) and Camerer *et al.* (2004b, 2005). Fudenberg and Levine (2006) is a recent dual-self model of self-control. Schelling (1984) and Bernheim and Rangel (2007) provide interesting contrasts on the implications of multiple selves for measuring welfare. On addiction, the paper by Bernheim and Rangel (2004) is recommended, and Kalivas and Volkow (2005) provide more on the neuroscience of addiction. For more on the debate over whether neuroeconomics is a good or a bad thing for economics, see Caplin and Schotter (2008).

9.7 Review questions

9.1 Why does the brain interpret money as a reward? Is it a primary or a secondary reinforcer?

9.2 Do you think the brain's reward systems react to expected value or 'expected utility'?

9.3 When does Rob feel the value of winning at roulette: when the wheel stops, when he collects his money, or when he eats the chips he buys with the money? Relate this to hedonic editing.

9.4 Why is reward prediction error relevant in interpreting Figures 9.4 to 9.7?

9.5 Relate reward prediction error to reference dependence.

9.6 Given that brain activation is constrained to fall within a fixed range, how can activation be in proportion to the reward? What does this suggest about our differing ability to distinguish relative from absolute magnitudes?

9.7 Why might it be consistent with forward-looking behavior that people want to quit smoking? What if I tell you that only 26 percent of people said they wanted to quit smoking because of financial reasons (ONS 2004), but 86 percent said they wanted to quit because of health reasons?

9.8 What policy should the government adopt to stop people doing drugs or smoking?

9.9 Why is addiction different to habit?

9.10 Is a multiple-self model helpful in modeling economic behavior?

Part IV

Welfare and policy

10 Happiness and utility

> The great source of both the misery and disorders of human life seems to arise from overrating the difference between one permanent situation and another. Avarice overrates the difference between poverty and riches: ambition that between a private and a public station: vain-glory, that between obscurity and extensive reputation.
>
> Adam Smith, *The Theory of Moral Sentiments*

Having looked at how people behave, and why, we shall now start to look at the welfare and policy implications of that behavior. The basic question I want us to look at in this chapter is whether people make the economic choices that will give them greatest satisfaction and happiness, and if not would they rather someone else make choices for them? To answer that question we need to know what makes people happy, whether people know what makes them happy, and how much people value choice. In the next chapter we shall make the logical next step in asking what role policy can play.

10.1 What makes us happy?

The story throughout the book has been one of people trying to maximize utility. For the most part we can think of utility as a measure of happiness, so, if people maximize utility, they maximize happiness. The standard economist's answer to the question 'What makes us happy?' is, therefore, simple: 'Whatever we do!' If we observe Emma going to the cinema, then we could infer that going to the cinema makes Emma happy; why else would she go? If we observe Alan buying car insurance, then we infer that this makes him happy; why else would he buy it? This is called **revealed preference**, because Emma's and Alan's actions reveal their preferences.

Can we be sure, however, that a person's choices truly reveal what makes them happy? To answer that question we need to have an alternative measure of what makes people happy. One alternative is to ask people how happy they are, and see how their answer changes as things happen in their life. For example, if we observe Emma getting a job, then a revealed preference argument would suggest that having a job makes her happier. If we know how happy Emma said she was before she got the job, and how happy she says she is after getting the job, then we can check whether she really is happier.

Fortunately, there is a lot of data on how happy people say they are. For example, a question in the World Values Survey asks respondents: 'All things considered, how satisfied are you with your life as a whole these days?' Many other surveys ask similar questions. There are pertinent issues about how much we can rely on this data (see Research Methods 10.1 and 10.2), but the data does throw up some consistent results and so we'll assume that it is reliable. This means we can check whether choices really do reveal what makes people happy. Before we do that, though, it is useful to have a look first at what people say makes them happy.

Research Methods 10.1

The law of large numbers: Can we trust happiness data?

Two ways we can measure happiness are to ask people questions like: 'How satisfied are you with your life as a whole these days?', or to ask them to look back at an event and try to recall the pleasure, pain, or utility they felt during the event. Do people give a reliable answer to such questions?

We know that people's answers to such questions can be affected by current mood and how the question is framed. This was amply demonstrated in an experiment by Norbert Schwarz, where half those surveyed were 'lucky enough to find a dime' before being surveyed. Those who found the dime reported higher 'life satisfaction'. We also know that the same people can give quite different answers to how happy they are if they are asked two or more weeks apart. Clearly, therefore, we need to be a little skeptical of happiness measures.

So, should we be using happiness data at all? It will probably suffice for our purposes. That is because we will aggregate the data of many people. For example, we will be interested whether unemployed people are less happy than employed people. If we ask lots of unemployed and employed people whether they are happy and average out the responses, we should get a reliable measure of whether those who are employed are happier. If the data is a little unreliable or noisy, then we may have to ask more people, but we can still get reliable information.

Research Methods 10.2

An alternative measure of happiness

The **day reconstruction method** involves participants filling out a diary summarizing episodes that occurred the day before. They should describe what they did, how long they did it for, etc., and also how they felt during each event of the day. A study by Kahneman and co-authors (2004) used the method on a sample of 909 working women in Texas. Some of the data is given in Table 10.1. Net affect measures positive minus negative experience, and there are not too many surprises in what gives relatively high and low net affect.

One way to use the day reconstruction method to measure happiness is the U-index. The **U-index** asks how much of the time a person spends doing unpleasant activities. There is no simple definition of when an activity is unpleasant, but one possibility is to count any event where the most intense feelings are negative. In Table 10.1 there is the U-index for the various daytime activities. So, for example, 28 percent of the time spent commuting was unpleasant.

Figure 10.1 compares the U-index with the standard measure of happiness and household income and age, and we see a strong correlation between the two measures. The U-index does, however, have one big advantage over the standard measure: interpersonal comparisons are more plausible. Interpersonal comparisons are hard to believe when focusing on satisfaction questions, because how people choose to rate themselves on, say, a ten-point satisfaction scale can vary widely from person to person without any difference in their happiness. So, that Maria rates herself seven and Alan six does not convincingly tell you that Maria is happier than Alan. The U-index is intuitively a more objective measure. People may more reliably remember whether or not an event is unpleasant, and the time spent doing unpleasant events is a readily understandable measure.

Table 10.1 The day reconstruction method. Net affect is a measure of positive minus negative emotions. All responses were on a six-point scale, so six is the most positive and zero the most negative

Activity	*Time spent (hours)*	*Net affect*	*U-index*
Intimate relations	0.23	4.83	0.040
Socializing after work	1.14	4.15	0.073
Relaxing	2.17	3.96	0.078
Dinner	0.81	3.94	0.074
Lunch	0.57	3.91	0.078
Exercising	0.22	3.85	0.088
Praying/worship	0.45	3.78	0.105
Socializing at work	1.12	3.78	0.100
Watching TV	2.19	3.65	0.095
Phone at home	0.93	3.52	0.126
Napping	0.89	3.35	0.131
Cooking	1.15	3.27	0.138
Shopping	0.41	3.23	0.157
Computer (non-work)	0.51	3.22	0.165
Housework	1.12	2.99	0.161
Childcare	1.10	2.99	0.199
Evening commute	0.61	2.77	0.209
Working	6.89	2.68	0.211
Morning commute	0.47	2.09	0.287

Source: Kahneman *et al.* (2004).

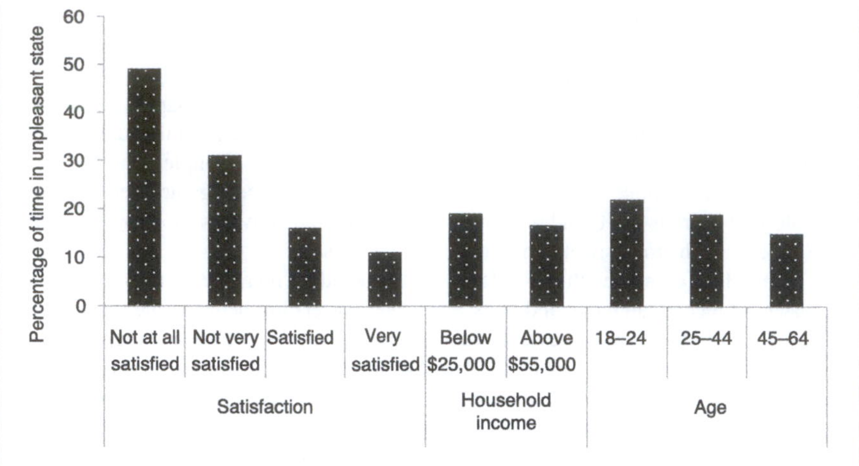

Figure 10.1 The U-index compared to life satisfaction. The lower was life satisfaction, the less time people spent in an unpleasant state.

Source: Kahneman and Krueger (2006).

10.1.1 Happiness is relative

When we look at how happy people say they are, or how satisfied they say they are with their life, we get some surprises. Two studies in the 1970s, one in economics and one in psychology, first highlighted the issues, and it is interesting to look at both.

Brickman and co-authors (1978) compared the happiness of lottery winners, accident victims, and a control group of people randomly selected from the phone book. The lottery winners had won between $50,000 and $1 million on the Illinois State Lottery. The accident victims were either paraplegic or quadriplegic as a result of their accidents.

The main results of the study are given in Figure 10.2. The first thing we see is very little difference in reported happiness between the lottery winners and control group. Winning the lottery does not seem to make people any happier. Being in an accident does have a more pronounced effect and, not surprisingly, lowers present happiness and increases the perception of past happiness. What is surprising is that the drop in happiness is not very large, and predictions of future happiness are no different to those of the lottery winners. Winning $1 million or becoming paraplegic is clearly a life-changing event, but this study suggests neither change life satisfaction as much as we might expect.

Easterlin (1974) looked at whether happiness correlates with income. Figure 10.3 reports data from a 1970 survey of the US population. As we might expect, those with higher income reported being happier. No surprises so far. If,

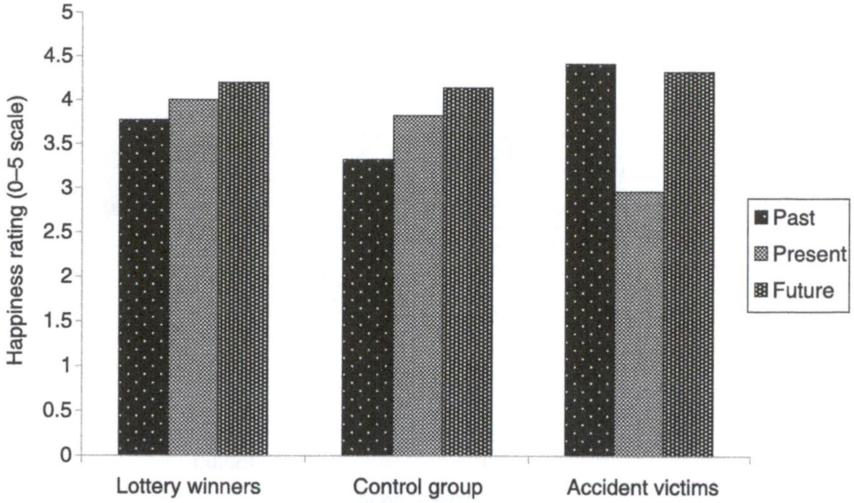

Figure 10.2 The change in reported life satisfaction following a life-changing event.

Source: Brickman *et al.* (1978).

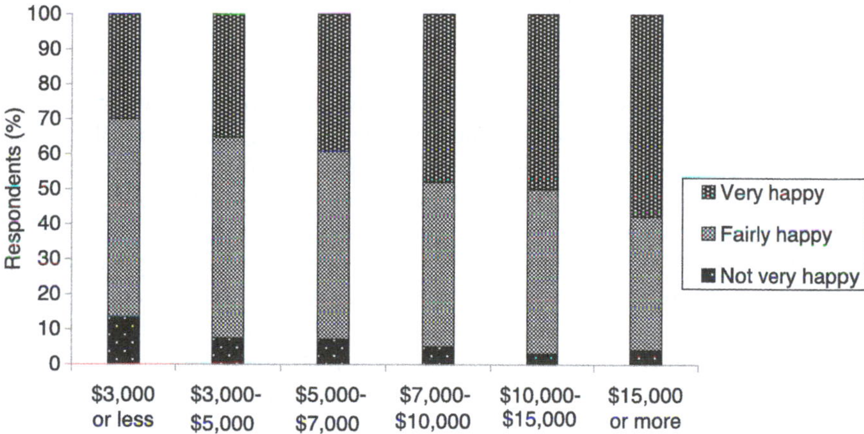

Figure 10.3 Life satisfaction and income. Those with higher income report higher life satisfaction.

Source: Easterlin (1974).

however, increased income leads to increased happiness, then it seems logical that: (i) people should be happier, on average, in countries with higher income, and (ii) people should become happier, on average, if incomes increase over time. The curious thing that Easterlin pointed out is that neither of these things happens!

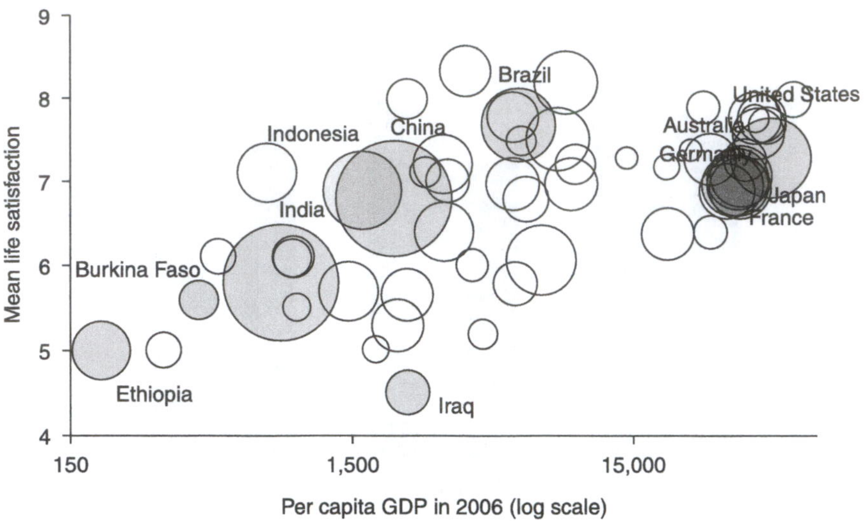

Figure 10.4 Life satisfaction and GDP per capita in different countries in 2006. There is a positive correlation between the average income in a country and satisfaction. Size of bubble reflects population size.

Source: World Values Survey (2009), World Bank.

Whether or not growth in average income leads to greater happiness remains a controversial topic. The findings of Easterlin have, however, largely survived the test of time. I say 'largely' because modern data does suggest that people are, on average, happier in countries with higher income. Figure 10.4, for example, provides a recent cross-country comparison of reported happiness relative to per capita GDP. There is a positive correlation. The correlation, though, is not particularly strong, and lower GDP tends to correlate with war, despotic governments, and lots of other reasons why people might be unhappy. More convincing is to look at changes in income within country. Figure 10.5 shows reported happiness in the US over time, and despite real income tripling over this period, reported happiness changed little. The story is the same in other countries. Increases in average income do not seem to cause increases in happiness.

Since the two pioneering studies discussed above there have been many more, some of which we shall look at below, and most confirm these early findings. Happiness, and unhappiness, it seems, can be a little elusive. Before we start to look at the important implications of this, we need to ask how such findings can be explained. The leading explanation is reference dependence. If happiness depends on the relative rather than the absolute level of things like income and health, then changes in the absolute level need not change happiness. The two most likely reference points here are what others have, and what the person used to have. I will primarily focus on the latter of these two in the rest of the chapter, and so let's briefly think about the implications of the first.

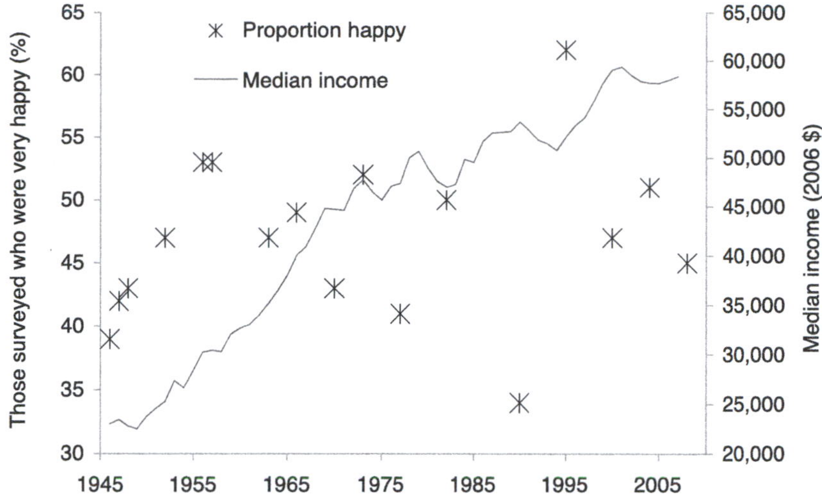

Figure 10.5 Life satisfaction and income over time. Median income increases a lot but reported satisfaction does not.

Source: Easterlin (1974), Gallup and US Census Bureau.

If people want to earn as much income as relatives and friends (and we saw evidence in Chapters two and seven that they do), then those earning relatively more will be relatively happier than those earning relatively less. This is consistent with Figure 10.3. Logically, however, there must always be some in a society that are earning relatively more, and some earning relatively less. This can explain why we see no correlation between average happiness and income over time. That people judge their own income relative to others can, therefore, explain a lot. But it cannot explain everything, as we shall now see.

10.1.2 Adaption and habituation

Looking back at Figure 10.2 we can see that happiness does not depend solely on circumstances relative to others. The lottery winners should be relatively wealthy, but are not happy. The accident victims should have relatively ill health, and were less happy when asked, but did not expect to be less happy in the future. To explain this, we need to introduce the ideas of adaption and habituation.

To illustrate and motivate these concepts we can look at some data on how people reported happiness or satisfaction changes in response to other 'life-changing' events. Clark and co-authors (2003, 2008) analyze data from Germany that tracks people's life satisfaction over the period 1984 to 1997. They use the first five or seven years of the panel to obtain a person's baseline level of satisfaction and then look at how satisfaction changes in the years leading up to and after events like marriage, divorce, a first child, and unemployment. Most of these

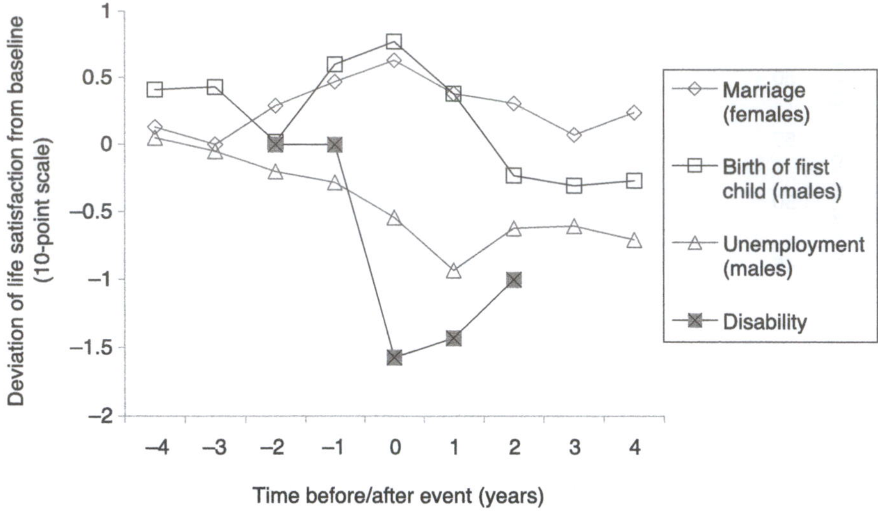

Figure 10.6 Changes in happiness relative to the baseline in, before, and after life-changing events.

Sources: Clark *et al.* (2003), Oswald and Powdthavee (2008).

events are predictable, and so it is also useful to have some data on an event that is more unpredictable. For that, we can look at data by Oswald and Powdthavee (2008) from the UK on the consequences of disability.

I am not going to look at all of the data, but Figure 10.6 plots a representative sample. In terms of marriage, the birth of first child, and layoff, we appear to see **anticipation**, in that happiness increases or decreases prior to the event. Disability, as we might expect, causes a more sudden jump in happiness, because it is less predictable. After the event, in the case of marriage and the birth of a first child, we see **adaption** in that happiness returns to the baseline level. There is some evidence of adaption in the case of disability, but not for being unemployed.

Adaption is a fascinating possibility because it implies that happiness will bounce back to baseline after a good or a bad life event. This has profound implications for policy, and how we look at life. So, why does it happen? There are lots of interrelated possible causes, all with different interpretations, of which I will mention four.

We can distinguish two effects that result from a real change in utility. In terms of negative events, there may be **readjustment** whereby the person finds new ways to fulfill their life. For example, someone who liked to play football but becomes paraplegic might learn to play wheelchair basketball. In this case the utility function or reference level has not changed, but the person has had to relearn how to maximize utility. **Habituation** is where a person becomes accustomed to their new life. For example, the lottery winner becomes accustomed to buying expensive things, and the accident victim becomes accustomed to being in a wheelchair. This would imply a change in the reference level and/or a change in the utility function (similar to that which we looked at in section 4.5.1).

We can next distinguish effects that focus more on how satisfied people feel they are. One is a **contrast effect** whereby an extreme good or bad event changes the scale by which all future events are judged. For example, nothing might seem 'as good' as winning the lottery or 'as bad' as being in an accident. Taking this one stage further, we get an **aspiration treadmill**, where a person adjusts aspirations to the satisfaction they normally experience. Consequently, the lottery winner is likely to downplay current satisfaction and the accident victim to overplay current satisfaction, given what they experienced before.

Readjustment and habituation suggest that utility regains its former level. The contrast effect and aspiration treadmill suggest that utility may not regain its former level, but people's answer to the question how satisfied they feel does. This is a crucial distinction. Unfortunately we do not yet have good answers to what best explains adaption. It does not necessarily follow, therefore, that utility bounces back to the baseline.

What we do know is that adaption only seems to happen some of the time. For some types of event, adaption can be incomplete and/or take a very long while. For instance, in Figure 10.6 we see little evidence of adaption after being unemployed. To illustrate this further, Figure 10.7 plots the estimated effect of unemployment on life satisfaction for males. We see that being unemployed has long-run effects and so any adaption is very weak.

We will come back to the consequences of adaption soon enough, but I now want to return to the question of whether a person's choice reveals what makes them happy.

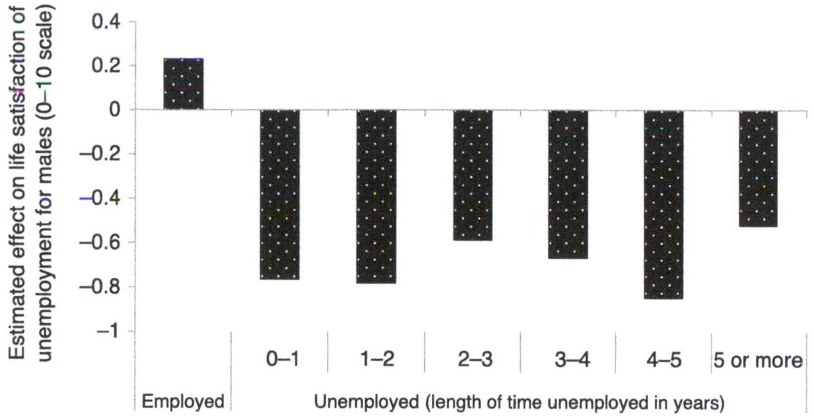

Figure 10.7 Estimated effect on life satisfaction of being employed versus unemployed. There is no evidence of adaption to being unemployed.

Source: Clark *et al.* (2008).

10.2 Do we know what makes us happy?

To illustrate some of the issues, imagine that someone called Ian has just come back from his annual summer holiday to Italy and we want to find out how happy he is and why he chose to go.

Thinking about things from a revealed preference perspective, we work back from the fact that Ian went on holiday. We would say that his decision utility for a holiday in Italy was greater than that for a holiday in France, or staying at home and not spending the $2,000 he spent on flights and hotels. We know this because we know that he decided to go for a holiday in Italy. More generally, **decision utility** is revealed by a person's behavior. Whenever I have referred to utility in this book up until now I was really talking about decision utility.

Thinking about things from a slightly different perspective, we can start with the concept of instant utility. **Instant utility** measures the pleasure or pain that Ian experienced at specific points in time. Figure 10.8 plots what this might look like over the course of his holiday. Like any good holiday we see some ups, a nice walk in the mountains, and some downs, mild food poisoning. From this we can calculate **total utility**, which is basically the sum of instant utilities. In the example, this would be the area under the instant utility curve, distinguishing between the positive area above the axis and the negative area below the axis. The bigger the positive area and the smaller the negative area, the greater is his total utility.

When we ask people how happy they are, we get a snapshot of their instant utility at that point in time. From this we could estimate total utility. Happiness data gives us, therefore, a means to measure total utility, and this looks like a good measure of happiness. The question we need to think about is whether total utility

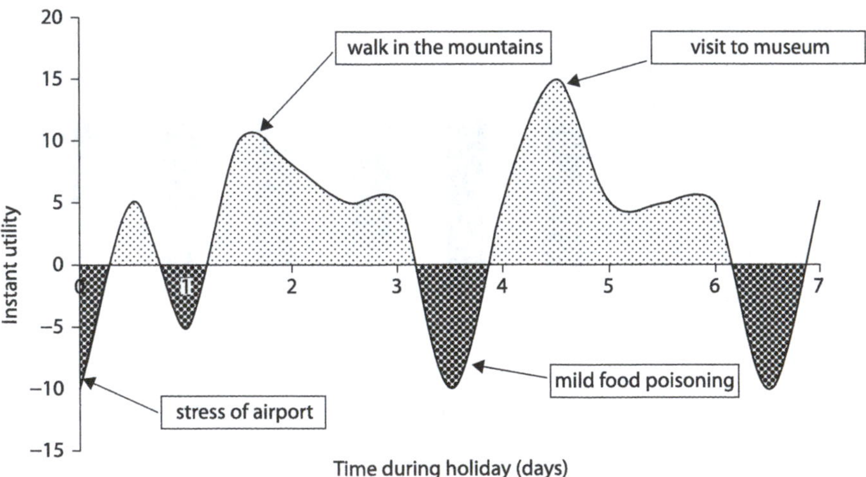

Figure 10.8 The instant utility over time of Ian on a holiday in Italy.

and decision utility coincide. If they do, then Ian's choice reveals what makes him happy, and so he must know consciously or subconsciously what makes him happy. Everything works nicely. But what if decision utility and total utility are different? Then things become less simple, and there are two good reasons why they can be different. I will look at each in turn.

10.2.1 Remembered utility

When looking back on past experiences, it seems that people typically do not remember total utility. I shall illustrate this with a study by Kahneman and co-authors (1993). The study involved subjects experiencing and evaluating pain. Subjects were first asked to immerse their hand in cold water for 60 seconds. The water was kept at 14 °C. Seven minutes later subjects were asked to put their other hand in cold water for 90 seconds. This time the water was kept at 14 °C for 60 seconds and then gradually increased to 15 °C. Seven minutes later each subject was told that they would be asked to put their hand in water a third time, but they could choose whether to repeat the first, 60-second trial, or the second, 90-second trial.

After all this was done, subjects were asked to plot their level of discomfort during the trials. If we convert this to instant utility, we get something like Figure 10.9. The first thing to note is that the reported discomfort was the same in the 60-second trial as the first 60 seconds of the 90-second trial. This means that total utility had to be less for the 90-second than for the 60-second trial, because there is an extra 30 seconds of discomfort. Surely, therefore, people prefer to repeat the 60-second rather than the 90-second trial? In fact 69 percent of subjects said that they would prefer to repeat the 90-second trial!

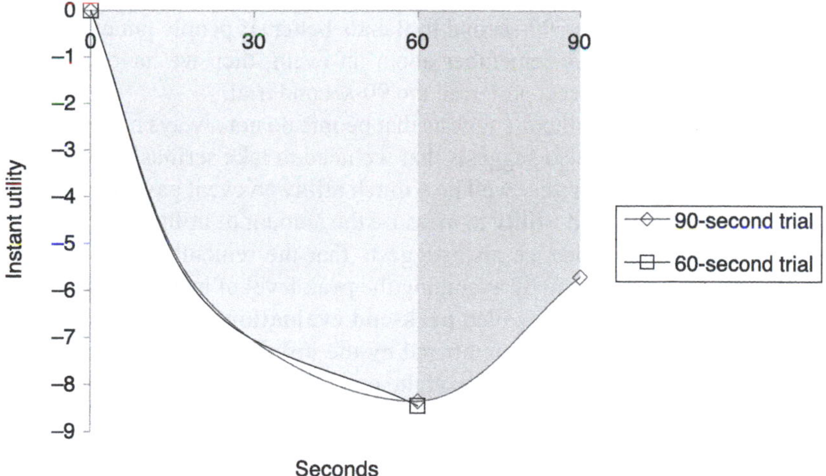

Figure 10.9 Instant utility while hand is immersed in cold water for 60 or 90 seconds.
Source: Kahneman *et al.* (1993).

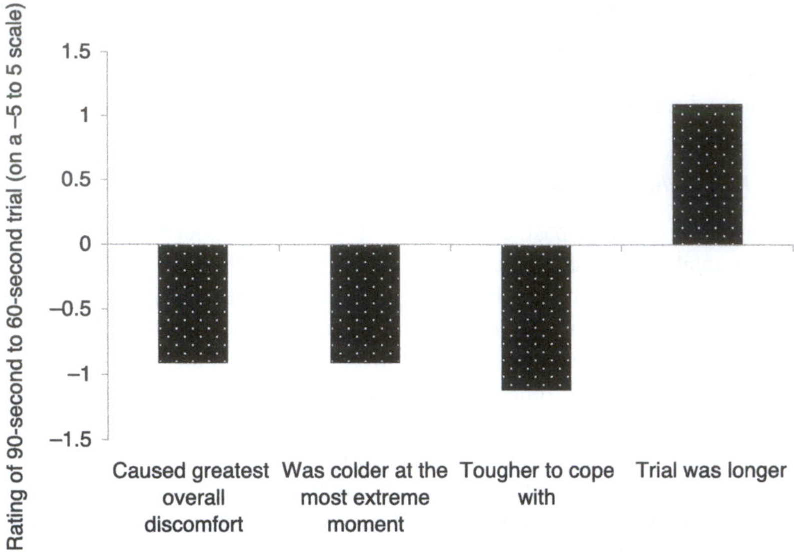

Figure 10.10 How the 90-second trial was rated compared to the 60-second trial. The 90-second trial was rated better on everything except length.

Source: Kahneman *et al.* (1993).

Figure 10.10 looks at how subjects rated the 90-second trial relative to the 60-second trial on several criteria. We see that subjects did correctly realize the 90-second trial was longer, but otherwise remember it as less bad. Why would they do that? The only difference between the two trials, and the only thing that could explain it, is that the 90-second trial ends better. If people put extra weight on the last thing that they remember about an event, then we have a plausible explanation for why subjects preferred the 90-second trial.

This study, and many others, suggests that people do not always make decisions based on total utility. It also suggests that we need to take seriously the idea that people may not remember very well how much utility an event gave them. We can use the term **remembered utility** to measure the amount of utility a person thinks an event gave them. Evidence also suggests that the remembered utility of an event is accurately predicted by averaging the peak level of instant utility and end level of instant utility. This is called **peak-end evaluation**.

Ian's holiday will thus be remembered by the instant utility at the best and/or worst moment, and the instant utility at the end of the holiday. It is clear that this can mean a significant difference between remembered utility and total utility, or between decision utility and total utility. Do not necessarily expect, therefore, that people choose things that will give them highest total utility. Maybe Ian should have stayed at home and saved $2,000?

Thanks to a study by Wirtz and co-authors (2003) we can answer this question a bit more definitively. They tracked 41 students as they went on their spring

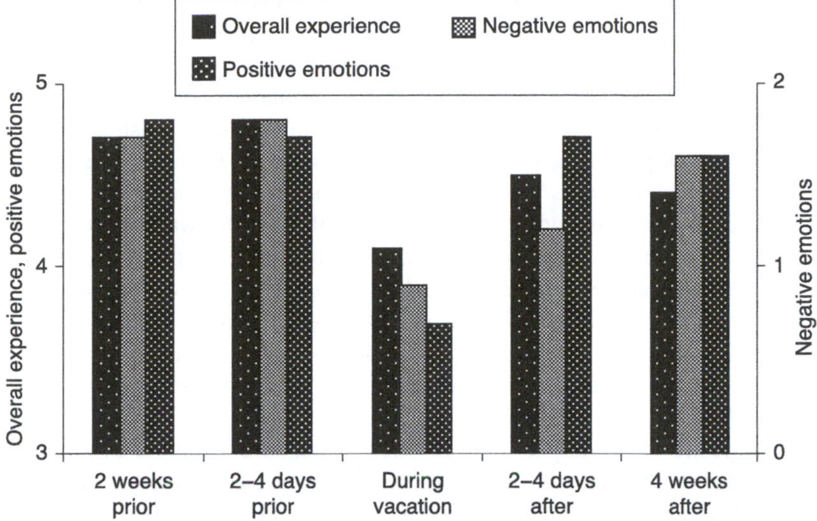

Figure 10.11 Students' expectations before, experience during, and recollections after a spring vacation.

Source: Wirtz *et al.* (2003).

vacation. The students filled in a questionnaire at various times before, during, and after the vacation. Figure 10.11 summarizes the results. Consistent with the earlier discussion, we find a mismatch between total utility and remembered utility. The interesting, new thing is that subjects overplayed both the positive *and* negative emotions experienced on the vacation. This illustrates how expectations and memories tend to be more intense than reality. Ian will not only remember the holiday as better than it really was, he will also remember it as worse than it really was!

Such differences between total and remembered utility raise some difficult but fascinating questions. For instance, peak-end evaluation implies there will be duration neglect. **Duration neglect** is where the duration of an event does not influence someone's memory of how good or bad the event was. This means that people can forget lots of good, or bad, moments and remember an event based on only a few instances. So, what is best: an event that gives higher total utility, or an event that will give higher remembered utility? Was the 60-second trial better because subjects suffered less total discomfort, or was the 90-second trial better because subjects remember less discomfort? What if we are talking about 60 or 90 days, months, or years, rather than seconds?

10.2.2 Projection bias

Having seen that people may not be accurate in looking back at their past, we next ask whether they are good at predicting the future. Adaption raises the possibility that people may not be good at this either. We need to question whether people will predict the extent to which their tastes and preferences adapt over time. The simple answer seems to be that most people correctly predict the direction of change, but not the magnitude. This leads to **projection bias** in which people overestimate how much future preferences and tastes will resemble current preferences and tastes. Projection bias can show up various different ways that I want to discuss and distinguish.

There is an **impact bias** if a person expects an event to have a bigger effect than it subsequently does. To illustrate, we can look at a study by Smith and co-authors (2008) that surveyed patients as they were waiting for a renal transplant, and again 12 months after they had had the transplant. Figure 10.12 summarizes the main results. An impact bias is shown by the patients predicting a greater increase in quality of life than actually occurred. We also see that patients remembered their quality of life as worse than it was. This could be because after the transplant we observe remembered utility, while beforehand we observe instant utility.

The opposite of the impact bias is when a person expects an event to have no effect but it subsequently does. One possible cause of this is the endowment effect that we looked at in Chapter two. Recall that the endowment effect causes people to value an item more when they own it. Do people predict this effect? Loewenstein and Adler (1995) asked this question in a study that involved subjects valuing a mug before and after they were given it. Figure 10.13 summarizes the results. We can see that, before they got the mug, subjects said they would be

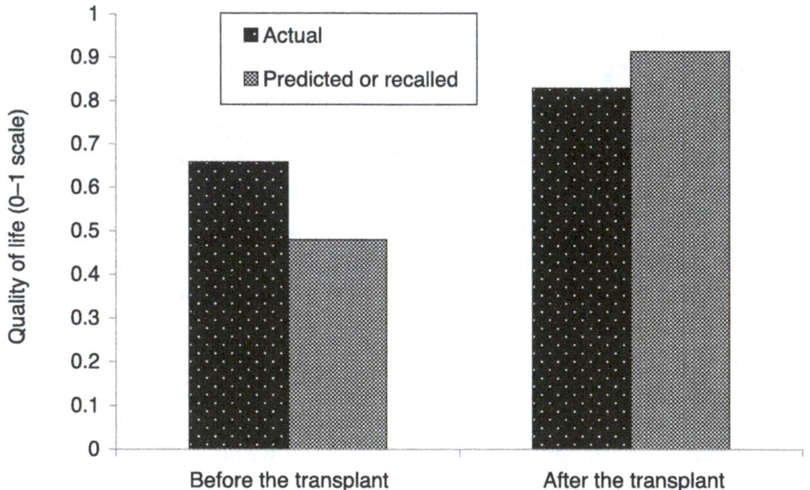

Figure 10.12 Predicted or recalled quality of life compared to actual before and after a renal transplant. Quality of life increases less than expected. People recalled quality of life being worse than it was.

Source: Smith *et al.* (2008).

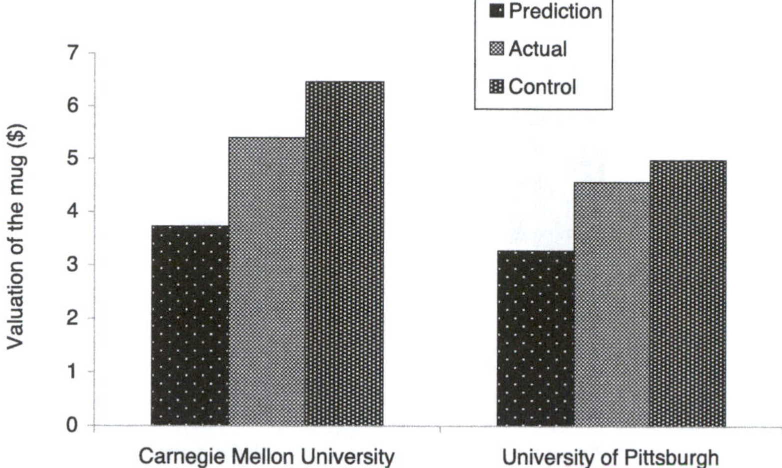

Figure 10.13 The endowment effect. Subjects failed to predict how ownership of a mug would increase their valuation of the mug.

Source: Loewenstein and Adler (1995).

willing to sell it for around $3.50 to $3.70. Having been given the mug, subjects increased their asking price. The control group, who were not influenced by giving a prediction before receiving the mug, provide a good measure of willingness to sell the mug once owned, and valued it at 50 to 100 percent more. This means that subjects underestimated what effect ownership of the mug would have on their willingness to sell.

The impact bias and a failure to predict the endowment effect suggest that people are poor at predicting how they will adapt to events and how their reference level may change over time. The accident victim may overestimate the long-run effects of disability, and the lottery winner may underestimate how much his reference level will increase as he becomes accustomed to his new wealth. The final effect I want to look at shows that people can underestimate the effect of short-run mood.

I will illustrate with a study by Read and van Leeuwen (1998). They asked 200 office workers in Amsterdam to choose what, from a range of healthy and unhealthy snacks, they would want to get in one week's time. The workers were asked either after lunch or late afternoon and were told that they would be given the snack after lunch or late afternoon. The expectation was that people would be hungry late afternoon but satiated after lunch, and this would affect choice. The results in Figure 10.14 suggest that it did. There is no good reason why current hunger should affect what the person will want in one week's time. For many, however, it seemed that current hunger affected what the person expected they would want in one week's time. Those who were relatively hungry when asked were relatively more likely to choose the unhealthy snack.

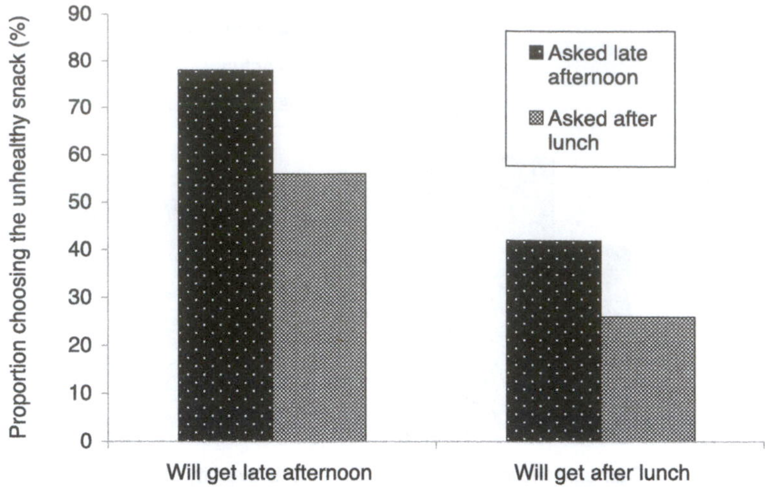

Figure 10.14 The proportion who chose an unhealthy snack for one week's time depends on current hunger.

Source: Read and van Leeuwen (1998).

In summary, we observe a projection bias in which people overestimate how much future preferences and tastes will resemble current preferences and tastes, underestimate how much they will adapt to events, and are influenced by current mood.

10.3 Choice and commitment

Projection bias and the difference between decision and remembered utility suggest that people may not know what is best for them. We have already seen elsewhere in this book that, even if people do know what is best for them, they may not make the best choices because of, say, present bias. Things do not look, therefore, very promising. But can people overcome projection bias and time-inconsistency? One way they might is by pre-commitment, either by pre-committing themselves to a plan of action or by allowing someone else to choose for them. What I want to do in this section is explore how well this could work.

To get us started on this question, let's stick with the subject of food a bit longer. After one week the workers in the study by Read and van Leeuwen were found and reoffered the choice of snacks. This time they got the snack they chose. As we can see in Figure 10.15 a lot of those who said they would want the healthy snack actually chose an unhealthy snack. This looks like the dynamic time inconsistency problem that we saw in Chapter four. Interestingly, however, it seems that many stuck by the choice of a healthy snack that they knew they made before. This would explain why the time they were initially asked affected subsequent choice.

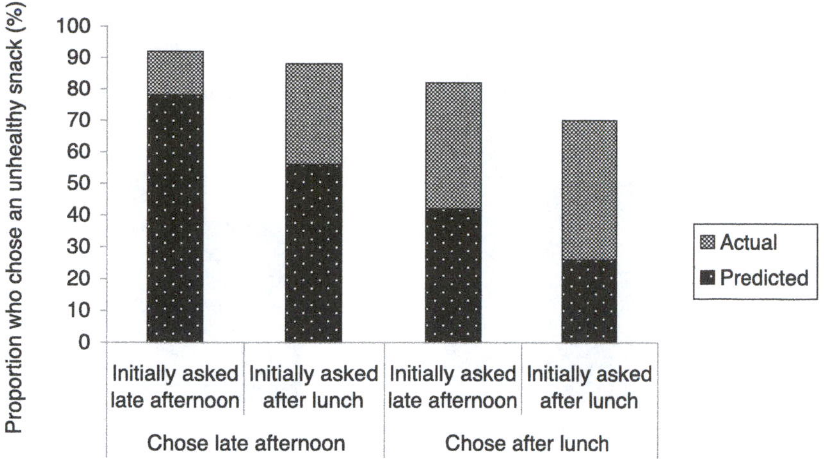

Figure 10.15 More chose an unhealthy snack than predicted they would, but fewer chose the unhealthy snack if they said they would choose a healthy snack.

Source: Read and van Leeuwen (1998).

We can follow this up with a study by Gilbert and co-authors (2002) that looked at the effect of hunger on grocery shopping. Shoppers in a grocery store were asked to take part in a survey in which they had to list their planned shopping. Some were given back the list and some were not, and some were given a muffin to try before shopping and some not. The number of unlisted items that the shopper subsequently bought was recorded. Figure 10.16 summarizes the main result. Not surprisingly shoppers purchased more items than they put on the list. Consistent with projection bias, we see that those who were relatively hungry, because they did not eat the muffin, bought more unplanned items. Interestingly, however, those with the shopping list to hand were seemingly much less affected by their current mood.

In both of these examples, behavior seemed to be influenced by a loose pre-commitment. In the first case, knowing that they said they would eat a healthy snack seemed enough to persuade some to stick with their choice. In the second case, having what they said written down, in the form of a shopping list, made people stick closer to what they planned. Potentially, therefore, pre-commitment is a good thing.

10.3.1 Does present bias matter?

Before we look in more detail at whether pre-commitment can work, it seems pertinent to take a step back and ask whether things like projection bias and present bias do really lower utility. In section 10.6.1 I will show you that projection bias can seriously lower utility. Here, I want to look at present bias and ask whether present bias lowers utility.

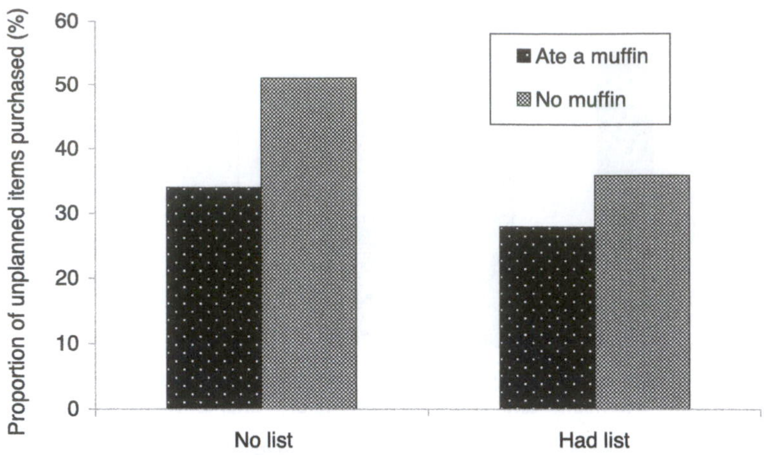

Figure 10.16 How many unplanned items shoppers bought depended on whether or not they ate a muffin and whether or not they had a shopping list to hand.

Source: Gilbert *et al.* (2002).

The first problem we have in answering this question is how to evaluate utility. The measure I am going to use takes a long-run perspective in which we ignore any present bias, and say the total utility, if utility in periods one to T is u_1 to u_T, is

$$U^0(u_1, u_2, ..., u_T) = u_1 + \delta u_2 + ... + \delta^{T-1} u_T = \sum_{\tau=1}^{T} \delta^{\tau-1} u_\tau$$

where δ is the long-run discount factor. This definition has its problems, which you might want to think about, but it's as good as we have.

Now imagine that Ian, fresh from his holiday, is deciding when to finish his dissertation. It's first of April today and the work has to be handed in by 30th April. It plays on his mind that it is not done, and so his utility is 99 on every day it is not done and then 100 a day once it is finished. He knows that it would take just one day's work to finish it, and on that day his utility would be zero. Table 10.2 illustrates how things look on the first of April. It is clear that Ian gets the highest total utility if he does the dissertation immediately. But what if he has present bias?

Recall (you might want to look back at Chapter four to refresh your memory) that we can write decision utility as:

$$U^T(u_1, u_2, ..., u_T) = u_1 + \beta\delta u_2 + ..., + \beta\delta^{T-1} u_T = u_1 + \beta \sum_{\tau=2}^{T} \delta^{\tau-1} u_\tau$$

where β measures the present bias. Let us assume β = 0.98, meaning Ian has only a very slight present bias. We can see that this present bias is enough that the

Table 10.2 Ian's utility depends on when he finishes the dissertation. Total utility ignores any present bias, while decision utility takes into account present bias. Assuming that $\delta = 1$ and $\beta = 0.98$, total utility is highest if he does the dissertation immediately, but present bias means he will constantly put it off until tomorrow and do it on 30 April

Plan	*Utility on each day*					*Total utility*	*Decision utility*	
	1st	*2nd*	*3rd*	*4th*	*30th*		*Today*	*Tomorrow*
Do it today	0	100	100	100	100	2900	2842	—
Do it tomorrow	99	0	100	100	100	2899	2843	2744
Do it on 3rd	99	99	0	100	100	2898	2842	2745
Do it on 30th	99	99	99	99	0	2871	2816	2719

decision utility is higher for doing the dissertation tomorrow. This, in itself, looks not too bad, because total utility is only one lower if he does it tomorrow. The problem is that tomorrow he will want to put it off until the next day, and so on. This means that, if he is naïve about his present bias, he will actually do it on 30 April and lose 29 in total utility.

Ian's naïve present bias will reduce his total utility by 1 percent. Nothing can be gained from arguing whether that is big or small; the main point we need to take from this is that a little bit of present bias can accumulate into a large loss in total utility. On any one day Ian is only willing to sacrifice one unit of total utility because of present bias. Unfortunately, he does not realize that he will end up sacrificing one unit every day, over lots of days, and so the total loss will be larger than he thought.

If Ian was sophisticated, and so knew about his present bias, he would do the dissertation straight away. Sophistication, however, does not mean he always avoids the welfare costs of present bias.

To illustrate, we can think about Emma who is sophisticated and eager to buy the latest book by her favorite author. As soon as she buys it she will read it and have utility 100. To complicate matters, the bookstore has a deal whereby the price of the book decreases by $1 every day, starting at $29. Table 10.3 summarizes the choice that Emma faces, again assuming $\beta = 0.98$. The best thing that Emma can do is wait until the price has gone down to $0. If she was naïve, that is what she would do, but because she is sophisticated she will buy today! That's because she can predict that on the 29th she will buy, which means on the 28th she should buy, and so on back to today. Again small day-to-day losses accumulate to a much bigger total loss.

It turns out that these examples are representative of what happens in general. If the costs are immediate and benefits later, then there can be a big loss in total utility from present bias for someone who is naïve. If the benefits are immediate and the costs later, then there can be a big loss in total utility from present bias for someone who is sophisticated.

Clearly, therefore, present bias is a potential problem. If someone keeps on putting something off, or bringing something forward, the losses will accumulate. And being sophisticated is not enough to avoid such losses; it can make them worse.

Table 10.3 Emma's utility depends on when she buys the book. Assuming that $\delta = 1$ and $\beta = 0.98$, total utility is highest if she waits to buy the book. Present bias means she knows she will buy it earlier than that, so ultimately she buys it today

	Utility on each day					*Total utility*	*Decision utility*	
	1st	*2nd*	*28th*	*29th*	*30th*		*on 28th*	*on 29th*
Buy it today	71	0	0	0	0	71	—	—
Buy it on 28th	0	0	98	0	0	98	98	—
Buy it on 29th	0	0	0	99	0	99	97	99
Buy it on 30th	0	0	0	0	100	100	98	98

10.3.2 Pre-commitment

Now we know that present bias and projection bias really are a problem it becomes even more relevant to see whether pre-commitment can work. In principle it can. Ian might commit to doing the dissertation by, say, making a bet with his friend that he will do it today. Emma might pre-commit by putting her money in a 'safe place' until the end of the month. In Chapter four (see, for example, section 4.2.3) I already argued that people may want to pre-commit. Here, and in the next chapter, I want to take that argument a bit further, and look at some data. I will start with a study by Ariely and Wertenbroch (2002).

In the study people were recruited to take part in a proofreading task that involved reading three texts of around ten pages. Recruits were paid for every error that they spotted, but had $1 deducted for each day of delay beyond a deadline. Recruits were randomly assigned to one of three conditions: an evenly spaced deadline condition, where deadlines were set at seven-day intervals for each of the texts; an end-day condition, where all three texts were to be handed in at the end of 21 days; or a self-imposed deadline condition, where recruits were invited to make their own deadlines for when to hand in the three texts over the next 21 days, with these deadlines subsequently being enforced.

If a person has no present bias, then they should prefer the end or self-imposed condition as this gives maximal flexibility when they do the task. If someone has a present bias and is sophisticated, then they should prefer the self-imposed condition as they can commit to a plan that is optimal for them. Figure 10.17 illustrates what happened. We see that in terms of performance those in the evenly spaced condition do better than those in the self-imposed condition, who do better than those in the end condition.

These results illustrate again that people can benefit from pre-commitment. A desire to pre-commit suggests that people are sophisticated to some extent about their present bias. Maybe, however, they do not choose the best plan when they do commit. The subjects in the previous study that self-impose a plan did not do as well, for instance, as those with an evenly spaced plan.

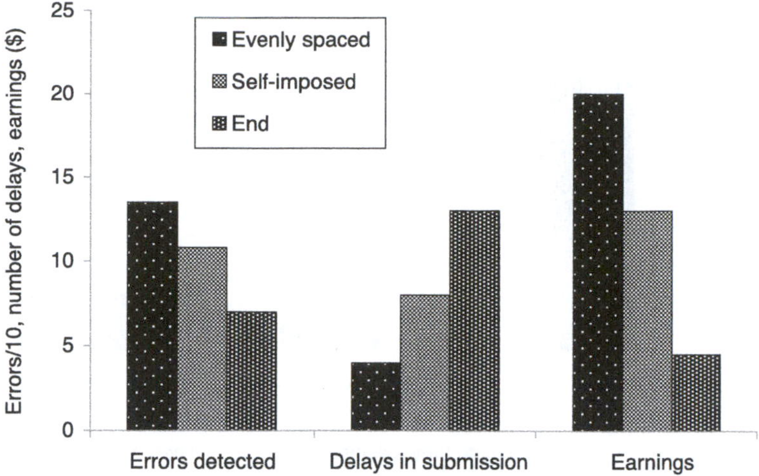

Figure 10.17 Performance in a proofreading task. Performance depended on whether the deadlines were evenly spaced, self-imposed, or all at the end.

Source: Ariely and Wertenbroch (2002).

To illustrate the consequences of this, recall the gym example in Chapter four. Buying membership may be a way that Ian could try to overcome his present bias by pre-committing to going to the gym. The problem is, he might underestimate the strength of his present bias and so still not go to the gym. He has ended up paying a lot of money for a pre-commitment device that does not work! Pre-commitment, therefore, is not a panacea for present bias. It might work for some people in some situations. But sometimes it might make matters worse, like for Ian not going to the gym.

If people do not always make great choices, and others could potentially make better choices, it seems natural to let those others decide. Indeed, even if people can make great choices, they might still prefer someone else to decide so that they can avoid the psychological costs of temptation and the like. This seems to go partly against ideals of liberty and free choice, but if people would choose not to choose, then the ideal of free choice becomes somewhat confused. To progress on this issue, it's useful to ask whether people like having choice or not.

10.3.3 Do people like having choice?

To illustrate how people respond to choice I am going to look at a study by Iyengar and Lepper (2000). In the study, subjects were asked to select one chocolate from a selection of either six, a limited choice, or 30, an extensive choice. Half the subjects then got to taste the chocolate they chose, and half got to taste a chocolate selected by the experimenter. On leaving the experiment, as payment

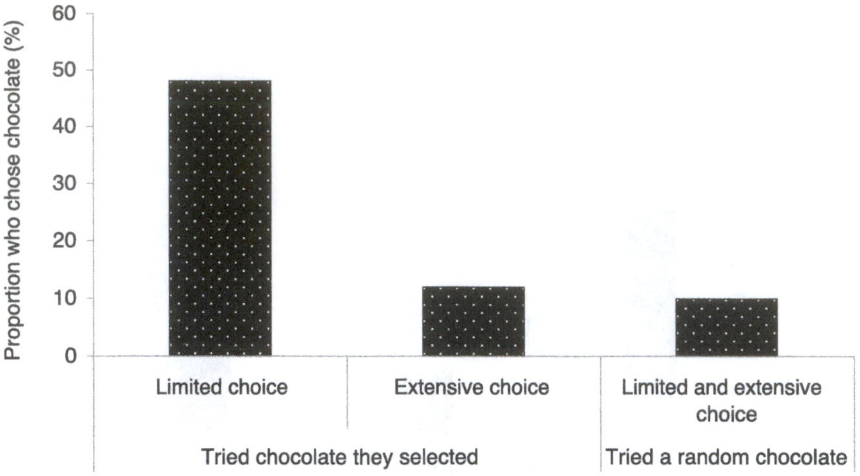

Figure 10.18 The proportion who chose chocolate rather than money depending on whether there was a limited or extensive choice, and whether they got to taste a chocolate they chose or the experimenter chose.

Source: Iyengar and Lepper (2000).

for participation, subjects were given the choice of receiving $5 cash or a box of chocolates worth $5. The main result is clear from Figure 10.18, where we see that the proportion choosing chocolate over cash was far higher for subjects asked to choose from a limited number of chocolates and allowed to taste the one they selected.

Why is there such a difference? Figure 10.19 offers some clues. There are significant differences in perceptions of the participants depending on whether they had a limited or extensive choice. Interestingly, participants did appear to enjoy choosing more when there was a more extensive choice. On all other measures, however, participants seemed to benefit from a more limited choice: it was quicker, less difficult, less frustrating, and they were more satisfied with their choice.

An experiment about chocolate seems a long way from us making conclusions on the benefits of free choice, but I like this study because it nicely illustrates two results observed much more generally. The first result is that more choice is not always a good thing. More choice can be bad because it complicates the decision and can lead to temptation and a need for self-control. This is consistent with what we saw in Chapter two, where many preferred to delay a difficult decision, or seemed overwhelmed when there were too many choices on offer.

Should we, therefore, be taking choice away from people? No, because the second result is that people like having a choice. We see this in the study by Iyengar and Lepper, where subjects were more likely to want a box of chocolates rather than cash if they had tasted the chocolate they chose during the experiment,

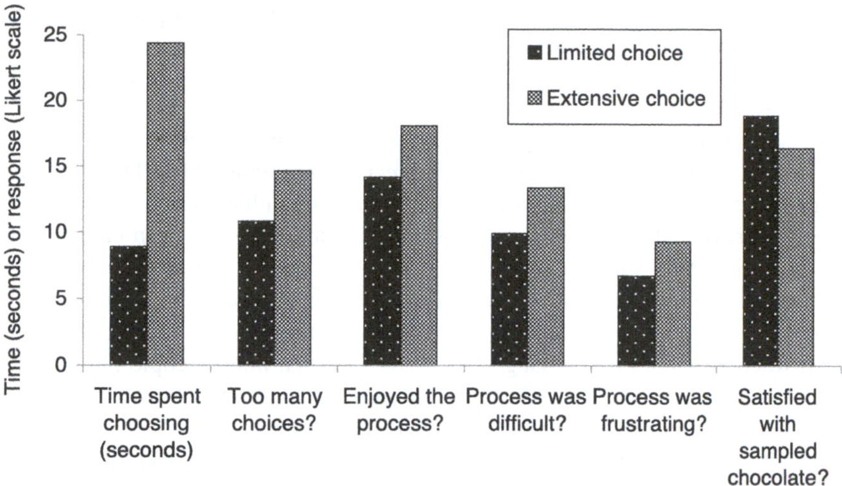

Figure 10.19 How opinions and behavior changed if subjects had a limited choice or extensive choice of chocolates.

Source: Iyengar and Lepper (2000).

i.e. their choice mattered. More generally, the evidence is strong that people do like to make choices. One explanation is that people have a greater interest and motivation in things that they have **self-determined** through their own actions.

So, when faced with an increased choice of options, many people defer making a decision or feel less satisfied with the decision they make. This is called **choice overload**. People do, however, like to have some control and choice.

Putting these things together gives a somewhat bizarre conclusion. People like having choice, but do not like difficult choice. What people should like most, therefore, are easy choices! There's not much evidence to say whether this is a fair conclusion or not, but what we do have is largely supportive. That's because choice seems to lead to the largest increases in motivation in experiments when the choice is largely irrelevant, such as choosing what color pen to use, or what name to give a game character. This raises some interesting policy implications that we can come back to in the next chapter.

10.4 Summary

Instant utility is how much utility a person gets at a specific point in time, and can be thought of as a measure of happiness. We saw that a person's instant utility, or level of happiness, appears to depend on their position relative to others and relative to what has happened to them in the past. In particular, we see varying degrees of adaption to life-changing events.

We then distinguished between decision utility, total utility, and remembered utility. Roughly speaking, decision utility is how much utility a person thought they would get from doing something, when they decided to do it. Total utility is how much utility they actually got from doing it. Remembered utility is how much utility they think they got from doing it.

We saw that decision utility, total utility, and remembered utility can be different because of things like duration neglect and projection bias. This suggests that people may not know what things would make them happiest.

We then revisited the issue of present bias and showed that it can cause a big drop in utility. This suggests that people may not choose the thing that would make them happiest even if they know what they should choose.

Given the suggestion that people may not always make good choices, we questioned whether people like having choice. We saw that many people like to pre-commit and do not appear to like difficult choices. Generally, however, people appear to enjoy some level of choice and self-determination.

We get, therefore, an interesting picture of people not always knowing what makes them happy, or will make them happy. We also see people willing to pre-commit or delegate choice to others, provided they retain some freedom of choice. This seemingly provides a clear rationale for policy intervention, if, of course, we can trust policymakers to know any better what makes people happy!

10.5 Health and happiness

Health care is one context where it can be vital to understand what makes people happy, because the potential benefits or costs of being ill and getting treated can be so large. In this section I shall look at two possible applications of what we have learnt about the nature of happiness and utility.

10.5.1 Measuring the value of treatment

Valuing the costs and benefits of medical treatments is fundamental to allocating health care resources efficiently and most effectively. This is particularly the case in state-financed health care systems like the National Health Service in the UK. Given the limited resources available, priority should be given to treatments that have higher net benefits than others. This notion is often controversial because it means denying treatment to some patients. In particular, patients are denied treatment if the net benefit of treating other patients is higher. Such economic logic is a hard sell when it comes to denying cancer patients much-needed drugs. The logic behind such rationing is, however, sound enough given the limited resources available. More difficult is accurately measuring the net benefit of treatments, and that's what I want to look at in more detail here.

To calculate the net benefit of a treatment we need some measure of its cost and benefits. The cost is a relatively objective thing to measure in principle. For example, the cost of a drug or the cost of a physician's time can easily be calculated. Much harder is to measure the benefits. There are two possible dimensions to any benefit: a treatment could improve the quality of life or prolong the length of life. How can we possibly measure the value of an improvement in quality of life, or an extra year of life?

One widely used way to do so is the QALY. Each year of perfect health is counted as one **quality adjusted life year** (QALY). A year of less than perfect health is given a QALY value of less than one. The lower the quality of life, the lower the value, with zero being equivalent to death. To get the overall value of a treatment we follow the QALY of a treatment over the subsequent life of the patient. To illustrate, Figure 10.20 tracks the quality of life of a patient if they have no treatment or two possible treatments, A and B. Without treatment, the quality of life deteriorates. With treatment A, the patient is stabilized and their life extended. With treatment B, the patient's quality of life initially deteriorates, because of the side effects, but subsequently increases to a relatively high level.

Without treatment, the patient gets 1.5 QALYs because there are 0.5 QALYs in the first year, 0.4 in the second year, and so on, adding up to 1.5. With treatment A, the patient gets 2.4 QALYs and with treatment B, they get 2.7. The net benefit of treatment A is, therefore, 2.4 − 1.5 = 0.9 QALYs, and that of treatment B is 1.2 QALYs.

In this example it looks like treatment B is better than treatment A. We do, however, need to take into account the cost. Suppose treatment A costs $10,000 and treatment B costs $20,000. Then, with treatment A each QALY costs $4,167, but with treatment B costs $7,407. In a publicly funded health service someone

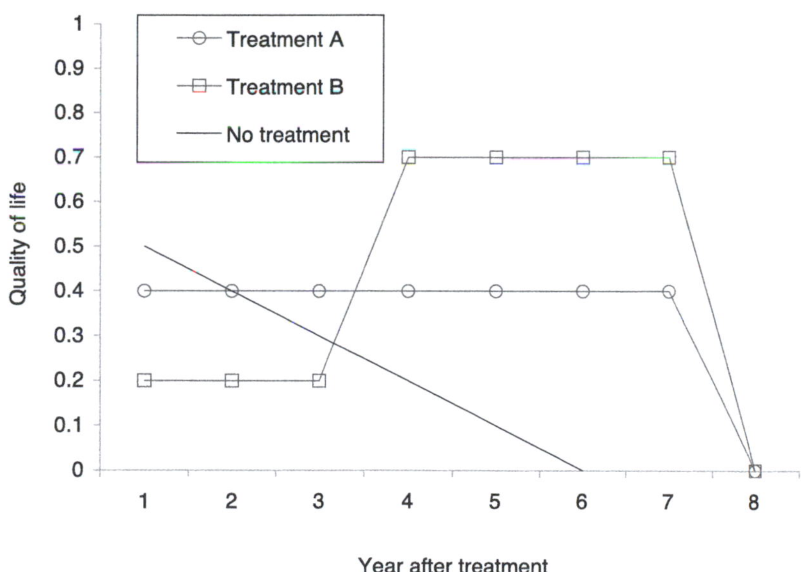

Figure 10.20 Changes in quality of life following two possible treatments, A and B, or no treatment.

has to decide whether these amounts of money are worth paying. In the UK an organization called the National Institute for Health and Clinical Excellence (with the sometimes unfortunate acronym, NICE) does that, and treatments below $45,000 a QALY are usually funded.

In order to get the data to calculate QALYs, the EQ-5D system is often used. Patients are asked to fill out a questionnaire that asks five questions about mobility, pain, self-care, anxiety, and ability to do normal activities. There are three possible answers to each question. A formula is then used to convert these answers into a QALY value. Table 10.4 gives some examples. If patients are tracked and fill in the EQ-5D questionnaire over time, then we can obtain the data to draw Figure 10.20. So, everything looks in place to make things work. The whole process, however, hinges on the formula used to derive the numbers in Table 10.4, and this is where the things that we have learned can start proving useful.

The formula used to calculate a QALY measure is derived using a **time trade-off valuation technique** or **visual analogue scale**. In both cases a random sample of people are asked to imagine a particular quality of life, like those in Table 10.4. The time trade-off technique then asks them to say what length of time in full health they consider to be equivalent to a longer period with this quality of life. The visual analogue scale directly asks them to rate the quality of life on a linear scale. Are people able to make accurate judgments of this sort?

Given what we know about adaption and habituation, the answer is probably no. People who are relatively healthy are likely to underestimate the quality of life of those in poorer health than them. Conversely, people who are relatively unhealthy are likely to overestimate the quality of life of those who are healthier than them. This matters if people find it easier to adapt to some states of ill health than others, and we have seen that adaption rates can vary. To illustrate the problem, Figure 10.21 plots how a person might adapt to treatment. We see that the person adapts very well to the health state resulting from treatment B and so

Table 10.4 Examples of QALY measures using the EQ-5D system

Description	*QALY*
No problems.	1.000
No problems walking about; no problems with self-care; some problems with performing usual activities; some pain or discomfort; not anxious or depressed.	0.760
No problems walking about; some problems washing or dressing self; unable to perform usual activities; moderate pain or discomfort; extremely anxious or depressed.	0.222
Confined to bed; unable to wash or dress self; unable to perform usual activities; extreme pain or discomfort; moderately anxious or depressed.	−0.429

Source: Phillips and Thompson (2009).

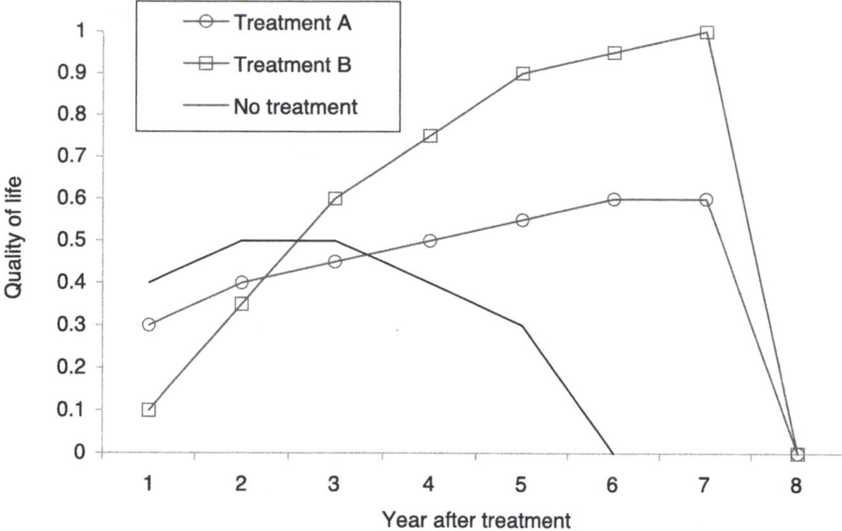

Figure 10.21 Changes in quality of life following two possible treatments, taking into account adaption.

would eventually report a quality of life near to full health. They adapt less well to the health state resulting from treatment A or no treatment.

If we ask non-patients to think what it would be like to have such treatments we are likely to get the low numbers that patients really do feel one year after treatment. This ignores the possibility of adaption and makes treatment A look better. If we ask patients after six or seven years of treatment, they would be more positive and feel particularly positive about treatment B. This ignores the fact that they have adapted. The key thing we need to do is not only rate health states like those in Table 10.4 but also to think how quickly patients will likely adapt to these health states. This should then enter the calculation for working out QALYs.

Unfortunately, it is not current practice to take into account adaption when calculating QALYs. One reason is probably that the notion of adaption can seem a little controversial because it raises the question: if people will adapt to ill health, then why do they need treatment? This looks a tricky question until we compare Figures 10.20 and 10.21. If we look at what happens with no treatment, then adaption does indeed improve the quality of life. The crucial thing, however, is that adaption increases the quality of life from having the treatment by even more! So, yes, people may adapt to their poor health state but they might also adapt to the potentially less than perfect health state that results from treatment. Adaption does not, therefore, mean that we are any more or less likely to recommend treatment.

Valuing improvements in quality of life is controversial and difficult, but if we are to make the best health choices we need these measures. I have only touched on the issue here but, hopefully, you have seen how the ideas we have looked at in this chapter, particularly adaption, can help inform the debate.

10.5.2 Improving the remembered utility of treatment

For effective prevention of health problems it is important that people turn up for relevant screening procedures. For example, colonoscopy is a screening procedure for colorectal cancer, one of the leading causes of cancer-related death. Colonoscopy saves lives, but only if patients are willing to undergo the fairly unpleasant procedure. Whether or not they are willing will depend to some extent on their recollections of previous treatments or procedures. Someone who remembers their last colonoscopy as painful and unpleasant may be less likely to turn up for a subsequent colonoscopy, and that could be very bad. This means that anything which can improve the remembered utility of the procedure should be a good thing. Redelmeier and co-authors (2003) investigated whether this can be done.

In the study, outpatients who were due for a colonoscopy were asked to take part. During the procedure patients were given a hand held device with which they could indicate their discomfort on a scale of 0 to 10. Afterwards patients and physicians were asked questions about how much pain and discomfort was experienced during the procedure. The procedure can last anything from a few minutes to over an hour. The striking thing was, however, that patients' recollections of pain and discomfort did not depend on how long the procedure lasted. Instead they depended on the peak and end pain. This is further evidence of duration neglect.

Duration neglect and peak-end evaluation suggests that extending the duration of a procedure while decreasing the end pain could make patients remember it less negatively. To test for this, a randomized trial was done in which the colonoscopy procedure was extended by three minutes for selected patients (see Research Methods 10.3). During the extra three minutes there would have been discomfort, but less than during the main part of the procedure. Figure 10.22 summarizes some of the data. Consistent with peak-end evaluation, end pain is less with the prolonged procedure and the retrospective evaluation of pain is less. Patients were subsequently tracked to see whether they returned for a repeat colonoscopy, where the median follow-up time is around five years. Those who took part in the prolonged procedure were marginally more likely to return.

The effect on the proportion of patients who returned for a repeat colonoscopy was not huge in this study; but, if it comes from waiting just three extra minutes, and if it means one or two people suffer less from cancer, then that is a big gain. We do not know whether other more significant changes could have larger effects, but it is an intriguing possibility. This possibility arose from distinguishing between remembered and total utility.

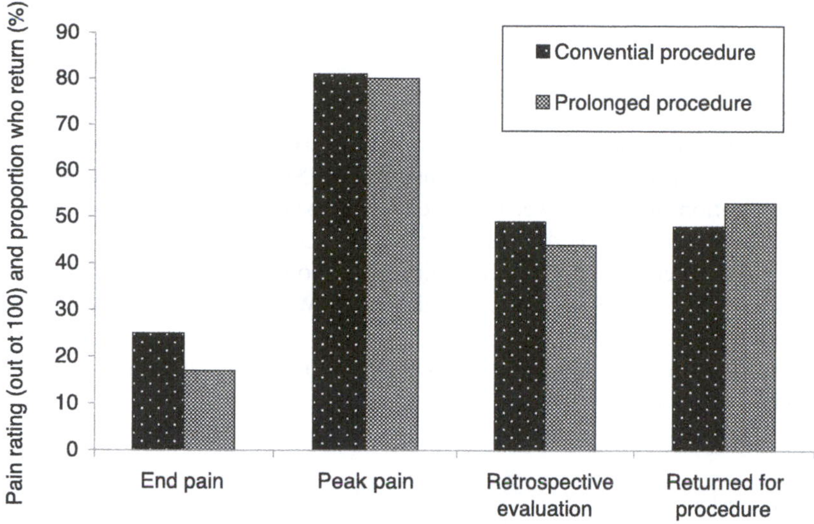

Figure 10.22 Measures of pain and rate of return for a repeat colonoscopy depending on whether the procedure was prolonged or not.

Source: Redelmeier *et al.* (2003).

Research Methods 10.3

Double blind experiments

In an experiment with multiple treatments it is sometimes a concern that the researcher knows what treatment a particular subject is in. If, for instance, the clinicians, in the study by Redelmeier and co-authors, know that a particular patient is in the treatment with a prolonged procedure, then they may treat the patient differently during the procedure. We need to avoid this because it can clearly affect the results.

A **double blind experiment** is one in which the researcher does not know what treatment is being run during an experimental session. Generally, this is not very simple to achieve, but there are ways to make it happen. In this particular study the treatment that a subject was assigned to was randomly determined and written down on a piece of paper in a sealed envelope. Only when the colonoscopy procedure was near to completion would the envelope be opened and the clinicians know whether to extend the procedure or not: a neat way to obtain double blindness.

10.6 Saving and retirement

In Chapters two and four we spent some time looking at the implications of choice and time-inconsistency for saving, borrowing, and the life cycle. It is natural to pick up these topics again in this chapter. I will start by looking at the implications of projection bias.

10.6.1 Projection bias in saving

In Chapter four we looked at a model of habit formation in which Maria would become habituated to past levels of consumption. Such habituation is representative of adaption, and we showed that it could lead to an increase in saving following an increase in income. At that stage we did not need to assume any present bias. In the last chapter, when looking at addiction, we looked more at how present bias can matter once someone becomes habituated. What I want to do now is add projection bias to the story.

To see why projection bias matters, we can work through an example. Suppose that Ian's utility in year t is:

$$u(c_t, h_t) = \begin{cases} \sqrt{c_t - h_t} & \text{if } c_t \geq h_t \\ -\sqrt{h_t - c_t} & \text{if } c_t < h_t \end{cases}$$

where c_t is his consumption and

$$h_t = c_{t-1}$$

is the reference level of consumption to which he is habituated. So, Ian's reference level adapts every year to his consumption of the previous year. I leave you to think about how this relates to the model we looked at in section 4.5.1.

Suppose that, because of projection bias, Ian underestimates how much his reference level will adapt. Specifically, suppose he believes that:

$$h_t = \alpha h_{t-1} + (1 - \alpha)c_{t-1}$$

where α is some parameter. If $\alpha = 0$, Ian does not have projection bias, but if $\alpha > 0$, he does.

Table 10.5 illustrates what consequences a projection bias could have. We see that Ian's income is going to increase in the next two years and then fall in year 3. You could think of this as a condensed version of working and then retiring. How can Ian best smooth his consumption? The best he could do would be to increase his consumption slowly. This is what he will do if $\alpha = 0$, and so he has no projection bias. What if he does have a projection bias?

The easiest case to look at is where he has a very strong bias because $\alpha = 1$. In this case Ian completely fails to realize that he will adapt to increased consumption and so increases consumption as much as possible relative to his current reference level. This does not work very well because he does adapt, and so, while he is happy in year 1, he is not so happy in years 2 and 3.

Table 10.5 The consequences of projection bias in a simple example. Ian's income will fall in year 3. If he has no projection bias he would choose a gradually increasing consumption profile and get total utility 3. With projection bias he chooses a flatter consumption profile and gets less utility than he expects

	Time				*Projected utility*	*Actual utility*
	Year 0	*Year 1*	*Year 2*	*Year 3*		
Income	1	4	4	1	—	—
Planned consumption						
$\alpha = 0$	1	2	3	4	3.00	3.00
$\alpha = 1$	1	3	3	3	4.23	1.41
$\alpha = 0.5$ and in year 0	1	2.33	3	3.67	3.47	2.79
$\alpha = 0.5$ and in year 1	1	2.33	3.14	3.53	2.94	2.68

More realistic is the case where $\alpha = 0.5$ and so Ian knows that he adapts but underestimates how much he adapts. He would now choose a plan intermediate between those he would choose when $\alpha = 0$ and $\alpha = 1$. The consumption profile is increasing, but flatter than optimal. The most interesting thing is what happens after one year. At this point Ian realizes that he underestimated how much he would adapt and so changes his plan. What's interesting is that the new plan that he comes up with is worse than the original one! Basically, he knows that he needs to increase his consumption more now than he thought he would have to in order to be above his reference level.

Stylized though it is, this example illustrates two key implications of projection bias for saving and retirement. First, Ian saves less for retirement than he should have done. Second, he will be time-inconsistent and save less for retirement than he planned to do. We see this in the 0.14 difference between how much Ian thinks he will save in year 2 and how much he actually will save.

Both of these implications are bad, and can accumulate over many years to a real shortfall in savings for retirement. Could we avoid this? In principle the second problem should, at least, be avoidable because Ian might be willing to pre-commit to a savings plan that does not allow him to change his mind. In the next chapter we shall see how such plans may work. The first problem could be avoided by 'forcing' Ian to save more, but this brings us back to the issue of choice and autonomy.

10.6.2 Investor autonomy

One way to 'nudge' people like Ian to save more for their retirement is to automatically enroll them in a savings plan. We are going to look at this in the next chapter, but you could probably guess from what we did in Chapter four that people usually stick to such plans. Even if they wanted to withdraw, present bias means they 'put if off until tomorrow' and never do get around to changing. So, let's imagine for now that automatic enrollment is like 'forcing' Ian to save.

This might be a good thing, but we encounter a problem. If we are going to automatically enroll Ian in a savings plan, then we have to decide where to invest, how much to invest, and so on. Should we also decide that, or let Ian choose? This is a fascinating situation to question whether choice is good or not. Let's look at a study by Benartzi and Thaler (2002).

In the first part of the study they collected information about people enrolled in the UCLA retirement plan. There is no default option in this plan, so participants have to choose their own portfolio. Based on this information they predicted the retirement income a person could expect if invested in (a) the portfolio he or she was invested in, (b) the average portfolio, and (c) the median portfolio. (Just to clarify, the median portfolio will be significantly different to the average portfolio, because many invested a lot in cash and so the average portfolio is skewed towards investing more in cash.) Participants in the study were then asked to rate, on a scale of 1 to 5, how attractive a portfolio appeared, without knowing which one was theirs. As we can see in Figure 10.23 the median portfolio received a higher rating than their own portfolio. Indeed, only 21 percent of participants rated their own portfolio highest!

In the second part of the study Benartzi and Thaler surveyed employees at SwedishAmerican Health Systems. Employees at SwedishAmerican are automatically provided with an individual portfolio selected by an investment management

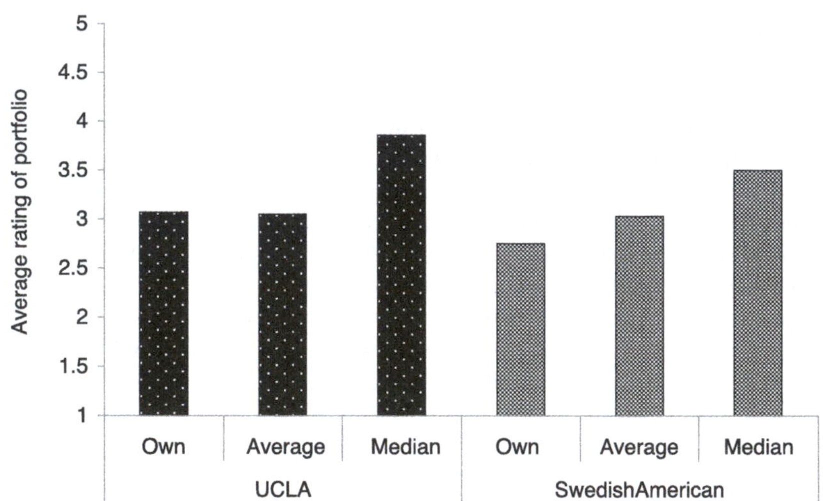

Figure 10.23 The average rating of portfolios at UCLA and SwedishAmerican.
Source: Benartzi and Thaler (2002).

firm, but have the possibility to opt out and choose their own portfolio. Focusing only on employees who had decided to opt out, they again predicted retirement income and asked participants how they would rank (a) their own portfolio, (b) the average portfolio, and (c) the default portfolio suggested by the investment management firm. This time we see in Figure 10.23 that the default portfolio gets the highest ranking. Only 20 percent preferred their own portfolio, and recall that participants had specifically opted out of the default option in order to choose their own portfolio!

These results suggest that investor autonomy is not worth much. In both cases participants rated higher a portfolio that was not chosen by them. We might be concerned that this is due to them having different expectations about what might happen to the stock market, etc. When surveyed, however, most participants expressed no strong beliefs about what would be likely to happen. The more plausible explanation seems to be that participants did not have the skills and information to pick the best portfolio for their preferences.

So, should we be letting people choose where they invest? The simple answer given these results would seem to be no, but we do need to be careful. First, there is the problem of deciding where best the money should be invested and how. Twenty percent of those in the study were most happy with the portfolio they chose, and can we justify taking choice away from these to benefit the other 80 percent? Second, is the problem that people may like making a choice, even if they make a bad choice. The potential costs of investing unwisely are huge, so people would really have to like making a choice for this to matter much. Even so, it suggests that we might want to think about giving investors some choice.

10.7 Welfare trade-offs

In this final section I want to start talking more explicitly about policy. One fundamental issue in policymaking is to measure the welfare consequences of different policies. After all, the objective is to pursue policies that increase overall welfare and to do that we need to measure welfare. Here, I shall look at two very different examples of measuring the welfare consequences of policy. There are lots of other examples I could have given, but I think these are two nice examples to illustrate what we have learnt can be useful. The first example shows how we can fill in some of the blanks of existing theory. The second example shows how we can open up new issues not considered in existing theory.

10.7.1 The inflation–unemployment trade-off

It is common in macroeconomics to think of a government trying to maximize a social welfare function. Two things usually thrown into the welfare function are inflation and unemployment, with high inflation and unemployment associated with lower social welfare. The textbook story would be that a government wishes to reduce inflation, which will cause unemployment in the short run, and so wants to find the disinflationary path that minimizes the loss in social welfare. For this approach to make sense we need to have some idea of the relative loss in social welfare if there is unemployment or inflation.

A standard approach would be to assume a one-to-one trade-off, so the welfare function would look something like:

$$W = -(Y - \bar{Y})^2 - (\Pi - \bar{\Pi})^2$$

where $Y - \bar{Y}$ is the deviation of national income from the optimum and $\Pi - \bar{\Pi}$ is the deviation of inflation from the optimum. The reason to assume a one-to-one trade-off seems to be the lack of any better idea! Happiness data can potentially give us a better idea because we can estimate how much unemployment and inflation decrease reported happiness, and observe the trade-off.

Di Tella and co-authors (2001) did this, looking at data from 12 European countries over the period 1975 to 1991. Table 10.6 summarizes some of the numbers they come up with. Unemployment causes two negative effects on happiness. There is a direct effect due to people who are unemployed being on average less happy. There is an additional indirect effect, what we could call 'the fear of unemployment', that lowers happiness of people still employed. Inflation has only an indirect effect.

With the numbers in Table 10.6 we can calculate the trade-off between inflation and unemployment. A 1 percent increase in the unemployment rate lowers the average satisfaction of everybody by 0.02 and lowers the satisfaction of the 1 percent who become unemployed by 0.33. Overall, therefore, average satisfaction decreases by $0.33 \times 0.01 + 0.02 = 0.0233$. To find the fall in inflation needed to compensate for this decrease in happiness, we calculate $0.0233/0.014 = 1.66$. So, a 1.66 percent fall in inflation increases average satisfaction by as much as a 1 percent increase in unemployment decreases average satisfaction. Thus, the unemployment–inflation trade-off is 1.66 and we might want a social welfare function

$$W = -1.66\,(Y - \bar{Y})^2 - (\Pi - \bar{\Pi})^2.$$

This is not the end of the story, because, for example, unemployment and inflation may influence different parts of society differently, and we might want to take account of that. We also know that being unemployed can have long-term effects on satisfaction, while a change in the inflation rate is unlikely to. The specific number 1.66 should not, therefore, be taken as definitive. But 1.66 does have more

Table 10.6 Changes in reported life satisfaction (on a 1–4 scale) if there is unemployment or inflation

	Change in life satisfaction
If unemployed	−0.33
If 1% rise in unemployment rate	−0.02
If 1% fall in inflation	+0.014

Source: Di Tella *et al.* (2001).

justification than the standard assumption of 1. This illustrates how we can use measurements of happiness and life satisfaction to better inform on optimal policy. We have focused on the inflation and unemployment trade-off but a similar idea can be applied to a wide range of other policy questions such as the optimal level of unemployment benefit and optimal tax rates.

Before moving on I think it is interesting to briefly mention a study by Di Tella and MacCulloch (2005) that asked whether people on the political right had a different inflation–unemployment trade-off to those on the political left. Why would they? Typically we would associate right-wingers with policies that focus on reducing inflation rather than unemployment. By contrast, left-wingers would be associated with policies that focus on reducing unemployment rather than inflation. Figure 10.24 illustrates that those who rated themselves to the political right did have a relatively low trade-off and those to the left a relatively high trade-off. This is not due to them being rich or poor. Recall that these numbers are estimated by looking at how satisfied people say they are. So, these differences do not mean that those on the political right say they care more about inflation than those on the political left. It means that the life satisfaction of those on the political right really does depend more on inflation than of those on the political left!

10.7.2 Tax saliency

One other thing that it is important to have a welfare measure of is the deadweight loss caused by taxes. I will finish this chapter with an example of how a seemingly irrelevant change in the framing of a tax can potentially change the associated welfare loss.

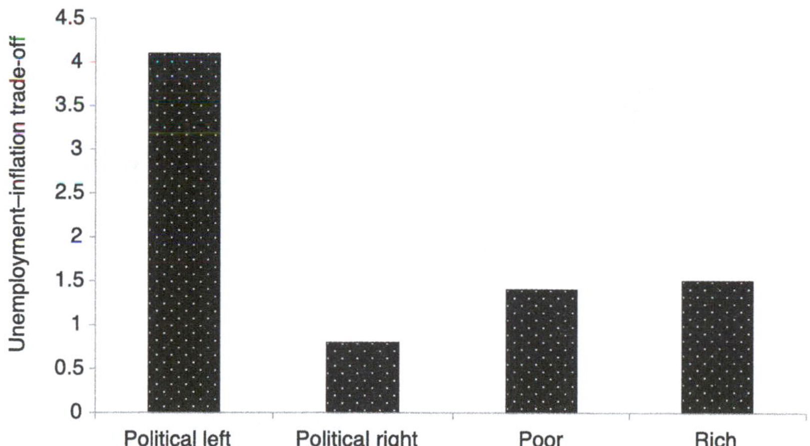

Figure 10.24 The inflation–unemployment trade-off of those on the political left is higher than of those on the political right, and this is not because of differences in income.

Source: Di Tella and MacCulloch (2006).

In Europe the advertised price of a product includes any relevant taxes. In the US and Canada it is normal for the price of a product to not include the sales tax. To work out the full price of an item a customer would, therefore, have to calculate and add on the sales tax of 4 to 10 percent. Cognitively this is not an easy thing to do, even if he carries around a calculator to do the math, because some things are subject to sales tax, some not, etc. A study by Chetty and co-authors (2009) questioned the consequences of not including the sales tax in the advertised price.

The first part of the study involved an experiment carried out in a large grocery store in California. On some of the products they placed a label, in addition to the main label, giving the price of the good including the tax. This does not change the price of the good but does change the appearance of the price to the customer.

It may be that customers would be more likely to buy such a product because the label allows them to avoid the cognitive cost of working out the tax. On the other hand, they may be less likely to buy the product because the label makes the product appear more expensive. What do you think happened?

By way of comparison, the study looked at the change in demand on goods that did have the amount of sales tax displayed (treated goods in the treatment store) versus the change in demand for similar goods in a similar part of the store (control goods in the treatment store) and those same goods in a different store (control and treated goods in the control store). Figure 10.25 summarizes what happened. The story is fairly clear: demand fell on goods that had the tax included in the price. This fall is also relatively large at 6 to 8 percent, depending on what is used as the comparator.

To check this result, the second part of the study looked at demand for alcohol. Alcohol is subject to two taxes: an excise tax that is included in the price, and the sales tax that is not. This allows for a natural experiment in which we can track

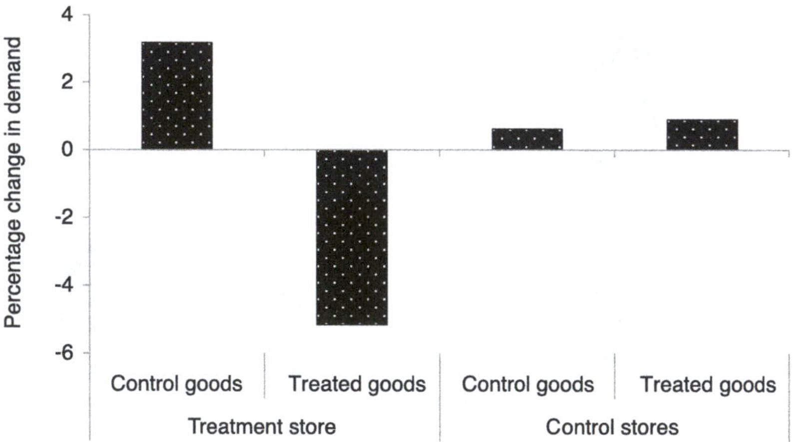

Figure 10.25 Change in demand if sales tax is displayed.

Source: Chetty *et al.* (2009).

changes in the two tax rates and changes in demand. Chetty and co-authors looked at data from 1970 to 2003 and found that changes in the excise tax cause a much larger change in demand than changes in the sales tax. This is consistent with the story that customers focus on the price on the label, which includes excise tax, and largely ignore the sales tax that will be added at the till.

The clear suggestion is that the advertised price is salient. If the price on the label is higher, then consumers buy less, even though the actual price is the same. What are the consequences of this? To answer that question I shall work through a model of consumer choice.

Suppose there are two goods, bananas and money. If Ian buys b bananas and has $\$y$ left, his utility is:

$$u(b, y) = 2\alpha\sqrt{b} + y$$

where α is some parameter. Further suppose that he has $\$m$ to start with and the price of a banana is p ignoring the tax and $p(1 + t)$ taking into account the tax.

[Extra] If Ian takes into account the tax, he would maximize his utility subject to the budget constraint $y = m - p(1 + t)b$. The optimum is where the marginal utility from consuming bananas equals the price and so where:

$$\frac{\alpha}{\sqrt{b}} = p(1+t) \quad \text{or} \quad b_T = \left(\frac{\alpha}{p(1+t)}\right)^2 \quad \text{and} \quad y_T = m - \frac{\alpha^2}{p(1+t)}.$$

If Ian does not take into account the sales tax he would maximize his utility subject to the budget constraint $y = m - pb$. The optimum in this case is where:

$$\frac{\alpha}{\sqrt{b}} = p \quad \text{or} \quad b_N = \left(\frac{\alpha}{p}\right)^2 \quad \text{and} \quad y_N = m - (1+t)\frac{\alpha^2}{p}.$$

In both cases Ian pays the sales tax, as seen when we calculate y. With this we can work out the difference in utility $\Delta = u(b_T, y_T) - u(b_N, y_N)$ whether Ian does or does not take into account the sales tax. It is:

$$\Delta = 2\alpha\left(\frac{\alpha}{p(1+t)}\right) + m - \frac{\alpha^2}{p(1+t)} - \left[2\alpha\left(\frac{\alpha}{p}\right) + m - (1+t)\frac{\alpha^2}{p}\right]$$

which we can simplify to:

$$\Delta = \frac{\alpha^2}{p(1+t)} - \frac{\alpha^2(1-t)}{p} = \frac{\alpha^2 t^2}{p(1+t)}. \tag{10.1}$$

Whether you followed the algebra or not, the main thing to know is that equation (10.1) tells us the amount Ian will lose if he does not take into account the sales tax. This difference will be small if t is small. For instance, if $t = 0.07375$, which is the relevant figure for California, we get:

$$\Delta = 0.0051\frac{\alpha^2}{p}.$$

This is not going to be a big number unless α is big, meaning Ian really likes bananas. For example, if $\alpha = 10$, $m = 200$ and $p = 1$, then ignoring the sales tax, he will buy 100 bananas and spend \$107.38. If he was to take into account the sales tax his utility would be \$0.51 higher. That does not look like much of a gain, and so he does not lose much by ignoring the sales tax.

It turns out that this is quite a general result and not restricted to the functional form for utility that I assumed. Primarily this is because by maximizing his utility, even if at slightly the wrong price, Ian reaches a point where he is relatively indifferent to changes in his consumption. So, if he were to take account of the tax, it might change his behavior but would not much change his utility. If ignoring the tax means little welfare loss for the consumer, then it is no surprise that we rarely see shoppers with calculators working out the tax on a good.

We can see the implications for the government with the help of Figure 10.26 and Table 10.7. These work through the consequences of a 5 and 10 percent tax.

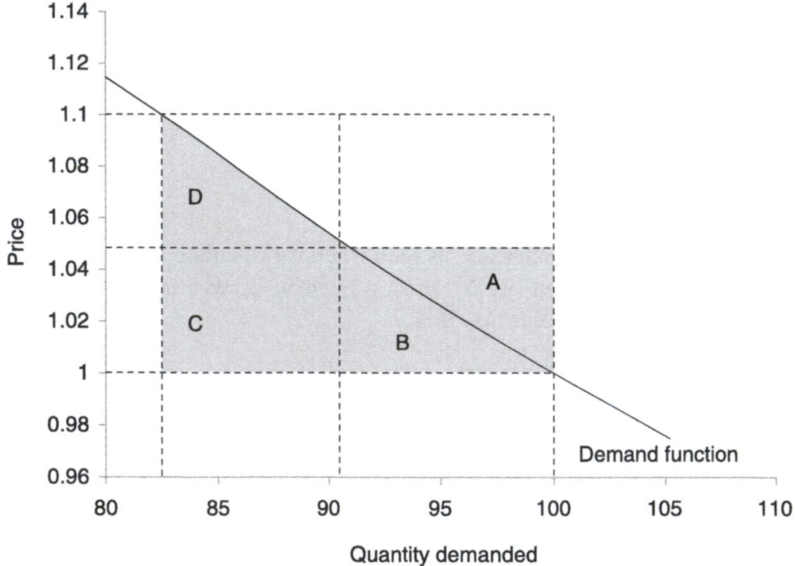

Figure 10.26 The consequences of ignoring the sales tax. If Ian takes account of the tax, there is a deadweight loss of B and D + C + B. If he does not take account of the tax, there is no deadweight loss but A + B is transferred from Ian to the government.

Table 10.7 The consequences of a 5 and 10 percent tax when $\alpha = 10$, $m = 200$, and $p = \$1$

	Is the tax salient?							
	No	*Yes*	*No*	*Yes*	*No*	*Yes*	*No*	*Yes*
Tax rate	*Bananas bought*		*Money left*		*Utility*		*Tax revenue*	
t = 0	100	100	\$100.00	\$100.00	300	300	\$0.00	\$0.00
t = 0.05	100	91	\$95.00	\$104.45	295	295	\$5.00	\$4.55
t = 0.1	100	83	\$90.00	\$108.70	290	291	\$10.00	\$8.30

If there is no tax, Ian will buy 100 bananas, have \$100 left, and have total utility 300. For a higher tax we can compare his utility and the tax revenue if he does or does not take account of the tax. Simplest is to measure welfare as utility plus the tax revenue, so it is \$300 with no tax.

If the tax is 5 percent and Ian takes account of it, then there is a deadweight welfare loss because some consumer surplus is lost. This is given by area B in Figure 10.26 and comes to \$0.21. If the tax were 10 percent, the deadweight loss would be equal to areas B + C + D and amount to \$0.79. You might argue that these are not big numbers. If, however, there are 1,000 or 10,000 consumers like this, then the overall welfare loss of the tax starts to add up.

What if Ian does not take account of the sales tax? He continues to buy 100 bananas. This means that, if the tax is 5 percent, we no longer lose area B. Instead area A + B gets transferred to the government in tax. We can see this by the fact that consumer utility goes down by five but tax revenue goes up by \$5. There is no deadweight loss of the tax, just a redistribution of welfare in which Ian becomes relatively worse off.

This is important because it suggests that taxes are not as bad as we might think in terms of efficiency, but are possibly worse in terms of equity. Ultimately, however, it is good for overall welfare that Ian does not take account of the tax. This suggests that care is needed to not push the tax beyond the threshold and that the consumer does take note of it. For example, if Ian ignores a 5 percent tax but takes note of a 10 percent tax, then increasing the tax from 5 to 10 percent would cause a big deadweight loss of B + C + D.

This example illustrates how it is important to take account of the likely behavior of people in designing policy. You might say that this is obvious, but the example shows that things can be a little subtle. In the next chapter I want to develop a more general framework with which to think through how behavioral economics can effectively inform policy.

10.8 Further reading

The literature on happiness gets ever larger and so you should not be short of places to find out more. Books include that by Frey (2008) and survey articles those by Frey and Stutzer (2002), Di Tella and MacCulloch (2006), and Kahneman and Krueger (2006). See also Easterlin (2013). Two nice papers that did not get a mention when talking about experience utility and projection bias are Kahneman *et al.* (1997) and Loewenstein *et al.* (2003). The implications for policy are discussed by Loewenstein and Ubel (2008), and a paper by Patall *et al.* (2008) provides a comprehensive survey of the psychology literature on whether choice is good or not. I also want to mention a classic paper by Laibson (1997) that looks at savings, commitment, and time-inconsistency. Finally, a useful source of information for more on how QALYs are measured and used is the website of the National Institute for Health and Clinical Excellence. The paper by Dolan and Kahneman (2008) provides a good overview of the issues.

One thing that I did not talk about, but is of current interest, is incorporating measures of happiness into measures of economic output. In February 2008, French President Nicolas Sarkozy asked Joseph Stiglitz to create a Commission, subsequently called 'The Commission on the Measurement of Economic Performance and Social Progress', to identify the limits of GDP as an indicator of economic performance and social progress. The Commission website has a copy of the committee's report and videos of various speeches made.

10.9 Review Questions

10.1 Explain why peak-end evaluation causes duration neglect.
10.2 Should a person choose the thing that maximizes decision utility, total utility, or remembered utility?
10.3 If a person has done something before, should we expect that remembered utility equals decision utility?
10.4 Why do you think a high national output does not translate to higher levels of life satisfaction? What are the implications of this for how we measure economic performance?
10.5 Suppose you are taking a course in behavioral economics that involves doing three assignments. Would you rather that the course organizer gives staggered deadlines for handing in the work, or that you merely need to hand in the work before the end of the course? Why?
10.6 How can we take account of adaption when calculating QALYs?
10.7 Given adaption and projection bias, are patients informed enough to decide what medical treatments are best for them?
10.8 Explain why projection bias is different to present bias. How does this show up in people's decisions to save for retirement?
10.9 Should we take account of adaption, or the lack of adaption, to unemployment when calculating the unemployment–inflation trade-off? What effect would this have?
10.10 Should Europe change policy and not require firms to include the sales tax when advertising price?

11 Policy and behavior

> A government agency will be set up to paint contour lines on to hills and colour roads the same as on maps. This will help people know where they are.
>
> The Official Monster Raving Loony Party 2010, UK General Election Manifesto

In this final chapter I want to look at whether behavioral economics can be used by policymakers to help people make better choices. For instance, Maria might buy gym membership but then never go to the gym. Alan might not save enough for retirement. Can we change things so that they make better choices? This question raises some tricky issues, that I will get to, but has to be a major objective of behavioral economics. It allows us to apply what we know in trying to make the world a better place where people are a little bit (or a lot) happier.

In looking at how behavioral economics can inform policy, I think it's useful to distinguish two broad categories of economic policy. The first is about designing institutions so that good things happen. The second is about manipulating individual incentives so that good things happen. There is inevitably some overlap between the two. For example, in designing a good institution we need to provide good individual incentives. The distinction is, however, a useful one and so I will look at each category in turn, beginning with the design of institutions.

11.1 Designing good institutions

An economic **institution** is basically the means and rules by which people interact. We have already seen plenty of examples of institutions in this book, and seen plenty of examples of why institutions matter. For example, in Chapter two we saw that whether the market is a double auction, posted offer, or negotiated price format will likely matter. In Chapter six we saw that whether the auction is an English, Dutch, or first or second price format might matter. We also saw that whether there is leadership, communication, and things like rebates or refunds can help people coordinate in providing, say, a threshold public good. Finally, in Chapter seven we saw that the threat of punishment can help sustain cooperation.

What I want to do here is look at three very different examples of institution design. As well as further illustrating the importance of institutions, this will take us into the world of practical policy design and intervention. I'll briefly mention that institutions can be of two basic kinds: **formal institutions**, like markets, and **informal institutions**, like social norms. The first example I want to look at is more about informal institutions and the latter two more about formal institutions.

11.1.1 The tragedy of the commons

To get us started, consider a lake used for fishing. Anyone who wants to go fishing is free to do so, and can fish as much as they want. What's going to happen? What might happen is **overuse** or **overexploitation** of the resource, whereby too many fishermen come along, catch too many fish, and leave the stock of fish too low to be sustainable. We don't want that to happen.

A fishing lake is one example of a common pool resource. A **common pool resource** is any good that it is difficult to exclude people from consuming, but one person's consumption lowers the possible consumption of others. It might, for instance, be hard to stop people fishing in the lake, and one fisherman's catch cannot be another's. Other examples include forests, water systems for drinking or irrigation, and the global atmosphere. As this list suggests, common pool resources are immensely important in thinking about environmental issues.

The **tragedy of the commons** is that we should expect overuse of common pool resources. That is, we should expect the worst. To see why, we can look at a specific version of a common pool resource game, used in some experiments.

Suppose that there are eight people, including Anna, who each have ten tokens. They can invest their tokens in something that yields a 'safe return', or spend it on extracting goods from a common pool resource. I will think of people deciding whether to harvest food in their garden, for a safe return, or go fishing in the local lake, where the return will depend on what others do. Tokens could represent money, time, or a combination of both, but I will think of time here. Table 11.1 summarizes

Table 11.1 Some of the possible payoff combinations in a common pool resource game involving Anna and seven others

Hours spent in extracting goods from the common pool resource						
Anna	*The other seven*					
	0	*14*	*28*	*42*	*56*	*70*
0	50	50	50	50	50	50
2	85	78	71	64	57	50
4	118	104	90	76	62	48
6	149	128	107	86	65	44
8	178	150	122	94	66	38
10	205	170	135	100	65	30

some of the possible payoff combinations. For example, if Anna spends four hours fishing and the others spend 14 hours fishing, she gets a payoff of 104.

To make some sense of the numbers in Table 11.1, note that Anna gets 50 for sure if she spends all her time in the garden, which is why it's a safe return. If the others do relatively little fishing, then her payoff will be higher if she spends time fishing, because the lake is full of fish. By contrast, if the others do relatively a lot of fishing then her payoff will be lower if she spends time fishing, because the lake is already empty of fish.

A good outcome is that each person spends four hours fishing to get a payoff of 90. If the others are going to fish a total of $7 \times 4 = 28$ hours, however, Anna does best to spend ten hours fishing. It looks unlikely, therefore, that people would stick to fishing for only four hours. More plausible is that they each spend eight hours fishing to get a payoff of 66. Why? If the others are going to fish a total of $7 \times 8 = 56$ hours, then Anna does best to spend eight hours fishing, and so everything fits a bit better. This is all captured by the fact that 'everyone fish four hours' is the Pareto optimum, while 'everyone fish eight hours' is the Nash equilibrium.

If everyone did fish for eight hours, then we would observe a version of the tragedy of the commons. People would be fishing too much and getting a lower payoff than they could do by fishing a bit less. This would not be good, but what happens in reality?

The evidence suggests that the tragedy of the commons can be avoided, sometimes. Indeed Elinor Ostrom won the Nobel Prize in Economics in 2009 because she: 'Challenged the conventional wisdom by demonstrating how local property can be successfully managed by local commons without any regulation by central authorities or privatization.' Examples of successful use of common pool resources include grazing land in the Swiss Alps and Japan, irrigation systems in Spain and the Philippines, and use of the ground water basins around Los Angeles. In each of these cases, users of the resource found some way to maintain use of the resource at the efficient level, or, at least, below the level of overuse.

To give a specific example: in 1995 Alaska's halibut fisherman decided to use something called **individual fishing quotas**. The basic idea is that individuals are given ownership over a share of the total amount that can be fished. The change was dramatic. The length of season went from a dangerous, three-day race to get as many fish as possible, to an eight-month, demand-led, sustainable solution.

For every success story though, there is an example where the news is not so good. For instance, the bluefin tuna has reached dangerously low levels in the Mediterranean, but there is little consensus on how the decline could be halted, especially given that attempts to use individual fishing quotas in international waters have largely failed.

The pertinent question, therefore, is why the tragedy of the commons can be averted in some cases and not others. Ostrom addressed this question by looking at case studies of common pool resources with the objective of seeing what distinguished the successes from the failures. An up-to-date list of the differences is given in Ostrom (2010) and includes things like: clear and locally understood boundaries between users and non-users, users of the resource have some say in how the resource is managed, and rules for using the resource are designed to include punishment for excessive use.

Such a list, providing as it does a neat dividing line between likely success and failure, is incredibly useful. For instance, it can help inform a policymaker when intervention is needed to avoid the tragedy of the commons, and when it is not. It can also help policymakers set things up so that users of the resource can help themselves, such as with individual fishing quotas. Clearly, however, this only works if the list is the right one, i.e. we have the right dividing line between likely success and failure. And case studies necessarily involve some worrying comparisons, such as Alaskan and Spanish fisherman. One way to supplement case studies, and make sure we have things right, are lab experiments.

Lab experiments are useful because they allow specific elements to be varied one at a time. To illustrate, I will look at a study by Ostrom *et al.* (1992). Subjects were involved in a common resource problem, like that in Table 11.1, for 20 rounds. In the first ten rounds, subjects independently had to decide how much to spend extracting goods from the resource, and in most cases there was overuse. Subjects were then given various means to try and avoid overuse in the ten subsequent rounds. Figure 11.1 summarizes the results. It looks a bit messy so let's go through it slowly.

In the baseline case, subjects were not given any means to avoid overuse and profits remain well short of those possible. In some treatments, subjects were

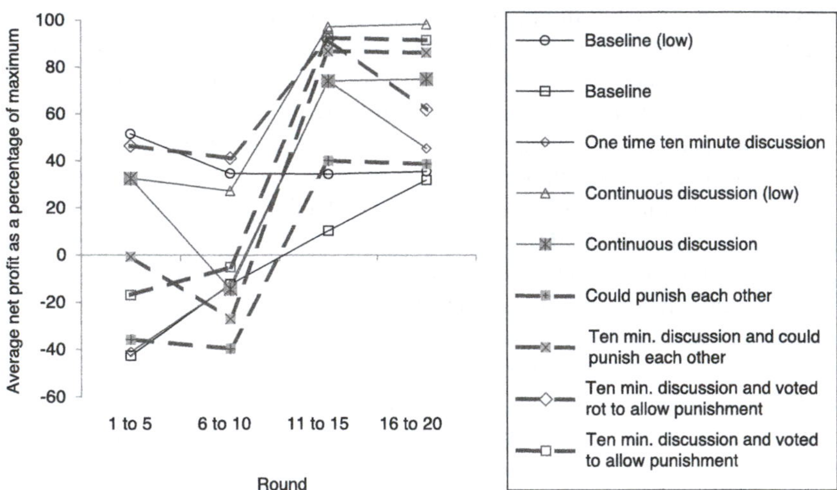

Figure 11.1 The average net profit as a percentage of the maximum over 20 rounds of a common resource problem. A negative percentage indicates that subjects would have done better to invest in the asset with a safe return. 100 percent is the Pareto optimum. The (10) and (25) indicates whether subjects were given 10 or 25 tokens at the start of each round.

Source: Ostrom *et al.* (1992).

given the chance to communicate with each other either though a one-off ten-minute discussion or through repeated communication before every round (see Research Methods 11.1); discussion seemed to have a positive impact and repeated discussion led to a sustained increase in profits.

In another treatment, subjects were given the chance to punish others (in a similar way to that in the public good game of Chapter seven); this seemed to have less of an impact. A further treatment combined the chance to communicate with the opportunity to punish others; this did appear to have a positive impact. In a final treatment, subjects voted, after discussion, on whether or not to allow punishment. Whatever the outcome of the vote we again see a positive impact.

Research Methods 11.1

Communication

As a general rule, experimental economists seem averse to letting subjects communicate with each other. There are good theoretical reasons for doing this because economic activity often takes place between people who simply cannot communicate with each other. There are also good practical reasons for doing this because it stops the experimenter losing control; for example, one subject with a 'strong' personality could end up biasing a whole experiment. In theory, communication should not matter anyway, at least according to the standard economic model!

People do, though, often communicate, and intuitively it makes a difference, so we do need to take account of it. There are various different ways that subjects can be allowed to communicate in experiments.

The most restrictive way is to let a subject say what action he plans to take. So, before a subject chooses, say, an effort level in the weak link game he gets the chance to say to others what he plans to choose. This can be done in a way such that the experimenter loses no control of the experiment, and so is the preferred way of many.

A step up from this is to let subjects chat via computer (see Research Methods 7.4). Now the experimenter starts to lose control because a subject is free to say anything. But, at least all that is said is recorded and relatively easy to analyze.

The final step, as in the experiment by Ostrom and co-authors (1992), is to let subjects talk to each other face to face. Now the experimenter loses a lot of control, and trying to record what happens is essentially impossible; we might be able to record what was said, but recording body language and the like is clearly difficult.

The latter type of experiment is very rare in economics, but I'm not sure that's a good thing.

The lesson from this study was that repeated communication in combination with some threat of punishment or sanction helped people avoid the tragedy of the commons. Other studies have shown that the benefits of communication are less if there are 'outsiders' who do not take part in the communication. This is reassuringly similar to what we see in case studies. A combination of case studies and experiments can give us, therefore, important insights into when and how the tragedy of the commons can be avoided. The crucial things necessary to avoid the tragedy of the commons seem to be communication, a threat of sanctions, an ability to exclude outsiders, and a sense of ownership.

11.1.2 Matching markets

In Chapter two when we looked at markets we contrasted double auction, posted offer, and negotiated price institutions. The basic objective of these institutions is to **match** buyers and sellers so that they can do mutually beneficial deals. Recall that in a double auction market there is an auctioneer who accepts bids and asks, and matches a seller to a buyer if the bid is higher than the ask. In a posted offer market, sellers advertise their prices and buyers walk around and find a price they like. In a negotiated price market, sellers and buyers walk around and ask each other what they are willing to sell or buy. What we hope to see is buyers being matched to sellers whenever the seller is willing to supply at a price a buyer is willing to buy.

In Chapter two I suggested that double auction markets are typically efficient. What that basically means is that we get the best match of buyers and sellers. Great! Our focus, however, was on a market where each seller had the same thing to sell; the goods were **homogeneous**. Often this seems appropriate; for instance, one share in a company, or one can of a particular brand of cola, is as good as any other, so a buyer should be relatively indifferent as to who they buy from. In many other cases, however, goods are not homogeneous. For example, no two houses, restaurant meals, or used cars are exactly alike. This makes it much more difficult to match buyers and sellers efficiently.

To illustrate the problem, we can look at the problem of matching workers to employers. In many professions, newly trained graduates simultaneously try to find entry-level jobs with employers. What we hope to see is the best match between the worker or supplier of labor and the employer or demander of labor. Workers, however, will have different preferences over where they would rather work, and employers will have different preferences over who they would rather hire. It is very easy for this to become a bit of a mess with great candidates getting no offers, and great employers finding that no one accepts their offers. Obtaining the best match is far from easy. One profession that has tried hard to tackle this problem is the medical profession.

The problem in the medical profession is to match newly trained doctors with hospitals willing to employ them. To demonstrate the problems there can be, we can look at the experience of the US. Before 1945 the market for new doctors was decentralized, like a negotiated price market. The outcome was an **unraveling of contract dates**, in which the best students were being hired earlier and earlier as hospitals tried to get the best candidates before anyone else did. In the end, students were being hired two years before graduation. This meant that hospitals were hiring students before they had a chance to see how good they really were, or students had a chance to see what type of medicine they would most want to practice. This is inefficient.

In 1945 medical schools banded together to try to improve matters, but a new problem arose. This time candidates who had offers from one place would wait to see if they would get an offer at a preferred place. This might sound reasonable but, if everyone is doing it, then everyone is waiting for everyone else to make a decision. Nothing happens until the deadline for acceptance, and then there is a last-minute rush and decisions are being made with little time to think. This is also inefficient.

In 1952 the National Resident Matching Program was set up as a central clearinghouse for applications. They needed to find a way to match doctors with hospitals that would avoid the previous problems. Since 1998 the program has used a **matching algorithm** designed by economists, notably Alvin Roth, and the process is a lot more efficient. Let's look first at the algorithm used.

After a process of interviews and visits, doctors submit a ranking of their preferred hospitals, and hospitals submit a ranking of their preferred doctors. Table 11.2 gives an example to work through. Something like a **deferred acceptance algorithm** is then used. The algorithm is as follows: each doctor is assigned to his or her first choice of hospital. Table 11.3 keeps track of who is assigned where in the example. The posts at each hospital are then filled

Table 11.2 An example of possible preferences of junior doctors looking for work and hospitals looking for junior doctors

		Preference		
		First	*Second*	*Third*
Doctors	Bill	Birmingham	New York	Boston
	Carol	Birmingham	Boston	New York
	Emma	Boston	New York	Birmingham
Hospitals	Birmingham	Bill	Carol	Emma
	New York	Bill	Carol	Emma
	Boston	Bill	Carol	Emma

Table 11.3 The deferred acceptance algorithm allocating doctors to hospitals for the example

	Doctors assigned			*Doctors rejected*
	Birmingham	*New York*	*Boston*	
Round 1	Bill and Carol	—	Emma	Carol
Round 2	Bill	—	Emma and Carol	Emma
Round 3	Bill	Emma	Carol	—

with the most preferred doctors assigned to them, and other doctors are rejected. In the example, Carol is rejected because Birmingham prefers to hire Bill. Any doctor rejected at this stage is assigned to his or her second choice of hospital. The posts of each hospital are then refilled with the most preferred doctors assigned to them, and other doctors rejected. This time it is Emma who is rejected, because Boston prefers Carol. This process goes on until no doctors are rejected.

Things are a bit more complicated than this because, for example, there might be couples who want to work in a similar location. The basic idea, however, remains the same. The crucial thing about the deferred acceptance algorithm is that it leads to a **stable matching**, in the sense that no candidate or hospital can look back and wish they had done a different ranking.

Not all possible algorithms are stable. For instance, consider a **priority matching algorithm** that works as follows: the priority of a match is measured by the product of the two rankings. For example, if a doctor ranks a hospital first and the hospital ranks the doctor third, the product is $1 \times 3 = 3$; if a doctor ranks a hospital fourth and the hospital ranks the doctor second, the priority is $4 \times 2 = 8$. Posts are filled in order of priority. Thus, priority one matches are filled first, where both doctor and hospital ranked each other first, then priority two matches are filled, and so on, until all vacancies are filled. To see why this algorithm need not be stable, we can look back at the example. The matching between Emma and Boston has priority three while the matching between Carol and Boston has priority four. This means that Emma will end up at Boston and Carol at New York. Once they know this, Boston can ring Carol and ask her to come, and she will accept. The assignment begins to unravel.

If the outcome of an algorithm is likely to not be stable, then we can expect unraveling of contract times, because applicants and hospitals like Carol and Boston will be reluctant to trust the algorithm. The UK provides a nice field experiment, because different regions have over time used different algorithms. Table 11.4 summarizes what happened. I will not explain what the linear programming algorithm is, but you can see that it provides something of a

Table 11.4 Different methods used in the UK

Regional market	*Algorithm*	*Stable*	*Unraveled*
Edinburgh	Deferred acceptance	Yes	No
Cardiff	Deferred acceptance	Yes	No
Birmingham	Priority matching	No	Yes
Newcastle	Priority matching	No	Yes
Sheffield	Priority matching	No	Yes
Cambridge	Linear programming	No	No
London Hospital	Linear programming	No	No

Source: Kagel and Roth (2000).

puzzle because it is, in principle, unstable, yet did not lead to an unraveling of contract times.

One way to try to answer this puzzle is to replicate each matching algorithm in the experimental laboratory and see what happens. That is what Kagel and Roth (2000) and Unver (2005) did. The experiments they ran lasted for 25 rounds. In each round, subjects, playing the role of worker and employer, tried to find a good match and were paid between \$14 and \$4 depending on who they matched with. To capture the possibility of unraveling, each round was split into three periods called −2, −1, and 0. If a worker and employer agreed a match in period −2 they each had to pay a fine of \$2, and if they agreed in period −1 they had to pay a fine of \$1. What we want to see is whether things unravel in the sense that subjects agree matches in periods −2 and −1, despite the cost that this entails.

Figure 11.2 summarizes what happened in the experiments. Start by focusing on the first ten rounds, where matching was decentralized and so there was no matching algorithm used. We see that subjects paid the fine to get a good match early, and so there was an unraveling of contract time. From round 11 onwards the matching algorithm was used. It was used in period zero for those workers and employers who had not matched so far in periods −2 and −1. We see that the fine subjects were willing to pay fell quite dramatically, and became almost zero with the deferred acceptance algorithm.

This shows that the deferred acceptance algorithm is working well. The priority and linear programming algorithm work less well in that the costs remain significant. The suggestion would be, therefore, that it is something of an accident that the linear programming algorithm worked for Cambridge and London Hospital.

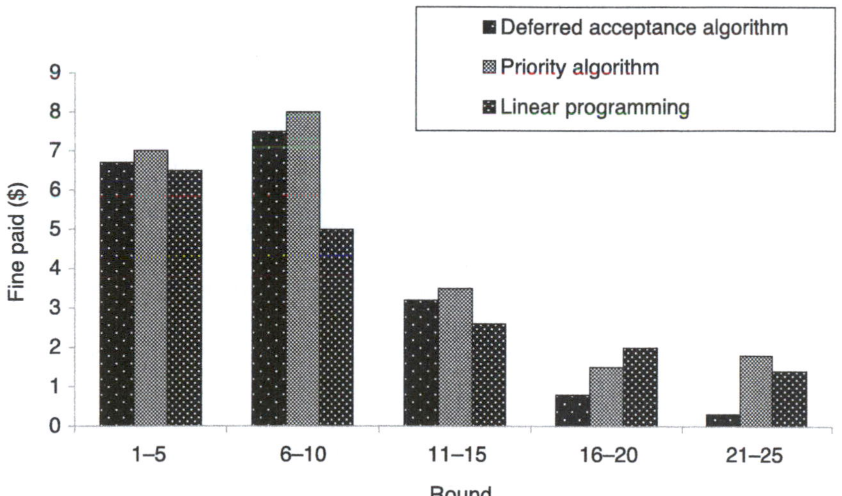

Figure 11.2 Matching algorithms compared.

Source: Unver (2005).

The main thing, however, is that these experiments confirm the advantages of the deferred acceptance algorithm. The deferred acceptance algorithm looks like it does a good job both in theory and the experimental laboratory. This has translated into success in the real world. The algorithm has proved successful in matching doctors to hospitals and is now being used in other areas as well, such as matching prospective students with schools. (The biggest mystery is why economists have not used it in their own profession to match junior faculty to departments!) In 2012, Alvin Roth won the Nobel Prize in Economics 'for the theory of stable allocations and the practice of market design'.

11.1.3 Spectrum auctions

The final example I want to look at is auction design. In particular I want to look at the so-called **spectrum auctions**. Before getting into the economics of these auctions, we need to know a bit about what is up for sale.

The electromagnetic spectrum is the name given to the range of electromagnetic frequencies that exist, from gamma rays, with a relatively high frequency, to long waves, with a relatively low frequency. Towards the low frequency end of the spectrum are radio waves with a frequency of around 9KHz to 300GHz. Television, radio, mobile phone signals, wireless networking, emergency communications, the signal for the door to open when someone presses a car key fob, and lots of other things, are all transmitted via radio waves.

This creates a competition for a portion of electromagnetic spectrum. For example, if a television channel is transmitting its programs on a certain frequency, then it does not want anyone else transmitting on that same frequency, causing interference. Somehow, therefore, the spectrum needs to be split and allocated in such a way that television, radio, and everything else can work.

To illustrate, the frequencies between 470MHz and 862MHz are typically set aside for television. These are then split into 49 chunks, or frequency channels, of 8MHz each, giving the frequency channels 21 to 69. A frequency channel is enough space to broadcast a television channel, or six to eight channels using digital television. Potential broadcasters who are allocated a frequency channel can broadcast without fear of interference. But how to decide which potential broadcaster gets allocated a frequency channel?

In many instances, governments directly allocate portions of the spectrum to companies. For example, a government committee might decide who gets what after companies have applied for, or tendered for, the right to use a portion of the spectrum. An alternative, that has become increasingly common, is to auction portions of the spectrum. We saw in Chapters two and six how auctions can work, and the basic rationale behind auctioning spectrum is that the market, rather than the government, decides who gets what. This could be more efficient, and raise more revenue for the government.

Auctioning spectrum is, however, quite complicated, and much more complicated than the auctions I looked at in Chapter six. That's why designing the spectrum auctions is no simple matter. To get some intuition for why things are so complicated, we can look at something called a chopstick auction.

I will start with a very simple version of the **chopstick auction**. Imagine that someone called Mathan goes to his favorite Chinese restaurant one evening and finds that the restaurant owners have come up with a game. At the start of the evening they are going to simultaneously auction ten sets of chopsticks. They will do so using a first price sealed bid auction. So, Mathan needs to write down how much he bids for the first set of chopsticks, how much for the second set, and so on. If he bids the highest amount for a set of chopsticks, then he wins that set. If Mathan wins a set of chopsticks, then he can enjoy his meal, but if he does not he will struggle to eat his meal. He wants, therefore, to win one and only one set of chopsticks, and does not care which one he wins.

The bidding for each set of chopsticks in isolation is very similar to the auctions we looked at in Chapter six. The complication here is that there are ten sets being sold simultaneously. For this reason it is called a **multi-unit auction**. How much should Mathan bid for each set?

This turns out to be a difficult question to answer. To see why, first imagine that there are ten diners in the restaurant. In principle this looks promising, because there are ten sets of chopsticks available, and ten diners wanting chopsticks. If Mathan bids $1 for set one and $0 for the others, Emma bids $1 for set two and $0 for the others, and so on, they will all get a set of chopsticks for $1. Somehow, however, the diners need to coordinate. How can Mathan know that he is supposed to bid $1 for set one and not sets two, or three? If the restaurant owners do not allow the diners to communicate with each other, there is no way he could know and so we will likely get coordination failure. This makes it hard to know how Mathan should bid. If there are 20 diners after the ten sets of chopsticks, or some chopsticks are more valuable than others, his task becomes ever more complicated.

We find these complications in auctioning spectrum. To demonstrate I will look at the spectrum auctions that have received most attention, namely those used to allocate spectrum to mobile phone companies. A mobile phone company needs a portion of spectrum in order to operate. For instance, around the year 2000, with the introduction of 3G or third-generation mobile standards, phone companies needed a new portion of spectrum to start running these services. In most Western countries, governments ran auctions to allocate it.

To be specific, I will look in more detail at the UK auction. The UK government decided to offer five licenses, which you can think of as five portions of spectrum. Figure 11.3 illustrates that license A consisted of a total of 35MHz. By comparison, license B consisted of a total of 30MHz, and the other three licenses a total of 25MHz. It was decided that license A would only be available to a new entrant in the UK mobile phone market (which excluded BT, One2One, Orange, and Vodafone). How does this compare to the chopstick auction?

There were five licenses or five sets of chopsticks up for sale. A company would want one and only one license but the more spectrum the better, so license A is

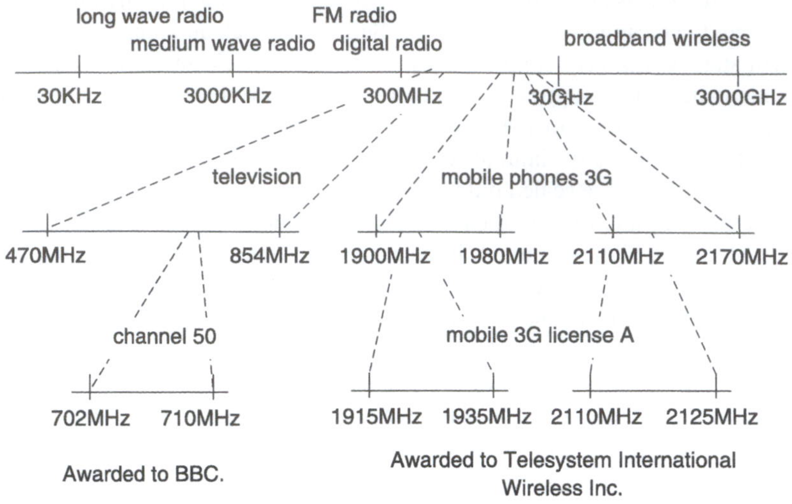

Figure 11.3 The radio wave portion of the electromagnetic spectrum and how it is allocated in the UK.

better than license B, which is better than licenses C to E. Overall there were 13 companies that bid, and so demand clearly exceeded supply, but remember four of these could not bid for license A. It is very hard to know how a company should bid in such circumstances. That makes it far from obvious whether auctions are a better way to allocate the spectrum than a government committee. In order to work well, auctions need to be well designed.

That is where economists can hopefully be of some use. The UK government employed a team of economists including Ken Binmore and Paul Klemperer to advise on the design of the UK 3G spectrum auction. The design eventually used was a simultaneous ascending auction. I will go into the details of what that entails when I look at the US example below. What I want to highlight first is that the auction was a big success. The total raised from the five licenses was £22.5 billion, which was way in excess of what many had expected. It was also far more than was raised from auctions in other European countries, as Figure 11.4 shows.

Figure 11.4 illustrates quite starkly how the success of an auction can depend a lot on the design of that auction. The UK, German, and Danish auctions were considered a success, others not so. The Netherlands, for example, used the same auction format as in the UK but had five incumbents compared to the UK's four. With five incumbents bidding for five licenses, other potential bidders stayed away and much less revenue was raised than expected. A similar thing happened in Switzerland. Things can, therefore, go badly wrong. An auction in 1990 in New Zealand of television spectrum is particularly notorious. A sealed bid second price auction was used, and only NZ$36 million was raised compared to a predicted NZ$250

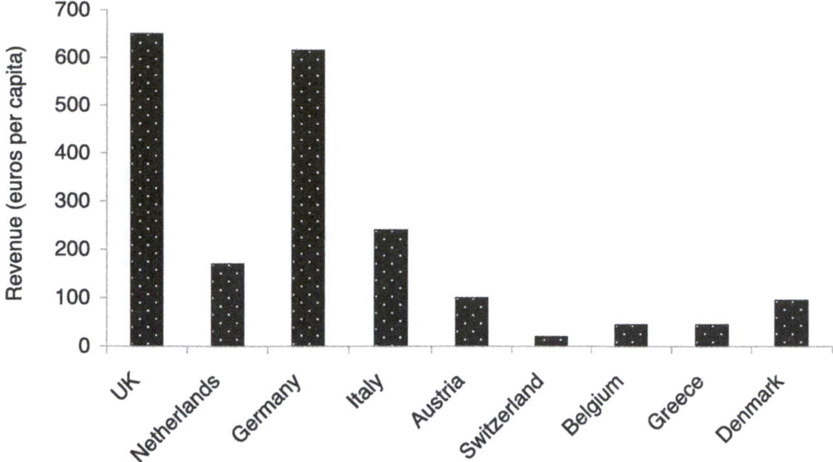

Figure 11.4 The revenue in euros per capita from the 3G spectrum auctions in different European countries in date order. The UK, German, and Danish auctions were considered a success.

Source: Klemperer (2004).

million. One lucky company bid NZ$100,000 but only had to pay the second highest bid of NZ$6, and another bid NZ$7 million but only had to pay NZ$5,000!

If things can go so wrong, then it is clearly crucial to design the auction well. The most successful auctions have generally been simultaneous ascending auctions. The first significant use of an ascending auction was by the Federal Communications Commission in the US in 1994, based on ideas of economists Paul Milgrom, Bob Wilson, and Preston McAfee. The basic idea behind the **simultaneous ascending auction** is that there are a number of rounds in which bidders make sealed bids for any items, or portions of spectrum, that they want to bid on. At the end of each round the **standing high bid** for each item is posted as well as the minimum bid for the item in the next round. In order to give bidders an incentive to bid early, an **activity rule** means that a bidder can only bid if they have bid in earlier rounds. Table 11.5 illustrates how the bidding progressed in the UK 3G spectrum auction.

The main benefit of an ascending auction is that bidders can coordinate over time by seeing how bids progress. This was particularly important in the auctions run in the US, and those in Germany. To see why, think back to the chopstick auction and imagine that, instead of auctioning ten sets of chopsticks, the restaurant owner auctions 20 chopsticks. Now Mathan wants to win two and only two chopsticks, and his task seems even harder than before. Having the auction run over successive rounds can allow bidders to coordinate a little better. Mathan can be surer to get the two chopsticks he wants, rather than end up paying for one that he does not want, or three, which is excessive.

Table 11.5 Bidding over the rounds in the UK 3G spectrum auction. The standing high bid for each round is given in millions of pounds

	License				
Round	*A*	*B*	*C*	*D*	*E*
1	TIW £170.0 m	Orange £107.4 m	—	Crescent £89.3 m	Epsilon £89.3 m
2	NTL Mobile £178.5 m	Telefonica £113.1 m	WorldCom £90.2 m	Crescent £89.3 m	Epsilon £89.3 m
3	NTL Mobile £178.5 m	TIW £176.5 m	Worldcom £90.2 m	3GUK £93.8 m	One2One £93.8 m
4	NTL Mobile £178.5 m	Orange £186.7 m	Telefonica £95.3 m	3GUK £93.8 m	One2One £93.8 m
5	Spectrumco £187.5 m	TIW £196.1 m	Telefonica £95.3 m	WoldCom £99.2 m	Epsilon £100.1 m
150	TIW £4,384.7 m	Vodafone £5,964.0 m	BT3G £4,030.1 m	One2One £4,003.6 m	Orange £4,095.0 m

Source: Ofcom.

Splitting things up like this, and selling chopsticks rather than sets of chopsticks, might seem like an unnecessary complication. It can, however, make sense in spectrum auctions, because it lets the market decide how many firms there will be. For example, in Germany the 3G spectrum auctions involved 12 portions of spectrum (compared to the five in the UK) that in blocks of two or three were enough to operate a viable network. The number of firms in the market could therefore have ended up as four, five, or six. Designing auctions where bidders may want to win multiple items does, however, pose a new set of challenges. This has led to the use of **package** or **combinatorial auctions** in which bidders can bid on combinations of items. For example, Mathan might be able to bid $1 for chopstick one, $5 for chopsticks one and two, $3 for chopsticks four, five, and six, and so on.

11.1.4 Behavioral economics and institution design

Hopefully you have seen that institutions matter, and designing good institutions is not easy. For example, avoiding the tragedy of the commons, matching doctors to hospitals, or designing an auction that will work efficiently when there are multiple items to sell is tricky. The tragedy of the commons is avoided in some situations and not in others. Some matching markets and auctions have gone badly wrong and others have been very successful. The question I want to finish with is what institution design has to do with behavioral economics.

At first glance one might say, not too much. Auction design, for example, draws heavily on game theory and the economics of industrial organization. We would not need behavioral economics to predict the poor performance of the 3G spectrum auctions in the Netherlands and Switzerland; a bit of industrial organization theory would be enough. Look a little deeper, however, and behavioral economics does seem a vital tool in institution design.

This is easiest to see in designing institutions to solve things like the tragedy of the commons. There, an understanding of social preferences and the ability to coordinate is crucial to understanding what will work and what will not. The case for behavioral economics is weaker in the design of auctions or matching markets, which are more like a combinatorial mathematical problem. Even here, though, behavioral economics can prove crucial. One reason is that the practicalities of institution design far exceed our theoretical ability; so, laboratory experiments can prove useful alongside theory to give an idea of how different institutions will perform. We saw this in looking at designing matching markets. Both the teams designing the UK 3G spectrum auction and the first FCC auctions in the US also used laboratory experiments to test possible auction designs.

Behavioral economics is, and has proved to be, therefore, a useful tool in institutional design, both in informing how people can realistically be expected to behave, and as an important test bed for possible institutions. In many ways this seems inevitable, because institution design forces us to step outside the comfort of the standard economic model. It forces us to recognize that it does not always make sense to assume people are like homo economicus. Behavioral economics gives us the tools and techniques to step with confidence beyond the standard economic model.

11.2 Nudge and behavior change

The second category of government policy I distinguished earlier was that of manipulating individual incentives. In recent years there has been much excitement that behavioral economics can change the way in which policy is viewed when it comes to individual incentives. To understand why there is such excitement, it is worth pointing out first something obvious: a policy focus on individual behavior is nothing new. For example, why would a central bank or government increase the interest rate? The answer might be that they want to reduce inflation, but for this to work they need individuals to respond to the change in interest rate. For instance, they need Mathan, who has a mortgage, to reduce his consumption because he knows he will have to pay more interest on his mortgage debt. To give a second example, why would a government give tax relief on saving for retirement? Presumably, they want to increase saving for retirement. Again, for this to work, they need people like Mathan to change his consumption plans and save more because the tax relief makes saving look a better deal.

So, how can behavioral economics change the way we look at policy? The traditional role for economics and policy has been about changing **incentives for homo economicus**. The focus has been on incentives that would matter to someone who maximizes utility without any mistakes or biases. A change in the interest rate or changes in tax relief are like this. Behavioral economics suggest that **incentives for homo sapiens** can also matter. Account should be taken of incentives that matter to someone who is biased in a predictable way. It seems best to illustrate with some examples. I will look at two related to saving and time-inconsistency.

11.2.1 Savings accounts

If people are time inconsistent when it comes to saving decisions, then properly tailored saving plans may be able to influence behavior. A number of field experiments have now shown this to be the case. I shall illustrate with a study by Ashraf and co-authors (2006).

The study was done in partnership with the Green Bank of Caraga, a rural bank in the Philippines. In the first part of the study, a household survey was done on 1,777 existing or former clients of the bank. One part of this survey involved hypothetical time preference questions (similar to those we looked at in section 4.1.2). This allowed respondents to be classified as time-consistent, time-inconsistent, or more patient now (meaning their discount factor decreased further into the future). In the second part of the study, half of those surveyed were offered a new SEED (Save, Earn, Enjoy Deposits) account. Of the remaining people, half received no further contact (a control group) and half were encouraged to save more using existing accounts (a marketing group).

The SEED account was specifically designed so that a client had to specify a goal. This could be date based, such as to save for a birthday, or amount based, such as to save for a new roof. The client had complete flexibility in setting the goal, but having set the goal they had no access to their money until the goal was reached. This meant very restricted access to funds. Also, the interest rate of a SEED account was no higher than that of a normal savings account.

For a person who is time-consistent the SEED account looks like a bad deal because she has no access to her money and gets no higher interest rate. For someone who is time-inconsistent the SEED account may look attractive because it is a strong commitment device to save and overcome the short-term impulse to spend.

In all, 202 SEED accounts were opened, of which 147 were date based. After 12 months, 116 of the accounts reached maturity or met the goal and all bar one opted to take out a new SEED account. Clearly, the SEED account proved relatively popular. The most fascinating thing is that a reliable predictor of who would take up a SEED account was time-inconsistent preferences. Women who exhibited time-inconsistent preferences were 15.8 percent more likely to take up the SEED product than those with time-consistent preferences. In men the figure was 4.6 percent. This is consistent with the idea that the account would appeal to those who needed to commit to saving because of present bias.

The final thing we need to check is whether people saved more if they opened a SEED account. The simple answer seems to be yes. After 12 months, savings for those offered the SEED account was estimated to be 82 percent higher than those in the control group, and also much higher than those in the marketing group. This increase in saving seems to be because the SEED product offers consumers incentives to save. In particular, those who took up a SEED account saved a lot more than anyone else. This is clearly apparent in Figure 11.5.

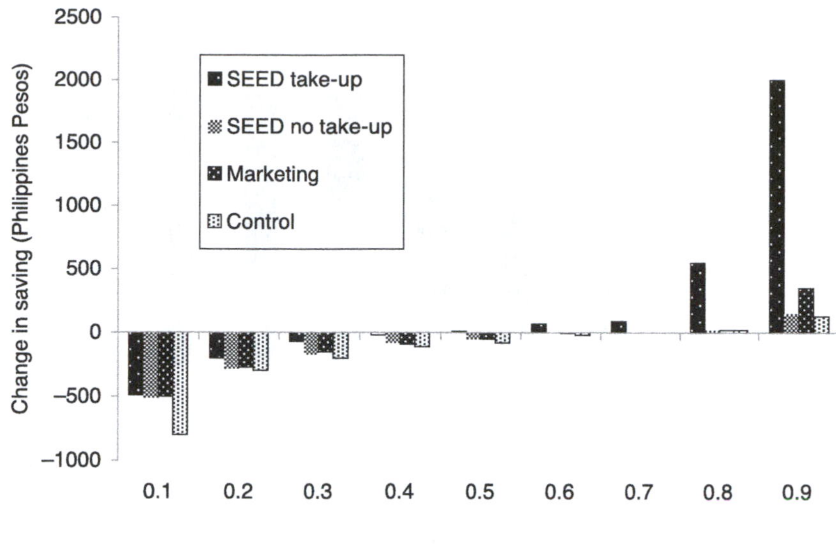

Figure 11.5 Changes in saving behavior after one year. The majority of those taking up the SEED account increased saving. For many, the increase in saving was very large.

Source: Ashraf *et al.* (2006).

The SEED account thus seemed to be popular and successful. It provided no incentives that would tempt homo economicus because there was no higher interest rate, or anything that should have appealed to someone who is unbiased. The account did, however, provide incentives for homo sapiens to save and seemingly did appeal to those with present bias who wanted a means to pre-commit to more saving.

11.2.2 A default to save

Accounts that restrict access to funds may help some overcome the urge to spend. They should work well for the consumer who is time-inconsistent but sophisticated and so looking for some way to commit for the long term. What about the consumer who is time-inconsistent and naïve? Such a consumer would never choose a restrictive savings account, so another solution is needed. One option is to automatically enroll him in a savings plan and thus put the emphasis on him to opt out of saving rather than opt in. To see how this could work we can look at a study by Madrian and Shea (2001).

The study looks at data from a large US company that changed enrollment and eligibility for the 401(k) retirement savings plan on April 1, 1998. Before this date, employees were only eligible to enroll in the plan after one year of employment,

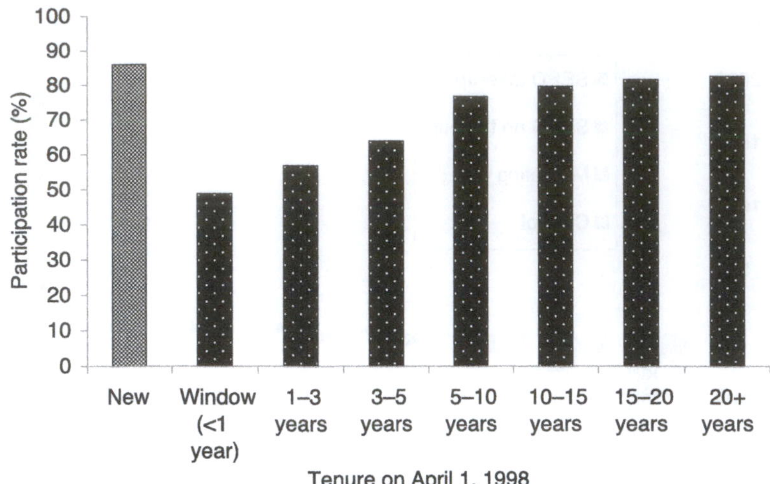

Figure 11.6 Participation rate in 401(k) retirement savings plan. There was a dramatic increase in the participation rate once the default was to be enrolled in the savings plan.

Source: Madrian and Shea (2001).

and had to choose to enroll. After the change, all employees were immediately eligible to enroll, and new employees were automatically enrolled unless they chose to stay out. Figure 11.6 shows how dramatic the changes proved. The participation rate of employees hired after the change was above that of any subset of current employees. The most telling comparison is between new employees and those employed less than a year before the change (the window group). The only substantive difference between these two groups is that enrolment was the default for one and non-enrolment the default for the other.

Clearly, making enrolment the default option increased participation, and we might consider this a good thing. There is, however, one problem. If employees are automatically enrolled, then their investment choices also need to be set automatically. In this particular instance there were two choices to make: how much to contribute, and whether to invest in stocks, bonds, or some other type of investment. The default chosen was a contribution rate of 3 percent of income invested in a money market fund. Basically, no one chose this combination before the change, but of those automatically enrolled, 71 percent stayed with this default option. Figure 11.7 illustrates the big contrast between the window group and the new group of employees.

Clearly, new employees tended to stick to the default, despite this probably not being the best thing they could do. This provides something of a conundrum. While the increased participation looks like a good thing, that people follow the default investment choices looks like a bad thing. Indeed, an employee who would

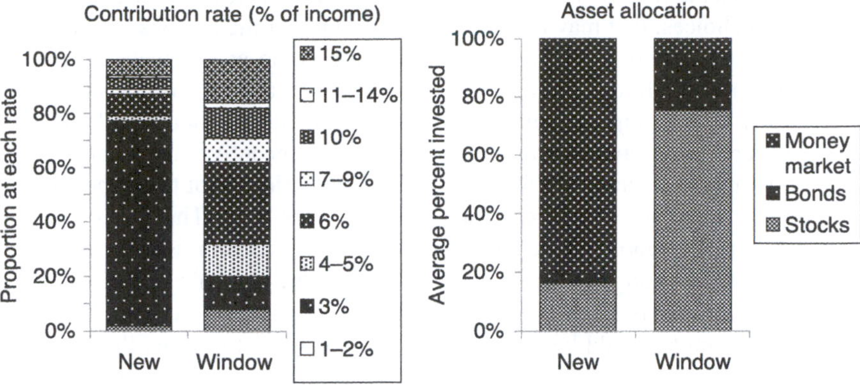

Figure 11.7 Contribution rate and asset allocation in the new and window groups.
Source: Madrian and Shea (2001).

have chosen to opt into the savings plan with different investment options may end up being worse off if he is enrolled in the plan by default.

I will come back to this conundrum shortly. For now, I want you to see again the distinction between incentives for homo economicus and those for homo sapiens. Changing the default option should make no difference to homo economicus. Whatever the default, he would have worked out his optimal savings plan and enacted it. For homo sapiens who are time-inconsistent or have other biases, the change can, and we see does, matter. Someone with present bias, for example, may procrastinate and never get around to changing their savings choices despite a desire to do so.

11.2.3 Nudge

In both of the previous examples we see changes, namely the introduction of a new account and a default of enrollment in a savings plan, that made a big difference. To calm, calculating homo economicus they should not have made a difference, but it probably came as little surprise that they did make a difference for normal people. This opens up interesting new ways to think of economics and policy, informed by behavioral economics.

The two examples illustrate two different possibilities. In the first example, where a new account is created, something 'real' was changed in that people had different choices. Ideas from behavioral economics suggested that these different choices may prove popular and worthwhile. In the second example, where the default is changed, nothing really changes, in that everyone still has the same choices as before. The framing of those choices is, however, changed and ideas from behavioral economics suggest why this change in framing may matter.

So, behavioral economics can suggest changes to choices, and changes to the framing of choices, that may make a difference. One of the reasons why this has excited interest in policymaking is that both can come at relatively little cost! Changing the default, or administering a new account, are relatively cheap to do, particularly when compared with the things governments might normally do, like change tax relief on savings. Basically, changing the incentives for homo sapiens is a lot cheaper than changing them for homo economicus. But to put behavioral economics to best use we need a framework to work with. The idea of nudge, made popular in a book by Richard Thaler and Cass Sunstein, is one way to go. To explain what a nudge is, we first need to explain the idea of a choice architect. A **choice architect** is anyone responsible for framing a decision that others will take. One example would be a sales assistant explaining to Emma the merits of different products that she might buy. The assistant has discretion to frame the choices in different ways by maybe emphasizing the good points of one product and the bad of another. A second example would be the way that share prices are listed when Alan looks up how well his investments are doing. Investments could be listed in alphabetical order, or performance order, declining stocks could be highlighted in bright red, or left in normal font, and so on.

This book has been full of examples where differences in framing have mattered. For instance, whether the sales tax is included or not in the price and whether the default is to be enrolled or not enrolled in the savings plan are classic examples of where framing matters. We can be pretty confident that how the sales assistant talks to Emma and how Alan's investments are displayed on the screen will also matter.

Now I want to move beyond saying that framing matters, to asking whether we can change the framing of a decision in a way that helps people make better choices. This brings us to the idea of **nudge**. To quote from Thaler and Sunstein (2008),

> A nudge, as we will use the term, is any aspect of the choice architecture that alters people's behavior in a predictable way without forbidding any options or significantly changing their economic incentives. To count as a mere nudge, the intervention must be easy and cheap to avoid.

So, something that changes the incentives of homo economicus cannot be a nudge. Something that changes the incentives of homo sapiens can. Changing the default option to that of being enrolled in a savings plan rather than being not enrolled is a fantastic example of a nudge. The options and economic incentives of the person are exactly the same whatever the default. All we have done is change the choice architecture or the framing of the choices in a seemingly small way. Even so, we get a predictable and big change in behavior.

Can policymakers harness the power of nudge and nudge people into making better choices? To answer that question it's useful to think about two subsidiary questions: When do people need a nudge? And how can people be most effectively given a nudge?

The first question is relatively easy for us to answer, given what we have already covered in this book. We have seen that people are pretty clever, most of the time, and do learn with experience. So, nudges should only be needed sparingly, but there are four good reasons why we may need to nudge someone like Alan: (i) Alan may face a very complicated choice and, clever or not, can easily get it wrong; (ii) He has had very little experience or chance to learn what is best; (iii) He is relatively uninformed about what he should choose; (iv) He has self-control problems and so may not make the choices he would have wanted himself to make.

If something ticks all four boxes, then it looks a good place for a nudge. Saving for retirement is one clear example: it involves complicated choices; Alan is only going to get old once, so has no chance to go back and start again having learnt from experience; he may have no real idea what savings he will need in 30 or 40 years time; present bias may also mean he puts off doing things that he knows he should be doing. In the US, health care is another thing likely to tick all four boxes.

This gives us a framework to think about when nudges might be needed. The next thing we need to think about is how to most effectively use nudges. This means that it's time for our first mnemonic. Table 11.6 briefly describes the six principles that Thaler and Sunstein (2008) suggest for good choice architecture. Only the first of these would get much attention in thinking about pushing homo economicus. The basic idea, therefore, is to supplement incentives with things that take account of why the nudge is needed: to lessen the complexity (structure complex choices), create experience (give feedback), improve information (understand mappings), and work around biases (defaults, incentives; and expect error).

This might look fine in principle, but can it work? Things are not necessarily so easy. For example, we have seen that making it the default option for people to be opted into a savings plan may not be enough. We also need to encourage

Table 11.6 Principles for good choice architecture, spell Nudges

Principles	*Brief description*
iNcentives	People do respond to incentives like price and cost, but only if these are salient.
Understand mappings	People may need help understanding the mapping, from the choices they may make to the outcomes they will get.
Defaults	Defaults matter a lot because of present bias and choice overload, so think carefully about them.
Give feedback	People do learn, so give feedback on when things are going well or badly.
Expect error	People make mistakes, so we need something that is as forgiving as possible to mistakes they may make.
Structure complex choices	The more complex the choice, the more problems a person has, and the more likely context effects will matter. So, keep things simple.

Source: Thaler and Sunstein (2008).

participants to choose the best contribution rate and stock options. Nudging people is, therefore, not simple, and can leave some worse off than they might have been. But there are some basic nudges that can move things in the right direction for most people. For example, most would probably agree that making it the default option for people to be opted into a savings plan is a good thing.

Thaler and Sunstein suggest various other nudges, and you can probably come up with some yourself. Before we move on, I want to look at one of these, which I think is pretty neat. It's called **save more tomorrow**. The idea is that a saver, like Mathan, can commit himself to save more tomorrow, in the sense that his contributions to a savings plan will automatically increase every time his pay increases. Why does this make sense? Mathan might learn that he is saving too little but not want to increase his current savings, because that would lower his income, and we know from Chapters two and four that people don't like that. If he says, 'I will save more tomorrow', we also know that this is probably not going to happen, because of present bias. The save more tomorrow plan means that Mathan commits to saving tomorrow.

If he knows he has a present bias, then this looks like a great commitment device that helps Mathan to save and overcome any time-inconsistency. So, does it work? Thaler and Benartzi (2004) report on successful first implementation of the plan; employees chose the save more tomorrow plan and stuck with it, and their savings rate almost quadrupled over the sample period. It's safe to say that this would not have happened without the plan, and many large employers have now adopted the idea. So, this is one nudge that does look as though it works.

11.2.4 Nudge and behavior change

One concern that many express about nudge is that it sounds a bit too much like big brother. It sounds a bit too much like the policymaker deciding on someone's behalf, and can we trust policymakers to know what is best?

An important aspect of nudge is that it should not involve sacrifice of liberty. This was clear in the quote I gave above from Thaler and Sunstein: 'without forbidding any options or significantly changing their economic incentives . . . the intervention must be easy and cheap to avoid'. In principle, therefore, a nudge should not impact on personal liberty. This, however, is a bit different to saying that a nudge is not about changing behavior in the way a policymaker thinks is best. Basically, a nudge should not change the set of options someone like Mathan has, but its very objective is to change the option that Mathan will choose.

There is no escaping the fact, therefore, that nudge does require us to think about whether the policymaker knows best. It is about **behavior change**. That's one reason to think through, as we have done, when people will most need a nudge. Is that enough? Well, we saw in the last chapter that most people might be comfortable with behavior change, and others making difficult decisions on their behalf, provided they retain some choice and self-determination. A nudge retains choice and so looks reasonable enough on this count. Even so, you may be wondering whether we should be trusting that policymakers know what's best. The crucial point I want to make here is that we have no choice but to do this.

Recall that in Chapters two and nine I argued that framing and context effects are inevitable: context influences perceptions and intuition, which influence reasoning, which influence behavior. What that means is that behavior change is an inevitability of policy. To quote from a report published by the UK's Institute for Government (Dolan and co-authors 2010):

> We may not agree on how we would like policymakers to change our behaviour. But whether we like it or not, the actions of policy-makers, public service professionals, markets and our fellow citizens around us have big, and often unintended, impacts on our behaviour. 'Doing nothing' is rarely a neutral option: we are always busy shaping each other's behaviour.

It's the lack of a neutral option that is key here. Is the neutral option that Mathan be not put in a savings plan, put in a savings plan, or put in a save more tomorrow plan? Quite simply, there is no neutral option; something has to be chosen. This means that policymakers have no choice but to change behavior. The key thing is to try to change behavior in the right direction.

That means it is time for our second mnemonic: The UK's Institute for Government came up with the idea of MINDSPACE. The basic idea is to provide a practical means to think about behavior change and apply insights from behavioral economics and psychology in policymaking. This is being used by policymakers in the UK and so gives one great example of policymakers using behavioral economics to try to change behavior in the right direction. Table 11.7 gives a brief overview of the main principles underlying MINDSPACE, and most of these are things that we have looked at in this book.

The MINDSPACE principles are designed to help policymakers better understand how possible policies might change behavior; they are a kind of checklist of things to think about. The interesting thing that I want to finish with is how this

Table 11.7 An overview of MINDSPACE

Principle	*Description*
Messenger	We are heavily influenced by who communicates information.
Incentives	Our responses to incentives are shaped by predictable mental shortcuts, such as strongly avoiding losses.
Norms	We are strongly influenced by what others do.
Defaults	We 'go with the flow' of pre-set options.
Salience	Our attention is drawn to what is novel and seems relevant to us.
Priming	Our acts are often influenced by subconscious cues.
Affect	Our emotional associations can powerfully shape our actions.
Commitments	We seek to be consistent with our public promises, and reciprocate acts.
Ego	We act in ways that make us feel better about ourselves.

Source: Dolan *et al.* (2010).

checklist can serve different purposes. I will quote again from the report (Dolan and co-authors 2010):

> **Enhance**. MINDSPACE can help policy-makers understand how current attempts to change behaviour could be improved.
> **Introduce**. Some of the elements in MINDSPACE are not used extensively by policy-makers, yet may have considerable impact.
> **Reassess**. Government needs to understand ways it may be changing the behaviour of citizens unintentionally. It is quite possible that the state is producing unintended – and possibly unwanted – changes in behaviour. The insights from MINDSPACE offer a rigorous way of assessing whether and how government is shaping the behaviour of its citizens.

The nice thing about this is that it illustrates the three different ways in which behavioral economics can have a positive impact on policy. It can help us come up with new ideas, like the save more tomorrow nudge; an example of 'introduce'. It can help us improve current policy, like changing the default to automatic enrollment; an example of 'enhance'. Finally, it can help us realize the problems with current policy, such as appreciating why a default of no automatic enrollment does not work; an example of reassess.

I would argue, therefore, that behavior change is not only inevitable, but is also something to be embraced as a positive means by which policymakers can design policies that work and avoid policies that do not.

11.2.5 Consumer protection, health, and the environment

The focus of this section so far has been primarily on encouraging saving. This is no accident. Saving is one area of life where many people need a nudge, and simple nudges can make a huge difference. If you read the general literature on nudge you could easily get the impression, however, that nudge is only about encouraging saving. All the good examples seem to be saving examples! To dispel such thoughts, I want to finish by highlighting some areas other than saving where nudge can make a difference.

In order to do this, I will point you in the direction of the UK government's Behavioural Insights Team, or nudge unit. Set up in 2010, the team will save the UK government an estimated $1.4 billion over five years. Suitably impressed, other governments, including the US, are looking to set up similar teams. The policy papers produced by the UK's team are an indication of how widely nudge can be applied. The papers include 'Applying behavioural insights to charitable giving', 'Fraud, error and debt', 'Behaviour change and energy use', 'Better choices: better deals', and 'Applying behavioural insight to health'. Let us delve a little deeper into two of the papers.

I shall start with the 'better choices: better deals' paper. My plan is not to go through the policy prescriptions in full, but merely illustrate some of the issues. (The full papers are well worth a read, and freely available on the team's website.)

The basic aim of better choices: better deals is to empower consumers to make better choices, get better deals, better value, better customer service, and better support when seeking help.

To understand the issues at stake, consider Mathan deciding which bank to use. Clearly Mathan wants to find the best match for his preferences; he will search around to see what the different banks have to offer in terms of fees, interest rates, accessibility, and so on. In Chapter two we looked at some search heuristics that Mathan might want to use when doing this, and one of the key things we learnt is that framing and context matter. The most successful banks are going to be keenly aware of the importance of framing and take this into account when designing their products.

One common trick is the use of hidden charges. These are charges that are 'hidden' but will almost certainly have to be paid at some point, such as a charge for going overdrawn, or for missing a credit card payment. Another trick is to offer a tempting, but short-term deal. For example, the bank might offer a higher interest rate for the first six months after opening a savings account. In this case the bank is hoping for naïve present-day bias; Mathan opens an account to take advantage of the great deal but then leaves his money in the account well after the great deal has expired.

For fairness' sake, I should point out that banks are not the only companies doing this. Indeed, it is hard to find companies that are not doing it! Consider, for example, an airline that offers a great fare, until you add on the fuel surcharge, taxes, fee for hold luggage, and charges for food and drink. (One airline recently floated the idea of charging passengers to use the toilet!) Or, consider a hotel that offers a great rate, but then charges for breakfast, and use of the internet and swimming pool.

Ruses such as hidden charges and joining offers would not fool homo economicus; they do fool us. The idea of better choices: better deals is to put more power in the hands of consumers. What does this mean in practice?

One key raft of policy proposals is about making sure that consumers have access to all relevant information in an easy-to-understand format. For example, credit card companies are now obliged to issue an annual statement that clearly states all fees and costs incurred on the card during the year; no more hidden charges. To give a second example, energy suppliers have agreed to simplify their tariffs and provide customers with clear information about the lowest available tariff; no more short-term great deals.

A second raft of proposals focuses on making it easier for consumers to learn from each other's experiences. For example, online consumer feedback is to be encouraged, as are comparison websites. In order to maintain the integrity of such sites, the Office of Fair Trading will monitor for manipulation by companies (and a number of companies have already been prosecuted). Performance and complaints data will also be made more transparent.

The basic rationale behind all of these proposals is to give companies less room to hide. That can, hopefully, nudge consumers to make better choices. This is clearly good news for consumers. It is not so obvious that it is good news for companies. Note, however, that manipulation of consumers can be something of a race to the bottom: if one company starts playing dirty, it is very hard for others to survive unless they go down the same route. The companies that are offering the best deal, rather than making it look as though they are offering the best deal, should welcome any proposals to make consumers more informed. So, this can be a win-win outcome for consumers and good firms.

Let us look next at applying behavioral insight to health. To understand the issues in this case consider Table 11.8. The table lists the main risks for lost years of healthy life as measured by the World Health Organization. In high-income countries we see that the top ten risks are full of things that an individual can avoid. You might rejoinder that a person has to die of something, and so why not die of tobacco or alcohol. The risks are ranked, however, using QALYs (see Chapter ten) and so the losses are very real; people are missing out on a higher quality of life. Given what we have seen about addiction and habit, it is hard to believe that this is optimal in any sense (except perhaps for the tobacco companies).

This somewhat depressing picture suggests that we need ways to encourage healthy behavior. The policy paper of the Behavioural Insights Team sets out some possibilities. They consider ways to help people quit smoking, eat more healthily, exercise more, and so on. One example is the Department of Health's Change for Life campaign with the slogan 'eat well, move more, live longer'. The campaign advocates simple but potentially effective things like always using a shopping list. We do not know yet what nudges are going to be effective, and so a lot more research is needed, but the hope is that simple nudges can make a big difference.

And nudge can not only help people improve their own life, it might also help them improve the lives of others. To illustrate, consider organ donation. The UK has traditionally used a system of **informed consent** for organ donation; this means that the default option is no organ donation. Other countries, such as Austria, use a system of **presumed consent**; this means that the default option is

Table 11.8 The leading risks for lost years of healthy life ranked from highest risk, one, to tenth highest risk

Rank	*High income*	*Low income*
1	Tobacco	Childhood underweight
2	Alcohol	Unsafe water and sanitation
3	Overweight	Unsafe sex
4	High blood pressure	Suboptimal breastfeeding
5	High blood glucose	Indoor smoke from fuel
6	Physical inactivity	Vitamin A deficiency
7	High cholesterol	High blood pressure
8	Illicit drugs	Alcohol use
9	Occupational risks	High blood glucose
10	Low fruit and vegetables	Zinc deficiency

Source: WHO (2009).

organ donation. It will probably come as no surprise that organ donation rates appear higher in countries with presumed consent.

The UK, like many other countries, needs more organ donors. The trend, therefore, is to move away from informed consent. Wales, for instance, will adopt a presumed consent policy in 2015. Presumed consent is, however, controversial and so a more neutral policy such as **prompted choice** may be desirable. In this case, people are required to decide, when filling in something like a driving license application, whether they want to become an organ donor; most do. Several US states, including Texas and California, have recently introduced such a policy. Thus, the simplest of nudges can save lives.

11.3 Summary

I started by looking at how behavioral economics can help design good institutions, looking at the tragedy of the commons, matching markets, and auctions as examples. We saw that insights from behavioral economics can be useful in better predicting behavior. We also saw that experiments can be a useful testing ground to see how institutions will perform.

Next we looked at how behavioral economics can help inform on policies that are directed at changing individual behavior. Two examples showed that small changes could have big, and desirable, consequences. This leads us to the concept of nudge and behavior change. We saw that behavioral economics can help us come up with new ideas, like the save more tomorrow program, and can also help us reassess why existing policies may not be working.

An important point in looking at both institution design and changing individual incentives is that context and framing will matter. This means that policy-makers cannot be neutral. What they do is going to influence behavior and/or the success of the institution. They need, therefore, to come up with the policies that have the most positive impact and, for that, they need behavioral economists to come up with the guiding principles, like those in Tables 11.6 and 11.7.

It's testament to the development of behavioral economics that it is now making an impact on policymaking. But hopefully this is only the beginning. Behavioral economics has the power to completely change the way we think about all aspects of the economy and economic behavior. What's more, I believe it gives us a much better way to think about and understand economic behavior. That's why my hope is that behavioral economics will soon become something that all economists do some of the time, rather than something some economists do all of the time.

11.4 Further reading

The book by Ostrom (1990) and article (2010) are a good place to start for more on the tragedy of the commons. See also Schmitt *et al.* (2000). For more on matching markets, see Roth (2002, 2008). On auction design there are lots of good resources. The books by Klemperer (2004), and Milgrom (2004) are good places to start. The web is also a great source of information. For more on the UK spectrum allocation, see the Ofcom website, and for more on the US spectrum allocation, see the Federal Communications Commission (FCC) website. Thaler and Sunstein (2008) is the obvious place to read more about nudge, and there is a lot more about MINDSPACE on the Institute for Government website, including the full report and interviews with the authors.

11.5 Review questions

11.1 What is the difference between a weak link game, threshold public good game, and common pool resource game?

11.2 Why is it easier to achieve sustainable fishing for national, inshore fishing than international, offshore fishing?

11.3 Do you think subjects should be allowed to communicate with each other during experiments?

11.4 Should the objective of a government running a spectrum auction be to raise as much money as possible?

11.5 Why is it useful to distinguish between policies about institutions and about individual behavior? You might want to contrast saving choices with interactive situations like a threshold public good game.

11.6 Why might people need a nudge in deciding what insurance to buy, or health care provider to use in the US? Where else might nudges make sense?

11.7 How could a charity or private firm exploit the save more tomorrow idea?

11.8 Is there any difference between a nudge that works at a conscious or subconscious level?

11.9 Should governments ask citizens whether they agree with behavior change, or just get on with it?

11.10 Come up with some nudges of your own.

Bibliography

Abbink, K., Irlenbusch, B., and Renner, E. (2006) 'Group size and social ties in microfinance institutions', *Economic Inquiry*, *44*(4), 614–628.

Agarwal, S., Liu, C., and Souleles, N. S. (2007) 'The reaction of consumer spending and debt to tax rebates – evidence from consumer credit data', *Journal of Political Economy*, 115: 986–1019.

Alberti, F. and Cartwright, E. (2010) 'Does endowment size matter in threshold public good games?', School of Economics, University of Kent working paper.

Allcott, H. (2011) 'Social norms and energy conservation', *Journal of Public Economics*, *95*(9), 1082–1095.

Allcott, H. and Mullainathan, S. (2010) 'Behavioral science and energy policy', *Science*, *327*(5970), 1204–1205.

Alm, J. (2012) 'Measuring, explaining, and controlling tax evasion: lessons from theory, experiments, and field studies', *International Tax and Public Finance*, 19: 54–77.

Alm, J., Cherry, T., Jones, M., and McKee, M. (2010) 'Taxpayer information assistance services and tax compliance behavior', *Journal of Economic Psychology*, *31*(4), 577–586.

Alpizar, F., Carlsson, F., and Johansson-Stenman, O. (2008) 'Anonymity, reciprocity, and conformity: Evidence from voluntary contributions to a national park in Costa Rica', *Journal of Public Economics*, 92: 1047–1060.

Anderson, L. R. and Holt, C. A. (1997) 'Information cascades in the laboratory', *American Economic Review*, 87: 847–862.

Andreoni, J. (1990) 'Impure altruism and donations to public goods: A theory of warm-glow giving', *Economic Journal*, 100: 464–477.

Andreoni, J. (1993) 'An experimental test of the public-goods crowding-out hypothesis', *American Economic Review*, 83: 1317–1327.

Andreoni, J. (2006) 'Philanthropy', in Kolm, S. C. and Ythier, M. (Eds.), *Handbook of the Economics of Giving, Altruism and Reciprocity: Foundations*, 2, 1201–1269, Amsterdam: Elsevier.

Andreoni, J. and Miller, J. (2002) 'Giving according to GARP: An experimental test of the consistency of preferences for altruism', *Econometrica*, 70: 737–753.

Antonakis, J. and Dalgas, O. (2009) 'Predicting elections: Child's play!', *Science*, *323*(5918), 1183.

Ariely, D. and Wertenbroch, K. (2002) 'Procrastination, deadlines, and performance: Self-control by precommitment', *Psychological Science*, 13: 219–224.

Ariely, D., Loewenstein, G., and Prelec, D. (2003) 'Coherent arbitrariness: Stable demand curves without stable preferences', *Quarterly Journal of Economics*, 118: 73–105.

Artavanis, N., Morse, A., and Tsoutsoura, M. (2012) 'Tax evasion across industries: Soft credit evidence from Greece', *Chicago Booth Research Paper*, 12–25.

Ashraf, M., Karlan, D., and Yin, W. (2006) 'Tying Odysseus to the mast: Evidence from a commitment savings product in the Philippines', *Quarterly Journal of Economics*, 121: 635–672.

Baicker, K., Buckles, K. S., and Chandra, A. (2006) 'Geographic variation in the appropriate use of cesarean delivery', *Health Affairs*, 25: w355–w367.

Ballew, C. C. and Todorov, A. (2007) 'Predicting political elections from rapid and unreflective face judgments', *Proceedings of the National Academy of Sciences*, *104*(46), 17948–17953.

Banerjee, A. V. (2013) 'Microcredit under the microscope: What have we learned in the past two decades, and what do we need to know?', *Annual Review of Economics*, 5: 487–519.

Banerjee, A. V. and Duflo, E. (2008) 'The experimental approach to development economics', National Bureau of Economic Research, w14467.

Banerjee, A. V., Cole, S., Duflo, E., and Linden, L. (2007) 'Remedying education: Evidence from two randomized experiments in India', *The Quarterly Journal of Economics*, *122*(3), 1235–1264.

Banerjee, A., Duflo, E., Glennerster, R., and Kinnan, C. (2013) 'The miracle of microfinance? Evidence from a randomized evaluation', MIT Working Paper in Economics, 13–09.

Barber, B. and Odean, T. (2008) 'All that glitters: The effect of attention and news on the buying behaviour of individual and institutional investors', *Review of Financial Studies*, 21: 785–818.

Barberis, N. and Xiong, W. (2009) 'What drives the disposition effect? An analysis of a long-standing preference-based explanation', *The Journal of Finance*, *64*(2), 751–784.

Bardsley, N., Cubitt, R., Loomes, G., Moffatt, P., Starmer, C., and Sugden, R. (2010) *Experimental Economics: Rethinking the Rules*, Princeton, NJ: Princeton University Press.

Bateman, I., Kahneman, D., Munro, A., Starmer, C., and Sugden, R. (2005) 'Testing competing models of loss aversion: An adversarial collaboration', *Journal of Public Economics*, 89: 1561–1580.

Battigalli, P. and Dufwenberg, M. (2009) 'Dynamic psychological games', *Journal of Economic Theory*, *144*(1), 1–35.

Becker, G. and Murphy, K. (1988) 'A theory of rational addiction', *Journal of Political Economy*, 46: 675–700.

Benartzi, S. and Thaler, R. (1995) 'Myopic loss aversion and the equity premium puzzle', *Quarterly Journal of Economics*, 110: 73–92.

Benartzi, S. and Thaler, R. (1999) 'Risk aversion or myopia? Choices in repeated gambles and retirement investments', *Management Science*, 45: 364–381.

Benartzi, S. and Thaler, R. (2002) 'How much is investor autonomy worth?', *Journal of Finance*, 57: 1593–1616.

Benartzi, S. and Thaler, R. (2007) 'Heuristics and biases in retirement savings behavior', *Journal of Economic Perspectives*, 21: 81–104.

Benzion, U., Rapoport, A., and Yagil, J. (1989) 'Discount rates inferred from decisions: An experimental study', *Management Science*, 35: 270–284.

Berg, N. and Gigerenzer, G. (2010) 'As-if behavioral economics: Neoclassical economics in disguise?', *History of Economic Ideas*, *18*(1), 133–166.

Berg, J., Dickhaut, J., and McCabe, K. (1994) 'Trust, reciprocity, and social history', *Games and Economic Behavior*, 10: 122–142.

Berg, J., Dickhaut, J., and Rietz T. (2010) 'Preference reversals: The impact of truth-revealing monetary incentives', *Games and Economic Behavior*, 68: 443–468.

Bergstrom, T. (1996) 'Economics in a family way', *Journal of Economic Literature*, 34: 1903–1934.

Bergstrom, T. (2002) 'Evolution of social behaviour: Individual and group selection', *Journal of Economic Literature*, 16: 67–88.

Bernheim, D. and Rangel, A. (2004) 'Addiction and cue-triggered decision processes', *American Economic Review*, 94: 1558–1590.

Bernheim, D. and Rangel, A. (2007) 'Toward choice-theoretic foundations for behavioral welfare economics', *American Economic Review*, 97: 464–470.

Bertrand, M., Mullainathan, S., and Shafir, E. (2004) 'A behavioral-economics view of poverty', *American Economic Review*, *94*(2), 419–423.

Bewley, T. (2007) 'Fairness, reciprocity, and wage rigidity', in Diamond, P. and Vartiainen, H. (Eds.), *Behavioral Economics and its Applications*, Princeton, NJ: Princeton University Press.

Bikhchandani, S., Hirshleifer, D., and Welch, I. (1998) 'Learning from the behavior of others: Conformity, fads, and informational cascades', *Journal of Economic Perspectives*, 12: 151–170.

Binmore, K. (2008) 'Review of behavioral economics and its applications', *Economic Journal*, 118: F248–F251.

Binmore, K. and Shaked, A. (2010) 'Experimental economics: Where next?', *Journal of Economic Behavior & Organization*, *73*(1), 87–100.

Blinder, A. S. and Morgan, J. (2005) 'Are two heads better than one? Monetary policy by committee', *Journal of Money, Credit and Banking*, 789–811.

Bolton, G. and Katok, E. (1998) 'An experimental test of the crowding out hypothesis: The nature of beneficent behavior', *Journal of Economic Behavior and Organization*, 37: 315–331.

Bolton, G. and Ockenfels, A. (2000) 'ERC: A theory of equity, reciprocity, and competition', *American Economic Review*, 90: 166–193.

Bornstein, G. and Yaniv, I. (1998) 'Individual and group behavior in the ultimatum game: Are groups more "rational" players?', *Experimental Economics*, *1*(1), 101–108.

Bortolotti, S., Devetag, G., and Ortmann, A. (2009) 'Exploring the effects of real effort in a weak-link experiment', SSRN working paper, no. 1355444.

Bowles, S. (2006) 'Group competition, reproductive leveling and the evolution of human altruism', *Science*, 314: 1555–1556.

Boyd, R. (2006) 'The puzzle of human sociality', *Science*, 314: 1560–1563.

Brandts, J. and Holt, C. A. (1992) 'An experimental test of equilibrium dominance in signaling games', *American Economic Review*, 82: 1350–1365.

Brandts, J. and Cooper, D. (2006) 'A change would do you good . . . An experimental study on how to overcome coordination failure in organizations', *American Economic Review*, 96: 669–693.

Brandts, J. and Cooper, D. (2007) 'It's what you say, not what you pay: An experimental study of manager–employee relationships in overcoming coordination failure', *Journal of the European Economic Association*, 5: 1223–1268.

Breiter, H., Aharon, I., Kahneman, D., Dale, A., and Shizgal, P. (2001) 'Functional imaging of neural responses to expectancy and experience of monetary gains and losses', *Neuron*, 30: 619–639.

Breitmoser, Y. (2012) 'Strategic reasoning in p-beauty contests', *Games and Economic Behavior*, *75*(2), 555–569.

Brickman, P., Coates, D., and Janoff-Bulman, R. (1978) 'Lottery winners and accident victims: Is happiness relative?', *Journal of Personality and Social Psychology*, 36: 917–927.

Brown, R. (1995) *Prejudice: It's Social Psychology*, Hoboken, NJ: Wiley-Blackwell.

Browning, M. and Crossley, T. F. (2001) 'The life-cycle model of consumption and saving', *Journal of Economic Perspectives*, 15: 3–22.

Bruni, L. and Sugden, R. (2007) 'The road not taken: How psychology was removed from economics, and how it might be brought back', *Economic Journal*, 117: 146–173.

Brunner, C., Camerer, C. F., and Jacob, K. (2011) 'Stationary Concepts for Experimental 2 x 2 Games: Comment', *American Economic Review*, *101*(2), 1029–1040.

Buehn, A. and Schneider, F. (2012) 'Shadow economies around the world: Novel insights, accepted knowledge, and new estimates', *International Tax and Public Finance*, *19*(1), 139–171.

Cadsby, C. and Maynes, E. (1999) 'Voluntary provision of threshold public goods with continuous contributions: Experimental evidence', *Journal of Public Economics*, 71: 53–73.

Caginalp, G., Porter, D., and Smith, V. L. (2000) 'Overreactions, momentum, liquidity, and price bubbles in laboratory and field asset markets', *Journal of Behavioral Finance*, 1: 24–48.

Camerer, C. (2003) *Behavioral Game Theory: Experiments in Strategic Interaction*, Princeton, NJ: Princeton University Press.

Camerer, C. (2007) 'Neuroeconomics: Using neuroscience to make economic predictions', *Economic Journal*, 117: C26–C42.

Camerer, C. and Weber, M. (1992) 'Recent developments in modelling preferences: Uncertainty and ambiguity', *Journal of Risk and Uncertainty*, 5: 325–370.

Camerer, C. and Thaler, R. (1995) 'Anomalies: Ultimatums, dictators and manners', *Journal of Economic Perspectives*, 9: 209–219.

Camerer, C. and Ho, T-H. (1999) 'Experience-weighted attraction learning in normal form games', *Econometrica*, 67: 827–874.

Camerer, C. and Loewenstein, G. (2004) 'Behavioral economics: Past, present and future', in Camerer, C., Loewenstein, G., and Rabin, M. (Eds.), *Advances in Behavioral Economics*, Princeton, NJ: Princeton University Press.

Camerer, C., Ho, T-H., and Chong, J-K. (2004a) 'A cognitive hierarchy model of games', *Quarterly Journal of Economics*, 119: 861–898.

Camerer, C., Loewenstein, G., and Prelec, D. (2004b) 'Neuroeconomics: Why economics needs brains', *Scandinavian Journal of Economics*, 106: 555–579.

Camerer, C., Loewenstein, G., and Prelec, D. (2005) 'Neuroeconomics: How neuroscience can inform economics', *Journal of Economic Literature*, 43: 9–64.

Campbell III, C. and Kamlani, K. (1997) 'The reasons for wage rigidity: Evidence from a survey of firms', *Quarterly Journal of Economics*, 112: 759–789.

Caplin, A. and Schotter, A. (2008) *The Foundations of Positive and Normative Economics*, Oxford: Oxford University Press.

Cardenas, J. C. and Carpenter, J. (2008) 'Behavioural development economics: Lessons from field labs in the developing world', *The Journal of Development Studies*, *44*(3), 311–338.

Carroll, C., Overland, J., and Weil, D. (2000) 'Saving and growth with habit formation', *American Economic Review*, 90: 341–355.

Cartwright, E., Gillet, J., and van Vugt, M. (2013) 'Leadership by example in a weak-link game', *Economic Inquiry*, 51: 2028–2043.

Cassar, A. and Friedman, D. (2004) *Economics Lab: An Introduction to Experimental Economics*, London: Routledge.

Chamberlin, E. H. (1948) 'An experimental imperfect market', *Journal of Political Economy*, 56: 95–108.

Charness, G. and Rabin, M. (2002) 'Understanding social preferences with simple tests', *The Quarterly Journal of Economics*, *117*(3), 817–869.

Charness, G. and Dufwenberg, M. (2006) 'Promises and partnership', *Econometrica*, *74*(6), 1579–1601.

Charness, G. and Sutter, M. (2012) 'Groups make better self-interested decisions', *The Journal of Economic Perspectives*, *26*(3), 157–176.

Chaudhuri, A., Schotter, A., and Sopher, B. (2009) 'Talking ourselves to efficiency: Coordination in inter-generational minimum effort games with private, almost common and common knowledge of advice', *The Economic Journal*, *119*(534), 91–122.

Chetty, R. (2006) 'A new method of estimating risk aversion', *American Economic Review*, 96: 1821–1834.

Chetty, R., Looney, A., and Kroft, K. (2009) 'Salience and taxation: Theory and evidence', *American Economic Review*, 99: 1145–1177.

Cheung, Y-W. and Friedman, D. (1997) 'Individual learning in normal form games: Some laboratory results', *Games and Economic Behavior*, 19: 46–76.

Clark, A.E., Diener, E., Georgellis, Y., and Lucas, R.E. (2003) 'Lags and leads in life satisfaction: A test of the baseline hypothesis', DELTA working paper, 2003–14.

Clark, A.E., Diener, E., Georgellis, Y., and Lucas, R.E. (2008) 'Lags and leads in life satisfaction: A test of the baseline hypothesis', *Economic Journal*, 118: F222–243.

Clotfelter, C. and Cook, P. (1991) 'Lotteries in the real world', *Journal of Risk and Uncertainty*, 4: 227–232.

Coats, J., Gronberg, T., and Grosskopf, B. (2009) 'Simultaneous versus sequential public good provision and the role of refunds – An experimental study', *Journal of Public Economics*, 93: 326–335.

Cohen, A. and Einav, L. (2007) 'Estimating risk preferences from deductible choice', *American Economic Review*, 97: 745–788.

Conlisk, J. (1996) 'Why bounded rationality?', *Journal of Economic Literature*, 34: 669–700.

Cooper, D. (2006) 'Are experienced managers expert at overcoming coordination failure?', *Advances in Economic Analysis and Policy*, 6: 1–30.

Cooper, D. and Kagel, J. (2005) 'Are two heads better than one? Team versus individual play in signaling games', *American Economic Review*, *95*(3), 477–509.

Coricelli, G. and Nagel, R. (2009). 'Neural correlates of depth of strategic reasoning in medial prefrontal cortex', *Proceedings of the National Academy of Sciences*, *106*(23), 9163–9168.

Costa-Gomes, M. and Crawford, V. (2006) 'Cognition and behavior in two-person guessing games: An experimental study', *American Economic Review*, 96: 177–1768.

Costa-Gomes, M., Crawford, V., and Iriberri, N. (2009) 'Comparing models of strategic thinking in van Huyck, Battalio, and Beil's coordination games', *Journal of the European Economic Association*, 7: 365–376.

Crawford, V. (1995) 'Adaptive dynamics in coordination games', *Econometrica*, 63: 103–143.

Crawford, V. and Iriberri, N. (2007) 'Level-k auctions: Can a non-equilibrium model of strategic thinking explain the winner's curse and overbidding in private value auctions?', *Econometrica*, 75: 1721–1770.

Croson, R. and Marks, M. (2001) 'The effect of recommended contributions in the voluntary provision of public goods', *Economic Inquiry*, 39: 238–249.

Croson, R. and Gneezy, U. (2009) 'Gender differences in preferences', *Journal of Economic Literature*, 47: 448–474.

Dana, J., Weber, R., and Xi Kuang, J. (2007) 'Exploiting moral wiggle room: Experiments demonstrating an illusory preference for fairness', *Economic Theory*, 33: 67–80.

Darley, J. M. and Gross, P. H. (1983) 'A hypothesis-confirming bias in labeling effects', *Journal of Personality and Social Psychology*, 44: 20–33.

DellaVigna, S. (2009) 'Psychology and economics: Evidence from the field', *Journal of Economic Literature*, 47: 315–372.

Della Vigna, S. and Malmendier, U. (2004) 'Contract design and self-control: Theory and evidence', *Quarterly Journal of Economics*, 119: 353–402.

DellaVigna, S. and Malmendier, U. (2006) 'Paying not to go to the gym', *American Economic Review*, 96: 694–719.

De Martino, B., Kumaran, D., Seymour, B., and Dolan, R. J. (2006) 'Frames, biases, and rational decision-making in the human brain', *Science*, *313*(5787), 684–687.

De Quervain, D. J. F., Fischbacher, U., Treyer, V., Schellhammer, M., Schnyder, U., Buck, A., and Fehr, E. (2004) 'The neural basis of altruistic punishment', *Science*.

Diamond, P. and Vartiainen, H. (2007) *Behavioral Economics and its Applications*, Princeton, NJ: Princeton University Press.

Diekhof, E. and Gruber, O. (2010) 'When desire collides with reason: Functional interactions between anteroventral prefrontal cortex and nucleus accumbens underlie the human ability to resist impulsive desires', *Journal of Neuroscience*, 30: 1488–1493.

Di Tella, R. and MacCulloch, R. J. (2005) 'Partisan social happiness', *Review of Economic Studies*, 72: 367–393.

Di Tella, R. and MacCulloch, R. J. (2006) 'Some uses of happiness data in economics', *Journal of Economic Perspectives*, 20: 25–46.

Di Tella, R., MacCulloch, R. J., and Oswald, A. J. (2001) 'Preferences over inflation and unemployment: Evidence from surveys of happiness', *American Economic Review*, 91: 335–341.

Dolan, P. and Kahneman, D. (2008) 'Interpretations of utility and their implications for the valuation of health', *Economic Journal*, 118: 215–234.

Dolan, P., Hallsworth, M., Halpern, D., King, D., and Vlaev, I. (2010) 'MINDSPACE: Influencing behavior through public policy', Cabinet Office publication.

Dufwenberg, M. and Kirchsteiger, G. (2004) 'A theory of sequential reciprocity', *Games and Economic Behavior*, 47: 268–298.

Dufwenberg, M., Lindqvist, T., and Moore, E. (2005) 'Bubbles and experience: An experiment', *American Economic Review*, 1731–1737.

Easterlin, R. (1974) 'Does economic growth improve the human lot? Some empirical evidence', in David, P. A. and Reder, M. W. (Eds.), *Nations and Households in Economic Growth: Essays in Honour of Moses Abramovitz*, New York: Academic Press.

Easterlin, R. A. (2013) 'Happiness, growth, and public policy', *Economic Inquiry*, *51*(1), 1–15.

Eckel, C. and Grossman, P. (2001) 'Chivalry and solidarity in ultimatum games', *Economic Inquiry*, 30: 171–188.

Ellison, G. (2006) 'Bounded rationality in industrial organization', in Blundell, R., Newey, W., and Persson, R. (Eds.), *Advances in Economics and Econometrics: Theory and Applications, Ninth World Congress, Volume II*, New York: Cambridge University Press.

Ellsberg, D. (1961) 'Risk, ambiguity, and the savage axioms', *Quarterly Journal of Economics*, 75: 643–669.

Engelmann, D. and Strobel, M. (2004) 'Inequality aversion, efficiency, and maximin preferences in simple distribution experiments', *The American Economic Review*, 94: 857–869.

Falk, A. and Fischbacher, U. (2006) 'A theory of reciprocity', *Games and Economic Behavior*, 54: 293–315.

Falk, A., Fehr, E., and Fischbacher, U. (2003) 'On the nature of fair behavior', *Economic Inquiry*, 41: 20–26.

Falk, A., Fehr, E., and Fischbacher, U. (2008) 'Testing theories of fairness – Intentions matter', *Games and Economic Behavior*, 62: 287–303.

Farber, H. S. (2005) 'Is tomorrow another day? The labour supply of New York City cabdrivers', *Journal of Political Economy*, 113: 46–82.

Farber, H. S. (2008) 'Reference-dependent preferences and labor supply: The case of New York City taxi drivers', *American Economic Review*, 98: 1069–1082.

Fehr, E. and Falk, A. (1999) 'Wage rigidity in a competitive incomplete contract market', *Journal of Political Economy*, 107: 106–134.

Fehr, E. and Schmidt, J. (1999) 'A theory of fairness, competition, and cooperation', *Quarterly Journal of Economics*, 114: 817–868.

Fehr, E. and Gächter, S. (2000a) 'Cooperation and punishment in public goods experiments', *American Economic Review*, 90: 980–994.

Fehr, E. and Gächter, S. (2000b) 'Fairness and retaliation: The economics of reciprocity', *Journal of Economic Perspectives*, 14: 159–181.

Fehr, E. and Fischbacher, U. (2004) 'Third-party punishment and social norms', *Evolution and Human Behavior*, 25: 63–87.

Feri, F., Irlenbusch, B., and Sutter, M. (2010) 'Efficiency gains from team-based coordination – Large-scale experimental evidence', *American Economic Review*, *100*(4), 1892–1912.

Fobian, C. S. and Christensen-Szalanski, J. J. (1993) 'Ambiguity and liability negotiations: The effects of the negotiators' role and the sensitivity zone', *Organizational Behavior and Human Decision Processes*, *54*(2), 277–298.

Forsythe, R., Horowitz, J., Savin, N., and Sefton, M. (1994) 'Fairness in simple bargaining experiments', *Games and Economic Behavior*, 6: 347–369.

Frank, R. (1991) *Passions within Reason*, New York: WW Norton and Co.

Frank, R. (2007) 'Behavioral economics and health economics', in Diamond, P. and Vartiainen, H. (Eds.), *Behavioral Economics and its Applications*, Princeton, NJ: Princeton University Press.

Frank, R. and Hutchens, R. (1993) 'Wages, seniority, and the demand for rising consumption profiles', *Journal of Economic Behavior and Organization*, 3: 251–276.

Frank, R., Gilovich, T., and Regan, D. (1993) 'Does studying economics inhibit cooperation?', *The Journal of Economic Perspectives*, 7: 159–171.

Frederick, S., Loewenstein, G., and O'Donoghue, T. (2002) 'Time discounting and time preference: A critical review', *Journal of Economic Literature*, 40: 351–401.

Frey, B. (2008) *Happiness: A Revolution in Economics*, Cambridge, MA: MIT Press.

Frey, B. and Stutzer, A. (2002) 'What can economists learn from happiness research?', *Journal of Economic Literature*, 40: 402–435.

Friedman, M. (1953) *Essays in Positive Economics*, Chicago, IL: University of Chicago Press.

Fudenberg, D. and Levine, D. (2006) 'A dual-self model of impulse control', *American Economic Review*, 96: 1449–1476.

Fudenberg, D., Levine, D. K., and Maniadis, Z. (2012) 'On the robustness of anchoring effects in WTP and WTA experiments', *American Economic Journal: Microeconomics, 4*(2), 131–145.

Gabaix, X., Laibson, D., Moloche, G., and Weinberg, S. (2006) 'Costly information acquisition: Experimental analysis of a boundedly rational model', *American Economic Review*, 96: 1043–1068.

Gächter, S. and Falk, A. (2002) 'Reputation and reciprocity: Consequences for the labour relation', *Scandinavian Journal of Economics*, 104: 1–26.

Gächter, S., Herrmann, B., and Thöni, C. (2010) 'Culture and cooperation', *Philosophical Transactions of the Royal Society B – Biological Sciences*, 365: 2651–2661.

Geanakoplos, J., Pearce, D., and Stacchetti, E. (1989) 'Psychological games and sequential rationality', *Games and Economic Behavior, 1*(1), 60–79.

Genesove, D. and Mayer, C. (2001) 'Loss aversion and seller behaviour: Evidence from the housing market', *Quarterly Journal of Economics*, 116: 1233–1260.

Gilbert, D. T., Gill, M. J., and Wilson, T. D. (2002) 'The future is now: Temporal correction in affective forecasting', *Organizational Behavior and Human Decision Processes*, 88: 430–444.

Gilboa, I. and Schmeidler, D. (1995) 'Case-based decision theory', *Quarterly Journal of Economics*, 110: 605–639.

Gillet, J., Cartwright, E., and van-Vugt, M. (2010) 'Leadership in the weak link game', School of Economics, University of Kent working paper.

Gilovich, T., Vallone, R., and Tversky, A. (1985) 'The hot hand in basketball: On the misperception of random sequences', *Cognitive Psychology*, 17: 295–314.

Gintis, H., Bowles, S., Boyd, R., and Fehr, E. (2005) *Moral Sentiments and Material Interests*, Cambridge, MA: MIT Press.

Glewwe, P., Kremer, M., and Moulin, S. (2009) 'Many children left behind? Textbooks and test scores in Kenya', *American Economic Journal: Applied Economics, 1*(1), 112–135.

Glimcher, P. (2004) *Decisions, Uncertainty, and the Brain: The Science of Neuroeconomics*, Cambridge, MA: MIT Press.

Gneezy, U. (2005) 'Deception: The role of consequences', *American Economic Review, 95*(1), 384–394.

Gneezy, U. and Rustichini, A. (2004) 'Gender and competition at a young age', *American Economic Review*, 94: 377–381.

Gneezy, U. and List, J. (2006) 'Putting behavioral economics to work: Field evidence on gift exchange', *Econometrica*, 74: 1365–1384.

Gode, D. K. and Sunder, S. (1993) 'Allocative efficiency of markets with zero-intelligence traders: Market as a partial substitute for individual rationality', *Journal of Political Economy*, 101: 119–137.

Goeree, J. K. and Yariv, L. (2007) 'Conformity in the lab', California Institute of Technology working paper, 902.

Goldfarb, A. and Xiao, M. (2011) 'Who thinks about the competition? Managerial ability and strategic entry in US local telephone markets', *American Economic Review, 101*(7), 3130–3161.

Grosskopf, B. (2003) 'Reinforcement and directional learning in the ultimatum game with responder competition', *Experimental Economics*, 6: 141–158.

Gruber, J. and Köszegi, B. (2001) 'Is addiction "rational"? Theory and evidence', *Quarterly Journal of Economics*, 116: 1261–1303.

Gul, F. and Pesendorfer, W. (2001) 'Temptation and self-control', *Econometrica, 69*(6), 1403–1435.

Güth, W. and Yaari, M. (1992) 'An evolutionary approach to explain reciprocal behavior in a simple strategic game', in Witt, U. (Ed.), *Explaining Process and Change – Approaches to Evolutionary Economics*, 23–34, Ann Arbor, MI.

Güth, W., Schmittberger, R., and Schwarze, B. (1982) 'An experimental analysis of ultimatum bargaining', *Journal of Economic Behavior & Organization, 3*(4), 367–388.

Halevy, Y. (2007) 'Ellsberg revisited: An experimental study', *Econometrica*, 75: 503–536.

Harbaugh, W. T., Krause, K., and Liday, S. G. (2003) 'Bargaining by children', University of Oregon Economics Working Paper, 2002–40.

Hare, T., O'Doherty, J., Camerer, C., Schultz, W., and Rangel, A. (2008) 'Dissociating the role of the orbitofrontal cortex and the striatum in the computation of goal values and prediction errors', *Journal of Neuroscience*, 28: 5623–5630.

Harrison, G., List, J., and Towe, C. (2007) 'Naturally occurring preferences and exogenous laboratory experiments: A case study of risk aversion', *Econometrica*, 75: 433–458.

Hashimzade, N., Myles, G. D., and Tran-Nam, B. (2013) 'Applications of behavioural economics to tax evasion', *Journal of Economic Surveys*.

Heath, C. and Soll, J. B. (1996) 'Mental budgeting and consumer decisions', *The Journal of Consumer Research*, 23: 40–52.

Henker, J. and Owen, S. (2008) 'Bursting bubbles: Linking experimental financial market results to field market data', *Journal of Behavioral Finance*, 9: 5–14.

Henrich, J., Boyd, R., Bowles, S., Camerer, C., Fehr, E., and Gintis, H. (2004) *Foundations of Human Sociality*, Oxford: Oxford University Press.

Herrmann, B., Thöni, C., and Gächter, S. (2008) 'Antisocial punishment across societies', *Science*, 319: 1362–1367.

Ho, T-H., Camerer, C., and Weigelt, K. (1998) 'Iterated dominance and iterated best response in experimental "p-beauty contests"', *American Economic Review*, 88: 947–969.

Hoffman, E., McCabe, K., and Smith, V. (1996) 'Social distance and other-regarding behavior', *American Economic Review*, 86: 653–660.

Hoffman, E., McCabe, K., Shachat, K., and Smith, V. (1994) 'Preferences, property rights and anonymity in bargaining games', *Games and Economic Behavior*, 7: 346–380.

Hogarth, R. M. and Reder, M. W. (1987) *Rational Choice: The Contrast between Economics and Psychology*, Chicago, IL: University of Chicago Press.

Holt, C. and Laury, S. (2002) 'Risk aversion and incentive effects', *American Economic Review*, 92: 1644–1655.

Hsu, M., Bhatt, M., Adolphs, R., Tranel, D., and Camere, C. (2005) 'Neural systems responding to degrees of uncertainty in human decision-making', *Science*, 310: 1680–1683.

Huberman, G. and Jiang, W. (2006) 'Offering versus choice in 401(k) plans: Equity exposure and number of funds', *Journal of Finance*, 61: 763–780.

Huck, S., Müller, W., and Normann, H. T. (2001) 'Stackelberg beats Cournot – On collusion and efficiency in experimental markets', *The Economic Journal, 111*(474), 749–765.

Huck, S., Müller, W., and Normann, H. T. (2002) 'To commit or not to commit: Endogenous timing in experimental duopoly markets', *Games and Economic Behavior, 38*(2), 240–264.

Huettel, S. Stowe, J., Gordon, E., Warner, B., and Platt, M. (2006) 'Neural signatures of economic preferences for risk and ambiguity', *Neuron*, 49: 765–775.

Hussam, R. N., Porter, D., and Smith, V. L. (2008) 'Thar she blows: Can bubbles be rekindled with experienced subjects?', *American Economic Review*, 93: 924–937.

Institute of Medicine (2001) *Crossing the Quality Chasm*, Washington, DC: NAS Press.

Iyengar, S. S. and Lepper, M. R. (2000) 'When choice is demotivating: Can one desire too much of a good thing?', *Journal of Personality and Social Psychology*, 79: 995–1005.

Jehiel, P. (2005) 'Analogy-based expectation equilibrium', *Journal of Economic Theory*, 123: 81–104.

Jensen, K., Call, J., and Tomasello, M. (2007) 'Chimpanzees are rational maximizers in an ultimatum game', *Science*, *318*(5847), 107–109.

Jianakoplos, N. and Bernasek, A. (1998) 'Are women more risk averse?', *Economic Inquiry*, 36: 620–630.

Johnson, D. S., Parker, J. A., and Souleles, N. S. (2006) 'Household expenditure and the income tax rebates of 2001', *American Economic Review*, 96: 1589–1610.

Kagel, J. H. and Roth, A. E. (2000) 'The dynamics of reorganization in matching markets: A laboratory experiment motivated by a natural experiment', *Quarterly Journal of Economics*, 115: 201–235.

Kahneman, D. (2003) 'Maps of bounded rationality: Psychology for behavioural economics', *American Economic Review*, *93*(5), 1449–1475.

Kahneman, D. (2011) *Thinking, Fast and Slow*, London: Macmillan.

Kahneman, D. and Tversky, A. (1973) 'On the psychology of prediction', *Psychological Review*, 80: 237–251.

Kahneman, D. and Tversky, A. (1979) 'Prospect theory: An analysis of decision under risk', *Econometrica*, 47: 263–291.

Kahneman, D. and Tversky, A. (1983) 'Choices, values, and frames', *American Psychologist*, 39: 341–350.

Kahneman, D. and Krueger, A. B. (2006) 'Developments in the measurement of subjective well-being', *Journal of Economic Perspectives*, 20: 3–24.

Kahneman, D. and Dolan, P. (2008) 'Interpretations of utility and their implications for the valuation of health', *Economic Journal*, 118: 215–234.

Kahneman, D., Knetsch, J., and Thaler, R. H. (1986) 'Fairness as a constraint on profit seeking: Entitlements in the market', *American Economic Review*, 76: 728–741.

Kahneman, D., Wakker, P., and Sarin, R. (1997) 'Back to Bentham? Explorations of experienced utility', *Quarterly Journal of Economics*, 112: 375–405.

Kahneman, D., Fredrickson, D. L., Schreiber, C. A., and Redelmeier, D. A. (1993) 'When more pain is preferred to less: Adding a better end', *Psychological Science*, 4: 401–405.

Kahneman, D., Krueger, A. B., Schkade, D. A., Schwarz, N., and Stone, A. A. (2004) 'A survey method for characterizing daily life experience: The day reconstruction method', *Science*, *306*(5702), 1776–1780.

Kaiser Family Foundation (2008) '2008 update on consumers' views of patient safety and quality information', report no. 7819.

Kalivas, P. and Volkow, N. (2005) 'The neural basis of addication: A pathology of motivation and choice', *American Journal of Psychiatry*, 162: 1403–1413.

Kaplan, H., Hill, K., Lancaster, J., and Hurtado, A. M. (2000) 'A theory of human life history evolution: Diet, intelligence, and longevity', *Evolutionary Anthropolgy*, 9: 156–185.

Karlsson, N., Loewenstein, G., and Seppi, D. (2009) 'The "ostrich effect": Selective attention to information about investments', *Journal of Risk and Uncertainty*, 38: 95–115.

Ketcham, J., Smith, V. L., and Williams, A. W. (1984) 'A comparison of posted-offer and double-auction pricing institutions', *Review of Economic Studies*, 51: 595–614.

Kilbanoff, P., Marinacci, M., and Mukerji, S. (2005) 'A smooth model of decision making under ambiguity', *Econometrica,* 73: 1849–1892.

Klemperer, P. (2004) *Auctions: Theory and Practice*, Princeton, NJ: Princeton University Press.

Knack, S. and Keefer, P. (1997) 'Does social capital have an economic payoff? A cross-country investigation', *Quarterly Journal of Economics*, 112: 1251–1288.

Knoch, D., Pascual-Leone, A., Meyer, K., Treyer, K., and Fehr, E. (2006) 'Diminishing reciprocal fairness by disrupting the right prefrontal cortex', *Science*, 314: 829–832.

Knutson, B., Fong, G., Adams, C., Varner, J., and Hommer, D. (2001) 'Dissociation of reward anticipation and outcome with event-related fMRI', *NeuroReport*, 12: 3683–3687.

Kocher, M. G. and Sutter, M. (2005) 'The decision maker matters: Individual versus group behaviour in experimental beauty-contest games', *The Economic Journal*, *115*(500), 200–223.

Kooreman, P. (2000) 'The labelling effect of a child benefit system', *American Economic Review*, 90: 571–583.

Kőszegi, B. and Rabin, M. (2006) 'A model of reference-dependent preferences', *Quarterly Journal of Economics*, 121: 1133–1165.

Kőszegi, B. and Rabin, M. (2007) 'Reference-dependent risk attitudes', *American Economic Review*, 97: 1047–1073.

Kube, S., Maréchal, M., and Puppe, C. (2006) 'Putting reciprocity to work – Positive versus negative responses in the field', University of St Gallen Department of Economics working paper series 2006–27.

Kugler, T., Bornstein, G., Kocher, M. G., and Sutter, M. (2007) 'Trust between individuals and groups: Groups are less trusting than individuals but just as trustworthy', *Journal of Economic Psychology*, *28*(6), 646–657.

Laibson, D. (1997) 'Golden eggs and hyperbolic discounting', *Quarterly Journal of Economics*, 112: 443–447.

Laibson, D. (2001) 'A cue-theory of consumption', *Quarterly Journal of Economics*, 116: 81–119.

Laibson, D., Repetto, A., and Tobacman, J. (2007) 'Estimating discount functions with consumption choice over the lifecycle', NBER working paper 13314.

Laland, K. and Brown, G. (2005) *Sense and Nonsense*, Oxford: Oxford University Press.

Landsberger, M. (1966) 'Windfall income and consumption: Comment', *American Economic Review*, 534–539.

Larrick, R. and Blount, S. (1997) 'The claiming effect: Why players are more generous in social dilemmas than in ultimatum games', *Journal of Personality and Social Psychology*, 72: 810–825.

Larrick, R. P. and Soll, J. B. (2008) 'The MPG illusion', *Science*, *320*(5883), 1593.

Levitt, S. and List, J. (2007) 'What do laboratory experiments measuring social preferences reveal about the real world?', *The Journal of Economic Perspectives*, 21: 153–174.

Lichtenstein, S. and Slovic, P. (1971) 'Reversals of preference between bids and choices in gambling decisions', *Journal of Experimental Psychology*, *89*(1), 46.

Lichtenstein, S., Slovic, P., Fischhoff, B., Layman, M., and Combs, B. (1978) 'Judged frequency of lethal events', *Journal of Experimental Psychology: Human Learning and Memory*, 4: 551–578.

List, J. (2004) 'Neoclassical theory versus prospect theory: Evidence from the marketplace', *Econometrica*, 72: 615–625.

List, J. (2007) 'On the interpretation of giving in dictator games', *Journal of Political Economy*, 115: 482–493.
Loewenstein, G. and Prelec, D. (1992) 'Anomalies in intertemporal choice: Evidence and an interpretation', *Quarterly Journal of Economics*, 107: 573–597.
Loewenstein, G. and Prelec, D. (1993) 'Preferences over sequences of outcomes', *Psychological Review*, 100: 91–108.
Loewenstein, G. and Adler, D. (1995) 'A bias in the prediction of tastes', *Economic Journal*, 105: 929–937.
Loewenstein, G. and Ubel, P. A. (2008) 'Hedonic adaption and the role of decision and experience utility in public policy', *Journal of Public Economics*, 92: 1795–1810.
Loewenstein, G., O'Donoghue, T., and Rabin, M. (2003) 'Projection bias in predicting future utility', *Quarterly Journal of Economics*, 118: 1209–1248.
Loomes, G. and Sugden, R. (1982) 'An alternative theory of choice under uncertainty', *Economic Journal*, 92: 805–824.
Loomes, G. and Sugden, R. (1983) 'A rationale for preference reversal', *American Economic Review*, 73: 428–432.
Loomes, G. and Sugden, R. (1986) 'Disappointment and dynamic consistency in choice under uncertainty', *Review of Economic Studies*, 53: 271–82.
Loomes, G., Starmer, C., and Sugden, R. (1991) 'Observing violations of transitivity by experimental methods', *Econometrica*, 59: 425–439.
Lord, C. G., Ross, L., and Lepper, M. R. (1979) 'Biased assimilation and attitude polarization: The effects of prior theories on subsequently considered evidence', *Journal of Personality and Social Psychology*, 37: 2098–2109.
Lucking-Reiley, D. (1999) 'Using field experiments to test equivalence between auction formats: Magic on the internet', *American Economic Review*, 89: 1063–1080.
Luhan, W. J., Kocher, M. G., and Sutter, M. (2009) 'Group polarization in the team dictator game reconsidered', *Experimental Economics*, *12*(1), 26–41.
McCall, T. B. (1996) *Examining your Doctor: A Patient's Guide to Avoiding Harmful Medical Care*, New York: Carol Publishing Corporation.
McClure, S., Laibson, D., Loewenstein, G., and Cohen, J. (2004) 'Separate neural systems value immediate and delayed monetary rewards', *Science*, 306: 503–507.
McKelvey, R. and Palfrey, T. (1995) 'Quantal response equilibria for normal form games', *Games and Economic Behavior*, 10: 6–38.
McKelvey, R., Palfrey, T., and Weber, R. (2000) 'The effects of payoff magnitude and heterogeneity on behavior in 2x2 games with unique mixed strategy equilibria', *Journal of Economic Behavior and Organization*, 42: 523–548.
Madrian, B. C. and Shea, D. F. (2001) 'The power of suggestion: Inertia in 401(k) participation and savings behavior', *Quarterly Journal of Economics*, 116: 1149–1187.
Marks, M. and Croson, R. (1998) 'Alternative rebate rules in the provision of a threshold public good: An experimental investigation', *Journal of Public Economics*, 67: 195–220.
Mazar, N., Amir, O., and Ariely, D. (2008) 'The dishonesty of honest people: A theory of self-concept maintenance', *Journal of Marketing Research*, *45*(6), 633–644.
Mehra, R. and Prescott, E. (2003) 'The equity premium puzzle in retrospect', in G. M. Constantinides, M. Harris, and R. Stulz., *Handbook of the Economics of Finance*, Amsterdam: North-Holland.
Mehta, J., Starmer, C., and Sugden, R. (1994) 'The nature of salience: An experimental investigation of pure coordination games', *American Economic Review*, 84: 658–673.
Miguel, E. and Kremer, M. (2004) 'Worms: Identifying impacts on education and health in the presence of treatment externalities', *Econometrica*, *72*(1), 159–217.

Milgrom, P. (2004) *Putting Auction Theory to Work*, Cambridge: Cambridge University Press.

Miravete, E. (2003) 'Choosing the wrong calling plan? Ignorance and learning', *American Economic Review*, 93: 297–310.

Mullainathan, S. and Thaler, R. H. (2000) 'Behavioral economics', in *International Encyclopedia of the Social and Behavioral Sciences*, Cambridge, MA: MIT Press.

Nagel, R. (1995) 'Unraveling in guessing games: An experimental study', *American Economic Review*, 85: 1313–1326.

National Drug Intelligence Center (NDIC) (2010) 'National drug threat assessment 2010', report.

Neumark, D. and Postlewaite, A. (1998) 'Relative income concerns and the rise in married women's employment', *Journal of Public Economics*, 70: 157–183.

Niederle, M. and Vesterlund, L. (2007) 'Do women shy away from competition? Do men compete too much', *Quarterly Journal of Economics*, 122: 1067–1101.

Northcraft, G. B. and Neale, M. A. (1987) 'Experts, amateurs, and real estate: An anchoring-and-adjustment perspective on property pricing decisions', *Organizational Behavior and Human Decision Processes*, *39*(1), 84–97.

Nowak, M. (2006) 'Five rules for the evolution of cooperation', *Science*, 314: 1569–1572.

Odean, T. (1998) 'Are investors reluctant to realize their losses?', *Journal of Finance*, 53: 1775–1798.

O'Doherty, J., Deichmann, R., Critchley, H., and Dolan, R. (2002) 'Neural responses during anticipation of a primary taste reward', *Neuron*, 33: 815–826.

O'Doherty, J., Kringelbach, M., Rolls, E., Hornak, J., and Andrews, C. (2001) 'Abstract reward and punishment representations in the human orbitofrontal cortex', *Nature Neuroscience*, 4: 95–102.

O'Doherty, J., Dayan, P., Schultz, J., Deichmann, R., Friston, R., and Dolan, R. (2004) 'Dissociable roles of ventral and dorsal striatum in instrumental conditioning', *Science*, 304: 452–454.

O'Donoghue, T. and Rabin, M. (1999) 'Doing it now or later', *American Economic Review*, 89: 103–124.

O'Donoghue, T. and Rabin, M. (2000) 'The economics of immediate gratification', *Journal of Behavioral Decision Making*, 13: 233–250.

O'Donoghue, T. and Rabin, M. (2006) 'Incentives and self control', in Blundell, R., Newey, W., and Persson, R. (Eds.), *Advances in Economics and Econometrics: Theory and Applications, Ninth World Congress, Volume II*, New York: Cambridge University Press.

Office for National Statistics (ONS) (2004) 'Smoking related behavior and attitudes', research report.

Olson, M. (1971) *The Logic of Collective Action: Public Goods and the Theory of Groups*, Cambridge, MA: Harvard University Press.

Oskarsson, A. T., Van Boven, L., McClelland, G., and Hastie, R. (2009) 'What's next? Judging sequences of binary events', *Psychological Bulletin*, 135: 262–285.

Ostrom, E. (1990) *Governing the Commons: The Evolution of Institutions for Collective Action*, New York: Cambridge University Press.

Ostrom, E. (2006) 'The value-added of laboratory experiments for the study of institutions and common-pool resources', *Journal of Economic Behavior and Organization*, 61: 149–163.

Ostrom, E. (2010) 'Beyond markets and states: Polycentric governance of complex economic systems', *American Economic Review*, 100: 641–672.

Ostrom, E., Walker, J., and Gardner, R. (1992) 'Covenants with and without a sword: Self-governance is possible', *American Political Science Review*, 86: 404–417.

Oswald, A. and Powdthavee, N. (2008) 'Does happiness adapt? A longitudinal study of disability with implications for economists and judges', *Journal of Public Economics*, 92: 1061–1077.

Patall, E. A., Cooper, H., and Robinson, J. C. (2008) 'The effects of choice on intrinsic motivation and related outcomes: A meta-analysis of research findings', *Psychological Bulletin*, 134: 270–300.

Phelps, C. E. and Mooney, C. (1993) 'Variations in medical practice: Causes and consequences', in Arnould, R., Rich, R., and White, W. (Eds.), *Competitive Approaches to Health Care Reform*, Washington, DC: Urban Institute Press.

Phillips, C. and Thompson, G. (2009) 'What is a QALY?', Hayward Medical Communications.

Porter, D. P. and Smith, V. L. (2003) 'Stock market bubbles in the laboratory', *Journal of Behavioral Finance*, 4: 7–20.

Post, T., van den Assem, M. J., Baltussen, G., and Thaler, R. H. (2008) 'Deal or no deal? Decision making under risk in a large-payoff game show', *American Economic Review*, 98: 38–71.

Pradel, J., Euler, H., and Fetchenhauer, D. (2009) 'Spotting altruistic dictator game players and mingling with them: The elective assortation of classmates', *Evolution and Human Behavior*, 30: 103–113.

Pratt, J. W., Wise, D. A., and Zeckhauser, R. (1979) 'Price differences in almost competitive markets', *Quarterly Journal of Economics*, 93: 189–211.

Preuschoff, K., Bossaerts, P., and Quartz, S. (2006) 'Neural differentiation of expected reward and risk in human subcortical structures', *Neruon*, 51: 381–390.

Proctor, D., Williamson, R. A., de Waal, F. B., and Brosnan, S. F. (2013) 'Chimpanzees play the ultimatum game', *Proceedings of the National Academy of Sciences*, *110*(6), 2070–2075.

Purves, D., Brannon, E., Cabeza, R., Huettel, S., LaBar, K., Platt, M., and Woldorff, M. (2008) *Principles of Cognitive Neuroscience*, Sunderland, MA: Sinauer Associates.

Rabin, M. (1993) 'Incorporating fairness into game theory and economics', *American Economic Review*, 83: 1281–1302.

Rabin, M. (1998) 'Psychology and economics', *Journal of Economic Literature*, 36: 11–46.

Rabin, M. (2000) 'Risk aversion and expected-utility theory: A calibration theorem', *Econometrica*, 68: 1281–1292.

Rabin, M. (2002) 'Inferences by believers in the law of small numbers', *Quarterly Journal of Economics*, 117: 775–816.

Rabin, M. and Schrag, J. (1999) 'First impressions matter: A model of confirmatory bias',*Quarterly Journal of Economics*, 114: 37–82.

Rapoport, A. and Budescu, D. V. (1997) 'Randomization in individual choice behavior', *Psychological Review*, 104: 603–617.

Rapoport, A., Seale, D. A., and Winter, E. (2002) 'Coordination and learning behavior in large groups with asymmetric players', *Games and Economic Behavior*, *39*(1), 111–136.

Read, D. and van Leeuwen, B. (1998) 'Predicting hunger: The effects of appetite and delay on choice', *Organizational Behaviour and Human Decision Processes*, 76: 189–205.

Redelmeier, D. and Kahneman, D. (1996) 'Patients' memories of painful medical treatments: Real-time and retrospective evaluations of two minimally invasive procedures', *Pain*, 66: 3–8.

Redelmeier, D., Katz J., and Kahneman D., (2003) 'Memories of colonoscopy: A randomized trial', *Pain*, 104: 187–194.

Ribar, D. and Wilhelm, M. (2002) 'Altruistic and joy-of-giving motivations in charitable behavior', *Journal of Political Economy*, 110: 425–457.

Ridley, M. (1997) *The Origins of Virtue*, London: Penguin.

Robson, A. (2001a) 'The biological basis of economic behavior', *Journal of Economic Literature*, 39: 11–33.

Robson, A. (2001b) 'Why would nature give individuals utility functions?', *Journal of Political Economy*, 109: 900–914.

Robson, A. (2002) 'Evolution and human nature', *Journal of Economic Perspectives*, 16: 89–106.

Robson, A. and Kaplan, H. (2003) 'The evolution of human life expectancy and intelligence in hunter-gatherer economics', *American Economic Review*, 93: 150–169.

Robson, A. and Samuelson, L. (2009) 'The evolution of time preference with aggregate uncertainty', *American Economic Review*, 99: 1925–1953.

Rodrik, D. (2008) 'The new development economics: We shall experiment, but how shall we learn?', HKS working paper, no. 08-055.

Roth, A. (1995) 'Introduction to experimental economics', in Kagel, J. and Roth, A. (Eds.), *Handbook of Experimental Economics*, Princeton, NJ: Princeton University Press.

Roth, A. (2002) 'The economist as engineer: Game theory, experimentation, and computation as tools for design economics', *Econometrica*, 70: 1341–1378.

Roth, A. (2008) 'Deferred acceptance algorithms: History, theory, practice, and open questions', *International Journal of Game Theory*, 36: 537–569.

Roth, A. and Erev, I. (1995) 'Learning in extensive-form games: Experimental data and simple dynamic models in the intermediate term', *Games and Economic Behavior*, 8: 164–212.

Roth, A., Prasnikar, V., Okuno-Fujiwara, M., and Zamir, S. (1991) 'Bargaining and market behavior in Jerusalem, Ljubljana, Pittsburgh, and Tokyo: An experimental study', *American Economic Review*, 81: 1068–1095.

Sanfey, A., Rilling, J., Aronson, J., Nystrom, L., and Cohen, J. (2003) 'The neural basis of economic decision-making in the ultimatum game', *Science*, 300: 1755–1759.

Schelling, T. (1984) 'Self-command in practice, in policy, and in a theory of rational choice', *American Economic Review*, 74: 1–11.

Schelling, T. (1990) *Strategy of Conflict*, Cambridge, MA: Harvard University Press.

Schmidt, U., Starmer, C., and Sugden, R. (2008) 'Third generation prospect theory', *Journal of Risk and Uncertainty*, 36: 203–223.

Schmitt, P., Swope, K., and Walker, J. (2000) 'Collective action with incomplete commitment: Experimental evidence', *Southern Economic Journal*, 66: 829–854.

Schunk, D. (2009) 'Behavioral heterogeneity in dynamic search situations: Theory and experimental evidence', *Journal of Dynamics and Control,* 33: 1719–1738.

Selten, R. (1994) 'Biographical', available on the Nobel Prize website, www.nobelprize.org/nobel_prizes/economic-sciences/laureates/1994/selten-bio.html.

Selten, R. and Chmura, T. (2008) 'Stationary concepts for experimental 2x2 games', *American Economic Review*, 98: 938–966.

Selten, R., Abbink, K., and Cox, R. (2005) 'Learning direction theory and the winner's curse', *Experimental Economics*, 8: 5–20.

Sent, E-M. (2004) 'Behavioral economics: How psychology made its (limited) way back into economics', *History of Political Economy*, 36: 735–760.

Shafir, E. and Thaler, R. (2006) 'Invest now, drink later, spend never: On the mental accounting of delayed consumption', *Journal of Economic Psychology*, 27: 694–712.

Shafir, E., Simonson, I., and Tversky, A. (1993) 'Reason-based choice', *Cognition*, 11–36.

Shang, J. and Croson, R. (2009) 'A field experiment in charitable contribution: The impact of social information on the voluntary provision of public goods', *Economic Journal*, 119: 1422–1439.

Shapiro, M. D. and Slemrod, J. (2003) 'Consumer response to tax rebates', *American Economic Review*, 93: 381–396.

Shefrin, H. M. and Thaler, R. H. (1988) 'The behavioural life-cycle hypothesis', *Economic Inquiry*, 26: 609–643.

Shiller, R. J. (2003) 'From efficient markets theory to behavioural finance', *Journal of Economic Perspectives*, 17: 83–104.

Shiv, B. and Fedorikhin, A. (1999) 'Heart and mind in conflict: The interplay of affect and cognition in consumer decision making', *The Journal of Consumer Research*, 26: 278–292.

Shogren, J. F. and Taylor, L. O. (2008) 'On behavioral-environmental economics', *Review of Environmental Economics and Policy*, *2*(1), 26–44.

Siemens, J. C. (2007) 'When consumption benefits precede costs: Towards an understanding of "buy now, pay later" transactions', *Journal of Behavioral Decision Making*, 20: 521–531.

Simon, H. (1955) 'A behavioural model of rational choice', *Quarterly Journal of Economics*, 69: 99–118.

Simon, H. (1991) *Models of my Life*, London: Basic Books.

Simonsohn, U. and Loewenstein, G. (2006) 'Mistake #37: The effect of previously encountered prices on current housing demand', *Economic Journal*, 116: 175–199.

Simonson, I. and Tversky, A. (1992) 'Choice in context: Tradeoff contrast and extremeness aversion', *Journal of Marketing Research*, 29: 281–295.

Slonim, R. and Roth, A. (1998) 'Learning in high stakes ultimatum games: An experiment in the Slovak Republic', *Econometrica*, 66: 569–596.

Smith, D., Loewenstein, G., Jepson, C., Jankovich, A., Feldman, H., and Ubel, P. (2008) 'Mispredicting and misremembering: Patients with renal failure overestimate improvements in quality of life after a kidney transplant', *Health Psychology*, 27: 653–658.

Smith, V. L. (1962) 'An experimental study of competitive market behavior', *Journal of Political Economy*, 70: 111–137.

Smith, V. L. (1991) 'Rational choice: The contrast between economics and psychology', *Journal of Political Economy*, 877–897.

Smith, V. L. (1998) 'Experimental economics: Behavioral lessons for microeconomics theory and policy', in Jacobs, D., Kalai, E., Kamien, M., and N. Schwartz (Eds.), *Frontiers of Research in Economic Theory: The Nancy L. Schwartz Memorial Lectures, 1983–1997*, Cambridge: Cambridge University Press.

Smith, V. L. (2002) 'Markets, institutions and experiments', in L. Nadel (Ed.), *Encyclopedia of Cognitive Science*, London: John Wiley & Sons.

Smith, V. L. (2003) 'Constructivist and ecological rationality in economics', *American Economic Review*, 93: 465–508,

Smith, V. L., Suchanek, G. L., and Williams, A. W. (1988) 'Bubbles, crashes, and endogenous expectations in experimental spot asset markets', *Econometrica*, 56: 1119–1151.

Sobel, J. (2002) 'Can we trust social capital?', *Journal of Economic Literature*, 40: 139–154.

Sobel, J. (2005) 'Interdependent preferences and reciprocity', *Journal of Economic Literature*, 43: 392–436.

Solnick, S. (2001) 'Gender differences in the ultimatum game', *Economic Inquiry*, 39: 189–200.

Spitzer, M., Fischbacher, U., Herrnberger, B., Grön, G., and Fehr, E. (2007) 'The neural signature of social norm compliance', *Neuron*, 56: 185–196.

Starmer, C. (2000) 'Developments in non-expected utility theory: The hunt for a descriptive theory of choice under risk', *Journal of Economic Literature*, 2000: 332–382.

Stern, N. (2006) *Review on the Economics of Climate Change*, London: HM Treasury.

Strotz, R. H. (1956) 'Myopia and inconsistency in dynamic utility maximization', *Review of Economic Studies*, 23: 165–180.

Sugden, R. (1995) 'A theory of focal points', *Economic Journal*, 105: 533–550.

Sutter, M. (2005) 'Are four heads better than two? An experimental beauty-contest game with teams of different size', *Economics Letters*, *88*(1), 41–46.

Sutter, M. (2009) 'Deception through telling the truth?! Experimental evidence from individuals and teams', *The Economic Journal*, *119*(534), 47–60.

Sutter, M., Czermak, S., and Feri, F. (2013) 'Strategic sophistication of individuals and teams: Experimental evidence', *European Economic Review*.

Sydnor, J. (2010) '(Over)insuring modest risks', *American Economic Journal: Applied Economics* 2: 177–199.

Terrell, D. (1994) 'A test of the gambler's fallacy: Evidence from pari-mutuel games', *Journal of Risk and Uncertainty*, 8: 309–317.

Thaler, R. H. (1981) 'Some empirical evidence on dynamic inconsistency', *Economics Letters*, 8: 201–207.

Thaler, R. H. (1988) 'Anomalies: The ultimatum game', *Journal of Economic Perspectives*, 2: 195–206.

Thaler, R. H. (1990) 'Anomalies: Saving, fungibility, and mental accounts', *Journal of Economic Perspectives*, 4: 193–205.

Thaler, R. H. (2008a) 'Mental accounting and consumer choice', *Marketing Science*, 27: 15–25.

Thaler, R. H. (2008b) 'Mental accounting and consumer choice: Anatomy of a failure', *Marketing Science*, 27: 1–14.

Thaler, R. H. and Shefrin, H. M. (1981) 'An economic theory of self-control', *Journal of Political Economy*, 89: 392–406.

Thaler, R. H. and Benartzi, S. (2004) 'Save more tomorrow™: Using behavioral economics to increase employee saving', *Journal of political Economy*, *112*(S1), S164–S187.

Thaler, R. H. and Sunstein, C. R. (2008) *Nudge: Improving Decisions about Health, Wealth, and Happiness*, London: Yale University Press.

Todorov, A., Mandisodza, A. N., Goren, A., and Hall, C. C. (2005) 'Inferences of competence from faces predict election outcomes', *Science*, *308*(5728), 1623–1626.

Tricomi, E., Rangel, A., Camerer, C., and O'Doherty, J. (2010) 'Neural evidence for inequality-averse social preferences', *Nature*, 463: 1089–1092.

Tversky, A. and Kahneman, D. (1974) 'Judgment under uncertainty: Heuristics and biases', *Science*, 185: 1124–1131.

Tversky, A. and Kahneman, D. (1981) 'The framing of decisions and the psychology of choice', *Science*, 211: 453–458.

Tversky, A. and Kahneman, D. (1983) 'Extensional versus intuitive reasoning: The conjunction fallacy in probability judgment', *Psychological Review*, 90: 293–315.

Tversky, A. and Kahneman, D. (1986) 'Rational choice and the framing of decisions', *Journal of Business*, 59: S251–S278.

Tversky, A. and Kahneman, D. (1992) 'Advances in prospect theory: Cumulative representation of uncertainty', *Journal of Risk and Uncertainty*, 5: 297–323.

Tversky, A. and Shafir, E. (1992) 'Choice under conflict: The dynamics of deferred decision', *Psychological Science*, 3: 358–361.

Tversky, A., Kahneman, D., and Choice, R. (1981) 'The framing of decisions', *Science*, *211*, 453–458.

Tversky, A., Slovic, P., and Kahneman, D. (1990) 'The causes of preference reversal', *American Economic Review*, 80: 204–217.

Unver, U. (2005) 'On the survival of some unstable two-sided matching mechanisms', *International Journal of Game Theory*, 33: 239–254.

van Huyck, J., Battalio, R., and Beil, R. (1990) 'Tacit coordination games, strategic uncertainty, and coordination failure', *American Economic Review*, 80: 234–248.

Venkatraman, V., Payne, J., Bettman, J., Frances Luce, M., and Huettel, S. (2009) 'Separate neural mechanisms underlie choices and strategic preferences in risky decision making', *Neuron*, 62: 593–602.

Walker, M. and Wooders, J. (2001) 'Minimax play at Wimbledon', *American Economic Review*, 91: 1521–1538.

Wang, J. T. Y., Spezio, M., and Camerer, C. F. (2010) 'Pinocchio's pupil: Using eyetracking and pupil dilation to understand truth telling and deception in sender-receiver games', *American Economic Review*, 984–1007.

Warner, J. and Pleeter, S. (2001) 'The personal discount rate: Evidence from military downsizing programs', *American Economic Review*, 91: 33–53.

Weber, R. A. (2003) " 'Learning" with no feedback in a competitive guessing game', *Games and Economic Behavior*, 44: 134–144.

Webley, P. (2004) 'Children's understanding of economics', in Barrett, M. and Buchanan-Barrow, E., *Children's Understanding of Society*, Hove: Psychology Press.

Weizsäcker, G. (2010) 'Do we follow others when we should? A simple test of rational expectations', *American Economic Review*.

Wirtz, D., Kruger, J., Scollon, C. N., and Diener, E. (2003) 'What to do on spring break? The role of predicted, on-line, and remembered experience in future choice', *Psychological Science*, *14*(5), 520–524.

World Health Organization (WHO) (2009) *Global Health Risks: Mortality and Burden of Disease Attributable to Selected Major Risks*, Geneva: WHO Press.

World Values Survey 1981–2008 (2009) Official Aggregate v.20090901, World Values Survey Association (www.worldvaluessurvey.org). Aggregate File Producer: ASEP/JDS, Madrid.

Index

Voicing the Popular

On the Subjects of Popular Music

Richard Middleton

Routledge
Taylor & Francis Group
New York London

Routledge is an imprint of the
Taylor & Francis Group, an informa business

Published in 2006 by
Routledge
Taylor & Francis Group
270 Madison Avenue
New York, NY 10016

Published in Great Britain by
Routledge
Taylor & Francis Group
2 Park Square
Milton Park, Abingdon
Oxon OX14 4RN

Routledge is an imprint of Taylor & Francis Group

Printed in the United States of America on acid-free paper
10 9 8 7 6 5 4 3 2 1

International Standard Book Number-10: 0-415-97589-1 (Hardcover) 0-415-97590-5 (Softcover)
International Standard Book Number-13: 978-0-415-97589-6 (Hardcover) 978-0-415-97590-2 (Softcover)
Library of Congress Card Number 2005031321

Library of Congress Cataloging-in-Publication Data

Middleton, Richard.
Voicing the popular : on the subjects of popular music / by Richard Middleton.
p. cm.
Includes bibliographical references and index.
ISBN 0-415-97589-1 (hb) -- ISBN 0-415-97590-5 (pb)
1. Popular music--History and criticism. 2. Music--Philosophy and aesthetics. I. Title.

ML3470.M53 2006
781.6409--dc22 2005031321

Taylor & Francis Group
is the Academic Division of Informa plc.

Visit the Taylor & Francis Web site at
http://www.taylorandfrancis.com

and the Routledge Web site at
http://www.routledge-ny.com

Contents

Acknowledgments

Much of the work for this book was done during a year's research leave in 2003–04. This was funded partly by the University of Newcastle, partly by the Arts and Humanities Research Board of Great Britain, and I am grateful to both. The research benefited greatly from the efficiency and helpfulness of staff in the Robinson Library at the University of Newcastle, and in the British Library in London (including the National Sound Archive). I owe specific debts, for assistance in chasing up material or references, to Paul Attinello, Helen Barlow, Jan Fairley, Jim Garretts, and Trevor Herbert. David de la Haye kindly put the music examples through the mysterious processes of Sibelius notation software.

Parts of the book were presented, in earlier versions, to seminars in Newcastle, Liverpool and Berlin, to a British Forum for Ethnomusicology conference at Goldsmiths, London in 2003, to the International Association for the Study of Popular Music conference at Montreal in 2003, and to the Nordic Musicology Conference at Helsinki in 2004. My thanks to all participants for comments and discussion. A different version of part of Chapter 1 will be published in the journal *Popular Music* in 2006, and I am grateful to the editors and their readers for comments on this material. A different version of part of Chapter 5 is included in *Frispel: Festskrift till Olle Edström*, edited by Alf Björnberg, Mona Hallin, Lars Lilliestam and Ola Stockfelt (Göteborgs Universitet, 2005).

If my last book, *Studying Popular Music*, was in large part a product of my time at the Open University, this one is my "Newcastle University book." It is difficult to find words to express what I owe to colleagues at the International Centre for Music Studies at Newcastle since I moved there in 1998. ("International Centre," by the way, although an accurate enough label in many ways, is neo-Blairite waffle for what was previously a "Music

Department"; but "departments" are so last year.) Certainly the book would be very different without the impact of their eye- and ear-opening intellectual companionship and the benefits of working with them in such a creative and collegial setting. If I single out Ian Biddle, David Clarke, Bennett Hogg, and Goffredo Plastino, it is because they work in areas close to mine and I owe them quite specific debts; but I would want to acknowledge the profound effects that all ICMuS staff—and students too—have had upon my thinking, often to an extent and in ways, I suspect, beyond anything they realize. Particular thanks are due, too, to our two Visiting Professors, Phil Bohlman and Larry Kramer, who have read or heard several parts of the book, and whose own work and presence in Newcastle have been an inspiration. I hope the book will be seen as a component in a broader scholarly, pedagogical and creative enterprise which is taking shape at Newcastle in what I believe is a quite remarkable way (I can say this in a semi-detached spirit since, as I write, I have just retired).

This debt sits at the tip of a pyramid whose foundations go deep and wide. My most obvious intellectual obligations are documented in the endnotes; but who could draw, in all their detail, the full dimensions of his biographical intertext? I have been thinking a lot recently about the significance of such interconnections and dependencies. It is a significance germane to the politics of this book. At a time when the word "socialism" has been consigned to museums or reduced to distorting mythologies, many people—and not exclusively the young—need reminding that our lives actually contain important pockets and models of socialistic practice. To adapt Marx: we may not know it but we are doing it. While academic and intellectual life is of course often sullied by petty competition, egotism, and assertion of property rights, there is here as well, at best, a collective network—a commons of the mind—within which we not only stand on the shoulders of giants but work with them daily. Given the reifying effects of "isms" and "ologies," and the totalizing "solutions" to which they have often led, perhaps we would indeed do better to put the word "socialism" to one side, look to and engage with the multifarious desires teeming around the political unconscious, and concentrate on the laborious critical work of transforming practice in specific spheres.

As important an arena for this as any is the home. My largest debt of all is to my dear wife and partner, Jane, who has responded with good humor (and sometimes with humor) to an assortment of often bizarre ideas, sprung on her at the least predictable moments (including the middle of the night); at the same time, getting on with her own work, which has probably achieved more good than I could ever claim.

CHAPTER **1**

Introduction

"We're Low, We're Low, We're Very, Very Low"

"The voice of the people is the voice of God:" so proclaimed the British Chartists in the revolutionary year of 1848.[1] The singularity of the grammar — one god, one people — obscures the political reality of contestation: where was this voice to be located, who owned it? While for many Chartists the slogan no doubt simply implied that "God is on our side" — a position memorably satirized a century later by Bob Dylan — or perhaps that democracy can claim divine inspiration, readers today can hardly fail to note the motif of usurpation: the authority vested in what the psychoanalyst Jacques Lacan called the "Name-of-the-Father" is claimed by a new god, the People, a transposition concretely pursued by many post-Chartist socialists and communists.[2] But not always with one voice; nor, often, without drowning out alternative sounds. Who, then, is entitled to this voice of the people? And what do they have to tell us?

Ernest Jones, the "Chartist poet laureate," was one who certainly laid claim to it, for instance, in the political soirées (or "evenings for the people") he organized in London in 1856, at which such pieces of his as "The Song of the Lower Classes" were sung by his composer friend John Lowry.[3]

We plough and sow — we're so very, very low
    That we delve in the dirty clay,
Till we bless the plain — with the golden grain,
    And the vale with the fragrant hay.
Our place we know — we're so very, very low,
    'Tis down at the landlord's feet:
We're not too low — the bread to grow,
    But too low the bread to eat.

Chorus: We're not too low — the bread to grow,
    But too low the bread to eat.

Down, down we go — we're so very low,
    To the hell of the deep sunk mines,
But we gather the proudest gems that glow,
    When the crown of a despot shines.
And whenever he lacks — upon our backs
    Fresh loads he deigns to lay:
We're far too low to vote the tax,
    But not too low to pay.

Chorus: We're far too low [etc.]

We're low — we're low — mere rabble, we know,
    But, at our plastic power,
The mould at the lordling's feet will grow
    Into palace and church and tower —
Then prostrate fall — in the rich man's hall,
    And cringe at the rich man's door:
We're not too low to build the wall,
    But too low to tread the floor.

Chorus: We're not too low [etc.]

We're low — we're low — we're very, very low,
    Yet from our fingers glide
The silken flow — and the robes that glow
    Round the limbs of the sons of pride.
And what we get — and what we give,
    We know, and we know our share:
We're not too low the cloth to weave,
    But too low the cloth to wear!

Chorus: We're not too low [etc.]

We're low — we're low — we're very, very low,
    And yet when the trumpets ring,
The thrust of a poor man's arm will go
    Thro' the heart of the proudest King.
We're low — we're low — our place we know,
    We're only the rank and file,
We're not too low — to kill the foe,
    But too low to touch the spoil.

Chorus: We're not too low [etc.]

Version 1
We're low, we're low, we're so ve - ry, ve - ry low That we delve in the dir - ty
Version 2
Marcato
We plough and sow we're so ve - ry, ve - ry low that we delve in the dir - ty
clay. Till we bless the plain with the gol - den grain, The vale with the new mown
clay, Till we bless the plain with the gol - den grain, And the vale with the fra - grant
hay. Our place we know, we're so ve - ry ve - ry low, 'Tis
hay Our place we know we're so ve - ry low, 'Tis
down at the land - lord's feet; We're not too low the bread to grow But too
down at the land - lord's feet, we're not too low the grain to grow, But too
low the bread to eat.
Chorus
low the bread to eat. We're not too low the
bread to grow, But too low the bread to eat.

Example 1.1

The discursive territory is familiar, and was so at the time Jones wrote, organized as it is around the opposition of rich and poor, property and labor. While it would have had enormous resonance in the 1840s, the theme was ancient (as John Ball's couplet from the time of the fourteenth-century Peasants' Revolt put it, "When Adam delved and Eve span/Who was then the gentleman?"), and there is nothing in the words to tie it specifically to the turmoil accompanying the birth of the world's first industrial working class: none of the categories of work (farming, mining, building, weaving, soldiering) is new, and the language is hardly "proletarian," rather "poetic," even biblical. Similarly, the style of Lowry's tune, as János Maróthy points out, derives from that of the bourgeois marches that developed out of song-types typical of the vaudeville, comic opera, and pleasure-garden repertories of the late eighteenth century. (Papageno's music in Mozart's *Die Zauberflőte* offers the most familiar example today.) At the same time, the initial $\hat{5}$-$\hat{1}$ upbeat — a call to attention, or to arms — recalls the beginning of the *Marseillaise* (a model followed by innumerable other marches and political songs of the nineteenth century). Moreover, Maróthy argues that the lyrical, balanced shapes of the melody — typical of song patterns in the emergent bourgeois culture — are broken up rhythmically and energized by slogan-like repetitions ("we're low, we're low"), internal rhyme and variation, and "heavy," even "stamping," or "smashing" crotchets ("our place we know"), which, as a musical tactic, he finds to be at the same time characteristic of nineteenth-century worker's song and typical of a plebeian song lineage traceable as far back as the Middle Ages. The figure of the Low conjured up here, then, faces in several directions: towards the people constructing themselves as the revolutionary citizenry of the *Marseillaise*; as an emergent working class, poised to smash the bourgeois system; as representatives of long-suffering yet resilient plebeian forces recently conceptualized by Romantics like Jones as a *Vőlk*.[4]

Interestingly, Maróthy takes his version of the song (Version 1 in Example 1.1) from a Workers Music Association pamphlet published much later. Comparing this to the first song sheet (Version 2), we find that the "smashing crotchets" are less evident in Lowry's original tune (see bars 8–10, for example), which contains a level of lyrical decoration that is simplified out in the later version (bars 6–7, 15). Presumably a process of folklorization has taken place. The slogan-like rhymes and heavy rhythm on which Maróthy comments are certainly present in Jones's text, and it is as if the music — probably as a result of its performance history — has been made to "catch up" (most of Lowry's other extant compositions fall into the category or style of drawing-room ballad). Perhaps this is also why the chorus indicated in the original publications — implying solo performance of the verses — has disappeared in the WMA version: by now, the music suggests collective delivery throughout.[5]

Still, even if we detect a slight mismatch in the original between text and tune, the prettiness of the melody finds its complement in Jones's romanticized language and imagery. As a comparison between the "dynamizing" dotted notes of the *Marseillaise* [♪♪ ♪♩] and the Mozartian lyrical quavers of "We're Low" suggests, this "people" is, whatever qualifications might be entered, quite well-bred. Jones's "evenings for the people" were, as he put it, "an attempt to combine elevating Recreation with Political Instruction — to raise Politics from the Sphere of the Tavern, by associating them with the refinements of Music of the choicest character, the finest Professional Talent, Vocal and Instrumental, being engaged for each Soirée."[6]

Raised and educated in rural northern Germany, Ernest Jones was deeply influenced by *Vőlkisch* conservatism, and by the German and English early Romantics on whom, in diluted forms, this tendency drew. On his return to England in 1838, he studied law, moving in aristocratic London circles, and also broke through as a writer of verse and romances. An increasing sense of social mission in the early 1840s led to his conversion to the Chartist cause, but, despite a friendship with Marx and Engels (beginning in 1847), Jones's basic historical picture, rooted in a vision of lost pastoral harmony, disrupted by industrialism and a ruling-class usurpation, never left him. It was a mythic construction not untypical of the Chartist leadership. "If these histories had a 'people' as their subject, then the people were simple peasant folk… Primitive rebels perhaps, but nothing more."[7] In the early 1850s, as some elements in a now declining Chartism were moving left, Jones's main cause, promoted in novels and in the newspapers he was producing, was land nationalisation; and by the 1860s he had moved into mainstream reform politics.

This is not to denigrate Jones's devotion to the people's cause, which was generous and unstinting. Rather, this example draws attention to some important scene-setting points. First, "the people" was searching for, and to some extent, finding a voice. In the era of democratic and industrial revolutions, this was not surprising. Second, this voice was *plural*; it was, implicitly or explicitly, internally contested. In a period when social and political formations were in flux, this too was not surprising. Third, this contestation was overdetermined by the effects of the larger social nexus, which we can begin to think of in terms of *class*; most notably, the people's voice was often, to a greater or lesser extent, spoken for it from elsewhere — or, at least, was forced to move within an orbit conditioned by "higher" cultural forces.

None of these features, considered separately, was completely new. What was novel, in the century or so leading up to 1848, was their combination, which was both the result and the motivating force of a new sense of *social space* — a space we must understand as "theatrical," that is, set on a stage peopled by social actors whose self-presentations can be grasped only in terms of their interactions. On one level this trend finds its manifestation in the new or reformed political assemblies, and the theories of, and debates over, representation of the various social interests that accompanied them. In the cultural sphere, the key genre was musical theater: opera, of course, but also lower forms such as pantomime and then music hall and (in the United States) minstrel show, and even pleasure garden and dance hall, where, in a sense, patrons, with the aid of the musical and other entertainments, "played themselves." Small wonder that nontheatrical popular songs in the nineteenth century often drew on musical theater repertoires for their tunes, a tendency that continued in the relationship between Broadway and Hollywood on the one hand, Tin Pan Alley on the other, in the earlier part of the twentieth century. It is on this stage — a social stage in a broad sense — that the "Song of the Lower Classes" airs its voice.

What was developing was a new type of musical semiotics of the social, a new mode of musical representation, replacing even as, to some extent, it drew upon, the older, more abstract codes associated with the relatively enclosed worlds of court and church music. The principal source, from the early eighteenth century, lay in the range of comic opera genres — *opera buffa*, ballad opera, *opéra comique*, *Singspiel*, and so on — genres which opened up the possibility, and also required, that composers should develop ways of putting "low" characters and situations on the stage and of representing their relationships with their betters. Mozart's *Die Zauberflöte* provides the classic case.

First performed in 1791, a mere two years after the beginning of the French Revolution, Mozart's *Singspiel* is shot through with ideals of deistic rationalism and universal fraternity; its hymn-like moments, indeed, can be heard as transposing the voice of God into a context marked by visions of secular illumination: enlightenment, potentially, for all. But the work does much more. In peopling his stage with representatives of interlocking social hierarchies — of gender and race as well as class — Mozart not only tells a story with universalistic claims, he also points (at least for those familiar with twentieth-century deconstructions of Enlightenment narratives) to the contradictions and foreclosures on which these claims were built. For there is, it seems, only one way to the truth and it comes from on high. I have written elsewhere[8] on the way that Mozart constructs, through musico-narrative structure and contrasts of musical style, a series of intersecting, alteritous relationships in which identities (of class, gender, race) are represented in terms of their others; for example, the birdcatcher Papageno is presented not only as a peasant simpleton (in relation to the heroic Tamino) but also as "girlish" — and yet at the same time capable of both learning (from his betters, the female heroine Pamina as well as Tamino) and of achieving patriarchal normality (marrying the equally low-class Papagena in the end), and also of mastering *his* other, the Moorish villain Monostatos and his black slaves.

The ideal selfhood, to which Tamino and Panima ultimately win through, is possible only through a set of distinctions which at the same time function as constitutive relationships: hierarchies that are always tending towards binary simplification. Crucially, the terms that occupy the "other" positions in this formation — the multivalent yet interlocking voices of what has been called the Low-Other — are portrayed as attractive as well as dangerous, enticing as well as subordinate. They possess magical powers, alien to Enlightenment norms, and yet require magic, good magic, to control them.

We have arrived here at a fairly developed stage in "the formation of the cultural Imaginary of the middle class in post-Renaissance Europe," a process involving (especially by the late eighteenth century) "an internal distancing from the popular which was complex and often contradictory in its effects."[9] Internal distance of course assumes external contiguity, that is, a shared social theater — a condition that the liberal bourgeoisie of Europe, watching as the events of the French Revolution unfolded, hearing of the world's first black anti-colonial revolution (led by Toussaint L'Ouverture in Haiti in 1791), reading Mary Wollstonecrafts's *Vindication of the Rights of Woman* (1792), could not escape.

Mozart's opera was only one in a huge repertoire of racy, spectacular, and exotic entertainments popular in the late eighteenth and early nineteenth centuries, drawing on many of the same themes. *Omai, or A Trip round the World,*[10] produced in London in 1785, shifts its focus further towards the black-other (not surprising in a country now confident of its status as the world's leading colonial power), and locates this figure not in Mozart's "Moorish" orient but in the South Seas — specifically Tahiti, recently explored by Captain James Cook. *Omai*, a proto-operatic masque-cum-pantomime, was a collaboration between the Irish playwright John O' Keeffe, the composer William Shield, and the designer Philippe de Loutherbourg, whose extraordinarily elaborate sets and apparatuses, bringing together innovatory design, lighting, sound effects, and theater machinery, were already celebrated; they gave "natural motion to accurate resemblance," according to one contemporary description.[11] The eponymous hero was based on a real Omai — a "prince" from Tahiti, brought back and shown around England by Cook's colleague, the botanist Sir Joseph Banks, in 1774–76, and quickly feted as a perfectly gentlemanly Noble Savage. Tahiti, discovered in 1768, had been speedily assimilated to existing images of exotic paradise. But in *Omai* the exoticism is presented as not only titillating but also dangerous: there is black magic as well as white. This exoticism is one side of a coin whose verso portrays the island's politics, of both statecraft and gender, as surprisingly similar to those of Europe, and gives to its leading characters — the king, Otoo, and the witch/goddesses, good and bad, Towha and Oberea — musical styles drawn from European high-art genres.

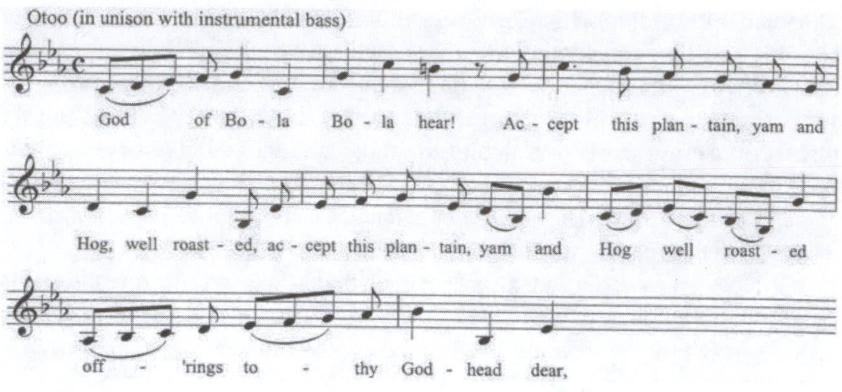
Otoo (in unison with instrumental bass)
God of Bo - la Bo - la hear! Ac - cept this plan - tain, yam and
Hog, well roast - ed, ac - cept this plan - tain, yam and Hog well roast - ed
off - 'rings to - thy God - head dear,

Example 1.2

Consider, for example, the Purcellian mode of awestruck grandeur in Otoo's initial appeal to his gods (he wants them to confirm his son Omai as his successor). (See Example 1.2, above.)

Or Towha's response, after the high-flown manner (one that can be found in Mozart) of Italian *opera seria*. (See Example 1.3, below)

Towha
My A - riel Band art rea - dy to run to swim to fly at
my com - mand to run to swim to
fly at my com - mand

Example 1.3

Whether we are to attribute this connection to natural good breeding (as in Rousseauian ideas of primitive nobility) or to Europe's civilizing mission is a question decided in this musical assimilation as much as in the opening and closing set-piece tributes to Britannia's benign political role. At the start, Omai, appointed his successor by Otoo, is sent off to Britain to claim his bride Londina by a vision of Britannia conjured up by the goddess Towha.

Britannia: Mark, votive Islander, thy fate is mine
For mine
The Queen of Isles, the mistress of the main!
Upon my sea-girt shore, by Neptune fenc'd,
Kind greeting, pleasure, welcome sweet receive;
Still shall my sons, by Cook's example taught,
Thy new-found world protect and humanise,
In soft alliance bound, this British maid
Be thine, and Love, a radiant throne shall fix
Firm as my rock, where sits bright Liberty.

And in the final scene, as Cook's death is mourned (by a Chorus of Indians) and his immortality saluted, the imperial assimilation is completed.

Captain: Accept of mighty George our sovereign lord,
In sign of British love, this British sword.
Oberea: Oh joy! Away my useless spells and magic charms,
A British sword is proof against the world in arms.

A sentiment sealed in the Captain's final air.

He [i.e., Cook] came, and he saw, not to conquer, but save;
The Caesar of Britain was he;
Who scorned the ambition of making a slave
While Britons themselves are so free.

Within three years, William Wilberforce would establish the British movement to abolish slavery. But the rulers of Britain, flushed with their emergent European hegemony, would resist both French and American ideas of freedom, and would impose their patronage on many millions overseas; mastery, liberty, and difference were not so easy to conjoin — a point that would shortly be given theoretical richness by the philosopher Hegel in his discourse of master and slave.[12]

It is perhaps not surprising, then, that the representations of the lower characters in *Omai* are more interesting than those of their masters; nor that the musical styles chosen for examples of British low-life and for foreign others tend to run together. In the songs of a comic Water Cress Woman and Raffling Toy Shop Man, there is an alternation between a "folky" style, indebted to the contemporary taste for "Irish" music, and a pared-down "clockwork" style similar to that in some of Papageno's songs.[13] (See Example 1.4 and Example 1.5, next page.)

In the closing "English Sailor's Song," these two lineages fuse in a way that both harks back to an existing national-patriotic ("roast beef and naval

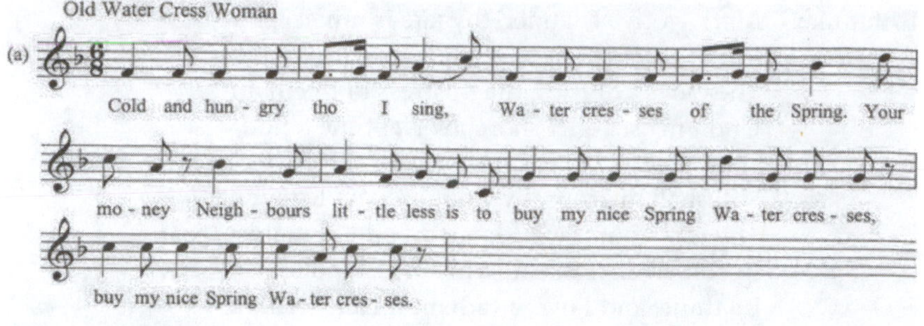

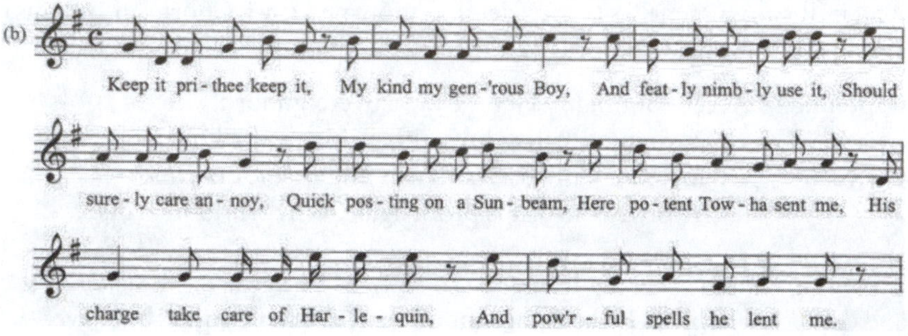

Example 1.4

Example 1.5

Old Tune
When I come back to bon - ny Shad - well Dock. Fol de rol lol de ra Fol de
rol lol la How the Girls will stare at their friend Jack Block, with his
chip chow, Cher - ry chow, Fol de lid - dle la de do, Fol lol la.

Example 1.6

supremacy") repertoire, and outlines the route that would carry us to the world of the "Song of the Lower Classes" (note the $\hat{5}$-$\hat{1}$ upbeat). (See Example 1.6, above.)

Compare now two songs heard during Omai's return from London to the South Seas, courtesy of a geographically bewildering but no doubt scenically entertaining itinerary (a Cook's Tour, one might say); first, a Chorus of Villagers of the Friendly Islands (see Example 1.7, next page).

And second, a song of an Otaheitean Traveller (see Example 1.8, page 13).

The latter, like the second strain of the "Toy Shop Man's" song, is described explicitly in the score as an "Irish Tune"; but its style — with its lopsided harmonic grammar (chord-changes in the "wrong" place) and unfinished structure, which refuses a perfect cadence — also looks forward to a song-type that would shortly become familiar in the blacked-up voices of the minstrel show: a connection cemented further by the equally cock-eyed grammar of the lyrics ("Teach me sail no paddle") and their liberal use of caricatured pronunciation ("de" and "den"; and later in the lyrics, "dis" and "dat" too). In the final verse, the Traveller, telling of his stay in London, describes how his attempted wooing of a "lady fine" (who called him an "ugly devil") was interrupted by her husband, who "give my head a tump" crying "get out dam Negar." Admittedly, these two songs move somewhat more unequivocally towards the folky end of the spectrum (even though this is "Irish" as much as "black"); but this marks a relational difference within a structure of family resemblance: a powerful alteritizing impulse brings together the English street, Ireland, the African diaspora, and the exotic South into an interchangeable cast of others.[14]

Within this structure, the triangular trade linking Africa, Europe, and America is particularly interesting. The blackface performance genres of proto-minstrelsy would not get under way in the United States for another fifteen years or so; but the representational mode heard in Shield's "Traveller's Song" was already familiar, both in Britain and in America. Charles Dibdin's

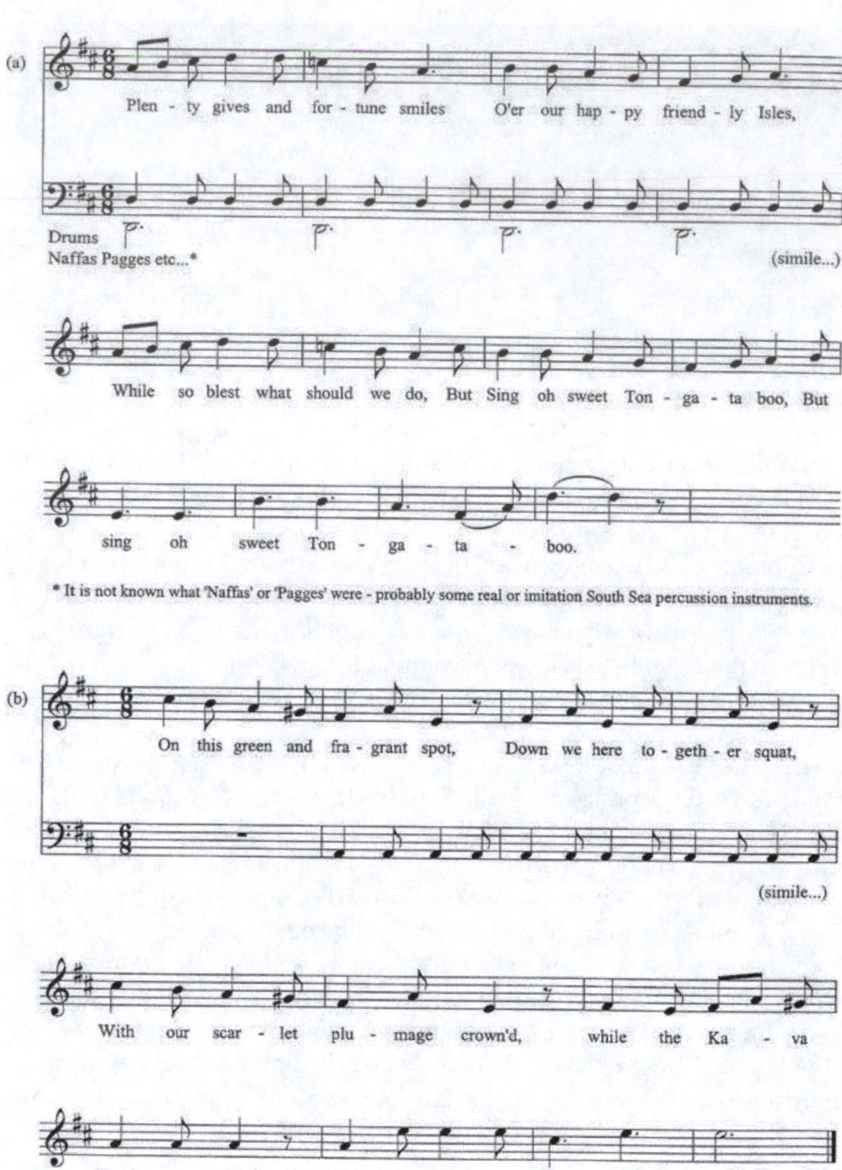
(a)
Plen - ty gives and for - tune smiles O'er our hap - py friend - ly Isles,
Drums
Naffas Pagges etc...*
(simile...)
While so blest what should we do, But Sing oh sweet Ton - ga - ta boo, But
sing oh sweet Ton - ga - ta - boo.
* It is not known what 'Naffas' or 'Pagges' were - probably some real or imitation South Sea percussion instruments.
(b)
On this green and fra - grant spot, Down we here to - geth - er squat,
(simile...)
With our scar - let plu - mage crown'd, while the Ka - va
bowl goes round while the Ka - va bowl goes round.

Example 1.7

Example 1.8

The Padlock was the first opera to feature a blackface character — Mungo, whose two songs are in the clockwork style previously described[15] — and this crossed the Atlantic only a year after its London premiere (1768). The transatlantic traffic in musical theater was brisk (as far as we know, *Omai* was not performed in the United States, but fifteen other works by Shield were); and, given the huge amount of blackface performance in the American theater following *The Padlock*, it is tempting to speculate that the influence in this specific respect may have traveled westward as well as eastward. The musical similarities between the style of many early minstrel show songs and that of contemporary "Scots" and, especially, "Irish" songs has often been noticed; Shield's "Irish" "Traveller's Song," for example, inhabits the same musical world as the famous "Jump Jim Crow," introduced by Thomas D. Rice around 1828 — provocative travel indeed![16]

This connection can be explained away as a product of white bourgeois condescension: a self-consciously crude style doing service for a whole range of backward cultures, whose differences are too trivial to require representation. But, while such assimilation may indeed have served bourgeois purposes, we should be careful about reducing agency too far: W. T. Lhamon sees the early minstrel style as marking the formation of a "plebeian Atlantic," and Dale Cockrell , who agrees with Lhamon that the songs were performed and enjoyed by a cross-racial proletariat, argues that "the meaning of 'Jim Crow' is thus slippery — all contestation and ambiguity"; Eric Lott suggests that "It was through 'blackness' that class was staged... blackface... *figured* class — ... its languages of race so invoked ideas about class as to provide displaced maps or representations of 'working-classness.'"[17] For Lhamon, "blackface developed distinct responses to 'amalgamation' — not by attacking but my enacting miscegenation." Is this how we should interpret English music hall singers, Joe Cowell and his son Sam, singing blackface songs in the Unites States in 1829–30 and then taking them back to Britain; in which direction was this trade running?[18]

The interface of race and class is not the only ambiguity within the exchange economy of *Omai.* The Water Cress Woman is the only solo female role, except for Towha and Oberea — whose contending magics pursue Omai on his journey home — and the rather pathetic Oedidee, Omai's childhood (male) friend and rival for the kingship, whose part is marked to be sung (pantomime-style presumably) by a woman. Thus the space of Woman is either filled by the supernatural, the comic, the sentimental (Oedidee's song of friendship and submission, "O'er Groves of Coral," is close to the low style already described), or is left blank.[19] Interestingly, the character of Omai is also something of a blank: throughout the work, he never speaks or sings. In a provocative reading, Christa Knellwolf[20] suggests that, although the story presents his visit to Britain as a civilizing process, the context of pantomime laughter would have rendered any exoticism unstable; his silence, then, is deliberate, "demanding that the audience should acknowledge its inability to understand who he is and what he stands for." We should note, however, that, like most pantomimes of the time, *Omai* was a harlequinade, and in this tradition Harlequin was always played as a silent mime. Yet in the sources, it is Omai's servant (it is he who is addressed by the Water Cress Woman in Example 1.4b) who is given the role of Harlequin; presumably, then, Omai acts as his double, mimicking his appearance and behaviour, silenced to the power two. The *commedia dell'arte* character of Harlequin had always been played in a black mask, and Knellwolf argues that Omai must have blacked up, too; thus "he acquires Harlequin's uncanny power to play with make-believe." But this power is at one remove, relayed through his *Doppelgänger* servant. By mingling with characters from English low-life and European fantasy (not to mention women and cross-dressers), Omai becomes an odd one out who is at the same time familiar; he takes over "their carnivalesque right to challenge hierarchies," and so, while subsumed by the end into "a celebration of Cook and by extension, the British Empire," he also retains "a subversive presence."[21] This problematic, in which the low-other questions its place and *answers back* — whether in play, on license, or for real — would go on to have a long history, even if, at times, it is dumbness or a loud invisibility which bespeak its presence.

The role of magic, in both *Omai* and *Die Zauberflöte*, is telling. It is as if reasonable men can banish the old superstitions, and safeguard their own identity and power, only through a superior magic, while restricting these transactions (so it seemed) to the fanciful spaces of art and entertainment. Thus in Mozart's opera, the manly magic of the Enlightenment sees off the black arts of the Queen of the Night, while in *Omai* the battle of unreason is removed back to the South Seas, where it serves to usher in Britannic rule. Marina Warner notes that within the genre of fantastic entertainments to which *Omai* belonged, great play was often made of the theme of the *genie*, the "slave of the lamp" in the highly popular pantomime *Aladdin* (first staged — in a work by, once again, Shield and O'Keefe — in London in 1788).[22] This figure, devoid of will and feeling, was often compared adversely to the free citizens of Europe and just as often transmutes, in the imagery, into a caricatured African. In *Omai* the magic talisman given to Omai by Towha, which causes involuntary sneezing, yawning, whistling, laughing, and crying, serves a similar role. In societies building their identity on the basis of forced labor, at home and abroad, to imagine summoning a slave by rubbing Aladdin's lamp, and banishing him at will, must have possessed striking symbolic value — even if, for later observers, it brings out the irony of a lamp of enlightenment guaranteed by irrational belief and imposed at the point of a sword. This is the mark of what Slavoj Žižek has called the "invisible master" — the belief that "behind the public Master (who, of course, is an impostor), there is a hidden Master who effectively keeps everything under control."[23] Indeed, as Warner explains,[24] this is exactly how it works in the Aladdin stories, where the ultimate master of the genies rarely appears. But if this Master is invisible, he is by no means silent. As "dictator" — the voice of authority within the subject (in the unconscious) — he runs the show, the author-function in *Omai*, for example, working its magic through a complex series of relays enabling it to stand in not only for the bourgeois self, but for a spectrum of positions with the imperatives of the British state at one end, the otherness of the South Seas (Africa, blackface, the Celtic margins) at the other. Yet, as Steven Connor reminds us, this manifestation of ventriloquism assumes a relationship that is potentially bidirectional: Omai the ventriloquist's dummy (not invisible but silent) asks of his masters if they are not also dummies, not only pulling the strings but also being pulled.[25]

In a sense, then, theatrical magic mirrored the magic of enlightenment — and also, we might add, of capitalism. The extraordinary development in the theater of mechanized effects such as Loutherbourg's conjured up, and controlled, nature — and at the same time exploited this entertainment as a newly accessible leisure commodity. The term "phantasmagoria" was coined to describe a new, more sophisticated type of magic lantern show put on in London in 1802, with immediate success. The name was subsequently applied widely to a variety of illusionist entertainments, and, metaphorically, to other phenomena with similar features: hallucination (usually with the frisson of the supernatural — spectre and ghost) and mutability (shifting, dissolving images).[26] But such entertainments had an ancestry going back as far as the sixteenth century, part of a broad, developing interest in representational technologies that were not without their religious ambivalence: the Devil was supposedly a skilful mimic, and image-making itself could be considered problematical, yet representation — producing accurate, useful or affecting maps of reality — might also be considered an important part of secularizing humanity's increasing mastery of nature. Small wonder that Marx would take up this discourse in order to probe the seemingly magical representational system of the commodity form under capitalism:

> The mysterious character of the commodity-form consists... simply in the fact that the commodity reflects the social characteristics of men's own labour as objective characteristics of the products of labor themselves... It is nothing but the definite social relation between men themselves which assumes here, for them, the phantasmagoric form of a relation between things. In order, therefore, to find an analogy we must take flight into the misty realm of religion. There the products of the human brain appear as autonomous figures endowed with a life of their own... So it is in the world of commodities... I call this the fetishism which attaches itself to the products of labor as soon as they are produced as commodities...[27]

We can pursue the lineaments of this phantasmagoric economy, in which a magical movement of exchange via processes of representation courses through the production apparatuses of human subject, social body, and political economy alike, back to an earlier emergent moment: back to the England of the South Sea Bubble of 1720, followed a few years later by a musical theater work that sketched many of the elements of the new economy — John Gay's *The Beggar's Opera* of 1728.[28]

Gay's work was the first ballad opera, remaining popular and influential throughout the eighteenth century (and beyond).[29] At this early stage in the development of the new representational economy, differentiation of social personae is much less than would become possible later. Indeed, by setting the whole of the opera in the criminal world of London low-life, while at the same time holding this world up as a mirror of the corruption of contemporary high society, Gay leaves the parallelisms between high and low that we observed in *Die Zauberflöte* and *Omai* — the "similitude of manners in high and low life," as his Beggar describes it — at a largely implicit level. The plot — revolving around the betrayal and imprisonment of Macheath, leader of a band of thieves, and the competition between the jailer's daughter, Lucy Lockit, and the fence's daughter, Polly Peachum, for his affections — mimics typical operatic narrative *topoi*. But all the music for Gay's songs comes from preexisting sources, the majority from popular songs current at the time, to be found on song sheets, broadsides, and, in many cases, two famous published tune collections from the seventeenth- and early-eighteenth centuries, *The Dancing Master* and *Wit and Mirth: Or Pills to Purge Melancholy* — the popularity of which already reflected a burgeoning aristocratic and bourgeois interest in vernacular music.[30] The vigor and expressive simplicity of these tunes must have seemed attractive across the political spectrum of elite society, even though Gay's purpose in deploying them to attack the skulduggery of the Whig ascendancy as it cashed in on economic expansion exemplifies a specifically conservative/aristocratic mode of identification with the common people (Gay moved in Tory circles).

If this is an appropriation — an opera that we must imagine written and put on by beggars — it is one that works by a sort of inversion: the audience must locate itself wholesale in the rough and salacious world of thieves and whores, from where it is then invited to appropriate — or de-appropriate? — at any rate, lampoon itself. Only, of course, to distance itself at the play's end, for this is but make-believe, as the Beggar's ironic introduction and closing scene make clear. Although, he says, "I have not made my Opera throughout unnatural, like those in vogue," he has included the poetic language and "pathetic" prison-scene required by the genre, and consents at the end to the necessary "absurdity" of a happy ending, for "an opera must end happily . . . to comply with the taste of the town."[31] The audience, then, is a character in the drama, which, on one level, is *about* the technology of representation; and in this sense, it is what Jonathon Swift suggested his friend should write, a "Newgate pastoral," the arcadian pretenses of court ritual transposed to the grubby world — and urban romanticism — of mercantile capitalism.

From this perspective, Gay's musical strategy, bringing together popular tunes from a range of contexts — dance, theater, ballad — and periods — from the sixteenth century to the present — is holistic: they are all tied together to form one world, whose ambivalence — is it high or low? — is unsettling only up to the limit imposed by the sense of cultural closure. Nowhere is this unifying move clearer than in the remarkable medley of song-fragments sung by the (anti-) hero, Macheath, as he meditatively contemplates his expected execution. He segues quickly (Airs 58–67) through snatches of recent theater song tunes, Carey's "Sally in Our Alley," sixteenth- and seventeenth-century ballads, including "Chevy Chase," dance tunes based on sixteenth-century grounds, such as the *passamezzo antico*, ending with the immortal "Greensleeves," in a scene that works both as stream of consciousness and as a fantasy of national cultural identity: the internal structures of self and of society are conjoined.

Perhaps it is not quite so simple, though. It appears that the songs had very simple accompaniments — continuo, including new bass parts written by the composer Johann Christoph Pepusch, together with violins doubling the voice — and this arrangement continued to be popular, despite the subsequent appearance of more elaborate settings, right down to the early nineteenth century. The contrast between this sound-world and that of contemporary *opera seria* may have had something of the same impact as that associated with the top-and-bottom crudity of rock 'n' roll textures in their confrontation with the more harmonically filled out arrangements of Tin Pan Alley ballads. At the same time, Pepusch did "civilize" the tunes. For the later music historian, Charles Burney, writing in 1789, he "furnished the wild, rude, and often vulgar melodies with bases so excellent that no sound contrapuntist will ever attempt to alter them."[32] This suggestion of ambivalence between high and low is intensified by the fact that Gay uses, alongside all the vernacular tunes, a few by contemporary opera composers, Italian as well as English. Admittedly, these seem as a rule to have a satiric purpose: a heroic march from Handel's *Rinaldo* serves to carry our troop of thieves into action (Air 20); and aria tunes by Handel, Bononcini, and Sandoni are used for Mrs. Peachum's meditation on female love (Air 4), Lucy's fury at Macheath's betrayal of her (Air 28), and Polly's despair at his betrayal of her (Air 34); but this mockery of high-flown sentiment begins to open up the social space.

Of the many "Scottish" tunes, several (including some of the most Scots in character, melodically and rhythmically) are reserved for Polly and Lucy at poignant moments of lament and parting (Airs 17, 40, 49, 52).[33] (See Example 1.9, below.)

Example 1.9

The first (17) is part of a triptych, Lucy's lament being preceded and followed by duets with Macheath, the second of which is, again, to a Scottish tune, the first to the very modal "Over the Hills and Far Away," with imagined exotic settings summoned in the words ("Were I laid on Greenland's coast . . . "; "Were I sold on Indian soil . . . "). Similarly, a sexy pastoral of cock and hens (Air 23) is set to "an excellent North-Country tune," "All in a Misty Morning" (also known as "The Fryar and the Nun"), while by contrast (or perhaps not), female comedy (Air 36 for Lucy and Polly: "I'm bubbled — I'm bubbled. Oh how I am troubled! Bamboozled, and bit! — My distresses are doubled") is given an "Irish Trot" ("a Scotch Song made to the Irish Jigg").

It seems that for moments of lament, of ribaldry, or of comedy (especially if associated with women), Gay looks to the uncouth margins of the British state. If so, this might prompt an ethnic interpretation of his use (Air 44) of the anti-papist tune, "Lillibulero," favorite song of the Whiggish Glorious Revolution, to lampoon the "modes of court" under the Whig government: who is speaking here through this "new Irish tune" (perhaps, though not definitely, composed by Purcell)? It might even license an interpretation of Lucy's "South Sea Ballad" (Air 42) that links the tune to the "Irish blackface clockwork" style found in many of the "low" songs in *Omai*, with which it shares technical characteristics:

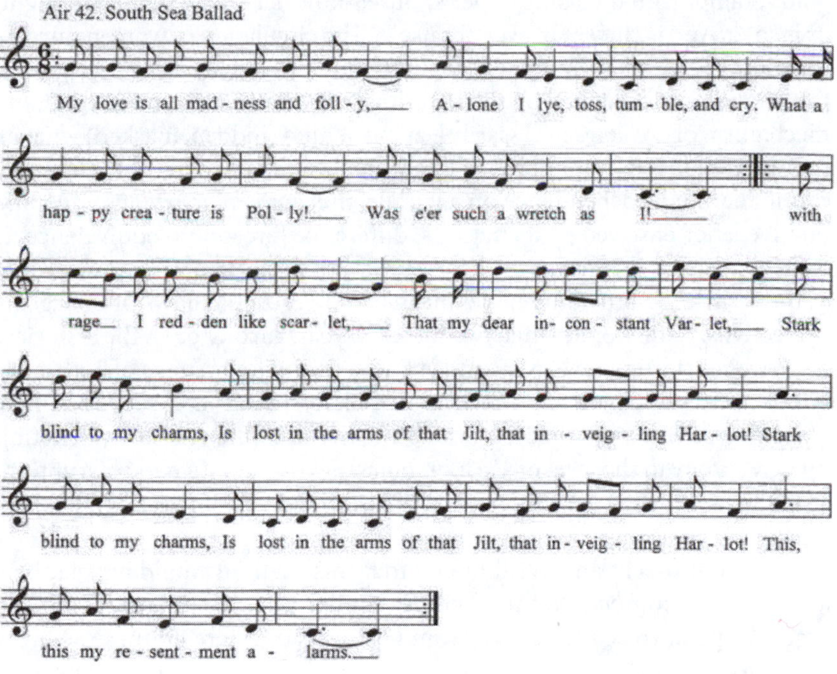

Example 1.10

Several songs had been written on the subject of the South Sea Bubble, and Gay's lyric implicitly compares losses in love with those in business: immediately before, Lucy's father, the jailer Lockit, has told her, "If you would not be looked upon as a fool, you should never do anything but upon the foot of interest. Those that act otherwise are their own bubbles";[34] and the tune's mechanical but hypnotic circulation of the same interchangeable figures might be read as an image of exchange — of both wealth and of transgressive subjective desire — the two sides brought together in the trope of the "inveigling Harlot."

It is at this point of convergence between the registers of representation and commodity that *The Beggar's Opera* becomes particularly interesting to us. For Marx, commodities represent the social relations of their production in phantasmagoric form. In Gay's work — itself a successful commodity — all social relations are reduced to the status of property, as the whole of society, including its musical representation, is brought under the rule of exchange. Stolen goods make the opera's world go round (as, by implication, they do the capitalist world of elite society), including even the relation of love, persistently figured in terms of profit and loss: as Mrs. Peachum puts it, "All men are thieves in love, and like a woman the better for being another man's property," immediately following up with a song: "A wife's like a guinea in gold,/Stampt with the name of her spouse;/Now here, now there; is bought, or is sold;/And is current in every house."[35] The circulation of women mirrors that of property and of money — and of *tunes*. As Marx's metaphor suggests, this movement, mediated by the high/low reflection, works by illusion, the mechanism of *exchange* necessarily leaving behind (hidden, masked) what its representations (its "autonomous figures endowed with a life of their own") cannot admit: its dependence on a parallel mechanism of *exploitation*, productive labor enslaved by its masters, difference forced into equivalence. It is this apparatus that lies at the heart of Gay's musical appropriations, while at the same time providing novel means to energize the flows of bourgeois subjectivity. Little wonder that, two hundred years further on in the historical cycle we see starting up here — and at a crisis point for systems of both capitalism and representation — Brecht and Weill reworked Gay's project in their *Die Dreigroschenoper* (1928), marking the depth of the crisis by ratcheting up Gay's irony to the level of *Verfremdungseffekt* — a systematic disruption, at the level of artistic production, of the mechanisms of identification, the passages of exchange, themselves.[36]

No doubt Brecht and Weill hoped that this method would enable their low-life to *answer back* to their betters. Similarly, Gay's work is of course a *beggar's* opera, voiced (it seems) from below.[37] But where do these answers come from? From "the people"? Surely, it might be objected, ventriloquism is at work — just as, in *Omai*, the potentially subversive blank space occupied by our dumb hero is provided by Shield and O' Keefe, and is at the interpretative mercy of his audience; just as the low-others of *Die Zauberflöte* are ultimately Mozart's creatures; just as the Chartists' song of the lower classes is put into their mouths by the well-meaning but inevitably superior Ernest Jones. Is this all that answering back can amount to? The question should not be taken to disparage the bourgeois populism of these pieces, nor to dismiss the progressive potential of their multivalent voicing, which, as we have already begun to see, takes on a particular richness if the directionality of the ventriloquial state — who speaks and to whom? — is made an issue.

The blank space surrounding Omai is particularly interesting. William Shield was a Tyneside man who, after his move to London in 1773 (he became house composer at Covent Garden in 1784), continued with an active interest in the popular songs of his native North-East England. He helped his friend Joseph Ritson — lawyer and antiquary — with his song-collecting and publishing work, almost certainly providing tunes for Ritson's *A Select Collection of English Songs* (1783) and for *The Bishoprick Garland; or Durham Minstrel* (1784). Ritson's inclusion in his collections (to a small extent, admittedly) of songs collected orally from working people was innovatory; both he and Shield were political radicals (they visited France together in 1791 and found the revolutionaries "more than a match for all the slaves in Europe."[38]) *The Northumberland Garland*, which came out in 1793, at the height of Jacobin agitation in the North-East, contained three such songs, associated with the miners ("The Collier's Rant") and the keelmen ("Weel May the Keel Row," "Bonny Keel Laddie"). In his theater work, Shield undoubtedly drew on the vernacular repertories that his association with Ritson, and others (O' Keefe, for example) opened up; but, this music is placed into contexts that would attract his bourgeois audiences: contemporary songs of industrial workers could not yet be voiced on the London stage. It is tempting to hear Omai's blank space as filled in, on his behalf, by the sounds of the array of exotic others the work contains; but might we go further and imagine them as standing in for that other voice — the one that would have been the most transgressive of all — which Shield could not represent? To place the work in its political context in this way is to reveal Omai's silence as positively deafening.[39]

Still, silence, however resonant, might seem second best. Steven Connor, though, makes a crucial point which we can use to link the ambivalence inherent in the ventriloquial relationship (as manifested in the "blackface exchange") and the structure of the new representational economy itself. Before the eighteenth century, Connor argues, ventriloquism was largely to do with "possession" — the subject divided by an invasive supernatural voice. Now, however, there was a shift — prompted by a scientific interest in the body as a "talking machine" — to the idea of the *projected* voice, the voice thrown elsewhere; translating the technology of vocal appropriation into a clearly spatialized social theater — the voice, so to speak, presented to and by the gaze — "the ventriloquist [now] effects his art by taking on invisibility, and by abstracting himself from the scene of which he is the unrecognised dramaturge." Yet the exchangeability of interior and exterior locations remains. Indeed, far from the Master's invisibility allowing him really to leave the scene, the new techniques were connected to, precisely, a rising interest in, and demand for, self-performance: "a new social dramaturgy, and...a performative understanding of selfhood." It is the contemporary debates over representation — political, social, cultural — that provide the essential context for this new sense of ventriloquism. Connors's discussion of the English entertainer Charles Matthews is particularly interesting here. Working in the theater from around 1795, Matthews evolved a highly successful one-man show format from 1818. This combined elements of impersonation, mimicry, and ventriloquism, including — once Matthews traveled to the United States in 1822 — influential "nigger" imitations. In these performances, a range of characters came and went, sharing space on and off stage with their Master, the circulation of voices raising the question whether he was playing them or they him. "In a sense...the monopolylogue [Matthews's term for these shows] reduces all the characters to the condition of dummy"; yet at the same time Matthews was celebrated as a performer who could *animate* his characters, not just mimic them.[40]

These developments mightily complicate our understanding of the social-semiotic space within which popular voices circulated. We can be certain that in the eighteenth and early nineteenth centuries the Low was not without its own voices. But they come to us through the screens of class and historical distance, and may often seem hard to hear; all that is documented are hybrids and mediations. This is true even when the lower classes appear to speak, in a less equivocal way, on their own account — in "The Collier's Rant," for instance — as, over the course of the next century (in music hall, industrial song, minstrel show, vaudeville, and Tin Pan Alley song, blues, jazz, and rock 'n' roll), was increasingly the case. Even here the positions occupied have always already been infiltrated by forces from outside, defined by their location in the field as a whole and by the interplay between them and their socio-musical protagonists. This is as true for the seemingly most archaic "folk song," which will generally turn out to have among its ancestry connections with the print world of the towns, as it is of the *Dreigroschenoper*'s jazzy lumpen-cabaret knowingness. The well-known couplet Brecht gave to his Peachum — "We would be good instead of so rude, if only the circumstances were not as they are" — is not only wonderfully cynical (the Low excusing its vulgarity with a deft appeal to vulgar-Marxist theory) but also realistic: We are here, and like this (so rude, so low), because, perforce, we are *here*.[41]

Four crucial points follow:

- There is no pure popular music; rather, the voice of the people is always plural, hybrid, compromised.
- This is so because this voice's identity is defined in relation to its position in a broader field, within which its starting-place (to put it no higher) is always one of subservience, its mode of existence one of dialogue.
- Indeed, this voice owes its very existence, and historical potential, *as* "popular" to a machinery (economic, cultural) put in place by those superiors whom it would then want to usurp: Show business shows us ourselves (in some imaginary guise) but must also show value for money.
- The voice of the people, then, is best conceived (to draw on Paul Gilroy's terminology) as a "counterculture of modernity"; it is *constitutive* of modernity itself (modernity as it actually developed), its role not only reactive but also productive, not only responsible to but also responsible for (that is, dialectically implicated in) its own apparent negation.

Thus this structure does not silence the Low — not even when it is silent — nor prevent the activation of (to use Cockrell's happy phrase) its "demons of disorder."[42] Answering back cannot happen from a self-sufficient position but only in dialogue with a protagonist. For "popular music" even to have an identity within the semantic space which it has come to inhabit under modernity *means* that it takes up a place within this formation. In this sense, popular music only exists when it *knows its place*; only on that basis can it then consider answering back (the move is some sort of shift from an in-itself to a for-itself state, as dialecticians would put it). Moreover, as it progressively struggled towards a greater prominence in the field — its quest for mastery going in conjunction with the waves of democratization marking, however ambivalently, the history of the past two centuries — it took over many of the same representational techniques as its superiors had used, and continue to use, to imprison it, appropriating, exploiting, distancing itself in its turn from its own others.

Much of the interpretative challenge for understanding twentieth century popular music is to find ways of confronting this complex field of forces of power and identity within which "the people" can be figured as both servant and master. For if, in the broader politics, the claims of popular hegemony have been made — "we are the masters now," to quote a member of the 1945 British Labour government — this is necessarily to reintroduce the question of representation (for who is this "we"?). If popular sovereignty has appeared only in mediated form, sited in the reifying figures of Party, Nation, Leader, Class, Market (etc.), and equally cited through the foreclosures of musical style, cultural location, star-persona, and vocal positioning, this returns us to the Lacanian issue of the "voice of God" — a vehicle of invisible authority, claims to which might seem to install the people musically as heirs to an old foundational fraud. Is this where voicing the popular ends up — mimicking a premodern imperium, "people" and "market" conflated as sovereign representative of divine law, the bathetic echo of Gay's knowing swagger all too aptly cashed in, in the two-bit cheapness of such early twenty-first century pop names as those of bling rapper 50 Cent and Tory boy band Busted?

******

But this is to move too fast. And is also more pessimistic than I want to be. This book is certainly about the popular music of the twentieth century — or, at least, some aspects of it. So why, then, start off so far back? My purpose is to establish the importance of that moment — a moment focused in the later eighteenth century, but reaching somewhat further back and forward, as we have seen — and to sketch the new regime of representation that emerged at this time.[43] My argument is that this moment saw both the "invention" of the people — as political subject, as economic agent, as cultural actor — and the working out of a new apparatus that enabled its (self-) representation. In essentials, every later development in the popular music system stems from this.

To suggest that this regime was the product of an economic as well as a discursive machine is not new. In Jacques Attali's political economy of music, the moment of what he calls "representation" is described in just this way, so that the new "theatrical" mode of musical production not only exemplifies the system of commodity production itself — for "already in the eighteenth century, music-turned-commodity was announcing the future role of all commodities under representation: a spectacle in front of silent people" — but at the same time generates its own, equivalent aesthetic, in which the functions of tonal harmony represent the new order of exchange:

> The entire history of tonal music, like that of classical political economy, amounts to an attempt to make people believe in a consensual representation of the world... music became the locus of the theatrical representation of a world order, an affirmation of the possibility of harmony in exchange... [It] is exchanged for what it is not and is used as a simulacrum of itself. All of the rest of production is also a simulacrum of order in exchange, of harmony... [For] representation leads to exchange and harmony. It requires a system of measurement, an autonomous value for the work, and hierarchy.[44]

And, Attali goes on, the same principle transformed political theory:[45] as we can readily agree, from Locke to Montesquieu, Condorçet and Sièyes, Jefferson, Madison, and Paine, the question of how disparate social and economic interests should be represented (and reconciled), in parliamentary assemblies and in other ways, was at the forefront of radical thought, just as — in a parallel movement on the level of political economy — Adam Smith showed how "to make the well-being of private individuals coincide with the public interest, reducing all social functions and labouring activities to one measure of value... The political transcendental of the modern state is defined as an economic transcendental."[46]

Attali's stress on harmony can mislead unless we add that harmony comes at a price, in the musical as much as in the political-economic realm, for difference must be refused (assimilated, smoothed over, foreclosed, repressed, projected elsewhere) in the interest of identity. This is as true internally — for the subject — as externally — for society. The modern subject coming into being in this way is defined precisely through such splitting processes, just as their externalizations — on the stage, in the concert hall, in the commodity exchanges, shopping arcades, and political assemblies — actually create the picture of "society." To put this in psychoanalytical language, representation, like any act of foreclosure, inevitably leaves a residue: something (whatever will not fit) is left out, and this must be dealt with somehow — displaced, suppressed, sublimated, or shifted into a counter-representation (an other, which guarantees, through difference, the subject's integrity). The secret of modern subjectivity, from this point of view, is that what seems to be inside has already happened outside — and vice versa. And on both territories, residues are not destroyed: they are always liable to return, often unbidden and unrecognized — and in any case their unbound or at least incompletely assimilated energies arguably constitute a sphere that actually underpins, *drives*, the symbolic work of the representational machine.[47]

In Attali's historical phase of "representation," one such residue, we might suggest, is *repetition*, which in Attali's scheme becomes the name of the phase that succeeds it, organised, he argues, around mass reproduction, especially through recordings. He offers each of his four phases as to some extent interpenetrating the others. Yet it is clear that there is an irreducible sequentiality in his scheme. Although it is true that repetition became problematical in the era of representation,[48] and that representation no longer means the same thing under the rule of repetition, it is vital to hang on to an awareness of their inter-relation throughout the modern age. Thus, just as eighteenth-century representations such as *The Beggar's Opera* were churned, repetitively, out of the printing presses, so the moments of repetition that remained in the music were made to signify: to represent subjectivity to itself, in a movement of what has been called the "acoustic mirror" — the capacity of sound to double back narcissistically from mouth to ear, re-presenting imagined identity to itself. Similarly, Attali's argument that the repetitions inherent in mass reproduction technology destroy use-value completely — that "the stockpiling of use-time in the commodity object is fundamentally a herald of death"[49] — disregards the psychoanalytic insight that, although repetition indeed rides on the death-drive, it does so in incessant negotiation with Life: a negotiation between the spheres of eye and ear, gaze and voice, within which records endlessly spin out a supply of sightless but lively voices in contrary motion with the specular (and deadening?) mirror-economy of the representational work.[50]

It is easy, perhaps too easy, to reduce the operation of this economy to a function of reification: Across the spectrum of scientific, social, political, and aesthetic epistemologies, "nature" is captured, pictured, laid out for display — systematically re-presented. To summon the eighteenth-century language of Sièyes, the image of the *ré-publique* (public thing) slips readily into that of the *ré-total* — a move that is "fatal for freedom,"[51] and which would subsequently be theorised in relation to the reification of consciousness itself by Lukács and, under his influence, by the critical Marxists of the Frankfurt School. In a longer historical perspective, however, representation should be seen as part of a much broader epistemological economy, which, after Michael Taussig, we might refer to as mimesis. For Taussig, "the mimetic faculty" is "the nature that culture uses to create second nature, the faculty to copy, imitate, make models, explore difference, yield into and become other." Mimesis takes us into alterity, and it does this through a "chain of sympathy" — "bodily involvement . . . in the image," or "sympathetic magic" even — which potentially has the effect of "reanimating" the object-other. But mimesis, in this large sense, even if it may be a human universal, has a history. An important moment in this history comes with the Enlightenment impulse to bring multiplicity into generalizing systems of abstraction — precisely the movement seized upon by Adorno and Horkheimer in their critique of Enlightenment Reason: mimesis as a "practice for living with nature" turns into "an instrument for dominating nature, the 'organisation of mimesis' necessary to that long march culminating in Enlightenment civilisation"; and this is inseparable from the hegemony of commodity-form: "Before, the fetishes were subject to the law of equivalence . . . Now equivalence itself has become a fetish." Still, the "magic" does not disappear. Pushed underground, it persistently shows its albeit hidden power, most obviously in modernity's obsession with primitivisms of various kinds — with its Low-Others, we might say; popular voices — "the ape aping [elite] humanity's aping" — touch precisely those "magical" (and often repetitive) springs that circulate identity and difference.[52]

An important issue throughout this book is the question: what might music be like "after representation"? I will not answer the question, at least not directly; but I strongly suspect that the key lies in the territory figured in the Gramscian notion of *articulation*, developed further by Hall and by Laclau and Mouffe, and which responds to the sense of fixity in the concept of representation with an emphasis on *connectivity*: which in turn brings back an interest in the full range of mimetic technologies.[53] But it is impossible to engage adequately with this potential without a grasp of what it would seek to supersede. Even if we accept Bruno Latour's critique[54] of the particularistic claims of modernity — on the grounds that the "purity" and "objectivity" of the representational systems (political and scientific) could only maintain their distinctiveness by denying the messy hybridities that underlie them, which actually link modern culture to every other, and which continue, although suppressed, to work their mediating magic — it remains the case that this economy of separation, with all the psychocultural distortions that come with it, does constitute the modern moment as specific. Hybridity was *ordered* in accord with a hierarchy of social interests: "From the eighteenth to the twentieth centuries, the great historical constructions of gender, race, and class were embedded in the organically marked bodies of woman, the colonized or enslaved, and the worker"[55] — bodies whose voices would struggle to be heard outside the roles which the representational schemas had prepared for them. This is Teresa Brennan's point too. "Modernity," she suggests, is "the ego's era," marked by the ego's quasi-psychotic "foundational fantasy" of complete self-containment on the one hand, complete mastery of nature, made possible by technology, on the other, and finding a point of focus in the commodity, where "the social and psychical converge."[56] The pac(ss)ification of nature is most obviously engineered through the fantasy of Woman, but other lower forms figure as well. Brennan looks to Lacan's idea of the mirror-stage for an appropriate psychoanalytical theory. What is striking here is the emphasis on *spatialization* in the historical development, at the expense of the temporal: for the ego, the world is laid out for control by the gaze, both inner and outer (as well as for exploitation by capital).

Here is a clue to understanding an otherwise paradoxical move in the contemporaneous musical history. Along with the new regime of representation comes the rise of so-called absolute music — music which, supposedly, offers the play of pure sounds, portraying nothing external at all. The problem vanishes if we grasp this shift as an attempt to *spatialize* and *interiorize* the social theater, displacing the drama to the sphere of silent listening, laying out the sound-architecture for compositional control, and shifting the attention to the internal flows of idealized feeling — abstract subjectivity, or subjective flow as such. This move is part and parcel of what Friedrich Kittler calls the 1800 discourse-network, in which, in the context of the expansion of literacy, the *Bildung* of bourgeois society was organized around the silent reading and educated interpretation of literary texts — preeminently poetry; "if one reads in the right way," Novalis wrote, "the words will unfold in us a real, visible world."[57]

But the modelling of absolute music after poetry was only one pole of what was happening. At the other pole we find the displacement of what the absolute could not admit, and its projection onto a range of others — exotics, women, peasants, and workers — whose voices (however qualified, mediated, appropriated) gave expression (in program music as well as in the popular genres) to what was suppressed in the nineteenth-century concert-hall and drawing-room repertories of *Symphonischerkunst*. On both sides, the apparatus of control is patent: what on one side acted as an absolutely concrete supplement doubled back to function as supplement in the Derridean sense as it forever threatened to disturb the "harmony" of abstract representation with a transgressive proliferation of possible selves.[58] What had in the eighteenth century been socio-musical theater had turned into drama of the soul: the bourgeois subject's fantasy of origins and self-development.[59] When Adorno proclaimed that after Mozart high and low impulses in music split apart into separate spheres — "the last instance of their reconciliation, utterly stylised and teetering as on a narrow mountain bypass, was *The Magic Flute*"[60] — he was only partly right. More to the point is to grasp both the whole musical field after Mozart and the inner workings of subjectivity itself as constituting an intricately warrened-out territory on which high and popular would work through their relationship in new ways.[61]

The question might be asked whether it is legitimate to deploy psychoanalytic concepts in discussing historical developments up to a hundred years and more before Freud (this is of course part of a wider issue of hermeneutic method). While the discursive integrity of specific historical (and cultural) moments should be respected, I am impatient with attempts to push this argument to the point where it forecloses on the possibility of dialogue and critique. The idea that pre-Freudian society possessed a political and cultural unconscious with which we can engage is an intellectual advance that we owe to Freud, even if at the same time it illuminates (backwards, as it were) the conditions out of which Freudian (and Lacanian) thought could emerge. The *longue durée* of the "ego's era" laid down the soil that he would till for us, revealing (to use psychoanalytic language) an "always already" which (putting to one side the intriguing question of human constants, absolute or relative) we can ascribe (using Benjaminian language) to the need to "brush history against the grain."[62] The significance of Freud — like that of Marx — lies less in any new dispensation that might be implied by the theories than in the defensive stratagems summoned up at "a moment of danger";[63] as Hegel put it, the owl, Minerva, flies at dusk (and not before).

This tutelary role shared by these two architects of modern self-understanding finds a crucial point of convergence in the concept of *symptom*, a concept "invented," according to Lacan and Žižek, not by Freud but by Marx.[64] ("If…Marx invented the symptom," asks John Mowitt, "might it not also follow that capitalism invented psychoanalysis? In this sense, capitalism also invented Marxism…" Yes, and yes.[65]) In Žižek's Lacanian reading of Marx, money — the most abstracted form of the exchange function of commodities — operates as a "real abstraction;" that is, as a framework for social interaction whose "misrepresentation" of social relations is the very condition (albeit a repressed condition) for social activity. Moreover (under capitalism), the same structure produces subjects: the "real abstraction" of social exchange, situated in the unconscious, generated by something like Althusser's apparatuses of interpellation, creates the illusion of subjective autonomy (hence the "ego's era").[66] The fetish-quality of both commodity and the social authority modelled upon it — the irrational "belief before belief" on which subjective consistency under this regime depends — is what constitutes this structure as ideological symptom, "a formation whose very consistency implies a certain non-knowledge on the part of the subject."[67] Freud then picked up the idea of this structure — in which the fetish (now a sexualized object) stands in for, represents, a socialized human labor (of desire) that cannot be recognized — and situated it within his symptomatology of transgression, neurosis, and perversion. It is entirely appropriate, then, that Hayden White's virtuosic reading of *The Communist Manifesto* as a theatrical "scene" points to the importance of the idea that the downfall of the bourgeoisie will come at the hands of the commodified "refuse" of the system — the low, the dirty and transgressive, the proletariat, "recruited from all classes of the population," the wretched of the earth, "in a condition of total dispersion." Moreover, this historical "plot" (White suggests) hinges on an analogy between the structure of representation (ideological mystification of real relations) and that of the commodity, in which the role of labor *as* commodity, whose destiny is to throw off the shackles of this structure, will be crucial.[68]

In Freudian theory fetishism is primarily a male condition, and the fetish is, ultimately, a substitute for the maternal lack: the mother's missing penis. Here there pretty clearly is a historical specificity masquerading as normative theory, all the more so if we follow through on Lacan's rereading of Freud, which is more concerned with the (symbolic) phallus than the (real) penis, and which correlates this phallus with authority as such — the real abstraction of the Name-of-the-Father. Potentially this "phallic" authority might be thought open to contestation, although Lacan does not raise this possibility: indeed, for him the asymmetry of power that it inhabits — either *having* or *being* the phallus — is mapped conclusively to the hierarchy of sexual difference: man has it, woman is it. At this point in my argument, the interest of this formulation lies in the way that this structure of property and being — production/reproduction, penetration/penetrated, active/passive, capital/labor, master/slave, or at bottom of course, culture/nature — dramatized by the representational work of the exchange economies, can be seen to traverse the whole range of social registers: not only gender but also race and, needless to say, class. If this is a universal, it took the "theatrical" epistemology of modernity to show it to us.[69]

I puzzled for some time over why, in the design of this book, I did not seem to want a separate chapter on class. Here is the answer (I think). It is not (only) that class has become, notoriously, difficult to theorize, with the blurring of distinctions between production and consumption, productive and nonproductive labor, and economic and other registers of inequality; nor (simply) that the extradiscursive reality of objective class positions can no longer be credibly maintained.[70] Class still matters; but its dispersal across the social terrain, as one key formulation of a broader having/being dichotomy, points to a condition that was always already there, but had been obscured by the nineteenth-century rigidifying movement towards a potentially apocalyptic bifurcation of capital and labor (with its own specific discourse of class). What tended to disappear behind this movement was an earlier more fluid and contested moment, with a discourse centered more on a concept of "people" — a concept, nevertheless, which itself was not immune from similar reifying pressures. For Hobbes, as Hardt and Negri point out, "the people is somewhat that is one, having one will, and to whom one action may be attributed; none of these can be properly said of the multitude."[71] Thus the potential openness of the democratic multitude would become fixed — "Married to the concepts of nation and people, the modern concept of sovereignty shifts its epicenter from the mediation of conflicts and crises to the unitary experience of a nation-subject and its imagined community"[72] — a shift that would in its turn be followed by an assault on this community on behalf of the new sovereignty of "class," either bourgeois or worker/proletarian. But if the discourse of class points beyond its own historical specificity, towards a more deeply embedded nexus of power, it also expresses the particular democratic gamble inherent in the Enlightenment stress on human production and self-production — the sense that the individual human subject, the subject as such, might be capable of transcending the fetters of racial and gender subjectification, of actualizing an equality beyond kith and kin, an international brother (and sister) hood of labor superseding the psychosocial attachments of family.[73] While the fact that these attachments are always already inscribed explains precisely why "class" in this pure sense can never exist, this *Telos* also explains (I hope) why this book, with no class chapter,[74] is nevertheless all about class.

It is also — and this follows — all about slavery. In an era that insistently thematized freedom, it is hardly surprising that the *topos* of slavery, and the anxieties that surrounded it, should be central to many of the discourses of modernity. "Britons never shall be slaves" ran the song, and Americans neither, as their revolutionary war attested; yet "industrial slavery" — labor as, inevitably, forced labor — powered economic transformation, mirroring within the body politic proper a relationship more starkly configured without, in the juridical category of slave, a category which in turn was often compared to the status of women.[75] Slavery through surveillance, exemplified in nineteenth-century panopticism,[76] led to ever growing anxieties for the subject, as the seemingly deterministic implications of the ideas of Darwin, Freud, genetic science, and artificial intelligence seemed to reduce agency to mechanism. With the secularization of authority and the dramatization of the quest for freedom, it was inevitable that these questions — whom would the subject serve? How would he master himself? Could he escape his own (imposed) representations? — would become the very questions at the center of modernity. Small wonder that the slave must at all costs continue to be controllable by Aladdin's lamp! Yet paradoxically (or perhaps not) the society within which the freedom discourse took this crisis turn was of course *built* on the profits of slavery.

At the turn of the eighteenth and nineteenth centuries, the products of slave labor in the Americas amounted to around one-third of the value of European commerce, while at the same time the "purity" of national identities was dependent on its alteritous protagonist: "The dark Other of European Enlightenment stands at its very foundation just as the productive relationship with the 'dark continents' serves as the economic foundation of the European nation-states."[77] The slave is the ultimate commodity — freely exchangeable labor-power, naturalized completely (slave as beast), reproduced at the lowest possible cost; at the same time, as embodiment of nature, enslaved labor-power is *itself* treated here as a mysterious fetish standing in for: *itself*, for it is this circle of reproduction which constitutes the commodity-process as natural.[78] Bearing in mind the dark secrets of primitive cross-racial desire within which this reproductive process went on, the fetish-theories of Marx and Freud converge again. Moreover, for Americans especially (but perhaps not exclusively) this slave was *within* — within the social system, and even the blood (it may be that for Europeans too, their slaves were felt to be within the national-imperial families); this was a *verna*, a native-born slave, the subject-other within the household itself, the supplement who made it possible to think both "family" and "fraternity" at all. From this point of view, the discourse of class represents a distorted writing of a myth that would overthrow this family in the name of "the people:" a fantasy to explain the (utopian) idea of freedom — a new twist to the Freudian "family romance."

For "the people" is also a *verna*, and "popular music," the music of the vernacular traditions, is a slave music, the voice of the skivvy within the household — or perhaps more precisely, of the slave who longs to be free, or even, to be master. I suggested earlier that popular music only exists when it knows its place. But in the light of this state of radical indeterminacy, one might add, perhaps: *and not even then*. Following Žižek's deployment of Lacan's rather notorious aphorism about the (non) existence of Woman, we might say that actually "(The) popular music does not exist." The logic here (which Lacan derives from Hegel) is that of the "non-all" set as it operates in a social field structured by antagonism. (Non-all set: a set which, so to speak, posits itself as universal — a move that, paradoxically, depends upon the expulsion of a particularity (here "popular music") to act as a boundary-forming exception.[79]) Of course, this does not mean that individual beings/objects/practices (women; popular songs) located under the relevant concept do not have empirical existence, but that the category as such covers over an internal blockage (it can never fully be what its nominalization would want to be, as it were); this lack stands in for the equal (but disavowed) lack of its antagonistic Other ('Man'; 'Music'), and is hence in some sense always spoken from the position of that Other, from elsewhere. (My parenthesis around the definite article — in Lacan and Žižek it is a bar through the word — marks this structure of lack.) Žižek often also uses the example of the class struggle. This can never appear as such, as a social totality, but only in terms of its effects which go to produce antagonistic and incompatible modalities.[80] The idea of "the people" (and hence of "popular music") operates within a similar field.

But although these antagonisms are mobilized by an absent cause (that is, an impediment in the symbolic system which prevents totalization), this does not rule out a bid for mastery, on the part of the bourgeoisie (positing itself as the universal class) or of "art" (hence "art music"), any more than an analogous move is ruled out on the part of "man" (in the field of sexual difference), or indeed of "white man" (in the field of race). This is why, just as (in another notorious Lacanianism) "Woman is the symptom of man," so popular music is the symptom of its Other, and the moment around 1800 when this relationship emerges can be regarded as a pre-echo of that symptomatic structure which Marx and Freud would go on to theorize.[81] On one level, there is a symmetry and in principle it is possible to try to invert the relationship (thus feminists can say, "Man is the symptom of woman"), but such inversions do not destroy the binary structure, which, for Žižek, is in any case at bottom asymmetrical: one side (the Master) is constructed as universal, the other (the Slave) as that particularity which makes the Master possible. Whether this position should be read as tough-minded realism (which would help explain, for example, why feminism has not yet triumphed and why most university music departments and degree courses are still given the universalistic title "music" while "popular music" courses have to be given their own marker) or as a problematic foreclosure of politics is an important question to come back to. In any case, just as significant are slippages round the chain of subaltern positions: as Woman is to Man (i.e., symptom), so Popular is to Elite, and Black to White — a triangular trade indeed (sometimes rough, sometimes conducted with feminine smoothness). What "stands up" here? An (exchangeable) master-signifier (together with its lacks) with distinctly phallocentric overtones? But which should also be thought in the context of what, in later Lacan, is considered to "stand out," to "ex-sist" (stand out[side]): a meaningless bit of the Real, that grit in the symbolic system which, he argues, is the foundation of the subject as such.

Interestingly, we have in a sense been here before — in Adorno's celebrated aphorism, to the effect that "popular" and "serious" musics are "torn halves of an integral freedom, to which however they do not add up":[82] not as in a simplistic reading (the two sides have split apart and for historical reasons cannot be stuck together again) but in the sense that they represent mutually contradictory conceptualizations *of the same field*. How appropriate, then, that at a crucial moment Adorno's theorization of popular music should itself live out this dialectic. As is well known, in Adorno's standard (not to say, classic) text of 1941, "On Popular Music," the standardization he finds in popular music is what excludes it from the field of good music, which is defined, in his view, by a commitment to the production of freshly-composed, individuated works.[83] Buried away in a footnote, where Adorno gnomically alludes to the definitional difficulties around the terminology of "standard/ization," we find a reference to a 1939 text, *How to Write and Sell a Song Hit*, which, it seems to me, may well be the source of many of Adorno's views, but which anyway certainly presents a pre-echo of them, as it were, by inversion.[84] Silver and Bruce, the authors of the 1939 book, accept completely the terms of Adorno's comparison ("the melody and the lyric of a popular number are constructed within a definite pattern or structural form, whereas... a standard number [they mean here a 'serious song'] has no structural confinements... [and] allows the composer freer play of imagination and interpretation"); but they invert the perspective: formulaic construction is not only *natural* to the popular song ("a popular melody, if properly constructed, should naturally conform to one of... three patterns"), but, because "a popular song is, in its broad sense, a musical composition whose words and melody appeal to the people as a whole," this makes it *better* ("A popular song is sold on its own merit... The names of the writer and publisher of a standard composition, on the other hand, constitute two of its greatest selling points").[85]

The binary division of the musical field also mirrors Adorno's method, in which any genre or practice failing to gain admittance to his category of "serious music" is lumped together as "popular" or "commercial;" thus, for Silver and Bruce, "Popular music has already been defined... Standard music is everything else" (and they mean *everything*: from symphonies to instrumental tutors, from church music to opera).[86] It hardly comes as a surprise, then, to find that all the main qualities that Adorno attributes to popular song — simplistic harmonies, over-regular melodic shapes, purely decorative orchestration — are described in the earlier text in almost identical terms, but with a positive rather than negative spin. Might we see Silver and Bruce, presented in Adorno's article "below stairs" (in a footnote), as servants in his patrician household, even (perhaps) doing his listening for him? When we bring the two pictures together, they appear clearly as mirror-images which are however quite incompatible: each is the supplement of the other, each from its own point of view stands the other on its feet (or head), while taken together they strenuously voice particular positions that attempt to cut up in antagonistic ways a neutral field which could not exist outside the perspective of an impossible totalizing gaze. In this world, (the) popular music can indeed not exist.

Is this Žižekian position, then, simply a rerun of the cul-de-sac we find in Adornian negative dialectics? Žižek does not seem to think so: for him, the "negation of the negation" does not freeze the dialectic but reveals negation as a sort of positivity referring back to the constitutive contradiction in the object itself; "synthesis" repeats "negation" but with a twist of perspective which locates it as what positively enabled the original problem.[87] Does this answer the question of how political movement might be possible? I suspect the answer is to found, somehow, in the status of that void — that lack which lies behind Adorno's "do not add up," that which "falls out," which cannot be symbolized when the constitutive antagonism forms — which Žižek presents as a condition of subjectivity itself.

However "popular music" is articulated, whatever we try to make it mean, the people as subject is embedded somewhere within it, and with an emotional charge that will apparently just not go away. We need to account for that investment as well as the (necessary) mutability of content. And here the word itself must come to the fore. Žižek's position is grounded, more broadly, in an anti-descriptivist theory of naming. Names ("the people," "music," "popular music"), he argues, do not acquire meaning through reference to given properties but through a "primal baptism" followed up in a "chain of tradition." To the question, what is popular music? the answer in the end is indeed: "I know it when I hear it!" — or rather (since hearing is not necessary), "I know it when I know it." (This is testable: are there any properties whatsoever that would rule out by definition a given musical experience from the category "popular music"? I think the answer is: no.) Thus, "popular music" is just: *that*. But the moment of the baptism is mythical: it appears with the act of naming itself, an always already, implied retroactively by its effects once we are in the Symbolic. The name, qua master-signifier (the Lacanian *point de capiton*, or quilting-point), is *empty*; yet it does have a sort of objective correlative, namely, the famous Lacanian *objet a* — Žižek's "sublime object," a little bit of the Real, what is in the object more than itself, what the symbolic process must exclude if it is to function at all, the object-cause of desire. This object corresponds, on the side of the subject, with the "belief before belief" which makes subjectivation (the articulatory play of contesting subject-positions) possible. Popular music interpellates its listeners (at least it does if they turn round when it says "Hey!"); but why should they *want* to turn — or, more precisely, *what* is it that turns? Žižek's answer is: that meaningless piece of stuff, that object in the subject, which alone ensures its consistency; it is the Real which responds.[88]

What, in our context, is this object-cause of desire but "the people" — or rather, that meaningless and impossible site of *jouissance* underlying and supporting all social fantasies of the popular?

But where does this leave politics? Lacan's answer is: traverse the fantasy; the final stage of ideological critique is to "go through" the fantasy, achieve distance from it, and identify with its underlying mode of *jouissance* (the "*Sinthome*" as Lacan neologistically calls it, to distinguish it from the ideological symptoms which it supports). A radical politics of the popular might require a more precise theorization of the relationship between symptom and *Sinthome*. It could, for example, work at the possibility that rearticulation of meaning might be able to transform the stratum of meaninglessness on which, according to Žižek, it depends; that Symbolic work could change the Real, that (to use older, Freudian terms) consciously articulated activity might restructure the (social and political as well as individual) unconscious, not just identify with it.

******

What follows falls into four lengthy chapters, each focusing on what I take to be a key aspect of the overall topic of the book. The first two are organized around specific social registers of analysis — first race, then gender — while the second pair tackle more general issues of subject construction, first the subject conceived as a structure of repetition, then questions of authenticity, truth, and ideology. Most music examples come from the first three decades of the twentieth century or from the 1960s and 1970s, but the significance of this is purely that these are periods of intricate resettlement in the musical field, following moments of profound change. Thus this book is in no sense a history. (A comprehensive history of the popular in music in the period of late modernity is a definite lack; but it will not be written in one volume, nor, probably, by a single author.) I would be happy if readers responded to the structure in the same way as Ernesto Laclau responded to that of Žižek's *The Sublime Object*. This

> is certainly not a book in the classical sense; that is to say, a systematic structure in which an argument is developed according to a pre-determined plan. Nor is it a collection of essays, each of which

> constitutes a finished product and whose 'unity' with the rest is merely the result of its thematic discussion of a common problem. It is rather a set of theoretical interventions which shed mutual light on each other, not in terms of the *progression* of an argument, but in terms of what we could call the *reiteration* of the latter in different discursive contexts... But as this process of refinement is not the result of a necessary progression, the text reaches a point of interruption rather than conclusion, thus inviting the reader to continue for him- or herself the discursive proliferation in which the author has been engaged.[89]

As to theory, I hope that this has by now come sufficiently into view that further (no doubt tedious) scene-setting is unnecessary. I can again do no better than quote a model, this time John Mowitt's remarkable book, *Percussion*, which seems to me to outline in exemplary fashion a method I was trying to follow myself (although not necessarily with the same success):

> What is at stake in putting it [theory] to work? How must it be written when it responds to the call of musical practice...?...I want to stress the importance of proliferating and diversifying music's claims on theory. Specifically, what is going on in music...must be granted the authority to provoke theorizing – that is, to provoke a reading of theory that challenges its integrity, that obliges theory to submit to the same, often violent scrutiny that its detractors claim is visited on those practices to which it has been applied. In this sense, theory 'responds' to the 'call' of music not by smothering it like a salve, but by discovering in this encounter other possibilities of elaboration, other orientations...By the same token, if what is going on in musical practice solicits the work of theorization, it is because music, too, is in need of the diversification of critical attention that theory can provoke as well as the conceptual rigor with which judgments about it can be debated.[90]

Such diversification should not be random. Historical writing (and, even more, images) has placed before us a range of views of "the people." Pictures of, say, Chartist marches, placed alongside photos of recent manifestations of "the people in motion" (the *mobile vulgus*; e.g., anti-war demonstrations), embody many differences of course, as well as certain commonalities. However, such sightings taken as a whole inevitably tend to freeze the action, silencing the protagonists, or at best translating their voices into words on a page. This is where songs can come to the fore — expecially once the new reproduction technologies of the twentieth century prolong and renew their sounding lives. If songs do in some sense voice the popular, how are these voices to be understood? Where do they come from and what do they have to say?

CHAPTER 2

Through a Mask Darkly

Voices of Black Folk

Chicago, 1893: the World's Columbian Exposition (or Chicago World's Fair), celebrating (if a year late) the 400th anniversary of Columbus's "discovery" of a new world. Drawing visitors from even the remotest parts of the country to gaze in wonder at the marvels of contemporary knowledge, industry, and culture, the Exposition stands as a convenient marker for the decisive transformation of a rural, premodern society into a unified, powerful state dominated by urban, modernizing trends — a "flight," as the later African-American writer Alain Locke would put it, "not only from countryside to city but from medieval America to modern."[1]

The World's Fair was seized upon by many African Americans as an opportunity to proclaim their own part in — and claims on — this advance. Although many of their leaders (e.g., the aged Frederick Douglass) were there, it was difficult for black musicians to make much headway on the official program. The musical content of Colored American Day was organized by the young composers, Harry T. Burleigh and Will Marion Cook, among others;[2] but the program they designed was dominated by opera. The Fisk Jubilee Singers and the Hampton Quartet were prominent, and their cultivated performances of spirituals were well received by both blacks and whites. What was probably the first musical show with black performers, *The Creole Show*, was on at the Opera House (though it drew on blackface minstrelsy conventions). Otherwise African-American musicians seem to have been confined to the peripheries of the entertainment area (the Midway Plaisance), where there was a vibrant red light district. This was where ragtime "got a running start," according to Cook — we know that Scott Joplin, among many other piano players, was there — and it is hard to believe that "cakewalks" and "coon songs," genres just emerging into mass popularity, were not heard in the bars, streets, and brothels (even though the whole idea of a Colored American Day had been opposed by many African Americans precisely because they feared it would include such "demeaning" music as the cakewalk — "race luggage," as one reverend described it). There would not have been blues — but blues-ballads, one of this new-genre-in-waiting's progenitors, would surely have drifted in from St. Louis, Memphis, and more remote spots lower down the Mississippi Valley.[3] (And Hawaiian musicians *were* there: the fashion for Hawaiian guitar often supposed to have influenced slide guitar techniques in blues.) There was a concert by jubilee singers from South Carolina with their own orchestra of "way-down-south fiddlers and a double bass that rasped like a Kansas cyclone"; they performed "characteristic camp meeting and plantation ballads, queer of dialect and jamful of jumpy music." And there was African music. Among the many foreign pavilions was a "Dahomey Village" where a company of Fon from West Africa drummed, sang, and danced, to the fascination of anthropologist Franz Boas, folklorist Henry Krehbiel, and some African-American musicians — Will Marion Cook, for example (though most middle-class blacks, seeing danger to their modernizing ambitions, appear to have been at least as dismissive of these backward primitives as whites). Among the most popular exhibits were phonographs and gramophones, which were already beginning to disseminate all these musics (or some of them; others would have to wait for their market) in quite new ways. Many of the visiting musicians, including some from the "South Sea Islands," were recorded, the 103 cylinders that resulted being the first recordings ever made of "world music."[4]

Fast forward to New York, February 1919: the troops coming home from the War in Europe, the parade up Broadway led by James Reese Europe's all-black Hellfighters Band, key protagonists in the transition from ragtime to jazz. Andy Razaf, who would figure prominently in the renaissance of black musical theater set off in 1921 by the show, *Shuffle Along*, and who wrote lyrics for Eubie Blake, James P. Johnson, and Fats Waller among others, composed a song in their honor: "The 15th Regiment." Two days later, the writer, scholar, and political leader, W. E. B. Du Bois, whose 1903 book, *The Souls of Black Folk*, had cemented the idea of the "sorrow songs" as the folk heritage of the race (but whose own musical tastes ran for the most part to German classical music), opened the Pan-African Congress in Paris.[5] A year later, the first blues record by a black singer was issued; but three years before, the all-white Original Dixieland Jazz Band from New Orleans, now working in New York, had put out the records that first placed jazz on the popular musical map. Back again in 1919, George Gershwin had his first song hit with "Swanee," a catchy number redolent with the blackface myths of the minstrel-show South. Accompanying these developments were the most serious race riots yet to have taken place in U.S. cities, the worst being in Chicago in 1919. But they could hardly stop the initiation of the "jazz age," an explosive culmination of three decades of musical activity in which music by, appropriated from, influenced by, or otherwise about "black folk" redrew the picture of what a modern popular musical culture might be.

These snapshots — for they are little more — at least point towards the main issues for any consideration of the development of "black music" in the early twentieth century: issues that would reverberate throughout the century. First, at the heart of this development lay a racial encounter: white investment and participation in, and response to, black music helped delimit, define, and valorize it. Second, this encounter — which was also a symptom, at the level of world (post)colonial history, of a larger tension — was heavily mediated by class difference, not least on the African-American side, and this variously affected the range of genres as these were aligned with distinct social groups and cultural and political positions. And third, this generic network was significantly organized and differentiated by a divergence of racial imagery, one lineage — quintessentially represented by the spirituals — projecting the suffering nobility of an ill-used, backward but resilient folk, the other — an entertainment tradition, rooted in the nineteenth-century minstrel show — disseminating a repertoire of caricature centered on stereotypes of sensuality, violence, indolence, and grinning stupidity, the legacy of which spread through vaudeville, theater and film, jazz, and even blues. Although this bifurcation was real, it was not absolute, partly because of cross-influence (spirituals, for example, were often performed in ways that drew on blackface convention), and partly because the two discursive clusters were equally mythological, owing their origins and power to structures of white desire, fear, and self-defense, that is, to their unasked-for place as Others of white subjectivity in a great drama of "love and theft."[6]

Du Bois's celebrated notion of African-American "double consciousness" laid out the ground on which these relationships operated: "the Negro is…born with a veil, and gifted with second sight in this American world," he wrote, "a world which yields him no true self-consciousness, but only lets him see himself through the revelation of the other world."[7] But the veil is also a (blackface) mask — and mirror, in which what is double on the black side is reflected, in distorted form, in a doubling structure on the white. It is as if a hybridity that cannot be admitted is forcibly refashioned as a hegemony (which, in spite of itself, will be a sort of hybrid anyway): "Produced through the strategy of disavowal, the *reference* of discrimination is always to a process of splitting as the condition of subjection: a discrimination between the mother culture and its bastards, the self and its doubles, where the trace of what is disavowed is not repressed but repeated as something *different* — a mutation, a hybrid."[8] At stake in our particular case is the question just how a modern self, in a (post)colonial Western society, could speak; what sort of voice(s) might represent it?

******

A good place to start is with the blues, a genre commonly regarded as central to representation of African-American experience but also one with huge significance for whites. Consider three events from the beginning of the twenty-first century:

First, the White Stripes, a guitar-based duo from Detroit, emerge as "the most exciting rock band in the world" (*The Guardian*, March 29, 2003), on a platform of emotional truth, pared-down simplicity, recall to tradition. Their style is centered on musical influences and an aesthetic of authenticity drawn from blues; their first two albums are dedicated to blues singers Son House and Blind Willie McTell, respectively. The White Stripes are only the most prominent of a number of likeminded bands. We seem to have yet another blues revival on our hands.

Second, in 2002 Alan Lomax, arguably the first significant folklorist to look for blues in the field (as distinct from tripping over them among other types of song), dies, and his book, *The Land Where the Blues Began*, which recounts his fieldwork experiences in the 1940s, '50s, and '60s, is republished.

And third, the Coen Brothers' movie, *O Brother, Where Art Thou?*, set in the 1930s and organized around the nostalgic appeal (but also the political potency) of "old timey" music, is an unexpectedly huge hit.[9] Although the focus of the soundtrack is on early hillbilly music — and it triggers another revival, this time of bluegrass — a racial theme, with a blues strand, is crucial. Early in the film, the three white heroes led by Everett Ulysses Grant are joined on their travels (which are part escape from prison, part search for "treasure") by an African-American singer-guitarist modeled on a real bluesman of the time (whose name he carries), Tommy Johnson. Part of the fun is that the initial meeting takes place at a crossroads, where, paying due homage to legend, Tommy has just met the Devil (he was white and had a "mean look") — and, presumably, traded his soul for musical prowess. Tommy is on his way to Tishomingo; the real Johnson would more likely have been on his way to Jackson — but close enough.[10]

Our four heroes miraculously form themselves into a band, and their version of "Man of Constant Sorrow," featured on local radio, is a smash hit, subsequently securing their pardons after they perform it at a political campaign rally in support of Governor Pappy O' Daniel. This song is a "white blues": the standard I-IV-V chord-sequence is truncated into a ten bar verse, with a four-bar refrain after each two-verse segment; the vocal follows familiar melodic shapes and drips with blue notes; Tommy's bluesy, riff-heavy guitar anchors the song "down home." In another important episode in the film, Tommy is rescued from the clutches of the Ku Klux Klan; the KKK's Grand

Wizard is revealed to be O'Daniel's racist political opponent, who, appalled, describes our boys as a "miscegenatin' band." (The point is confirmed when, in the performance at the rally, Tommy's guitar fits effortlessly into the marvelously intricate textures of a full bluegrass band sound — a sound which, by the way, did not yet exist, any more than did the label "bluegrass.")

These three events, though distinct in many ways, have several aspects in common. First, "revival:" the past is conjured up, brought into the present, re-configured (reinvented even, as the point about bluegrass dating suggests). At the same time, this past is a "folk" past: what is conjured up is "tradition," a home that has been lost. And finally, these transactions are unavoidably racialized: white rock musicians, white scholars, white filmmakers drawing on black roots — only to find (at least in the movie) a white investment already in place, right back down home.

Much is at stake in this way of picturing the blues past, as we can see if, approaching from a different direction, we take up Charles Keil's scandalous suggestion[11] that, far from fitting the "folk" paradigm, blues in its origins was urban and modern rather than rural and archaic, was circulated and developed on records as much as (perhaps more than) through live performance and oral dissemination, and was from the beginning an interracial phenomenon — that, in a sense, it was even a white invention, with which black musicians then had to come to terms, which they reconfigured. Writing at a time when the claims of African-American identity politics were being shouted from the rooftops, Keil would probably be less than surprised that his speculations have not been widely pursued.[12] Of course we know (e.g., from the work of Tony Russell[13]) that in the vernacular musical practice of the South there was a cross-racial "common stock" of tunes, songs, and vocal and instrumental techniques going back at least to the nineteenth century and including features and songs that we would now associate with blues (hence, for instance,"Man of Constant Sorrow"). But although this is important and relevant (it provides the broader historical backdrop to Keil's more specific point), it is not the same argument. We may quibble with the idea of origin (where in the endless relays of cultural practice does anything begin, and how could such an *ex nihilo* claim justify its authority?), but nevertheless when a genre is *named* and a certain cultural place discursively established, then we identify a moment possessing a particular historical power.

There is no significant historical evidence for the existence of a discrete blues genre before 1902–03, the period when Gertrude "Ma" Rainey, Jelly Roll Morton, and W. C. Handy all claim to have heard (or in Morton's case, made up) blues songs for the first time; all, however, were speaking (and naming the genre) with the benefit of hindsight.[14] During the next few years, several folklorists included verses resembling blues in published collections,[15] but they did not identify them as such nor show any special interest in them. The big moment came in 1912 with the first publications of blues compositions, including Handy's "Memphis Blues." In fact, Handy (a trained, middle-class musician, far from "the folk") had put together his tune in 1909, as "Mr Crump" (as yet without words), for his band to play in a political contest (another!) in Memphis; but he was beaten to publication by the white bandleader, Hart Wand, with his instrumental, "Dallas Blues" — just as he was closely followed in 1913 by Leroy "Lasses" White's "Nigger Blues" (White, who was also associated with Dallas, was, ironically but appropriately, white and a blackface minstrel), which in turn became one of the first blues to be recorded (in 1916).[16] A torrent of publications followed.

From the start, the blues craze set off by these publications involved white bands as well as black, and (preponderantly) white singers — Gilda Gray, Blossom Seeley, Marion Harris — until Mamie Smith's "Crazy Blues" of 1920 (which is as much a torch song as a blues, actually). The female black singers following in Mamie Smith's wake, singing "vaudeville blues," were part of this rich interracial culture of commercial song, including but not limited to blues, and they also, arguably, played the single biggest role in establishing a black performing presence within it, touring the South and disseminating their records there as well as in the Northern cities. But in the 1920s blues were also a key part of the repertoires for many white singers, for dance bands, both black and white, and for theater and jazz musicians. The first significant blues recordings by a male singer came out in 1924, from the banjo-playing, minstrel-show songster, "Papa" Charlie Jackson. No "folk blues" records appeared until Blind Lemon Jefferson's in 1926, and, although his success initiated a down-home blues recording boom during the late twenties and early thirties, the most commercially successful male blues singers at this time were the jazzy Lonnie Johnson, and Leroy Carr — sophisticated in a different way, based in Indianapolis, with a style locating itself far from the cotton fields and levees.

This story is familiar enough. But the inferences that Keil would draw are less so. What had happened, it would seem, is that whites (together with a good number of middle-class and ambitious blacks such as Handy and Perry Bradford, composer of "Crazy Blues"), working in a context defined increasingly by a sequence of black-tinted music fads — coon song, ragtime, jazz — and by conventions of blackface performance, had crystallized a new commercial song genre out of their appropriations of a bundle of African-American vernacular practices. As part of this process, white singers, drawing on images of black style, had created models of blues vocality, which black performers could not evade.

From this point of view, "Nigger Blues," usually dismissed as a wooden travesty, becomes interesting. Recorded by an up-market white "character" singer from Washington, D.C., George O'Connor, its meanings flow when placed where it belongs, in a metropolitan drawing-room.[17] Like many of Handy's compositions, White's song jams together an assortment of lyric clichés, familiar from many other songs, and puts them to a formulaic blues melody over the standard twelve-bar changes. It is O'Connor's delivery that speaks to the regulative norms of the culture within which "blues" would now exist. Whose voice(s) do we hear? Two at least, I would suggest, or even three: the singer's, itself split between that of the white elite, to which he belongs and which he addresses, and that of an imaginary object that he strives to imitate; and second, that of the object itself — or rather, the object wanting to subjectivise itself, to make its own desire heard, conjured up in our imaginations now. Here is the "plantation South" transplanted to the white drawing room (and then to our ears), the exotic reified (in dialect, in rhythm, in melodic gestures): desire, and lack, coursing through the gaps between the voice we actually hear, the voice O'Connor wants us to imagine, and the voice blotted out but that we know is there, somewhere, could we but find it.[18]

The "nigger" has been, precisely, folklorized, a blues revival set in train even before its source has been sufficiently established to copy. (Cecil Sharp, who would shortly make his fieldwork visit to the Appalachians, where he would collect, among many other songs, a version of "Man of Constant Sorrow," would certainly have recognized what was going on.) The full blues folklorization process comes later, however, starting in the 1950s. Thus the historical schema that follows from pursuing Keil's proposal is striking. The blues Golden Age[19] — when black reappropriation gives the music sufficient relative autonomy to produce its moment of condensed historical force — is very short, running from the 1920s to the 1950s. It is preceded by a period when blues as an emergent pop fad covers over, but at the same time provides a hazy refraction of, a no doubt rich, multivalent vernacular practice. It includes two even shorter peaks of down-home assertiveness (Mississippi, late-'20s/early '30s; Chicago, late '40s/early '50s), which would subsequently provide the core sources for the (mostly white) pattern of folklorization and revival that constitutes one pole of the afterglow, the other pole marked by the marginalization of blues for African Americans. The Golden Age coincides with a period of enormous tension, shaped by forces promoting the modernization of the South on the one hand, and explosive racist reactions, centered on such organizations as the Ku Klux Klan, on the other. *O Brother* sits in the middle of this period, exploring the tensions with a comedy as black as it is hilarious. "Real" blues, it confirms, is a construction always mediated by white desire — which thus also enfolds blacks within this structure. Despite the pressures of identity politics, this position does not rob blacks of the blues: the music's political potential as a cultural resource remains, but inescapably embedded in a larger racial dialogue.[20]

In *O Brother*, Governor O'Daniel, rushing into the radio station to do a show immediately after our heroes have made their record there, declares excitedly for modernity: he is "mass communicatin'," he boasts. Communicatin' what? Well, the past: "culture 'n' heritage," to use a well-worn and rather suspect Southern phrase, also deployed by O'Daniel's KKK opponent, disgustedly describing the "miscegenating band": "This ain't *my* culture 'n' heritage," he asserts. Blues too points both forward and back; it is modern, as we have seen, but from the start also sounds old.

As a genre, blues comes into being with sheet music and records, and registers the social effects of Reconstruction and its failure, followed by the profound economic shifts — industrialization, urbanization — of the late nineteenth- and early twentieth centuries. It speaks of culture shock: mobility, deracination, alienation, freedom — both sexual and more general. Even in the core of down-home territory, the Mississippi Delta, the social and economic geography was the result of quite recent developments — large-scale migration from the surrounding hill-country, drainage projects through levee building, settlement of new land, the coming of the railways, producing "the conditions of an urban ghetto spread out over a rural landscape."[21]

Yet from the beginning blues *sounds old*: "back then" is built into its aesthetic ("Times ain't now nothing like they used to be...I done seen better days but I ain't putting up with these...": Rabbit Brown's "James Alley Blues" (1927)); and "going back" (to that same old used to be, etc.) is as common as "going to" (Chicago, Kansas City, etc.). As Tommy Johnson puts it, "Crying, Lord, will I ever get back home" ("Cool Water Blues" (1928)), and "Well, I'm going back home, gon' fall down on my knees" ("Lonesome Home Blues" (1930)). The motif is still there — indeed, not surprisingly, intensified — when Muddy Waters records such songs as "I Believe I'll Go Back Home" in Chicago in 1948. At the same time it cannot be entirely separated from a much older trope: the mythological "dear old Southland" of the minstrel-show plantation, still clearly present in many early commercial blues songs (for example, Spencer Williams's "Tishomingo Blues" (1917) and "Basin Street Blues" (1928) and Handy's "Way Down South where the Blues Began" (1932)).

From this point of view, blues, as Houston Baker puts it, is the "always already" of African-American music: "the song is no stranger...I been here before", and blues offers an ancestral voice, "an anonymous (nameless) voice issuing from the black (w)hole."[22] In Paul Oliver's words, "Blues had come from way back, but no one knew then, or even knows now, quite where, when or how they sounded."[23] And blues is "always already" revived, bringing back up something already lost. Race record marketing commonly appealed to an "original" authenticity. For example, Paramount advertised Blind Lemon Jefferson's first release as "a real old-fashioned blues by a real old-fashioned blues singer...old-time tunes...in real southern style," while earlier, in 1924, they had announced the first issues by Ma Rainey in a style that reads like an ethnographer's celebration of finding a lost tribe: "Discovered at Last — 'Ma' Rainey, Mother of the Blues!"[24] A 1923 advertisement in *The Metronome*, probably placed by the music publishers E. B. Marks, states that "Mechanical companies are tumbling over each other in their eagerness to discover 'real blues.' There are bushels of inferior compositions on the market labeled 'blues,' but the genuine article by born writers of 'blues' is as scarce as the proverbial 'hen's teeth.' A 'real blues'...sways the hearer almost with every note, and underneath it all there is the wail of the aborigine."[25] In his Introduction to W. C. Handy's 1926 anthology of blues music sheets, white enthusiast Abbe Niles, while locating blues as a new genre, insists on its status as folk music, and describes his task as digging out "their folk source," hidden in a range of previous folk genres, from beneath their popular success.[26] Handy himself, in his autobiography, consistently portrays these pre-blues folk materials as "rough diamonds," which he, as a skilled composer, had refined into more rounded and varied pieces; blues, then, is part of his "mother tongue" and writing blues songs "cannot be delegated outside of the blood."[27]

First-generation blues singers interviewed later in life sometimes bring out the moment early in the century when they encountered the new genre. Tommy Johnson's brother, LeDell, recalls family music-making in the early years of the century as based on "love songs" and "jump ups," but "when all these late blues come out, that's all I studied"; similarly a blind Clarksdale songster told Alan Lomax how his repertoire of the early 1900s, jump ups and reels, gave way to blues: "we were entering the jazz age and the old world was being transformed." Just as often, however, they refer to deep, mysterious pre-twentieth century origins: thus, for Memphis Slim, also talking to Lomax, "Blues started from slavery," while for John Lee Hooker, "it's not only what happened to you — it's what happened to your foreparents and other people. And that's what makes the blues."[28] No sooner had blues exploded into popular consciousness, it seems, than it was mythologized as "old time." The interplay of "modernity" and "folkloric" deeply embedded in blues discourses maps this dialectic of old and new.

The folklorization process assumed the force of a movement in the 1950s and '60s, but this is prefigured by the collecting and publishing work of John Lomax, and especially his son Alan, in the 1930s and '40s, and to some extent, with a rather different sort of focus, by activities associated with the Harlem Renaissance of the later 1920s. There is a clear lineage, constructed through the wider "folk revival", via the Lomaxes, the Seegers, and their associates, leading to young revival singers of the 1960s such as Bob Dylan, along with the British "blues boom" of the same period.

The iconic figure of Leadbelly has an important transitional status. Discovered in 1933 by the Lomaxes in Angola state prison, Louisiana, his songs published three years later,[29] promoted as a "folk singer," Leadbelly (Huddie Ledbetter) became a key point of focus within the early white American folk revival. Leadbelly was a songster, but he sang blues and, so he claimed, had worked with Blind Lemon Jefferson; more importantly perhaps, he seemed to carry a disappearing culture (the Lomaxes' aim in 1933 was "to find the Negro who had had the least contact with jazz, the radio, and with the white man").[30] Moreover, he had charisma, not least because of his fearsome reputation for violence, which had led to several imprisonments for assault and murder.

It is hard not to suspect that, for many middle-class whites, here was the body of a noble savage on to which forbidden desires and anxieties could be projected,[31] a suspicion intensified by many of Alan Lomax's later descriptions of similar experiences to those on the 1933 trip. His romantic account of a Son House performance at the moment of his "discovery" in deepest Mississippi in 1941 (actually House had made commercial records some ten years earlier) can stand for many:

> His voice, guttural and hoarse with passion, ripping apart the surface of the music like his tractor-driven deep plow ripped apart the wet black earth in the springtime, making the sap of the earth song run, while his powerful, work-hard hands snatched strange chords out of the steel strings the way they had snatched so many tons of cotton out of brown thorny cotton bolls in the fall... Son's whole body wept, as with eyes closed, the tendons in his powerful neck standing with the violence of his feeling and his brown face flushing, he sang in an awesome voice the *Death Letter Blues*.[32]

Alan's father had described his response to the music at a Texas dance on their 1933 field trip: "I felt carried across to Africa, and I left as if I were listening to the tom-toms of savage blacks."[33] But Leadbelly was no savage, nor a rural simpleton. He actually discovered blues (as distinct from other song genres) in the early 1900s, working in the red-light district of Shreveport; and at the same time he was picking up contemporary vaudeville and Tin Pan Alley songs as well, a process that continued throughout his career: established as a folk singer, he added pop, jazz, and country songs to his repertoire, including Jimmie Rodgers yodels. The Lomaxes tried to dissuade him, arguing that he should stick to "older folk songs." For John Lomax, Leadbelly "was a 'natural,' who had no idea of money, law or ethics and who was possessed of virtually no self-restraint" — which posed both a problem and an opportunity, for "his money value is to be natural and sincere"; unlike contemporary commercial African-American singers, "Leadbelly doesn't burlesque. He plays and sings with absolute sincerity. To me his music is real music." On the occasion of Leadbelly's folkloric debut — at a Modern

Languages Association conference in Philadelphia in 1934, at which he was scheduled along with a performance of "Elizabethan Ayres to the virginals" — Lomax was complimented on his "talented aborigine" who produced "a treat of uncontaminated 'original' music."[34]

Such primitivism was there from the time of the first surge in white enthusiasm for "authentic" folk blues in the mid-1920s. Carl Van Vechten — critic, writer, socialite, "undisputed downtown authority on [black] uptown night life"[35] and tireless supporter of all forms of African-American culture — begged blacks to pursue the "primitive" blues back to their sources in the South, to value their "wealth of eerie melody, borne along by a savage, recalcitrant rhythm," rather than reject these in the interests of upward cultural mobility; his description of a Bessie Smith concert homes in on her "rich, ripe beauty of southern darkness," "the monotonous African pounding of the drum," "her strange rhythm rites in a ... wild, rough Ethiopian voice, harsh and volcanic, but seductive and sensuous too."[36]

A little later, Big Bill Broonzy, though a very different character from Leadbelly, underwent a similar transformation. Mississippi born, Broonzy moved to Chicago as early as 1920, and played a key part in the evolution there, in the 1930s, of a citified, commercially orientated band-based blues style. With his career in decline after the war, he was picked up by the revivalists, toured Europe, and was remade as a "folk" artist. In Lomax's account, based on interviews with Broonzy, his 1930s trajectory was a forced response to the demands of "villainous" and "vulgar" record company bosses demanding "slavish and uncreative imitation," "cheap 'novelty' blues," "drowning the poignant and often profound poesy of the earlier country blues in oceans of superficial swill." Charles Edward Smith's picture in his Foreword for the 1964 edition of Broonzy's memoir is similar, presenting the singer's later career as a *release* into renewal of an earlier rural identity that mentally he had never left. Yet, as Charters points out, this renewal was *also* a response — a response to Broonzy's sense of a new market, and many of his new recordings were transformations of songs that had first been recorded in band formats, or even picked up from records by others or from songbooks.[37] What is interesting here, though, is that in both his Lomax interview and his own memoir Broonzy goes along with the revival narrative. He defends his "old time blues," describing them as "the real blues,"[38] and traces many of his songs back to youthful experiences in the South; it is as if he himself is "inventing" a musical past that would substantiate his folk persona.[39] There is, it appears, a double consciousness at work here — a mask that can always turn but that, from both directions, casts a particular light on the more obvious screen constituted by the blackface cork.

Black involvement in the folklorization process can be traced back to the early decades of the century. As mentioned previously, at that time folklorists (including a few African Americans as well as whites) paid little attention to blues, despite booming interest in African-American folk song. This is not surprising. Conceptions of folk culture were conventional. Dorothy Scarborough's viewpoint, though perhaps rather cruder than most, gives the drift: she writes of songs with a "rough, primitive charm," which "show us the lighter, happier side of slavery, and recreate for us the rustic merry-making of the slaves"; this results from the fact that the Negro "is closer to nature" — but this will not last, and there is an urgent need to collect these songs "before the material vanishes forever, killed by the Victrola, the radio, the lure of cheap printed music." It was hard to fit blues, "that peculiar, barbaric sort of melody… sung in vaudevilles everywhere," into this paradigm.[40] The usual line was that blues were a regrettable commercial product with buried folk origins, but this product could in turn be taken back and folklorized. As Newman White put it, blues, "which were originally folk material but which come back to the Negro, through phonographs, sheet music, and cabaret singers, as a factory product whose dubious glory may be attributed to both white and Negro 'authors,'" have now reached a stage where the "folk blues and the factory product are… almost inextricably mixed." White also points out that African Americans, as they emerged from the folk stage (that is, as an aspect of modernization), were starting to appreciate their own folk heritage — but so far their perspective was little different from that of white folklorists.[41]

A shift in educated African-American attitudes only came with the Harlem Renaissance, although it was the subject of fierce dispute. By now, spirituals had been accepted as folk heritage; Roland Hayes and the young Paul Robeson (who was friendly with Van Vechten and his circle, and with many Renaissance figures) were singing them, along with other black folk songs, on the concert stage. As we have seen, W. C. Handy, with Abbe Niles's support, insisted on the folk sources of blues but also on the need for professionals to aestheticize these sources. (George Gershwin was pursuing a parallel policy — Paul Whiteman's celebrated Aeolian Hall concert, which included the premiere of Gershwin's *Rhapsody in Blue*, took place in 1924 — a policy congruent also with the "uplift" approach to folk materials of Renaissance vanguardist, Alain Locke.) Renaissance intellectuals such as Sterling Brown, Waring Cuney, and Langston Hughes began to deploy phraseology, themes, and diction drawn from blues in their poems. B. A. Botkin's *Folk-Say* (1930) included several of these and also Brown's critical study, "The Blues as Folk Poetry," perhaps the first fully worked out scholarly attempt by an African American to assimilate current recorded blues to the criteria of folk song. (Van Vechten had followed a similar line, although in much less detail, in an article published in 1925, and the white scholars, Howard Odum and Guy Johnson, put the same argument in their 1926 book, *Negro Workaday Songs*;

much the same turn is apparent in Langston Hughes's poems and supporting critical writings from the same period, although Hughes was more interested in the urban realism of the blues than in any romantic folk origins.)[42]

Brown describes the border between "authentic" blues and "urbanized fake folk things" as vague, the work of Rainey and Bessie Smith as "of the folk," and current blues songs in general, "at their most genuine," as "accurate, imaginative transcripts of folk experience."[43] By the time of the appearance of *The Negro Caravan* (1941), a landmark collection of African-American literature of all kinds, partly edited by Brown, we find not only spirituals, traditional ballads, work songs, and two of Langston Hughes's blues poems, but a whole section devoted to blues which includes examples by Handy and Morton, songs drawn from the Lomaxes' Leadbelly collection, and also transcriptions from records by Ma Rainey, Bessie Smith, Bill Broonzy, Lonnie Johnson, Memphis Minnie, and Ida Cox. In a move typical of a modernist outlook, blues has been situated as on the one hand, folk culture, on the other, a source for art.[44] Around the same time that *The Negro Caravan* came out, Harry Smith was starting to assemble the interracial repertory for his celebrated *Anthology of American Folk Music,* a collection that would act as a basic archive for the 1950s/1960s folk revival, documenting that "old weird America," as Greil Marcus has called it.[45] In effect, Smith turned earlier entrepreneurs like Ralph Peer into folklorists, for, in an innovative and revealing move, he sourced his anthology from (by then almost forgotten) commercial records of the pre-Depression era.

In fact, this moment (the moment that Smith and *The Negro Caravan* can stand for, running from the late 1930s through the 1940s, roughly speaking) saw a veritable explosion of revivalism (down-home blues, in Chicago; "traditional" jazz; bluegrass; folk-blues and other folk musics), although in a sense the moment simply folds a further phase into an already established recessive pattern. This is also the moment in which *O Brother Where Art Thou?* is set, and, as far as the structure of revival is concerned, the film is exemplary: it enacts through its own success a revival of a culture that is already, in the film narrative, reviving its own past. The story seems to be set around 1937, but O'Daniel's campaign-song, "You Are My Sunshine," written in 1940 by country musician Jimmie Davis, was actually used in Davis's campaign for the Louisiana state governorship in 1944.[46] By contrast, an unknown Tommy Johnson is most likely to have been encountered traveling to Tishomingo (Jackson) during his early period of recording, in the late '20s or early '30s. Like a dream, then, the film diagesis condenses several periods in a historical transition on to a mythical moment, which can then serve as a node within an even longer pattern. The lynchpin song, "Man of Constant Sorrow," is "traditional." It had been first published around 1913, in a pocket songster by the blind (white) Kentucky singer, Richard Burnett, collected in the field in the Appalachians in 1918 by Cecil Sharp, who published it as "In Old Virginny," and first recorded in 1928, by hillbilly singer Emry Arthur (who knew Burnett). It was revived by bluegrass group, the Stanley Brothers, and influentially recorded by them at the Newport Folk Festival in 1959, which led to a spate of revivalist versions in the early 1960s, by Bob Dylan, Peter, Paul & Mary, and others. In the wake of *O Brother*, it became a hit all over again, together with the elderly Ralph Stanley himself. In this structure, the object of revival forever recedes from view.

Ironically (it might seem), this lost object is disseminated in the film by *modern* technology. However, records, far from destroying what we have lost, are better seen (like photographs) as producing this loss itself — or rather, as contributing to a momentous reconfiguration of the interrelations of loss, memory, and presence. Records circulate disembodied voices: spectral emanations that at one and the same time seem to come from *beyond* (beyond the grave?) and to be contained *within* an object, reanimating it in a novel form of mimesis. Friedrich Kittler among others has exhaustively explored the associations of the early phonograph and gramophone with figures of death, memorial, and the supernatural — and the striking conjunction of the technological changes with the birth of Freudian psychoanalysis (in which the unconscious is taken to write itself, its losses, memories, and desires, in an equally uncanny way).[47] Ethnographers were quick to take up the new technology, and tales of their subjects' uneasy reactions to its supernatural power are legion.[48] Both Erika Brady and Michael Taussig, though, note that urbanized Westerners were equally likely to fall into a magical interpretation, suggesting a projective/introjective structure that reflects a strange reciprocity between primitivism and modernity.[49]

But if records refigured otherness — the rush to preserve creating the very gap it recorded, in a move that Lacan's neo-Freudian theory would shortly enable us to interpret in terms of the "object voice," that voice situated uncannily outside any locus of subjectivity[50] — they built on long-established foundations. The link between disembodied voice (as in echo, for example) and supernatural power is an anthropological commonplace; the use of totemic ritual masks designed to enable the actor to represent godlike authority not only visually but also vocally has been widely documented. "Primitive" responses to the new technology from rural African Americans actually seem to be rather rare: Alan Lomax tells of an old farmer who, on hearing the recording of his friend that Lomax has just made, exclaims, "That's a ghost... It purely a ghost"; but he is immediately slapped down by the musician as "old-fashioned."[51] Was this acceptance because, even in remote areas of the South, blacks were actually *moderns*? Lomax's anecdote is set in 1942, but even in the late 1920s, when the first blues recordings to be made in the South were produced, people were familiar with technology (railways, steamboats, cotton gins, radio — and phonographs).[52] In Ma Rainey's stage act, she used to emerge from a huge cardboard Victrola, reconnecting the voice to the body and marking this easy acceptance.[53] Or was this acceptance a residue of neo-African superstition — voodoo voices, hauntings, and the familiarity of the doubling strategies offered by masking (not least in the secular parody laid out by blackface performance)? Or a combination of both, perhaps? On this account, Edison's "fugitive sound waves"[54] — always receding from grasp — represent a reconfiguration of an old dynamic, whereby fetishes externalize human powers (at the same time as making nonhuman nature speak). When, in *O Brother*, as the moment for Tommy's lynching approaches, the Grand Wizard mimes Ralph Stanley's spine-chilling song, "Oh Death," through the mask of his (oh-so-white) shroud, the layers of cultural meaning run very deep.

This structure — the lost object forever fleeing through the psychocultural strata — maps precisely to the structure of nostalgia. Densely layered, without clear origin, or else with an origin repressed from view, the nostalgic moment in its typical obsessive repetition may be identified, using Freudian-Lacanian terminology, as a species of *fantasy*, its object located within the acting out of a *fantasy scene*. In this sense, nostalgia is actually emblematic of modernity, for it is the fracturing of tradition that brings forth this particular figuring of loss, even though the effect when it emerges, as part of the psychoanalytic excavation of the modern subject, is to reveal what was always already there — a structure built around a lost object, which is in one form or another a human constant. (For psychoanalysis, the quintessential mark of this structure is of course the metaphor of castration which in turn stands as a model for a range of other separations [from the breast, the womb, etc.]: a point not without specific interest given the importance in blues of the thematic interplay between phallic insistence and its defeats.) The novelty brought by recording technology is that the object lost is now itself objectified, fetish fetishized, the commodity-totem supplementing a already existing phantasmatic cathexis. And this process happens — time is compressed — with such force that the investments are at once obscured and placed at exceptionally high risk.

But what exactly is the object of nostalgia in blues? *Loss* is the genre's main topos, usually *a propos* of love or a lover. But this is widely understood as a metonym for a broader loss — a "defiant discontent,"[55] or a "state of being as well as a way of suffering" in the words of Alan Lomax, who acutely links this both to alienation and racial terror in the Deep South in the early twentieth century and, more broadly, to the rootlessness of modern life.[56] In this context, even the more celebratory aspects of blues — sexualized boogie-woogie rhythms, the ribald fun of "hokum," the rock-solid grooves of later, urbanized musicians like B. B. King, even the good-humored dance-rhythms of jump bands such as Louis Jordan's — take on a quality of fragility: almost an out-of-time, out-of-place "as-if," experienced against a background of historical flux and racio-sexual neurosis. If the blues is "devil music," the loss it figures has the familiarity of the everyday — it is accepted, even embraced — while at the same time inhabiting a marginal moment, forming an endless dialogue of disempowerment and self-assertion. For Tony Russell, blues offers, for whites as well as blacks, an invitation to enter a different space: "to step out in the guise of the blues is to step out of line. Blues confers a license to break rules and taboos, say the unsayable, create its own dark carnival."[57]

One way into this territory is via the classic "bad man" ballad, "Stagolee," based on real events taking place in St. Louis in 1895, which, however, quickly formed themselves into a legend generating hundreds of song versions, associated with both blacks and whites, and a myth with a potency, especially for African Americans, that has lasted to gangsta rap. Common to most versions is that Stagolee shoots his antagonist in cold blood over the theft of his hat, and that the bragging machismo of this anti-hero produces awe-struck respect. Cecil Brown stresses the racial dimension.[58] The real murderer, Lee Shelton, was a black pimp working in a red light district of St. Louis, a marginal area where blacks and whites could mingle, and was also involved in political struggles around the issue of the black vote. Attempts by "progressive" politicians to clean up such areas went side by side with exoticising descriptions by slumming white journalists, drawing on blackface discourse (for instance, the "razor-toting coon"). It is easy to see why Stagolee could be a hero to the growing black lumpen class; but many early versions were associated with whites (including the first recordings), even though Brown traces the main thematic elements back into stories about anti-slavery rebels, and points out that many black versions end with the hero's descent into hell, where usually he throws out the Devil (variably figured as a white man or another "bad nigger") and takes over. Shelton knew Tom Turpin, composer of the first published rags, and Brown speculates that Turpin may have created the first "Stagolee" song, but it first surfaces as a holler from ex-slaves moving into Mississippi levee camps; although not formally a blues, it is often described as such in song titles, and its macho theme certainly fed into blues traditions.[59]

It seems possible that the blues nexus emerged in the early years of the century precisely through a graft of such highly charged and often morally ambivalent themes on to the evolving pool of proto-blues vernacular and commercial musical developments: a "dark carnival" indeed. Mississippi banjo player Lucius Smith, who started performing in 1902, playing old-style (pre-blues) dance music with Sid Hemphill's string band, had fascinating views on the advent of blues:

> The blues done ruined the country... It just make 'em go off at random, I'd say, frolicking, random, you see. More folks have got killed since they start playing the blues than ever been. It's just a, you know, just a out of order piece... the "Memphis Blues" and all that, it done brought about a whole lots of it, you know, I'd say, trouble... Makes a racket, you know, with young folks, you see... The blues ain't nothing but a racket. A whole lot of drunk folks, you know, don't care for nothing, and they just bring eternity, the blues do. Heaps of folk love to hear it, but it just brings eternity...[60]

Intriguingly, this sort of historical shift is exactly what Newman White outlined in 1928: he saw Handy's mediating role as crucial, but "folk blues," he speculated, originated in the "Negro underworld" of cities like Memphis and St. Louis, from where it passed through the streets and levees to construction gangs and rural workers.[61] In "Stagolee," the fixing of the themes of loss, race, and violence to the specific topos of sex is still loose; the hero fights over a symbol of his manhood, his Stetson.[62] In blues, this knot is tied, with a vengeance. Blues foregrounds the knowledge that human beings have always needed, tried, sometimes failed to learn, that the sexual relationship always falls short (in Lacan's more radical aphorism, "There is no sexual relationship.")[63]; quarrels, mistreatment, break-up, absence dramatize this essential core, which situates the sexual act as always a species of nostalgia, a reference to a fulfillment forever lost — a reference, therefore, that can stand in for all other disappointments and deprivations. The obsession with sex in blues marks out a territory where a particular topology of desire and rupture (specified culturally and historically) overlays and stands for the founding deprivations of subjecthood itself — at the limit, the cry of the fallen creature as such. As in all manifestations of nostalgia, the true object of desire is veiled — an absence fantasized as a presence which, however, is never quite there. The blues condition is often personified ("Mr. blues, how do you do?"), but comes upon the singer unawares, appears behind one's back, in dreams, a ghostly presence; it is a specter — a *conjuration*. (Some singers, including Tommy Johnson, have described their music as "air music," referring to its mysterious, apparently supernatural source.)[64] In Lacanian terms, it is an *objet a*, object-cause of desire, around which actual movements of desire can only circle, which will always be missed.

Does the blues drama truly represent a desire to confront the loss on which it is built? For Lacan, the fantasy scene functions as a repetitive image, protecting the subject from trauma (ultimately, from the terror of castration). It is located in a framed, theatrical space (that is, within the sphere of the Symbolic), which, however, invokes an unknowable Real, a space lying beyond the frame; and it is "acted out" (performed) in response to an alienation — the other's refusal to listen (that is, it stands for a blockage). What is the trauma that is silenced here? Surely, the murderous scene "down home."[65] For blacks, this is obviously rooted in the history of slavery and since, but for whites too there is an investment via mechanisms of guilt, projection, and appropriation. But for both groups, might not these specific symptoms also be standing for something deeper — for a primal structure, made raw by the effects of modernity that find their point of most intense focus in images of black bodies, commodified by capitalism in its crudest form (slavery) and now at one and the same time simulated, evacuated, and fetishized all over again in the objects of mass reproduction technology?[66] This scene is a family scene, and the structure is of course oedipal; but it is also fratricidal (Cain and Abel, black and white, Oh Brother!), rooted in a particular horror, fear, and guilt engendered by a competitive resistance, but also a secretly complicit accommodation, to the primal castration threat: a sado-masochistic fratricidal embrace, for "there is no *racial* relationship" either, and blues is devil's music because, in its exemplary determination to stare secularity straight in the face, the "Name-of-the-Father" is forever at issue, forever displaced. After all, the union of these United States had been consummated through the fratricidal strife of the Civil War, within which African Americans were located as both object and subject (at least in part, or in waiting). At the same time, on a broader historical canvas, brother-trouble, along with the woman-problem that is its inevitable issue, surely stands at the core of a key cultural problematic of the nineteenth and twentieth centuries, its stain running through a range of fractures constituted by racial, colonial, and class difference as well as by the alienated psychologies of the urban masses. Blues trauma stands for no little local difficulty.[67]

The figure of blues nostalgia, and the traumatic hinterland it covers, thus locates us in an historical structure of meaning, allied on the one hand to the layered pattern of revival, but condensed also on to a concrete sexualized metonym that in turn relates to a network of racialized projections, introjections, and abjections. If, after the fashion of Lacanian algebra, we write nostalgia as N, this is to locate it as a specific aspect of O — the Big Other, the Symbolic system as such. But N is forever fractured by the impossible claims of O (because there can be no final signifier, justifying its authority), forever as a result splitting off symptoms of n (*object petit n)* in the incessant coursing of subjective desire: unassimilable, spectral, allied to the founding trauma located in the Real. Thus:

$$\frac{\emptyset}{N} \rightarrow n(\$)$$

that is, N, "divided into" the barred (incomplete) Big Other, splinters off infinite numbers of n, which in turn help structure the barred (split) subject:

a formula that should be given the dynamics of a vortex in which intersecting tropes of modernity, tradition, and subjectivity pull us giddily towards an uncertain future.

N can be privatized, that is, move towards purely personalized lament; this is what happens in some white song genres (Broadway/Tin Pan Alley blues, torch songs), so that, where personal loss in blues is understood to stand for a larger structure, it now takes center stage. The reverse trajectory is what produces (the mythical) "real blues," the howl of down-home melodrama. Actually existing blues (black and white) are then squeezed out between these two pressures.

How might we read these processes in songs? I will focus my brief excursus on one particular moment — the first down-home peak in the late '20s and early '30s — when the spread of a recording culture had enabled the down-home style to take its place within a broad, intricately differentiated blues territory. First, though, I will outline a hermeneutic model appropriate to the cultural analysis offered already.

Fantasy-scenes, we might suggest, are animated by attaching "looks" and/or "voices" to other subjects, creating imagined dialogues, and hence symbolic fictions. This process involves also eliding, repressing, or misrepresenting object gaze and object voice: symptoms of the Real. But if the pressures are sufficiently strong, subversions of the scene and its dialogues may appear, bending them to the force of the *objet a*, disrupting consistency. Slavoj Žižek theorizes two particular fantasy-modes, each of which skews these mechanisms in a distinctive direction.[68] In *pornography*, he argues, the viewing (and, we may add, the listening) subject assumes the position of object of instrumentalized arousal, that which is acted upon for the pleasure of the other. In *nostalgia*, by contrast, the subject, rather than being objectified, is *over-subjectified*, or, to put it another way, doubled: the viewing (and listening) subject half-identifies with (but also distances itself from) a mythical, naïve viewer who we can imagine still believes in the fantasy that at the same time we know to be impossible. (This is how *O Brother* works: our self-conscious retrospective knowledge acts as a bracket as we allow the characters to watch for us; the bracketing devices — the naiveté of many of the songs (as they sound to us now), the cartoon-ish, slapstick gestures, the various framing techniques that locate the action in an inaccessible past — are the source of the humor.) In both cases, however, these structures can be disrupted, subverting the pleasure of perversion (in the first case), unveiling hidden trauma (in the second). For Žižek, discussing film examples, disruption is produced through a surplus of the Real left over from the operations of montage — that is, a space implied by, but left out of, the screen image, something "uncanny" that "sticks out." In songs, the equivalent is voices (sung or played) that do not belong.

To the degree that blues references a mythic source, a lost state (that is, approximates the structure of nostalgia), the blues listener follows the singer in, as it were, inhabiting that gap, watching that gaze and imagining it, in an act of appropriation, as the (illusory) object gaze itself (this is what the famous "objectivity" of blues, identifiable even in the most fraught of songs, amounts to). But the moment an unexpected or dissonant voice enters the scene, the fiction may unravel. In George O'Connor's "Nigger Blues," this dissonance is conjured up in relation to an absence; it is the product of the listener's retrospective knowledge (which stands in for the putative black response — if there was one — in 1916). By the late 1920s, when the "montage" of blues repertoire had developed a much bigger (interracial) range, the issues had become starker and more convoluted.

From 1928, when he recorded "How Long, How Long Blues" with guitarist Scrapper Blackwell, through to his death in 1935, pianist and singer Leroy Carr was commercially the most successful bluesman of the period.[69] The tone of his best-known records — "How Long," "Midnight Hour Blues," "Blues Before Sunrise," "Hurry Down Sunshine" — has often been described as, in a straightforward way, nostalgic:[70] his warm, lyrical singing, suffused with a mood of introspective melancholy, the typically slow, rather dragging tempi, the warm, blurry piano chording, combine to create an effect analogous to that of an old photograph, an effect given precise expression in many of the lyrics — "My mind is running back to days of long ago"; "I've been sitting here thinking with my mind a million miles away"; "How long has that evening train been gone?" — to the last of which the follow-on point is that his departed lover will be sorry someday, but "it will be too late": it is, so it seems, always too late in Carr.

Yet, at the same time, Carr is an intensely *modern* artist. A key influence on the emergence of a citified male blues in the 1930s, especially in Chicago, he is notable for the regularity of his musical formats (square phrases, clearly measured time, square melodic shapes with "rhyming" cadences, and a focus, often, on major-pentatonic or triadic arpeggios with few blue notes). Of course, it is ironic that the modernity implied by this move towards Tin Pan Alley norms is fixed to themes of loss — as if it were always a mirage. Moreover, it is for ever going awry — in guitar figures that do not quite fit harmonically or rhythmically, and lyric phrases that Carr struggles to fit into the metric scheme (unlike a down-home singer, he is not able to stretch the rhythm to accommodate the words) — while at the same time it is undercut by elements of bluesiness and of boogie-woogie rhythm.

As has often been pointed out, these latter elements are particularly associated with the contribution of Blackwell, whose incisive guitar lines offer an astringency that acts, perhaps, as an ironic commentary on Carr's daydreams. They do more than this, however. Blackwell's riffing around blue notes and his typical triplet-based phrasing, conjuring images, at whatever distance, of dancing bodies, reference somewhere down-home — an "if only" (we could remember, could get back there . . .). Carr is not deaf to this other voice. There are faster pieces — "Barrelhouse Woman," "Good Woman Blues," "Sloppy Drunk Blues" — in which, despite the tone of regret still there in the voice, an energy associated with the memory of an older culture is summoned. But this energy does not just operate as a contrasting backdrop to the core repertory; it crosses the gap. Quite often there are hints in Carr's piano of (as-it-were almost forgotten) boogie rhythmic and bass patterns — as if glimpsed through a veil — and, most movingly, on occasions these gather themselves into halting, transient double-time passages in a boogie rhythm; the codas of "Blues Before Sunrise" and "Hurry Down Sunshine" are examples. Listening to Carr's music against a knowledge of these examples, one starts to hear the piano as "wanting" to break into a boogie shuffle, even when it fails to do so. In two of his last recordings, made just two months before his death, "Going Back Home" and "Six Cold Feet in the Ground," the intense melancholy at very slow tempos does not prevent the inclusion in each piece of a solo piano chorus with hazily contoured double-time boogie effects; the eroticism for which boogie-woogie rhythm stands will not be stilled, even by the grave.[71]

The tissue of voices in Carr's songs is still more intricate, however. In his most lyrical records, the vocal timbre together with the phraseology and intonation often suggest comparison with contemporary white hillbilly singers. (His recording career coincides almost exactly with that of Jimmie Rodgers, the first hillbilly star, who was equally prominent and influential within his own musical milieu; perhaps it is no accident that some of Carr's tunes carry hints in their shapes of white folk tunes.) At the same time, the intimacy of his vocal production — unlike many down-home records, Carr's sound as if they come out of a studio and there is no attempt to "transcribe" live performance — also brings to mind the approach of contemporary crooners. In "Prison Bound Blues," for example, as his eloquent farewell to his sweetheart moves towards the privatized nostalgia of straight-forward romance, one could almost identify the missing voice — spectrally invoked but hardly available to an African American at this date — as that of Bing Crosby.

To fully grasp the "scene" within which Carr's records were heard means to place him within this network of voices, another strand of which was the "hokum blues" initiated by Tampa Red's enormous hit, "It's Tight Like That," recorded (like Carr's "How Long") in 1928.[72] This genre of good-time, humorous party blues, with lyrics that were usually ribald going on obscene, became a second important foundation for emergent city blues (and, as that tradition developed in the 1930s, there are occasions when — recalling Žižek's terms — nostalgia moves towards pornography). Tightly written and performed, produced in response to a new, urban market, this song-type was, again, a clearly modern one (and the flood of covers and imitations of Tampa Red's song speaks to the effects of commercial music production norms); yet, as Davis has argued, it also has an intensely nostalgic air: the rhymes and risqué humor go way back, the ambience of good-humored nonsense suggests roots in minstrelsy and coon song (the stereotype tempered, as so often by mirth), and the raggy, happy-go-lucky performance style locates us at an imagined country dance as much as a city rent-party.[73] This is music that was *meant* to seem old: the couplet-and-refrain form points back towards the disappearing world of the songsters, while the rigid instrumental formulae, especially at turnarounds, not only fit right into the requirements of commercial mass production but also add to the sense of eternal repetition associated with social dance-song; but of course it is this — the music's nostalgic always-already quality — that gives away its modernity. The apparent naiveté of the musicians only half-masks their self-awareness — less than that in the remake of the initial hit, a few months later, by the Hokum Jug Band, in which Tampa Red's guitar and Georgia Tom Dorsey's piano are supplemented with washboard, kazoo, and jug, the lyrics are cut right down, and the "live" social context is knowingly represented by background chat and laughter. Pointing themselves to a "dialogue" with Leroy Carr, the same band also recorded a version of "How Long How Long Blues." The jug band accompaniment puts flesh on Carr's skeletal pointers to a disappearing culture. But the most striking feature is the extraordinary vocal by female impressionist Frankie "Half-Pint" Jaxon, whose falsetto plaint to "her" missing "daddy" reverses the gender positioning of Carr's original — but with a twist: as Jaxon's technique moves increasingly towards grotesquerie, he speaks also, and perhaps out of a moment that was particularly fraught for urbanizing masculinity, to the female blues singers of the time, satirizing it would seem (with a comedy that is quite scary) their sexual demands.[74]

Of course, the contribution of those female singers constitutes an essential backdrop to the work of all the male blues performers of the later 1920s, even though their popularity was beginning to fade by the end of the decade. They had dominated the process of establishing blues as a commercial song genre, set many of the structural and performance norms, and disseminated a good deal of repertoire. They dominated partly because they were *there*; that is, there was an established tradition of female professional popular singing, available to black women, within which songs of romance featured heavily (by contrast, commercial singing for black men had typically been limited to comic roles). Moreover, even within blackface contexts, women could offer strong personae (however caricatured); this was a lineage that was there to be exploited. (The racial negotiations were actually quite delicate: it was risky for black men to sing about sex unless the object of their desire were clearly designated as black, whereas black women could be less inhibited. Indeed, for white listeners an enjoyable frisson might attach to racially ambiguous expressions of their demand.) This structural difference between the genders meshed neatly with the upheaval in sexual mores in the earlier part of the decade (which in turn may help explain why the female repertoire tended to shift subsequently towards torch song, as this upheaval was quashed). Thus, to the extent that the women were at the forefront of representing pent-up feelings of sexual desire and demands for greater independence — the most forthright of them, such as Ma Rainey and Bessie Smith, certainly were — they can be seen as asking questions with which, in one way or another, all the male blues singers of the time had to come to terms.

Rainey and Smith — Southerners, schooled professionally on the Southern minstrel show circuit — also mediated between the cultures of the down-home South and of Northern big-city vaudeville. When Mississippi singer, Charley Patton, recorded his song about the widespread floods of 1927, "High Water Everywhere" (1929), he would certainly have had in his mind Bessie Smith's 1927 hit on the same subject, "Back Water Blues." Similarly, he clearly modeled his "Tom Rushen Blues" (1929) and "High Sheriff Blues" (1934) on Ma Rainey's "Booze and Blues" (1924). Both Smith and Rainey sang humorous songs and hokum, too. Ma Rainey, who often included Tampa Red and Georgia Tom in her bands, also recorded vaudevillian duets with Papa Charlie Jackson ("Ma and Pa Poorhouse Blues," "Big Feeling Blues," both 1928), not to mention the ribald "Shave 'Em Dry" in 1924. "Nobody in Town Can Bake a Sweet Jelly Roll Like Mine" (1923), "Put It Right Here (or Keep It Out There)" (1928), and "I'm Wild about That Thing" (1929) exemplify similar categories for Bessie Smith. Convincing anecdote, for both Smith and Rainey, suggests that their sexual appetites were stimulated by women as well as men, a sisterly deviation celebrated in riotous fashion in the latter's "Prove It on Me" (1928). If the fantasmatic exchanges articulated in blues dialogue are taken to reference, at one level, the dynamics of a (racially distorted) brotherhood, the precarious foundations of this fraternal struggle are exposed by any threat of exchange between (rather than with or of) women. But the racial warping of any sisterly embrace is signaled in turn by the shift from blues to torch song — or, to put it in explicitly racial terms, by the "transfer" from Ruth Etting, Helen Morgan, Libby Holman, Fanny Brice (all white) to Billie Holiday.

Within this wider, always gendered context, blues dialogue between men — among "brothers" — could only be multifaceted. Carr and Blackwell could do hokum as well as their more celebrated lyrical numbers ("Papa Wants a Cookie," "Carried Water for the Elephant"), though there is always a suspicion of incongruity between the material and Carr's vocal aesthetic. These songs function as yet another aspect of what, in Carr's universe, can only be invoked in fantasy. Indeed, in "Papa Wants," the perfectly tuned (rather than blue) flat thirds and sevenths sound like nothing so much as what we might hear in a concert rendition of a published blues (one of Handy's, for instance) or even, the reified form they assume in O'Connor's "Nigger Blues": an extraordinarily ironic allusion across the blackface mask. In fact, hokum — or what "hokum," once designated, grew out of — featured in many blues singers' repertories — even those categorized as the most intense, emotional, and uncompromising of down-home singers, such as Charley Patton, the personification of Mississippi Delta blues for subsequent blues folklorists, and a mentor for a whole group of influential musicians, including Tommy Johnson. Patton's "Shake It and Break It," for example, with its seemingly never-ending supply of verses, happily lewd lyrics, and a dance rhythm with suggestions of raggy fiddle and banjo, locates us in the world of a country picnic. Yet its style is what lies behind the extraordinary "Spoonful Blues," which is structured like a country rag (an endless circle of VI-II-V-I chord-changes), but played on slide guitar with a lurching, other-worldly effect, and "sung" in a multiplicity of voices, sung and spoken, delivering fragmentary, often uncompleted lyrics. This is a drug song (the "spoonful" is of cocaine — although as the song goes on it appears to stand in as well for any desirable intoxicant, such as sex), and if it presents a nostalgic fantasy scene, this is a surreal nostalgia passed through the eye of a decidedly modern form of alienation.

This marks Patton as a modern. And his most celebrated recordings, with their musically very different style, confirm it. This style is often described as the most "primitive" of all recorded blues styles. And to be sure, in such songs as "Pony Blues," "Down the Dirt Road Blues," "Screamin' and Hollerin' the Blues," "High Water Everywhere," and "Green River Blues," the harsh, abrasive vocal tone, held vowels often tightening into a rasp, the guttural diction with words sometimes indecipherable, the percussive accompaniments (the guitar body often used as a drum), the flexible treatment of chord changes and metre, the treble guitar figures often running in almost heterophonic parallel with the voice, challenge the norms of contemporary mainstream popular song to their core. But the *rage* this style portrays (an emotion plentifully documented in Patton's own life) delineates a very modern sense of alienation — one encapsulated as well in his deployment of multiple voices.[75]

It is impossible to pin down the Patton persona. In addition to the spoken asides and falsettos, even his "own" voice possesses such extreme timbral shifts, as vowels mutate, that it is as if there were another voice inside there somewhere. This technique reaches an extraordinary pitch in "High Water Everywhere," where the voice is pushed so hard that we seem to hear a chest voice plus a tighter throat voice an octave higher in an uncanny doubling effect, as if imitating the kazoo he liked to play (though not on records), and which we might link (according to David Evans) to the use of such instruments in Africa to supply a voice for masks in ritual performances.[76] It seems highly appropriate that at one stage Patton was marketed by Paramount as "The Masked Marvel"; examining his masked portrait, customers were invited to compete to name his identity.

Patton's ancestry was racially highly mixed (African American/white/native American). His performances were popular with many whites and he was well respected by some of them. He was ambitious as artist and entertainer, and Evans suggests that he saw an international reputation as not beyond him. His outrage at the inescapability of his racial categorization was, not surprisingly, as acute as his insistence on an independent life was unshakeable. He was the epitome of marginality: his "'niche' in the system consisted of placing himself *outside* the system and actually *avoiding* a niche, never permanently accommodating..."[77] He recorded some songs that seem to derive from pop numbers. But "Runnin' Wild Blues" turns Tin Pan Alley's "Runnin' Wild" into something midway between a hymn and a country dance, while "Some These Days I'll Be Gone" puts words stemming from Sophie Tucker's hit, "Some of these Days" to a lyrical, hymnlike melody invoking hillbilly. Both are extraordinarily evocative, melding contemporary pop and an image of a (cross-racial) folk past into an ambivalent whole in which the elements refuse to separate out. Patton's output is full of archaic references ("Frankie and Albert," "Elder Greene Blues," which is the old rag "Alabama Bound," popularized by Charlie Jackson — not to mention his many spirituals and gospel hymns), and when he incorporates contemporary material, it turns into something already past; it is as if *this* sort of modernity refuses to "come out." Similarly, in "Tom Rushen Blues," Patton can sing a tune that Leroy Carr would appreciate (it is in fact very similar to "Midnight Hour Blues"), but his vocal timbre drags it back to the Delta. His very status as an entertainer — he was famous for his clowning — looks both back and forward, speaking to his commercial nous but at the same time conjuring memories of minstrelsy, just as the hybridity of his repertoire links him, as a songster, to a pre-blues world "before history" but also to the exigencies of modern cultural markets.

The extent to which things do not fit in Patton is very high, and this is perhaps as close as blues comes to unveiling the trauma underlying its fictive landscapes. Yet his determination to survive in this new, modern world renders complete "honesty" — which after all would implode the subject — impossible, while on the other hand old worlds, layer upon layer, are constantly brought up through the mists of cultural memory. There is always another voice, another position, threatening to disrupt the scene, but at the same time confirming the essential ambivalence of blues fantasy; and when Patton, as he often does, leaves lines in his lyrics unfinished or completes them with a guitar phrase, he reserves both a position and a distance (for us, for himself): He assumes we know the missing words for they have already been heard, the original has already gone (a nostalgic naiveté, this, which is more knowing than Žižek's theory can allow). And, on a broader level, this exteriority is then doubled, as Patton plays the missing other to Leroy Carr and Tampa Red — just as they do, in return, for him.

Further out still, what do we hear, faintly but insistently, but "white blues": above all Jimmie Rodgers, the rambling "singing brakeman" from Mississippi, whose "blue yodels" established the genre in country music. In, for example, his first blue yodel, "T for Texas" (1927), his singing sounds rather like a more nasal version of Leroy Carr's — or, more precisely, like a cross between this and the sound of Tommy Johnson. Small wonder, perhaps, that Rodgers started off his career in blackface, playing traveling medicine shows (was *he* the Masked Marvel? Well no, but . . .). Debate over the origins of yodeling in country music shows no sign of concluding, but is immaterial here: in the context of blues singing in the late 1920s, Rodgers's blue yodels could hardly help but suggest distorted images of the falsetto effects common in black blues. (Tommy Johnson was well known for this device; it occurs in, for instance, his "Canned Heat Blues" and throughout "Cool Drink of Water Blues.") More interesting for us is that in African-American blues singing falsettos are almost always transient effects, usually at the end of a phrase, whereas Rodgers constructs entire yodeled refrains. The difference is between a hint of another voice *within* (perhaps with implications for gendering) and a throwing of the voice, as it were, *without*: a ventriloquistic objectification (as with alpine yodeling, one of the putative sources of the technique). Is this the mark of a power differential — the white voice assuming an alignment with the authority of the object gaze — or, to the contrary, a shriveling of the self virtually to the status of thing (as, perhaps, in the tradition of the black field holler, one of the other putative sources)?[78] Or both (a play with the longing for a reciprocal exchange of masks)?

What is in any case clear is that this network of blues voices constitutes an intricately tied cultural knot in which racialized identity is continually at stake, both for blacks and whites, the knot always at risk of unraveling.[79] A similar analysis could no doubt be applied to the second great nub in the history of the blues Golden Age — the '40s and early '50s. The down-home passion of the Mississippi "deep blues" was revived by Delta émigrés, Muddy Waters and Howlin' Wolf; Leroy Carr's position was occupied by B. B. King (who acknowledged Carr's influence on his singing, along with that of Lonnie Johnson and country star Gene Autry); hokum took on a new lease of life in the good-time R&B of Louis Jordan; while white investments were represented by, for example, Hank Williams in country music and, above all, if a few years later, by Elvis Presley. In both cases, what is at issue is the dialogue of voices, including voices from elsewhere, which may indeed not even be heard: the absences without which the songs would shrivel. These dialogues together with these absences — interruptions and prompts from off stage — constitute the theatrical field for the *always already blackface subject*, through whose circuitry blues is unavoidably mediated.

For Žižek, following Lacan,[80] such absence, the mark of the object gaze, is a "blot," "stain," or "spot" on the image, the gaze's implied point of origin which, by definition, the subject — limited to a specific perspective — can never see. By analogy, the object voice is inaudible, forever located outside that scene within which voice began to carry meaning, to function for a subject. In "miscegenating" blues, this spot, this impossible trace, is surely the "mark of Cain," whose hermeneutic shiftiness — is it black or white? a mark of authority, exile or guilt? what governs its visibility? how does it relate to the mask? — has been outlined by W. T. Lhamon in his wonderful book *Raising Cain*. The significance of this figure to the fratricidal conflict of the blues family is clear. But in a wider context, it goes far beyond the historical specifics of Southern racism. In *O Brother, Where Art Thou?*, the cross-racial band of Odysseans are saved in the end by a flood which perhaps represents modernity (it initiates a hydro-electric scheme: "the South is changing," as Everett tells us), or equally, in the longer perspective of mythological history, a broader moral challenge. This challenge is surely to be located in the perpetual (always transmuting, always reviving) need to dislodge the (political and representational) colonial state — the dialectic of slavery.

******

Blues was far from being the only musical arena within which the interconnected dramas of black and white, and of modernity and tradition, were played out in the 1920s and '30s. In 1927, a show opened in New York which, one could imagine, might have been called "O Sister, Where Art Thou?" if its authors, Jerome Kern and Oscar Hammerstein II, had not more conventionally followed the title of the 1926 Edna Ferber novel from which they drew their story — *Show Boat*. Like the novel, the musical is explicitly concerned with history, nostalgia, and modernity, and also with race: it is a miscegenating story, both in theme and, as it turned out, in production, for not only does it, unusually for the period, contain significant roles for black characters, it also includes black and white choruses which at times sing together — a move that was probably without precedent.[81]

The central storyline of *Show Boat* is conventional enough. Magnolia Hawkes, daughter of the showboat's owners, falls in love with the Southern aristocrat, Gaylord Ravenal, whose looks and manners are as convincing as his fantasies. She achieves success on the stage, but the marriage collapses as Gay's gambling ruins them — only for this to be reversed in a final reunion, accompanied by the stage success of their daughter, Kim. But this is "make-believe," to quote the words of the show itself — "Only make believe I love you," as the duet that initiates the romance puts it. On this level, *Show Boat* is about the mechanisms of representation itself (Attali's *faire croire*), together with the strategies of performance through which (self-) convincing identities can be presented. To an extent this is generic to the musical as such, of course, but Hammerstein seems to have believed in the truth-content of fantasy for particular reasons as well: "the enchantment of theater, however primitive, is what holds a community together," he thought; "theater is good for democrats."[82] The question that follows, though, is what the price of such "truth" might be; what might be the incongruities, the too-real elements that refuse to fit, which have to be excluded if make-believe is to weave its spell? Here the subplot — the doomed relationship between Julie and Steve, the initial leads in the showboat cast, who are replaced by Magnolia and Gay, and whose story forms a distorted mirror-image of their narrative — will be crucial.

Romance here (as in blues, although in a context governed by very different generic conventions) is a metonym standing for the wider theme of "history." The plot moves through half a century, starting in the late 1880s (on the riverside at Natchez Mississippi, and in the showboat tied up there to put on performances), through the World Exposition in 1893 Chicago, and Chicago some years later (1904), to end back in Natchez in the present (1927). Nostalgic appeal was built in, for showboat theater, which dated back to the early nineteenth century, enjoyed its golden age in the period from the Civil War to the First World War, and by 1927 it was all but dead. The narrative articulates an interplay between the resulting sense of loss and a sequence of historical shifts that continually push the characters into modernity. (By bringing together in the figure of the showboat the themes of *mobility* and of *show* [representation, especially performative self-representation], it also encapsulates a central American dynamic of the period — as, in its own way, blues did too.) It maps this structure to both geography (from South to North and back again: a projected unity but also a tension) and to the generational rhythm lived out by the Hawkes-Ravenal family, in which cultural shifts are projected against the backdrop of a mighty continuity, that of "Ol Man River" (the Mississippi) itself. This historical layering follows, once again, the structure of nostalgic fantasy.

The musical depiction of this historically mutating landscape is neatly done.[83] The overture and opening chorus intersperse the expected Romantic style markers with off-beat banjo plunks, pentatonic melodic figures, oom-pah, slightly syncopated two-four rhythms, and "barbershop" chord-slides, conjuring up memories of minstrelsy, ragtime, spiritual, and work-song.[84] (The words with which black Natchez welcomes the showboat — "Niggers all work on the Mississippi" — contain potential political ambivalence; but if the 1936 movie is any guide, the overall atmosphere is jolly, with only the most cursory push on the odd cotton bale: the happy Southland [so far].)

The "glittering" orchestration suggests comparison with the similar effects that Gershwin uses for exoticising scene-setting in *Porgy and Bess*, and the prominent tuba bass (march, rag, early jazz) helps confirm the specific cultural location.

Similarly, our move to the Chicago World Exposition is authenticated by two slices of appropriate exotica: "Fatima's Dance," a piece of orientalism actually popularized at the Fair by the dancer "Little Egypt" for the "Streets of Cairo" pavilion; and Kern's own "In Dahomey," a "barbaric" dance for the "Zulus" [*sic*] of the Dahomey Village, whose pounding drum-beat, relentless ostinati, modest dissonance, and mumbo-jumbo lyrics suggest a kind of Everyman's *Le Sacre*. Later (in 1904), the scene is set for Magnolia's audition at the Trocadero (Gay has left and she needs to find work again) by Sousa's *Washington Post March* (1889); and she is asked to update her test-piece by "ragging" it. In the following scene (which stages her first Trocadero performance), the music is almost all diagetic. Magnolia sings an "old favorite": Charles Harris's "After the Ball" (1892). She is preceded by her old colleagues from the showboat, Frank and Ellie, performing the coon song "Goodbye My Lady Love" (Joseph E. Howard, 1904) and the cakewalk "At a Georgia Camp Meeting" (Kerry Mills, 1897), and the scene is closed out with a snatch of "(There'll Be) A Hot Time in the Old Town Tonight" (Theodore Metz, 1896). Finally, towards the end (in 1927), Queenie, the showboat's black cook, sings a hot "flapper" number; and Kim performs a jazzed-up version of her parents' earlier romantic "Why Do I Love You?"[85]

This "music history" works. As one reviewer in 1927 put it (somewhat simplistically), "he [Kern] has blended the Negro spirituals of the Southland with jazz of today . . . he has caught the subtle distinction that exists between jazz and the ragtime of twenty or twenty-five years ago . . . "[86] But there are interesting creaks. The opening overture and chorus certainly position us "back then" and "down there," but the style specifics are mashed together: this is *mythic* history. The key song, "Can't Help Lovin' Dat Man," is presented, even when set in the late 1880s, as embedded in black tradition; to Kreuger, it is a "pseudo-Negro folk tune."[87] Yet it actually sounds like a 1920s torch song (which is, indeed, what it is). Immediately before Magnolia's Trocadero audition, her old friend from showboat days, Julie, tries out a new number. This is "Bill," actually written by Kern, but with P. G. Wodehouse, in 1918. Again, especially in performances by the first Julie, Helen Morgan, this comes over as a torch song. The initial version of "Why Do I Love You?" (set in 1893) is performed first with prominent banjo in the accompaniment (historically fine), then transformed into a waltz (okay), but then into a foxtrot (which did not emerge as a dance genre until about 1912).

Perhaps there is a clue to the ground of these vacillations in Kern's World's Fair exotica. These function as historical color, clearly. But at the same time, they may be regarded as embedding the work's racial theme in a broader structure of neo-colonial exoticism, within which historical accuracy is of distinctly secondary importance. The Zulu/Dahomey dancers, once they have frightened the whites off the stage, switch musically to ragtime and lyrically into English, identifying their real home as New York; this is an amusing deconstruction (although the ragtime style is about a decade before its time), but in its equivocation (a primitivism within modernity? modernity's construction of primitivism?) it points, I think, towards a deeper ambivalence around the representation of black otherness.[88] There is an added piquancy here. Kern's piece is, we can surely assume, making reference to the highly successful, all-black 1902 musical show, starring the celebrated vaudeville blackface team, Bert Williams and George Walker, and composed (mostly) by Will Marion Cook, *In Dahomey*. The plot of this show satirizes a contemporary interest among some blacks in returning to Africa (it is set partly in Florida and partly in "Dahomey"), lampooning both African-American class pretensions and myths about savage Africa — not to mention white ambivalence. ("On Emancipation Day," runs one song, "All you white folks clear de way/ . . . When dey hear dem ragtime tunes/ White folks try to pass fo' coons/ On Emancipation Day.") Compared to this, Kern's piece, while on one level shifting the theme back ten years to populate the (real) Dahomey Village in 1893 Chicago, appears from the standpoint of 1927 as a weak echo, turning sly comedy into assimilated nostalgia.[89]

For the *Show Boat* "make-believe" is fantasy for *white* folks. Blacks have a role — if whites are to progress into modernity, this role, it turns out, is indispensable — but it is presented as basically supportive; it can be read in the gaps of Kreuger's enthusiastic endorsement: "The depiction of the innocent South of the nineteenth century, the roistering gaiety of old Chicago . . . and the depiction of the modern theater all rang true . . . "[90]

The miscegenation theme is key to understanding these gaps. Julie (emotionally the real heroine of the show, it might be argued) has racially mixed parentage. Her marriage to the white Steve is illegal in the state of Mississippi, and they are forced to leave the showboat. But not before she has passed on what she knows — and she "knows more than she should"[91] — to the youthful Magnolia. In the pantry scene, early in Act 1, Julie launches into "Can't Help Lovin' Dat Man," a song she should not know (because, according to Queenie, it is a "colored folks" song), but which, Magnolia tells us, Julie often sings on their walks together. Queenie takes up the song, and then the whole group (including her husband, Joe, and the other black servants, male and female), while Magnolia performs a (black) "shuffle" dance. A transfer of knowledge, a cultural and racial relay, is put in motion here, that will reverberate through the entire work; and this knot is pointedly tied at the beginning of the song verse, when Julie sings (by implication to Queenie) "Oh, listen sister."[92]

Ironically, "Can't Help Lovin' Dat Man" is musically a "white woman's blues." The main chorus strain starts off with pentatonic, yet richly harmonized phrases (with innocent Nature imagery: "fish gotta swim, birds gotta fly"[93]), but ends with a chromatic lurch in the harmony and a blue (that is, minor) third in the tune (to represent the irrational, aching inescapability of love).

Example 2.1

This language shifts us into torch song territory — and it is, in part, the cultural bridge-crossing that moves us there.[94] The verse is a "Tin Pan Alley blues": a twelve-bar structure with chromatic passing chords and written-in "blue notes" (that is, major/minor oscillations or even clusters) in both vocal and accompaniment. (Once again, we think of "Nigger Blues" — although specifics of performance are important. In the 1936 movie, Morgan uses plenty of pitch inflection — and not just on the third — and [the very black] Hattie McDaniel as Queenie takes this even further.)[95] There is a mapping together of (irrational) love, blackness, and Nature — Queenie loves Joe despite his "shiftlessness" and liking for gin — a conjunction sealed in the concluding ensemble choruses, which "un-torch" the mood. The men join in with the women (replacing torch-song gendering with a universalizing shrug: love, with all its problems, is just *natural*), and the tempo increases to create a feel (with forceful tuba bass) of a rather jolly marchlike dance: a further naturalization effect (love is in the body, after all). Magnolia's shuffle, with prominent banjo in the accompaniment, signs off the transaction that has taken place with a blackface flourish.

In the film, the dance transformation starts early, as Queenie's body begins involuntarily to twitch to Julie's singing. Magnolia starts her shuffle with an almost catatonic air, as if absorbing this cultural knowledge into her very body. At the same time, we see shots through the windows of onlookers on the levee gradually gathering to listen, and by the final chorus joining in. As the camera takes us in closer, we see a crowd of blacks, singing, swaying, dancing, hand-clapping (on the back-beat, of course); torch song has turned into something more like gospel. The viewpoint then switches to outside and, as we see the characters emerge from the boat (and *into* the broader black culture that has been laid out for us) to take a bow, a network has been put in place, visually as well as musically: Magnolia connected into a layered structure (Julie — Queenie/Joe — the black South) that will in due course carry her to success.

After Julie's forced departure from the boat, Magnolia takes over her lead role in the company (while Ravenal takes over as leading man), and their rise to success begins. We are shown part of a performance (typically for showboat theater, a melodrama), given some three weeks later. It is followed (equally typically) by an Olio, that is, a sort of variety sequence, derived from the minstrel show. What we see, in the original production, is a "Villain's Dance" for Frank, but by the 1936 film this has been changed to "a little Southern song" for Magnolia. It is a coon song, "Gallivantin' Aroun'," which she sings in full blackface and "plantation" costume, pretending to accompany herself on banjo, ending with a cakewalk-style dance with a blackface group. This builds a springboard that will catapult her to Chicago and the next stage of the "blackface cycle."[96] In the original stage show, much the same function is served by the Finale to Act 1, where the marriage festivities for Magnolia and Gay are twice interrupted: once for a "buck and wing" dance, accompanied by syncopated banjo, and again by a full choral version (for both blacks and whites) of "Can't Help Lovin' Dat Man," an apotheosis that wonderfully maps the romance theme to that of racial transfer. (Mordden asks[97] how a song that is supposedly hidden black property can now be sung by everybody, whites and blacks, together; but that is precisely the point of the cultural work that is being done.) For her audition at the Trocadero, Magnolia, who specializes, she says, in "Negro songs," sings — yes, "Can't Help Lovin' Dat Man" ("one of the songs I taught her," comments Julie, who, unknown to her protégé, is listening in). Her attempt to modernize (rag) the tune is half-hearted, despite the frantic encouragement of the dancing Frank, whose robotic twitching in the 1936 film recalls Magnolia's earlier catatonic shuffle, the auto-motoric body acting out modernity's imitation of the primitive. But she gets the job, and, although her triumph at her first appearance is with the old-time "After the Ball," this is encased within blackface numbers, as we have already seen; from this point, her career is unstoppable, a point amplified by yet another generational transfer, when at the end Kim demonstrates the hot style of "today." Meanwhile, Julie — down and out, drinking heavily — has consciously sacrificed her career to give Magnolia her chance (again); as she slips from the stage in the audition scene, she also disappears from the story (the only important character not to be involved in the final reunion).

But although Act II is largely about white folks moving into the modern world, Julie's disappearance does not mean there is no longer a black presence; indeed, this (but black, not miscegenating) is a constant. After the Trocadero, we move back to Natchez, and forward to 1927 — only to hear Joe still singing his key song, "Ol' Man River," first heard back in Act I Scene I: for "New things come, 'N ol' things go, But all things look de same to Joe"; or, as a 1928 newspaper cartoon put it, "Despite ragtime and jazz music, poor old Joe sings 'Ole Man Ribber' right through the years from 1880 to 1928."[98] And it is this tune, hummed by Joe and the chorus, that closes the show, behind the final reunion of Magnolia and Gay. (The film ending is different, but still the reunion gives way to a concluding snatch of "Ol' Man River" in voice-over to a shot of the Mississippi.) Indeed, this tune accompanies many of the crucial moments of the story, for example, Ravenal's proposal of marriage (an off-stage chorus humming the tune, Magnolia having just identified herself by whistling a phrase!), and Julie's departure from the show-boat. (In the movie, it replaces "Can't Help Lovin' Dat Man" in the wedding festivities, and features in the montage that bridges Acts I and II, replacing the World's Fair scene.)

Joe's part is relatively small (it is extended somewhat in the film through the addition of a new song, "Ah Still Suits Me," which also features in this montage; this is a "ragtime-blues," minstrelized, with banjo accompaniment, a hymn to Joe's good-natured laziness); but his role is crucial. It is easy to see that the river (and by extension, Joe) represents constancy (as against the flux of modernity), reality (as against white folks' fantasies), Nature (as against the stresses of labor, the anxieties of change, the traumas of culture). For Mordden, "The musical harmonizes the races, perhaps because music is the only language both white and black can speak. The very center of this transaction is 'Ol' Man River,' a white man's spiritual — written by white men out of a white woman's book, to be performed by a black character."[99] Again we need to ask, however, what the price of such harmony might be. The part of Joe was written for Paul Robeson, and, although as it turned out he did not appear in the first New York run, he took the part in the London production, followed by the 1932 New York revival and then the 1936 film; "Ol' Man River" quickly became, indelibly, his song. Robeson was emerging at this time as perhaps the outstanding, multiply talented young African-American male of his generation — an heroic figure indeed; but, as Joe, he was Natural Man incarnate, whether he liked it or not.[100]

Joe introduces the song at the close of the first scene. He has just observed Magnolia falling for Ravenal and scents trouble ahead. The main strain of the tune (a hymn to the river's eternal qualities) is a plausible spiritual imitation: pentatonic, with modest half-beat syncopations, set very low in the bass register for (one imagines) exotic manly "depth" (in the film, it is transposed down a further tone, to intensify this effect).

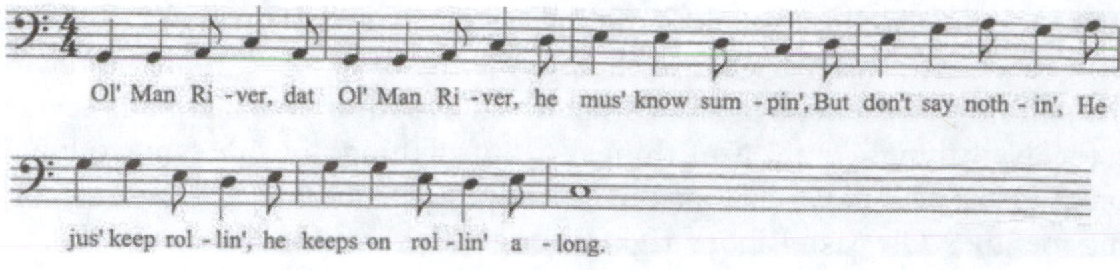
Ol' Man Ri -ver, dat Ol' Man Ri -ver, he mus' know sum -pin', But don't say noth - in', He
jus' keep rol - lin', he keeps on rol -lin' a - long.

Example 2.2

But this strain is folded into a standard Tin Pan Alley 32-bar structure, with modulating bridge and preceding verse (it is a "white man's spiritual"). Admittedly, the bridge, and the second verse, are concerned with human troubles — specifically the tribulations of labor and racialized economic injustice — but the function of the main chorus theme is to absorb these worries and sublimate the emotion into quasi-religious ecstasy. As the choir takes it up, in jubilee style, with Joe first interpolating comments between their phrases, like a preacher, then joining in with them, the music swells to deliver a vision in which the Mississippi turns into "dat stream called de river Jordan, Dat's de ol' stream dat I long to cross." One might say that in a way this representation is accurate for a certain strand of nineteenth-century black sentiment. Yet to set this in the late 1880s, after the failure of Reconstruction (even bracketing, for the sake of the nostalgic view, the audience perspective from 1927), is, to say the least, *partial*. The concluding musical apotheosis performs out Joe's initial wish — "Dere's an ol' man called de Mississippi, Dat's de ol' man dat I'd like to be"; history has been frozen as myth, and Joe as it were *becomes* Ol' Man River — the ceaseless and unchanging current of black labor on which white civilization is built, in eternal dialogue with the consolations of Nature and religion.

The 1936 film's take on this moment supports this interpretation. The camera first makes a slow, almost complete circle round Joe, lingering longingly on Robeson's impressive body, before closing in on his face. This both places this body in its context — the river and the naturalized world of black labor — and locates it as what houses this voice (equally impressive: deep, manly, reverberant — a force of Nature). In the bridges, montages are cut into the visual flow, showing off-stage scenes of (mostly male) black labor. The loads are superhuman, the movements almost in slow motion, the figures huge, shot from below in semisilhouette; these are moments "out of history," their nobility — produced by mapping the dignity of labor on to the almost fetishistically shot heroic physiques — as much a constant as the river. During the second verse, a chorus of (male) workers assembles to form a backdrop for Joe — a frieze (it *is* almost frozen, like a social-realist tableau celebrating collective labor) — and for the final chorus, the film cuts between shots of this frieze, closer images of Robeson (often shot from a low position, looking up at his heroic head and torso), more montage of off-stage labor, and shots of the river; a filmic semiotic chain, running: Joe — the black male body — manual labor — Nature seals the music's message. The final shot is of Joe smiling, trouble all washed away.

We understand now what is necessary if whites are to enter modernity: first, blacks must continue to function as an Other — a constant river that (second) must continue to supply cultural food for white consumption; and third, they should then disappear — either metaphorically (by accepting a supporting role) or, if necessary, literally: Julie (the sister who goes missing) refuses to follow the code encapsulated in the first and second injunctions, she *comes between*, muddying the racial water, and consequently must be written out. What would happen, one wonders, if an audience tried to experience the final scenes of *Show Boat* from Julie's point of view? Her absence during these scenes, pressing on the spectator, is the "blot" without which the fantasy cannot function: without this disappearance, the happy ending will not come out. Her off-stage gaze, we can imagine, stands for the impossible object gaze: she would see *everything*, including what we are not allowed, within the confines of the show, to more than glimpse. Similarly, her silenced voice, standing in again for the impossible (vocal) object, is heard now only spectrally, through the ventriloquisms of Magnolia and Kim. And within that silence we may also hear the ghostly strains of those voices that Kern could not, it would seem, find any way at all to represent: the blues that, actually, were all around Natchez in 1927; the music that, really, meant it was "getting hotter in the North" in the late 1920s — not the imitations of "symphonic jazz" that Kern produced for his final scene but the work of Armstrong, Ellington, and Waller.[101]

******

I have written elsewhere about the role of George Gershwin's "folk opera," *Porgy and Bess* (1935) in this same apparatus of negotiations with the black-other.[102] I approach the structure of relations there through the concepts of *assimilation* (which I would now prefer to write as the politically stronger *appropriation*) and *projection*, the first pursuing mastery of the other by incorporating (digesting, reconstituting, refining) it, the second by locating it (or rather, what is both forbidden and desired in it) elsewhere. Through this "here and there" formation, "the aim of both . . . strategies is to manage the threat posed by potentially infinite difference to the authority of the bourgeois self, by reducing such difference to a stable hierarchy."[103] It is not difficult to think of "Can't Help Lovin' Dat Man," as it effects its transfer through the racial categories, in terms of appropriation, and "Ol' Man River," with its mythic images of natural man, in terms of projection. But each song contains aspects of the other concept too; and because we are exploring musical (and dramatic) texts, which by their very nature project aspects of authoriality while at the same time offering these back for appropriation as figures of identity, meaning, and control, a hermeneutic based on figures of dialogical circulation seems entirely apt.

The concepts of appropriation and projection can be found in several different areas of theory, but stem most clearly from the psychoanalytic pair, introjection and projection (which are themselves linked to the operations of condensation and displacement respectively in the Freudian dream-work, and thence to the distinction between the functions of metaphor and metonymy within the processes of signification). While in Kleinian theory, projection and introjection are regarded as related by reciprocity, Lacan insists that they operate in different registers. Projection, he suggests, is part of the mechanisms of the Imaginary whereby the ego defines its identity in relation to its ideal image and its others; introjection, by contrast, works on the Symbolic level, in relation to superego functions of Law: it "is always the introjection of the speech of the other."[104] While we do not need to follow this dichotomy rigorously — if songs, for example, stage fantasy scenes, and fantasy, by Lacan's own argument, deploys images in the service of signifying structure, then imaginary and symbolic functions are always intermingled — it offers a useful corrective to facile "market equality:" the dialogic exchange here is always skewed by power, and what is at stake is not just imagined identities but the right to lay down the Law — the "paternal" authority of the Master.

Operas and musicals — songs too, for that matter — are multiauthored texts, more especially so in performance. In *Show Boat* there are not only Kern and Hammerstein, and behind them, Edna Ferber, but also conductors, designers, and producers, including the impresario Florenz Ziegfeld, and (for the movie) film director John Whale — before even the singers get to work (not to mention the orchestra). *Porgy and Bess*, I suggest, is unified by Gershwin's intense authorial control, linked to the constraints of genre and historical period: it "both exposes and exploits to the utmost the limits imposed on its project by genre convention and cultural situation," with the result that, despite the dialogic potential offered by the elements of stylistic eclecticism, in the end "difference was effaced, as projection and assimilation merged in the assertion of authority: he had to be master."[105] *Show Boat* is a bit looser, and there are certainly possibilities for subversion; but the work's reputation as the first American musical to subordinate dance, song, and spectacle to coherence of plot and theme tells its own story. The themes picked out above, and their foundations in the racialized cultural architecture I have described, are without question those of the (white) authors. Still, the uncertainties surrounding several moments in the work, manifested in the many cuts and changes made between 1927 and 1936, suggest a lower level of confidence than Gershwin's. The conclusion, for instance, was always a problem, either taking us (along with New York, symbolically) back to Mississippi or (in the movie) taking us and the South (in the form of "hot music") to New York, and running in successive productions through a series of musical numbers, none of which seems quite to work (perhaps because the symphonic jazz with novelty effects — trombone and clarinet glissandi, for example — which is common to most of them fails to convince us of its cultural *savoir faire*).[106] For the film, Kern planned a grand set-piece, based on the music of "Gallivantin' Aroun'," which would demonstrate the history of "jazz" from the 1860s to the present through a sequence of stylistic shifts with appropriate accompanying dances; but almost all of this was cut. The overall aim — to find a way of carrying us confidently into the modern world, and to do it through a trajectory based on "black" music — is clear, but the uncertainty as to how exactly to make this credible is revealing.

The key *Show Boat* songs appeared quickly on records, casting interesting light on the opportunities for performers to intervene in the construction of meaning.[107] Helen Morgan can be heard singing "Bill" on records from 1928 and 1932, and an air-shot from 1938; and she put out records of "Can't Help Lovin' Dat Man" in 1928 and 1932. In both cases (and bearing in mind the 1936 film as well), there is a clear trajectory. Morgan sings quite straight in the early versions but becomes gradually freer in later ones: the tone becomes more "colored" and variable, the phrasing and tempo more fluid, even fragmentary, and pitch inflection much more widespread. In relation to blues aesthetics, this represents a sort of privatization — exactly what torch song was about — but, for those with knowledge of Julie's story on the one hand, Morgan's personal decline and foreshortened career on the other, was there also a way of reading this shift in terms of the broader context of the racialized structure of song culture in this period? Comparison with Billie Holiday is inevitable.

In Holiday's 1937 recording of "Can't Help Lovin' Dat Man,"[108] she sings only one chorus (none of the verse), and literally recomposes the tune; the pentatonic folkiness is obliterated, while the "blue" effects are de-localized and spread right across the performance. No longer a "white woman's blues," this is now a bluesy ballad, presented, in an act of de/re-appropriation, through a particular jazz optic with its home far from the plantation. The contrast with the 1928 releases by English music theater star Marie Burke (from the London cast) and by Tess Gardella is startling. Burke gives a suboperatic performance, with trilling vibrato, dramatic surges of articulation, and elongated English vowels ("that m-e-e-n"), blue effects smoothed over as far as possible; Deep South becomes Home Counties, any signs of blackness entirely picturesque (her "Bill" is similar). Gardella sings with a well-trained (Italianate) voice, which is "blacked up" with the occasional effect — an extravagant smear, a telegraphed blue note — and commercial blues cliché. Her novelty jazz accompaniment orients the record as a sort of Dixieland tribute to the blues women of the 1920s: all sisters behind the mask.

Norma Terris, the original Magnolia, described Robeson's Joe as "brooding," Jules Bledsoe's (in the first production) as "happy,"[109] but this is hard to square with the available recordings of "Ol' Man River." Bledsoe's 1931 release is sung very straight, in terms of voice production and pronunciation, but the approach is much more dramatic than Robeson's: this is an operatic rather than a concert performance. Robeson's first version (one of the London cast recordings) came out in 1928 and is simpler but also comes across now as very straight, virtually with Received Pronunciation. If the song as composed is regarded as a projection of exotic otherness, then arguably such a classicizing performance (lifting the Race, as discourse of the time might have had it) could be heard as subversive; yet there is evidence to suggest that Robeson's approach was heard at the time as refreshingly "natural." According to his wife, Essie, his "regal, 'typically Negro' physique, his 'unspoiled Negro voice . . . full of over and undertones,' and its 'peculiar husky coloring,' enabled him 'through some deep racial instinct' to identify more deeply with the spirituals than could other black singers of the day, whose overly cultivated technical training and repertoire of European art songs kept them at a distance from those 'simple songs.'"[110] Robeson himself seems to have believed, certainly at this stage, in a sort of African essence with which American blacks could (and should) connect. A few months later, back in New York, Robeson recorded another version, with Paul Whiteman's orchestra. His two choruses are sung much the same as before, but they are accompanied, and indeed encased (at length), by Whiteman's orchestra at its most gimmicky: multiple arbitrary tempo changes, sophisticated chromatic harmonies, expanded orchestral palette (vibraphone chords, fast banjo versions of the tunes, a "heavenly" backing choir), a quotation of the famous "New World Symphony" theme. Whatever he does, Robeson cannot escape being presented as an exhibit in Whiteman's modernistic symphonic jazz (perhaps the sort of "jazz" that Kern was aiming at in his initial endings for *Show Boat*).

Robeson's subsequent records (1932, 1936) follow a similar trajectory to Morgan's: both phrasing and pronunciation become more flexible. The meaning of this shift is hard to read. But perhaps it amplifies the sense one has in watching his 1936 film performance of a certain tension between a dignity, even an assertiveness, which wants, but is not quite sure how, to come out (there is more "dat" and "dere" and "de" than on the 1928 records but even so the "d"s are unobtrusive, as if resisted), and the filmic and musical processes that are inescapably objectifying him. According to Duberman, by 1935 Robeson had taken to singing (in concerts, presumably) "There's an ol' man called the Mississippi; that's the ol' man I *don't* like to be" (my emphasis); he does not do this in the film performance. In public, he was skilled at "dissembling" performances of race (to both whites and blacks), and seldom dropped the mask of amiable respectability — but could do so in private, when comfortable. At the same time, he was ambivalent about the roles of "training" and of "instinct"“in his own theater and musical work, sometimes complaining that he was portrayed as nothing more than an instinctive performer (because he was black), at other times falling back himself — perhaps as a preemptive move — on the image of a "mere" folk singer, noble but simple.[111]

These tensions take on extra meaning when Robeson's performances are heard in the context of two extraordinary versions released in 1928 by Bing Crosby and Al Jolson respectively. Crosby sings one chorus with Whiteman's orchestra, at a swinging dance tempo twice that favored in Robeson's 1930s recordings. He croons his vocal, with an uninvolved, light, intimate sound and some jazzy phrasing; the effect is of technical mastery. In that sense, Crosby fits right into Whiteman's modernistic approach, projection definitively re-appropriated into "something that would show that jazz had progressed"[112] — although an alternative interpretation, drawing on contemporary objections to crooning as representing the "emasculation" of the male voice, might hear it differently.[113]

Al Jolson's approach is at an opposite extreme, or so it seems at first hearing. Over a more conventional accompaniment, designed to showcase his voice, he turns the song into a piece of wildly emotive rhetoric. All his typical vocal features are here: strangulated vowels, overextended and articulated consonants, sense-disrupting (but heavily emoting) breaths and breaks, extravagant glissandi and vibratos, mordents on climactic notes, heightened (quasi-cantorial) parlando effects, his trademark phrase-end (sliding $\hat{3}$-$\hat{1}$ descent on the final strong beat). This is "Yiddish-blackface": Jolson used the cork mask to mediate his own sense of (Jewish) marginality, creating room for "feeling" by associating himself with, but at the same time distancing himself from, a space identified with the irrational black other. One can readily imagine him singing this song, on his knees, beseeching — who? His "Mammy"? "Ol' Man River"? (are they the same?). This is an appropriation that appears to be at the other end of a spectrum from Crosby, folding an insistent spotlit assertion of self back into a narcissistic projection of need on to a feminized Other;[114] and yet both might be heard, in their different ways, as raising those questions about noble black masculinity that seem to have troubled Robeson but that he could not settle.

As with blues, *Show Boat* gives up more meaning when placed within this broader network of voices. Indeed, ideally, it should be understood in the context of the lengthy process of African-American assimilation into show business, and particularly musical theater, since the late nineteenth century (in fact, since the minstrel show). We should imagine the relationship between the "plantation ballads" of the white songwriter Stephen Foster (1826–64) and those, slightly later, by James Bland (1854–1911) — the first black song composer to achieve commercial success — as a dialogue. Similarly, in the sphere of coon song, Ben Harney, self-styled "inventor of ragtime" (in 1897), speaks to Ernest Hogan, black composer of the hit, "All Coons Look Alike to Me" (1896). (There is an added piquancy here, in that, although Harney passed for white, there are many reports of his mixed-race ancestry. Meanwhile, Hogan refused to use cork.) Around the same time, Bert Williams became the first black vaudeville star, drawing on performance patterns rooted in the caricatures developed in the minstrel show; and from 1910 for ten years, he appeared annually in Florenz Ziegfeld's *Follies* revues. We can imagine him in dialogue with white vaudeville singers like Jolson and Sophie Tucker — all three performed in blackface — and all of them with "the Black Patti," Sissieretta Jones, whose touring company, the Black Patti Troubadours, offered programs mixing opera extracts, skits, and popular songs for about twenty years starting in 1896.[115] Bob Cole (musician, writer, actor, playwright) put on the first all-black full-length musical comedy, *A Trip to Coontown*, in New York in 1898 (he appeared in *whiteface*!);[116] and Will Marion Cook followed with *In Dahomey* (starring Williams and his vaudeville partner, George Walker). Both Cook and Cole (the latter often in collaboration with composer J. Rosamund Johnson and his brother, James Weldon Johnson, writer and later politician) went on to produce many musical shows and hit songs (the Johnsons also published key collections of arrangements of spirituals in 1925 and 1926). Many of these songs found their way into the repertoires of white vaudeville singers. White songwriters, such as Irving Berlin, responded to the stimulus. From 1905, James Reese Europe was giving concerts of syncopated dance music in New York with all-black bands, and in 1910 he founded the Clef Club, which organized and provided black dance bands for all purposes; we should picture the hugely successful Europe during the subsequent dance-crazy decade as in dialogue with white peers such as Vincent Lopez.

This sketches something of the ambience within which the theatrical success of Kern and Hammerstein's Magnolia is to be imagined — and, as already pointed out, which provided the context for the early development of blues. (W. C. Handy was involved in many of its strands, for instance, as minstrel-show performer, band-leader, song composer and publisher.)[117] The racial dialogue was at the core of popular music history in this early twentieth-century period — a feature only intensified by the successive waves of ragtime and jazz — bringing with it, always, an acute psycho-cultural charge related to the particular configuration of power by which this dialogue was structured. By the 1920s, the black influence within mainstream popular song was almost too obvious to need mention; and, rightly, Alec Wilder makes this a defining quality in the emergence of a specifically American style. Charles Hamm's criticism of Wilder's argument is based on an untheorized hierarchy of musical parameters — black features such as syncopated rhythm are described as "exotic seasoning," while the "chief stylistic features," notably harmonic structure, are ascribed to Euro-American sources — but also fails to register the *charge* that must have accompanied such "miscegenation," however it is described technically.[118]

Given the effects of postcolonial historical revisionism (such as Paul Gilroy's), one would think this dispute settled by now (in Wilder's favor), were it not that Hamm's argument was in effect reproduced more recently by music theorist, Allan Forte.[119] Forte is more inclined than Hamm to acknowledge the significance of African American sources in the style of the mainstream popular ballad, but his characteristic gesture is to efface the element of dialogue (or even, as it sometimes appears, of shock) by stressing the *integration* of these elements into an overall coherence — a gesture to which he is predisposed by his neo-Schenkerian analytical assumptions (and the aesthetic that goes with them: he sees these songs as "American Lieder"). Thus the shift from pentatonic to bluesy in the main phrase of the chorus of "Can't Help Lovin' Dat Man" is interpreted in terms of how the melodic moves fit into the overall voice-leading structure of the tune, and the *frisson* of this moment is lost. (Forte does not even discuss the verse, an important element in some recorded versions of the song, as we saw earlier; but he is not particularly interested in performance anyway.)[120]

African-American musical theater was reborn after World War I through the spectacular success of the Eubie Blake/Noble Sissle revue, *Shuffle Along* (1921; including the young Paul Robeson), which was followed by a host of black shows, including Sissle and Blake's *Chocolate Dandies* (1924) and James P. Johnson's *Runnin' Wild* (1924). In 1926, two white writers, Lawrence Stallings and Frank Harling, brought out *Deep River*, a "native opera with jazz" and an integrated cast including Jules Bledsoe; and in 1927 DuBose and Dorothy Heyward put on their dramatization (with music) of *Porgy*, based on the former's 1925 novel, with Bledsoe playing the part of Crown (until replaced by Robeson in 1928). The revue, *Blackbirds of 1928*, by white writers Jimmy McHugh and Dorothy Fields (who over the next few years also wrote material for the Cotton Club, with house bands led by Duke Ellington and then Cab Calloway), included a host of black stars, and a *Porgy* sketch. "It's fascinating to consider what might have happened if not Gershwin [who no doubt was familiar with all these shows] but the authors of *Shuffle Along* or *Blackbirds* had written *Porgy: The Musical*."[121] Or, indeed, if Paul Robeson, to whom Gershwin offered the part of Porgy, had not turned it down.

In my discussion of Gershwin's opera, I argue that his need finally to control the black-others to which he was so attracted wins the day. The structures of cultural power predispose the blackface mask to turn in that way. But I also explore ways in which black subjects could seek to "answer back," the subaltern find ways to "speak" (to use Gayatri Spivak's terms),[122] notably in the contemporaneous music of Duke Ellington. Partly this revolves around the subversive potential of performance, for if representations have to be continually performed in order to maintain their credibility, there is always the possibility they might be de/re-formed; we found glimpses of this potential in some recordings of songs from *Show Boat,* and the entire blues tradition, on the black side oriented strongly towards a performance aesthetic, can be seen in this light. But this is an aspect of a deeper problematic, in which the performance culture of Afro-diasporic groups — now theorized in terms of Gates's Signifyin(g), itself a rewriting of Du Bois's concept of "double consciousness"[123] — connects up to the still broader currents of modernism *tout court*, with its predilection for "doublings" of various sorts (alienation, irony, hybridity, etc.). I want to suggest that "Harlem modernism" (it is not limited to Harlem, but this was its spiritual center in the 1920s and '30s) constitutes a particular variant within these currents, one indelibly marked by the specific doubling mechanisms of the blackface mask, which, as a species of what Homi Bhabha calls "colonial mimicry," are "constructed around an *ambivalence*; in order to be effective, mimicry must continually produce its slippage, its excess, its difference... [It is therefore both] a complex strategy of reform, regulation and discipline, which 'appropriate' the Other... [but] also the sign of the inappropriate, a difference or recalcitrance which... poses an immanent threat to both 'normalised' knowledges and disciplinary powers."[124]

But slippage may push further. According to Houston Baker, what is at work in this modernist variant is a continuous interaction of two strategies: on the one hand, *mastery of form* — the "liberating manipulation of masks" — and on the other, *deformation of mastery* — an act of deterritorialization, an assertion of selfhood that is "never simply a coming into being, but always, also, a release from a BEING POSSESSED" — and a release into what Baker calls "new territory" — a place that "exists on no map."[125]

In 1932 Brunswick put out what amounted to the first album (four two-sided records) devoted to music from a single show: *Show Boat.*[126] They followed this with a twelve-sided set featuring numbers from *Blackbirds of 1928*, including performances by the Ellington and Calloway bands, the Mills Brothers, Ethel Waters, and Adelaide Hall, among others. Not surprisingly, the Ellington recordings draw from the aesthetic developed over the preceding five years at the Cotton Club, where fashionable white negrophiles were offered an oh-so-up-to-the-minute pseudo-primitive revue-style ambience.[127] They are not among his key records, but they do broach many of the core issues in Harlem modernism. "Diga Diga Doo" is an up-tempo dance tune in the "jungle" style that was so important to Ellington's emergent originality at this time; yet its repeated minor-key chords and pounding beat stand in a (blackface) history going back to *In Dahomey*, as we have seen. Ellington's innovation (actually the contribution of trumpeter Bubber Miley and trombonist Joe "Tricky Sam" Nanton, interpreting blues vocalism with the aid of the plunger mute) is the "growling" brass, heard here both in ensemble and in Cootie Williams's trumpet solo. The Mills Brothers sing the trite lyrics in their first chorus straight, in innocent close harmony, but in their second, move into scat, locating a connection between this modernistic technique and "jungle" instrumentalism on the one hand, the mumbo jumbo lyrics of the cod-African tradition on the other.[128] The blues/jungle elements permeate even a straightforward love-song like "Baby," which Adelaide Hall sings as if it were a blues, backed by bluesy trombone commentary from Lawrence Brown, and followed by another growled Cootie Williams solo.

More striking, though, is Hall's torch song, "I Must Have that Man." Her first chorus, sung beautifully but fairly straight, is preceded by a double-time introduction from Ellington and saxophonist Johnny Hodges and followed by an interlude with double-time stride piano from Ellington; this leads to her second chorus which is comprehensively scatted (the meaning scattered), over jungly muted brass chords, in a vocal displaying Hall's extraordinary range together with occasional implied excursions into double-time phrasing, especially in her end-of-phrase breaks. Is it far-fetched to hear the tempo oscillations as a commentary (take-off? lesson?) on Magnolia's failure to bring this off in her Trocadero "Can't Help Lovin' Dat Man" audition? Anyway, it sets up an internal dialogue (red hot mama/torch song victim?) that undercuts the song's surface message (and offers divergent gender interpretations, no doubt), while at the same time delineating a particular modernistic territory (the body slipping through language).

Dialogue is even more overt (along with gender issues) in "I Can't Give You Anything but Love (Baby)," sung by Ethel Waters. The first chorus is conventional enough, both in vocal and accompaniment, but the second is taken by an unidentified *male* singer (presumably one of the band), who however sings mostly in falsetto as well as introducing scat phrases and what sounds like occasional parodic diction (especially on the word "Baby"). This chorus (and the performance) ends with a surreal semitonal vocal ascent, in a clipped staccato, very high in register, over rising chromatic chords — a device that clinches what we have already been coming to suspect, that this is a dialogue with (parody of?) Louis Armstrong's style, indeed of his 1929 recording of this song, which also contains a vocal full of surreal scat and which ends, in what was by now an Armstrong trademark, with a very similar ascent, on trumpet. But the dialogue may reach even wider. Ellington had recorded a version of this tune for Victor in 1928. Here (the male) Irving Mills sings the first chorus and (the female) "Baby" [*sic*] Cox the second, with scat and growls, in a performance that is notably couldn't-care-less up-tempo. (Similarly, there are two 1928 Ellington recordings of "Diga Diga Doo." The Okeh version is relatively orthodox, with Irving Mills taking the vocal. But the Victor version is taken at a frenetic tempo; the vocal duo — Mills and the female Ozzie Ware — is less prominent than the extravagant growled solos from Nanton and Miley, the second over pounding four-to-the-bar slapped bass; and the performance ends with garishly voiced, wah-wah reed/brass interchanges: a jungle feast (as it were), which Ellington offers, one might think, with a knowing "Man, look how primitive we are!")[129]

We can now begin to sketch out the features of Harlem modernism: first, jungle instrumentalism; second, freak vocalism (as in scat, but going much wider in range of effects); and third, primitivist rhythm. This is a voice-plus-drums aesthetic, for which a key model is — blues.[130] But instrumental and vocal varieties of grotesque (or eccentric performance, as it was often termed at the time) share the same roots: semiotically, the prelinguistic voice; historically, blackface typologies of character portrayal, not to say caricature — laughing trombones, whistling coons, animal masquerades, etc.[131] This ventriloquistic territory is also where blues makes its home; and it was precisely when Ellington assimilated the jungle gobbledy-gook of Miley and Nanton into the "high-class" perspectives of his Washington, D.C., youth and installed blues vocality at the heart of his style that he was enabled to set sail for new lands. Blues vocality, with its deeply-layered, uncompromising dialogics, pitched from the margin, a modernism in waiting that speaks from underneath: it is this location, not just the specifics of form, feeling, or articulation, that led jazz musicians to claim possession and to position blues at the heart of whatever gave their innovations a life outside the mainstream. The key moment for Ellington came in 1927 when (not long before the opening of *Show Boat*) he recorded the two classics, "Black and Tan Fantasy" and "Creole Love Call," for the first time:[132] the first with its definitive jungle instrumental solos, the second built around Adelaide Hall's wordless vocal, full of scat, growl, smear, and blue notes; both, as it happens, constructed around twelve-bar blues sequences; both pointing to racial ambivalence. ("Black and tan" alludes to the racial mix in clubs like the Cotton Club as well as the cultural mix in music of the period, reflected in the piece itself when the "black" blues theme is contrasted with sweeter "tan" material; the "love call" was intended, apparently, as a tribute to [the very black] Bessie Smith, but Adelaide Hall, who came from a professional family background, sings in a higher register altogether, and is surrounded by clarinet, the quintessential instrument of New Orleans Creoles.)

This dialogic ambivalence could turn in many different ways, depending on the material and the moment: this, after all, is what one would expect of an expressive mode that hides as it reveals, displays and displaces, seeks and secretes — an aesthetic of mask and mimicry. As Ellington explores its potential, through such pieces as "Jungle Blues," "Jungle Nights in Harlem" (both 1930), "Echoes of the Jungle" (1931), and then longer pieces like "Creole Rhapsody" and "Crescendo and Diminuendo in Blue" down to the concert suite, *Black, Brown and Beige*, we should be ready to grant an equivalent degree of interpretative openness. White jazz critics of the time, for obvious reasons, found it hard to do this, but also hard to agree. As we read Roger Pryor Dodge's view of jazz from 1929 — "It is a musical form produced by the primitive innate musical instinct of the Negro and those lower members of the white race who have not yet lost their feeling for the primitive" — we can imagine his response to "Black and Tan Fantasy"; yet his later analysis of the piece located a "purity" that he validated through reference to Bach and Palestrina. R. D. Darrell's review starts by locating its blackface grotesquerie — "I laughed like everyone else over its instrumental wa-waing and garbling and gobbling" — but then comes under its spell as "the whinnies and wa-was began to resolve into new tone colours, distorted and tortured, but agonisingly expressive … a twisted beauty that grew on me more and more and could not be shaken off"[133] — new territory indeed.

Nevertheless, most Harlem modernists, including Ellington, produced some pieces where blackface deconstruction seems a clear intent. Ellington's 1933 version of "Dear Old Southland,"[134] a 1921 song by the African-American writers Layton and Creamer that is based on the melodies of two spirituals, "Deep River" and "Sometimes I Feel Like a Motherless Child," turns plantation fantasy and folk pathos into a rather woozy dream, extravagantly mellifluous reed voicings blurred by the merest of jungle hints from muted brass. Trumpeter Louis Bacon, buried deep in the texture, reduces the vocal (in the original, full of minstrelesque references) to a series of ruminations ("I want to be … ", "I love to see … "), each of which relapses into almost inaudible scat, their completions (but what do they mean?) to be heard in Nanton's accompanying growled trombone commentary and the Hodges solo that follows. (Ellington's recording dates from 1933, and can be heard now, piquantly, as a deconstructive pre-echo of George Gershwin's evocation of Southern folk bliss in "Summertime" from *Porgy and Bess* — the melody of which was clearly derived from "Sometimes I Feel Like a Motherless Child.")[135] In 1938, Ellington followed up this tinted portrait of the "sorrow songs" with a more clearly tongue-in-cheek recording of "Ol' Man River"; here, only two years after Robeson's iconic film performance, an absurdly up-tempo rhythm turns nobility into slapstick, while Cootie Williams's over-the-top jungle-trumpet growls its way through the lyrics at top speed and the vocal chorus (by the little-known female singer, Jerry

Kruger, all jaunty sweetness) comprehensively reconstructs them: not, for example, getting a little drunk and landing in jail but more a case of "smoke a little tea, and sing 'O Sole mee-oh.'"[136]

Louis Armstrong was, it might seem, rather more accommodating to blackface convention; certainly he recorded — apparently fairly straight — several songs with demeaning lyrics, such as his theme-tune, "When It's Sleepy Time Down South" (1931), and suffered criticism for apparently ingratiating performance behavior. But listen to his duet (a racial as well as musical interchange) with Jack Teagarden on another Deep South fantasy, Hoagy Carmichael's "Rockin' Chair" (1929): as they swap phrases, eliding words, moving towards scat, the caricatures offered in the lyrics splinter and they end the vocal almost in laughter. Or listen to "Shine" (1931), generically a coon song (by African Americans Ford Dabney and Cecil Mack), linking "Negro work" (shoe-shining) with Uncle Tomming (a shiny, ingratiating smile). As Appel's excellent analysis points out, Armstrong's vocal, after a straight first chorus, gradually leaves the words behind as it moves into ever wilder scat, setting up a coruscating trumpet solo full of wipe-the-floor, ground-clearing glissandi; and this de(con)structive tour de force takes place at doubled tempo, with a texture thinning out to emphasize Armstrong on the one hand, a powerful rhythm section on the other — voice and drums, "a sharp irony inasmuch as 'primitive' (nonverbal or preverbal) vocalizing [on voice and trumpet] has been able to dispatch 'civilized' (verbal) discourse."[137]

Armstrong's friend, Thomas "Fats" Waller (in 1929 Armstrong had his biggest hit to this point with Waller's "Ain't Misbehavin'"), was less selective in his targets. As both Appel and Alyn Shipton have pointed out, anything with blackface content was fair game: "Mandy," "Floatin' Down to Cotton Town," "Old Plantation," "My Window Faces the South," "Darktown Strutters Ball." His lampooning could even extend to *blues*, its folk grittiness already stereotypical enough in some guises to warrant a parody in Waller's "Original E Flat Blues," where it is undermined by a loping piano bass shuffle, suggestive of Hollywood cowboys, and quite unsuitable pseudo-classical scale figuration behind the final riff chorus.[138]

But Waller, the period's greatest master of vocal masks — cross-cutting register, timbre, accent, articulation (sung and spoken), and expression — could take aim at *any* style, and is celebrated for his send-ups of Tin Pan Alley banality. Underlying this stance is a sideways look at modernity (including its entertainment) derived from the blues margins: black performers, positioned as "primitives," can, once they have "seen through" this image, turn a gaze back on a lesser modernism than they are now entitled to claim. In the first significant (and highly influential) scat vocal, by Armstrong in his 1926 "Heebie Jeebies,"[139] he celebrates a dance ("do the heebie jeebies") but also a condition, one that is both modern (the term was recent coinage, for a tense, nervous, jumpy state) and primitive ("someone with juju," according to the lyric): the body possessed (is this what Magnolia was after?). He does this by subverting (re-writing, by-passing) language, a technique inviting comparison with the Surrealists' "automatic writing" and the Dadaists' "word salad," but, of course, with its own provenance too in a neo-African (whether historically real or not) double-take on the white man's lingo and its black embodiment. But scat, as I have already suggested, is part of a wider "jungle" of vocal (and vocalizing instrumental) techniques. In "Mean Old Bed Bug Blues," recorded by Billy Banks and His Rhythm Makers in 1932,[140] the monstrous beast at issue draws from Banks a high-register wail of a vocal; but this is topped by a female-impersonating falsetto chorus rumored (though never with confirmation) to have been delivered by Fats Waller, pianist on the date. Meanwhile, the scat is in effect transferred to Henry "Red" Allen's fantastical trumpet commentaries.

Shipton has pointed out Banks's stylistic debt to Cab Calloway. And certainly it is Calloway, more than any other performer, who brought together all the strands of Harlem modernist vocality.[141] As bandleader, he was a showman extraordinary (his persona part clown, part streetwise hepster,[142] pushing past minstrelesque resonances on both sides) and as singer, his exceptional range — from baritone up to falsetto — and capacity for mimicry enabled him both to lampoon and to create a sound-world whose enormous popularity is matched by its ambivalences. "Is That Religion" is spoof gospel, with preaching vocal and ecstatic vocal responses and spoken interjections (some in falsetto) from the band. But the parody is warm: nothing has been destroyed. Calloway's "St. Louis Blues" puts Handy's venerable tune through the mincer — his vocal cuts, often abruptly, between long held notes and quick-fire gobbled diction and scat, between high tenor and baritone registers, mixing in huge glissandi and gabbling imitations of freak instrumental techniques — but it comes up smiling if splintered into multiple dimensions. In the latter part of the piece, the band plays staccato chords in formulaic riff patterns, as if slicing up the tune, and ends each chorus with an extravagant, whinnying held chord, the false endings holding up the form to scrutiny, as if to say, "what on earth are we doing here?" This is cubist (or perhaps Joycean) blues. As Calloway sings, "I'm gonna leave this town, walking, talking to myself" — and he does, mumbling and shrieking (but who is this self and what world is he in?). Shipton suggests that Calloway's gabbling-on-a-note is a takeoff of Jolson-esque cantorial chanting, and the declamatory register shifts and glissandi may reference this source too. In his recording of "Yaller," an affecting plaint on behalf of the "miscegenated," he sings in clear imitation of Al Jolson (given Jolson's complex dealings with blackface, the irony is exquisite); and his debt to Jolson appears elsewhere too, in ballads such as "So Sweet" and even in "Blues in My Heart," a sinuously chromatic, Ellingtonian but heartfelt blues.

"Black Rhythm" is a blues telling of a red-hot piano player "down in Louisiana." He plays, Calloway tells us, what may sound like a wonderful "symphony" but actually he is just improvising on a "Southern mammy melody"; still, "the blues that he'll compose will thrill you to your toes," because he has "black rhythm" in his hands ("he can lay on the white ones [keys], can play on de black ones with ease").[143] Calloway's vocal cuts between serious baritone and over-the-top high tenor bordering falsetto; and the arrangement again "cuts up" the piece with an assortment of sophisticated breaks, some in double-time, some with modernistic harmonies or modulations, others pointedly illustrative (stride piano, New Orleans clarinet, plunking banjo) — all of them caricatures in some sense of "black rhythm." But when all the winks have been winked, damn it, the piece *is* hot: the swing is infectious, the interlacing of materials and splicing of rhythms so precise, so *masterful* (pregnant word in this context), that blues rhythm, blues voices, come out on top of all misuse. It is as if blackface has been picked up, given a good shake, and then, still spinning, re-turned under new management.

This is Calloway's secret, and that of Harlem modernism as a whole. The middle section of "Black Rhythm" is in his "moanin'" style — his version of the jungle mode. Calloway followed Ellington into the Cotton Club in 1930 and undoubtedly absorbed much from the Ellington model, although the band — known as The Missourians before Calloway took over its leadership — was already a "primitive" (noisy, hard-driving, bluesy) outfit from the way-out-west frontier jungle of St. Louis. The series of pieces he developed in this style, locating it in an exoticised depiction of a bohemian Harlem drug subculture, with its own esoteric practices and language, became the largest factor in his exploding popularity, disseminating a secret culture that was no doubt titillating for whites (even if one did not quite understand) at the same time as fitting perfectly with the equally secret languages of scat and jungle instrumentalism.[144]

In the first of these pieces, "The Viper's Drag," the usual jungle features — minor key, heavy 4/4 beat and repeated band chords, growled solos, but with added "orientalist" chromatics in places — also incorporate a wordless Calloway vocal whose moans and shrieks, swooping eerily between registers, give them a real nightmare power. The classic "Minnie the Moocher" adds a (dreamlike) story to the mix. Each verse is followed by a refrain of responsorial gobbledy-gook between Calloway and the band's blurry vocal echoes: and they *are* echoes, mimic-acts, an unconscious writing from a hallucinatory place that seems to ask just what "story" or "words" might be. In style, the song (and its successors in the "Minnie" series) recalls the blues-ballads of the turn of the century (indeed, it is modeled on one of them, "St. James Informary," which Calloway had recorded three months earlier).[145] It is as if, after the turbulent blues history of the intervening decades, with all its racio-sibling contestation, Stagolee reappears through a dreamlike haze: a knowing inversion (a bad man feeling good, in a telling reversal of blues cliché), which responds to the struggles of the disappearing jazz age with a surreal black comedy appropriate to the Depression.

Many of the elements in Calloway's vocalism can be found also later in the 1930s in the work of Leo Watson, of the vocal/string group, The Spirits of Rhythm, and that of the idiosyncratic singer and multi-instrumentalist (and tap dancer), Slim Gaillard. Gaillard recorded mostly at this time in small bands including the remarkable bassist, Slam Stewart.[146] Like Calloway, Gaillard invented his own jive language (he called it "vout"), and his vocals present a surreal flow of nonsense, humor, and scat, set in a bouncing, boogie-influenced musical style that shows how small-group swing would move towards the 1940s rhythm 'n' blues of Louis Jordan on the one hand — an equally comedic, good-time style with clear proto-minstrelesque elements, but also links back to the legacy of hokum blues — and the hard-edged but often surreal modernism of be-bop on the other. (Gaillard recorded, briefly, with Charlie Parker and Dizzy Gillespie in 1945. Listen too to Charlie Parker's "Now's the Time" [1945] and then the R&B hit "The Hucklebuck," based on Parker's riff and recorded by several bands in 1949.) The first hit record by "Slim and Slam," "Flat Feet Floogie" (1938), displays all these features, together with Stewart's innovatory vocal harmonizing (an octave higher) with his own bowed bass playing, an effect that as it were seals the vocal/instrumental exchange at the heart of the jungle aesthetic at the same time as it renews the vocal multiphonics of blues tradition. (Recall Charley Patton's kazoolike voices; or think of a weirdly pitch-shifted yodel, the distinct registers compressed into simultaneity.) Several of Gaillard's pieces are about food: "Matzoh Balls," "Tutti Frutti," "Groove Juice Special" ("about" may be the wrong word — but anyway the food/music conjunction, located in the grooving body, gives a new meaning to "gob-bledy-gook"). Many play explicitly with language: "Boot-Ta-La-Za," which sounds like cod-Greek; "My Chinatown," which brings out the connection between scat nonsense and conventions of orientalist mumbo-jumbo. "Laughin' in Rhythm" laughs *at* (or with?) the "rhythm changes" by superposing lyrics made up entirely of laughter.

The up-tempo quick-fire phrasing of Gaillard's "Ra-Da-De-Da" points clearly towards be-bop. Dizzy Gillespie made his early reputation playing in Cab Calloway's band (1939–41); the clowning showmanship he developed as a bandleader, and the scat vocals he introduced, come out of the Calloway/Gaillard lineage, just as be-bop's esoteric hipsterism and surreal approach to language ("be-bop spoken here" was the publicity tag) are inconceivable without it. This strand interlacing blues and jazz is sutured by an approach to voice (in the broadest sense) that body-swerves right through the caricatures rooted in blackface traditions; be-bop as a whole, with its expanded vocabulary of pitch-inflection, intensely vocalized concept of instrumental articulation, and para-linguistic sense of rhythm, is saturated with this approach. Gillespie is often described as not a natural blues player (unlike, so the story generally goes, the more "emotive" Charlie Parker).[147] It is truer to say that he played a splintered, modernistic blues, edgy with self-aware comedy, a blues that, like Ellington's, Waller's, and Calloway's, locates down-home in a jungle that is urban as well as implicitly postcolonial.

It is the move represented by this multi-braided strand — a sort of double turn, first laughing at "folk roots" stereotypes, then exploiting the freedom which that creates to rehabilitate them — that powers the neo-African music Gillespie helped to pioneer, in collaboration with the Cuban percussionist Chano Pozo. "Cubana Be/Cubana Bop," for instance, with its "African black magic chanting. Heavy mysterious folk music," can accommodate Afro-Cuban primitivism because it grows out of, first, Afro-*cubist* blues.[148] Duke Ellington, having done his share of deconstructing pseudo-spirituals, was entitled to re-create (or create?) the "real thing" in the "Black" movement of his suite *Black, Brown and Beige*.[149] From this perspective, Louis Armstrong had earned the right to offer us his vision of "Sleepy Time Down South," even with all the risks attached. This "new territory" could not be innocent or free of conflict, as the controversies surrounding all three of these examples indicate. The race-related struggles also mediate gender issues, as has become apparent at various points; and class tensions too: the role of blues here was to *ground* ambitious middle-class black musicians in a position far enough beneath the underdog (as the title of Charles Mingus's autobiography has it)[150] to enable them credibly to talk black (and therefore back). It is worth comparing Ethel Waters's bluesy recording of the Fields-McHugh ballad "Porgy," accompanied by the Ellington band, with the more "cultivated" operatic music that George Gershwin composed for his Bess; and asking what effect it may have had that Paul Robeson would not (perhaps could not) sing blues (his one attempt at the twelve-bar form is an embarrassment).[151] The Black-Other is never more a Low-Other than when it is blue.

******

Black, Brown and Beige sets out to tell the story of "the race," an ambition that Duke Ellington had nurtured since the 1920s; one, indeed, that was deeply embedded in socially ambitious African-American circles in the early twentieth century, but that — not surprisingly, given its prominent up-from-slavery trope — could be traced back to the nineteenth, for instance to ex-slave autobiographies. (It is found too, in a rather different register, in such shows as *In Dahomey*; and in the set of six songs by Cole and Johnson, frequently interpolated into their shows, entitled *The Evolution of Ragtime*, which also starts its history in Africa.[152] This brings to mind as well Kern's original intention to tell the history of jazz in the finale of *Show Boat* — a work that, as a whole, could be regarded as offering a white gloss on these dark strivings.) But music not only played a part in telling the story; it *constructed* one (or rather, many), performing out the negotiation of desire, loss, and power. And such negotiation has continued: slavery is not so easily superseded (nor is mastery readily freed from its grip).

Voices of black(face) folk: out of the mouth of — *Elvis Presley*?! Whose "culture 'n' heritage" was this? Elvis was at least dimly aware of what was at stake: as Robert Fink points out,[153] in his performances of, for example, "Hound Dog" he purposely exaggerated what he took to be typical black gestures to the point of caricature — part of an in-built ironic stance that allies him with a specifically blues comedy. By contrast, Mick Jagger, blessed with lips that rendered him born into blackface, was after a romanticized vision of "roots." In "Jumpin' Jack Flash," the specter of Stagolee reemerges, but Jagger's exaggerated vocal mannerisms — deeply serious and self-absorbed in their stud-hustler sneer — suggest a desperate search for authenticity, set off, however, by the rather crude half-beat guitar syncopations and almost marchlike up-beat figures: "square" and "hip" jammed (hardly jamming) together (does this help explain why in later years Jagger could accept the embrace of the white Establishment so easily?).

Meanwhile, Jimi Hendrix, at least in the early stage of his British career, was knowingly playing up to his hysterical media reception as "the wild man from Borneo," performing out gestures of rapacious but ever so cool and dandified sexual power: a "psychedelic Uncle Tom" (for some), a "mirror-image of our own inner darkies" (for others). But he was also developing his own variant of that specific modernistic territory which enabled maneuvers behind and beyond the mirror. Listen, for instance, to "Voodoo Chile," which traverses (as it constructs) a history linking Charley Patton's guitar/vocal heterophonies to the rebellious noise of new wave jazz, passing the spectral shiver of its supernatural imagery through the landscape of a space-age jungle: "Delta blues . . . on Mars."[154]

Around the same time, a young Michael Jackson was starting out on a trajectory that would eventually give new meaning to the term "passing" (in relation to sexuality as well as race), exploring in much of his mature work some of the key tropes of blackface tradition (I will discuss this in the next chapter). But by this time, rap was already taking over the lead in articulating black folks' concerns. Lhamon has drawn attention to the roots of much hip-hop performance gesture in minstrelsy,[155] and it is a commonplace to note the music's debt to long-established blackface stereotypes of machismo, male narcissism, and racially charged violence, not to mention heavy white investment, emotional and financial, in the culture, its styles and commodities. Class-related tensions within the African-American community emerge in differing hip hop attitudes to politics, life-style, and gender. Not the least irony is that one of the most impressive rappers at the turn of the century is poor white trash, Eminem — the Jimmie Rodgers (or Jimmie Davis) of his day? — among whose many voices is, appropriately, that of his alter ego, Slim *Shady*.[156] The irony only increases when Eminem duets with the black Kirk Jones on the latter's track, "What If I Was White," where race-linked stereotypes are gleefully guyed both in the lyrics and the music; rhythmically complex, multivoiced dialogues are contextualized by a painfully banal, martial four-four thump for the hook, "What if he was white" (Example 2.3a), which becomes a nightmarishly repetitive foreground in the refrains (Example 2.3b). Can white men (not) jump?[157]

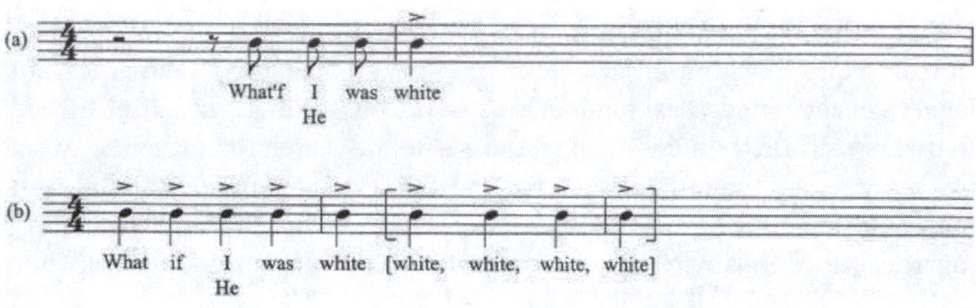

Example 2.3

Early in *O Brother, Where Are Thou?*, the heroes (as yet only three, all white) meet a mysterious blind black prophet (Polyphemus in the Coen Brothers' Odyssean schema). He has no name (unlike the slaves, who lost their own and gained the master's; unlike Eminem, who hides the master's — Marshall Mathers — within his sobriquet, while adopting a shady substitute). On hearing that the heroes seek a treasure, the prophet — accompanied by a guitar blues — tells them: "You will find a fortune, though it would not be the fortune you seek." Many diverse fortunes have been sought by those writing (interpreting, constructing, performing) the history of the voices of black folk and their white others. Whether what was found was really fortunate depends on true recognition of the "moment of danger" on which, suggests Walter Benjamin, the writing of history rests. The moment of danger today is no less acute than it was a hundred years ago when blues (perhaps) began. Indeed, in many ways it is not dissimilar: a new phase in the reach of global capital, driven in part by a leap in technology (now digitization, which, among other things, enables Moby and Tangleeye to sample Alan Lomax's field recordings); labor divided by race, now on a global scale; the resulting fractures finding a metonymic focus in the sexual relationship (e.g., in rap); in music a deluge of revivals, most notably in the new category of "world music," into which blues and bluegrass are partly assimilated, and which, like early blues, constitutes itself as a revival without a source — or rather with a mythic source which world music itself brings into being.

The postcolonial fetters have been weakened — but how much? Would a new *Show Boat*, as one might assume, be impossible today? Homi Bhabha points us towards both the inevitability of rupture and the haunting uncertainties of the new: "The paranoid threat from the hybrid is finally uncontainable because it breaks down the symmetry and duality of self/other, inside/outside. In the productivity of power, the boundaries of authority — its reality effects — are always besieged by 'the other scene' of fixations and phantoms."[158] Beyond the mask — what?

CHAPTER 3

Appropriating the Phallus?

Female Voices and the Law-of-the-Father

Voice; phallus: two radically distinct bodily objects (it would seem). What are they doing, coupled together here in this disorienting conjunction — one, moreover, that can hardly help but conjure up the couplings of sex?

The bodily locations and representations of popular voices situate them in an irreducibly gendered universe. Vocality is always sexualized, and this quality comes to us through the screen of gender difference, albeit a screen rendered less than stable in recent years through feminist and queer critiques. The discipline of popular music studies developed over much the same period as second-wave feminism, and it is not surprising that feminist perspectives have inflected a good deal of work in the discipline. Much of this has been pretty straightforwardly sociological. The question of how women's subordinate roles within the music industry and the social relations of popular music production can be addressed is indeed a vital one, alongside the equally important, and interlinked, question of how the stereotypes governing female participation can be countered.

But if the analysis is allowed to rest at that point, two dangers follow.[1] The first is that the work of songs in reproducing the broader structures of the symbolic economy is left unexplored; it is as if an old-style vulgar materialist approach is still in charge, assuming that if only the relations of production are revolutionized, changes in patterns of identity, representation, and expression will automatically follow.[2] The second danger is political and follows from the first: If social change fails to lead to radical change on the symbolic level, there is nowhere to turn for help. The stalling of the broader feminist project at the so-called postfeminist stage, with its concomitant in the musical sphere of Madonna-lite girl groups and scantily clad wannabe-divas, suggests that this is the historical point we have reached in the early twenty-first century. The much advertised "crisis of masculinity," with similarly confused relationships between the advent of "new men" on the social level and panics around representation (e.g., as in gangsta rap), points in the same direction. Even when scholars have paid more attention to performance images and strategies, and their related identity politics, the focus has often been on moments of allegedly subversive play — repertories of cross-dressing and gender-bending — which, all too often, seem easily assimilable to mainstream music industry marketing. In this case it is as if the notorious banality of cultural studies translates quite readily into wishful victory claims in the gender wars.

While acknowledging the problems inherent in the psychoanalytic account of Woman, I aim to take seriously the argument that her subordination is deeply embedded in the historically constituted structures of socialized subjectivity and will not easily be overturned; "appropriating the phallus," or indeed subverting its power, is an enterprise where much is at stake. As Barbara Bradby and Dave Laing point out, the "impossibility [apparently] of the female self within patriarchal society or phallocentric discourse" still haunts the feminist imagination; "this 'I who wants not to be' of Kristeva's (1974) essay on female suicides conflicts with the happy assertiveness that assumes we can retrain our selves, and sets up a powerful undertow of feminist nihilism."[3]

"To approach woman as a symptom" in this way, according to Kaja Silverman, "is not to suggest that she is no more than the afterimage of male subjectivity... Woman is inscribed not only on celluloid [and on records] and on the surfaces of the male subject's imaginary register, but in the psychic, material, and social conditions of the female subject's daily existence."[4]

But why look at women? Why not men? Carolyn Abbate pushes this question even further, skewering the "unappetizing figure of the male critic who takes up 'feminist' interpretation...as a politically correct or, more reprehensibly, professionally profitable move," and reserving particular scorn for male critics' interpretations of "phallic women." My own investments, as a straight male, will, I hope, emerge in what follows (though not necessarily in ways I can predict). If to position "masculinity" analytically as *what comes after* risks, as a critical structure, perpetuating a political stasis — Woman as, still, the exception that enables male universalism — the contrary possibility, that such a move might have the capacity to put the gender structure, precisely, at risk, seems worth holding on to.[5]

I am interested here especially in voice. This focus straightaway lays out an insistently sexuated territory. Not only is the voice felt to be a key marker of identity, representing a person and (usually) carrying the machinery of (always gendered) subject-positions embedded in language, but its site of production — mouth, throat, vocal tract — is associated with a range of sexing tropes. As an apparatus that organizes the passage of energy from inside the body to outside — "desire as articulated air"[6] — this site bears obvious comparison to sexual organs. The mouth, from childhood an important erogenous zone, both sucks in and ejaculates, opens and closes, articulates flows and reproduces them endlessly. In this sense, voice can be figured as standing for, that is, metonymically representing, our sense of sexuality as such.

But the sexual positioning of voices is not fixed. Rather, as Wayne Koestenbaum points out,[7] the ideology of voice works within a complex discursive formation where entry into the field of sex and gender is both represented and constituted on the level of vocal articulation, through the operation of sets of regulatory ideals that are powerful but never conclusive. Nevertheless, there are strong tendencies to think voice, on the level of the historical *longue durée*, in two overarching but apparently conflicting ways. In the first it is a site of masculine authority. Considered as a self-validating "fingerprint (or larynx-print) impossible to steal,"[8] its role as carrier of spoken language marks voice within the traditions of Western thought as vehicle of self-authoring metaphysical presence, hence, as the special property of the patriarchal sources of *logos*. In the second tradition, by contrast, voice is persistently coded as female. This is partly because as an organ it is *inside,* hidden, indeed as a rule invisible, while at the same time the laryngeal organs (once they *can* be seen, via the nineteenth-century invention of the laryngoscope) might seem to have a structure uncannily similar to that of female genitalia; and partly because the movement of air through the vocal apparatus from deep within the body up to the head can easily be pictured as facilitating a two-way bodily traffic: either an escape from genital tyranny (where voice, "sublimely independent of the place below,"[9] can be thought of as gender-free or androgynous, or, more commonly, can be associated with feminine lack), or, by contrast, an embedding of voice within the body's reproductive machinery, an "invagination," to use Derrida's metaphor.[10] Whether invaginated or phallicized, the site of vocal production can be imagined as a sort of "column," or better, a "vocalimentary canal," carrying energy flows between the head on the one hand, and, on the other, *that place down below.*[11]

Of course, this ideology of voice needs to be overlaid on a different (but related) binary structure, that governing the relationship of language to *music*. Music here is persistently figured as language's Other, in a familiar inside/outside, centre/margin topography, which, once again, is always gendered. How might singing be placed within this structure of interlocking binaries?

As Koestenbaum makes clear, it is important to register the intricate dynamics formed within this discursive structure by the intersecting metaphors of "nature" and "discipline." One searches for a "true" voice — but this is an exercise in self-formation, requiring the acquisition of "control." The voice "natural" to a specific gender, age, race, class is, at least in a Foucauldian perspective, an effect of normative performance-acts "inscribed" on (and hence bringing into being) particular types of body.[12] Inhabiting and manipulating specific vocal registers (chest, throat, head); passing between them naturally (or not); deploying appropriate (or other) timbres and articulations: all contribute. Such frameworks are constituted, but can also be challenged, by particular cultural formations. Thus, while disciplinary norms are most clearly laid out in the textbooks of the classical (and especially the so-called *bel canto*) tradition, they can be put in question or even subverted by other vocal regimes, that is, through an articulation of class or ethnic difference. In her 1918 publication, *How to Sing a Song*, the French cabaret artist Yvette Guilbert presents not the system of technical (and moral) discipline familiar from the history of classical singing manuals but rather "guidelines for a kind of self-invention," an explicit system of *mimicry* centered on portrayal of a range of personalities.[13] This approach became an important strand in twentieth-century vernacular singing; but so too did a new kind of naturalism: the "true," "authentic" voice of a rock or blues singer (male or female) forms its realism through very different techniques from those of the *bel canto* stars.

Performance acts; portrayal; mimicry: these terms point towards a further obvious factor — singers *perform*. All performers are, in a particular, codified way, on display, objects of consuming attention; but singers stand naked, their bodies not mediated by external instruments. *Display,* in this context, is an already sexualized site, heavily coded feminine (which means that men who sing, especially in live situations when their bodies are on display, are already in danger of being seen as feminized or queer). The signifying chain (voice–body–sex–woman–display–prostitute), although commonly activated via metaphoric links to the natural (embodiment, sexual availability, mother-love, etc.), fastens on a procedure of objectification, or alienation (in the philosophical sense) — one that Lucy Green discusses in terms of a *mask* separating but also mutually implicating performer and spectator/listener in a variety of relationships of power, desire, and imaginary identifications.[14] Of course, masquerade has commonly been seen as the privileged strategy of female sexuality *tout court*. Indeed, as Abbate reminds us, Nietzsche saw Woman as precisely "a being without visible essence, an unseeable core, concealed by a sheen of adornments…you undrape her at your peril"; for what you may unveil, so fantasy suggests, is: a secret maleness! — a property that, in psychoanalytic terms, is no more than an inversion of that male lack which must on no account be revealed and which had therefore been displaced on to Woman in the first place.[15] The female body is fixed in its place — as too are the bodies of feminized racial and class groups, such as dandified blacks and working-class teddy boys — through a technology of adornment, which maintains a central, albeit ambivalent role for the imaginary, vivifying presence of voice.

Abbate's larger point is to argue that in opera (and by extension, we might add, in other genres where female singers deliver narratives typically scripted by male composers, such as popular songs) we find a certain dispersal of authoriality, as women performers, conventionally regarded as objects both of compositional manipulation and of audience spectatorship, in effect "re-sex" themselves into positions of creative agency. Although Abbate draws on Roland Barthes's theory of a "second semiology" of voice — a bodily (hence, by implication, female or perhaps castrated) voice in the performed text, as against the signifying voice of the (male-authored) work — her own approach to Richard Strauss's opera *Salome* is deconstructive, opening to view subversive voices hidden within the score, which singers can exploit. Indeed, a limitation of her analysis is that, against the drift of her own project, she does not discuss any actual performances; instead, the capacity of the character Salome to "slide[…] into the male subject-position"[16] and compose her own trajectory emerges from fractures that, wittingly or unwittingly, have been composed into the work by the male author.

This issue becomes even more interesting when we consider recorded rather than live performance (bearing in mind, of course, that the recording has become the normative performance mode for popular music, to the point where the "Is it 'live' or is it Memorex?" question[17] has become a permanently constitutive issue for listening, both to live and recorded musical sources). When we listen to recorded music, the sound of the voice is, obviously, separated from the body that is, putatively, its physical source, at once making available new routes of imaginary identifications and evacuating the too-easy conflation of sight and sound characteristic of live performance. Just as photographic and filmic images offer, it would seem, access to a reality that is in fact always elsewhere and is therefore at the same time with-held, so a recorded voice promises a body we can never hold, opening up a gap between desire and object that can never be closed. But this reveals what was always already there (albeit remediated, amplified, doubled): "the moment we enter the symbolic order, an unbridgeable gap separates forever a human body from 'its' voice. The voice acquires a spectral autonomy, it never quite belongs to the body we see."[18] What, in performance, normally covers over this gap was in any case only a mask, a masquerade, which is now just given new and added powers (like the photograph, the recording cannot lie — which means that it lies more convincingly; like the photograph, it is both lifelike and already dead and gone).

The recorded voice is therefore particularly difficult to pin down in gender terms, stretched as it is on a screen framed by intersecting axes running between mask and realism, embodiment and virtuality, presence and absence; which, however, makes it all the more open to gender trickery. If women traditionally have been positioned as objects of the gaze and men as those who both look and speak, then the upheavals in the interplay of the impulses of looking and hearing occasioned by developments in the mass media (film, records) restructure this nexus of semiotic and psychoanalytic interest as a site of intense ideological tension. What is important here is not only the parallels in the roles of voice and gaze — both act as *mirrors*, playing out the dramas of reflection, identity, and difference that construct subjects and their others — but also the differences — the "acoustic mirror," as it has been called, loops back to the ears of the vocalizing subject in a narcissistic short-circuit — and the interplay between them. When, as with film and recorded music, representation is twice removed — a display of a display — this interplay takes on an additional intensity, even (or especially) when one aspect is left to the imagination.[19]

Both Abbate and Koestenbaum fix on the figure of the castrato to focus their arguments. For Koestenbaum, the falsetto voice, epitomized *in extremis* by the castrato, stands for whatever escapes the disciplinary codes of natural singing; its "effeminacy" is linked to the *frisson* aroused by fantasies of "the missing phallus," and, as the result of "breath that took the wrong exit out of the body," heard as "a species of ventriloquism," it potentially queers any established settlement of the relationships of gender, sex, and body.[20] Abbate points out that this foregrounding of the *constructed* status of gender clears ground for assertions of a "maleness" within women. Drawing on Barthes's analysis of the castrato disguised as a woman in Balzac's *Sarrasine*, she suggests that to find female agency in opera, we should "look for the castrato" (that so-called man who sounds unnaturally like a woman). And her interpretation climaxes at the moment of Jochanaan's execution at Salome's request, when Salome's voice is accompanied by a solo double-bass, playing unnaturally high and sounding (according to the composer's instructions in the score) like "the suppressed groaning of a woman"; this "unknowable sound," like "nothing (on earth)," represents, Abate argues, a castrato, "another singer inside *Salome*" (and inside Salome, surely) who mobilizes the possibility of un-manning/re-manning gendered subject-positions.[21]

Castration is, of course, one of the key metaphors for psychoanalysis. It is the incest-taboo accompanied by attendant threats of punishment differentially applied to males and females that initiates both the binary structure of sex (because all subjects, in order to function as subjects, are required — so it seems — to line up under one gender or the other) and the differential structures of what Lacan calls the Symbolic Law (because language, staging the encounter with the Other in exchanges of words rather than of women, forever seeks but fails to make good the originary loss figured in the cut of castration, at the same time positioning subjects by gender within its own rules, and excluding what cannot be allowed to be even thought so that what is thereby included can function to reproduce meaning and identity). In this developmental logic, the phallus operates as a token of symbolic authority (the Paternal Law, for it is men who assume themselves to *have* it), although this can never be more than a ruse (for men are always afraid to *lose* it, and the forbidden zones of homosexuality are there, for both men and women, to shore up the link between sexual deviance and loss of symbolic identity). Within this perspective, women's quests to subvert or appropriate phallic power can never reduce to the question, who does the washing up — or who plays the guitar. Indeed, in the psychoanalytic tradition, the sex/gender cut (the nexus of male/female, hetero/homo oppositions) is implicated in, or even foundational for, a whole range of elaborated binaries: public/private, mind/body, lack/supplement, inside/outside (e.g., of culture), which consolidate a structure of symbolic as well as social power.

The possible historical contingency of this way of thinking is raised in many of the critiques of psychoanalysis (and I shall return to it). Koestenbaum, in a provocative excursion into cultural history, points out that the term *bel canto*, as a formulation nostalgically fixed to a lost vocal culture epitomized by the disappearing castrato, appeared at almost exactly the same time (the 1860s) that "homosexuality" as a sexual pathology was first named; and that both usages gave rise to intensely anxious pseudo-scientific medico-ethical panics — about "decadent" singing, "decadent" sexual behavior — climaxing in the 1890s and the early 1900s. Psychoanalysis and hysteria emerged as characteristic discourses during the same period — and so, we might add, did interlinked discourses of racial and class hygiene, as those with most to lose rushed to man [*sic*] the redoubts of élite, racial, and gendered power. This period (the 1880s to the 1920s) was also the moment of first-wave feminism; of recording and, towards the end, the sound film, putting the embodiment of voice in question as never before; and of new kinds of voice — from below (music hall, cabaret, and political song) and beyond (the dark continent of black America, not to mention the Jewish diaspora). Exploration of popular voices of this period from this point of view — female blues singers and other powerful "mammy" figures, blackface whites, male impersonators from Vesta Tilley to Marlene Dietrich, torch singers, feminized male heart-throbs (Al Jolson) and closeted puffs (Noel Coward, Cole Porter), yodeling cowboys (Jimmie Rodgers) — would pay rich dividends.

Equally inviting is the period of second-wave feminism, particularly the 1960s and 1970s when feminist critiques were becoming widely disseminated, in an intoxicating if uneasy relationship with the so-called counterculture, but when at the same time emergent rock music was, according to the terms of those very critiques, often re-inscribing the values of an entrenched male chauvinism within its expressive and representational repertoire. This was also a time marked by class upheaval and resettlement, racial conflict (especially in the United States) and postcolonial struggle (Algeria, Vietnam, Congo, Ireland), and a renewed interest in psychoanalysis, especially re-readings, extensions, and critiques of Freud, by Jacques Lacan and many others. It is to this period that, bearing in mind the need to situate the gender issue within this broader context, I want first to direct my attention.

******

I will start with a record by the American singer-songwriter, Patti Smith, from her 1975 album *Horses*, a cover of Van Morrison's 1965 garage-rock classic, "Gloria."[22] And although the thrust of my approach is Lacanian, I want to reckon with some of the issues in the psychoanalytic account by building the theory in historically evolving stages — as if, one might say, moving through three sessions on the couch, each superintended by a different analyst: Sigmund Freud, Jacques Lacan, and Slavoj Žižek.

The original "Gloria," by the Belfast R&B band Them, with Van Morrison singing the leering vocal, is a classic example of what became known, after Frith and McRobbie,[23] as "cock-rock," in which a strutting male voice, dripping with demand, imposes his phallic authority on a female object of desire. While there may appear to be a certain passivity about the way he describes her approach to his room and what she does to him, this conforms to the pattern of male scopophilic control (she "make me feel so good"), just as his performance conforms to the cock-rock vocal conventions ("explicit, crude... aggressive... loud, rhythmically insistent, built around techniques of arousal and climax... shouting and screaming... swagger untrammeled by responsibility... ").[24]

Patti Smith's cover, as Mike Daley has pointed out,[25] comprehensively reworks the original.

> Jesus died for somebody's sins but not mine
> Meltin' in a pot of thieves/ Wild card up my sleeve
> Thick heart of stone/ My sins my own
> They belong to me
> People say beware/ But I don't care
> The words are just/ Rules and regulations to me
>
> I walk in a room/ You know I look so proud
> I move in this here atmosphere where/ Anything's allowed
> And I go to this here party/ And I just get bored
> Until I look out the window see a sweet young thing
> Humpin' on the parking meter leaning on the parking meter
> Oh she looks so good/ Oh she looks so fine
> When I got this crazy feeling/ That I'm gonna make her mine
> Put my spell on her

Here she comes/ Walkin' down the street
Here she comes/ Comin' through my door
Here she comes/ Crawlin' up my stair
Here she comes/ Waltzin' through the hall
In a pretty red dress and
Oh she looks so good/ Oh she looks so fine
And I got this crazy feeling/ That I'm gonna make her mine
And I hear this knockin' at my door/ And I look up at the big tower clock and say
"Oh my god it's midnight/ And my baby is walkin' through the door"
Layin' on my couch/ She whispers to me
And I take the big plunge and
Lord, she was so good/ Lord, she was so fine
And I'm gonna tell the world/ That I just made her mine
I said "Darling tell me your name"/ She told me her name
She whispered to me/ She told me her name
And the name is/ G-L-O-R-I-A (*Gloria*)

It was at the stadium where twenty thousand girls call their name out to me
Marie Ruth but to tell you the truth/ I didn't hear them I didn't see
I let my eyes rise to the big tower clock/ And I heard those bells chimin' in my heart
Going ding dong ding dong....
Early the time when you came in my room/ When you whispered to me
And we took the big plunge
And oh you were so good/ Oh you were so fine
And I gotta tell the world/ That I made you mine
G-L-O-R-I-A (*Gloria*)

Oo the tower bells chime/ Ding dong they chime
I say that Jesus died for somebody's sins but not mine
(*Gloria*) G-L-O-R-I-A (repeat to fade)
[Italics = band responses]

Only the basic narrative shape together with a few key ideas (to do with feeling good and feeling fine) and the chorus line (G-L-O-R-I-A, *Gloria*) survive from Morrison's lyrics. Smith encases this in new material — actually a version of a poem she had written some years before called "Oath" — which foregrounds the moral dangers of her lustful desires; and she pushes her appropriation of Morrison's vocal persona to an extreme. Daley rightly brings out the way that Smith's vocal extremes — the switching of registers, which confuses gender norms, the vast range of vocal effects, the barely coherent climaxes — seem both to parody the conventions of cock-rock and appropriate them, thereby inverting the traditional structure of sexual positioning. A straightforwardly feminist critique of oedipal norms, then?

There is no lack of biographical material to fuel a Freudian analysis. (I am putting on hold for the moment the familiar question of how the subject of the biography might be thought to relate to the subject of the song.) Brought up by a mother who was a religious fanatic and an atheistic, blaspheming father whom she adored, Smith rebelled as a teenager against her earlier religiosity, substituting the religions of art and of rock 'n' roll, particularly its sexual permissiveness. An unmarried mother at twenty-one, she gave the baby up for adoption — refusing, one might say, the Freudian cure for penis envy. Adolescent hallucinations appear to have mingled religion and sex: "I used to dream about getting fucked by the Holy Ghost," she later said.[26] Although as a child she fiercely resisted feminine type-casting, subsequently, as she struggled to make it in bohemian New York in the years after 1967, she seems to have worked through relationships with a succession of father-figures, including artist and photographer Robert Mapplethorpe, Bob Dylan's friend Bobby Neuwirth, playwright Sam Shepard, musicians Allen Lanier and John Cale, who produced *Horses*, and, at least in fantasy, Jim Morrison and Jimi Hendrix.[27] These men, she herself said, she looked to for "discipline." Her performance style became celebrated for performative excess and sexual frisson, and among her specialities was the appropriation of songs associated with dominant male singers, not just "Gloria" but The Who's "My Generation," the Stones' "Paint It Black" and Hendrix's "Hey Joe." Mapplethorpe's iconic cover photo for the *Horses* album portrays her ambiguous in gender but undoubtedly masterful and in control. "I write to seduce a chick," she said, "I write to have somebody."[28] Plenty of evidence here, then, Freud might say, of unresolved oedipal business.

What Freud might have paid less attention to is the wider context. In the early '70s, a specific New York rock music was coalescing — a sort of arty, avant-garde punk — built on foundations provided by the twisted street-realism of Velvet Underground, with John Cale and Lou Reed to the fore, and the tradition of mostly unknown garage bands of the 1960s, continued by MC5, and Iggy Pop and the Stooges. Backed by the writers of the new rock magazine, *Creem*, with writers like Lester Bangs, Dave Marsh, and Lenny Kaye (who became Patti Smith's lead guitarist), bands such as Suicide, the New York Dolls, Wayne County, Television, Blondie, and the Ramones put together a provocative antihippie aesthetic characterized by noise, shock, avant-garde excess, and self-proclaimed trash. Important to them also were gender inversion and a playing with sexual marginalities — both Wayne County and the Dolls, for instance, cultivated transvestite imagery — which were to feed through into later punk's gender-bending. Influential in the wider background were free jazz and the performance art of Fluxus, Lamonte Young, and John Cage — and indeed the whole bohemian New York scene: William Burroughs; Mapplethorpe, celebrating in his photos the gay S&M subculture; Andy Warhol, whose Factory was a center of a "postmoral" philosophy of sexuality and of a brand of performativity — a sort of cool, indeed blank narcissism — clearly influential on Smith.

The attempted shooting of Warhol in 1968 by Valerie Solanas, founder of SCUM (the Society for Cutting Up Men), reminds us that this was also the moment of second-wave feminism. Betty Friedan's *The Feminine Mystique* had come out in 1963, and, much more radical in tone, Mary Ellman's *Thinking about Women* in 1968, Evelyn Reed's *Problems of Women's Liberation: A Marxist Approach* in 1969, and both Germaine Greer's *The Female Eunuch* and Kate Millett's *Sexual Politics* in 1970. The women's movement, intricately related to New Left politics and the civil rights struggles, was in ferment, especially in the United States, and was also entwined with the gay rights movement: the Stonewall Riots had taken place as recently as 1969; in 1972 David Bowie came out as a self-proclaimed bisexual, and by the mid-'70s an image of bisexuality was decidedly cool.

Notoriously, of course, feminists had (still have) problems with Freud — specially with his alleged phallocentrism. From this perspective, one can readily interpret Smith's "Gloria" as an attempt to rewrite the Freudian story: that is, as an attempt to invert the traditional relations of sexual power, and to lay claim to an active, quasi-masculine pleasure — with (assuming her vocal persona is unproblematically female — which we should perhaps not assume) a possibly lesbian tonality. (In the light of this latter strand, it is intriguing to note the interplay in the lyric between public and private spaces, whispered trysts and an exultant telling of the world, which it would be easy to interpret in terms of Eve Kosofsky Sedgewick's "epistemology of the closet.") And listeners who know their Barthes will then have no difficulty in associating the fracturing of linguistic coherence, the extravagant graininess of the vocality, as symptoms of *jouissance*.[29] This analysis would certainly go with the historical grain. The 1966 book *Human Sexual Response*, by Masters and Johnson, setting out the results of their exhaustive research into sexual practice in the United States, seemed to establish "the myth of the vaginal orgasm," a conclusion seized upon by feminists, including Anne Koedt in her book with that title published in 1970, and Shere Hite in her best-selling *The Hite Report on Female Sexuality* (1976).

But if the clitoris were now the thing, this upset Freud's theory, according to which infantile genital activity common to little boys and girls must give way, in the female, to acceptance of lack and of a proper sexual passivity. In this theory, female adolescent fantasies of masochism or narcissism are assuaged only when vagina replaces clitoris as focus, and impregnation and motherhood come to provide a substitute fulfillment for the lost phallic object; continuing clitoral activity, by contrast, produces neurosis or perversion. Millett's critique of Freud argues for an "equalling up" of sexual autonomy (later twists to this approach would theorize a "lesbian phallus");[30] Greer's proposes rather a softening of penile aggression and a rehabilitation of vaginal authenticity — a sort of generalizing of Eros, after the manner put forward in Herbert Marcuse's sociological revision of Freud, *Eros and Civilisation*, which, in its 1966 second edition, had become a core text for both feminists and the New Left in general.

Either way, on this reading, Patti Smith's "Gloria" has Freud — at least the Freud of caricature — retreating in some confusion; although he is probably muttering as he goes something about hearing signs of anxiety as well as lust in her performance, and speculating about neurotic tendencies.

On this first level of analysis, the exchange taking place — the appropriation — is figured as one simply of a body part. But surely sex happens (also) in the head? For Freud, sexuality is always psycho-sexuality, and the phallus functions on the symbolic as well as the biological level — an approach pushed much further in Lacan's rereading of Freud.[31] We might ponder whether the analysis so far is adequate to the sense of religious angst in Smith's recording — or indeed, to its representation of sexuality. Is there not something deeper than we have grasped? Desire seems both *over*coded here — almost hysterically insistent — and *under*coded — not quite there musically, as if, in line with the Warholian voyeuristic tendencies of the New York avant-garde, it is being "looked at" rather than felt gesturally, "acted out" rather than grooved out. These are terms that might point towards one of Lawrence Kramer's "hermeneutic windows."[32] With the help of Lacan, let us see if we can push through it.

Lacan's concept of the phallus is complex and by no means stable. The key point, though, is that, although he does keep a place for the real phallus — the penis as it functions in the register of the Real — in his mature thought this is far less important than the phallus as *image* (in this Imaginary register, it mirrors or reflects back desire) and as *symbol* (in the register of the Symbolic, it comes to stand for the whole structure of Law, the Law of the Signifier). Simplifying, we may locate the phallic image in the sphere of Lacan's *objets petits a* — the famous Freudian part-objects, for Lacan, object-causes of desire; and the phallic symbol in the sphere of the Lacanian Big Other — that radical alterity, the locus of language, culture, law, which precedes all individual subjectivity. The importance of *castration* is as a marker of the paternal threat. This is not necessarily associated with a real person but is a metaphorical function, which Lacan therefore calls the Name-of-the-Father. The threat — whose authority is essentially a sham, because there is no final signifier in the Big Other — institutes the superego and founds culture itself; and is mapped, in an asymmetrical structure, on to the field of sexual division: the possession or lack of a real phallus is taken retroactively as a figure for the unequal positioning of men and women in the symbolic field. Sexual difference, on this account, is thus entirely contingent — it stands for an inscription of a differential schema of subjection to a phallogocentric law — but it is nonetheless deeply rooted in history.

The figure of *jouissance*, for Lacan, stands for a quasi-orgasmic bliss, a transgressive ecstasy, which it is the role of the normative pleasure-principle inscribed under the sign of castration to forbid, and which is therefore also associated with pain. For Lacan, as for Freud, *jouissance* is essentially phallic; perhaps we may think of this powerful image-fantasy as standing at the head of the whole family of part-objects — *objets petits a* — and in that sense the signs of *jouissance* we noticed earlier in Patti Smith's vocal mark the coursing of her desire around Gloria's "bits." Indeed, "voice" — along with "gaze" — is Lacan's addition to Freud's list of part-objects; and the "object-voice" is defined precisely as that impossible (because inaudible) surplus left over when the symbolic stratum of the vocal stream has been accounted for — the excess, the "indivisible remainder," which can be at best disturbed when the subject is temporarily not at home, the signifiers not in place. To the extent that Smith's vocal performance approaches objectivity in this sense, it is the terrifying *jouissance* associated with an invocation of the object-voice that is at issue. Most revealing in this respect, perhaps, are the high-pitched octave leaps into a sort of female falsetto with which she sprinkles her performance, most notably on the final "A" of her spelling out of Gloria's name; in these "impossible" sounds, "ventriloquized" (to use Koestenbaum's term), the subject we expect to be inhabiting our image of Smith's body definitely seems to be missing, and what unsettles it, we might imagine, is something like the castrato within it.

Applications of the *jouissance* idea usually link it to subversion of patriarchal law — the law of the Symbolic. This is the drift of Barthes's theory of geno-song — and still more of Julia Kristeva's theory of a presymbolic level of "semiotic," which she associates explicitly with a prephallic developmental phase centered on the mother. These applications arguably oversimplify their Lacanian source, even though in his later years Lacan himself came to speculate about the possibility of a specifically feminine *jouissance* — a rather mysterious bliss "beyond the phallus" that women may experience but know nothing of; and that is the point: this *jouissance* can appear only through breaks and slippages in the order of knowledge, only as a fantasy projection. For Lacan, there is no prediscursive reality, no presymbolic body; for him, *jouissance* (what escapes in sexuality) and *signifiance* (what shifts within language) are inseparable, and the excess is therefore radically undecideable in its orientation. It can subvert the Law but it can also stick to it, the terrifying, superhuman, disembodied voice of the patriarchal god acting precisely as what lends a spurious authority to the dicta of the superego — "*le-père-jouissance*," as Lacan calls it — the obscene ecstasy of control as such.[33] It seems there are two object voices, "voice against voice," as Mladen Dolar puts it. Or rather, because we are here in the territory not of complement but of supplement, "the secret is maybe that they are both the same; that there are not two voices, but only one object voice, which cleaves and bars the Other in an ineradicable 'extimacy'"[34] ("extimacy" being Lacan's coinage for the "outsideness" of the "inside," in the final analysis, the lack in the big Other that voids its guarantee of self-sufficiency). This means, Lacan speculates, that one might "interpret one face of the Other, the God face, as supported by feminine *jouissance*... [and] while this may not make for two Gods, nor does it make for one alone."[35]

Even so, we might think, this does not entirely answer all our questions about the meaning of Patti Smith's "Gloria." We are left wondering whether the glimpses of object voice mark a *subversion* of the phallic order; or rather an attempted *theft* of the phallus, an *appropriation*; or again, an eruption — between the lines — of feminine *jouissance*; or alternatively, a same-sex masquerade traversing the routes between all of these (on a relatively banal level, the repeating-climax structure of the recording, a common technique with Smith that she herself compared to the rhythms of female orgasm, might be taken to back up the apparently lesbian narrative setting).[36] In one sense, these choices can readily be left open for listeners to respond. The ground they sketch out organizes itself around a series of tactics of subversion which may not be mutually exclusive alternatives: *occupation* (of the place of the phallus); *displacement* (of this place to other sites); *disruption* (of the phallic system as such). The issues involved have often been articulated, with acute insight, by Judith Butler; for example: "What is 'forced' by the symbolic... is a citation of its laws that reiterates and consolidates the ruse of its own force. What would it mean to 'cite' the law to produce it differently, to 'cite' the law in order to reiterate and co-opt its power, to expose the heterosexual matrix and to displace the effect of its necessity?"[37]

But although such choices — of interpretation and of political tactic — may be undecideable in the abstract, our excursions around the landscape of Patti Smith's "Gloria" have exposed something of the forces shaping this field, hence revealing more pressingly what could be at stake. This is a song of desire, but also one of *blasphemy*: the Law-of-the-Father is rejected (or, perhaps, co-opted, the phallus appropriated), but the looming tower, the tolling bells ("ding dong"), the half-time day-of-judgment moment are marks of terror and guilt, and the initial declaration of moral autonomy is delivered in tones that manage to suggest both the cocky, more-than-human self-staging of the rock god,[38] and, it would seem, the barely suppressed sense of trauma marking an awareness of what is being hazarded; the defenses against the void opening up beyond the Law itself are only just maintained. "Extimacy" is also excommunication — even if we cannot be sure whether the abyss is a site of patriarchal anathema or of the horror lying beyond Law *tout court*.

Lacan has been little better received by feminist critics than Freud.[39] But psychoanalysis stands not for utopias but for understanding. It is this realism — its "always already" is its reading of original sin — that prompts Lacan's notorious aphorism, "Woman does not exist:" by which he means to point to the particular subjected status — her unavoidable "bar" or split veiled in the interest of male hegemony — of the discursive figure Woman, qua phantasmatic Absolute, within the phallogocentric symbolic order.[40] While criticism of this position, on both theoretical and political grounds, is entirely in order (and I will return to it), for the moment this clarity has the merit of enabling us to recognize the sheer weight of *risk* entailed in Patti Smith's performance. This is no simple claim for equality of sexual pleasure; to challenge the ordering of desire is to challenge also the authority of Law itself.

Does this mean that biology is irrelevant? By no means. Lacan's point here is precisely that deadlock in the symbolic order — the asymmetrical layout of masculine and feminine modalities — is grafted in an entirely contingent way on to the "facts" of anatomy and reproduction (although these facts, as constructionist commentators have pointed out, are themselves constituted in this graft, as the subject's bodily morphology takes on a particular, culturally sanctioned identity). Sexual difference is a nonnatural suture sited at this point of disjunction. At one and the same time, this widens the space available to cultural work, including interpretive and political critique, both for Smith and for the listener, and enables a proper respect for the ambition, the sheer *danger*, of the performance.

And what about the listener? So far, the performative dimensions of the recording have been somewhat underplayed; I have discussed "Gloria" essentially as a text — to use a linguistic terminology, as an *énoncé*. But there is also an *énonciation* — albeit, as a recording, this is a complex type, its staging of a quasi-live performance at the same time objectified by a technology that mortifies as it disseminates. There is a literature about this deadening quality of the phonograph, notably Friedrich Kittler's book *Gramophone, Film, Typewriter*: the phonograph, this medium which brings up ghosts, voices of the living dead, disembodied traces of an uncertain humanity, an *énoncé* always carrying the label, "anon"; and, as suggested earlier, it surely can be no coincidence that this medium achieved a cultural centrality over the same period as Freud and Lacan were developing the theory of the part-object, the *objet petit a,* including most importantly here, the object-voice. But this mortifying effect is to be read always in its dialogue with the vivifying quality of the *énonciation*, the performance-act as such.

In this intricately structured listening experience, then, who speaks? And to whom? And also, who looks? In both Van Morrison's original and Patti Smith's cover, "Gloria" has an intensely filmic quality; the story is told through the scopophilic gaze of the singer. We might recall that voyeurism was very much a theme of New York art-rock, probably derived in part from Warhol, whose description of visual images as "shots" testifies to more than just the standard photo-technical language: It is also a symptom of his general alienated and voyeuristic approach to both art and stardom. In this sense Valerie Solanas's shooting of him can be regarded as an attempted phallic reversal via an example of what Lacan calls a *passage à l'acte*; real gun replaces symbolic photo images, just as, in the Lacanian *acte*, an impulsive, quasi-psychotic action carries the subject temporarily out of the Symbolic altogether into the dimension of the Real, reaching for the status of an object. Although some moments are suggestive (what might happen after the final fade?), "Gloria" as a whole does not go that far — even if, according to one biographer, Smith welcomed the suggestion that she might become a "sex-object."[41] Lacan makes a distinction between "act," where the subject qua subject goes missing, exiting the theatrical set-up of reality, and "acting out," which takes place within the scene. Smith's track has very much the structure of *fantasy* as Freud and Lacan describe it: a quasi-theatrical staging of a scene within which the subject's unconscious desire is obsessively acted out, and which functions as a defense against trauma — veiling the unavoidable insatiability of desire, ultimately the lack in the Other.

To explore this further, we turn to our third shrink, Slavoj Žižek; but, because much of his writing focuses on analyses of film, he will probably take us for our consultation to the cinema (not inappropriately, given that in a way this darkened fantasy-space relocates the individual psychoanalytic transference as a mass cultural practice). Critical theory has been here before, notably in Laura Mulvey's classic but much-criticized article, "Visual Pleasure and Narrative Cinema,"[42] in which Mulvey draws on Lacan's account of the origins of the Imaginary order in the child's so-called "mirror phase" to offer a gendered theory of the pleasures of the cinematic gaze in terms of relationships of identification and scopophilia. But Žižek, like Lacan, insists that fantasy, including film fantasy, inscribes images in structures of meaning as well as identification; and that this operation must be understood in terms of the interplay of *énoncé* and *énonciation*, and its role in the splitting of the subject. *Énoncé* writes the subject into existence through the structures of the text, while *énonciation* points to the site from where the unconscious speaks — the place where the leftovers of the subject's encounters puts identity at risk.

In a first approach, we could draw on Brian Currid's adaptation of Barthes's theory of photographic pleasure in his book *Camera Lucida*, for his discussion of house music.[43] For Barthes, the pleasures of authorship (the Operator) and of reception (the Spectator), which in any case implicate and configure each other, are "triangulated" by a third position, that of the Spectrum, "that which is photographed, which serves as the ghostly materiality of the pleasures of both the Operator and the Spectator."[44] Currid gives as an example of Spectrum pleasure the "spectacular" consumption of the house club scene (the interplay of authoriality and listener/dancer participation being conceived as a "cruising of the other in the space of the dance floor"),[45] and compares this with Kobena Mercer's analysis of Robert Mapplethorpe's photos of black men, where an initial fetishistic structure is supplemented by a deconstructive "third gaze" from the position of a black queer.

In "Gloria," the interplay of voices (both vocal and instrumental) and the gazes they suggest can, at one level, certainly be thought of as helping to put in place the structure of the fantasy scene, constructing that symbolic fiction which we know as reality, speaking for characters to imaginary listeners whose putative replies can be felt as citing those normative responses which in turn help constitute the stage from which the voices speak. (This might represent a circulation of the phallus.) And we could then imagine a position further beyond this, a metalevel, from where this dialogue is queered. But arguably, Currid's interpretations overpositivise this position, falling slightly short of the full scope of Barthes's suggestion — the *objectivity* of the Spectrum (which is therefore also spectral). On this level, that of object-voice, the voices in "Gloria," and their imagined visual positions, disrupt the fiction of the fantasy-scene. With Lacan, Žižek argues that, as objects, both voice and gaze occupy a place from which the subject is always already excluded, simply by virtue of his partiality of positioning; rather than a "thing that sees" or a "thing that sounds," he has become an "I," a looking, vocalizing subject. Žižek's advance is to suggest that these two partial objects can supplement each other, the one filling the hole left in the field of the other, acting as the other's *objet petit a*: "we hear things," he says, "because we cannot see everything,"[46] and vice versa. And in film, he argues, this can happen when the structure of montage — the network of intersecting gazes — necessarily implies a missing space — what has been excluded — which may be filled by an uncanny, unexpected voice, a sound that does not belong, or even a voice we strive to hear but cannot.[47]

It is easy enough to hear the interplay of Smith and the boys in the band as they combine to name Gloria in terms of an exchange of voiced gazes: a phallic exchange, centered on their joint, almost pornographic objectification of Gloria.[48] In terms of film theory, we expect the boys to come on as though off-stage — authoritative deployers of disembodied voiceover — and this is indeed how their measured "Gloria" riff strikes us; while Smith's gabbled, falsetto-ing responses insistently raise the question of how to see her (castrated?) body. But where is Gloria herself? She is "veiled" (as women should be) and silent (or almost: she whispers — or so we are told; that is, not to us). In the network of "camera angles" created by the exchange of voices and instrumental figures throughout the song, she is present only in her gestures — a moving point or "spot," covering a hole in the recording space, a hole waiting, perhaps, for its voice. Is she, then, the surplus left over from the montage process, her voice traceable only in the senseless scream stratum of Smith's vocal, or alternatively in the force of her own voice's almost palpable absence — as that silent scream which, for Žižek, represents object-voice in its purest form? Or, is she to be read, again within Smith's vocal itself, but simply as a symptom of narcissistic (perhaps homosexual) fantasy; and, by extension, as the sound of voiceless feminine *jouissance*? (The "big plunge" is seen — that is, described — but not heard, in an inversion of the patriarchal norm, which generally authenticates female orgasm through sounds, in both porn and dance music.)[49] Or, given that the boys unveil her, speak for her, name her, is she standing for the passages of subjectivity itself?

Silverman, writing about the (male) voice-off in classic cinema, talks about its "theological status."[50] Žižek, following Hegel, regards the naming power of language as the very mechanism whereby "pure self" — the void that represents the "night of the world" — moves into the symbolic order and assumes the trappings of subjectivity.[51] But what frightening figure is unveiled, and where does it live? Behind this process, it would appear, sanctioning it through the figure of castration, stands the Big N, the Name-of-the-Father, which Smith tries to, but cannot, speak coherently, which the recording makes to fragment and to circulate inside and outside of the (gendered) subject, but which is written unequivocally in the song title in an appropriate theologic: "Gloria in excelsis deo."[52]

In a song called "Ain't It Strange" from the 1976 album *Radio Ethiopia*, Smith challenges God: she sings, "Turn around God, make a move!" In an interview she said of this, "I wanna be God's daughter. No... I wanna be God's mistress... I wanna be fucked by God. Not just once, a thousand times." On January 26, 1977, while singing this song — "its after a part where I spin like a dervish and I say 'Hand of God I feel the finger, Hand of God I start to whirl, Hand of God I don't get dizzy, Hand of God I do not fall now.'" — she fell dangerously off the stage, seriously damaged her neck, and was laid up for three months. "I fell... I did feel the finger push me right over...[53] And her music started to become more subdued, less turbulent, more feminine.

In 1979 Smith retired and married ex-MC5 guitarist Fred "Sonic" Smith. She raised a family and lived quietly, in apparent domestic tranquility, for some years amid persistent rumors of how she was subservient to Fred, deferred to him in everything, and even whispers that she suffered domestic violence.

In terms of conventional therapy, this might look like some sort of cure. In terms of gender politics, it looks like a relapse. From the point of view of the analysis presented here, though, its most important meaning is surely to signal the pressures attendant on Smith's challenge and the difficulties, at the level of localized cultural activity, of sustaining this challenge. Yet it is worth adding to this halfway judgment Judith Butler's broader challenge to the foundations of the Lacanian position.[54] While castration stands as a powerful metaphor for the prohibitions necessary to human sociality and culture, for Butler, Lacan's mapping of sexual division — itself universalized out of historical contingency — to a master-slave dialectic taken from Hegel serves to immobilize identity and meaning in a "structure of religious tragedy" rooted in Old Testament guilt and played out between nostalgia for a lost plenitude on the one hand and a masochistic idealization of failure before the Law on the other. This morality play — which Lacan, if guilty, would appear to share with Patti Smith — should, Butler argues, come under a Nietzschian critique, in which a deconstructive will-to-power uncovers the perversions underlying the creation of an externalized theocratic Law: an intoxicating prospect, no doubt, but one where the outcome of Nietzsche's own project, not so much in itself as for what it may symbolize of the moral and epistemological crises afflicting modernity as a whole, might give us reason for caution.

******

Patti Smith is not only female but white (and Van Morrison is not only male but white);[55] yet "Gloria," in both versions, calls up references to African-American music.[56] How, if at all, might this affect our understanding of its sexual politics, and how might we position this racial dimension within the cultural economy of the period? Van Morrison and his band, Them, emerged out of British R&B, and this movement, as well as cock rock as a whole, in its sexual politics as well as in many other respects, looked back to African-American models, particularly the reformulation of blues machismo carried through in postwar Chicago, most influentially by Muddy Waters ("I Can't Be Satisfied," "Mannish Boy," "Hoochie Coochie Man," "I'm Ready," etc.). Patti Smith, brought up in a predominantly black area in New Jersey, worshipped American performers in the same lineage (Hendrix, Morrison) as well as the Rolling Stones[57] — although the New York white rock scene to which she came to belong developed a notable ambivalence towards black influences, especially to rhythmic grind and groove (widely thought in the white popular culture as a whole to offer models of sexual freedom); and this ambivalence was part in fact of its critical stance towards traditional gender representations. The "hermeneutic window" offered by her "Gloria" recording, with its under/overcoding of sexual desire, probably has its source in this problematic, and this may provide the essential context to the ambivalences we have located in the performance.

Relations between the black civil rights and feminist movements in this period were much debated but difficult — and indeed in much of the Black Power movement of the time attitudes to gender roles and sexual politics were equally as unreconstructed as in most of the contemporary white counterculture: the message for black women, according to bell hooks, was that they should "breed warriors for the revolution."[58] At the same time, the idea of a structural correspondence between the subordinate positions of blacks on the one hand and women on the other (not to mention homosexuals) was widespread, cropping up in such varied sources as Marcuse, sociologist Gunnar Myrdal, feminist readings of Genet, and John Lennon (in his song, "Woman is the Nigger of the World," from 1972).[59] When Patti Smith took on a song like "Gloria," therefore, she was inescapably engaging a point in the contemporary culture that was particularly fraught, as well as a long history in which specific patterns of African-American gender roles and sexual attitudes were inextricably entangled with white investments in images of black sexuality. The uncertainties over sexual representation in the recording speak to the freight carried in this engagement as well as the specific ambivalences foregrounded in New York rock — just as my own silence so far on the racial dimension no doubt reflects a linked anxiety.

Breaking this silence is difficult. If Woman is, according to Lacan, the symptom of Man, then Black Woman, from this perspective, could be regarded as the symptom not only of Man but of Black Man and, with variants, of White Man too (and indeed of White Woman). Black female voices come bearing the marks of the stereotypic positions in which their history has located them, and it is just as foolish to ignore the discursive force of this positioning as to fail to engage the deconstructive efforts provided by feminist and race-theoretic critiques. Hortense Spillers acknowledges the inescapability of the images — "Let's face it. I am a marked woman… 'Peaches' and 'Brown Sugar,' 'Sapphire' and 'Earth Mother,'… [etc.]… a locus of confounded identities, a meeting ground of investments… My country needs me, and if I were not here, I would have to be invented."[60] — even as she notes that this is the effect of a *mis*-naming. And in a similar way, Nina Simone in her song "Four Women" paints in the historical realities behind the stereotypic figures — "Aunt Sarah," "Sweet Thing," "Saphronia," and "Peaches."

It seems hardly possible to discuss Simone's voice — that large, rich chest voice, resonant, sometimes enveloping, sometimes intimidating, throughout her entire range — without resorting to the trope of "maternity." It is not just a question of voice quality but also of the cultural lineage centered around figures of the powerful black matriarch, which, as manifested through singers, runs from Gertrude "Ma" Rainey and Bessie Smith, through "Big Mama" Thornton, Rosetta Tharpe and Mahalia Jackson, to Aretha Franklin and Simone herself. As these names suggest, the lineage has both secular and sacred (blues and gospel) wings; and Simone was often described in both hieratic terms ("high priestess of soul") and Amazonian metaphors (Bernice Johnson Reagon, herself an African-American singer, described the "warrior energy" of her sound).[61] But if this is a maternal sound, it is one of a very specific sort, both from the point of view of cultural history, and musically. There is always an *edge* to Simone's voice as well as a resonant power: one is not allowed to just sink into it, and it certainly does not summon up fantasies of comfort, safety, or womblike bliss. At the same time, on a more generic level, the "powerful cultural fantasy" of the maternal voice, "first voice of love," prefiguring and potentially subverting the phallic authority of the symbolic sphere, has been foregrounded by feminist psychoanalysis as a politically empowering trope for women.[62] Within the matrix formed through these intersecting discourses, and against the background of Patti Smith's ambivalent relationship with the phallus, it becomes intriguing to consider Nina Simone in the context of the function of what Lacanian psychoanalysis has termed the "phallic mother."

The story of an African-American matriarchate is well entrenched, with sociological research apparently confirming populist stereotype, the message widely accepted within black culture as well as white. As a result of the slavery system and experience, backed up subsequently by the economic effects of racial discrimination — so the story goes — black women were forced to take on huge responsibilities, both as workers and in the household, while their men were on the one hand often separated and exiled from them, and on the other demeaned and emasculated by white oppression. With men often a weak influence or absent, women assumed a headship role in the family — and in strong versions of the myth, they appear as a castrating force. For conventional political wisdom in the 1960s, encapsulated in Daniel Moynihan's widely influential *The Negro Family* (1965), the moral to draw was that the problem of the "dysfunctional" African-American family could be solved only if it acceded much more to the norms of (white) patriarchy. And black (male) radicals largely agreed; indeed, many black women seem also to have done so.

Black nationalists, needing to reject the heritage of slavery, accepted the historicity — and also the destructive effects — of the matriarchate, constructed a masculinist myth of Africa, and stressed the need for strong black men. Angela Davis, herself a revolutionary closely involved with the Black Panther Party, was forced to confront its masculinism and, in her letters to the imprisoned George Jackson, challenged his male chauvinism.[63] Amiri Baraka stressed the need to address the "separation" of black men and black women not through the "devilish" idea of "equality" but through "complementarity" ("the divine complement the black woman is for her man") — a complementarity rooted in "nature."[64] Malcolm X justified his time as a pimp as a way of asserting his masculinity. And Eldridge Cleaver called for the rape of white women as an "insurrectionary act"; "four hundred years minus my balls" must come to an end: "we shall have our manhood." It is Cleaver who offers the clearest example of how such "radicalism" could accede to both the myth of the emasculating black matriarch and that of the super-virile black male. In "The Allegory of the Black Eunuchs," he lays the blame at the door of the "nigger bitch [who] seems to be full of steel, granite — hard and resisting, not soft and submissive [like the white woman]"; and in response to the white man's confident expression of superior (brain) power — "My prick will excel your rod... [your] big Nigger dick" — asserts a Lawrenceian faith that his phallic power will prevail, "if I never betray[...] the law of my rod."[65]

Clearly this late 1960s moment was one of extreme racio-sexual tension. But it was also the moment when feminist critique of precisely the positions outlined above began.[66] Angela Davis was driven by her militant opposition to black patriarchalist attitudes to embark on historical research into African-American women under slavery, and first published on the subject in 1971.[67] Her example was followed a few years later by bell hooks.[68] For both writers, black women's resilience was resistant, not compliant; they held families together rather than acting as agents of their disruption, and were forced by economic circumstances to become community leaders. Fault for the plight of their men should be laid not with them but squarely with white racism. Nevertheless, the degree of strength and relative autonomy exercised by many women, no matter how historically contingent, was real: hooks approvingly quotes Maya Angelou on how African-American women's social leadership roles create a distinction between black and white American communities; and Davis, with similar approval, quotes the eminent African-American leader and philosopher, W. E. B. Dubois: "Our women in black had freedom contemptuously thrust upon them."[69] But these were not signs of a matriarchate, for which the requirements of social and economic power were quite lacking. Rather, what we see is a pattern of gender relations that is in one way an inversion of the white norm and in another its diseased extension (we might say that here the Law-of-the-Father is over-determined by the Law-of-the-Man), with the matriarchy theory developed as an ideological distortion to cover for this situation.

Despite their critiques, both Davis and hooks see the feminist potential of the historically constituted role of African-American women. In a more recent work, on female blues singers, Davis links this tradition of relative economic independence with the capacity of Ma Rainey and Bessie Smith to act as social role models — "Sexuality and travel provided the most tangible evidence of freedom"[70] — and with the vocal modalities of their songs. By this time she is also prepared to connect a gender politics that was "radically different from those operating in the dominant culture" with the Mother trope; she quotes jazz musician Danny Barker on Ma Rainey: "Ma Rainey was *Ma* Rainey. When you said 'Ma,' that means mother. 'Ma' that means the tops. That's the boss, the shack bully of the house, Ma Rainey. She'd take charge. 'Ma.' Ma Rainey's coming to town, the boss blues singer. And you respect Ma, Grand 'Ma,' my 'Ma,' and ma 'Ma.' That's 'Ma.' That's something you respect. You say mother. That's the boss of the shack. Not papa, ma-ma."[71]

But it is Hortense Spillers who pursues the political potential of these links most imaginatively. Accepting the thrust of the Davis/hooks critique, she nevertheless faces the effects clearly: "the 'Negro family' has no Father to speak of — his Name, his Law, his Symbolic function... and it is... the fault of the Daughter, or the female line. [But] This stunning reversal of the castration thematic, displacing the Law of the Father to the territory of the Mother as Daughter" offers fruitful ground for the cultivation of radical possibilities, both for men and women:

> the African-American male has been touched... by the *mother, handed* by her in ways that he cannot escape, and in ways that the white American male is allowed to temporize by a fatherly reprieve... the African-American woman, the mother, the daughter, becomes historically the powerful and shadowy evocation of a cultural synthesis long evaporated — the Law of the Mother — only and precisely because legal enslavement removed the African-American male not so much from sight as from *mimetic* view, as a partner in the prevailing social fiction of the father's name, the Father's law.

Spillers's program is to build on this historically contingent heritage, to seek "the *insurgent* ground as female social subject. Actually *claiming* the monstrosity (of a female with the potential to 'name'), which her culture imposes in blindness."[72] I want to suggest that within Nina Simone's musical trajectory is to be found something analogous to the conjoining of race and gender critiques initiated by Angela Davis and carried on by bell hooks and Hortense Spillers — and even, perhaps, something comparable as well to Spillers's adventurous political project.

Clearly we have moved close here to the territory marked by the psychoanalytic concept of the "phallic mother" — dangerous territory indeed. When Peter Antelyes writes about the "red hot mama" of the 1920s, exemplified by Ma Rainey and Bessie Smith, as "'red hot' in her sexual appetite, and maternal in her authority, her allure, and her dangerously enveloping possessiveness," it is hard not to feel the force of familiar patriarchal fantasies; and when he quotes musicians Art Hodes and Danny Barker to the effect that Bessie Smith "don't need a mike; she don't use one... she could fill up Carnegie Hall... she could fill it up from her muscle and she could last all night," the conflation of voice, mike, and (phallic) muscle is equally telling.[73] As Judith Butler points out, male anxieties around figures of phallicized femininity often construct the phallic mother misogynistically as a terrifying, devouring (castrating) force;[74] and mothers who "will not let go" are also implicated strongly in homophobic panics (although this does prevent the "omnipotent, unknowing mother" assuming, perhaps by way of reaction, a deeply rooted function in gay culture).[75]

For psychoanalytic theory, though, the phallic mother does have an important, albeit circumscribed role to play in "normal" (heterosexual) development. Lacan's view of the preoedipal stage, the initial phase of the mother-infant relationship (which he often calls the "first time" of the Oedipus complex), appears to grow out of his interest in the picture of the mother as a devouring, engulfing force developed by object relations theorists such as Melanie Klein. In this first stage, the mother's attempt and failure to satisfy her desire through the child, and the child's attempt and failure to satisfy that desire, sets up a reciprocal movement that Lacan characterizes as the circulation of an imaginary phallus. The mother seems to the child to be omnipotent — at this point she is the Law — yet she is also patently lacking (otherwise she would not desire). The entire game can be thought of as an oscillation of having and being the phallus for the other (a binary which, according to Lacan, will later come to settle, albeit asymmetrically, on the partners of the heterosexual couple). In any case, this phase is destined to come to an end, through the intervention of the (imaginary) father — that is, via the incest taboo — who "castrates" the mother (that is, forbids access to and by the child), enabling the child's entry into the social (symbolic) world. From this point of view, later appeals to images of a maternal phallus can only have the status of regressive fantasy.

Arguably, if ironically, feminist constructions of a presymbolic maternal voice offer no challenge here. According to Silverman, whether such constructions are marked positive (Guy Rosolato's "sonorous envelope," Didier Anzieu's "bath of sounds," Julia Kristeva's "mobile receptacle," or *chora*) or negative (entrapment in "umbilical night": Michel Chion), they stand together in infantilizing the mother (displacing childish babble to her), and transferring her symbolic power to the father, whose intervention is installed as an originary moment restricting the role of the preoedipal phase to what becomes forever lost, and that of the mother to a purely foundational function (invisible, underneath the ground on which the Symbolic is constructed).[76] Kristeva in particular is taken to task for positioning the presymbolic *chora* where, whatever its disruptive potential subsequently, it must constantly be abjected by the mature subject (although we might also note in passing the resonance between her notion of a "homosexual facet" to the "choric fantasy," that is, a narcissistic transfer of desire/knowledge between the female generations via the cycle of birth, and Spillers's thematizing of the "female line").[77] By contrast, Silverman draws attention to the *symbolic work* performed at the preoedipal stage, particularly by the voice. Its role as acoustic mirror, circulating aural images between mother and infant, initiates the identity work subsequently taken up on the visual level in Lacan's mirror stage (and one wonders how this relatively unrestricted circulation of voice, later of course to be much more tightly disciplined and gendered, relates to circulation of the imaginary phallus).[78] The maternal voice, considered as an *objet a*, represents an early splitting of self, standing for rupture as well as bliss, and hence functioning as an early "voice-off" (in Silverman's theory of film voices, the abstracting, disembodied voice-off will normatively be identified with a (phallic) male).[79] And even the superego, already understood by Freud as formed through the internalization of authoritative voices (in contrast to the spatial imaginary associated with formation of the ego), can be regarded as beginning its life in the imperatives the child absorbs from the (phallic) mother.[80] Small wonder, perhaps, that the "voice of the law" we detected in the vocal *jouissance* of Patti Smith's "Gloria" proved so difficult to gender!

Silverman's critique is congruent with several other feminist receptions of Lacan. Judith Butler, for instance, focuses on the way that Lacan fixes the *process* of castration, conceived metaphorically as the figure of lack, hence as the inescapable gateway into subjectivity, to a specific *moment,* which, through its oedipal structure, fastens subject-position inexorably and asymmetrically to a heterosexual binarism. He does this, she argues, through an unacknowledged slippage of registers, from (real) penis to the (imaginary) phallus, as guarantor of bodily totality, and then to the (symbolic) phallus, as "privileged signifier"; "what operates under the sign of the symbolic may be nothing other than precisely that set of imaginary effects which have become naturalized and reified as the law of signification," for "by changing the name of the penis to 'the phallus'... the part status of the former [is] phantasmatically and synechdochally overcome through the inauguration of the latter as 'the privileged signifier.'"[81]

But if the phallus/castration matrix is regarded as the effect of a continual performatively maintained imaginary (which is Butler's position), then it becomes potentially mobile, as between genders and sexualities, as among imagined body parts, and as instantiated in a variety of moments. And this, in a way, is no more than to follow up the hints in Lacan himself: the metaphoric (rather than purely developmental) status of castration is clear, and so is that of the Law-of-the-Father (it is a "paternal metaphor," which is not dependent on any actual father). Indeed, the circulation of the phallus in the preoedipal phase implies, for Lacan, that the symbolic father is already operative there; thus (for example) the *fort-da* game, which Freud interprets as the young child's dramatization of the mother's absence, is seen by Lacan as an early (preoedipal) point of entry into the structure of signifying lack which is constitutive of the symbolic itself. These materials provide internal deconstructive pointers, one might think, although this potential is at the same time disavowed by Lacan's core insistence on the importance of the oedipal moment, which forever ties (hetero)sex and symbolic positioning together. It is a matter of interpretative choice whether one sees this disavowal as a phallogocentric relapse (perhaps with theocratic overtones, as Butler does) or a "realistic" acceptance of a relative universal grounded, however contingently, in anthropo-historical phylogeny.

Whichever way that argument goes, we are certainly entitled by the debate to envisage the return of the phallic mother from her dismissal as no more than regressive fantasy, and to put her, very definitely, in question. And the point is in the question: it is a matter not only of how, in what guise, with what associations and authority, this persona might appear, might construct herself (including her voice(s)), in relation to her others, but also how the sex of this persona is articulated with other markers of identity — here most especially with race. If, tendentially, "the symbolic is not merely organized by 'phallic power' but by a 'phallicism' that is centrally sustained by racial anxiety and sexualized rituals of racial purification,"[82] how would this articulation play out in the work of an African-American "ethnic maternal" voice fighting both to confront and to draw sustenance from a collective history deeply embedded in quite specific racial as well as gender myths?

There is suggestive biographical material in Nina Simone's life and career (although one would not want, any more than in the case of Patti Smith, to allow suggestion to turn into psychologistic explanation: I am trying to position both life and music, considered as performed texts, within a set of partly intersecting, partly overlapping, constitutive discourses).[83] Its trajectory can be regarded as being articulated around motifs of ambition, success, and failure: from a middle-class family, she learned classical piano and aimed at the concert platform, failed, became an entertainer, succeeded, aligned her work with the burgeoning civil rights/black nationalist movement, which by the end of the 1960s seemed to her a failure, moved abroad, where, for the rest of her life, a combination of exile, neo-Africanism and diva-like remoteness seems to have resulted both in a sense of personal confusion and a reputation as difficult and demanding. These motifs were mediated by an oscillation of private and public energies: a succession of relationships and sought-after relationships with men intersected (at least in her self-construction) with her discovery and assertion of public authority (musical and political: it was a revelation when she realized the political utility of the "power and spirituality," the "state of grace," she could create in performance, and she compares this to her memory of revivalist church services in childhood).[84]

These processes were always mobilized in contexts structured by gender and race: for example, her rejection as a piano student by the elite Curtis Institute was, she was convinced, motivated by racial prejudice; and by the early 1960s she "started thinking about myself as a black person in a country run by white people and a woman in a world run by men."[85] Class was important too. Starting out with a "superior" attitude to popular music and the venues and audiences she encountered (they are "dumb," "stupid," "disrespectful"), she realized with her first political songs, such as "Mississippi Goddam" (1963), that she could direct this "dirty" quality into political persuasion; and this propaganda for "freedom," this pulpit as it were, this "insurgent ground" where, to recall Hortense Spillers's words, she claimed "the monstrosity of a female with the potential to 'name,'" made the music more worthy of her respect, even, than the elite music she preferred aesthetically.[86] All this seems to have resulted in a persona that was intensely *mobile*, even marginal — she crossed musical, social, and racial borders readily — but the sense of directed self-production is tinged with regret: "Sometimes I think the whole of my life has been a search to feel the one place I truly belong."[87]

Simone's mother was a powerful figure — a church minister — but also somewhat forbidding; she found it difficult to acknowledge Nina's success, and as a child, Nina felt she lacked mothering, regarding her piano teacher as a substitute "white momma."[88] It seems possible that the melancholia induced by this early withdrawal from the maternal scene resulted in a phantasmatic self-identification with the lost (internalized) phallic mother, especially because her father, though worshipped by Nina when a child, appears to have been an at times remote and even "weak" presence. Later, Simone "disowned" him after overhearing him apparently lying about the centrality of his family role; and an almost Old Testament ruthlessness stopped her from responding to his deathbed appeals to see her again: "I was helpless because of the vow I had made, the vow I had to obey."[89] The personal and the political ran together as she contemplated exile: "America was Daddy, and he got under my skin."[90] Reconciliation came eventually, at least with Daddy (or rather his "spirit"), but only with the intervention of an African "witchdoctor." Meanwhile, she still got swept off her feet by other men, for example the seventy-year-old Liberian C. C. Dennis (who told her, "In Africa men are the boss," to which she responded that "Faced with a man like this, I had no choice; he was my Liberian Rhett Butler"),[91] though at the same time they never lasted: "Malcolm [X]; Martin [Luther King]; Daddy; C. C.; all the greatest men I have known have died, taken away before I was ready to leave them." "Daddy," she concludes, "would be my only companion until a man his equal came along, and we both knew that meant I might have to wait a long, long time."[92]

During this wait (which in truth lasted the whole of Nina Simone's career), she filled the gap with a "vocal phallus," circulated between herself and her listeners; but this, as the ambivalences of her life suggest, could never be more than part of a story within which the figures of a normative sexual-symbolic matrix constantly exerted their own pressures. The qualities of the voice itself are pretty well a constant, traversing a wide range of material. Much of this was composed by others (often, almost by definition, male), so this transfer can be regarded as already a kind of authorial gesture, pulling the material into her own orbit where it very much circles round this voice. But the material comes from right across the spectrum of African-American genres — spiritual, gospel, blues, jazz, soul — and to some extent, too, from black-influenced genres (popular standards, rock), building up a sort of composite black music tradition on which her persona sits, drawing on the authority invested in that history and in the contribution to it of strong women singers.

Simone's usual performing style produces an intensely *focused* tone with minimal (sometimes effectively no) vibrato (which is usually a vibrato as much of rhythm as of pitch). The effect is to center the performance on her, claim attention, demand the "camera" — and for listeners there is, one might think, nothing to do except to return this gaze. Although in one sense this might seem to entrap the voice in a normative position — adapting Kaja Silverman's model of cinematic voice, we could see the voice as fastened to (our strong imaginary projection of) Simone's body, contained there in the standard female performance position, ceding ultimate authority to an unseen, disembodied male source — Simone's refusal to play along with the usual concomitants of this structure (markers of feminine lack, subjection, or a mindless erotic) suggest that an inversion is in train: a phantasmal investment in a quasi-maternal *objet a*, which, as it sites the phallus in another place, the mouth, might also be thought to cite the dynamic of what Judith Butler calls the "lesbian phallus."

Indeed, the edge in the voice, forever standing in the way of maternal envelopment, is also continually to be reckoned with: this rattle in the throat, this grating in the vocal stream. On one level, this can be read as a mark of a refusal — a refusal of complete identification with the material; it opens a space for reflexivity, for critique, but also for representations of dissatisfaction, anxiety, loss, rupture. It is this that stamps Simone as a "jazz" or "blues" singer (even though she objected strongly to the label "jazz singer" on the grounds that this typecasted her racially: the refusal, then, is doubled), rather than a more straight-ahead "soul" singer. On another level, this edge can be read in relation to the inheritance of phallic motherhood, that is, as the remainder of an old ejaculate, a marker of penetration, tongue and teeth working within the (quasi-vaginal) mouth. If we are hearing a maternal voice, it is one whose antipaternal music, "at once dispersed and unary," according to Barthes, is turned in the direction of critique, becoming — as Barbara Engh's extrapolation from Barthes has it — "distorted, displaced, noisy, activated, put into discourse."[93]

What is in play seems to be a grating of the Symbolic against a too easy completion of an Imaginary, but interpretatively what is at issue is where this phallic content is located and how it is deployed — and the latter condition varies with the musical material. In ballads and torch songs, for example, where Simone is placed in relatively conventional feminine positions ("I Loves You Porgy," "Ne Me Quitte Pas"),[94] the impetus is towards a realizing, a making-real, of our fictive expectations — bringing home to us, as good jazz singers do, what this ache of desire and lack feels like. In political songs like the excoriating "Mississippi Goddam," by contrast, the edgy authority is turned in the direction of political work. The historical irony in this song is hard to miss: this is a "show tune" — Simone tells the (live) audience this, and it is confirmed by the soft-shoe shuffle of the piano vamp, summoning up images of blackface Uncle Toms and accommodating mammies. But the drive of the vocal performance, with stabbingly clear diction and unapologetic blasphemy ("Goddam"), performs out an ethico-political inversion, and this is pursued to the extent that at times her normal unity of vocal persona fragments momentarily, or rather collectivizes, demanding antiphonal responses from the band ("too slow!" they shout, in relation to faint-hearted moves towards racial equality). What happens here, it would seem, as our identification oscillates, is a circulation of (maternal) Law around the introjection/disavowal chain typically put in place by superego demands. (How many mothers have not commanded "Hurry up! You're too slow!" The disavowal may be heard in the audience's embarrassed laughter.)

There are many songs in Simone's repertoire where this *vocal command* is directed in more straight-forwardly positive ways to (often cultural-) political ends. Many fall into what may be termed her black power style, which draws on soul-jazz models ("Work Song," "I'm Going Back Home," "Gimme Some"), and the whole category is grounded culturally in a display of mastery of the tradition: spiritual ("Take Me to the Water"); blues ("Backlash Blues," "The Gin House Blues"); even "Africa" ("See-Line Woman" is an ecstatic hymn to black female sexuality which brings together minor-pentatonic holler, similar flute responses, vocal antiphony and 3+3+2 dance-rhythm percussion: it is as if Simone had been listening to the "neo-African" fife-and-drum dance music that Alan Lomax had recorded a few years earlier in the Mississippi hill-country).[95]

Sometimes this *négritude* style is explicitly coded to "freedom." This is the case in her version of Billy Taylor's "I Wish I Knew How It Would Feel to

Be Free" and in her appropriation of "Ain't Got No — I Got Life" from the rock musical, *Hair*. The latter is particularly interesting here, considered as a parable of new, politicized identity-formation. After listing all the possessions and social goods that she lacks, Simone enumerates what she does have, namely the parts of her body; and taken together — and given life by galvanic rhythm and gospel phrasing — these add up to, precisely, *life*, or, as she immediately translates this, freedom. But how exactly is this body (this life, freedom) to be grasped? After all, it is not really there, in the sounds — and nor was it really there, for the audience, in live performance (for it was "displayed," acted out). Judith Butler is helpful: "The linguistic categories that are understood to 'denote' the materiality of the body are themselves troubled by a referent that is never fully or permanently resolved or contained by any given signified. Indeed, that referent persists only as a kind of absence or loss... This loss takes place in language as an insistent call or demand that, while *in* language, is never fully *of* language."[96] The song lyric works like a mirror-scene, in which the *corps morcelé* is gradually brought into an apparent whole: even though the genitalia, indeed none of the traditionally eroticized body parts (except, significantly perhaps, the mouth), or even any definitely gendered body parts, are named. The completion of the body-image, its sense of reality, is an illusion brought about by the gaze, which the recording process attracts squarely on to Simone; but the focal point of that gaze is of course the *voice*, which here performs the phallic gesture of control and unification. It is an acoustic mirror that carries out the conjuring trick, gendering an identity (which, as Butler reminds us, also implies a loss of a possible identity), and assuring us that in this case the body in question is not castrated.[97]

In this repertoire, Simone appears to offer an authority that a Patti Smith could only pitch for. But at least as interesting are the songs where the ambivalences inherent in the maternal legacy come to the fore. I will concentrate on two stunning, and contrasting, recordings: "I Put a Spell on You" (1965) and "Sinner Man" (1967).

Like Patti Smith's "Gloria," "I Put a Spell on You" is a female cover of a male R&B song, in this case written and first recorded by Screaming Jay Hawkins in 1956.[98] Hawkins's song is itself a parody (to a manic extreme) of a strand of "magic phallicism" deeply embedded in blues history, a strand which in the 1950s was most strikingly cultivated by Muddy Waters ("Got My Mojo Working," "Hoochie Coochie Man"; not surprisingly, this rhetoric is normally male-oriented — although there is at least one female example, in Bessie Smith's "Red Mountain Blues").[99] In Hawkins's hands, this voodoo machismo goes completely maniacal, with bizarre screams and ghoulish laughter, accompanied (in live performance) with a surreal takeoff of horror-film rituals (flaming coffins, etc.). At first sight, then, Simone's appropriation is akin to Patti Smith's; and we notice that, not only do Smith's lyrics "put my spell on her," but also her triumph (or fantasy) — "I made her mine" — is paralleled by Simone's "Because you're mine." The property thematic is familiar enough: it is after all what normatively positions women under the exchange economy of the oedipal system. What is striking here is, of course, the inversion, and also the religious reinforcement. Once again, Law (here property law) is its own (superstitious) justification — perhaps because, in a way, what is "mine" is actually *mine*, that is, introjected, inside as well as out, and the *jouissance* is sado-masochistic.

To *hear* Simone's recording, however, comes as a shock. Far from following Smith's disruptive, transgressive strategy, she turns the song into a slow, intense blues-ballad, accompanied by large orchestra complete with "romantic" (if bluesy) strings. The voice is its usual huge, resonant, centered self — but its authoritative command in the first verse (her lover is "running around," but she has put a spell on him, "because you're mine") incorporates in the second an element of torch song submissiveness ("I love you... I don't care if you don't want me... I'm yours"). Just who is in control? The first half of verse two is given over to a tenor sax solo which clearly is imitating her singing in its tone, phraseology, intense centrality. From here to the end, instrument and voice chase each other in imitative, intertwining phrases, the doubling effect made all the more striking by the way that Simone's occasional excursions into intricate jazzy scatting (a technique she had already introduced in verse one) bridges the relationship, as language is temporarily evacuated. The effect is not so much of call-and-response as a splitting identity — indeed, a mirror. And the ecstatic sound of Simone's scat phrases suggests nothing so much as that "jubilation" which, according to Lacan, accompanies the child's first sight of (what he thinks is) himself in the mirror phase — unless it be the wordless "semiotic" associated with the (allegedly) presymbolic mother. But which mirror? What bubbles up here, one might think, is a tension associated with the relationship between an acoustic mirror — which, particularly in the preoedipal stage, produces a quasi-narcissistic circulation of pleasure and desire between child and phallic mother — and the visual (glass) mirror, which, as it sets up the ego, its ideal, and its others, introduces the child to the sexuating problematic of completion organized around the unifying phallus or its lack. An adult sexual anxiety, codified musically in the ballad/torch/blues conventions, overlaid on an "earlier" (maternal) nexus, throws up a fantasy deeply marked by the sado-masochistic impulses associated (at least by Lacan) with the most archaic functions of voice in its guise as irrational authority (its command after all devolves to the law of pure magic), as these are displaced to a "later" scene of recognizable heterosexual trauma.

The terrifying "Sinnerman" is quite different, musically and (it would at first seem) thematically. But it is also rooted in trauma, and acts as a religious complement to the previous song's secular setting. Based on a traditional spiritual, "Sinnerman" is a parable of judgment running with apocalyptic imagery (rivers that bleed and a sea that boils), but crucially the identities of those populating this last-day drama are never entirely clear. The sinner begs God for help; God is implacable. The sinner runs to "the rock," to the river, to the sea, and (at God's command) to the Devil, who is "waiting" (but who, judging by what happens subsequently, provides no lasting respite). But, although for most of the song Simone takes the sinner's part, as an "I" in the lyric, she not only reports God's responses in the third person ("He said go to the Devil," for instance) but also appears to assume his persona at the beginning and end: at least, she voices there an impersonal, god-like presence that one feels should have been a voice-off ("Sinnerman, where you gonna run to," "Sinnerman, you oughta be prayin'").

While the most obvious interpretation, within the recording's late-1960s historical context, is that the "sinnerman" stands for the forces of (especially male) white racism (and there is textual evidence to support this, which I will come to in a moment), Simone's own apparent involvement on that side of the dialogue seems to push her vocal performance to an extreme unusual for her. She is much less consistently centered, in tone and in intonation, than normal; the edge sometimes turns into a snarl; and occasionally her voice shoots upward in falsetto breaks reminiscent of those in Patti Smith's "Gloria." It might seem fanciful to see the rock and the river/sea tropes as images of paternal and maternal refuge, respectively. But the whole thrust of the performance is to set up an imaginary place for a Law that lies beyond the relatively feeble law of the secular Symbolic: as if to say, no matter how much you seek to transgress, there will always be a limit beyond which what is foreclosed is not to be questioned. The implacable effect of the repeating I-♭VII piano vamp, almost unbroken throughout the recording, and of the ruthlessly on-the-beat rhythm section, forces the pressure of this image on the listener.

The performance is divided into two, each part giving way to an extended break that stands outside the narrative recounted in the traditional lyrics. The breaks certainly situate us in a different place, summon up a different scene; it is as if there are two fantasies colliding, but also intersecting, commenting on each other. Each narrative part is organized around a build-up in emotional tension, produced through gradual increases in dynamic, texture, and vocal tessitura (upwards). In the first break, we hear — over the vamp — a repeated vocal interchange between Simone and the (male) band, a shouted statement (demand?) of "Power." Whose power is at issue? Black Power, and/or its white antagonist, we think ("It was certainly time for some Old Testament justice," Simone remarked of the mid-1960s)[100] — though feminists or queers might have heard it differently, even in 1967. Yet the exchange is abruptly terminated with a dissonant piano crash, followed by what sounds like a new start: a fragmentary guitar riff and solo, then, as the band reduces almost to nothing, handclaps and a foot-stamped beat, over which a freely improvised piano solo enters — leading via wordless gasps from Simone to an "Oh Yeah," and then to part two. The music has been pared back to the sounds of — the *body*; with Simone almost certainly (although one cannot be sure just from a recording) starting the handclaps off and "handing" them (as Spillers might say) to the men, like a mother teaching a clapping game to her children. Something dramatic has surely happened in this moment, though it is hard to be certain what it is, exactly. In the second break, the "Power" interchange returns and this time is interrupted by an out-of-time wordless shriek, crashing piano, then an extended passage in free rhythm with occasional dissonant, free-jazz style piano flurries supporting an extraordinary improvised vocal which can best be described as *glossolalic*: speaking *in* tongues rather than without one. Occasional words pop out of the scat babble, eventually culminating, as language reemerges, in the distraught demand, "Don't you know I need you, Lord?" — answered only by a drum-kit conclusion of Old Testament severity. Again the drama is palpable — but to what effect?

The song presents a "show" — a show that (as Simone remarks in "Mississippi Goddam") has not been written yet, but on another level one that, so the performance suggests, we are condemned to live anyway. The specifics are as important as the broader readings that emerge so readily. God and the Devil change places (there is a long tradition in African-American folklore of the Devil as an admirable trickster figure who can be lined up against a white God); there is both patriarchal and matriarchal imagery, in the music and in the lyrics. The song is certainly about Law — its imposition, dissolution, occupation, renovation — but also, it seems, its multiple sources. As such, its pleasures are harsh indeed. If the spirit of "Daddy" hovers over the question, "Don't you know I need you, Lord?" — his loss and the empty place this left forcing a prolonged take-up of the maternal phallocentric baton — the lesson is one not only of political empowerment (an "insurgent ground") but also of accompanying loneliness and pain.

******

It would be simplistic to reduce the tactics considered so far to two positions — occupation/appropriation of the locus of a male phallus on the one hand, exploitation of a maternal phallic legacy on the other — and to distinguish rigidly between them, let alone to suggest that subsequent excursions by female singers can be clustered neatly into these two categories. Nevertheless, it is useful to think of them as influential models to which many late-twentieth century repertoires can be related. They are often associated tendentially with the garage/punk/metal and soul/funk/dance lineages respectively, which, on a broader level of genre topography, comprise the two most prominent routes of insurgence within Anglo-American popular music of the later twentieth century. This already begins to suggest how, in this context, a class-linked insurgence — energies inseparable from representations and experiences of some sort of social Low — is always seen through optics formed on registers of race and gender.

But with some performers, it is often impossible to separate out definitively signs of the two models. This is the case, I think, with Diamanda Galás. Although Galás is often thought of as an avant-garde figure or (to her annoyance) a "performance artist," she draws deeply on vernacular, especially African-American, materials and techniques, and could be considered as standing in a place towards which both Patti Smith and Nina Simone, from their different starting-points, might have pushed had they worked in less commercially oriented contexts. Her album *The Singer*[101] is a collection of blues, gospel songs, and originals built from similar materials. The blues are all songs associated with male singers, mostly in the down-home Chicago lineage, and Galás picks up the extreme vocality associated with this tradition and pushes it so much further as to disappear, virtually, over the edge of meaningfulness.[102] What we hear is in effect an impossibility: the emotional insistence of this vocal tradition — embodied in its cries, moans, shrieks, noise — is not belittled, but it is rendered as if quite arbitrary, unhinged from its normal masculinist bearings. Her approach — an "unmatrixed production of vocal sounds," as she calls it[103] — seems, as this rejection of any "matrix" suggests, to set out to establish lawlessness as a rule. And we are justified in linking this approach with her (anti-) theology: in response to Michael Flanagan's description of her as in a sense on the side of the Devil, "as accuser, avenger of the oppressed, and anathema," she points out: "When a witch is about to be burned on a ladder in flames, who can she call upon? I call that person 'Satan'... It's that subversive voice that can keep you alive in the face of adversity... I am the shit of God!... I am the Antichrist... I am all these things you are afraid of."[104]

Galás's material typically brings together an obsession with Old Testament themes of taboo and transgression, and the plight of contemporary oppressed groups: the mad, tortured, imprisoned, and socially exiled (especially AIDS victims). Flanagan describes *The Singer* as a "voodoo hymnal."[105] Small wonder that in her version of "I Put a Spell on You" the unearthly quality of her extreme sounds enables her to comprehensively out-voodoo Screaming Jay Hawkins.

On one level, this clearly suggests a subversion, or inversion, of the authority of the patriarchal God. Extremes of register, timbre, and (dis)continuity (e.g., drastic disruptive vowel shifts within a long-held "note") are put to work on "natural" sounds (shrieks, moans, rasps, etc.) and denaturalize them. They seem to come at us from all points of the sonic space, as if Galás were projecting her voice through the multiple points of an immense ventriloquistic apparatus — an object gaze we could never see but picked out in shards of sound. For such a palpable presence, the voice is rendered strangely bodiless — an "extroversion of the soul through the voice, so to speak."[106] This is definitely a voice-off — a terrifyingly authoritative imposition — but if it is taken to be occupying the place of the phallus, what it finds there is a field that is both a wreckage (a modernistic deconstruction of "natural" male desire) and a madness. To quote Galás herself: "My vision is as cold as any man's... I can take a situation and look at it as dispassionately as anyone. On the other hand, who is anyone to be able to say that he or she can look at a situation dispassionately, especially when attempting to be most dispassionate? So what the fuck does that mean?"[107]

As this suggests, on a second level, this occupation is also part of a right of passage, a passing through; and this movement — a familiar quasi-maternal dispersal of phallic authority around the sonorous body — is mapped by the whirling mobility of vocal placement. This reading is authenticated not only by the African-American references in the vocal style but also by Galás's acknowledged debt to traditional Greek women's lament (*moirologia*), a genre that David Schwartz reads as a ritual assertion of female power (often incorporating calls for revenge), separated in gender terms from, and posited against, the patriarchal authority of the state.[108] We might think that the madness Galás's voice seems to discover as it passes through the phallic site is given many of the conventional codings of *hysteria*, that disease produced, according to ancient Greek medicine, by the female seat of reproduction, the womb, wandering through the body, and classified by psychoanalysis as that neurosis generated (most typically in women) by the question of sexual position, that is, by the question, "'Am I a man or a woman?' or, more precisely, 'What is a woman?'"[109] In "I Put a Spell on You" this sexual confusion is revealed to be the outcome of a misogynistic framing of female authority as witchcraft, and figured visually on the CD sleeve through a splitting of Galás's image: she is dressed in black leather and appears on one side in a powerful, indeed intimidating head-and-shoulders shot, with the words "We are all HIV+" showing on the fingers of one hand, and on the reverse from the waist up, with her coat open to reveal, S/M style, tightly laced (abjected?) breasts. That the flow of phallic energy somehow goes "wrong" is suggested musically as well, especially by her piano self-accompaniment. Like the vocal stream, the piano takes familiar signifiers — here, typical blues melodic turns, rhythmic figurations, and harmonic moves — and refuses their projected continuities, splintering them into meaningless fragments through dissonance and disjunction, and detaching them from normal physical references through rhythmic dislocation (there is no groove) and "incorrect" registers, textures, and articulation (use of classical keyboard touch, for instance). Taking voice and piano together, the effect is of a body falling apart — a *corps re-morcelé*

— as if the mutation of phallic energy towards a quasi-maternal locus is at the same time problematized, even foreclosed.

Schwartz reads Galás's noise, transgressions of normal sound-categories and blurrings of sound/language boundaries as markers of abjection; but what exactly is abjected? Surely it is the "phantasy" of the maternal body, its symbolic power opened up at the same time as its messy sustenance is subjected to, imprisoned within, the force of dispassionate moral outrage. (Galás performs her *Plague Mass* naked from the waist up, covered in blood or stage blood; other works are performed surrounded by razor wire or from within a cage.) This is a *hystericized* abjection, neither the integrity seemingly promised in the bodily ego-image nor that associated with the memory of the matriarchal acoustic mirror proof against the pressures accompanying a re-imagined anatomy. The hysteric's typical loss of bodily synthesis and control — where has the phallus gone now? might be the question here — marks out the territory where, in Diamanda Galás's music, the consequences of the threat posed to the Law-of-the-Father are registered.

Galás's militantly antihomophobic stance, channeled especially though not exclusively through her interventions in the AIDS crisis, might remind us that an only partly visible narrative strand — that of gay transgression — has been running continuously through the discussion so far. It is intriguing to speculate what queer readings of the music considered here might look like, not least because Patti Smith has sometimes been claimed as an influence and inspiration by radical lesbian musicians and the diva tradition represented by such performers as Nina Simone and Diamanda Galás has attracted a large male gay audience for many years. On the other hand, maybe my readings already are queer in some respects; how might one tell?

The radical undecideability of this question, in the abstract, points towards the fact — too little noticed in the scholarly literature — that the entire history of modern popular music (i.e., since the birth of Tin Pan Alley) has provided privileged territory for posing the gender question, and for answering it in particularly complex and often disruptive ways. The potential is built into the nexus of typical subject-matter (love) and its modes of performance (body/voice/dance). At first sight, it seems surprising, given the prominence of gay rights struggles over the period since the 1960s, that relatively little music that one might describe as distinctive to gay sensibilities has emerged from out of its subcultural settings. Most prominent, at least in the Anglo-American world, would be the "women's (or rather womyn's) music" developed by lesbian separatists and the various manifestations of queercore. But even here, connections with mainstream styles such as folk and punk are evident — as, for example, in the politically and stylistically complex location of 1990s riot grrrl music.[110] Much more audible has been a whole array of gay appropriations. Good examples can be found within gay usages of dance music, where a dichotomy between masculinist styles and modes of consumption (high-energy, with fetishizing of the active, displayed male body) and feminized styles and consumption practices (identification with the emoting vocalizations of female diva-queens, for instance) is well developed.[111] What happens here seems to be a transplantation and distorted reproduction of familiar straight binaries — a "bad copy," to use Butler's terms, but one that, as such, exposes the fact that "gender is a kind of imitation for which there is no original," or in other words that its heterosexual source is itself a "bad copy" of what can be no more than a normativizing yet performatively anxious ideal.[112] A parallel strategy appears in the rise of apparently androgynous (cross-dressing, gender-bending) performance styles associated with such artists as Boy George, Annie Lennox, David Bowie, k.d. lang and Prince, except that here appropriation is left as more like ambivalence. An alternative strategy is to cultivate, not so much ambivalence, as ambiguity: associated mostly with "sensitive" male performers (the Pet Shop Boys, Michael Stipe of R.E.M., David Byrne, Morrissey), this tends to offer a clearly antimacho image of masculinity but one that leaves sexual identification blurred.[113]

But is this rather confused picture so surprising? If the normative mapping of heterosexual coupling to the stereotypical gender pair is no more than a performatively enacted fiction, held in place through foreclosures on alternative gender ideals and forbidden homosexual desires, it is predictable that subversion of the boundaries would lead not to the discovery of new continents but to permanent de-stabilization of what already existed — of the map itself. Sedgewick points out that we are dealing with the superimposition of two explanatory schemas. The first organizes the dynamic of hetero/homo desire around the relationship between a "minoritizing" view (there is a minority and it is really, intrinsically gay) and a "universalizing" view (desire is always, in every human subject, potentially ambivalent in its object); the second covers the relation of the structure of desire to gender and is again organized around a binary, this time of "inversion" (norms are unstable: a man may *feel* like a woman, or vice versa) as against "separatism" (each gender desires its own).[114] That destabilization of the boundaries might involve both appropriations, subversions, inversions of familiar positions within the phallic economy and attempts to reshape, recenter, or even undermine that economy, with a multiplicity of effects on the mechanisms of symbolic authority as well as those of gender representation, was to be expected — all the more because the force of general social and cultural change was here reinforcing a long-established historical dynamic in a particular expressive sphere (popular music) where mainstream norms had been extensively shaped by modes of performative display predisposed to the attractions of camp.

A perhaps negative aspect of this predisposition, against which Bradby and Laing have already warned us (see p. 92), is that it is all too easy for the diversions of musical gender play to be safely corralled in places of licensed carnival, such as dance clubs. When feminist artists — Diamanda Galás, P. J. Harvey, Sinéad O'Connor — have "gone too far," they have found the going tough. And the general drift, even within the context of postfeminist pseudo-liberalism ("whatever…"), has been quite sufficient to provoke the predictable backlash, most notably in the misogyny and homophobia found in a good deal of gangsta rap and dancehall, and, correspondingly, in the return of young female singers with love (that is, fetishized flesh) to sell. Desire and meaning are here buttoned back into their lawful places, the mechanisms of castration reasserted. What happened to the *castrato*? What happened to serious *drag*?

To explore the effects for men of female appropriations of the phallus, no more fascinating case exists in popular music than that of Michael Jackson. I want to consider briefly his identity shift from black child star, complete with giant Afro and angelic voice, to (so the images suggest) a simulacrum of white middle-class woman, a trajectory that can be seen as a dramatic and extended exercise in drag performance — and as a thematic transition to his trans-located apotheosis: the Israeli "transsexual," Dana International.[115]

In point of fact, the childishness of the youthful Jackson voice in his Jackson Five period (late '60s/early '70s) can be exaggerated. It was not long before a strength, an expressivity and a rich vibrato were apparent, with a tone of aching desire in ballads, which positioned the voice within a category developed by the female singers of Motown (by the early 1980s, Jackson even looked like Diana Ross). With maturity, the fundamentals hardly changed, except for an extension of technical and expressive scope. The lower range reaches a bit further down; the spectrum of vocal effects broadens (to include a husky tone; a sharp, aggressive tone); he develops his characteristic (often off-the-beat) vocal "pops," gasps, and squeals (they recall the conventional sonic markers of female orgasm), which sometimes shoot up into what, in the context, can only be conceptualized as a female falsetto. But nowhere does Jackson sound "like a man" (nor much like a phallic mother, for that matter). There is never, even in the low register, much depth of resonance; the sound comes from the top end of the body, suggesting perhaps the vocalizing phallus wandering experimentally up the body. Overall the markers of a "natural" voice are in place (that is, of a "natural woman"), but they are also classified, insistently, as *un*natural (he is not a woman — is he?).

This weirdness should not surprise us: he is "wacko Jacko" after all. As Cynthia Fuchs has pointed out, his threatened transgressions, manifest in the surgical and cosmetic transformation of his body, his retreats to his "Neverland" ranch, the rumors and court cases concerning alleged abuse of children, the gender-confusing gestures in his performances, the oscillation between imagery of violence and of innocence, find a thematic center in the inescapable, obsessive focus on his *penis*, represented equally in media discourse (What is his sexuality? Where does he *put it*?) and in his performances (notably his crotch-grabbing choreography).[116] But this focus is on an absence as much as a presence: in the music as in his (hypermediated) life, it shrinks from view into an image of virginity. Fuchs, drawing on Homi Bhabha, treats this as a "productive ambivalence": his crotch-grabbing is "a sign of autoerotic sexuality (read: perverse, unreproductive, and homosexual), his unseen penis resists visibility, that prevailing emblem of Western Cultural Truth."[117] Jackson comes across, then, as in effect a transsexual — but one who cannot come out. For Fuchs, his repertoire of uncertainty, anxiety, perpetually repeating self-reference, strung out between registers of private and public, marks an "epistemology of the closet." The "real" Michael Jackson promises to appear, in brackets between the endless mutations and dissipations of gender and racial identity, but promptly disappears, as just another image. He is best read, Fuchs argues, as a drag performance. But what lies beneath the drag is just another performance: "Under the binary phallocratic myth by which Western bodies and subjects are constituted, only one body per gendered subject is 'right'...but Jackson never gets it 'right.'"[118] For Lacan, woman's lack of possession of the phallus is itself a kind of possession (while actual [male] possession is always, through castration, already lost); in Jackson's drag performance, though, the clarity of this symmetrical heterosexual logic goes wacko.

The penile focus is foregrounded in Jackson's virtuosic dancing — not just the choreographed crotch-pointing and grabbing, which forms its gestural core, but the dance style as a whole. The pelvic movements, especially the typical forward thrusts; the body spins; the repertoire of leg kicks, bends, and walks, including the celebrated "moon-walk"; the "bicycling" side-shot; the X-shaped (crucifixion?) pose and the arm straight up in (self-?) salute: all cohere around a clearly outlined right-angled double axis, in which the vertical and horizontal axes cross at the hip area, dragging the eye to *that place*. The gestures are also often jerky and mechanical: the limbs move as if by themselves. (When asked to explain his crotch-grabbing, Jackson turned for answer to a song title by the equally queer disco-queen, Grace Jones, saying he was a "slave to the rhythm.")[119] One feels this is how a robot would move if programmed well (but not quite well enough) to look "natural." Taking dance and voice together, we sense the construction of a perverse flow between phallic and vocal regions inscribed on a body that is never quite clear. Is this "sexy"? If so, it is a sexiness we can think of — by analogy with the cyborgian "fembot" — as that of a "queerbot." And, of course, the queerness disrupts the boundaries of race as well as those of sex and gender.

Jackson's performances engage both sides of the myth of black male sexuality — on the one hand, rapaciously potent, on the other, an emasculated husk. His album titles (*Thriller, Bad, Dangerous*) form a context for his obsessive pointing towards the area of the black phallus, a theme colored in as well in such allegorical self-presentations as a black panther ("Black or White"), werewolf, and vampire ("Thriller").[120] But this deep-rooted fantasy, at once satisfying and troubling, represents a transgression that is no sooner raised than erased; in a perpetual double movement, the threat is at the same time cancelled by images of Jackson's femininity, his innocence, the ubiquitous narrative of his victimization, confirmed by the embrace of his adoptive mothers: Elizabeth Taylor, Oprah Winfrey. Canceled too by his constant retreat along the chain of (dis-)simulacra (here, life and music constitute a single, multi-instantiated text): the lip-synching morphs in the *Black or White* video and the construction of narratives within narratives, here and in the *Thriller* video, always transplanting the "real" Jackson to somewhere outside the previous scene, somewhere other, provide compelling examples of a constant tendency in his work.[121] It comes as little surprise that Jackson was involved with the film *E.T.* (he spoke the narrative on the soundtrack album) and was photographed with this other child-like alien of uncertain sex and gender. Fuchs reads this photo, of Jackson with his arm round E.T., as resembling "nothing so much as a boy and his oversized penis" — a metaphor of his confused incorporation/excorporation of sexual difference; then revises this to a pose "with a big plastic dildo" — that is, to use Butler's terms, a lesbian phallus.[122] But does Jackson *have* a phallus at all?

As we have seen, the signifiers — of desire, control, power, transgression — are ever-present, but always already disavowed, or barred: at the heart of Jackson's music is a curious blank, or passivity, an absence that cannot confess itself. There is, so to speak, a *missing organ* (one reading of the Lacanian "bar" is that it is the symbolic phallus; for Lacan, this can never itself be barred, or divided, but Jackson suggests otherwise). Might we sense here one of Kristeva's suicides (incarceration on child abuse charges has more than once seemed a possibility; but in any case the rhythm of the life — a procession of new selves, periodic disappearances to Neverland — points in the same direction)? It would be the suicide of a *male*: this particular "I who wants not to be" is perhaps macho man, specifically, the murderous black rapist of racist myth, and we might read the monstrous transformations in the *Black or White* and *Thriller* videos as attempts to exorcise this figure.[123] If so, Kobena Mercer's point, that *Thriller* in particular stands in the music-horror lineage initiated by Screaming Jay Hawkins's "I Put a Spell on You,"[124] suggests that what Jackson is about is putting a stake through that misogynistic persona and what, in the more general politics of gender, he might stand for. But, on the other side, Jackson's femaleness is illicit — virtual, queer, impossible to verify; it has no real power. If he *is* a castrate, then, it is the woman (specifically, perhaps, the phallic mother) who has been castrated (and — biography again — the role of Jackson's allegedly violently abusive father might be relevant here). Which, within the economy in question here, leaves what? The phallus: the *infant* phallus or rather the infant as phallus, offered to the forever-absent mother, proving its presence through its always-traumatic cancellations, but somehow emptied out, pure metaphor circulating endlessly but hopelessly and meaninglessly around the repertoire of signifiers. If Michael Jackson is this phallus (rather than having it), it appears as pure supplement, desire with no definite object.

Who is this phallus for? In my fantasy, for — Dana International. (A more conventional answer would be, Madonna; but since she became a mother, her need — according to Dr. Freud — is less.)

If Michael Jackson "never gets it right," Dana International would seem to have made every effort to do so. Born Yaron Cohen in Tel Aviv, and first developing a reputation in the early 1990s as a drag performer in the dance clubs of Israel's burgeoning gay music scene, s/he underwent gender reassignment surgery in 1993, changing her name to Sharon, enjoyed her first hits the same year under the stage name Dana International, and carried on to win, famously, the Eurovision Song Contest of 1998 in Birmingham.[125] A quick glance at the media reception for her E.S.C. win confirms — in every drooling cliché ("enviably curved," "spectacular cleavage," "luscious lips," etc.) — perceptions of her womanliness. As a TV cameraman is reported to have commented, "We all agreed she was the sexiest singer. I can't believe she was once a bloke."[126] At the same time, she has been careful to draw a veil over the precise details of her medical treatment and over her sex life (in one interview, she asserts she still has a penis),[127] as if to tease her multi-stranded audience about her sexual undecideability. The visual completeness — which, for the vast majority of her audience, is of course a media simulation-effect — is presented as a reality which, we know (don't we?), conceals a scar (how deep, in what zone of self-formation, we cannot tell); but what appears to traumatize Michael Jackson has here become a plaything.

The richness of the cultural setting belies the apparent superficial transience of the E.S.C. moment; play here has had real, if limited, political effects. The figure of Woman, in the Middle East, comes to us enmeshed in the trappings of orientalist myth, a trajectory with a particular sheen in the case of a Jewish tradition that combines a rigid patriarchalism with a specific sentimental place for the clichéd Jewish mother. At the same time, late-nineteenth century European racist thought created the figure of the feminized Jewish male: a (circumcised) "third" version of the masculine, not straight, not gay, but nevertheless predisposed to, and aligned with, homosexuality.[128] The overall picture is a distorted reproduction of that which sexed/desexed the African-American family — a point, perhaps, of some significance for our understanding of the development of American popular music.[129] It also contextualizes the upsurge in queer politics in Israel in the 1990s along with the rabid response of the religious orthodoxy.[130] But the intersection of gender and sexuality with race goes still deeper: it is mediated by the racialized hierarchy well established in Israeli society — again a distorted reflection, this time of European imperialism — which places an Ashkenazi elite in charge and Mizrahi Jews almost at the bottom, with only Israeli Arabs below them.[131] The class implications are unsurprising: the working class is dominated by Mizrahi and Arabs. Dana International's parents were working-class immigrants from Yemen. She was, then, a subalternized Other three times over: by race, sexuality, and class. Yet her music had a particular appeal — again, not surprisingly, perhaps — to (rebellious or bored) middle-class Ashkenazi youth, especially (but not exclusively) gays. At the same time, her initial celebrity was built just as much, maybe more, in the surrounding Arab world, especially Egypt, where (despite opposition from the cultural and moral elites) bootleg recordings sold by the million.[132]

In Jewish religious tradition, the *Shechinah* or "feminine presence of God" arrives (metaphorically) in the synagogue at a specific moment on the Sabbath eve, transforming a masculine space into a feminine sacred space. Yemen is seen as the quintessential site of authentic tradition and Jewish difference — but has also given rise to a particularly strong women's song culture which, ironically, stresses themes of the secular everyday. For Philip Bohlman, this has given these women singers (with their "double doubleness") a special role in subverting gender identities through popular song.[133] One way of reading Dana International would be that she appropriates and mangles the gendered significance of religious and musical traditions. On the one hand she challenges the Law: "They claim I'm an insult, corrupt, doomed to death. Well, then… let God do his work if I'm so bad. Let God deal with me. But if anyone laid a finger on me, millions of people would murder him." (Murder whom? God?) On the other hand, "I do not need the rabbis to tell me I am acceptable to God. I have my own romance going on with the Lord."[134] This might throw a new light on her status as diva — a secularized divinity. Her E.S.C. performance of the song, "Diva," conforms to the stereotypes: glittery, figure-hugging gown, much sexy swaying and hip-wiggling, extending later in the performance to distinctly orientalist arm and hand gestures. One can readily understand the (racially marked) heterosexual appeal. But this is an *over*performance, surely, locating itself in the tradition of gay drag. Although the image — manufactured for and by the TV simulation-machine — might seem to pull towards "fembot" norms, we know (don't we?) that there is something *queer* going on, *really*, under the surface. Something we might term "post-human," perhaps. But "how exactly do the over-the-top sexual theatrics of the posthuman diva dis-organize gender?"[135]

For Dana International's second E.S.C. performance of "Diva," to celebrate her victory and close out the show, she reemerged in a different, even more extravagant gown, designed by Jean-Paul Gaultier (whose previous subjects had included the equally though differently queer Madonna and Grace Jones). The surrealistically feathered arms, on her amazonian frame, could not help but suggest mythological alongside maternal themes (would this freakish mother-bird take flight?). Is this monster — her too-perfect, silicone-suggestive shape points this way too — one of Donna Haraway's cyborgs: a nonnatural "creature in a post-gender world… a fiction mapping our social and bodily reality and… an imaginative resource suggesting some very fruitful couplings"?[136] We should take the outrage of the orthodox seriously ("an abomination," "worse than sodomy," "some kind of crossbreed," "a mutant," etc.).[137] Rather than look for Abbate's castrato within, we recognize here the castrato without: the wound is broadcast (discursively) to the world. The lyrics of the song turn her body inside out: she is a body politic, "larger than life," with "senses nobody else has," on "a stage which is all hers"; she is "hysteria," "an empire," identifying with a string of mythic queens: Aphrodite, Victoria (the British Queen?), Cleopatra. The voice is flexible and powerful,[138] magnified by double-tracking, backing female singers, and, especially in an out-of-time break before the out-chorus, in massively reverberant, digitally echoing, repeats of "Diva!" This is not so much a patriarchal voice-off — it is presented as insistently if ambivalently embodied — but more the voice of a fantasy world-body which saturates the sonic space, voc-animating (vocalimenting) an imagined object gaze. Just as Homi Bhabha sees his gender (like the penis-phallus-dildo itself, we might add — not to mention the voice) as a prosthesis,[139] so we can sense (hear/see) in this performance an inversion (an intrathesis), the energy folded back, following new contours "down there" and emerging in a cyborgian phallus of a voice which — the prosthetic properties of recording technologies working at warp speed — forever problematizes its own fit in any particular gendered body. Of course, many of the musical details draw from a clichéd house music repertoire for diva deployment;[140] and no doubt a stereotypical straight "fembot"-oriented reception is available. But for most listeners, I think, the drama will be too camp, our intimate knowledge too pressing, for this; I hear Dana International saying, with Donna Haraway, "I would rather be a cyborg than a goddess."[141]

If we return to Bohlman (the *agency* attributed to the *Shechinah*) and other commentators, it becomes clear why Dana International's intervention could create such political waves, not only in Israel but in the wider Middle

East, where she was widely heard as offering an alternative modernity to that on offer from either the West or local state elites.[142] In many songs, she hybridizes disco/house and Arab pop elements more obviously than in "Diva" ("Danna International," "Sa'ida Sultana"). She "queers" romantic ballads. She performs soldiers' songs tongue in cheek ("Yesnan Banot") and parodies heroic nationalism ("Going to Petra," where a motif of "penetrating" Asia is turned into a critique of Ashkenazi patriarchalism). In her unsuccessful entry for the 1995 E.S.C. Israeli preliminary contest, "Good Night Europe," she celebrates Africa and America dancing and Asia "ascending," but for (Ashkenazi) Europe.... By contrast, "Another Kind of Sex" and "Power" are musically more conventional house tracks, with "cyborgian" vocals. Often she mixes between languages (Hebrew, Arabic, English, sometimes with a bit of "esperanto"), producing a Babel that, as with other transgressions in linguistic clarity we have encountered, seems to stand for a relapse in symbolic authority — an insanity most fully realized in "Magnuna" ("Crazy"). Similarly, she exploits the potential for ambiguity created by the fact that Hebrew is a fully gendered language (e.g., there is no neutral pronoun). In "Danna International" the conflation of sexual and political border crossings is particularly clear, as a flight from Saudi Arabia to Israel is made to stand also for a sexual journey.[143]

This, of course, is "cheap" (i.e., no expense spared) pop music — but its trashiness is the seat of a power seen in the Middle East as linked to subversive class and ethnic interests; laughing at or refusing the authority of the Father — "dragging" it down, one might say — appears to work well when covered in sequins. It is equally clear that the political point is blunted on the wider stage of the European Song Contest. The popular voice here (for the first time in 1998 the results were voted by the TV viewers) is squeezed through a paternally run imitation of "market democracy," then broadcast back to an audience imagined as a convivial mass whose differences are reduced to friendly national rivalry, subsumed in a ubiquitous acceptance of African-American musical norms. Is this no more than play assimilated to the banal pleasures of titillating consumption?

******

Perhaps Dana International's performance of "Diva" is best read as a *mime* of a certain kind of freedom ("freedom" was certainly the term she used when talking about the significance of the result). As Philip Bohlman explains, the Jewishness of the *Shechinah*, unlike that of the male sacred "that is 'seen'... that is 'just there,'" is one "that is heard... that must be performed into existence"; like the singer in "Danna International," it "returns like the Sabbath bride from exile," over and over again — but now as a force for a new freedom in society.[144] Of course, as we know (don't we?), Jews — like blacks, like women — have a special talent for mimicry; that is to say, what we all must do, generally unwittingly, every day, is for them forced to the surface of their otherness.

Judith Butler, in her critique of Luce Irigary's theory of femininity, seizes on Irigary's concept of miming. This is seen as a tactic to expose what the binary distinctions and exclusions of the heterosexual gender system attempt to cover over, namely a deeper metonymy — "a closeness and proximity which appears to be the linguistic [and musical] residue of the initial proximity of mother and infant. It is this metonymic excess in every mime, indeed, in every metaphorical substitution, that is understood to disrupt the seamless repetition of the phallogocentric norm." But this tactic only doubles what is really there anyway; Irigary "mimes mimesis itself," refusing "the notion of resemblance as copy" and promoting an erotics of contiguity and surface rather than one of repetition, penetration, and displacement. Butler rejects, on epistemological grounds, Irigary's characterization of what the phallogocentric system excludes as the site of an unfigurable "feminine." (Her more open image of this "elsewhere," as an infinite series of displaced foreclosures has, to my mind — although she would reject this, I think — more in common with Žižek's understanding of the Lacanian Real.) Nevertheless, her preferred strategy of subversion is not dissimilar, installing permanent slippage along a long front of positions as the mechanism to deconstruct the heterosexual matrix.[145]

For Lacan, the mirror phase marks a privileged moment in this mimetic drama. But Butler reveals the sleight of hand whereby a (real) body part, inflated into the imaginary phallus, is then translated into a status guaranteeing the authority of symbolic law as a whole; this is, precisely, performative mime cloaking its metonymic and metaphoric shifts under a rubric of developmental necessity. There are ample grounds — as Silverman too reminds us — for proposing to work back, and forward, along the lines of an ontology of the phallus that is broader and more variegated. We might end up doubting *any* originary moment for culture: Haraway's cyborgianization of man, and of woman ("It's not just that 'god' is dead; so is the 'goddess'"),[146] carries with it a denaturing of nature, embedding the symbolic all the way down. The role of sound has in general been underplayed. We notice, for example, that mime is *silent* (as is the imaginary phallus and its penile model). Voice, though, is of course *noisy* — and can vocalize the phallus as it traverses the routes offered (phantasmatic but also material) by the vocalimentary canal. But a visual emphasis rooted in the assumptions of Aristotelian and Cartesian science ensured that psychoanalysis hardly noticed. An aurally aware theory of miming might skip right past the accident of physical genital difference, all the way back to the sonorous symbolic of the (denatured) womb.

This might start to unpick the monolithic role attributed to sexual difference, which actually "is not prior to that of race or class in the construction of the subject."[147] Spinning between mirrors, the emerging subject grasps itself as not only gendered but also bearing the lineaments of race and of a class culture. Again, sound/music may show this more readily than language or images. If the heterosexual binary is read, not as foundational, but as symptomatic of a broader master-slave dialectic that at once permeates all levels of the subject's economy (manifest in structures of activity/passivity, ingestion/excretion, desire/lack, *fort/da*, subject/object, production/reproduction, etc.) and brings into being a fantasized elsewhere of never-forgotten plenitude, then musical processes offer rich resources for articulating imagined subject positions within the fully delineated web of social and symbolic relations; for their basic mode of operation, arguably, is to articulate patterns of metonymy (repetition and resemblance) with hierarchies of difference, creating both an economy of desire and labor, and a skeletal framework inviting schemas of imaginary embodiment through attachments of voicing and identification. To think this through does not of itself clear away the long-accumulated effects of the heterosexual matrix on the resources and interpretations of popular songs. It does, however, reconfigure the territory for subversion, both multiplying the points of attack (dispersing the metaphorical phallus) and mounting a de-binarizing assault on the master/slave structure of position (having and being that phallus).

A political strategy might then revolve around an aim that we should work towards *being* the phallus for each other. But, so long as society continues to be structured in antagonism (that is, as far as we can possibly imagine), a topography of possession seems inescapable, especially while antagonism centers on a political and representational economy based on property. To put it this way represents a secularized (depatriarchalized) version of the Lacanian-Žižekian insistence that some- (metaphorical) one must wield the knife (and probably explains my choice — unconscious at first — of songs to discuss that have a thread of Old Testament reference). The best vision, then, is a *radical democratisation* of the whole having/being problematic, both dispersing ownership and continually displacing the bar. The root of domination remains deep and strong: my starting point in this chapter. Yet it seems likely that the vocal liberatory gestures identified here relate to social, economic, and ideological changes that are, in variable, uneven but noticeable ways, restructuring kinship patterns, feminizing employment, slowly decolonizing subaltern imaginations, and, as Haraway tells us, denaturing nature. Passive beings low in the gender, racial, and class hierarchies have begun to find voices. For Haraway, "the symbolic system of the family of man — and so the essence of woman — breaks up."[148] Shaping the cultural work demanded of us devolves on to the negotiation of knowledge, specifically, the intelligent analysis of the differences on offer: "some . . . are playful; some are poles of world historical systems of domination. 'Epistemology' is about knowing the difference."[149]

CHAPTER **4**

Memories Are Made of This

On the Subjects of Repetition

Ceasing to repeat is to die: this is true for individual organisms, for genes and species, for cultures and languages. Yet repetition is also a kind of death: repetition extinguishes the original, and extinction (replication, fading, displacement, doubling) on one level is the condition for renewal on another. In Lacanian thought, reproduction represents the victory of the species over the individual — precisely the *subjection* of the subject to death, or, put another way, to the endless circulation of both the drive and the signifier, in a "topological unity of the gaps in play."[1] Repetition, then, *grounds* us in more than one sense. And nowhere more than in music, the art of iteration, whose multiple periodicities choreograph our every level of self-reproduction, life and death. At the same time, it is a commonplace that, with the industrialization of culture, the mass reproduction of musical commodities takes the repetition process to another level. Increasingly, music's cycling grooves are carried into every geographical, social, and psychic corner, and carried on the replications and exchanges inscribed in the commodity form itself. Thus, while musical repetition would appear to be a universal, there is a specific history of the recent period that has the effect of compressing both the temporal and spatial cycles of sociomusical practice with a quite particular intensity. Standing on this global ground, can we grasp what repetition is doing for and to us?

Starting from a different point, if we follow Judith Butler and other theorists of performativity, repetition is the mode of subject construction itself. The "original" (the subject) is produced in the process of its repetition, and we continually perform out (cite, quote, mime) the markers of gender and sexuality, race and ethnicity, class and generation, sustaining subjectivity through a "regularized and constrained repetition of norms."[2] (This does not mean that the social relations configured through these norms are not real, only that to be configured at all — that is, to have meaning for us — requires internalization of discursively articulated formulae through which we can live them.) Conventionally, these normative matrices work through an either/or logic in which a series of excluded others sustains, by difference, the autonomy of the self. Equally conventionally, in the Western system, these others serve as marked inferiors, validating by contrast the un-marked self (its superiority taken as read: male as against female, white as against black, master as against slave, capital as against labor); and this schema (itself sustained through repetition) is grounded (rooted, planted deep) in the overarching binary of *having* over *being*, *culture* as against *nature*. From this point of view, what Butler does, drawing on Derrida and Foucault, is to deconstruct the either/or logic by problematizing the self-justification of the mimes — by, in a sense, inserting into the "gaps" in the "topological unity" an *excess*, an insistence of a repetition *of* a difference that turns either/or into and/and. At the same time, this reveals norms as fictions, nature as always already culture — that is, as *naturalized*. And as part of this, the binary construction of repetition with which we started — on the one hand, a ground, an aspect of nature, on the other, an apparatus of culture, indeed of an alienation inherent in culture, intensified through the circuits of industrialized mass reproduction — is itself revealed as a (repetitive) trope subject to the nature/culture schema.

Ironically, as Donna Haraway points out, the moment when this deconstructive momentum has appeared is also the moment when technological developments, particularly in relation to a "cyborgianization" of culture, threaten to tear man loose altogether from nature. "In a sense," she writes,

> the cyborg has no origin story in the Western sense — a final irony since the cyborg is also the awful apocalyptic *telos* of the "West's" escalating dominations of abstract individuation, an ultimate self untied at last from all dependency, a man in space. An origin story in the "Western," humanist sense depends on the myth of original unity, fullness, bliss and terror, represented by the phallic mother from whom all humans must separate, the task of individual development and of history, the twin potent myths inscribed most powerfully for us in psychoanalysis and Marxism.[3]

Is the binary logic of individuation/unity (for which read culture/nature; mind/body; *telos*/stasis; production/reproduction; renewal/repetition) giving way to a "permanent slippage along a long front of positions," a tactic of *contiguity*? How then should we read the effects for musical processes of repetition? What attention should we pay to the contemporaneous shift in social and cultural theory whereby a political-economic category of (naturalistic) *need* has expanded or even given way, via an intermediate biologistic or part-biologistic concept of *instinct* or *drive*, to the psychoanalytic category of *desire*: the multiply directed, always-already socialized, forever deferred and displaced movement around a *lack*?[4] Is this a corollary of a shift in the prevailing social mode of production from a focus on, precisely, production to one oriented more obviously round the continual excitation of consumption? Does it a mark the moment when the cement in the wall separating animal needs from the sphere of reason began to crumble, revealing the traverses of a single human economy in which the repeating springs of desire and lack, life and death, forever overflow?

I have written about repetition before,[5] obsessively perhaps, to the point that one might suspect some Freudian compulsion to be in play. If I respond to this sense of neurosis with the Lacanian question, *che vuoi?* (what do you want from me?), this should be addressed above all to the discourse of the Other in its place nearest to home, that is, in the Unconscious: where the ceaseless insistence of the signifiers, and their equally inevitable failure to reach the mark, are at their most productive — but also, perhaps, their most traumatic. As with my discussion of "Gloria," my discourse here must incorporate a stand-in role for the absent shrink, on to whom my obsession might otherwise be transferred. The structure of the chapter constantly folds back (or, more hopefully, spirals back) on itself — the only way I could find to write it.

Freud's core understanding of repetition (his thinking on this develops an added complexity in the 1920s, a point to which I shall return) is that when we repeat psychic material it is as a defense. Especially when repetition is obsessive or compulsive (that is, more insistent than surrounding circumstances would seem to justify), it marks the repression of material that is too painful or troubling to remember. Repetition and recollection are offered here as alternatives, and it is the function of psychoanalysis to help the patient to work through the repetition compulsion and integrate what was repressed into memory.[6] It is worth noting in passing that this conception seems at first sight to be diametrically opposite to the common sense picture derived from empiricist psychology according to which repetition of data (e.g., in rote learning) is seen as, precisely, a route to remembering. Even in this perspective, however, it turns out that the most successful aids to memory lie in the embedding of information in larger structures and schemata; the role of repetition here lies purely in enabling recognition by making the elements familiar.

In a sense, then, Freud and the empiricists agree: psychological maturity requires integration; repetition is at most a (childlike) tool or marks a relapse or problem. In this they stand in a venerable tradition: for ancient philosophers such as Plato and Pythagoras, the preservation of knowledge through memory work was essential to avoid the blandishments of Lethe, to escape the cycle of rebirth, the flux of meaningless repetition, entropy into inanimate matter; only memory, honed by constant effort, enables ascent from base repetitive nature. At the same time, the explosion of interest in the repetition/memory *topos* in the late nineteenth century (when both psychoanalysis and the empirical study of memory began) is striking. It surely marks a cultural–historical knot; the infantilizing of "mere repetition," for instance, would become a repeating [*sic*] trope of mass culture critique (so many identical consumer products pouring off the assembly lines; so many records, all sounding the same; so many people, all wanting an equal share...).

A plethora of other, related terms are tangled up in this knot: reproduction, regeneration, representation, and (coming further to the fore later in the twentieth century) replication, simulation, regulation (especially in the Foucauldian thematic) and Althusserian interpellation, with its concomitants of *mis*representation and *mis*recognition. Intense debates around these terms have characterized one strand by which we recognize the lengthy history of Western modernity itself, punctuated by particularly explosive moments (the Enlightenment; the moment of modernism and mass culture; more recently the moment of digitization and cyborgianization), and together have formed the contours of a politics of re-presentation[7] as it has been configured in this lineage. The implications for science, philosophy, political economy, and the arts, in relation to epistemology (the subject/object dialectic), personal identity, social relations of the body politic, and the articulation of time and space, are familiar. As we note the historical contingency of this problematic, we might also note the irony — a true philosophical circularity — that "history" itself comes into being as one of its effects; but so too, on the level of spatial awareness, does the encounter with cultural others,[8] others who dwell elsewhere (and put norms, identities, assumptions in question).

Within musical practice, this entire constellation revolves around articulations of time and of space within which a subject is positioned in relation to multiple elsewheres: what lies behind, ahead, beyond, within, without, now here, now there. And these movements operate both intratextually and intertextually (not to mention inter-generically and interrepertorially), marking the importance within the Western tradition of the concept of the musical work — conceived as the whole within which, normatively, the constellation of representation techniques are worked out, on a range of structural levels — and, along with this, the critique of the work concept coming from spheres of vernacular practice.[9]

Such critique (usually unwitting: scepticism, qualification, supplementation or substitution, sometimes autochthonous, would often be better terms) revolves to a significant extent around usages and understandings of repetition. Particularly since the establishment of Tin Pan Alley hegemony and of recording technology in the late nineteenth century, with pressures on both the production and the stylistic sides towards the intensification of economies of repetition, popular music has been widely seen as the music that does the same again, over and over: "From Edison's primitive phonograph cylinders all the way to popular music, the true poetry of the present, everything has gone like clockwork."[10] This may be presented as positive or negative; a force of nature (e.g., in the form of dance-groove) or a force of society (capital accumulation, serial production, passive consumption); as driven by technology (mass reproduction) or by culture (the decolonization — which can also be figured in this case as an exploitation — of the African diaspora and its characteristic modes of musical expression). In any case, the shortest of walks through today's musical soundscape — physically, or figuratively through our home-based media — is sufficient to remind us of the inescapability of the multiple frames of repetition. Its grip is the only possible explanation for the otherwise extraordinary fact that the extraordinary quality of this triumph — in a world that seems in many other ways to be bent upon tropes of change (progress, individuation, modernization, and personal growth) — goes for the most part unnoticed.[11]

It seems important to disentangle different moments of interpretation, levels of understanding, flows of causality; for instance, it is possible to distinguish, certainly for the period up to the most recent past, repetition in popular music at the level of signifiers (intratextual repetition) and repetition at the level of the song (intertextual repetition, which, as one manifestation, produces the practice of covering an existing record). However, developments since the 1980s have tended to render this distinction problematical. The rise of digitized sampling and looping techniques — borrowing within and between texts as a multi-faceted principle — appears to represent a new paradigm, marked by an increased blurring of the distinction between musical work and musical field. Similarly, while older analytical approaches, applied to Tin Pan Alley and rock songs, found little difficulty in distinguishing between the level of political economy and that of culture, including the effects that might be attributed to repetition on these different levels, it is no longer so clear how we might do this. Even models more subtle than vulgar Marxist perspectives — for example, Adorno's critique of Benjamin's account of the mass reproduction of art, where the nub is precisely that, for Adorno, consciousness *does not (nor should not) necessarily follow* where socio-technical relations point — fall short in the present stage of capitalist development, where digitally repeating musical loops feed back on the economic level (e.g., via Internet distribution and multiple mix production), stimulating new spirals of exchange value creation. "History" and "repetition" (each the alter ego for the other in the established system) continue, we might suspect, to intersect in the contouring of structures at every level of both discourse and practice, across the configurations of both genre and performance, at both micro and macro levels; yet the suspicion is that they are increasingly crashing together. If repetition is both a salve of subjectivity (at once healing ointment and salvation ritual) and a symptom of its disease (forever threatening to open up its sutured wounds),[12] how can we assess its effects at a moment when the end of history has, it turns out, been indefinitely delayed?

Refrain 1[13]

That the history of repetition (constructed across the changing musical field) and the repetitions of history (constructed in the individual performance) constantly intersect, is a subset of a still broader nexus, in which history dances with re-presentation (or, to use Michael Taussig's term, with "mimesis"). If mimesis "is a faculty," Taussig suggests, "it is also a history, and just as histories enter into the functioning of the mimetic faculty, so the mimetic faculty enters into those histories."[14] Whether and in what sense repetition is a form of mimesis, and/or vice versa, is itself an historical variable.

This historicizing impulse suggests an initial, simple point which may be introduced by reference to three examples. Susan McClary draws on Monteverdi's "Zefiro Torna" (1632) to illustrate her discussion of the *ciaccona* and the impact of its importation into Europe from the Americas in the early seventeenth century.[15] She argues that the effect of the *ciaccona*'s repeating ground bass pattern here is orgiastic, not only for early-seventeenth century dancers (which she demonstrates) but also, it seems, for her: "the *ciaccona* proliferates its dance pattern with reckless abandon, each temporary conclusion breeding only the desire for yet another repetition . . . one truly does not want that groove to stop, even if civilization itself is at risk."[16] Of course, the effect is created by the whole texture, not just the repeating bass (not to mention the words, which pit the poet's inner anguish against a repeating celebration of the joys of spring); but the repetition does seem to be inextricably tied to the sensuality: "What *compels* the repetitions is a groove of jazzy cross-rhythms that engages the entire body," and this repeating structure elides this body with "the carefree, seductive *ciaccona* rhythms of 'nature.'"[17] Does a repeating bass always have this effect? No — and McClary does not say so. Indeed, she is careful to point out that, as Europeans modified the *ciaccona*, the genre came to be used for "static [i.e., 'timeless'] formal rituals" and for "depicting obsessive states of mind."[18] Late in the seventeenth century, Purcell's "Evening Hymn," again with a repeating chaconne bass, creates an effect very different from that of Monteverdi's piece. It is about night, sleep, repose of the soul with God, and is usually taken by listeners to be elegiac, spiritual, perhaps even a farewell to bodily existence. Yet the rhythmic phrasing of the vocal line, while lyrical, is sharp and (I find) energizing — a "good night" to the world, but also an ecstatic invitation to the arms of God. The differences of meaning between the two pieces need careful technical explanation, no less than the technical link, in the form of the repetitive structure, requires its significance to be theorized.

McClary also draws a parallel between the reception of the *ciaccona* and that of African-American music by American and European whites in the 1960s. Again the differences need as much attention as the similarities. Her example is Wilson Pickett's "In the Midnight Hour." But there are songs that are technically closer to the baroque genre: Percy Sledge's "When a Man Loves a Woman," for instance,[19] which has a repeating bass that is very similar in shape to that of the "Evening Hymn" (in both cases the ground bass is a descending tetrachord, falling by step from tonic to dominant — one of the most common types). However, many listeners might hear links not only with Purcell's piece but also with Monteverdi's "Zefiro Torna" — soul ballads such as this are often considered both sexy *and* lyrical, sensual *and* spiritual, located in the sphere of the body *and also* in that of romance. Sure enough, Sledge's song is about the obsessive romantic love of a (generic) Man for an (equally generic) Woman (she is so generic, so mysterious, so unreasonably demanding, as to qualify as an example of the Lacanian object of "courtly love"),[20] yet sets this to the triploid groove characteristic alike of the chaconne and the bump-and-grind of the African-American slow drag, here translated from blues dive to uplifting soul stage.

It would be bizarre to neglect those features of all three pieces that situate them in cultural and historical moments that are quite distinct. Yet something seems to hold them together: the repeating basses not only ground but also *bind* the different voices with which they are in dialectical relationship, subjecting them to basic discipline. A Lacanian interpretation might hear the ground basses as insistent, unrelenting representatives of the Other — for Monteverdi, Nature, for Purcell, God, for Percy Sledge, the unapproachable Lady — against which desire twists and turns. More specifically, they function perhaps as an anamorphic Object, standing in the place of an impossible totality (impossible because foreclosed by the "self-retracting Real which, in a way, grounds the Ground itself"); anamorphic because its true shape could only be perceived in an absent mirror, a possibility forever postponed by the diversions pursued in the rhythmic and melodic play of the upper voices. "This elevation of a particular moment of the totality into its Ground" represents a "hubris" perpetually unraveled by the play of desire and suffering that energizes the textures, resulting in a bittersweet pleasure with distinctly masochistic qualities.[21]

But still, this a-historicizing reduction is not quite right. After all, the poetic imagery and allusions are distinct in the three songs, the sound worlds are different, and the conventions of phrasing and articulation are quite specific. Even on the psychoanalytic level, we might think that "Zefiro Torna" is oriented more towards Eros (the life-drives: the desire and desolation of the subject in the lyric are contrasted with the verdant fertility of Nature), the "Evening Hymn" more towards Thanatos (the death-drives), "When a Man Loves a Woman" more towards Masoch (standing for narcissistic accession to the will of the Other, in a particular intersection of life and death). Admittedly, located in our later-than-late-modern space, our three examples (and all the more so if we add to them from the huge stock of ground bass pieces available, through Bach's chaconne for solo violin and the finale of Brahms's fourth symphony to Procul Harum's "A Whiter Shade of Pale") feel as if they come to us in the guise of what Lawrence Kramer calls "revenants" — uncanny, spectral "returns" from who knows where, producing difference through iteration and supplementarity (*différance*), problematizing origin and all sense of linear sequence.[22] In this sense, their relation to any (hidden) point of unity is itself a figure of "temporal anamorphosis," one that Kramer represents in spatial terms in the entrée he metaphorically constructs for the ghostly "revenant" in the multiply mirrored changing rooms of the clothing store.[23]

Yet, at the same time, history clings to them. "Zefiro Torna" comes from the early stages of a history when the problematic of "re-presentation" in music was forcing itself on to the attention. On one level the ground presents just itself, in a conventional introversively functioning figure of technical mastery, but it also affixes the sensuality of its dance-rhythm to particular images of Nature's fertility in the lyrics, so that we are confronted with the question, "Whose bodies are seen to be dancing here?" The answer must encompass an awareness of those (just discovered) exotic bodies of the New World: sixteenth-century Spanish literary sources consistently associate the *ciaccona* with slaves, servants, and Amerindians, with an enticing if dangerous sensuality and hence with moral threat; small wonder that they also often describe the genre as "*mulata*" and "*amulatada*."[24] McClary is, quite properly, keen to emphasize this history. But her description reveals more than the geo-historical facts, for her language ("proliferates . . . reckless abandon . . . breeding . . . desire . . . ") wants to associate the music with bodily gestures that are both "natural" and a threat to Western reason (they put "civilization itself . . . at risk").[25] Her point subsequently is to link this threat with an analogous subversion coming more than three hundred years later. But Percy Sledge comes after in more than just chronological terms: by the 1960s the black body *knows* far more than anything that could be imputed to it by early-seventeenth century Europeans. How can we hear him without having this in mind?

In this light, what could be the force of McClary's use of the term "groove"? As a technical-cum-critical term, referring to the characteristic repeating rhythmic patterns that give a particular performance or style its distinctive gestural feel, this is familiar usage, among fans and critics as well as musicians.[26] It has rich associations and history, though. As a musical term, it originated in jazz slang of the 1930s and came of age in the esoteric hipster language coined by the be-boppers. (Dizzy Gillespie's tune, "Groovin' High," dates from 1944, for instance.)[27] From this context, it acquired connotations both of *fashion* (an up-to-date, often in-group cultural knowledge so cool as to require no spelling out) and *pleasure*, perhaps with narcotic connections (an ecstatic automaticity, halfway between "natural" and "mechanical:" in the groove, and *high*).[28] These associations spread out from musical reference to the spheres of culture generally and of the body; thus "groove," "groovy," or "grooving" could be applied to any activity or object regarded with approval or as chic, to social cooperation, or to making love. In the 1940s, it was also still possible for older, apparently contrary usages — groove as routine and by extension as suggesting staidness and lack of novelty or originality — to resurface: one of many criticisms of the allegedly over-repetitive riff style of the swing bands referred to "groove beat as an end in itself," and, in a similar vein, one writer celebrating the apparent death of swing applauded the end of "the Benny Goodman groove."[29]

For centuries, the most familiar nonmusical examples of grooves would have been furrows in the ground — pregnant signs of potential new life, giving rise to a metaphorical linkage with processes of human procreation: male seed sown into female grooves. (Note, however, that in many early usages, from the fourteenth century, a groove is a seam or drift in a mine, and also that etymologically "groove" is linked to "grave"; the plough buries as well as cultivates, and the human relationship to the ground here is penetrative, extractive, reproductive, and deadly all at the same time.) In American slang from the 1920s, "groove" could refer to the vagina (compare earlier parallels: "furrow" from the nineteenth century, "agreeable rut" from the eighteenth, and of course "ploughing" this ground is a common metaphor in traditional song). But by the early twentieth century, an equally likely image would be found in the technology of recording: many early dictionary references are taken from record reviews, and by the 1960s one American meaning of a "groove" was as a synonym for "record."[30]

Overall, the tenor of most music and music-cultural usages from the 1930s on suggests some sort of reproducing pattern, usually agreeable or even ecstatic, and the sense of a background in cultural awareness of technological reproduction is strong. The contemporary deployment of the term, which McClary's text exemplifies, stands in this lineage, summoning up a host of images, not only, perhaps, of dancing bodies but also of circling discs and even the never-ending routines typical of both everyday life and popular culture under modernity. Here, where the stylus and with it the listener faithfully follow the spiral groove cut in the disc,[31] is His Master's Groove, drawing the listening subject inexorably towards that central disappearing-point (which, in due course, the technique of the fade-out would attempt to deny), in a movement that irresistibly suggests both an auditory equivalent to the invisible but all-seeing gaze of Foucault's panopticism, and a Lacanian mirror-function, already foreseen in the 1920s by the young T. W. Adorno: "What the gramophone listener actually wants to hear is himself, and the artist merely offers him a substitute for the sounding image of his own person . . . The mirror function of the gramophone arises out of its technology . . . ".[32]

McClary does not want Monteverdi's groove to stop. With modern recording technology, it need not. The panauditory discipline exerted by this technology — the source of the voice hidden from us, its power at once radiating out ubiquitously and drawing us in magnetically — is also an enticement to bodily fulfillment. The way that, in the record form, tropes of nature and of machine are overlaid — reification shot through with renewal, grave with reproduction, subjective death with cultural survival — is nowhere better caught than in Adorno's early writings on the subject.[33]

For Adorno, the record has no form of its own. It is "empty," mirroring back the listener's often narcissistic needs with tedious fidelity and eliding authorial intention: "the 'modernity' of all mechanical instruments gives music an age-old appearance — as if, in the rigidity of its repetitions, it had existed for ever, having been submitted to the pitiless eternity of the clockwork."[34] At the same time, if the record tends to write out the authorial subject, it also writes in the music itself, or rather music begins to write itself, to reveal itself as akin to writing. In the indexical relationship of the record groove to the sounds — its status as a kind of encrypted repetition rather than a representation, image, or system of signs — Adorno (following Benjamin)[35] finds a utopian glimpse of what the Romantics had searched for: a way to understand the mysterious meanings of the hieroglyphs of Nature, lost with the fall into semiotic babel. Ironically, it is "merciless" technology that reveals music's own potential as a universal language: "this writing can be recognized as true language to the extent that it relinquishes its being as mere signs: inseparably committed to the sound that inhabits this and no other acoustic groove," this language attempts "to name the name itself," in a form of "demythologized prayer."[36]

If Adorno seems, unusually, to approach here a kind of identity-thinking, this is forgivable: the risk of confusing — to use Lacanian terms — *objet petit a* and Big Other (here a quasi-theological naming power) is always hard to escape. McClary uses the language of "want" to describe her feelings about the *ciaccona* groove. She is referring, it would seem, to subjective desire, and, truly, this is endless — a burden killing us slowly yet which, masochistically, we would not wish away even if we could. For Lacan, "want" expresses "appetite," not "desire"; it works on the level of "need." Adorno, though with opposite trajectory to McClary's, speaks this language too (and in both cases, there is, it must be said, a danger of overreading the details of their rhetoric). "The phonograph record," he writes, "is an object of that 'daily need' which is the very antithesis of the humane and artistic, since the latter can not be repeated and turned on at will but remain tied to their place and time."[37] Both, perhaps, displace desire on to the level of "need/want," where a mythology of Nature as Other (however technologically mediated) holds sway.[38] The subject stands or falls — or rather, stands *and* falls — in the shadow of this very modern problematic.

******

Any "archaeology" of the ground of musical repetition must, then, account both for historical and cultural difference, and for historical and cross-cultural links; but also needs to deal with the specific insistence of this *topos* itself in the twentieth-century structure of feeling and the shapes it has assumed in this structure: Adorno and McClary offer, as we have seen, two examples of how these pressures have been engaged. It is certainly the case (to repeat myself) that, across the board, repetition processes pick up a distinct charge in twentieth-century music; and this charge is negative as well as positive. In the vernacular genres, the cult of novelty progressively increases its grip and its velocity as the century unfolds — the industry obsessively searching for "the next big thing," consumers for new distractions and stimulations — as if an inoculation is required against a disease of entropy: the awareness that actually songs are driven by groove and riff, repertoires by formula and intertextual reference, music cultures by social technologies of file-sharing.

On the other side of the High/Low fence too, where novelty is understood as a valorization of originality, and where individuation of technical profile, works, and artistic career development are given an enormous premium, these qualities can be grasped in terms of a terrified flight from the implications of techniques whose motif of stasis nevertheless cannot be gainsaid; they are there, for example, in serialism, in Stravinsky's and Bartók's neoprimitivism, in minimalist and process music, and even, in an inverted sort of way, in the apparently opposite tendency, the search for total differentiation — for instance, John Cage's all-inclusiveness, where infinite difference ends up sounding all the same. For David Toop, this is an "environmental" tendency, originating in an ambient aesthetic and resulting in the replacement of an older style of artistic purposiveness with an "ocean of sound": "Music not going anywhere... drifting or simply existing in stasis... is one of the most fertile developments of the twentieth century"; it "can suggest (on the good side of boredom) a very positive rootlessness. At the same time, a search for meaningful rituals recurs again and again, surely a response to the contemporary sense that life can drift towards death without direction or purpose." But drifting can also suggest a simple escapism: so the choice might be — to use Toop's words — "blankness" or "openness"; though it is possible that such an either/or formulation is less than what is required by the politics of this situation.[39]

As in popular music, this sense of stasis can be located in the overall style-formation as well as in individual pieces. Despite the continuing influence of modernism's insistence, with Marx, that "all that is solid melts into air," and that music must continually be made anew, the feeling that a purpose and a center have been lost, that a teleological sense of music history no longer holds, is widespread. Leonard Meyer has even given this situation a name, "fluctuating stasis, a sort of dynamic steady-state," as well as his approval.[40] Similarly, standing back from the bewildering surface of style change in twentieth-century Anglo-American popular music and looking intently at the beginning and the end — at, for instance, ragtime, blues and coon song, on the one hand, R&B, hip-hop and "dance," on the other — would the question, "How much has *really* changed?" necessarily have the apparently obvious answer?[41]

Twentieth-century music as a whole can be seen as obsessed with this problematic: doing the same, or avoiding it. Moreover, the obsession is replicated in critical theory, where topographical and cybernetic metaphors have tended to take over from temporal ones, fields and networks contending with logics and dialectics, the poststructuralist focus on infinite diffusion overshadowing Hegelian, Marxist or, for that matter, positivist teleologies. According to Gilles Deleuze, writing in 1968, "difference and repetition have taken the place of… identity and contradiction," due to a "generalized anti-Hegelianism" which had by then become hard to miss.[42] If the Dialectic were now our tottering Hero, his usurping Other could most obviously, in this sphere, be identified as Derrida (not to mention Deleuze himself) — though, to locate the debate in a somewhat longer-established trajectory, Bakhtinian dialogics had already set out important markers. Whether (once again) such a binary opposition is the most fruitful way of constructing the repeating antiphonies of theory is a question to return to, along with the contributions of Derrida and Deleuze (and we might note in advance that to Lacan and Žižek, both Hegel and — at least in Žižek's case — Marx remain important). First, though, it will be useful to retrace our steps to the moment out of which Hegel's dialectics grew — the beginnings of late modernity — and the distinct notion of history that accompanied it.

"History," in the sense constituted by and constituting modern experience, certainly looks at repetition with a suspicious eye. This is hardly surprising:

the self-understanding of modernity cannot be grasped outside of the establishment of a dominant sense of time as sequential, Newtonian, linear, secular — a sense that *time has a direction,* which underpins the teleological project of Enlightenment Reason itself.[43] For traditional Western music aesthetics, as it emerged from the Enlightenment period, the individuality of each successive work should aim to guarantee what the artist's creative method is set upon, namely, a means of exploring, modeling, representing *development* — personal, social, technical.[44] This *Bildungsroman* mentality, not without power, still, even in pop music criticism, gave rise in the nineteenth century to two predominant interpretative models: music being related to *narrative,* on the one hand, *organicism* on the other, with both cases governed by the Leitmotif of evolutionary change. (Lyric moments in this repertory seem to be felt as an always subordinate Other: a dream of escape or a [feminized] domestic enclave marked by reproducibility.)[45]

How could such teleonomic thinking deal with repetition — especially given the undeniable tendency of musical forms to articulate themselves through repeats, and listeners' equally undeniable fondness for such strategies? One way was to reject repetition as such. This was widespread in criticisms of the narrative absurdity of the Da Capo aria in opera (and one can see how this line of criticism would inform nineteenth-century attitudes to popular songs, where similar refrain-based repetition was commonplace). In the sphere of instrumental music, the force of the criticism was all the greater. As the composer, Grétry put it, "A sonata is a discourse. What would one think of a man who, after cutting his discourse in two, would repeat each half?... That is just about the effect repeats in music have on me."[46] Another response was to cover repetition up, to articulate it as much as possible through screens of developmental detail; this was common, especially in large-scale movements. A third approach is associated with Kant who, by inventing a *wallpaper* model of music aesthetics, discovered affinities between the patterns of instrumental music and the symmetries of decorative design which had the happy effect (for him) of confirming music's lowly placing in his aesthetic hierarchy.[47] Hanslich, similarly, compared music to *arabesque* and *kaleidoscope.* But wanting, unlike Kant, to save music for "creativity," he decided that it is "an arabesque that is not lifeless and static, but perpetually renewing itself... Thus the design grows steadily... [It is] the active production of an artistic imagination, ceaselessly transfusing its whole wealth into the veins of this organism"; it is a kaleidoscope of patterns that is "always self-consistent yet always new," rather than just "an ingenious mechanical toy." Symmetry on its own is "worthless," "lifeless," "hackneyed" (again a whole lineage of popular music criticism came to be built on such phrases).[48] At the end (perhaps) of this tradition we find Pierre Boulez justifying his compositional emphasis on processes of continual mutation through a critique of the redundancies of previous European music, where repetition (such repetition as there was) "was plainly designed to support perception by 'sedating' it with memory."[49] Truly, as John Chernoff writes in his book on African music, this European tradition is "not yet prepared to understand how people can find beauty in repetition" (of course, for Hegel, repetition in African culture was precisely what located it outside history).[50] To give a more concrete (if also slightly tongue-in-cheek) example: in a 1993 British court case, one Helen Stephens was jailed for the effect on her neighbors of playing Whitney Houston's "I Will Always Love You" continually for six weeks. The testimony of a music psychologist, who said that the song's four-chord structure, repeated day and night, could probably count as psychological torture, seems to have been decisive[51] — although, admittedly, six weeks of repetitive groove might be excessive even for an African festivity.

The aesthetic discourse intersects with social and cultural criticism. From the later nineteenth century onwards, critiques of mechanized routines, formulaic production, the tedium and ennui associated with contemporary life, leisure, entertainment, and culture became commonplace, and they have not let up since. Of the many proponents, Adorno is one of the most formidable, particularly for musically focused investigations. Popular music scholars (including myself) have made us familiar with his (arguably rather blinkered) account of formulaic production in popular music, and its corollary, "fetishized" or "regressive" listening, which asks only for what it is going to get anyhow, resists whatever might disturb, consumes over and over what it has already been taught how to digest, indeed what has been predigested as part of the production process. In Adorno's well-known phrase, this is repetition as "social cement." But what is important here is that his account of popular music is part of a broader critique of modern music as a whole which, in turn, depends for its coherence on a still larger-scale intellectual position: a critical Marxism turned sour by the apparent endgame reached in the "dialectic of enlightenment" — the contradictions embedded in the historical movement itself reach their own limits — ruling out the promised outcome of revolutionary change. Thus, when Adorno writes, for example, of an "'I know already' [which] insults musical intelligence,"[52] he could have been discussing not only Mahler's resistance to such predictability (as he was), not only (from a different point of view) any number of types of popular music (such as "dances composed of dull repetitions filling dull hours"),[53] but also Stravinsky — or, much later, Steve Reich. Similarly, Adorno's notorious alignment of Stravinsky's "neo-primitivism" with totalitarian political impulses (via the "collectivism" and "sado-masochism" implied by his frenzied repetitions) could in essence have been applied as well to interwar popular music — and, in his writings on mass culture, it was.[54] But Adorno's point was not that repetition should simply be abjured: he was well aware that music could not help but respond to the repetitive qualities of contemporary life and social technologies ("the current historical state of the works themselves to a large extent requires them to be presented mechanically").[55] The issue was the nature of the response.

Indeed, Adorno's whole philosophy of music positions it in relation to a dialectic of Nature and History, which forms consciousness and shapes musical language precisely through the inter-mediation of sameness and difference. Nature is always presented as "second nature" — a historical construct standing for naturalized cultural convention, invariance, "what-has-always-been": history is the qualitatively new, that which individuates. But as conventions are increasingly rationalized, instrumentalized, and commodified, ending up in a Weberian "iron cage," the progressive composer, responding to the pressure of the historical demands of the musical material, accedes ever more rigorously to a "ban on repetition."[56] Or more precisely, although "there is no lack of invariants... in serious music... in good pieces even the clichés acquire changing values, depending on the configuration in which they are placed... Eventually, in the historical unfolding of this tendency, the invariants kept dissolving more and more; in essence the history of great music over the past 200 years has been a critique of those very elements which complementarily claim absolute validity in popular music."[57] For Adorno, the model for such critique was offered by Schönbergian serialism (where the row functions as a kind of "dissolving invariant") and by the post-serial avant-garde; thus it remained true that "wherever music articulates itself meaningfully, its inner logicality is tied up with overt or latent repetitions," but the contradictions must be faced: "the articulation of time through repetition, through stasis, and the Utopia of the unrepeatable penetrate each other."[58] The key division is between those who face the contradictions and those who ignore them. By this point, under the reign of the culture industries, the musical field has split into "two torn halves of an integral freedom, to which however they do not add up:"[59] modernism's cult of extreme individuation on the one hand, the standardized clichés of commodity music — almost a "third nature" — on the other. Repetition, at least unmediated repetition, now stands for a self-willed conformism, a regression at once mechanized and pseudonaturalized, a closure of history. And, ironically, the dialectic as a whole appears to grind to a teeth-gritting, unreconciled stasis.

Adorno often tells this story in terms of a conflict between *production* and *reproduction*; and increasingly reproduction triumphs. One critical issue arises precisely here because, despite his dialectical conception of nature, Adorno does implicitly follow Marx and Engels in mapping a (heavily gendered) conception of the production/reproduction pair to the economic flows of culture. What difference might it make to his picture of (feminized) mass culture if the increasingly mechanized nature represented by its invariances were to be refigured as, precisely, a *production* — if, that is to say, the status of reproduction as, not a passive escape from history, but a historically contingent discursive construct were to be taken fully into account?[60] As it is, reproduction in the mode to which it has been condemned in Adorno's system can only appear as one in which life-sustaining returns are reified into seriality, where the creative force of production is realized wholly in the fetishized form of exchange. Similarly, the cycles of daily life, as they previously appeared (however deceptively) under cultures of self-management, are transformed into the blank "routines" of "everyday life," according to Henri Lefebvre[61] a category of experience quite particular to modern industrialized society. Routine harnesses body-cycles to industrial time-discipline — and the quiescent subject can do nothing except lie back in her allotted role — lie back to be grooved.

Refrain 2

In his specific discussions of popular music,[62] Adorno's approach finds its focus in his concept of standardization. Modeled on his understanding of Fordist methods of assembly-line industrial production, this pictures popular song production as governed by all-powerful formulae, which generate their structures, thematic typology, rhythmic patterns, and harmonic frameworks; individual details possess no intrinsic necessity — they can be substituted by equivalents with no significant effect — and no structural relationship to the whole; any impression of novelty is the result of "pseudo-individualization," a sort of surface, ersatz differentiation that actually works through deployment of an equally stereotyped repertoire of gimmicks merely embellishing (and hence substituting for) the standard framework itself. In this picture, the subject of popular song — the sense of subjective consciousness located by producers and listeners in the song experience — is coextensive with the standardized schemas, and any diversions, mutations, subversions of this quasi-transcendental core are written off as symptoms of false consciousness. Production for the people (for the masses, as Adorno would have it) has been redrawn as reproduction *of* the people: "the tendency of an over-accumulating society to regress to the stage of simple reproduction" results in an image of the world "that enables it to serve as a mythical mirage of eternity."[63]

It is worth thinking more closely about the term "standard/ization." A standard is, first of all, something that stands out, stands tall, ex-tends (a flag or other military standard; a tree left to grow tall). From this stems the sense of a standard as an exemplar, criterion, authoritative model, and thence as a level of excellence or basis for measurement or classification, at first physical, then moral and aesthetic (standards of taste). Already, at this point (the fifteenth to eighteenth centuries), the particular, with its unique aura, its *extension* above the surroundings, is spinning off copies in a move towards universality; and this move is completed with the emergence in the nineteenth century of the sense of a standard form as a norm (often a prescriptive norm, as in "standard English"), and then, in the late nineteenth century and even more the twentieth, of standardization as denoting uniformity. It is not surprising that this shift should occur in association with the triumph of industrial production. In terms of music history, it is connected to the shift away from a sequential model, in which unique works follow each other in linear time, towards a genealogical model based on family resemblance. The transition is precisely caught in the tension within music-critical discourse between "standards" — original songs that stand the test of time and are worthy of frequent reperformance — and "standardization."

The Adorno of "On Popular Music" was writing at a time when the transition marked by this tension was in full swing. He was aware of the shift. In the tantalizing footnote, already cited, referring to the guidebook, *How to Write and Sell a Song Hit*, he quotes the authors' distinction between "popular songs" and "standard songs," and remarks that what they "call a 'standard song' is just the opposite of what we mean by a standardized popular song."[64] This is tantalizing because what might have functioned as a reminder to himself to historicize his analysis is not picked up. While there are occasional hints of historically aware interpretation in Adorno's text (he explains standardization as a kind of monopolistic "freezing" of "standards" — successful innovations — previously established through competition, and argues that this explains the appeal of "revivals": "the breath of free competition is still alive within them"),[65] for the most part he conforms to the category depicted in Raymond Williams's ironic observation that those who resist standardization are often also the same as those who vociferously deplore the loss of "standards" (for Adorno, the standards set by Austro-German modernism), without acknowledging that "standards" here operates as what Williams calls a "plural singular": a range of values (standards) in the actual history is surreptitiously reduced to a single, authoritarian measure.[66]

We may regard the standard/ization nexus as marking an historical territory where a use-value (auratic singularities, repositories of cultural capital) and an exchange function (mass reproduction exerting market pressures on production) mediate each other, on the way to an economy of the simulacrum, where inter-penetration of the two (full inter/intratextual conflation) would in principle void the distinction. Except that simulacra — copies with no original, in Baudrillard's celebrated aphorism — have to reckon with their continual *performance*: each copy can only be a re-presentation; and in the process "origins" (that is, locations where authority could appear — manifestations in the aesthetic sphere of the self-authorizing ruses employed by the Name-of-the-Father) are also continually set up. Adorno was deaf to the significance of performance. Improvisation is his prime example of pseudo-individualization; it fabricates spontaneity in order to disguise the hegemony of the schema. And to be sure, in the era of recorded sound, the concept of performance needs to be widened so that it accommodates the full range of "instantiations" forming the economy of re-presentation: "networks of interconnected moments, coalescing into temporary hierarchies," in which the sense of originating moments is regarded not as "a 'first cause,' more a transiently privileged *moment of departure* within networks of family resemblances."[67] In this economy, the *cover version* plays an important role. If we attend to the function of covers, and the relationships they set up within the networks of family resemblance, what light might this throw on the question of standard/ization? And would the passages of subjectivity then appear less like moments of self-identical reification, more like a perpetual slippage "sideways" through the potential positions in the family networks?

Percy Sledge's "When a Man Loves a Woman" became one of the most familiar soul standards, put out after its first appearance in 1966 on innumerable reissues and compilations, copied by innumerable tribute singers, used in TV commercials and film soundtracks. On this level, the repeated phrases and implacable bass ground of the song itself as it were spill out and spin off into the everyday patterns of the "simulaculture." The song has also been covered by many other soul singers. Sledge's vocal is a wonderful fusion of lyricism and passion, its cascading phrases full of Gospel-derived melisma. Some covers stay fairly close to Sledge's original (e.g., Solomon Burke's, recorded twenty years later), some move further away (Lou Rawls's is much cooler, jazzier, more controlled), while at least one is intriguingly odd: James Brown incorporates a few phrases, delivered with characteristic screams, towards the end of a nineteen-minute live version of his own "It's a Man's Man's Man's World"; an intertextual scenario is thus brought inside the structure of the performance itself, and it is organized around the gender question, for "It's a Man's World" sets up the classic patriarchal binary in the context of which the interpolated phrases, pointing towards male *dependency*, can function only as a disquieting comment.

Interesting issues are bound to arise when female singers cover the song. Natalie Cole's rock/R&B version leaves the lyrics intact, thus singing from a more definite third-person position, as if on the man's behalf. Laura Lee, by contrast, prefaces her performance of the lyrics with a new introduction in which, explicitly addressing "girls" who have "taken enough," she advises them to ditch unsatisfactory men; but then, having found a faithful lover in the main body of the song, she extends it with new material, encouraging her listeners to be grateful for this gift and to "treat him good"; so a moderately feminist inversion is re-assimilated into the old gender norm. Organist Shirley

Scott recorded the tune as a solo instrumental — slow, atmospheric, with funky right-hand runs. Is she appropriating the song for female instrumental prowess, demonstrating (rather than merely describing) female control?

The song has traveled much further stylistically, however. There are not only the predictable dreary easy-listening versions (from pianist Richard Clayderman to flautist James Galway, and even jazz guitarist Wes Montgomery, whose string-backed doodle is something he would want to forget), but also recordings by country musicians (Kenny Rogers's voice, for instance, replaces soul passion with country "honesty"), folk groups (De Danaan demonstrate that a pentatonic tune over a repeating chord-sequence can be turned readily enough into something sounding Irish), and singer-songwriters (Art Garfunkel's slow, meditative soft-rock performance, with breathy, double-tracked crooned vocal, removes all soul timbre and pitch inflection, locating the scene somewhere like a (white) New York City loft — surrounded, though, by atmospheric jungle noises from time to time!). Gregorian's chill-out version — with choral, pseudo-plainsong tune, backed by churchy strings and restrained dance groove — manages to turn the song into something "sexless." By contrast, Bette Midler produces a hysterically over-the-top live performance (for the film *The Rose*, in the persona of rock singer Janis Joplin), in a slick showtime arrangement (complete with tension-screwing key shifts), for an almost equally hysterical audience. She sings the lyrics pretty straight — but, given her status as gay icon, how straight is that?[68]

These examples scratch the surface of what seems like a conversation (sometimes, admittedly, of the deaf) between family members. As Dai Griffiths puts it (with an appropriate allusion to the other worldly metaphors of old-time religion: it is easy to experience these records, especially when they emerge unexpectedly out of a radio, as *revenants* or specters): "The circle . . . seems unbroken, but the journey . . . says so much to the time and attitudes that these versions traverse — the cover version has become part of . . . a 'songline,'" the reference here suggesting a cartographic and navigational function which can point both forwards and — in moves of cultural archaeology — back as well.[69]

One type of (particularly conversational) cover is the "answer song." Who knows if the writers of Percy Sledge's hit (Calvin H. Lewis and Andrew Wright) had in their mind an earlier song written in 1934 by Harold Arlen, Bernard Hanighen, and Gordon Jenkins, entitled "When a Woman Loves a Man," which was memorably recorded by Billie Holiday in 1938? But the link is irresistible — the, so to speak, inverted torch song theme of "When a Man Loves a Woman," with its love-struck, slave-like male, turns the traditional torch song pattern evident in Arlen's lyric upside down (and may thereby have something to tell us about shifts in gender rhetoric, especially among African Americans). Adorno would have recognized the earlier song's dependence on "primitive harmonic facts," just as predictable in their way as the later song's bass line. This is a circle-of-fifths tune. The main phrase in the 32-bar structure (which, correctly, Adorno treats as the norm in this period) is organized around a VI-II-V-I approach to the cadence, and the middle eight extends this pattern further into a highly conventional III-VI-II-V bridge.

Rather than pursue this song further — the nagging discipline of the harmonic structure, forever circling round the same ground, seems highly appropriate to the fatalistic tenor of the torch song genre — I would like to move to a still earlier song which also relies heavily on a circle-of-fifths pattern but which, intriguingly, puts it to a different expressive purpose. This is "There'll Be Some Changes Made," put out by African-American writers Billy Higgins and Benton Overstreet in 1921 and first recorded in the same year by Ethel Waters. (See Example 4.1, next page.)

The tune of the chorus follows an earlier, but equally formulaic, pattern: a 16-bar AA^1 with two-bar extension, and the rhythms have a ragtime bounce familiar since the 1890s. The two cadences divide the structure conventionally into an open-closed (V-I) binary. But the circle-of-fifths formula, repeated in each eight-bar phrase, tantalizes the listener by starting out of key, on a chromatic G^9, then working in an extension of the sequence: VI-II-III-VI-II-V-(I). The tonic chord is not heard until the final cadence, and this spins off the two-bar extension by immediately leaping again to VI and running once more round the VI-II-V-I circle. The effect of the chromatics (all the chords are of the dominant seventh type, each therefore pulling strongly to the next) together with the open quality of the cycle (the end of a chorus, in performance, leads straight on to the next, with a leap from the tonic B♭ to the out-of-key G^9) is to modulate the repetitiveness with a refusal to stop and stabilize. At the same time, the melody focuses around the most yearningly dissonant notes — A (the ninth over the G chord) and D (the ninth over the C chord), creating plentiful opportunities for singers to smear the pitch. These notes "happen" to be the seventh and third of the key, that is, those notes most commonly smeared in blues: pools of potential bitter-sweetness tempering the bright-eyed bounce of the rhythm and the ever-onward cycling of the harmonies. The overall effect is of a quite particular take on repetition, one familiar in African-American ragtime/early jazz tunes, and which maps beautifully to the lyrics: human change is placed in the context of natural cycles ("change in the weather . . . change in the sea"),[70] and seems to be driven by a desire to make the most of the present before an equally natural cycle fulfils itself ("Cause nobody wants you when you're old and grey"); but it out-reaches these cycles in scope ("My walk will be diff'rent, my talk and my name, Nothing about me is going to be the same") and in

G9
For there's a change in the wea - ther, there's a change in the sea,

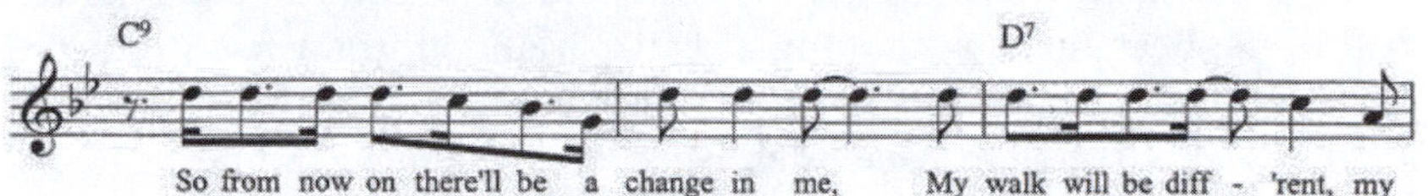
C9
D7
So from now on there'll be a change in me, My walk will be diff - 'rent, my

G7
C7
F7
talk and my name, Noth - ing a - bout me is goin' to be the same, I'm goin' to

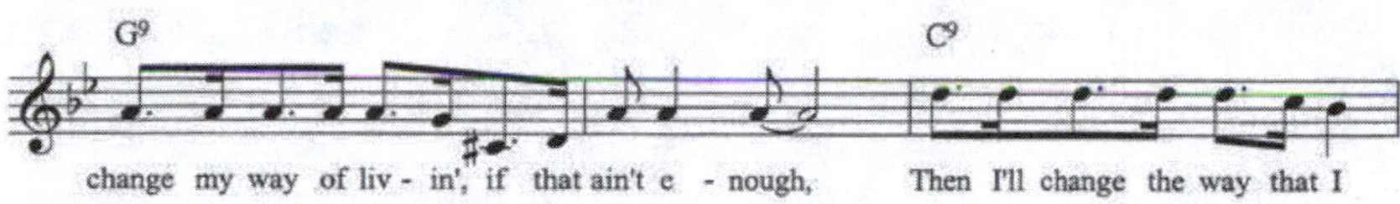
G9
C9
change my way of liv - in', if that ain't e - nough, Then I'll change the way that I

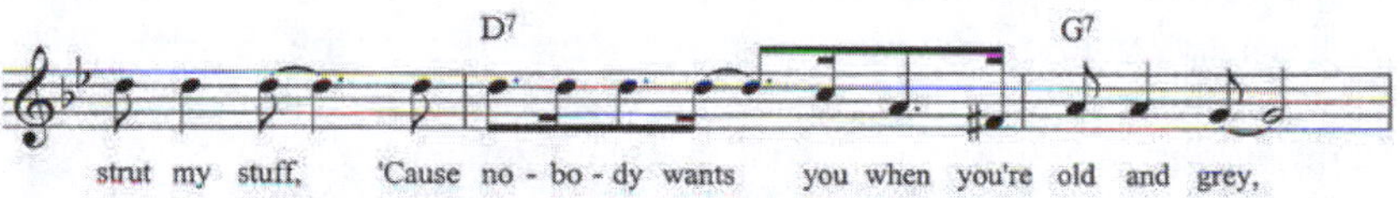
D7
G7
strut my stuff, 'Cause no - bo - dy wants you when you're old and grey,

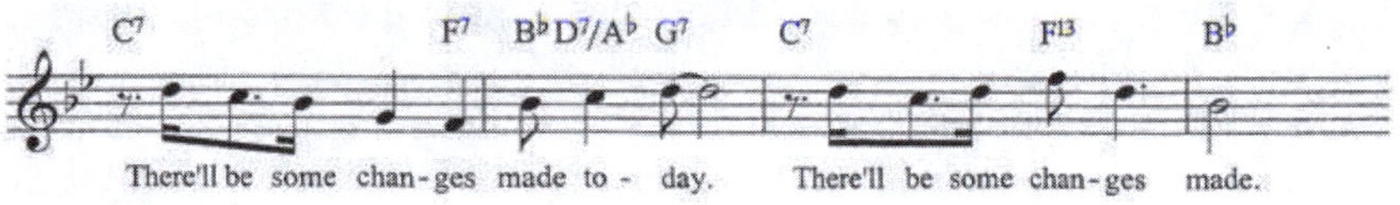
C7
F7
B♭D7/A♭ G7
C7
F13
B♭
There'll be some chan - ges made to - day. There'll be some chan - ges made.

Example 4.1

determined agency ("There'll be some changes made"). Placed in an historical context when potential changes in race and gender relations seemed, however overoptimistically, to be in the air — and coming after the verse, in which the singer tells us she has been dumped by her long-time lover — the result is poignant.

Ethel Waters's 1921 recording, accompanied by a small jazz group led by Fletcher Henderson, is polished but also decidedly feisty, confident diction, before-the-beat phrasing, and some semi-parlando throwaways producing the effect of a young woman's (and an optimistic early jazz age?) performance.[71] This seems to have established one strand in the performance tradition: Mildred Bailey's 1939 version, although somewhat more laid-back and with a band playing in a swing style, is very much in the same mold. In between (in 1927) Sophie Tucker, bringing a blackface slant,[72] gets to a similar place — but with more difficulty. Tucker's first run through the chorus is slow, in free rhythm and with a piano accompaniment that interpolates strings of semitonally moving parallel seventh-chords, a technique that has the effect of subverting the "changes" posited by the harmonic structure: Can she actually do what she sings she will? The second chorus — up to tempo and with driving stride piano — suggests she can, only for the tempo to drop back again for the ending, which turns affectingly personal — "nobody wants *me*..." (rather than "you"); the "red hot momma," vulnerable after all. Billie Holiday's recording comes from her very last session (1959). But even without this biographical subtext, one would hear in the slow tempo, tremulous vocal timbre, and minimal change of register (it is all middle) a performance implying that she does not believe *anything* will change.

Holiday cuts the verse, as had become the norm for performance of standards (in this case, excising the then-and-now narrative has the effect of placing even more emphasis on the repetitiveness of the chorus). This is the usual practice when mainstream singers take on the song: Peggy Lee, for example, with a bouncy, up-tempo, confident version; or (in what might be heard as a riposte, in gender terms) Tony Bennett, who starts off slow and halting but then doubles the tempo and belts out the changes with supreme self-assurance. In this form (i.e., as a set of changes derived from the chorus) the tune became a jazz standard and can be heard in innumerable versions, down to Charlie Byrd's virtuoso small-group version and Dave Brubeck's accompaniment for Jimmy Rushing, which underpins his vocal with the percussive, syncopated, added-note chords typical of his piano style. Glenn Miller's 1941 recording offers a rather surreal take on mainstream confidence (confidence in *change*). In this smoothest of medium-tempo swing, all smooching saxes and soporific four-to-the-bar, set in a context of war-time escapism, the signal is that nothing must be *allowed* to change.

In a way, a more recent equivalent to this, relocated into the territory of country music and from the register of gender to that of age, is provided by Chet Atkins's duet with Mark Knopfler. Jokily rewriting the lyrics for an aging country star under threat from change (from youth, from rock), our two protagonists self-indulgently swap virtuosic guitar licks, smoothly absorbing the threat (maybe tomorrow, not today, sings Atkins) into the stereotypic conservatism of country. Sometimes this mood generates a full-blown retroactive move: change, yes, but backwards. Russ Conway included the tune in a medley of early Tin Pan Alley hits, feeding nostalgia through the high-octane Liberace-esque glitz of his "pub piano plus"; this is "more twenties than the twenties." Mezz Mezzrow's revivalist-jazz version, with a band including Muggsy Spanier and Sidney Bechet recorded live in 1947, also harks back to the twenties — in this case to New Orleans and Dixieland; but there is a racial misfire here, condensed into the contrast between Mezzrow's own well-meaning but static noodling (Mezzrow has often been described as the purest example of Norman Mailer's "White Negro") and Bechet's explosive playing, with modernistic touches, playing that surges out of the loudspeaker, forcing the past into the future. This blackface negotiation casts an interesting light on the fact that it is has often been white musicians who have made a point of exploring the bluesy elements in the tune. Italian-American guitarist Eddie Lang recorded it in 1928 under the name of Blind Willie Dunn (probably adopting this persona in order to allow him to target the race record market), turning it into a slow and melancholy rumination pervaded by blue notes. The Boswell Sisters's 1932 version, with the Dorsey Brothers Orchestra, is even more remarkable. Their first chorus is sung in up-tempo close harmony, slowing to a half-time close; but this is followed by three slow twelve-bar blues choruses (published lyrics, new tune), which in turn leads to a final fast chorus in the minor mode. White girls singing (but also contextualizing) the blues — changes indeed.

For both "When a Man Loves a Woman" and "There'll Be Some Changes Made" the picture that emerges is far from the prefabricated stampers for the mass reproduction of reified subjectivity that Adorno imagines; rather, what we hear, flickering around particular constellations of historical time-space, at once exploding and imploding, is the continuous production of difference — of mutating subject potential — out of apparent repetition. At this point, the predictable, but nevertheless intriguing, move would be to wonder how Adorno's sparring partner, Walter Benjamin, might have responded to these examples. Writing in 1936, the Benjamin of "The Work of Art in the Age of Mechanical Reproduction"[73] famously argued that the new technologies of mass reproduction and dissemination, and their feedback on to production methods, tended to dissolve aesthetic aura, that quality which, inverting

Baudrillard, belongs to an original without a copy. The result, Benjamin suggested, was to break the hold of tradition and install art in the sphere of politics, with the specific benefit — vital for him — that fascist appropriations of auratic techniques could be resisted. The limitations of this view have been well rehearsed, starting with Adorno's own critique: for example, a technologized form of aura is readily reinstated, with glossy, endlessly circulating star images mystifying ego-identifications all over again; not to mention the way that the cultic origins of aura, with their resonances of fetishistic authority, are drawn upon to power the phantasmagoric effects of commodity circulation itself. But the argument cannot be regarded as closed, especially given the vacillations in Benjamin's own writings.

In "The Work of Art," aura appears, one might say, on the side of the object: it is "the unique phenomenon of a distance, however close it [the aesthetic object] may be."[74] In Benjamin's classic study of Baudelaire, published three years later, the account is focused much more on the side of the subject. Now, aura is "the associations which, at home in the *mémoire involontaire*, tend to cluster around the object of a perception." This process is part of the dialogics of subject-construction: "The person we look at, or who feels he is being looked at, looks at us in turn. To perceive the aura of an object we look at means to invest it with the ability to look at us in return. This experience corresponds to the data of the *mémoire involontaire*... This designation has the advantage of clarifying the ceremonial character of the phenomenon. The essentially distant is the inapproachable..."[75] Moreover, as John Mowitt has pointed out, the political reading has changed.[76] Mass reproduction still destroys aura, but far from being politically advantageous this is now regarded as, on the one hand, something to regret, on the other, a process that the modernist artist (such as Baudelaire) can show us how to resist. The key seems to be that elements of aura, deposited in the unconscious (the *mémoire involontaire*) as fragments of socialized memory, can function as a kind of protection mechanism — a shield against the shocks of modernity. This begins to mesh with Benjamin's theory of reception as formed in the mode of *habit* (for "technology has subjected the human sensorium to a complex kind of training");[77] that is, what constitutes the subject's dialogue with the world at the level where it is automatic.

We might think that something of an aporia opens up in Benjamin's thought here. For habit is precisely the mode he recommends for the mass reception of the new media.[78] And this mode is surely characterized precisely by its repetitive quality: the uniqueness of aura, in this sense, is a myth that must constantly be *performed*, and it is the function of tradition to sustain the originary fraud. Perhaps because his focus is on literary and visual works, Benjamin neglects the "repetition compulsion" necessary to sustaining aura even at its cultic stage, a mechanism which greater attention to the performed arts, such as music, would have revealed. If aura is not so much repetition's opposite but is actually carried on the repetitive patterns of memory, then memory-traces can (*pace* Freud) be regarded as integral to the subject's perpetual self-reproduction. To be sure, this process would be mediated by the contingencies of changing technology. If, then, we attend to the antinomies of aura no less than to those that Adorno detected in the dialectic of reason (or indeed those of repetition), we will not miss the historical specificities of Benjamin's discourse. Writing (like Adorno) against the background of the fascist threat, he reads Proust (and Bergson and Freud) against the context of their early-twentieth century moment, and, through Proust, reads back to Baudelaire's mid-nineteenth century Paris. In doing this, his discourse itself works through (to use a Freudian phrase) a layered structure of memory — and, at the same time, lays out the method whereby we can extend it into the future.

Benjamin's sensitivity to this rhythm appears in his studies of nineteenth-century Paris, where teleology gives way to intricate interdependencies: the urban crowd and the solitary individual; ennui and compulsive novelty; the cult of fashion and social discipline; boredom and factory production; chance and mechanicity.[79] His understanding of repetition (not least his discussion of Nietzschian "eternal recurrence") is at once rooted in the precise moment — the moment we recognize as marking the beginnings of many of the still familiar patterns of modern life — and clearly prefigures twentieth-century developments. In the emergence of electronic techniques of reproduction — sampling, looping, remixing — we can identify a further stage in this narrative, with the saturation of the soundscape producing production itself as always already a sort of cover, together with a model of subjectivity in continual (cyborgianized) dispersion for which Freud's *Erinnerungsspuren* (to which Benjamin refers in his Baudelaire study) are no longer just traces (*Spuren*) but also spurs (tracks, branches) extending out into the social landscape.[80]

The ambivalence is there, often enough, in Benjamin's formulations themselves. He writes of "novelty," "This semblance of the new is reflected, like one mirror in another, in the semblance of the ever recurrent"; and again, on progress and stasis, "The belief in progress — in an infinite perfectibility understood as an infinite ethical task — and the representation of eternal return are complementary. They are the indissoluble antinomies in the face of which the dialectical conception of historical time must be developed. In this conception, the idea of eternal return appears as precisely that 'shallow rationalism' which the belief in progress is accused of being, while faith in progress seems no less to belong to the mythic mode of thought than does the idea of eternal return."[81] But it is his insistence on the ambivalence of his "interdependencies" — these "dialectical images," as he called them — that frees them for historical thought and political work. As Benjamin puts it, "precisely the modern, *la modernité*, is always citing primal history. Here this occurs through the ambiguity peculiar to the social relations and products of this epoch. Ambiguity is the manifest imaging of dialectic, the law of dialectics at a standstill. This standstill is utopia, and the dialectical image, therefore, dream image."[82]

Ironically, while Adorno's commitment to the historical logic of reason could result only in its negative moment, its freeze-up, Benjamin's theory of history — opposed to all concepts of progress, drawing as much on Jewish mysticism as historical materialism, and hinging on the attempt to summon past moments into a timeless Now, whose "flash" of recognition is pregnant with potential for future action — built on the idea of history's *end* through revolutionary rupture (almost a dream-equivalent of the Lacanian *passage à l'acte*). As Andreas Huyssen has noted, to read Adorno against the grain — following up the hints of historical flexibility mentioned earlier, levering open the occasional theoretical fissure — reveals more signs of hope there too than Adorno himself is ready to claim. "Because human beings, as subjects, still constitute the limit of reification," Adorno wrote, "mass culture has to renew its hold over them in an endless series of repetitions; the hopeless effort of repetition is the only trace of hope that the repetition may be futile, that human beings cannot be totally controlled."[83] And if repetition qua mechanism *were* to fail, this could breach the walls of the reified, self-identical subject which is its home and effect, "shak[ing] up that invariant of bourgeois society understood in its broadest sense: the demand of identity. First, identity had to be constructed, ultimately it will have to be overcome." And at that point, Adorno even hazards, "The dawning sense of freedom feeds upon the memory of the archaic impulse not yet steered by any solid I."[84] But these hints are stymied by the requirement of the theory for an *Aufhebung* which the theory itself has rendered impossible — a postautonomous subject generated out of autonomy, as if by virgin birth.

Of the two, then, it is Benjamin, with his greater sense of premodern, mythic residues within bourgeois subjectivity and his feel for the new contours of sociotechnological space in mass culture, who better helps us to grasp the spacious territory of repetition in modern societies: forever generating would-be standard(izing) models, standing proud of the field (but already strangely familiar), which however immediately copy with a programmed fidelity both built-in and impossible; auratic emblems (military and potentially militant) wanting to be sign machines, which are however doomed to misfire; and always flickers, coming and going, of memories, memories... (are made — where? — in the unconscious, wherever that is...), memories are made of this.[85] Perhaps, then, a politics of the *standard(izing) moment* — those moments which *ex-tend*, *ex-sist*, *stand out or up* (to be counted) within the ceaseless circulating flow, and which, as such, are actually coextensive with the subject — would be one that enabled those moments to be productively articulated together.

******

These examples suggest something of the *complexity* of the nineteenth- and twentieth-century history of repetition. Yet this only fills out the more evident point that the cultural dominant of this period lies elsewhere: in, precisely, history; and against this background, repetition is positioned for hegemonic modes of theory as a subaltern figure. Although its challenge emerges more strongly as the twentieth century unfolds, its status as somehow other, backward, or negative has been hard to shake. Whatever reconfigurations can be detected, it is clear that overall the matrix of thought of which repetition is part under modernity continues in place; understanding repetition in this sociohistorical moment means, inescapably, grasping it in this matrix.

"Only modernity... gives ontological weight to history and a determining sense to our position within it," writes Gianni Vattimo.[86] But the signifer "history," within the self-understanding of modernity, has been by no means univocal, as we have seen — particularly once modernism began to enter its critical points of view. In cartoon sketch, we might register, on the one hand, the arrow of time, the telic imperative, the solid ceaselessly melting into air; yet, ironically, these are also bound by the conveyor-belt of capital accumulation and Fordist seriality into the reproductive treadmill of mass society — itself subjected, on both its time and space axes, to a remorseless succession of compressions suggesting a putative state of equilibrium.[87] On the other hand, modernist artists mark these features, however variably (in, for instance, an incessant quest for the new, a focus on the fragment or a flirtation, sometimes fascistic, with the aestheticization of stasis), yet at the same time are typically to be found rebelling against the predictabilities of normative culture — even if this might involve a provocative deployment of repetition, a rebellious refusal to rebel (as in Satie's *Vexations*). In this (by no means monolithic) lineage, repetition as such is never innocent. Even when indulged, it is deeply scarred with marks of negation. From Baudelaire and Marx to Barthes and Baudrillard, the sign of freedom, the moment of *jouissance*, is (variably) critique, rupture, a break with the code, silence — at any rate, a *transgression*. The terms of debate are set, it would seem, with repetition at one side, shock at the other. Benjamin's classic epigram about Baudelaire starkly outlines the typical modernist line: "He indicated the price for which the sensation of the modern age may be had: the disintegration of the aura in the experience of shock."[88]

But is repetition doomed to be a junior partner, a shadowy double, a disturbing symptom of a normativity that, for human fulfillment, demands to be unsettled? Is it only to be associated with a ground, a code, a predictability (of the subject, of social formation, of the body, of a *plaisir* that can always be accommodated)? Or might this ground be susceptible to opening up, to a certain *loss*? The musical examples discussed so far, together with the historical, technological, and social variables surrounding them, certainly suggest that repetition is less an ontological datum than a discursively construed operationality. And, while the historically constituted sphere of musical practice as such — based as it is, in striking fashion, in all its parameters, on periodicities — may be regarded as influential in the more general play of repetition going to form culture itself, at the same time it offers a quite specific case: for here repetition is always wanting to, as it were, put itself forward, through markers of iteration, transformation, variance and return, even while this very instinct lays the ground for an intensive variability of application (including, of course, resistance to this very instinct). Elsewhere,[89] I have tried to begin the task of analyzing types of musical repetition. One distinction I have put forward is between *musematic* and *discursive* forms, the first built on repetition of musemes — short units such as riffs — the second on repetition of phrases or sections. I suggested that such distinctions could be followed through at the level of subject formation, for example, in terms of affirmation or dissolution of subject identity, *plaisir* or *jouissance*. If we return now to the history of modernity's troubled engagement with repetition, we will find that such variability played a bigger role than we have recognized so far.

Poststructuralist *jouissance* is often indebted as an idea to the Romantic concept of the Sublime, influentially explored in the mid-eighteenth century by Edmund Burke and further developed by Kant. The Sublime offered a powerful opening to irrationality in which images of terror, awe, and natural grandeur invited readers, viewers, and listeners to an enticing but threatening pleasure of self-extinction. This was an aesthetic of excess, of transgression, its theatre constituted by figures that, in one way or another, lay beyond the norms familiar to predictive consciousness. But as early as 1805, the Kantian philosopher C. F. Michaelis saw self-loss in the musical Sublime as accessible not only through "too much diversity, as when innumerable impressions succeed one another too rapidly and the mind being too abruptly hurled into the thundering torrent of sounds" but also through "uniformity so great that it almost excludes variety: by the constant repetition of the same note or chord, for instance." What most critics of the time would have read as tedious was here figured as offering entry to a particular pleasure, and the story of the mysterious link between boredom and ecstasy got under way.[90] More than a century-and-a-half later, minimalist composer Terry Riley struck a similar note: "You can get high by getting in one groove . . . You can get high by staying on one note, there's different ways but that's definitely a way to ecstasy."[91] In both examples, ecstasy-through-repetition is clearly thought of as signaling abnormality; it gets you high. But the transgression motif itself (whether driven by rupture or repetition) may, at least in this rather melodramatic form typical of the Romantic-Modernist tradition, be historically contingent. To suggest that the whole bivalent *topos* of conformity versus transgression may now have had its day — is it perhaps analogous, and even linked, to other binaries, in such spheres as gender, sexuality, race, and aesthetic hierarchy? — would be premature, and certainly to jump ahead of my argument; but at least it enables me to emphasize the need to locate it, where it belongs, as specifically a trope of the modernity narrative.

This narrative is less unilinear than many accounts imply. It is particularly useful here to think modernity with full attention to the place within the modern Western world of the Afro-diasporic presence, notably, but by no means exclusively, in the Americas. Which requires us to double back to Paul Gilroy's influential argument[92] that it is impossible to grasp adequately the shape of that history without understanding that this presence was integral; in other words, that black culture, far from being a purely foreign body, played a constitutive role in the evolution of modernity itself. At the same time, Gilroy insists on the specificity of African-American cultures, and this two-sided approach enables him to figure their role as that of a *counterculture of modernity* — dependent, participative but relatively autonomous — which significantly colors the whole to form a "black Atlantic."

Writing before Gilroy, James Snead nevertheless is on a similar track, albeit focusing his attention specifically on repetition.[93] Pointing out that repetition is fundamental to culture as such, functioning as protection against disruption and loss of identity, but that different cultures vary in how they deal with it, Snead describes the European picture of African practice as an "absolute alterity" constructed against its own usages.[94] For Europe, repetition must be managed and controlled, worked into processes of growth and accumulation; for Africa (at least in this picture), it is celebrated, as equilibrium or apparently accidental "cut" (arbitrary return to a previous moment, as in James Brown's cuts).[95]

The fulcrum of Snead's argument is provided by Hegel. He fixes Hegel's critique of Africa in his sights and then inverts it. Hegel, Snead points out, defines historical Europe through opposition to its Other — history-less Africa. For Hegel:

> In this main portion of Africa there can really be no history. There is a succession of *accidents and surprises*... The Negro represents the Natural Man in all his *wildness and indocility*: if we wish to grasp him, then we must drop all European conceptions. What we actually understand by "Africa" is that which is without history and resolution, which is still fully caught up in the natural spirit,... [so] terrifyingly close to the cycles and rhythms of nature.[96]

Inevitably, then, Europe — at the cutting-edge of the developing spirit of world history — is Master, Africa condemned to be Slave, in Hegel's notorious dialectical figure. But Snead argues that Hegel's description is right, and only his valuation wrong: "The written text of Hegel is a century and a half old, but its truth still prevails, with regard to the tendencies, in the present-day forms…, of the cultures that Hegel describes… Hegel was almost entirely correct in his reading of black culture."[97] The awareness and acceptance of the unavoidable repetitiveness of life is a wisdom: "everything that goes around comes around." This argument enables Snead to describe the widespread cultivation of repetition in black music, from Africa to James Brown, as a positive, and to welcome its influence on a twentieth-century West gradually releasing repetition from previous repression — for example, in Stravinsky: "The outstanding fact of late twentieth-century European culture is its ongoing reconciliation with black culture."[98]

At about the same time as Snead was writing, literary theorists Houston Baker (1984) and Henry Louis Gates (1988) were developing the theory of "Signifyin(g)," which is congruent with Snead's approach and also fleshes out Gilroy's.[99] Signifyin(g), as found right across black culture, is "repetition and revision, or repetition with a signal difference":[100] the continual paradigmatic transformation — inter- or intratextual — of given material, the repetition and varying of stock elements, the aesthetic of a "changing same," to use a phrase invented by Leroi Jones/Amiri Baraka. The theory is a vernacular theory, derived from the cultural practice itself, and posed explicitly against the goal-oriented aesthetics of the official culture — even though Gates is at pains to stress that in essence it belongs to a broader practice: "all texts signify upon other texts."[101] But Signifyin(g) has its own specificity: it also Signifies on the official process of signification, on its syntagmatic narrative chains — "The absent *g* is a figure for the Signifyin(g) black difference"[102] — and it is thus "double-voiced," acting as oral subversion of the textual, in a process that constantly undercuts not only meanings but also meaning as such. So there is not only otherness but also relation: a running commentary, giving voice to those "outside the groove of history" and constituting Signifyin(g) as a strand of counterculture; a "slaves's trope" that contains but covers over the "master's trope" — a "trope reversing trope."[103]

It is not difficult to see the force of the theory of Signifyin(g) for understandings of African-American music. For example, tonal chord sequences are often turned into riffs and looped to create repetitive frameworks, undercutting the received significance of such sequences as prime sources in European music of, precisely, sequential, goal-oriented logic. Blue thirds and sevenths probably stand in an analogous relationship to their diatonic equivalents. Arguably, this is exactly how the circle-of-fifths sequences in "There'll Be Some Changes Made," and the blue notes brought out in many performances, function. This analytic potential has begun to feed through into musical interpretation, notably in David Brackett's study of James Brown's "Superbad," where Signifyin(g) is revealed as working on a host of levels: lyrics, textural patterns, vocal structure, harmony, rhythmic relationships.[104]

Hovering around all these theories, sometimes explicitly, is the figure of Mikhail Bakhtin, who categorically rejected Hegelian dialectics, and for whom meaning lies in the dialogue of utterance and the always already said: no *Aufhebung*, only heterology — a double-voiced, or multi-voiced circling around changing sames. But we need to look further at the identity of these multiple voices.

Snead identifies a counter-current in Western thought, running from Vico through the Counter-Enlightenment, Kierkegaard and Nietzsche, to aspects of modernism — a current where cyclic theories of history and valorizations of repetition can be found. But the *purchase* of this lineage on the surrounding culture is never really engaged. Similarly, Snead's treatment of repetition in the bourgeois music of this period is simplistic. On both levels, although he wants to insist that European music and thought could not avoid repetition and pursued a damage-limitation strategy of absorbing it into processes of differentiation and growth, he presents their relationship with black culture as a simple alterity. Above all, he makes nothing of the fact that, actually, Hegel was wrong, not right, about the history-less state of Africa, as actual historical work has shown; it is Hegel's picture, not its object, that is mythic. The dangers of a simple Nature/History dualism are manifest in Snead's account of the renaissance of repetition in twentieth-century music as a reconciliation, a simple return. Such thinking is not uncommon. Steve Reich, for example, connects process music to age-old, ritualistic, prehistorical compositional methods. He wants a dance music that rejoins an ancient consensus on the rhythmic regularity and predetermined structures of dance. He describes playing his own music as "imitating machines" but claims that this is akin to Yoga breathing exercises: "the kind of attention 'mechanical' playing calls for, which is related to sitting and counting one's breaths, is something we could do with a great deal more of right now."[105]

Similarly, something of a consensus seems to have emerged within cultural studies over what is almost a *separatist* notion of black difference. Tricia Rose, in her book on rap music, rightly remarks on the essential role of repetition, often highly technologically mediated, in rap.[106] She reviews the Adornian view of repetition but plays down its relevance to black music, where repetition can draw on "long-standing black cultural forces" in order to function as "collective resistance" to industrialized patterns. The Adornian critique (whose tentacles she finds in Attali and Jameson as well) is a "massive misreading."[107] But this conflict of interpretation is not related to musical, social, or cultural mechanisms that could explain it. Rose asks the very good question, "If we assume that industrial production sets the terms for repetition inside mass-produced music, then how can alternate uses and manifestations of repetition that are articulated *inside* the commodity market be rendered perceptible?" An equally good question, though, would be, if we assume that black difference sets the terms for repetition in black music, whenever it may occur, or even if we assume (as Rose does) the importance of attending to "multiple histories and approaches," how can we demonstrate these terms, histories, approaches, unless we identify the factors that govern the interpretative choices (as Rose does not)?[108] Crucial here will be the recognition of black culture as, not separate, but a counter-culture, and the "black Atlantic" as always also a plebeian and contested one.

Of course, it is very hard to think past the baleful influence of alterity, with its essentializing structures of projection. Even Brackett, in his study of "Superbad," ends up presenting the "critical difference" between black and European musics in a way that threatens (though he draws back) to absolutize it, rather than placing both dialogically within Gilroy's transatlantic culture of modernity. In more recent work,[109] he has moved on, suggestively, to put forward a way of understanding black difference discursively, that is, in terms of a historically contingent sequence of constructs in which the structures of projection are animated by social changes. This advance is one that has yet to be engaged by most commentators, for whom — as the debates around hip-hop in fact attest — "black music" still occupies its traditional role in the theatre of alterity. It is a theatre summoned up, with different actors, by Seán Ó Riada, romantically describing the circular processes of traditional Irish music as "the graph of real life. Every day the sun rises, every day it sets. Every day possesses the same basic characteristics, follows the same fundamental pattern, while at the same time each day differs from the last in its ornamentation of events."[110] However apposite it may be on some level, a description of this kind is, one feels, mainly there to fulfill *his* mythology of a folk-other. How much use, if any, might such an image be to understanding the role of repetition today?

In many of these models, repetition is imagined as somehow natural — or at least it is close to nature, goes with the flow of natural cycles and limits, etc.[111] But repetition within a cultural practice is a *production*; it is, precisely, *practiced* and, equally, always *cultural*. And to emerge in discourse, including theoretic discourse, it has to be *recognized* — in much the same way that resemblance (acceptance or assertion of representational likeness) is not innate in the objects but is the product of a performative act.[112] (Discursive recognition is not necessarily conscious; it may even be that some sort of "dispersed" act of recognition performs repetition into existence at the level of somatic operations, and that the discursive consequences subsist at an unconscious level.) Just as "the folk" was invented (probably by Herder), along with "savages" and "primitives" (in ancient Greece, in the Age of Discovery, in the Enlightenment, and so on — over and over), not to mention ideas of cyclic existence (which, within the West, may be traced back to Pythagoras and Ovid, and, according to Marina Warner, go on to form a constantly active quasi-pagan belief-system in continual tension with the Judaeo-Christian emphasis on the teleology of individual identity),[113] so, as an identifiable issue within the context of aesthetic, political, and social philosophy, "repetition" had to be invented — performed into awareness by those who found it at once suspect and enticing: at any rate, who could imagine themselves as standing somehow outside its sway.

A spate of such recognitions emerged in the later eighteenth century. We might suppose that this represented [*sic*] a precipitation forced by the trajectory of Teleological Reason. It is therefore no surprise that repetitive qualities were so often projected on to subhuman, supernatural, or other inferior figures — machines, robots, zombies, women, primitives, puppets, and mimics of all kinds; that they became, precisely, objects of representation, while the voice of controlling, reasoning subjectivity went unmarked.[114] Those positioned within the economy of repetition have little choice, for reasons of disparity of power, but to live within it, even if they struggle against its absolutes — that is, as others, strive to answer back. Meanwhile, as this historical trajectory continues, what is repressed (or projected out) by the dominant stratum will often return; we recognize it, for instance, in "civilization's" perverted mime of the primitive, in that "organisation of mimesis", that "mimesis of mimesis," which Adorno identified in the magic of fascist rituals (or, we might add, those of the Ku Klux Klan).[115]

What happens in that eighteenth-century moment, at least in the musical sphere, is that relations of equivalence (an aesthetic of metonymic contiguities, recalling Irigary's model of gender miming) are, so to speak, turned sideways, creating relations of metaphoric representation. Repetition is turned into representation — or rather, repetition is *represented*. The semiotics of this difficult intersection — representations are and need to be repeatable, but repetitions (including repetitions of representations) in a sense represent themselves to each other[116] — calls for a historical anthropology of the entire nexus, which, as a totality, we scarcely yet possess, but which would surely agree on the specificity of the moment of modernity. What arises is a specific economy of reference — an attempt to *picture* something beyond the practice, whether internal emotion or external scene, story or object. As Heidegger puts it:

> the fact that the world becomes a picture at all is what distinguishes the modern age... The word "picture" now means the structured image that is the creature of man's producing which represents and sets

> before. In such producing, man contends for the position in which he can be that particular being who gives the measure and draws up the guidelines for everything that is.[117]

What is copied, that is to say, is brought under the rubric of a universalizing point of view, nature laid out for domination. Moreover (to expand Heidigger's point), the "nature on display" can be inner as well as outer, laying out the self rather than the territory of otherness for exploration and development (the bifurcation may be related to the twin aesthetic tracks in nineteenth-century art music — narrative, organicism — described earlier). In contrast, repetition as *practice* can be thought of as more like a facilitator of conversation or, in Michael Taussig's terms, an operator of mimetic magic, a "chain of sympathy."[118] In so many descriptions of folk-repetition — whether celebratory or patronizing — what happens is precisely the turning of a practice (a performative) into a representation: a reified portrait of otherness. For those portrayed, such *misrepresentation* is, in this sphere, the inevitable concomitant of being a counterculture of modernity.

At the same time, the detailed history is complex and does not always fall into the simple alteritous structure that the protagonists often imagine. Warner's study of modes of metamorphic reproduction — mutating, hatching, splitting, doubling — argues that pagan themes continue to energize thought and expression in the modern West, mutating under the impact of successive waves of encounter with congruent tropes associated with colonial and imperial Others, drawing on old motifs to represent new conditions. But she resists the logic of opp/repression in favor of "more direct intellectual and cultural exchanges" that produced "rich new materials to think with."[119] Although she arguably understates the effects of colonial power structures,[120] Warner's view of Otherness as a sign not only of "a cultural bipolar disorder" or "a return of the repressed, a counter-Enlightenment negation of sense and rationality," but also "an extension of the spirit of empirical inquiry," an "incubus" born of "the imperial enterprise itself,"[121] produces rich interpretative dividends, especially in her explorations of "zombies" and "doubles" in eighteenth- and nineteenth-century literature (where they are usually linked to themes of alienation and fragmentation of subjective identity). Her accounts of Coleridge's "doubles" as phantasmatically traversing inner and outer space, and of "hatching" themes as a metaphor for narrative representation (like a butterfly emerging from a cocoon, "doing the work of making the real, of making it up," bringing together apparently disparate moments into a "single creature"),[122] offer stimulating ways into understanding nineteenth-century art-music. For this is a music where narrative often emerges out of reproductive mutation in exactly this way, and where a representational economy based on the transcription of subjectivity's inner movements and its external portraiture, working through a deployment of repetitions, transformations, and detours, seems to be precisely how this repertoire acquired its reputation as the quintessential art-form of the period.

Against this background, it is instructive to read, say, Lawrence Kramer's studies of nineteenth-century music for the light they throw on modes of management of repetition. In *Musical Meaning*, for instance, chapters on Beethoven, Schubert, Schumann, and Liszt can all be read this way.[123] Similarly, Anthony Newcomb sees the narrative in Mahler's Ninth Symphony as a "spiral quest" in which the multiple, often unexpected, even jarring repetitions (many of them of material with vernacular origins or allusions) fold the past, through strategies of recall and transformation, into a search in which "repetition has to do with finding the proper ending." Drawing on Freud's theory of repetition and memory, Newcomb argues that the key here is that "the past needs to be incorporated *as past* within the present, mastered through the play of repetition in order for there to be an escape from repetition."[124] Across the (black as well as white) Atlantic, and unknown to Freud no doubt, the case of Ives offers an American parallel to Mahler's (of course, different in many ways, including those that would have had Freud licking his lips). The sources of vernacular repetitions here lay in American white, and to some extent black, popular musics.[125]

This Freudian moment, the moment of modernist crisis (not to mention of Proust, Bergson, and Einstein), presents us with the most fraught historical example to this point of the rewriting of the sense of time, against the clatter and chatter of the present, the felt loss of the past (this is the moment of the institutionalization and "mass production" of "tradition"),[126] and an insistent gaze at the future heightened by its threatened collapse. A key preliminary shift occurred, as Benjamin noticed, when the serialities of secular urban existence and mass production found that they had to realise themselves through the novel means of — *novelty*, "the quintessence of that false consciousness whose indefatigable agent is fashion."[127] The aimless circlings in the crowded Parisian Arcades marked a new sense of time — a kind of "industrialized eternal return." The inception of this self-validating "everyday life" coincided with what would shortly be termed the "death of God," one effect of which was to imply the secularization and politicization of cultural memory, as religious ritual began to give way to vernacular knowledges and institutions. Ian Hacking argues[128] that memory only became an object of scientific knowledge in the late nineteenth century, when the sciences of memory — including Freudianism — began to supplant the idea of the soul as the key discourse of the modern self. Modernism probed this cultural knot. At the same time, everyday men and women learned to live within its new structure of hopes and fears. The teleological journey of the soul, together with the ritual structures marking its passages, metamorphosed into the secular dreams, memories, and self-constructions of contemporary experience; and, at the same moment, provoked by the tedium of their never-ending repetition, Nietzsche invented the secular religion of "eternal return."

Stretched by the pressures of this extreme moment, the collective cultural psychology of the Western elites drew upon the full range of its traditional projections, helped as ever by the continuing presence of objects of dubious desire in the system itself: "imperial consciousness provided a screen on which these fantasies could be projected."[129] African Americans could not help but assume their role as one such object, along with other folk-others. The "masses" and their culture, at once uncivilized and frighteningly modern, were also often figured in terms of repetition — as standardized workers, reproductive machines, unreflective consumers, devoid of historical grandeur — and so was Woman, so close, apparently, to the rhythms of natural cycles.[130] The sensual passivity attributed to "orientalized" exotics achieved a new level of potency within the European imagination.[131] And giving an added twist to the explosive spirals of doubling were the new mass reproduction technologies. For Taussig, these "modern mimetic machines" kick-start a historical back-wave, "recharging and retooling the mimetic faculty"; the fact that Walter Benjamin, above all, registered its significance, was, he argues, what enabled him to identify primitive magic within the technologically modern.[132] Warner traces the prehistory of the cinema's mimetic "image magic," through magic lantern, phantasmagoria, diorama, and photograph, back as far as the seventeenth century. But from the "mirror point" of 1900 — with film illusion supplemented by the acoustic mirror mechanisms of the phonograph, the Model T rolling off the assembly-line as if by mirror magic, psychoanalytic patterns of identification and splitting (which would shortly give rise to the theory of the mirror stage) finding an apotheosis in the fetishizing effects, conjoining Marx and Freud, of the glittering store windows, reflecting back to bourgeois, imperial subjects their colonial possessions — she also looks forward, putting the changes in the context of an overall theory of representation:

> representation itself acts as a form of doubling; representation exists in magical relation to the apprehensible world, it can exercise the power to make something come alive, *apparently*. The figure of the other you inside you threatens to escape, not only in states of trance… but in actuality, and become another, usurping your being as someone else: the idea of the clone is probably most frightening because even if it looks and acts like a copy, it cannot and will not be one.[133]

As this cyborgian trajectory suggests, replication is here installed at the core of representation, reproduction at the heart of production; we struggle to tell them apart, as they mimic each other.

African Americans were not spectators to these developments. As piano rolls and gramophones span out the "primitive" iterations of ragtime, coon song, foxtrot, tango, and early jazz, they played a leading role in the industrialization of repetition. And, as songwriters created ways of managing musematic repetition by folding it into longer-breathed formal articulations — a small-scale equivalent of the procedures in nineteenth-century art music — blacks were among them.[134] Characteristically modern themes of loss, nostalgia, and disruption helped form early blues (see chapter 2), while spirituals were historicized, creating the sense of a folk past within African-American music culture itself. Boogie-woogie overwrote its hypnotically repeating images of erotic body rhythms with those — congruent but other — of the railway, penetrating the folk hinterland even as it carried former slaves into modernity.[135] Equally, though, blacks could rarely escape objectification. Warner describes how the figure of the "zombie" was derived from Afro-diasporic sources and subsequently affixed to varied images of "possession" and slave-consciousness, often associated with exotic groups,[136] and this association can be traced through to popular images (including Adorno's) of jazz.

Above all, the intricate maneuvers of blackface — a kind of reifying caricature of Signifyin(g) in which black and white alike looked into a mirror that both misrecognised and misrepresented each to the other — formed the inescapable framework for all black performance. From this point of view, Al Jolson's blacked-up appearance in the first sound movie, *The Jazz Singer* (1927), represents a key moment, an iconic albeit "cracked" image reflected in multitudinous if equally crackly cinematic projections around the world. Another, perhaps, lay in Louis Armstrong's indulgence (arguably) of stereotype when he adopted the 1931 tune "When It's Sleepy Time Down South" as his theme tune, ensuring its continued recycling as a blackface standard (although he had undercut the image two years earlier in his moving recording of Fats Waller's "What Did I Do to Be So Black and Blue?" — and, as suggested earlier, there may be more, interpretatively, to his "Sleepy Time" than first hearing assumes).[137]

But such twists and turns went way back. For example, to the early nineteenth century when the "blackface turn"[138] emerged in New York as a symptom not only of racist projection but also potential plebeian agency. W.E.B. Du Bois, whose theory of "double consciousness" underlies subsequent models of Signifyin(g), was in many ways a Hegelian — a tendency that in later years took him towards Marxism — and he developed the theory out of existing ideas in European Romanticism, American Transcendentalism, and late-nineteenth century psychology.[139] But, of course, the teleology of the master-slave dialectic would, for him, have to work itself out in a very different way from anything Hegel envisaged. As repetition began to be commodified in the arcades of Paris, the view from the plantations of the South would have looked very different, even though the two sites were intimately connected economically: the slaves *were* commodities, objects (rather than subjects) of fetishistic effects both as factors of production and (as breeding machines) of reproduction. This gives the repeating cycles of work songs a very specific edge; and when those familiar pendular thirds (usually, though not always, joining tonic and minor third above) resonate through the riffs of later African-American song repertories, the edge remains: in, for example, "Baby Please Don't Go," or, even more forcefully, Howlin' Wolf's "Spoonful," where their ambivalent force (the body as it were imprisoned but — all the same — powerful) is transplanted to a sexual theatre; or Public Enemy's "Black Steel in the Hour of Chaos" (1988), where a speeded up bass version of the riff underpins a transplantation to the fantasy-scene of a prison break-out (that is, an escape, as the lyrics put it, from "a form of slavery organized under a swarm of devils").[140] What this lineage seems to point to is the inscription of repetition on a collective body that has been positioned in a place not outside the cycles of capitalist accumulation but, in a very specific way, right at their center.

As many of these examples suggest, however, Others can in principle "answer back." Objects forced to reflect projections are not necessarily condemned to be forever dumb, and in speaking back, can Signify on, and in that sense work with, aspects of the myths. But in deconstructing the apparatus of projection, we need to recognize not only the right of its objects to self-definition but also the weight of historical interweavings which alteritous maps have misrepresented. Deconstruction — rather than simple negation — should lead not to the inversion of a previous duality but to the recognition of an open-ended *spread* of experience and position, defined through the specific vectors of historical pressures. Marina Warner notes a postcolonial twist to the figure of the zombie in which it is reimagined as a power, not an emptiness; as the spirit of dead slaves protecting their descendants, "a figure not of servitude, but of occult and diffuse potency for the very regions where the concept arose in its reduced, subjugated, even annihilated character."[141] Is this what Ishmael Reed is about when in his novel *Mumbo Jumbo* he answers back to white pretension: "They are after themselves. They call it destiny. Progress. We call it Haints. Haints of their victims rising from the soil of Africa, South America, Asia..."?[142] And among these Haints do we hear the figures conjured up by the uncanny, uncompromising declamations of both Howlin' Wolf and Public Enemy: specters that, by virtue of special knowledge, haunt modernity from within? What might this tell us about the robotic qualities of Michael Jackson's dancing, whether he is dancing with zombies or not?[143]

In our own would-be postcolonial moment, it sometimes feels as if, at least in the developed societies, we are haunted *all the time*; the repeat/shuffle buttons are on full-time, and saturation via ring-tone, computer bleep, holding music, mall Muzak — as well as music in its more old-fashioned guise — approaches. If formerly repetition in music had to be *recognized* before it could be discursively linked to experience on other levels, now these levels are increasingly interpreted — apprehended, sorted, processed — in the light of the soundscape. Musical and nonmusical time slide together. Until relatively recently, music punctuated life; often the performed time of the musical event stood in a dissociated, even liminal relationship to the experienced time of surrounding existence.[144] The shift is not absolute: complete dislocation between music and life is impossible, and in general, we may surmise, to recognize in music the shape of temporal contours known from elsewhere is an experience equally familiar as to be carried out of any such contours into a distinct temporal realm. The second no more constitutes music as separate (cut off) from the rest of life than does the first: musicalized life and lived music interact. Nevertheless, the *specialness* of the musical event that we can recognize in many traditional contexts — its capacity to interrupt — has been attenuated by the vernacularization of musical experience in modern societies.

The transition from the bourgeois concert to today's pop-drenched soundscape reveals the auratic music-ritual as part of the historical wreckage that Benjamin's Angel of History leaves behind[145] — and the late-twentieth century "rave" as its after-shock. Even the tranciest techo-high bleeds out into secular life-values. The critical impulse that, typically, is attached to music's autonomy in the bourgeois aesthetic paradigm is, in post-Benjaminian culture, thoroughly dispersed and at the same time politicized: *representation* wants to turn towards *action*, recollection (in a reverse-Freudian movement) towards repetition, even as we cannot stop, in vertiginously compulsive images (a sort of generalized transference), watching each other act. But the objects of recollection (memories) are increasingly located *outside*, in mediated texts: whereas we used to hear our own voices, "media dissolve such feedback loops,"[146] recording these voices for us, placing the internal voice of consciousness in crisis. For the later Freud, the subject is in effect a prosthesis of social memory: "consciousness arises at the site of a memory trace"; "this is the temporal contradiction of the subject, its displacement by a reproductive apparatus that precedes it," and the discontinuity, Freud suspects, "lies at the bottom of the origin of the concept of time."[147] Today, more clearly than ever, these glints of consciousness cling to repeating flashes of technically mediated memory like clouds of gas to shooting stars, refractive shards in an ever mobile kaleidoscope. If in a certain light this might look a bit like a technologized Spinozan pantheism, it stands to the philosopher's holistic utopia — with individual selves fading into a single mind/body *sub specie aeternitatis* — much like the market of consumer capitalism (to which it no doubt has a certain Benjaminian "correspondence") stands to democracy.

In this conjuncture, the connections are multiple. Thought may mirror music as well as vice versa. Fed by certain strands in ecological and feminist thought, and by the sense of an end of grand narratives, there is certainly a renewed awareness of the relative constants of human limitations, death, and intergenerational repetitions. As Kierkegaard puts it, "every generation begins again from the beginning... No generation has learned how to love from another, no generation begins at any other point than the beginning, and no subsequent generation has a shorter task than the generation that preceded it." This leads him to the view that "Repetition is reality, and it is the seriousness of life. He who wills repetition is matured in seriousness."[148] Consider, in a similar vein, Nietzsche:

> the world, as force, may not be thought of as unlimited, for it *cannot* be so thought of... Thus — the world also lacks the capacity for eternal novelty... [A]s a certain definite quantity of force... it must pass through a calculable number of combinations. In infinite time, every possible combination would at sometime or another be realized... And since between every combination and its next recurrence all other possible combinations would have to take place... a circular movement of absolutely identical series is thus demonstrated...[149]

Or, in the twentieth century, Jean Wahl:

> We are in this world limited in our very being. The only way to take our destiny upon ourself... is to want ourselves to be limited by death. It is therefore by way of dread and the thought of death that we arrive at repetition. We must take what we are upon ourselves... [we must] live our own death in advance. We overcome our failure by becoming conscious of that failure.[150]

Yet are Kierkegaard, Nietzsche, and Wahl altogether right? Wahl is glossing Heidegger, whose response to the speed-up of modern life was, it might be argued, to ontologise contemporary anxiety into a theory of human Being as such; which subject is it who is consumed by dread in this way? Nietzsche, arguably, confuses potential infinity with actual, historically contingent infinitudes in particular spheres, forgetting as well the determinate effects that one "combination" may have on the chances of a subsequent "combination." Similarly, Kierkegaard's moving vision of human love catches the effort this capacity demands but absolutizes it. There is more than one kind of beginning, and configurations and understandings of love are always historically contingent.

The conjuncture today — *our* combination — is in many ways unique. *Telos* collapses for the very specific reason that, so to speak, after Auschwitz it cannot face the world. At the same time, the ever accelerating tempo of "time-space compressions" fundamentally alters the social matrix within which repetitions take place. Benjamin's flood of reproductions circulates in an ever-shrinking world, against an ever-shortening horizon, and by the time of the later Baudrillard appears (at least to him) to have left all distinction between original and copy behind, so that "simulacra surpass history."[151] But the collapse of *telos* does not require the end of history. The end signaled here is inscribed only in an ideology congruent, to say the least, with neoliberal apocalyptics. And Baudrillard misses the Benjaminian insight that simulation not only uproots meaning but also, through the reinternalizing of repetition, the decontextualizing of representation, potentially frees practice.

Not the least singularity of the contemporary moment is what I think of as the "dual world system" governing today's music regime: the astonishing confluence, in a twin triumph, of global capital circulation in the political economy, African musical diaspora in the sign economy — modernity and its counterculture, relatively autonomous still, but symbiotic. Is this a joke by the World Spirit at Hegel's expense? Frederic Jameson's concern[152] that postmodern ecstasy represents a false Sublime, powered by the giddy cycles of commodity circulation, might worry us that the Slave is now complicit with the Master; but such either-or melodrama, itself complicit with an outworn paradigm, is sounding tired. Chernoff's insistence[153] that the effect of multiple repetitions in African music is not frenzied but refreshing, that "ecstasy" would be seen as tasteless, is a useful caution. Similarly, Morton Marks, in his study of African-American religious music, takes issue with Victor Turner's theory that liminality strips participants of their identities: the ritual structures he discovers do not disrupt but rather reconfigure existing systems of order; they are "rule-bound but liminal,"[154] their mechanisms depending on switching — successive or contrapuntal — between different repetition patterns.

Kierkegaard,[155] while carefully distinguishing different modes of repetition and recollection, nevertheless finds them overlapping. Similarly, Deleuze defines *true* repetition, counter-intuitively, as "repetition of difference," which takes place in "another dimension, a secret verticality"; but it is always in disguise, intermingled with, on the one hand, "brute repetition" — what Deleuze calls mechanical repetition-of-the same — and, on the other hand, with resemblance: the grouping of differences under a concept, or in another word, representation: "It is always in this gap, which should not be confused with the negative, that creatures weave their repetition and receive at the same time the gift of living and dying."[156] Kristeva's program for a reconstruction of "women's time" promotes a tactic of interweaving the (male) cursive time of production and the (female) recursive, cyclic time of reproduction. This process, she argues, needs to be recuperated to the internal structure of the subject, in an "interiorization of the founding separation of the socio-symbolic contract":[157] that is, in a shifting of socially oriented splitting, scapegoating and projections to the *interior* of identities, social or individual, putting them into a new fluidity.

We should be wary of totalizing visions. As a political tactic, Kristeva's proposal is strong. Yet there is the danger of ontologizing the "founding separation" and leaving the female time of reproduction where the split forced it to dwell, *before* culture — a place from which it will be hard to rescue it. Similarly, applications of Deleuze's metaphysics risk confusing an inspiring yet ultimately phantasmatic attempt to (in Lacanian terms) represent the Real — something that, inescapably, can take place only on *this* side of representation — with a political program. But memory, even if in shreds, is everywhere; repetition here has only a figurative link with Nature, and has, still, to be *produced*; difference, no less than repetition, can at this stage in history not operate — the machinery will not start up — except in relation to representations, including representations of difference and repetition themselves.

Refrain 3

What, then, does repetition-practice look like at the turn of the twentieth and twenty-first centuries? An adequate answer would require an attention to difference of Deleuzian proportions. My snapshot from the 1990s selects a few examples that simply offer some interpretative contrasts, while locating popular voices in a musical context sufficiently broad to enable us to take a fix on them.

The Third Symphony (*Symphony of Sorrowful Songs*) by Polish "holy minimalist," Henryk Gorecki, was composed in 1976 but achieved celebrity in the early 1990s, when it was heavily promoted by British radio station Classic FM and topped the classical album chart.[158] At the start of the second movement, we hear the hallowed tonic-subdominant move, repeating over and over, I and IV chords bleeding into and overlapping each other, the progression unclosed (it is followed by a setting of a text discovered on a concentration camp wall). The cadential pull alluded to maps a narrative structure (the *telos* of modernity?), while its religious associations (I-IV = Amen) root this narrative in its Christian sources. In a symphony linked to mourning for Nazism and the Holocaust, this is indeed historical debris; it seems to summon up a skein of memory reaching right back into the heart of European civilization. What can the composer do with its teleonomic and at the same time ritualistic potential but rehearse and at the same time refuse it? — except, perhaps, use it for prayer: "…art is prayer," says Gorecki, "…But it is difficult to understand: one has to mature to this thought. It seems to many people that prayer means to 'recite the Hail Mary' — but someone may recite 'Hail Mary' as many times as one wants and it will not be prayer."[159] The old repetitions no longer work; the new will be at best tentative, built from the wreckage.

John Adams, who achieved considerable popularity around the same time, has also sometimes (if wrongly) been classified as a minimalist. His "On the Dominant Divide," from his *Grand Pianola Music* (1981–82), scored for chamber orchestra with two pianos and voices, also deals in historical debris, in this case the I-V progression (there is also more specific allusion, in the piano figuration and the main theme, to Beethoven's *Emperor Concerto* and *Hammerklavier Sonata*).[160] The initial dominant pedal is comically over-extended, and the repeating I-V chords of the theme are bathetic. Adams is obviously having fun at the expense of the hoary old perfect cadence (more particularly, its crucial role in the developmentalism of Beethovenian form); perhaps too at the expense of a particular grandiose nineteenth-century manner, and even the style of Hollywood epic theme-tune that grew out of it. But the naiveté seems to transfigure these overused materials, the aimless repetition to cancel the narrative weight of the cadence.

Yet if this suggests a historical burden lifted, Adams's aim seems to have been far more than postmodernist goofing. He describes the composition as having "started with a dream image in which while driving down Insterstate 5, I was approached from behind by two long, gleaming, black stretch limousines. As the vehicles drew up beside me, they transformed into the world's longest Steinways…twenty, maybe even thirty feet long. Screaming down the highway at 90 mph, they gave off volleys of B flat and E flat arpeggios."[161] The conflation of mechanicity (the modern grand associated with military rounds [volleys], with a pianola-like automaticity and with time-space compressions induced by the effects of the automobile industry) and Beethovenian subjectivity (the *Emperor* and the *Hammerklavier* are celebrated warhorses of heroic pianism) is telling. It is not difficult to imagine the limos containing the specters of Beethoven and his retinue of history-making descendants (but is this a VIP convoy or a high-speed funeral?) and our Hero as given the impossible task of bridging the two sides of Enlightenment Reason, critical and instrumental. This, then, is a fantasy of Adornian negative dialectics turned sunny side up (and if the music celebrates its own "corn," this is stylistic grist to a mill that — as it fed the magic music industry goose — had, over a long period, certainly resulted in many golden eggs).[162]

Rock music dwells in a world that, while it overlaps and is inseparable from that inhabited by Gorecki and Adams, is not identical. The bourgeois concert hall, and its virtual simulations on radio and record, mimic an autonomy on one side of a divide that rock — situating itself in a mythical street-scene, at once everyday and impossibly highly colored — crosses only in ironic or mutant forms, if at all.[163] Lawrence Grossberg has argued that, given the transformation of the cyclicities of daily life into the *routines* of everyday life, rock for the most part lives within these routines, accepting them as a confining framework, but at the same time imagining the possibility of escape, if only through identifications with Others (especially black-Others). Thus the rhythms of routine are de-territorialized, serving as a way to imagine Saturday-night "fun" as permeating the everyday.[164] Reducing freedom to transient fun is the price paid to the forces of alienation and to the continuing potency of the structure of projections: the repetitions both set the limits of this strategy and point still, perhaps, towards a certain utopian moment. But this is, so to speak, a default position, from which individual instances may well stand out; it does not mean that repetitions in rock do not carry heavy and specific historical freight, all the more so because repetition is generally much more powerfully foregrounded here than in the musical lineages that Gorecki and Adams deconstruct. In heavy rock it is put to uses that, often, are not free from their own complicity with hegemonic discourse — particularly through its association with the grindingly insistent structures of patriarchal demand. How to deal with — rather than simply reproduce — this?

Earlier, we saw something of how Patti Smith addressed this issue, in her version of "Gloria"; the management of repetition there (particularly the harmonic underpinning: an unchanging I-♭VII-IV riff which emerges out of a slimmer I-♭VII introductory version) plays an important role in the representation of desire, its unresolvable frustrations, ecstasies, and terrors. P. J. Harvey, often compared to Smith and stylistically indebted in a similar ambivalent way to blues-rock's hard men (Wolf, Hendrix, Plant, et al.), works much the same territory in her "blues album," *To Bring You My Love* (1995).[165] The tracks reassemble a bagful of familiar heavy rock/R&B riff-types — harmonic, melodic, rhythmic — but the vocal focus (which, despite the generally low tessitura and excursions into shriek and growl, is clearly marked "female," albeit often "phallic" in orientation) resexes them, leaving a thematic that combines sexual obsession, sado-masochism, religious imagery ("It's my voodoo working"), and brazen boasting ("Laid with the devil") to negotiate as best it can a territory deeply marked with raced and gendered histories. In "Send His Love to Me," for example, the relentless harmonic riff (I-♭VII — again, although the tonic chord is broodingly minor) and repeating vocal phrases (breaks, whoops and growls fragmenting the chilling force of the core timbre) mark out a space where loss ("How long must I suffer?"), religious appeal ("I'm begging, Jesus, please/Send his love to me"), and oedipal bewilderment ("Mummy, daddy, please/Send him back to me") combine to summon images of Nina Simone as much as Patti Smith and the "magic phallicism" of Muddy Waters. When backing strings enter, part way through, memories of ballad and torch song are added, and, as their repeated phrases fade out the track, the overall impression, in comparison to Smith and Simone, is of a controlled, hopeless anguish — a turn-of-the-century feminism that, however daunted, will not give up.[166]

The contemporaneous album by trip-hop star Tricky — *Maxinquaye* — is also largely about love and is also dark and complex.[167] But in most other ways, it offers a radical contrast. This is very much a studio album, the vocals (by Tricky and girlfriend Martine) laid over textures produced mostly out of looped samples. In "Suffocated Love," for instance, this is made up of virtually unchanging drum and bass tracks, plus subtly varied string and guitar phrases, almost all descending, mostly chromatically, halfway between lyricism and the effect of fingers scratching a blackboard. The tempo is moderate, the mood subdued, the texture dense, intricate, mysterious. At this level, the track seems to pass a whole aesthetic tradition of atmosphericism, running from Romanticism and expressionism to pop ballad and ambient music, through the filter of trancy dance loops. The repetitions slip between images of relaxing physical gesture, everyday urban dread, and the babble of inner consciousness. A heritage of *angst* is relocated, but at the same time somehow dissipates between the multiple points in the texture with its varied positions for listener identification, its circling loops of reassurance.

From another point of view, the style constitutes itself as a response to American rap: laid-back rather than aggressive, implicit rather than explicit. In this sense, the cycles of repetition have the effect of a distorting mirror, angled across the black Atlantic.[168] At the same time, the sexual theater, while understated rather than militant, plays to similar themes as those familiar in American hip hop: Tricky raps (that is, deploys the controlling male power of speech) while Martine sings (lyrically, expressively, from the body), even though both seem to have much the same view of the sexual relationship as a space of suffocating love, a prison of misunderstanding and exploitation as much as a bed of pleasure. ("Will you spend your life with me/And stifle me?") It is as if the potential to pioneer an increased sexual equality which Hortense Spillers found in the distorted relations of the historical African-American family has been generalized, in the context of a widespread, late-twentieth century weakening of patriarchal family forms — albeit with negative as well as positive results (Tricky, it might be noted, seems much exercised by his mother's premature death when he was four, an event that perhaps created a powerful maternal fantasy).[169] This brings us to the specifically *black* dimension of the music, not only in many aspects of its style but also its provenance in the black community of Bristol, a key center of the British slave trade, only recently starting to come to terms with its part in this history. One of the images on the CD sleeve, which overall presents a surreal collage depicting a "jungle," part urban, part natural, shows the two vocalists (one assumes) roped together at the wrists, with overtones that are disturbing both sexually and racially. Once this aspect is raised, against the background of a musical style that is druggy while at the same time conjoining figures of black embodiment and of cyborgian production,[170] the trope of the *zombie* comes irresistibly to mind, albeit a postcolonial zombie in the business of inverting previous stereotype. A trip hopping across history indeed.

What does this highly selective group of examples have to tell us? I hear a range of "changing sames" as they intersect with the magnetic images — wired positive or negative — of varied historical force fields, themselves groaning with memory-traces. Freud might want to ask what traumas are being hidden beneath these repetitions. But the traumas emerge readily enough; indeed, it is more the case that the deployments of repetition here seem to usher them into the light. Listening in a world where we have, literally, repetitions constantly in our ears, we encounter a flow of memory that is both dispersed and temporally disjointed.

Yet *these* traces are for the most part disturbing ones. Are the hermeneutic windows I have tried to open dependent on an unacknowledged preference, a rubric of *critique*? Would this not be to take us back to the antinomies of Adornian critical theory, which, I have been suggesting, has grown cold? And in any case, under that rubric does the *popular acceptability* of these pieces not devalue them? This perspective seems wrong. Its plausibility arises in the first place, I think, because of the important role played here by familiarity — by historical debris, all of it pregnant with the wash of inherited representational fields. Yet to varying extents this debris is mobilized in forms of dialogical practice — while (also to varying extents) retaining and refracting the representational backwash. Besides, the binary logic of dialectical critique seems foreign to the giddy whirl of mimes flying about here. This is not to say that the spirit of such critique is dead in contemporary music, only that to find it, we must look elsewhere — to late-modernism.

Alastair Williams does precisely this,[171] searching the post-Webern repertory for ways of working *within* the apparent impasse represented by Adorno's road-blocked dialectic: a Hegelian dialectic with the *Aufhebung* missing, as Williams describes it. He finds them in Ligeti's interanimations of stasis and movement, repetition and difference, which can be regarded, he argues, as a form of immanent critique; there is no *outcome,* but still we hear glimpses of the possibility of a utopian immediacy. That the critique remains immanent marks its limitations, however. In the third movement of Ligeti's Chamber Concerto, multiple intersecting and overlapping clock-like mechanical repetitions layer and cut up the otherwise fragmentary motion. The idea seems to be to signal at once the unacceptability of "the same" and the impotence of "difference." But the music refuses the vernacular; any familiar gesture is treated as worn out, a frozen aesthetic mark, in a strategy that guarantees the really worn out ideology of musical autonomy; comprehensibility functions only as an ironic opposite to the modernist norms of dissonance and irregularity. The music's bracketing of historical narrative cannot shake off the horror that results from an inability to break with the authors of the plot (from Hegel and Beethoven to Schönberg and Cage); its "contained extremism" forgoes the possibility of dialogue, to remain mired in a "non-supercessionary dialectic."[172]

Georgina Born points out that, as the negative becomes familiar, it always itself becomes repetitive. Moreover, it cannot explain the appeal of constant variation of the same. Most of all, it insists on structuring the musico-political field around a center, so that difference can only be heard as negative to a positive, rather than as difference-in-repetition — just "difference without any necessary antagonism, another form of positively constitutive identity."[173]

Even so (the argument might continue), the examples I have just discussed are all characterized by considerable compositional *finesse*, which arguably makes it easy to bestow approval. What about Deleuze's "brute repetition"? What about music that just repeats — Satie's *Vexations*, for example? Or where the change is minimal and, perhaps, governed by an apparent mechanicity — in early minimalism, for instance, or in some dance music? If we compare, say, Steve Reich's *Come Out* (1966) and Prodigy's "Everybody in the Place" (1992),[174] we find some technical features in common, in terms of the types of electronically mediated sound but also the repetition processes, built on looped chains of superimposed short riffs. (Of course, there is dissimilarity too, to do with the way difference is incorporated: Reich builds imperceptible change into the compositional system, while Prodigy cut arbitrarily from one textural matrix to another.) Is the effect likely to be an ecstatic loss of self or a state of boredom? How would one decide, and which is preferable? Reich has written about his music of that period in terms of its capacity to bring on a sort of "ecstasy" through subversion of "personality."[175] Terry Riley, another minimalist (and one whose influence can be heard in some dance music), made similar comments, as we saw earlier. The discourse around dance is full of references to childlike, oceanic states which the music is supposed to induce.

Toop distinguishes within early minimalism between the "knitting-machine repetitiveness" that he hears in Reich and Glass, and the "more expansive" quality of the "more open" works of Riley and LaMonte Young. He relates techno's "machine-age coldness" to an inhuman Fordist economy which, in its inevitable breakdown, created the urban wastelands of America's urban ghettos; and he has "serious doubts" about claims by some rave adherents that their music produces states equivalent to neoshamanistic trance. While welcoming an ecologically motivated return to "hearing the world," he argues that a music based just on observing the periodicities of nature and "ignoring the social" is "oppressive": its "rigid, formulaic exclusion of representation, drama, contrast, variety or direct reference" excludes "the wicked body, the human voice." If human discontents are painted over in the interests of "white-light bliss, then the musicians are mere functionaries, slaves to cool the brows of overheated urban info-warriors . . . The demand that sound should bow to escapist needs is a rejection of the potential implicit in music's unfolding permeability over the past hundred years."[176]

John Rahn goes further. Distinguishing between different types of musical repetition, he puts his faith in what he calls "lively" repetition, "whose telos is not given . . . but is in the process of being formed." Such repetition "is transformation . . . and all transformation rests on the possibility of repetition, of repeatable qualities and patterns . . . Sense is dependent on repetition, without which nothing can be recognized . . . This process of continual repetition . . . creatively folding a life back over its traces as it unfolds, is a source of great satisfaction . . . for without this process, without hope of telos, there would be no life. Who among us is ready to die?" How, then, can repetition be *boring*? In two ways — either through a mode of "slavery" (repetition "without final cause; nothing is happening; they have no future, no exit") or through the "wan glow of pseudo-life" produced by "repetition in the presence of a given global telos," a preestablished schema (re-presentations are here just "re-animated, a zombie or *revenant*").[177]

I myself intuitively prefer to either Reich or Prodigy work such as Abdullah Ibrahim's, about which I have written elsewhere.[178] Typically, an Ibrahim performance or recording grounds itself on a harmonic loop (often a two-bar sequence: I-IV-I$^6_4$-V, a cornerstone of the South African jazz/jive repertory, but also a favored cadential progression of composers like Mozart and Rossini), but then Signifies on this cliché of Western musical modernity, opens it up to process, repeating it as the foundation for lengthy stretches of improvisation, constantly sprouting forth new generations of melody whose ancestors we feel we have heard somewhere before. Rahn might account this no more than a "re-animation" — yet Ibrahim refuses the closure embedded in the cadential formula; closure — narrative control of difference, finding a "proper end," the presumptions of *telos* — has become literally incredible. Paradoxically, the proposal here is that it is repetition — repetition-in-and-of-difference, representing nothing but itself — that can best open up the future, freeing difference from narrative and re-presentation from the Law of the Master.

What is at stake in these differences of preference? Is it any more than a case of three anachronistic critics — Toop, Rahn, myself — refusing to give up humanistic remnants that have actually been rendered inoperable by technological, social, and epistemological changes?

******

For answers (assuming they are to be found at all) we might look again to the topology of contemporary subjectivity — perhaps to an imaginary conversation between Lacan, Derrida, and Deleuze (with interjections from others).

In *Beyond the Pleasure Principle* (1920), Freud revisited his earlier theory of repetition, having realized that the idea of blockage seems inadequate. Repetition, he now observed, appears to be associated with a pleasure of its own, or at least, when carrying unpleasurable material, it appears to have a distinctive drivelike character giving "the appearance of some 'daemonic' force at work." Freud's interpretation of the celebrated *fort-da* game, in which his grandson mimicked his mother's disappearance and return in repeated manipulations of a cotton reel, attributes the boy's pleasure to the "great cultural achievement" of instinctual renunciation; but the pleasure itself must have its source in a separate energy, which he christens the Death drive. This force — Thanatos — becomes the antagonist of the Life or sexual drives — Eros — in a redrawn psychic economy. It stands for an "inertia inherent in organic life... an urge... to restore an earlier state of things." But Eros and Thanatos are intertwined in their operations from the beginning ("the aim of all life is death" yet Eros, through reproduction, ensures a "potential immortality"), and both are at work in the operation of the pleasure-principle, for instance in the repeating rhythm (excitation/discharge) of coitus.[179]

Derrida's critique seizes on the idea of repetition's cultural work. Deconstructing Freud's role (as *father* both of the boy's mother and of psychoanalysis) in his description of the *fort-da* game, Derrida argues that Freud is himself playing *fort-da* in his text: "The writing of a *fort/da* is always a *fort/da*, and the PP [Pleasure Principle] and *its* death drive are to be sought in the exhausting of this abyss."[180] But, while this has the merit of exposing the attempted closure in Freud's analysis (which is grounded in the biologistic remnant in his theory), it tends to bypass repetition's psychic *threat*, which means that, for Freud, repetition is both a cultural mechanism and a figure of potential dissolution. Lacan is alive to both sides of this vacillation.

He stresses the *fort-da*'s ludic character. The reel is an *objet a*, a small piece of the subject, which functions as a mark of alienation but also a first step into the symbolic sphere, the shortest possible narrative. As Lacan puts it, "the game of the cotton-reel is the subject's answer to what the mother's absence has created on the frontier of his domain — the edge of his cradle — namely a *ditch*, around which one can only play at jumping... The activity as a whole symbolizes... the repetition of the mother's departure as cause of a *Spaltung* [split] in the subject — overcome by the alternating game, *fort-da*... whose aim, in its alternation, is simply that of being the *fort* of a *da*, and the *da* of a *fort*..."[181] But repetition is part of a complex — repetition/remembering — which as a whole is concerned with recall up to a limit — the limit of the Real, defined as "that which always comes back to the same place" and which the subject can therefore never meet up with. Repetition here is an *act* (Lacan uses Freud's term *Vorstellungsrepräsentanz*, interpreting this as what stands in for a [missing] representation, but we can also translate it as the performance [precisely the *act*] of a representation that has gone missing): an act of *resistance*, with a symbolic structure created through its relation to the Real. What looms is an "endless repetition... that... reveals the radical vacillation of the subject"; "if the... subject can practice this game..., it is precisely because he does not practice it at all, for no subject can grasp this radical articulation" — which is why the object, the *objet a*, is required. In the interplay between "the encounter with the real" and "the return, the coming-back, the insistence of the signs," we find the structure of repetition; and while this rhythm marks the "pulsative function" of the unconscious as such, its insistence puts "reality" "in abeyance."[182]

It is an insistence of "something that occurs... as if by chance." Rejecting any biologism, Lacan sees repetition in this sense not as "a return of need... directed towards consumption placed at the service of appetite" but as what "demands the new." The strictest, most ritualized of repetitions proceeds on the basis that the presence (re-presentation) of sameness is impossible, and that at the same time mimetic variance (the play of memory and thought) conceals "the true secret of the ludic, namely the most radical diversity constituted by repetition in itself."[183] Repetition on this account appears as "empty," as an "emptying out" — or rather, as perpetually eluding the attempts of representation to "fill" it. One can see how music itself, especially "at the limit" of its repetitive tendencies, can be regarded as an (the?) exemplary *fort-da,* and hence how a Lacanian account such as Guy Rosolato's can see musical repetition, at that limit, as a source of subjective rupture: "rhythmic obstinacy, reiteration to excess... obliterates organization and variety: a hypnotic abandon to this energy is also the expression of an energy" for "if the drive can be considered like the metaphoric play of music, the latter becomes the metaphoric representation of the drive substituted for the subject."[184]

There is much in Lacan's analysis with which both Derrida and Deleuze would agree. For Derrida, repetition is the principle of the Symbolic — of signification — itself.

> For us there is no word, nor in general a sign, which is not constituted by the possibility of repeating itself. A sign which does not repeat itself, which is not already divided by repetition in its first time, is not a sign.

> The signifying referral must therefore be ideal — and ideality is but the assured power of repetition — in order to refer to the same thing each time. This is why Being is the key word of eternal repetition, the victory of God and Death over life.[185]

While this account has general force, we might again regard music as possessing a certain privilege. As Paul de Man puts it:

> On the one hand, music is condemned to exist always as a moment, as a persistently frustrated intent toward meaning; on the other hand, this very frustration prevents it from remaining within the moment. Musical signs are unable to coincide: their dynamics are always oriented toward the future of their repetition, never toward the consonance of their simultaneity. Even the potential harmony of the single sound, *à l'unisson*, has to spread itself out into a pattern of successive repetitions; considered as a musical sign, the sound is in fact the melody of its potential repetition.[186]

But, as with Lacan, repetition is here a mode of difference — or rather, *différance*: that endless division, spacing, deferral in the signifier that makes of repetition both a condition of meaning and an impossibility: "This iterability (*iter*... comes from *itara, other* in Sanskrit, and everything that follows may be read as the exploitation of the logic which links repetition to alterity) structures the mark of writing itself, and does so moreover for no matter what type of writing..."[187]

The effects for subjectivity are radical (and are related, we might say, to the relations of Eros and Thanatos, and the economy of *plaisir* and *jouissance*):

> The same, precisely, is *différance*... as the displaced and equivocal passage of one different thing to another... And on the basis of this unfolding of the same as *différance*, we see announced the sameness of *différance* and repetition in the eternal return... How are we to think simultaneously, on the one hand, *différance* as the economic detour which, in the element of the same, always aims at coming back to the pleasure or the presence that has been deferred by (conscious or unconscious) calculation, and, on the other hand, *différance* as the relation to an impossible presence, as expenditure without reserve, as the irreparable loss of presence, the irreversible usage of energy, that is, as the death instinct, and as the entirely other relationship that apparently interrupts every economy?[188]

Derrida's answer — that we cannot because the unconscious always defers itself — is hard to deny, but also points towards the debilitating aspect of deconstruction itself, which exposes the false closures underpinning the traditions of Western thought but leaves the matter there, with no more than a shrug, at the same time refusing to take seriously the necessity (but also the manifest impossibility) of deconstructing itself. Caught in an opposition (as negation of all systems of presence), which contradicts his own anti-foundationalist premises, Derrida (like Barthes, Kristeva, and so many poststructuralists) looks for a (partial) alternative only towards the transgressive, decentering refusal of repetition found in certain strands of avant-garde art.

We can pursue this a bit further through Derrida's own figure of the *hymen*, which for him functions as a double-sided organ, "at once screen and mirror,"[189] situated between the two aspects of mimesis in Western thought: on the one hand, a movement of memory (an unveiling of truth, a representation), on the other, a movement of simulation (a copy whose original has always been displaced, a repetition). Standing for both veil and closeness, deferral and promise of consummation, the hymen is precisely an *entre*; the mirror is never passed through, the veil never torn. But in the real social world, such passages *must* take place (*entre* doubles as *entrée*) — the Name-of-the-Father must be installed, the mirror must give back its object, castration must circulate, the Real will have its effects in its encounters with the Symbolic, Lacan's *points de capiton* must button down the circling drive at particular moments of meaning (however provisional) — if subjectivity is to function.

Thus, for example, the mirror function — remembering that all sorts of objects in the world can have this function — both repeatedly "plates" the subject within its identity-ideals and threatens their (mis)representations with dissolution in the territory of the Other. As we saw earlier, the Imaginary and the Symbolic twist and articulate each other in this operation, in a process reaching right back to maternal, indeed fetal territory, where the echoing dialogues of the acoustic mirror rule. The hymen opens the way to this territory — to the womb, "the mimetic organ par excellence, mysteriously underscoring in the submerged and constant body of the mother the dual meaning of reproduction as birthing and reproduction as replication."[190] Even the genetic inheritance repeats genealogical narratives that go back to the dawn of human culture (and still inform the kinship dramas of the psychic theater). But plenitude has always already gone. Just as, Taussig points out, the many origin myths that deploy the maternal body as the source of mimesis do so with immense variety — so that, "in bringing together . . . copying, reproduction, and origin, as so many moments of the mimetic, what we find is not only matching and duplication but also slippage which, once slipped into, skids wildly"[191] — so musical repetitions not only switch us into these circuits, as on one level the "voice of the body" (the organs wired up, e.g., to cyborgian dance-beats), but also, as they do so, cannot help but invoke our bodily *mis*-identifications, the ego's imaginings represented to itself. And as Lacan reminds us, "The ego is structured exactly like a symptom. At the heart of the subject, it is only a privileged symptom, the human symptom *par excellence*, the mental illness of man."[192]

In some ways this picture is reminiscent of Kristeva's *chora*, a "rhythmic space," "nourishing and maternal," anterior to the Symbolic and to representation, where the maternal body mediates the play of primary drive-processes in an "infinitely repeated separability":

> The death drive is transversal to identity and tends to disperse "narcissisms" . . . But at the same time and conversely, narcissism and pleasure are only temporary positions from which the death drive blazes new paths. Narcissism and pleasure are therefore inveiglings and realizations of the death drive. The semiotic *chora*, converting drive discharges into stases, can be thought of both as a delaying of the death drive and as a possible realization of this drive, which tends to return to a homeostatic state.[193]

But Kristeva not only genders the semiotic/symbolic dichotomy, fixing the heterosexual hierarchy as inescapable, but also installs what arguably are variable tendencies into an ontologically fixed developmental sequence. In a sense, Deleuze carries this ontologizing tendency still further.

As we saw earlier, Deleuze distinguishes between "radical" repetition — which is repetition *of* difference — and repetition-of-the-same, and between both of these and representation. He agrees with Freud that the source of repetition is to be found in the death instinct, which is a "transcendental principle"; but he thinks Freud wrong to associate this with the "brute repetition" of "inanimate matter." Rather, "repetition is truly that which disguises itself in constituting itself, that which constitutes itself only by disguising itself," and "natural phenomena are produced in a free state, where any inference is possible among the vast cycles of resemblance: in this sense, everything reacts on everything else, and everything resembles everything else," in "a swarm of differences, a pluralism of free, wild or untamed differences." Hence "Eros and Thanatos are distinguished in that Eros must be repeated, can be lived only through repetition, whereas Thanatos . . . is that which gives repetition to Eros, that which submits Eros to repetition."[194] This works itself out in the relationship of the two repetition types, for "brute repetition," repetition-of-the-same, forms a sort of casing within which true repetition is hidden: "One is a static repetition, the other is dynamic. One results from the work, but the other is like the 'evolution' of a bodily movement."[195]

This is a picture that might be assimilated to the Lacanian *fort-da* (as well as Taussig's mimetic "chain of sympathy," which yokes together *copy* and *contact*, infusing the mimetic relationship with the "breath" of bodily participation), except that Deleuze seems to embed it in a theory of things as they really are:

in an ontological principle which, so he tells us, distributes difference between the two types of repetition, "a repetition of *ungrounding* on which depend both that which enchains and that which liberates, that which dies and that which lives within repetition"; for "The domain of laws must be understood, but always on the basis of a Nature and a Spirit superior to their own laws, which weave their repetitions in the depth of the earth and of the heart, where laws do not yet exist."[196] But how could this "ungrounding" ontology be grounded epistemologically? And how could any human being survive, as a subject in any recognizable sense, in Deleuze's world of wild difference, which, surely, constitutes itself as phantasy: language's other, constructed, in language, by a subject on this side of representation?

What Lacan, Derrida, and Deleuze share is an opening up of the field of the Other — installing repetition somehow *there* — by so to speak clipping the wings of the over-mighty subject and his systems of representation. Utopically, this might suggest the kind of "electricity" of which Taussig writes:

> an ac/dc pattern of rapid oscillations of difference... a magnificent excessiveness over and beyond the fact that mimesis implies alterity as its flip-side. The full effect occurs when the necessary impossibility is attained, when mimesis becomes alterity. Then and only then can spirit and matter, history and nature, flow into each others' otherness.[197]

But, bearing in mind the historical moment — one of *crisis* for the subject — circumspection is in order. Would digital looping be likely to follow Taussig's program, or to present itself as a limit case of Deleuze's repetition-of-the-same? Warhol's defense of boredom comes to mind:

> I've been quoted a lot as saying "I like boring things." Well I said it and I meant it. But that doesn't mean I'm not bored by them... if I'm going to sit and watch the same thing I saw the night before, I don't want it to be essentially the same — I want it to be exactly the same. Because the more you look at the same exact thing, the more the meaning goes away, and the better and emptier you feel.[198]

Can the meaning go away? Derrida is content (nay, forced) to leave the question hanging, within the insubstantial traces — "memory" without origin — of the archi-writing. Deleuze, reversing Freud, declares that "We are not... healed by simple anamnesis, any more than we are made ill by amnesia. Here as elsewhere, becoming conscious counts for little... It is in repetition and by repetition that Forgetting becomes a positive power while the unconscious becomes a positive and superior unconscious."[199]

What is conspicuously absent in both Derrida and Deleuze is anything fulfilling the function of the Lacanian Real — the rock of the Real, as Žižek likes to call it, the hard kernel that resists both the Imaginary and the Symbolic but, at the same time, is their source. The Real, Lacan suggests, is raw matter, unbounded and undifferentiated; yet as subjectivity emerges, erecting a barrier against the Real that is essential to normality, what is thereby excluded leaves a void which will be covered by the subject's *objets a* (gaze, voice, cotton reel — perhaps repetition as such), but which nevertheless cannot prevent the Real's subversive effects in the unconscious. The later Lacan, increasingly emphasizing the role of the Real, insists on its structural relation to the Symbolic both outside and inside the subject, suggesting that successful inter-subjective communication depends on an "answer of the real" (a "bit of the real" inside the subject guaranteeing its consistency). This "bit" equates to the subject's specific mode of *jouissance*: a meaningless "That," more than the subject itself (its *sinthome* — as distinct from its *symptom*, which by contrast operates in the Symbolic), an "open wound of nature," forever liable to throw up a proliferating "undergrowth of enjoyment."[200]

Is this what repetition brings back from its encounters with the Real — that element of "blindness" which guarantees "good faith"; a blindness dependent on pure chance, that is, on whether there is an "answer," as signifier binds on to a bit of real-stuff — a glob of memory, a floating image, a tremor of mimesis? Certainly Žižek's analyses (of films, Rothko paintings, fictions by Ruth Rendell and Patricia Highsmith) bring out the repetitive loops through which the Real — "that which returns as the same" — emerges. He also suggests that the *sinthome* manifests itself in *rendu*: moments (typically of acousmatic sound, detached from any visible source) that render reality directly, demonstrating the "lack of a lack" (that is, of castration) in the Real. However, this suggestion seems to run counter to the overall thrust of the Lacanian project, which found its final figure of the indissolubility of the three orders of the subject in the topology of the Borromean Knot. Indeed, in Žižek's specific analyses, mediated meanings of the *rendu* — interpretations of the representations that have apparently gone missing — instantly flood in.[201]

In fact, the Lacanian theorization of this knot is, one might suppose, exactly what explains its relevance to the crisis of the contemporary subject, a subject which, for all the efforts of deconstructionists, has not yet effaced itself. As Taussig argues, in response to the theoretical advances of constructionism, subjectivity needs "more invention," not less.[202] We have seen that the moment of this crisis is historically contingent, as are the modes of its inscription within reconfigured understandings of repetition. Jacques Attali has expertly explained the undermining of the system of representation in the late-nineteenth and early-twentieth centuries (though his dystopian picture of its replacement, repetition, is less convincing, outdoing even Adorno in negative focus); but this sweeps far wider than the two spheres he explores — music and political economy — covering literature and the visual arts as well as social and political formations, with effects that are still recognizable today. (Where, after all, would we look to find modes of democratic representation adequate to the locuses of power in the ruthless neoliberal global economy of the early twenty-first century?) Yet arguably mimesis did not disappear so much as change its orientation and significance. The *fort-da* game could not have been recognized earlier; Freud's description marks a moment when mimesis begins to move towards a new self-understanding. Warhol's boredom is inscribed in and by an "I" who represents it for others. Toop's "wicked body" and "human voice" beg the question of their discursive construction. Rahn's "lively" repetition, "creatively folding a life back over its traces," and my own "improvisation, constantly sprouting forth new generations of melody, whose ancestors we feel we have heard somewhere before" betray historical debts to rich tropological complexes ("undergrowths of enjoyment"?) that demand redemption.

Subjectivity, to be sure, bathes itself in a sea of objects, circuits of simulation and mimicry, all speaking back, switching on and off, and requiring new modes of perception (Benjamin's assimilation by *habit*?).[203] But, far from rendering memory anachronistic, this re-sites it in a hugely expanded sociotechnological extimacy offering the Real a global, multi-media archive (of both material subject-markers — voices of the "people," the "low," the "black," etc. — and object-images) to play with. The Real becomes at once more pressing (how could it not in an era of secularization, vernacularization, and totalitarianism, barbaric or apparently benevolent) and more elusive (hiding within the simulations of hyperreality). The repetition embodied in each encounter brings its inevitable miss providing the space where, precisely, consciousness continues to arise, memory to spiral, mimesis to explode… If quantum theory, with its uncanny metaphors of doubling, finally succeeds in reanimating nature for modernity, this space is where quanta must nevertheless turn into qualia.[204]

As we saw earlier (pages 103–4), the structure of *jouissance* is double, not only subverting Law but also supporting it: "while this may not make for two Gods, nor does it make for one alone,"[205] and, like object-voice, repetition qua *objet a* possesses an orientation that is radically undecideable. As many of Žižek's examples demonstrate, for example, repetition structuring "mindless enjoyment" (that is, marking the passages of the *sinthome*) can underpin fetishistic, totalitarian authority as well as invoking the absolute alterity of the presymbolic object.[206] If nature is to be reanimated, therefore, it will not be through a simple return to primitive "sympathetic magic"; more plausible, as Taussig suggests, is a future transformation of what has become mimetic magic's most characteristic modern form: fetishism of the commodity (a transformation foreseen, he argues, by Marx).[207] The contemporary musical object, circulating magic in the forms of infinitely multiplying images and sound-loops, now accumulates copies and variants in such fast and complex ways as to suggest it might approach a point where, paradoxically, it would begin to *de*accumulate abstract exchange value, revealing the concrete life within (perhaps illicit copying and sampling — ghostly premonition of a future gift economy? — already point in this direction); once again, repetition, its "emptiness" laid bare, would so to speak undo itself, even while at its most powerful. What would it take for fetish-power to metamorphose into a figure standing in for this apparently missing (but in reality, spectral) representation? — a *Vorstellungsrepräsentanz* which might take on the shape of Benjamin's Angel of History, commodities endlessly emptying themselves out around her feet, whose very dumbness can be read as a plea to humanity to take up its proper burden. Here, beyond a *politics of the standard(izing) moment* proposed earlier, we glimpse its necessary supplement — necessary but always incomplete, as that Derridean term implies — namely a *politics of performance,* of *performance-work*:[208] one that, in the course of articulating and rearticulating such (infinitely repeating) moments, would seek not just to follow Freud's interpretative approach to the economy of "dream-work" and reveal their "attachments" (*Repräsentanzen*) but actively to attach and reattach these, to enact them (perform them out); to fill their "emptiness" with meaning, memory and life, their "blindness" with (yes) sound; and in so doing to pursue the essential if finally impossible goal of representing repetition to itself and thus, perhaps, bursting the carapace of fetishism.

(In Lieu of a) Final Refrain

At this point, musical evidence seems both obligatory and, in practice, no more than a token: any attempt at comprehensive documentation would betray the very density and mobility of the field — a representation too far! A sample, then (appropriately): a few moments in the life of one out of this cybeast's many tentacles, and not in the form of argument so much as a tentative stream of feeling.[209]

Example 4.2

and so on . . . : the outline of the famous drum riff from "Funky Drummer," recorded by James Brown and the James Brown Orchestra in 1970 (the drums by Clyde Stubblefield). James Brown, the most sampled musician in the world (so we are told); "Funky Drummer," perhaps his most sampled figure (FD from now on). It's *everywhere*, then, almost literally; yet in rhythmic outline how many legions of ancestors, going back to who knows when or where — so a multivalent simulacrum, and how!

On the record, the drum riff only emerges after lengthy preparation: a long first part with a syncopated horn riff decorating a I-IV alternation enriched by several jazzy/bluesy instrumental solos (Abdullah Ibrahim would like this: Brown certainly does judging by his vocal effects, urging, responding, commenting); then cut to a second part over a different chord sequence (I-Vm-ish, but the voicing is obscure, the harmonic dimension fading from the attention) with rhythm riffs on guitar and organ, over and over: setting up — the drum break. So here's the famous loop, solo, then the band quietly reenters, mostly guitar, very rhythmic, but still drum and bass foregrounded, with Brown making sure we understand: "Ain't it funky? ain't it funky? ain't it funky?" . . . and fade.

Now we can feel the journey we have traveled: starting out in a rich field of repetitions, soulful, embroidered, gradually narrowing the focus, until we end up with (almost) just rhythm, the nitty-gritty, the gesturing body, the wiring emerging, the cyborg connecting . . . From a field to a *spot* — inside or outside? — a self-mirroring acoustic trace pointing towards the impossible object-gaze. There's a blindness here, an emptiness, pulling us in towards the "radical diversity" concealed in the increasing identity of the repetitions. But hang on: *empty*? (Brown wouldn't think so. Just as his innovations, in shifting Soul towards Funk, towards a more pared-down rhythmic emphasis, brought criticisms of reductiveness, so, in a mirror-image, Brown himself criticized appropriations of his style in disco: "Disco is a very small part of funk. It's the end of the song, the repetitious part, like a vamp. The difference is that in funk you dig into a groove, you don't stay on the surface. Disco stayed on the surface."[210] Surface, depth, digging — what does he mean? Digging into a groove, ground, grave . . . ? What's down there — a *sinthome*?)

So, is this really empty? "Funky Drummer": think of "drumming," think of "funky," and the rich discursive fields that open. Here, from whichever direction you look at it, is a *black body*; and the journeys of the sample take that imagery with them. They also carry James Brown's ego, as his concerns over widespread pilfering of his records in disco and then hip-hop demonstrate. Authorship in question; riffs as mirror-images sustaining ego. But what about Stubblefield, what about the other guys in the band? Brown, notorious for authoritarian control (you can hear it on the records, as he orders, organizes, directs out loud), his bands disputatious, forever subject to splitting; so, on another level, ego splits (clones?) musically, as bits of Brown circulate around the media-archive, most graphically in the myriad samples of his vocal effects (screams, grunts) — vocalized body-parts or *objets a* available to all. For a price. As an exemplary black capitalist, Brown — considered as fetish-object (visual, gestural, sonic) — focuses for us the industry work going into extracting maximum exchange-value from his repetitions (his record company has an entire department devoted to tracing license infringements relating to Brown). As a black body, though, the weight of a certain inversion can be felt: might this fetish, emerging from within the bowels of capitalism, have the smell of a force that could have the wind of history in its sails?[211]

Particularly strong sightings of Brown samples appear in the early waves of hip-hop, thus enveloping them in the debates around rap politics (black power, misogyny, gangsta violence, parody consumerism). Public Enemy, for example, deploy the FD loop (admittedly, in slightly different variants) in several tracks, including "Bring the Noise," "Terminator X to the Edge of Panic," and "Rebel without a Pause." (Public Enemy: first record, "Public Enemy Number 1" (c. 1984), the title also of a 1972 release by Brown. But the hip-hop soundscape here, with voice collage, aggressive scratching, and synthesizer noise, no longer funks but *screams*.) FD also finds its way into dance music, for instance, the Stone Roses' 1989 acid-house hit, "Fool's Gold" — speeded up, with added bongos and tambourines, plus "spaced out" vocal and wah-wah guitar (1960s psychedelia with a hint of Motown passed through the filter of ecstasy-driven Manchester hedonism); from where it was in turn sampled for Future Sound of London's 1992 hit, "Papua New Guinea" (so-called "intelligent house": the loop is placed in a context of vaguely exotic, vaguely other-worldly electronic collage; how to feel at one with the planet).

But in broad terms — thinking of the FD loop as parent of a whole family of rhythms — it's pervasive in dance music vocabularies; many commercial presets — for example, the Propellerheads's Reason software — although they cannot include the actual FD break for obvious reasons, contain an emulation of it.[212] The genre of Drum 'n' Bass as a whole can be heard as a hyper-speed mutant (again evading simple imitation for financial reasons). For a different way to out-maneuver the cycle of capital accumulation, listen to electronica artist John Oswald's *Plunderphonics* CD (1989). On "black" and "brown" [*sic*], Brown samples, including FD, are splintered into fragments, mixed into high-speed collages with guest appearances too from Prince, Charlie Parker, and others; a sort of modernism, but one that reassembles tradition (here "black music") rather than dynamiting it, denaturing grooves, so to speak, before good-naturedly replacing them on the archive shelves, but at the same time evacuating a sense of authorial center just as it deconstructs the Brown ego. Oswald sought no copyright permissions, offered the disc free, with encouragement to copy, but was forced to withdraw it under threat of legal action; you can still download it from the Web, however.[213]

Meanwhile (1990), Sinéad O'Connor was recording "I Was Stretched on Your Grave": drum track constructed entirely from the FD sample; dub-reggae bass from Jah Wobble; newly composed vocal melody very much in an Anglo-Irish tradition (formally that old AABA, with its "discursive repetition," summoning memories of Tin Pan Alley ballads but also of long lineages of folk tunes, probably influenced by earlier bourgeois variants of this structure),[214] sung with decorative melismata very much in an Irish style (but also blue notes) — then giving way to a fiddle melody, with more closely focused repetitive figures, the various repetitive schemas (drums, bass, fiddle) then proceeding in parallel and in cultural diversity not to a fade but an arbitrary cut finish. A track full of references, then, exploding with memory traces, outlining one might say the shape of a black-Irish Atlantic; and full too of historical depth: the source of the lyric is a twelfth-century Gaelic poem, and in the mysterious narrative the protagonist (who is she?) grieves for someone (who?) on a grave that is also implicitly a bed in a text full of nature references ("I smell of the earth"). Knowledge of O'Connor's fraught negotiations around religion, gender, nation, and maternity might color our feeling that the FD groove, along with the deep dub bass, is pulling us through the hymen of the grave, while the angelically pure vocal floats soul-like above and the dancing fiddle reminds us of what has been lost. Eros and Thanatos, in a somber but somehow restful *jouissance*.[215]

And so the mimetic spiral goes on. And all the examples I have picked out, one might say — playing with difference as they do — seem to position themselves in a field constructed against a most pressing absence; which I hear as the *reductio* of the hardcore techno beat, machine-tooled out of the four-beat framework of funk and disco, originating in the *Bladerunner* wastelands of post-industrial Detroit, matured in turn-of-the-century European nihilistic hedonism. Here we find an uncanny alliance (which is at the same time a shift) between James Brown's "The One" (its significance both sociopolitical — everybody together — and musical — on the first beat of the four) and the late Lacan's "*Y a de l'Un*" — a one "which is not one-among-others" but "precisely the One of *jouis-sense*, of the signifier not yet enchained but still floating freely," the *sinthome*, "nucleus of an enjoyment that simultaneously attracts and repels us." Entrance via the *Abfahrt* — which "in German techno slang means immediate abandon, the inescapable command of the music, the brutal violence" of pounding beat plus industrial noise: "Submission as the realm of freedom, in which one breathes, dances, works, lives and loves to the beat, and in which one becomes a slave to the rhythm."[216] But, listen again to "Everybody in the Place." Long stretches of four-four techno kick drum, certainly. Submit? To sameness? Or to a deferral hinting at a diversity then elaborated by the rich surrounding polyrhythmic layers, the sectional cuts ushering in material we have heard before but not quite like this....?

This radical interpretative uncertainty has the feel of collective fantasy into which the individual listener intrudes. Has this whole discussion perhaps been a dream? If so, how should we read it, what would it mean to "go through," to "traverse" the fantasy? More specifically, how would we identify the missing *Repräsentanz* of this *Vorstellung*? What ghostly representation lies hiding, threatening to return? Mediator between "reality" and the Real, repetition is both subjectivity's greatest support — its mimetic screen — and the ground of its self-questioning. In our time of crisis, what manner of subject might be emerging from this vacillation?

CHAPTER 5

The Real Thing?

The Specter of Authenticity

"Rock 'n' roll was real, everything else was unreal... You recognize something in it which is true, like all true art." John Lennon's *cri de coeur* says something about the 1960s of course, and, more broadly, about certain strands in popular music culture developing out of rock 'n' roll; but his language has much deeper historical roots. Here is Henry David Thoreau, writing in 1854:

> Let us settle ourselves, and work and wedge our feet downward through the mud and slush of opinion, and prejudice, and tradition, and delusion, and appearance... till we come to a hard bottom and rocks in place, which we can call *reality*, and say, This is, and no mistake... Be it life or death, we crave only reality. If we are really dying, let us hear the rattle in our throats and feel cold in the extremities; if we are alive, let us go about our business.[1]

The idea of the rock of reality would no doubt summon a different interpretation from Žižek than was Thoreau's intention (I will return to this), just as the suggestion of a death-or-life-drive antinomy would interest psychoanalytically inflected criticism generally (the drives too, as always, will return). But the genealogy goes back as well as forward. Thoreau — his withdrawal to Nature and his civil disobedience alike built on opposition to both consumerism and slavery and, overall, on a characteristic individualism of the unfettered self — appealed to many twentieth-century counter-culturalists, at the same time as calling up legacies of earlier Romantic subjectivities, of Enlightenment quests for genuine rather than false knowledge — and, indeed, of an insistent concern with the troubling relationship between "reality" and "truth" going back to ancient philosophy.[2]

If this is the background to Lennon's rhetoric, it is worth picking up his key terms and applying them to concluding moments in previous chapters. If it is the case, then, that "the postcolonial fetters have been weakened," revealing new fractures and hybridities, what is it exactly that is uncovered, "beyond the mask," and in what sense is it real? If "passive 'beings' low in the gender, racial and class hierarchies have begun to find voices," demanding of us "the intelligent analysis of the differences on offer," how can we *know* which voice is true? If the nexus of differences and repetitions in the music mediate "between 'reality' and the Real," what manner of subjectivities are conjured up, "what would be the missing *Repräsentanz* of this *Vorstellung*"? Or are popular music's reality-effects — its "collective fantasy" — no more than illusion, devoid of aesthetic veracity, epistemological credibility, and political efficacy alike?

It is not as if truth is a foreign concept here. Within popular music culture, the discourse of authenticity is familiar. Typically, it is taken to mark out the genuine from the counterfeit, the honest from the false, the original from the copy, roots from surface — oppositions which in turn often map on to further distinctions: feeling as against pretence, acoustic as against electric, subculture as against mainstream, people as against industry, and so on. As Simon Frith has shown,[3] the roots of this discourse lie in the bourgeois appropriation of folk music, constructed as an Other to commercial pop, and in debates over jazz and blues, where, in a similar fashion, "authentic" strands were promoted over allegedly ersatz derivatives. On the level of scholarship — within cultural studies, subcultural theory, ethnic studies, and ethnomusicology — the music features within grids of distinction and political position clearly indebted to older discourses in folkloristics, anthropology, and Romantic *Kulturkritik*. Throughout this history, both people and music were involved: authentic music came from (perhaps even generated) authentic communities; the bogus stuff was produced by cynics and aimed at (perhaps even created) consumers mired in false consciousness — dope for dupes.

Feedback between the spheres of interpretation on the one hand, and music production and dissemination on the other is common. Indeed, we might say, in Foucauldian fashion, that music industry institutional practices — distinctions between record labels, music genres, radio channels, sales charts, and within the discourses of artist and repertoire departments and popular music journalism — make it almost impossible to think outside the terms of this problematic. We can see John Lennon as an exemplary figure. Almost as soon as the Beatles became successful, Lennon was beginning to formulate his creative ambitions along the lines of a search for the "real me" — "John Lennon" as opposed to "John Beatle," to use his own labels, an authentic self as opposed to the commodified, fetishized icon that he came to loath. Musically, culturally, politically, this search was articulated through a set of oppositions in which a series of Others was lined up against the inauthentic. As we have seen, this started with rock 'n' roll, but this was already being linked to a larger topography of difference, because rock 'n' roll, in Lennon's words, "is primitive enough and has no bullshit... Go to the jungle and they have the rhythm and it goes throughout the world and it's as simple as that." So "rock and roll was real, everything else was unreal. And the thing about rock and roll, good rock and roll, whatever good means, is that it's real, and realism gets through to you despite yourself. You recognize something in it which is true, like all true art. Whatever art is, readers, OK? If it's real, it's simple usually, and if it's simple, it's true, something like that."

Subsequently, in Lennon's musical trajectory, the search took in singer–songwriter honesty and psychedelic visions, avant-garde iconoclasm and conceptual art, transcendental meditation and primal scream therapy, political anthems and politicized happenings, hymns to feminism and to black pride. The search for the real Lennon, it would seem, could only proceed through the cultural peripheries — through the Other. In a familiar figuration, these Others were conceived as attractively unreflective — models of *action*, in the face of over-intellectualized sophistication: the blues, for example, is better [than jazz] "Because it's real, it's not perverted or thought about, it's not a concept, it is a chair, not a design for a chair, or a better chair, or a bigger chair, or a chair with leather or with design... It is the first chair. It is a chair for sitting on, not chairs for looking at or being appreciated. You sit on that music." This simplicity, this cult of origin ("the first chair"), is then linked, intriguingly, to the music's aesthetic challenge, its modernity: "'Tutti Frutti' or 'Long Tall Sally' is pretty avant-garde."[4]

Lennon's 1970 album with the Plastic Ono Band[5] stands as a highpoint in the articulation of this dialogue between self and other, inside and outside. Consider, for example, his song "God," which is actually, in a fairly direct way, *about* authenticity. The lyric lists a collection of authorities and myths, including religious icons (Jesus, the Buddha, the Bible, the I-Ching), secular leaders (kings, Kennedy, Hitler) and even rock musicians (Elvis, Zimmerman — i.e., Bob Dylan) whose god-claims are punctured, climaxing in: "the Beatles." "The dream is over" (a statement with both a historical reference — the '60s counterculture that is finished — and an epistemological claim); and what is left? "Me," sings Lennon: the self — or the loved self: "Yoko and me"; "and that's reality." But this inner reality is secured through a musical reference outwards to a "real" music — a self-grounding through the Other, here a black-Other speaking in the signifiers of Gospelized Soul, marked most obviously by the slow twelve-to-the-bar groove, Billy Preston's piano phrasing, and Lennon's vocal melismas, but going right down to the "Stand by Me" chord-sequence used as the main harmonic foundation for the verse.[6]

The negotiation of authenticity implied by the inner/outer dialogue is paralleled rhetorically, negation (the lengthy recital: "I don't believe in..." — all the discredited authorities) giving way, at the crucial hinge of the song's form, to affirmation: "I just believe in me," sung unaccompanied, close to the mike, previous reverb stripped away — the voice (this tells us) of a real person, singing direct to us.[7] Yet the shift is hardly straightforward. For his refusal of external authority, Lennon chooses a musical style more resonant with religious connotations than any other in twentieth-century popular music; and his quasi-liturgical recitation of anathemas (to a repeated phrase of a "marking time" character, moving harmonically between VI and IV, a giant interrupted cadence, building tension) resolves into revelation, if only of the self: stand by *me* indeed. As part of this process, the voice quality shifts too, at the same point, from throat-tearing rock 'n' roll shout (the old religion?) to Lennon's '70s soul-ballad voice, the voice of "Imagine," silky, fluid, intimate, domestic. Which me, then?

In "Working Class Hero," from the same album, the vocal ambivalence is harder to tease out, though no less suggestive. The complex of authority and authenticity is again split. It is represented here partly by those oppressive forces — bitterly rejected by Lennon — destroying working-class culture and hopes, and partly, if only by hesitant implication, by the class itself and its demand for leadership, a role that — Lennon's experience equally bitterly tells him — can only offer false status: "A working class hero is something to be," as he puts it, with a purposeful ambiguity; "If you want to be a hero, just follow me." In this song the musical style draws from that same Zimmerman whose authority had been rejected in "God," a style that, originating with Woody Guthrie, had been pulled by folk-revivalists and leftist radicals into one that could (they hoped) speak for [*sic*] the workers. In Lennon's song, ambivalence surrounding lyric shifters (who are "I," "me," "we," "they"?) is paralleled by the way that the forbidding vocal tone (the tone of patriarchal laborism?) threatens from time to time to fracture, exposing the "feminine" voice of Yoko Ono's domestic-to-be.[8]

In the fractures of these songs — no less than in the protective self-deprecation of Lennon's contemporaneous comments ("whatever good means...whatever art is...") — we can hear, better perhaps than in any other music of the period, the incipient crisis of the authenticity concept. The album, if read as an implied response to the Beatles phenomenon and beyond that to the '60s more broadly, can also act as a pointer towards the historical force-field constituting this period, framed on the one hand by the Cuban missile crisis of 1962, when instrumentalized Reason, projecting the authority of the hegemonic Self on to the level of state paranoia, came close to destroying the whole human species, and on the other hand by the "events" of 1968 and their aftermath, when subversions and reconfigurations of Western

Reason — proposed, co-opted, neutralized, marginalized — ended up initiating the decisive turn towards the formations of narcissism and consumer capitalism — the self obsessively cultivated but also privatized — within which we still find ourselves. Within vernacular philosophy, derivatives of existentialism and of situationism were strong — representing moves of the self inward into *angst* and outward into absurdist action — and both were influential on Lennon. But in the intellectual wings, currents of poststructuralist thought were poised, against a backdrop of despair over political failure, to carry Western thought towards the problematic of relativism so familiar today.

Here (that is, when we reach today) we encounter a striking disjunction. Despite the passage of some pop music styles since the 1970s through various aesthetics of irony and self-deconstruction, the discourse of authenticity within the music culture still holds much of its critical primacy, as dismissive response to turn-of-the-century "manufactured pop" and "corporate hegemony" makes clear. And who is to say that this stubbornness does not reflect a continuing (if often unacknowledged) quotidian adherence, throughout social practice, to the claims of intuitive judgment? Yet within the academy, and, at the level of considered argument, among the intelligentsia more widely, this perspective has become an embarrassment. According to Georgina Born and David Hesmondhalgh, authenticity is a concept that "has been consigned to the intellectual dustheap,"[9] outmoded in a culture ruled by the simulacrum, an epistemological regime run through by anti-foundationalism, and a politics governed by pragmatism, at a moment marked, we are told, by the "end of history." The Czech "velvet revolution," focused on Václav Havel's attempt to bind together artistic and ethical commitments to truth, looked increasingly like a last gasp as, after 1989, in an Americanized world, the stakes were reduced to a crude antinomy of power — with or against? — in which the hegemonic authority's attempts to hide its instrumentalism, whether in political, economic, or cultural arenas, floundered between flimsy and disingenuous. Just at the moment when "speaking truth to power" could scarcely be more necessary, the intellectual tools to guide and justify this have gone missing.

Or are they actually right there, but in hiding, struggling for a footing? For, in an irony of world-historical proportions, the intellectual collapse of authenticity concepts has coincided with its opposite on the level of the political economy: a phase, unprecedented in its reach and force, in which an irrational fundamentalism has imposed itself across the planet, the norms of neo-liberal capitalism once again given the status of natural law but now with the backing too of divine authority — "one market under God."[10] Here the political weakness of anti-foundationalist views is as striking as their moral necessity. "Difference" is certainly everywhere in the people's musics, which, however, are also inextricably positioned within structures maintained and manipulated by monolithic corporate power (well practiced, of course, in the profitable exploitation of difference). Understanding how the trope of authenticity works within this culture demands that we tease out an understanding of its commodification, at a moment when the project of the self so clearly enunciated in Lennon's therapeutic trajectory has largely devolved upon a subject that struggles to define itself beyond the function of consumption: discourses of empowerment through work, and through the ever-growing consumption work makes possible, increasingly drive each other; "selling yourself" brands individuals with, precisely, a self, which their purchase of (musical and other) brands at the same time guarantees.

Staying, for now, at the level of intuition, though, authenticity does continue, apparently, to do its job. The commitment of the White Stripes strikes a chord. The Dixie Chicks stand up to threats generated by their opposition to the Iraq invasion, while Steve Earle goes further and releases "John Walker's Blues," a sympathetic portrait of the American Taliban recruit. Ms Dynamite and Dizzee Rascal rap, not for bling and big bucks, but for community, reality, and mutual respect, and it seems right. Mike Skinner (The Streets) sings from, precisely, there — a romanticism that is supposed to have been discredited — while punk bands such as The Others put on impromptu "guerrilla gigs" actually *on* the streets (perhaps including their anthemic song, "This is for the Poor"), the purpose of which is precisely to outflank music industry commodification. Israeli jazz musician, Gilad Atzmon, with Palestinian singer Reem Kelani, aims his outrageous post-orientalist hybrids at Ariel Sharon's fundamentalism: who giggles? Back in the Anglo-American pond, the youthful Joss Stone has an extraordinary success in the United States with an album of covers drawn from a repertory that provides the touchstone of authenticity for many (as it did, apparently, for Lennon) — African-American soul — and is nominated for the British Mercury Music Prize. (Subsequently, her first hit single is "Fell in Love with a Boy" by the White Stripes.) Yet with Stone the doubts immediately appear as well. Can a white seventeen-year old from Devon really sing black? Can she, so young, "own" such songs of experience and pain? Is covering not a confession of creative inadequacy — of inauthenticity? What would happen if she were to win a MOBO (Music of Black Origin) award?[11]

With the other cases listed here too (and many more that could have been), we are driven to ask if the authenticity-effects we see are somehow just mystifications, or manifestations of nostalgia or solipsism. I want to ask whether the idea of authenticity can be, if not rehabilitated, at least refitted in a way appropriate to a supposedly postmodern age, in which the apparatus of Western Reason is in disarray, and all notions of origin, foundation, absolute truth have become suspect. But in doing this we also need to ask where this concept came from — to sketch in a genealogy, that is, an excavation of the historically specific institutional and discursive passages whereby authenticity was molded into an ethical and cultural, even disciplinary force.

This might seem to raise the issue of *ideology*. Except that, for deconstructionists and poststructuralists alike, ideology subsides into the epistemologically weaker sphere of discourse. Foucault, for example, conceives power, the solvent of knowledge, as simply everywhere, an inescapable horizon of evaluation. But the truth-claims inherent in the historically formulated concept of authenticity invite us to at least consider the arbitrariness or alternatively the normativity of values. Although we could decide to just follow Foucault's lead and assign such issues to the machinery of an entirely contingent discursive regime, unless we also follow him in the illogicality of supposing that his figure of "so-called man" can simply choose to cancel himself, we shall need to take the historical *Telos* of the authenticity problematic (i.e., its utopian ambition) seriously. Cancellation could take place only from a position beyond that occupied by the humanistic experiment, either super- or sub-human; there seems every reason why the cyborgian hybrids we now know we always were should favor the former: as Taussig argues (see page 191), we need more invention, not less. For this reason I will be doubling back later to the question of ideology.

Part of the disjunction between vernacular and academic discourses stems from the fact that, although the idea of authenticity seems to retain much of its purchase within the popular music culture, its formulation there, and even to some extent within popular music studies and ethnomusicology, is not particularly well developed. Ask a student of pop — let alone a pop fan — what authenticity is, and almost certainly the answer will instance musical types: it is rock (rather than commercial pop), blues (rather than disco), early (rather than late) Elvis, Badly Drawn Boy (rather than well-groomed boy bands). Similarly, ethnomusicologists, though less so than used to be the case, might talk about rural rather than urbanized, traditional rather than commercial, local rather than international, indigenous rather than hybrid, and so on. Or, at a more sophisticated level, the discourse might be about the effects on musical practice of cultural imperialism, the trans-national music industry corporations, postcolonial subalternity, new border-crossing identities, etc. Generally, in any case, the focus is on music; it is *music* that is authentic (or not) — or at least, music is taken to stand metonymically for a rather inchoate sense of some wider territory. As I have already suggested, this territory needs to come more clearly into view. Allan Moore has started to engage with this requirement.[12] He argues that authenticity is not inscribed in music but *a*-scribed, *by* people; and that it is they who are authenticated (or not), not the music as such. Actually, as we have seen, it is both. We talk about people being true or false to themselves, and we worry about whether our actions, feelings, and views are really, authentically our own; and we also wonder if music expresses or represents us, or other subjects, in an honest way. And the interplay is important. Authenticity is a quality of selves and of cultures; and they construct each other: which is another way of saying that the question here is not so much what or where authenticity is, but how it is produced.

We should not expect stability, as the etymology itself confirms. The root is the Greek, *authentikos*, carrying senses of both "authority" and "original." Development of these meanings — authoritative, legally valid, reliable, factual, original, genuine, real — predominated from the Middle Ages down to the eighteenth century, with applications largely, it would seem, to aspects of the external world. From the eighteenth century they were joined by more inward-pointing usages: the authentic could become now what is truly a product of its reputed source or author; what belongs to oneself, is proper; what acts of itself, is self-originating or self-generating (and we remember that, according to some dictionaries, the root of *authentikos* itself was in *autos* (self).

This historical shift retrospectively meshed with an earlier (fifteenth-century) assimilation of the semantic territory of authenticity to that deriving from the Latin *auctor* (agent), giving us the agency associated with authorship (*auctor* is the root of "author") but also the chain, author — authority — authoritarian (joining up with the sense of authority already present in authenticity). From around the same (medieval) date, *auctor* had become confused as well with *actor*, also an agent but one who in subsequent predominant usage definitely *acts for* (another), particularly on a stage, in a way that seems opposed to the idea of self-generation, but which the concept of performativity in more recent theory would wish to situate, problematically, exactly in the midst of that idea.

The semantic trajectory of the term autonomy (etymologically "self" plus "law") followed a similar course to that of authenticity: from the external, political sphere (having one's own laws) to the subjective (having freedom of the will), which in the late eighteenth century, especially under the influence of Kant, became the prominent usage. However, an *Oxford English Dictionary* citation from 1765 could be taken to gloss this trend in an intriguing fashion, defining authenticity in the sense of self-generation as the "spontaneous or authentic motions of clockwork." It is worth recalling that *autos* means same as well as self, and this self-same stuff, product of structures (but also performances) of repetition, may on the one hand claim autonomy but on the other may be suspicious of its own sense of automaticity. Is the self-movement of cyborgs authentic or authoritarian?

We need to keep the full complexity and historicity of this formation in mind. In particular, its tendency to fall into a binary shape — subject and object, internal and external, self and other — should prompt us to be sure to hang on to both sides of the coin but also, perhaps, to query whether currency (a metaphor whose appearance here is by no means accidental, as we shall see) really does circulate in ways that ring true or false in quite that simple manner. Is this truly the best approach to our search for "the real thing"?

Two recent texts discussing examples of musical authenticity offer illuminating pointers to the implications and difficulties of such a search for reality. The Spice Girls' 1996 hit, "Wannabe,"[13] which launched them to fame, seems on one level to be about precisely this search: "I'll tell you what I really, really want"; but, along with the surrounding publicity, it also established them, among critics, as a model for the emergent phenomenon of the "manufactured band" — a cynically assembled, talent-less group of puppets: inauthentic fakes. My own previous analysis of the song focused on how dialogues between the individual girls and between the two musical modes structured into the song (rock/rap against pop; "girl power" demand against fantasy and romance; "black" against "white") dissolve into fluid similarity. Thus, I argued,

> the bridging of individual empowerment . . . and collective feeling . . . is meant to target and construct girl power's own community . . . But . . . Just as girl power offered a fake individual and collective empowerment at the extreme end of Thatcherism . . . , so "Wannabe" rehearses a simulacrum of difference, a wannabe teleology, a fantasy in which nobody fails and nothing is left out: rock and pop, romance and raunch, black (rap) and white (singalong), past and future are seamlessly stitched together.[14]

By contrast, Elizabeth Leach, having (rightly) traced the popular music authenticity trope back to the formations of nineteenth-century Romanticism and identified its post-punk inversion (when self-conscious artifice became the new authenticity), describes "Wannabe" as following up that history through a knowing play with a range of markers for authenticity itself. In particular, the various videos into which the song was inserted exploit further the "playful use of musical signs connoting traditional authenticity" in the original record — signs bridging "ordinariness" and "stardom," "talent" and "busking," "spontaneous creativity" and "artistic craft" — so that:

> manipulating the discourse of authenticity enables the Spice Girls to use a re-branded version of the post-Madonna feminism with which their audience was familiar, without the lack of originality (usually a marker for "inauthenticity") forming an obstacle to their success. [Thus] The Spice Girls' contribution to *fin-de-siècle* pop music is to upset the clarity of authenticity markers by presenting a polysemy which allows different

> collectives to construct the kind of authenticity that they require, based on the assumptions that they bring to their listening and thus to find their own meanings in the group... This polysemous presentation of authenticity enables listeners who see and enjoy the contradictions in these markers to understand that the opposition between commercialism and authenticity is itself a commercially constructed one.[15]

My use of the term *fake* was provocative, at least if it is taken to imply a putative standard of the real. It points, rather, to a certain "trick" by which a representational regime is cracked open but at once closed up again, its fictionality occluded as its apparently generous offer to articulate differences into an equivalence is at the same time gathered up into a rounded whole — precisely the definition, one might say, of a commercial brand.[16] Leach's interpretation, skillful though it is, strikes me as a postmodernist reading of a text whose own postmodernist claims are written in tabloid headlines, and as therefore acceding too readily to the terms set out by its object. All records are simulacra (the original by definition lost, even when we are given sonic indices of live performance, as is the case with "Wannabe")[17]; but here this "lie" is not only knowingly celebrated, as Leach suggests (there is no attempt to deny that the girls do not play instruments; the issue of authorship is made not to matter; different aural and visual modes of verisimilitude are montaged together), it is at the same time covered over, limited in scope and put in its place with glossy production values. Camera and microphone collude in eliding differences of subject position, so that the resulting simulacrum of community, although admittedly interpretatively malleable, amounts to little more than the multiple choices of a tick-box questionnaire, circumscribed by the overriding message, "This is all there is" (or as Margaret Thatcher used to put it, "There Is No Alternative"). By the time of the Spice Girls' successors, Girls Aloud ("discovered" in a TV talent competition), the spice of feminist noise has been frankly if punningly reduced to an acknowledgement of the need for permission.

In contrast to Leach's deconstructive approach, Terry Castle's tribute to saxophonist Art Pepper attempts to rehabilitate, albeit equally knowingly, an older mode of critical response which celebrates rather than demystifying authentic expression.[18] Like Leach, Castle is an academic, but, unlike her, she is not a musicologist; she writes as a fan, although a fan with considerable intellectual pedigree. For Castle, Pepper was "an authentic American genius"; and this quality permeated not just his music, but also his writing (she is enraptured by his autobiography, *Straight Life*, its title no doubt intended to suggest telling the story straight as well as alluding ironically to life without the heroin he found it almost impossible to leave alone) and indeed his life, bohemian to a romantic and fatal extreme — three aspects which she cannot really separate: "Like his music, Pepper's verbal style was thrilling: licentious, colloquial, and so painfully human . . . Pepper offered himself up with such astonishing vulnerability . . . In spite of the torments he suffered, Art, you would have to conclude, was blessed by life . . . [and] on account of his honesty . . . he was granted a second life . . . [for he] was also blessed by having a language. Not just one language but two. He could play and he could talk." A hero in the Romantic tradition, then.

But Castle is no *naïf*. She knows that Pepper's honesty was constructed. She quotes him describing how he "arranged" his self-image by looking in the mirror when high in order to "cancel" his older, hateful self. She knows that *Straight Life* was dictated to Pepper's partner of the time, Laurie, who by chance was an anthropologist, giving it something of the quality (and problems) of an ethnographic document. She is well aware that autobiographers, especially those as "loose and crazy in print" as Pepper, are often guilty of "distorting or embellishing the facts" (perhaps not aware enough, though: letters responding to her article pointed out that she was misguided in accepting Pepper's romantic falsification of the details of one celebrated recording session).[19] Pepper was "upfront . . . about yearning to imitate the flip, dandyish, hipster style that . . . black postwar players cultivated so effortlessly"; "what I wouldn't give," he wrote, "to just jump in and say those things." And Castle's own yearning for such naturalism — "the mortifying craving I (still) had for a certain uncensored verbal fluency" — followed his. But although she acknowledges the delusions and the clichés in Pepper's self-writing ("wet blankets everywhere will be saying, *This is all such a load of crap* . . . what a . . . self-deluding bastard Art Pepper must have been"), she insists still on her "own readerly intuition: the faith . . . that . . . it is still possible to locate some core emotional truth"; "in order to succeed at either [writing or music] you have to stop trying to disguise who you are. The veils and pretences of everyday life won't work," or as Pepper observes, "jazz musicians really only play themselves": "I've realized," she quotes him as writing, "that if you don't play *yourself* you're nothing."[20]

But which self is really at issue here? Castle identifies with Pepper, at first sexualizing their relationship through her consumption of the persona constructed in his music, writing, and photos, then assimilating his early life-story into a parallel with her own. Eventually she reveals that in a sense Pepper is standing in for her dead, seemingly psychotic stepbrother, Jeff, who was a sort of Pepper with no language to communicate his equally tortured self; Art speaks for Jeff (and therefore also for and to Terry). In the end, Castle's essay is about *her* search for honesty, and Pepper has been used as "a manikin or decoy," a "mummified icon," safely distanced by ventriloquism. His authenticity retains its value, in itself, but also functions via an appropriation/projection mechanism to mark her weariness with the hypocrisies of the

French rococo — her scholarly specialism — in favor of the "close-packed human chaos" of the present and of her own life. The contradictions in Castle's account make an easy target, but there is also a bravery in her insistence that the level of reality can be measured, even while — in a characteristic modernist gesture — real expression is always imagined as being *elsewhere*. Against this, the (equally modernist) aestheticism of one her critics — "this [Pepper's] honesty is a purely aesthetic quality. It has something to do with not sparing yourself. It has nothing to do with telling the truth" — seems to come a poor second.[21]

Leach and Castle not only represent contrasting methodological stances — the one in the intellectual swim, the other defiantly unfashionable — but also carry us a bit deeper into the layering of the authenticity problematic. There is first of all the level of the musical texts, by the Spice Girls and by Art Pepper; and in both these cases the texts are actually more than musical, being surrounded by writing and visual images. The questions at this level concern the authenticity of these texts: are they true to... (their authors, their moment, an expressive intention, a conception of truth, a political purpose, or whatever)? At a second level, there are the interpretations, by Leach, by Castle; the questions here concern *their* fidelity: are they true to their objects (which includes the question whether and how deconstruction might count as truth), and also to the authors, moment, intention, etc. of these objects? (Even when no published commentaries exist, this level is in play, for as soon as music comes into being, verbal interpretation comes with it. Indeed, to some extent interpretation comes first: commentary has always already been prepared and will immediately make its truth-to claims.) At a third level come my critiques of Leach and of Castle; the question here, of *my* fidelity — to the music, to the interpretations, to the relationships set up between them — is one for my readers, but also, to the extent that "I" can interrogate "myself" in this text, one for "me." And, of course, this process proliferates endlessly, spiraling around the circuits of repetition and representation — precisely the setting where, we may suppose, authenticity sparks into life (and fades away).[22]

Is fidelity also complicity? The question returns, like a specter haunting the gaze of all representational sciences, from older theoretical formations — the dilemmas of the ethnographic encounter, the dialogic circles troubling hermeneutics and historiography — in all cases, raising issues rooted in the problematic meetings of selves and others. But the fidelity-stakes take on a new slant with the advent of recordings, which would come to make claims to be both repositories of fidelity (to remembered performance) and objects of faith (with originary authority). The anxieties pervading the practices of ethnographic recording and the controversies surrounding records in music cultures where live performance is highly valued, such as jazz, are typical. At first glance, recording technology might seem to edit out the subject of performance or to elide it with the subject of the record text; to turn *énonciation* into *énoncé*, in a definitive freeze-up of subjectivity into iconic object. In practice, however, it is just as much the case that technological disembodiment has the effect of releasing multiple specters of *énonciation* into the textual arena, and, as we have seen in previous chapters, their potential work can actually intensify the dialogues of voices. At one extreme, the alienation of the record from an authorial subject can gear up an already existing mirror-function, enabling the listener to, as it were, insert him/herself into the imaginary role of (narcissistic) uttering subject; at the other, the record's capacity to act as a repository of socially constituted subjective memory-traces, to constitute a kind of prosthesis of imagined vocal bodies, and to act out such fantasies through technical trickery, can result in a complex fissuring of apparently coherent textual statements.[23]

If Leach and Castle are in some way complicit with their subjects (and which of us could claim total innocence in this respect?), it may be in part because they pay insufficient attention to these tensions. Leach, for instance, seems to follow the claims of polysemy apparently inscribed in a Spice Girls web of ironic subject positions, while missing the extent to which, at a higher level of technical process, the recorded texts displace a conventional gender binary on to an internally differentiated structure of femininity (powerful girls against others), which cannot in the end resist reflecting back the familiar phallogocentrically organized gaze.[24] Castle, by contrast, arguably conflates Pepper's written and musical *énoncés* into a single persona and is content to invest his account of his records — as the spontaneous (if drugged up) transcription of the insights of authentic genius — with phantasmatic power, indeed to locate herself emotionally within this process, even though this requires bracketing out both the complex negotiations of multiple positions and the intertextual social learning involved in any successful jazz performance.[25] In both cases, we can say that an over-simplification of the recording's fidelity stands metonymically for a broader problem in which authenticity is displaced from its true, and truly fraught location at the heart of the problematic of enunciation: Who speaks?

Leach is after the "subject of deconstruction" — although, as we have seen, on my account she stops short of following the process right through.[26] But in any case her analysis exposes limitations in the concept. For her, authenticity resides with the listener (she identifies a "polysemy which allows different collectives to construct the kind of authenticity that they require, based on the assumptions that they bring to their listening"); but not only does this position deny the authoriality that actually circulates around the text (the author here is certainly *not* dead), it also stops at a point where the theory itself should push it on: if "this polysemous presentation of authenticity enables listeners who see and enjoy the contradictions in these markers to understand that the opposition between commercialism and authenticity is itself a commercially constructed one," this understanding should surely generate a process with no end. Authenticity must recede for ever, in the typical deconstructive move which, through complete deterritorialization of subjectivity, evacuates the political field in favor of a view from everywhere.

Castle, on the other hand, is after the "subject of psychoanalysis" — although, arguably, she makes the classic error (in Lacanian terms) of displacing the transference process from the level of the Symbolic (Pepper clearly should function as Lacan's "subject supposed to know," of whom the analyst is the exemplary case) to that of the Imaginary, where Pepper functions as object of desire. This subject, though fragmentary, mutable, dishonest, and as much social as inner, implies acknowledgement of a situated knowledge that goes with both embodiment and a specific psychic history, a history which, if denied or disavowed, will simply return in other shapes. Castle's essay could be read as an (incomplete) attempt to "traverse the [her] fundamental fantasy"; but, if there is no more an end to this process than to that of deconstruction (just as "the emergence of the subject from the transference is…postponed *ad infinitum*"), what continues is not deconstruction but dialogue ("it is natural to analyze the transference"), which has, therefore, a specific contour and, at least potentially, an ethical point.[27]

The question now becomes how and where this process might be paused, so that some sort of authentic *agent,* one who can plausibly claim the authority to act and to interpret this action, can emerge. For Nicholas Spice:

> We've grown adept at seeing more than meets the eye, to hearing more than meets the ear. But for life to go on, for action of any kind to be possible, we have to stop the interpretative machine at some point and settle for definite meaning…Psychoanalysis is still feared…because it invites us into a world with more variables than we can cope with…So we keep sane with an idea of integrated selfhood which we derive from our experience of the dazzling individuation of other people…But beyond this, psychoanalysis does something altogether breathtaking. Out of the unworkability of its own project, and as though to upbraid us with the comfortable dishonesty of our ordinary human bonds, it fashions an image of pure trust: not trust based on the appetitive deal-making of friendship and love, but a groundless, purposeless, unjustifiable trust between two human beings holding a conversation on the edge of the abyss.[28]

What sort of trust — of fidelity — would this be? Is the price of authenticity then *insanity*? And the price of politics, musical or other: *dishonesty*, comfortable or not?

******

The existential quality of these troubling questions is impossible to grasp outside an awareness of the historical trajectory that has projected them into contemporary consciousness. As my brief archaeology of the term "authenticity" suggested, the earlier history is lengthy. It takes us back most obviously to the eighteenth century: to the Enlightenment, to Rousseau, Herder and Kant. But this moment itself has an important prehistory.

In his authoritative study,[29] Charles Taylor begins his story with the Greeks. He points out that although Plato posited a unitary model of the virtuous person against the multifaceted Homeric *psychē*, centered on an ideal of self-mastery through reasoned reflection, this did not imply a modern sense of interiority, rather the search for accord with a more general quality of Reason — the Idea of the Good. For a more radical reflexivity, betokening a first-person standpoint — a "proto-cogito," as Taylor calls it — we must wait for Augustine, whose Christianized Platonism located the presence of God within, in self-experience, as well as without, in the created universe. Augustine's move was then picked up and developed further, in the sixteenth and seventeenth centuries, by Descartes and Locke on the one hand, Montaigne on the other. Descartes in effect scientized the cogito; the self, disengaged from reality (now conceived as mechanistic extension), nevertheless has the capacity to construct more or less correct *representations* of this reality. In Locke, this disengaged self — a "punctual self" in Taylor's phrase, a self as disconnected *point* — reached a new level of mastery, reifying itself in the interests of control, both of the individual and of the world. In parallel with this trend, however, was a movement towards, not so much self-discipline, as self-exploration. For Montaigne, as reflected in his autobiographical "Essays" (themselves harking back in form to Augustine's *Confessions*), the self is mutable, incompletely known and often frightening; the interior move in this case results less in universality (e.g., some conception of human nature) than in difference.

These exemplars, particularly Cartesian rationalism and Lockean empiricism, can be taken to represent the most important foundations on which the eighteenth-century Enlightenment built its (albeit variegated) discourses of the self and its objects. At their most soothing, these discourses, against a background of apparently beneficent commerce, imperial expansion, and universal improvement, seemed to promise a harmonious civil society in which an agreed agenda of human freedom, rights, and capacities might unite inner and outer nature in a narrative of endless progress. But Rousseau, looking within, found not harmony but discord. Nature, he thought — including human nature — is intrinsically good, but culture estranges men from nature; conscience "speaks to us in the language of nature," but few hear it. Rousseau's dramatization of the depths and struggles of authentic identity, whose "inner voice," if only uncovered beneath the babble of social conditioning, is what we should be true to, strikes a recognizably modern note: "I long for the time," he wrote, "when, freed from the fetters of the body, I shall be myself, no longer torn in two, when I myself shall suffice for my own happiness." And if the original locus of this voice of nature was most clearly identified — projected, we might say — in the figure of the Noble Savage, Rousseau had nevertheless a political and educational project for rediscovering it. (We might note the counterargument of Rousseau's contemporary, Diderot, whose insistence — following Montaigne — on the constant and confusing interaction within the self of reason, desire, and fantasy "leaves us," in Richard Rorty's words, "with the need to construct a self to be true to, rather than, as Rousseau thought, the need to make an already existent self transparent to itself.")[30]

Rousseau's stress on inwardness, self-expression, and a freedom guaranteed in nature led in an obvious way to the Romantics. But this motif of autonomy was drawn upon too, in his distinctive manner, by Kant, who also defined freedom in terms of action according with man's true nature but for whom this nature lay in a quality of rational agency with universal application. Kant offered "a prospect of pure self-activity" in which such activity itself possesses autonomy, for "rational nature" — man's highest nature — "exists as an end in itself," even if many human actions are in practice "crooked."[31] The Romantics preferred to ground individuation in an expressivist conception of nature (including inner nature), in which the artist (who "is become a creator God" [Herder], a "true priest of the Highest" [Schleiermacher]) led the way in showing how "creative imagination" could reveal what lies beyond the senses, completing and transfiguring reality even as it is put before us. Yet in the work of many of the most penetrating thinkers of the early nineteenth century (Schiller, Schelling, Hegel) these two tendencies were brought together, not without tension but with a belief that this historical phase would in due course give way to a new stage in which man would return to nature in a higher synthesis (a belief that would influence the young Marx). This *Telos* was influentially articulated by Hölderlin:

> There are two ideals of our existence: one is the condition of the greatest simplicity, where our needs accord with each other, with our powers and with everything we are related to, *just through the organisation of nature*, without any action on our part. The other is a position of the highest cultivation, where this accord would come about between infinitely diversified and strengthened needs and powers, through the organisation which we are able to give to ourselves.

But it had already been anticipated in Kant: "Perfected art becomes nature again; which is the final goal of the moral destiny of the human race."[32]

The foregrounding of *art*, emerging with the mid-eighteenth century field of aesthetics, is important. For Kant, Beauty (as embodied in "fine art" — high art, as we might now call it) has moral import, for the Romantics, revelatory significance. For both, such art possesses its own autonomous quality (Kant's "purposiveness without a purpose"; Schiller's "aesthetic state," defined as one of "free play"), and its standards are of universal application: thus, just as "men work themselves gradually out of barbarity if only intentional artifices are not made to hold them in it . . . [and thus] the propensity and vocation to free thinking . . . works back upon the character of the people, who thereby stepwise become capable of managing freedom," so properly aesthetic judgments — as distinct from "barbaric" standards of taste dependent on the partiality of emotion — assert "universal" validity; such a judgment "requires the same liking from others . . . *demands* that they agree."[33]

Placed within a context of contemporaneous institutional innovation — public concerts, organs of critical discourse, conservatoires, and other educational provision — this aesthetic interlinks (though by no means in an entirely homologous manner) with the elements of a familiar constellation, elements whose aspirant universalism, seen through the optic made available by later critiques, can be identified as making up the emergent bourgeois music culture: the concept of the (score-based) musical work; the Great Man theory of production (genius, according to Kant, being "the talent (natural endowment) . . . [or] innate mental predisposition . . . through which nature gives the rules to art"); the collection of great works into a canon (for "the products of genius must also be models, i.e., they must be exemplary"); the ascription of truth-value to art; the practices of "detached," "structural," and "contemplative" listening.[34] If authenticity is to be found, it seemed, works of art, including art music, would be a key place to look.

However, the critique of this culture's universalizing claims implied by the specification "bourgeois" already raises a problem: How would this discourse deal with *difference*?[35] J. G. Herder, ethnographer, philosophical anthropologist, and early folk-song collector as well as writer and historian, was probably the first to speak (in the late eighteenth century) of cultures in the plural — ways of life distinctive of particular peoples (*Vőlker*), each valid, all incommensurate with the others. A key marker of these distinctions was language — the voice of a *Volk*. This view, indebted to Rousseau's expressivist theory of the common origin of music and language (the "voice of nature") in the articulation of feeling, would help power nineteenth-century nationalism (as Rousseau put it, "the locus of sovereignty must be a people . . . something more than a mere 'aggregation'").[36] But Herder, now looking inwards rather than outwards, also insisted that each individual person had his own way of being human: "Each human being has his own measure (*Mass*), likewise his own tuning (*Stimmung*) of all his own sensual feelings to each other."[37] Even though Herder negotiated a coherence out of such difference through a theory of empathy that looks suspiciously like a kind of appropriation strategy ("every nation, every age, every individual judges music and poetry by widely different criteria... yet the materials of art are none the less inseparably linked by empathy to the person who enjoys them... an emotion that is always purely *human*... even if the masters of the art from various eras and peoples did not wish to deny their individuality, the intellect's musical ear will still correlate them, appreciating each in its individuality and raising it to the sphere of the universal"),[38] this is still a remarkably modern model of cultural pluralism.

Herder's negotiation was clearly motivated by his dialogues with musical, poetic, linguistic, and cultural others. There was, nevertheless, a prehistory to this important moment. Indeed, the archaeology takes us back to the Age of Humanism — the period of Montaigne, for example — which was also, of course, the Age of Discovery, when emergent topoi of travel, exotic others, center and periphery, empire and colony, represent the impact of rapidly expanding cultural horizons, and at the same time, arguably, dramatize through formations of difference the uniqueness of the equally emergent Western self. From our perspective — now speeding forward from Herder's moment — such "encounters," as Philip Bohlman calls them, form the history within which, from the Age of Discovery down to the present, changing images of "world music" play out. Montaigne, for instance, as well as exploring the inner self, also wrote an essay "On Cannibals," drawing on accounts from 1578 by the missionary Jean de Lery of what Bohlman describes as "the first encounter between the musics of old and new worlds."[39] At each such moment, whether the meeting was with diasporic Africans in the Americas, with "the Orient" in Egypt, Turkey or India, or with the polyglot folk singers of Herder's expansive Europe, musical norms were challenged by encounters with difference, disrupting but also reshaping both cultural politics and musical subjectivity.[40]

Encounters were constitutive, for both cultures and subjects, and with dynamics both positive and negative (i.e., working through trajectories of both appropriation and projection) — though these poles are themselves ambivalent. But the history was not simply cumulative. As the upward curve of Western bourgeois expansion — geopolitical, economic, and also philosophical and cultural — reached a certain peak in the later eighteenth century, the pressures exerted by and on its authoring subject stiffened noticeably, one symptom being the urgent and difficult issues of representation, as these related to the Enlightenment conflicts over universality and difference. Quite apart from the obvious political content of the work, Mozart's *Die Zauberflöte*, whose lofty idealism is inseparable from its alteritous portrayal of class, race, and gender difference, speaks both to the partiality of the democratic revolutions in America and France, and to the tensions in the philosophy of Kant. (For Kant, enlightenment was available in principle to all, but in practice, at the present moment, was considered "very dangerous by the far greater portion of mankind (and by the entire fair sex)," not to mention "the great unthinking masses." Similarly, he distinguished rigorously between high art, with its cognitive and reflective element, and the merely "pleasurable," "entertaining," and "enjoyable.")[41] Nor is it surprising that at much the same time blackface performance was starting up in the United States (in a sort of inverted relation with the slavery abolition movement), or that, as much recent musicology has revealed, novel techniques for portraying subordinate or illicit gender and sexual identities were emerging (alongside the first shoots of radical feminism). Transgression, feared, policed, and indulged, would become a leitmotiv of the culture in the nineteenth century, intimately connected with the dramas of self-mastery. Rousseau's claim in the *Social Contract*: "Man is born free, and everywhere he is in chains. One man thinks himself the master of others, but remains more of a slave than they are," was worked up by Hegel into his celebrated discourse of Master and Slave, which points both inward and outward, mapping together dialectics of history, philosophy, and psychology. The background here lies in the increasingly powerful discourses of imperialism, orientalism, raciology, and sexual orthodoxy; and of class — what I have been calling the problematic of the Low-Other. Even Herder, who had a place for "light music," drew the line at street song: "The people (*Volk*) are not the mob (*Pőbel*) of the streets, who never sing or compose but shriek and mutilate,"[42] initiating a discourse that traversed the nineteenth century (at the end of which, in 1899, the composer Hubert Parry inaugurated the English Folk Song Society with a comparison between "true folk-songs" — "treasures of humanity ... with no sham, no got-up glitter, and no vulgarity" — and the "insidious ... repulsive ... rowdyism ... the musical slang" of the "common popular songs of the day"), and still energized debates over the value of Tin Pan Alley song, jazz, and rock in the twentieth.[43]

The authenticity trope was deeply embedded in this problematic, for at the heart of the issue lay the question of what a subject true to itself would be like and how such subjectivity would be represented musically. And this question was historically variable, which is to say that it is inseparable from, and an engine of, the on-going drama of modernity itself. The critique of too-easy authenticities is thus part of a wider critique of Enlightenment certainties with which we have become so familiar. Could the concepts of autonomy, self-direction, and the unitary self withstand the impact of Darwin, Marx, and Freud? How would the belief in endless progress respond to Schopenhaurian pessimism? Could the locus of civilization in a specific geo-historical space, represented in canons of self-validating texts, survive attacks from feminism, the objects of colonialism, and other peripheries? Above all, perhaps, what would happen to notions of the objectivity and universality of reason after Nietzsche's devastating critique?

If the nineteenth century, looked at from this point of view, presents itself as the period when a certain conception of the authentic subject puffed itself up to the point of incipient explosion, the twentieth appears as the time when the resulting crisis, addressed in differing ways by positivism, critical Marxism, structuralism and poststructuralism, feminism, postcolonial critique, phenomenology, and existentialism, demanded to be worked through, or at least on. By the middle of the century, the good ship authenticity — under threat not only from philosophical critiques but also the baleful lessons of fascism and Stalinism — seemed definitely holed below the water; and yet so pressing, still, appeared its demands, as God, reason, progress lay dead or at least unconscious, that in another way it steamed ahead even faster, into the turbulence of the '60s, folk revivals, rock purism, punk nihilism, and world beat just some of its musical manifestations. Taylor points out that, while the negative side of Nietzsche's critique had by the second half of the century achieved a pervasive influence, the positive aspect — his "yea-saying" will to, despite everything, affirm — was less acknowledged (even though, he suggests, the most coruscating critics of the Enlightenment — Foucault, Derrida — do themselves nevertheless maintain an implicit ground for evaluation: in their case, "freedom").[44] This reluctance is understandable, given the Nazi misuse of Nietzschian discourse — but can we hear an echo in the voices of the Beatles, known throughout Europe as the "Yeh-Yeh-Yehs"? The most important of the early postcolonial critics, Franz Fanon, still spoke this language too: "Let us try to create the whole man, whom Europe has been incapable of bringing to triumphant birth."[45]

This is the language of "culture." But, as Fanon's appeal implies, the idea of culture — the idealized figure of the human subject, made whole by its own creative work — originated within the Enlightenment project itself. This idea, in its distinctive modern sense, arose with Herder and the German Romantics in response to the perceived failures or banality of actual civilization. It would go on to assume a range of forms, variously emphasizing moral demands, aesthetic standards, or anthropological plurality — or indeed, subversive difference, from the Parisian *bohèmes* to the Black Atlantic as counterculture of modernity. But in whatever guise, culture is conceived as *critical*; it answers to lack. From this point of view, authenticity fills out the absence that culture anxiously diagnoses.

But culture is also a response to the secularizing tendencies of the society, to the disenchantment of the world. In this sense it is normative: it tells us what we *should* think or feel or do, what art *should* be like, how society *should* work, when divine revelation is unavailable and unreflexive tradition seems insufficient. From this point of view, authenticity is precisely *un*critical: it offers itself as *natural* (which is, of course, one of the standard definitions of ideology). Squeezed forth in this way, authenticity appears as, so to speak, a byproduct of secular culture's political ambition and the drama of the modern subject's self-construction that accompanies this. Its materials can be both introjected (as superego commands and modes of signification assimilated from elsewhere) and projected (on to desirable others); but they coexist or struggle there with their opposites, forever drawing the distinctions by which we live, by which cultural values — in music, for instance — have their effects. For the young Marx, "Man... practically and theoretically makes the species... History is the true natural history of man";[46] that is, we become human when we get to work on nature, enter history, and produce ourselves as the human species. But this historical movement (self-production, self-knowledge) comes with a cost: the sense of alienation.[47] As Terry Eagleton puts it, culture in all its guises is a response to "the failure of culture as actual civilization — as the grand narrative of human self-development... It [culture] is itself the illness to which it proposes a cure."[48] Authenticity, as a name for value-claims positioned within the alteritously structured social and psychological fields of action where the cultural body is formed, is a symptom of this disease.

The crisis of authenticity thus represents both a cultural crisis - which needless to say runs through all forms of signifying practice, including music — and also a crisis of subjectivity. In both spheres, foundations seem to have been knocked away — foundations of, on the one hand, subjective agency and schemas of representation (of both self and others), and, on the other hand, of cultural legitimacy and power. And yet, the language of authenticity, and many of the assumptions on which it was built, refuse to die. This legacy is still clear in the texts by Leach and Castle, embroiled as they are in debates around identity, community, art, and politics which thread their way through the entire history of twentieth-century popular music, with roots going back still further — ultimately, indeed, to the familiar Enlightenment tropes of expression, authorship, and truth.

As I pointed out at the start of this chapter, discourses associated with folk music, blues, and jazz played a key role in this history, establishing terms that were subsequently taken over in rock and other late twentieth-century genres such as rap and world music. Intriguingly, in all these cases, authenticity has been negotiated not only in terms of the *Völkisch* but also those of Art: the construction of canons has vied with the celebration of ways of life, Kant with Herder, in the validation of what is to count in the negotiation of distinction. This is a negotiation, moreover, that projects forth for us one image of modernity itself, together with its critiques — a point that would not be lost on those modernists (from Stravinsky to Picasso, Bartók to Brancusi) whose re-imaginings of the dialogues of mastery with its slave-others, canonic tradition with neo-primitivism, left the legacy of artistic autonomy at once more forthcoming and more anxious about its own heteronomous underpinnings.

It may clarify our understanding of this history to look at a case from the earlier twentieth century, when many of the patterns of argument were set. An obvious choice would be blues, appropriated early to the criteria of folk music yet performed, especially in the 1920s, by singers who seemed to many to possess artistic stature; and at the same time, always at risk — or so it seemed to some — of dilution into an inauthentic commercial derivative.[49] Fans during the 1960s blues boom, when the genre was helping to power the new rock music and seemed to run over with exotic otherness, were familiar with its paradigmatic folk status; yet many of them also knew that the female singers of the twenties had performed something called "classic blues." Why "classic"? In the first study of this subgenre,[50] Derek Stewart-Baxter expresses bewilderment, pointing out that the eclecticism of the blues repertoire makes this epithet highly inappropriate. The best he can do is to quote critic George Melly, who had written in 1969: "At their best the 'classic' blues represent that fragile but precious moment in a developing art form when feeling and technique are in perfect accord, and in Bessie Smith the times provided the necessary genius to give this moment concrete expression."[51] But where does this term, classic blues, come from? How does it relate to blues, as folk, and what has this relationship to say about the interplay of tradition, modernity, and authenticity?

Classic blues seem to have been first named by Rudi Blesh in his 1946 book, *Shining Trumpets*, which might plausibly claim to be the first general history of jazz.[52] Blesh, an art critic and jazz writer, was a leading ideologue in the "traditional jazz" revival movement that had begun in the late 1930s, and, as such, a combatant in the "jazz wars" which consumed many critics and fans for the next decade or so. This conflict was fought over the territories of, precisely, tradition, authenticity, and modernity, and between three battalions, associated with New Orleans jazz, swing, and bebop, respectively. The politics went wider than those of the music culture itself (although there was no neat map of attachments): most revivalists were romantic leftists, often with close associations with protagonists in the contemporary folk music revival such as the Lomaxes.[53]

Blesh's history of blues puts forward a three-stage model. The first stage, beginning around 1870, is "archaic" or "preclassic." It is identified retrospectively — it is "prior to the fullest development of the form" — and the discourse here clearly derives from folklore traditions. This is "authentic blues in every sense," and the songs are "stark and simple," with a "simple and heartfelt style" and a "lack of self-consciousness and a naturalness almost naïve"; Blesh's imagery ("sprouting," "seedlings," "vitality") is all natural. In the second stage, starting about 1900, "classic" blues emerge. Here Blesh's writing moves towards an art discourse. The songs "still have spiritual simplicity, greatness, and natural poetry, to which are added the clarity and power with which greater singers infuse the form"; this brings "growth in expressive means and in communicated power," while the introduction of more complex band polyphony, including players such as Louis Armstrong, results in "an integrated musical whole." From around 1920, "postclassic" blues appear, and Blesh's discourse adopts elements from mass culture critique. He divides this stage into three types: "contemporary" (associated with male singers influenced by the classic women but turning their style into cliché: there is a "falling off in power but not in sincerity"); "decadent" ("an empty recital of dead history" characterized by "spurious elements of insincerity . . . grasping for easy success in the pornographic, the theatrical, or the merely clever"); and "eclectic" ("no more than a sophisticated revival," as represented in the work of Billie Holiday, an "agreeable but enervated voice" peddling "uncreatively repeated mannerisms").[54]

Of course, three-part historical schemas with this rise-and-fall shape are familiar, in music historiography and more widely. Perhaps the first examples come from narrative constructions (including to some extent contemporary self-understandings) of the Classical Greco-Roman period itself; but more recently what would become the conventional mold for music historiography of the canon (Preclassical, Classical, Romantic) offered a telling model. As is commonly the case, Blesh's rhetoric is organicist: "From the endless, seemingly aimless movement and mutation of cells, from the ceaseless counterpoint of natural forces, there sometimes emerges a form that endures, a generic form . . . the sonnet, the sonata, and the blues."[55] This has the effect of naturalizing the teleology: the second stage, the classic, becomes generic — the *Ur*-form.

Blesh's blues schema is embedded within a broader but similar model for jazz. Folk progenitors, from "memories of life on the Dark Continent" to "archaic street jazz," led, through a process of "selective assimilation," to a second phase beginning in the 1890s and marked by "stabilization" — "a more developed, classic stage," localized in New Orleans and centered on a genealogy running from Buddy Bolden through Freddie Keppard, Bunk Johnson, and King Oliver to Louis Armstrong and Jelly Roll Morton. But "a quick degeneration occurred when this extraordinarily pure and vital music was transplanted, killing a part, deforming some of the growth, yet not striking quite to the roots"; leading, nonetheless, to "dilution and deformation," setting in from about 1920 and marked by processes of commercialization, individualization, and Europeanization. These developments were especially clear in swing, some parts of which were "a completely devitalized, sentimental hodgepodge," others, "nihilistic, cynically destructive, reactionary . . . devoted to the superinducement of a wholly unnatural excitement" — both tendencies to be found in the work of the "decadent . . . reactionary," Ellington.[56]

So the question now becomes, why "classic jazz"? Although this trope has become part of a familiar jazz discourse (jazz as America's classical music, with variable understandings of what the canon comprises, albeit always with an essentializing movement), it was fairly recent coinage in 1946. Alain Locke used the phrase "classic jazz" in his 1936 book, *The Negro and His Music*, but in reference to "symphonic jazz," that is music such as Paul Whiteman's, influenced by classical music — a trend that Blesh abhorred. But Locke did refer to a "golden age" of jazz, in the mid-twenties, before artistry had been swamped by commerce. A similar paradigm is operative in writings from the 1930s and early 1940s by Hughes Panassié, Winthrop Sargeant, Charles Edward Smith, and Frederic Ramsey — and even earlier in the first critical writings of Roger Pryor Dodge, dating from the mid-1920s.[57] For some of these writers — and certainly for Blesh — this usage clearly represented a revivalist need to mark out the qualities of that golden age as against those of contemporary swing.

Blesh himself links the blues and jazz schemas. "The blues, developed," he writes, "could provide a nucleus for New Orleans jazz"; Ma Rainey and Bessie Smith fused them "into a single greater form." This relationship is gendered in an interesting (and very familiar) way, for "the blues of the classic period . . . are pre-eminently the music of Negro women as jazz is the lusty music of Negro men. The one seems to embody healing, maternal sympathy, which gestates and conserves life; the other externalizes the vitality and power of male procreativeness." And it is also mediated by race: true blues and jazz are alike "Negroid" — "To this day, with rare exceptions, only New Orleans Negroes can play real jazz"; "it is the survival . . . of an informing spirit, a racial consciousness," and Blesh systematically charts jazz "deformation" in terms of the baleful effects of white influence. This combination is enough to see off Bix Beiderbecke: "real jazz is a strong music. Objectively considered, Beiderbecke's playing is weak and weakness characterized his life." Similarly, "hybridity" (a term that Blesh worries at throughout the book, and that we can surely read here as in part a euphemism for miscegenation) is a source of "decadence"; "[classic] jazz is no musical hybrid" but "a miracle of musical synthesis" (which is presumably why it is classic), whereas swing is a "hybridized popular music rather than a fine-art form . . . Negroid only in surface manner." This is enough to dismiss Ellington's "ridiculous and pretentious hybridizing," and poor Billie Holiday was lost because she "recorded with effete Negroes like . . . Teddy Wilson."[58]

So far, Blesh's perspective seems to fit unproblematically into the terms of a long-established aesthetic position. It comes essentially from the traditions of *Kultur,* with a distinct leftist orientation (the attempt to ground the music in an African aesthetic of collective participation gives it the status, or at least potential, of a "people's art"),[59] and its racist and phallocentric elements are not unfamiliar. But Blesh's construct is complex and unstable, marked by a number of discursive binaries which are always in danger of contradicting one another.

Völkisch language, with its characteristic tropes of "spontaneity" and "nature," is everywhere: "a music, improvised freely ... sounds a summons to free, communal, creative living"; blues is such a music, for "the real blues grew spontaneously" and, as a "naturally evolved form ... [,] sophistication acts like a blight upon them"; "the music seems like a phenomenon of nature itself." And these qualities are linked to ethnicity: "primitivism at each crucial point saves jazz." Against this discourse, however, runs a language of classicism, with tropes of "discipline," "purity," and "control," where the talk is of "a generic art form ... universal in expressive scope ... essentially an abstraction, a flexible framework built up of directives and limitations ... no longer haphazard and capricious ... but formulated in a cogent and fateful repetition, a ceaseless but controlled variation," with "purity of line and ... rigid avoidance of the decorative." In effect the discourse of authenticity — urgently, even anxiously present throughout the book — faces two ways. The attempt to bridge them is not ignoble: a chance observation of a folk dance-song in the South sets Blesh to musing that "music which comes directly from the people need never thread its way from Elysian fields, down Olympic slopes to the Thessalonian plains. It begins on the plains, stays on the plains, and high above the rural revelry the high sounds float, to settle like dew on the parched heavenly groves." But it *is* awkward: "while jazz is a fine art, it has not been recognized as such ... and has been forced to subsist as a folk art." But does this tension not bring out what is always a condition of constructions of the classic, at least in post-Enlightenment societies: that it depends on the folk as its other side? Each authenticity speaks in the name of a reified and naturalized transcendental subject (the people; *Kultur*) in a binary dance of otherness. And the gendering and racializing of this maneuver — the so-called oedipalized construction of the canon — has had deep-rooted effects that are still with us.[60]

The folk/classic conflict spins off a related binary, concerning authoriality. Blues and jazz are people's arts and the stress on participation means that authorship has to be in one sense collective. Thus in classic jazz "the group becomes a single individual in the throes of creation," and Blesh criticizes Louis Armstrong in particular for, after 1926, becoming an individualist. At the same time, though, the story is told in terms of the deeds of Great Men: it "centers around a comparatively few great figures"; "in New Orleans ... the history of jazz is written in biography. As it moved to Chicago ... its story is still that of men of genius who worked together," so that "a personal style becomes definitive in a whole music." Blesh's way round this contradiction is to suggest that the individual, notably the lead trumpet player, stands *symbolically* for the whole front-line, or even the whole band. (Oh, the stresses and strains of bourgeois subjectivity!)[61]

Which exclamation might lead us to the "class" hidden in "classic." Blesh wants classic to be a conceptual not a stylistic term, so that classic blues and jazz are seen as aesthetically *equivalent* to classical music, not as influenced by it. But he constantly slides towards more specific comparisons, which make upwardly mobile claims. The relationship of blues to jazz is similar to the way that "European music of the latter half of the eighteenth century developed from the earlier dance suite"; he compares the "pregnant grandeur" of the blues to that of Beethoven's Fifth Symphony; and, most bizarrely of all, suggests that in classic blues "the piano or guitar may occasionally reach the equality of importance with the voice that the piano attains in Beethoven's violin sonatas." The viewpoint here is that of a liberal élite — and sure enough, black musicians turned out mostly to betray his patronage.

It is possible that this problem had its origins in Blesh's knowledge of ragtime (his pioneering book on the subject, coauthored with Harriet Janis, appeared in 1950).[62] Here, once again, he wanted to stress that the "classic ragtime" of Scott Joplin and a few others was classic in its own way (starting with a folk genre, "gifted composers…carried the music to a level that can only be termed classical," but this just meant that the music was "highly articulated and developed along ragtime's own proper lines"); yet at the same time he was deeply impressed by Joplin's own "seriousness" and artistic ambition, and by his insistence on notational precision and discipline. In this case he found the "classicizing" discourse in the music culture itself — in titles of pieces, sheet music advertisements, and surrounding commentary — where, however, claims to quality ("high class rag") were thoroughly mixed up with more specific attempts to accumulate cultural capital ("We have advertised these as classic rags… They have lifted ragtime from its low estate and lined it up with Beethoven and Bach": advertisement by John Stark in *Rag Time Review* [1915]). Joplin's alliance with (white) publisher, John Stark, clearly marks what is anyway apparent, that his project was part of the contemporary movement of black self-improvement (whose legacy was there in the Harlem Renaissance, with its ambivalent attitudes to low-class musics). For Blesh, this relationship reveals a cross-racial "mirrorlike correspondence" (he notes their palindromic initials: SJ-JS), with Stark the "alter ego of a Negro genius"; and this transposes to another level the fact that Stark himself was already "two men in one: the pioneer and the man of the new cities, the farmer with folk music in his veins and the new man of culture with opera in his head." This trajectory took concrete form in the drive to *publish*, to textualize the vicissitudes of performance (for musical scores, after all, also reflect back the interpellative mirror-strategies of [self-] authoring); and this drive took a pronounced pedagogic (disciplinary) shape in Joplin's *School of Ragtime — Six Exercises for Piano* (1908), in which an uncompromising Preface ("That all publications masquerading under the name of ragtime are not the genuine article will be better known when these exercises are studied. That real ragtime of the higher class is rather difficult to play is a painful truth...") introduces a welter of fierce instructions with the individual pieces (the music is to be "played as it is written," "giving each note its proper time and... scrupulously observing the ties"; "never play ragtime fast"; those "prone to vamp" are enjoined to avoid "careless or imperfect rendering" in order "to complete the sense intended").[63]

For Stark — and probably for Joplin, too — these scruples went along with opposition to the crass (as distinct from old-fashioned, gentlemanly) commercialism of Tin Pan Alley.[64] Blesh shared this view too. Classic jazz, he wrote, "was a fine art transcending its surroundings" but then brought low by "the dry rot of commercialization"; this "cheapening and deteriorative force" produced "increasing banality," "a product that can be put together by hacks, ...profitably sold to the people" and "unobtrusively substituted for what the people already wanted and had," demanding "aural activity devoted to neurotic excitement and the cliché."[65] The language will be familiar to readers of Adorno's (roughly contemporary) mass-culture critique; and it roots Blesh's folk/classic ambivalence in an established modernist position.

Which brings us to a final binary conflict: in tension with blues/jazz classicism is Blesh's insistence that they are also modern. As a revivalist, he "wanted to take it [jazz] back to 1926, when it had reached its highest point and then stopped... It was modern then — when it captivated yet thwarted a Milhaud and a Stravinsky; it is modern still." By contrast, swing "sacrifices the truly modern tendencies of polyphonic jazz." He compares jazz's "free-melodic" technique, its "improvised polyphony," to medieval and baroque music and to twentieth-century neoclassicism, all of which stand against the "harmonic-chromatic process" typical of the nineteenth century.[66] But where does this leave its classicism?

The answer lies in the way that Blesh's three-stage historical schema[67] is overlaid with two binaries: a quarrel of ancients and moderns, together with a quarrel within the modern that sets modernism against commercial mass culture. But he has the really modern as also ancient, going back, via the "folk," to Africa — an act of political utopianism (or fantasy) which only works by freezing the contradictions, and through an authoriality trick: conflating the multiple voices (individual/collective; transcendent/vernacular; low/high) into a single teleologically confident narration, orchestrating the various binaries so that they can turn difference into a self-sustaining circle of representations. Is this the classic classicizing move — the way this particular authenticity-work works?

In the second edition of *Shining Trumpets* (1958), Blesh added a Postscript. Now he regrets the jazz revival's conservatism. It should have built, organically, on its peak moment, not rested as an "anachronism." Drawing on his still active ethnic distinctions, he now legitimates bebop, and funky post-bop (Blakey, Rollins), and even soul (Ray Charles), and rock 'n' roll (Elvis) because they "go back," back to "drum-rhythms," "cries," "wailing" — to *blues*: "jazz is a fine art that sprang from a people... it will not cease being a folk art... Its people will not give it up." But this is still to reduce blues/jazz modernism to a single narrative — to *synthesis*, rather than hybridity: "It has its own primitive sources — which have always been the real elements of its modernness. Its Gabon masks are built in. The blues are such a mask... like the tragic mask of Greek drama..., the face of reality. The true likeness of the race, for the individual to wear."[68]

Blesh would surely have regarded Bessie Smith's version of "St. Louis Blues" — a tune certainly assembled out of folk elements, as his own attack on Handy's "fatherhood" points out, but accompanied now by expressionistic twists and turns from Louis Armstrong's cornet, and set in some dusty tin church by Fred Longshaw's harmonium — as classic: a definitive mask whose tragic cast is at once statuesque and raw.[69] Yet in blues — the blues that is always already modern — the voice is always seeking to speak round the edges of the mask (which is precisely what Armstrong's cornet does). What happens, then, when Cab Calloway — as I believe — rips the mask away from Smith?[70] In his "cubist" version, what emerges is: more masks, more voices — an authenticity not destroyed but dismantled, its shards unsure how to authenticate their own voice, yet with a modernity beyond all classicizing.

Placing Blesh in this way suggests how a sense of the combination of under- and over-determinations in his account can open up the authenticity problematic in its actual historical development to more subtle scrutiny, at the same time as it points back to the discursive beginnings of the art/folk/mass nexus at the turn of the eighteenth and nineteenth centuries, and forward to subsequent extrapolations from the terms of his argument in discourses around rock, rap, and world music.[71] Three interlinked territories of debate emerge especially strongly from thinking about Blesh's book. First, there is the issue of the self or subject; can we still say there is a self to be true to, and what might be the nature of this subject? (To think about Armstrong or Ellington as coherent musical subjects immediately makes clear the extent of Blesh's problem here.) Second, we might ask how and where such a subject is to be found in musical texts and practices; what is the nature of creative agency, and what, now, can be the status of authoriality? (We saw how confused Blesh becomes on this question.) And third, there is the problem of how this author-subject is to be identified; what is the nature of the dialogue, the encounter, between the subject-in-music and its interlocutors (us — as readers, listeners, speakers back)? (Blesh drew on anthropology, written historical sources, interviews, and recordings, and the results appear, mostly but not exclusively in his voice, in the form of words, discussions of musical performances, and transcriptions into staff notation; the question how historical and ethnographic others are to be represented is famously difficult.) It is to these three territories of debate that I turn in initiating the final section of this chapter.

******

Charles Taylor followed up his historical study of the "sources of the self" with *The Ethics of Authenticity*, a more polemical work on the plight of selfhood in the late twentieth century and one of the more impressive philosophical attempts to rescue authenticity from its apparent fate.[72] His focus is on precisely the mutation I have outlined: the self has seemingly shrunk, its supports weakened or discredited, but at the same time its response, from within its smaller, inward-looking world, has often been to shout its demands all the louder. For Taylor, this narcissism describes one of the effects of the "soft relativism" into which the *topos* of the authentic self has now so often sunk, accompanied by privatization of the subject and the shrinking of the scope of agency in the face of systemic "iron-cage" instrumentalism. His answer to this decline is: conversation — or to use his term, dialogics. He insists that outside of dialogue with significant others, no sense of a real me can have meaning. Difference only registers against a "horizon" of existing values, and authenticity thus demands, as a condition of existence, reference to schemas located beyond the isolated self. Identity depends on recognition, and oppression can be defined as recognition denied.

This account of identity has enough in common with Lacan's to justify comparison — the roots of both lie in Hegel, via Heidigger — but Taylor lacks Lacan's tragic sense of what is foreclosed and imposed in these negotiations; both social antagonism and the unconscious are relative absentees in his theory. He does respond to poststructuralist critiques by — paradoxically but plausibly enough — aligning the poetic, rhetorical qualities of the Nietzschean legacy with the same source in Romantic aesthetics — the will to self-creation — as also generated the authenticity paradigm, which they have been used to deconstruct. Hence, he suggests, the denial of foundations inevitably becomes itself a foundation — unending "free play" — a point virtually accepted in the late Foucault's emphasis on the aesthetic cultivation of the self (but less clearly acknowledged by Derrida). But, by so to speak eliding Dionysus with Prometheus, Taylor arguably underplays the *fictive* and *phantasmatic* quality of the poststructuralist self: the constant canceling which renders the subject "as if," forever lost, incomplete, or elsewhere. Similarly, his heroic strategy to break the bars of the iron cage, through re-harnessing instrumental reason to moral choices open to (dialogically constructed) real agents in the service of concrete political projects, is on one level inspiring but falls short of the necessary acknowledgement of the possible effects of the prison state itself on the very structures of self-understanding and self-construction. Something important is missing: self and other, subject and society, are made to ground each other, and the movements of authenticity articulate that process; but the point of leverage from which the entire picture comes into view — the larger field of articulation that is undoubtedly implied — is present only through its absence.

If the fully constituted, let alone the self-constitutive subject is at issue, what can we say about the statements to which its name is attached? Roland Barthes's celebrated answer is clear: The author is dead; the meaning of texts — of songs, let us say — is the creation of the reader (the listener).[73] Like all binary inversions, this simply transfers authority rather than upsetting the order within which it operates. More productive has been Foucault's historically oriented account of author-functions. Like Barthes, Foucault cuts the link between text and biographically substantiated individual. His aim, however, is not to destroy the author but to disclose the changing modes of his or her construction, as a figure with particular discursive properties, within both a body of "works" and particular social conditions of existence (e.g., the commodity status of these works). In taking account of the full range of discursive practices within which authorship operates, he comes up to the point where the modes of existence of the subject as such appear: "It is a matter of depriving the subject (or its substitute) of its role as originator, and of analyzing the subject as a variable and complex function of discourse."[74] In songs, such functioning is complex and variable indeed — although, if we substitute for the concept of origination that of instantiation, this suggests immediately that the possibility of the former has been too quickly foreclosed. Foucault foresees the end of the author-function — "discourses . . . would then develop in the anonymity of a murmur" — a prophecy paralleled in some excited claims about the production of music within a culture of digital sampling; but even here, so far at least, new forms of author-function continue to circulate.[75]

These functions are spoken (enunciated, uttered: *voiced*) as well as inscribed. Taking advantage of the dialogical space this distinction opens up, Kaja Silverman has intriguingly pursued the issue of authorship in film in a way that insistently foregrounds the vital question (vital for music, too): Who speaks?[76] Although she hardly refers to Foucault, Silverman's argument is congruent with his. Subject-positions and identifications, associated with characters or with the operations of the camera, are constructed in the film discourse, and, if sufficiently coherent, produce an "author-inside-the-text," which then projects for us the sense of a (nonbiographical) "author-outside-the-text." But Silverman goes further. To the extent that this relationship represents a play of "authorial identification" and "authorial desire," indeed a "*mise-en-scène* of [authorial] desire," its manifestation in the filmic text will reveal a split subjectivity — a "text inside the author" structured around a particular fantasy scenario.[77] It is not difficult to see how this approach could be transferred to analysis of songs, where authorship often refers to the playing out of an (individually or collectively owned) fantasy scene. While Silverman declares that she does not want to bracket the biographical author altogether, her author-outside-the-text is a textual projection, and she barely looks beyond it — only, in fact, to touch on the implications for gender position when the gender of the biographical author and that of the author-outside-the-text differ. But the biographical author, albeit always discursively mediated, does exist — under the unifying function of a name — and exists too in other places than the film (or musical) text. Perhaps our sense of her solidity depends upon a sort of cross-checking between the fantasy-scenarios circulating in this intertext; and, as corollary, perhaps her own sense of reality depends upon what seems to support this structure. Something, again, is missing — something without which analytic movement cannot pause and authoriality risks shooting right past the demands of practice.[78]

One way to explore this broader territory within which musicians, and others, author their utterances might be through the methods of ethnography — which, since the "reflexive turn" of the last twenty years apparent in both anthropological and historical branches of this discipline, has applied itself with some force to the problematic of subjectivity, notably the subject in its relations with the other, and both in relation to the practices of representation and writing. By "ethnography" I mean here not only ethnomusicologists' recordings of their encounters, which have proliferated in this period, but also reports of analogous expeditions, literal and metaphorical, by popular music scholars, and by historical anthropologists (Philip Bohlman, Gary Tomlinson et al.) — and even by historical musicologists reconstructing past performance practices: all our attempts, in fact, to make sense of, to represent, to fashion a story — a *true* story — about what is foreign but must also become familiar — the music of others and our engagement with it. At this point in the argument, the various levels of the authenticity formation — structures of selfhood, interactions of participants, truth-claims of authorship, aesthetic or ethical values of musical objects and practices — tend to intersect in particularly complex ways. It is convenient to focus on Michelle Kisliuk's brief but classic exposition of an ethnographic method appropriate to the post-reflexive moment: "(Un)Doing Fieldwork: Sharing Songs, Sharing Lives."[79]

Kisliuk rejects any pseudo-objectivity, but at the same time she knows very well that her subject — music cultures of the BaAka in central Africa — is not just "there for her." (In her book-length study of the BaAka, *Seize the Dance*, she is very careful to distance herself from previous stereotypes of so-called pygmy culture, and exoticizing exploitations of it.)[80] What is persuasive about her method is precisely her insistence on writing herself in: her determination to present the encounter as shared, a conversation, yet to acknowledge, even foreground, her own inescapable authoring role. In the impulse to share, in fact, she seems to put her very identity at risk: "Self-Other boundaries are blurred... our very being merges with the 'field.'" But this self-conscious constructionism has a purpose. Ethnographers "create themselves," as, in fieldwork, "the process of identity-making surges to the forefront of awareness"; and in a sense her aim is to define herself as she wants the BaAka to see her — in particular, to differentiate herself from tourists and missionaries. Here the intense difficulties in her project begin to emerge; they are, actually, the difficulties always associated with the Lacanian *Che vuoi?* — the "What do you want from me?" addressed to the Big Other — but further complicated by a doubling of the position addressed.[81] She sides with the locals in their refusals to play along with stereotypes and in their essays in modernization; but she cannot avoid having an agenda of her own (one inextricably implicated in her relations with a different other — her readers). She too has a sense of what is real in BaAka culture, and ironically, to defend this, she has to risk her own authenticity, to *perform* the role she wants to represent her (for the BaAka; for her readers) in the encounter. Although she is aware of the history she brings with her, and of the history going to create BaAka culture as she finds it, the foregrounding of "experience" ("I tried to keep an open mind...," she writes — perhaps as a tactic to help manage the difficulties of her two-sided position) effectively brackets this out. She knows, and she knows that we know, that she is (unavoidably) selective; but her criterion for selection — we should "ask ourselves whether an experience changed us in a way that significantly affected how we viewed, reacted to, or interpreted the ethnographic material" — pushes ethnography in the direction of *Bildungsroman*. In the end, BaAka music becomes, against her will as it were, "for her." In the conjunction, Kisliuk and the BaAka, each term is in danger of becoming the mere ground for the other; something has gone missing, and it is in this unacknowledged absence that the images of authenticity — of experience, of representation, of belonging — spring up.[82]

One term for the missing element might be *ideology*. The indispensable names of the game in play, as they are for Kisliuk, Taylor and, in a somewhat different register, Silverman, are exchange, encounter, intersubjectivity, dialogue — even if in many circumstances we would need to think in terms of Spice's "groundless... conversation on the edge of the abyss," with all the phantasmatic positions this might conjure up. Yet power is the lubricant for this game. Even in the scriptural texts of dialogics — the writings of

Bakhtin and his circle — the dialogic exchange, within the operation of signifying practices or of the structures of subjectivity, is commonly written in the language of ideological conflict. And the concept of authenticity, born in the same Enlightenment moment as that of ideology, lives within that world — the world of truth and falsehood, reality and illusion, and the struggles between them. This does not mean it is easy to stitch the assumptions of Bakhtinian dialogics into the dialectical framework within which the mainstream Hegelian-Marxist tradition of ideology theory developed — although Žižek's rereading of Hegel does outline a "dialecticized dialogics" that puts this intriguing goal on the agenda. In this approach, negation, the antagonistic response to an initial proposition of the subject, "preserves all its disruptive power" but at the same time turns back on this propositional moment, revealing itself as its guarantee; "negativity as such has a positive function" and the "negation of the negation," far from performing a sublation, turns out to be the prior (retroactive) condition of the subject's only identity, namely his constitutive lack. "Contradiction which appears at first as an unresolved question is already in itself a solution": an idea that could stand as a certain kind of definition of ideological work, as well as indicating the dialogical conditions of an experience of truth.[83]

But we have moved too fast. Let us take a step back. If a dialogical stance is the starting point for any attempt to refigure authenticity for a world where foundational authority must be regarded as humanly constructed, then there are several versions available — including some, and not just Žižek's, that factor in a role for ideology. The best-known is Jürgen Habermas's model of "communicative reason": "action oriented to reaching understanding" in which "the unforced force of the better argument" is counted on to bring interlocutors into alignment, always subject to "third-party" judgment of validity-claims (that is, ideology critique in the interests of "undistorted communication").[84] Habermas derives his model from what he identifies as a counter-discourse within Enlightenment reason itself — thus he distances himself from the exclusionary tactics he associates with Foucault and Derrida — and indeed he can be criticized for a neo-Kantian return of universalism: "intersubjective understanding" exerts a "binding force," setting up a "dialectic of betrayal and avenging force" that is ultimately indebted to a religious motif of faith — a "covenant" with truth.[85] At a distance from such universalism stands the unalloyed pragmatism of Richard Rorty, whose refusal to look beyond an interests-oriented account of truth, again pursued through intersubjective negotiation, links his politics with Taylor's liberalism.[86] In both cases, however — Rorty and Habermas — one is struck by the sheer *reasonableness* of the approach — as if "authenticity" can just be neatly stitched back in to an unfortunately disrupted coffeehouse conversation. But if authenticity appears historically exactly in the moment when the modern dialogics of Self and Other emerge, then to identify dialogue as the mechanism *on its own* that can save it is to take as input what was in the beginning an effect. Authenticity was born in shock. Its conjoining of ethical and aesthetic imperatives — law with pleasure, a "you should" with a "you want" — introjects a turbulence into the signifying dialogues forming the subject that goes along with the withdrawal of the Father (for God is dead). The resulting trauma is what requires to be brought to light.

We shall not get far without the concept of ideology. The difficulty, though, is that this concept has long since been moved beyond its earlier character of tying values to specific interests — typically, those of social classes — so that, especially since the poststructuralist turn, it is most often now conceived as pervading discourse in general.[87] According to Žižek, in his article "The Spectre of Ideology," "We are within ideological space proper the moment this [any] content — 'true' or 'false' (if true, so much the better for the ideological effect) — is functional with regard to some relation of social domination ('power,' 'exploitation') in an inherently non-transparent way."[88] But if "truth," as Lacan puts it, "has the structure of a fiction," what then marks out ideology as different? For Žižek, this is the wrong question. Indeed, the denial of a nonideological reality is the ultimate ideological move, the too-easy "it's all ideology" acting as the verso of the vulgar-relativist "it's all true (from its own point of view)." In Žižek's words:

> Although ideology is already at work in everything we experience as "reality," we must none the less maintain the tension that keeps the *critique* of ideology alive... ideology is not all; it is possible to assume a place that enables us to maintain a distance from it, *but this place from which we can denounce ideology must remain empty, it cannot be occupied by any positively determined reality* — the moment we yield to this temptation, we are back in ideology.[89]

We *can* after all, then, ground ideology, and hence truth also — but only in an absence, an impossibility. And how is this place to be specified? Žižek takes a fix on it through the dualities of inside and outside, spirit and body, one ideology over against another, ideology as external force (institutionalized in the Ideological State Apparatuses of Althusserian theory, for example) and ideology as internal spontaneity. This dialogics introduces a "reflective distance:" ideology is always "ideology of ideology," and we can think perhaps of chains or triangulations of authenticities in this way, such that all binaries are always overrun (the case of Rudi Blesh comes to mind). But this is no comfortable conversation. Its issue is a ghostly presence, for which Žižek adopts Marx's term, *specter*: an elusive pseudo-materiality that subverts the classic ontological opposition of reality and illusion. Specter, indeed, *supplements* what can be represented, covering for what is missing from our symbolizations of reality. It is, then, "the pre-ideological kernel, the formal matrix, on which are grafted various ideological formations" — and the specter (e.g., of authenticity) stands for the return of just what cannot be represented. Žižek is of course drawing here on the Lacanian concept of the Real — defined as what always escapes from, is foreclosed by, the orders of the Symbolic (ruled by the signifier) and the Imaginary (where the identities of Self and Other are played out), which brings them along with itself into being in the very act of foreclosure. For Žižek, then, specter appears in the gap between reality and the Real; "the pre-ideological 'kernel' of ideology thus consists of the spectral apparition that fills up the hole of the Real."[90]

Why do we — we the subjects constituted in this ideological space — go along with this? Or rather, what is the nature of this "we" in relation to the mechanisms Žižek has described? Approaching from this direction, Žižek's argument[91] has a post-Althusserian cast, picking up the theory of interpellation from where the intervening phase dominated by Foucauldian and other poststructuralists had (too quickly) dropped it. But the question here is, why do we even respond to the interpellative hail, that hail on behalf of authority which, according to Althusser, encapsulates the mechanisms of ideological subjectivation? Why does the hailed individual *turn* — or better: what is it that turns? Žižek's answer, in effect, is that in the turn — in that "Who? Me?" — there is already *desire*: "the externality of the symbolic machine... is ... not simply external... When we subject ourselves to the machine, ... we already believe *unconsciously* because ... [the machine] exercises its force only in so far as it is experienced, in the unconscious economy of the subject, as a traumatic, senseless injunction... a residue, a leftover": a "dead letter."[92] We turn because we *want* to, and this desire — Pascal's "belief before belief" — is what marks the subject, not as "what makes ideology work... [but as what] emerges where ideology fails"[93] — an empty space, a meaningless kernel, a rock of the Real around which (ideologically structured) reality is built. This object is of course an *objet petit a*, what Žižek terms a "sublime object," what Lacan calls — to distinguish it from ideological symptoms — *sinthome*: the subject's "only substance," "a certain signifying formation penetrated with enjoyment: it is a signifier as a bearer of *jouis-sense*, enjoyment-in-sense."[94] If this belief is a "bad faith," it is not because of "betrayal" — at this level nothing substantive has yet been established that could be betrayed — but because it gives way on "freedom:"[95] yet it is all we have (our "only substance").

This object at the heart of the subject marks the subject's constitutive alienation, its thing-ness, whose symbolic impossibility (or "hole") supplies the very condition of the subject's consistency (or whole). Žižek thinks this impossibility in terms of *antagonism*, a concept certainly important to Lacan but which Žižek takes in more politically developed form from Laclau and Mouffe, for whom, as Žižek points out, "Society does not exist" (any more than

"Woman" does, or "The Sexual Relationship" — or, for that matter, "Popular Music").[96] For Laclau and Mouffe, the protagonists in a social antagonism overlap and interpenetrate each other, each constituting the other's condition but also the impossibility of its completion:

> antagonism constitutes the limits of every objectivity, which is revealed as partial and precarious *objectification*. If language is a system of differences, antagonism is the failure of difference: in that sense, it situates itself within the limits of language and can only exist as the disruption of it — that is, as metaphor ... [Thus] antagonism, as a witness of the impossibility of a final suture, is the 'experience' of the limit of the social.[97]

In other words, the totality, the absolute, which, by definition, our socially constructed symbolizations can never encompass, is necessarily riven by social antagonisms (e.g., class struggle), the representation of which is always already distorted ("objectified"), even as the protagonists concerned lay claim to the whole symbolic terrain — to the totality, as it were. What is necessarily excluded, "the 'repressed' real of antagonism,"[98] to use Žižek's phrase, can never emerge because it would mean the mutual canceling of incompatible visions — one authenticity and another, working-class and bourgeois, self and other — whose thoroughly ideological self-presentation as *polarities* inserts a third term, a neutral context — truth, God, social harmony — to ground them. It is in the traumatic gap between these "realities" and the repressed Real that the apparitions of authenticitity — "real music," "honest expression," "people's culture," "truthful performance," etc. — emerge: spectral fetishes, fetishized specters that are the subject of our worship and our haunting — not true but not false either. We can begin to glimpse what is missing from Kisliuk, Taylor, and Silverman: just that antagonism — that cut between what is and what can be conceived — whose exclusion makes possible the appearance of an ordered symbolic whole, social reality as such, throwing up in the process the specters associated with the authenticity trope: truth to self, representations of the other, a quasi-universalistic human sympathy, and so on.

Both subject and other are holed, that is, are constituted around an exclusion; indeed, these holes are mutually constitutive: this is the meaning of the Lacanian concept of extimacy. It is at this level, where the void at the heart of the subject provides the support for the symbolic realities which structure it, that the circuits of ideology and those of *jouissance* meet up — meet up in those webs of *jouis-sense* we call fantasy. (Lacan's formula for fantasy is $\$\lozenge a$: the barred subject in relation to its *objet a*; and I take the Žižekian specters to be particular, socially referenced figures of fantasy.) As Žižek puts it: "The subject (of the signifier) and the (fantasy-)object are correlative or even identical: the subject is the void, the hole in the Other, and the object the inert content filling up this void; the subject's entire 'being' thus consists in the fantasy-object filling out his void." Such fantasy-objects make ideology not only operative but desirable. Fantasy covers over what ideology cannot admit to; it "is a means for an ideology to take its own failure into account in advance." At this level — the level "beyond interpellation" — "we find only drive, its pulsation around the *sinthome*. 'Going-through-the-fantasy' is therefore strictly correlative to identification with a *sinthome*."[99]

Here we might pause to think further about the concept of fantasy. John Mowitt has made the important point, in relation to both mechanisms of fantasy and those of interpellation, that Freud and Lacan (in the first case) and Althusser (in the second) over-emphasize the role of vision at the expense of sound. For Althussser (following Lacan's theory of the mirror-phase), subjectivation takes place in the field of specularity, while for Lacan (following Freud), fantasy has a "freeze-frame" form designed to protect the subject from the sounds of memory (i.e., from trauma). Mowitt wants to reinstate the aural dimension of the interpellative hail in order to construe subjectivation as a "discontinuous space" at the level of the sensorium; and to stress how, within the visual stasis of fantasy, "sound breaks in on the hearer," enabling us to "see how the theatrical character of fantasy... is also decisively mediated by hearing." Drawing on Laplanche and Pontalis's rereading of Freud's theory of fantasy, Mowitt points to the temporal ambivalence of the relationship between fantasy and reality: in effect, fantasy is the origin of what it installs, in so-called reality, as its own origin (just as, we might add, the Symbolic as such is the origin of what it installs as its own foundation, the Real). Fantasy is "originary", and "originary fantasy is thus indexed to the psychical process through which the subject 'stages' the history of its own formation." Moreover, "if a temporal delay structures the relation between reality and fantasy, then this delay is in some sense part of our experience of both reality and fantasy... This means that, in what makes reality seem original to us [we might say, what makes it seem *authentic*], fantasy is at work."[100]

Curiously, Mowitt does not link his account of temporality with his theory of the interpellative sensorium, even though the vocal stream carrying the hail, unlike the visual self-image to which it gives rise, is inescapably temporally organized. By the time of the "You!", we might say, the "Hey!" has already installed itself as the originary source of interpellative acquiescence, the vocal surplus — the voice as object, or that which escapes the sense of the signifier — correlating precisely with the subject's *sinthome*, that which makes the identification stick, sustains the phantasmatic investment, hence makes reality real. Moreover, the temporal ambivalence *within* the acoustic signifier — both in terms of the structure of the signifier itself, where oscillation between repetition on the one hand and movement forward and back on the other is built in, and in terms of the structure of subjective identification, where the feedback loops and relay mechanisms characteristic of the acoustic mirror distinguish it from its visual equivalent — remind us of Kaja Silverman's crucial point: that the symbolic work performed by voice goes all the way down through the developmental phases of the subject, with a particularly important focus on the (originary? phallic?) role of the mother.[101] As part of this complex work, it is (perhaps) object voice — the meaningless stratum of the interpellative "Hey," first constituted in the maternal babble — which deposits *sinthome* in the heart of the subject. If sound, then, is what on this "primordial" level goes to constitute the real-impossible kernel of ideology, then the key exemplar of this mechanism would be the *fort-da*, understood as a model of senseless (self-) interpellation; here ideology is constituted, authorized, and enjoyed in the very pulsations of the subject itself, in the movements of repetition and (self-) representation — and in the constitutive delays of fantasy and truth. Is this trajectory where we should look to find the passages of the *sinthome*? And, in thinking through the role of fantasy, should we reserve a special importance to the intersection of voice and gaze, as Žižek himself suggests?

Bearing these suggestions and questions in mind, let us return to the general account of ideology but with a more methodological cast of mind. How would we carry on, now, the practice of ideology critique?[102] Žižek himself has helpfully outlined a procedure:[103]

1. "The first task... is... to isolate, in a given ideological field, the particular struggle [it is useful to gloss this as antagonism] which at the same time determines the horizon of its totality."
2. The second task is to locate the field's *point de capiton* (Lacan's "quilting-point") — an "empty" yet richly performative master-signifier that ties the field together: "The crucial step... is thus to detect, behind the dazzling splendour of the element which holds it together ('God,' 'Country,' 'Party,' 'Class'...) this self-referential, tautological, performative operation."
3. The third task is to unveil the interplay, set in motion by the ideological performance, between ideal ego and ego-ideal, imaginary and symbolic identification, subjective lack, acting as cause of desire, and lack in the Other, articulated in the *Che vuoi?*, which together provide the setting for fantasy. (We should add to Žižek's discussion that the interplay of voice and gaze, as objects/routes of identity/identification, should feature here.)
4. The fourth and last (?) task — bearing in mind that "'Beyond interpellation' is the square of desire, fantasy, lack in the Other and drive pulsating around some unbearable surplus-enjoyment" — is to uncover

> this "non-sensical, pre-ideological kernel of enjoyment . . . structured in fantasy," to "detect, in a given ideological edifice, the element within it which represents its own impossibility," that is, "what is excluded from the Symbolic . . . [and which] returns in the Real." This is to "traverse the fantasy" and identify with the *sinthome*.[104]

How might this procedure work in relation to, say, the Spice Girls' "Wannabe"? The determining struggle is presumably a gender struggle, but one specific to young women in an allegedly postfeminist consumer society, a relationship metonymically condensed to the ambitions of young, female pop performers in a male-dominated, mass-market music industry. The *point de capiton* is, most obviously, "girl power," encapsulated musically in the chorus hook, "If you wanna be . . . ," which fades the record out, and which — both in terms of its rather inchoate message of want and its musical materialization — disseminates its power throughout the song: the continuity of the underlying groove, the multiple repetitions of this particular musical idea, the links between the two fundamental musical modes in the song, the articulation of the individual voices into a collective position — all combine to perform out the quilting function. Relatively empty in themselves, these signifiers, tautologically repeated, demonstrate how the self-referential quality common in music as such can be put to particularly powerful ideological use.

The articulations of formal units, of voices and of stylistic references already suggest how structures of identification are animated. A theatrical scene peopled by "I," "you," "lovers," "friends," "giving and taking," is activated through the interplay of these musical positions, and given corporeal form — both desired (from here) and envisaged (from there) — in the injunctions to "slam down," "wind around," and "zig-a-zig" the body. Needless to say, the fantasy put in play takes variable shape, depending on listener position, a variability only enhanced when structures of video or film gazes intersect with the network of voice positions. (But this intersection is there even when just listening to the record, to the extent that a simulacrum of performance is built in to the listening experience implied by the form of the recording.)

At this point in the analysis, we would certainly be permitted to associate this "ideological edifice" with a certain authenticity — what is really, really wanted, what we "gotta" do, insisted upon to the point where its reality seems close enough to inhabit. We could even (with Elizabeth Leach) identify a knowing traverse of authenticity-markers, although this would not significantly affect the ideological analysis because, as Žižek points out, cynicism here simply rewrites Marx's "They do not know it, but they are doing it" with a "They know very well what they are doing, but still, they are doing it."[105] Indeed, the latter eventuality reveals all the more clearly that the authenticity here can only be *spectral*: even if its untruth is acknowledged, we still want it, and we want it all the more because this phantasmatic version is all we have — what has been excluded from symbolization (genuine gender revolution) by the antagonistic structure that depends on its denial (marked by the commodification of feminism) "returns in the Real." For the power invoked, and given voice in the intoxicating drive [*sic*] of the music, bodies forth a nonsensical *jouissance* without which, "unbearable" though it is, the edifice of sense would crumble. It is an enjoyment with distinct sado-masochistic elements, the power of the Thatcherite whip re-enacted *après la lettre* (a "dead letter" indeed), the Spice Girls playing out as (lucrative) comedy the tragedy of the first time.

What next? If we have now outlined a way of "going through" the fantasy implicated in this particular signifying formation and identifying with its *sinthome*, is the job done? Žižek's approach successfully rehabilitates the critique of ideology for a non-foundational world and is good at accounting for ideological pleasures, but it is open to the criticism that, just as traversing the fantasy marks for Lacan the limit stage of the transference — we can only identify with, and hence repeat the *sinthome*, not dissolve it — so it is for Žižek at the level of politics. The fundamental antagonism can at best be managed, not escaped, because "all culture is in a way a reaction-formation, an attempt to limit, canalize — to *cultivate* this imbalance, this traumatic kernel, this radical antagonism through which man cuts his umbilical cord with nature, with animal homeostasis."[106] Does identifying with the *sinthome* not reconcile us with untruth? How, then, might social change come about? How, to be more specific, might the people's interests be pursued?

If the object at the heart of the subject — the meaningless bit of the Real underpinning reality — is impossible to symbolize, its content by definition un-representable, then it would appear to be out of the question to shift its position, let alone rearticulate it. Yet it is part of the Enlightenment legacy — that legacy claimed by Lacan and Žižek themselves (not to mention Marx, Freud, and Nietzsche) — that what is forbidden should be taken as what is to be unveiled (even if we know that we shall never fully succeed). The *sinthome*, we are told, is (the meaningless) part of a signifying formation, and comes "afterwards," as an originary effect. If, then, the sense of the signifiers shifts as a result of rearticulative work, so too surely, in some indefinable way, will the *sinthome*. This will be all the more the case if we take seriously the idea that the symbolic work of subjectivity *goes all the way down*, so that *sinthome* and symptom, Real and Symbolic, are always already articulated together. Identifying with the *sinthome* might then have the effect of releasing its potential meaning (yet another in the line of interpretations of Freud's "*Wo es war, soll ich werden*," which I am reading here to indicate where the subject of the Symbolic must go — into the place occupied by the impossible Thing). This move will, of course, displace or re-articulate the underlying antagonism rather than abolishing it, but also *enables history* — a history conceived, moreover, as the proper territory of the fully constituted subject of both meaning and desire.

In other words: the concept of the *sinthome* must be radically secularized, socialized, and grasped historically if it is not to become a fetish.[107] To the extent that we can see it as social substance — and the argument that the unconscious is socially constituted, in a field of *extimité*, implies that we must — we should think, perhaps, of *sinthomaticity*: a function of collective subjectivities. Moreover, such a socialized field of sinthomaticity would also certainly be itself split, divided against itself as a manifestation of social antagonism, and hence susceptible to the labors of political struggle. This process of division, producing ever-new remainders, relates in one direction to the deep-rooted symbiotic struggle between *sinthome* and Symbolic, and in another (for the struggle is life or death) to the dialogics of the drives, pulsing forever between, precisely, Life and Death. Lacan himself can be read as hinting in this direction, for at the topmost level of the graph of desire, "beyond interpellation," where the sphere of meaning is intersected by the forces of enjoyment, we find the functions of *jouissance* on the one side, castration on the other. Incarnated pleasure, evacuated by the cut of the Symbolic (the body dismembered) survives in pockets, as *sinthome*, in relation to drive on the one hand (including the scopic and invocatory drives), lack in the Big Other (correlating to the subject's own constitutive lack) on the other. To put this another way, the Lacanian bar — as figured in the symbolic phallus, marker of the castration metaphor — can itself (contrary to many readings) be barred, its remainder *sinthomatised*; or (a different way again) it can be construed as a movable point: *fort/da* goes all the way down (senseless repetition intersects with representational meaning as far down as one can see). It is just this mobility and permeability of the bar that makes politics possible.

The historicity of *sinthome* in "Wannabe" already started to come into view — indeed (perhaps indicatively), forced itself on our attention. If, by definition, we can only speak here in hint and metaphor, it seems clear nonetheless that the pleasures of power that are at stake are specified, first, in relation to the powers that were available to girls and to others identifying, and identifying with, them in this society at this time, and, second, in relation to an intersection between this sphere of collective girlhood and a more individualized, fetishistic power associated with the contemporary sphere of stardom. The exchanges insistently played out between the girls may invoke fantasies of both sisterhood and of the "lesbian scene" — fantasies that, needless to say, will be variably occupied depending on gender and sexual position — but sinthomaticity here is irrevocably riven by an undecideability of *jouissance*, revolving around the alternative pleasures of having and being: lesbian phallus, or oedipal exchange of women? For Brennan, an important aspect of "the ego's era" is the gradual decline of traditional patriarchal social forms, a transition to a more "liberal" social system, and a consequent transfer of authority from external god-figures to the male self, in effect displacing the social contract to one between brothers (who then take out their increasing insecurities on an all-the-more stereotyped category of Woman).[108] If this is true, it casts the pleasures of sisterhood, as these have been posited and claimed more recently, in a light both fraught (politically) and specific (historically) (remember *Showboat*!).

But in reckoning with this master/slave split in the "Wannabe" *sinthome* (having, being, being had…), we need to factor in the effects of other collective fantasies as well. Racial difference, smoothed into a faint blackface oscillation in the musical material with a visual focus on the minority black presence (Mel B); class hierarchy, articulated in a space bounded by middle-class ("Posh Spice") Victoria on the one hand, working-class Mel C on the other, and similarly smoothed into a celebration of individuality as togetherness: these disavowals show just enough of a repressed Real to titillate while marking the effects of underlying social antagonisms the suppression of which is the enabling condition for the pleasures — celebrating collectivity and celebrity in apparent contradiction — of the song. To add that the principle of *exchange* links the musico-ideological level of the record to the political economy within which it was disseminated — the Spice Girls, the individual girls, girl power, and the record itself all commodified and subjected to the laws of exchange-value — is to amplify the point that sinthomaticity here is contoured in a way specific to its moment: vocal life, frozen by the mortifying gaze of money, turns the trick of a particular pleasure — equivalence enjoyed as apparent difference.

At this level — the pleasures of exchange in consumption, given their own symbolic representations in the forms of sales charts — sinthomaticity is systemic, anchored to a particular phase of capitalism. If we return to the John Lennon songs discussed earlier, "God" and "Working Class Hero," the analysis on many levels will of course be different from that of "Wannabe." The formation of the *sinthome* here is transected by figures of external authority (religious and political, from Jesus to the working class), and their sadistic destruction turns the focus of the fantasy inwards to a narcissistic imaginary, abjected in the one song, reconstituted by quasi-maternal embrace in the other. (To hear "God" after "Working Class Hero" is to hear suicide followed by rebirth, a trajectory completed in "Imagine," where — so the images circulating around the song suggest — the world is saved, the people's peace secured, by John, Yoko, and a white grand piano.) But the antagonism underlying the "impossible" overlay of social fantasy and solipsistic cocoon points towards a confusion of collective and individual investments similar to that in the Spice Girls' anthem — even if the heroism of celebrity is apparently rejected in "Working Class Hero." The list, in "God," of disavowed but mutually substitutable authorities; the reduction of workers, in "Working Class Hero," to a homogenous mass of "fucking peasants"; the traverse of difference, in "Imagine," to produce a singular "all the people," living "as one": these provide the setting for the endless circulation of the musical commodities themselves, which offers exchange as and of fetish as a Real underlying the reality Lennon's patent sincerity constructs. "The dream is over," he sings; to the contrary, it had simply mutated, its authenticity relocated — and its Real foundation (the "dream within the dream")[109] had changed also, just enough and no more, and come along with it.

It might seem that this analysis has the effect of reconstructing a dichotomous formation — ideology/commodity equating to Symbolic/Real (or even, heaven help us, superstructure and base). Not so. Žižek develops his theory of *sinthome* on the basis of Lacan's claim that it was Marx (rather than Freud) who invented the idea of symptom, and he derives his figure of the specter from Marx's theory of the commodity-fetish, which of course also confounds the false (that is, real) abstractions of exchange with the nonetheless real (i.e., spectral) presence of the consumer good. We can add another twist to the approach if we remind ourselves that this is not just an analytic model but also as an historically specific condition; for authenticity arose *on the back of* commodity-fetishism: the two figures are codependent, each the under- or over-side of the other. These specters are *Doppelgänger* — and the authenticity claims of musical commodities, such as Lennon's album, gleam through a dense and ghostly mist.

Žižek's argument, we recall, is that the system of commodity exchange is a "real abstraction," that is, a framework whose social efficacy — for we act as if we believe in the material reality of money even if we know this to be "nonsensical" — belies its abstraction, all the more so because it is covered over by the fetishistic appeal of the commodity itself. This "sublime object" installs itself, within the conditions of this social regime, in the foundations of the subject: it is, indeed, *sinthome* — a "form of thought whose ontological status is not that of thought, that is to say, [it is] the form of thought external to the thought itself," a form that in effect announces to the subject, "there, in the external effectivity of the exchange process, is your proper place; there is the theatre in which your truth was performed before you took cognizance of it."[110] Within this theater, where inside and outside interpenetrate each other, symptoms marking both the contours and the limits of particular ideological formations — their constitutive imperfections vis-à-vis the abstract universality implied in the principle of exchange — correlate, at the level of subjectivity, to those marking the illusory value of commodities, at the level of the object. Covering these fissures, we can then say, the specters or fantasies of truth, value, origin — of, let us say it, *authenticity* — match up to the fetish-power in consumption, each the verso of the other in a socio-ideological figure of *genuine coinage*.

Žižek pushes his argument further, pointing out that the principle of exchange penetrates not only relations between things but also those between human beings. Just as the value of a commodity depends on its exchange-relationship with another, so it is with human subjects: "only by being reflected in another man [*sic*] . . . can the ego arrive at its self-identity; identity and alienation are thus strictly correlative"[111] — the formula of the Lacanian mirror stage. Extrapolating from Žižek's extension of this argument to the master-slave dialectic, we can readily see how not only women but also racial subalterns (slaves and their blackface descendants) and workers (differentiated labor-power reduced to substitutable exchanges of labor-time) are subjected to this mechanism of equivalence. For Žižek, under capitalism (as compared to feudalism) fetishism is displaced from social relationships to the sphere of commodities; human subjects are defined (if only nominally, we might add) as just as "free and equal" as the factors in market production (and indeed, this is precisely the context for the advent of a new type of "autonomous" subject). Yet it would surely be truer to say that, with the increasing alienation (or "thingness") of subjectivity in this period, fetishism is also displaced into the interior of the subject, where fraught relationships with its others (of gender, sexuality, race, class, etc.) stake out ground on which the master-slave dialectic is reconstituted. The dependence of these imaginary others for their representation on the objectification of real (if misrecognized) social actors marks the way in which modernity itself in its capitalist articulations performs out its founding antagonism — which is why its most revealing symbolic mode is that of the mask, across the range of techniques of masquerade, mimicry, and blackface. The space created here is where the regime of representation and that of exchange (across symbolic and political-economic registers, in both cases) meet up: the subject's authenticity is guaranteed — so long as the credit is good — by its (self- and other-) representations and their exchangeability; in the dream-world of capitalism, the repetitive *vorstellen* (*fort/da*) of *Repräsentanzen* (present, absent, spectral) sets the stage. This is also, we might hazard, where social substance bodies forth the *sinthome* — where it is, precisely, fleshed out, contouring our objects (of desire, identity, meaning) in historically specific ways.

If this locates the apparatus of ideology (correctly) as specific to a particular historical phase — at least "ideology" in this understanding of the term — then it does the same for sinthomaticity.[112] Returning now to our methodological agenda for ideology critique — asking again how this might offer ways of exploiting openings revealed in the previous song-analyses for productive political effect — we can see the need to proceed on two, interlinked levels. The techniques are there to de- and re-articulate what Laclau and Mouffe call "moments" of discourse, or "relations of representation":

> every relation of representation [even the most "authentic"] is founded on a fiction: that of the presence at a certain level of something which, strictly speaking, is absent from it. But because it is *at the same time* a fiction and a principle organising actual social relations, representation is the terrain of a game whose result is not predetermined from the beginning.[113]

Rearticulation can thus, potentially, have political as well as symbolic effects — perhaps through un-pinning the *points de capiton*, releasing the differences of the signifiers (including constitutive absences) and reknotting them in new points of equivalence; not, however, an equivalence of exchange and substitution but one of "slack" overdetermination (what a rearticulated Deleuze might be persuaded to categorize as repetition of difference as against repetition of the same; or what a Butler might think of in terms of subversive mutation of the performative mime). But the critique will fall short, politically, if we do not at the same time *stand in the place of the sinthome*; that is, identify with the fantasy-object filling out the foundational void of the formation, enjoy (however guiltily) its pleasures (however dirty), and sense/make sense of the *jouis-sense*. If this puts "integrity" at risk, the transaction takes place, on all sides, *in history*; overflow thus has practical limits, and in any case simply acknowledges the critic's own dependent lack. It is hard to see that to articulate figures of the people musically can today have any other starting point.

This argument may have something to say to the problematic of what Donna Haraway (among others) has called "situated knowledge." Because "only partial perspective promises objective vision,"[114] the concept of situated knowledge is a *sine qua non* for any epistemological regime that takes seriously the essential fraudulence of any fixed Name-of-the-Father. Haraway's stress on the need for contestational connectivity between different points of view, in full awareness of their technological mediations, is not too far from a politics of articulation, as formulated by Laclau and Mouffe (though it needs to be supplemented with a broader theory of mediality: ear as well as eye). It is difficult to see, though, that situational analysis can cope with the full trickery of ideology and its base of antagonism without building in Žižek's impossible "empty place" of ideology critique. But what is this place, one might ask, if not that which is always already reserved for *sinthome*? To occupy this place — or rather, to assume it, in a move that is also necessarily a refusal — is to "sinthomatise" it: which is to say, to engage its void in a structure of desire, to wrestle, not with the angel, but with the god-like *saint-homme* (who is also doubting Saint Thom, as well as cyborgian synth-man).[115] What is at issue is objectivity itself. Haraway argues that "embodiment is significant prosthesis; objectivity cannot be about fixed vision when what counts as an object is precisely what world history turns out to be about."[116] Her vision offers a world of objects reanimated by human modesty (a reanimation engineered, we might think, by that "re-tooling [of] the mimetic faculty" through technological innovation of which Michael Taussig writes).[117] If the era of the *sinthome* is the era of the death of God — or rather, the era when God moved progressively inside — then its climactic moment might well lie in the current emergent political phase of "Empire," where the gathering of every element into relationship with a de facto systemic whole marks the point at which, on the one hand, a constitutive territorial exterior of the type that has legitimized all previous social ideologies disappears (or rather, is forced to move into the *interior* of the body politic), and, on the other hand, the *sinthome* is divided against itself. Just as the existence of matter, it seems, depends on assuming an invisible anti-matter, so the price of identification with the impossible-real object, in an apparently single social universe, may be acceptance of a permanently mutating anti-*sinthome*. Somewhere in this murky territory lies the remake of nature that so many recent writers, from Benjamin down to Haraway, Taussig, and Brennan, have sensed — a remake that, in its dethroning of the imperial subject, reveals that (as Bruno Latour has it) we were never really modern anyway.[118]

At this point I find myself in a dilemma. This book has centered its arguments on musical materials drawn from the period of Western late modernity, with a particular focus on its Anglo-American popular-music dominant. To pursue these arguments into the phase of "Empire" demands a shift into the framework of "world music": not just the commercial category but the entire late-twentieth/early twenty-first century context marked out as the territory of popular musics of the whole world. This is beyond my scope. Might it be possible, though, to outline some of the questions that would need to be asked, and to relate them to a specific world music product — say, the unexpectedly successful 1997 album of old-time Cuban *son*, *Buena Vista Social Club*?[119]

If we were to look for a symptom of Empire, located in the interstices of its plural formations, it would be hard to find a more resonant example: a music originating (in style, in much of the repertoire) from the old Cuba (a lost territory, from before the Revolution); recorded towards the fag-end (?) of Castro's reign, under conditions of U.S. blockade (including the baleful glare of a militantly right-wing exile community a few miles across the water in Florida); but recorded through the intervention of celebrated American roots musician and "animator of world music,"[120] Ry Cooder; and shot to success through the imperial mechanisms of the global music system (first world record label, Grammy award, sell-out concerts around the world, Wim Wenders's documentary film, etc.).[121] In a sense the music is pre- and post-Cold War at the same time, but also — stemming from Cuba — comes from its aging heart, marking a place that stands as one of the few remaining "blots" troubling the otherwise triumphant neoliberal world system. Yet the elderly musicians who were catapulted to fame owed this to the circuits of that very system, and on that level the *Buena Vista* brand — manifested in nostalgic visual images and musical grooves that circulated, so it seemed at one time, around every bourgeois living-room, every trendy café and bar, in the world — functioned like any other. For this audience, the appeal of the music — like that of early blues, hillbilly, and New Orleans jazz — related, it seems, to its prelapsarian innocence, an authenticity lost to the musical mainstream. But by the 1990s such credibility drained out of the product much more quickly, and these listeners knew all along, one suspects, that this was an authenticity that could only work as dream — a point mirrored, from the other side, by the ambivalent reception of the phenomenon in Cuba itself, where, certainly for many of the youth, tastes ran more to styles influenced by contemporary dance music and rap, often conjoined emotionally with revolutionary weariness and a pent-up desire for consumer goods which, for them, could only be misrepresented by the Buena Vista success.[122]

Within this context, the ideological field and the particular struggles marking its contours are extraordinarily multi-leveled. But the *point(s) de capiton* is/are situated in, or cluster around, some notion of a "real popular" — the people as reality, or an authentic reality that is here represented in a popular music form. Many references in the songs are to a certain peasant imaginary rooted in early twentieth-century Cuban society (including religious allusions from the cult of *Santería*).[123] But the racial divisions and hybridities in this society — glancingly signaled in the term Afro-Cuban — without which the music is inconceivable, are smoothly covered over; and the patriarchal gender positions go without question. Multiple alterities (of race, of class) are, arguably, assimilated within a latin-masculinist dominant. The exclusions driving both left- and right-wing appropriations (and negations), from positions outside the Cuban theatre itself, are no less clear, if different. And the even starker "repressed Real" going to found predominant modes of "world music" reception may be read easily enough in, for instance, Ry Cooder's quasi-anthropological claim that this music was "nurtured" in "an atmosphere sealed off from the fall out of a hyper-organized and noisy world" (this despite the clear influences from American jazz); or in the suggestion by a Miami film festival director that "The [Wenders] film succeeds because music transcends politics" (a claim always identifiable as the most political of all).[124] The dialogues of identification set up by this multi-leveled discourse are complex and variable indeed (many are delineated in the intersections of voice and gaze, bridging worlds, that are caught in Wenders's movie).[125]

Given this, sinthomaticity here can only be equally heterogeneous. My own enjoyment of the music (which is intense) relates, I suspect (but what do I know?), to a fantasy of social interaction that seems to underlay the grace and dialogic interplay running through the vocal/instrumental ensembles; and this in turn seems rooted in a "natural" submission of subjectivity to an automatism of the body, for, as Cooder puts it (yes, I am susceptible too), "the music flows like a river. It takes care of you and rebuilds you from the inside out." But, while there is (I hope) something in this spectral memory that, with appropriate articulative work, is not necessarily dead to a future politics, it is certainly dependent on crippling exclusions (marked by the gender and sexuality strai[gh]tjacket, for instance). Moreover, this sinthomatic trajectory is in inescapable competition with other structures of desire founded on their own exclusions (bracketing, for example, any socialist potential, or racial antagonism). Sinthomatic struggle here is irreducible — and in a world of Empire this is what we would expect: "When we see [or hear] it [the album], we feel heart-stopping nostalgia for something *we did not realize we had been missing*. That something is Cuba" (my italics) — but Cuba as spectral *Vorstellung* of a *Repräsentanz* that was always already inside, already conflicted, an *infection* within the body of the global imaginary.[126]

Where, then, with "the people"? The authenticity of *Buena Vista*, and of the other music discussed in this chapter, is through-and-through *historical*. It is "the real thing" precisely to the extent that, in the particular case, a sound-signifying-formation is constructed with sufficient skill, integrity, and engagement to constitute itself as a popular object-cause of desire capable of supporting a convincing fiction, the result carrying its listeners along in a direction that is, in the broadest sense, politically productive. This does not abolish antagonism, nor therefore the struggle between musics. Nor does it render the music's truth-effects anything other than intrinsically contingent (for the status of whatever we can imagine them to be true to is necessarily floating, while that of even the meaningless stuff embodying their sinthomatic foundations is historically situated); contingent but not disabled, either on the level of performativity (where power, persuasiveness, subversiveness are at issue) or on the level of critique (where articulation, re-connection, re-identification are the names of the game). Somewhere along this trajectory, at an (impossible) point in the future, we may imagine a *buena vista* to end all others; for this is where the specter of authenticity (decommodifed, defetishized) is leading us. The view from there would be truly "social"; for, with society demystified (we would *know* that "it" does not exist), "clubbing" (by class, gender, race, whatever) would lose all association with violence, real or symbolic — in short, with enforced hierarchy — turning instead towards a radically self-inventing democracy which we might tentatively characterize as a state of freedom.[127] At that (utopian) moment, the people will dissolve itself, its need for collective voice superseded. But not yet.

Notes

Chapter 1

1. The slogan was prominent in the procession to the great Chartist meeting on Kennington Common, London, in April 1848: "The body of the car [a horse-drawn cart carrying the Chartist leaders] was inscribed on the right side with the motto, 'The Charter. No surrender. Liberty is worth living for and worth dying for;' on the left, 'The voice of the people is the voice of God;' while on the back of the car was inscribed, 'Who would be a slave that could be free?' 'Onward, we conquer; backward, we fall'" (*Illustrated London News*, April 14, 1848).
2. Lacan's trope will be discussed in more detail later. It points toward the metaphorical status of patriarchal authority-claims typically vested, in their originary mythic forms, in divine figures.
3. The song text given here in full comes from Ernest Jones, *Songs of Democracy*, published in *The People's Paper,* "the organ of the working classes" (London: John Lowry, 1856–57). As for the music, version 2 is taken from a song sheet, "The Song of the 'Lower' Classes" (London: John Lowry, n.d. [1856]), while version 1 is from a pamphlet published by the Workers Music Association (WMA; n.d.) and reproduced in János Maróthy, *Music and the Bourgeois, Music and the Proletarian* (Budapest: Akadémiai Kiadó, 1974), 475. The pamphlet cannot date from before 1936, the year the WMA was formed. However, the metamorphosis of the tune that it documents (discussed below) may reflect a process which had been going on for some time.
4. See Maróthy, *Music of the Bourgeois* (cf p. 288 n. 213), 1974, 474–75 and passim. In a lecture from 1867 (the time of the second Reform Act), Jones, writing about the fusty building that was the British constitution, declares that "public opinion, like a clear breeze, shall come pouring through its halls with the breath of heaven, the people's voice, which is the voice of God" (quoted in Miles Taylor, *Ernest Jones, Chartism, and the Romance of Politics 1819–1869* [Oxford: Oxford University Press, 2003], 237). Was Jones, who was involved in, and indeed arrested at, the Kennington meeting, recalling it some twenty years later? The slogan, "The people's voice is the voice of God," was deeply embedded in nineteenth-century radical discourse. A title search of the British Library catalog, with the keywords *voice*, *people*, and *God*, brings up some twenty publications issued between the 1830s and the 1880s. *The Voice of the People* was a trade union newspaper of the 1830s (and similarly *Die Stimme des Volks* was a German communist paper of the same period, referred to by Marx). At the same time, ownership of the phrase was contested: Gladstone liked to think of himself as the voice of the people, and that people as the voice of God (see Patrick Joyce, *Visions of the People: Industrial England and the Question of Class 1848–1914* [Cambridge, UK: Cambridge University Press, 1991, 50]). And the idea was older: the Kintilloch Weavers Reform banner, from 1832, is inscribed "The Voice of the people is the supreme" — as in the Supreme Being of eighteenth-century Deism, and of Robespierre's revolutionary civic religion? See Nick Mansfield, "Why Are There

No Chartist Banners? — The 'Missing Link' in 19th Century Banners," *Journal of the Social History Curators Group* 25 (2000): 35–44, 40.

The phrase itself was also far older, familiar in debates about political and religious freedom in the seventeenth and eighteenth centuries and even before — especially in its Latin version, "Vox populi, vox Dei." For example, Daniel Defoe — novelist, journalist, and campaigning dissenter, imprisoned in 1702 for publishing a satire on the Anglican establishment's attitude to nonconformity — was the probable author of a 1709 pamphlet with this title. It circulated widely for some time, and was drawn upon later in the century by the American revolutionaries. The Vox populi, Vox Dei slogan was well known in the Middle Ages; indeed, the first written record dates from the eighth century AD — a letter from the theologian Alcuin to the emperor Charlemagne (advising him to pay no attention to it). It was rooted in still earlier Christian critiques of Classical elitism (for all true Christians were to be regarded as God's People), and even in the Old Testament: when, for instance, the people ask Samuel to give them a king, God's advice to Samuel is (in the language of the Vulgate), "Audi vocem populi" (I Samuel 8:7).

5. The Workers Music Association, closely associated with the Communist Party of Great Britain, brought together several already existing labor movement choirs, and devoted much of its energy to the encouragement of choral singing. The march trope to be found in "We're Low" has a historical complexity too great to be explored in detail here. Bearing in mind the connection of marching and drumming, John Mowitt (*Percussion: Drumming, Beating, Striking* [Durham, NC: Duke University Press, 2002], 91–115), draws attention to a rich nexus of connotations in nineteenth- and twentieth-century musical and political practice: the disciplining of bodies (as explored by Foucault); the specific disciplines of (black) slavery, and the possibility that African-American drumming answered back to these disciplines; the noisy processions associated with "rough music" (charivari) in both Europe and America; the similar practices developed in the organized labor movements: for instance, antiscab sloganeering, and the rhetoric of the industrial strike. Maróthy's "smashing crochet" arrays itself across this historical terrain. I shall have occasion to come back to the labor–slavery articulation; for the moment it is perhaps enough to note that in this perspective "We're Low" points not only back to the *Marseillaise* and forward to a lineage of industrial conflict, but also to the "marching" rhythms of ragtime and jazz, and, through the link between its tone of mockery and that of "rough music," to the parodistic march-dance of the turn-of-the-century cakewalk.
6. Taylor, *Ernest Jones,* 2003, 179.
7. Ibid., 95.
8. Richard Middleton, "Musical Belongings: Western Music and Its Low-Other," in *Western Music and Its Others: Difference, Representation, and Appropriation in Music*, ed. Georgina Born and David Hesmondhalgh (Berkeley: University of California Press, 2000a), 59–85.
9. Peter Stallybrass and Allon White, *The Politics and Poetics of Transgression* (London: Methuen, 1986), 193.
10. I owe my awareness of this work to Marina Warner, *Fantastic Metamorphoses, Other Worlds: Ways of Telling the Self* (Oxford: Oxford University Press, 2002), 142–44. My interpretation, starting out from hers, is based on the primary sources: John O'Keefe, *A Short account of the new pantomime called Omai, or, A trip round the world… With the recitatives, airs duets… and choruses… a new edition* (London: T. Cadell, 1785; and William Shield, *Omai or A Trip round the World. A Pantomime… The Words written by J. O'Keefe* (London: Longman & Broderip, [1786]). See also Roger Fiske ("A Covent Garden Pantomime," *Musical Times* 104 (1963): 574–76.
11. *European Magazine* (1782), 182, quoted in Richard D. Altick, *The Shows of London* (Cambridge, UK: Cambridge University Press, 1978), 121. For Loutherbourg's *Omai* designs, and his work more generally, see ibid., 118–27. On Shield's theater music, see Roger Fiske, *English Theatre Music in the Eighteenth Century* (Oxford: Oxford University Press, 1973), 453–73.
12. See G. W. F. Hegel, *Phenomenology of Spirit*, trans. A. V. Miller (1807, Oxford: Oxford University Press, 1977), 111–19.
13. Mozart shared the widespread fascination of his time for automata, and wrote pieces for mechanical instruments. A "slave" can be not only a dependent human being but also that component of a mechanical system (later also a computer system) which is "driven" by a master; that is, which simply obeys.
14. Among Shield's many operas and other theater pieces, there are examples of music drawn

from, or imitating, Irish, Scottish, Sicilian, Russian, and Turkish traditional repertories, as well as tunes from the English collections that John Gay had plundered earlier in the century in *The Beggar's Opera*. There may also be vernacular tunes that Shield had heard while growing up in the Northeast of England (he was born in Swalwell, near Gateshead, on the south bank of the River Tyne); Roger Fiske ("A Covent Garden Pantomime," 1963, 576) speculates that he may have picked up the tune of the "Sailor's Song" in *Omai* while working as an apprentice shipbuilder in South Shields. For a selective list of musical borrowings (including of many folk tunes) in English operas produced between 1760 and 1800, see Fiske, *English Theatre Music,* 1973, 600–12.

15. In one of the two, "Let Me When My Heart A-Sinking," reproduced in Hans Nathan, *Dan Emmett and the Rise of Early Negro Minstrelsy* (Norman: University of Oklahoma Press, 1962), 23, pizzicato violins and bass, imitating the "clinking" of Mungo's guitar ("When de tring peak... I soon am cur'd of tinking"), might be heard as initiating a trajectory that would lead, a century and a half later, to Porgy's banjo in the equally minstrelized "I Got Plenty of Nuttin'" from Gershwin's opera, *Porgy and Bess.* It is difficult to believe that a later song by Dibdin, "The Negro and His Banjer" (from his one-man show of 1790, *The Wags, or The Camp of Pleasure*), did not include a banjo imitation, although the vocal score gives no clue.
16. For information on American music theater production, see Julius Mattfeld, *Handbook of American Operatic Premieres 1731–1962* (Detroit: Detroit Information Service, 1963), and Oscar G.T. Sonneck, *A Bibliography of Early Secular American Music (18th Century)*, rev. William T. Upton (1905) (Washington DC: Library of Congress, 1945). For estimates of the extent of blackface performance in the second half of the eighteenth century, see Dale Cockrell, *Demons of Disorder: Early Blackface Minstrels and Their World* (Cambridge, UK: Cambridge University Press, 1997),13–29. For comment on the musical connections between the early minstrel and the contemporary "Scots" and "Irish" repertories, see ibid.; Nathan, *Dan Emmett,* 1962, 59–213; Charles Hamm *Yesterdays: Popular Song in America* (New York: Norton, 1979), 109–18; Robert Toll, *Blacking Up: The Minstrel Show in Nineteenth-Century America* (New York: Oxford University Press, 1974), 26–28.
17. W. T. Lhamon, Jr, *Raising Cain: Blackface Performance from Jim Crow to Hip Hop* (Cambridge, MA: Harvard University Press, 1998); Cockrell, *Demons of Disorder*, 1997, 89; Eric Lott, *Love and Theft: Blackface Minstrelsy and the American Working Class* (New York: Oxford University Press, 1993), 64, 68. Lhamon is of course alluding to, and expanding on, Paul Gilroy's influential concept of the "Black Atlantic"; see *The Black Atlantic: Modernity and Double Consciousness* (London: Verso, 1993).

    Charles Hamm (*Yesterdays*, 1979, 118) is one who argues that the clockwork-Irish-blackface style reflects the ignorance of white bourgeois composers, referring to a complexity in "real" African and African-American music which they were unwilling or unable to recognize. This is an argument that either treats black culture at this time as a pure object of history with no possibility of agency, or appeals to a folkloristic model that assumes the existence of a *hidden* culture. In fact, the evidence for racial interaction and hybridity is overwhelming — there *was* trade, even if the terms (as in all so-called free markets) were skewed. Rice is supposed, according to legend, to have learned "Jim Crow" from an elderly black man; so why is the tune so "Irish"? Because, perhaps, black musicians — slave and free — had been assimilating the white traditional repertories of the South (English, Irish, Scots) for years, and giving them back to whites with a twist; and had also more recently been picking up (and feeding into) the early blackface repertory as well. Nathan (*Dan Emmett,* 1962, 166, 171–72) gives "Jim Crow" alongside similar tunes from the Irish folk tradition and the English stage. Lhamon (*Raising Cain,* 1998, 180–86) locates it in part within a long-established black folk repertory, while Cockrell (*Demons of Disorder,* 1979, 76–89) roots it on the one hand within a tradition of corn-shucking songs, black as well as white, and on the other in the noisy lineages (again, biracial) of antimusical, carnivalesque charivari or "rough music." Lott (*Love and Theft*, 1993, 59–60) quotes a report of an occasion when Rice overheard a "Negro version" of "his song," learned it, and paid its singer; was this "black" or "blackface"? Lott provides the richest and most subtle account of the irreducible hybridity of the early minstrel repertoire in general (see especially 94, 177–82).

    The wider social context is important too. In the late eighteenth and the nineteenth centuries, Irish immigrants and African Americans were often thrown closely together, both located at the bottom of the heap but also, incipiently and in due course actually, in competition. For many "superior" white Americans, the Irish were "white Negroes," the blacks, "smoked Irish"; see Noel Ignatiev, *How the Irish Became White* (New York: Routledge, 1995); Lott, *Love and Theft*, 1993, 71, 94–96. The musical evidence suggests that this relationship may be rooted in a complex of attitudes with earlier, European origins — hence Lhamon's "plebeian Atlantic."

Peter van der Merwe (*Origins of the Popular Style: The Antecedents of Twentieth-Century Popular Music* [Oxford: Clarendon Press, 1989]) traces the outlines of a similar triangular trade going into the evolution of blues. The results of this would not become fully visible until the twentieth century; but it is intriguing to think that it may have been paralleled by an analogous economy operating more visibly on the bourgeois/popular stage — and indeed, that the two may have intersected.

18. Lhamon, *Raising Cain*, 1998, 42; Cockrell, *Demons of Disorder*, 1997, 63.
19. The Water Cress Woman is actually a fairy in disguise, an emissary from Towha. Thus the three categories of "womanhood" are interconnected. Moreover, she is played by a man (a pantomime Dame?). The element of cross-dressing, here as in the case of Oedidee, adds its usual frisson to the role of gender in the drama of alterity.
20. Christa Knellwolf, "Comedy in the OMAI Pantomime," in *Cook and Omai: The Cult of the South Seas* (Canberra: National Library of Australia, 2001), 17–21.
21. Ibid., 18, 20, 21. The actor John Rich had influentially developed the genre of harlequinade earlier in the eighteenth century at Covent Garden, playing Harlequin as a dumb acrobat, a comic figure who was, however, endowed with magical powers. According to Roger Fiske (*English Theatre Music*, 1973, 472), the actor David Garrick reveals in a letter of 1775 that he had thought of putting Omai on the stage as an "'arlequin sauvage."
22. Warner, *Fantastic Metamorphoses*, 2002, 144–50; *The Pantomime of Aladin, or the Wonderful Lamp... the Poetry by J. O' Keefe Esq. the Music selected from the Works of Handel, Giordini, Carolan & Shield, by Mr A. Shan, the Songs by W. Shield* (London: G. Goulding, n.d. [1788?]). Among Shield's pieces are several "Irish" tunes, and dances (a "Turkish Dance," and dances for "Zoreb the little slave," and for "Mustapha") in typical "clockwork" style. Another popular example is *Aladdin or The Wonderful Lamp, A Fairy Opera... Composed by Henry R. Bishop* (London: Goulding & D'Almaine, 1826); much of Bishop's music for the genies is significantly repetitive and drone-based — but overall his score, compared to earlier works, is in a more homogeneous early Romantic ("fairy") style: the bourgeois ego settling into a greater degree of (self-) control?
23. Slavoj Žižek, "'I Hear You with My Eyes'; or, The Invisible Master," in *Gaze and Voice as Love Objects*, ed. Renata Salecl and Slavoj Žižek (Durham NC: Duke University Press, 1996), 90–126, 97.
24. Warner, *Fantastic Metamorphoses*, 2002, 144, 149.
25. Steven Connor (*Dumbstruck: A Cultural History of Ventriloquism* [Oxford: Oxford University Press, 2000], 23) remarks that the etymology of the word *dictator* reminds us of the priority of *voice* in the apparatus of authority; he quotes St. Paul (Romans 10:17): "Ex auditu fides" (from hearing, belief). He also comments (275–77) on how, in the classic ventriloquist–dummy setup, the ventriloquist is himself often constructed as a stooge, sharing the same mechanical, childlike discourse as his dummy.
26. See Warner, *Fantastic Metamorphoses*, 2002, 166–79.
27. Karl Marx, *Capital*, vol. 1, trans. Ben Fowkes (Harmondsworth, UK: Penguin, 1976), 164–65; translation slightly modified. Marx's word was not *phantastische*, as the translation in this edition suggests, but *phantasmagorische*. His concept was later significantly developed, in relation to the specific sphere of cultural production, by the critical Marxists, Walter Benjamin and T. W. Adorno; see Max Paddison, *Adorno's Aesthetics of Music* (Cambridge, UK: Cambridge University Press, 1993),124, 244–45.
28. The South Sea Bubble was one of the earliest examples — and is still the most notorious — of irrational speculative investment and crash. The South Sea Company was awarded a trade monopoly in return for taking over most of the National Debt. An overheated rise in share value was matched only by its precipitous fall. The situation was rescued only by the intervention of the politician Sir Robert Walpole, who became First Minister the following year on the strength of his achievement. Gay was an investor, and lost heavily — not the least of the ironies inherent in the title of *The Beggar's Opera*, along with the fact that the corruption of Walpole's administration is among the objects of satire in the work.

Although the phantasmagoric value of South Sea capital dissolved in 1720 when the bubble burst, one might suggest that it returned later, as cultural capital, in the forms offered for consumption by Cook, Omai, and others. "O my!" seems a suitable exclamation to mark the magical effects of both moments (especially since property, financial or cultural, was involved in both).

29. This popularity extended to America. It was first performed there, in New York, in 1750. It was preceded by performances of other English ballad operas (starting in 1735), and followed by many more (see note 16 above).
30. *The Dancing Master*, eighteen editions, with changing content, published by John Playford (1651–89), Henry Playford (1690–1703), and John Young (1706–c. 1728). *Wit and Mirth*, ed. Thomas D'Urfey, various editions, 1699–1720. It is not known if Gay took tunes directly from these collections but many of the tunes he uses can be found there. Also important in this period were Allan Ramsey's collection of Scottish songs, *The Tea-Table Miscellany* (1724), Alexander Stuart's *Musick for Allan Ramsey's Collection of Scots Songs* (1725), and William Thompson's *Orpheus Caledonius* (1725). Again it is not known if Gay took tunes from these sources, but he does use some tunes that are found there. For Gay's tunes, and discussion of their sources, see Jeremy Barlow, *The Music of John Gay's The Beggar's Opera* (Oxford: Oxford University Press, 1990).
31. John Gay, *The Beggar's Opera* (New York: Dover, 1999), 1, 57.
32. See Barlow, *The Music of John Gay's The Beggar's Opera*, 1990, ix–xi; for the Burney quotation, p. x.
33. This point is made by Barlow, ibid., 109. Quotations in the rest of this paragraph describing tunes come from sources listed in ibid., 109–16.
34. Gay, *Beggar's Opera*, 1999, 40.
35. Ibid., 7. In one of the many parodies of *The Beggar's Opera* — *The Metamorphosis of the Beggar's Opera*, presented at the Little Theatre in London in 1730 — all the male parts were played by women and vice versa — an interesting subversion (perhaps) of the gendered structure of exchange in the work (cf. note 19 above); see Fiske, *English Theatre Music*, 1973, 102.
36. That the crisis was at the same time economic (hyperinflation, crash, depression), political (totalitarianism), and discursive (modernist assaults on "representation" as such) marks out the interpenetration of systems which I have been outlining, but by negation: "exchange" itself, as a social and epistemological principle, was in question — and has remained so.

    A different but also intriguing comparison would be between *The Beggar's Opera* and a novel which came out one year before the South Sea Bubble, by that arch-dissenter Daniel Defoe — *Robinson Crusoe*, no less: whose guileless location of mercantile enterprise within man's natural state itself, as celebratory as Gay is mordant, provided ample grounds for the political economists' theorizing (and, later, for Marx's ironic comment on their romantic "Robinsonades": see, e.g., Karl Marx, *Grundrisse: Foundations of the Critique of Political Economy*, trans. Martin Nicolaus (Harmondsworth, UK: Penguin, 1973), 83.
37. According to Fiske (*English Theatre Music*, 1973, 102), at the moment of McHeath's (deliberately absurd) reprieve, the gallery (i.e., the lower elements in the audience) "cheered hysterically."
38. Shield in a letter to Ritson, cited in Bertrand H. Bronson, *Joseph Ritson: Scholar at Arms* (Berkeley: University of California Press, 1938), 146; according to Fiske (*English Theatre Music*, 1973, 544–46), Shield's pantomime of 1790, *The Picture of Paris*, is full of such lines as "The gay Monsieur, a slave no more."
39. On Ritson and Shield, see Bronson, *Joseph Ritson*, passim; Fiske , *English Theatre Music*, 1973, 544–46; and Dave Harker *Fakesong: The Manufacture of British "Folksong" 1700 to the Present Day* (Milton Keynes, UK: Open University Press, 1985), 15–37. On "The Collier's Rant" and its contemporary context, see A. L. Lloyd, *Folk Song in England* (London: Panther, 1969), 331–37; Ritson was the first to print this iconic song, but most specialists agree that it is almost certainly of much older provenance. Shield's textbook, *An Introduction to Harmony*, in its first edition (London: G. and J. Robinson, 1800), already contained a few "national" tunes together with advice to accompany them "simply" (for, as Shield wrote to Ritson, both preferred "simple national melody" to florid Italian stuff: quoted, Bronson, *Joseph Ritson*, 1938, 87); in the second edition (London: J. Robinson, n.d. [1815]) Shield added an Appendix containing an extensive selection of model harmonizations of folk tunes — Scots, Irish, Welsh, Canadian, and "Border tunes" said to have been learned "during my infancy" (35). Among the last category is "The Keel Row," in arrangements for piano, harp, fiddle, and "small Northumberland pipe," and a dance tune called "The Running Fitter," described as being associated with the "Hopping

Musicians" (the "hoppings" is still the local (North East England) name for annual carnival). Ritson's publications referred to in the main text are: *A Select Collection of English Songs*, 3 vols. (London: J. Johnson, 1783); *The Bishoprick Garland; or Durham Minstrel* (Stockton, 1784); and *The Northumberland Garland; or, Newcastle Nightingale: A Matchless Collection of Famous Songs* (Newcastle: Hall and Elliot, 1793).

40. See Connor, *Dumbstruck*, 2000, 191–225, 249–89; quotations from 200, 197–98, 231, 277.
41. My translation (helped by Ian Biddle) of "Wir wären gut — anstatt so roh/Doch die Verhältnisse, sie sind nicht so" (Bertold Brecht. *Die Dreigroschenoper, Versuche*, 3 [Berlin: Suhrkamp Verlag, 1959], 175). Literally, *roh* means "raw" or "crude" and *Verhältnisse* means "relations;" the latter casts an interesting extra light on the "Marxism" of Peachum's point: it is the word that Marx often uses when he is talking about "relations of production."
42. Cockrell (*Demons of Disorder*, 1997) takes the title of his book from an 1833 Philadelphia newspaper description of "rough music" (78), and links its function to Jacques Attali's association of "noise" with disorder. See Jacques Attali, *Noise: The Political Economy of Music*, trans. Brian Massumi (Manchester, UK: Manchester University Press, 1985); I come to Attali's theory in a bit more detail shortly. Describing early blackface songs, Cockrell writes: "This music assaulted sensibilities, challenged the roots of respectability, and promised subversion, a world undone…" (82).
43. This dating should not be taken too tightly. In England, the period of Civil War and Commonwealth (1642–53) marked a moment of great popular agitation, and between then and the end of the seventeenth century, Milton and Locke among others laid the foundations of democratic political theory. This half century was also the period that saw the beginnings of an organized music business, manifested in public concerts, pleasure garden entertainment, and music publishing enterprises such as Playford's, which to some extent began to bring vernacular music into this new public space. In Raymond Williams's terms, this early Enlightenment period was an *emergent* phase in a process that would reach its peak in the second half of the eighteenth century. We could go even further back, say, to Shakespeare's "All the world's a stage," at a time when an initial expansionist phase of mercantile capitalism coincided, intriguingly, with consciousness-shifting encounters with foreign "others," in the New World and elsewhere. But, despite the invention of opera at this time, with its *stile rappresentativo,* music was not yet to an equivalent level of development; for some time to come, the subjects of opera would be confined to gods, kings, and mythic heroes.

    This "archaeology" is congruent with Foucault's — even though (with apparent perversity) he presents the "modern" episteme (beginning around 1800) as breaking with the representationalism of the earlier period (which he terms the "classical" episteme); see Michel Foucault, *The Order of Things: An Archaeology of the Human Sciences* (London: Tavistock, 1974).
44. Attali, *Noise*, 1985, 81, 46, 57, 61, 62.
45. Ibid., 64–65.
46. Michael Hardt and Antonio Negri, *Empire* (Cambridge, MA: Harvard University Press, 2000), 86.
47. Readers may recognize, lying behind this paragraph, the outlines of Lacan's psychoanalytic economy. The three "orders" of this economy are: the Symbolic, the sphere of the signifier, where subjects are positioned in relation to the overall system governing the structures of semiotic difference (or Big Other); the Imaginary, the sphere of identification, where the ego finds its ideals and (self-/mis-) representations (typically through such processes as those associated with the so-called mirror stage) and its objects of desire (*objets petits a*); and the Real, that stratum of brute materiality which is foreclosed, rendered impossible, by the initiation of the Symbolic and the Imaginary, whose existence can only be supposed but whose unknowability is absolutely necessary if particular meanings and identities are to function. For more detailed discussion, see Dylan Evans, *An Introductory Dictionary of Lacanian Psychoanalysis* (London: Routledge, 1997), to which (rather than clutter up my text with over many citations of Lacan's own writings) I shall often refer.
48. The same is true in the political theory as well: repetition here, it was considered by many writers, turned representatives into mere ventriloquizing delegates.
49. Attali, *Noise,* 1985, 126.
50. Referring to Merleau-Ponty's phenomenology, Steven Connor (*Dumbstruck*, 2000) has argued that vocal gesture "is not a form of representation, or mimicry of pre-existing thoughts, but a

way of bringing the speaker's [or singer's] world into being" (4). Connor's first chapter (3–43) eloquently outlines the sensorial structure of voice/gaze interaction. I shall return to the topic of this structure quite often, particularly in the context of its technological reconfiguration.

51. Cited in Hardt and Negri, *Empire,* 2000, 113.
52. Michael Taussig, *Mimesis and Alterity* (New York: Routledge, 1993), xiii, 72, 21, xiii, 47, 45, xviii; the quotation beginning "Before, the fetishes..." is from Horkheimer and Adorno's *Dialectic of Enlightenment.* When Taussig invented his "aping" trope, he may have had in his mind Marx's aphorism, "Human anatomy contains a key to the anatomy of the ape" (Marx, *Grundrisse,* 1973, 105). Marx's point is that critical self-understanding at a "higher" stage is a condition for explaining the differences and similarities of the "lower," and hence the process of historical development; Taussig stands this insight on its head — or at least reveals the mimetic circle underpinning the relationship.

   The "magical" (irrational) power which actually supports the generalization of representation (the *ré-total*) is nowhere clearer than in the schemas of Marxist futurology — unless it be in Napoleonic confidence in the global applicability of French revolutionary law, or in the doctrine of the "manifest destiny" of the United States.
53. For an excellent critical summary of the post-Gramscian development of articulation theory, as worked out by Hall, Laclau, and Mouffe, see Jennifer Daryl Slack, "The Theory and Method of Articulation in Cultural Studies," in *Stuart Hall: Critical Dialogues in Cultural Studies,* ed. David Morley and Kuan-Hsing Chen (London: Routledge, 1996), 112–27. Returning to an earlier point in the argument (*Omai*), one might say that the desirable trajectory is from a relation of property ("Oh my... [whatever]") to one of wonder in the connectivity of difference ("Oh, *my*!").

   This "post-Marxist" development of articulation theory is only one of the ways in which attempts have been made to cut the hierarchical ties of representation. Derridean deconstruction is another. Perhaps Deleuze's "nomadic thought," constantly de- and reterritorializing itself, is closest — except that Deleuze's antipathy to even temporary formations of power seems to rule out all possibility of political agency; see Gilles Deleuze and Félix Guattari, *A Thousand Plateaux,* trans. Brian Massumi (London: Athlone Press, 1988). Curiously, Deleuze (along with some other poststructuralists — Barthes, for example) seems to see music itself — defined as "refrain" constantly deterritorializing itself — as a model of nonrepresentational practice, downplaying the hierarchical structures of mimesis which have developed here no less than in other signifying practices.
54. Bruno Latour, *We Have Never Been Modern,* trans. Catherine Porter (New York: Harvester Wheatsheaf, 1993).
55. Donna Haraway, *Simians, Cyborgs, and Women: The Reinvention of Nature* (London; Free Association Books, 1991), 210.
56. Teresa Brennan, *History After Lacan* (London: Routledge, 1993), 10.
57. Cited in Friedrich Kittler, *Gramophone, Film, Typewriter,* trans. Geoffrey Winthrop-Young and Michael Wutz (Stanford, CA: Stanford University Press, 1999), 9. For an application of Kittler's perspective to early nineteenth-century German music aesthetics (to which I am indebted here), see Ian Biddle, *Listening to Men: Music, Masculinity and the Austro-German Tradition, 1789–1914* (forthcoming), chapter 1, "Discourse Channels: Listening as a Cultural-Historical Category in the Austro-German *Frűromantik*."

   The spatialization of voice at which Novalis seems to hint might support an interpretation of this historical shift in terms of an interplay between the Lacanian part-objects — *objets petits a,* or objects of desire — of "gaze" and "voice." I see this Lacanian economy as an equivalent to the Derridean antimony of "speech" and "(archi-) writing" — except that in Lacan there is no presumption that "voice" (the carrier of "presence" in Derrida's scheme), is simply a metaphysical charlatan; rather, it retains a constant potential of disruption — of invoking the Real. One of the pioneers of phantasmagoria, Étienne-Gaspard Robertson, liked to project specters onto smoke, including the severed head of the recently guillotined Danton (see Warner, *Fantastic Metamorphoses,* 2002, 177–79); surely this head would be open-mouthed in the act of a (now silenced) final scream — just like the scream in Edvard Munch's famous picture, which Žižek has taken as a definitive image of "object voice" (Žižek, "I Hear You with My Eyes," 1996, 93–94). Munch wrote obsessively about this silent scream, seemingly conjoining the scream inside himself and that within nature: "One evening I walk down a hillside path… I felt a huge scream welling up inside me — and I really did hear a huge scream… The lines and colours quivered with movement. These vibrations of light caused not only the oscillation of my eyes. My ears were also affected and began to vibrate. So I actually heard a scream." And again: "I was walking along the road with two friends — then the sun set. The heavens turned a bloody red… and I was left trembling in fear. And I felt a huge endless scream course through nature" (quoted, Poul Erik Tøjner, *Munch in His Own Words* [Munich, London, and New York: Prestel, 2002], 96). The suggestion is that, as the reification and abstraction of gaze proceeded (including within the abstracted writing out of subjectivity in musical scores), so the disruptive, transgressive potential of voice — especially disturbingly disembodied voices — increased. Connor points out (*Dumbstruck*, 2000, 338–56) that the age-old fantasy of building a "talking head" — an apparently vocalizing automaton — took on new impetus in the eighteenth and nineteenth centuries, leading eventually to the development of telegraphy and phonography.

It is important to stress that the aesthetic shift I am pointing to here is concretely there in the detail of the music history: symphony and concerto grew most significantly out of opera, and their methods of representation of inner drama can be readily traced to operatic models, while the theatrical structures of chamber music add to this lineage the drama of the street (via the traditions of divertimento and serenade). However, this shift should not be seen as a simple displacement. The relationships that ensued were intricate and ambivalent: for instance, it would be possible to think of the imposition of monologic authorial control in autonomous musical works as a tactic in which voice so to speak takes over the spatializing function of gaze — "the composer's voice" (to use Edward Cone's famous formulation) *speaks for* the gaze. This complexity is such that, although the topic is enormously relevant to my overall argument, its full development would demand a different book, and I can only gesture here to some of the existing literature.

Gary Tomlinson ('Musicology, Anthropology, History,' in *The Cultural Study of Music: A Critical Introduction*, ed. Martin Clayton, Trevor Herbert and Richard Middleton [New York: Routledge, 2003], 31–44) traces the disciplinary divergence in the West between music historiography and music anthropology, beginning in this period, to the split between a conception of autonomous instrumental music, conceived as specific to the West, and a broader, intercultural category of *singing*. Elsewhere (*Metaphysical Song: An Essay on Opera* [Princeton, NJ: Princeton University Press, 1999]), Tomlinson explores the role of opera in this history as constituting a sphere where a sense of the "noumenal" — what lies beyond the territory of concrete representation — could be adumbrated; the modern operatic voice (dating from around 1800), for example, is seen as mediating between the structure of the Kantian transcendental subject ("The accord governing knowledge is now a harmony of faculties within the subject. The system of representation involved in knowing is folded wholly into the soul" (77)) and an emergent awareness of the *uncanny* ("This voice… is a place where the phenomenal world extends itself to a noumenal margin, so it holds out the hope of embodying before our ears, finally, a transcendental object" (84)). This is an area influentially discussed also by Carolyn Abbate (*Unsung Voices: Opera and Musical Narrative in the Nineteenth Century* [Princeton, NJ: Princeton University Press, 1991]), who argues for the importance of moments when the obvious operatic narrative, associated with the control exerted from an authorial distance, is disrupted by uncanny, other voices (e.g., instrumental enunciations; female characters who seem to sing "against" the compositional line), which have the effect of dividing subjectivity in a kind of "second hearing" (56) — precisely the "proliferation of possible selves" to which I refer shortly (see p. 28). Wagner is central to Abbate's argument, as he is too to Lydia Goehr's in her *The Quest for Voice* (Oxford: Clarendon Press, 1998): Wagner, whose operatic symphonism (out of Beethoven) is at the same time shot through with his highly theorized attempt (derived ultimately from Rousseau's account of the primordial relationship of melody, speech, and human feeling) to rebut the claims of musical formalism through a technique that would reanimate instrumental sounds themselves with the quality of "voice." Nietzsche, as quoted by Goehr (ibid., vi), catches precisely the essence of Wagner's mimetic counterthrust:

> One can say, as a general comment on Wagner, as a musician, that he has given a language to everything in nature that until now has made no attempt to speak; he does not believe that some things must inevitably be dumb. He plunges even into dawn and sunrise, into

forests, fogs, ravines, mountain peaks, the dead of night and moonlight and discovers a secret longing in all of them: they want a voice.

Finally (here), one should mention Richard Leppert (*The Sight of Sound: Music, Representation, and the History of the Body* [Berkeley: University of California Press, 1993]), who offers a broader account (broader both historically and in theme) of the interplay of the sight and sound of music, in the context of *embodiment*, and, in particular, the gendering of this whole nexus; within this history, music as such, at least in its sensuous presentations (as against rational theorizations), was always tending to be feminized, a tendency that reached a peak of anxious insistence in the nineteenth century.

In the face of this impressive body of work, by a collection of remarkable scholars, I have only one further comment to add: that a still fuller picture of this discursive field as a whole will not be available until more account is taken of the contemporaneous and more clearly palpable contributions of *popular* voices.

58. Musicological excavation of this "supplement" is now well established. One excellent example, by Lawrence Kramer ("The Musicology of the Future," *Repercussions* 1 [1992]: 5–18), reads the textures of a Mozart Divertimento "as a staging of the 'civilising' effort needed for an artistic distancing from the palpable body of the Low" (Richard Middleton, "Who May Speak? From a Politics of Popular Music to a Popular Politics of Music," *Repercussions* 7–8 [1999–2000]: 77–103, 98n). But how should we animate the voice of this body? To use Taussig's terms, how should we represent (*sic*) its aping of Mozart's aping? "My question for Kramer [it is a question for all of us] would be: what would it mean to hear this music from the vantage-point not of the drawing-room but of the street?" (idem.).
59. This fantasy spread widely down through the social layers in the nineteenth century, and is still powerful. Two examples: the hugely influential essays on self-development by Ralph Waldo Emerson, and the extraordinarily popular *Self-Help* (influenced by Emerson) by Samuel Smiles (first published in 1859).
60. T. W. Adorno, *Introduction to the Sociology of Music*, trans. E. B. Ashton (New York: Seabury Press, 1976), 22.
61. Attali's somewhat misleading dating may come back into the picture at this point. His picture of the bourgeois concert as representation — a "spectacle in front of silent people" — actually only became typical in the second half of the nineteenth century (later still in America: see Lawrence Levine, *Highbrow/Lowbrow: The Emergence of Cultural Hierarchy in America* [New Haven, CT: Yale University Press, 1988]). The process of interiorization took place gradually, unevenly, and partially, and even then retained an exterior (that is, a social) dimension in the intraclass ritual enacted in the concert-event. See Christopher Small, "Performance as Ritual: Sketch for an Enquiry into the True Nature of a Symphony Concert," in *Lost in Music: Culture, Style and the Musical Event*, ed. Avron Levine White (London: Routledge and Kegan Paul, 1987), 6–32,
62. Walter Benjamin, "Theses on the Philosophy of History," in *Illuminations*, trans. Harry Zohn (London: Fontana, 1973), 255–66, 259. Benjamin also writes:

> Historicism contents itself with establishing a causal connection between various moments in history. But no fact that is a cause is for that very reason historical. It became historical posthumously, as it were, through events that may be separated from it by thousands of years. A historian who takes this as his point of departure stops telling the sequence of events like the beads of a rosary. Instead, he grasps the constellation which his own era has formed with a definite earlier one. (Ibid., 265)

63. Ibid. 257: "To articulate the past historically does not mean to recognise it 'the way it really was' (Ranke). It means to seize hold of a memory as it flashes up at a moment of danger."
64. See Slavoj Žižek, "How Did Marx Invent the Symptom?," in *The Sublime Object of Ideology* (London: Verso, 1989), 11–53.
65. Mowitt, *Percussion*, 2002, 205. Mowitt goes on (205–6) to turn his question into a critique of Žižek, diagnosing (symptomatically) a "naturalism" at odds with the method of historical materialism. But the material process of discursive invention surely has an important role in such a method.

66. The idea is already adumbrated (complete with an embryonic mirror-stage theory) by Marx himself: "after a fashion, it is with the human being as with the commodity. Since the human being does not come into the world bringing a mirror with him, nor yet as a Fichtean philosopher able to say 'I am myself,' he first recognises himself as reflected in other men" (Marx, *Capital,* 1976, 1:23).
67. Žižek, *Sublime Object,* 1989, 21.
68. Hayden White, *Metahistory: The Historical Imagination in Nineteenth-Century Europe* (Baltimore: John Hopkins University, 1973), 309–17. The quotations here are taken by White from *The Communist Manifesto* itself.
69. Here it is, clearly signaled in Marx: "The division of labour . . . which in its turn is based on the natural division of labour in the family, and the separation of society into individual families opposed to one another, simultaneously implies the *distribution*, and indeed the *unequal* distribution, both quantitative and qualitative, of labour and its products, hence property, the nucleus, the first form of which lies in the family, where wife and children are the slaves of the husband." (Karl Marx, *The German Ideology* [New York: Prometheus Books, 1998], 51–52.)
70. The first point has been concisely explored by Teresa Brennan (*History After Lacan*, 1993, 160–65), among others. The second has been most incisively put in Ernesto Laclau and Chantal Mouffe's devastating critique of economic essentialism, *Hegemony and Socialist Strategy: Towards a Radical Democratic Politics* (London: Verso, 1985). In their "post-Marxist" position, "objects appear articulated not like pieces in a clockwork mechanism, but because the presence of some in the others hinders the suturing of the identity of any of them" (104).
71. Hobbes, quoted in Hardt and Negri, *Empire,* 2000, 105.
72. Ibid., 103.
73. Compare Marx:

> human beings become individuals only through the process of history. He appears originally as a *species-being, clan being, herd animal* — although in no way whatever as a 'political animal' in the political sense. Exchange itself is a chief means of this individuation. It makes the herd-like existence superfluous and dissolves it. Soon the matter [has] turned in such a way that as an individual he relates himself only to himself, while the means with which he posits himself as individual have become the making of his generality and commonness. (Marx, *Grundrisse,* 1973, 496)

74. Unless, of course, this *is* that chapter — the chapter that cannot speak its name (and what might this silence be a symptom of?).
75. It is quite hard for us to think ourselves back into a situation in which huge proportions of populations, in every continent of the world, were in conditions of slavery or related forms of servitude (serfdom, peonage, debt-bondage, indentured service). In many parts of the Americas, Africa, and Asia, during the period around 1800, the proportions were over 50 percent. It is worth noting too that the possibility of slavery for *Britons* had been a worry, and sometimes a reality, within recent memory. At least 20,000 Britons were captured by "Barbary corsairs" between 1600 and 1730, and many were enslaved in north Africa; see Linda Colley, *Captives: Britain, Empire and the World 1600–1730* (London: Pimlico, 2003). Similarly, American ideology celebrated the new world as a refuge from European systems of religious and economic "slavery," even though large numbers of white Americans had been indentured or enslaved (including by Native Americans). Yet in both cases (Britain and the United States), freedom was founded, economically and arguably psychologically, on enslavement of others. It is as if "freedom" cannot even be conceptualized — its absolute promise is too terrifying — unless it is given an anchorage in the palpable nonfreedom of another.

    A piercing light is thrown on this problematic by Eric Lott's brilliant dissection of the economy of blackface as "love and theft": a traffic in representations and another in commodities (both human and musico-theatrical), each mediating the other, both finding a focus in fetishizing exchanges of the black male body, with its (more or less off-stage) setting in the "peculiar institution" itself; see Lott, *Love and Theft,* 1993, 55–62. Bearing in mind the complex dynamics here of both (mis-)recognition and of property, this appears — translating now into my terminology — as a prime case of a *being*(,) *had.* Lott (ibid., 226–33) is also illuminating on the tortured discursive knot around which the concepts of slavery and wage-slavery chased each other in nineteenth-century America.

What might be the significance of the fact that both "slavery" and "the people" (hence "popular music") took on a dramatically new discursive force — that is, became issues in a new way, became problematized — at around the same time? Is it, perhaps, because in both cases (and in interlinked ways, actually) they became "others," their specificity thrown into new light by alteritous relationships? Robin Blackburn ("Slavery — Its Special Features and Social Role," in *Slavery and Other Forms of Unfree Labour*, ed. Léonie Archer [London: Routledge, 1988], 262–79) outlines the interrelations (as well as differences) between various types of bondage. Basing his argument on the theory of early human history put forward by Marx and Engels, Blackburn also describes ways in which these types of bondage may have grown out of early developments in family and kinship structures; one can see, as I will shortly suggest, how "the people" could appear as a kind of "slave" within the political and cultural household.

76. See Michel Foucault, *Discipline and Punish: The Birth of the Prison*, trans. Alan Sheridan (London: Penguin,1979), 195–228. Foucault makes clear the "theatrical" character of panoptical systems: "They [the cells in which subjects are 'enslaved'] are like so many cages, so many small theatres, in which each actor is alone, perfectly individualised and constantly visible." And this triumph of the authoritarian gaze carries with it the *silencing* of those imprisoned actors, for it "made it possible… to avoid those compact, swarming, howling masses that were to be found in places of confinement [not only earlier forms of prison but all other locations of multitudinous connection]" (200). Foucault's "dummies" — unable to make themselves heard, ventriloquized even without their knowledge — find a twentieth-century apotheosis in the inhabitants of Debord's "society of the spectacle"; see Guy Debord, *Society of the Spectacle* (Detroit: Black and Red, 1970).
77. Hardt and Negri, *Empire*, 2000, 121, 115.
78. Marx's stress on the role of *circulation* (*Grundrisse*, 1973, 401–743, for example) comes inescapably to mind. Thus "The exchange of substance and of form subordinated to human need through human labour appears from the viewpoint of capital as its own reproduction. It is at bottom the constant reproduction of labour itself" (742). But the dialectic of property and being is central to this process: "The exchange of labour for labour — seemingly the condition of the worker's property — rests on the foundations of the worker's propertylessness" (515).
79. "This, then, is the basic paradox of the Lacanian logic of 'non-all' [*pas-tout*]: in order to transform a collection of particular elements into a consistent totality, one has to add (or to subtract, which amounts to the same thing: to posit as an exception) a paradoxical element which, in its very particularity, embodies the universality of the genus in the form of its opposite." (Slavoj Žižek, *For They Know Not What They Do: Enjoyment as a Political Factor*, 2nd ed. [London: Verso, 2002], 44.) Thus "The Woman [Woman qua universal] does not exist," whereas Man, having universalized himself via the exception, "Woman," does.
80. "…in so far as every position within social totality is ultimately overdetermined by class struggle, no neutral place is excluded from the dynamics of class struggle from which it would be possible to locate class struggle within the social totality" (Slavoj Žižek, "The Spectre of Ideology," in *The Žižek Reader*, ed. Elizabeth Wright and Edmond Wright [Oxford: Blackwell, 1999c], 53–86, 75). "Class struggle" is "a certain limit, a pure negativity, a traumatic limit which prevents the final totalisation of the social-ideological field. The 'class struggle' is present only its effects, in the fact that every attempt to totalize the social field, to assign to social phenomena a definite place in the social structure, is always doomed to failure." (Žižek, *Sublime Object*, 1989, 164).
81. Here is cultural historian Jacob Burckhardt, grappling in the middle of the nineteenth century with the effects of this moment: "The word freedom sounds rich and beautiful, but no one should talk about it who has not seen and experienced slavery under the loud-mouthed masses, called 'the people,' seen it with his own eyes and endured civil unrest…. I know too much about history to expect anything from the despotism of the masses but a future tyranny, which will mean the end of history" (from *Letters*, quoted in White, *Metahistory*, 1973, 235).
82. Ernst Bloch, Georg Lukács, Bertold Brecht, Walter Benjamin, and Theodor W. Adorno, *Aesthetics and Politics* [London: New Left Books, 1977], 123.
83. It is only an apparent paradox that the effect of universalization here (i.e., the installing of "serious music" as a norm) is individuation — the (phallogocentric) power to "be oneself," to lay down a law. By contrast, of course, "all women are the same," and "all blacks look alike." It is no coincidence that Adorno persistently figures popular music in terms of feminization and emasculation; see Middleton, "Who May Speak"? 1999–2000, 89–92; Susan McClary,

Feminine Endings: Music, Gender, and Sexuality (Minneapolis: University of Minnesota Press, 1991), 65.

84. T. W. Adorno, "On Popular Music," in *On Record: Rock, Pop and the Written Word*, ed. Simon Frith and Andrew Goodwin (1941, London: Routledge, 1990), 301–14, see footnote on p. 314; Abner Silver and Robert Bruce, *How to Write and Sell a Song Hit* (New York: Prentice-Hall, 1939). Needless to say, both texts come from a moment that was just as much a "moment of danger" as was 1848 or the 1790s. I have no doubt that today, when Žižek is writing, qualifies to join this lineage.
85. Silver and Bruce, *How to Write*, 1939, 2, 55, 161–62.
86. Ibid., 159.
87. See Žižek, *Sublime Object*, 1989, 173–78.
88. For this paragraph, see ibid., 55–129. For Althusser's celebrated "parable" of interpellation, in which a subject is "hailed" ("Hey, you there!") by a policeman on the street, see Louis Althusser, "Ideology and Ideological State Apparatuses (Notes towards an Investigation)," in *Lenin and Philosophy and Other Essays*, trans. Ben Brewster (London: New Left Books, 1971), 121–73 (esp. 160–65).
89. Ernesto Laclau, "Preface," in Žižek, *Sublime Object*, 1989, xii.
90. Mowitt, *Percussion*, 2002, 12.

Chapter 2

1. Cited in Paul Allen Anderson, *Deep River: Music and Memory in Harlem Renaissance Thought* (Durham NC: Duke University Press, 2001), 1. For background on the Fair, see Christopher Robert Reed, *"All the World Is Here": The Black Presence at White City* (Bloomington IN: Indiana University Press, 2000); subsequent quotations from ibid., 186, 71 (Cook), 132, 103–4 (*Chicago Herald*, July 19, 1893 on "jumpy music").
2. Burleigh was a protégé of Dvořák (who was also there, promoting his view that a true "national" American music should be based on "Negro melodies"), and went on to write the first arrangements of spirituals for solo concert performance.
3. A young W.C. Handy, later to become "father of the blues," set off for the Fair with his vocal quartet, which sang contemporary popular and minstrel songs, but they arrived to find the event postponed for a year; see Handy, *Father of the Blues: An Autobiography* (1941, New York: Da Capo, 1991), 24–26. Handy would not "discover" blues for another ten years; see note 14 (p. 259). One wonders, however, if his youthful quartet included barbershop chords in their performances; according to Lynn Abbott and Doug Seroff ("'They Cert'ly Sound Good to Me': Sheet Music, Southern Vaudeville, and the Commercial Ascendancy of Blues," *American Music* 14 (1996): 402–54), who quote Handy on the subject, such "intuitive" chromatic harmonizing was one route whereby blue notes emerged (ibid., 404).
4. See Philip V. Bohlman, *World Music: A Very Short Introduction* (Oxford: Oxford University Press, 2002), 33, 112.
5. This oversimplifies Du Bois's views, but the effects of his hugely influential book perhaps justify this for my context; see W. E. B. Du Bois, *The Souls of Black Folk*, centenary ed., ed. Henry Louis Gates Jr, and Terri Hume Oliver (1903, New York: Norton, 1999). Ronald M. Radano ("Soul Texts and the Blackness of Folk," *Modernism/Modernity* 2, no. 1 (1995): 71–95), explores the complexity of Du Bois's view of the spirituals, as carrying meaning far beyond what could be associated with any "authentic" folk essence, a view that was absolutely demanded by his theory of "double consciousness" and its implications for the relationship of race, culture, and history. Du Bois's book was crucial in showing African Americans that they, no less (indeed, more) than whites, could assert an interest in the musical evidence of an earlier phase of their development rather than abandon it in embarrassment.
6. Lott, *Love and Theft*.
7. Du Bois, *Souls of Black Folk*, 1999, 10–11. Ronald M. Radano ("Denoting Difference: The Writing of the Slave Spirituals," *Critical Inquiry* 22 (1996): 506–44) demonstrates how the roots of the folklorization of the spirituals go back to the early nineteenth century, and also how the impulses behind this process and the contemporaneous white investment in blackface discourse were from the start thoroughly intermixed, in an affective nexus where desire,

envy, distancing, and mockery slide into each other. Du Bois's Herderian idea of the "slave songs" as part of a world folk heritage surfaced again, interestingly, when in the 1930s Paul Robeson visited Eastern Europe, Russia, and Spain, and began to theorize a universal folk music grounded in a common popular experience of suffering; see Martin Bauml Duberman, *Paul Robeson* (London: Bodley Head, 1989), 121, 129, 156, 176, 218. This is only one aspect of how we can see "black music" as linked to an emergent category of "world music." Radano's perspective on the always already hybrid nature of "black music," which is very close to my own, is more fully discussed in his *Lying Up a Nation: Race and Black Music* (Chicago: University of Chicago Press, 2003).

8. Homi Bhabha, *The Location of Culture* (London: Routledge, 1994), 111.
9. *O Brother, Where Art Thou?*, Universal MPO14V.
10. The Faustian bargain was a widespread blues trope. Tommy Johnson certainly made the claim: see David Evans, *Tommy Johnson* (London: Studio Vista, 1971), 22–23; Francis Davis, *The History of the Blues* (London: Secker and Warburg, 1995), 105–6.
11. Charles Keil and Steven Feld, "People's Music Comparatively," in *Music Grooves: Essays and Dialogues*, (Chicago: University of Chicago Press, 1994), 197–202. Keil's piece had been initially published in 1985 (in *Dialectical Anthropology* 10:119–30).
12. Francis Davis (*History of the Blues*) follows a somewhat similar, though not quite so radical line; but he does not list Keil's text in his bibliography. Otherwise, to the best of my knowledge, Keil's argument has not really been followed up.
13. Tony Russell, "Blacks, Whites and Blues," in *Yonder Come the Blues: The Evolution of a Genre*, ed. Paul Oliver, Tony Russell, Robert M. W. Dixon, John Godrich, and Howard Rye (1970, Cambridge, UK: Cambridge University Press, 2001), 143–242.
14. Rainey was speaking to John W. Work (*American Negro Songs and Spirituals: A Comprehensive Collection of 230 Folk Songs, Religious and Secular* [1940, New York: Dover, 1998] 32–33); she remarks that when, shortly after, she began to sing such songs in her act, they were not yet called "blues." Morton was speaking to Alan Lomax in his Library of Congress interviews of 1938 (*Mister Jelly Roll: The Fortunes of Jelly Roll Morton, New Orleans Creole and "Inventor of Jazz."* [1950, Berkeley CA: University of California Press, 1973]), 62; Morton also mentions other pieces that he heard, or created, around the turn of the century and that he refers to as "blues" — but the exact dating is unclear and in many cases the examples he gives suggest ragtime features as much as those of what would come to be understood as blues. Handy was writing in his autobiography (*Father of the Blues*, 1991, 74), telling the famous story of hearing a bottleneck guitarist at Tutwiler railroad station; Handy, admittedly, does also refer (142) to a one-line tune he heard in St. Louis in 1892, of a type that, later, he says, he would draw on to create his own blues songs. Clearly, then, elements which would later congeal into typical blues features were in play before 1900 — but that is a different point.

    For an overview of the few sources that describe blueslike music in the 1890s, see David Evans, *Big Road Blues: Tradition and Creativity in the Folk Blues* (New York: Da Capo 1987), 32–33, and, for similar references to the early twentieth century, ibid., 33–40. Some of the locations are rural but many are urban (including racially fluid New Orleans).

    Charles Keil ("People's Music Comparatively," 1994, 200) has a footnote referring to an unpublished master's dissertation including descriptions of sheet music, by white composers, that contains blueslike features and dates from the 1880s. On the other hand, Thomas L. Riis (*Just Before Jazz: Black Musical Theatre in New York, 1890 to 1915* [Washington DC: Smithsonian Institution Press 1989], 58) describes proto-blue notes — actually chromatic oscillations around the major/minor third — in songs from the "new" African-American musical theater of the early 1900s as part of what made it sound innovative at the time. But then Peter van der Merwe (*Origins of the Popular Style*, 1989), traces some such features back to sixteenth-century Europe…!
15. See Howard W. Odum,"Folk-Song and Folk-Poetry as Found in the Secular Songs of the Southern Negroes," *Journal of American Folklore* 24 (1911): 255–94, 351–96; E. C. Perrow, "Songs and Rhymes From the South," *Journal of American Folklore* 25 (1912): 137–55; 26 (1913): 122–73; 28 (1915): 129–90. The songs had been collected some years before publication. John A. Lomax does identify a blues (see note 61, p. 263) but treats it not as part of a genre but as just a song — one that lives in the larger category of secular songs ("reels"); see John A. Lomax, "Self-Pity in Negro Folk-Songs," *The Nation* 105 (1917): 141–45.

16. "Memphis Blues" was also an instrumental at first, not being given lyrics until 1913. The original "Mr. Crump" was modeled on a song already circulating on the streets of Memphis; see Abbott and Seroff, "'They Cert'ly Sound," 1996, 438. Handy's 1912 publication was also preceded, just, by "Baby Seals' Blues," composed by the black vaudeville artist, H. Franklin "Baby" Seals (ibid., 415–19); this did have lyrics. Four years earlier, in 1908, "I Got the Blues" by white New Orleans musician Antonio Maggio came out; this is a piano rag, but does have an opening strain in 12-bar blues form (ibid., 405–6). White's "Nigger Blues" had been copyrighted in 1912 under the title "The Negro Blues"; in that version it has fifteen verses, reduced in the 1913 publication to six (ibid., 409–11). The very first recording of a vocal blues seems to have been a version of "Memphis Blues" by the white minstrel Morton Harvey, put out by Victor in 1915 (ibid., 439).
17. For a typical, dismissive description of "Nigger Blues," see Robert Palmer, *Deep Blues* (New York: Viking Press, 1981), 105–6.

    George O'Connor (1874–1946) was a highly successful lawyer and businessman, a familiar figure in upper-class Washington, DC, society, an intimate of many top politicians, and well-known too in these circles as a singer of light opera and contemporary popular songs. Among a large amount of sheet music, his papers contain 63 "coon songs." Columbia put out quite a number of records by O'Connor, usually backed by other popular singers of the time, including Al Jolson; "Nigger Blues," for example, is backed by Jolson's "I'm Saving Up the Means to Get to New Orleans." See http://www.library-georgetown.edu/dept/speccoll/oconnor.htm. "Nigger Blues" was reissued on *Let's Get Loose*, New World Records NW290 (1978).
18. Intriguingly, the earliest known published account of blues singing on a public stage has it coming from the mouth of a ventriloquist's dummy (see Abbott and Seroff, "'They Cert'ly Sound," 1996, 413–14). The "ventriloquist" was black vaudeville performer Johnnie Woods from Memphis, whose blues voice seemed to come from his little wooden-headed doll, Henry. (Woods was also a female impersonator; cf. Frankie "Half Pint" Jaxon; see note 74, p. 264). From the start, it seems, and for blacks as well as whites, the blues voice was split — located somehow elsewhere.
19. As it might seem to us. For some in this period, the Golden Age was already gone, destroyed by "modernity" (sheet music, records, commerce). This pattern of infinite regression is part of the process of folklorization itself — and also, as we shall see, of the structure of nostalgia.
20. It is both an advantage and a disadvantage of speculative historiography that proof is impossible. In this case, presumably, it would entail establishing that all black blues singers were situated within chains of musical learning at earlier stages of which — perhaps beyond various mediating links — one would find white as well as black inputs. Walter Benjamin's advice ("Theses on the Philosophy of History," 1973, 257), which I find persuasive, that "To articulate the past historically does not mean to recognise it 'the way it really was' (Ranke). It means to seize hold of a memory as it flashes up at a moment of danger," does not license distortion of materials. We now have the sources to show the explosive development of a rich commercial music culture, involving blacks and whites, often in close proximity, from the 1890s to the 1920s; the spread of the new media technologies, including into rural areas, and the importance in the South of traveling shows and vaudeville theater; the important mediating role of white entrepreneurs (Ralph Peer; H. C. Speir; Frank Walker) in marketing blues from the South; and the inescapable presence across these developments and processes of blackface performance conventions. To assemble all the evidence would require a large book. (There is a useful summary of many of the strands, drawing on recent research, in Alyn Shipton, *A New History of Jazz* [London: Continuum, 2001], 30–71; Ted Vincent, *Keep Cool: The Black Activists Who Built the Jazz Age* [London: Pluto Press, 1995] is also useful, if due allowance is made for an overzealous black-nationalist viewpoint; Abbott and Seroff's "They Cert'ly Sound," 1996, is indispensable in documenting the establishment of an African-American vaudeville circuit in the South, and the important role played there from around 1910 by blues performance.) Such a book, however, still would not prove the point. What is at issue is a cultural unconscious that can be invoked, led to the couch, and encouraged to speak (through interpretations of its textual signifiers) but not reliably documented. I am not of course assuming that, for African-American actors within this unconscious, the signifiers unthinkingly replicate what has been heard, only that they are involved in a network of reference structured by differential power. I will come to the "moment of danger" presently.

21. David Evans, quoted in Davis, *History of the Blues*, 1995, 47. See also Lomax, *The Land Where the Blues Began* (New York: Pantheon, 1993), 64–70; Evans, *Big Road Blues*, 1987, 169–74.
22. Houston Baker Jr., *Blues, Ideology and Afro-American Literature: A Vernacular Theory* (Chicago: University of Chicago Press, 1984), 4, 64, 65, 5. We should add (with Radano, "Soul Texts," 1995, 72), that blues is also always already *different* (from itself: that is, internally differentiated), and that such differences are to be historically situated. Still, although on one level it is indeed vital to insist on such differentiation (and the operation of intrablues dialogics will be important later in my argument), on the level of myth it is precisely the fact that "blues" can present itself as a "(w)hole" that explains its nostalgic appeal.
23. Paul Oliver, Tony Russell, Robert M. W. Dixon, John Godrich, and Howard Rye, *Yonder Come the Blues: The Evolution of a Genre* (Cambridge, UK: Cambridge University Press, 2001), 2.
24. Quoted, Samuel B. Charters, *The Country Blues* (1959, New York: Da Capo Press, 1975), 63; Oliver et al., *Yonder Come the Blues,* 2001, 262–63.
25. Quoted, Evans, *Big Road Blues*, 1987, 63.
26. W. C. Handy *Blues: An Anthology*, ed. Abbe Niles (1926, New York: Da Capo, 1990), 12, 20.
27. Handy, *Father of the Blues,*1991, 231; and see 137–51.
28. Evans, *Tommy Johnson*, 1971, 18, 19; Lomax, *Land Where the Blues Began,* 1993, 55, 460; Oliver et al., *Yonder Come the Blues,* 2001, 203.
29. John A Lomax and Alan Lomax, *Negro Folk Songs as Sung by Leadbelly* (New York: Macmillan, 1936).
30. John A. Lomax and Alan Lomax, *American Ballads and Folk Songs* (New York: Macmillan, 1934), xxx.
31. The *New Yorker* (January 19, 1935) published a "ballad" by noted poet William Rose Benet to mark Leadbelly's arrival in New York with John Lomax. It includes the words: "He was big and he was black/And wondrous were his wrongs/But he had a memory travelled back/Through at least five hundred songs./When his fingers gave those strings a twang/Like a very god in heaven he sang." (Accompanying booklet, Leadbelly, *The Library of Congress Recordings*, comp. Lawrence Cohn, Elektra EKL-301/2, ND). See Charles Wolfe and Kip Lornell, *The Life and Legend of Leadbelly* (London: Secker and Warburg, 1993), 167–68; and for further evidence of the frisson surrounding Leadbelly's arrival in New York, ibid., 1–4, 136–42. On Leadbelly as primitive, see also Davis, *History of the Blues,* 1995, 164–71.
32. Lomax, *Land Where the Blues Began,* 1993, 18.
33. Quoted, Wolfe and Lornell, *Life and Legend,* 1993, 112.
34. Ibid.,145, 141–42, 2, 130, 135.
35. Nathan Huggins, *Harlem Renaissance* (New York: Oxford University Press, 1971), 199.
36. In Bruce Kellner, ed., *Keep A-Inchin' Along: Selected Writings of Carl Van Vechten about Black Art and Letters* (Westport, CT: Greenwood Press, 1979), 48, 162.
37. Lomax, *Land Where the Blues Began,* 1993, 446, 447; Bill Broonzy (with Yannick Bruynoghe), *Big Bill Blues: Big Bill Broonzy's Story as Told to Yannick Bruynoghe* (1955, New York: Oak Publications), 1964), 11–25; Charters, *Country Blues*, 1975, 177–80.
38. Broonzy, *Big Bill Blues,* 1964, 31.
39. John Lee Hooker, speaking in 1968, was more straightforward: "My type of music, I got a variety — for the young folks and the older folks, and the folksingers… I have created about three different fields; a folk field, a blues field, and a jump field for the kids" (quoted in Evans, *Big Road Blues,* 1987, 84).
40. Dorothy Scarborough, *On the Trail of Negro Folk-Songs* (Cambridge MA: Harvard University Press, 1925), 128, 161, 264, 281–82.
41. Newman I. White, *American Negro Folk-Songs* (Cambridge MA: Harvard University Press, 1928), 25, 389, 5.
42. Sterling A. Brown, "The Blues as Folk Poetry," in *Folk-Say: A Regional Miscellany*, ed. B. A. Botkin (Norman OK: University of Oklahoma Press, 1930), 324–39; Carl Van Vechten, "The Black Blues," in Kellner, *Keep A-Inchin' Along,* 1979, 43–49 (first published, *Vanity Fair*, August 1925); Howard W. Odum and Guy B. Johnson, *Negro Workaday Songs* (Chapel Hill: University of North Carolina Press, 1926); Langston Hughes, "The Weary Blues," (1926) in *The Negro Caravan*, ed. Sterling A. Brown, Arthur P. Davis and Ulysses Lee (1941, New York: Arno Press, 1970), 367–68; Langston Hughes, "The Negro Artist and the Racial Mountain," *Nation,* June 23, 1926: 692–94.

43. Brown, "Blues as Folk Poetry," 1930, 324, 339.
44. I am most interested in, and have concentrated on, this folklorizing move. But, debate concerning the interpretive, historical, and policy significance of African-American music, especially spirituals, blues, and jazz, was fierce throughout Harlem Renaissance circles, reflecting its role in the contemporary drama of tradition, nostalgia, and modernization. For Du Bois, the spirituals had a special status as Herder-ish race heritage, whose destiny, he hoped, was to function as a complementary pole to a more developed artistic consciousness, leading to a Hegelian reconciliation; he had no time for more recent commercial products. Locke too regarded the spirituals as a stage in an evolutionary story, out of which a specific sort of formal art would develop, but one which would be part of his vision of a pluralistic cultural universalism: "Deep river; deeper sea!"; Locke valued early jazz, whose neofolk credentials he also wanted to see built on by more formally trained composers. (So far as performance of spirituals was concerned, Locke's taste was for Roland Hayes's "classicizing" style, while Du Bois preferred the more "natural" approach of Paul Robeson.) Hughes attacked the "race towards whiteness" of the black bourgeoisie on class grounds, and his defense of blues and jazz was on the basis that they, rather than spirituals, constituted the genuine poetic voice of contemporary working-class African Americans. Ethnographer and writer, Zora Neale Hurston, criticized Du Bois explicitly for imprisoning rural African Americans in a narrowly interpreted, mythologized past, and in a "double consciousness" which left them no alternative but a normative (white) idea of "progress"; for her, the complexity of contemporary rural musical culture — especially the full range of religious song — ruled out all primitivist interpretation and demanded recognition on its own terms (although she did not, perhaps, altogether escape the dangers of folkloric romanticism). On these debates, and for full references, see Paul Allen Anderson, *Deep River: Music and Memory in Harlem Renaissance Thought* (Durham NC: Duke University Press, 2001).
45. Greil Marcus, *Invisible Republic: Bob Dylan's Basement Tapes* (London: Picador 1997); *Anthology of American Folk Music*, comp. Harry Smith, Smithsonian Folkways FP 251, 252, 253 (1997) [1952].
46. Intriguingly, Davis also recorded white blues, was considerably influenced by black music, and even recorded with a black musician, Oscar Woods; see Tony Russell's account, "Blacks, Whites and Blues," 2001, 206–9.
47. Kittler, *Gramophone, Film, Typewriter*, 1999.
48. See Erika Brady, *A Spiral Way: How the Phonograph Changed Ethnography* (Jackson: University of Mississippi Press, 1999).
49. Ibid., 30–32; Taussig, *Mimesis and Alterity*, 1993, 208–11.
50. On this see Žižek, "I Hear You with My Eyes," 1996.
51. Lomax, *Land Where the Blues Began*, 1993, 9.
52. In John Lomax's account of his and Alan's 1933 recording trip (John Lomax, "Sinful songs of the Southern Negro," *Musical Quarterly*, 21 (1934), 177-87), the convicts they record seem to demonstrate absolutely no suspicion of the "singing machine."
53. Davis, *History of the Blues*, 1995, 72–73.
54. Brady, *A Spiral Way*, 1999, 1.
55. Abbe Niles in Handy, *Blues*,1990, 40.
56. Lomax, *Land Where the Blues Began*, 1993, ix–x, and see 472.
57. Russell, "Blacks, Whites and Blues," 2001, 233.
58. Cecil Brown, *Stagolee Shot Billy* (Cambridge, MA: Harvard University Press, 2003).
59. In tracing the genealogy of the archetype represented by Stagolee, it is difficult to avoid romanticizing an outlaw culture. Howard Odum published a trilogy of "novels" (the best known being the first, *Rainbow Round My Shoulder: The Blue Trail of Black Ulysses* [1928, New York: Krause, 1972]) recounting the nomadic, womanizing, often violent life of a fictional bluesman. Odum undoubtedly drew on his fieldwork, in particular his relationship with a real hobo-songster called John Wesley "Left Wing" Gordon; but in speaking for his Homeric hero — the narrative is in a highly dialectized first person — Odum cannot resist introducing each chapter with a scene-setting, purple-prose slab of "romantic sociology." Alan Lomax described one of his "discoveries," James "Ironhead" Baker, as a "black Homer" (Wolfe and Lornell, *Life and Legend*, 1993, 112). Like the Coen Brothers' similar movie — the story of *O Brother* is loosely based on that of Homer's *Odyssey* and Everett Grant's middle name is Ulysses — both Odum's and Lomax's conceit can perhaps be seen as a powerful cultural inversion in the inter-

est of the Low: the hero no longer a king but an outcast. At the same time, one might ask if this overromanticizes a certain marginality in a way that is absolutely standard in bourgeois culture. Do the Coen Brothers do this too? Do I?

60. Cited in Evans, *Big Road Blues*, 1987, 47–48.
61. White, *American Negro Folk-Songs*, 1928, 389. It is interesting to compare Langston Hughes, for whom "the decisive modernity of the blues — the music he read as *city* songs rising from the crowded streets of big towns — in no way threatened its authenticity as folk music" (Anderson, *Deep River*, 2001, 194).

    John Lomax ("Self-Pity in Negro Folk-Songs," 1917, 143) gives a blues which, he says, he has heard many times under many different names (usually referring to a particular place: e.g., "The Dallas Blues"), but first of all in a levee camp in Texas that was using imported Mississippi labor. The lyric contains a huge number of familiar blues phrases, many of which can be found in published songs such as Handy's and in later recordings, and some of which appear in White's "Nigger Blues." According to David Evans (sleeve notes, *Let's Get Loose*), "Nigger Blues" entered the southern white and black folk repertoires and was recorded under a number of titles; no doubt the traffic went both ways.
62. See Brown, *Stagolee*, 2003, 98–105.
63. Meaning that sexual difference functions not in terms of complement but of supplement: the two partners do not add up to a whole; rather, each represents a different modality (which, in both cases, fails — that is, as one might say, contains a hole). Part of the failure is that the relationship will always be asymmetrical. Lacan's patriarchalism weights this asymmetry in a predictable direction, one which we do not need to accept and on which the fraught and distinctive history of African-American gender relations offers a sharp commentary. Dylan Evans (*Introductory Dictionary*, 1997, 181–82) gives a concise explanation of Lacan's thinking on this subject.
64. See Evans, *Big Road Blues*, 1987, 114–15.
65. Which is not quite always silenced: "Every day seem like murder here" (Charley Patton, "Down the Dirt Road Blues," 1929).
66. The discourse of commodity-fetishism is not used idly here. I have already noted John Lomax's remark about Leadbelly's "money value." It is clear that female blues singers in the 1920s made a much bigger contribution to the composition of their songs than is recorded in the copyrights; what they were called to supply was their bodies (as Van Vechten's tribute to Bessie Smith's implies). Male singers were often exploited even more comprehensively while, at the same time, many were refused recording opportunities because they were considered not to possess sufficient "original" (that is, copyright) songs (even if they made creative use of common-stock material). W. C. Handy was inspired to compose blues not only by the Tutwiler incident (see note 14, p. 259) but also when he observed the success of an unknown local band in Cleveland, Mississippi, playing what sounds like dance-blues; describing the shower of cash thrown by the ecstatic dancers, Handy notes, "Then I saw the beauty of primitive music" (*Father of the Blues*, 1991, 77). Advertising images for blues records often fetishize singers' bodies, especially the women's, if only via the distortions of blackface caricature, while in the 1930s the flood of semipornographic hokum blues records certainly paid dividends.
67. For Lacan, "the true formula of atheism is not *God is dead* — even by basing the origins of the function of the father upon his murder, Freud protects the father — the true formula of atheism is *God is unconscious*" (Jacques Lacan, *The Four Fundamental Concepts of Psycho-Analysis*, ed. Jacques-Alain Miller, trans. Alan Sheridan [Harmondsworth, UK: Penguin, 1979], 59) — a formula confirmed throughout the blues, where God is a very present absence. Lomax acutely points out that many singers of the most agonized blues were actual orphans, but that this also stands for a broader sense of orphanage from society (*Land Where the Blues Began*, 1993, 361–62). In this context, the racialized discourse of (black) "boys" and (white patriarchal) "bosses" of course takes on a particular meaning. Teresa Brennan has drawn attention (*History After Lacan*, 1993, 171–72) to the argument that, with the social–historical shift from feudalism to liberalism, there was a gradual decline in the symbolic power of external authority (the Father, in a chain running from patriarch through lord and monarch to God) and a transfer inwards to the level of the fraternal (that is, God becomes increasingly unconscious). The fierce fraternal rivalry that resulted had particularly fraught consequences for women, as she points out. On one level, blues emerges out of just such a shift from feudal to liberal social relations — but one where everything is intensified by the effects of slavery

and racial subjection. At the same time, the relationship of this specificity to a quasi-universalistic level where song as such seems to have a privileged function for the psychodynamics of loss, is nicely caught by Nathaniel Mackey: "Song is both a complaint and a consolation dialectically tied to that ordeal, where in back of 'orphan' one hears echoes of 'orphic,' a music that turns on abandonment, absence, loss. Think of the black spiritual 'Motherless Child.' Music is wounded kinship's last resort" ("Sound and Sentiment, Sound and Symbol," in *The Jazz Cadence of American Culture*, ed. Robert G. O'Meally [New York: Columbia University Press, 1998], 602–68, 603).

68. Slavoj Žižek, "Pornography, Nostalgia, Montage: A Triad of the Gaze," in *Looking Awry: An Introduction to Jacques Lacan through Popular Culture* (Cambridge, MA: MIT Press, 1991), 107–22.
69. All tracks mentioned are on *Hurry Down Sunshine: The Essential Recordings of Leroy Carr*, Indigo IGOCD 2016 (1995).
70. For example, Davis, *History of the Blues*, 1995, 138–39.
71. For more detailed exploration of this relation (in Freudian terms, between the life and death drives) see chapter 4.
72. All records discussed in this paragraph are on *Tampa Red — Volume 1 (1928–1929)*, Document DOCD-5073 (1991).
73. Davis, *History of the Blues*, 1995, 137–38.
74. Jaxon was active in vaudeville from around 1910 and became closely involved in the hokum/jive scene, especially in 1930s Chicago, where he had his own radio show from 1933. I will pick up this element of "modernistic" grotesque, which was typical of that scene, later in this chapter.
75. Evans (*Big Road Blues*, 1987, 190–93) describes how racial tension and violence were particularly high, even for Mississippi, in and around the town of Drew, where Patton and many of his blues associates spent much of their careers.
76. David Evans, "Charley Patton, The Conscience of the Delta," in *Screamin' and Hollerin' the Blues: The Worlds of Charley Patton*, Revenant Album No 212 (ND), 14. All Patton recordings mentioned are also found in this reissue collection (whose label name could hardly be more appropriate for Patton's ghostly vocal doublings!). Patton's recording career ran from 1929 to 1934.
77. Ibid., 10.
78. For an early example of a "phono-photographic" representation of a yodeled African-American holler, clearly showing the division of the voice produced by sudden register breaks, see Odum and Johnson, *Negro Workaday Songs*, 1926, 257–63 (the graphs were the work of Carl Seashore and his associates).

    The black lineage may not have been straightforward, however. The vaudeville performer, Charles Anderson, was singing combinations of blues and "lullaby yodels" from 1913, as part of his female impersonation act (see Abbott and Seroff, "'They Cert'ly Sound Good to Me,'" 1996, 421.
79. Although I have often represented voices in this network as present in a particular recording only by their absence, the network had solid material existence, via common stock cross-racial repertory, travel, and migration, and above all dissemination of records. The records of Carr and Blackwell, and of Tampa Red's various hokum groups (which later in the 1930s, incidentally, often included Bill Broonzy), circulated widely, in the South as well as the North. Tommy Johnson adapted songs from records of both Tampa Red and Leroy Carr (see Evans, *Big Road Blues*, 1987, 253), and, according to Alan Lomax (*Land Where the Blues Began,* 1993, 411–12), Muddy Waters — protégé of Son House, who was in turn part of the circle around Johnson and Charley Patton — claimed that the first song he tried to learn was Carr's "How Long Blues." The Chatmon family, neighbors of the Pattons, produced many musicians and groups, including the Mississippi Sheiks, whose best-selling hokum was marketed in both old time and race record catalogs (see Russell, "Blacks, Whites and Blues," 2001, 184–87); their 1930 hit, "Sittin' on Top of the World," was covered by Patton as "Some Summer Day" (and by many others, including country performers). Equally, down-home records by such artists as Charley Patton would have been familiar to city-based performers in the North. Jimmie Rodgers traveled widely, and is known to have listened to and learned from many black musicians, just as it is clear that many of them listened to his recordings (see e.g., the evidence given by Russell in ibid., 188–95); Howling Wolf, who learned his falsetto from Tommy Johnson,

claims he was given his name by Rodgers when he met him in the 1920s (ibid., 194). I have already mentioned connections between Patton and both Bessie Smith and Ma Rainey, and that Rainey recorded with Tampa Red. Versions of "Tight Like That" appeared from (among many others) Leadbelly, Duke Ellington, and Louis Armstrong — who also recorded with Jimmie Rodgers... (and so on).

80. Lacan, *Four Fundamental Concepts of Psycho-Analysis,* 1979, 67–119; Žižek, "Pornography, Nostalgia, Montage," 1991; "'I Hear You with My Eyes'," 1996.
81. The race theme was awkward for many from the start. Nomenclature ("nigger," "colored," "Negro," etc.) was always controversial and subject to change in later productions. Both the original productions (New York, 1927; London, 1928) and the first important film version (1936) received a good deal of criticism from blacks for their portrayals of African Americans (see e.g., Duberman, *Paul Robeson,* 1989, 114–15, 203). The first *Show Boat* film (1929) tactfully excised the miscegenation element of the plot and cast the comedian Stepin Fetchit as Joe, symbol of the mighty "Ol' Man River," a part originally intended by Kern and Hammerstein for the heroic Paul Robeson; see Miles Kreuger, *Show Boat: The Story of a Classic American Musical* (New York: Da Capo, 1990), 76–98.
82. Cited in Ethan Mordden, *Make Believe: The Broadway Musical in the 1920s* (New York: Oxford University Press, 1997), 213.
83. The main source for my musical interpretations is the "authentic" recording supervised by John McGlinn, the first to be based on the 1927 full score and sketches rediscovered in 1982 (*Show Boat,* EMI CDS 7 49108 [1988]). This recording includes the whole work in its 1927 version, with the original orchestrations, together with numbers discarded before the New York opening and several others added for the 1928 London production and the 1936 film. I also refer to this film, available on video as MGM/UA M301757 (1990).
84. On the banjo, cf. Walt Whitman: "American opera — put three banjos (or more?) in the orchestra..." (quoted in Lott, *Love and Theft,* 1993, 89.
85. This was the ending in the first New York production, at least. It replaced an earlier attempt at a finale, containing a new number, equally "jazzy," called "It's Getting Hotter in the North," and was in turn replaced by a variety of alternatives in later productions. There was clearly a problem here, to which I will return — although the aim throughout this production history was to mark the moment musically as *now* — the "jazz age."
86. Quoted in Kreuger, *Show Boat,* 1990, 55.
87. Ibid., 65.
88. Bessie Smith put out a record of "A Hot Time in the Old Town Tonight" early in 1927, while Kern and Hammerstein were working on *Show Boat*. It is intriguing to wonder if they heard it. Whether they did or not, comparison of Smith's bluesy version with the raggy march style of the snatch that ends the Trocadero scene points up the question what "hot" could mean for them and for their white characters in 1927, and what this had to do with blackness.
89. Another black composer, Bob Cole, had included a song called "In Dahomey," with a similar debunking theme to Cook's, in the show, *A Trip to Coontown* (1898); and his 1901 song, "A Castle on the Nile," follows a similar theme, with music displaying "the clichés of jungle depiction — a minor key, drone fifths, and pulsating eighth-notes" (see Riis, *Just Before Jazz,* 1989, 87–88). With this description in mind, it is worth thinking ahead not only to Kern's "In Dahomey" (which displays all these techniques), but also to Duke Ellington's "jungle style" developed in the late 1920s and 1930s (see below), and at the same time comparing the style to that of the "Caboceer's Entrance" in Cook's *In Dahomey* (reproduced in Riis, *More than Just Minstrel Shows: The Rise of Black Musical Theatre at the Turn of the Century*. ISAM Monograph No 33 [New York: Institute for the Study of American Music, 1992], 29), which deploys the same "jungle" clichés. The tune for "On Emancipation Day" is in a bluesy major-pentatonic, with major/minor third oscillations and raggy syncopations (cf. note 14, p. 259). On the *In Dahomey* show, see Riis, *Just Before Jazz,* 1989, 91; Riis, *The Music and Scripts of "In Dahomey."* Recent Researches in American Music, vol. 5 (Madison, WI: A&R Editions, 1996, 104); John Graziano, "Images of African Americans: African-American Musical Theatre, *Show Boat* and *Porgy and Bess,*" in *The Cambridge Companion to the Musical*, ed. William A. Everitt and Paul R. Laird (Cambridge, UK: Cambridge University Press, 2002), 63–76.

All the clichés of this "jungle style" circulated across a broader style spectrum freely attached to depictions of cultural exoticisms; they all appear, for instance, in Derek Scott's list of "orientalist" style-markers (Derek Scott, "Orientalism and Musical Style," *Musical Quarterly* 82

[1998]: 309–35, 327). But it is clear that, within American music at this time, they had formed into a specific subset. This ambivalence (it may be compared to that in early minstrelsy: see pp. 11–14 above), as well as supporting my argument about Kern's equivocation, explains how Duke Ellington could, in his usual sly manner, parody the "orientalist" style from *within* his "jungle" stance: see Middleton, "Musical Belongings, 2000a, 71–72.

90. Kreuger, *Show Boat,* 1990, 64.
91. Mordden, *Make Believe,* 1997, 209.
92. We should think here of the "sisterly discourse" in 1920s female blues to which I have already referred, and which has been discussed by Angela Davis and Hortense Spillers among other writers. They link such discourse to the transmission of (black) knowledge along female genealogical lines. See also pp. 112–13 below.
93. Compare John Lomax: "[Black] folk singers render their music more naturally in the easy sociability of their homes and churches and schools, in their fields and woodyards, just as birds sing more effectively in their native trees and country" (quoted in Wolfe and Lornell, *Life and Legend,* 1993, 111).
94. According to John Moore ("'The Hieroglyphics of Love': The Torch Singers and Interpretation," in *Reading Pop: Approaches to Textual Analysis in Popular Music,* ed. Richard Middleton [Oxford: Oxford University Press, 2000], 262–96), although the torch song genre in the 1920s was white, many of the singers were *regarded* as "blues" singers, as exotic and even as racially marginal. Helen Morgan, who created the part of Julie, was often thought (mistakenly) to be of mixed race, and Noel Coward wrote "Half-Caste Woman" for her (264–71).
95. The first Queenie was Tess Gardella, who was Italian and whose career had been built as a blackface performer with the stage-name of "Aunt Jemima." She was billed as "Aunt Jemima" for the 1927 and 1932 New York productions. The nuances this must have brought to the relationship with Julie/Helen Morgan, especially in the playing of the pantry scene, boggle the mind! It is clear from photographs reproduced by Kreuger (*Show Boat,* 1990, 31, 47) that she did not play Queenie in blackface (although she must have been heavily made up, and she did wear her stereotypic Aunt Jemima costume); however, in both the souvenir program (68) and several contemporary newspaper cartoons (66–67) she is portrayed in full blackface caricature. One wonders what blues singer Alberta Hunter made of the part in the 1928 London production (she is not featured in the London cast recording of "Can't Help Lovin' Dat Man," where "Julie" [Marie Burke] sings Queenie's part as well as her own). Hattie McDaniel, although she also had been a blues singer, was by the 1930s better known for stock "Mammy" roles in films, including *Gone with the Wind* (1939), and (ironically) as an "Aunt Jemima" who advertised cake mix. In a further connection, Frankie "Half-Pint" Jaxon (see above, p. 58) got his start around 1910 in a touring show run by McDaniel's father.
96. The concept, which homes in on the dialogical "turning" of the blackface mask/dance through the generations and between the races, is Lhamon's; see his *Raising Cain.*
97. Mordden, *Make Believe,* 1997, 229.
98. *Sketch,* October 5, 1928, quoted in Duberman, *Paul Robeson,* 1989, 115.
99. Mordden, *Make Believe,* 1997, 212.
100. Robeson nearly always had trouble finding theater and film roles that would not compromise his politics. By the mid-1930s, these were becoming increasingly militant, coupling pan-Africanism with a leftism that would shortly carry him into Communist Party circles. His parts portraying African "natives" in the films, *Sanders of the River* (1934) and *King Solomon's Mines* (1936), which he later deeply regretted, may cast an interesting light on his role in the *Show Boat* movie. Duberman (*Robeson,* 1989, 196, 203) suggests that, though he was happy with the filming, his part was significantly cut and changed in the final version, which he was not allowed to preview.
101. It is equally interesting to imagine spectators experiencing *O Brother, Where Art Thou?* from Tommy's point of view. Although the Coen Brothers soften the burden of representational hegemony through comedy (as against the naively credulous romance of *Show Boat*), the difficulty of even imagining a racial inverse of *O Brother*'s narrative dynamic raises the question of how much has actually changed between 1927 and the early twenty-first century.
102. Middleton, "Musical Belongings," 2000a, 66–70.
103. Ibid., 62.
104. Lacan, quoted, Evans, *Introductory Dictionary,* 1997, 90.
105. Middleton, "Musical Belongings," 2000a, 70.

106. The first attempt was "It's Getting Hotter in the North," but this was abandoned in favor of a jazzed-up "Why Do I Love You?" (1927), then a new song called "Dance Away the Night" (London, 1928), and then a "Gallivantin' Aroun'" sequence (film, 1936), most of which never made it into the film. Interestingly, the "hot" quotient gets steadily less as we move through this sequence (the "black" contribution more and more taken for granted?). Stills reproduced from the cut "Gallivantin' Aroun'" material can be seen in Kreuger, *Show Boat,* 1990, 148–50.
107. All records referred to in this section are from *The Ultimate Show Boat: Original Casts, Revivals, Film and Radio Productions and Significant Performances 1928–47*, Pearl GEMS 00600 (1999), except those taken from the 1928 London cast recordings (*Jerome Kern's Showboat and Sunny*, World Records SH 240 [ND]), or where otherwise indicated.
108. On *Lady Day: The Complete Billie Holiday on Columbia 1933–1944*, Columbia CXK 85470 (2001).
109. Kreuger, *Show Boat,* 1990, 74.
110. Duberman, *Robeson,* 1989, 79.
111. Ibid., 604, note 14; 270, 290, 428.
112. Whiteman on Gershwin's *Rhapsody in Blue*, quoted in Neil Leonard, *Jazz and the White Americans: The Acceptance of a New Art Form* (Chicago: University of Chicago Press, 1962), 80.
113. Allison McCracken ("'God's Gift to Us Girls': Crooning, Gender, and the Re-Creation of American Popular Song, 1928–1933," *American Music* 17, no. 4 [1999]: 365–95), explores the widespread association of early crooners with homosexuality and the panic that ensued: "The contrast of their widely publicized white male bodies with their thin, pleading voices marked crooners as sissies who had no right to the adulation they received from white women" (366). She also draws attention to the racial lineages of this association: previously it was only blacks and women, particularly black women and blackface minstrels, who could be described as "crooning."
114. Many of Jolson's listeners in 1928 would have seen him the previous year, blacked up, in this beseeching, kneeling pose, singing "Mammy" in the film *The Jazz Singer* — a moment, according to Lawrence Kramer (*Musical Meaning: Toward a Critical History* [Berkeley: University of California Press, 2002]), 194), which "dramatizes the power of European immigrants, represented by their pariah figure par excellence, a Jew, to assimilate into the social mainstream by establishing their difference from America's blacks.... The result 'is that [*The Jazz Singer*] contains no jazz' [Michael Rogin] — only minstrelsy." Yes — but there is not only difference but also a strange (masked) identification, and the distinction between "jazz" and "minstrelsy" was at this point (if it ever was) by no means entirely clear. On Jolson's singing style, see Stephen Banfield, "Stage and Screen Entertainers in the Twentieth Century," in *The Cambridge Companion to Singing*, ed. John Potter (Cambridge: Cambridge University Press, 2000), 70–72. Lhamon (*Raising Cain,* 1998, 102–15) is good on Jolson's place in the blackface cycle. The relationship between the paternal metaphor — the introjection of the Law-of-the-Father — and the nexus of narcissism and maternal desire and authority (the field of the so-called phallic mother), especially in the context of race, is something I pursue in chapter 3.
115. On Jones, see Riis, *Just Before Jazz,* 1989, 146–49, *More Than Just Minstrel Shows*, 1992, 8–11.
116. Riis, *More Than Just Minstrel Shows,* 1992, 13.
117. Shipton (*New History of Jazz,* 2001, 42–62) stresses the importance of the black theater, including the touring outfits and networks, to the early development of both blues and jazz.
118. Alec Wilder, *American Popular Song: The Great Innovators 1900–1950* (New York: Oxford University Press, 1972), 3–28; Hamm, *Yesterdays,* 1979, 358 (and see 357–90 passim).
119. Allan Forte, *The American Popular Ballad of the Golden Era, 1924–1950* (Princeton NJ: Princeton University Press, 1995).
120. Ibid., 55–59; for my critique of Forte's book, see Richard Middleton, "Pop Goes Old Theory," *Journal of the Royal Musical Association* 122 (1997): 303–20 (for his treatment of "Can't Help Lovin' Dat Man," 311–12).
121. Mordden, *Make Believe,* 1997, 145.
122. Gayatri Chakravorty Spivak, "Can the Subaltern Speak?" in *Marxism and the Interpretation of Culture*, ed. Cary Nelson and Lawrence Grossberg (London: Macmillan, 1988), 271–313.
123. On Signifyin(g) — the aesthetic of the "changing same" — see Henry Louis Gates Jr., *The Signifying Monkey: A Theory of African-American Literary Criticism* (New York: Oxford University Press, 1988); on double consciousness, see above, p. 39.

124. Bhabha, *Location of Culture*, 1994, 86.
125. Houston Baker Jr., *Modernism and the Harlem Renaissance* (Chicago: University of Chicago Press, 1987), 15, 25, 56; Alfred Appel Jr., *Jazz Modernism from Ellington and Armstrong to Matisse and Joyce* (New York: Knopf, 2002), 204.
126. All eight sides are on *The Ultimate Show Boat*, and those by Morgan and Robeson were discussed earlier.
127. The recordings discussed here, together with Ethel Waters's recording of "Porgy" discussed later, are on *The Complete Duke Ellington*, vol. 5, CBS 88082 (1974). On the Cotton Club at this time, see Middleton, "Musical Belongings, 2000a, 70–73; Nathan Huggins, *Harlem Renaissance* (New York: Oxford University Press, 1971); Leonard, *Jazz and the White Americans*, 1962; Jim Haskins, *The Cotton Club* (New York: Random House, 1977); Gilbert Osofsky, *Harlem: The Making of a Ghetto* (New York: Harper and Row, 1968). Cab Calloway describes the Cotton Club as "a replica of a Southern mansion.... The waiters were dressed in red tuxedos, like butlers in a southern mansion... and the whole set was like the sleepy-time-down-south during slavery.... I suppose the idea was to make whites who came to the club feel like they were being catered to and entertained by black slaves" (Cab Calloway and Bryant Rollins, *Of Minnie the Moocher and Me* [New York: Thomas Y. Crowell, 1976], 88) .
128. However, according to Shipton (*New History of Jazz*, 2001, 576–77), scat had a white as well as black provenance, within vaudeville performance; but where did that come from — the minstrel show?
129. This is my speculative reading of Ellington's blackface wink in such performances; see Middleton, *Musical Belongings*, 2000a, 72.
130. And which would bear further fruit in the emergence of rock 'n' roll, the subject of John Mowitt's analysis of drum voicing in his book, *Percussion* (2002).
131. It is no doubt this that James Reese Europe is referring to in his description (1919) of a four-piece band from New Orleans, which he seems to have heard there around 1904, and which subsequently came to New York. This "Razz's Band" (from whose name the term *jazz* derives, he rather dubiously claims) "had no idea at all of what they were playing; they improvised as they went along, but such was their innate sense of rhythm that they produced something that was very taking.... The Negro loves anything that is peculiar in music, and this 'jazzing' appeals to him strongly.... I have to call a daily rehearsal of my band to prevent musicians from adding to their music more than I wish them to. Whenever possible they all embroider their parts in order to produce new, peculiar sounds" (quoted in Vincent, *Keep Cool*, 1995, 211–12). On "circus trombone" and its origins in cakewalk band music, see William J. Schafer and Johannes Riedel, *The Art of Ragtime* (New York: Da Capo Press, 1977), 112–15. The techniques fed through to New Orleans jazz; for example, the trombone tiger growls in "Tiger Rag" (which, interestingly, would become a key piece, along with blues, in the repertoire of The Missourians, Cab Calloway's band: see below).
132. The Victor recordings, from October 1927, are on *The Works of Duke/Complete Edition*, vol. 1, RCA 731043 (ND).
133. Dodge (1929), quoted in Shipton, *New History of Jazz*, 2001, 210; Roger Pryor Dodge, "Harpsichords and Trumpets" (1934) in *The Duke Ellington Reader*, ed. Mark Tucker (New York: Oxford University Press, 1993), 105–10; R. D. Darrell, "Black Beauty" (1932) in *The Duke Ellington Reader*, 1993, 57–65, 58.
134. *The Works of Duke/Complete Edition*, vol. 8, RCA 741114 (ND).
135. On Ellington's "Dear Old Southland," see Appel, *Jazz Modernism*, 2002, 213; David Metzer, "Shadow Play: The Spiritual in Duke Ellington's 'Black and Tan Fantasy,'" *Black Music Research Journal* 17, no. 2 (1997): 137–58, 138–39, note 4. (Metzer's article focuses on the derivation of the main theme in "Black and Tan Fantasy" from a "spiritual" — actually a black mediation of a "sacred song," "The Holy City," by a *white* composer.) On the derivation of "Summertime," see Samuel A. Floyd Jr., "Troping the Blues: From Spirituals to Concert Hall," *Black Music Research Journal* 13, no. 1 (1993): 31–51.
136. Cootie Williams and His Rug Cutters, "Ol' Man River," *The Duke's Men*, vol. 2, *1938–1939*, Columbia C2K48835 (1993); and see Appel's excellent discussion (*Jazz Modernism*, 2002, 218).
137. Appel, *Jazz Modernism*, 2002, 143; and see ibid., 31–32, 140–43. These three recordings are on *Louis Armstrong V.S.O.P.* 6, 7, CBS 62475, 62476 (1974).
138. See Appel, *Jazz Modernism*, 2002, 26–27, 91–114; Shipton, *New History of Jazz*, 2001, 594–97.

All the Waller tracks discussed here are on Fats Waller, *Great Original Performances 1927–1940*, Jazz Classics RPCD 619 (1993).

139. On *Louis Armstrong, V.S.O.P.*, vol. 1, CBS 62470 (ND).
140. On *Billy Banks and His Rhythmakers*, CBS 52732 (1970).
141. Shipton, *New History of Jazz,* 2001, 593. All pieces discussed here are on *Cab Calloway and His Orchestra 1930–1931*, Classics 516 (1990). Calloway and his band went on performing in his style right through the thirties and beyond, but the main elements are all there in the early recordings of 1930 and 1931. Shipton's discussion of Calloway (583, 590–93) is useful, and so is Gunther Schuller's: *The Swing Era: The Development of Jazz, 1930–1945* (New York: Oxford University Press, 1989), 326–50.

    According to Calloway, "music… should keep up with the pace and feeling of life.… The Missourians were closer [than the Alabamians, his previous band] to what was going on in New York, but they still needed to work at keeping up with the times. That was exactly what I tried to get them to do… to stay hip with it" (Calloway and Rollins, *Of Minnie,* 1976, 84).
142. Arguably, he more than anyone invented the hepster language of "jive" which became so popular at this time, although he drew on existing scat vocabularies such as Armstrong's; see Calloway, *The New Cab Calloway's Cat-ologue* (New York: Calloway, 1938); *The New Cab Calloway's Hepster's Dictionary: Language of Jive* (New York: Calloway, 1944). Small wonder that Gershwin intended the character of Sportin' Life in *Porgy and Bess* for him, and that in later years he made a great success of the part (though he did not play it in the first production).
143. "De black ones" is what he sings; this is how to do it, Paul!
144. Much of the drug-related argot concerned marihuana or opium, and there are often "oriental" references (e.g., snake imagery: a "viper," for instance, was a marihuana user; Minnie the Moocher's downfall takes place in Chinatown, and she is described as a "red hot hootchie coocher"). A piece like "The Levee Low-Down" demonstrates that Calloway could readily do the jungle style without the drug references — but even here, in one of the growled brass solos, there is a quotation from "Fatima's Dance"! So much for "primitivism," this seems to say (but then again, *how* much?). The "orientalism" in Calloway's moaner repertoire may cast light on the participation of African-American musicians at this time (including Ellington) in fashionable "Arabian" motifs, as well as on Calloway's debt to Jolson.
145. See Calloway and Rollins, *Of Minnie,* 1976, 111.
146. See Slim Gaillard and Slam Stewart, *Complete Columbia Master Takes*, Definitive Records DRCD11190 (2001).
147. See, e.g., Alyn Shipton, *Groovin' High: The Life of Dizzy Gillespie* (Oxford: Oxford University Press, 1999), 158–62, 173.
148. George Russell, who contributed to the composition, quoted in ibid., 200. "Cubana Be/Cubana Bop" is reissued on Dizzy Gillespie, *The Complete RCA Victor Recordings*, Bluebird 07863 66528-2 (1995).
149. *The Duke Ellington Carnegie Hall Concerts, January 1943*, Prestige P-34004 (1977); the core theme of the "Black" movement is Ellington's "spiritual," "Come Sunday."
150. Charles Mingus, *Beneath the Underdog* (Harmondsworth, UK: Penguin, 1975). Nowhere is the pathology of the race/sex interplay in America more powerfully represented. Nobody in the 1950s and 1960s played more "cubist blues" than Mingus.
151. This is "King Joe," a 1941 tribute to boxer Joe Louis, with words by novelist Richard Wright, music by the Basie Band, and production by white impresario John Hammond. Robeson sings the simple blues formulae in standard English, with full "operatic" voice production, wooden phrasing, and blue notes that scream their discomfort. He also recorded "St. Louis Blues" in much the same style (but without the advantage of backing from the Basie Band); but of course only one of this tune's three strains is in the twelve-bar form. Both recordings can be heard on *The Paul Robeson Collection*, Hallmark 390692/3 (1998).
152. Riis, *Just Before Jazz*, 1989, 67–68.
153. Robert Fink, "Elvis Everywhere: Musicology and Popular Music Studies at the Twilight of the Canon," *American Music* 16 (1998): 135–79. Fink tells a more complicated story, however, arguing that Presley's live performance of "Hound Dog" started off as comedy ("a witty multiracial piece of signifyin' humor, troping off white overreactions to black sexual innuendo") but that, angered by media panic and censorship when he sang this version on TV, he transformed it for his recording into a "menacing, rough-trade version of the song" (169). I confess I cannot hear the contrast as being this extreme; but in any case both versions are

"performative" — Fink, I think, errs in distinguishing the recorded version as being "fierce, angry, and real" (171), as if coming from some inchoate emotional core of authenticity — and each encapsulates a form of blackface caricature. Fink makes a good point in noting that in the process of developing the recorded version, elements of the rhythm become more "square," rigid, and "Beethovenian," and the connection to my discussion (below) of "Jumpin' Jack Flash" and "What If I Was White?" is intriguing (see note 157). But white reification of "black rhythm" is as old (at least) as notations of the spirituals, as Radano makes clear ("Denoting Difference," 1996, 506–44).

154. Charles Shaar Murray, *Crosstown Traffic: Jimi Hendrix and Post-War Pop* (London: Faber, 1989), 82, 83, 138; and see 45, 68–71, 78–79 (on Hendrix's blackface negotiations) and 145–49 (on "Voodoo Chile"). "Voodoo Chile" is on The Jimi Hendrix Experience, *Electric Ladyland*, Track 613 017 (1968).
155. Lhamon, *Raising Cain*, 1998, 218–26.
156. I discuss Eminem's "My Name Is" from his *The Slim Shady LP*, Interscope 490 287-2 (1999) in Richard Middleton, "Locating the People: Music and the Popular," in *The Cultural Study of Music: A Critical Introduction*, ed. Martin Clayton, Trevor Herbert, and Richard Middleton (New York: Routledge, 2003), 251–62, 259–60.
157. Sticky Fingaz, "What If I Was White," *[Black Trash] The Autobiography of Kirk Jones*, Universal 012 157 990-2 (2001). The answer to my question, the music seems to suggest (but the subtleties in the lyrics, not to mention the participation of Eminem, to query) is: no (despite the claims of Jumpin' Jack Flash). The hook's first rhythm (Ex. 2.3a) insistently recalls the initial, and famous, "fate" or "V for Victory" motive of Beethoven's Fifth Symphony, its continuation (Ex. 2.3b) Beethoven's equally celebrated tendency to hammer his triumphs to death, usually in marcato four-four, e.g., at the end of the same symphony. The mind then moves on, deliciously in view of blackface phallic myth, to Susan McClary's notorious analysis of such Beethovenian moments as standing for male desire, penetration, and even rape; see McClary, *Feminine Endings*, 1991, 12–16, 68–69, 124–30.
158. Bhabha, *Location of Culture*, 1994, 116.

Chapter 3

1. There is good work that does not stop at this point; for example, Sheila Whiteley, ed., *Sexing the Groove: Popular Music and Gender* (London: Routledge, 1997); Stan Hawkins, *Settling the Pop Score: Pop Texts and Identity Politics* (London: Ashgate, 2002); and relevant parts of Philip Brett, Elizabeth Wood, and G. C. Thomas, ed., *Queering the Pitch: The New Gay and Lesbian Musicology* (London: Routledge, 1993), of Leslie C. Dunn and Nancy A. Jones, ed., *Embodied Voices: Representing Vocality in Western Culture* (Cambridge: Cambridge University Press, 1994), and of McClary, *Feminine Endings*, 1991.
2. Not that the converse position is less problematic: the exploration in punk rock of new female voices did not of itself lead to transformation in women's economic and social power within the music industry.
3. Barbara Bradby and Dave Laing, "Introduction," in "Gender and Sexuality," special issue, *Popular Music* 20 (2001): 295–300, 299. Kristeva's essay is included in Julia Kristeva, *About Chinese Women*, trans. Anita Barrows (London: Marion Boyars, 1977).
4. Kaja Silverman, *The Acoustic Mirror: The Female Voice in Psychoanalysis and Cinema* (Bloomington IN: Indiana University Press, 1988), 41.
5. Carolyn Abbate, "Opera; Or, the Envoicing of Women," in *Musicology and Difference: Gender and Sexuality in Music Scholarship*, ed. Ruth A. Solie (Berkeley: University of California Press, 1993), 225–58, 239, n. 257. Do I dare go further and draw attention to the common observation that it is men who know best what it means to behave (walk, talk, flirt, etc.) "like a woman"? This is the transvestite or *Some Like It Hot* argument, and it can also be applied, mutatis mutandis, to the register of race (the "blackface" argument).
6. Wayne Koestenbaum, "The Queen's Throat: (Homo)sexuality and the Art of Singing," in *Inside/Out: Lesbian Theories, Gay Theories*, ed. Diana Fuss (London: Routledge, 1991), 205–34, 211.
7. Ibid., 206–7.

8. Ibid., 205.
9. Ibid., 214.
10. For an excellent summary of the contradictory values forming the field of voice, see Silverman, *The Acoustic Mirror*, 1988, 42–45; and for a discussion of the construction in some psychoanalytic traditions of the mouth as an "organ hole," entry-point to the "dark continent" of female sexuality, concluding with the Derridean deconstruction, see ibid., 66–71.
11. Steven Connor (*Dumbstruck*, 2000), has a not dissimilar figure — the "vocalic body," which "is the idea . . . of a surrogate or secondary body, a projection of a new way of having or being a body, formed and sustained out of the autonomous operation of the voice" (35). "Having or being": the gendered articulation of this body is already implicit in this formulation; and, while I like the "alimentary" metaphor in part for its active quality — its insistence on the voice's in-, di-, and e-gestive functions in a process that is always both production and consumption — Connor's discussion also moves in this direction. Pointing to the assumption in Classical Greece that the ventriloquial voice is located in the stomach (as the etymology suggests), he describes how this topography was extended to take in the female genitals, seen as offering an "opening" to the workings of the *earth*'s breath, an operation "which parallels ingestion . . . but differs from ingestion in that . . . speech adds something to the breath which it exhales; breathing has utterance as its fruit" (57). These ideas, including the myth of the "speaking womb" and of "incarnation itself as a kind of ventriloquism, the emission of a word from the genital regions" (92, 93), remained current to the eighteenth century. They go far, perhaps, to provide mythic embodiment for the structure of phallogocentricity: man — born as Logos from Woman — in turn speaks her, ventriloquist to her dummy.
12. On the body as an "inscriptional site" for performative fabrications of gender identity, see Judith Butler, *Gender Trouble: Feminism and the Subversion of Identity* (London: Routledge, 1990), 134–41.
13. Koestenbaum, "The Queen's Throat," 224.
14. See Lucy Green, *Music, Gender, Education* (Cambridge, UK: Cambridge University Press, 1997), 21–46.
15. Abbate, "Opera; Or, the Envoicing of Women," 1993, 226–27. On displacement of male lack to the female through the classic techniques of cinematic projection (and, we might add, similar techniques in recorded music), see Silverman, *The Acoustic Mirror*, 1988, 24.
16. Ibid., 251.
17. John Mowitt starts with this question in "The Sound of Music in the Era of Its Electronic Reproducibility," in *Music and Society: The Politics of Composition, Performance and Reception*, ed. Richard Leppert and Susan McClary (Cambridge, UK: Cambridge University Press, 1987), 173–97.
18. Žižek, "'I Hear You with My Eyes,'" 1996, 92. In this sense, we might say that *all* voices are ventriloquial; the issue is just who (or where) is the ventriloquist, who (where) the dummy.
19. The "acoustic mirror" is a phrase of Guy Rosolato's. His ideas, together with the roles of voice and gaze in subject construction more generally, are discussed in Silverman, *The Acoustic Mirror*, 1988.
20. Koestenbaum, "The Queen's Throat," 1991, 223, 217.
21. Abbate,"Opera; Or, the Envoicing of Women," 1993, 236, 248, 252.
22. Van Morrison, "Gloria," *The Story of Them, Featuring Van Morrison*, Deram 844 813-2 (1997); Patti Smith, "Gloria in Excelsis Deo"/"Gloria," *Horses*, Arista 07822 18827 2 (1975).
23. Simon Frith and Angela McRobbie, "Rock and Sexuality," in *On Record: Rock, Pop, and the Written Word*, ed. Simon Frith and Andrew Goodwin (London: Routledge, 1990), 371–89.
24. Ibid., 374.
25. Mike Daley, "Patti Smith's 'Gloria': Intertextual Play in a Vocal Performance," *Popular Music* 16, no.3 (1997): 235–53.
26. Victor Bockris, *Patti Smith* (London: Fourth Estate, 1998), 20.
27. Goffredo Plastino kindly brought to my attention a Hendrix version of "Gloria," issued on an Italian single (Polygram 2311 014 Jimi 1) in 1979. I have not come across this recording elsewhere. This stretched-out psychedelic-rock version is even more "monolithic" in its effect than Morrison's, dominated by the unceasing chordal riff and Hendrix's vocal and guitar. His guitar solos leave very little (that is, everything) about his encounter with Gloria to the imagination.

28. Bockris, *Patti Smith*, 1998, 7.
29. See Eve Kosofsky Sedgewick, *Epistemology of the Closet* (Hemel Hempstead, UK: Harvester, 1991); Roland Barthes, "The Grain of the Voice," in *Image-Music-Text*, trans. Stephen Heath (London: Fontana, 1977a), 179–89.
30. This is Judith Butler's term for that subversive process which "opens up anatomy — and sexual difference itself — as a site of proliferative resignifications," at once "deprivileging" the phallus and "recirculating and reprivileging it"; see Butler, *Bodies that Matter: On the Discursive Limits of "Sex"* (London: Routledge 1993), 88, 89.
31. Actually Freud hardly ever uses the word *phallus* (though he does use the adjective *phallic* rather more). His preference for *penis* is a symptom of his reluctance to abandon biologism completely.
32. See Lawrence Kramer, *Music as Cultural Practice 1800–1900* (Berkeley: University of California Press, 1990), 5–11; *Classical Music and Postmodern Knowledge* (Berkeley: University of California Press 1995), 20–21.
33. One way of putting this, drawn from a particular current in Lacan's thought, is that there are *two* laws: the law of the superego is one of irrational, tyrannical command and is actually at odds with the normative law governing the subject's position in the Symbolic order. The destructive character of the superego — it stands for the *jouissance* of the Other within the subject — means that it represents loss as such.
34. Mladen Dolar, "The Object Voice," in *Gaze and Voice as Love Objects*, ed. Renata Salecl and Slavoj Žižek (Durham NC: Duke University Press, 1996), 7–31, 27.
35. Lacan, quoted in ibid., 27–28.
36. The tempo increases continuously through the first set of verses to create an initial climax at the first chorus, then builds to a second climax at the second chorus, drops to half-time for the chiming of the tower bells, then jumps back to full speed for the final chorus — which fades to incompletion.
37. Butler, *Gender Trouble*, 1990, 15.
38. Note how, with the strange episode in the lyrics where "twenty thousand girls call their name out to me" "at the stadium," there is a conflation of modes of *jouissance* attaching to sex, religion, and rock stardom.
39. Butler is perhaps the most incisive. However, there have long been intelligent feminists prepared to defend, or at least work with, Lacan's ideas — not just within the rather specific tradition of French feminist psychoanalysis (Kristeva, Irigary, Cixous) but also in the Anglophone world; the first important publication in the latter category, dating from not long after Patti Smith's "Gloria," is Juliet Mitchell and Jacqueline Rose, eds., *Feminine Sexuality: Jacques Lacan and the Ecole Freudienne* (London: Macmillan, 1982).
40. For a stimulating account, see Slavoj Žižek, "Otto Weininger, or 'Woman Doesn't Exist,'" in *The Žižek Reader*, ed. Elizabeth Wright and Edmond Wright (Oxford: Blackwell, 1999b), 127–47 — a critique of Otto Weininger's misogynistic tract of 1903, *Sex and Character*. A comparison between Germaine Greer's treatment of Weininger (*The Female Eunuch* [London: Paladin, 1971], 119ff.), which straightforwardly attacks his misogyny, and Žižek's, which unpicks his extremism in order to lay the foundations for a "realistic" but "knowing" feminist counterposition, is telling.
41. Apparently, she used to "jerk off" to her own photo — not to mention the Bible (Bockris, *Patti Smith*, 1998, 160); and on one level her work often has some of the quality of pornography — the objectification of the watching subject-voyeur (see Žižek's exploration of this territory, in his "Pornography, Nostalgia, Montage," 1991). At the same time, her general attitude to performance is more like that associated with acting — an "acting out."
42. Laura Mulvey, "Visual Pleasure and Narrative Cinema," *Screen* 16, no. 3 (1975): 8–18.
43. Brian Currid, "'We Are Family': House Music and Queer Performativity," in *Cruising the Performative: Interventions into the Representation of Ethnicity, Nationality, and Sexuality*, ed. Sue-Ellen Case, Philip Brett, and Susan Leigh Foster (Bloomington: Indiana University Press, 1995), 165–96.
44. Ibid., 177.
45. Ibid., 179.
46. Žižek, "I Hear You with My Eyes," 1996, 93.
47. See Žižek, "Pornography, Nostalgia, Montage," 1991, 116 ff.; "I Hear You with My Eyes," 1996, 92ff.

48. Lacan took the idea of Woman as "object of exchange" most directly from Lévi-Strauss, but it was already well entrenched in physical anthropology and Freudian psychoanalysis. In both of these discourses, it is regarded, taken together with the incest taboo which it accompanies, as a founding moment in the emergence of human society. Gayle Rubin's celebrated critique applies a Marxist analysis to the implications of this for the history and structure of the heterosexual gender system (see "The Traffic in Women: Notes on the Political Economy of Sex," in *Toward an Anthropology of Women*, ed. Rayna Rapp Reiter [New York: Monthly Review, 1975], 157–210). For an excellent survey of feminist work on gender, from a Marxist point of view, see Haraway, "'Gender' for a Marxist Dictionary," in *Simians, Cyborgs, and Women*, 1991, 127–48.
49. See John Corbett and Terri Kapsalis, "Aural Sex: The Female Orgasm in Popular Sound," *The Drama Review* 40, no.3 (1996): 102–11.
50. Silverman, *The Acoustic Mirror,* 1988, 49.
51. Zizek, "Otto Weininger," 1999b, 136.
52. That a Big N might stand both for the Name-of-the-Father and for Nostalgia (see above, pp. 54–55) may be no accident.
53. Bockris, *Patti Smith,* 1998, 125; Clinton Heylin, *From the Velvets to the Voidoids* (London: Penguin, 1993), 198.
54. See, e.g., Butler, *Gender Trouble,* 1990, 35–78.
55. And, adding a further register of analysis, it is worth noting that both originated from working-class backgrounds and moved, along one of the classic popular-music routes, into a certain sort of bohemia. More about class in due course.
56. Jimi Hendrix's version, referred to in note 27 above (p. 271), brings these references right up front, especially given his (racist) image as a "black stud."
57. "I never really liked white stuff" (Bockris, *Patti Smith,* 1998, 13); "the Rolling Stones redeemed the white man forever" (ibid., 28).
58. bell hooks, *Ain't I a Woman: Black Women and Feminism* (London: Pluto Press, 1982), 5.
59. See Kate Millett, *Sexual Politics* (1970, London: Virago, 1977), 57, 80–81; Greer, *Female Eunuch*, 1971, 343. hooks (*Ain't I a Woman,* 1982, 138ff) attacks this "correspondence" as equating "women" with "white women" and "blacks" with (implicitly) black men, and hence itself a construct of patriarchy. Angela Davis (*Women, Race and Class* [London: The Women's Press, 1982], 33–34, 42–45) points out that the "correspondence" can be traced back to the nineteenth century, when it led to actual political alliances (but also disputes) between feminists and abolitionists.
60. Hortense Spillers, "Mama's Baby, Papa's Maybe: An American Grammar Book," *Diacritics* (summer 1987): 65–81, 65.
61. Quoted in Brian Ward, *Just My Soul Responding: Rhythm and Blues, Black Consciousness and Race Relations* (London: UCL Press, 1998), 302.
62. See, e.g., Dunn and Jones, *Embodied Voices*, 1994, 11–13. The quoted phrases here are taken by Dunn and Jones from Kaja Silverman and Hélène Cixous respectively.
63. See Angela Davis, *The Angela Y. Davis Reader*, ed. Joy James (Oxford: Blackwell, 1998a), 7, 12.
64. Baraka, quoted in hooks, *Ain't I a Woman,* 1982, 95. Baraka's masculinism at this time was also, entirely typically, homophobic: unlike "effeminate" white men, the virile black was a "real" man; see ibid., 96.
65. Eldridge Cleaver, *Soul on Ice* (London: Panther, 1970), 26, 184, 65, 146, 151, 152. Like Baraka's, Cleaver's neoprimitive masculinism was also homophobic: in his critique of James Baldwin, he equates Baldwin's alleged intellectual integrationism with his homosexuality; he "bends over" for the white man (100).
66. Interestingly, Cleaver's *Soul on Ice*, including "The Allegory of the Black Eunuchs" (143–59), was first published in 1969, only a year before Germaine Greer's *The Female Eunuch.*
67. "Reflections on the Black Woman's Role in the Community of Slaves," reprinted in Davis, *The Angela Y. Davis Reader*, 1998a, 111–28. See also Davis, *If They Come in the Morning: Voices of Resistance* (London: Orbach and Chambers, 1971), and her later work, *Women, Race and Class* (London: The Women's Press, 1982).
68. bell hooks, *Ain't I a Woman,* 1982. See also Michele Wallace, *Black Macho and the Myth of the Super Woman* (New York: Dial Press, 1978).
69. bell hooks, *Feminist Theory: From Margin to Center* (Boston MA: South End Press, 1984), 69–70; Davis, *Angela Y. Davis Reader,* 1998a, 116.

70. Angela Davis, *Blues Legacies and Black Feminism* (New York: Pantheon, 1998b), 67.
71. Quoted in ibid., 121–22 (emphasis added).
72. Spillers, "Mama's Baby, Papa's Maybe," 1987, 66, 80.
73. Peter Antelyes, "Red Hot Mamas: Bessie Smith, Sophie Tucker, and the Ethnic Maternal Voice in American Popular Song," in *Embodied Voices: Representing Vocality in Western Culture*, ed. Leslie C. Dunn and Nancy A. Jones (Cambridge, UK: Cambridge University Press, 1994), 212–29, 213, 216. At the same time, Antelyes makes use of the same Danny Barker quotation as Angela Davis, see note 71 above.
74. Butler, *Bodies that Matter,* 1993, 102–3.
75. Sedgewick, *Epistemology of the Closet,* 1991, 248–49. There is a specific genealogy behind such images. Just as feminism and abolitionism danced together in complex ways in the nineteenth century, so too the more transgressive side of the racio-sexual imaginary was prefigured in the cross-dressing fantasies of the early minstrel show: see Lott, *Love and Theft*, 1993, 159–68. The two lineages intersected in the "feminization" of minstrely associated with Stephen Foster (ibid., 187–201).
76. See Silverman, *Acoustic Mirror,* 1988, 72–100.
77. Ibid., 101–26. For another critique of Kristeva, on similar lines, see Butler, *Gender Trouble,* 1990, 79–91.
78. Silverman, *Acoustic Mirror,* 1988, 79–84
79. Ibid., 84–86.
80. Ibid., 98–100.
81. Butler, *Bodies that Matter,* 1993, 79, 80.
82. Ibid., 184
83. See Nina Simone (with Stephen Cleary), *I Put a Spell on You: The Autobiography of Nina Simone* (London: Ebury Press, 1991). As a ghosted autobiography, this source is, of course, likely to be performing a particular kind of act of self-construction.
84. Ibid., 92.
85. Ibid., 87.
86. Ibid., 65, 90–91.
87. Ibid., 113.
88. Ibid., 24.
89. Ibid., 125.
90. Ibid., 141.
91. Ibid., 144.
92. Ibid., 150, 164
93. Barbara Engh, "Loving It: Music and Criticism in Roland Barthes," in *Musicology and Difference: Gender and Sexuality in Music Scholarship*, ed. Ruth A. Solie (Berkeley: University of California Press, 1993), 66–79, 74, 79. One is reminded of the ancient fantasy of "speaking without a tongue" — part of the myth of a female-genital voice (Connor, *Dumbstruck*, 2000, 182); but Simone decisively inverts the feminizing implications of this fantasy.
94. All the Simone recordings discussed in any detail here can be found on Nina Simone, *Gold,* Universal Classics and Jazz 9808087 (2003).
95. Maybe she had. Lomax's field trip was in 1959, and many of the recordings were issued on Atlantic Records in 1960. Simone's recording of "See-Line Woman" dates from 1964.
96. Butler, *Bodies that Matter*, 1993, 67.
97. Koestenbaum ("The Queen's Throat," 1991, 222) reminds us that "Marcel Garcia's laryngoscope — a device made of two mirrors — assured him that he had a larynx, and, by extension, a phallus and a self."
98. Screaming Jay Hawkins, "I Put a Spell on You," Okeh 7072 (1956), reissued on *Radio Gold 4*, Ace CDCHD 810 (2001).
99. See Davis, *Blues Legacies*, 1998b, 156.
100. Simone, *I Put a Spell,* 1991, 110.
101. Diamanda Galás, *The Singer*, Mute CDSTUMM103 (1992).
102. Galás is Greek-American and her father is said to have sung Rebetika, the "Greek blues." See David Schwartz, *Listening Subjects: Music, Psychoanalysis, Culture* (Durham NC: Duke University Press, 1997), 197, note 3.
103. Galás, quoted in ibid., 134.
104. Michael Flanagan, "Invoking Diamanda," in *Life Sentences: Writers, Artists, and Aids,* ed. Thomas Avena (San Francisco: Mercury House, 1994), 161–75, 164.

105. Ibid., 173.
106. Galás, quoted in Thomas Avena, "Interview with Diamanda Galás," in *Life Sentences: Writers, Artists, and Aids,* ed. Thomas Avena (San Francisco: Mercury House, 1994), 177–97, 180.
107. Quoted in ibid., 188.
108. See Schwartz, *Listening Subjects,* 1997, 134–38.
109. Evans, *Introductory Dictionary*, 1997, 78.
110. See Mary Celeste Kearney, "The Missing Links: Riot Grrrl — Feminism — Lesbian Culture," in *Sexing the Groove: Popular Music and Gender*, ed. Sheila Whiteley (London: Routledge, 1997), 207–29.

    Kearney's objection to the reduction of Riot Grrrl to stereotypic positions within existing patriarchal discourse (e.g., as "girl punks") is well made. But the fact that no "separatist" movement can escape such conflicts demonstrates that the structure of gender politics is an interactive web to which there is no outside.
111. See Currid, "'We Are Family,'" 1995; Susana Loza, "Sampling (Hetero) Sexuality: Diva-ness and Discipline in Electronic Dance Music," *Popular Music* 20 no. 3 (2001): 349–57 ; Stephen Amico, "'I Want Muscles': House Music, Homosexuality and Masculine Signification," *Popular Music* 20, no. 3 (2001): 359–78; Barbara Bradby, "Sampling Sexuality: Gender, Technology and the Body in Dance Music," *Popular Music* 12 no. 2 (1993): 155–76.
112. Judith Butler, "Imitation and Gender Insubordination," in *Inside/Out: Lesbian Theories, Gay Theories*, ed. Diana Fuss (London: Routledge, 1991), 13–31, 17, 21.
113. See Fred E Maus, "Glamour and Evasion: the Fabulous Ambivalence of the Pet Shop Boys," *Popular Music* 20, no.3 (2001): 379–93.
114. Sedgewick, *Epistemology of the Closet,* 1991, 86–90.
115. I draw on *The Best of Michael Jackson and Jackson Five*, Polygram 530 804-2 (1997); Michael Jackson, *Number Ones*, Epic 2 513800 (2003); and Michael Jackson, *Video Greatest Hits*, Sony SMV 50123 2 (1995).
116. Cynthia Fuchs, "Michael Jackson's Penis," in *Cruising the Performative: Interventions into the Representation of Ethnicity, Nationality, and Sexuality*, ed. Sue-Ellen Case, Philip Brett, and Susan Leigh Foster (Bloomington: Indiana University Press, 1995), 13–33.
117. Ibid., 17.
118. Ibid., 26.
119. Ibid., 18.
120. Fuchs (ibid., 13) quotes Fanon: "One is no longer aware of the Negro, but only of a penis; the Negro is eclipsed. He *is* a penis."
121. On the narrative structures of his videos, see Kobena Mercer, "Monster Metaphors: Notes on Michael Jackson's *Thriller*," in *Sound and Vision: The Music Video Reader*, ed. Simon Frith, Andrew Goodwin, and Lawrence Grossberg (London: Routledge, 1993), 93–108. A good example of the interinscription of "life" and "music," pointed out by Mercer, is the way that the transformation of Jackson in the *Thriller* video into a werewolf, enacted through special effects before our eyes, can be seen as "a metaphor for the aesthetic reconstruction of Michael Jackson's face" —that is, of his face in "real life" (105).
122. Fuchs, "Michael Jackson's Penis," 1995, 19–20.
123. In one celebrated sequence in *Black or White*, Jackson, portrayed as an angry ghetto youth, wrecks a car with a crowbar while clearly (it would seem) masturbating. It seems wonderfully appropriate both that Jackson cut this sequence, in response to apparent Moral Majority outrage, and that it is now restored: his decision "to excise the masturbatory member that remains not-seen, [which] imitates his continuing surgical reconstruction," doubles the castration that the exorcism has already put in play, while the return of "the painful, aching, unseen penis" performs out, as in all structures of disavowal, an insistence of what has been denied (ibid., 24).
124. Mercer, "Monster Metaphors," 1993, 106–7.
125. I have drawn on the CD single of her E.S.C. song, "Diva," CNR Music 5300295 (1998); the album *Diva*, IMP 2048 (1998); and a privately produced video of the BBC broadcast of the 1998 Eurovision Song Contest.

    Although there appears to be no connection between Dana International's choice of name and that of the 1970 E.S.C. winner, the Irish singer Dana, the coincidence is piquant. Dana epitomized the wholesome values of a traditional "feminine" singing style — as in her winning song, "All Kinds of Everything" — and subsequently went on to stand, unsuccessfully, for the

Presidency of the Irish Republic, and, successfully, for election to the European Parliament on a Catholic, antiabortion, family values ticket.

126. For a cross-section of media reports, see http://home.online.no/geskogse/media_press_uk.html
127. Ted Swedenburg, "Saida Sultan/Dana International: Transgender Pop and the Polysemiotics of Sex, Nation, and Ethnicity on the Israeli-Egyptian Border," *Musical Quarterly* 81, no.1 (1997): 81–108, 98; 107, note 59.
128. See Sander Gilman, "Damaged Men: Thoughts on Kafka's Body," in *Constructing Masculinity*, ed. Maurice Berger, Brian Wallis, and Simon Watson (New York: Routledge, 1995), 176–89.
129. Peter Antelyes, reasonably enough, discusses Bessie Smith and the Jewish Sophie Tucker side by side (see "Red Hot Mamas," 1994). The interplay of African-American and Jewish elements — East and South penetrating (or "invaginating"?) the "West," as it were — sets the essential framework for the development of American popular music right through the twentieth century.
130. See Yael Ben-Zvi, "Zionist Lesbianism and Transsexual Transgression," *Middle East Report* (Spring 1998), 26–28, 37.
131. Ashkenazi Jews are those of European origin. Mizrahi Jews originate in Africa or Asia, and especially Middle Eastern countries other than Israel.
132. See Swedenburg, "Saida Sultan," 1997. There was by this time a tradition of Mizrahi music in Israel, including a lineage of female Yemenite singers; Dana International's immediate predecessor, Ofra Haza, who stemmed from this background, came second in the 1983 E.S.C. See Motti Regev, "*Musica Mizrakhit*, Israeli Rock and National Culture in Israel," *Popular Music* 15, no.3 (1996): 275–84.
133. See Philip Bohlman, "The *Shechinah*, or the Feminine Sacred in the Musics of the Jewish Mediterranean," accessed at http:/home.online.no/~geskogse/bohlman.pdf. The quotations are from pp. 1 and 9 respectively. See also Liora Mariel, "Dana International: A Self-Made Jewish Diva," *Race, Gender, and Class* 6, no.4 (1999): 110–24.
134. From interviews in *The Guardian* (June 26, 1998) and the *Jewish Telegraph* (June 19, 1998) respectively; accessed on the web (see note 126). Dana International's selection as Israeli candidate for the E.S.C. certainly disturbed the order of the patriarchal state: the government almost fell as far-right religious parties threatened to walk out.
135. Loza, "Sampling (Hetero) Sexuality," 2001, 354.
136. Haraway, *Simians, Cyborgs, and Women*, 1991, 150.
137. Mariel, "Dana International," 1999, 116; Swedenburg, "Saida Sultan," 1997, 97.
138. It is intriguing, if inconclusive, to compare it to the recordings of the last castrato (dating from 1902 and 1904): Alessandro Moreschi, *The Last Castrato: Complete Vatican Recordings*, Opal CD 9823 (1987). The radical gap opened by the different recording technologies leaves any parallel (which I certainly sense) tantalizingly faint. My colleague, Paul Carding, Professor of Voice Pathology at the University of Newcastle, thinks it unlikely, on the basis of aural evidence alone, that Dana International has undergone surgical "tightening" of the vocal folds. It is of course amusing that the first and last institution known to have employed castrato singers was the Vatican; *il Papa*'s little joke?
139. Homi Bhahba, "Are You a Man or a Mouse?" in *Constructing Masculinity*, ed. Maurice Berger, Brian Wallis, and Simon Watson (New York: Routledge, 1995), 57–65.
140. See Currid, "We Are Family," 1995, 186–92.
141. Haraway, *Simians, Cyborgs, and Women*, 1991, 181.
142. Bohlman, "The *Shechinah*"; Swedenburg, "Saida Sultan," 1997, 93–97, 99–101; Mariel, "Dana International," 1999, 117, 122.
143. For more detail on these songs, and on the language issue, see Ben-Zvi, "Zionist Lesbianism," 1998; Swedenburg, "Saida Sultan," 1997; Liora Mariel, "Diva in the Promised Land: A Blueprint for Newspeak?" *World Englishes* 17, no.2 (1998): 225–37.
144. Bohlman, "The *Shechinah*," 11, 12.
145. See Butler, *Gender Trouble*, 1990, 36–53; the quotations are from 48, 45.
146. Haraway, *Simians, Cyborgs, and Women*, 1991, 162.
147. Butler, *Gender Trouble*, 1990, 130.
148. Haraway, *Simians, Cyborgs, and Women*, 1991, 160; see also Barbara Ehrenreich, "The Decline of Patriarchy," in *Constructing Masculinity*, ed. Maurice Berger, Brian Wallis, and Simon Watson (New York: Routledge, 1995), 284–90.
149. Haraway, *Simians, Cyborgs, and Women*, 1991, 161.

Chapter 4

1. Jacques Lacan, quoted, Mitchell and Rose, *Feminine Sexuality*, 1982, 35.
2. Butler, *Bodies that Matter*, 1993, 95.
3. Haraway, *Simians, Cyborgs, and Women*, 1991,150–51.
4. In ad hominem terms, this is a passage from Marx through Freud and Lacan to Žižek — though I would want to avoid thinking this historical staging in overly reductive terms.
5. For example, in Richard Middleton, *Studying Popular Music* (Buckingham, UK: Open University Press, 1990), chapter 7.
6. Sigmund Freud, "Recollection, Repetition and Working Through," in *Therapy and Technique*, ed. Philip Rieff (1914, New York: Collier Books, 1963), 157–66.
7. "Re-presentation": I intend the use of this style here to signal the significance of the temporal (and often spatial) gap which enables us to group all of these terms under this general concept. There are important differences between them. For example, "to represent" (to place before, again) and "to repeat" (to seek again), even in the etymology, seem to have radically different tones, related perhaps to claims of epistemological certainty. Jacques Attali's rich account of the relations between "representing" and "repeating" is relevant, though arguably it oversimplifies the relationship (see pp. 25–26 above).
8. The idea of "encounter," as a trope articulating the emergence and development of a sense of "world music" within the culture of Western modernity, from the Renaissance to the present, is brilliantly presented by Philip Bohlman in his *World Music* (2002). I use the term *history* here in a particular sense, one contingent upon the self-understanding of "modernity" itself; this understanding will, I hope, become clear as the discussion proceeds.
9. On the "work concept," its critique and its historical career, see Michael Talbot, ed., *The Musical Work: Invention or Reality?* (Liverpool: Liverpool University Press, 2000).
10. Kittler, *Gramophone, Film, Typewriter*, 1999, 94.
11. Not entirely: Attali (*Noise*, 1985, 120-21) suggests that "It is not the least of the paradoxes of our research that we have detected uniformity in such multiform music, repetition in a society that talks so much about change, silence in the midst of so much noise, death in the heart of life. Everywhere, in fact, diversity, noise, and life are no longer anything more than masks…" We may not want to accept his pessimistic tone uncritically.
12. We might think that repetition in music is always in the act of saying, "*Salve*!" — "Be well (or else…)."
13. The concept of "refrain" is crucial to Deleuze's privileging of music in his theory of rhizomatic thought; thus: "Music is a creative, active operation that consists in deterritorializing the refrain. Whereas the refrain is essentially territorial, territorializing, or reterritorializing, music makes it a deterritorialized content for a deterritorializing form of expression" (Deleuze and Guattari, *A Thousand Plateaux*, 1988, 300; and see 299–350 passim). I introduce the concept here partly in acknowledgment of this intriguing idea, but also as a prelude to my critique of Deleuze which will come later.
14. Taussig, *Mimesis and Alterity*, 1993, xiv.
15. Susan McClary, "Same as It Ever Was: Youth Culture and Music," in *Microphone Fiends: Youth Music and Youth Culture*, ed. Andrew Ross and Tricia Rose (London: Routledge, 1994) 29–40. For a similar argument, including much of the same material, but in a different context, see Susan McClary, "Music, the Pythagoreans, and the Body," in *Choreographing History*, ed. Susan Leigh Foster (Bloomington: Indiana University Press, 1995), 82–104.
16. McClary, "Same as It Ever Was," 1994, 38.
17. Ibid., 37, my emphasis; 38.
18. Ibid., 40.
19. Sledge's record was first issued on Atlantic 2326 (1966).
20. In Žižek's account of the Lacanian story, the Lady of "courtly love" is an emptied-out, sublimated object standing in for the traumatic Thing — the impossible Real that can never appear — imposing randomly unreasonable demands on her masochistic (male) slave. See Slavoj Žižek, "Courtly Love, or Woman as Thing," in *The Žižek Reader*, ed. Elizabeth Wright and Edmond Wright (Oxford: Blackwell, 1999a), 148–73.
21. See ibid., 150–60; the quotations are from 158, 159.
22. See Kramer, "Ghost Stories: Cultural Memory, Mourning and the Myth of Originality," in *Musical Meaning*, 2002, 258–87.
23. Žižek, "Courtly Love," 1999a, 156; Kramer, *Musical Meaning*, 2002, 258–59.

24. Stanley Sadie, ed., *New Grove Dictionary of Music and Musicians*, vol. 5, 2nd ed. (London: Macmillan, 2001), 410–15 (entry on Chaconne); Willi Apel, *Harvard Dictionary of Music* (Cambridge, MA: Harvard University Press, 1961), 126–28 (entry on Chaconne and Passacaglia). McClary's references ("Same as It Ever Was," 1994, 36–37) document the European reception, and link the musical style of the seventeenth-century European *ciaccona* to long-lasting norms in a range of American vernacular dance-song genres.
25. I do not want to misrepresent McClary. She is clear that the body gestured into existence here is a *constructed* body and that music is one of the cultural technologies through which this process happens. Nevertheless, the metaphors in her descriptions are striking in their rhetorical passion.
26. See John Shepherd, David Horn, Dave Laing, Paul Oliver, and Peter Wicke, eds., *Encyclopedia of Popular Music of the World*, vol. 2, *Performance and Production* (London: Continuum, 2003), 610 (entry on Groove).
27. According to anecdotal evidence (gleaned over a pint at the Brecon Jazz Festival in the 1970s), hipster Slim Gaillard claimed to have "invented" the new usage of "groovy." Source: Bennett Hogg. Cab Calloway might well have disputed this: see the definition he quotes (Calloway and Rollins, *Of Minnie*, 1976, 256) from his own *Hepster's Dictionary* (1944) — "fine. Ex., 'I feel groovy.'"
28. The dimension of fashion is highlighted if one attends to the historical staging of changes in meaning: in the late nineteenth century, the main metaphorical meaning of "groove" was "routine"; by the 1930s, at least in slang musical usage, this had turned right around, as we have seen; but then in the 1980s, we find a further (ironic) inversion, in which "groovy" can be used, by adolescents to whom earlier "groovy" styles have become discredited, as meaning, precisely, passé. These, and subsequent, definitions are taken from the *Oxford English Dictionary*; Jonathan Green, ed., *Cassell's Dictionary of Slang* (London: Cassell, 1998); and Tony Thorne, *Dictionary of Contemporary Slang* (London: Bloomsbury, 1999).
29. Quoted in Bernard Gendron, *Between Montmartre and the Mudd Club: Popular Music and the Avant-Garde* (Chicago: University of Chicago Press, 2002), 134, 148; the sources date from 1944 and 1947 respectively.
30. The earliest *OED* reference to a record "groove" dates from 1902. My colleague Bennett Hogg has drawn my attention to the wealth of references in early twentieth-century literature to qualities of routine, tedium, or mechanicity in modern life which draw on phonographic metaphors. For example, T. S. Eliot's typist in *The Waste Land* (1923), after desultory sex: "She smoothes her hair with automatic hand/ And puts a record on the gramophone." Of course, many such metaphors have stuck (as it were): "stuck in a groove," "the needle's stuck," "change the record!".
31. The phenomenological effects are not set in stone (or rather wax, shellac, vinyl…), but shift with the technology; the artisanal or agricultural image of "cutting" gives way, with CD technology, to that of "burning" — the unseen but powerful (panoptical?) eye of the laser? — and thence to the cybernetic imagery of computer memory.
32. T. W. Adorno, "The Curves of the Needle" [1928], trans. Thomas Y. Levin, *October* 55 (1990b): 48–55, 54; the translation is of a revised version (by Adorno) first published in 1965.
33. See Adorno, ibid.; Adorno, "The Form of the Phonograph Record" [1934], trans. Thomas Y. Levin, *October* 55 (1990c): 56–61; and Thomas Y. Levin, "For the Record: Adorno on Music in the Age of Its Technological Reproducibility," *October* 55 (1990): 23–47, which acts as an introduction to these.
34. Adorno, "Form of the Phonograph Record," 1990c, 58,
35. Though Benjamin, typically, goes further: in Taussig's extrapolation from Benjamin, what matters is not so much the "clockwork" as the *animistic* quality in such mimetic technologies as the "talking [*sic*] machine"; revealing the primitive magic within technology, the gramophone is an object that speaks, re-creating "mystical participation" between consciousness and "nature" (Taussig, *Mimesis and Alterity*, 1993, 193–211). Connor's history of ventriloquism picks up this interpretation: "Matter which has… been given a voice — the radio, or the telephone, for instance — still retains a tincture of the old supernatural explanations, and indeed begins to bring about a kind of re-enchantment of the world. In technological modernity, the dead and dumb world of matter begins to speak, though now not as the voice of nature or the breath of God, but on its own" (Connor, *Dumbstruck*, 2000, 42).
36. Adorno, "Form of the Phonograph Record," 1990c, 59; Adorno (1953), quoted, Levin, "For the Record," 1990, 41.

37. Adorno, "Form of the Phonograph Record," 1990c, 58.
38. Levin ("For the Record," 1990, 41) argues that for Adorno this functions not as "nostalgic origin" but as utopian "regulative ideal"; but this does not seem to reduce its metaphysical status.
39. David Toop, *Ocean of Sound: Aether Talk, Ambient Sound and Imaginary Worlds* (London: Serpent's Tail, 1995), prologue [unpaginated]; 12.
40. Leonard. B. Meyer, *Music, the Arts, and Ideas: Patterns and Predictions in Twentieth-Century Culture* (Chicago: University of Chicago Press, 1967), 170.
41. My response would be: "No, it would not"; but this would not mean that the opposite conclusion — that history has stopped — is right either.
42. Gilles Deleuze, *Difference and Repetition*, trans. Paul Patton (London: Athlone Press, 1994), ix.
43. See, e.g., Joyce Appleby, Lynn Hunt, and Margaret Jacob, *Telling the Truth about History* (New York: Norton, 1994); Matei Calinescu, *Five Faces of Modernity* (Durham NC: Duke University Press, 1987), including his bald statement that "Modernity and the critique of repetition are synonymous notions" (66).
44. As Lawrence Kramer puts this, "A requirement was widely accepted: such music had to testify at every moment to its own originality. In practical terms, this meant that the music could contain none of the conventionalised 'filler' common in earlier eras" (*Musical Meaning*, 2002, 277).
45. Interpretation along these lines is now well-established. As well as the work of Susan McClary and Lawrence Kramer, see, e.g., Ruth A. Solie, "Whose Life? The Gendered Self in Schumann's *Frauenliebe* Songs," in *Music and Text: Critical Inquiries*, ed. Steven Paul Scher (Cambridge, UK: Cambridge University Press, 1992), 219–40.

    Solie, discussing Schumann's *Frauenliebe* songs, begins by quoting D. H. Lawrence: "[A woman] is the unutterable which man must forever continue to try to utter," and goes on to comment, in light of the way the composer stresses in his settings, "the endless repeatability of the woman's experience," that "though Lawrence is undoubtedly right to deem woman 'unutterable,' she clearly is *iterable*" (219, 228). Lawrence's aphorism, of course, offers an exemplary instance of the phallogocentric formulation of the "vocalic body"; see p. 271, note 11 above.
46. Quoted in Peter Kivy, *The Fine Art of Repetition: Essays in the Philosophy of Music* (Cambridge, UK: Cambridge University Press, 1993), 335.
47. Ibid., 344–45.
48. Eduard Hanslick, "On the Musically Beautiful," in *Music in European Thought 1851–1912*, ed. Bojan Bujić (1854, Cambridge, UK: Cambridge University Press, 1988), 11–39, 19, 29.
49. Pierre Boulez, *Orientations*, ed. Jean-Jacques Nattiez, trans. Martin Cooper (London: Faber, 1986), 93.
50. John Miller Chernoff, *African Rhythm and African Sensibility* (Chicago: Chicago University Press, 1979), 55.
51. Reported in *The Guardian*, December 31, 1993. Maybe I should not be so flippant: Jon Ronson (*The Men Who Stare at Goats* [London: Picador, 2004]) has documented how elements in U.S. intelligence have developed the use of endlessly repeated, and repeating, pop tunes as a "disorienting" interrogation technique; the link between such repetition and psychosis is clear in their theorizing, and the techniques seem to have been widely deployed in the "war on terror."
52. From Adorno's book on Mahler, quoted in Anthony Newcomb, "Narrative Archetypes and Mahler's Ninth Symphony," in *Music and Text: Critical Inquiries*, ed. Steven Paul Scher (Cambridge, UK: Cambridge University Press, 1992), 118–36, 118.
53. Adorno, "Form of the Phonograph Record," 1990c, 58, 118.
54. See, e.g., T. W. Adorno, *Philosophy of Modern Music*, trans. Anne G. Mitchell and Wesley V. Bloomster (London: Sheed and Ward, 1973); "Perennial Fashion — Jazz," in *Prisms*, trans. Samuel and Shierry Weber (1953, Cambridge, MA: MIT Press, 1983), 120–32; "On Popular Music," 1990a. Adorno was not alone: Bernard Gendron has described (*Between Montmartre and the Mudd Club*, 2002, 135–36) how in the 1930s and 1940s jazz revivalists excoriated the swing bands for their militaristic, riff-based discipline and connected these qualities to fascistic tendencies. Rudi Blesh, for example, writing in 1946, explicitly linked the "rabble-rousing" repetitions of riff-swing to the techniques of political demagoguery (*Shining Trumpets: A History of Jazz.* 2nd ed. [1958, New York: Da Capo Press, 1976], 290–91). Such critiques of repetition, then, have not been confined to elite cultural discourse; and much the same line of

attack could be found at later moments in popular music critical discourse, applied to other repetition-heavy styles, such as disco and techno.

55. Adorno in 1929, quoted in Levin, "For the Record," 1990, 29.
56. Max Paddison, *Adorno's Aesthetics of Music* (Cambridge, UK: Cambridge University Press, 1993), 179.
57. Adorno, *Introduction to the Sociology of Music*, 1976, 28, 29.
58. Adorno, quoted in Paddison, *Adorno's Aesthetics*, 1993, 178, 179.
59. Adorno, in Bloch et al., *Aesthetics and Politics*, 1977, 123.
60. On this problematic, see Donna Haraway's "'Gender' for a Marxist Dictionary," in Haraway, *Simians, Cyborgs, and Women*, 1991, 127–48.
61. Henri Lefebvre, *Everyday Life in the Modern World*, trans. S. Rabinovitch (1971, New Brunswick NJ: Transaction Books, 1990).
62. The classic text is his article "On Popular Music" (Adorno 1990a), first published in 1941.
63. Adorno, "Perennial Fashion," 1983, 125.
64. Adorno, "On Popular Music," 1990a, 314. See above, p. 33.
65. Ibid. 306–7. Similarly, Adorno stresses that songwriting (as distinct from production and promotion of song carriers — sheet music, records) only pretends to industrialization and is really at a handicraft stage; but, as Bernard Gendron has argued ("Theodor Adorno Meets the Cadillacs," in *Studies in Entertainment: Critical Approaches to Mass Culture*, ed. Tania Modleski [Bloomington: University of Indiana Press, 1986], 18–36), he does not allow this to disturb an assembly-line analogy for standardization in music which is badly in need of a more historically and analytically nuanced discussion. For a concise outline of the historical processes through which standardized types of popular song emerged as a result of "competition," see Paul Charosh, "Introduction," in *Song Hits from the Turn of the Century* (New York: Dover, 1975), ix–xii. The magical conjunction of novelty and repetition is nicely caught in Charosh's quotation (xi) from *Music Trade Review* (July 14, 1900): "The song of the moment constantly touches a great popular chord and this song can never die."
66. Raymond Williams, *Keywords: A Vocabulary of Culture and Society*, rev. ed. (London: Fontana, 1988), 298. Williams's essay on "Standards" (296–99) informs my discussion here.
67. Richard Middleton, "Work-in(g)-Practice: Configuration of the Popular Music Intertext," in *The Musical Work: Reality or Invention?*, ed. Michael Talbot (Liverpool, UK: University of Liverpool Press, 2000b), 59–87, 84, 83.
68. Recordings from: Solomon Burke, *A Change Is Gonna Come*, Rounder REU 1004 (1986); Lou Rawls, *Classic Soul*, Magmid MMO 19 (1986 [1969]); James Brown, *Live at the Apollo* vol. *2*, Polydor 314 549 884-2 (2001 [1967]); Natalie Cole, *Happy Love*, Capitol EST 12165 (1981); Laura Lee, *Two Sides of Laura Lee*, Hot Wax SHW 5009 (1972); Shirley Scott, *The Very Best of Jazz After Dark 2*, Global TV RADCD 156 (2000); Richard Clayderman, *Les Musiques de L'Amour*, Delphine 174 052-2 (N.D. [1977]); James Galway, *I Will Always Love You*, RCA Victor 7432 1 26221 2 (1995); Wes Montgomery, *The Legendary Wes Montgomery*, Music for Pleasure MFP 50436 (N.D. [1967]); Kenny Rogers, *Always and Forever*, Recall SMDCD 199 (1998); De Danaan, *Welcome to the Hotel Connemara*, Hummingbird HBCD 0025 (2000); Art Garfunkel, *The Best of Art Garfunkel*, Columbia 491450 2 (1998 [1988]); Gregorian, *Masters of Chant*, Edel 0114042 ERE (2000); Bette Midler, *The Rose*, Atlantic 7567-82778-2 (1979).
69. Dai Griffiths, "Cover Versions and the Sound of Identity in Motion," in *Popular Music Studies*, ed. David Hesmondhalgh and Keith Negus (London: Arnold, 2002), 51–64, 59; the "songline" reference is to Bruce Chatwin's *The Songlines* (London: Jonathon Cape, 1987) — see ibid., 61–62.
70. Walter Benjamin pointed out the significance in the mid-nineteenth century of the connection between weather and *boredom;* see Benjamin, *The Arcades Project*, trans. Howard Eiland and Kevin McLaughlin (Cambridge MA: Belknap Press, 1999), 101–5.
71. Recordings of "There'll Be Some Changes Made" from: Ethel Waters, *An Introduction to Ethel Waters: Her Best Recordings 1921–1940*, Best of Jazz 4013 (1994 [1921]); Mildred Bailey, *That Rockin' Chair Lady*, Topaz TPZ 1007 (1994 [1939]); Sophie Tucker, *Some of These Days*, Digimode GO 3821 (N.D. [1927]); Billie Holiday, *Last Recording*, Verve 817 802-1(1959); Peggy Lee, *A Portrait of Peggy Lee*, Gallerie GALE 442 (N.D. [1947]); Tony Bennett, *Have You Met Miss Jones?*, Recall SMDCD 353 (2001 [1976]); Charlie Byrd, *Byrd-Love*, Concorde SMDCD 270 (2000 [1997]); Dave Brubeck, *The Essential Dave Brubeck*, Columbia 5105942000 (2003 [1960]); Glenn Miller, *Glenn Miller in Concert*, RCA NL 89216 (1982); Chet Atkins, *The Best*

of Chet Atkins, Columbia 504420 2 (2001 [1990]); Russ Conway, Columbia SEG 7957 (N.D.); Mezz Mezzrow, *"Really the Blues" Concert*, Jazz Archives JA 39 (1978 [1947]); Eddie Lang [Blind Willie Dunn], *A Handful of Riffs*, Living Era CDAJA 5061 (1989 [1928]); The Boswell Sisters, *Jazz Age! Hot Sounds of the 20s and 30s*, Past Perfect PPCD 78131 (1998 [1932]).

72. Tucker — a white but Jewish "red hot momma" — had begun her career performing in blackface.
73. Walter Benjamin, "The Work of Art in the Age of Mechanical Reproduction," in *Illuminations*, trans. Harry Zohn (London: Fontana, 1973b), 219–53.
74. Ibid., 224.
75. Walter Benjamin, "On Some Motifs in Baudelaire," in *Illuminations*, trans. Harry Zohn (London: Fontana, 1973a): 157-202, 188, 190; "*Mémoire involontaire*" was Proust's term for (in effect) the unconscious.
76. Mowitt, *Percussion*, 2002, 20–28.
77. Benjamin, "Some Motifs in Baudelaire," 1973a, 177.
78. Benjamin,"The Work of Art," 1973b, 241–43.
79. See Benjamin, *Arcades Project*, 1999, esp. "Convolute D [Boredom, Eternal Return]," 101–19.
80. Mowitt's incisive discussion of the Adorno–Benjamin dispute traces some of the implications of post-Benjamin technological innovations for formations of subjectivity (see "The Sound of Music, 1987, 173–97). Dai Griffiths ("Cover Versions," 2002, 58) points out that basing a song on a sample of a previous record's key riff effectively turns the later song into a new kind of cover.

    The "traces" (*Spuren*) of Freud's "memory traces" (*Erinnerungsspuren*) can also refer to tracks (such as animal tracks) and branches (such as railway branch lines or mountain spurs). A further enticing word-play is available in English, introducing elements of both temporality and agency, if we think of subjects spurred into action, on the spur of the moment.
81. Benjamin, *Arcades Project,* 1999, 11, 119; Adorno could make similar points: cf. his "The eternity of fashion is a vicious circle" ("Perennial Fashion," 1983, 127).
82. Benjamin, *Arcades Project*, 1999, 10.
83. Quoted in Andreas Huyssen, *After the Great Divide: Modernism, Mass Culture, Postmodernism* (Bloomington: Indiana University Press, 1986), 26.
84. Ibid., 27.
85. As Mowitt ("The Sound of Music," 1987) is keen to point out, memory is always socially organized and subjectivity forms on its foundations. Arguably, Adorno's misrecognition of the sociotechnological conditions of musical memory under high capitalism goes far to explain the impasse in which his autonomous subject finds itself. Following Mowitt, we may suggest that a key part of this misrecognition lies in a continuing visual orientation: the ego initiated through a process of (mis)representation in the mirror phase is modeled in the relationship between the contemplative listening subject and the imaginary totality pictured in the notated score; a reweighting of subject formation toward sound and the dialogic repetitions constituted via the acoustic mirror may be deciphered not only in recent theory but also in the techno-collectively constructed memory formations of cyborg culture, of which the subject may be a prosthesis: "cover, riff and sample" as Phallic Mother?
86. Gianni Vattimo, *The End of Modernity*, trans. J. R. Snyder (Cambridge, UK: Polity Press, 1988), 4.
87. In *The Condition of Postmodernity* (Oxford: Blackwell, 1989), David Harvey provides a detailed account of the sequence of time–space compressions.
88. Benjamin, "Some Motifs in Baudelaire," 1973a, 196.
89. Notably in Middleton, *Studying Popular Music*, 1990, chapter 7.
90. Christian Friedrich Michaelis, *Berlinische musikalische Zeitung* (1805), in Peter Le Huray and James Day, eds., *Music and Aesthetics in the Eighteenth and Early-Nineteenth Centuries* (Cambridge, UK: Cambridge University Press, 1981), 290; see also 5–6.
91. Quoted in Toop, *Ocean of Sound,* 1995, 185.
92. Gilroy, *The Black Atlantic*, 1993.
93. James A. Snead, "Repetition as a Figure of Black Culture," in *Black Literature and Literary Theory*, ed. Henry Louis Gates Jr. (London: Routledge, 1984), 59–80.
94. Ibid., 63.
95. An irony of this picture is that the African's apparent predeliction for repetition could be

used to explain his tendency (so it was thought) to "imitation," including imitation of what in itself had been positioned as opposed to mere repetition (i.e., European cultural forms). Henry Louis Gates Jr. gives eighteenth- and nineteenth-century examples of this trope of black "mimicry" (*The Signifying Monkey*, 1988, 66–68).

96. Hegel, quoted in Snead, "Repetition," 1984, 62, 63; the translation is Snead's own. For the passage from which his quotations come, see G. W. F. Hegel, *Lectures on the Philosophy of World History. Introduction: Reason in History*, trans. H. B. Nisbet (1830, Cambridge, UK: Cambridge University Press, 1975), 174–90. Hegel's short diversion through "Africa" ends with the magisterial dismissal: "We shall therefore leave Africa at this point, and it need not be mentioned again. For it is an unhistorical continent, with no movement or development of its own" (190).
97. Snead, "Repetition," 1984, 63, 64.
98. Ibid., 75.
99. Baker, *Blues, Ideology and Afro-American Literature*, 1984; Gates, *The Signifying Monkey*, 1988.
100. Gates, *The Signifying Monkey*, 1988, xxiv.
101. Idem.
102. Ibid., 46.
103. Ralph Ellison, quoted in ibid., 62; ibid., 52
104. David Brackett, "James Brown's 'Superbad' and the Double-Voiced Utterance," in *Reading Pop: Approaches to Textual Analysis in Popular Music*, ed. Richard Middleton (Oxford: Oxford University Press, 2000), 122–40. For other examples of the application of the theory of Signifyin(g) to music, see Matthew Brown, "Funk Music as Genre: Black Aesthetics, Apocalyptic Thinking and Urban Protest in Post-1965 African-American Pop," *Cultural Studies* 8, no.3 (1994): 484–508; Samuel A. Floyd, *The Power of Black Music: Interpreting Its History from Africa to the United States* (New York: Oxford University Press, 1995); Middleton, "Work-in(g)-Practice," 2000b; Gary Tomlinson, "Cultural Dialogics and Jazz: A White Historian Signifies," *Black Music Research Journal* 11, no. 2 (1991): 229–64.
105. Steve Reich, *Writings about Music* (New York: Universal Edition, 1974), 53. Paul Allen Anderson (*Deep River*, 2000, 211–17) has suggested that the debate about repetition in black music can actually be traced back, within African-American thinking itself, to the Harlem Renaissance and even before — to the difference between, for instance, Du Bois and Hurston; Du Bois's insistence that the simplicities of the "sorrow songs" needed to be developed in the context of more worked-through musical forms — what Alain Locke would call a "path of progress" — was couched in explicitly Hegelian terms, while Hurston's innovative characterization of African-American rhythmic technique as a "rhythm of segments," asymmetrical, cut up, foreshadows not only Snead but also Gates, as well as offering implicitly a neo-Bakhtinian perspective. At issue here, of course, is the politics — dialectical? dialogical? — of "double consciousness."
106. Tricia Rose, *Black Noise: Rap Music and Black Culture in Contemporary America* (Hanover, NH: Wesleyan University Press, 1994), 65–72.
107. Ibid., 70, 72.
108. Ibid., 72. Rose takes me to task (ibid., 198–99, note 24) for discussing musematic repetition in *Studying Popular Music* without grounding the analysis of "black practices in African traditions… [in] an alternative approach to cultural production." This observation is fair comment, although it ignores the fact that such cultural grounding is not provided for the white examples either, and is not the point of the discussion. I hope it is not racist to contest the idea that the theorists to whom I refer — Freud, Lacan, Barthes and others, as well as Adorno — are necessarily less relevant to examples of commercial popular music produced by African Americans than to examples produced by white Americans or Europeans. Interestingly, Snead, on whom Rose's account of repetition in black culture is based, also refers approvingly to Freud and Lacan.
109. David Brackett, "What a Difference a Name Makes: Two Instances of African-American Music," in *The Cultural Study of Music: A Critical Introduction*, ed. Martin Clayton, Trevor Herbert, and Richard Middleton (New York: Routledge, 2003), 238–50. This might also be read as a riposte to Kofi Agawu's piece in the same book, whose heuristic program of starting interpretation with a presumption of *sameness* between African and European music would no doubt interest Tricia Rose! (See Agawu, "Contesting Difference: A Critique of Africanist

Ethnomusicology," in *The Cultural Study of Music: A Critical Introduction*, ed. Martin Clayton, Trevor Herbert, and Richard Middleton [New York: Routledge, 2003], 227–37.)

110. Quoted in Nuala O'Connor, *Bringing It All Back Home: The Influence of Irish Music* (London: BBC Books, 1991), 67.
111. Cf. Wagner, writing to August Rőckel in 1854: "[No one] can [ever] again surpass that act whereby he became human through love; he can only repeat it… and it is this repetition which alone makes possible the unique nature of this love whereby it resembles the ebb and flow of the tides, changing, ending, and living anew." (Quoted in Kramer, *Music as Cultural Practice*, 1990, 135). As Kramer points out, Wagner's *Tristan und Isolde* has been seen in this light from the moment in the composer's own program note when he writes of its representation of desire as "forever renewing itself, craving and languishing" (147). Kramer also shows, however, that the point of the work is at the same time to suggest how desire can overflow all natural boundaries.
112. See Kramer, *Classical Music*, 1995, 68–71.
113. Warner, *Fantastic Metamorphoses*, 2002, 1–17.
114. Taussig (*Mimesis and Alterity*, 1993, 212–20), drawing on Alexander Buchner's *Mechanical Musical Instruments* (1978), points out that the automata in eighteenth-century mechanical musical instruments are almost never modeled on white males; they are animals, birds, blacks, or women. This re-creation of primitive mimicry through mechanism — the clockwork of Newtonian Nature — is then picked up later in the famous His Master's Voice logo for the early gramophone, where the faithful dog, Nipper, continues the theme: fidelity, both to the Master and to what is copied. Taussig also quotes Zora Neale Hurston on African-American mimicry: "The Negro, the world over, is famous as a mimic. But this in no way damages his standing as an original. Mimicry is an art in itself [and] he does it as the mocking-bird does it, for the love of it, and not because he wishes to be like the one imitated" (68). And he gives an anecdote concerning dancer Josephine Baker dancing privately for a German count in 1926, imitating his demonstration of the new dance he has created for her but going beyond the original in an "excess" that serves as an example of the possibilities of "answering back"(68–69). At the same time, we should note the irony that many nineteenth-century African-American writers were known as the "mockingbird school" on account of their alleged inability to rise above imitation — perhaps a measure of white neurosis where "repetition" was concerned.
115. See ibid., 45–47, 63–68; the quoted phrases are from Horkheimer and Adorno's *The Dialectic of Enlightenment*, and Taussig gives them on pp. 47 and 63.
116. The latter is what Roman Jakobson called "introversive signification," but in the specific context of black culture is Signifyin(g). The gaps which appear all over the entire nexus are, in Derridean terms, the trace of the supplement. I discuss (*Studying Popular Music*, 1990, 183, 214–17) the fact that in music, much more than in any other signifying practice, *difference* is filtered through the screen of *equivalence* (that is, introversive signification); this in turn points to the importance of *contiguity* (as against *distinction* and *opposition*); which in turn points us back to the *acoustic mirror*. Even the best studies of mimesis/doubling (Taussig's, Warner's) tend to pay little attention to sound, which often leads to a downplaying of the significance of the specific mimetic processes of repetition.
117. Martin Heidigger, *The Question Concerning Technology* (New York: Harper and Row, 1977), 149, 150.
118. Taussig, *Mimesis and Alterity*, 1993, 72.
119. Warner, *Fantastic Metamorphoses*, 2002, 21.
120. Taussig, whose historical scheme is similarly shaped, is less inclined to do so, although he is at least as intrigued by the interplay of mimicking between colonizers and colonized as by structures of repression. He describes a "colonial mirror of production," a "crucial circulation of imageric power between… selves and… anti-selves, their ominous need for and their feeding off each other's correspondence — interlocking dream-images guiding the reproduction of social life no less than the production of sacred powers" (*Mimesis and Alterity*, 1993, 66, 65).
121. Warner, *Fantastic Metamorphoses*, 2002, 24, 25.
122. Ibid., 102.
123. So could Kramer's quotation from Carl Dahlhaus on the subject of Schumann's *Carnaval*, which is exemplary of a traditional attitude to repetition in nineteenth-century music less self-aware than Kramer's own: "Almost invariably, the motive has a distinctive rhythm while the pitch content remains open and variable. Thus the 'four notes,' instead of *quickly cloying*

by frequent repetition and manipulation, merely serve as an initial impetus to the pieces. At the same time, the pitch content, by merely alluding to the opening of the movement, could be taken up *again and again* without *courting monotony* or 'unpoetic' pedantry" (Kramer, *Musical Meaning*, 2002, 101; emphasis added).

124. Newcomb, "Narrative Archetypes," 1992, 120, 133, 134 (the last a quotation of Peter Brook); Newcomb is drawing on Freud's earlier theory of repetition, not the later development which I shall come to presently.

    Mahler and Freud were of course contemporaries in Vienna. They knew each other; Freud admired Mahler's sensitivity to psychoanalytic ideas; Mahler approached Freud for an analysis, and Freud produced one. The connection surely points to a cultural knot of larger scale. Interestingly, Newcomb at one point refers to "Jekyll-and-Hyde" intercutting between different materials in the Ninth Symphony; Robert Louis Stevenson's more or less contemporary Jekyll and Hyde story is treated by Warner as a key example of late-nineteenth century uncanny "doubling"; see Warner, *Fantastic Metamorphoses*, 2002, 185–87.

125. See Kramer, *Classical Music*, 1995, 174–200; *Musical Meaning*, 2002, 194–215 (esp. 194–201). The transatlantic anamorphic mirror constructed between Mahler and Ives here — (Euro-) Jewish on the one side, (African) American on the other — might recall the one I erected earlier between Michael Jackson and Dana International. As in that case, there are, for both protagonists, Mahler and Ives, important gender and class dimensions to their "pathologies." Kramer goes into Ives's; for Mahler, see Biddle, *Listening to Men*, forthcoming, chapter 5, "'*... man sagte bloß, es tanze jemand*': Mahler, Kafka and the Male Jewish Body at the Habsburg fin de siècle."

126. See Eric Hobsbawm and Terence Ranger, eds., *The Invention of Tradition* (Cambridge, UK: Cambridge University Press, 1983), esp. chapter 7, Eric Hobsbawm, "Mass-Producing Traditions: Europe, 1870–1914" (263–307).

127. Benjamin, *Arcades Project*, 1999, 11.

128. Ian Hacking, *Rewriting the Soul: Multiple Personality and the Sciences of Memory* (Princeton NJ: Princeton University Press, 1995). This conjunction is also dependent on the fact that new media could record memory; see Kittler, *Gramophone, Film, Typewriter*, 1999, passim but esp. 78–94.

129. Warner, *Fantastic Metamorphoses*, 2002, 156.

130. On this see Huyssen, *After the Great Divide*, 1986, 44–62; Tania Modleski, "Femininity as Mas(s)querade: A Feminist Approach to Mass Culture," in *High Theory, Low Culture*, ed. Colin McCabe (New York: St Martin's Press, 1986), 37–52.

131. See, e.g., Kramer, *Classical Music*, 1995, 201–25. Kramer draws attention to the conjunction in Ravel's work of exoticism, a spectacularly modern technique, and a consumerist attitude to the massing of sensations, all of which on one level come to be centered on Ravel's "techniques of reproduction, iteration, similitude — techniques, we might suggest, strikingly similar to those by which commodities are identified and distributed" (216), and which may also be linked with the "sensational" mass reproduction of images in the early cinema and its technological predecessors (217).

132. Taussig, *Mimesis and Alterity*, 1993, 23, xix; and see 19–43, 193–249.

133. Warner, *Fantastic Metamorphoses*, 2002, 165.

134. I discuss this process in Middleton, *Studying Popular Music*, 1990, 275–78.

135. Interestingly, Danny Barker's reminiscences of early twentieth-century New Orleans suggest that, there at least, the imagery of "honky-tonk trains" was preceded by such expressions as "playing the horses" and "rolling the horses," "because it was the same thing over and over and sounded like a gang of horses trotting" (Barker, *Buddy Bolden and the Last Days of Storyville*, ed. Alyn Shipton [London: Continuum, 2000], 103). This (preindustrial, "natural") imagery comes up in the context of an anecdote about the young Barker accidentally but excitedly observing activity in a brothel, featuring a naked woman dancing to the accompaniment of boogie-woogie.

136. Warner, *Fantastic Metamorphoses*, 2002, 119–41.

137. Cf. p. 86 above.

138. An emblematic phrase derived by W. T. Lhamon (whose theory this is: see *Raising Cain*, 1998) from the lyrics of Thomas "Daddy" Rice's minstrel hit, "Jump Jim Crow": "Weel about, and turn about, And do jis so; Eb'ry time I weel about, I jump Jim Crow."

139. See Henry Louis Gates Jr., Preface, ix, and Introduction, xxvii–xxxiii; Dickson D. Bruce Jr.,

"W. E. B. Du Bois and the Idea of Double Consciousness" (236–44); all in Du Bois, *The Souls of Black Folk*, 1999. Gates also points out (x) that the idea was subsequently taken up in such a way that the African-American case could be treated as exemplary for a broader sense of the human condition under modernity. On Du Bois's debt to (and transformation of) Hegel, see Gilroy, *The Black Atlantic*, 1993, 111–45, esp. 134ff.

140. I take the phrase "pendular thirds" from Peter van der Merwe (*Origins of the Popular Style*, 1989, 131), who in turn took it from Nigerian ethnomusicologist, J. H. Nketia. For examples of work songs that use the tonic-minor third riff, see: "Po' Lazarus" (discussed in ibid, 192–93; this tune is heard at the start of the movie, *O Brother, Where Art Thou?*, where it marks not only what is escaped in the search for modernity but also the bedrock state against which this search is measured and to which the heroes might just have to return [they almost do]); "I Be So Glad When the Sun Goes Down" (*Sounds of the South*, Atlantic 1346, ND [c. 1960]); "Eighteen Hammers" (*Roots of the Blues*, Atlantic 1348, ND [c. 1960]). All these were recorded by Alan Lomax in 1959 from inmates of the Parchman State Penitentiary in Mississippi. "Baby Please Don't Go" can be heard in many versions; also see Harold Courlander, *Negro Folk Music U.S.A.* (New York: Columbia University Press, 1963), 108–9. Howlin' Wolf's "Spoonful" (1960) is on *His Best*, Chess MCD 09375 (1997). Public Enemy's "Black Steel in the Hour of Chaos" is on *It Takes a Nation of Millions to Hold Us Back*, Def Jam 527 358-2 (1988). Admittedly, this record was a careful choice to fit my argument; but many Public Enemy, and other, rap tracks use very similar bass riffs; they can often be heard as speeded up work songs, as if produced by hyperactive cyborgs (from the point of view of technology, they literally were).
141. Warner, *Fantastic Metamorphoses*, 2002, 159.
142. Quoted, Snead, "Repetition," 1984, 64.
143. Cf. p. 129 above. Jodi Brooks ("Ghosting the Machine: The Sounds of Tap and the Sounds of Film," *Screen* 44, no.4 [2003]: 355–78) discusses the cultural politics of tap dance in the contexts of Fordist machine-rhythm, minstrelized performance conventions, and Hollywood genre formulae, focusing on "the Hollywood musical's barely repressed ghosts — the bodies, sounds, and steps of African American vernacular dance" (359), and concluding with an analysis of Michael Jackson's *Black or White* video from this point of view. Carol Vernallis (*Experiencing Music Video: Aesthetics and Cultural Context* [New York: Columbia University Press, 2004], 167) suggests that, in his *Thriller* video, the music tells us that the zombies (rather than Jackson) are actually warm-blooded: "it is the *zombies* who know the groove" (indeed yes — the *groove* from beyond the *grave*).
144. The most obvious example to cite would be music associated with possession experiences (obvious also in that quasi-possessive effects are often attributed as well to minimalist music, rock, and pop-dance — rave, techno, etc.). Gilbert Rouget ("Music and Possession Trance," in *The Anthropology of the Body*, ed John Blacking [New York: Academic Press, 1977], 233–39) reminds us, however, that even in this case the relationship is complex and variable, and he suggests that the purpose of possession music is precisely to "*socialize* trance" (238; my italics) — a point that, translated into the theory of ventriloquism, can also be taken to suggest that the development I am discussing here should be seen as yet another symptom of shifts in the ventriloquial possession economy.
145. The angel stands facing the past. The storm of History "irresistably propels him into the future to which his back is turned, while the pile of debris before him grows skyward. This storm is what we call progress" (Benjamin, "Theses on the Philosophy of History," 1973c, 260).
146. Kittler, *Gramophone, Film, Typewriter*, 1999, 22–23. And compare Kittler's quotation of the philosopher Jean-Marie Guyau (1880): "The soul is a notebook of phonographic recordings" (30).
147. Sigmund Freud, "Beyond the Pleasure Principle," in *On Metapsychology: The Theory of Psychoanalysis* (1920, London: Penguin, 1991b), 269–338, 296–97; Mowitt, "The Sound of Music," 1987, 183; Freud, "A Note upon the 'Mystic Writing Pad,'" in *On Metapsychology: The Theory of Psychoanalysis* (London: Penguin, 1991a), 429–34, 434. I have modified the Penguin translation of Freud's famous "memory trace" phrase ("*das Bewußtsein entstehe an Stelle der Erinnerungsspur*": see *Jenseits des Lustprinzips*, in *Gesammelte Werke*, vol. 13 [Frankfurt: Fischer Taschenburg Verlag, 1999], 25); "at the site of" (*an Stelle der*) appears in some other translations but the Penguin translation has "instead of." The ambiguity is in the German phrase itself, and perhaps points to an unacknowledged uncertainty in Freud's thinking, still, about the relationship between consciousness, memory, and the unconscious

(and hence also, of course, repetition). (Thanks to Thomas Rutten for advice on interpreting the German phrase.)

148. Søren Kierkegaard, *Fear and Trembling*, trans. Robert Payne (1843, London: Oxford University Press, 1939), 183–84; *Repetition: An Essay in Experimental Psychology*, trans. W. Lowrie (London: Oxford University Press, 1942), 6.
149. Friedrich Nietzsche, *The Will to Power*, trans. Walter Kaufman and R.J. Hollingdale (New York: Vintage, 1968), 547, 549.
150. Quoted, Baker, *Blues, Ideology and Afro-American Literature, 1984*, 217.
151. Jean Baudrillard, "Symbolic Exchange and Death," trans. Charles Levin, in *Selected Writings*, ed. Mark Poster (Cambridge, UK: Polity Press, 1988), 119–48, 138.
152. Frederic Jameson, "Postmodernism: The Cultural Logic of Late Capitalism," *New Left Review* 146 (1984): 53–92.
153. Chernoff, *African Rhythm*, 1979, 140–50.
154. Morton Marks, "Uncovering Ritual Structures in Afro-American Music," in *Religious Movements in Contemporary America*, ed. I. Zaretsky and M. P. Leone (Princeton, NJ: Princeton University Press, 1974), 60–134, 112.
155. Kierkegaard, *Repetition*, 1942, passim.
156. Deleuze, *Difference and Repetition*, 1994, 18, 21.
157. Julia Kristeva, "Women's Time," in *The Kristeva Reader*, ed. Toril Moi (Oxford: Blackwell, 1986b), 188–213, 210.
158. Henryk Gorecki, Symphony No 3, Warner Classics 0927498212 (2003).
159. Interview with Maja Trochimczyk, 1997, accessed at http://www.edu/dept/polish_music/composer/gorecki.html
160. John Adams, *Grand Pianola Music*, Nonesuch 7559-79219-2 (1993).
161. http://www.schirmer.com/composers/adams_bio.html
162. If the auto-piano figure functions as a fetishized *objet a*, we might recall that for Lacan all such objects are representatives of "the libido, *qua* pure life instinct, that is to say, immortal life, or irrepressible life, life that has need of no organ [nor piano] ... precisely what is subtracted from the living being by virtue of the fact that it is subject to the cycle of sexed reproduction." If the repetitions of Adams's music are "sexy," it is in this reduced (and here mechanized, alienated) sense. And appropriately, what is subtracted — this transfinite libido which "flies off" at the moment of birth — is figured by Lacan, in a yolky joke, as an eggy lamella: the *l'hommelette,* which represents "the relation between the living subject and that which he loses by having to pass, for his reproduction, through the sexual cycle. In this way I explain the essential affinity of every drive with the zone of death, and reconcile the two sides of the drive — which, at one and the same time, makes present sexuality in the unconscious and represents, in its essence, death" (Lacan, *The Four Fundamental Concepts*, 1979, 197, 198, 199). I am anticipating my argument somewhat here (see p. 185ff. below), but repeat the question: Does Adams's fantasy-object represent a triumph of phallic authority or a funeral?
163. There is a postmodernist argument that denies this difference; see, e.g., Fink, "Elvis Everywhere," 1998. For convincing rebuttals of this position, both drawing on Bourdieu's theory of capital (cultural/economic), see Gendron, *From Montmartre to the Mudd Club*, 2002, 1–23, and Georgina Born, "Afterword: Music Policy, Aesthetic and Social Difference," in *Rock and Popular Music: Politics, Policies, Institutions*, ed. Tony Bennett et al. (London: Routledge, 1993), 266–92. If (as Fink's title suggests) Elvis *is* everywhere, it strikes me this is less a symptom of the end of cultural hierarchy than one of a multiplicity of highly differentiated *revenants*; see Kramer, *Classical Music*, 1995, 227–42.
164. See Lawrence Grossberg, "Is Anybody Listening? Does Anybody Care? On the 'State of Rock,'" in *Microphone Fiends: Youth Music and Youth Culture*, ed. Andrew Ross and Tricia Rose (London: Routledge, 1994), 41–58.
165. P. J. Harvey, *To Bring You My Love*, Island CID 8035 (1995).
166. Mark Mazullo locates the feminism and the anguish in a topos of suicide ("Revisiting the Wreck: PJ Harvey's *Dry* and the Drowned Virgin-Whore," *Popular Music* 20, no.3 [2001]: 431–47). On the sleeve of *To Bring You My Love*, Harvey is depicted floating, Ophelia-like. On the back insert, she is shown climbing some stairs (like Gloria?) — but the stairs, claustrophobic as they are, are lit from above by a shaft of quasi-heavenly light, and they have no end that we can see. The comparison with Kristeva's female suicide problematic (see p. 92 above) is obvious.

167. Tricky, *Maxinquaye*, Island BRCD 610 (1995).
168. "Black Steel," on the same album, is a cover of Public Enemy's "Black Steel in the Hour of Chaos" (see above, p. 174), but the lyrics are regendered (transferred to Martine), sung rather than rapped, and in any case largely disappear into the pulsating sound mix.
169. This is not to suggest that one can simply read across from the specifics of African-American history to the situation in the Caribbean, let alone its aftermath in Britain — although it seems likely that slavery created similar pressures. Looking into the black Atlantic mirror, Martine, in "Suffocating Love," quotes the title of Maya Angelou's first volume of autobiography, *I Know Why the Caged Bird Sings*.
170. On another track, "Aftermath," Tricky samples a phrase from a replicant in the film *Blade Runner*: "Let me tell you about my mother."
171. Alistair Williams, "Music as Immanent Critique: Stasis and Development in the Music of Ligeti," in *Music and the Politics of Culture*, ed. Christopher Norris (London: Lawrence and Wishart, 1993), 187–225.
172. Ibid., 216, 217.
173. Born, "Afterword," 1993, 285.
174. Steve Reich, *Come Out*, *Early Works*, Nonesuch 979 169-2 (1987); Prodigy, "Everybody in the Place," *Best of Rave*, vol. 1, Low Price Music LOW CD 115 (1993).
175. Reich, *Writings about Music*, 1974, passim.
176. Toop, *Ocean of Sound*, 1995, 183, 214, 278, 257, 258, 259, 275, 279–80.
177. John Rahn, "Repetition," *Contemporary Music Review* 7 (1993): 49–57, 50, 53, 50. The discourse of "slavery," "zombies," and "*revenants*" is revealing in its lack of historical self-consciousness!
178. Middleton, "Musical Belongings, 2000a, 76–77.
179. Freud, "Beyond the Pleasure Principle," 1991b, 307, 285, 308, 311, 312.
180. Jacques Derrida,"To Speculate — On Freud," in *A Derrida Reader: Between the Blinds*, ed. Peggy Kamuf (Hemel Hempstead, UK: Harvester Wheatsheaf, 1991d), 518–68, 549.
181. Lacan, *The Four Fundamental Concepts*, 1979, 62–63.
182. Ibid., 49, 239, 53, 54, 43, 56.
183. Ibid., 61.
184. Guy Rosolato, "*Répétitions*," *Musique en Jeu* 9 (1972): 33–44, 40, 43, 41.
185. Jacques Derrida, *Writing and Difference*, trans. Alan Bass (Chicago: University of Chicago Press, 1978), 246.
186. Quoted in Christopher Norris, "Utopian Deconstruction: Ernst Bloch, Paul de Man and the Politics of Music," in *Music and the Politics of Culture*, ed. Christopher Norris (London: Lawrence and Wishart, 1993), 305–47, 339.
187. Jacques Derrida, "Signature Event Context," in *A Derrida Reader: Between the Blinds*, ed. Peggy Kamuf (Hemel Hempstead, UK: Harvester Wheatsheaf, 1991b) 82–111, 90.
188. Jacques Derrida, "*Différance*," in *A Derrida Reader: Between the Blinds*, ed. Peggy Kamuf (Hemel Hempstead, UK: Harvester Wheatsheaf, 1991a), 61–79, 70, 72.
189. Jacques Derrida, "The Double Session," in *A Derrida Reader: Between the Blinds*, ed. Peggy Kamuf (Hemel Hempstead, UK: Harvester Wheatsheaf, 1991c), 171–99, 193.
190. Taussig, *Mimesis and Alterity*, 1993, 35.
191. Ibid., 115.
192. Quoted in Evans, *Introductory Dictionary*, 1997, 51.
193. Julia Kristeva, "Revolution in Poetic Language," in *The Kristeva Reader*, ed. Toril Moi (Oxford: Blackwell, 1986a), 90–136, 94, 126, 128.
194. Deleuze, *Difference and Repetition*, 1994, 18, 17, 3, 50, 18.
195. Ibid., 20.
196. Ibid., 292–93, 25.
197. Taussig, *Mimesis and Alterity*, 1993, 192.
198. Quoted in Van M. Cagle, *Reconstructing Pop/Subculture: Art, Rock and Andy Warhol* (London: Sage, 1995), 62.
199. Deleuze, *Difference and Repetition*, 1994, 19, 7–8.
200. See Slavoj Žižek, "The Undergrowth of Enjoyment: How Popular Culture Can Serve as an Introduction to Lacan," in *The Žižek Reader*, ed. Elizabeth Wright and Edmond Wright (Oxford: Blackwell, 1999d), 11–36; quotations on 24, 30, 31.
201. Ibid.; quotations on 34, 28.

202. Taussig, *Mimesis and Alterity,* 1993, xvi.
203. Taussig's gloss is very fine: "only at the depth of habit is radical change effected, where unconscious strata of culture are built into social routines by bodily disposition. The revolutionary task... could thus be considered as one in which 'habit' has to catch up with itself. The automatic pilot that functions while asleep has to be awakened to its own automaticity..." (ibid., 25).
204. See Peter Pesic, *Seeing Double: Shared Identities in Physics, Philosophy and Literature* (Cambridge, MA: MIT Press, 2002).
205. Lacan, quoted in Dolar, "The Object Voice,"1996, 28.
206. See Žižek, "The Undergrowth of Enjoyment," 1999d, 16–17.
207. Taussig, *Mimesis and Alterity,* 1993, 96–99. Elaine Scarry's reading of Marx in this respect is similar; see Scarry, *The Body in Pain: The Making and Unmaking of the World* (New York: Oxford University Press, 1985), 286 (but also passim).
208. The term "performance-work" is indebted to the idea of "song-work" put forward by Barbara Bradby and Brian Torode (in "Song-Work: The Musical Inclusion, Exclusion and Representation of Women," unpublished conference paper, British Sociological Association, Manchester, 1982). They in turn are drawing on Freud's concept of "dream-work"– the mental labour through which, in dreams, "latent content" is translated into, and disguised by, "manifest content": a process that the psychoanalyst (and by analogy the analyst of musical performance) will try to reverse. For Lacan's gloss on Freud, in which he adopts Freud's term *Vorstellungsrepräsentanz* and applies it not only to the economy of the dream but also that of repetition, see Lacan, *The Four Fundamental Concepts*, 1979, 53–64.
209. Details of records discussed in this section: James Brown, "Funky Drummer," King K6290 (1970); Public Enemy, "Bring the Noise," "Terminator X to the Edge of Panic," and "Rebel without a Pause," *It Takes a Nation of Millions to Hold Us Back*, Def Jam 527 358-2 (1988); Stone Roses, "Fool's Gold," Silvertone ORE13 (1989); Future Sound of London, "Papua New Guinea," *Papua New Guinea*, Jumpin and Pumpin CDTOT52 (2001); John Oswald, *Plunderphonics* (1989); Sinéad O'Connor, "I Am Stretched on Your Grave," *I Do Not Want What I Haven't Got*, Ensign CDP32 1759-2 (1989).
210. James Brown (with Bruce Tucker), *The Godfather of Soul* (London: Macmillan, 1986), 242; Ulf Poschardt, who quotes this (*DJ Culture*, trans. Shaun Whiteside [London: Quartet Books, 1998], 117), has a useful discussion of the issue.
211. The allusion is not only to Benjamin's Angel but also to his view of dialectics generally: "having the wind of history in one's sails.... What is decisive is knowing the art of setting them" (Benjamin, *Arcades Project,* 1999, 473).
212. I am indebted to Suade Bergemann for this information. Bergemann also confirms, through personal acquaintance with one of those involved, the "Fool's Gold" FD sample, even though this has been queried by some commentators.
213. http://www.plunderphonics.com, which also contains a wonderfully tasteless picture of "Michael Jackson" (subject of another track, "dab"), resexing him and with a clearly missing penis. For Oswald's well-argued case against copyright, and in favour of sampling, see http://www.halcyon.com/robinja/mythos/plunderphonics
214. János Maróthy (*Music and the Bourgeois*, 1974) has magisterially documented this lengthy history.
215. On this track, see Keith Negus, "Sinéad O'Connor — Musical Mother," in *Sexing the Groove: Popular Music and Gender*, ed. Sheila Whiteley (London: Routledge, 1997), 178–90.
216. Žižek, "The Undergrowth of Enjoyment," 1999d, 30; Poschardt, *DJ Culture,* 1998, 318, 116.

Chapter 5

1. Henry David Thoreau, *Walden*, ed. Christopher Bigsby (1854, London: Everyman, 1995), 78.
2. The condition of slavery, actual and metaphorical, is a theme that runs right through *Walden*. It is intriguing to note that at the same time Thoreau was experimenting with self-sufficiency in his Walden cottage (1845–47), and not so very far away, the minstrel show was also dramatizing the issues around, and symbolized by, slavery, albeit in very different ways. The crisis both were addressing was the moment of the "American 1848," as it has been called; see Lott, *Love and Theft*, 1993, 86–88, 105–7, 169–210.

3. Simon Frith, "'The Magic that Can Set You Free': The Ideology of Folk and the Myth of the Rock Community," *Popular Music* 1 (1981): 159–68; "Playing with Real Feeling – Jazz and Suburbia," in *Music for Pleasure: Essays in the Sociology of Pop* (Cambridge: Polity Press, 1988), 45–63.
4. Jann Wenner, *Lennon Remembers: The Rolling Stone Interviews* (Harmondsworth, UK: Penguin, 1972), 100–1, 103.
5. *John Lennon/Plastic Ono Band*, Apple PCS 7124 (1970).
6. The main chord-sequence of Ben E. King's 1961 Soul hit, "Stand By Me" — I-VI-IV-V — was familiar enough from previous soul and doo-wop tunes but became iconically associated with King's song (much as George Gershwin's "I Got Rhythm" sequence became "the rhythm changes"). Lennon would have a minor hit with "Stand By Me" in 1975.
7. Cf Thoreau once again: "it is, after all, always the first person that is speaking" (*Walden*, 1995, 3).
8. For a somewhat longer discussion of "Working Class Hero," see Middleton, "Locating the People, 2003, 256–57.
9. Georgina Born and David Hesmondhalgh, *Western Music and Its Others: Difference, Representation, and Appropriation in Music* (Berkeley: University of California Press, 2000), 30.
10. The phrase comes from Thomas Frank, *One Market Under God: Extreme Capitalism, Market Populism and the End of Economic Democracy* (London: Vintage, 2002).
11. All these questions were raised in a profile published in *The Guardian* by Caroline Sullivan (July 23, 2004, 13). We might add that in the histrionic performance culture of soul music epitomized by James Brown, "authenticity" is, precisely, performed, and when singers sweat out their commitment to "telling it like it is" and "'keeping it real," through an arsenal of well-tried stage techniques, knowing listeners may well smile. In this sense, the "doubts" raised in the Stone case are built into the culture.
12. Allan Moore, "Authenticity as Authentication," *Popular Music* 21, no.2 (2002): 209–23.
13. Spice Girls, "Wannabe," *Spice*, Virgin CDV 2812 (1996).
14. Middleton, "Locating the People," 2003, 258.
15. Elizabeth Eva Leach, "Vicars of 'Wannabe': Authenticity and the Spice Girls," *Popular Music* 20, no. 2 (2001): 143–67, 151, 149, 161–62.
16. On representation as an unstable field, always marked by the search for a final (impossible) suture of representative (here the musical/filmic texts) and represented (the differential structure of the girl power community), see Laclau and Mouffe, *Hegemony*, 1985, 119–22; and on New Right (Thatcherite) populism as an example, see ibid., 169–71. "Wannabe" offers a case where the two extremes of Laclau and Mouffe's "unstable oscillation" seem to meet up, a knowing "literalization of the fiction" (this is just a polysemic game) giving rise to "a dissolution of the fictitious character of representation" (the Spice Girls really are like this, and you [other girls] are/could be too). This defines the aesthetic mechanism of populism.
17. The stage is set with the sound of footsteps approaching the mike, followed by a laugh.
18. Terry Castle, "My Heroin Christmas," *London Review of Books*, December 18, 2003: 11–18.
19. For example, letter from Don Locke (*London Review of Books*, January 22, 2004, 5): "addictable to everything and anything, self-deluding as well as self-destructive, Pepper tells it not as it is, but as he needs it to be."
20. A nice symptom of Castle's knowingly ironized credulity (as well as being a commentary on authenticity as acting) is the way she implicitly plays (*sic*) with the connection between her enjoyment of Pepper's "playing" and her own professional standing as a scholar of eighteenth-century literature specializing in masquerades.
21. Locke, letter. Quotations from Castle's essay ("Heroin Christmas," 2003) come, in order, from: 11, 14, 18, 16, 14, 15, 16, 18.
22. Many questions are begged — at least for now — in this way of putting things, not least the epistemological status of the construction, "true to." One of them is the status of music as, so to speak, an object or a subject of discourse. If "every object is constituted as an object of discourse, insofar as no object is given outside every discursive condition of emergence" (Laclau and Mouffe, *Hegemony*, 1985, 107), musical objects will come under this rubric; but if music also (arguably) operates as a quasi-discursive signifying practice (I think it does), it also constructs conditions of emergence for its own objects (at the same time as doing so within the regime of linguistic discursivity). This complicates musical truth-claims somewhat.
23. For differing versions of the "mirror" argument, by Adorno and Silverman respectively, see pp. 96, 115 and 146 above. For record dialogics, see pp. 95–96, 105–6 and 159–60 above.

24. Elsewhere ("Locating the People," 2003, 258) I have suggested that the binary structure of "Wannabe," articulated through the contrast of musical modes and its artful closure, not only maps to a conventional masculine/feminine dichotomy but also conjures up "specters" of paired dance-forms from earlier European music history and of an *antico/moderno* negotiation intrinsic to the self-understanding of Western modernity itself. These relationships help root/route the record in/to the structure of a familiar binary subjectivity.
25. In the exemplary case, Castle defends the essential truth of Pepper's account of how he made the *Art Pepper Meets the Rhythm Section* recordings, against incontrovertible historical evidence, because of its "ludic genius"; but Pepper's (false) insistence that he "was forced to pull the music out of himself" because he had not played for six months, had no decent mouthpiece, and was wrecked by drugs simply airbrushes from history his own professionalism, training, and stock of musical knowledge — not to mention the contributions of the other musicians ("Heroin Christmas," 2003, 16).
26. To put it differently (and perhaps better): Leach signals a deconstructive enterprise, but this is applied to an autodeconstructive text; what a deconstructive analysis really demands, therefore, is an exposure of the constructive intentions hidden beneath the wannabe-deconstructions of the song.
27. The phrase "situated knowledge" comes from Donna Haraway ("Situated Knowledges: The Science Question in Feminism and the Privilege of Partial Perspective," in *Simians, Cyborgs, and Women*, 1991, 183–201). Subsequent quotations from Evans, *Introductory Dictionary*, 1997, 61; Jacques Lacan, *Écrits: A Selection*, trans. Alan Sheridan (London: Tavistock, 1980), 231, 271.
28. Nicholas Spice, "I Must Be Mad," review of *Wild Analysis*, by Sigmund Freud, *London Review of Books*, January 8 2004, 11–15, 15.
29. Charles Taylor, *Sources of the Self: The Making of Modern Identity* (Cambridge, UK: Cambridge University Press, 1989). Taylor's account is particularly informative but, in essentials, the same story is told by many other authors; Teresa Brennan's genealogy of "the ego's era," for instance (in *History After Lacan*, 1993), makes many of the same points as Taylor, and refers to many of the same sources.
30. Jean-Jacques Rousseau, quoted, Taylor, *Sources of the Self*, 1989, 357–58, 362; Richard Rorty, "To the Sunlit Uplands," review of *Truth and Truthfulness: An Essay in Genealogy* by Bernard Williams, *London Review of Books*, October 31, 2002, 13–15, 15.
31. Taylor, *Sources of the Self*, 1989, 364; Kant, quoted, ibid., 365.
32. Herder and Schleiermacher, quoted, ibid., 378; Hölderlin, quoted, Laclau and Mouffe, *Hegemony*, 1989, 94; Kant, quoted, Taylor, *Sources of the Self*, 1989, 385.
33. Immanuel Kant, *Critique of Judgment*, trans. Werner S. Pluhar (Indianapolis: Hackett, 1987), 65; Friedrich Schiller, *On the Aesthetic Education of Man*, trans. Reginald Snell (London: Routledge and Kegan Paul, 1954), 137; Kant, "What Is Enlightenment?" in *Foundations of the Metaphysics of Morals*, trans. Lewis White Beck (Upper Saddle River, NJ: Prentice-Hall, 1997), 83–90, 89–90; Kant, *Critique of Judgment*, 1987, 55, 56, 69.
34. Kant, *Critique of Judgment*, 1987, 174, 175. On the musical work concept, see Lydia Goehr, *The Imaginary Museum of Musical Works: An Essay in the Philosophy of Music* (Oxford: Oxford University Press, 1992); Talbot, ed., *The Musical Work*, 2000; David Clarke, "Musical Autonomy Revisited," in *The Cultural Study of Music: A Critical Introduction*, ed Martin Clayton, Trevor Herbert and Richard Middleton (New York: Routledge, 2003), 159–70.
35. The authoritative critique of Kant's aesthetic universalism is Pierre Bourdieu, *Distinction: A Social Critique of the Judgment of Taste*, trans. Richard Nice (Cambridge MA: Harvard University Press, 1984).
36. Rousseau, quoted, Taylor, *Sources of the Self*, 1989, 415.
37. Herder, quoted, ibid., 375; translation modified. *Stimmung* can also mean "tune," from *Stimme*, "voice."
38. Herder, from *Allgemeine musikalische Zeitung* (1813), in Le Huray and Day, eds., *Music and Aesthetics*, 1981, 252.
39. Bohlman, *World Music*, 2002, 2.
40. Accounts from the Americas, from the seventeenth century on, are plentiful; see, e.g., Eileen Southern, *The Music of Black Americans: A History* (New York: Norton, 1971); *After Africa: Extracts from British Travel Accounts and Journals of the Seventeenth, Eighteenth, and Nineteenth Centuries Concerning the Slaves, their Manners, and Customs in the British West Indies*

(New Haven: Yale University Press, 1983). For one eighteenth-century "orientalist" account, with references to many others down to that of Guillaume-André Villoteau, sent to Egypt by Napoleon, see Amnon Shiloah, "An Eighteenth-Century Critic of Taste and Good Taste," in *Ethnomusicology and Modern Music History*, ed. Stephen Blum, Philip V. Bohlman, and Daniel M. Neuman (Urbana: University of Illinois Press, 1991), 181–89. Herder's folk-song collections, published in 1778–79, included songs sent back from Latin America as well as European material from as far away as Estonia and Latvia.

41. Kant, "What Is Enlightenment?" 1997, 83, 84; Kant, quoted in Le Huray and Day, eds., *Music and Aesthetics*, 1981, 220–23.
42. Herder, from *Kalligone* (1800), in Le Huray and Day, eds., *Music and Aesthetics*, 1981, 255; Herder, quoted in Peter Burke, *Popular Culture in Early Modern Europe* (London: Temple-Smith, 1978), 22.
43. Hubert Parry, "Inaugural Address to the Folk Song Society," *Journal of the Folk Song Society* 1 (1899): 2–3. On the twentieth-century debates, see Richard Middleton, "The 'Problem' of Popular Music," in *The Twentieth Century*, vol. 6 of *The Blackwell History of Music in Britain*, ed. Stephen Banfield (Oxford: Blackwell, 1995), 27–38.
44. Taylor, *Sources of the Self*, 1989, 487–90.
45. Franz Fanon, quoted in David Caute, *Fanon* (London: Fontana, 1970), n.p.
46. Karl Marx, *Economic and Philosophical Manuscripts*, in *Early Writings*, trans. Rodney Livingstone and Gregor Benton, intro. Lucio Colletti (Harmondsworth, UK: Penguin, 1975), 279–400, 327, 391.
47. A term that in most nineteenth-century formulations, such as the young Marx's, implies an essentialized conception of human subjectivity, against which "alienation" marks a loss — a conception which is of course very much part of what is at issue now. Yet, psychoanalysis, unlike most poststructuralist currents, retains the concept, and although "alienation" for psychoanalysis is not the same — it marks not so much a fall as the condition of a coming to be (of any subject) — there is a certain continuity, which will turn out to be important later in this chapter.
48. Terry Eagleton, *The Idea of Culture* (Oxford: Blackwell, 2000), 23, 31.
49. On blues as art see, e.g., Carl Van Vechten on first hearing Bessie Smith live: "we felt as we might have felt before going to a Salzburg Festival to hear Lilli Lehmann sing Donna Anna in *Don Giovanni*" (Kellner, ed., *Keep A-Inchin' Along*, 1979, 162). Or similarly, pianist Teddy Wilson: "She had the dynamic range of an opera singer and the same control and power of voice" (quoted in Shipton, *New History of Jazz*, 2001, 54). (But these are not just *ad feminem* references, for they stand in a lengthy history initiated by the widespread nineteenth-century conception of the minstrel show as "Ethiopian opera".) On the early commercialization of blues, see Evans, *Big Road Blues*, 1987, 59–70 (he sees the relationship in terms of a "dual aesthetic").
50. Derek Stewart-Baxter, *Ma Rainey and the Classic Blues Singers* (London: Studio Vista, 1970).
51. Ibid., 7. Interestingly, in his book on pop culture, first published in the same year as Stewart-Baxter's book on classic blues, Melly adopts a very similar line on the Beatles: "Nostalgically we may regret the simple cocksure days of Rock… but there has never been a way of preventing an art form from developing. The compensation for the loss of innocence, of simplicity, of unselfconscious energy, is the classic moment. In pop this belonged to the Beatles. It's there on record. You can play it any time" (George Melly, *Revolt into Style: The Pop Arts in Britain* [Harmondsworth, UK: Penguin, 1972], 124).
52. Blesh, *Shining Trumpets*, 1976.
53. It is no accident that Alan Lomax, as well as collecting, researching, and publishing blues and other folk genres, conducted and published (in 1950) the Library of Congress interviews with celebrated (but "outmoded") New Orleans musician, Jelly Roll Morton (Lomax, *Mister Jelly Roll*, 1973). On the "jazz wars," see Gendron, *Between Montmartre and the Mudd Club*, 2002, 131–57. The articulation of discursive binaries with a triangulated territory produced interesting effects. Many of the terms of debate characterizing the initial conflict between revivalist jazz and swing were transferred subsequently to those between swing and bebop and between traditional and modern jazz.
54. Blesh, *Shining Trumpets*, 1976, 108, 110, 113, 114.
55. Ibid., 98.

56. Ibid., 3, 5, 6, 156, 227, 290, 321.
57. On Locke's usage, see Vincent, *Keep Cool*, 1995, 173, 184; and on his views as a whole, see Anderson, *Deep River*, 2001, 113–166. On Dodge, see ibid., 247–56. See also Hughes Panassié, *Le jazz hot* (1934), published in English as *Hot Jazz: The Guide to Swing Music*, trans. Lyle and Eleanor Dowling (New York: Witmark, 1936); Winthrop Sargeant, *Jazz: Hot and Hybrid* (New York: Dutton, 1938); Frederic Ramsey Jr. and Charles Edward Smith, eds., *Jazzmen* (New York: Harcourt, 1939); Hughes Panassié, *The Real Jazz*, trans. Anne Sorelle Williams (New York: Smith and Durrell, 1942). Here is Panassié in 1936, for example: in 1926, jazz, especially through the agency of Louis Armstrong, who "brought hot style to a peak," "attained its stable form… ceased to falter and became a definite, balanced musical form" (*Hot Jazz*, 1936, 27, 38). There are some differences, however: Sargeant is more inclined to a neoprimitivist picture, stability being attributed to folklike tradition; Panassié moves toward this position in his *The Real Jazz*. On this nexus in jazz criticism, see Scott DeVeaux, "Constructing the Jazz Tradition: Jazz Historiography," *Black American Literature Forum* 25, no. 3 (1991): 525–60.
58. Blesh, *Shining Trumpets,* 1976, 100, 134, 6, 176, 95, 230, 3, 6, 134, 143.
59. See, e.g., ibid., 25–27.
60. Ibid., 4, 146, 109, 108, 378, 98, 99, 102, 124, 97, 15. I owe my understanding of the oedipal construction of the canon to my colleague, Ian Biddle. One of the problems for Blesh is that, whereas the black-other is usually feminized (in relation to the white Law-of-the Father), his inversion of the racial hierarchy means that the black-other has to encompass both "maternal sympathy" and "lusty male procreativeness"; this can only work by casting "effete Negroes" like Teddy Wilson as effectively white: homosexuality is always available to shore up Oedipus!
61. Ibid., 241, 242, 252; on the symbolic status of the star individuals, see 257.
62. Rudi Blesh and Harriet Janis, *They All Played Ragtime*, 4th ed. (1950; New York: Oak Publications, 1971).
63. Ibid., 8, 253, 36, 48–49, 141, 142, 144. According to Blesh and Janis (ibid., 8), the term *classic ragtime* was first used early in the twentieth century by Stark and was "commonly accepted" by 1912–13.
64. Stark on Tin Pan Alley songs: "The methods of selling them are wide of our own conception of how the 'art divine' should be dispensed. They are hurled across the country with a whoop and hurrah, while the songs that teach and thrill the purer souls too often lie silent on the shelf" (quoted, ibid., 253–54); and on his opposition to the new monopolistic practices, see ibid., 240–41. Compare Joplin: "Syncopations are no indication of light or trashy music" (ibid., 141).
65. Blesh, *Shining Trumpets,* 1976, 11, 12.
66. Ibid., 346, 289, 8.
67. Which is itself incipiently binary, of course: there is peak, and there is not-peak, each side guaranteeing the other.
68. Blesh, *Shining Trumpets,* 1976, 344, 375, 378.
69. Ibid., 146; Bessie Smith, "St. Louis Blues" (1929), *Bessie Smith 1928–1929*, Classics 897 (1996).
70. For Calloway's version of "St. Louis Blues," see above, p. 83.
71. It is certainly vital to take due account of historical specificity. Thus, while in the later twentieth century the canonizing impulse spread right across the range of musical genres — to the extent that in 2004 I noticed a reference to "classic gangsta" — this move tended to overlay the qualitative criterion with a quantitative one. Drawing on the semiotics of "charting" — which arose precisely as a way of ordering difference (and its absence) when received values come into question — the ubiquitous phenomenon of *lists* (favorite rock albums, best disco tracks, etc.) suggests a cultural shift marked by the difference between the psychology of collecting and that of enumerating, between the private library and the rewriteable disk, between bourgeois and populist consumerism. Though we can thread our way back from here to John Stark's commitment to high-class musical commodities, the distance traversed presses the question, can maximum exchange value now possess its own kind of authenticity?
72. Charles Taylor, *The Ethics of Authenticity* (Cambridge, MA: Harvard University Press, 1991). Rescue-philosophy on the subject of "truth" has been quite common in recent anglophone writing; see, for example, Bernard Williams, *Truth and Truthfulness: An Essay in Genealogy* (Princeton, NJ: Princeton University Press, 2002), which also discusses the thematic subset clustered under "authenticity" quite extensively. I concentrate on Taylor's book here because "authenticity" is his focus.

73. Roland Barthes, "The Death of the Author," in *Image-Music-Text*, ed. and trans. Stephen Heath (London: Fontana, 1977b), 142–48.
74. Michel Foucault, "What Is an Author?" trans. Joseph V. Harari, in *Modern Criticism and Theory: A Reader*, ed. David Lodge (New York: Longman, 1988), 196–210, 209, 210.
75. See Middleton, "Work-in(g)-Practice," 2000; Elie During, "Appropriations: Deaths of the Author in Electronic Music," in *Sonic Process* (Barcelona: Museu d'Art Contemporani di Barcelona, N.D. [2002?]), 39–57.
76. Silverman, *The Acoustic Mirror*, 1988, 187–234.
77. Ibid., 193, 217, 216.
78. This is somewhat unfair to Silverman, who argues that "the fantasmatic… is always absorbing the world outside. I would go even farther, and argue that it is being continually drawn into new social and political alignments, which may even lead to important 'scenic' changes. It is thus important to ask of any authorial desire: How has it assimilated history? And how might it be seen to have acted upon history?" (ibid., 217–18). In part, this makes my point for me. But to the extent that this methodological rule is not followed up, it also supports my reservation. Moreover, the status of "authorial desire" seems to remain entirely contingent. What and where, exactly, is this "it" that is drawn into new alignments, that assimilates history and acts upon it, and how does it manage to imagine itself speaking?

    For an incisive study of poststructuralist conceptions of authoriality, see Seán Burke, *The Death and Return of the Author: Criticism and Subjectivity in Barthes, Foucault and Derrida*, 2nd ed. (Edinburgh: Edinburgh University Press, 1998). Burke not only discusses problems with these conceptions but also brings out the resistant passages of authoriality within the texts of these writers themselves, ending with an argument for a theory of "situated" (rather than transcendental or naively biographical) authorship. (This species of authorship is what I was looking for in my discussions of Charley Patton, Patti Smith, Nina Simone, and some others.) He also points out that to kill the author, one must first build him up — which is to maintain him: "the concept of the author is never more alive than when pronounced dead" (7) — just like that of God (of whom the Author is of course part).
79. Michelle Kisliuk, "(Un)Doing Fieldwork: Sharing Songs, Sharing Lives," in *Shadows in the Field: New Perspectives for Fieldwork in Ethnomusicology*, ed. Gregory F. Barz and Timothy J. Cooley (New York: Oxford University Press, 1997), 23–44. The contextualizing literature is vast. Many of the classic texts on the anthropological side involve James Clifford (*The Predicament of Culture: Twentieth-Century Ethnography, Literature, and Art* [Cambridge, MA: Harvard University Press, 1988]; "Travelling Cultures," in *Cultural Studies*, ed. Lawrence Grossberg, Cary Nelson, and Paula A. Treichler [New York: Routledge, 1992], 96–116; James Clifford and George E. Marcus, *Writing Culture: The Poetics and Politics of Ethnography* [Berkeley: University of California Press, 1986]). On the historiographical side, the work of Hayden White and of "new historicists" such as Stephen Greenblatt and Roger Chartier have been particularly important. For a useful introduction, see Peter Burke, ed., *New Perspectives on Historical Writing* (Cambridge UK: Polity Press, 1991). Bridging this entire field is the hugely significant work of Michel de Certeau.
80. Given the profile of "pygmy pop" over recent decades, such caveats were certainly necessary; on the exploitation of BaAka and other central African "pygmy" music, by a range of musicians from jazz and rock through to avant-gardists such as Brian Eno and dance music mixes like *Deep Forest*, see Steven Feld, "The Poetics and Politics of Pygmy Pop," in *Western Music and Its Others: Difference, Representation, and Appropriation in Music*, ed. Georgina Born and David Hesmondhalgh (Berkeley: University of California Press, 2000), 254–79.
81. In more detail: Lacan's theory of identification distinguishes between the imaginary level of the "ideal ego" and the symbolic level of the "ego-ideal," the first referring to the image the subject wishes to assume, the second to the point in the Other from which this image is to be seen, for which it is intended. The "*Che vuoi?*" marks the extent to which these can never completely correlate, that is, the subject's doubt as to the right answer. Kisliuk, as I try to suggest, is presenting herself for two different gazes. There is a clear explanation of Lacan's theory in Žižek, *Sublime Object*, 1989, 100–14.
82. Quotations in this paragraph from Kisliuk, "(Un)Doing Fieldwork," 1997, 23, 24, 25, 29, 39.
83. Žižek, *Sublime Object,* 1989, 176, 177. The question might be raised whether Žižek's move, as well as (or rather than) dialecticizing dialogics, has the effect of dialogicizing dialectics, and if so, whether this freezes the possibility of historical movement in a way that, arguably,

reinscribes the Adornian standstill of the negative dialectic. This is a question I will come to in due course.

84. Jürgen Habermas, *The Philosophical Discourse of Modernity: Twelve Lectures*, trans. Frederick Lawrence (Cambridge, UK: Polity Press, 1990), 296, 130.
85. Ibid., 324, 325. Žižek's response to Habermas's positing of the "ideal speech situation" brings out its neoreligious impulse, its "status as fetish": as an example of something that is "simultaneously denied and laid claim to," this ideal demonstrates the classic fetishist logic — "I know very well that communication is broken and perverted [that the phallus is not there; that this god has no power…] but still…(I believe and act as if the ideal speech situation is already realized)" (Slavoj Žižek, "Beyond Discourse-Analysis," in Ernesto Laclau, *New Reflections on the Revolution of Our Time* [London: Verso, 1990[, 249–60, 259). But this also reveals, in what is only apparently a paradox, Habermas's Enlightenment roots. For Žižek, Kantian Reason was free to operate, as Kant himself was aware, only on condition of an acceptance of contingent social law: "Only to the already enlightened view does the universe of social customs and rule appear as a nonsensical 'machine' that must be accepted as such." But further: Reason itself has its nonsensical side; the "categorical imperative is precisely a Law which has a necessary, unconditional authority, without being true," so that "we can free ourselves of external social constraints and achieve the maturity proper to the autonomous enlightened subject precisely by submitting to the 'irrational' compulsion of the categorical imperative" — in Kant's own formulation: "You can because you must!" (Žižek, *Sublime Object*, 1989, 79–84; quotations from 80, 81). Of course, this is to locate Habermasian Reason, including its commitment to "internal" ideology critique, as itself "irrational," to situate his truth-machine as, precisely, ideological at a deeper level. As we shall see, this is part of what Žižek's theory of ideology attempts to do.
86. See, e.g., Richard Rorty, *Objectivity, Relativism and Truth, Philosophical Papers*, vol. 1 (Cambridge, UK: Cambridge University Press, 1991).
87. The most convincing argument along these lines is Laclau and Mouffe, *Hegemony*, 1985; see p.109, for example, where the authors' radically antiessentialist concept of discursive overdetermination leads them to bracket the category of ideology altogether.
88. Žižek, "The Spectre of Ideology," 1999c, 61.
89. Ibid., 70. This empty place may, at first sight, look like the discredited Godlike "view from nowhere" of scientistic Reason. Its emptiness and its impossibility are designed to prevent this. Moreover, it can only be internal to the discursive formation, not above it — within, not outside, the territory of subjectivity. Admittedly, this raises the question whether, even if emptied of "positively determined reality," it might be thought to contain *something*; I come to this question below.
90. Ibid., 72, 73, 74.
91. Developed most notably in Žižek, "How Did Marx Invent the Symptom?" in *Sublime Object*, 1989, 11–53. For a concise and admirably clear account along similar lines, see Mladen Dolar, "Beyond Interpellation," *Qui Parle* 6, no.2 (1993): 75–96.
92. Žižek, *Sublime Object*, 1989, 43.
93. Dolar, "Beyond Interpellation,"1993, 78.
94. Žižek, *Sublime Object*, 1989, 75.
95. On freedom, not on *desire* (the subject should "ne pas céder sur son désir," according to Lacan), which is precisely what is brought into existence by this moment.
96. See Žižek, "Beyond Discourse-Analysis,"1990, 249. So Margaret Thatcher was right ("no such thing as society")! But not for the reason she thought. On the nonexistence of popular music, see pp. 32–34 above.
97. Laclau and Mouffe, *Hegemony*, 1985, 125.
98. Žižek, "The Spectre of Ideology,"1999c, 77.
99. Žižek, *Sublime Object*, 1989, 196, 126, 124.
100. Mowitt, *Percussion*, 2002, 42–58, 138–50; the quotations are on 56, 147, 148, 144, 142–43. See also Jean Laplanche and Jean-Bertrand Pontalis, "Fantasy and the Origins of Sexuality," in *Formations of Fantasy*, ed. Victor Burgin and Cora Kaplan (London: Methuen, 1986), 5–34.
101. On this aspect of Silverman's argument, see above, pp. 114–5, 135.
102. As will be obvious, I find this perspective broadly persuasive, as one that I believe measures up to the tragic dimension inherent in human existence without thereby giving way on desire (as Lacan puts it). But there are alternatives. Here are two:

John Mowitt (*Percussion*, 2002, 51–58), rejecting the Žižekian idea of the postinterpellative "remainder" as implying a nostalgic vision of subject-as-agent (rather than as system), puts forward a conception of subjectivity as a "discontinuous and uneven lamination of strata," an "unsteady locus of spatial and temporal discontinuities" (55), mediated by sensorial variability (hearing/seeing, for instance). His argument that the conditions of *sinthomicité* (as we might call it) have not been satisfactorily specified, is well made, and I will return to it. But nothing in Žižek's model necessarily construes the subject as agent rather than system (albeit system with an unspecified motor). Moreover, the "absent remainder" in Mowitt's more typically deconstructive model tends itself to get filled in with undertheorized "foundations" — "radical democracy," "resistance," "knowledge production." And without a "belief before belief," he has no answer to the question why the interpellated individual should even want to turn. (Interestingly, his distrust of subjective "solidity" has a correlate at the level of the musical object: by employing Christopher Small's concept of "musicking" to attribute those (necessary) moments when the flow of musical practice "solidifies" temporarily — we mark these moments with, for example, song-titles — to the fantasizing of "old musicology," he misses the degree to which a retroactive "as if" is installed here, just as it is in the space of the preideological subject. On "musicking," see Small, *Music of the Common Tongue: Survival and Celebration in Afro-American Music* [London: John Calder, 1987a]).

By contrast, Teresa Brennan (*History after Lacan*, 1993) — while she too in effect focuses on the moment of interpellation (she calls it the "founding fantasy" of the ego and her model draws on Melanie Klein as well as on Lacan's theory of the mirror phase) — certainly does specify a "foundation before the foundation" (16). Describing the destructive effects of "the ego's era," and connecting the "founding fantasy" to a misogynistic myth of Woman rooted in the objectification and passification of the mother, Brennan, drawing on elements from Spinoza, Deleuze, and Irigary, invokes a prior "foundation" in which the mother stands for a "natural reality" (21) marked by a "logic" based in the multitudinous differences and connections between beings and their environment, and the flows of energy that link them. The political program Brennan constructs from this model is powerful — not least because one of its bases is an ecologically sensitive revisionist account of Marxist political economy which brings natural resources, along with human labor-power, into the category of variable capital that can produce surplus value; but, although she acknowledges that the action called for — in which "the subject invests itself with the properties that animate the generative logical chain of nature" (17) — is built upon an unprovable foundation, it is hard to see her elision of the discursive constitution of "nature" as anything other than an originary fantasy of maternal origin masquerading as a godlike subject of science.

103. Žižek, *Sublime Object*, 1989, 87–129. The outline is structured around a remarkably clear interpretation of Lacan's "graph of desire," moving from the lowest (quasi-Althusserian) level of the graph to the upper levels ("beyond interpellation").
104. Ibid., 89, 99, 124, 125, 127. I will return to my questioning of the finality of the fourth step in the procedure.
105. Ibid., 28–30.
106. Ibid., 5.
107. Rather than "grasped historically," I might have written "historicized" - except that Benjamin, among others, has taught us the poverty of historicism as a method of articulating the past for productive political effect. According to Žižek, the problem with historicism (as opposed to what he terms "historicity") is that it relativizes all historical content and hence "evades the encounter with the Real;" "historicity differs from historicism by the way it presupposes some traumatic kernel which endures as 'the same,' non-historical; and so various historical epochs are conceived as failed attempts to capture this kernel." (Žižek, *For They Know Not What They Do*, 2002, 101, 102.)
108. See Brennan, *History after Lacan*, 1993, 169–72; and cf. above, pp. 53–54.
109. Žižek, "The Spectre of Ideology," 1999c, 82.
110. Žižek, *Sublime Object*, 1989, 19.
111. Ibid., 24.
112. If "ideology," qua concept, is specific to modernity, perhaps its changing phases can be mapped to the history of modern society. Thus it would begin, in the late eighteenth century, as the theory which identifies the attachment of specific worldviews to specific social interests, and then, as the discursive space gradually fills up with ideological work, would generate the

narrative (and problems) of Marxist, anti-Marxist, and post-Marxist theories. At the culmination of that process comes the point when Žižek's "empty place" is required. Again there is a relation between theory and social formation, for this empty place corresponds, perhaps, to the "non-place" occupied by power in the deterritorialized space of "Empire" (see Hardt and Negri, *Empire*, 2000). The question now becomes how this place can/should be occupied, without thereby installing the Godlike gaze of a new Master. I come to this question shortly.

113. Laclau and Mouffe, *Hegemony*, 1985, 119.
114. Haraway, *Simians, Cyborgs, and Women*, 1991, 190.
115. This rather fantastical etymology is given in Žižek, *Sublime Object*, 1989, 75.
116. Haraway, *Simians, Cyborgs, and Women*, 1991, 195.
117. Taussig, *Mimesis and Alterity*, 1993, xix.
118. This understanding of "Empire" comes from Hardt and Negri, *Empire*, 2000. They write:

> The passage to Empire emerges from the twilight of modern sovereignty. In contrast to imperialism, Empire establishes no territorial center of power and does not rely on fixed boundaries or barriers. It is a *decentred* and *deterritorialising* apparatus of rule that progressively incorporates the entire global realm within its open, expanding frontiers. Empire manages hybrid identities, flexible hierarchies, and plural exchanges through modulating networks of command. (xii–xiii)

They (and I) may be overstating things. It is an open question whether it will actually be possible for an ideological formation, and its accompanying apparatus of social command, to survive without a constitutive outside to act as an other (the potential of the extraterrestrial comes to mind; and "history," once completely spatialized, may be available for a similar function — although, in both cases, does the foreign not immediately get incorporated in the interior?). But the main drift — that territorializing divisions move inside — is unmistakable; as many commentators have pointed out, the perpetrators of 9/11 were in many senses creations of "the West" — "they" were already "us."

The idea that the modern subject of Reason never actually succeeded in escaping from nature comes from (inter alia) Bruno Latour (*We Have Never Been Modern*, 1993). Dethroning the objectifying subject of Empire reveals its "objectal" underside — as the Lacanian joke puts it, in rewriting the story of how the emperor's new clothes were seen through, "Look, under his clothes he is completely naked!"(see Žižek, *Sublime Object*, 1989, 29).

119. *Buena Vista Social Club*, World Circuit WCD050 (1997).
120. Michael Chanan, "Play It Again, or, Old-Time Cuban Music on the Screen," *New Left Review* 238 (Nov./Dec. 1999): 150–56,154. For an account of Cooder's role, in the context of a useful discussion of global and local forces in popular music, see Jan Fairley, "The 'Local' and 'Global' in Popular Music," in *The Cambridge Companion to Pop and Rock*, ed. Simon Frith, Will Straw, and John Street (Cambridge, UK: Cambridge University Press, 2001), 272–89.
121. Wim Wenders's film, *Buena Vista Social Club*, was a Road Movies production in association with Kintop Pictures and ARTE (1999). Wenders also made a film, *Until the End of the World* (1991), exploiting the "childlike" sounds of BaAka pygmies.
122. According to one Chanan source (quoted in "Play It Again,"1999, 154), "The youth consider them 'something like antediluvian monsters.'" For a study which presents the Buena Vista Social Club phenomenon as "revivalist" music for tourists (real and metaphorical), see Jan Fairley, "'Ay Díos, Ampárame' (O God, Protect Me): Music in Cuba during the 1990s, the 'Special Period'," in *Island Musics*, ed. Kevin Dawe (London: Berg, 2004), 77-97. The genre which really represented contemporary Cuban life, according to Fairley, was *timba*, the main focus of her piece.
123. Not the least resonant symptom of *Buena Vista Social Club*'s appeal — if "the era of the *Sinthome* is [indeed] the era of the death of God" — lies in the way that the religious references might be taken to mark the *rebirth* of religion in recent decades, most strikingly in Africa and Asia but also in the Americas, including the United States; has the script of modernity gone wrong? To investigate fully the factors involved in this seemingly bizarre development would demand another book. An intriguing question to raise, though, is whether, in a state of "Empire," what is happening is that a hitherto premodernist (superstitious) "outside" is being forced "inside," highlighting the irrationality inherent in modernity itself. It is clear that the rebirth is not a simple return or renewal but rather a fundamentalist reaction to a perceived

failure of modernity. And part of the context is the crisis, equally, of the People-idea, whether conceived as subject of democracy, agent of socialism, or image of the nation-state. There is a vacuum of authority asking to be filled.

124. Cooder quotation from album sleeve notes; the film director is Nat Chediak, quoted on http://www.salon.com/ent/music/feature/1999/03/09feature.html

125. Wenders cuts constantly between "here" and "there," "them" and "us," mediated by the traveling figure of Cooder, and setting up a "triangular trade" between Europe (the opening concert, in Amsterdam), (Afro-) Cuba, and the United States (the final sequence, and concert, in New York). His "innocent" documentary-style camera presents the musicians in interview like ethnographic subjects, and the occlusion of politics (except for a very occasional visual signifier referencing the Revolution), indeed, the relative lack of social context altogether, constructs a "Cuba" that in its way has as much of a fairy-tale quality as the hypermodern street scenes of New York patently do for the visiting, wonder-struck Cuban "old-timers" (as Cooder calls them). Similarly, there is no other music than that of the band — it inhabits its own universe, out of time — so that the way it flows round all three sites, always the same, a truly global sound, can cover over the fractures between worlds: the impossible "blot" in the object gaze which the admission of political antagonism would otherwise expose.

126. Critic Alma Guillermoprieto, quoted in Chanan, "Play It Again," 1999, 151; Cooder quotation again from album sleeve notes.

127. Some might hope that this moment would also see the end of labored punning — but, to the extent that it is inconceivable without an increase in *jouis-sense*, I cannot agree. I do, however, see this moment as redeeming the promise laid down in Raymond Williams's inspirational idea of a "common culture" — a promise weakened in the original vision by essentialist notions of human autonomy and of "the people" (see Raymond Williams, "The Idea of a Common Culture," in *Resources of Hope*, ed. Robin Gable [1968, London: Verso, 1989], 32–38). Williams rightly rejects his earlier formulation of a "culture in common," but we might rewrite this as a "culture of the commons," where "common" stands both for a postpopular understanding of the space of democratic subjectivity and for those ecosocial spaces where the writ of property does not run — where all may safely graze.

Hardt and Negri (*Empire,* 2000, 300–303) come up with the same metaphor for their utopia. (I read their book after drafting my note, an interesting sign of, precisely, common passages of thought.) Referring back to French revolutionary political theorist, Emmanuel-Joseph Sieyès, they want to push past his dismissal of "*ré-total*" (the totalizing "thing" of monarchical sovereignty) in favor of "*ré-publique,*" toward a "commons" where the "non-place" of Empire is populated by "the new place in the non-place, the place defined by the productive activity that is autonomous from any external regime of measure… [standing for] the incarnation, the production, and the liberation of the multitude" (357, 303). Their figure for this multitudinous inventiveness harks back even further historically, contrasting "the naked life of *homo tantum*" with the Renaissance trope of "*homohomo,* humanity squared, enriched by collective intelligence and love of the community" (204) (we might prefer humanity not so much squared as multiplied to the infinite power). However, in the end their search for an image to render this project more concrete seizes on the figure of the *posse* ("posse," from Latin, "to be able," "to have the *power*"), and finds a pointer in the social imaginary of U.S. rap groups. While this exemplar certainly offers pregnant figures of cooperative invention outside the law, if we pursue its fantasmatic prehistory into the Wild West, we are reminded that posses here (even if made up of gangstas) existed to enforce the Law, often with maximum violence — clubbing clubs indeed (and one wonders how far they are, in the rappers' imagination, if only by inversion, from the lynch mob). For Hardt and Negri, the posse is "a biopolitical unity managed by the multitude, organized by the multitude, directed by the multitude — absolute democracy in action" (410). It is the *absolute* that is the problem. Although the empty or nonplace should certainly be occupied — occupied by (conflicting) desire(s), that is, sinthomatized — on the level of content, it is essential that it remain *empty.*

Bibliography

Abbate, Carolyn. *Unsung Voices: Opera and Musical Narrative in the Nineteenth Century*. Princeton, NJ: Princeton University Press, 1991.

———. “Opera; Or, the Envoicing of Women.” In *Musicology and Difference: Gender and Sexuality in Music Scholarship*, edited by Ruth A. Solie, 225–58. Berkeley: University of California Press, 1993.

Abbott, Lynn, and Doug Seroff. “‘They Cert’ly Sound Good to Me’: Sheet Music, Southern Vaudeville, and the Commercial Ascendancy of Blues.” *American Music* 14 (1996): 402–54.

Adorno, T. W. *Philosophy of Modern Music*, translated by Anne G. Mitchell and Wesley V. Bloomster. London: Sheed and Ward, 1973.

———. *Introduction to the Sociology of Music*, translated E. B. Ashton. New York: Seabury Press, 1976.

———. “Perennial Fashion — Jazz.” In *Prisms*, translated by Samuel and Shierry Weber, 120–32. Cambridge, MA: MIT Press, 1983 [1953].

——— .“On Popular Music.” In *On Record: Rock, Pop and the Written Word*, edited by Simon Frith and Andrew Goodwin, 301–14. London: Routledge, 1990a [1941].

———. “The Curves of the Needle,” [1928] translated by Thomas Y. Levin. *October* 55 (1990b): 48–55.

———. “The Form of the Phonograph Record” [1934], translated by Thomas Y. Levin. *October* 55 (1990c): 56–61.

After Africa: Extracts from British Travel Accounts and Journals of the Seventeenth, Eighteenth, and Nineteenth Centuries Concerning the Slaves, their Manners, and Customs in the British West Indies. New Haven, CT: Yale University Press, 1983.

Agawu, Kofi. “Contesting Difference: A Critique of Africanist Ethnomusicology.” In *The Cultural Study of Music: A Critical Introduction*, edited by Martin Clayton, Trevor Herbert, and Richard Middleton, 227–37. New York: Routledge, 2003.

Althusser, Louis. “Ideology and Ideological State Apparatuses (Notes towards an Investigation).” In *Lenin and Philosophy and Other Essays*, translated by Ben Brewster, 121–73. London: New Left Books, 1971.

Altick, Richard D. *The Shows of London*. Cambridge: Cambridge University Press, 1978.

Amico, Stephen. “‘I Want Muscles’: House Music, Homosexuality and Masculine Signification.” *Popular Music* 20:3 (2001): 359–78.

Anderson, Paul Allen. *Deep River: Music and Memory in Harlem Renaissance Thought*. Durham, NC: Duke University Press, 2001.

Antelyes, Peter. “Red Hot Mamas: Bessie Smith, Sophie Tucker, and the Ethnic Maternal Voice in American Popular Song.” In *Embodied Voices: Representing Vocality in Western Culture*, edited by Leslie C. Dunn and Nancy A. Jones, 212–29. Cambridge: Cambridge University Press, 1994.

Apel, Willi. *Harvard Dictionary of Music*. Cambridge, MA: Harvard University Press, 1961.

Appel, Alfred, Jr. *Jazz Modernism from Ellington and Armstrong to Matisse and Joyce*. New York: Knopf, 2002.

Appleby, Joyce, Lynn Hunt and Margaret Jacob. *Telling the Truth about History*. New York: Norton, 1994.

Attali, Jacques. *Noise: The Political Economy of Music*, translated by Brian Massumi. Manchester: Manchester University Press, 1985.

Avena, Thomas. "Interview with Diamanda Galás." In *Life Sentences: Writers, Artists, and Aids*, edited by Thomas Avena, 177–96. San Francisco: Mercury House, 1994.

Baker, Houston, Jr. *Blues, Ideology and Afro-American Literature: A Vernacular Theory*. Chicago: University of Chicago Press, 1984.

———. *Modernism and the Harlem Renaissance*. Chicago: University of Chicago Press, 1987.

Banfield, Stephen. "Stage and Screen Entertainers in the Twentieth Century." In *The Cambridge Companion to Singing*, edited by John Potter, 63–82. Cambridge: Cambridge University Press, 2000.

Barker, Danny. *Buddy Bolden and the Last Days of Storyville*, edited by Alyn Shipton. London: Continuum, 2000.

Barlow, Jeremy. *The Music of John Gay's The Beggar's Opera*. Oxford: Oxford University Press, 1990.

Barthes, Roland. "The Death of the Author." In *Image-Music-Text*, edited and translated by Stephen Heath, 142–8. London: Fontana, 1977a.

———. "The Grain of the Voice." In *Image-Music-Text*, edited and translated by Stephen Heath, 179–89. London: Fontana, 1977b.

———. *Camera Lucida: Reflections on Photography*, translated by Richard Howard. New York: Hill and Wang, 1981.

Baudrillard, Jean. "Symbolic Exchange and Death." Translated by Charles Levin. In *Selected Writings*, edited by Mark Poster, 119–48. Cambridge: Polity Press, 1988.

Benjamin, Walter. "On Some Motifs in Baudelaire." In *Illuminations*, translated by Harry Zohn, 157–202. London: Fontana, 1973a.

———. "The Work of Art in the Age of Mechanical Reproduction." In *Illuminations*, translated by Harry Zohn, 219–53. London: Fontana, 1973b.

———. "Theses on the Philosophy of History." In *Illuminations*, translatd by Harry Zohn, 255–66. London: Fontana, 1973c.

———. *The Arcades Project*, translated by Howard Eiland and Kevin McLaughlin. Cambridge, MA: Belknap Press, 1999.

Ben-Zvi, Yael. "Zionist Lesbianism and Transsexual Transgression." *Middle East Report* (Spring 1998): 26–28, 37.

Bhabha, Homi. *The Location of Culture*. London: Routledge, 1994.

———. "Are You a Man or a Mouse?" In *Constructing Masculinity*, edited by Maurice Berger, Brian Wallis and Simon Watson, 57–65. New York: Routledge, 1995.

Biddle, Ian. *Listening to Men: Music, Masculinity and the Austro-German Tradition, 1789–1914*. Forthcoming.

Blackburn, Robin. "Slavery — Its Special Features and Social Role." In *Slavery and Other Forms of Unfree Labour*, edited by Léonie Archer, 262–79. London: Routledge, 1988.

Blesh, Rudi. *Shining Trumpets: A History of Jazz*, 2nd ed. New York: Da Capo Press, 1976 [1958].

Blesh, Rudi, and Harriet Janis. *They All Played Ragtime*. 4th ed. New York: Oak Publications, 1971 [1950].

Bloch, Ernst, Georg Lukács, Bertold Brecht, Walter Benjamin, and Theodor W. Adorno. *Aesthetics and Politics*. London: New Left Books, 1977.

Bockris, Victor. *Patti Smith*. London: Fourth Estate, 1998.

Bohlman, Philip V. "The *Shechinah*, or the Feminine Sacred in the Musics of the Jewish Mediterranean," available at http://home.online.no/~geskogse/bohlman.pdf.

———. *World Music: A Very Short Introduction*. Oxford: Oxford University Press, 2002.

Born, Georgina. "Afterword: Music Policy, Aesthetic and Social Difference." In *Rock and Popular Music: Politics, Policies, Institutions*, edited by Tony Bennett et al., 266–92. London: Routledge, 1993.

Born, Georgina, and David Hesmondhalgh (eds.). *Western Music and Its Others: Difference, Representation, and Appropriation in Music*. Berkeley: University of California Press, 2000.

Boulez, Pierre. *Orientations*, edited by Jean-Jacques Nattiez, translated by Martin Cooper. London: Faber, 1986.

Bourdieu, Pierre. *Distinction: A Social Critique of the Judgment of Taste*, translated by Richard Nice. Cambridge, MA: Harvard University Press, 1984.

Brackett, David. "James Brown's 'Superbad' and the Double-Voiced Utterance." In *Reading Pop: Approaches to Textual Analysis in Popular Music*, edited by Richard Middleton, 122–40. Oxford: Oxford University Press, 2000.

———. "What a Difference a Name Makes: Two Instances of African-American Music." In *The Cultural Study of Music: A Critical Introduction*, edited by Martin Clayton, Trevor Herbert, and Richard Middleton, 238–50. New York: Routledge, 2003.

Bradby, Barbara. "Sampling Sexuality: Gender, Technology and the Body in Dance Music." *Popular Music* 12:2 (1993): 155–76.

Bradby, Barbara, and Dave Laing. "Introduction to 'Gender and Sexuality special issue.'" *Popular Music* 20:3 (2001): 295–300.

Bradby, Barbara, and Brian Torode. "Song-Work: The Musical Inclusion, Exclusion and Representation of Women." Paper presented to conference of the British Sociological Association. Manchester, 1982.

Brady, Erika. *A Spiral Way: How the Phonograph Changed Ethnography.* Jackson, MS: University of Mississippi Press, 1999.

Brecht, Bertold. *Die Dreigroschenoper, Versuche*, 3. Berlin: Suhrkamp Verlag, 1959.

Brennan, Teresa. *History After Lacan.* London: Routledge, 1993.

Brett, Philip, Elizabeth Wood, and G. C. Thomas (eds.). *Queering the Pitch: The New Gay and Lesbian Musicology.* London: Routledge, 1993.

Bronson, Bertrand H. *Joseph Ritson: Scholar at Arms.* Berkeley: University of California Press, 1938.

Brooks, Jodi. "Ghosting the Machine: The Sounds of Tap and the Sounds of Film." *Screen* 44:4 (2003): 355–78.

Broonzy, Bill (with Yannick Bruynoghe). *Big Bill Blues: Big Bill Broonzy's Story as Told to Yannick Bruynoghe.* New York: Oak Publications, 1964 [1955].

Brown, Cecil. *Stagolee Shot Billy.* Cambridge, MA: Harvard University Press, 2003.

Brown, James (with Bruce Tucker). *The Godfather of Soul.* London: Macmillan, 1986.

Brown, Matthew. "Funk Music as Genre: Black Aesthetics, Apocalyptic Thinking and Urban Protest in Post-1965 African-American Pop." *Cultural Studies* 8:3 (1994): 484–508.

Brown, Sterling A. "The Blues as Folk Poetry." In *Folk-Say: A Regional Miscellany*, edited by B. A. Botkin, 324–39. Norman: University of Oklahoma Press, 1930.

Brown, Sterling A., Arthur P. Davis, and Ulysses Lee (eds.). *The Negro Caravan.* New York: Arno Press, 1970 [1941].

Burke, Peter. *Popular Culture in Early Modern Europe.* London: Temple Smith, 1978.

Burke, Peter (ed.). *New Perspectives on Historical Writing.* Cambridge: Polity Press, 1991.

Burke, Seán. *The Death and Return of the Author: Criticism and Subjectivity in Barthes, Foucault and Derrida.* 2nd ed. Edinburgh: Edinburgh University Press, 1998.

Butler, Judith. *Gender Trouble: Feminism and the Subversion of Identity.* London: Routledge, 1990.

———. "Imitation and Gender Insubordination." In *Inside/Out: Lesbian Theories, Gay Theories*, edited by Diana Fuss, 13–31. London: Routledge, 1991.

———. *Bodies that Matter: On the Discursive Limits of "Sex."* London: Routledge, 1993.

Cagle, Van M. *Reconstructing Pop/Subculture: Art, Rock and Andy Warhol.* London: Sage, 1995.

Calinescu, Matei. *Five Faces of Modernity.* Durham, NC: Duke University Press, 1987.

Calloway, Cab. *The New Cab Calloway's Cat-ologue.* New York: Calloway, 1938.

———. *The New Cab Calloway's Hepster's Dictionary: Language of Jive.* New York: Calloway, 1944.

Calloway, Cab and Bryant Rollins. *Of Minnie the Moocher and Me.* New York: Thomas Y. Crowell Co., 1976.

Castle, Terry. "My Heroin Christmas." *London Review of Books*, December 18, 2003: 11–18.

Caute, David. *Fanon.* London: Fontana, 1970.

Chanan, Michael. "Play It Again, or, Old-Time Cuban Music on the Screen." *New Left Review* 238 (Nov./Dec. 1999): 150–56.

Charosh, Paul. "Introduction." In *Song Hits from the Turn of the Century*, ix–xii. New York: Dover, 1975.

Charters, Samuel B. *The Country Blues.* New York: Da Capo Press, 1975 [1959].

Chernoff, John Miller. *African Rhythm and African Sensibility.* Chicago: Chicago University Press, 1979.

Clarke, David. "Musical Autonomy Revisited." In *The Cultural Study of Music: A Critical Introduction*, edited by Martin Clayton, Trevor Herbert, and Richard Middleton, 159–70. New York: Routledge, 2003.

Cleaver, Eldridge. *Soul on Ice*. London: Panther, 1970.

Clifford, James. *The Predicament of Culture: Twentieth-Century Ethnography, Literature, and Art*. Cambridge MA: Harvard University Press, 1988.

———. "Travelling Cultures." In *Cultural Studies*, edited by Lawrence Grossberg, Cary Nelson, and Paula A. Treichler, 96–116. New York: Routledge, 1992.

Clifford, James, and George E. Marcus. *Writing Culture: The Poetics and Politics of Ethnography*. Berkeley: University of California Press, 1986.

Cockrell, Dale. *Demons of Disorder: Early Blackface Minstrels and Their World*. Cambridge: Cambridge University Press, 1997.

Colley, Linda. *Captives: Britain, Empire and the World 1600–1730*. London: Pimlico, 2003.

Connor, Steven. *Dumbstruck: A Cultural History of Ventriloquism*. Oxford: Oxford University Press, 2000.

Corbett, John and Terri Kapsalis, "Aural Sex: The Female Orgasm in Popular Sound." *The Drama Review* 40:3 (1996): 102–11.

Courlander, Harold. *Negro Folk Music U.S.A*. New York: Columbia University Press, 1963.

Currid, Brian. "'We Are Family': House Music and Queer Performativity." In *Cruising the Performative: Interventions into the Representation of Ethnicity, Nationality, and Sexuality*, edited by Sue-Ellen Case, Philip Brett and Susan Leigh Foster, 165–96. Bloomington: Indiana University Press, 1995.

Daley, Mike. "Patti Smith's 'Gloria': Intertextual Play in a Vocal Performance." *Popular Music* 16:3 (1997): 235–53.

Darrell, R. D. "Black Beauty" [1932]. In *The Duke Ellington Reader*, edited by Mark Tucker, 57–65. New York: Oxford University Press, 1993.

Davis, Angela Y. *If They Come in the Morning: Voices of Resistance*. London: Orbach and Chambers, 1971.

———. *Women, Race and Class*. London: The Women's Press, 1982.

———. *The Angela Y. Davis Reader*, edited by Joy James. Oxford: Blackwell, 1998a.

———. *Blues Legacies and Black Feminism*. New York: Pantheon, 1998b.

Davis, Francis. *The History of the Blues*. London: Secker and Warburg, 1995.

Debord, Guy. *Society of the Spectacle*, Detroit: Black and Red, 1970.

Deleuze, Gilles. *Difference and Repetition*, translated by Paul Patton. London: Athlone Press, 1994.

Deleuze, Gilles and Félix Guattari. *A Thousand Plateaux*, translated by Brian Massumi. London: Athlone Press, 1988.

Derrida, Jacques. *Writing and Difference*, translated by Alan Bass. Chicago: University of Chicago Press, 1978.

———. "*Différance*." In *A Derrida Reader: Between the Blinds*, edited by Peggy Kamuf, 61–79. Hemel Hempstead: Harvester Wheatsheaf, 1991a.

———. "Signature Event Context." In *A Derrida Reader: Between the Blinds*, edited by Peggy Kamuf, 82–111. Hemel Hempstead: Harvester Wheatsheaf, 1991b.

———. "The Double Session." In *A Derrida Reader: Between the Blinds*, edited by Peggy Kamuf, 171–99. Hemel Hempstead: Harvester Wheatsheaf, 1991c.

———. "To Speculate - On Freud." In *A Derrida Reader: Between the Blinds*, edited by Peggy Kamuf, 518–68. Hemel Hempstead: Harvester Wheatsheaf, 1991d.

DeVeaux, Scott. "Constructing the Jazz Tradition: Jazz Historiography." *Black American Literature Forum* 25:3 (1991): 525–60.

Dodge, Roger Pryor. "Harpsichords and Trumpets" [1934]. In *The Duke Ellington Reader*, edited by Mark Tucker, 105–10. New York: Oxford University Press, 1993.

Dolar, Mladen. "Beyond Interpellation." *Qui Parle* 6:2 (1993): 75–96.

———. "The Object Voice." In *Gaze and Voice as Love Objects*, edited by Renata Salecl and Slavoj Žižek, 7–31. Durham, NC: Duke University Press, 1996.

Du Bois, W. E. B. *The Souls of Black Folk* (Centenary Edition), edited by Henry Louis Gates Jr., and Terri Hume Oliver. New York: Norton, 1999 [1903].

Duberman, Martin Bauml. *Paul Robeson*. London: Bodley Head, 1989.

Dunn, Leslie C. and Nancy A. Jones. (eds.) *Embodied Voices: Representing Vocality in Western Culture*. Cambridge: Cambridge University Press, 1994.

During, Elie. "Appropriations: Deaths of the Author in Electronic Music." In *Sonic Process*, 39–57. Barcelona: Museu d'Art Contemporani di Barcelona, N.D. [2002?].

Eagleton, Terry. *The Idea of Culture*. Oxford: Blackwell, 2000.

Ehrenreich, Barbara. "The Decline of Patriarchy." In *Constructing Masculinity*, edited by Maurice Berger, Brian Wallis, and Simon Watson, 284–90. New York: Routledge, 1995.

Engh, Barbara. "Loving It: Music and Criticism in Roland Barthes." In *Musicology and Difference: Gender and Sexuality in Music Scholarship*, editd by Ruth A. Solie, 66–79. Berkeley: University of California Press, 1993.

Evans, David. *Tommy Johnson*. London: Studio Vista, 1971.

———. *Big Road Blues: Tradition and Creativity in the Folk Blues*. New York: Da Capo, 1987.

———. "Charley Patton, the Conscience of the Delta." In *Screamin' and Hollerin' the Blues: The Worlds of Charley Patton*, Revenant Album No 212 (ND): 6–34.

Evans, Dylan. *An Introductory Dictionary of Lacanian Psychoanalysis*. London: Routledge, 1997.

Fairley, Jan. "The 'Local' and 'Global' in Popular Music." In *The Cambridge Companion to Pop and Rock*, edited by Simon Frith, Will Straw, and John Street, 272–89. Cambridge: Cambridge University Press, 2001.

———. "'Ay Díos, Ampárame' (O God, Protect Me): Music in Cuba during the 1990s, the 'Special Period.'" In *Island Musics*, edited by Kevin Dawe, 77–97. London: Berg, 2004.

Feld, Steven. "The Poetics and Politics of Pygmy Pop." In *Western Music and Its Others: Difference, Representation, and Appropriation in Music*, edited by Georgina Born and David Hesmondhalgh, 254–79. Berkeley: University of California Press, 2000.

Fink, Robert. "Elvis Everywhere: Musicology and Popular Music Studies at the Twilight of the Canon." *American Music* 16 (1998): 135–79.

Fiske, Roger. "A Covent Garden Pantomime." *Musical Times* 104 (1963): 574–6.

———. *English Theatre Music in the Eighteenth Century*. Oxford: Oxford University Press, 1973.

Flanagan, Michael. "Invoking Diamanda." In *Life Sentences: Writers, Artists, and Aids*, edited by Thomas Avena, 161–75. San Francisco: Mercury House, 1994.

Floyd, Samuel A., Jr. "Troping the Blues: From Spirituals to Concert Hall." *Black Music Research Journal* 13:1 (1993): 31–51.

———. *The Power of Black Music: Interpreting Its History from Africa to the United States*. New York: Oxford University Press, 1995.

Forte, Allan. *The American Popular Ballad of the Golden Era, 1924–1950*. Princeton, NJ: Princeton University Press, 1995.

Foucault, Michel. *The Order of Things: An Archaeology of the Human Sciences*. London: Tavistock Publications, 1974.

———. *Discipline and Punish: The Birth of the Prison*, translated by Alan Sheridan. London: Penguin, 1979.

———. "What Is an Author?" translated by Joseph V. Harari. In *Modern Criticism and Theory: A Reader*, edited by David Lodge, 196–210. New York: Longman, 1988.

Frank, Thomas. *One Market under God: Extreme Capitalism, Market Populism and the End of Economic Democracy*. London: Vintage, 2002.

Freud, Sigmund. "Recollection, Repetition and Working Through." In *Therapy and Technique*, edited by Philip Rieff, 157–66. New York: Collier Books, 1963 [1914].

———. "A Note upon the 'Mystic Writing Pad.'" In *On Metapsychology: The Theory of Psychoanalysis*, 429-34. London: Penguin, 1991a [1925].

———. "Beyond the Pleasure Principle." In *On Metapsychology: The Theory of Psychoanalysis*, 269–338. London: Penguin, 1991b [1920].

Frith, Simon. "'The Magic that Can Set You Free': The Ideology of Folk and the Myth of the Rock Community." *Popular Music* 1 (1981): 159–68.

———. "Playing with Real Feeling — Jazz and Suburbia." In *Music for Pleasure: Essays in the Sociology of Pop*, 45-63. Cambridge: Polity Press, 1988.

Frith, Simon, and Angela McRobbie. "Rock and Sexuality." In *On Record: Rock, Pop, and the Written Word*, edited by Simon Frith and Andrew Goodwin, 371–89. London: Routledge, 1990.

Fuchs, Cynthia. "Michael Jackson's Penis." In *Cruising the Performative: Interventions into the Representation of Ethnicity, Nationality, and Sexuality*, edited by Sue-Ellen Case, Philip Brett, and Susan Leigh Foster, 13–33. Bloomington: Indiana University Press, 1995.

Gates, Henry Louis, Jr. *The Signifying Monkey: A Theory of African-American Literary Criticism*. New York: Oxford University Press, 1988.

Gay, John. *The Beggar's Opera*. New York: Dover, 1999.

Gendron, Bernard. "Theodor Adorno meets the Cadillacs." In *Studies in Entertainment: Critical Approaches to Mass Culture*, edited by Tania Modleski, 18–36. Bloomington: University of Indiana Press, 1986.

———. *Between Montmartre and the Mudd Club: Popular Music and the Avant-Garde.* Chicago: University of Chicago Press, 2002.

Gilman, Sander. "Damaged Men: Thoughts on Kafka's Body." In *Constructing Masculinity*, edited by Maurice Berger, Brian Wallis, and Simon Watson, 176–89. New York: Routledge, 1995.

Gilroy, Paul. *The Black Atlantic: Modernity and Double Consciousness.* London: Verso, 1993.

Goehr, Lydia. *The Imaginary Museum of Musical Works: An Essay in the Philosophy of Music.* Oxford: Oxford University Press, 1992.

———. *The Quest for Voice: On Music, Politics, and the Limits of Philosophy.* Oxford: Clarendon Press, 1998.

Graziano, John. "Images of African Americans: African-American Musical Theatre, *Show Boat* and *Porgy and Bess.*" In *The Cambridge Companion to the Musical*, edited by William A. Everitt and Paul R. Laird, 63–76. Cambridge: Cambridge University Press, 2002.

Green, Jonathon (ed.). *Cassell's Dictionary of Slang.* London: Cassell, 1998.

Green, Lucy. *Music, Gender, Education.* Cambridge: Cambridge University Press, 1997.

Greer, Germaine. *The Female Eunuch.* London: Paladin, 1971.

Griffiths, Dai. "Cover Versions and the Sound of Identity in Motion." In *Popular Music Studies*, edited by David Hesmondhalgh and Keith Negus, 51–64. London: Arnold, 2002.

Grossberg, Lawrence. "Is Anybody Listening? Does Anybody Care? On the 'State of Rock.'" In *Microphone Fiends: Youth Music and Youth Culture*, edited by Andrew Ross and Tricia Rose, 41–58. London: Routledge, 1994.

Habermas, Jűrgen. *The Philosophical Discourse of Modernity: Twelve Lectures*, translated by Frederick Lawrence. Cambridge: Polity Press, 1990.

Hacking, Ian. *Rewriting the Soul: Multiple Personality and the Sciences of Memory.* Princeton, NJ: Princeton University Press, 1995.

Hamm, Charles. *Yesterdays: Popular Song in America.* New York: Norton, 1979.

Handy, W. C. *Blues: An Anthology*, edited by Abbe Niles. New York: Da Capo, 1990 [1926].

———. *Father of the Blues: An Autobiography.* New York: Da Capo, 1991 [1941].

Hanslick, Eduard. "On the Musically Beautiful." [1854] In *Music in European Thought 1851–1912*, edited by Bojan Bujić, 11–39. Cambridge: Cambridge University Press, 1988.

Haraway, Donna. *Simians, Cyborgs, and Women: The Reinvention of Nature.* London: Free Association Books, 1991.

Hardt, Michael, and Antonio Negri. *Empire.* Cambridge, MA: Harvard University Press, 2000.

Harker, Dave. *Fakesong: The Manufacture of British "Folksong" 1700 to the Present Day.* Milton Keynes: Open University Press, 1985.

Harvey, David. *The Condition of Postmodernity.* Oxford: Blackwell, 1989.

Haskins, Jim. *The Cotton Club.* New York: Random House, 1977.

Hawkins, Stan. *Settling the Pop Score: Pop Texts and Identity Politics.* London: Ashgate, 2002.

Hegel, G. W. F. *Lectures on the Philosophy of World History. Introduction: Reason in History*, translated by H. B. Nisbet, 174–90. Cambridge: Cambridge University Press, 1975 [1830].

———. *Phenomenology of Spirit*, translated by A. V. Miller. Oxford: Oxford University Press, 1977 [1807].

Heidigger, Martin. *The Question Concerning Technology.* New York: Harper and Row, 1977.

Heylin, Clinton. *From the Velvets to the Voidoids.* London: Penguin, 1993.

Hobsbawm, Eric and Terence Ranger (eds.). *The Invention of Tradition.* Cambridge: Cambridge University Press, 1983.

hooks, bell. *Ain't I a Woman: Black Women and Feminism.* London: Pluto Press, 1982.

———. *Feminist Theory: From Margin to Center.* Boston, MA: South End Press, 1984.

Huggins, Nathan. *Harlem Renaissance.* New York: Oxford University Press, 1971.

Hughes, Langston. "The Negro Artist and the Racial Mountain." *Nation*, 23 June 1926: 692–4.

Huyssen, Andreas. *After the Great Divide: Modernism, Mass Culture, Postmodernism.* Bloomington, IN: Indiana University Press, 1986.

Ignatiev, Noel. *How the Irish Became White.* New York: Routledge, 1995.

Jameson, Frederic. "Postmodernism: The Cultural Logic of Late Capitalism." *New Left Review* 146 (1984): 53–92.

Joyce, Patrick. *Visions of the People: Industrial England and the Question of Class 1848–1914.* Cambridge: Cambridge University Press, 1991.

Kant, Immanuel. *Critique of Judgment*, translated by Werner S. Pluhar. Indianapolis: Hackett Publishing Co., 1987 [1790].

———. "What Is Enlightenment?" In *Foundations of the Metaphysics of Morals*, translated by Lewis White Beck, 83–90. Upper Saddle River, NJ: Prentice-Hall, 1997.

Kearney, Mary Celeste. "The Missing Links: Riot Grrrl — Feminism — Lesbian Culture." In *Sexing the Groove: Popular Music and Gender*, edited by Sheila Whiteley, 207–29. London: Routledge, 1997.

Keil, Charles. "People's Music Comparatively." In Charles Keil and Steven Feld, *Music Grooves: Essays and Dialogues*, 197–202. Chicago: University of Chicago Press, 1994.

Kellner, Bruce (ed.). *Keep A-Inchin' Along: Selected Writings of Carl Van Vechten about Black Art and Letters.* Westport, CT: Greenwood Press, 1979.

Kierkegaard, Søren. *Fear and Trembling*, translated by Robert Payne. London: Oxford University Press, 1939 [1843].

———. *Repetition: An Essay in Experimental Psychology*, translated by W. Lowrie. London: Oxford University Press, 1942.

Kisliuk, Michelle. "(Un)Doing Fieldwork: Sharing Songs, Sharing Lives." In *Shadows in the Field: New Perspectives for Fieldwork in Ethnomusicology*, edited by Gregory F. Barz and Timothy J. Cooley, 23–44. New York: Oxford University Press, 1997.

Kittler, Friedrich. *Gramophone, Film, Typewriter*, translated by Geoffrey Winthrop-Young and Michael Wutz. Stanford: Stanford University Press, 1999.

Kivy, Peter. *The Fine Art of Repetition: Essays in the Philosophy of Music.* Cambridge: Cambridge University Press, 1993.

Knellwolf, Christa. "Comedy in the OMAI Pantomime." In *Cook and Omai: The Cult of the South Seas,* 17–21. Canberra: National Library of Australia, 2001.

Koestenbaum, Wayne. "The Queen's Throat: (Homo)sexuality and the Art of Singing." In *Inside/Out: Lesbian Theories, Gay Theories*, edited by Diana Fuss, 205–34. London: Routledge, 1991.

Kramer, Lawrence. *Music as Cultural Practice 1800–1900.* Berkeley: University of California Press, 1990.

———. "The Musicology of the Future." *Repercussions* 1 (1992): 5–18.

———. *Classical Music and Postmodern Knowledge.* Berkeley: University of California Press, 1995.

———. *Musical Meaning: Toward a Critical History.* Berkeley: University of California Press, 2002.

Kreuger, Miles. *Show Boat: The Story of a Classic American Musical.* New York: Da Capo, 1990.

Kristeva, Julia. *About Chinese Women*, translated by Anita Barrows. London: Marion Boyars, 1977.

———. "Revolution in Poetic Language." In *The Kristeva Reader*, edited by Toril Moi, 90–136. Oxford: Blackwell, 1986a.

———. "Women's Time." In *The Kristeva Reader*, edited by Toril Moi, 188–213. Oxford: Blackwell, 1986b.

Lacan, Jacques. *The Four Fundamental Concepts of Psycho-Analysis*, edited by Jacques-Alain Miller, translated by Alan Sheridan. Harmondsworth: Penguin, 1979.

———. *Écrits: A Selection*, translated by Alan Sheridan. London: Tavistock Publications, 1980.

Laclau, Ernesto and Chantal Mouffe. *Hegemony and Socialist Strategy: Towards a Radical Democratic Politics.* London: Verso, 1985.

Laplanche, Jean, and Jean-Bertrand Pontalis. "Fantasy and the Origins of Sexuality." In *Formations of Fantasy*, edited by Victor Burgin and Cora Kaplan, 5–34. London: Methuen, 1986.

Latour, Bruno. *We Have Never Been Modern*, translated by Catherine Porter. New York: Harvester Wheatsheaf, 1993.

Le Huray, Peter, and James Day (eds). *Music and Aesthetics in the Eighteenth and Early-Nineteenth Centuries.* Cambridge: Cambridge University Press, 1981.

Leach, Elizabeth Eva. "Vicars of 'Wannabe': Authenticity and the Spice Girls." *Popular Music* 20:2 (2001): 143–67.

Lefebvre, Henri. *Everyday Life in the Modern World*, translated by S. Rabinovitch. New Brunswick, NJ: Transaction Books, 1990.

Leonard, Neil. *Jazz and the White Americans: The Acceptance of a New Art Form*. Chicago: University of Chicago Press, 1962.

Leppert, Richard. *The Sight of Sound: Music, Representation, and the History of the Body.* Berkeley: University of California Press, 1993.

Levin, Thomas Y. "For the Record: Adorno on Music in the Age of Its Technological Reproducibility." *October* 55 (1990): 23–47.

Levine, Lawrence. *Highbrow/Lowbrow: The Emergence of Cultural Hierarchy in America.* New Haven: Yale University Press, 1988.

Lhamon, W. T., Jr. *Raising Cain: Blackface Performance from Jim Crow to Hop Hop*. Cambridge, MA: Harvard University Press, 1998.
Lloyd, A. L. *Folk Song in England*. London: Panther, 1969.
Lomax, Alan. *Mister Jelly Roll: The Fortunes of Jelly Roll Morton, New Orleans Creole and "Inventor of Jazz."* Berkeley: University of California Press, 1973 [1950].
———. *The Land Where the Blues Began*. New York: Pantheon, 1993; republished, New York: The New Press, 2003.
Lomax, John A. "Self-Pity in Negro Folk-Songs." *The Nation* 105 (1917): 141–5.
———. "Sinful Songs of the Southern Negro." *Musical Quarterly* 21 (1934): 177–87.
Lomax, John A. and Alan Lomax. *American Ballads and Folk Songs*. New York: Macmillan, 1934.
———. *Negro Folk Songs as Sung by Leadbelly*. New York: Macmillan, 1936.
Lott, Eric. *Love and Theft: Blackface Minstrelsy and the American Working Class*. New York: Oxford University Press, 1993.
Loza, Susana. "Sampling (Hetero) Sexuality: Diva-ness and Discipline in Electronic Dance Music." *Popular Music* 20:3 (2001): 349–57.
Mackey, Nathaniel. "Sound and Sentiment, Sound and Symbol." In *The Jazz Cadence of American Culture*, edited by Robert G. O'Meally, 602–28. New York: Columbia University Press, 1998.
Mansfield, Nick. "Why Are There No Chartist Banners? — The 'Missing Link' in 19th Century Banners." *Journal of the Social History Curators Group* 25 (2000): 35–44.
Marcus, Greil. *Invisible Republic: Bob Dylan's Basement Tapes*. London: Picador, 1997.
Mariel, Liora. "Dana International: A Self-Made Jewish Diva." *Race, Gender, and Class* 6:4 (1999): 110–24.
———. "Diva in the Promised Land: A Blueprint for Newspeak?" *World Englishes* 17:2 (1998): 225–37.
Marks, Morton. "Uncovering Ritual Structures in Afro-American Music." In *Religious Movements in Contemporary America*, edited by I. Zaretsky and M. P. Leone, 60–134. Princeton, NJ: Princeton University Press, 1974.
Maróthy, János. *Music and the Bourgeois, Music and the Proletarian*. Budapest: Akadémiai Kiadó, 1974.
Marx, Karl. *Grundrisse: Foundations of the Critique of Political Economy*, translated by Martin Nicolaus. Harmondsworth: Penguin, 1973.
———. *Economic and Philosophical Manuscripts*. In *Early Writings*, translated by Rodney Livingstone and Gregor Benton, 279–400. Harmondsworth: Penguin, 1975.
———. *Capital*, vol. 1, translated by Ben Fowkes. Harmondsworth: Penguin, 1976.
———. *The German Ideology*. New York: Prometheus Books, 1998.
Mattfeld, Julius. *Handbook of American Operatic Premieres 1731–1962*. Detroit, MI: Detroit Information Service, 1963.
Maus, Fred E. "Glamour and Evasion: the Fabulous Ambivalence of the Pet Shop Boys." *Popular Music* 20:3 (2001): 379–93.
Mazullo, Mark. "Revisiting the Wreck: PJ Harvey's *Dry* and the Drowned Virgin-Whore." *Popular Music* 20:3 (2001): 431–47.
McClary, Susan. *Feminine Endings: Music, Gender, and Sexuality*. Minneapolis: University of Minnesota Press, 1991.
———. "Same as It Ever Was: Youth Culture and Music." In *Microphone Fiends: Youth Music and Youth Culture*, edited by Andrew Ross and Tricia Rose, 29–40. London: Routledge, 1994.
———. "Music, the Pythagoreans, and the Body." In *Choreographing History*, edited by Susan Leigh Foster, 82-104. Bloomington, IN: Indiana University Press, 1995.
McCracken, Allison. "'God's Gift to Us Girls': Crooning, Gender, and the Re-Creation of American Popular Song, 1928–1933." *American Music* 17:4 (1999): 365–95.
Mercer, Kobena. "Monster Metaphors: Notes on Michael Jackson's *Thriller*." In *Sound and Vision: The Music Video Reader*, edited by Simon Frith, Andrew Goodwin and Lawrence Grossberg, 93–108. London: Routledge, 1993.
Melly, George. *Revolt into Style: The Pop Arts in Britain*. Harmondsworth: Penguin, 1972.
Merwe, Peter van der. *Origins of the Popular Style: The Antecedents of Twentieth-Century Popular Music*. Oxford: Clarendon Press, 1989.
Metzer, David. "Shadow Play: The Spiritual in Duke Ellington's 'Black and Tan Fantasy.'" *Black Music Research Journal* 17:2 (1997): 137–58.
Meyer, Leonard. B. *Music, the Arts, and Ideas: Patterns and Predictions in Twentieth-Century Culture*. Chicago: University of Chicago Press, 1967.

Middleton, Richard. *Studying Popular Music*. Buckingham: Open University Press, 1990.

———. "The 'Problem' of Popular Music." In *The Blackwell History of Music in Britain. Vol. 6: The Twentieth Century*, edited by Stephen Banfield, 27–38. Oxford: Blackwell, 1995.

———. "Pop Goes Old Theory." *Journal of the Royal Musical Association* 122 (1997): 303–20.

———. "Who May Speak? From a Politics of Popular Music to a Popular Politics of Music." *Repercussions* 7–8 (1999–2000): 77–103.

———. "Musical Belongings: Western Music and Its Low-Other." In *Western Music and Its Others: Difference, Representation, and Appropriation in Music*, edited by Georgina Born and David Hesmondhalgh, 59–85. Berkeley: University of California Press, 2000a.

———. "Work-in(g)-Practice: Configuration of the Popular Music Intertext." In *The Musical Work: Reality or Invention?*, edited by Michael Talbot, 59–87. Liverpool: University of Liverpool Press, 2000b.

———. "Locating the People: Music and the Popular." In *The Cultural Study of Music: A Critical Introduction*, edited by Martin Clayton, Trevor Herbert, and Richard Middleton, 251–62. New York: Routledge, 2003.

Millett, Kate. *Sexual Politics*. London: Virago, 1977 [1970].

Mingus, Charles. *Beneath the Underdog*. Harmondsworth: Penguin, 1975.

Mitchell, Juliet and Jacqueline Rose (eds.). *Feminine Sexuality: Jacques Lacan and the Ecole Freudienne*. London: Macmillan, 1982.

Modleski, Tania. "Femininity as Mas(s)querade: A Feminist Approach to Mass Culture." In *High Theory, Low Culture*, edited by Colin McCabe, 37–52. New York: St Martin's Press, 1986.

Moore, Allan. "Authenticity as Authentication." *Popular Music* 21:2 (2002): 209–23.

Moore, John. "'The Hieroglyphics of Love': The Torch Singers and Interpretation." In *Reading Pop: Approaches to Textual Analysis in Popular Music*, edited by Richard Middleton, 262–96. Oxford: Oxford University Press, 2000.

Mordden, Ethan. *Make Believe: The Broadway Musical in the 1920s*. New York: Oxford University Press, 1997.

Mowitt, John. "The Sound of Music in the Era of Its Electronic Reproducibility." In *Music and Society: The Politics of Composition, Performance and Reception*, edited by Richard Leppert and Susan McClary, 173–97. Cambridge: Cambridge University Press, 1987.

———. *Percussion: Drumming, Beating, Striking*. Durham, NC: Duke University Press, 2002.

Mulvey, Laura. "Visual Pleasure and Narrative Cinema." *Screen* 16:3 (1975): 8–18.

Murray, Charles Shaar. *Crosstown Traffic: Jimi Hendrix and Post-War Pop*. London: Faber, 1989.

Murray, James, A. H. (ed.) *Oxford English Dictionary*. Oxford: Clarendon Press, 1933.

Nathan, Hans. *Dan Emmett and the Rise of Early Negro Minstrelsy*. Norman: University of Oklahoma Press, 1962.

Negus, Keith. "Sinéad O'Connor — Musical Mother." In *Sexing the Groove: Popular Music and Gender*, edited by Sheila Whiteley, 178–90. London: Routledge, 1997.

Newcomb, Anthony. "Narrative Archetypes and Mahler's Ninth Symphony." In *Music and Text: Critical Inquiries*, edited by Steven Paul Scher, 118–36. Cambridge: Cambridge University Press, 1992.

Nietzsche, Friedrich. *The Will to Power*, translated by Walter Kaufman and R. J. Hollingdale. New York: Vintage, 1968.

Norris, Christopher. "Utopian Deconstruction: Ernst Bloch, Paul de Man and the Politics of Music." In *Music and the Politics of Culture*, edited by Christopher Norris, 305–47. London: Lawrence and Wishart, 1993.

O'Connor, Nuala. *Bringing It All Back Home: The Influence of Irish Music*. London: BBC Books, 1991.

Odum, Howard W. "Folk-song and Folk-poetry as Found in the Secular Songs of the Southern Negroes." *Journal of American Folklore* 24 (1911): 255–94, 351–96.

———. *Rainbow Round My Shoulder: The Blue Trail of Black Ulysses*. New York: Krause, 1972 [1928].

Odum, Howard W., and Guy B. Johnson. *Negro Workaday Songs*. Chapel Hill: University of North Carolina Press, 1926.

Oliver, Paul, Tony Russell, Robert M. W. Dixon, John Godrich, and Howard Rye. *Yonder Come the Blues: The Evolution of a Genre*. Cambridge: Cambridge University Press, 2001.

Osofsky, Gilbert. *Harlem: The Making of a Ghetto*. New York: Harper and Row, 1968.

Paddison, Max. *Adorno's Aesthetics of Music*. Cambridge: Cambridge University Press, 1993.

Palmer, Robert. *Deep Blues*. New York: Viking Press, 1981.

Panassié, Hughes. *Hot Jazz: The Guide to Swing Music*, translated by Lyle and Eleanor Dowling. New York: Witmark, 1936 [1934].

———. *The Real Jazz*, translated by Anne Sorelle Williams. New York: Smith and Durrell, 1942.
Parakilas, James. "Classical Music as Popular Music." *Journal of Musicology* 3 (1984): 1–18.
Parry, Hubert. "Inaugural Address to the Folk Song Society." *Journal of the Folk Song Society* 1 (1899): 2–3.
Perrow, E. C. "Songs and Rhymes from the South." *Journal of American Folklore* 25 (1912): 137–55, 26 (1913): 122–73, 28 (1915): 129–90.
Pesic, Peter. *Seeing Double: Shared Identities in Physics, Philosophy and Literature.* Cambridge MA: MIT Press, 2002.
Poschardt, Ulf. *DJ Culture*, translated by Shaun Whiteside. London: Quartet Books, 1998.
Radano, Ronald M. "Soul Texts and the Blackness of Folk." *Modernism/Modernity* 2:1 (1995): 71–95.
———. "Denoting Difference: The Writing of the Slave Spirituals." *Critical Inquiry* 22 (1996): 506–44.
——— *Lying Up a Nation: Race and Black Music.* Chicago: University of Chicago Press, 2003.
Rahn, John. "Repetition," *Contemporary Music Review* 7 (1993): 49–57.
Ramsey, Frederic, Jr., and Charles Edward Smith. *Jazzmen.* New York: Harcourt, 1939.
Reed, Christopher Robert. *"All the World Is Here": The Black Presence at White City.* Bloomington: Indiana University Press, 2000.
Regev, Motti. "*Musica Mizrakhit*, Israeli Rock and National Culture in Israel." *Popular Music* 15:3 (1996): 275–84.
Reich, Steve. *Writings about Music.* New York: Universal Edition, 1974.
Riis, Thomas L. *Just Before Jazz: Black Musical Theatre in New York, 1890 to 1915.* Washington, DC: Smithsonian Institution Press, 1989.
———. *More than Just Minstrel Shows: The Rise of Black Musical Theatre at the Turn of the Century.* ISAM Monograph No 33. New York: Institute for the Study of American Music, 1992.
———. *The Music and Scripts of "In Dahomey."* Recent Researches in American Music, vol. 5. Madison, WI: A&R Editions, 1996.
Ritson, Joseph. *A Select Collection of English Songs*, 3 vols. London: J. Johnson, 1783.
———. *The Bishoprick Garland; or Durham Minstrel.* Stockton, 1784.
———. *The Northumberland Garland; or, Newcastle Nightingale: A Matchless Collection of Famous Songs.* Newcastle: Hall and Elliot, 1793.
Ronson, Jon. *The Men who Stare at Goats.* London: Picador, 2004.
Rorty, Richard. *Objectivity, Relativism and Truth, Philosophical Papers Volume 1.* Cambridge: Cambridge University Press, 1991.
———. "To the Sunlit Uplands." [review of Bernard Williams, *Truth and Truthfulness: An Essay in Genealogy*, Princeton, NJ: Princeton University Press, 2002] *London Review of Books*, 31 October 2002, 13–15.
Rose, Tricia. *Black Noise: Rap Music and Black Culture in Contemporary America.* Hanover, NH: Wesleyan University Press, 1994.
Rosolato, Guy. "*Répétitions*," *Musique en Jeu* 9 (1972): 33–44.
Rouget, Gilbert. "Music and Possession Trance." In *The Anthropology of the Body*, edited by John Blacking, 233–9. New York: Academic Press, 1977.
Rubin, Gayle. "The Traffic in Women: Notes on the Political Economy of Sex." In *Toward an Anthropology of Women*, edited by Rayna Rapp Reiter, 157–210. New York: Monthly Review, 1975.
Russell, Tony. "Blacks, Whites and Blues." In *Yonder Come the Blues: The Evolution of a Genre*, edited by Paul Oliver, Tony Russell, Robert M. W. Dixon, John Godrich, and Howard Rye, 143–242. Cambridge: Cambridge University Press, 2001 [1970].
Sadie, Stanley (ed.). *New Grove Dictionary of Music and Musicians.* 2nd ed. London: Macmillan, 2001.
Sargeant, Winthrop. *Jazz: Hot and Hybrid.* New York: Dutton, 1938.
Scarborough, Dorothy. *On the Trail of Negro Folk-Songs.* Cambridge, MA: Harvard University Press, 1925.
Scarry, Elaine. *The Body in Pain: The Making and Unmaking of the World.* New York: Oxford University Press, 1985.
Schafer, William J., and Johannes Riedel. *The Art of Ragtime.* New York: Da Capo Press, 1977.
Schiller, Friedrich. *On the Aesthetic Education of Man*, translated by Reginald Snell. London: Routledge and Kegan Paul, 1954.
Schuller, Gunther. *The Swing Era: The Development of Jazz, 1930–1945.* New York: Oxford University Press, 1989.

Schwarz, David. *Listening Subjects: Music, Psychoanalysis, Culture.* Durham, NC: Duke University Press, 1997.
Scott, Derek. "Orientalism and Musical Style." *Musical Quarterly* 82 (1998): 309–35.
Sedgewick, Eve Kosofsky. *Epistemology of the Closet.* Hemel Hempstead: Harvester, 1991.
Shepherd, John, David Horn, Dave Laing, Paul Oliver, and Peter Wicke (eds). *Encyclopedia of Popular Music of the World*, Vol. II, *Performance and Production*. London: Continuum, 2003.
Shield, William. *An Introduction to Harmony*. London: G. and J. Robinson, 1800; 2nd ed., London: J. Robinson, ND [1815].
Shiloah, Amnon. "An Eighteenth-Century Critic of Taste and Good Taste." In *Ethnomusicology and Modern Music History*, edited by Stephen Blum, Philip V. Bohlman, and Daniel M. Neuman, 181–9. Urbana and Chicago: University of Illinois Press, 1991.
Shipton, Alyn. *Groovin' High: The Life of Dizzy Gillespie.* Oxford: Oxford University Press, 1999.
———. *A New History of Jazz.* London: Continuum, 2001.
Silver, Abner, and Robert Bruce, *How to Write and Sell a Song Hit.* New York: Prentice-Hall, 1939.
Silverman, Kaja. *The Acoustic Mirror: The Female Voice in Psychoanalysis and Cinema.* Bloomington, IN: Indiana University Press, 1988.
Simone, Nina (with Stephen Cleary). *I Put a Spell on You: The Autobiography of Nina Simone.* London: Ebury Press, 1991.
Slack, Jennifer Daryl. "The Theory and Method of Articulation in Cultural Studies." In *Stuart Hall: Critical Dialogues in Cultural Studies*, edited by David Morley and Kuan-Hsing Chen, 112–27. London: Routledge, 1996.
Small, Christopher. *Music of the Common Tongue: Survival and Celebration in Afro-American Music.* London: John Calder, 1987.
———. "Performance as Ritual: Sketch for an Enquiry into the True Nature of a Symphony Concert." In *Lost in Music: Culture, Style and the Musical Event*, edited by Avron Levine White, 6–32. London: Routledge and Kegan Paul, 1987.
Snead, James A. "Repetition as a Figure of Black Culture." In *Black Literature and Literary Theory*, edited by Henry Louis Gates, Jr., 59–80. London: Routledge, 1984.
Solie, Ruth A. "Whose Life? The Gendered Self in Schumann's *Frauenliebe* Songs." In *Music and Text: Critical Inquiries*, edited by Steven Paul Scher, 219–40. Cambridge: Cambridge University Press, 1992.
Sonneck, Oscar G .T. *A Bibliography of Early Secular American Music [18th Century]*, revised by William T. Upton. Washington, DC: Library of Congress, 1945 [1905].
Southern, Eileen. *The Music of Black Americans: A History.* New York: Norton, 1971.
Spice, Nicholas. "I Must Be Mad." [review of Sigmund Freud, *Wild Analysis*, London: Penguin, 2002] *London Review of Books*, 8 January 2004, 11–15.
Spillers, Hortense. "Mama's Baby, Papa's Maybe: An American Grammar Book." *Diacritics* (Summer 1987): 65–81.
Spivak, Gayatri Chakravorty. "Can the Subaltern Speak?" In *Marxism and the Interpretation of Culture*, edited by Cary Nelson and Lawrence Grossberg, 271–313. London: Macmillan, 1988.
Stallybrass, Peter and Allon White. *The Politics and Poetics of Transgression.* London: Methuen, 1986.
Stewart-Baxter, Derek. *Ma Rainey and the Classic Blues Singers.* London: Studio Vista, 1970.
Swedenburg, Ted. "Saida Sultan/Dana International: Transgender Pop and the Polysemiotics of Sex, Nation, and Ethnicity on the Israeli-Egyptian Border." *Musical Quarterly* 81:1 (1997): 81–108.
Talbot, Michael (ed.). *The Musical Work: Invention or Reality?* Liverpool: Liverpool University Press, 2000.
Taussig, Michael. *Mimesis and Alterity.* New York: Routledge, 1993.
Taylor, Charles. *Sources of the Self: The Making of Modern Identity.* Cambridge: Cambridge University Press, 1989.
———. *The Ethics of Authenticity.* Cambridge, MA: Harvard University Press, 1991.
Taylor, Miles. *Ernest Jones, Chartism, and the Romance of Politics 1819–1869.* Oxford: Oxford University Press, 2003.
Thoreau, Henry David. *Walden*, edited by Christopher Bigsby. London: Everyman, 1995 [1854].
Thorne, Tony. *Dictionary of Contemporary Slang.* London: Bloomsbury, 1999.
Tøjner, Poul Erik. *Munch in his own Words.* Munich, London and New York: Prestel, 2002.
Toll, Robert. *Blacking Up: The Minstrel Show in Nineteenth-Century America.* New York: Oxford University Press, 1974.

Tomlinson, Gary. "Cultural Dialogics and Jazz: A White Historian Signifies." *Black Music Research Journal* 11:2 (1991): 229–64.
———. *Metaphysical Song: An Essay on Opera*. Princeton, NJ: Princeton University Press, 1999.
———. "Musicology, Anthropology, History." In *The Cultural Study of Music: A Critical Introduction*, edited by Martin Clayton, Trevor Herbert, and Richard Middleton, 31–44. New York: Routledge, 2003.
Toop, David. *Ocean of Sound: Aether Talk, Ambient Sound and Imaginary Worlds*. London: Serpent's Tail, 1995.
Vattimo, Gianni. *The End of Modernity*, translated by J R. Snyder. Cambridge: Polity Press, 1988.
Vernallis, Carol. *Experiencing Music Video: Aesthetics and Cultural Context*. New York: Columbia University Press, 2004.
Vincent, Ted. *Keep Cool: The Black Activists Who Built the Jazz Age*. London: Pluto Press, 1995.
Wallace, Michele. *Black Macho and the Myth of the Super Woman*. New York: Dial Press, 1978.
Ward, Brian. *Just My Soul Responding: Rhythm and Blues, Black Consciousness and Race Relations*. London: UCL Press, 1998.
Warner, Marina. *Fantastic Metamorphoses, Other Worlds: Ways of Telling the Self*. Oxford: Oxford University Press, 2002.
Weber, William. "Mass Culture and the Re-Shaping of European Musical Taste, 1770-1870." *International Review of the Aesthetics and Sociology of Music* 8:1 (1977): 5–22.
Wenner, Jann. *Lennon Remembers: The Rolling Stone Interviews*. Harmondsworth: Penguin, 1972.
White, Hayden. *Metahistory: The Historical Imagination in Nineteenth-Century Europe*. Baltimore: John Hopkins University Press, 1973.
White, Newman I. *American Negro Folk-Songs*. Cambridge, MA: Harvard University Press, 1928.
Whiteley, Sheila (ed.). *Sexing the Groove: Popular Music and Gender*. London: Routledge, 1997.
Wilder, Alec. *American Popular Song: The Great Innovators 1900–1950*. New York: Oxford University Press, 1972.
Williams, Alistair. "Music as Immanent Critique: Stasis and Development in the Music of Ligeti." In *Music and the Politics of Culture*, edited by Christopher Norris, 187–225. London: Lawrence and Wishart, 1993.
Williams, Bernard. *Truth and Truthfulness: An Essay in Genealogy*. Princeton, NJ: Princeton University Press, 2002.
Williams, Raymond. *Keywords: A Vocabulary of Culture and Society*. Rev. ed. London: Fontana, 1988.
———. "The Idea of a Common Culture." [1968] In *Resources of Hope*, edited by Robin Gable, 32-38. London: Verso, 1989.
Wolfe, Charles, and Kip Lornell. *The Life and Legend of Leadbelly*. London: Secker and Warburg, 1993.
Work, John W. *American Negro Songs and Spirituals: A Comprehensive Collection of 230 Folk Songs, Religious and Secular*. New York: Dover, 1998 [1940].
Žižek, Slavoj. *The Sublime Object of Ideology*. London: Verso, 1989.
———. "Beyond Discourse-Analysis." In Ernesto Laclau, *New Reflections on the Revolution of Our Time*, 249-60. London: Verso, 1990.
———. "Pornography, Nostalgia, Montage: A Triad of the Gaze." In *Looking Awry: An Introduction to Jacques Lacan through Popular Culture*, 107–22. Cambridge, MA: MIT Press, 1991.
———. "'I Hear You with My Eyes'; or, The Invisible Master." In *Gaze and Voice as Love Objects*, edited by Renata Salecl and Slavoj Žižek, 90–126. Durham, NC: Duke University Press, 1996.
———. "Courtly Love, or Woman as Thing." In *The Žižek Reader*, edited by Elizabeth Wright and Edmond Wright, 148–73. Oxford: Blackwell, 1999a.
———. "Otto Weininger, or 'Woman Doesn't Exist'." In *The Žižek Reader*, edited by Elizabeth Wright and Edmond Wright, 127–47. Oxford: Blackwell, 1999b.
———. "The Spectre of Ideology." In *The Žižek Reader*, edited by Elizabeth Wright and Edmond Wright, 53–86. Oxford: Blackwell, 1999c.
———. "The Undergrowth of Enjoyment: How Popular Culture Can Serve as an Introduction to Lacan." In *The Žižek Reader*, edited by Elizabeth Wright and Edmond Wright, 11–36. Oxford: Blackwell, 1999d.
———. *For They Know Not What They Do: Enjoyment as a Political Factor*, 2nd ed. London: Verso, 2002.

Song Index

This is a list of all songs and similar musical pieces referred to in the text and notes. Numbers in bold type indicate significant discussion of the piece. For larger works (operas, films, albums, etc.) see the General Index.

General Index

Q